The
RED BOOK

on Real Estate Contracts in

GEORGIA

By Seth Weissman & Ned Blumenthal

PUBLISHED BY **THE GEORGIA ASSOCIATION OF REALTORS®**

ISBN-10: 0-9886178-0-3
ISBN-13: 978-0-9886178-0-3
Copyright ©2012
Weissman, Nowack, Curry & Wilco, P.C.
All rights reserved.

DISCLAIMER AND TERMS OF USE

This book is designed to provide accurate and authoritative information with regard to real estate sales contracts in Georgia. Since each transaction is unique and the facts and circumstances will vary from one transaction to another, no representations are made, however, regarding the appropriateness of the sample Special Stipulations and other information contained herein to specific real estate transactions. Additionally, the authors note that the Georgia Association of REALTORS® ("GAR") Forms are frequently updated and modified. Accordingly, it is important to confirm whether the content of any particular GAR Form has changed as such may significantly impact the commentary relative thereto or the appropriateness of any particular sample Special Stipulation. This book is sold with the understanding that neither the authors, publishers, Georgia Association of REALTORS® nor Weissman, Nowack, Curry & Wilco, P.C. are engaged in rendering specific legal or other professional advice. If specific legal or other expert assistance is required, the services of a competent professional should be sought.

DEDICATION

Dedicated to the memory of
Rosalind M. Weissman
May 8, 1930 –July 6, 2012

ACKNOWLEDGMENTS

The authors would like to thank Donna Beezhold and Belishe Pompey for their extraordinary efforts in making this edition of *The Red Book* a reality. Donna served as our research assistant and did a great job in editing the book, reorganizing its content, researching many new topics covered in the book and tracking down obscure points of law about which the authors had questions. Belishe spent countless hours typing the book, looking for typographical errors and providing technical assistance in formatting the book.

ABOUT THE AUTHORS

Seth Weissman is a founding partner of the real estate and litigation firm of Weissman, Nowack, Curry & Wilco, P.C. He received his undergraduate degree summa cum laude from the University of Pennsylvania, a master's degree in city and regional planning from the University of North Carolina at Chapel Hill, and a juris doctor degree from Duke University.

Mr. Weissman is general counsel to the Georgia Association of REALTORS® and is actively involved in representing real estate brokerage firms, developers, builders, lenders and institutional owners of real property throughout Georgia. He is a former Chair of the Real Property Law Section of the State Bar of Georgia and a member of the American College of Real Estate Lawyers. Mr. Weissman is a Professor of the Practice of City Planning in the College of Architecture at the Georgia Institute of Technology. Mr. Weissman is an author and lecturer on a wide variety of real estate and real estate brokerage subjects.

Ned Blumenthal is a partner with the real estate and litigation firm of Weissman, Nowack, Curry & Wilco, P.C. He received his undergraduate degree from Emory University in 1987, and his juris doctor degree from Emory University School of Law in 1990.

Mr. Blumenthal is actively involved in representing and defending REALTORS® and real estate brokerage firms in civil actions, administrative proceedings, HUD investigations, regulatory compliance and commission claims. Mr. Blumenthal is a former REALTOR® and lectures and writes frequently on many real estate brokerage topics, including risk reduction, claims avoidance, RESPA and fair housing. He is admitted to practice in Georgia, Florida and Maryland.

FOREWORD

This edition of *The Red Book* is so different from previous editions you will hardly recognize it. A lot has obviously happened in real estate over the five (5) years since the last edition of The Red Book was published. *The Red Book* has been completely rewritten to address all of the industry shattering changes we've experienced and includes hundreds of new topics and sample special stipulations. My favorite part of *The Red Book* is a new chapter on the hundreds of things that can go wrong in real estate transactions and how to guard against them. This chapter alone is worth the price of the book.

As a real estate broker for more than 30 years, *The Red Book on Real Estate Contracts in Georgia* has become an indispensable resource for me and my agents. It is the first place we go to get questions answered about contracts. It is also our first line of defense when we find ourselves in the middle of disputes over a real estate contract. Since most agents and brokers treat *The Red Book* as the final word on real estate contracts, we have resolved many a dispute over the years by simply pointing out the section of *The Red Book* that addresses the issue at hand.

I have known and worked with Seth Weissman and Ned Blumenthal since they first began to devote their real estate practices to protecting real estate licensees against claims. During that time, Seth and Ned have had a hand in rewriting our state's laws to give real estate licensees greater legal protections. Seth along with the GAR Forms Committee has also written the GAR Forms with that same goal in mind. Unlike many lawyers who explain things in legalese, Seth and Ned have a remarkable way of explaining things in ways I can understand. They both also give practical legal advice that reflects a keen understanding of our industry. *The Red Book* reflects these values and I highly recommend it.

John R. Barnes

Sr. Vice President/Managing Broker
Harry Norman, REALTORS®

TABLE OF CONTENTS

CHAPTER 1: CREATING A BINDING CONTRACT

CHAPTER 2: TITLE

CHAPTER 3: PARTIES TO THE CONTRACT

CHAPTER 6: PURCHASE PRICE

CHAPTER 7: METHODS OF PAYMENT AND FINANCING

CHAPTER 8: APPRAISAL AND OTHER CONTINGENCIES

CHAPTER 9: DISCLOSURES

CHAPTER 10: INSPECTION, CONSTRUCTION AND REPAIR ISSUES

CHAPTER 11: NOTICE

CHAPTER 12: CLOSING AND POSSESSION

CHAPTER 15: RISK ALLOCATION IN REAL ESTATE CONTRACTS

CHAPTER 17: LEASING

CHAPTER 18: SPECIAL TYPES OF CONTRACTS

CHAPTER 19: THE GEORGIA BROKERAGE RELATIONSHIPS IN REAL ESTATE TRANSACTIONS ACT

CHAPTER 20: CONDOMINIUMS, HOMEOWNER ASSOCIATIONS AND OTHER FORMS OF COMMON INTEREST COMMUNITIES

CHAPTER 21: MORTGAGE FRAUD

CHAPTER 23: *AD VALOREM* TAX ON REAL PROPERTY

CHAPTER 24: WATER RIGHTS

CHAPTER 25: FAIR HOUSING ACT AND AMERICANS WITH DISABILITIES ACT

CHAPTER 26: REAL ESTATE SETTLEMENT PROCEDURES ACT ("RESPA")

CHAPTER 27: BANKRUPTCY

TABLE OF SPECIAL STIPULATIONS

INDEX

The **RED BOOK**

CHAPTER 1

CREATING A BINDING CONTRACT

OVERVIEW

This chapter on creating a binding contract addresses some of the thorniest issues that arise in real estate transactions, including how various time periods in the contract are calculated, when offers can be withdrawn, the effect of a party making a counteroffer when the offer has already expired, and the effect of a party refusing to sign a "clean" copy of the contract. This chapter also includes a discussion on the basics of contract formation, letters of intent, and the common mistakes in filling out pre-printed form real estate contracts.

§ 1.1   OFFER AND ACCEPTANCE

To form a binding contract there must be mutual agreement by all of the parties to all of the terms.[1] Such a mutual agreement is established when one party makes an offer which the other party accepts unconditionally and without any changes.[2] A qualified or conditional acceptance, or one that adds a new material term, is a counteroffer. Therefore, if a party accepts all of the terms of the offer but places a condition or adds a new term in the acceptance, a mutual agreement is not established and there is no binding contract.[3] So, for example, adding an e-mail address of a party or the party's broker and providing that notices can be sent by e-mail would likely be the addition of a new term because it changes the manner in which notice may be sent.[4] Thus, the Georgia Court of Appeals found that when a party signs an offer as it was presented but changes the closing date (because the original closing had passed) this was a counter offer.[5]

In another case, a seller made an offer to sell certain property in which the closing would take place no later than July 30, 1981.[6] The buyer attempted to accept the seller's offer but stipulated that the closing would take place by August 25, 1981. The seller treated the buyer's offer as a counteroffer and refused to accept it. The court held that no contract existed between the parties because the buyer made a counteroffer, not an acceptance, when she changed the closing date of the original offer.

§ 1.1.1   Letters Of Intent

In commercial transactions, a letter of intent will often precede the delivery of an offer to purchase real property. The purpose of a letter of intent is for the buyer to express in writing an interest in purchasing the property and under what terms.[7] Since the preparation of an offer to purchase commercial property can be time consuming, the thought behind a letter of intent is to see if the parties are in general agreement on the basic terms of the transaction.[8] If they are, the parties then proceed to have a purchase and sale agreement prepared based upon the terms of the letter of intent.

There are a few rules for letters of intent. The parties to them will often include in them as many specific deal points as possible to limit issues to be negotiated later. However, the major risk with a letter of intent is that it not be so specific and detailed that it is misconstrued as an offer to purchase property which, if accepted, creates an enforceable purchase and sale agreement. The more the parties agree to in a letter of intent, the greater the risk that one of the parties may claim that the letter of intent is an enforceable contract.

---

1   O.C.G.A. § 13-3-1.

2   *Lamb v. Decatur Fed. Sav. & Loan Ass'n.*, 201 Ga.App. 583, 411 S.E.2d 527 (1991); *Harry Norman & Assoc., Inc. v. Bryan*, 158 Ga.App. 751, 282 S.E.2d 208 (1981); *Butler v. Household Mortg. Services, Inc.*, 266 Ga.App. 104, 596 S.E.2d 664 (2004).

3   *Harry Norman & Assoc., Inc. v. Bryan*, 158 Ga.App. 751, 282 S.E.2d 208 (1981).

4   *Benton v. Shiver*, 254 Ga. 107, 326 S.E.2d 756 (1985) (varying closing date); *Stubbs v. Tattnall Bank*, 244 Ga. 212, 259 S.E.2d 466 (1979) (varying original price offered); *Panfel v. Boyd*, 187 Ga.App. 639, 371 S.E.2d 222 (1988); *Harry Norman & Assoc., Inc. v. Bryan* 158 Ga.App. 751, 282 S.E.2d 208 (1981); *Clover Realty Co. v. Gouyd*, 153 Ga.App. 64, 264 S.E.2d 547 (1980); *Frey v. Friendly Motors, Inc.*, 129 Ga.App. 636, 200 S.E.2d 467 (1973) (varying means of acceptance).

5   *Panfel v. Boyd*, 187 Ga.App. 639, 371 S.E.2d 222 (1988) (holding that original contract had expired where closing date was past and changed to new date from original contract).

6   *Benton v. Shiver*, 254 Ga. 107, 326 S.E.2d 756 (1985).

7   *Garner v. Boyd*, 330 F.Supp. 22 (D.C. Tex. 1970).

8   *Garner v. Boyd*, 330 F.Supp. 22 (D.C. Tex. 1970).

The Georgia Court of Appeals confirmed that "the failure to agree to even one essential term means that there is no agreement to be enforced" but that "a deferral of agreement on a nonessential term does not invalidate an otherwise valid contract."[9] The question of what is an essential term is dependent upon the circumstances of the specific sale in question. In this particular case the letter of intent was clear on the identification of the property involved, the purchase price, earnest money, and certain conditions of closing. However, the letter of intent clearly contemplated a deed restriction regarding use of the property, the exact terms of which the parties could never agree upon. The court held that the deed restriction was an essential term, that the parties had never reached a meeting of the minds on that issue, and that the letter of intent could therefore not be enforced as a binding contract.

In the following case, however, the Georgia Supreme Court upheld the letter of intent as an enforceable agreement.[10] Beller & Gould, a partnership, executed a letter of intent to acquire the Lisenbys property. The letter of intent gave Beller & Gould the option to purchase the property by November 15 and when they tried to exercise the option and enter into a formal agreement, the Lisenbys refused. Beller & Gould then sued for specific performance to enforce the letter of agreement. The court found the letter of intent was sufficient to support the creation of a binding agreement because the letter (i) identified the parties and their assent, (ii) described the subject matter of the contract, and (iii) set forth the terms of the consideration.[11] The court went further and stated that even if the parties discussed other terms which were not included in the letter of intent, the absence of such terms does not render the letter of intent unenforceable.[12] The court determined that all the material terms of the agreement had been established in the letter of intent.[13] To avoid the risk of having a letter of intent be considered an enforceable contract, most letters of intent contain specific language stating that it is only intended as a letter of intent and not as a real estate purchase and sale agreement. Such a provision states something like the following:

> **Special Stipulation 01: Letter of Intent**
> *Notwithstanding any provision to the contrary contained herein, all parties acknowledge that this Letter of Intent is not intended as an offer to purchase real property which, if accepted, shall create an enforceable agreement between the parties. This Letter of Intent shall be subject to the parties agreeing to a separate written purchase and sale agreement subsequent to the Letter of Intent being accepted.*

Parties should not underestimate the value of a well written letter of intent. While the letter of intent is generally not legally binding[14], it establishes the basis of what will eventually be included in the purchase and sale agreement between the parties. If there has been an agreement or a particular point in the letter of intent, few parties will agree to alter that term in the purchase and sale agreement. Therefore, deal points that are particularly important to a party are often set out in a letter of intent to avoid disputes on that point at a later time.

§ 1.1.2   Time Limit Of Offer

Most form real estate contracts include a provision limiting the time period during which the offer can be accepted. If the offer is not accepted within this time period, the offer then expires. The idea behind this type of provision is to limit the time period that a party has to accept or reject an offer see if a more attractive offer is made.

One question that regularly arises with such provisions is what must the person receiving the offer do prior to the end of the time limit of the offer to prevent the offer from expiring? Must the person receiving the offer merely accept it before

---

9   *Miami Heights LT, LLC v. Home Depot U.S.A, Inc.*, 283 Ga.App. 779, 643 S.E.2d 1 (2007).

10   *Beller & Gould v. Lisenby*, 246 Ga. 15, 268 S.E.2d 611 (1994).

11   *Beller & Gould v. Lisenby*, 246 Ga. 15, 268 S.E.2d 611 (1994).

12   *Beller & Gould v. Lisenby*, 246 Ga. 15, 268 S.E.2d 611 (1994).

13   *Beller & Gould v. Lisenby*, 246 Ga. 15, 268 S.E.2d 611 (1994).

14   *Garner v. Boyd*, 330 F.Supp. 22 (D.C. Tex. 1970).

the time limit of the offer expires or must the person also deliver the accepted offer back to the offeror prior to the end of the time limit? The GAR Contract requires that the offer be both accepted and delivered back to the offeror prior to the expiration of the time limit of the offer to prevent the offer from expiring. Not all form contracts are as clear as the GAR Contract on this point.

If the offer is silent as to time given for acceptance, the offer will be considered open for a "reasonable time."[15] The law does not define what constitutes a reasonable time, and it will likely vary with the facts and circumstances of different transactions. However, it will probably be interpreted as being a longer period than the day or two most parties give each other to accept an offer or counteroffer. This is because if the intent of the offeror was to limit the time period to accept an offer, the offeror would presumably have done so.

One scenario that frequently occurs in real estate sales transactions is the party making a counteroffer forgets to change the time limit of the offer. Sometimes this means that the counteroffer is made after the time for it to be accepted has already expired. While there is no case law on this point, it is likely that a court would allow such counteroffers to be accepted for a reasonable time thereafter on the theory that the party would not have made a counteroffer which was incapable of being accepted.

When the offer contract contains an express time limit for the offer to be accepted, if the offer is not accepted within the stated time, no contract is formed. If the offer is accepted after the stated time[16], the late acceptance is generally considered a counteroffer which the original offeror may accept or not.[17] If the original offeror timely accepts this counteroffer and delivers it back to the original offeree, prior to the expiration of the time limit, a binding contract is formed.

Sometimes the court will find that a contract exists based upon the actions of the parties, even though there is technically no timely acceptance of an offer. In one Georgia case, the offer expired on March 10, 1956, but the offeree did not accept the offer until March 27, 1956.[18] Even though the offeree did not accept the offer prior to the expiration, both parties operated as if there was a contract for several months. For this reason, the court found that the offeror had waived the deadline for acceptance of the offer, through the offeror's actions and, thus the parties had formed a valid and binding contract.

In another Georgia case, the time for acceptance of the buyer's offer expired on February 23, 1976.[19] The seller rejected the buyer's offer on February 23, but submitted a counteroffer which the buyer accepted on March 9, 1976. The buyer later tried to back out of the contract and argued that the contract was not binding because it was entered after the offer expired. The court held that the buyer waived the February 23 limitation when the buyer accepted the seller's counteroffer on March 9. Therefore, the late acceptance of the counteroffer created a binding and enforceable contract.

§ 1.1.3 Binding Agreement Date Or Effective Date

As a general rule in real estate, a binding contract is created only when it has been signed by both parties and a fully-executed copy of the same is delivered back to the party who made the offer that was ultimately accepted. The date the offer is first made is normally referred to as the Offer Date.[20] The date that the signed acceptance is delivered back to the offeror is known as the Binding Agreement Date.

---

15   *Simpson & Harper v. Sanders & Jenkins*, 130 Ga. 265, 60 S.E. 541 (1908).

16   *Century 21 Pinetree Properties, Inc. v. Cason*, 220 Ga.App. 355, 469 S.E.2d 458 (1996); *Crawley v. Sexton*, 207 Ga.App. 360, 427 S.E.2d 804 (1993), *cert. denied*.

17   *Century 21 Pinetree Properties, Inc. v. Cason*, 220 Ga.App. 355, 469 S.E.2d 458 (1996); *Achour v. Belk & Co.*, 148 Ga.App. 306, 251 S.E.2d 157 (1978); *B. L. Montague Co., Inc. v. Somers*, 94 Ga.App. 860, 96 S.E.2d 629 (1957).

18   *W.B. Leedy & Co. v. Shirley*, 97 Ga.App. 801, 104 S.E.2d 580 (1958).

19   *Achour v. Belk & Co.*, 148 Ga.App. 306, 251 S.E.2d 157, 158 (1978).

20   GAR Form F20.

Let's look at the example below to better understand the Binding Agreement Date. A buyer makes an offer to purchase a seller's property, which is accepted by the seller on a Sunday, but not delivered back to the buyer until Wednesday. In this case, the Binding Agreement Date would be Wednesday. In the GAR Contract, the obligations of the buyer to apply for financing or inspect the property are all measured from the Binding Agreement Date. The GAR Contract requires the offeror to notify the offeree when notice of acceptance has been received. In other words, if the buyer receives the signed, accepted contract back on Wednesday, the buyer or her agent is then obligated under the contract to notify the seller that Wednesday is the Binding Agreement Date.[21] This was included in the GAR Contract to avoid disputes between the parties regarding the Binding Agreement Date since most of the obligations in the contract are tied to this date.

The GAR Contract provides that notice to the broker or sales agent representing a party in a client relationship is notice to that party. Therefore, if the accepted offer is first delivered to the broker representing a party as a client, the Binding Agreement Date would be the date of that delivery. One exception to this rule is where the broker is acting in a designated agency capacity. In this case, notice to the sales agent designated to represent the party as a client is deemed notice to that party while notice to the broker is not.[22]

If the broker is acting as a transaction broker (and is therefore not representing either party in the transaction), notice of acceptance given to the transaction broker is not effective to the buyer. Only when notice of acceptance is delivered to the buyer will the Binding Agreement Date be established. This can, however, be modified with the following special stipulation.

> **Special Stipulation 02:   Notice to Broker Working with Customer is Deemed Notice to Customer**
>
> *Notwithstanding anything to the contrary contained herein, all parties agree that all notices sent to [Insert name of broker or agent] shall, for all purposes herein, be deemed to be good and simultaneous notice to [Seller/Buyer] provided that such notice is delivered in accordance with the requirements set forth in this Agreement. [Seller/Buyer] acknowledge that even though [Insert name of broker or agent] has been designated to receive notice on behalf of [Buyer/Seller], [Insert name of broker or agent] is not representing [Buyer/Seller] in this transaction in a client relationship.*

Until delivery of the signed contract is completed, the buyer's time-restricted obligations under the contract do not commence.

§ 1.1.4   Delivery Of Acceptance Required

The party accepting an offer must deliver written notice of the acceptance to the offeror before expiration of the offer. This means that the notice must be received by the offeror before the offer expires.[23] A party cannot accept an offer and form a binding agreement until the acceptance has been delivered back to the offeror.[24] The GAR Contract explicitly states in the time limit of the offer section that the accepted offer must be delivered back to the party who made the offer prior to the end of the time limit of the offer.[25] The following example illustrates this point.

Example: A buyer makes an offer and states that the offer expires at 11:00 a.m. on May 1. The seller accepts the offer before 11:00 a.m. on May 1 and signs the contract. However, the seller does not deliver the acceptance to the buyer

---

21   It is a violation of Georgia law for a real estate broker to fail to deliver, within a reasonable time, a completed copy of the purchase agreement. O.C.G.A. § 43-40-25(a).

22   *See* § 1.7 (Common Mistakes In Filling Out Pre-Printed Form Real Estate Contracts) of this work for further information regarding notice requirements.

23   *Holland v. Riverside Park Estates, Inc.*, 214 Ga. 244, 104 S.E.2d 83 (1958).

24   *Federal Farm Mortgage Corp. v. Dixon*, 185 Ga. 466, 195 S.E. 414 (1938); *Hartford Fire Ins. Co. v. Steenhuis*, 115 Ga.App. 625, 155 S.E.2d 690 (1967)).

25   GAR Form F20.

(or the buyer's authorized agent) until 11:00 a.m. on May 3. In this example, no binding agreement would be formed because while the offer was timely accepted, it was not timely delivered back to the buyer. Under the GAR Contract, the accepted offer must be delivered back to the person who made the offer before it expires. The rationale for this is that if a contract were found to exist in this situation, the buyer could end up in the unfortunate position of being under contract without knowing about it. Such a buyer could go out and purchase another house having thought that her offer had expired. If the seller could enforce a contract accepted prior to the end of the time limit of the offer, but delivered back after the time limit had expired, the buyer would never have any certainty in being able to move on to look at other houses. Such a result would be highly inequitable and not likely to be the judgment of any court.

A phone call to the other party or a note saying that the contract will be forwarded shortly is generally not sufficient. In one Georgia case, for example, the buyer submitted an offer to the seller which provided that the offer would be open for acceptance by the seller until 3:00 p.m. on July 5, 1957 "by which time written acceptance of such offer must have actually been received by the purchase."[26] The seller told her broker over the telephone that she would accept the offer and she authorized the broker to accept the offer on her behalf. However, the seller never gave her broker or the buyer written acceptance of the offer. The broker wrote the buyer a letter on July 2, 1957 stating, "Your offer to purchase the [Seller's] property has been accepted," and further stated that the "signed contract will be forwarded to you shortly." The court found that these communications did not constitute written acceptance pursuant to the terms of the contract, and because the seller did not deliver to the buyer the signed contract by July 5, there was no mutually binding contract.

Many parties rely on their real estate brokers to complete the delivery of the accepted contract for them. This is because real estate licensees are required to deliver all offers or counteroffers entrusted to them within a reasonable time.[27] A broker's license may be revoked or suspended for failing to do so and the broker may also be subject to a fine or other sanctions.[28]

§ 1.1.5 Sample Problems Regarding Time Limit Of Offer

The following hypothetical situations illustrate some of the common problems related to the time limit of the offer.

Situation #1: The buyer makes an offer to the seller which provides that the offer expires at 10:00 a.m. on May 1. At 8:30 a.m. on May 1, the seller delivers to the buyer the offer, with several terms changed, but fails to change the time limit of the offer from 10:00 a.m. Does the buyer have to accept the counteroffer by 10:00 a.m. in order to reach a binding agreement?

Answer: Yes. While the time period to accept the contract is short, the buyer will have to accept it and deliver the acceptance back to the seller before 10:00 a.m. pursuant to the express terms of the counteroffer submitted by the seller which has incorporated the time limit of the original offer. In all likelihood, however, the seller's failure to change the time limit of the offer is due to an oversight (since in most cases but not all, the seller would give the buyer more than one and one-half hours to accept the counteroffer). The buyer may want to contact the seller to discuss increasing the time period in which the counteroffer may be accepted. If the buyer accepts the counteroffer after the time limit expires, however, the acceptance becomes a counteroffer by the buyer, and the seller would be entitled to reject it or would have to formally accept it in order for a binding contract to be created. If the parties, however, operate under the contract as if it were binding, they would likely be deemed to have waived any objections to the validity of the contract.

---

26   *Holland v. Riverside Park Estates*, 214 Ga. 244, 104 S.E.2d 83 (1958).

27   O.C.G.A. § 43-40-25(b)(19), O.C.G.A. § 10-6A-5, O.C.G.A. § 10-6A-7.

28   O.C.G.A. § 43-40-25(a).

Situation #2: The buyer makes an offer to the seller which provides that the offer expires at 10:00 a.m. on May 1. At 3:00 p.m. on May 1, the seller delivers a signed acceptance back to the buyer. Does the seller's acceptance after the expired time limit create a binding agreement?

Answer: No. The seller's delivery of an acceptance after the time limit of the offer had expired operates as a counteroffer which the buyer may accept or reject.

Situation #3: The buyer makes an offer to the seller which provides that the offer expires at 10:00 a.m. on May 1. At 3:00 p.m. on May 1, the seller makes a counteroffer, but fails to change the original time limit of the offer from 10:00 a.m. In other words, the seller makes a counteroffer which is incapable of being accepted within the time limit provided. If the buyer accepts the seller's counteroffer and delivers it back to the seller, has a valid contract been formed?

Answer: While arguments can be made on both sides of this question, the answer is probably yes. Presumably, the seller would not have made a counteroffer which the buyer was incapable of accepting. A court in this case would likely look to what the intent of the seller was in making the counteroffer with an expired time limit on the offer. If the court concluded that the intent of the seller was to make a counteroffer, the court would likely effectuate the intent of the seller and reform the contract to give the buyer a reasonable time period to accept the seller's counteroffer.

Situation #4: The buyer makes an offer to the seller which provides that the offer expires at 10:00 a.m. on May 1. At 3:00 p.m. on May 1, the seller delivers a signed acceptance back to the buyer. The seller does not object to the buyer having delivered the acceptance after the time limit expired. The parties begin operating under the contract, and the buyer has an inspection done and applies for financing. The parties also begin negotiating over what repairs are to be made to the property through a series of offers and counteroffers during the Due Diligence Period. Several days later the seller receives a better offer. The seller looks for a way out of the contract and argues that she and the buyer never reached an enforceable contract because the seller accepted it after the time limit expired. Can the seller escape the contract with the buyer?

Answer: While arguments can be made on both sides of this question, the best answer is probably no. Once the seller delivered the executed contract back to the buyer and the parties began acting upon it as a binding agreement, the seller likely her right to object to the acceptance having been made after the time limit had expired.

Situation #5: The buyer makes an offer to the seller which provides that the offer expires at 10:00 a.m. on May 1. At 3:00 p.m. on May 1, the seller delivers a signed acceptance back to the buyer. The seller does not object to the buyer having delivered the acceptance after the time limit expired. The parties begin operating under the contract, and the buyer schedules an inspection to be done for May 3. At 5:00 PM May 2 the seller receives a better offer. The seller looks for a way out of the contract and argues that she and the buyer never reached an enforceable contract because the seller accepted it after the time limit expired. Can the seller escape the contract with the buyer?

Answer: This is a tough call. here is not yet much evidence that the seller has waived the time limit of the offer. There is no good way to predict how a judge or jury may rule on this one.

§ 1.1.6 Confidentiality In Residential Real Estate Transactions

Confidentiality agreements are typically used in a residential real estate transaction for a different reason than in a commercial real estate transaction. In residential real estate transactions, one of the major goals of a confidentiality agreement is to prevent the seller or the seller's broker from shopping the offer to other prospective buyers. Unfortunately, it is often difficult to prove that such a breach has occurred or the damages resulting from a breach. The GAR Form Confidentiality Agreement[29] can be entered into between the buyer and seller before the buyer then presents and offer to purchase the seller's property. The form basically provides that the terms of any offers, counteroffers and other communications made by the buyer to the seller will be kept confidential by the seller and the listing broker and shall not be revealed to third parties. This is to try to prevent the seller and/or the listing broker from shopping the offer to other prospective buyers.

§ 1.2 TERMS OF OFFER AND ACCEPTANCE MUST BE THE SAME

The terms of the offer as proposed by the offeror (the party making the offer) and accepted by the offeree (the party receiving the offer) must be the same in order for the parties to have a binding contract.[30] In fact, the consent of all of the parties to all of the terms is essential, and without such a "meeting of the minds" no binding contract will exist. So, for example, if a seller signs an offer for her property but changes the purchase price by $1 or the closing date by only one day, the writing would likely be considered a counteroffer rather than an acceptance of an offer. Similarly, let's say that a seller is using a GAR Contract and receives an offer in which the listing agent's e-mail address is included for the receipt of notices to the seller. If the only change to the contract is that the listing broker strikes the e-mail address, it would also likely be viewed as a counteroffer because the method of receiving notices has been changed.

In making the offer and acceptance, the parties must also strictly abide by the time limitations and notice requirements of the contract.[31] Disputes often arise in transactions with multiple offers and counteroffers where the parties either: (a) forget to change the offer date in the contract, causing the offer or counteroffer to expire prematurely, or (b) otherwise fail to meet the time and notice requirements in the contract. For these reasons it is important for parties to understand what makes a binding contract, the principles of offer and acceptance, and the time and notice requirements for reaching a binding agreement.

§ 1.2.1 Mutuality Requirement

The terms of the offer and the acceptance must not only be the same to create a binding agreement,[32] but there must also be sufficient consideration to support the creation of a contract.[33] Such consideration can either be mutual promises (also known as mutuality) or some other form of consideration.[34] An example of mutuality might be a promise to sell the property in exchange for a promise to pay money to purchase the property.

Mutuality, often referred to as a "promise for a promise," is essential to support a binding agreement when no other consideration is present.[35] A mere unilateral promise, unsupported by consideration or mutuality, does not create a binding contract.[36] However, a seller's promise to convey property at a fixed price to a buyer, combined with a buyer's promise to purchase the seller's property at the fixed price, creates a binding agreement because there is mutuality of contract (*i.e.*, a promise for a promise).

Georgia courts have held that whether promises are mutual is determined at the time the agreement is to be enforced.[37] Therefore, if at the closing, the agreement contains mutual obligations binding both the seller and the buyer equally, the

29   GAR Form F20.

30   *Lamb v. Decatur Fed. Sav. & Loan Ass'n.*, 201 Ga.App. 583, 411 S.E.2d 527 (1991); *Harry Norman & Assoc., Inc. v. Bryan*, 158 Ga.App. 751, 282 S.E.2d 208 (1981).

31   *Holland v. Riverside Park Estates, Inc.*, 214 Ga. 244, 104 S.E.2d 83 (1958); *Century 21 Pinetree Properties, Inc. v. Cason*, 220 Ga.App. 355, 469 S.E.2d 458 (1996).

32   *Lamb v. Decatur Fed. Sav. & Loan Ass'n.*, 201 Ga.App. 583, 411 S.E.2d 527 (1991); *Harry Norman & Assoc., Inc. v. Bryan*, 158 Ga.App. 751, 282 S.E.2d 208 (1981).

33   *Brack v. Brownlee*, 246 Ga. 818, 273 S.E.2d 390 (1980).

34   *Brack v. Brownlee*, 246 Ga. 818, 273 S.E.2d 390 (1980.)

35   *Johnson v. Unified Residential Dev. Co., Inc.*,285 Ga.App. 852, 648 S.E.2d 163 (2007)).

36   *Brack v. Brownlee*, 246 Ga. 818, 273 S.E.2d 390 (1980).

37   *Jones v. Quigley*, 169 Ga. App. 862, 315 S.E.2d 59 (1984)

agreement will satisfy the mutuality requirement and thus be enforceable.[38] In cases where the promise of one party is relied upon as consideration for the other, the mutual promises must impose their obligations at the same time in order to create a binding agreement. So, if the buyer promises to purchase the seller's property at the closing and the seller promises to sell her property to the buyer at the closing, these mutual promises impose their obligations at the same time thus meeting the mutuality requirement.

§ 1.2.1.1   Agreements With Discretionary Contingencies

Generally, agreements that are subject to contingencies, which give a party the right to buy or not buy in the sole discretion of the buyer or give the seller the right to sell or not to sell in the sole discretion of the seller, do not meet the mutuality requirement.[39] Rather, the existence of such a discretionary contingency creates a lack of mutuality and thus results in an unenforceable illusory promise.[40] An illusory promise is an offer which a party can renege on in their sole and absolute discretion.[41] Essentially, the existence of a discretionary contingency creates an unenforceable illusory promise because the agreement is lacking the necessary consideration to be binding upon the parties.[42]

For example, let's say that a buyer contracts to purchase a seller's property. The purchase and sale agreement provides that the buyer may obtain a survey of the property at any time before the closing and may terminate the agreement if she is not satisfied with the survey for any reason whatsoever. This discretionary contingency arguably creates a lack of mutuality because the buyer has the sole power to judge her own satisfaction. Since the buyer is not actually bound to any obligation, the agreement is an unenforceable illusory promise.[43]

Let's look at another example. The seller contracts to sell her property to the buyer. The agreement states that the buyer only has to purchase the seller's property if she gets approval from a railroad company to run a spur line on the property at a location satisfactory to the buyer. This discretionary contingency creates a lack of mutuality because again the buyer is the sole judge of her satisfaction irrespective of whether objectively reasonable and sufficient grounds exist for dissatisfaction.[44] The buyer may never find a satisfactory location and is not technically bound to the agreement, thus this discretionary contingency creates an unenforceable illusory promise.

It is possible to draft an agreement with discretionary contingencies without creating a lack of mutuality if the contingency is subject to being objectively interpreted by a court, based upon the reasonableness of the standard.[45] For example, making a purchase contingent upon a home inspector's satisfactory inspection of the property has been upheld. This is because the decision of whether the contingency is met (*i.e.*, whether the home inspector is satisfied with the inspection) is not within the control of the buyer. Rather, it is left to the presumably independent judgment of a third party. By contrast, making the purchase subject to the buyer's satisfactory inspection of the property will likely fail because the buyer is in complete control of her satisfaction.

The existence of a discretionary contingency should not to be confused with an option contract. An option contract is an agreement in which the seller is paid separate consideration[46] to give the purchaser an "option to purchase the land" within a specified time frame on mutually agreeable terms and conditions.[47] This type of agreement gives the buyer a

---

38   *Jones v. Quigley*, 169 Ga. App. 862, 315 S.E.2d 59 (1984).

39   *Johnson v. Unified Residential Dev. Co., Inc.*, 285 Ga. App. 852, 648 S.E.2d 163 (2007).

40   *Jakel v. Fountainhead Development Corp., Inc.*, 243 Ga. App. 844, 534 S.E.2d 199 (2000).

41   *Clayton McLendon Inc. v. McCarthy*, 125 Ga. App. 76, 186 S.E.2d 452 (1971).

42   *Schaffer v. Wolbe*, 113 Ga.App. 448, 148 S.E.2d 437 (1966).

43   *Lee v. Green Land Co., Inc.*, 245 Ga.App. 558, 538 S.E.2d 189 (2000).

44   *Stone Mountain Properties, Ltd. V. Helmer*, 139 Ga. App.865, 229 S.E.2d 779 (1976).

45   *Johnson v. Unified Residential Dev. Co., Inc.*, 285 Ga. App. 852, 648 S.E.2d 163 (2007).

46   *Pargar, LLC v. CP Summit Retail, LLC*, 2012 WL 2626905 citing *Hewatt v. Leppert*, 259 Ga. 112, 376 S.E.2d 883 (1989).

47   *Johnson v. Unified Residential Dev. Co., Inc.*, 285 Ga. App. 852, 648 S.E.2d 163 (2007).

unilateral right and complete discretion to purchase the seller's property. If the purchaser decides to exercise her option and purchase the property, the seller is obligated to sell the property to the purchaser.[48] On the other hand, a discretionary contingency obligates a party to perform only if the contingency has been satisfied or waived.[49] For this reason, a discretionary contingency generally creates a lack of mutuality. However, the discretion given to the purchaser in an option contract does not create the same problem because the seller is still obligated to sell her property if the option is ever exercised. Option contracts are discussed in further detail in § 18.1 (Option Contracts).

§ 1.2.1.2   Payment Of Earnest Money Eliminates Mutuality Requirement

If an agreement is supported by any form of valid consideration other than mutual promises, mutuality of obligation is not required to create a binding agreement.[50] In other words, if the promisor obtains any benefit from the promisee or the promisee incurs any loss, trouble or disadvantage by providing the consideration to the promisor, such consideration would be considered sufficient.[51] There is no bright line test for determining what constitutes sufficient consideration to eliminate the mutuality requirement. Each situation will depend on the facts and circumstances surrounding the contract at the time it was made. However, the Georgia Supreme Court has held that an earnest money payment (even if such payment is refundable[52]) in exchange for the seller's promise to sell to the buyer provides sufficient consideration for a real estate contract and thus mutuality of obligation is not required.[53] Ultimately, the earnest money payment eliminates the requirement for mutuality.[54] There is at least one case in Georgia that suggests that the existence of a discretionary contingency would not render an agreement unenforceable for lack of mutuality if the agreement is supported by the payment of earnest money.[55] However, there has not been one case following that court's ruling since the decision was rendered in 2007. Moreover, since earnest money is typically paid in almost every transaction, it is unlikely that the existence of an earnest money payment would allow a party to back out of an agreement based on her sole discretion. As a practical matter, discretionary contingencies should not be placed in an agreement regardless of whether earnest money is paid because the existence of such would likely create an unenforceable agreement, even in light of case law suggesting the contrary.[56]

§ 1.2.1.3   Recital of Consideration Eliminates Mutuality Requirement

As stated above, if no mutuality is present, the agreement must be supported by some other form of consideration.[57] Typically, parties use the payment of money (such as an earnest money deposit) to replace and eliminate the need for mutuality of promises.[58] However, a recital of consideration in the agreement may be sufficient to support an enforceable

48   *Swinks v. O'Hara*, 98 Ga.App. 542, 106 S.E.2d 186 (1958).

49   *Krogh v. PARGAR, LLC*, 227 Ga.App. 35, 625 S.E.2d 435 (2005).

50   *Johnson v. Unified Residential Dev. Co., Inc.*,285 Ga.App. 852, 648 S.E.2d 163 (2007).

51   *Hayes v. Alexander*, 264 Ga.App. 815, 592 S.E.2d 465 (2003).

52   *Grier v. Brogdon*, 234 Ga.App. 79, 505 S.E.2d 512 (1998).

53   *Brack v. Brownlee*, 246 Ga. 818, 273 S.E.2d 390 (1980).

54   *Brack v. Brownlee*, 246 Ga. 818, 273 S.E.2d 390 (1980).

55   *Johnson v. Unified Residential Dev. Co., Inc.*, 285 Ga. App. 852, 648 S.E.2d 163 (2007).

56   *Johnson v. Unified Residential Dev. Co., Inc.*, 285 Ga. App. 852, 648 S.E.2d 163 (2007). The court held that the existence of a discretionary contingency placed in an agreement for the buyer's protection would not render the agreement unenforceable if the agreement was supported by payment of earnest money. However, this seems contrary to well-established principles in Georgia and it is likely that this principle of law is just dicta. Since this case has never been followed and the practice of the industry is to the contrary, it is believed by the authors of this book that this decision would be reversed if it was ever challenged.

57   *Brack v. Brownlee*, 246 Ga. 818, 273 S.E.2d 390 (1980).

58   *Brack v. Brownlee*, 246 Ga. 818, 273 S.E.2d 390 (1980).

agreement in certain circumstances. Generally, a consideration recital will support an option contained in an agreement[59] and a sealed contract,[60] even if the stated consideration has not been paid.[61]

The payment of the consideration recited for an option is not necessary because the recital gives rise to an implied promise to pay which can be enforced by the other party.[62] Typically, this type of consideration recital is seen in an agreement giving a party an option to terminate during a specified Due Diligence Period. For example, let's say that a buyer contracts to purchase the seller's property subject to a Due Diligence Period. During the Due Diligence Period, the buyer may terminate the agreement for any reason, effectively turning the purchase and sale agreement into an option contract. To create this option, the agreement contains the following consideration recital: "For and in consideration of the additional payment of Ten Dollars ($10) by the Buyer to Seller, the receipt and sufficiency of which is hereby acknowledged, Seller does hereby grant Buyer the option of terminating the Agreement, for any reason, for a 30 day period from the Binding Agreement Date." In this instance, even if the ten dollars is never paid, the agreement is still enforceable because the obligation for payment is enforceable by the party to whom the consideration is presumably paid.[63]

A sealed contract may also be supported only by a consideration recital.[64] In Georgia, sealed contracts are considered to have been entered into with more solemnity, and consequently of higher dignity, than ordinary, simple contracts.[65] In other words, contracts under seal are considered to be more formal than standard written, signed contracts.[66] For this reason, sealed contracts are presumed to have sufficient consideration.[67] Sealed contracts typically include bonds and property deeds.[68] Real estate contracts may also be sealed.[69] To create a sealed agreement, there must be both a recital in the body of the instrument for an intention to use a seal and the affixing of the seal or scroll after the signature.[70]

Although consideration in a contract under seal is presumed, a party may still assert a claim that a contract is non-binding for failure of consideration.[71] However, such a claim is unlikely to prevail because any nominal consideration recited in a sealed contract will be considered sufficient as a matter of law.[72] As such, so long as the document meets the requirements to constitute a sealed contract, the contract will not be unenforceable for failure of consideration even if no consideration is actually paid.[73]

---

59   *Jones v. Smith, 206 Ga*, 162, 56 S.E.2d 462 (1949).

60   *Jolles v. Wittenberg*, 148 Ga.App. 805, 253 S.E.2d 203 (1979).

61   *Thomas Mote Trucking, Inc. v. PCL Constructors, Inc.*, 246 Ga.App. 306, 540 S.E.2d 261 (2000). The court held that even if it is shown that the recited consideration was not paid, it does not void a contract, and the recital of consideration merely gives rise to an implied promise to pay, which can be enforced by the other party; see also O.C.G.A. § 13-3-40(a).

62   *Thomas Mote Trucking, Inc. v. PCL Constructors, Inc.*, 246 Ga.App. 306, 540 S.E.2d 261 (2000).

63   *Jones v. Smith*, 206 Ga, 162, 56 S.E.2d 462 (1949). The court held that the option in the agreement in this case, reciting a consideration of one dollar, the receipt of which was acknowledged, cannot be held to be invalid for lack of consideration, although the sum may not have been actually paid.

64   *Jolles v. Wittenberg*, 148 Ga.App. 805, 253 S.E.2d 203 (1979). The court held that consideration is essential to a contract and without such, a contract will be unenforceable. Consideration is presumed, however, in contracts under seal. In these types of contracts, recital of consideration, even if the consideration has not been paid, will be sufficient to support the agreement.

65   O.C.G.A. § 13-1-4.

66   2 Ga. Proc. Considerations in Initiating Suit § 2:26.

67   *Jolles v. Wittenberg*, 148 Ga.App. 805, 253 S.E.2d 203 (1979).

68   2 Ga. Proc. Considerations in Initiating Suit § 2:26.

69   *Warthen v. Moore*, 258 Ga. 198, 366 S.E.2d 666 (1988).

70   *McCalla v. Stuckey*, 233 Ga.App. 397, 504 S.E.2d 269 (1998).

71   *Jolles v. Wittenberg*, 148 Ga.App. 805, 253 S.E.2d 203 (1979).

72   *Jolles v. Wittenberg*, 148 Ga.App. 805, 253 S.E.2d 203 (1979).

73   *Milde v. Harrison*, 162 Ga.App. 809, 293 S.E.2d 56 (1982).

§ 1.3   COUNTEROFFERS

The acceptance of an offer must be unconditional and identical in order to create a binding agreement between the parties.[74] A counteroffer occurs if one party makes an offer and the other party either changes the terms of the offer or creates a condition for her acceptance.[75] Changing merely one term in the original offer will constitute a counteroffer.

Some parties describe their counteroffers as conditional acceptances in an effort to avoid appearing to reject the offer outright. However, such a conditional acceptance is still a counteroffer if it contains terms different from what was contained in the original offer. When a party makes a counteroffer, intentionally or not, the counteroffer operates to reject the offer and terminates the party's power of acceptance of the original offer.[76] The fact that a person did not intend to make a counteroffer is irrelevant.[77] In some cases, a party will reject a counteroffer only to then realize that she may have been too hasty. In an effort to try to resurrect the counteroffer, the buyer will try to withdraw her rejection. However, once an offer or counteroffer has been rejected or countered, the offer or counteroffer is revoked and cannot be revived. Buyers and sellers should appreciate that every time they reject or counter an offer, the offer goes away with no guarantee that the other party will ever make another offer. This is the case even if the party rejecting the offer or making the counteroffer then makes a new offer that is identical to the one they rejected. If buyers and sellers fully realized the potential finality of their rejections, some of them might think more carefully about countering over minor inconsequential issues.

A counteroffer will not necessarily end negotiations. When a counteroffer has been made, the original offeror becomes the offeree and the offeree becomes the new offeror. In a sense, the negotiations start over and the new offeree must accept the all the terms and conditions of the counteroffer to create a binding agreement.[78]

Generally, the offeror may withdraw her counteroffer up until the point of acceptance.[79] For example, the seller offers to sell her property to the buyer for $100,000. The buyer makes a counteroffer to purchase the property at $99,000 with the seller paying an additional $5,000 towards the closing costs. Before the seller accepts the buyer's counteroffer, the buyer rescinds the counteroffer and terminates negotiations. Since the seller had not yet given her acceptance, the buyer may properly rescind the counteroffer without incurring liability.

The acceptance of a counteroffer must be in writing to create a binding agreement since under what is known as the Statute of Frauds, an agreement for the sale of land or property must be in writing in order to be binding upon the parties.[80]

§ 1.3.1   Counteroffers And The GAR Contract

The GAR Counteroffer form[81] provides a convenient method for either the buyer or seller to counter an offer from the other. The GAR Counteroffer references the original offer to purchase real property made by one of the parties in a purchase and sale agreement ("Offer"). The Counteroffer form goes on to state that the provisions of the Counteroffer control over any conflicting or inconsistent provisions set forth in that original Offer, and supersedes all previous counteroffers. The terms of the original offer set forth in the purchase and sale agreement are incorporated into the

---

74   O.C.G.A. § 13-3-2.

75   *Morrison v. Trust Co. Bank*, 229 Ga.App. 145, 493 S.E.2d 566 (1997).

76   *Duval & Co. v. Malcom*, 233 Ga. 784, 214 S.E.2d 356 (1975); *Lamb v. Decatur Fed. Sav. & Loan Ass'n.*, 201 Ga.App. 583, 411 S.E.2d 527 (1991).

77   *Morrison v. Trust Co. Bank*, 229 Ga.App. 145, 493 S.E.2d 566 (1997).

78   O.C.G.A. § 13-3-2.

79   O.C.G.A. § 13-3-2.

80   O.C.G.A. § 13-5-30.

81   GAR Form F22.

Counteroffer form by reference and are accepted, subject to whatever changes modifications deletions and additions are set forth in the Counteroffer form. The parties also acknowledge and agree that the Offer, as modified by the Counteroffer, reflects the entire agreement of the parties. Accordingly, in order to create a binding agreement, the original Offer must be signed by one of the parties and the Counteroffer form must be signed by both of the parties.

The Counteroffer form then states that all terms and conditions of the original offer are agreed to and accepted by the parties with the express exception of "the following." The party making the counteroffer then spells out in the counteroffer the changes she is seeking to make to the original Offer. Regardless of the number of counteroffers made in a transaction, every counteroffer is modifying the first written offer made in the transaction. As such, each counteroffer made on the GAR form must state everything that is different from the original offer.

So, for example, let's assume that an Offer set forth in a Purchase and Sale Agreement is signed only by the buyer and states a purchase price of $210,000. The seller signs and delivers a counteroffer changing only the purchase price to $215,000. If the buyer signs the counteroffer and returns it to the seller, a binding contract will be created at a sales price of $215,000, regardless of whether or not both parties signed the original Offer set forth in the Purchase and Sale Agreement. This is because the GAR Counteroffer form specifically states that having both parties sign the counteroffer and deliver it to the other party will create a binding agreement between the parties. Thus, the original offer does not need to be signed by both parties. However, the GAR Counteroffer form also provides that if requested to do so, the parties will to sign a conformed or "clean" copy of the Purchase and Sale Agreement (or any exhibits included as part of that Agreement) incorporating therein the terms of the counteroffer.

Again, each and every counteroffer using the GAR Counteroffer form should reflect all terms and conditions that are different from the original Offer. This is because the GAR Counteroffer form does not incorporate the terms of any prior counteroffers into the current counteroffer, and in fact specifically states that "no prior representation, inducement or agreement … not contained in the Offer, as modified by this Counteroffer, shall be binding upon the parties." This includes any previous Counteroffers. The following examples illustrate this point.

The buyer's initial offer states a purchase price of $150,000, with a closing date of June 1. The seller does not accept this offer, but rather transmits a GAR Counteroffer form showing a purchase price of $160,000, and a closing date of May 15. The buyer then makes a counteroffer on a GAR Counteroffer form, stating a purchase price of $155,000 with no reference whatsoever to a closing date. If the seller accepts this counteroffer, the terms of the contract will be a purchase price of $155,000 and a June 1 closing date. This is because the accepted counteroffer never modified the original closing date, even though a previous counteroffer had changed the date. The simple rule of thumb is that the original Offer and the last accepted counteroffer should constitute the entire agreement of the parties with no consideration given to intervening counteroffers which were not accepted by all parties.

A question that sometimes arises with the use of the GAR Counteroffer form is whether exhibits referenced in the Counteroffer should also be attached to the Counteroffer and initialed by the parties. If the exhibit is not a part of the original Offer, it should always be attached as an exhibit to the counteroffer and initialed by the party making the counteroffer. If further counteroffers are made, the exhibits that are not a part of the original Offer should be brought forward and included in each subsequent counteroffer. However, if an exhibit is part of the original Offer, it does not need to be referenced in the Counteroffer form unless there are proposed changes to that exhibit. It should be noted that while exhibits in the original Offer do not need to be initialed if the buyer and seller both sign the GAR Counteroffer form, some lenders will nevertheless require that all documents which are part of the contract be signed or initialed as a condition of making the loan.

In some transactions involving the use of GAR Contracts, the parties make one or more counteroffers directly on the Purchase and Sale Agreement, and then make further counteroffers on the GAR Counteroffer form. For example, let's say that a buyer makes an initial offer and requests that the seller pay $10,000 in closing costs. The seller makes a counteroffer directly on the GAR Purchase and Sale Agreement by striking the reference to the payment of $10,000 in the offer and signing and dating the revision. The parties then make further counteroffers on the GAR Counteroffer form, none of which reference whether or not the seller is going to be paying $10,000 in closing costs. The likely intent of the seller in this situation is not to pay the $10,000 in closing costs. However, the GAR Counteroffer form provides that the initial Offer and the accepted counteroffer constitute the entire agreement of the parties. Since the first Offer provided that the seller was to pay $10,000 in closing costs and the accepted counteroffer did not alter this request, a good argument can be made that the seller must pay the $10,000 in closing costs (even though this was not likely her intent).

The best way to avoid this problem is to be consistent in the method of making counteroffers. For example, if the parties make their initial counteroffers on the GAR Contract, subsequent counteroffers should similarly be made on the GAR Contract. The same approach is equally applicable if counteroffers are first made using a GAR Counteroffer form – all subsequent counteroffers should also use a GAR Counteroffer form.

§ 1.3.2   Counteroffers Not Using The GAR Contract

Some buyers and sellers will make counteroffers on the face of the contract itself. So, for example, a seller may cross out the purchase price that is being offered for the property and counter with a higher price. In this example, all such proposed changes to the original offer should be initialed by the seller and the date and time it is initialed by the seller should be written below the initials. To avoid any confusion regarding the seller's intent to make a counteroffer, the seller in transmitting the counteroffer to the buyer may also want to send a written note saying something like the following:

> *"Attached please find a counteroffer to your offer. I have modified the terms of your offer by striking through the unacceptable terms and replacing them with terms that are acceptable to me. I then initialed each such change and time-dated my initials. Please signify your acceptance of my counteroffer by initialing each such change, time-dating your initials and returning a copy of the same to me."*

The GAR Contract now has all of the blanks to be filled in on the contract on the first page of the contract. Moreover, the first page of the GAR Contract now has an initial block on the bottom of the first page. Some real estate licensees have asked whether they can make a counteroffer by merely substituting a new first page to the contract. My recommendation is to avoid this practice and to continue to use the GAR Counteroffer form since this form has become the industry standard for making counteroffers. However, if a party chooses to make a counteroffer by substituting a revised first page of the GAR Contract my recommendation is to initial the new first page (which, at the time the counteroffer is made, should only have the initials of one party on it) and send it to the other party with a note that says something like the following:

> *Enclosed please find a counteroffer to your offer. I have substituted a new first page of the contract which reflects different terms than those set forth in your offer. If the terms in this counteroffer are acceptable to you, please so signify by signing your initials in the initial block on the first page and timely return a coy to me. I have not made any other changes to your offer other than what is set forth on the first page of the contract.*

By doing this, the party is clearly stating her intention to make a counteroffer and as such should avoid any question or dispute regarding her intentions.

§ 1.4   CREATING AN ENFORCEABLE REAL ESTATE CONTRACT

§ 1.4.1   Real Estate Contract Must Be In Writing

Georgia law requires that any contract for the sale of real estate or any interest in real estate must be in writing and signed by the person against whom the contract is being enforced or someone authorized by him.[82] This is based on English common law known as the "Statute of Frauds" which requires certain types of contracts to be in writing to prevent fraud and abuse. The law is codified in Georgia at O.C.G.A. § 13-5-30. The written contract must also express all of the essential terms of the agreement.[83] These requirements invalidate most verbal agreements for the purchase and sale of real property. At a minimum the written contract should identify the buyer and seller, describe the property, state the price to be paid for the property, and how that price is to be paid.[84]

Georgia statutory law provides several exceptions to the requirement that a contract for the purchase and sale of real property be in writing. Real estate contracts may be held to be enforceable, even though not written, when:

(a) a contract has been fully performed;

(b) one party performs her part of the contract and that performance is accepted by the other party in accordance with the contract; or

(c) there is partial performance by one party that would amount to fraud by the party refusing to comply if the court did not give effect to the contract.[85]

§ 1.4.2   Enforceability Of Verbal Real Estate Contracts

Verbal contracts are referred to as "parol contracts". Even when a parol contract does not fit one of the exceptions noted above (and therefore would still normally be required to be in writing), Georgia law allows courts to order specific performance of such a contract in the following circumstances:[86]

(a) if both parties admit that there is a verbal contract and agree as to its essential terms;

(b) if one party has performed the contract to such an extent that the party could not be restored to her previous position if the contract is not enforced; or

(c) if (i) the seller has accepted either full payment or (ii) partial payment accompanied by the buyer taking possession, or (iii) the buyer has taken possession and made valuable improvements to the property.[87]

One of the exceptions to the statute of frauds is when there has been a partial performance of the contract such that it would be a fraud if the court did not compel performance by the other party (see Section 1.3.1(c) above).[88] O.C.G.A. § 23-2-131 sheds some light on what will be considered sufficient partial performance to justify a decree of specific performance. Specifically, the law provides that there must be: (1) full payment accepted by the vendor or (2) partial payment accompanied by possession; or (3) possession alone with valuable improvements to the property.

---

82   O.C.G.A. § 13-5-30(4); *Fraser v. Jarrett*, 153 Ga. 441, 112 S.E. 487 (1922).

83   *Engram v. Engram*, 265 Ga. 804, 463 S.E.2d 12 (1995); *Smith v. Cox*, 247 Ga. 563, 277 S.E.2d 512 (1981); *Stonecypher v. Georgia Power Co.*, 183 Ga. 498, 189 S.E. 13 (1936).

84   *Powell v. Adderholdt*, 230 Ga. 211, 196 S.E.2d 420 (1973); *Pierce v. Rush*, 210 Ga. 718, 82 S.E.2d 649 (1954); *A.S. Reeves & Co., Inc. v. McMickle*, 270 Ga.App. 132, 605 S.E.2d 857 (2004).

85   O.C.G.A. § 13-5-31.

86   O.C.G.A. § 23-2-131.

87   *Masters v. Redwine*, 279 Ga. 432, 615 S.E.2d 118 (2005); *Stephens v. Trotter*, 213 Ga.App. 596, 445 S.E. 2d 359 (1994); *Braddy v. Boynton*, 271 Ga. 55, S.E. 2d 411 (1999)

88   *Edwards v. Sewell*, 289 Ga.App. 128, 656 S.E.2d 246 (2008).

The Georgia Court of Appeals addressed the question of when specific performance of an oral contract may be appropriate in the case of *Edwards v. Sewell*.[89] In that case, Mr. Sewell, Sr. and his sister, Joan Ledbetter, inherited property consisting of four apartments. One of the apartments was rented to Mr. Edwards for a number of years. Mr. Edwards inquired about buying the property. Mr. Sewell and Ms. Ledbetter were willing to sell, and Mr. Edwards signed two documents to consummate the deal. One was a "Fixed Rate Note" payable to OJS Properties providing for payment of $40,000 principal at a fixed rate of interest, with specific monthly payments over a period of 12 years. The second document was a "Notice of Right to Cancel" which gave Edwards the right to cancel the transaction under certain circumstances by notifying OJS Properties. Unfortunately, OJS Properties did not own the property. The documents also did not reference the real property that Mr. Edwards was allegedly buying, and they were not signed by the sellers. Mr. Edwards made all of the payments to OJS Properties for the full 12 years, remained in possession of the property, and made several improvements to the property at a cost of over $35,000.

OJS Properties was incorporated by Ledbetter and Sewell, Sr. for the purpose of holding title to this and other properties, but title to the subject property was never transferred to OJS Properties. Title remained in Ledbetter and Sewell, Sr. Ms. Ledbetter handled all the books and finances of OJS Properties, accepted all of Mr. Edwards' payments, and although Mr. Sewell was aware that payments were being made to OJS Properties, she never requested that she refuse to accept payments to OJS.

After all payments had been made, Ms. Ledbetter executed a quitclaim deed transferring her one-half interest in the property to Mr. Edwards. By that time, however, Mr. Sewell, Sr. had died. The administrator of his estate had transferred his one-half interest in the property to his heirs, who refused to honor the alleged oral contract with Mr. Edwards. Mr. Edwards then filed a lawsuit seeking an order of specific performance.

Sewell's heirs relied, of course, on the statute of frauds and claimed there was no written enforceable contract. However, as noted, Mr. Edwards paid the full purchase price for the property, resided on the property for more than 12 years, and made significant improvements to the property. Based on this, the Georgia Court of Appeals found that refusal to honor the oral contract would be a fraud against the buyer. As such, the court ordered the property to be transferred to Mr. Edwards.

In another case, the plaintiff and the defendant were co-owners of a certain property.[90] One co-owner moved out and allegedly entered into an oral agreement with the other co-owner that she could have the property if she made all the payments for it. Although the co-owner who moved out disputed the existence of any oral agreement, the co-owner who stayed was able to prove that she paid off the mortgage, made improvements to the property, and remained in possession of the property after the alleged oral agreement. The co-owner who moved out did not make any mortgage payments, which was consistent with the alleged oral agreement. The court held that based on these facts there were grounds to support a claim for specific performance seeking to have one co-owner convey the property to the other.

On the issue of proof, the party trying to enforce the oral agreement must prove that their actions were done according to the oral agreement. In addition, the party must show that there was an agreement on the essential terms of the contract. For example, in one case two partners entered into an oral partnership agreement to purchase, renovate, and sell properties.[91] One partner's role was to purchase the properties, while the other partner was to supervise the renovation in return for 50 percent of the profits upon the sale of the properties. The court held that the partnership agreement was unenforceable because the parties did not agree on several essential terms of the contract, including the duration of the agreement, the manner of selecting homes for renovation, the time period during which renovations were to be completed, or the compensation for renovations that were unprofitable.

---

89   *Edwards v. Sewell*, 289 Ga.App. 128, 656 S.E.2d 246 (2008).

90   *Vaughn v. Stoenner*, 276 Ga. 660, 581 S.E.2d 543 (2003).

91   *Razavi v. Shackelford*, 260 Ga.App. 603, 580 S.E.2d 253, (2003).

§ 1.4.3   Initialing Changes To Contract

Any changes in the terms of the contract must also be in writing and agreed to by all of the parties.[92] For this reason, parties should be careful when making changes directly on a written contract. Parties sometimes alter the terms of the contract by striking over terms, stating new terms, and initialing the changes on the contract. In such cases, it is good practice for the parties to initial and time-date any such alterations to reflect the parties' assent to the changes. In this way a judge interpreting the contract can more easily follow the order in which offers and counteroffers were made by the parties to the contract. If the contract does not clearly reflect that all of the parties agreed to the changes, the changes may not be binding against a party who did not initial them. In one case where multiple counteroffers were exchanged between the parties, the court held that it was not clear whether there was indeed a meeting of the minds. The multiple documents signed and/or initialed by the parties were confusing, and the question of whether a valid contract was formed was left to a jury to decide.[93]

§ 1.4.4   Initialing Every Page Of A Contract

Real estate professionals frequently ask if it is a good idea to have their customers and clients initial every page of a contract. There are pluses and minuses to this approach.

On the plus side, when a party initials every page of a contract, it is an acknowledgement that she has seen every page of the document. This makes it harder for an unscrupulous individual to perpetrate a fraud upon a party by substituting a page in a contract that the other party has not seen. Of course, this risk is minimized if the party keeps a complete copy of all documents which she has signed.

On the negative side, if a party inadvertently fails to initial each and every page, a question can arise whether the page was seen by the parties even though it was. Absent a showing of fraud, a contract signed by the parties would likely be upheld even if a page or section that was intended to be initialed was not, so long as the contract complies with the Statute of Frauds.[94] Nevertheless, the absence of the initials would raise a question of fact as to why the mistake took place and whether it reflects a failure of the parties to reach a meeting of the minds.

§ 1.4.5   Substituting Pages In A Contract

In an effort to simplify the process of amending a contract, the parties or their real estate brokers will sometimes simply substitute a new page or pages rather than prepare a formal amendment to the contract. This should never be done unless both parties have signed and preferably time-dated the portion of the contract that is being changed. Otherwise, there is no written evidence that the change is acceptable to all parties. Moreover, if a real estate licensee removes and replaces a page that has not been signed by all parties, the licensee is at risk of being sanctioned by the Georgia Real Estate Commission for being a party to the falsification of a real estate contract.[95]

§ 1.4.6   Effect Of Writing "Clean" Or Conformed Contract After Agreement Reached

When the initial offer is made on a purchase and sale agreement, it is common for subsequent counteroffers to be made on a separate counteroffer form. As a result, the final contract is on more than one document. Some lenders in this situation, particularly in short sale transactions, will insist that the parties sign one "clean" or conformed copy of the purchase and sale agreement reflecting all of the terms agreed to by the parties. In other cases, counteroffers are made

---

92   *Sanders v. Vaughn*, 223 Ga. 274, 154 S.E.2d 616 (1967); *Re/Max Specialists, Inc. v. Kosakai*, 202 Ga.App. 871, 415 S.E.2d 698 (1992).

93   *Re/Max Specialists, Inc. v. Kosakai*, 202 Ga.App. 871, 415 S.E.2d 698 (1992); *Target Properties, Inc. v. Gilbert*, 192 Ga.App. 161, 384 S.E.2d 188 (1989), cert. denied.

94   O.C.G.A. § 13-5-30; *Johnson v. Sackett*, 256 Ga. 552, 353 S.E.2d 326 (1986).

95   O.C.G.A. § 43-40-25(b)(25).

directly on the Purchase and Sale Agreement itself. Once the parties reach a binding agreement, a "clean" or conformed contact is often prepared for ease of reference as to the final agreement of the parties.

The purpose of the conformed contract is to merely create a legible version of the original agreement. Therefore, the conformed contract should not change any provision in or the substance of the final negotiated contract. Since a conformed contract is a "clean" version of the original contract, the date on the conformed contract should be the same date as on the original contract even though it is signed at a later date. If one party refuses to sign the conformed contract, the parties would still have a binding agreement so long as the original contract was signed by the parties and delivered back to the party making the last offer. GAR Counteroffer Form F22 specifically requires all parties to sign a conformed copy of the contract. As such, a party failing to do so would be in breach of contract.

What happens if the conformed contract is different from the original contract? Technically, this is an amendment to the contract rather than a conformed copy of the contract. However, most contracts, including the GAR Contract, include language that the contract is the entire agreement of the parties and supersedes all previous agreements of the parties. While the last contract signed by all the parties normally takes precedence over an earlier contract, this may not always be the case and the courts will review the circumstances of each case to ascertain the intention of the parties. The best way to prevent this problem is to state in the conformed contract that it is intended to be a conformed copy only and, in the event of conflict between the conformed contract and original contract, the original contract will take precedence. An example of this type of special stipulation is set forth below.

Special Stipulation 03: Original Agreement Takes Precedence Over "Clean" or Conformed Copy

This Agreement is intended to be a conformed or "clean" copy of the existing contractual agreement between the parties. In the event of any discrepancy, conflict or difference between the original Agreement and this conformed copy, it is the express intent of the parties that the original Agreement shall control.

If this special stipulation is included in the conformed copy of the contract, it should be initialed and time-dated by all parties since it is a change to the original contract. Of course, there are times when changes and amendments are agreed upon by the parties and intended to be included in a conformed copy of the contract. In such an instance the conformed copy should control over the original copy. An example of this type of provision is set forth below.

Special Stipulation 04: Conformed Agreement Takes Precedence Over Original Contract

This conformed or "clean" copy of this Agreement contains amended or modified provisions not included in the original Agreement. It is therefore the express intention of the parties that this conformed Agreement shall amend, take precedence over and supersede the original Agreement entered into between the parties.

Our recommendation is to have the conformed contract only reflect the final agreement of the parties and for a separate amendment to be executed to reflect changes to that final agreement.

§ 1.4.7 Dealing With Multiple Offers

There are some properties that, either because of their location or price, generate multiple purchase offers. What is the best strategy for dealing with multiple offers?

For the listing broker, the first step is to timely present all offers to the seller.[96] The seller should then decide how best to respond to the multiple offers because there are business risks involved with every possible response with multiple offers regardless of the strategy the seller decides to employ in responding to them. For example, notifying all of the potential buyers that multiple offers have been received on a property may cause each of them to withdraw their offers to avoid getting into a bidding contest with the other potential buyers of the property. As a result, a multiple offer situation can in some situations turn into a no offer situation. Similarly, if the seller counters one of the offers, the other parties who made offers may move on to other properties if there is too long a delay in hearing from the seller.

If the response to multiple offers causes all potential buyers to terminate negotiations, it is obviously much better from the prospective of mitigating the broker's legal risks, if the seller decided on the response. From the seller's perspective, the two most common strategies for dealing with multiple offers are to (1) notify all potential offers that there are multiple offers and to invite each potential buyer to submit their highest and best offer by a specific date and time, or (2) negotiate with the buyer whose offer appears to be the most attractive while trying to keep the other interested prospective buyers in reserve.

If the seller decides to negotiate with just one of the interested buyers, many sellers will let this chosen prospective buyer know that other offers remain outstanding. In this way, the seller can negotiate from a position of strength, state in a counteroffer the terms that are acceptable to the seller and then give the buyer a short period of time to either accept or reject the offer. If the buyer does not accept the offer within the specified time frame, the seller may then still have time to negotiate with the other buyers who made offers.

Some listing agents have expressed uncertainty as to whether they owe an affirmative disclosure obligation to all offerors and their brokers when multiple offers have been made. The answer to this question is "no." Of course, if a buyer specifically asks whether multiple offers have been received, a real estate licensee is at risk of violating license law[97] if she falsely answers this question. However, a simple response of "I am not at liberty to discuss that" allows the licensee to answer the question without being untruthful.

§ 1.4.7.1 Call For Final And Best Offers

As discussed above, one strategy that a seller may pursue when multiple offers are made is to contact all of the prospective buyers and give them all an opportunity to make their final and best offer by a particular date and time. Since the seller is requesting to receive offers rather than making an offer, there is no risk of creating an enforceable contract without the seller accepting one of the new offers that is made. Calling for offers and calling for best and final offers is particularly common in the sale of commercial real estate after it has been on the market for a sufficient period of time for prospective buyers to become familiar with the property.

---

96 O.C.G.A. § 44-3-25(b)(19). Providing that a real estate licensee may be sanctioned for "failing to deliver within a reasonable time a completed copy of any purchase agreement or offer to buy or sell real estate to the purchaser and to the seller."

97 O.C.G.A. § 44-3-25(b)(21). Providing that real estate licensees may be sanctioned for "making any substantial misrepresentations."

A sample notice calling for final and best offers is set forth below.

> **Sample Notice: Call For Final and Best Offers When Multiple Offers Have Been Received**
>
> *Re:*   *Property located at the following address:*
>
> _____
>
> _____ *("Property")*
>
> *This is to notify you that multiple offers have been made to purchase the above referenced Property. Seller wants to give each interested, prospective buyer the opportunity to make his or her highest and best offer to purchase the Property. All offers should be submitted on a purchase and sale agreement that when signed by the seller and returned to the offeror will create a binding agreement.*
>
> *Therefore, this notice is to serve as a formal call for all final and best offers to be submitted to the undersigned listing agent (at the FAX number, email address, or office address of the listing agent listed below.) by _____ o'clock ___m on the _____ day of _____, 20___.*
>
> *In making your final and best offer, please be aware that all things being equal, the offers in which the following issue(s) have been addressed by the prospective buyer will be at an advantage over those that do not:*
>
> _____
>
> _____
>
> _____
>
> *Listing Agent Contact Information:*
>
> _____
>
> _____

In looking at the Call For Final and Best Offer form above, it should be noted that there is a blank space where the seller can identify special issues of concern to her or her in considering final and best offers. For example, the seller may fill in things like the following in that space:

1. *Seller needs to close no later than _____, 20_____. Therefore, offers with a quick closing date included in them will be considered more favorably than offers with a delayed closing; or*

2. *Having the financial ability to get the transaction closed is of utmost concern to the seller. Therefore, offers which demonstrate that the buyer has the financial strength and ability to get the transaction closed will be considered more favorably than those that do not.*

While it is not uncommon to request highest and best offers in a multiple offer situation, the psychology of how to make that request is something that should be given careful consideration. Some buyers and their brokers are suspicious when they are told that multiple offers have been made and may not believe that the seller or listing broker is telling the truth. Buyers and their brokers may view the call for final and best offers as a ploy to simply get a higher sales price for the property. Taking the time to explain the circumstances of the multiple offer situation to each prospective buyer or their broker usually helps convince the prospective buyers that the transaction is a genuine multiple offer situation.

§ 1.4.7.2   Making Counteroffers To Multiple Buyers

Another approach is to make the same counteroffer to all of the buyers who made an offer but restrict the terms under which it can be accepted. This approach is generally not recommended because of the potential for conflicts over who first accepted a counteroffer made to multiple buyers. However, the following is an example of such a special stipulation.

> **Special Stipulation 05:   Counteroffer to Multiple Buyers**
>
> *This Counteroffer is being made to more than one prospective buyer. Notwithstanding any other provision to the contrary contained elsewhere in this Counteroffer or the original Offer, acceptance of this Counteroffer will not create an enforceable contract between the Buyer and Seller herein unless it is accepted and delivered back to the Seller prior to the following: (1) the time limit of the Counteroffer, and (2) prior to the acceptance and delivery back of this Counteroffer by any of the other prospective buyers to whom this Counteroffer has been made.*
>
> *This Counteroffer may only be accepted in writing delivered to Seller's Listing Broker by facsimile at the following number: _____. Notice to Seller's Listing Broker shall be deemed to be notice to Seller. Listing Broker shall maintain a list of the prospective buyers and determine which prospective buyer, if any, is the first to accept and deliver back this Counteroffer. All parties agree that the determination of the Listing Broker in this regard shall be final and binding upon Seller and all prospective buyers. Upon the receipt by the Listing Broker of the first acceptance of this Counteroffer meeting the terms and conditions specified above, the Listing Broker shall promptly notify said buyer that that a Binding Agreement has been formed between said Buyer and Seller. The Listing Broker shall also promptly notify the other prospective buyers that a binding agreement has been formed with another party.*

§ 1.4.7.3   Multiple Offers From A Buyer's Perspective

If the buyer is concerned that multiple offers will be made on a property, there are several things the buyer can do to maximize the likelihood of being the high bidder. The first is for the buyer to immediately put her best offer on the table in hopes of outbidding the competition. Normally such an offer is coupled with a short period of time to accept or reject the offer to help ensure that the seller does not shop the offer to other prospective buyers.

Buyers facing the risk of multiple offers will also normally want to make their offers as easy for the seller to accept as possible. So, for example, buyers who are in a position to buy "as-is" for all cash with few or no contingencies have a significant advantage in a multiple offer situation than buyers without such options. While some buyers retreat in the face of multiple offers, the level of interest of some buyers will increase as a result of other buyers also wanting the property. Buyers in such situations are encouraged to go slow to ensure that they do not get buyer's remorse once the bidding war is over.

§ 1.4.8   Signing A Contract In Multiple Counterparts

There are some circumstances where a buyer and seller cannot easily sign the same document to create a binding contract. As a general rule, it is permissible to have two duplicate original contracts,[98] (*i.e.*, photocopies or emailed, faxed or scanned copies of the same document), where the buyer signs one and the seller signs the other, and each signed contract is then delivered to the other party.

---

98   O.C.G.A. § 24-10-1001(3).

Many contracts specifically provide that the agreement may be executed in multiple counterparts. This type of provision is often referred to as a "counterparts provision."

A counterparts provision is particularly useful when the parties in the transaction are in different locations and are unable to sign the same physical signature page of the purchase and sale agreement. However, in this age of emails and facsimile transmissions, the likelihood that the buyer and seller not being able to sign the same contract is increasingly small. Nonetheless, including a provision that reminds buyers and sellers that they have the option to sign counterparts of the same contract can be helpful.

The absence of a counterparts provision will not invalidate an agreement that has been signed in this fashion because the statute of frauds generally allows an agreement to be executed in more than one writing.[99] Therefore, if two parties execute and exchange two different, but identical agreements, a court should find that the two agreements are treated as one final and enforceable agreement.[100] Although there is no law in Georgia requiring this provision to be included in an agreement, it is typically placed in the boilerplate section of any purchase and sale agreement out of an abundance of caution.

The GAR Contract provides that it may be signed in such multiple counterparts.[101] If using a non GAR form, the following special stipulation will allow for multiple counterparts.

> **Special Stipulation 06: Signing Contract in Multiple Counterparts**
>
> *This Agreement may be executed in any number of counterparts, each of which shall be deemed to be an original. The execution and delivery of the agreement in multiple counterparts shall create a binding agreement between the parties to the same extent as if the parties executed and delivered one (1) complete and original copy of the Agreement.*

§ 1.4.9 Signing Different Documents

As discussed in § 1.4.8 (Signing A Contract In Multiple Counterparts), it is permissible for parties to each sign a separate copy of the same document. Georgia courts have also made it clear that the offer and acceptance of a contract do not have to be on the same document and that one document does not have to expressly incorporate the others. The law states that binding contracts may consist of several writings provided there is no conflict between the various parts.[102] Thus, if one party signs one form and the other party signs another form, but the terms contained in each form are the same, the parties have entered a binding and enforceable contract. So, for example, if the buyer makes an offer using a GAR Contract and the seller responds in writing to the buyer on the back of a napkin with "I accept your offer of January 3, 2012 to purchase 123 Smith Street, Atlanta 30355" the parties have a binding contract.

§ 1.4.10 Contracts Consisting Of Multiple Documents

The Statute of Frauds does not require the purchase and sale agreement to be contained in one singular signed writing.[103] Georgia law allows multiple documents to be considered together as a single contract as long as all the necessary terms are contained in signed contemporaneous writings.[104] The Supreme Court of Georgia has rejected the notion that the whole agreement must be contained in one writing signed by all of the parties.[105] The court specifically ruled that "as long as all

---

99 *Baker v. Jellibeans, Inc.*, 252 Ga.458, 314 S.E.2d 874 (1984).

100 *Harris v. Baker*, 287 Ga.App. 814, 652 S.E.2d 867 (2007).

101 GAR Form F20.

102 *Cassville-White Assoc., Ltd. v. Bartow Assoc., Inc.*, 150 Ga.App. 561, 258 S.E.2d 175 (1979).

103 *Baker v. Jellibeans, Inc.*, 252 Ga.458, 314 S.E.2d 874 (1984).

104 *Board of Regents of the University System of Georgia v. Tyson*, 261 Ga. 368, 404 S.E.2d 557 (1991); *Baker v. Jellibeans, Inc.*, 252 Ga. 458, 314 S.E.2d 874 (1984). Contemporaneous does not necessarily mean perfect or absolute coincidence in point of time. Georgia courts have interpreted one thing to be contemporaneous with a given transaction when it is so related in point of time as reasonably to be said to be a part of such transaction. *Manry v. Hendricks*, 66 Ga.App. 442, 18 S.E.2d 97 (1941).

105 *Baker v. Jellibeans*, 252 Ga. 458, 314 S.E.2d 874 (1984).

the necessary terms are contained in signed contemporaneous writings, the statutory requirements and purpose of the Statute of Frauds have been met, whether or not the writings are cross-referenced."[106]

In another case, the Georgia Court of Appeals explained, "[w]hen an agreement consists of multiple documents that are executed at the same time and during the course of a single transaction, those documents should be read together."[107] In *Baker v. Jellibeans, Inc.*, a buyer offered to purchase two of the seller's properties. The seller was only willing to sell one of his properties to the buyer. However, the seller agreed to give the buyer a lease on the second property with an option to purchase at a later date. The buyer and seller entered into two separate contracts, one for each property. The first agreement was a purchase and sale agreement in which the buyer purchased the first property for $100,000. The second agreement was a lease for the second property giving the buyer an option to purchase no later than August of that year. Both agreements were entered into at the same time by the parties. When August came, the buyer tried to exercise his option to purchase the second property, but the seller refused and tried to sell the second property to someone else. In this case, the court allowed both agreements to be considered as one purchase and sale agreement and ordered the seller to sell the second property to the buyer. Since the writings were contemporaneous with each other and signed by both parties, the court found that the whole transaction was for the sale of both properties.[108]

In using the GAR Counteroffer form, the parties are agreeing to all of the provisions in the original offer subject to what the parties have additionally agreed to in the Counteroffer form. This is an example of a single contract consisting of multiple documents.

§ 1.4.11 Reconciling Conflicts Within A Contract, Or Between The Contract, Special Stipulations And Exhibits

§ 1.4.11.1 Hierarchy Of Provisions In GAR Contract

The GAR Contracts create a hierarchy for resolving disputes between provisions in the contract, special stipulations and exhibits. Exhibits control over the main body of the contract in the event of a conflict between the contract and an exhibit. Special stipulations control over exhibits and any other portion of the contract in the event of a conflict between the special stipulation and either the contract or an exhibit. Since special stipulations are at the top of the hierarchy, persons using the GAR forms should always include provisions as special stipulations if they are at all concerned about whether they will take precedence over inconsistent provisions contained anywhere else in the contract.

§ 1.4.11.2 Ambiguities In Contracts

Absent rules internal to the contract to reconcile conflicts, our courts apply their own rules for the interpretation of conflicts or ambiguities in contracts. First, the court has to decide if the contract is ambiguous, that is, capable of more than one interpretation. If the contract is clear, the court will enforce the contract as written. It is not at liberty to re-write the contract under the pretext of "interpreting" it.[109] In other words, unless there is some ambiguity, the court will scrutinize the four corners of the contract to determine what the parties intended and will not permit the parties to testify as to their intentions.

It should also be noted that verbal or parol evidence will not be admissible to *add* missing elements of a contract that are required to be in writing or to *change* the terms of a contract.[110] For example, if an adequate legal description of property being sold is not included in the written contract, outside evidence will not be admitted. To do so would go beyond

---

106 *Id.*, at 460.

107 *Sofran Peachtree City LLC v. Peachtree City Holdings L.L.C.*, 250 Ga.App. 46, 550 S.E. 2d 249 (2001).

108 *Baker v. Jellibeans, Inc.*, 252 Ga. 458, 314 S.E.2d 874 (1984).

109 *Brigadier Industries, Corp. v. Pippin*, 148 Ga.App. 145, 251 S.E.2d 114 (1978).

110 O.C.G.A. § 13-2-2(1).

resolving an ambiguity to re-writing an unenforceable contract to make it enforceable.[111] In another case, the court ruled that parol evidence was not admissible to supply the interest rate at which purchasers would obtain their financing, since the interest rate is an essential element in the contract, rather than merely an ambiguity.[112]

If the contract is ambiguous, the court will try to ascertain the intention of the parties and interpret the contract accordingly.[113] The court will look at the whole contract when deciding on the meaning of any part of the contract,[114] and will favor an interpretation of the contract that will uphold the contract as a whole.[115] There are several rules the court will apply when it must interpret contracts, including:

(a) typewritten or handwritten provisions normally prevail over printed provisions;[116]

(b) specific provisions will prevail over conflicting but more general provisions on the same issue;[117]

(c) words will be given their plain and literal meaning, unless they are "words of art," in which case the court will use their technical meaning in the sense required by the contract;[118] and

(d) the court will try to find a reasonable interpretation which will uphold the contract in its entirety, rather than uphold only one part while invalidating another;[119]

If after the application of all the rules described above the contract is still ambiguous, then the ambiguity must be resolved by jury.[120] Generally, any ambiguity in the contract is construed by a court against the drafting party.[121] The theory behind this approach is that all other things being equal, the party who created the confusion in the contract should suffer the consequences of having done so.[122] However, when an agreement contains an explicit provision providing that any ambiguity will not be construed against the drafting party, a court will honor the intent of the parties.[123] Most purchase and sale agreements, including the GAR Contract,[124] include such a provision.

If a non GAR Contract is being used, a stipulation similar to the following special stipulation can be used when trying to avoid the court interpreting ambiguities against the drafter of the contract.

---

111 *Sawyer v. Roberts*, 208 Ga.App. 870, 432 S.E.2d 610 (1993).

112 *Bulloch South, Inc. v. Gosai*, 250 Ga.App. 170, 550 S.E.2d 750 (2001).

113 *Grier v. Brogdon*, 234 Ga.App. 79, 505 S.E. 2d 512 (1999); *Ali v. Aarabi*, 264 Ga.App. 64, 589 S.E.2d 827 (2003).

114 *Alimenta (USA), Inc. v. Oil Seed South, L.L.C.*, 276 Ga.App. 62, 622 S.E.2d 363 (2005).

115 O.C.G.A. § 13-2-2(4).

116 *Hibbard v. P.G.A., Inc.*, 251 Ga.App. 68, 553 S.E.2d 371 (2001).

117 *Tower Projects, LLC v. Marquis Tower, Inc.*, 267 Ga.App. 164, 598 S.E.2d 883 (2004).

118 O.C.G.A. § 13-2-2(2).

119 O.C.G.A. § 13-2-2(4).

120 *Auldridge v. Rivers*, 263 Ga.App. 396, 587 S.E.2d 870 (2003).

121 *Auldridge v. Rivers*, 263 Ga.App. 396, 587 S.E.2d 870 (2003).

122 Restatement (Second) of Contracts § 206. "Where one party chooses the terms of a contract, he is likely to provide more carefully for the protection of his own interests than for those of the other party. He is also more likely than the other party to have reason to know of uncertainties of meaning. Indeed, he may leave meaning deliberately obscure, intending to decide at a later date what meaning to assert. In cases of doubt, therefore, so long as other factors are not decisive, there is substantial reason for preferring the meaning of the other party."

123 *Auldridge v. Rivers*, 263 Ga.App. 396, 587 S.E.2d 870 (2003).

124 GAR Form F20.

Special Stipulation 07:   Contract Shall Not Be Interpreted More or Less Favorably Against the Drafter

The parties have cooperated and participated in the drafting and preparation of this Agreement. Accordingly, the rule that any ambiguity in a document shall be construed against the party drafting the document shall not apply to this Agreement. The parties hereto shall jointly be deemed to be the drafters of this Agreement and agree that this Agreement shall not be construed or interpreted in favor of or against any party by virtue of the identity of any alleged drafter.

§ 1.4.11.3   Missing Terms

Sometimes a real estate agreement will be missing an important term. The question in such a situation is whether the court will declare the contract unenforceable. The answer depends on what provision is missing and how easy it is for the court to supply the missing term. For example, assume that an agreement does not state a specific closing date. In these types of situations, the court will generally provide that the closing date will occur within a reasonable time frame.[125] Generally, courts will not declare a contract unenforceable on the grounds of uncertainty if it is possible to determine the reasonable intention of the parties.[126] The absence of a required time or date will not destroy an agreement since a "reasonable time" can be read into the agreement by the court.[127]

However, in some cases, if the agreement is missing an essential term, the court will find such agreement too indefinite and vague to be enforceable.[128] An example is if an agreement does not state the type of deed that will be used to transfer the property. Unless there is some evidence as to what the parties intended, courts are usually reluctant to supply terms where there is no evidence to guide the court.[129]

Similarly, in a contract for the purchase of real estate, if the agreement is missing the interest rate in a buyer's financing contingency, the court will not enforce the agreement.[130] The absence of the required interest rate is considered an essential term in the agreement, rather than an ambiguity. As stated above, the court will not add essential terms to the parties' agreement.[131] Furthermore, the court will not enforce an agreement when it is left to determine the intention of the parties.[132] As stated above, parol (or verbal) evidence may be admissible to explain any ambiguity in the contract.[133] The reasoning behind allowing this evidence to be introduced is that the ambiguity creates two different meanings or an uncertainty of meaning, and thus the court has an ability to interpret the agreement.[134] However, the Statute of Frauds requires every essential element of a sale for real property to be in writing; therefore, a court will generally not allow parol (or verbal) evidence to supply a missing essential element for an agreement required to be in writing.[135]

---

125 *Read v. GHDC, Inc.*, 254 Ga. 706, 334 S.E.2d 165 (1984).

126 *Bulloch South, Inc. v. Gosai*, 250 Ga.App. 170, 550 S.E.2d 750 (2001).

127 *Read v. GHDC, Inc.*, 254 Ga. 706, 334 S.E.2d 165 (1984).

128 *Bulloch South, Inc. v. Gosai*, 250 Ga.App. 170, 550 S.E.2d 750 (2001).

129 *Kitchen v. Insurameria Corp.*, 296 Ga.App. 739, 675 S.E.2d 598 (2009).

130 *Bulloch South, Inc. v. Gosai*, 250 Ga.App. 170, 550 S.E.2d 750 (2001).

131 *Bulloch South, Inc. v. Gosai*, 250 Ga.App. 170, 550 S.E.2d 750 (2001).

132 *Kitchen v. Insurameria Corp.*, 296 Ga.App. 739, 675 S.E.2d 598 (2009).

133 *Bulloch South, Inc. v. Gosai*, 250 Ga.App. 170, 550 S.E.2d 750 (2001).

134 *Bulloch South, Inc. v. Gosai*, 250 Ga.App. 170, 550 S.E.2d 750 (2001).

135 *Bulloch South, Inc. v. Gosai*, 250 Ga.App. 170, 550 S.E.2d 750 (2001).

§ 1.4.12   Resolving Conflicts

One question that frequently arises in interpreting contracts is whether one provision completely overrules another provision or merely supplements it. The answer usually depends on whether the provisions are compatible or incompatible.

Courts are required to attempt to interpret the provisions of a contract in a manner that will harmonize the provisions and not render one of them void.[136] A conflict in a contract exists where two provisions of the contract are in opposition to one another and cannot be harmonized with one another. An example of incompatible provisions is where the contract provides that the purchase price is $400,000 in one section of the main body of the contract and $415,000 in another section of the main body of the contract. The two provisions are clearly in conflict with one another. However, if the higher price is contained in the special stipulations section of the contract and the contract is a GAR Contract, the higher price would control because the GAR Contract provides that special stipulations override the main body of the GAR Contract. If provisions appear at first glance to be conflicting with one another, the court will normally look for a reasonable interpretation that will make them compatible with one another.[137] For an example, a contract includes a Due Diligence Period that extends beyond the closing date. In this case, the Georgia Court of Appeals extended the closing date until after the Due Diligence Period had ended on the theory that this must have been what the parties intended.[138] While obtaining financing is normally done during the Due Diligence Period, inclusion of a longer financing contingency period evidences an obvious intent for the financing contingency period to extend beyond the Due Diligence Period.

Similarly, what if a GAR Contract includes both a 10 day Due Diligence Period and a 30 day Property Sold With Right to Request Repair of Defects Exhibit? While the nature of these two provisions might initially appear to conflict with one another, most courts would likely interpret the two provisions as being compatible and hold that the buyer has an absolute right to terminate the contract during the Due Diligence Period, and then only a limited right to terminate if the seller does not agree to repair or replace defects identified by a home inspector.

The GAR Contract includes its own rules to help avoid conflicts. Specifically, an exhibit controls over the main body of the contract and a special stipulation controls over both.

§ 1.4.13   Effect Of Mistakes In The Contract

The types of mistakes made in real estate contracts can be grouped into two categories: unilateral mistakes and mutual mistakes. The legal consequences of a mistake will depend on its type. A unilateral mistake is a mistake made by only one party to a contract. For example, a buyer contracts to purchase a property on the mistaken belief that she will be able to install a septic system on the property when it is not possible due to its lot size. Subject to limited exceptions, a party is not able to cancel or reform a contract based on a unilateral mistake.

A mutual mistake is a mistake that is shared and relied on by both parties to a contract. A court will often revise or nullify a contract based on a mutual mistake involving a material term in the contract. The legal effect of each type of mistake is discussed below.

---

136   *Guaranty Trust Life Ins. Co. v. Davis*, 149 Ga.App. 826, 256 S.E.2d 76 (1979).

137   *Guaranty Trust Life Ins. Co. v. Davis*, 149 Ga.App. 826, 256 S.E.2d 76 (1979).

138   *Yargus v. Smith*, 254 Ga.App. 338, 562 S.E.2d 371 (2002). The court held that when an unskillfully drafted contract in computing time to perform the duties of the parties must be construed to resolve any conflict in terms, it is the court's duty to discover and to give effect to the intent of the parties to the contract.

§ 1.4.13.1   Effect Of A Mutual Mistake

If both the buyer and the seller entered into a purchase and sale contract under a mistake, as to the subject matter of the contract, so that the contract does not express the true intention of the parties, the court may (1) reform the contract to correct the parties' mutual mistake[139] or (2) allow one or both of the parties to rescind the contract.[140]

In one case, a grandmother instructed her attorney to prepare a deed conveying property to her grandson.[141] When she signed the deed, the space for the property description was blank. The attorney added a description and made a mistake, describing an adjoining lot instead, and delivered the deed to her grandson. Neither the grandmother nor the grandson read the deed at any time. The grandson recorded the deed and built a mechanic shop on the property. After the grandmother was declared incompetent, her son was appointed her guardian and sought to eject the grandson. The Georgia Court of Appeals held that the grandson was entitled to reformation of the deed because any error in the deed was a mutual mistake of both parties.

In another case, both the seller and the buyer were unaware, at the time the contract was signed, that the wall and patio attached to the house were situated on an adjoining property instead of the property that was being sold.[142] The court held that since there was a mutual mistake, the buyer was entitled to sue for rescission of the sale contract and obtain a refund of the earnest money.

Not all contracts made under a mutual mistake can be rescinded. In a purchase and sale transaction, the buyer is still required to exercise due diligence to try to prevent a mistake from occurring. For example, the Georgia Court of Appeals refused to allow a contract to be rescinded even though there was mutual mistake as to the size of the property because the mistake could have been easily discovered had the buyer exercised due diligence.[143] The seller's sign had mistakenly listed the size of the property as 1.5 acres. However, a recorded plat identified the property as being 0.8 acres. The description of the property in the contract made specific reference to the plat and the contract was given to the buyer to read before its execution. The court found, that if the buyer had given the contract more than a cursory review, she could have discovered the discrepancy. The court stated the buyer could not seek rescission of the contract based on mutual mistake of fact if she failed to exercise due diligence to protect her self against the mistake.

Once a party discovers facts that would give them the right to rescind (*i.e.*, once they discover the mutual mistake), the party needs to act promptly to seek rescission of the agreement. While there is no bright line rule on how fast the party needs to act, the sooner the better. If parties are found to have waited too long, or to have done anything inconsistent with the repudiation of the contract, they are likely to be held to have waived the right to seek rescission.[144]

§ 1.4.13.2   Effect Of A Unilateral Mistake

A unilateral mistake, even if it pertains to a material term, will generally not support the reformation or rescission of the contract.[145] For example, if the buyer mistakenly believes that the property is 2.2 acres, or is in a particular school district, and there is no evidence that this mistaken belief was shared by the seller, the buyer will not likely be able to seek reformation or cancellation of the contract.

---

139   *W. P. Brown & Sons Lumber Co. v. Echols*, 200 Ga. 284, 36 S.E.2d 762, (1946); *Timeless Architectural Homes, Inc. v. Jones*, 270 Ga.App. 406, 606 S.E.2d 635 (2004).

140   O.C.G.A. § 13-5-4 (If the consideration upon which a contract is based was given as a result of a mutual mistake of fact or of law, the contract cannot be enforced); O.C.G.A. § 23-2-22 (an honest mistake of the law as to the effect of an instrument on the part of both contracting parties, when the mistake operates as a gross injustice to one and gives an unconscionable advantage to the other, may be relieved in equity).

141   *Curry v. Curry*, 267 Ga. 66, 473 S.E.2d 760 (1996).

142   *Lundin v. Hill*,105 Ga.App. 449, 125 S.E.2d 105, (1962).

143   *Simmons v. Pilkenton*, 230 Ga.App. 900, 497 S.E.2d 613 (1998).

144   *Ben Farmer Realty Company v. Woodard*, 212 Ga.App. 74, 441 S.E.2d 421 (1994).

145   O.C.G.A. § 23-2-27. (Mere ignorance of the law on the part of the party himself, where the facts are all known and there is no misplaced confidence and no artifice, deception, or fraudulent practice is used by the other party either to induce the mistake of law or to prevent its correction, shall not authorize the intervention of equity.)

There are limited exceptions to this rule. A unilaterally mistake may support a claim for rescission when there is fraud or inequitable conduct on the part of the other party.[146] In such cases, the person claiming the mistake bears the burden of proving that: (1) the mistake is of such consequence that enforcement would be unconscionable; (2) the mistake relates to the substance of the consideration; (3) the mistake occurred regardless of the exercise of ordinary care; and (4) permitting rescission will not harm the other party and the mistaken party has given prompt notification of the mistake and his intent to rescind.[147]

A good illustration of this point is that a seller's property is listed for $150,000. The buyer, intending to submit a full price, inadvertently transposes figures so the offer reflects a price of $510,000. The seller, realizing the buyer has obviously made a mistake, attempts to capitalize upon this and immediately accepts the offer. Under these circumstances (a typographical error which was recognized as such by the seller), the court will likely allow the buyer to rescind.[148]

§ 1.4.14 "Agreement To Agree" Generally Unenforceable

If a contract fails to establish an essential term, allows the parties to agree on that term at a future date and fails to include some mechanism for resolving the dispute if the parties cannot come to some agreement, the document amounts to a mere "agreement to agree" and is likely not a valid contract at all. For example, an agreement to transfer assets where "[d]ivision is to be by mutual agreement" was held to be unenforceable.[149] Likewise, an agreement where a loan officer assured a borrower that "something will be worked out" with respect to additional loans was held to be an unenforceable agreement to agree in the future. The court held that unless an agreement is reached as to all terms and conditions and nothing is left to future negotiations, an agreement to enter into a contract in the future is of no effect.[150]

Many builder contracts contain provisions that the buyer will make design selections for a new home after the contract has been entered into. These provisions are not viewed as agreements to agree because absent an agreement on design selections, the builder is normally authorized to unilaterally make choices from the builder's standard selections. As such, the contract provides a solution to the parties reaching an impasse in the event they cannot agree on an issue.

The same principle applies to option contracts. In one case, a landlord granted an option to a tenant to renew the lease where "[t]he rental rate for the renewal term shall be the fair market rental with fair market escalations. Fair market rental rate and fair market escalations being that rate and escalation found within comparable premises in comparable properties within the Northwest office submarket, taking into account any concessions being offered at that time."[151] The court held that the above provision was unenforceable because the provision did not define an objective method of ascertaining the fair market rental rate, comparable premises, comparable properties, nor the Northwest office submarket. The rent was an essential part of the contract upon which there must be a meeting of the minds and even though the negotiations showed a complete willingness or determination to agree in the future upon such term, there was no binding contract. The court stated that unless all the terms and conditions are agreed on, and nothing is left to further negotiations, an agreement to reach an agreement in the future is of no effect.

In contrast, the court in another case upheld an option contract to purchase improved real property in five years for "the appraised value of the property at time of purchase based on an MAI Appraisal." The court found this agreement to be valid because the contract defined an objective method by which the value could be ascertained.[152]

---

146 *Caudell v. Toccoa Inn, Inc.*, 261 Ga.App. 209, 582 S.E.2d 180 (2003).

147 *First Baptist Church of Moultrie v. Barber Contracting Co.*, 189 Ga.App. 804, 377 S.E.2d 717 (1989).

148 *Id.*

149 *Kreimer v. Kreimer*, 274 Ga. 359, 552 S.E.2d 826 (2001).

150 *Bridges v. Reliance Trust Co.*, 205 Ga.App. 400, 422 S.E.2d 277 (1992).

151 *Insurance Industry Consultants, Inc. v. Essex Inv., Inc.*, 249 Ga.App. 837, 549 S.E.2d 788 (2001).

152 *Miller v. McCullough*, 236 Ga. 666, 224 S.E.2d 916 (1976).

In addition to the price of the contract, the obligations of the parties must be clearly set out for a contract to be enforceable. If any essential term is left open for future consideration, there is no binding contract. For example, a buyer intending to build a service station-convenience store on the subject property sued the seller to obtain specific performance of a provision in the sales contract. The provision required the seller to execute a covenant restricting seller's development of adjoining property the seller still owned, such that the buyer would have the only service station-convenience store on the property.[153] When various conditions were not met by the closing date, including the signing of the restrictive covenants, the parties executed an addendum providing that the restrictive covenant provision would survive the closing and would not be subject to merger. The seller argued that the agreement to later sign restrictive covenants that had not yet been drafted was a mere "agreement to agree" and was therefore unenforceable. The Court of Appeals disagreed, stating that there were no terms that were lacking or otherwise indefinite (the contract spelling out the terms required in the restrictive covenant), and held that such an obligation was not a mere "agreement to agree" but an enforceable contract.

§ 1.4.15   Facsimile Copies And Electronic Signatures

Georgia law provides that any contract for sale of real estate, or any interest in or concerning real estate, must be in writing and signed by the party against whom it is being enforced.[154] Does a real estate sales contract which contains only faxed or electronic signatures satisfy this requirement? The answer is yes.

Under the Georgia Uniform Electronic Transactions Act, when the law requires something to be in writing, an electronic record such as a faxed signature or electronic signature, satisfies that legal requirement.[155] The Act only applies to transactions that the parties have agreed to conduct by electronic means.[156] Therefore, a faxed or electronic signature may not satisfy the statutory writing requirements for certain types of agreements[157] if the agreement does not provide for these types of signatures. Whether the parties have agreed to conduct a transaction by electronic means is determined from the context and surrounding circumstances, including the parties' conduct.[158]

Once the parties have agreed to execute the agreement by electronic means, a faxed or electronic signature is just as valid as a physical signature.[159] A contract will not unenforceable merely because the signature is electronic rather than ink.[160] Therefore, faxed or electronic signatures may be used to execute real estate documents including, but not limited to, purchase and sale agreements, options, leases, deeds, easements, and deeds to secure debt.[161] Most purchase and sale agreements, including the GAR Contract,[162] are now including provisions that allow parties to conduct a transaction by electronic means. More specifically, the GAR Contract allows the use of electronic means to execute an agreement and explicitly provides that faxed and electronic signatures are treated as original signatures. In addition, a party may request a conformed copy of the agreement with physical signatures if the party so desires. To allow the agreement to be executed by electronic means, the following special stipulation can be used.

Special Stipulation 08:   Facsimile or Electronic Signatures

For all purposes herein, an electronic or facsimile signature shall be deemed the same as an original signature; provided, however, that all parties agree to promptly re-execute a

---

153 *Neely Development Corp. v. Service First Investments, Inc.*, 261 Ga.App. 253, 582 S.E.2d 200 (2003).

154 O.C.G.A. § 13-5-30.

155 O.C.G.A. § 10-12-4(a) and (c).

156 O.C.G.A. § 10-12-5(b).

157 O.C.G.A. § 13-5-30.

158 O.C.G.A. § 10-12-5(b).

159 O.C.G.A. § 10-12-7(a).

160 O.C.G.A. § 10-12-7(a).

161 Ga. Real Estate Sales Contracts § 3:16 (6th ed.); O.C.G.A. § 10-12-7(c).

162 GAR Form F20.

conformed copy of this Agreement with original signatures if requested to do so by the buyer's mortgage lender or the other party.

Popular software systems, such as DocuSign®, allow parties to easily sign an agreement electronically. These types of software programs offer a secure online system in which the parties can sign the agreement using the curser on their computer. DocuSign®, for example, allows a party to upload an agreement and enter the name and email address of the party whose signature is required. An email is then sent to the signing party instructing the party to sign the agreement online through the DocuSign® website. Once the agreement is signed, the party confirms her signature and may save the signed document to her records.

§ 1.5   WHEN AN OFFER CAN BE WITHDRAWN

A binding contract is formed only when the parties mutually agree to all the terms of the contract and the accepted offer is delivered back to the offeror. Until then, each party may withdraw her offer or counteroffer.[163] The offeror may withdraw her offer even if the time limit has not expired.[164] For example, if a seller makes a counteroffer which is open for acceptance until 5:00 p.m. on May 1, but on April 29 the seller gets a better offer for her property, the seller may withdraw the counteroffer if the first buyer has not yet accepted it.

A party may also withdraw an offer before there has been actual delivery of an accepted offer back to the offeror. For instance, if a seller accepts a buyer's offer and the seller gives the executed agreement to her broker, the seller can withdraw her acceptance anytime before her broker delivers the acceptance to the buyer or the buyer's broker. Similarly, if the listing broker who is representing the seller calls the selling broker to inform her that the seller has accepted the buyer's offer in writing, the listing broker then tells the selling broker that she will drop off the signed offer the following morning at the selling broker's office. The selling broker calls the buyer to let her know the good news only to discover that the buyer has changed her mind about wanting to buy the property. If the buyer immediately withdraws the offer before the buyer receives delivery of the seller's acceptance, no contract should be formed.

A withdrawal of an offer should always be in writing and should clearly state the intentions of the party withdrawing the same. A sample notice to withdraw an offer is set forth below:

Notice To Withdraw Offer or Counteroffer

Re: Offer or Counteroffer made by: _____*[Buyer/Seller] to [purchase/sell] real property located at the following address:* _____

_____

_____ *("Property").*

Notice is hereby given by [Buyer/Seller] that the last [offer/counteroffer] [Buyer/Seller] made to [purchase/sell] the above-referenced Property is hereby withdrawn and revoked.

It is the intent of [Buyer/Seller] that no present [offer/counteroffer] shall remain open for acceptance and that no binding contract between the parties shall be capable of being created.

_____

[Buyer/Seller]

Date: _____

Time: _____

---

163   *Harry Norman & Assoc., Inc. v. Bryan*, 158 Ga.App. 751, 282 S.E.2d 208 (1981); *Vlass v. Walker*, 86 Ga.App. 742, 72 S.E.2d 464 (1952).

164   *Camp Realty Co., Inc. v. Jennings*, 77 Ga.App. 149, 47 S.E.2d 917 (1948); *Blanchard v. Sachs*, 74 Ga.App. 727, 41 S.E.2d 326 (1947).

§ 1.5.1 Option Contracts To Prohibit Withdrawal Of Offer

In order to avoid having an offer withdrawn before the offer expires, the parties may enter into an option contract in which, in exchange for some consideration paid by the buyer to the seller, the seller absolutely commits to sell the property to the buyer for a defined period of time.[165] By agreeing to the option, the seller may not withdraw the offer during the stated time period and the buyer may or may not proceed with the purchase of the property. The following special stipulation may be used to provide for such an option.

> **Special Stipulation 09:   Seller Not to Withdraw Offer for a Stipulated Period**
>
> *Notwithstanding any other provision in this Agreement to the contrary, in consideration of the payment by Buyer to Seller of $_____ which shall be nonrefundable and immediately paid to Seller, this Agreement shall operate as an irrevocable option to purchase the Property on terms and conditions set forth in the Agreement for a period of _____ days until _____, 20___ ("Option Period"). During the Option Period, Buyer may convert this option to purchase into a purchase and sale agreement upon written notice to Seller, in which case the consideration for the granting of the option shall not be applied to the purchase price at closing. If the Buyer does not exercise this option in writing during the Option Period, all rights hereunder shall lapse.*

§ 1.6   EXPLANATION OF TERMS RELATED TO TIME

Many real estate contracts contain time periods within which something has to be done. The most significant time period is the period within which the offer must be accepted. In most real estate transactions, time is of the essence.

When the transaction requires something to be done within a specific period, it is critical to state in no uncertain terms exactly when that period ends. This section explains the definitions of words commonly used in reference to time.

§ 1.6.1   Definitions Of Dates And Times

A **day** means an entire 24 hour day beginning immediately after midnight and ending 24 hours later. For example, if the buyer signs the contract at 3:00 p.m. on January 1 and delivers it back to the seller at 4:00 p.m. on January 1, the binding agreement date would be January 1. If the seller has 7 days from the binding agreement date to terminate the contract, the time does not end at 4:00 p.m. on January 8. Instead, it would run through the end of the day on January 8.[166]

A **week** means 7 days. means 7 days. Therefore, a week from Monday is 7 days from Monday, therefore ending on Monday, not Sunday. However, "**calendar week**" means the specific period of time starting on Sunday and ending on Saturday.

A **month** means calendar month, regardless of whether the month consist of 28, 29, 30 or 31 days. Therefore, if a tenant wishes to renew the lease by giving one month's notice, this normally means the number of calendar days in the month in which the notice is given.

A **year** usually means January 1 to December 31, inclusive.[167] However, if a contract states that offer to open for acceptance for a year commencing, say January 1, 2012, the term ends on January 1, 2013.

---

165 *Mattox v. West*, 194 Ga. 310, 21 S.E.2d 428 (1942).

166 O.C.G.A. §1-3-1(d)(3) provides that when any time (except hours) is prescribed for the exercise of any privilege or the discharge of any duty, the first day shall not be counted but the last day shall be counted.

167 O.C.G.A. § 1-3-3.

§ 1.6.2 Definitions Of Other Words Commonly Used For Time

There are words, such as "from," "within," "until," "continue through," that are used when referring to time. Georgia statutes state that "until" a certain date includes that day when used in a statute.[168] The Supreme Court of Georgia held that the same meaning should be used in contracts unless the parties to the contract clearly intended otherwise.[169] Therefore, the word "until" as used in a purchase and sale agreement includes the stated date. Of course, the drafter of the contract can use the phrase "until and through" as a way to be clear that the date the agreement ends includes that date.

If there is any ambiguity, the courts will look to the intention of the parties to decide when the time expires. An example is in the case where the tenants had a lease commencing December 1990 and continued "until December 1993" and were given an option to purchase the property for the same period.[170] The court held that since the lease terminated in November the option would be ineffective beyond the term of the lease. Therefore, the time period of "until December 1993" for the tenants to exercise the option terminated at midnight on the last day of November. To avoid any ambiguity, it is best to specify an exact time and date in which something has to be done.

If a contract states that the seller has 30 days "from" the offer date to accept the offer, it likely means 30 days exclusive of the offer date.[171] In other words, the day after the offer date is the first day from that day. If the offer day is Tuesday, January 12th, seven (7) days from that date would be Tuesday, January 19th. If the contract states that the seller has to accept the contract "by" July 1, the time period includes July 1. The meaning of "within" is "no later than." Therefore, if the seller has to accept the offer within 15 days from January 1, the seller has 15 complete days from midnight of January 1; this expires at midnight January 16. When the contract states the tenant has 15 days prior to the expiration of the lease to exercise the option to purchase, the notice to exercise the option has to be given 15 whole days before sale of the property, excluding the date of lease expiration.

§ 1.6.3 Meaning Of Banking Day, Business Day, And Legal Holiday

A banking day is defined under Georgia law as "the part of a day on which a bank is open to the public for carrying on substantially all of its banking functions."[172] Therefore, in theory, what constitutes a banking day could vary from one financial institution to another. However, for most banks Saturdays, Sundays and holidays are not banking days because even if certain branches are open, the bank is not open to the public for carrying on substantially all of its banking functions. There are a few banks, however, where Saturdays are banking days because they carry on substantially all of their banking functions. An officer of the bank should be able to answer questions regarding which days the bank treats as official banking days.

By comparison, the term "business day" means "Monday through Friday, excluding any legal holiday."[173] "Legal holiday" means "all days which have been designated as of January 1, 1984, as public and legal holidays by the federal government and all other days designated and proclaimed by the Governor [of Georgia] as public and legal holidays or as days of fasting and prayer or other religious observance."[174] Since legal holidays other than those recognized by the federal government must be declared by the Governor, holidays declared only by a county or city (*i.e.*, Good Friday) are still generally considered business days.[175]

---

168 O.C.G.A. § 1-3-3.

169 *Brooks v. Hicks.*, 230 Ga. 500, S.E.2d 711 (1973).

170 *Burns v. Reves*, 217 Ga.App. 316, 457 S.E.2d 178 (1995).

171 *Dobbs v. Conyers*, 36 Ga.App. 511, 137 S.E.298 (1927).

172 O.C.G.A. § 11-4-104(a)(3).

173 O.C.G.A. § 1-3-1(d)(3); *Georgia Receivables, Inc. v. Welch*, 242 Ga.App. 146, 529 S.E.2d 164 (2000).

174 O.C.G.A. § 1-4-1.

175 *In Re Estate of Dasher*, 259 Ga.App. 201, 576 S.E.2d 559 (2002).

§ 1.6.4   Meaning Of Banking Hours And Business Hours

There is little case law defining business hours. In the abstract this appears to be a reference to 9:00 a.m. to 5:00 p.m.[176] Presumably with reference to a specific business, the phrase means the normal operating hours for the referenced business. Similarly, banking hours presumably means the bank's normal hours of operation. However, banks are permitted by statute to fix the hour of 2:00 p.m. or later as a cutoff hour for the handling of money.[177] As a result, question could arise if a contract makes reference to banking hours. Due to the uncertainty in this area, the safest course of conduct is to state the actual time in the contract (*i.e.*, 3:30 p.m.) rather than referencing banking hours or business hours.

§ 1.6.5   Time Expiring On A Saturday, Sunday, Or Public Holiday

The general rule is that if the last day an event may occur falls on a Saturday, Sunday or public holiday,[178] then the last day will be extended to the next business day. For example, if a lease requires the tenant to give notice of extension by certified mail by a certain date, which happens to be a Sunday, it would be impossible to send a certified letter on Sunday. Therefore, the tenant can send the notice on Monday.[179] This is only the case if the performance cannot take place on a Saturday, Sunday or holiday.[180] Accepting an offer only requires notice to be delivered pursuant to the contract, which is possible on a Sunday or public holiday. Therefore, an offer which remains open for acceptance through Sunday would need to be accepted prior to the end of Sunday. On the other hand, if the closing date falls on a Sunday or public holiday, it will be postponed to the next business day when lenders can disburse funds and attorney firms are open.

§ 1.7   COMMON MISTAKES IN FILLING OUT PRE-PRINTED FORM REAL ESTATE CONTRACTS

There are certain mistakes that are made with some regularity by real estate licensees in filling out pre-printed form real estate contracts. One way to avoid mistakes is to compare the contract the licensee is filling out against a checklist of questions designed to avoid mistakes. A sample checklist of questions, designed to avoid mistakes in filling out contracts, is set forth below.

Questions to Ask to Avoid Making Common Mistakes in Filling Out Form Contracts.

> *1. Has the contract been signed by all buyers and all sellers?*
>
> *2. Are the names of parties spelled correctly?*
>
> *3. Is the address of the property correctly spelled and filled in?*
>
> *4. Have parties needing to sign in a representative capacity done so correctly?*
>
> *5. Have all places in a contract requiring the parties' initials been filled in?*
>
> *6. Have all of the other blanks in the contract been filled in, crossed out or marked not applicable?*
>
> *7. Does contract reflect the entire agreement of the parties?*

---

176 *Thornton v. National American Insurance Co.*, 269 Ga. 518, 499 S.E.2d 894 (1998).

177 O.C.G.A. § 11-4-108.

178 *See* § 1.6.3 (Meaning Of Banking Day, Business Day, And Legal Holiday) for the definition of legal holidays.

179 *Target Properties, Inc. v. Gilbert*, 192 Ga.App. 161, 384 S.E.2d 188 (1989) *cert. denied*. The contract in Target Properties also provided that notice could be hand-delivered; however, the address for notice was post office box, making hand-delivery impossible.

180 *Brooks v. Hicks*, 230 Ga. 500, 197 S.E.2d 711 (1973).

8. *Are all exhibits referenced in the contract attached?*

9. *Is the legal description of the property attached?*

10. *Is an address where a party can receive notice included?*

11. *Do the time deadlines in the purchase and sale agreement make sense? For example, is the closing date after the end of any financing contingency?*

12. *Has any earnest money referenced in the contract as having been paid been paid?*

13. *Is the Seller's Property Disclosure Statement attached? Is it up to date?*

14. *If required, is a lead-based paint exhibit attached to the contract?*

15. *Does the closing date falls on a weekend or holiday?*

16. *Are special stipulations written clearly enough to be understood by a stranger to the contract?*

17. *Is the time limit of the offer filled in and realistic?*

18. *If the purchase and sale agreement references that a survey is attached to the agreement, has it been attached?*

19. *Has the closing attorney been identified?*

20. *Are the names of the real estate licensees and their GREC license numbers correctly identified on the contract?*

21. *Has the licensee identified the correct facsimile number and/or email address for receiving notice on behalf of a client?*

22. *Have any amendments to the contract been signed by all buyers and all sellers?*

§ 1.7.1   Missing Time Deadlines In Real Estate Transactions

Time deadlines in real estate contracts are also sometimes missed because of a lack of attention to such deadlines. Creating a checklist of key dates in the real estate transaction is one way to avoid missing such deadlines. A sample timeline checklist is set forth below.

Timeline of Key Dates in a Real Estate Transaction.

   a. Offer Date:_____

   b. Date and Time Offer Expires: _____

   c. Binding Agreement Date: _____

   d. Date By Which Additional Earnest Money Must Be Paid: _____

   e. Date By Which Financing Must Be Applied For: _____

   f. Date That Due Diligence Period Ends: _____

   g. Date That Any Appraisal Contingency Ends: _____

   h. Date That Any Financing Contingency Ends: _____

   i. Other Key Date: _____

   j. Closing Date: _____

The **RED BOOK**

CHAPTER 2

TITLE

OVERVIEW

Would you like to buy the Brooklyn Bridge? You had better be sure the seller can deliver good title. Title is the means by which the owner of lands takes possession of them. This chapter discusses title, title insurance and a variety of title defects, easements and other encumbrances that can have an impact upon how one is permitted to use property in which they have an ownership interest.

§ 2.1 WHAT THE GAR CONTRACT PROVIDES

The GAR Contract requires the seller to convey good and marketable title (with certain exceptions that will be discussed below) to the property. The buyer has until closing to examine title and furnish the seller with a written statement of objections that affect the marketability of title. The seller must satisfy all valid title objections prior to closing or the buyer may terminate the contract by giving written notice to the seller.[181] In commercial property sales, the contract may dictate another time period, for instance, by the end of the due diligence period, by when purchaser must provide seller with title objections. The contract may also have negotiated terms specifying which title objections the seller must clear by closing and which the seller may, but is not required to, to clear by closing. If a survey of the property is attached to the contract and a new survey obtained by the buyer is materially different from the one attached to the contract, the buyer may terminate the contract by giving written notice to the seller.[182]

The GAR Contract for residential property requires the buyer to notify the seller of title defects prior to closing.[183] This means that the buyer has up to and excluding the date of closing to give the notice of termination. There is no requirement that notice must be given in reasonable time, which is the case with some contracts. This helps the buyer because the title examinations may not be completed until days before closing. If the seller fails to satisfy valid title objections prior to closing, the buyer may terminate the contract upon written notice to the seller, in which case the earnest money must be refunded to the buyer. Alternatively, the buyer or seller may unilaterally extend the closing date by seven days for the seller to satisfy valid title objections.[184]

In most commercial purchase and sale agreements, the buyer has a certain number of days to review the title to the property and raise title objections. Normally this is done substantially in advance of the closing date. Under the GAR Commercial Purchase and Sale Agreement,[185] the buyer has a specified timeframe within which to make title objections, which must be given to the seller in writing.[186] If the title objection is a lien or other monetary encumbrance, the seller can cure the objection be making payment on or before closing. The seller must cure all other title objections within the timeframe specified in the GAR contract. If the seller fails to do so, the buyer has the right to the exercise the following remedies within 5 days of the expiration of the seller's 'cure period': (1) rescind the contract and obtain a refund of the earnest money; (2) waive the objection without any reduction in the purchase price or (3) extend the closing date for up to 15 days for the seller to cure any title objection. If the buyer fails to act within the 5-day window, the buyer will be treated as having waived these rights.

The concept of "permitted title exceptions" is also common in most commercial real estate transactions. These are title exceptions which the buyer agrees to accept without objection. They are normally provided to the buyer prior to entering into a contract and are typically attached as an exhibit to the purchase and sale agreement.

---

181 GAR Form F20.

182 GAR Form F20.

183 GAR Form F20.

184 GAR Forms F20 and F133 may be used to extend the closing date.

185 GAR Form CF2.

186 GAR Form CF2.

Once the period of time to raise title objections has run, sellers in many commercial contracts will often warrant title against new objections arising between that date and the date of the closing. In other contracts, such as the GAR Commercial Purchase and Sale Agreement, the buyer has the right to re-examine title and notify the seller of any new title objections arising between the end of the title objection period and the date of closing.

If a GAR Contract is not used, parties should state clearly when the buyer is entitled to terminate the contract due to title defects. For example, in one case the contract provided that the buyers had "until" the closing date to examine title defects and "in the event the Purchaser concludes in its sole discretion that Seller's title is such that Seller will be unable to or will elect not to cure the defects herein in with accordance to the Agreement, Purchaser may so notify the Seller…" to terminate the contract.[187] The contract also contained a termination provision, which stated the purchaser might terminate "if any or more of the following conditions or states of fact exist at the time of Closing…" The buyers argued that their right to terminate existed for the period until closing, while the seller argued that the buyer only could exercise the right to terminate at closing. The court looked at the contract as a whole and held that the buyer's right to terminate refers to the time prior to the closing date.

§ 2.2 NOTICE REQUIREMENTS FOR TITLE DEFECTS

The GAR Purchase and Sale Agreement[188] requires that the buyer give written notice of title objections to the seller. The objections must affect the marketability of title, which should be specifically stated in the notice, so that the seller can verify their validity and have sufficient information in order to satisfy the objections. All notices shall be deemed to be given as of the date and time they are received. The GAR Contract sets out the requirements for sending notices and that these requirements shall be strictly construed.[189]

Parties are expected to comply strictly with the notice provisions in the contract. In one case, two corporate real estate entities represented by attorneys entered into a contract for the purchase of property.[190] The contract required the seller to convey marketable fee simple title in accordance with Georgia law and the Title Standards of the State Bar of Georgia.[191] The buyer was required to give the seller written notice of objections affecting the marketability of the title. Those objections were to be mailed by registered or certified mail to a specific partner in a law firm representing the seller. On the final day for examination of title, the buyer's attorney hand-delivered a letter to an associate of the law firm representing the seller regarding "difficulty with chain of title" to 70 acres of the total acreage of 3,613. The letter asked for an opinion of that associate as to the title issues and indicated that she would continue to contact other parties to resolve hers questions.

The buyer failed to appear at closing so the seller kept $45,000 in earnest money. The court concluded that the letter did not comply with the specific provisions of the contract. It was hand-delivered, not mailed, and was not addressed to the party specified in the contract. In addition, the letter did not qualify as a notice of defect nor was it an objection raising an issue of marketability of title that would defer a sale of this magnitude. The court noted that neither the word "objection" nor the phrase "marketability of title" was mentioned in the letter.

In another case, the contract provided that notice of termination must be sent to the sellers by hand or Federal Express to a specified address.[192] The buyers sent the notice of termination to only one of the sellers and to an address other than the one indicated in the contract. The buyers also sent the notice to the sellers' agent. The court held that the sellers could

---

187 *Thornton v. Kumar*, 240 Ga.App. 897 , 525 S.E.2d 735 (1999).

188 GAR Form F20.

189 GAR Form F20.

190 *Real Estate World, Inc. v. Southeastern Land Fund, Inc.*, 137 Ga.App. 771, 224 S.E.2d 747 (1976), *overruled on other grounds*.

191 *See* § 2.9 (Title Standards) below for separate discussion of title standards.

192 *Thornton v. Kumar*, 240 Ga.App. 897 , 525 S.E.2d 735 (1999).

retain the earnest money because the buyers failed to give proper notice. Since the contract did not contain any provision that the agent was authorized to receive notice, the notice to the agent was also invalid.

§ 2.3   SELLER HAS OBLIGATION TO CONVEY MARKETABLE TITLE

If the property has defective title, the seller has an obligation to provide clear title even when the buyer fails to give written notice of the title defect. The buyer, by giving written notice of a title defect, gets the right to declare the contract null and void based on the failure to satisfy the stated title objection.

For example, in one case, the closing on a contract to purchase property never occurred because the title examination revealed the existence of a deed to secure debt on the property creating an indebtedness greater than the purchase price.[193] The sellers argued that the buyer's failure to present a written statement of objection to title, as contemplated by the terms of the contract, excused their failure to consummate the sale. In that case, the court noted that it was undisputed that the sellers were unable to remove the encumbrance created by the deeds to secure debt, since their proceeds were insufficient to pay the full amount of the indebtedness and they were unwilling or unable to pay the difference. The court held that it would not have made any difference if the sellers had been given written notice of the existence of the encumbrance because they still would not have been able to convey clear and marketable title to the buyers.

In another case, the court similarly held that the seller was required to convey marketable title even though written notice of the title problems was given after the date of closing.[194] In that case, the contract provided for closing within 31 days but gave the sellers 90 days after written notice from the buyer to cure any title defects. The day before closing was to take place, the buyer's attorney informed the sellers that there were several title problems. The sellers insisted that the sale be closed the following day. The day after the closing was to have taken place, the buyer's attorney responded with a letter in which she detailed eight title problems, including outstanding deeds to secure debt and interest, unpaid taxes and a judgment lien. At the end of the 90 days, the sale was not closed and the buyer demanded a return of the earnest money. The sellers argued they were entitled to the money on the theory that the buyer failed to give timely notice of any alleged title defects.

The trial court concluded that because the sellers were not able to tender marketable title, as was required by the contract, the buyer was entitled to judgment as a matter of law. The appellate court noted that the contract, which did not state that time was of the essence and merely specified a closing date, did not obligate the buyer to tender notice of title objections prior to the time set for closing.

§ 2.4   DEFINITION OF GOOD AND MARKETABLE TITLE

Even where title is not mentioned in a contract, the law implies that the seller agrees to furnish "good and marketable title." Good title generally means one which is clear of defects and encumbrances. Good title has been defined as "not merely a title valid in fact, but a marketable title which can be again sold to a reasonable buyer or mortgaged to a person of reasonable prudence as security for the loan."[195]

Under the GAR Purchase and Sale Agreement, "good and marketable title" means title which a title insurance company, licensed to do business in Georgia will insure at its regular rates, subject only to standard exceptions. Moreover, the GAR Contract requires that:

> Seller will convey good and marketable title to said Property by general warranty
> deed, subject only to (1) zoning; (2) general utility, sewer, and drainage easements of

---

193   *Hill v. McGarity*, 179 Ga.App. 788, 347 S.E.2d 679 (1986), *cert. denied*.

194   *Pollard v. Martin*, 191 Ga.App. 681, 382 S.E.2d 720 (1989).

195   *Atlanta Title & Trust Co. v. Erikson*, 67 Ga.App. 891, 21 S.E.2d 548 (1942), *cert. denied*.

record as of the Binding Agreement Date and upon which the improvements do not encroach; (3) declarations of condominium and declaration of covenants, conditions and restrictions of record on the Binding Agreement Date; and (4) leases and other encumbrances specified in this Agreement.[196]

Under the GAR Commercial Purchase and Sale Agreement, the seller is obligated to convey good and marketable fee simple title to the property by limited warranty deed.[197] This means that the seller is warranting the property against defects in title arising during that owner's tenure of ownership. A discussion of the different types of deeds sellers can use to sell real property in Georgia is set forth in § 2.17.2 (Types of Deeds) of this book.

The definition of what constitutes "good and marketable title" is different in the GAR Commercial Purchase and Sale Agreement than in the GAR Purchase and Sale Agreement used in residential transactions. In the latter contract, good and marketable title is defined as title that a title insurance company will insure at its standard rates. In the GAR Commercial Purchase and Sale Agreement, good and marketable, fee simple title means such title:

(a) is classified as "marketable" under the Title Standards of the State Bar of Georgia and

(b) is acceptable to and insurable by a title insurance company doing business in Georgia at standard rates on an American Land Title Association Owner's Policy.

Because property is insurable at standard rates by a title insurance company, it does not always mean that the property is free from title defects. In some cases, a title insurance company which has issued a title policy on a property with a title defect will issue a policy to the new buyer of the property knowing that the company's risk is no greater than if ownership of the property did not change hands. Defining marketability in terms of the Title Standards of the State Bar of Georgia is a more objective and less economically-based measure of marketability. The Title Standards, developed by real estate lawyers in Georgia over the decades, are commonly accepted principles as to what constitutes good title and how to solve title problems.

§ 2.4.1 Marketable Title And Economic Marketability

Title marketability relates to defects affecting legally recognized rights of ownership, such as liens or other types of encumbrances. Economic marketability generally relates to physical conditions affecting the use of property. For example, location of property in a flood plain may affect the economic marketability of property, but it does not affect the marketability of title.[198]

Covenants applying to the use of property may affect the economic marketability rather than the title marketability of the property. Case law in Georgia defines marketable title as title that is not merely a title valid in fact, but a marketable title that can again be sold to a reasonable purchaser or mortgaged to a person of reasonable prudence as security for the loan of money.[199]

This standard was applied in a case in which a religious organization exercised an option to purchase certain property intending to use it as a church or a school.[200] One of the conditions of the option was that if the property were not zoned for church or school purposes, the option money would be refunded. The title search revealed a recorded survey containing a restriction prohibiting use of the property for schools or churches. The organization sought the return of its option money on the basis that the seller could not give good and marketable title to the property.

---

196 GAR Form F20.

197 GAR Form CF2.

198 *Chicago Title Ins. Co. v. Investguard, Ltd.*, 215 Ga.App. 121, 449 S.E.2d 681 (1994).

199 *Ardex, Ltd v. Brighton Homes*, 206 Ga.App. 606, 426 S.E.2d 200 (1992).

200 *Swinks v. O'Hara*, 98 Ga.App. 542, 106 S.E.2d 186 (1958). For a more comprehensive discussion on the impact of covenants on the use of property, *see* Chapter 20 (Condominiums, Homeowner Associations and Other Forms of Common Interest Communities) of this work.

The court concluded that while the property had covenants running with the land which prevented it from being used as a site for a church or school, this would not prevent the title to the property from being marketable, because it could not be said that a reasonable man would neither purchase nor loan money on the property because of these restrictions. However, if the religious organization had argued that its option money should be returned because the seller did not meet the conditions of the option agreement, the court's decision probably would have been different.

It should be noted that statutory provisions set forth in covenants for certain types of communities (*e.g.*, pursuant to the Georgia Condominium Act and Georgia Property Owners' Association Act) must be complied with by the seller in order to convey marketable title.

§ 2.4.2   Marketable Title And Insurable Title

The Official Code of Georgia Annotated defines title insurance as follows:

> [I]nsurance of owners of real property or others having an interest in such real property, or liens or encumbrances on such real property, against loss by encumbrance, defective titles, invalidity, adverse claim to title, or unmarketability of title by reason of encumbrance or defects not excepted in the insurance contract, which contract shall be written only upon evidence or opinion of title obtained and preserved by the insurer.[201]

Title insurance is issued after a thorough examination of title and an analysis of any claims or encumbrances. An insurer can make the business decision to insure title that is not marketable or even not to insure marketable title. Consequently, marketable title and insurable title are not synonymous, even though most buyers equate the two.

Although marketable title does not necessarily mean that a title insurance company will insure it, the parties can agree to define marketable title in such a fashion.[202] The GAR Contract recognizes this common requirement and defines good and marketable title as "title which a title insurance company licensed to do business in Georgia will insure at its regular rates, subject only to standard exceptions."[203] If the GAR Contract is not being used, the following special stipulation can be included.

Special Stipulation 10:   Good and Marketable Title Must Be Insurable

Notwithstanding any other provision in this Agreement to the contrary, in order for Seller to meet her obligation to convey good and marketable title to Buyer, title to the Property that is the subject matter of this Agreement must be insurable by a title insurance company licensed to do business in the State of Georgia at the title insurance company's regular rates and subject only to standard title exceptions.

§ 2.4.3   Agreement To Provide Title Acceptable To Buyer

Some purchasers may attempt to avoid the issue of marketable versus insurable title by having the contract provide that title must be acceptable to the buyer. Buyers should be careful with such language, however, for a contract that bases acceptance on the subjective decision of one party is known as an illusory contract and may be void for lack of mutuality. Although language providing that title must be acceptable to the buyer has the potential to render the contract void, rejection by the buyer may still be upheld. One court, for example, upheld a buyer's rejection of title because her attorney failed to approve title for reasons that were specified in the attorney's written report. Since there was nothing in the

---

201 O.C.G.A. § 33-7-8.

202 *Green v. Sams*, 209 Ga.App. 491, 433 S.E.2d 678 (1993), *cert. denied*.

203 GAR Form F20.

attorney's report to indicate that it was capriciously or fraudulently made, or that the buyer's rejection of title based on that report was capricious or fraudulent, the rejection of title by the buyer was valid.[204]

§ 2.4.4 Threats Of Litigation Affect Title Marketability Of Property

Potential litigation concerning title to property may render the property unmarketable. An example of such a situation is described in the following case. The property being sold was described in previous conveyances referencing marble monuments and iron pins. The iron pins had been subsequently removed and no one could recall the purpose of the marble monuments. The adjacent landowner disagreed with the seller on the location of the property lines and the buyer refused to close. In this case, the court did not require the buyer to purchase the property because "[t]he law will not compel a party to purchase a lawsuit or accept a conveyance which a reasonably prudent man would refuse."[205]

§ 2.4.5 Some Survey Defects Do Not Affect Title Marketability Of Property But May Affect Economic Marketability

When a property description refers to monuments actually erected as the boundaries of property and the distance between such monuments is also part of the property description, Georgia law holds that if there is a discrepancy between the distances stated and the actual distance between the monuments, the actual distances between the monuments will prevail. The Georgia Supreme Court has stated:

> Whenever in a conveyance the deed refers to monuments actually erected as the boundaries of the land, it is well settled that these monuments must prevail, whatever mistakes the deed may contain as to courses and distances.[206]

For example, if a property description states that the distance between monument 1 and monument 2 is 125 feet, but when measuring the actual distance between the monuments the distance is discovered to be only 120 feet, the seller of the property will be warranting title to only 120 feet, the actual distance between the monuments.

A monument is a permanent landmark, natural (trees or water bodies) or artificial (fences, walls, stakes, pins or roads), established for the purpose of indicating boundaries of property. In a case where the length of a call line did not meet the buyer's expectations, but the monuments cited were accurate, a court held that the buyer received good and marketable title to the property in question based on the monuments and that the error in the call lines was of no consequence.[207] However, the buyer also argued that the title insurance company insured more than the marketability of title. The buyer claimed that the title insurance covered the length of the property lines as set forth in the property description and not just the property as measured between the monuments and as shown on the survey. The title insurance policy in this case did not contain an exception for defects in the survey, but the court held nonetheless that such defects were not insured since "the policy is silent regarding defects in the survey and, simply put, it does not insure against such risks." This situation was distinguished from a case in which the title insurance policy affirmatively stated that the survey was insured, which required a different result.

In situations where a current survey dated within six months of the closing is prepared, title insurance policies will insure the property subject to only the specific exceptions disclosed on the survey. If a current survey is not obtained, the title policy will contain an exception for matters which would be disclosed by a comprehensive survey of the property. It is almost always in the buyer's best interest to obtain a survey, even if the buyer's lender does not impose such a requirement.

---

204 *Youngblood v. Schwan*, 72 Ga.App. 86, 33 S.E.2d 26 (1945).

205 *Mrs. E. B. Smith Realty Co. v. Hubbard*, 130 Ga.App. 672, 204 S.E.2d 366, citing *Horne v. Rodgers*, 113 Ga. 224, 228, 38 S.E. 768, 770 (1901).

206 *Leverett v. Bullard*, 121 Ga. 534, 49 S.E. 591(1904), citing *Riley v. Griffin*, 16 Ga. 142 (1854); *Weathers Bros. Transfer Co. v. Loyd*, 224 Ga. 157, 160 S.E.2d 346 (1968).

207 *Lynburn Enterprises, Inc. v. Lawyers Title Ins. Corp.*, 191 Ga.App. 710, 382 S.E.2d 599 (1989), *cert. denied*, citing *Stewart v. Latimer*, 197 Ga. 735, 742, 30 S.E.2d 633 (1944).

§ 2.5   INCORPORATING SURVEY INTO CONTRACT

In earlier versions of the GAR Contract, buyers had the right to survey the property, but the survey itself was not a part of the contract. The legal description of the property was defined as "the same as is recorded with the Clerk of Superior Court of the county in which the Property is located."[208] Since most buyers do not have a title examination of the property performed prior to entering into a contract, they were contracting to purchase property based on a legal description they had never seen or examined.

The current GAR Contract provides that the full legal description of the property is either attached as an exhibit to the agreement (*i.e.* survey) or is "identical to the legal description for the property contained in the deed recorded in Deed Book _____, Page_____, *et seq.*, _____ County, Georgia records." The GAR Contract also contains a section which provides in part as follows:

> Notwithstanding any other provision to the contrary contained herein, Buyer shall have the right to terminate this Agreement upon notice to Seller if a new survey of the Property performed by a licensed Georgia surveyor is obtained that is materially different from any survey of the Property provided by Seller and attached hereto as an exhibit. The term "materially different" shall not apply to any improvements or repairs constructed by Seller in their agreed-upon locations subsequent to Binding Date Agreement. Matters revealed in any survey, including a survey attached hereto may be raised by Buyer as title obligations.[209]

Under this provision buyers can request that sellers provide a copy of their surveys of the property which the buyers can review prior to executing the contract. It should be noted, however, that the seller is not required to attach a survey to the contract absent an affirmative agreement between the parties to do so.

Even if there are no material differences between the survey and the legal description of the property found in the county land records, the GAR Contract provides that the seller will convey good and marketable title subject only to (1) zoning, (2) general utility, sewer, and drainage easements of record as of the Binding Agreement Date and upon which improvements do not encroach, (3) declarations of condominiums and declarations of covenants, conditions and restrictions of record on the Binding Agreement Date, and (4) leases and other encumbrances specified in this Agreement. Therefore, if the survey and the legal description in the county land records are the same, but the survey shows an improvement encroaching on an easement (like a house built on top of a county sewer line), the seller must remedy this title defect in order to convey good and marketable title to the buyer. In order to avoid this, the seller may incorporate the following alternative language in the contract.

Special Stipulation 11:   Buyer Agrees to Take Title Subject to Survey Matters

Notwithstanding the warranty of title provisions of Paragraph 6C of this Agreement, Buyer agrees to take title to the Property subject to all matters shown on the attached survey.

§ 2.5.1   Importance Of Attaching A Survey

A survey will show the actual boundary lines of the property being conveyed and will show easements and encroachments which may affect the buyer's interest in purchasing the property. If a survey is presented as part of the legal description of the property, the buyer can determine if there is any issue reflected on the survey which would affect the buyer's decision to purchase the property before signing the contract.

---

208   GAR Form F20, Purchase and Sale Agreement (1995 printing).

209   GAR F20.

For example, a buyer signs a contract for the purchase of property, intending to put a pool in the rear yard. The contract states that the property description is the same as what is found in the county land records. The buyer believes that the rear boundary of this property is a hedge. However, a survey obtained later shows that the rear yard is 20 feet closer to the dwelling than the hedge and that there is a county drainage easement running through the area in which the buyer intends to put the pool. Since the property being conveyed is the same as described in the land records, the buyer will be obligated to purchase it even though she thought the property extended all the way to the hedge. If a survey were part of the legal description, however, she would have discovered the easement that would prevent her from building a pool prior to executing the contract.

From a legal perspective, a contract that incorporates a recorded survey which provides the metes and bounds description, is treated as proof that what is being conveyed is what is stated on the survey. In other words, the buyer will be treated as having actual knowledge of the property being conveyed. The buyer will also be considered to have actual knowledge of any encumbrance, easement, or other defect that is shown on the recorded survey, since a recorded survey gives notice of any encumbrances to title whether or not the buyer knows of the record. Thus, the buyer will take title to the property, subject to any defect that is stated on the recorded survey.[210]

§ 2.5.2   Guidelines For One Survey "Materially Different" From Another

The GAR Contract states that if a new survey, which the buyer obtains, is materially different from the seller's survey, the buyer can terminate the contract.[211] Alternatively, the buyer can use the threat of termination as a basis to negotiate some mutually satisfactory resolution to the discrepancy. This provision gives a buyer the ability to terminate a contract based on concerns with the economic marketability of the property.

The GAR Contract does not define the term "materially different." It does, however, state that "materially different" does not apply to any improvements or repairs constructed by the Seller in their agreed-upon locations subsequent to the Binding Agreement Date. Generally, a matter is considered "material" if it relates to a matter which is so substantial and important as to influence a party. Whether a difference in surveys will be considered material is a question of fact. It is likely that if a new survey shows the property in a flood plain, the difference will be considered material, particularly if it means the buyer will be obligated to purchase flood insurance.

Similarly, if a fence or other structure has been erected which constitutes an encroachment, the difference may be material. If boundary lines vary between the surveys, the difference may or may not be material. For example, a one-foot difference along a 100 foot call of a 100 acre tract may not be material. On the other hand, a one-foot difference on a 1/4 acre lot may be material, particularly if it affects the setback and placement of the dwelling.

§ 2.5.3   Protection For Buyer If No Existing Survey Available

Many contracts identify the property as set forth in the county land records. However, there are many matters that a metes and bounds description will not show: whether a fence is within the boundary of the property; whether there is any encroachment onto a neighboring property; where easements of record may be located; whether the property is in a flood hazard area; or even to readily determine the shape of the property buyers are considering purchasing.

One possible solution to these problems is to provide in the contract that a survey acceptable to the buyer is attached by the seller. However, Georgia courts have held that a sales contract is voidable for lack of mutuality if the buyer is the sole judge of her satisfaction.[212] Below are several special stipulations that can be used in cases where a survey is unavailable at the time of contract, but the buyer still wants protection against possible survey problems in the future.

---

210   *Security Union Title Insurance Co,. v. RC Acres, Inc.*, 269 Ga.App. 359, 604 S.E.2d 547 (2004).

211   GAR F20.

212   *Lee v. Green Land Co., Inc.*, 245 Ga.App. 558, 538 S.E.2d 187, citing *Stone Mountain Properties, Ltd. v. Helmer*, 139 Ga.App. 865, 867, 229 S.E.2d 779 (1976).

Special Stipulation 12:   Seller Warrants There Are No Easements, Encumbrances or Septic Tanks on Property

Notwithstanding any provisions in this Agreement regarding title, Seller warrants that there are no easements, licenses, rights of third parties, septic fields, septic tanks or other buried tanks on, across, over, or under that portion of the property identified on Exhibit "__" to this Agreement and incorporated herein. All parties acknowledge that Buyer intends to put a pool in the area after Closing and that Buyer would not be buying the Property if Buyer cannot do so. This warranty shall survive the closing of the Property.

Special Stipulation 13:   Seller Warrants That Property is Not in a Floodplain

Seller warrants that no portion of any residential dwelling or garage on the Property is in a flood plain. If Buyer discovers prior to Closing that any portion of any residential dwelling or garage is in a flood plain, Buyer may terminate this Agreement without penalty upon notice to Seller.

Special Stipulation 14:   Seller Warrants Minimum Acreage of Property

Seller warrants that the Property contains at least ___ acres. If a survey reveals that the Property contains less than ___ acres, Buyer may terminate this Agreement without penalty upon notice to Seller.

Special Stipulation 15:   Seller Warrants Size of Front and Rear Boundaries

Seller warrants that the front and rear boundaries of the Property are a minimum of _____ feet in length and the side boundaries are a minimum of _____ feet in length. If a survey reveals boundaries of lesser dimensions, Buyer may terminate this Agreement without penalty upon notice to Seller.

§ 2.6   ZONING MATTERS DO NOT AFFECT MARKETABILITY OR QUALITY OF TITLE

It is generally recognized that the zoning status of property does not relate to title and cannot create a breach of a warranty of title. Georgia case law provides that the zoning status of property does not concern title.[213] Zoning ordinances are legislative enactments. Thus, the uses which may be made of land under the applicable law or ordinance is a matter of law and a buyer is presumed to know what zoning regulations do or do not permit on a certain property.[214]

The Georgia Title Standards state that "a title examiner must be careful to disclaim in her opinion any coverage as to the applicability of effect of zoning because it is settled in Georgia that such matters do not implicate the locus or quality of title."[215] That section of the Title Standards also states that title insurance companies operating in Georgia are not permitted to issue insurance as to "zoning matters," broadly conceived. Therefore, title opinions do not refer to "zoning matters" as exceptions. Although a seller is obligated to deliver marketable title to a buyer under the GAR Contract, zoning issues are specifically listed as an exception in this area because, by law, such issues do not affect title. If the buyer is purchasing the property for a particular use and wishes to make the contract conditional upon rezoning, the buyer should include the following stipulation in the contract.

---

213 *Sachs v. Swartz*, 233 Ga. 99, 209 S.E. 2d 642 (1974).

214 *Gignilliat v. Borg*, 131 Ga.App. 182, 205 S.E.2d 479 (1974), citing *Barton v. Atkinson*, 228 Ga. 733), 187 S.E.2d 835 (1972) and *Maloof v. Gwinnett County*, 231 Ga. 164, 166, 200 S.E.2d 749 (1973).

215 State Bar of Georgia Title Standards, section 34.1(a). *See* § 2.9 (Title Standards) below on Title Standards.

Special Stipulation 16: Rezoning Contingency

Buyer understands and agrees that Property is zoned _____ and that the improvements thereon do not meet Buyer's zoning requirements. The Buyer's obligation hereunder is conditional upon the Property being rezoned to _____by the appropriate (County/City) authorities by [date] subject only to zoning conditions that do not: 1) prohibit less than the following number of single-family residential dwellings or density of development on the Property: _____;

_____

_____

2) increase the cost of the development of the Property; and 3) impose side or rear setback requirements in excess of what is normally provided for in the above-referenced zoning category. In the event any of the above-referenced conditions are not met, Buyer shall have the right, but not the obligation, to terminate this Agreement upon notice to Seller. The Buyer ☐ or Seller ☐ shall be responsible for pursuing such rezoning and shall pay all the costs thereof. In the event said rezoning is not obtained by said date, then this Agreement shall become null and void and all earnest money shall be refunded to the Buyer. All rezoning applications shall be submitted to Seller for Seller's approval prior to filing, and approval shall not be unreasonably withheld. All parties agree to cooperate, to sign the necessary documentation and to support the rezoning application.

In some cases, real estate developers will want the right to terminate a purchase and sale agreement if any conditions of zoning are not acceptable to the developer "in the developer's sole discretion". This creates the potential argument that the contract is illusory or lacks mutuality because the developer is the sole judge of her satisfaction regarding the conditions of zoning. A better solution is to write the stipulation using an objective standard such as the one set forth in the special stipulation above. The buyer may want the seller to provide proof of zoning, in which case the buyer may include the following stipulation.

Special Stipulation 17: Seller to Provide Proof of Zoning

This Agreement is conditional upon Seller providing a letter from the city or county zoning authority stating that the Property is presently zoned for _____use. Seller shall have two weeks from the Binding Agreement Date. Should the Seller not present the letter within the above-stated time period, Buyer may terminate this Agreement without penalty upon notice to Seller.

Rezoning contingencies are discussed in further detail in § 8.8 (Rezoning Contingencies)

§ 2.6.1 Violations Of Zoning Ordinances Are Not Matters Affecting Title To Property

Zoning matters are not included with the general warranty of title contained in a general warranty deed. Therefore, the conveyance of land which is in violation of a zoning ordinance is not a breach of the covenants included in a general warranty of title.

This is illustrated by a case where a large parcel of property was subdivided. A one-acre lot was conveyed to successive buyers while in violation of the zoning ordinance regarding the minimum acreage of property. The ultimate buyer argued that the seller had breached his warranty of title because an existing violation of a zoning ordinance subjected the buyer to litigation and even to possible criminal penalties, resulting in title which was not marketable.[216] The Court of Appeals concluded that even though zoning is not a matter of title, the conveyance of land in violation of a municipal ordinance is an encumbrance and constitutes a breach of warranty of title because the buyer was exposed to litigation. However, the Georgia Supreme Court reversed the Court of Appeals, declining to extend the traditional scope of a general warranty of title to include zoning matters.[217] The commentary in the Title Standards states that even if a survey reveals that a building violates a "zoning" setback line, the title examiner may ignore the violation on the theory that "zoning matters" are not title matters, and title examiners may certify such titles as marketable.

Some of the most common zoning violations involve legal and illegal non-conforming uses, setback lines, historic preservation ordinances and stream buffer regulations. Although these matters do not affect the title to a property, an ongoing violation could result in an injunction,[218] civil fines[219] or even criminal penalties, depending on the violation.[220]

§ 2.6.1.1   Legal Non-Conforming Uses

In some cases, property will be zoned for a use other than that for which it is presently being used. For example, a single family residential dwelling may be located on property that is now zoned for an office use. Similarly, a property zoned for single-family residential use may have both a house and an apartment located on it. If a property is being used for something other than what the property is presently zoned for, it is referred to as a non-conforming use.[221] Georgia courts, however, have been very careful to distinguish between legal nonconforming uses and illegal nonconforming uses.[222]

A legal non-conforming use is one that lawfully existed prior to the enactment or amendment of a zoning ordinance.[223] These types of nonconforming uses are almost always capable of being "grandfathered." In other words, the nonconforming use will generally be permitted so long as the owner can be shown that the land was lawfully used prior to the ordinance's adoption and the use continues.[224] For example, a property owner currently uses his property as a landfill pursuant to a city ordinance. Shortly thereafter, the city amends the zoning ordinance and prohibits such use of the land. In this case, the property owner could "grandfather" his [now] nonconforming use by showing the local zoning authority the prior ordinance that permitted the lawful use of his land as a landfill.[225] As long as the property's use is continued, the nonconforming use will be permitted.[226]

However, prior (or grandfathered) nonconforming uses are not completely protected. Georgia law provides that a property owner may not move or transfer a "grandfathered" nonconforming use from one property to another.[227] In addition, if a nonconforming use is discontinued for the time period specified in the local zoning ordinance, the use will be abandoned and cannot be re-established.[228] For example, when a property was built, it lawfully contained two residences; a home and a basement apartment. Thereafter, the zoning ordinance was amended to provide that only one residence could be located on each property. As such, the basement apartment became "grandfathered" and its use was

---

216   *Decatur v. Barnett*, 197 Ga.App. 459, 398 S.E.2d 706 (1990).

217   *Decatur v. Barnett*, 261 Ga. 205, 403 S.E.2d 46 (1991).

218   *Hill v. Busbia*, 217 Ga. 781, 125 S.E.2d 34 (1962).

219   O.C.G.A. § 12-7-15.

220   O.C.G.A. § 44-10-30.

221   3 Ga. Jur. Property § 25-34.

222   *Corey Outdoor Advertising, Inc. v. Board of Zoning Adjustments of City of Atlanta*, 254 Ga. 221, 327 S.E.2d 178 (1985).

223   *BBC Land & Development, Inc. v. Butts County*, 281 Ga. 472, 640 S.E.2d 33 (2007); see also *Rockdale County v. Burdette*, 278 Ga. 755, 604 S.E.2d 820 (2004).

224   *Flippen Alliance for Community Empowerment, Inc. v. Brannan*, 267 Ga.App. 134, 601 S.E.2d 106 (2004).

225   *Flippen Alliance for Community Empowerment, Inc. v. Brannan*, 267 Ga.App. 134, 601 S.E.2d 106 (2004).

226   *Flippen Alliance for Community Empowerment, Inc. v. Brannan*, 267 Ga.App. 134, 601 S.E.2d 106 (2004).

227   *Thurman's Auto Parts & Wrecker Service, Inc. v. Cobb County*, 248 Ga. 826, 286 S.E.2d 707 (1982).

228   *Ansley House, Inc. v. City of Atlanta*, 260 Ga. 540, 397 S.E.2d 419 (1990).

permitted so long as it was continued. The ordinance also provided that if a nonconforming use was discontinued for more than one year, such use would be abandoned and could not be re-established. The house was then foreclosed on and remained vacant for almost two years. In this case, since the nonconforming use was abandoned for more than the statutorily prescribed period of time, any new owner of the property is prevented from re-establishing the nonconforming use without obtaining a variance from the local authority.[229]

It is not uncommon for properties with older improvements to have some development feature that is nonconforming with the current zoning ordinance.[230] One of the most typical nonconformities is the encroachment on the side, rear or front setback requirements. While such improvements may remain if they were built prior to the adoption of the zoning ordinance, the nonconforming aspects of the development cannot normally be expanded[231] or re-built[232] in the event they are destroyed or absent of the granting of a variance. As an example, there is an older residential home that has a detached garage which was built almost on the side property line. The present zoning ordinance requires a ten (10) foot setback from the side property line. If the garage is destroyed by fire, the new garage would have to be built in conformity with the zoning ordinance's ten (10) foot side setback requirement unless the property owner obtains a variance. Similarly, the owner would not be able to add onto the rear of the garage and encroach further into the side setback area without obtaining a variance.

§ 2.6.1.2 Illegal Non-Conforming Uses

An illegal nonconforming use is a property use by an owner that was never lawful to begin with and does conform to the current zoning ordinance.[233] Some of the most common illegal nonconforming uses occur when improvements are made to a property. For example, if a zoning ordinance permits only one residence on a single lot, but the owner adds an apartment above his garage, the garage apartment in this case is both illegal and nonconforming. The use of such apartment is illegal because the zoning ordinance only permitted one residence per lot when the apartment was constructed.[234] It is also nonconforming because the use of the apartment doesn't conform to the current zoning ordinance which prohibits more than one residence per lot.

Illegal non-conforming uses, if discovered, are subjected to an enforcement action by local government seeking their removal.[235] However, while the risk of an enforcement action is always present, such actions are usually a low priority for most local governments, particularly if the nonconformity has been there for many years.

Some cities in Georgia have even grandfathered illegal nonconformities when adopting their zoning ordinances.[236] For example, the city of Sandy Springs, Georgia has created an exception for any nonconformities existing prior to the adoption of the zoning ordinance.[237] The city allows any existing nonconforming uses to continue, subject to certain limitations, but it is the intent of the city that all nonconformities will be eliminated over time.[238] Some of the limitations include, but are not limited to, the following: the non-conforming use (i) shall not be expanded to occupy a greater area; (ii) shall remain in the original building structure or land area in which it was originally occupied; (iii) shall not

---

229 *Ansley House, Inc. v. City of Atlanta*, 260 Ga. 540, 397 S.E.2d 419 (1990).

230 *Flippen Alliance for Community Empowerment, Inc. v. Brannan*, 267 Ga.App. 134, 601 S.E.2d 106 (2004).

231 *Henry v. Cherokee County*, 290 Ga.App. 355, 659 S.E.2d 393 (2008).

232 *Fayette County v. Seagraves*, 245 Ga. 196, 264 S.e.2D 13 (1980).

233 *Troutman v. Aiken*, 213 Ga. 55, 96 S.E.2d 585 (1957).

234 *Corey Outdoor Advertising, Inc. v. Board of Zoning Adjustments of City of Atlanta*, 254 Ga. 221, 327 S.E.2d 178 (1985).

235 *Troutman v. Aiken*, 213 Ga. 55, 96 S.E.2d 585 (1957).

236 Sandy Springs Mun. Ord., 4.3.1.

237 Sandy Springs Mun. Ord., 4.3.1.

238 Sandy Springs Mun. Ord., 4.3.1.

be intensified or escalated, for example by increasing the number of deliveries, employees, etc.; and (iv) shall not be reinstated after it has been abandoned.[239]

Where an illegal nonconforming use has not been grandfathered into a zoning ordinance, obtaining a variance is normally the best way to eliminate any risk of an enforcement action.

§ 2.6.1.3   Setback Lines

A setback line is a zoning regulation that prohibits the construction of buildings or homes within a specified number of feet from the nearest street.[240] However, if the size and shape of the lot has already been established prior to the regulation's enactment and it is now impossible to build and comply with the ordinance, a variance may be granted.[241]

In one case, an owner was permitted to construct his home in violation of the set back regulation because the lot of record was too small to build a residence that conformed with the requirements.[242] The owner in this case bought a property intending to tear down the existing residence and rebuild another in its place. However, a zoning ordinance required any constructed home to be set back from the street a distance which is the average set back line of existing structures.[243] The average set back was 58 feet 6 inches from the street in front of the property and the home in question was only set back 25 feet. The lot of record, however, showed that the entire property was only 77 feet in depth and if the owner was required to set back the property 58 feet 6 inches, there would only be 18 feet or so to build the residence. In this case, since the property could not conform to the setback requirements due to the lot size, a variance was granted to exempt the property from compliance.[244]

Georgia law provides that actions which may accrue as a result of the violation of a building setback line must be brought within two years after the right of action accrues.[245]

Setback violations are of more concern with new construction since there is a greater risk of the local governing authority requiring that the violation be removed. As such, buyers may want to add the following special stipulation to new construction contracts.

> **Special Stipulation 18:   Seller Warrants no Setback Violations**
>
> *Seller warrants that all improvements on the Property comply with all setback requirements set forth in applicable local zoning ordinances. In the event Buyer notifies Seller of a setback violation and the same cannot be corrected prior to closing, Buyer may terminate this Agreement without penalty upon notice to Seller, in which event Buyer shall be entitled to a refund of all monies paid toward the purchase of the Property.*

For this reason, buyers should check whether the relevant zoning ordinance permits the present use of the premises, as well as any other different uses. A buyer should not simply assume that the existing use is a permitted violation because the authorities can enforce zoning laws despite that the violation has been in existence for a long time. Buyers should review ordinances, statutes, regulations, and the zoning map to determine the zone and the permitted use. Buyers should also enquire about any proposed amendments to the ordinances.

---

239 Sandy Springs Mun. Ord., 4.3.1(A).

240 Pindar's 1 Ga. Real Estate Law & Procedure § 3-19 (6th ed.).

241 *Hill v. Busbia*, 217 Ga. 781, 125 S.E.2d 34 (1962).

242 *Hill v. Busbia*, 217 Ga. 781, 125 S.E.2d 34 (1962).

243 *Hill v. Busbia*, 217 Ga. 781, 125 S.E.2d 34 (1962).

244 *Hill v. Busbia*, 217 Ga. 781, 125 S.E.2d 34 (1962).

245 O.C.G.A. § 9-3-29(a).

§ 2.6.1.4   Historic Properties And Historic Districts

Historic preservation ordinances can also restrict a homeowner's use of her property. Under the Georgia Historic Preservation Act,[246] local authorities may adopt certain zoning ordinances for designated historic properties or historic districts to protect and enhance the state's historical attractions.[247] These ordinances are placed on the official zoning map of the legal entity adopting it and describe each designated property or district, as well as a list of the names of each owner.[248]

The owners and occupants of each designated historic property are given written notification of such designation by the local governing authority.[249] The notice also contains the requirement that owners obtain a certificate of appropriateness prior to making changes to the appearance of the historic property.[250]

If an owner wants to make material changes to the appearance of a historic property, the owner must apply for a certificate of appropriateness from the historic preservation commission.[251] The application should include drawings, photographs or plans of the proposed changes.[252] Once the certificate of appropriateness has been approved by the commission, the owner may complete only the specified changes to the property.[253] Certain changes, however, do not require the approval of the historic preservation commission. For instance, the ordinary maintenance or repair of any exterior architectural feature in or on a historic property may be completed without the commission's approval, so long as the maintenance or repair does not involve a material change in the design, material or outer appearance of the property.[254]

An owner's failure to comply with the zoning ordinances enacted under the Historic Preservation Act could result in severe fines, civil penalties and even criminal action.[255]

§ 2.6.1.5   Stream Buffers

A stream buffer (also referred to as a riparian buffer) is a vegetated area near a body of water that protects the body of water from potentially harmful surrounding land uses. In Georgia, stream buffers are required for any land that abuts state waters to ensure the quality of water and protect the aquatic habitat.[256]

In 1975, the state of Georgia passed the Sedimentation Act to strengthen and extend the present erosion and sediment control activities, as well as conserve the state's waters and aquatic habitat.[257] The Act requires local governing authorities to adopt ordinances and regulations establishing minimum standards for protecting stream buffers within their respective boundaries.[258] All ordinances and regulations must, at a minimum, be as stringent as the state general permit.[259]

---

246   O.C.G.A. § 44-10-20 *et seq.*

247   O.C.G.A. § 44-10-26.

248   O.C.G.A. § 44-10-26(a).

249   O.C.G.A. § 44-10-26(c).

250   O.C.G.A. § 44-10-26(c).

251   O.C.G.A. § 44-10-26(a).

252   O.C.G.A. § 44-10-27(a).

253   O.C.G.A. § 44-10-27(a).

254   O.C.G.A. § 44-10-29.

255   O.C.G.A. § 44-10-30. "The municipal or county governing body or the historic preservation commission shall be authorized to institute any appropriate action or proceeding in a court of competent jurisdiction to prevent any material change in the appearance of a designated historic property or historic district, except those changes made in compliance with the provisions of an ordinance adopted in conformity with this article, or to prevent any illegal act or conduct with respect to such historic property or historic district."

256   O.C.G.A. § 12-7-6(b)(15)(A).

257   O.C.G.A. § 12-7-2.

258   O.C.G.A. § 12-7-4.

259   O.C.G.A. § 12-7-6(b).

The state general permit requires at least a 25-foot stream buffer between the bank of the water and the residence or building being constructed on the property.[260] Local authorities may, however, establish more stringent stream buffer requirements. For instance, the city of Atlanta has imposed a 75-foot minimum stream buffer between the water bank and any constructed residence or building, instead of the 25-foot minimum in the state permit.[261]

Once a stream buffer is in place, no land-disturbing activities[262] may be conducted within that area, unless an exception applies.[263] While a property is being constructed, the stream buffer must stay in its natural and vegetative state until all construction is completed.[264] Once the construction is finished, the buffer may be thinned or trimmed, so long as a protective vegetative cover remains to protect the water quality and aquatic habitat.[265]

The Act provides several exceptions to the stream buffer requirements. Some of the exceptions include: (1) when a variance is granted; (2) where a drainage structure or roadway drainage structure must be constructed, provided that adequate erosion control measures are incorporated into the project; (3) construction along any ephemeral stream[266]; and (4) where shoreline stabilization is installed in the construction of bulkheads and sea walls.[267]

Failure to comply with any stream buffer ordinance will result in civil action and significant monetary penalties.[268] For instance, any person who intentionally or negligently violates a stream buffer ordinance will be liable for up to $2,500 fine per day.[269] In addition, any court or magistrate is authorized to impose a penalty of up to $2,500 per violation.[270] Each day during which the violation or failure or refusal to comply continues constitutes a separate violation.[271]

§ 2.6.2 Special Stipulations Warranting Zoning Status Are Enforceable

Although zoning provisions do not affect title, the parties to a real estate contract can agree that a buyer may terminate the contract if the property is not zoned for a particular purpose.[272] The following special stipulation can be used for this purpose.

> **Special Stipulation 19: Right to Terminate if Property Not Zoned for Particular Purpose**
>
> *Notwithstanding any other provision in this Agreement to the contrary, if it is determined that the Property subject to this Agreement is not zoned for _____ (i.e., multi-family residential, office/industrial), Buyer shall have the right to terminate this Agreement without penalty upon notice to Seller.*

---

260 O.C.G.A. § 12-7-6(b)(15)(A).

261 City of Atlanta Ordinance § 74-303(a).

262 O.C.G.A. § 12-7-3(9). "Land-disturbing activity" means any activity which may result in soil erosion from water or wind and the movement of sediments into state water or onto lands within the state, including, but not limited to, clearing, dredging, grading, excavating, transporting, and filing of land but not including agricultural practices as described in O.C.G.A. § 12-7-17.

263 O.C.G.A. § 12-7-6(a)(15)(B).

264 O.C.G.A. § 12-7-6(a)(15)(B).

265 O.C.G.A. § 12-7-6(a)(15)(B).

266 O.C.G.A. § 12-7-6(a)(15)(A)(v). The term "ephemeral stream" means a stream: (i) that under normal circumstances has water flowing only during and for a short duration after precipitation events; (ii) that has the channel located above the ground-water table year round; (iii) for which ground water is not a source of water; and (iv) for which runoff from precipitation is the primary source of water flow.

267 O.C.G.A. § 12-7-6(a)(15)(A).

268 O.C.G.A. § 12-7-15.

269 O.C.G.A. § 12-7-15.

270 O.C.G.A. § 12-7-15.

271 O.C.G.A. § 12-7-15.

272 *Sachs v. Swartz*, 233 Ga. 99, 209 S.E. 2d 642 (1974).

Since warranty of the zoning status of the property is not a title issue, the notice requirements in the contract as to non-performance of a condition relating to title are not applicable.[273] The buyer would need to add a provision to the contract such as one of those that follow.

> **Special Stipulation 20: Seller Warrants Property Will be Properly Zoned by Closing**
>
> *Notwithstanding any other provision in this Agreement to the contrary, Seller warrants that at the time of closing, the Property shall be zoned for multi-family residential development. If at the Closing the Property is not so zoned, this Agreement may be terminated in Buyer's sole discretion, in which case all earnest money shall be immediately returned to Buyer.*

> **Special Stipulation 21: Seller's Warranty That There are no Zoning or Building Violations at Closing**
>
> *Notwithstanding any other provision in this Agreement to the contrary, Seller warrants that at closing, Seller shall deliver Property free from all violations of zoning and building ordinances.*

§ 2.7   COMMON ENCUMBRANCES ON PROPERTY

§ 2.7.1   Encroachments

An encroachment is generally defined as an illegal intrusion or projection of improvements either from or onto property. There are three general classifications of encroachments which may affect title to property: (1) encroachments upon abutting property; (2) encroachments upon the subject property; and (3) encroachments upon streets and alleys.

For title insurance purposes, encroachments related to property boundary lines, easements, minimum building setback lines or restricted areas without authority, are generally listed as title exceptions. This means that title insurers will not insure such encroachments on an owner's title policy. The extent of the encroachment and the length of time it has existed may impact an insurer's willingness to insure over such encroachments for lenders.

Title insurers generally distinguish between minor and major encroachments. Minor encroachments may be defined as improvements less than 10% over the minimum building setback lines and improvements onto public utility drainage easements. Encroachments of fences and gravel driveways onto easement areas or over boundary lines may be considered minor if they are less than three feet.[274] The length of time the encroachment over a building line has existed affects the enforcement of the violation.

§ 2.7.2   Boundary Line Agreements

The purchaser of property on which an encroachment exists or which encroaches on abutting property may want to obtain a boundary line agreement, even if not required by the title insurer, to avoid disputes in the future as to boundary lines or authority to move or remove improvements.

A boundary line agreement generally permits an encroachment to remain with each owner agreeing that the new boundary line specified in the agreement is the agreed-upon line and that neither owner will claim any interest in the other owner's property. It is recorded in the land records of the county where the property is located and should be cross-referenced to the deeds of both property owners. Once the agreement is recorded, it is enforceable against all

---

273   *Sachs v. Swartz*, 233 Ga. 99, 209 S.E. 2d 642 (1974).

274   United General Title Insurance Company Underwriting Guidelines.

future owners of both properties. There is no requirement that the lender holding a security deed to either parcel be a signatory to any boundary line agreement. However, if the lender subsequently forecloses, it will not be subject to any such agreement to which it was not a party. Accordingly, it is the better practice to have all lenders, and anyone else who may claim an interest in the properties, be a signatory to a boundary line agreement. The party having actual possession of property under a boundary line agreement for more than seven years will acquire title to that property.[275]

In the absence of a boundary line agreement, an owner with an improvement encroaching on another's property may be required to remove the improvement. For example, a property owner built a concrete garage which extended more than 11 feet over the property line. Neither party was aware of the encroachment, and it was not discovered for 17 years. After it was discovered, the neighboring owner brought an action to have the garage removed. The court concluded that the garage owner did not have a boundary line agreement and did not have title to the property on which the garage was located, so the garage owner was obligated to remove the trespassing improvement from the neighboring property.[276]

Boundary line agreements can be used to address a variety of encroachments including, but not limited to, fences, walls, garages and other improvements.

§ 2.7.3 Easements And Licenses

An easement is "an interest in land owned by another person, consisting in the right to use or control the land, or an area above or below it, for a specific limited purpose."[277] A license is merely a "permission, usually revocable, to commit some act that would otherwise be unlawful."[278] It is sometimes difficult to distinguish between an easement and a license.

Easements are generally distinguished from licenses in that easements are interests in property which: (1) are related to the property; (2) pass with the property from one owner to the next; (3) can be created only in writing or by the actions of the parties over time; and (4) are not revocable.

Licenses are a right given by the owner of property to do an act on her property which is created either orally or by implication. Also, under Georgia law, a parol or orally granted license to do something on another's property is revocable at any time if its revocation does no harm to the person to whom it has been granted. However, a parol license can become a non-revocable easement if the licensee has acted in reliance on the license and has incurred expense.[279] For example, if a property owner orally grants a person the right to construct a road over her property, and the person purchases an adjoining property in reliance upon such a parol license and spends money and labor to build and improve the road, the person holds an executed license which becomes an easement running with the land.[280]

The GAR Contract provides that recorded easements on which improvements do not encroach are exceptions to title.[281] In other words, the buyer cannot claim that such easements are title defects. However, if an improvement encroaches on the recorded easement, then a title defect does exist.

In some cases, easements may affect the buyer's use of the property purchased. If an abutting owner has a landscape easement on the buyer's property, the buyer may be precluded from putting a fence where she intended to put one. Similarly, a utility easement for a sewer line may preclude a buyer from placing an improvement (such as a pool) on a portion of the property. Since recorded easements are identified on the survey, these problems may be avoided if the survey is part of the contract.

---

275 O.C.G.A. § 44-4-7.

276 *Roe v. Doe*, 233 Ga. 691, 212 S.E.2d 854 (1975).

277 Black's Law Dictionary (8th ed. 2004); *Brown v. Tomlinson*, 246 Ga. 513, 272 S.E.2d 258 (1980).

278 Black's Law Dictionary 9 (8th ed. 2004).

279 O.C.G.A. § 44-9-4.

280 *Jordan v. Coalson*, 235 Ga. 326, 219 S.E.2d 439 (1975); *Waters v. Pervis*, 153 Ga.App. 71, 264 S.E.2d 551 (1980).

281 GAR Form F20.

The GAR Contract does not list unrecorded easements or licenses as permitted exceptions to title. Oftentimes, unrecorded easements are seen in land transactions involving the purchase of a property in a rural area. If a buyer discovers an unrecorded easement or license after examining the property, the buyer may object to these matters as title defects and the seller will have to remedy the defect before closing.

An example of an unrecorded easement is an easement acquired by prescription.[282] This means that title to an easement was acquired after a period of twenty years' use that was public, continuous, uninterrupted and peaceable. The general law on title acquired by prescription applies to easements.[283] Private ways (*i.e.* a road, path or driveway across property belonging to another party) are protected after seven years' use, which must be constant and uninterrupted.[284] The private way must not exceed 20 feet during the prescribed period and must be kept open and in repair by the applicant. Further, there must be an adverse claim and actual notice of the claim to the other party.[285]

Another example of an unrecorded easement is an implied easement. An easement is implied by law in favor of one owner when the easement is necessary, such as for light and air. One buyer purchased property that was land-locked by a tract retained by the seller. However, the buyers used a private way across the retained tract. The court held that although there was no written record of the private way or easement, the buyers had an implied easement in the private way for access to and exit from their property.[286]

Easements may contain express or implied obligations for maintenance and upkeep. One may not use an easement in a manner beyond its intended use so as to damage the property of another.[287] Similarly, the grantor of an easement must maintain their property so as to not interfere with the use of the easement.[288]

To avoid any issues with unrecorded easements, it is a good idea for the buyer to get an affirmative warranty from the seller that she is unaware of any unrecorded easements or other interests in the property. An example of such a provision is set forth below.

> **Special Stipulation 22:   Seller Warrants That Seller is Unaware of Unrecorded Records or Claims or Third Parties to the Property**
>
> *Seller warrants that Seller has no knowledge of any unrecorded easements over, across, or under the Property, and is unaware of any use of the Property or right or claim in or to the Property by any third party. This warranty shall survive closing.*

§ 2.7.3.1 Landlocked Property: Easements By Necessity

What happens when a property is landlocked? This issue often arises in a land transaction when a subdivision plat has not yet been recorded. The owner can, of course, approach neighboring owners and seek to purchase the right to access. But what happens if a neighboring owner refuses to sell? In most instances, the owner of property who has no means of access, ingress, and egress, has the right to petition the Superior Court for a private way to go through adjoining property to access their land.[289] This effectively forces the neighboring owner to sell an access right, whether he wants to do so or not.

282 O.C.G.A. §44-5-175.

283 *See* § 2.15 (Title By Prescription Or Adverse Possession) of this Chapter for a discussion of title by prescription.

284 O.C.G.A. § 44-9-54.

285 *Greer v. Piedmont Realty Investments, Inc.*, 248 Ga. 821, 286 S.E.2d 712 (1982).

286 *Burk v. Tyrell*, 212 Ga. 239, 91 S.E.2d 744 (1956).

287 *City of College Park v. Pichon*, 217 Ga.App. 53, 456 S.E.2d 686 (1995).

288 *Bishop Eddie Long Ministries, Inc. v. Dillard*, 272 Ga.App. 894, 613 S.E.2d 673 (2005).

289 O.C.G.A. § 44-9-40.

In such an action, the private way cannot exceed 20 feet in width and may be smaller depending upon what the Court determines is reasonably necessary. The recipient of any such easement is responsible for keeping the way open and in good repair.[290]

While the filing of such a petition is deemed to be a declaration of the necessity of the private way for access, the Court may deny the petition if it appears that the owner already has a right of access, ingress, and egress, even though it may not be the most direct or convenient, or if it would be "otherwise unreasonable" to grant the private way.[291]

The Georgia Courts have held that it is unreasonable for one to voluntarily landlock themselves. As a result, when an owner owns two adjacent parcels, sells one, and landlocks the remaining parcel she owns, a private way of necessity cannot be obtained.[292] Knowingly purchasing landlocked property, on the other hand, does not preclude a purchaser from obtaining a private way of necessity.[293]

If the buyer of a property wants assurances that the lot will have access to a public or private road, especially if the buyer is contracting to buy a lot for which a subdivision plat has yet to be recorded, the following special stipulation may be used to handle such situation.

> **Special Stipulation 23:   Access to Road**
>
> *Seller warrants that as of the date of Closing, Buyer shall have a permanent right of ingress and egress over a road abutting the Property by virtue of the following: [Select one. The sections not selected shall not be a part of this Agreement.]*
>
> ☐ *a. The road shall be a public road.*
>
> ☐ *b. The road shall be a private road owned and maintained by a homeowners association in which Buyer shall be a mandatory member and over which members shall have permanent easement rights for ingress and egress.*
>
> ☐ *c. Buyer shall have an easement of ingress and egress over a private road owned by a person or legal entity other than a homeowners association, which easement shall run in perpetuity with the title to the Property.*
>
> *This warranty shall survive the Closing of the purchase and sale of the Property.*

§ 2.7.3.2   Blocking Or Obstructing Easements

The rule in Georgia is that neither the landowner nor the beneficiary of an easement have the right to block or obstruct the easement (unless the easement agreement gives a party that right).[294] So, for example, a landowner whose property is burdened with a road easement cannot erect a fence or gate over the road or lock the same, even if the landowner gives the beneficiary of the easement a key for the lock.

§ 2.7.3.3   Underground Pipeline Easements

Many properties have pipeline easements crossing them for things such as gas, water and sewer lines. Obviously, the existence of such easements can significantly affect the ability of the landowner to construct pools, garages and other structures on the property.

---

290 O.C.G.A. § 44-9-40.

291 O.C.G.A. § 44-9-40.

292 *Dovetail Properties, Inc. v. Herron*, 287 Ga.App. 808, 652 S.E.2d 856 (2007).

293 *Dovetail Properties, Inc. v. Herron*, 287 Ga.App. 808, 652 S.E.2d 856 (2007).

294 *Williams v. Trammell*, 281 Ga.App. 590, 636 S.E.2d 757 (2006).

Disputes often arise between the owner of the property and the owner of the pipeline when the line needs to be repaired or replaced, or when the pipeline company wants to clear the area where the line is located to make inspection of the pipeline easier. Usually the terms of the easement agreement will control the rights of the parties. Georgia courts have ruled that a petroleum pipeline company has the right to remove shrubbery overhanging its easement area and to side cut tree limbs to make it easy for the lines to be inspected.[295]

§ 2.7.3.4   Shared Driveway Easements

In many older residential neighborhoods, it is common for there to be a shared driveway serving two properties. As the driveway recedes from the street, it will at some point branch out to connect with garages or carports on individual properties. These shared driveways may be all on the property of one owner or may straddle a property line between two owners. In either case, such situations call for the creation of an easement whereby the owner(s) of the land upon which the driveway sits would grant to the neighboring owner(s) an easement for ingress and egress over the driveway. Normally the easement is for ingress and egress only. Therefore, in theory, neither owner sharing the driveway should park on the common portion of the driveway since the same would interfere with the easement rights of the other owner.

§ 2.7.3.5   Easements Of Support

Neighboring property owners owe each other an easement of support. This most often arises in the case of party walls or trees that straddle the property line. In these instances, both owners have a duty to maintain the wall or tree and to take reasonable steps to guard against any hazardous conditions the structure or tree may pose.[296] Easements of support also prevent a property owner from removing the earth along a common property line in a manner which causes the neighbor's property to be undermined.

§ 2.7.3.6   Cemeteries

An issue which sometimes arises with the sale of large tracts of land is the existence of a cemetery on the property. If there are graves on a tract of land, an implied easement for ingress and egress in favor of the heirs of the deceased exists, allowing them to visit the graves and to maintain and decorate them.[297] The easement also includes the right to consent to the disinterment of bodies.[298]

There is a procedure in Georgia law whereby a permit can be obtained to remove and relocate graves from a property.[299] The applicant must contain detailed information (itemized in O.C.G.A. § 36-72-5) and overcome a presumption in favor of leaving the cemetery undisturbed by showing that the applicant's interest in disinterment outweighs the interests of the public and the heirs of the deceased in leaving the property undisturbed.[300]

§ 2.7.3.7   Water Rights: Prescriptive Easements

In much the same way as a person may obtain title to or an easement over property by way of prescription, water rights may also be obtained or lost by prescription. In one case, for example, a group of landowners agreed to share the cost of building and maintaining a dam on property owned by Mr. Tomlinson for the purpose of creating a pond.[301] The pond

---

295 *Avery v. Colonial Pipeline Co.*, 213 Ga.App. 388, 444 S.E.2d 634 (1998).

296 *Willis v. Maloof*, 184 Ga.App. 349, 361 S.E.2d 512 (1987).

297 14 Am. Jur. 2d, Cemeteries, § 36 and § 37.

298 *Rivers v. Greenwood Cemetery, Inc.*, 194 Ga. 524, 22 S.E.2d 134 (1942).

299 O.C.G.A. § 36-72-1, *et seq.* This law authorizes local cities or counties to permit the removal of graves, but also authorizes them to preserve and protect abandoned cemeteries.

300 O.C.G.A. § 36-72-8.

301 *Brown v. Tomlinson*, 246 Ga. 513, 272 S.E.2d 258 (1980).

was to be used primarily for recreational purposes. Mr. Brown owned 120 acres which were submerged to form the pond. Several other landowners then owned property with shoreline on the pond, in addition to Mr. Brown.

Over a period of 24 years the condition of the pond deteriorated due to water hyacinths clogging the pond. A committee of concerned landowners was formed to study the situation. Several advertised meetings were held, but Mr. Brown did not attend. The group decided to cut the dam on Mr. Tomlinson's property, drain the pond, dredge it, burn it out, refill and restock it. When Mr. Brown noticed the water level dropping significantly, he filed a lawsuit seeking a permanent injunction against cutting the dam. It was his position that since it had been in existence more than 20 years, he had obtained the prescriptive right to the continued existence of the pond on his land. Mr. Tomlinson, on the other hand, argued that he had the right to do as he wished with the dam on his property. The court disagreed with both positions.

The court explained that normally both riparian owners have easements: the upper landowner had the right to pass the water along unobstructed by the owner of the lower property, and the lower landowner had the duty to receive the water without obstruction from the owner of the property upstream. In this case, both had lost their respective rights by prescription. The existence of the dam for more than 20 years meant that Mr. Tomlinson no longer had the right to permanently drain the pond on Mr. Brown's property. But since the pond was only temporarily being drained and no irreparable injury was being done, the court allowed Mr. Tomlinson to cut the dam and drain the pond, provided that the plan to refill it was carried out.[302]

§ 2.7.4 Judicial Liens

Money judgments against an owner of property entered on the General Execution Docket of the county in which that owner's property is located, constitute a lien on all property owned by the owner in that county.[303] It should be noted that judgment creditors might file their judgments in counties other than the counties where the judgments are obtained, in order to perfect their lien rights on any property owned by the defendant in those counties. A judgment against a seller constitutes an encumbrance on the seller's property and must be satisfied before or at closing in order to convey clear title to a buyer.

In some cases, a seller may have a name which is the same as, or very similar to, a judgment defendant, but the seller may not be the defendant. In such cases, the closing attorney will have to be satisfied that the judgment defendant and the seller are not the same person, and the seller will usually have to execute an affidavit to that effect.

If there is a judgment recorded against a buyer, the judgment may affect the buyer's ability to obtain an approved loan for financing the transaction. In some cases, the buyer may be required to satisfy a judgment in order to obtain financing. If the buyer cannot do so, the contract may terminate because the buyer is unable to obtain a loan and therefore meet the financing contingency.

§ 2.7.5 Special Assessment Liens

The costs of grading, curbing, paving, laying sewer and water pipes, etc., are generally required to be assessed in some part against abutting landowners.[304] Such special assessments are not a tax but are a lien on the property.

§ 2.7.6 *Ad Valorem* Tax Liens

Ad valorem tax Fi. Fa.'s (writs of *Fieri Facias*) are general liens against all property owned by a taxpayer in addition to being a special lien on the taxed land.[305] Therefore, even if *ad valorem* taxes are not owed on the property being sold to a

---

302 *Id.*

303 O.C.G.A. § 9-12-80.

304 O.C.G.A. § 36-39-3, § 36-39-7, and many municipal ordinances.

305 O.C.G.A. § 48-3-5; for a more detailed discussion of *ad valorem* taxes and liens, *see* Chapter 23 (*Ad Valorem* Tax on Real Property) of this work.

buyer, if the seller owes taxes on another property in the same county, those taxes will constitute a lien on the property being sold. Unpaid taxes on other property, however, will usually be waived by the title insurance company insuring the property being sold because payment of the taxes is secured by the other liened property.

§ 2.7.7 Federal Tax Liens

Federal tax liens include liens for federal estate taxes, unpaid income taxes, gift taxes, excise, and other taxes. Such liens attach on the date of assessment to all the taxpayer's property, but a federal tax lien does not gain priority over other liens or interests until a notice or lien is filed in the public records. When property subject to a federal tax lien is sold at a foreclosure sale, the United States has 120 days from the date of the sale to redeem the property.[306]

§ 2.7.8 Mechanics' And Materialmen's Liens

Under Georgia law, mechanics, contractors, subcontractors, materialmen furnishing material, labors furnishing labor, architects, surveyors and engineers are given statutory liens for their contributions toward the improvement of real property.[307] These liens must be filed in the county land records where the property is located within three months after completion of the work or furnishing of services. In addition, the lien claimant must start an action in court for recovery of the amount of the claim within 12 months from the time the amounts became due.[308]

Since these liens are valid for three months before they are required to be recorded, they are an unrecorded encumbrance on the property during that period. For that reason, sellers will generally be asked by a closing attorney to sign an affidavit stating that no work has been performed on the property which may result in a lien being filed against the property in the three months preceding the closing and that all construction costs have been paid in full.

§ 2.7.9 Liens Under Georgia Condominium Act And Georgia Property Owners' Association Act

The Georgia Condominium Act and the Georgia Property Owners' Association Act both provide that condominium or homeowner assessments not paid when due constitute an automatic lien against the property.[309] This means that such liens automatically attach to the property and do not have to be physically filed in the land records. Since these liens are not recorded in the county land records, it is incumbent on the closing attorney, or the party charged with ensuring that title is clear, to contact the management company or the board of directors for the association to determine if assessments are due. Both statutes provide that a written statement can be requested from the association setting forth amounts due and that successors are not liable for any amounts in excess of the amounts set forth in the statement.[310]

§ 2.7.10 Deeds To Secure Debt

A deed to secure debt, also referred to as a security deed, constitutes an absolute conveyance of the property by the buyer to the lender with the lender having an obligation to reconvey the property to the buyer upon payment of the debt.[311] It is commonly said that the lender has legal title to the property and the buyer has equitable title while the debt or mortgage is being paid off by the buyer.

---

306 26 U.S.C.A.§ 7425(d)(1).

307 O.C.G.A. § 44-14-361(a).

308 O.C.G.A. § 44-14-361.1.

309 O.C.G.A. § 44-3-109, § 44 3 232.

310 O.C.G.A. § 44-3-80(e), 44 2 225(c).

311 O.C.G.A. § 44-14-60.

§ 2.7.10.1 Three Methods To Cancel Deed To Secure Debt

Unless the seller's loan or loans are being assumed by the buyer at closing, all loans to the seller secured by deeds to secure debt encumbering the property should be paid in full at closing and subsequently released by the lender. Georgia law sets forth three methods to cancel a deed to secure debt: (a) a cancellation upon the original deed to secure debt; (b) a quitclaim deed from the record holder of the deed to secure debt to either the current holder of record title, the person to whom title is to be conveyed, or the original grantor of the security; or (c) a cancellation document, in the event that the original deed to secure debt has been lost, stolen or mislaid.[312]

§ 2.7.10.2 Reversion Of title To Grantor Without Cancellation

Although Georgia law requires that the grantee of a deed to secure debt cancel the deed of record within 60 days of full payment of the debt,[313] there are cases where this does not happen. To address the problem of locating grantors of old deeds to secure debt, Georgia law provides that after a certain amount of time, title will revert to the grantor or her successors, even if the debt has not been satisfied of record.

Title to real property conveyed to secure a debt reverts to the grantor or her heirs, personal representatives, successors, and assigns at the expiration of seven years from the maturity of the debt or debts or the maturity of the last installment of the debt as stated in the record of the conveyance; provided, however, when the parties affirmatively state in the record of conveyance that they intend to establish an indefinite security interest, title reverts at the expiration of the later of (a) seven years from the maturity date of the debt or the maturity of the last installment as fixed in the record of conveyance, or (b) twenty years from the date of the conveyance as stated in the record.[314]

§ 2.7.11 Covenants

Covenants are restrictions on the way property may be used. In the 1970's, more elaborate sets of covenants began to be used as part of the development of condominiums and subdivisions. The covenants in these planned communities are contained in separate recorded legal documents typically known as a "declaration of condominium" in a condominium and a "declaration of covenants, conditions, and restrictions" ("CC&Rs") in a subdivision with a homeowners association. In addition to restrictions on the use of the property, the declarations typically address whether the owner must belong to the association of owners and pay assessments. They also generally give a developer special rights to develop the community and control the association.

Covenants are generally considered an encumbrance on property. However, although such covenants are in the chain of title to the property and may affect the economic marketability of title, they do not generally affect title marketability as that term is defined in the GAR Contract.

Under the GAR Contract, the seller must convey marketable title to the buyer, with the exception that declarations of condominium, declaration of covenants, and conditions and restrictions of record are permitted to be on the property so long as they were recorded on the property on or before the Binding Agreement Date of the contract.[315]

Earlier versions of the GAR Contract did not include declarations of condominium, declaration of covenants, conditions and restrictions of record, and the like within the warranty exceptions. Under those previous versions of the GAR Contract, if subdivision covenants were recorded against the property, the buyer could raise the existence of the covenants as a title defect.

---

312 O.C.G.A. § 44-14-67.

313 O.C.G.A. § 44-14-3.

314 O.C.G.A. § 44-14-80(a)(1).

315 GAR Form F20.

In any event, since an owner of such property has to comply with the covenants, it is important that a buyer obtain a copy of the covenants to review. Buyers are on legal notice of recorded covenants whether or not they read them and regardless of whether they agree to them in the contract. This is a concept known as constructive notice, and it applies to all documents recorded in the county land records. The declaration reviewed by a potential purchaser should be stamped by the clerk of court as having been recorded in the land records. This avoids the problem of purchasers being given an early, unrecorded draft of a declaration which is later changed to include provisions they find unacceptable.

Real estate brokers representing buyers as clients are well advised to ensure that the buyer reviews the covenants prior to signing a purchase contract. If a buyer signs the contract and then finds an unacceptable provision in the covenants, the buyer cannot use the provision as a basis for terminating the contract (unless the contract specifically provides for this). A special stipulation affording the buyer time to obtain and review the covenants is as follows.

> **Special Stipulation 24:   Agreement Subject to Acceptance of Covenants**
>
> *For and in consideration of the sum of $10 and other good and valuable consideration, the receipt and sufficiency of which is hereby acknowledged, Purchaser shall have _____ days from the Binding Agreement Date in which to review any declaration of covenants or declaration of condominium to which the Property is subject. If the terms of such declaration of covenants or declaration of condominium are not satisfactory to Purchaser, Purchaser may terminate this Agreement by providing written notice thereof to Seller within the stated time. In such event, the earnest money shall be returned to Purchaser.*

§ 2.7.11.1   Duration Of Covenants

Georgia law generally limits the term during which covenants apply to a piece of property in counties or municipalities that have adopted zoning laws to no more than 20 years,[316] subject to three exceptions. The first two exceptions relate to covenants on property subject to the Georgia Condominium Act[317] and the Georgia Property Owners' Association Act, which are perpetual.[318] The third exception is for subdivisions of 15 or more lots (that are not subject to the Georgia Property Owners' Association Act), where the covenants will automatically renew unless a majority of the lot owners execute and record an instrument terminating the covenants prior to their expiration.[319] This applies only to covenants recorded after 1993. Covenants recorded prior to 1993 may expire after 20 years, although some have provisions providing for their renewal.

In one case, a property owner sold property in a subdivision subject to covenants recorded on a plat. The covenants stated they would expire in 30 years. The covenants did not provide for renewal in any way. The purchaser acquired the property in 1973 after the covenants were recorded. The purchaser intended to develop the property that was shown on the plat as the recreation property for office or commercial use.[320] The court first held that the covenants expired in 20 years, not 30. The court further held that the purchaser relied on the plat and the law at the time of the purchase that the covenants would expire, and application of the statute would take away the purchaser's right to use the property. Therefore, the court held the statute would not apply retroactively to covenants recorded before 1993.

Many covenants recorded before 1993 limited the term to 20 years, but also contained provisions for automatic renewal for consecutive ten-year terms. The court's decision did not address the enforceability of such automatic renewal provisions in covenants recorded prior to the 1993 statute.

---

316 O.C.G.A. § 44-5-60(b).

317 O.C.G.A. § 44-3-116.

318 O.C.G.A. § 44-3-234.

319 O.C.G.A. § 44-5-60.

320 *Appalachee Enterprises, Inc. v. Walker*, 266 Ga. 35, 463 S.E.2d 896 (1995).

When buying a lot adjacent to or near undeveloped property designated by a developer for future recreational use, the buyer may want to consider adding the following provision to the sales contract to protect against the undeveloped property being used for non-recreational purposes in the future.

> **Special Stipulation 25:   Seller to Provide Covenant Against Property Being Developed for Non-Recreational Purposes**
>
> *This Agreement shall be contingent upon Seller, prior to closing, filing a restrictive covenant limiting the use of the property described on Exhibit "A" (legal description of recreation property) hereto recreational use only for the use and enjoyment of the owners in _____ subdivision.*

The provision and the requested restrictive covenant will be valid and enforceable only if the developer with whom the buyer is contracting also owns the undeveloped property.

§ 2.8   SPECIAL ISSUES: BUYING AND SELLING LAND WITH TIMBER OR CROPS

The sales price of agricultural land can vary widely depending on the value of crops on the land. This is particularly the case when there is standing timber on the property. If no agreement to the contrary has been reached, title to the standing timber passes with the title to the real estate.[321] In many situations, the ownership of the timber will be separated from the ownership of the underlying land.[322]

In many cases, the land will be sold subject to an existing timber lease. In such instances, the existing lease should be attached to the sales contract and incorporated therein.

In other cases, the seller will retain a right to come onto the property after it has been sold to cut timber. When this is the agreement of the parties, it is strongly recommended that this right not be described in a special stipulation to the contract, but that instead a separate timber contract be entered into in which the various issues which arise in timber contracts can be properly addressed. The timber contract can then be attached and incorporated into the sales contract and made contingent upon the closing of the sale of the land.

Alternatively, the seller may first have a cruise report done of the existing timber on the land and simply build the value of the timber into the sales price of the property. An example of a provision giving the seller the right to remove timber is set forth below.

> **Special Stipulation 26: Seller May Remove Timber after Closing**
>
> *Seller and Seller's agents shall have the right to come onto the Property for _____ days following the Closing of the sale of the Property to cut and remove timber. This right shall include the right to remove both pine trees and other softwoods and hardwoods. Any timber remaining on the Property at the end of the _____ period shall be the property of the Buyer.*
>
> *Seller acknowledges that Seller is as or more familiar than Buyer with the condition of the Property and any hazards or dangerous conditions located thereon, and Seller shall warn Seller's agents of all such hazards or dangerous conditions located on the Property. Seller agrees to indemnify and hold Buyer harmless from and against any and all claims, causes of action, suits, damages, and injuries, both to persons and property, arising out of or related to the performance of the timber removal work on the Property by Seller and Seller's agents.*

---

321 *Miller Lumber Co. v. Milan*, 57 Ga.App. 211, 194 S.E. 911 (1938).

322 *Kitchens v. Kirkland*, 215 Ga. 680, 113 S.E. 111 (1960).

Prior to commencing the timber removal work, Seller shall provide Buyer with a certificate of insurance from an insurance company licensed to do business within Georgia evidencing that Buyer has a current liability insurance policy in place with a single limit amount of at least $1,000,000 which names Buyer as an additional insured. Seller agrees to maintain the policy in full force and effect for the entire time period that Seller is removing timber from the Property, and to provide Buyer with a copy of the policy upon Buyer's request.

It shall be the Seller's responsibility to contact a utility locator service to mark the location of all utilities serving the Property. Seller shall be responsible for immediately repairing all utility lines damaged as a result of Seller's timber removal work. This provision shall survive the Closing.

§ 2.9 TITLE STANDARDS

The Title Standards adopted by the State Bar of Georgia are described as a "crystallization of the practice of title attorneys" and their purpose is to eliminate technical objections to title which do not impair marketability.

A title standard is a statement officially approved by a bar association which declares the answer to a question or a solution for a problem involved in the process of title examination. It is not a law, but acquires its authority from voluntary compliance by attorneys.

The Title Standards address a number of issues, including, but not limited to, the following: name variances; conveyances by co tenants; instruments executed by corporations; conveyances involving limited partnerships, general partnerships, and limited liability companies; title through decedents' estates; foreclosures; planned unit developments; bankruptcy; mineral rights; environmental issues; surveys; marital rights; conveyances by and to trustees; assessments for governmental improvements and services; federal tax liens; commercial real estate broker liens; zoning; and condemnation.

On occasion, good and marketable title will be defined in relationship to the title standards, as seen in the special stipulation below.

Special Stipulation 27:   Good and Marketable Title Based on Title Standards

At closing, Seller agrees to convey to Buyer good and marketable title to the Property by general warranty deed. For all purposes herein, "good and marketable" shall be determined in reference to the Title Standards of the State Bar of Georgia.

§ 2.10   TITLE INSURANCE AGAINST LOSSES ARISING THROUGH DEFECTS IN TITLE

Even if the title search is done perfectly, there may be encumbrances recorded between when the title examination is performed and the dates on which the warranty deed and deed to secure debt are recorded. This is called the "gap period" and is insured routinely by some, but not all, title insurers. Whether or not the gap is routinely insured may depend on the county in which the property is located and the county's timeliness in recording documents. Title insurance also protects against encumbrances not properly satisfied at closing and other claims of ownership caused by forged deeds, deeds by minors or incompetent persons, or the like.

Rather than a guarantee of marketable title, title insurance is generally described as an indemnity against unmarketability. Even though title insurance will not protect the owner against all risks associated with the purchase of property, buyers are well advised to purchase title insurance. It is a one-time expense that, if needed, can prove to be invaluable.

§ 2.10.1 Lender's Title Policy Does Not Protect Owner

Lenders require a title policy for their protection. The lender's policy insures against loss by the lender and its successors. It insures that the lender has an enforceable, valid lien on the property securing the loan. Since the lender's title insurance policy does not protect the buyer, the buyer should obtain a separate insurance policy, known as an owner's policy, to protect the buyer's ownership interest in the property.

Georgia courts have held that the duty of the insurer is only to its insured, not to one who is not a party to the contract, even though the buyer pays the premiums on the policies.[323] The cost of the title insurance policy is a closing cost which is often paid by the buyer. If the owner's title insurance is written at the same time as the lender's policy, a simultaneous issue rate is charged and the expense is less than if the buyer purchased an owner's title policy at a later date.

§ 2.10.2 Title Insurance Does Not Insure Against All Risks Of Ownership Of Property

The standard American Land Title Association (ALTA) owner's policy covers the following risks:

(a) Loss or damage resulting from title to the property being vested in someone other than the person listed on the policy;

(b) Loss or damage resulting from a lien or encumbrance on the title;

(c) Loss or damage resulting from a lack of right of access to the property;

(d) Loss or damage resulting from unmarketable title.

Title insurance is not the answer to every problem relating to property. There are five standard exceptions:

(1) Assessments and taxes from the year the policy is purchased;

(2) Rights or claims of parties in possession not shown by public records;

(3) Roadways, streams or easements not shown by public records, riparian rights and title to any filled-in land;

(4) Encroachments, overlaps, boundary line disputes and other matters that would be disclosed by an accurate survey or inspection; and

(5) Liens or rights to a lien for services, labor or material imposed by law and not shown in the public records.

Title insurance does not always cover the costs to correct the error in a faulty survey. In one case, a buyer brought an action against a title insurance company that denied coverage for what was described only as "2727 Spalding Drive" in the purchase contract.[324] The buyer walked the boundaries of the property with the seller, and the seller represented that he owned title to parcels one through four; but in fact, because of faulty surveys by predecessors in title, he owned only parcels two and three. The buyer claimed that he was led to believe that he was purchasing four parcels of land, but in reality, he paid for parcels two, three, and four and received a warranty deed describing only parcels two and three. The title insurance company reached a settlement with the buyer on parcel two because the warranty deed containing the property description insured included that parcel. The buyer then brought legal action against the title insurance company (among others), contending that the title policy did not include parcel four, which the parties intended to convey. Even though the court eventually found that the buyer had title to parcel four, the title insurance company was not responsible for any of the expenses because its policy did not insure that parcel.

Purchasers of title insurance should exercise caution in determining what is covered and what is excepted from the policy. For example, matters of survey are frequently excepted. If the warranty deed correctly describes the metes and bounds of the property, but the survey inaccurately shows more acreage than actually conveyed, the title insurance policy will

---

323 *Gaines v. American Title Ins. Co.*, 136 Ga.App. 162, 220 S.E.2d 469 (1975); *Sherrill v. Louisville Title Ins. Co.*, 134 Ga.App. 322, 214 S.E.2d 410 (1975).

324 *White v. Lawyers Title Ins. Corp.*, 197 Ga.App. 780, 399 S.E.2d 526 (1990).

not insure the shortage in area. On the other hand, if the survey is included under the policy, the shortage in area will be insured.[325] However, standard practice is for title insurers to specifically provide an exception that the exact acreage of the property is not insured.

§ 2.10.2.1 Other Excluded Risks

Other excluded risks are:

(a) Matters relating to building or zoning ordinances or regulations, environmental protection laws or any improper subdivision of property either current or back in the chain of title, and exercise of other governmental police power, unless there is notice in the "public records" at the date of the policy;

(b) Loss or damage relating to exercise of eminent domain;[326]

(c) Defects, liens, encumbrances, adverse claims or other matters including those resulting from those created, suffered, assumed or agreed to by the insured, those not known to the insurer or not recorded but known to the insured and not disclosed in writing to the insurer by the insured; those resulting in no loss or damage to the insured; those created after the policy date and those resulting in loss and damage because the insured did not pay value for the interest insured by the policy.

(d) Any fraud or preferential claim that is based on the current transaction and arising from the operation of federal bankruptcy, state insolvency or other creditors rights laws.

§ 2.10.3 Enhanced Title Policy

An enhanced title policy provides coverage for a range of different items that are not covered by the standard policy. The standard title policy protects the homeowner from certain limited risks of loss such as someone else having an ownership interest in the property and forgery or fraud in the chain of title. It also protects against other types of claims, such as a lien against the property due to an open security deed, a judgment, or a tax or special assessment. While this coverage is extremely important, title insurance companies began to receive requests for even better protection from homeowners who had suffered losses that were not covered by the standard title insurance policy. Hence, the Enhanced Title Insurance Policy was born. It was designed to provide the broadest protection currently available to homeowners. Although enhanced policies differ slightly from title insurance company to title insurance company, most offer similar coverage to protect against a range of unforeseen but more common title problems. In fact, there are approximately twenty-seven new coverage benefits in these policies.

One of the most important benefits is that the owner's coverage automatically increases in value by 10% per year for the first five years. This means that in five years coverage is 150% of the stated value of the policy with no additional fee. This protects a homeowner against large claims as his property increases in value.

Enhanced title insurance policies also protect against financial loss due to the lack of obtaining proper building permits and due to zoning violations. For instance, if a homeowner is forced to remove or amend an existing structure, including a boundary wall or a fence, because a previous owner did not obtain a proper building permit or because the structure violates a zoning ordinance, this coverage pays up to $25,000 after a small deductible. It also protects the homeowner if she is in danger of losing the title to his property, is unable to close a sale, or to obtain a loan because of the enforcement of restrictive covenant violations. The enhanced policy may also pay for rent for substitute land or facilities if that is deemed necessary. It also protects against loss from attempts of others to enforce covenant restrictions against the policyholder, subject to a small deductible.

---

325 *U.S. Life Title Ins. Co. of Dallas v. Hutsell*, 164 Ga.App. 443, 296 S.E.2d 760 (1983), *cert. denied*.

326 The right of the state to reassert its dominion over property for public exigency and public good.

Another significant benefit to the enhanced policy is that even if a buyer does not purchase a property survey, the policy still provides affirmative coverage against loss due to survey matters. This benefit is designed to cover problems such as improvements that do not conform to zoning requirements (for example, in the case of building set back requirements), encroachments upon the buyer's property or encroachments by the buyer upon a neighboring property, and the problems due to the placement of easements on the property.

The standard title insurance policy protects against legal lack of access to the property. That means as long as the property was granted an access easement, the owner was considered protected. However, if the access was obstructed with giant trees growing in the center of the path or if a deep ditch made the road impassable, the owner was on their own to resolve that problem. An enhanced title policy insures the homeowner's right to both pedestrian and vehicular access to his land. It even covers the owner if the subdivision was improperly subdivided prior to their purchase. Enhanced title insurance policies also cover the homeowner for loss against mechanics liens, or unrecorded liens, easements or leases.

One of the most advanced benefits of the enhanced policies is that they now cover post-issuance policy issues. This means that after the closing, if someone tries to forge a deed against the homeowner or if someone builds a structure (other than a boundary wall or a fence) which encroaches on the homeowner's land, he is covered against financial loss.

Additionally, the coverage for a living trust not only covers the trustees of a trust, but the beneficiaries as well. This important benefit expansion recognizes the growing popularity of living trusts as a wealth management tool, as well as addresses the concerns of trustors for those who will succeed them in ownership of real property.

Enhanced title policies are only available for one-to-four family residential structures and residential condominium units, but protect the homeowner and her heirs forever.

§ 2.10.4 "Insuring Over" Title Defects

Some defects can be "insured over" by a title insurance policy without having to correct the defect itself. When this happens, it is because the title insurer has agreed to insure the title in spite of the defect.

Title insurance companies will sometimes make the business decision to insure a title with a defect because the risk of an actual claim arising from the defect is small relative to the cost of curing the defect. In other cases, while the risk may be significant, it may be a risk that the title insurer is already bearing under an existing policy, and as such, the insurer is willing to continue to insure the risk going forward. In other cases, the title insurer will agree to insure a risky title to generate good will and enhance business relationships.

If the defect can be insured over, the transaction can go forward and the buyer is still able to purchase title insurance.

§ 2.10.4.1 Low Risk Issues

Some defects have a small risk. These are defects where no one is likely to come forward and challenge or make a claim on the title. These include such issues as an old open security deed. If the security deed was from a long time ago and was for a previous owner, the title insurance company may agree to insure over this defect if they think there is very little likelihood that the lender, who was the beneficiary of the security deed, will come back and make a claim. The title insurance company may look at several factors, such as how long ago the loan was taken out and whether or not it should have been paid off by now. If there is documentation from a previous closing showing that the loan was paid off, such as a settlement statement showing the payoff and/or a cancelled check, that may be sufficient to warrant insuring over the defect. The risk is clearly quite low.

Other defects may represent only small issues, or may not have a large monetary risk attached to them. In that case, the title insurance company looks at the amount of time that has passed since the defect occurred and the level of risk that they will have a claim made against the title. Time solves a lot of issues. For example, liens are usually only good for a certain amount of time before they expire. Old security deeds expire. Long lost heirs only have a certain amount of time to make a claim. Sometimes a defect may be small and not carry much risk, but also be quick and inexpensive to fix. In that case, the title insurance company may require the defect to be corrected.

§ 2.10.4.2 High Risk Issues

Some defects simply have too high of a risk and cannot be insured over. These are defects where the title insurance company determines there is too much likelihood that a claim would surface due to the defect and there is too much exposure for them to insure over. In those cases, there is no other option but to correct the defect, no matter how long it takes or how much it costs, or to walk away from the deal.

It would be wonderful to be able to clear up every title defect on every property and pass along pristinely clean title from owner to owner. In reality, though, this would be very time consuming and expensive and would lead to many cases where a closing could not occur because a very small defect could not be cleared off of the title. A mortgage company may have gone bankrupt 40 years ago and disappeared. There may be no way to get them to sign a Quitclaim Deed releasing their open security deed if they don't exist anymore. A person holding a small interest in a property from 40 years ago may be impossible to locate. If these defects can be insured over, due to the small risk involved, the transaction can go forward and the seller, the buyer and the agents can still have their closing.

§ 2.10.5 Title To Property Can Be Marketable And Still Be Worthless In Economic Sense

Title insurance is not a guarantee that the property is worth what the buyer paid for it, and it does not protect against a drop in fair market value of the property. The fact that property is in a flood plain is not considered a title defect.[327] However, the price the buyer paid for the property may be in excess of its worth if the buyer was not aware of the fact that the property was in a flood plain.

§ 2.11 BANKRUPTCY BY SELLER CAN AFFECT TITLE

Bankruptcy proceedings affect the conveyance and encumbrance of property and the enforceability of liens against property, but do not automatically extinguish all judgments and liens against a debtor's property. To convey marketable title, a seller in bankruptcy will have to follow certain procedures outlined in the Bankruptcy Code.[328] These procedures may vary depending on the type of bankruptcy action filed. Bankruptcy actions may fall under several chapters as follows: a Chapter 7 is a liquidation; a Chapter 11 is a reorganization for a corporation, or for an individual with unsecured debt in excess of $250,000 and secured debt in excess of $750,000 as of the date of filing of a bankruptcy; a Chapter 12 is family farmer bankruptcy; and a Chapter 13 is an individual reorganization for all other individuals.

Whenever property to be sold is owned by a person or entity in bankruptcy, the closing attorney should be notified as soon as possible, to give her time to verify that all necessary documentation is available so that the parties can be assured that marketable title can be conveyed. The conveyance will likely be subject to the approval of the bankruptcy judge, which may take time to obtain. Many bankruptcy issues can be complex and are beyond the scope of this book. Outlined below is a brief review of issues involved when property to be sold is part of a bankruptcy action.

§ 2.11.1 Property Of Debtor That Is Part Of Bankruptcy

The property of a bankrupt individual or entity is known as the bankruptcy estate or property of the estate. The bankruptcy estate consists of all property of the debtor at the commencement of the case.[329] Inheritance, property received through a property settlement or divorce decree, and life insurance benefits the debtor receives or is entitled

---

327 *Chicago Title Ins. Co. v. Investguard, Ltd.*, 215 Ga.App. 121, 449 S.E.2d 681 (1994).

328 11 U.S.C.A. § 101, *et seq.*

329 11 U.S.C.A. § 541(a)(1).

to receive within 180 days from the date the bankruptcy action is filed are also property of the estate.[330] Additionally, in a Chapter 13 case, property of the estate includes property the debtor acquires after commencement of the case but before the case is closed.[331]

§ 2.11.2   Purchase And Sale Agreement Can Be Rejected In Bankruptcy

If property is listed or a contract for sale of property is entered into before the bankruptcy is filed, the Bankruptcy Code allows the bankruptcy trustee to assume or reject any contract which has been signed, but not yet carried out (*i.e.*, an executory contract). In a Chapter 7 bankruptcy action, the contract is deemed rejected if not assumed (specifically agreed to) by the bankruptcy trustee within 60 days of the filing of the petition.[332] In Chapter 11 and Chapter 13 cases, the debtor generally retains possession of the property and has the power to assume or reject an executory contract at any time before confirmation of the bankruptcy reorganization plan.[333]

A listing agreement is an executory contract. Accordingly, if a real estate broker has property listed when the owner filed for bankruptcy the broker may request an order directing the debtor to decide within a specified time whether to assume or reject the listing agreement.[334] The attorney for the broker would normally file this request. In addition, the broker should file a motion with the bankruptcy court for approval of employment of a professional person. The broker's motion for approval of employment of a professional person, if granted, should ensure that when a motion to sell the property is filed with the court the commission will be paid to the broker directly out of closing.[335]

If the broker does not verify that the debtor has affirmed the listing agreement and if the broker does not apply to the court for appointment as a professional person, there is a risk that the property could be sold while listed, but that the broker would not receive any commission. In the alternative, the broker may have to file a lawsuit and make an equitable argument for entitlement to a commission in the event of a sale.

If the listing agreement or real estate contract is entered into after the owner files a bankruptcy petition, the issues above regarding executory contracts do not exist. However, in most cases the court must approve the sale, so the real estate broker is still going to need to pay attention to what is happening in the bankruptcy.

§ 2.11.3   Impact On Real Estate Transaction If One Co-Owner Files For Bankruptcy But Other Does Not

If one co-owner of property files a petition in bankruptcy, any property that is jointly owned will be affected, but any other property owned by the non-filing co-owner, individually or jointly with some other third party, will not be affected. If only one spouse files a bankruptcy action, property owned solely by the spouse who has not filed bankruptcy will not be affected. For example, if a wife owns property in her own name and her husband does not have any interest in the property, the property will not be affected if the husband files a bankruptcy petition.

If husband and wife own the property jointly, however, either as joint tenants or as tenants in common, the bankruptcy petition of the husband will affect the property even if the wife does not file. In some instances, the property may be released from the bankruptcy estate due to an exemption which the debtor may claim.

In certain cases where the non-bankrupt owner does not agree to the sale, the bankruptcy trustee has the authority to sell the entire property anyway, including the interest of the non-bankrupt owner. This can happen when: partition of the property between the bankruptcy estate and co-owner(s) is impracticable; the sale of the estate's undivided interest in the

---

330   11 U.S.C.A. § 541(a)(5).

331   11 U.S.C.A. § 1306.

332   11 U.S.C.A. §365(d)(1).

333   11 U.S.C.A. §365(d)(2).

334   11 U.S.C.A. §365(d)(2).

335   11 U.S.C.A. §327.

property would realize significantly less for the estate than sale of the property free of the interest of such co-owner(s); and the benefit to the estate of a sale of such property free and clear of the interests of co-owner(s) outweighs the detriments, if any, to the co-owner(s).[336] In such cases, the co-owner(s) may purchase the property at the price at which the sale is to be consummated.[337]

§ 2.11.4   Sale Of Property Under Protection Of Bankruptcy

In a Chapter 7 case, the bankruptcy trustee is the party who would sign a deed of conveyance, unless the trustee abandons her interest in the property because it has little or no value to the estate. If the trustee sells the property, marketable title may be conveyed if there is an order authorizing the sale of the property filed in the bankruptcy court showing notice given to all creditors and an opportunity for hearing, documentation of the appointment of the trustee, and proof that the property is property of the estate.[338]

If the trustee abandons the property in a Chapter 7 bankruptcy, the debtor may sell it; however, it is subject to all liens and encumbrances. In some cases the debtor may avoid a judicial lien on property to the extent that it impairs an exception;[339] however, the debtor may not avoid statutory and certain other liens against the property. The debtor may convey marketable title upon proof showing that the trustee has abandoned the property and upon satisfaction or release of liens which are not avoided under the Bankruptcy Code.[340]

Chapter 11 reorganization cases are generally more complex than Chapter 7 and Chapter 13 cases. In many Chapter 11 cases, a trustee is not appointed. In such a case, a debtor may sell estate property subject to certain notice requirements to creditors and an opportunity for a hearing.[341] If the sale is considered to be in the "ordinary business" of the Chapter 11 debtor, notice to creditors may not be necessary.[342] If the sale is authorized as part of the confirmed plan, marketability of the title to the property will not be impaired.[343]

In a Chapter 13 case, marketability of the title to the property will not be impaired if the debtor has obtained a final order authorizing the sale after notice to creditors and the opportunity for a hearing.[344] As in a Chapter 7 case where the debtor may sell the property, the sale of the property will be subject to outstanding liens and encumbrances unless the order from the court specifically provides that the sale is "free and clear of all liens."[345]

In most instances, the trustee or debtor conveying the property will obtain an order that the sale is free and clear of all liens. Generally, in order to obtain an order authorizing the sale, the sales contract must provide for sales proceeds to be used to pay liens that have not been avoided.

§ 2.12   EFFECT OF DIVORCE ON TITLE

Property owned by a spouse prior to marriage remains the separate property of that spouse.[346] However, both spouses acquire an equitable interest in property acquired after the marriage, even if the property is titled in the name of only one

---

336   11 U.S.C.A. § 363(h).

337   11 U.S.C.A. § 363(i).

338   State Bar of Georgia Title Standards, §21.2(B); 11 U.S.C.A. § 363.

339   11 U.S.C.A. § 522(f).

340   State Bar of Georgia Title Standards, §21.2(C).

341   11 U.S.C.A. §363.

342   11 U.S.C.A. §363(c)(1). A determination of what is in the "ordinary course of business" is not always plain and may require an order of the court.

343   State Bar of Georgia Title Standards, §21.2(d).

344   11 U.S.C.A. §363, State Bar of Georgia Title Standards, §21.2(e).

345   11 U.S.C.A. §363(f) and (g).

346   O.C.G.A. § 19-3-9; *Bailey v. Bailey*, 250 Ga. 15, 295 S.E.2d 304 (1982).

of the spouses. Such property is subject to later equitable division.[347] Third parties are not affected by the equitable interest of a spouse until an order or petition for divorce is filed in the county in which the property is located.[348]

§ 2.12.1   Transferring Title During Divorce Proceedings

If a notice of *lis pendens* has been filed in the superior court of the county where the land is located after a petition for divorce has been filed, neither party may transfer the property to avoid the vesting of title according to the final verdict in the divorce, except for a bona fide transfer in payment of preexisting debts.[349] Even if a notice of *lis pendens* is not recorded, both spouses' signatures should be obtained on real property transfers which occur while a divorce or separate maintenance action is pending.[350] When the broker is aware that property is being sold when a divorce is pending, she should advise the client to consult with her divorce attorney to determine if the property will be in dispute in the divorce and whether the client's spouse will need to consent to the sale.

§ 2.12.2   Title By Decree

Georgia law provides that a decree for specific performance operates as a deed to convey land or other property without any conveyance being executed by the vendor, if the decree is recorded in the superior court of the county where the property is located, and the decree "shall stand in the place of a deed."[351] Even when the decree is not recorded, the decree transfers the title to the property.[352]

The State Bar of Georgia Title Standards also provide that a divorce decree declaring title to be vested in one spouse is sufficient to vest title without the need of a deed, provided the decree contains a sufficient description of the property.[353] The Title Standards further provide, however, that if the decree calls for a deed but does not contain vesting language, then a deed must be obtained.[354] Georgia case law provides that when one spouse receives a percentage of the net proceeds, such award is not an interest in property and it is not necessary to obtain a quitclaim deed from the other spouse.[355]

§ 2.13   TITLE THROUGH DECEDENT'S ESTATE

When a person dies, the procedure for administering the estate is similar to the liquidation process that takes place when a corporation goes out of business. A personal representative is appointed to wrap up the affairs of the person who has died ("decedent"). If the decedent dies with a will, the representative is called the executor and may be named in the will. If the person dies without a will (intestate), the representative is called the administrator and is appointed by the court according to a statutory procedure.

The duties of the personal representative are to collect and conserve the assets of the decedent, pay claims of creditors and distribute any remaining assets of the decedent. The representative is under the control of and accountable to the Probate Court. To "go through probate" means to have an estate administered by the Probate Court.

---

347 O.C.G.A. § 19-5-13; *Stokes v. Stokes*, 246 Ga. 765, 273 S.E.2d 169 (1980).

348 State Bar of Georgia Title Standards, §27.2(a).

349 O.C.G.A. § 19-5-7.

350 O.C.G.A. § 19-5-7.

351 O.C.G.A. § 9-11-70. This code section also provides remedies against a party who fails to comply with an order for specific performance (*i.e.*, a requirement to execute a deed).

352 *Richardson v. Park Ave. Bank*, 173 Ga.App. 43, 325 S.E.2d 455 (1984).

353 State Bar of Georgia Title Standards, § 27.2; *Elrod v. Elrod*, 231 Ga. 222, 200 S.E.2d 885(1973).

354 State Bar of Georgia Title Standards, § 27.2.

355 *Sisk v. Sisk*, 214 Ga. 223, 104 S.E.2d 103 (1958); *Lawrence v. Smith*, 213 Ga. 57, 96 S.E.2d 579 (1957).

The State Bar of Georgia Title Standards set forth the criteria that must be met in order to have marketable title conveyed from an estate.[356] The methods used to determine what is necessary to convey title through a decedent's estate will depend on a number of factors including, but not limited to, the following: (1) whether the decedent died intestate or with a will; (2) how long ago the decedent died; and (3) if the decedent died with a will, how the will was probated and whether or not it authorizes sale of the property.

A surviving spouse or minor children may apply for a year's support, which is defined as that property or money set apart and assigned to the spouse and children, or children only, for their support and maintenance for 12 months from the date of death.[357] An application for a year's support will affect the ability of an administrator or executor to transfer property.

It is important to ascertain that the party executing the contract has proper authority to act on behalf of the estate. If the party does not have such authority, the contract will be null and void. The ability to convey good and marketable title to property out of an estate may be time-consuming and somewhat involved and goes beyond the scope of this book. Even if the party executing the contract has authority to enter the contract, the closing attorney should always be made aware as soon as possible that the property is being sold by an estate to give the attorney time to resolve issues and obtain the necessary verification that title is marketable. In some cases, for example, the Georgia Title Standards require the heirs to execute an affidavit renouncing their interest in the property. Obtaining such affidavits may be time-consuming because of the number of heirs. The closing attorney may refer certain situations to a probate attorney to handle unresolved issues before the closing may take place.

§ 2.14   TITLE THROUGH TRUSTEE

To ensure that marketable title is conveyed from a trust, the existence of the trust and the authority of the trustee must be verified.[358] Georgia law provides that an express trust must be in writing and must have each of the following elements, ascertainable with reasonable certainty: (1) an intention by a settlor to create a trust; (2) trust property; (3) a beneficiary; (4) a trustee; and (4) active duties imposed on the trustee.[359] A trustee has no authority to sell or convey the property of the trust estate unless expressly authorized by the instrument creating the trust or pursuant to an order of the superior court.[360] In many cases, verification as to the existence of the trust and authority of the trustee must be made by reference to facts or documents outside the record.

If a decedent conveys property to a trust by her will, the provisions of the Testamentary Additions to Trusts Act should be considered.[361] This statute provides that property conveyed by a testator under a will shall be part of the trust to which it is given, and shall be administered and disposed of in accordance with the provisions of the instrument or will setting forth the terms of the trust.[362]

§ 2.15   TITLE BY PRESCRIPTION OR ADVERSE POSSESSION

A possessor of property may acquire title to the property by prescription if the possession extends over the period of time prescribed by statute, commonly referred to as adverse possession. Georgia law provides that possession of real property for a period of 20 years shall confer good title against everyone with a few exceptions.[363]

---

356 State Bar of Georgia Title Standards, § 13.1 13.14.

357 O.C.G.A. § 53-5-2.

358 *See* Chapter 3 (Parties to the Contract) for capacity of trustee to execute a contract.

359 O.C.G.A. § 53-12-20.

360 O.C.G.A. § 53-12-257.

361 O.C.G.A. § 53-12-70, *et seq.*

362 O.C.G.A. § 53-12-71.

363 O.C.G.A. § 44-5-163. Title by prescription cannot be acquired in respect of public property. *City of Marietta v. CSX Transp., Inc.*, 272 Ga. 612, 533 S.E.2d 372 (2000). Other exceptions listed in O.C.G.A. § 44-5-170.

In order to acquire title by prescription, the claimant must be the party in possession of the property and the possession must be public, continuous, exclusive, uninterrupted, peaceable, and not obtained by actual fraud. The adverse possession must be continuous for more than twenty (20) years. If there has been more than one owner of the property during that time period, the owner bringing the adverse possession claim can add her period of ownership to that of prior owners in the chain of title, provided that collectively they add up to more than 20 continuous years of adverse possession. If the possession is by permission of the owner, the possession cannot amount to title unless the claimant has given actual notice of the claim to the owner.[364] Therefore, owners who discover that a neighbor is bringing an adverse possession claim should consider sending a letter to the claimant giving them a permissive right to occupy the property being claimed until the dispute is either resolved or the owner notifies the claimant that her possessive right is being terminated. In this way, the time period necessary to establish adverse possession is not running during the pendency of the dispute.

§ 2.15.1 What Constitutes Sufficient Possession

The possession of property that is grounds for an adverse possession claim may be by successive owners, provided that the requisite time period for adverse possession is achieved by "tacking" or adding together the periods of their possession.[365]

What constitutes sufficient possession of the property to have a claim for adverse possession ripen into legal title to the property is largely a question of fact. Examples of situations deemed sufficient to establish possession of the property include payment of taxes on the property claimed;[366] cultivating the land, harvesting trees, creating roads and keeping others off of the property;[367] construction of permanent buildings on the land when followed by occupancy of such buildings;[368] and erecting fences, walls and barriers.[369]

Examples of situations not deemed sufficient to constitute possession include: allowing livestock to roam on the land,[370] mowing of grass and occasionally cleaning up the property,[371] and posting signs forbidding trespassing and driving away hunters.[372]

§ 2.15.2 Possession Must Be Adverse To Interests Of Record Owner

If possession of the property is permissive, there is no claim for adverse possession. So, for example, if a property owner gives a neighbor written permission to erect a fence slightly over the property line onto the owner's property, no claim for adverse possession can be brought for the land enclosed by the neighbor's fence.

§ 2.15.3 Color Of Title

The prescribed time period is reduced to seven years if there is some written evidence of title, legally referred to as "color of title," which does not actually pass title but is sufficient evidence of the claim to title.[373] "Color of title" means a document that on its face appears to transfer title, but which fails to do so because the transferee does not have title or because the conveyance was defective in some way. In other words, that there is some form of written evidence showing at least the attempt to transfer title of property to the claimant.

---

364 *Love v. Love*, 259 Ga. 423, 383 S.E.2d 329 (1989).

365 O.C.G.A. § 44-5-172.

366 *Georgia Power Co. v. Irvin*, 267 Ga. 760, 482 S.E.2d 362 (1997).

367 *Cooley v. McRae*, 275 Ga. 435, 569 S.E.2d 845 (2002).

368 *Serritt v. Johnson*, 223 Ga. 620, 157 S.E.2d 484 (1967).

369 O.C.G.A. § 44-5-165.

370 *Fitzpatrick v. Massee-Felton Lumber Co.*, 188 Ga. 80, 3 S.E.2d 91 (1939).

371 *Friendship Baptist Church, Inc. v. West*, 265 Ga. 745, 462 S.E.2d 618 (1995).

372 *Fitzpatrick v. Massee-Felton Lumber Co.*, 188 Ga. 80, 3 S.E.2d 91 (1939).

373 O.C.G.A. § 44-5-164.

The conditions are that the property must be described so that it can be identified with certainty and the claimant must have claim to the property in good faith. The rationale of allowing a claimant to have good title despite only having "color of title" is to make a bad title good when the claimant has bought the property in good faith, and believing he has obtained good title, enters into possession and remains there uninterruptedly and peaceably. The date of the seven-year period begins to run from the date of the written color of title and not from the time of possession.

§ 2.15.3.1   Documents Which Qualify As "Color Of Title"

Set forth below are examples of documents which qualify as "color of title" which ripen into good title:

(a)   A deed from a partnership signed only by one partner;[374]

(b)   A sheriff's deed that is based on a void judgment;[375]

(c)   A deed purporting to transfer title which was void because of the failure to comply with divorce or probate law;[376]

(d)   A quitclaim deed;[377] and

(e)   A deed from a seller who did not have title to the property.[378]

§ 2.15.3.2   Examples Which Do Not Qualify As "Color Of Title"

The following are examples of situations which were held not to constitute "color of title":

(a)   A void mortgage;

(b)   The payment of taxes (held not to be evidence of title, but admissible as a circumstance tending to prove adverse possession);[379] and

(c)   A deed lacking a good legal description from which the property could not be identified.[380]

§ 2.15.4   Adverse Possession Claim Not Available In Certain Circumstances

As a general rule, adverse possession is ineffective against property owned by a governmental entity.[381] It will also not generally be effective when the owner is a minor, confined in prison, insane, or under some other similar disability.[382]

§ 2.16   EFFECT OF FORECLOSURE

Foreclosures in Georgia may be either by judicial procedure or by non-judicial procedure. Judicial foreclosures may be conducted pursuant to statutory procedures[383] or equitable procedures.[384] However, the method of foreclosure used by virtually all lenders in Georgia is foreclosure by non-judicial power of sale which is exercised under a deed to secure

---

374   *Tarver v. Depper*, 132 Ga. 798, 65 S.E. 177, 24 L.R.A.N.S. 1161 (1909).

375   *Rogers v. Smith*, 146 Ga. 373, 91 S.E. 414 (1917).

376   *Carpenter v. Booker*, 131 Ga 546, 62 S.E. 983 (1908); *Ponder v. Ponder*, 275 Ga. 616, 571 S.E.2d 343 (2002).

377   *Warlick v. Rome Loan & Finance Co.*, 194 Ga. 419, 22 S.E.2d 61 (1942).

378   *Gitten v. Lowry*, 15 Ga. 336 (1854).

379   *Chamblee v. Johnson*, 200 Ga. 838, 38 S.E.2d 721 (1946).

380   *Donaldson v. Nichols*, 223 Ga. 206, 154 S.E.2d 201 (1967).

381   *City of Marietta v. CSX Transp., Inc.*, 272 Ga. 612, 533 S.E.2d 372 (2000). The Georgia Supreme Court held that there can be no adverse possession against property owned by a city, county or state.

382   O.C.G.A. § 44-5-171.

383   O.C.G.A. § 44-14-180, § 44-14-210.

384   O.C.G.A. § 44-14-49.

debt.[385] Once a borrower has waived her rights to a judicial sale, the lender can foreclose on the property using a non-judicial sale. Although there is no statutory procedure for conducting non-judicial foreclosure sales, such sales must be advertised and conducted in the same manner as sheriff's sales[386] and notice must be provided to the debtor.[387]

Specifically, the lender is required to send the delinquent owner a 30-day letter giving the owner an opportunity to cure the mortgage default.[388] The lender is also required to advertise the property for sale for four consecutive weeks in an official legal newspaper of the county.[389] The 30-day cure letter can be sent at the same time that the property is being advertised for sale by the lender.[390] The property is then sold at public auction the first Tuesday of the month after the procedure has been followed. In states where only judicial sales are allowed, the length of time it takes a lender to foreclose can be measured in years, rather than the few months it typically takes to non-judicially foreclose on property in Georgia.

In order to convey marketable title through a foreclosure sale, all statutory and contractual requirements must be complied with and there must be no outstanding rights of redemption. In a non-judicial foreclosure sale, the security instrument and succession of transfers to the current holder should be recorded. This allows the examining party to verify the instrument under which the property was foreclosed and to verify that all contractual requirements are met.

For example, failure to pay intangible recording tax applicable to a security instrument is a bar to foreclosure.[391] This bar to foreclosure may be removed by payment of the tax plus penalty and interest. The security instrument should also outline the terms and procedures for conducting the foreclosure sale and these terms and procedures must be followed. Finally, the instrument must contain a valid power of attorney empowering the grantee to conduct the foreclosure sale and execute the deed under power of sale as attorney-in-fact for the grantor.[392]

Prior to commencing foreclosure, the foreclosing party should also ensure that, if applicable, the Servicemembers Civil Relief Act[393] has been complied with. This statute provides protection to people in the military service from loss of certain interests in property during the period in which they are involved in a military conflict and can preclude foreclosure.

A valid foreclosure sale generally terminates the debtor's interest in the property and there is no right of redemption in favor of the debtor or junior lien holders. If an IRS tax lien is properly filed more than 30 days prior to the foreclosure sale date, written notice of the foreclosure sale must be given to the Internal Revenue Service at least 25 days prior to the sale date. If such notice is not given, a federal tax lien is not eliminated by the foreclosure sale of a senior security instrument. If a federal tax lien is eliminated by the foreclosure sale, the United States has a period of 120 days from the date of the sale to redeem the property.

If the owner of the property filed a bankruptcy action, an automatic stay precluding creditors from proceeding against the debtor's property arises upon commencement of the bankruptcy case.[394] If a bankruptcy is pending on the date of foreclosure, there must be evidence that the foreclosing party complied with the provisions of the Bankruptcy Code.[395]

385 O.C.G.A. § 23-2-114.
386 O.C.G.A. § 44-14-162.
387 O.C.G.A. § 44-14-162.1 - 162.4.
388 O.C.G.A. § 44-14-162.2.
389 O.C.G.A. § 44-14-162.2.
390 O.C.G.A. § 44-14-162.2.
391 O.C.G.A. § 48-6-77(a).
392 State Bar of Georgia Title Standards, § 17.1.
393 50 App. U.S.C.A. § 501, *et seq.*
394 11 U.S.C.A. § 362.
395 11 U.S.C.A. § 101, *et seq.*

A foreclosing party must generally obtain from the bankruptcy court an order for a relief from stay to proceed with foreclosure. Oftentimes, the homeowner is at the bankruptcy court on the morning of the foreclosure. Even though the foreclosing lender is not aware of the filing of the bankruptcy, the automatic stay is nonetheless effective and renders the foreclosure void.

As an alternative to foreclosure, a conveyance of property in lieu of foreclosure may be made by quitclaim deed, limited warranty deed, or general warranty deed from the debtor to the lender. However, a deed in lieu of foreclosure does not eliminate junior security interests. Most lenders will therefore not accept a deed in lieu of foreclosure and will choose to exercise their rights under the deed to secure debt.

§ 2.17 TRANSFER OF TITLE BY DEED

A deed is a written instrument used to convey the ownership of property from one party to another. A party who executes a deed and relinquishes her interest in the property is called the grantor. The person receiving the grantor's interest in the property is the grantee.

§ 2.17.1 Requirements For Valid Deed

To be valid, a deed must be a written instrument purporting to convey title to the land.[396] Title to real estate cannot be conveyed orally but must be conveyed in writing.[397] A deed must also contain:

(a) A <u>grantor</u>, that is, a person or legal entity possessing the property and having the legal ability to convey title.[398]

(b) A <u>grantee</u>, a person or a legal entity capable of holding title to the conveyed property.[399]

(c) <u>Words of conveyance or granting clause</u>. Although a deed must contain language which has the effect of conveying title, no particular form of words is necessary. The granting clause must clearly express the grantor's intent to make a present or immediate conveyance of title to the grantee, not a future conveyance.[400] Phrases most commonly used are: "bargain, sell, and convey," "give, grant, and convey," "demise, quitclaim, and release," "transfer and assign."[401]

(d) <u>A description of the property sufficient to identify it</u>. The property being conveyed must be described so that it can be clearly distinguished from all other parcels of land. If the description is so indefinite that it cannot be identified with certainty, the deed is void.[402]

(e) <u>Signature of the grantor</u>. Although the names of both the grantor and grantee appear in the deed, only the grantor is required to sign it since it is the grantor who is conveying the title.[403]

(f) <u>Delivery and acceptance</u>. Title to real estate is conveyed when a properly executed deed is delivered to and accepted by the grantee or grantee's agent.[404] The grantee's acceptance need not be by express words, but may be by acts, conduct, or words showing an intention to accept the conveyance.[405] Acceptance may be inferred from such

---

396 O.C.G.A. § 44-5-30.

397 O.C.G.A. § 13-5-30.

398 *McCollum v. Loveless*, 187 Ga. 262, 200 S.E. 115 (1938).

399 *State Highway Dept. v. Williams Lumber Co.*, 222 Ga. 23, 148 S.E.2d 426 (1966); *Handy v. Handy*, 154 Ga. 686, 115 S.E. 114 (1922).

400 *Caldwell v. Caldwell*, 140 Ga. 736, 79 S.E. 853 (1913).

401 *Woodward v. LaPorte*, 181 Ga. 731, 184 S.E. 280 (1935).

402 *Allen v. Smith*, 169 Ga. 395, 150 S.E. 584 (1929); *Furney v. Dukes*, 226 Ga. 804, 177 S.E.2d 680 (1970). *See* Chapter 4 (Describing the Property) for an in-depth discussion of this topic.

403 O.C.G.A. § 44-5-30.

404 *Domestic Loans of Washington, Inc. v. Wilder*, 113 Ga.App. 803, 149 S.E.2d 717 (1966).

405 *Domestic Loans of Washington, Inc. v. Wilder*, 113 Ga.App. 803, 149 S.E.2d 717 (1966); *McKenzie v. Alston*, 58 Ga.App. 849, 853, 200 S.E. 518 (1938).

facts as retention of the deed, assertion of title, subsequent sale or encumbrance of the property, or bringing suit on the deed.[406]

There are two other elements that are usually included in a deed, even though the deed is valid between the parties in their absence:[407]

(g) A good or valuable consideration. This is defined as the inducement to a contract and must be something of value moving from the grantee to the grantor. As between parties, a deed without actual consideration may be valid if a nominal consideration is recited, or if the conveyance was intended as a gift.[408] Conveyances without actual consideration are termed "voluntary deeds" and are recognized as recordable.[409] A deed which recites the payment of a consideration is valid even though it is a nominal amount and may not in fact have been paid, since it could be sued for and recovered.[410]

(h) Attestation and/or acknowledgment is required in order for the deed to be recorded.[411] An attestation is the act of witnessing the actual execution of the paper and signing one's name as a witness to the execution. An acknowledgment is the act of a grantor going before a notary public and declaring the paper to be her deed. The deed is then accompanied by a certificate of the notary public stating that the acknowledgment was made.[412] In order for a deed to be recorded, it must be attested to by at least two witnesses, one of whom must be a notary, or attested to by two witnesses and acknowledged by a notary.[413] This requirement goes only to the recordability of the deed and a deed will not be invalid between the parties simply because there is no attestation.[414]

§ 2.17.2 Types Of Deeds

All deeds serve the same basic function, which is to convey the grantor's interest in property. This function is accomplished after a deed has been properly executed, delivered, and accepted. The distinctions between deeds are found in the extent of title protection the grantor promises the grantee, the identity of the grantor, and the circumstances under which the property is conveyed.

§ 2.17.2.1 General Warranty Deed

A general warranty deed offers the most comprehensive title protection of any deed. It contains covenants of title which are promises by the grantor that certain conditions of title exist. Typical covenants of title include: covenant of seisin, covenant against encumbrances, covenant of quiet enjoyment, covenant of warranty forever, and covenant of further assurances.[415] The covenants in a warranty deed apply not only to title defects occurring during the grantor's period of ownership but also to those occurring before she took title. The GAR Purchase and Sale Agreement provides that the seller will convey title by general warranty deed. Many builder contracts provide that title will be conveyed by limited warranty deed. When buyers receive title to a property by limited warranty deed, they will often want to convey title to the property by limited warranty deed when they sell the property. In this way, they are not warranting the title beyond the warranties they received when they purchased the property.

---

406 *Widincamp v. Brigman*, 166 Ga. 209, 143 S.E. 149 (1928).

407 O.C.G.A. § 44-5-30.

408 *Dodson v. Phagan*, 227 Ga. 480, 181 S.E.2d 366 (1971).

409 O.C.G.A. § 44-2-3.

410 *Thornton v. North American Acceptance Corp.*, 228 Ga. 176, 184 S.E.2d 589 (1971).

411 O.C.G.A. § 44-2-14.

412 *White & Co. v. Magarahan*, 87 Ga. 217, 13 S.E. 509 (1891), *overruled on other grounds*.

413 O.C.G.A. §§ 44-2-14, 44-2-15, 44-5-30.

414 *Domestic Loans of Washington, Inc. v. Wilder*, 113 Ga.App. 803, 149 S.E.2d 717 (1966).

415 O.C.G.A. § 44-5-62.

§ 2.17.2.2   Limited Warranty Deed

A limited warranty deed is distinguished from a general warranty deed in that the grantor warrants the property's title only against defects occurring during the grantor's ownership and not against defects existing before that time.[416]

For example, the purchaser in one case had purchased a property by way of a limited warranty deed.[417] The seller was the bank, which became the owner after foreclosing on the loan and obtaining a power of sale. The warranty provided that the " … Grantor will warrant and forever defend the right and title to the above described property unto the said Grantee against the claims of all persons claiming by, through or under Grantor, and not otherwise." The bank was not aware that there were unpaid taxes on the property, which constituted a lien on the property. The lien existed before the bank became the owner of the property.

The tax authority claimed the unpaid taxes against the buyer, who then sued the bank for reimbursement. The court stated that the limited warranty only protects the buyer against claims made after the conveyance by the bank or by some person claiming through or under the bank. The bank did not warranty anything else except as against itself and its own acts, or acts of third parties affecting the right to possession, which occur during the time of when the bank owned the property. Since the tax lien was imposed by the tax authority and not the bank or anyone claiming under the bank, the tax lien did not fall within the limited warranty.

§ 2.17.2.3   Quitclaim

A quitclaim is intended to pass any title, interest, or claim which the grantor may have in the property, but it does not guarantee the title is valid and does not contain any warranty or covenants of title.[418]

§ 2.17.2.4   Gift Deed Or Voluntary Deed

A gift deed conveys title without the exchange of valuable consideration.[419] Generally, the phrase "for love and affection" is stated in the deed and is sufficient to make the conveyance valid.[420]

§ 2.17.2.5   Deed To Secure Debt

This is a loan instrument used in Georgia in lieu of a mortgage or trust deed found in other states. It conveys equitable title as security for the debt as compared with a mortgage, which conveys merely a lien, not title.[421]

§ 2.17.2.6   Deed In Foreclosure Or Deed Under Power

A deed under power is used to convey title when the holder of a deed to secure debt forecloses on the property and sells the property to satisfy a lien.[422]

§ 2.17.2.7   Tax Deed

A tax deed is used to convey title to property that has been sold by the government because of non-payment of taxes.[423] The method of sale is the same as a judicial sale.[424] The property is advertised for a public sale, with notice of the sale

---

416 *McDonough v. Martin*, 88 Ga. 675, 16 S.E. 59 (1892).

417 *Creek v. First Nat'l Bank of Atlanta*, 154 Ga.App. 266, 267 S.E.2d 872 (1980).

418 Black's Law Dictionary (8th ed. 2004).

419 *Clayton v. Tucker*, 20 Ga. 452 (1856).

420 *Hobbs v. Clark*, 221 Ga. 558, 146 S.E.2d 271 (1965).

421 O.C.G.A. § 7-1-1000; *Pusser v. Thompson*, 132 Ga. 280, 64 S.E. 75 (1909).

422 O.C.G.A. § 44-14-160.

423 O.C.G.A. § 48-5-359.

424 O.C.G.A. § 48-4-1

published weekly for four weeks preceding the sale. Sales are made at public outcry at the courthouse of the county where the levy was made, on the first Tuesday in each month, between the hours of 10 A.M. and 4 P.M. At the sale, the purchaser must pay by cash or cashier's check and will take title at his/her own risk. A purchaser who acquires property in a tax sale does not acquire fee simple title to the property, but acquires only that title that was vested in the owner.[425]

Title obtained under a tax deed executed pursuant to a valid and legal tax sale before July 1, 1989 will ripen into fee simple title by prescription after a period of seven years from the date of execution of that deed. Similarly, title obtained under a tax deed executed on or after July 1, 1989, but before July 1, 1996 will ripen into fee simple title after four years from the execution of that deed. For tax deeds executed on or after July 1, 1996, title will ripen by prescription after a period of four years from the recording of that deed in the land records in the county in which said land is located.[426]

A tax deed which has ripened by prescription as described above will convey a fee simple title to the property described in that deed which will vest absolutely in the grantee in the deed or in the grantee's heirs or assigns.[427] Until then, any person having any right, title, or interest in or lien upon such property may redeem the property from the sale by the payment of the redemption price or the amount required for redemption.[428] The right of redemption may be exercised at any time within 12 months from the date of the sale or at any time after the sale until the purchaser bars the right to redeem. The purchase can bar the right to redeem by the giving notice after 12 months from the date of a tax sale giving the requisite notice required by statute.[429]

§ 2.17.2.8 Survivorship Deed

A survivorship deed is a deed conveying property to several grantees, often a husband and wife, for their joint lives with the survivor(s) entitled to the deceased party's interest. A survivorship deed conveys interest outside a will.

Joint tenancy with the right of survivorship is a creation of statute in Georgia: O.C.G.A. § 44-6-190. When property is held in joint tenancy and one of the joint tenants dies, the decedent's interest in the property immediately vests in the surviving joint tenants and never becomes part of the estate of the decedent. One part of Section 44-6-190 provides that a joint tenancy will be severed (extinguishing the "survivorship" aspect) if one of the joint tenants transfers "all or a part of [the grantor's] interest" to another.

In one recent case, the Georgia Supreme Court was asked to decide whether the execution by one joint tenant of a Deed to Secure Debt was a sufficient transfer of that joint tenant's interest to sever the joint tenancy.[430]

Here are the relevant facts. William and Linda, brother and sister, inherited a piece of property from their mother and decided to take title as joint tenants with the right of survivorship. Linda agreed that William could reside in the house, and William agreed to maintain it and pay all taxes on the property. Some time later, William married Dianne, and thereafter he signed a promissory note to Rita, his wife's sister. The loan from Rita was secured by a Deed to Secure Debt encumbering William's interest in the property, which was only signed by William.

When William died, Linda (his sister and the surviving joint tenant) filed a lawsuit seeking a declaration that she was the sole owner of the house, and that Rita had no interest in the property. Not surprisingly, Rita objected and sought repayment of the note. Rita argued that William's execution of the Deed to Secure Debt severed the joint tenancy, since it transferred to William's interest in the property. Neither the trial court nor the Supreme Court agreed.

---

425 A widow's life estate sold by a sheriff's deed was held to convey only her life estate and hence the purchasers were subject to ejectment subsequent to her death. *Allen v. Lindsey*, 1913, 139 Ga. 648, 77 S.E. 1054.

426 O.C.G.A. § 48-4-48.

427 O.C.G.A. § 48-4-48c.

428 O.C.G.A. § 48-4-40.

429 O.C.G.A. § 48-4-45.

430 *Biggers v. Crook*, decided January 28, 2008.

The court held that although a Deed to Secure Debt conveys the legal title to property, it does so only for the purpose of security. The conveyance carries "none of the incidents of ownership of the property." A Deed to Secure Debt is therefore the same as a mortgage with power of sale, which does not sever a joint tenancy. Since the joint tenancy was not severed but remained intact, William's death had the effect of vesting full ownership of the property in Linda, the surviving joint tenant. Since William's interest ceased immediately upon his death, so did Rita's security in William's interest. Linda had never signed the promissory note and was not obligated to repay it.

While this is a "case of first impression" in Georgia, the ruling follows the reasoning the California courts have followed on the subject for more than 40 years. It also lines up with existing Georgia law regarding survivorship rights in financial instruments. For example, a lien placed on a certificate of deposit by one joint tenant is extinguished when that joint tenant dies, since the entire ownership of the certificate of deposit is immediately vested in the survivor.[431]

What effect will this have on Georgia real estate transactions? You can count on lenders to be more cautious about accepting security in property that is held in joint tenancy, unless all of the joint tenants join in signing the Deed to Secure Debt and any underlying promissory note. And if a property is to be seller-financed, REALTORS® should caution sellers to have all buyers execute the note and deed to secure debt if the buyers are taking title as joint tenants.

§ 2.17.2.9 Difference Between "Tenants In Common" And "Joint Tenants With Right Of Survivorship"

Tenancy in common is created whenever two or more persons are entitled to the simultaneous possession of any property. Tenants in common may have unequal shares in the property, but they will be held to be equal unless otherwise stated.[432] If parties hold property as tenants in common and one of the parties dies, the decedent's interest in the property will be transferred through her will or as provided by the intestacy laws. For example, if Joe and Mary own property as tenants in common and Mary dies with a will that designates her daughter Sally as her sole beneficiary, Sally will acquire Mary's interest in the property and will become a tenant in common with Joe.

The Joint Tenancy Act of 1976 provided for joint tenancy in Georgia. Joint tenancy means that parties can take title to property jointly and when one party dies, the surviving party will have title to the entire property automatically without the property having to pass through the decedent's estate.[433] Any instrument of title in favor of two or more persons which expressly refers to the takers as "joint tenants," "joint tenants and not as tenants in common," or "joint tenants with survivorship" or as taking "jointly with survivorship," or language essentially the same as these phrases creates a joint tenancy estate or interest.[434] If the instrument does not contain such language, no joint tenancy is created. This form of ownership is typically used when property is titled in the names of spouses or others with close relationships. For example, if Joe and Mary own property as joint tenants with right of survivorship and Mary dies with a will that designates her daughter Sally as her sole beneficiary, Joe will take Mary's interest in the property because title to the property passes to Joe outside the will.

The statute as drafted in 1976 stated that if a joint tenant transferred all or part of her interest in the property to a third party during her lifetime, the joint tenancy would be severed. The Code section was amended in 1984 to protect bona fide purchasers from a severance by any lifetime transfer which is unrecorded. Survivorship deeds are not subject to these severance problems and have been upheld by case law.[435]

---

431 *Commercial Banking Co. v. Spurlock*, 238 Ga. 123 231 S.E.2d 748 (1977).

432 O.C.G.A. § 44-6-120.

433 Prior to 1976, Georgia law did not recognize joint tenancy. However, parties in Georgia could still create a right of survivorship. A right of survivorship meant that property could be owned by two persons so that they would hold the property as tenants in common until one of them died and then the survivor would take title to the whole in fee simple. *Williams v. Studstill*, 251 Ga. 466, 306 S.E.2d 633 (1983), citing Agnor, "Joint Tenancy in Georgia," 3 Ga. St. Bar J. 29 (1966).

434 O.C.G.A. § 44-6-190.

435 *Epps v. Wood*, 243 Ga. 835, 257 S.E.2d 259 (1979).

§ 2.17.2.10 Fiduciary Deeds

Fiduciaries who are grantors and are acting in a representative capacity generally have no power to warrant anything. They convey no more title or interest than that owned by the person or estate they represent.[436]

Examples of fiduciary deeds are a trustee's deed, a guardian's deed, an executor's deed, and an administrator's deed.

A trustee uses a trustee's deed in her representative capacity to convey property owned by a trust. It contains no warranties of title, as a trustee does not have the power to bind the trust by a warranty of title.[437]

A guardian's deed is used to convey a ward's interest in real property.[438] The property can be sold when it is presumed to be in the best interests of the ward. However, such sales are required to be consummated under supervision and direction of the probate court.[439]

An executor's deed conveys title to property of a decedent who died leaving a valid will.[440] For a decedent who died intestate, or without naming an executor in the will, an administrator's deed is executed to convey title for the purposes of payment of debts or for distribution.[441]

---

436 *Harrison v. Harrison*, 214 Ga. 393, 105 S.E.2d 214 (1958); *Smith Realty Co. v. Hubbard*, 124 Ga.App. 265, 183 S.E.2d 506 (1971).

437 *Moss v. Twiggs*, 260 Ga. 561, 397 S.E.2d 707 (1990).

438 O.C.G.A. § 29-2-3.

439 *Merritt v. D.O.T.*, 147 Ga.App. 316, 248 S.E.2d 689 (1978), *rev'd on other grounds*.

440 *Knowles v. Knowles*, 125 Ga.App. 642, 188 S.E.2d 800 (1972).

441 *Horn v. Wright*, 157 Ga.App. 408, 278 S.E.2d 66 (1981).

The **RED BOOK**

CHAPTER 3

PARTIES TO THE CONTRACT

OVERVIEW

This chapter explains the effect of a buyer or seller not signing a real estate sales contract or signing the contract in the wrong capacity. The technical requirements for signing real estate sales contracts by different types of entities are also discussed. Sample signature blocks are provided to illustrate how corporations, partnerships, limited liability companies and court appointed receivers should sign contracts. Signature blocks are also included to show how persons acting in representative capacities such as executors, administrators, trustees, guardians and persons holding powers of attorney should sign contracts.

Finally, this chapter discusses whether persons who are mentally incapacitated, intoxicated, or minors have the legal capacity to enter into real estate sales contracts. Issues including the death of a party to a contract are also discussed.

§ 3.1 PARTIES WHO MUST SIGN THE CONTRACT

§ 3.1.1 All Buyers And Sellers Must Sign Contract

In order for a real estate sales contract to be valid, the parties must sign the contract.[442] Courts will not enforce a real estate sales contract unless there is a definite and specific statement of the terms of the contract and the parties to the contract are clearly defined.[443] The names of all of the parties to the contract should be clearly printed or typed in the body of the contract or beneath the signature lines identifying each person as a buyer or seller. If two or more persons own the property, each name should be listed as a seller and each owner should sign the contract. Likewise, each individual buyer whose name will be listed on the title must be listed as a buyer on the contract and each should sign the contract.

§ 3.1.1.1 Possession As Notice Of Title

Purchasers may not rely solely upon the public records to determine who holds title to a property, and therefore who needs to sign the deed transferring title. When a person is in possession of a property, that possession constitutes notice to any prospective purchaser that that person has some title or, claim to, or right to be in possession of the property.[444] Buyers must investigate to determine the nature of the person's interest in the property or the basis for the person to be in possession of the property. The safest course of action in such instances is to obtain evidence of the rights of the person in possession of the property such as a lease or an affidavit establishing that the person in possession is claiming no interest in the title to the property.

§ 3.1.1.2 Signature By Both Husband And Wife

Similarly, even where the owner of record is listed as one individual, if that person is married at the time of the conveyance, both spouses will normally be asked to sign the deed transferring title to a buyer (with the non-owner spouse typically being asked to sign what is known as a quitclaim deed conveying whatever interest, if any, in the property that the spouse may have). Even though Georgia is not a community property state (in which title held by one spouse is automatically jointly vested in the other spouse), case law has established that spouses may have equitable rights to property held solely in the name of the other spouse.[445] For example, if the wife is the only title holder of record, the husband may nonetheless have an equitable interest in the property. As a precaution, most closing attorneys will require that the husband sign a quitclaim deed transferring whatever equitable interest the husband may have in the property.

---

442 O.C.G.A. § 13-5-30(4).

443 *Brega v. CSRA Realty Co.*, 223 Ga. 724, 157 S.E.2d 738 (1967); *Harris v. Porter's Social Club, Inc.*, 215 Ga. 687, 113 S.E.2d 134 (1960).

444 O.C.G.A. § 44-5-169.

445 *Stokes v. Stokes*, 246 Ga. 765, 273 S.E.2d 169 (1980).

§ 3.1.1.3 Signatures By Common Owners

It is becoming more common for unmarried persons to purchase real estate together. When two (or more) unmarried persons purchase property, both persons should (but are not required to) sign the purchase and sale agreement.[446] Most unmarried persons who purchase property together choose to sign the purchase and sale agreement to evidence their interest in the property. However, an unmarried person may ensure her interest in ways other than signing the purchase and sale agreement. For instance, the non-signing owner may enter into a separate agreement with the signing owner providing for common ownership of the property (known as a tenant agreement), or both persons can be listed on the purchase agreement and deed to the property.[447] Although both common owners are not required to sign the sale agreement when purchasing a property, this is not the case if the common owners are selling a property. When two persons sell a jointly owned property, each owner must sign the purchase and sale agreement to be obligated to convey title to the property.[448] One common owner does not have the authority to sell a jointly owned property on behalf of another owner.[449] If one common owner has not signed the purchase and sale agreement to sell the property, the agreement will be incomplete and unenforceable.[450] More information on unmarried persons who purchase property is discussed further below.

§ 3.1.2 Recourse Against Owner Who Signs Contract

If property is owned by more than one person and only one owner signs the sales contract and the other owners do not sign the contract, the party who signed the contract may be liable for damages to the buyer for failure to convey the whole property. In one Georgia case, a husband contracted to sell property that he and his wife owned as co tenants.[451] The wife never signed the sales contract. At the time of the scheduled closing, the wife refused to convey her one-half undivided interest to the buyer. The court held that the husband was liable for money damages to the buyer because the husband failed to convey title to the whole property.

If a non-GAR Contract is being used, the following special stipulation can be used to prevent the problem of one co-owner being liable for damages if the other co-owner does not sign the contract.

Special Stipulation 28: Contract Not Valid Until Signed by Both Co-Owners

The Property is owned by _____ and _____. Buyer and Seller agree that this Agreement shall not become a Binding Agreement until it has been signed by both co-owners of the Property.

This type of special stipulation may be particularly helpful where the sellers are a husband and wife getting a divorce, and one of the spouses is concerned that the other spouse may not sign the Agreement.

Real estate brokers may avoid some of the problems that arise by requesting the seller to produce a copy of the deed by which they obtained title to the property. This will help determine who needs to sign the sales contract.

The GAR Contracts now include a place in the body of the contract to list the names of the buyers and sellers. In addition, the GAR Contracts provide that there shall be no binding agreement if all of the parties listed in the body of the contract as buyers and sellers have not signed the contract. This was done to avoid the problem of the buyer or seller claiming that an enforceable contract exists when not all of the actual buyers and sellers have signed the contract.

446 *Johnson v. Sackett*, 256 Ga. 552, 353 S.E.2d 326 (1986).

447 *Pindar*, 1 Ga. Real Estate Law & Procedure § 7-77 (6th ed.).

448 *MacDonald v. Whipple*, 273 Ga.App. 409, 615 S.E.2d 150 (2005).

449 *MacDonald v. Whipple*, 273 Ga.App. 409, 615 S.E.2d 150 (2005).

450 *MacDonald v. Whipple*, 273 Ga.App. 409, 615 S.E.2d 150 (2005).

451 *Deal v. Mountain Lake Realty, Inc.*, 132 Ga.App. 118, 207 S.E.2d 560 (1974).

§ 3.1.3   No Recourse Against Owner Who Does Not Sign Contract

Owners who do not sign a real estate contract as sellers will not be required by the courts to convey their interest in the property.[452] For example, in the case discussed above where the husband signed the contract but his wife did not, the court required the husband to convey his one-half undivided interest in the property to the buyer. However, the court could not require the wife to convey her interest because she had not signed the sales contract. This results in the buyer becoming a tenant in common with the wife, each owning a half interest in the property.

In a similar case, the husband signed a sales contract to convey a piece of property to a buyer.[453] However, at the time of conveyance, the property was titled solely in his wife's name. The wife had not signed the sales contract and she would not convey the property to the buyer. The court would not order her to convey the property to the buyer because she never signed the contract. In this situation, like the others discussed above, the husband could be liable for money damages to the buyer.

§ 3.1.3.1   Protecting Buyers When Sellers Not Properly Listed On Contract

The GAR Contract allows buyers to conduct a title search on the property and to present to the seller a written statement of objections affecting the marketability of the title. Pursuant to the GAR Contract, the seller must satisfy all valid title obligations prior to closing, or the buyer can terminate the contract and obtain a refund of all her earnest money.[454] The buyer may also be able to recover additional money damages from the seller or sue the seller for specific performance of the contract. A buyer should obtain a title search to determine, among other things, the identity of the current legal owner(s) of the property.

As a practice tip, if the buyers know which attorney is going to handle the closing, they can retain that firm to run the title search for them. This may avoid some duplication of costs, since a title examination will also be required by the buyer's lender.

If all of the current title holders of the property are not listed as sellers in the contract, the buyer can request that the contract be re-executed to properly identify the sellers and/or the buyer can request that the sellers listed in the contract obtain legal title to the property before closing.

§ 3.1.3.2   Recourse Against Buyer Who Signs Contract

Sellers may enforce the terms of the contract against all buyers who sign the contract.[455] This means that if a buyer signs a real estate contract and later decides (improperly) not to purchase the property, the seller can sue the buyer for specific performance seeking to require her to purchase the property. However, courts will not enforce a real estate sales contract against a buyer who did not sign the contract. If a seller sues an individual to require her to purchase the property, the court will not require a closing on the property if the person being sued did not sign the contract to purchase the property.[456]

As a practical matter, however, specific performance claims against buyers who breach a contract are difficult claims for sellers to win. This is because specific performance is an equitable remedy that is normally not granted if the seller can be made whole through an award of money damages.

---

452 *Sandison v. Harry Norman Realtors, Inc.*, 145 Ga.App. 736, 245 S.E.2d 37 (1978).

453 *Pryor v. Cureton*, 186 Ga. 892, 199 S.E. 175 (1938).

454 GAR Contract.

455 *Golden v. Frazier*, 244 Ga. 685, 261 S.E.2d 703 (1979).

456 O.C.G.A. § 13-5-30; *Dickens v. Calhoun First Nat. Bank*, 189 Ga.App. 798, 377 S.E.2d 715 (1989).

§ 3.2   PARTIES MUST SIGN IN THE RIGHT CAPACITY

§ 3.2.1   Owner Signing In Wrong Capacity

If an individual owns a piece of property, she should execute the sales contract by signing just her name. If a corporation or some other entity owns the property, the person signing the contract on behalf of the company must reflect her representative capacity in the signature block of the contract. Parties will sometimes sign a contract in the wrong capacity. In one Georgia case, the buyer entered into a contract to purchase certain property from Holiday Builders, Inc.[457] The president of Holiday Builders, Inc. signed the contract on behalf of the corporation in his capacity as an officer of the corporation. The buyer later learned that the president owned the property individually and the corporation had no interest in the property.

The buyer sued both the corporation and its president to convey the property (*i.e.*, a claim for specific performance). The court held that neither the corporation nor its president was required to convey the property to the buyer because even though the corporation signed the contract it did not own the property, and the individual who did own the property signed the contract in the wrong capacity. Therefore, the true and proper owner of the property had never signed the sales contract. It is likely, however, that the corporation would be liable for monetary damages even though the purchaser could not maintain an action for specific performance.

§ 3.2.2   Authorized Agents Or Representatives

There are instances when someone other than the named party to the contract can sign the contract on the party's behalf. Authorized representatives may sign on behalf of corporations, partnerships, limited partnerships, and limited liability companies. In particular circumstances, executors, administrators, trustees, and guardians may sign real estate contracts for the estate, trust, or individual they represent.

The contract must identify the capacity in which a person is signing. It is important that when an agent, representative, trustee, guardian, or the like signs a contract on behalf of another, the representative names the person or entity being represented on the face of the contract and shows that she is signing the contract in a representative capacity. If the representative relationship is not clearly disclosed on the contract, the contract could be enforced against the individual acting as the agent, representative, trustee, or guardian and not against the person or entity being represented.

§ 3.3   PERSONS WHOSE NAMES HAVE CHANGED

In some cases, a person's legal name is no longer the same as it appears on a deed. For example, Sally Smith may have purchased a condominium unit in her own name when she was single and then changed her name to Sally Smith Jones upon getting married. A person whose name has changed by marriage or otherwise, may (but is not required to) petition a court of competent jurisdiction to obtain an order directing the clerk to note the name change in the title register.[458]

Generally, when a seller's name on the purchase and sale agreement is different from how it appears on the deed recorded in the land records, a closing attorney will require the seller to bring her marriage license, divorce decree or other official name changing document and a photo identification (reflecting the seller's new name) to the closing for verification. Once the name change is verified, a name affidavit stating that the named persons are one and the same is included in the recital section of property deed. An example of a name affidavit is as follows.

457 *Jolles v. Holiday Builders, Inc.*, 222 Ga. 358, 149 S.E.2d 814 (1966).

458 O.C.G.A. § 44-2-142.

Name Usage Affidavit for Deeds

Grantor named herein is one and the same person as Sally Smith, the grantee named in the warranty deed recorded in Deed Book _____ at page ____ in the Chancery Clerk's office of _____ county, and grantor named herein is one and the same person as Sally Jones Smith, the grantor in the deed of trust recorded in Book _____ at page ____ in the Chancery Clerk's office of _____ county.

Lastly, closing attorneys generally require that the seller sign the deed and purchase and sale agreement with her new legal name followed by "formally known as (or f.k.a.) _____ (previous legal last name)." The sample signature block set forth below may be used to indicate a name change.

Seller: */s/ Sally Smith Jones*

Sally Smith Jones, f.k.a. Sally Smith

§ 3.4   USING A POWER OF ATTORNEY

§ 3.4.1   Requirements For A Power Of Attorney

An individual who has been given a power of attorney may sign a contract on behalf of any individual party who has the capacity to enter into a contract.[459] Since a contract for the sale of land must be in writing, the power of attorney giving someone the authority to sign a real estate contract on someone else's behalf also must be in writing.[460] This is known in the law as the "equal dignity rule."[461] The standard Georgia form for a power of attorney as it appears in the Official Code of Georgia requires that the power of attorney be signed and sealed by a notary public and separately witnessed if the power of attorney is being given to buy or sell land.[462] This is because since a deed must be witnessed and notarized, the equal dignity rule requires the power of attorney to similarly be witnessed and notarized. Moreover, a party may (but is not required to) record a power of attorney.[463] If a party chooses to do so, the power of attorney may be recorded as a supporting document for the property deed.[464] Generally, a power of attorney to sign a contract is executed before a party signs a real estate agreement on behalf of an absent party. However, in some rare instances, a party who is not authorized to sign an agreement will do so on behalf of an absent party without a power of attorney. If such an instance occurs, the contract will generally be void and unenforceable because the signatory did not have the proper authority to consummate the transaction.[465] However, the party with the proper authority may ratify the contract after it has been signed by creating a power of attorney with a retroactive effect.[466] If a power of attorney to sign a contract is executed after the real estate sales contract, the power of attorney will not have a retroactive effect, unless the power of attorney contains an express intention to make the power of attorney retroactive.[467] For example, if the power of attorney is executed after the real estate contract is signed, the power of attorney must specifically provide that the representative had the authority

---

459 O.C.G.A. § 13-5-30(4).

460 O.C.G.A. § 10-6-2; *Turnipseed v. Jaje*, 267 Ga. 320, 477 S.E.2d 101 (1996); *Jones v. Sheppard*, 231 Ga. 223, 200 S.E.2d 877 (1973); *Dover v. Burns*, 186 Ga. 19, 196 S.E. 785 (1938).

461 *Augusta Surgical Center, Inc. v. Walton & Heard Office Venture*, 235 Ga.App. 283, 508 S.E.2d 666 (1998).

462 O.C.G.A. § 10-6-142.

463 *Doe v. Roe*, 27 Ga. 418 (1859). The court held that there is no Georgia statute that requires a party to record a power of attorney; however, a power of attorney may be recorded with the property deed made under it.

464 Doe v. Roe, 27 Ga. 418 (1859).

465 *Hubert Realty Co. v. Bland*, 79 Ga.App. 321, 53 S.E.2d 691 (1949).

466 *Hubert Realty Co. v. Bland*, 79 Ga.App. 321, 53 S.E.2d 691 (1949).

467 *Hubert Realty Co. v. Bland*, 79 Ga.App. 321, 53 S.E.2d 691 (1949).

to enter that specific real estate contract on behalf of the named party. In essence, a power of attorney with a specified retroactive effect would save a contract which would be otherwise unenforceable.[468]

Normally in closing real estate transactions, the closing attorney is going to ask for the documents evidencing the power of attorney's authority to execute the agreement on behalf of the absent party. Without this documentation, it is unlikely that a party will be able to sign the contract on behalf of an absent party. Therefore, it is important for the power of attorney to retain the document expressly empowering her to sign the purchase and sale agreement.

The recommended practice is for a party to grant the representative a formal power of attorney that expressly empowers the representative to execute a sales contract for a particular piece of property. If such a power of attorney is executed, the terms of the power of attorney should describe the property with the same specificity as the contract itself. Although the power of attorney may include only a general description of the property, title insurance companies are reluctant to accept such general authority for a representative to act. Therefore, merely having a general description of the property is not recommended.

The power of attorney does not have to set out the terms of the sale in detail. Instead, the law provides that representatives with a power of attorney are given the power to sell or buy property on such terms and conditions as the representative deems appropriate.[469] Nevertheless, it is best if the power of attorney state that the representative has the express power to sign mortgage loan documents if this is going to be the case.

Lenders and title insurance companies may have their own preferred form for powers of attorney and require that they be used. While any legally enforceable power of attorney should do, it may make the transaction smoother to first check with the lender's closing attorney or title insurance company to determine if they have a preferred form.

§ 3.4.2   Consequences Of An Insufficient Power Of Attorney

A party who signs a contract based on an insufficient or ineffective power of attorney is not bound to the contract. Individuals who deal with representatives in real estate contracts should carefully examine the representative's authority to act. If there is a written power of attorney, the party giving the power of attorney should be contacted, if possible, to confirm its authenticity. The parties may also attach a copy of the power of attorney to the sales contract.

A power of attorney must be effective at the time it is being exercised. If the power of attorney is very old, it is best to verify that it is still valid. The power of attorney must be signed by the property owners of record. Further, the power of attorney must contain a provision which allows the agent to execute a deed of transfer of ownership to the property as well as the power to negotiate the terms of the sale. A power of attorney terminates by express revocation,[470] by the appointment of a new agent, or by the death of the principal or agent.[471]

If a person acting in a representative capacity signs a contract based on a power of attorney and the power of attorney does not actually give the representative the authority to enter into the contract, the other party to the contract cannot sue the representative for a breach of authority if that other party could have protected herself by taking ordinary care, such as reviewing the power of attorney or contacting the party who gave the power of attorney.[472]

---

468 *Hubert Realty Co. v. Bland*, 79 Ga.App. 321, 53 S.E.2d 691 (1949).

469 O.C.G.A. § 23-2-115, O.C.G.A. § 23-2-116.

470 The instrument itself may provide that it remains in effect only until the deed for the transaction records in the appropriate county, or that it is effective only until a particular date.

471 O.C.G.A. § 10-6-33.

472 *Nalley v. Whitacker*, 102 Ga.App. 230, 115 S.E.2d 790 (1960).

§ 3.4.3   Real Estate Brokers With Power Of Attorney

Although real estate brokers can enter into contracts on behalf of their clients if the broker is given a power of attorney, doing so is not recommended for two reasons. First, brokers have a financial interest in the real estate transaction closing because they only get paid a commission in that event. This leaves the broker forever exposed to a claim by the party granting the power of attorney that the broker did something when acting as a power of attorney that was not in the best interests of the broker's principal and instead only benefitted the broker. In light of this potential for a conflict of interest, it is a better practice to have a third party, with no financial interest in the transaction, hold the power of attorney and execute the contract of behalf of the party.

Second, when a broker acts on behalf of a client based on a power of attorney, the broker arguably becomes a principal in the transaction. As such, the broker needs to disclose in writing that she is both a principal and a client in the transaction.[473]

§ 3.4.4   Spouse Has No Implied Power Of Attorney To Sign For Other Spouse

One spouse does not have a power of attorney by virtue of marriage to sign a real estate sales contract for the other spouse. If one spouse is going to be unavailable to sign a real estate sales contract, the spouse should execute a power of attorney in favor of the other spouse.

Some builders will include a provision in their contracts that once the contract is initially signed by both spouses, the signature of one spouse thereafter on any amendment or addendum to the contract will automatically bind the other spouse. This type of provision is particularly helpful when both parties may not be available when the buyers need to make multiple design selections for a new home after signing a contract. An example of this type of provision follows.

> **Special Stipulation 29:   One Buyer Has Power to Sign for Other Buyer**
>
> *Each undersigned Buyer, by signing below, does hereby appoint the other Buyer or Buyers herein to act as her authorized agent of and power-of-attorney of said Buyer(s) for the purpose of signing any amendments hereto and all other documents contemplated herein, including but not limited to any notices given hereunder, and authorizes the taking of all such actions on behalf of Buyer with respect to this Agreement. All parties agree that if any Buyer signs any document contemplated above, said Buyer shall be signing for himself or herself and for all other buyers, regardless of whether the Buyer indicates that she is acting in a representational capacity. This appointment and grant of this power-of-attorney may only be terminated upon written notice to Seller, and shall only be effective upon actual receipt of said notice.*

§ 3.5   WHEN CORPORATIONS SIGN CONTRACTS

§ 3.5.1   Individuals Signing On Behalf Of A Corporation

A contract with a corporation as a party should identify the corporation as the buyer or seller of the property, fully identify the officer executing the contract on behalf of the corporation, and clearly specify that the officer is acting as a representative for the corporation and not in an individual capacity. In order for the officer's signature to clearly reflect her representative capacity, the name of the corporation must precede or follow the name and office of the corporate representative.

---

473 O.C.G.A. § 43-40-25(b)(9).

If the corporation and its executing officers are not fully identified, the contract may not be enforceable. For example, in one case, Porter's Social Club, Inc. owned a piece of real property. The potential buyer of the property sued Porter's Social Club, Inc. asking the court to order the club to convey the property to him.[474] The buyer had signed a contract which had been executed by "Ezekiel Harvery" and "C. T. Brinson Treas." who were identified in the contract as the "Sellers." Nothing in the contract reflected that the sellers were acting on behalf of the club, and the name of the club was never mentioned in the contract. The court held that the contract was too indefinite to support an order requiring the club to convey the property.

In another case, a corporation owned a piece of property and an individual named Williamson represented to a buyer that he was the vice president of the corporation and was authorized to execute a sales contract for such property on the company's behalf.[475] The contract specified that the corporation was the seller of the property, but nothing in the body of the contract or at the signature line reflected that Williamson was acting as an agent for the company. When the buyer sued the company for conveyance of the property, the court found that Williamson had executed the contract in his individual capacity because he was not identified as an agent of the corporation anywhere in the contract and the court refused to order the company to convey the property. As discussed below, if Williamson had been identified as vice president but the contract did not include the signature of a secretary or a corporate seal, then unless other actions or conduct were present, there would not be apparent authority.[476] However, the signature by an identified chief executive officer or president would bind the company absent a provision in the corporate documents taking away such authority.

§ 3.5.2 Apparent Authority

Georgia law provides that a principal may authorize an agent to act on his behalf merely by a course of conduct whereby the principal holds that person out as an agent and induces others to rely on the agent's statements.[477] Such authority is called "apparent authority". It can become an issue when an agent so authorized, signs a real estate contract in her capacity as agent for a corporation or other principal. When a principal's conduct leads third parties to believe that its agent has authority, those third parties may bind the principal to the agent's acts.[478] Accordingly, where a corporation holds out a particular party as its agent authorized to bind it in contract, the agent's execution of a real estate contract as corporate agent binds the corporation.

Apparent authority is based on the conduct of the principal, not of the agent, and on the reasonableness of third parties' reliance thereon.[479] A party trying to show an agent's apparent authority must establish that he relied in good faith on the principal's conduct which would lead a reasonable person to believe that a principal-agent relationship existed.[480] A principal cannot deny that its agent has authority reasonably deduced from the principal's conduct.[481] If a corporation's actions reasonably induce a third party to believe its agent is authorized to enter into a real estate contract, and the agent does so in its capacity as corporate agent, the corporation is bound. The lesson here is that you need to be very careful about who you allow to act on your behalf and explain very clearly the limits on any representative's authority.

In many builder contracts, the builder will avoid disputes over whether an agent of the builder had the apparent authority to bind the builder by specifically disclaiming such authority. An example of such a special stipulation is set forth below.

---

474 *Harris v. Porter's Social Club, Inc.*, 215 Ga. 687, 113 S.E.2d 134 (1960).

475 *Brega v. CSRA Realty Co.*, 223 Ga. 724, 157 S.E.2d 738 (1967).

476 *See* § 3.5.2 (Apparent Authority) of this book.

477 *Ampex Credit Corp. v. Bateman*, 554 F.2d 750 (5th Cir. 1977).

478 *Morris v. Williams*, 214 Ga.App. 526, 448 S.E.2d 267 (1994).

479 *Addley v. Beizer*, 205 Ga.App. 714, 423 S.E.2d 398 (1992), *cert. denied*. Ga.App.

480 *APCOA, Inc. v. Fidelity Nat'l Bank*, 703 F. Supp. 1553, *aff'd*, 906 F.2d 610 (1988).

481 *Addley v. Beizer*, 205 Ga.App. 714, 423 S.E.2d 398 (1992), *cert. denied*. Ga.App.

Special Stipulation 30:   No Real Estate Broker or Licensee or Person Performing Construction Work on Property is the Agent of the Builder

Notwithstanding any provision to the contrary contained herein, no real estate broker or licensee or any person performing construction work on the Property shall have the authority, express, implied or apparent, to bind Seller. The only persons who have the authority to act for or bind Seller shall be the duly authorized officers and directors of Company acting in accordance with the Bylaws and Articles of Incorporation of Company. No other person shall have any apparent authority to act for Company.

§ 3.5.3   President May Sign For Corporation

The chief executive officer or president (if there is no chief executive officer) of a corporation has the authority to sign real estate contracts on behalf of the corporation if the sale does not require approval by the board of directors or shareholders.[482] However, when all or substantially all of the assets of a solvent corporation are involved, stockholder approval is required. The articles of incorporation, bylaws, or a resolution of the board of directors of a corporation may authorize other officers to execute contracts on behalf of the corporation.[483] Parties may rely on resolutions of the board of directors permitting other officers to execute contracts, unless all or substantially all of the assets of a solvent corporation are involved.[484] In order to protect themselves, parties should make a full inquiry as to what percentage of the corporation's assets are involved in the sale. Assets are deemed to be all or substantially all of a corporation's property if they exceed two-thirds of the fair market value of all of the assets of the corporation.[485]

Although the chief executive officer or president of a corporation may have the authority to sign contracts acting alone, it is better practice to have real estate sales contracts signed by two officers. Georgia law provides that the execution of a real estate contract on behalf of a corporation by the president or vice president and attested to or countersigned by the secretary, an assistant secretary, or other officer authorized to authenticate records of the corporation, conclusively establishes that: (1) the president or vice president of the corporation executing the document does in fact occupy the official position indicated; (2) the signature of such officer on the contract is genuine; and (3) the president or vice president is properly authorized to execute the document on behalf of the corporation.[486] The signature block below is an example of how a contract should be signed by a president on behalf of a corporation.

SMITH REALTY CO., INC.

By: */s/ John Smith*

John Smith, President

Attest: */s/ Jane Jones*

Jane Jones, Secretary

---

482 O.C.G.A. § 14-2-841, O.C.G.A. § 14-2-1202.

483 O.C.G.A. § 14-2-841.

484 O.C.G.A. § 14-2-1201.

485 O.C.G.A. § 14-2-1201.

486 O.C.G.A. § 14-2-151

§ 3.5.4   Effect Of Corporate Seal Affixed To Contract

If the board of directors of a corporation has passed a resolution authorizing an officer other than the president of its corporation to execute real estate contracts on behalf of the corporation, the corporate seal, or a facsimile thereof, should be affixed to the contract. It is preferable and provides further authority if the signature of the secretary, assistant secretary, or other authorized officer of the corporation is also included.

This second signature (called an attestation) provides evidence that: (1) the corporate seal or facsimile thereof affixed to the document is, in fact, the seal of the corporation or a true facsimile; (2) any officer executing the document does in fact occupy the official position indicated in the signature block; (3) an officer in that position is duly authorized to execute such document on behalf of the corporation; (4) the signature of the officer signing the contract is genuine; and (5) the person signing the contract on behalf of the corporation has been properly authorized by the board of directors.[487]

When the corporate seal is affixed to the contract or when the contract is executed by the president or vice president and attested by the secretary, assistant secretary, or officer authorized to authenticate corporate records, a buyer or seller entering a contract with that corporation may rely on the document and the signatures to the document as being valid unless the buyer or seller has knowledge or reason to know otherwise.[488] Although the corporate seal may be affixed to any document executed by a corporation, the absence of the seal does not automatically invalidate the document or invalidate any actions taken by a party in reliance on the contract.[489]

Where an officer of the corporation other than the president signs the contract, all necessary parties should complete the following signature block.

SMITH REALTY CO., INC.

By: /s/ *John Smith*

John Smith, President

Attest: /s/ *Jane Jones*

Jane Jones, Secretary

[CORPORATE SEAL]

§ 3.5.5   Unformed Corporations Have No Authority To Contract

Buyers and sellers should be careful not to enter a contract with an entity that may become, but that is not yet, a corporation. Corporations cannot act until they are chartered and organized. If a buyer or seller enters a contract with an entity she believes to be a corporation but the corporate entity is never properly created, the buyer or seller can still enforce the contract, but not against the non-existent corporation. The buyer or seller's only recourse is against the individuals who represented and acted on behalf of the unformed corporation. Such individuals could be personally and individually liable under the real estate contracts they sign.[490]

While parties entering contracts with purported corporations must be careful, people who intend to incorporate should also be wary of attempting to enter contracts on behalf of a corporation they have not yet formed. For example, the owner of a theater offered to lease the theater to a corporation once the corporation was organized.[491] The theater owner and incorporators drew up a written lease. Relying on the offer to lease the theater, the individual expended money and

---

487 O.C.G.A. § 14-2-151.

488 O.C.G.A. § 12-2-151(c).

489 O.C.G.A. § 14-2-151(d).

490 O.C.G.A. § 14-2-204; *Gifford v. Jackson*, 115 Ga.App. 773, 156 S.E.2d 105 (1967).

491 *R.A.C. Realty Co. v. W.O.U.F. Atlanta Realty Corp.*, 205 Ga. 154, 52, S.E.2d 617 (1949).

formed the corporation. Before the final incorporation of the company and before the company could legally accept the theater owner's lease offer, the theater owner withdrew his offer.

When the corporation sued for enforcement of the lease, the court held that the corporation was not entitled to enforcement because there was no enforceable lease contract. Although the theater owner had made an offer to lease, the corporation could not have accepted the offer until it had attained the legal status of a corporate entity by acquiring a charter and organizing the corporation. This did not occur until after the theater owner's offer was withdrawn. Because the offer was never legally accepted before it was withdrawn, no enforceable contract was ever created.

In order to avoid problems with corporations that are not yet formed, parties intending to form a corporation should sign contracts in their individual capacity with the right to assign the contract to the corporation once it is created. If the corporation is assigned a contract by a buyer, the contract should specify that the sale will be for cash, because a contract to purchase property on the credit of the person who enters into the contract is not assignable.[492] When the contract is assigned from the individual to the corporation, the assignment must be executed in the same way as a deed for an original conveyance of property.[493]

Individuals signing a contract that will later be assigned to a corporation will sometimes want to try to limit their personal liability if the contract is terminated. A good way to do this is to limit the other party's recourse to the earnest money deposited in the transaction. The following special stipulation allows for an assignment of the contract, but limits the recourse of the other party to the contract to the earnest money.

> **Special Stipulation 31:   Seller's Recourse Against Buyer if Buyer's Assignee Terminates this Agreement**
>
> *If Buyer assigns this Agreement to a third party and this Agreement is later terminated, for any reason whatsoever, Seller's sole remedy and recourse against Buyer and Buyer's assignees shall be the receipt of the Earnest Money held by _____ (Holder) as full liquidated damages, it being stipulated that this amount is a reasonable pre-estimate amount of Seller's actual damages and not a penalty.*

Alternatively, the following special stipulation can be used in contemplation of an assignment to a yet-to-be formed corporation.

> **Special Stipulation 32:   Seller's Consent to Assign to a Yet-to-Be Formed Corporation**
>
> *Seller acknowledges that Buyer intends to form a [corporation/ limited liability company] and that this Agreement will be assigned to the said [corporation/ limited liability company]. For and in consideration of the sum $10.00 and other good and valuable consideration, the receipt and sufficiency of which are hereby acknowledged, Seller agrees that should Buyer form said [corporation/ limited liability company] Seller shall permit the assignment of this Agreement from Buyer to said [corporation/ limited liability company] (provided that Buyer is a principal thereof) and Buyer will thereafter be released from and have no further personal liability under this Agreement.*

---

492 *Sims v. Cordele Ice Co.*, 119 Ga. 597, 46 S.E. 841 (1904).

493 O.C.G.A. § 44-5-32; *Pawn World, Inc. v. Estate of Sam Farkas, Inc.*, 218 Ga.App. 334, 461 S.E.2d 295 (1995). The assignment must be: (1) in writing; (2) signed by the party making the assignment; (3) signed by at least two witnesses; (4) delivered to the assignee; and (5) made for good or valuable consideration; O.C.G.A. § 44-5-30.

§ 3.6 WHEN PARTNERSHIPS SIGN CONTRACTS

§ 3.6.1 When A General Partnership Signs A Contract

Pursuant to the Uniform Partnership Act (the "Act")[494], it is not necessary to have all partners sign a real estate contract to convey partnership property, but it is best to do so. Generally, every partner is an agent of the partnership for the purpose of its business, including execution of real estate contracts.[495]

In some circumstances, however, a partner has no authority to act for the partnership.[496] Whether a partner has authority to act on behalf of the partnership can be ascertained from the statement of partnership that may be recorded in the office of the clerk of the superior court of one or more counties.[497] Although statements of partnership are not required, if they are filed they may state, among other things, what authority the partners have or if the partners' authority differs from what is listed in the Act.[498]

According to the Act, any partner may convey title to property held in the partnership name by a contract executed in the partnership name.[499] However, if the statement of partnership or other partnership documents do not give the contracting partner the authority to convey partnership property, the partnership may be able to regain title to its property. In order to recover its property, the partnership will have to show that the contracting partner did not have the authority to convey the property and that the buyer and any subsequent purchaser knew this.[500] Where title is held in all of the individual names of the partners, all the partners must execute the contract in order to transfer all of their rights in the property.[501]

In order to avoid problems regarding a partner's authority to sign a real estate contract, when entering into real estate contracts with general partnerships, a party should require all partners in the partnership to sign a Consent and Authorization. Since a joint venture is technically a general partnership, the rules pertaining to signatures for general partnerships should be followed. Generally, in real estate transactions, the closing attorney is going to ask for the documents evidencing the person's authority to execute the transaction. Below is an example of a signature block to be used when an individual partner signs a real estate sales contract on behalf of her partnership.

SMITH REALTY, a Georgia Partnership

By: /s/ *Janet Smith*

Print name: Janet Smith

Title: Partner

---

494   O.C.G.A. § 14-8-1 through O.C.G.A. § 14-8-64.

495   O.C.G.A. § 14-8-9, and O.C.G.A. § 14-8-10(a).

496   O.C.G.A. § 14-8-10.1.

497   O.C.G.A. § 14-8-10.1(a). The statement of partnership can be filed in any county in Georgia or in more than one county. However, Georgia law does not require that a statement of partnership be filed at all.

498   O.C.G.A. § 14-8-10.1(b)(5).

499   O.C.G.A. § 14-8-10.

500   O.C.G.A. § 14-8-10(a).

501   O.C.G.A. § 14-8-10(d).

§ 3.6.2 When Limited Partnerships Sign Contracts

Property owned by a limited partnership is titled in the partnership name and not the names of the individuals or entities that make up the limited partnership. Only the general partners of a limited partnership may execute real estate contracts on behalf of the limited partnership.[502] The Georgia Revised Uniform Limited Partnership Act[503] provides that general partners who sign a contract to convey property on behalf of limited partnerships are presumed to have the authority to do so, if the property is located in Georgia. The Partnership Agreement should address who the authority to sign on behalf of the partnership.

An exception to this presumption is when the general partner's authority is limited and the limitation is properly recorded in a certificate of limited partnership. To be valid, a copy of the certificate of limited partnership must be certified by the Secretary of State and filed with and recorded in the Superior Court Clerk's Office in the county where the property is located.[504] The certificate can be obtained by searching the land records of the county in which the property is located. Once the certificate is obtained, the other party to the contract can confirm the general partner's authority. Georgia limited partnerships created prior to January 1, 1988 were not required to file paperwork with the Secretary of State. Generally, a copy of the partnership agreements for limited partnerships created prior to January 1, 1988 were filed with and can be obtained from the land records in which the property is located.

If the general partner does not have the necessary authority, the contract may not be enforceable against the limited partnership. Like with general partnerships, when entering real estate contracts with limited partnerships a party should require that all general partners sign a Consent and Authorization. Normally in real estate transactions, the closing attorney is going to ask for the documents evidencing the person's authority to execute the transaction.

Below are two examples of a signature block to be used when a general partner signs a real estate contract on behalf of the limited partnership.

EXAMPLE 1

ABC Imports, LP,

a Georgia Limited Partnership

By: ABC Exports, Inc., its General Partner

By: */s/ John Smith*

Print Name: John Smith

Title: President

Attest: By: */s/ Jane Jones*

Print Name: Jane Jones

Title: Secretary

[CORPORATE SEAL]

---

502 O.C.G.A. § 14-9-403.

503 O.C.G.A. § 14-9-403.

504 O.C.G.A. § 14-9-106(c).

EXAMPLE 2

> ABC Imports, LP, a Georgia limited partnership
>
> By: */s/ John Smith* [SEAL]
>
> Print Name: John Smith
>
> Title: General Partner

§ 3.6.3 When Limited Liability Limited Partnerships Sign Contracts

A limited liability limited partnership ("LLLP") organized under the Georgia Revised Uniform Limited Partnership Act[505] operates just like a limited partnership. Similar to a limited partnership, property owned by a limited liability limited partnership is titled in the LLLP's name and not the names of the individuals or entities that make up the LLLP.[506]

Only the general partners of a limited liability limited partnership may properly execute real estate contracts on behalf of the LLLP.[507] Limited partners may not properly execute real estate contracts; however, a limited partner is not liable for the obligations of a LLLP by participating in the management or control of the business.[508]

Real estate contracts executed by the general partners for property located in Georgia are presumed to have been duly authorized and binding upon the LLLP.[509] The exception to this presumption is if the certificate of limited liability limited partnership contains contrary limitations on the authority of the general partner(s) and such limitations are properly recorded.[510] To be valid, a copy of the certificate of limited liability limited partnership must be certified by the Secretary of State and recorded in the office of the clerk of the superior court of the county where the real property is located.[511] Such certificate may be obtained by searching the land records of the county that the property is located in. Once the certificate is obtained, the other party to the contract can confirm the general partner's authority.

If it is determined that the general partner does not have the requisite authority, the contract may not be enforceable against the limited partnership. Like with limited partnerships, when entering real estate contracts with limited liability limited partnerships a party should require that all the general partners who have the requisite authority sign a Consent and Authorization for the transaction.

Below are two examples of a signature block to be used when a general partner signs a real estate contract on behalf of a limited liability limited partnership.

EXAMPLE 1

> ABC Imports, LLLP, a Georgia Limited Liability Limited Partnership
>
> By: ABC Exports, Inc., a Georgia corporation,
>
> its General Partner
>
> By: */s/ John Smith*
>
> Print Name: John Smith
>
> Title: President

---

505 O.C.G.A. § 14-8-62.

506 O.C.G.A. § 14-9-106(b).

507 O.C.G.A. § 14-9-403.

508 O.C.G.A. § 14-9-303.

509 O.C.G.A. § 14-9-106(c).

510 O.C.G.A. § 14-9-106(c).

511 O.C.G.A. § 14-9-106(c).

> Attest: By: /s/ *Janet Smith*
>
> Print Name: Janet Smith
>
> Title: Secretary
>
> [CORPORATE SEAL]

EXAMPLE 2

> ABC Imports, LLLP, a Georgia Limited Liability Limited Partnership
>
> By: /s/ *John Smith [SEAL]*
>
> Print Name: John Smith
>
> Title: General Partner

§ 3.7   WHEN LIMITED LIABILITY COMPANIES SIGN CONTRACTS

Unless the articles of organization provide otherwise, every member of a limited liability company is an agent of the company and may execute real estate contracts on its behalf.[512] Contracts signed by a member of a limited liability company on behalf of the company are binding on the company unless the contracting member of the company has, in fact, no authority to act for the company and the other party to the contract knows this.[513] The members' rights or limitations to bind the company in a real estate contract can be found in the company's articles of organization which are filed with the secretary of state.[514]

The articles of organization of a limited liability company may provide that all powers of management of the company are vested only in one or more manager(s).[515] If this is the case, no member, acting solely in her capacity as a member, may execute a real estate contract on behalf of the limited liability company. Instead, only the manager(s) may enter real estate contracts on behalf of the limited liability company.[516] The Operating Agreement should address who has authorization to sign contracts (member, manager, officers). The Operating Agreements are not public records although they can be recorded, for example, as an exhibit to a document.

Parties who deal with limited liability companies should be aware that if any limitations on the authority of any or all of the members or managers are set forth in the articles of organization and properly recorded with the secretary of state, the limitations will be conclusively binding against the party dealing with the limited liability company.[517] For example, if a member of a limited liability company contracts to sell property owned by the company to a buyer, and the articles of organization (properly filed in the Secretary of State's Office) prohibit the members from conveying property on behalf of the limited liability company, the buyer would not have any recourse against the limited liability company for conveyance of the property. In a situation like this, the buyer is deemed to have known that the member had no authority to sign the contract because the buyer could have obtained and reviewed the articles of organization. In order to ensure that the party signing a contract on behalf of the limited liability company has the authority to do so, a copy of the company's articles of organization can be obtained from the secretary of state.

In most real estate transactions, limited liability companies and other legal entities will be required to provide their governing documents to the closing attorney to confirm that the legal entity was properly formed, and that the person(s) signing on behalf of that entity are duly authorized to do so.

---

512   O.C.G.A. § 14-11-301.

513   O.C.G.A. § 14-11-301(a).

514   O.C.G.A. § 14-11-203.

515   O.C.G.A. § 14-11-301(b).

516   O.C.G.A. § 14-11-301(b).

517   O.C.G.A. § 14-11-302.

In order for restrictions on members' or managers' authority to be conclusively presumed against a grantee, a copy of the articles of organization certified by the secretary of state must be filed with and recorded in the superior court clerk's office where the property is located.[518] In such cases, anyone searching the land records can obtain a copy of the articles of organization and confirm the authority of the person contracting on behalf of the LLC. Examples of signature blocks for a contract being executed by a limited liability company are below.

EXAMPLE 1

> ABC Imports, LLC, a Georgia limited liability company
>
> By: /s/ *John Smith* [SEAL]
>
> Print Name: John Smith
>
> Title: Manager

§ 3.8 WHEN COURT APPOINTED RECEIVERS SIGN CONTRACTS

In some real estate transactions, the seller of property may be a court appointed receiver. Any party with an interest in a real property may petition a superior court of competent jurisdiction to appoint a receiver if the party believes that her rights are not being protected and there is a risk of harm to the property.[519] A mortgage lender is one of the parties who may seek the appointment of a receiver. Oftentimes, loan documents in commercial transactions will include language where the borrower consents in advance to the appointment of a receiver if there borrower is in default of the mortgage.

Once the petition is received by a superior court, the judge will decide if there are circumstances to support the appointment of a receiver.[520] The decision is within the sole discretion of the judge[521] and requires a showing of clear and urgent circumstances,[522] such as another party's waste, mismanagement, insolvency or other danger of loss to the property.[523] A receiver will generally not be appointed if the party's rights could be protected by a means other than appointing a receiver.[524] Ultimately, the receiver's goal is to preserve the property in dispute and protect the rights of the parties until all the issues surrounding the property are resolved.[525]

The receiver obtains her authority and obligations from an order of the court.[526] Generally, the superior court gives the receiver all necessary powers to operate the property.[527] Whether the receiver has other power, such as a right to sell the property, will vary from case to case depending on the situation. If the receiver is unclear about her under the court order, the receiver will normally request clarification from the court before taking any action.

---

518 O.C.G.A. § 14-11-302.

519 *Patel v. Patel*, 280 Ga. 292, 627 S.E.2d 21 (2006).

520 O.C.G.A. § 9-8-4.

521 *Patel v. Patel*, 280 Ga. 292, 627 S.E.2d 21 (2006).

522 O.C.G.A. § 9-8-4.

523 *Patel v. Patel*, 280 Ga. 292, 627 S.E.2d 21 (2006); *Warner v. Warner*, 237 Ga. 462, 228 S.E.2d 848. Appointment of a receiver was proper to protect the interests of the co-owners when one co-owner failed to distribute profits from the building, stopped making mortgage payments, urged the mortgagee to foreclose on the property, commingled the funds from the property with his personal funds, and deposited certain receipts from the property into an account maintained under a fictitious name.

524 *Patel v. Patel*, 280 Ga. 292, 627 S.E.2d 21 (2006)..

525 *Pittman v. State*, 288 Ga. 589, 706 S.E.2d 398 (2011).

526 O.C.G.A. § 9-8-8.

527 *Pittman v. State*, 288 Ga. 589, 706 S.E.2d 398 (2011).

Oftentimes, a receiver will be appointed to sell property on behalf of the owner.[528] However, a court will only authorize a receiver to sell a particular property if there is evidence that the sale is necessary due to clear and urgent circumstances.[529] Once it is determined that the sale is necessary, the receiver will be appointed to conduct the sale by court order.[530] Before the receiver signs an agreement for the purchase and sale of the property, the receiver must obtain confirmation or approval of the sale by the judge.[531] Without the judge's confirmation, the purchase and sale agreement will not give the buyer the property even if the receiver signs the agreement.[532]

The receiver acts in a fiduciary capacity.[533] In other words, once the receiver is appointed, the receiver has a duty to sell the property to receive the highest value for the benefit of the creditors or mortgagor.[534] As such, it is important to note that the receiver is an officer of the superior court[535] and not an agent of the party she is appointed to protect.[536] Therefore, a receiver's fiduciary and any other duties imposed by the court order are owed to the appointing court rather than the seller.[537]

When a receiver signs an agreement on behalf of a party, the receiver must include her name and the capacity in which she is signing.[538] In contrast to the some other signature blocks in this chapter, this signature block must include the capacity in which the receiver is signing. It is particularly important for the receiver to indicate her capacity to avoid any individual liability.[539] If the receiver's capacity is not included in the signature block, the receiver will be individually liable for the performance of or any liability arising out of the agreement.[540] The signature block should also include the name and county of the appointing court, as well as the case name and case number. This additional information is useful to the other party because it gives the specific legal information regarding the receiver's authority to sign the agreement.

When a court appointed receiver signs an agreement on behalf of a party, the following signature block should be used.

Seller: John Smith

By: ABC Incorporated, as Receiver

By: _____

Jane Brown, not in her individual capacity but solely in her capacity as Agent

---

528 O.C.G.A. § 44-6-140 Form 5.

529 *Kruzel v. Leeds Bldg. Products, Inc.*, 266 Ga. 765, 470 S.E.2d 882 (1996); *Coker v. Norman*, 162 Ga. 238, 133 S.E. 243 (1926). The court ordered the receiver to sell the property to pay accrued taxes and money borrowed to complete unfinished buildings on the property, even though there were conflicting claims over title and liens that were not yet resolved by the parties.

530 O.C.G.A. § 9-8-8.

531 O.C.G.A. § 23-4-35.

532 *Leggett v. Ogden*, 248 Ga. 403, 284 S.E.2d 1 (1981).

533 *Northeast Factor & Discount Co. v. Mortgage Investments, Inc. of Ga.*, 107 Ga.App. 705, 131 S.E.2d 221 (1963).

534 *Northeast Factor & Discount Co. v. Mortgage Investments, Inc. of Ga.*, 107 Ga.App. 705, 131 S.E.2d 221 (1963).

535 O.C.G.A. § 9-8-8.

536 *Anthony v. Anthony*, 143 Ga.App. 691, 240 S.E.2d 167 (1977).

537 O.C.G.A. § 9-8-8.

538 O.C.G.A. § 14-11-205.

539 O.C.G.A. § 11-3-402.

540 O.C.G.A. § 11-3-402.

for the court-appointed receiver ABC Incorporated, over specific assets of John Smith, et al as appointed by the Superior Court of Georgia, Fulton County in Smith v. White, Case No. 2012-CV-00000

[SEAL]

Normally in closing real estate transactions, the closing attorney will ask for the documents evidencing the receiver's authority to sign the purchase and sale agreement. Therefore, it is important for the receiver to retain the court order giving the receiver the power to sign the purchase and sale agreement to ensure no issues arise at closing.

Typically, receivers are appointed in commercial transactions involving a concerned lender or creditor. Lenders or creditors who are concerned about the possibility of destruction, damage, or loss of income from a mortgaged property may petition the court for the appointment of a receiver.[541] A mere lien on the property by the lender or creditor resulting from a debtor's nonpayment of a mortgage or debt will be insufficient to appoint a receiver.[542] The appointment will only be justified if the purpose is to protect the property for the repayment of debt that could be lost, destroyed, or wasted.[543]

In one case, a receiver was appointed to protect the interests of a party to a promissory note and security deed. In this instance, a partnership purchased an apartment complex from the seller by signing a promissory note and making monthly payments. The partnership also secured the payment of the purchase price by offering the property as collateral through a security deed. At first, the partnership made payments on the promissory note, but then stopped paying. After several demands, the seller had not received payment from the partnership in nine months. As such, the seller was worried that the apartment complex was in danger of being damaged because the partnership was not taking proper care of the property. The seller filed suit and requested the appointment of a receiver to protect his rights to the property under the security deed. The evidence presented to the court indicated that the partnership had not made monthly payments on the promissory note in nine months, the partnership made unauthorized distributions from the property, the property was in need of substantial repairs, and there were insufficient funds to pay the taxes and insurance.[544] Ultimately, the court upheld the appointment of a receiver to maintain the property based on the evidence of potential injury and damage to the property by the other party.[545]

A receiver will also be appointed to protect the rights of materialmen with a lien against a particular property if the property is in danger of being damaged.[546] In this case, the property owner entered in an agreement with a construction company to make certain improvements. The loan for financing the construction was through a residential mortgage lender. In addition, the owner secured the payment of the construction loan by offering the property as collateral through a security deed with the lender. Shortly after the construction begun, the owner stopped paying the construction loan and the mortgage lender went out of business. Several of the subcontractors and materialmen working on the improvements filed liens against the property. One of the materialmen brought suit requesting cancellation of the security deed with the lender and the appointment of a receiver to protect the property. The materialmen presented evidence that the repairs had stopped, the house had been vandalized and there were threats of further damage to the unoccupied house. The court found this evidence sufficient and ordered the appointment of a receiver to take possession of the property and complete the improvements. Ultimately, the purpose of the receiver was to preserve the property until the materialmen's claims, including the cancellation of the security deed, could be determined.[547]

---

541 *Lemans Associates Ltd. Partnership v. Lemans Apartments*, 268 Ga. 396, 489 S.E.2d 831 (1997).

542 *Kruzel v. Leeds Blgd. Products, Inc.*, 266 Ga. 765, 470 S.E.2d 882 (1996).

543 *Kruzel v. Leeds Blgd. Products, Inc.*, 266 Ga. 765, 470 S.E.2d 882 (1996).

544 *Lemans Associates Ltd. Partnership v. Lemans Apartments*, 268 Ga. 396, 489 S.E.2d 831 (1997).

545 *Lemans Associates Ltd. Partnership v. Lemans Apartments*, 268 Ga. 396, 489 S.E.2d 831 (1997).

546 *Kruzel v. Leeds Blgd. Products, Inc.*, 266 Ga. 765, 470 S.E.2d 882 (1996).

547 *Kruzel v. Leeds Blgd. Products, Inc.*, 266 Ga. 765, 470 S.E.2d 882 (1996).

Oftentimes, the appointment of a receiver is a more practical financial option for a lender or creditor than a traditional foreclosure action. Typically, when a receiver is appointed, the receiver maintains the property to protect the interested partys' rights until all the issues surrounding the property have been resolved.[548] However, the lender or creditor may also request the appointment of a receiver to generate income for the property by collecting rents and profits for the repayment of the debt or mortgage.[549] In this situation, the lender or creditor would receive profits from the property to pay down the debt or mortgage while the property is in litigation. Eventually, the property may be sold in a public or private sale or the property may be foreclosed on. Regardless of the end result, a lender or creditor should seek the appointment of a receiver to manage the property and collect rents or other profits in the meantime to repay any outstanding debt.[550] Once the proper grounds for appointment are shown, the lender or creditor could pay off more of the debt by asking that the receiver to manage the property and generate income during litigation than if the lender or creditor simply foreclosed on the property. Therefore, this option may be more attractive to a lender or creditor than a traditional foreclosure action.

§ 3.9 FIDUCIARIES: EXECUTORS, ADMINISTRATORS, TRUSTEES, AND CONSERVATORS

With the permission of the appropriate probate court, an executor, administrator, trustee, or conservator who has the power to sell property held by the estate of a deceased person, the trust, or the minor she represents, may sell the property privately instead of through auction, as is otherwise required.[551] So long as she has the consent of the probate court, the executor, administrator, trustee, or conservator may execute a real estate contract to sell the property or sign a power of attorney authorizing someone else to sell the property.[552]

In order to ensure that an executor, administrator, trustee, or conservator has the authority to sell property, a search of the court records should be conducted in the appropriate probate court. The probate judge should have signed an order of the court permitting the sale of the property and the signed order should be filed with the probate records. If no order is found, the other party to the contract should require that such an order be obtained prior to closing.

If the executor, administrator, trustee, or conservator sells property at a public sale, the contract to buy or sell the property becomes binding and subject to enforcement "upon the fall of the auctioneer's hammer."[553]

Neither an administrator nor an executor can bind the estate to any type of warranty in any real estate contract (including warranty of title) made on behalf of the estate. This means that when conveying property an executor or administrator does not sign a warranty deed or limited warranty deed. Rather, she signs a special executor's or administrator's deed to convey title to a buyer. The administrator or executor will not be personally bound by any such warranty unless the intent to create personal liability is expressly stated in the contract.[554]

§ 3.9.1 When Executors Sign Contracts

Executors of an estate may sell property owned by the estate upon the approval of the appropriate probate court judge.[555] Where there is more than one executor, each one should sign the real estate contract.[556] Unless the terms of a will provide otherwise, one executor cannot bind the estate to a real estate contract unless the co-executor(s) has also signed the contract.

---

548 *Shaw v. Caldwell*, 229 Ga. 87, 189 S.E.2d 684 (1972).

549 *Patel v. Patel*, 280 Ga. 292, 627 S.E.2d 21 (2006).

550 *Patel v. Patel*, 280 Ga. 292, 627 S.E.2d 21 (2006).

551 O.C.G.A. §23-2-115, O.C.G.A. § 23-2-116, O.C.G.A. § 53-8-10.

552 O.C.G.A. § 10-6-4, O.C.G.A. § 29-2-21.

553 *Stanley v. Whitmire*, 233 Ga. 675, 212 S.E.2d 845 (1975).

554 O.C.G.A. § 53-8-14.

555 O.C.G.A. § 53-8-10.

556 *First Nat'l Bank & Trust Co. v. McNatt*, 141 Ga.App. 6, 232 S.E.2d 356 (1977); *Harrison v. Carpenter*, 72 Ga.App. 149, 33 S.E.2d 274 (1945).

If an executor enters a contract on behalf of the estate without the signature(s) of the other executor(s), even though the estate might not be bound to the contract, the contracting executor could be obligated individually for the contract.[557] The signature block below should be used when contracting with an estate's executor. More than one of the following signature blocks should be drafted at the end of the contract if there is more than one executor.

> Robert Lance, Executor
>
> */s/ Robert Lance*
>
> As Executor under the Last Will and
>
> Testament of Mary Brown, Deceased

§ 3.9.2 When Administrators Sign Contracts

Administrators of an estate may also sell property belonging to the estate with a court order entered by the probate judge. A sale without an order from the probate court is void and conveys nothing to the buyer.[558] When an administrator signs a contract, the signature block should look like the following.

> Jan Baker, Administrator
>
> */s/ Jan Baker*
>
> As Administrator under the Last Will
>
> and Testament of Mary Brown, Deceased

§ 3.9.3 When Trustees Sign Contracts

Trustees may be expressly authorized by the instrument creating the trust to sell or convey property of the trust. If no statement of such authority is included in the documents, the trustee may sell the trust's property only upon an order issued by the appropriate superior court permitting the sale.[559]

Like executors and administrators, trustees may not be personally liable on any warranty made in any conveyance of property lawfully sold unless the trustee expressly undertakes such liability.[560] In conveying property from a trust the following signature block should be used.

> Bertram Harrington, Trustee
>
> */s/ Bertram Harrington*
>
> As Trustee for Samuel Brown

§ 3.9.4 When Conservators Of Minors Sign Contracts

Georgia law, with respect to the property of minor, was significantly changed in 2005. The court appointment of a guardian of a minor now places only the minor child in the guardian's custody; the minor's property is under the control of a conservator.[561] A conservator of a minor's property may sell, lease, encumber, or exchange her ward's property only by order of the appropriate probate court and upon such terms as the court may order.[562] To avoid personal liability, the conservator should sign a real estate contract in the following manner.

---

557 *First Nat'l Bank & Trust Co. v. McNatt*, 141 Ga.App. 6, 232 S.E.2d 356 (1977).

558 *Porter v. LaGrange Banking & Trust Co.*, 187 Ga. 528, 1 S.E.2d 441 (1939).

559 O.C.G.A. § 53-12-257.

560 O.C.G.A. § 53-12-199(a).

561 O.C.G.A. § 29-3-1(b).

562 O.C.G.A. § 29-3-35.

Janet Smith, Conservator

/s/ Janet Smith

As Conservator of the property of

John Barnes, a minor child

§ 3.10 CAPACITY OF THE PARTIES TO ENTER INTO CONTRACTS

For a valid sale of land, there must be a seller and buyer who must be persons or legal entities capable of contracting. The parties must have the legal capacity to act. Parties without the legal capacity to act include minors and mentally incompetent persons.

§ 3.10.1 Minors

The age of legal majority for all Georgia residents is 18 years; until that age, all persons are minors.[563]

§ 3.10.1.1 Students Residing In Georgia

An individual is not automatically a resident of Georgia if she is in Georgia for the purpose of attending school.[564] In fact, a person in Georgia only to attend school may be considered a minor in Georgia (even though he may be over 18 years old) if the student's home state has a legal age of majority that is beyond age 18.

The student's home state residence will be the state in which her parents reside if under the laws of that state she would still be considered a minor and if she is incapable of proving her emancipation.[565]

§ 3.10.1.2 Contract Of Minor Voidable Upon Majority

The age upon which a person reaches majority is significant because generally, when a minor reaches majority age, she can choose to void any contract she entered while still a minor.[566] A minor may similarly disaffirm a deed, security deed, bill of sale to secure debt, or any other conveyance of property or interest in property when she reaches majority.[567] However, if a minor receives property through a contract and after she reaches age 18 retains possession of the property or interest in the property, she shall have ratified or affirmed the original conveyance and it shall continue to be binding on her.[568]

Upon reaching majority, minors may take property that they had conveyed during minority back from certain purchasers.[569] Minors must reclaim such property within a reasonable time after attaining majority. If the minor fails to reclaim her property within a reasonable time, the right to do so will be lost. What constitutes a reasonable time depends on the facts and circumstances of each situation, but it will not be longer than seven years after the minor reaches majority.[570]

---

563 O.C.G.A. § 39-1-1(a).

564 O.C.G.A. § 39-1-1(b).

565 O.C.G.A. § 39-1-1(b).

566 O.C.G.A. § 13-3-20; *Clemons v. Olshine*, 54 Ga.App. 290, 187 S.E. 711 (1936).

567 O.C.G.A. § 44-5-41.

568 O.C.G.A. § 13-3-20, O.C.G.A. § 44-5-41.

569 *Ware v. Mobley*, 190 Ga. 249, 9 S.E.2d 67 (1940).

570 *Holbrook v. Montgomery*, 165 Ga. 514, 141 S.E. 408 (1928); *McGarrity v. Cook*, 154 Ga. 311, 114 S.E. 213 (1922).

§ 3.10.1.3   Contracting With A Minor

The right of a minor to disaffirm a contract is a personal privilege that the other party to the contract does not have. The other party to the contract cannot use the fact that she contracted with a minor to get out of the contract herself unless she did not know of the person's minority status at the time of the contract.[571] Accordingly, contracts by adults or other entities made with minors are generally enforceable against the adults or legal entities, but not against the minors.[572]

Before entering a real estate contract with a minor, parties should seek legal advice in order to determine how best to protect themselves from future loss as a consequence of the transaction.

§ 3.10.2   Mentally Incompetent Persons

The status of contracts entered into by persons who are insane, mentally ill, mentally retarded, or mentally incompetent varies. The status depends on whether a court has made a legal determination about the individual's mental competency and capability of managing their affairs and whether the court has appointed a guardian to handle the person's affairs.[573]

A person is mentally incompetent if she has a total deprivation of reason.[574] If someone is mentally incompetent, contracts which she enters are voidable,[575] which means that they are not automatically void but they are capable of being declared void at a later time, even if the other party to the contract had no notice of the person's incompetence.[576] The contract of a person who is mentally incompetent, even though not legally adjudged so, is voidable after her death upon the instance of her legal representative[577] or heirs at law.[578] Conversely, contracts entered into by a mentally incompetent person could also be determined to be enforceable at a later date.

§ 3.10.2.1   Contracting With A Mentally Incompetent Person With Guardian

Once a person is legally declared mentally incompetent and the affairs of the person are vested in a guardian, the power of the person to contract, even though the person is later restored to sanity, is lost for so long as the guardianship remains in place. Any contracts made by the mentally incompetent person are absolutely void until the guardianship is dissolved.[579] However, the guardian may enter contracts on the mentally incompetent person's behalf.

§ 3.10.2.2   Contracting With A Mentally Incompetent Person Without A Guardian

The validity and enforceability of a contract with someone adjudicated mentally incompetent but without a guardian is dependent upon the person's sanity at the time of the execution of the contract.[580] The law presumes that such a person continues to be mentally incompetent and the contract is void. It is the obligation of the person who contracts with someone who has been adjudicated as mentally incompetent to prove that the individual was sane at the time the contract was executed or that the person entered the contract during a lucid interval.[581]

---

571   O.C.G.A. § 13-5-3; *Smith v. Smith*, 36 Ga. 184 (1867).

572   *Hughes v. Murphy*, 5 Ga.App. 328, 63 S.E. 231 (1908).

573   O.C.G.A. § 13-3-24.

574   *Slaughter v. Heath*, 127 Ga. 747, 57 S.E. 69 (1907).

575   *Norfolk Southern Corp. v. Smith*, 262 Ga. 80, 414 S.E.2d 485 (1992).

576   *Sewell v. Anderson*, 197 Ga. 623, 30 S.E.2d 102 (1944); *Herrin v. George*, 183 Ga. 77, 187 S.E. 58 (1936).

577   O.C.G.A. § 13-3-24(a); *Morris v. Mobley*, 171 Ga. 224, 155 S.E. 8 (1930).

578   *Dean v. Goings*, 184 Ga. 698, 192 S.E. 826 (1937); *Warren v. Federal Land Bank*, 157 Ga. 464, 122 S.E. 40 (1924).

579   O.C.G.A. § 13-3-24.

580   *Strickland v. Chewning*, 227 Ga. 333, 180 S.E.2d 736 (1971).

581   *Id.*; *Georgia Power Co. v. Roper*, 201 Ga. 760, 41 S.E.2d 226 (1947)

A contract with a mentally incompetent person will automatically be considered valid and binding whenever it is shown that the terms of the contract have been subsequently ratified either expressly or by implication by words or conduct of the mentally incompetent person during a lucid interval, or if the mentally incompetent person's personal representative later confirms the contract.[582]

If you are unsure about a person's mental capacity to contract, you could request that a doctor examine the person. If it is determined that the person is mentally competent to sign the contract they are being asked to sign, the doctor's report can be used later to prove the validity of the contract. Short of a doctor's examination, you may want to ask the person some questions at the time the person is executing the contract.[583] The questions should be asked and answered in front of two or three witnesses who are not related to the transaction. The witnesses could also sign the contract under a statement showing that they attest to the mental capacity of the party being questioned.

§ 3.10.2.3   Voiding A Contract With A Mentally Incompetent Person

A party with whom an incompetent person contracts cannot get out of the contract simply because the other person is incompetent. Even though a party did not know the other party was mentally incompetent and entered the contract in good faith, the party may not be relieved of her obligations under the contract on the basis of the other party's incompetence. Parties contract at their own peril and must bear the loss if necessary.[584]

§ 3.10.2.4   Voided Contracts May Require Restitution From Mentally Incompetent Person

Generally, when the contract is voided by a mentally incompetent person, such person must restore the other party to the position she was in prior to entering into the contract. However, if the other party was aware that the person was incompetent at the time of the contract, such restoration is not required.[585]

Before entering a real estate contract with a person whose mental capacity is at issue, parties should obtain legal advice in order to determine how to best protect themselves from future loss as a consequence of the transaction.

§ 3.10.3   Intoxicated Persons

A contract made by a voluntarily intoxicated person is valid unless the intoxication was so great that the person was deprived of all reason and the other party had notice of this condition.[586] If the other party brought about the intoxication, the intoxicated person can avoid the contract. Alternatively, the intoxicated party can approve or ratify the contract either expressly or by acting in a way consistent with the terms of the contract.[587]

---

582   *Norfolk Southern Corp. v. Smith*, 262 Ga. 80, 414 S.E.2d 485 (1992); *Bunn v. Postell*, 107 Ga. 490, 33 S.E. 707 (1899); *Watkins v. Stulb & Vorhauer*, 23 Ga.App. 181, 98 S.E. 94 (1919).

583   Questions to ask the party you believe could be mentally incompetent should include: What is your birth date? Do you know how old you are? Do you know what the date is today? Do you want to sell your house? Do you understand that if you sign this document, you will be agreeing to sell your house? Do you understand how much money you are agreeing to sell your house for? Where do you live now?

584   *Norfolk Southern Corp. v. Smith*, 262 Ga. 80, 414 S.E.2d 485 (1992); *Williford v. Swint*, 183 Ga. 375, 188 S.E. 685 (1936); *Watkins v. Stulb & Vorhauer*, 23 Ga.App. 181, 98 S.E. 94 (1919).

585   *Metter Banking Co. v. Millen Lumber & Supply Co.*, 191 Ga.App. 634, 382 S.E.2d 624 (1989).

586   *Weldon v. Colquitt*, 62 Ga. 449 (1879); *Abbeville Trading Co. v. Butler, Stevens & Co.*, 3 Ga.App. 138, 59 S.E. 450 (1907).

587   O.C.G.A. § 13-3-25.

§ 3.10.4   Persons Who Do Not Speak (Or Read) English

The English language is the official language of the state of Georgia.[588] English must be used in all public records,[589] including documents, papers, letters, or other similar materials prepared and maintained or received by an agency or private person.[590] Based on the language of the statute, all contracts brought before a court in the state of Georgia must also be in English. A contract in a language other than English will prevent a court from interpreting the contract. Even if a court had the capability to read the contract written in a language other than English, there would likely be interpretation issues. For these reasons, all real estate agreements should be in the English language.

What should be done when the buyer or seller does not speak or read the English language? It is incumbent upon someone who does not read English to arrange for a translator to truly and accurately convey to them the terms of the sales contract and any other documents related to the transaction.

A real estate agent proficient in the seller's or buyer's native tongue may be tempted to act as the translator. While the agent can certainly assist in this regard, it is strongly recommended that the agent advise her client to have someone else, perhaps a friend, attorney, or professional translator, perform this function. English does not translate easily into some languages, and it is not unheard of for an unhappy buyer or seller to claim that the real estate agent either failed to accurately translate the contract or neglected to include some important point in the translation.

If a buyer or seller does not speak or read English but refuses to obtain the services of a qualified translator, it may be a good idea for the real estate agent to have the following warning translated into the client's native language and have it signed by the client:

> The sales contract you are about to enter into concerns your legal rights and liabilities
> related to the purchase and sale of (property address). Because this document is written
> in English, you are strongly encouraged to retain the services of an independent
> qualified translator. By signing below, you acknowledge that you have not relied upon
> _____ (name of agent or broker) to act as your translator in this matter.

Of course, an argument can be made that if the buyer does not understand English, the disclaimer will be of little benefit to them.

§ 3.11   ASSIGNMENT AND SUBSTITUTION OF PARTIES TO CONTRACT

§ 3.11.1   Assignment In General

Real estate sales contracts may provide for the future substitution of new parties.[591] The GAR Contract provides that it is binding upon the parties to the contract, their heirs, successors, legal representatives, and permitted assigns. Any assignment must be signed by all of the parties to the contract, and all of the terms and conditions of the contract will be binding upon the assignee.

Whether a contract is assignable depends upon the language in the agreement. If a real estate contract is silent as to whether it can be assigned, an assignment will generally be permitted.[592] However, such an assignment in no way releases the original party from her obligations. They remain fully liable to perform under the terms of the contact.[593]

---

588 O.C.G.A. § 50-3-100(a).

589 O.C.G.A. § 50-3-100(a).

590 O.C.G.A. § 50-18-70(b)(2).

591 *Pearson v. Courson*, 129 Ga. 656, 59 S.E. 907 (1907).

592 *Southern Concrete Co. v. Carter Const. Co.*, 121 Ga.App. 573, 174 S.E.2d 447 (1970).

593 *Id.*

A contract providing that it may not be assigned, or that consent for an assignment may be given or refused at a party's sole and absolute discretion, is assignable solely at the discretion of the other party.[594] In such a case, the non-assigning party can withhold her consent for any reason, or for no reason at all. There is no requirement that the party act reasonably in denying permission to assign the contract.

Alternatively, a contract may provide that it can be assigned upon the consent of the other party, which consent may not be unreasonably withheld. In such a case, the term "unreasonably" means that the party cannot act in an arbitrary or capricious manner or base consent merely upon personal preferences.[595] While "reasonableness" is often a jury question, the primary factor typically considered is the proposed assignee's financial ability to perform the terms of the contract.[596]

What if a contract simply provides that it is assignable upon the consent of the other party? Must the party from whom consent is sought act reasonably in this situation in granting or denying consent? Interestingly, the answer depends upon the type of contract. Nearly every contract in Georgia imposes upon each party a duty of good faith and fair dealing in its performance and enforcement. As a result, a general contract provision permitting assignment upon the consent of the other party is deemed to include the added provision that the party must act in good faith (*i.e.*, be reasonable) in granting or denying an assignment.[597] However, the Georgia courts have created a limited exception to this rule in the case of leases. In lease contracts, the courts have declined to read in a requirement of good faith or fair dealing, and have not forced landlords to be reasonable in permitting assignments absent contractual language calling for reasonableness.[598]

Most residential real estate purchase and sale agreements prohibit the assignment of the contract without the written consent of the seller. For instance, the GAR Purchase and Sale Agreement[599] provides that it may not be assigned by the buyer without the written permission of the seller.

Other types of purchase and sale agreements, however, provide more flexible assignment options. Commercial purchase and sale agreements and land contracts normally allow at least some limited form of assignment in recognition of the fact that many buyers will create a separate legal entity for the express purpose of owning the property being acquired. Both the GAR Commercial Purchase and Sale Agreement[600] and the GAR Land Purchase and Sale Agreement[601] provide a check box where the parties may select (1) that the buyer may not assign the contract without the seller's approval or (2) that the agreement may be assigned by the buyer to any legal entity of which the buyer owns at least a 25% interest.

In some cases, the seller may only want to allow an assignment without the seller's consent if the buyer assigns the agreement to a legal entity in which she owns a majority interest. In this case, the following special stipulation may be used.

> **Special Stipulation 33:   Seller's Consent to Assign to Legal Entity in which Buyer has a Significant Interest**
>
> *Notwithstanding any provision to the contrary contained herein, Seller does hereby consent to an assignment of this purchase and sale agreement to a legal entity in which buyer owns a majority interest.*

An alternative approach is to permit the buyer to absolutely assign the contract to an entity in which the buyer has any interest (regardless of the percentage) without the consent of the seller. An example of such a special stipulation follows.

---

594 *Tap Room, Inc. v. Peachtree-Tsg Associates, LLC*, 270 Ga.App. 90, 606 S.E.2d 13, (2004).

595 *Pakwood Industries, Inc. v. John Galt Associates*, 219 Ga.App. 527, 466 S.E.2d 226 (1995).

596 *Id.*

597 *Hunting Aircraft, Inc. v. Peachtree City Airport Authority*, 281 Ga.App. 450, 636 S.E.2d 139 (2006).

598 *Id.*

599 GAR Form F20.

600 GAR Form CF2.

601 GAR Form F34.

Special Stipulation 34:   Assignment Allowed to Legal Entity in which Buyer has an Interest

Notwithstanding any provision to the contrary contained herein, this Agreement may be assigned by the Buyer to a legal entity in which the Buyer has a legal interest without the consent of the Seller. Of course, even without a right to assign the contract, the buyer can still close and immediately sell the property to another purchaser. The right to assign the contract merely avoids a second closing.

§ 3.11.2   Releases

What happens if a party validly assigns their interest in a contract? Obviously, if the assignee performs the terms of the contract then there is no issue. However, what if the assignee fails to perform? Is the assignor released from liability?

The answer to these questions is that unless the contract expressly provides that the assignor is relieved of liability, she will remain fully liable to the other party in the event the assignee fails to perform.[602] This is the case even if the other party has consented to the assignment and deals exclusively with the assignee.[603]

Parties looking to be released from their contractual obligations upon an assignment can use the following special stipulation.

Special Stipulation 35:   Assignment Operates as Release of Assignor

Seller acknowledges that Buyer has the right to assign this Agreement as provided for herein. For and in consideration of the sum $10.00 and other good and valuable consideration, the receipt and sufficiency of which are hereby acknowledged, Seller agrees that should Buyer validly assign this Agreement, Seller will thereafter look solely to the assignee for performance hereunder rather than Buyer and that Buyer will be released from and have no further rights, obligations, duties and liabilities under this Agreement.

§ 3.11.3   Fictitious Names And Straw Parties

Sometimes it is to a party's advantage to conceal their real name in a transaction. For instance, a celebrity may wish to avoid having her identify or address become public. In other cases, for example, where a well-known corporation is the buyer, revealing the buyer's identity may drive up the cost of the property. After a divorce, one spouse may wish to purchase the marital residence, but knows that the ex-spouse will not sell to her. However, sometimes the use of a fictitious name is an indicator of mortgage fraud. See Chapter 21 (Mortgage Fraud) for a detailed discussion of that issue.

In legitimate (*i.e.*, non-fraudulent) transactions, persons wishing to conceal their identities have several options. First, they can create a corporation or limited liability company for the sole purpose of acquiring title to the property. Of course, most sellers will inquire who the principals are of this newly formed legal entity. Second, they can arrange for a trusted friend or business partner to acquire the property and purchase it from them after the fact. Third, they can provide that the contract is assignable, negotiate the transaction using a corporate name, and then take title in their own name at the last minute via an assignment. Finally, when negotiating the terms of the contract, the broker can state that they are not at liberty to reveal the name of the buyer and will not do so until the seller has made a counteroffer on the property that is acceptable to the buyer. Buyers can also insist that the seller sign a confidentiality agreement that they will not reveal the name of the buyer to third parties except with the permission of the buyer.

---

602 *Fagbemi v. JDN Realty Corp.*, 275 Ga.App. 540, 621 S.E.2d 765 (2005).

603 *Id.*

Real estate licensees need to remember that while there is no need to affirmatively disclose the true identity of the ultimate purchaser, they are prohibited under license law from making any substantial misrepresentations[604] regarding the identity of the purchaser.

§ 3.12 DEATH OF A PARTY TO CONTRACT

The GAR Contract provides that it shall be for the benefit of and binding upon the parties and their heirs, successors, legal representatives, and assigns. Therefore, when either a buyer or seller dies before the real estate contract she executed is consummated and where there is no administrator or executor appointed to represent the estate, the heirs at law may enforce the contract.

For example, in one Georgia case an individual contracted to purchase property and died before the closing. There was no legal representative or administrator for the decedent's estate. The court held that the heirs of the decedent could sue the seller and force the seller to execute a warranty deed to the decedent's estate for the property which the decedent had contracted to buy before his death.[605]

Georgia law allows the seller of property to enforce a real estate contract against a decedent's estate through the decedent's heirs at law, unless the contract executed by the seller and the decedent provides otherwise.[606] For instance, when a person contracts to sell her property and dies before the closing, the buyer may sue the heirs of the decedent/seller to force them to convey the property.[607] In another Georgia case, a seller entered an option contract with a buyer for certain property owned by the seller. The seller died before the sale was consummated, and the buyer sued the seller's surviving heirs because the seller died without a will. The court held that the contract was enforceable against the seller's heirs and they were required to comply with the terms of the contract and convey the property to the buyer.[608] Two stipulations that buyers can use to protect themselves in the event of the death of a buyer are set out below. The first makes the contract voidable in the event of the death of a buyer. The second results in the contract actually becoming void.

> **Special Stipulation 36: Death of a Buyer Makes Contract Voidable**
>
> *In the event any person who is a Buyer hereunder dies prior to the date of Closing, this Agreement may be terminated by the surviving Buyer(s) upon notice to the Seller, provided that the same is delivered within seven (7) days of the death of said person.*

> **Special Stipulation 37: Death of a Buyer Voids Contract**
>
> *In the event any person who is a Buyer hereunder dies prior to the date of Closing, this Agreement shall automatically terminate without penalty to Buyer.*

§ 3.12.1 Selling Property Not Yet Owned

In many purchase and sale agreements, the seller warrants that she has good and marketable title to the property as of the date of the purchase and sale agreement. Sellers who are interested in selling property that they do not yet own should carefully review the contracts they are signing to ensure that they are not breaching the purchase and sale agreement as of the date the agreement becomes binding.

---

604 O.C.G.A. § 43-40-25(b)(21).

605 *Gaskins v. Vickery*, 234 Ga. 833, 218 S.E.2d 617 (1975).

606 O.C.G.A. § 53-3-1, O.C.G.A. § 53-3-8 to O.C.G.A. § 53-3-14, 53-3-19, and O.C.G.A. § 53-3-20.

607 O.C.G.A. § 53-7-9; *Harper v. Georgian Villa, Inc.*, 222 Ga. 130, 149 S.E.2d 90 (1966).

608 *Harper v. Georgian Villa, Inc.*, 222 Ga. 130, 149 S.E.2d 90 (1966).

The GAR Contracts provide that the seller warrants that at the time of closing, the seller will convey to the buyer good and marketable title to the property. Thus, a seller is not prevented from contracting to sell property for which she does not have title at the time the contract is executed, so long as the seller obtains title before the specified time of conveyance in order to complete the sale.[609]

If the seller fails to obtain title to the property before the closing date, the seller will be liable in damages to the buyer for failure to convey the property.[610] In such a situation, the seller cannot be required to sell the property to the buyer because the seller does not own the property, but the seller could be liable to the buyer for money damages.[611]

The GAR Contracts provide that prior to closing the buyer may examine the title and furnish the seller with a written statement of objections affecting the marketability of the title. The seller must satisfy all valid title objections prior to closing or the buyer may terminate the contract and obtain a refund of all of her earnest money.

For this reason, some sellers will want to limit their liability in the event they are unable to convey good and marketable title to the buyer. The first special stipulation below limits the seller's liability to the return of the buyer's earnest money if the seller cannot convey good and marketable title to the buyer at closing. The second special stipulation listed below limits the seller's liability to the return of the buyer's earnest money and the reimbursement of any and all of the buyer's actual expenses.

> **Special Stipulation 38: Seller's Liability Limited to Return of Earnest Money if Seller Cannot Convey Title at Closing**
>
> *Holder is presently holding $_____ in earnest money in this transaction. Buyer acknowledges that Seller has not yet acquired title to the Property. In the event Seller cannot convey good and marketable title to the Property at closing, Buyer's sole remedy shall be to receive all funds deposited with Holder, plus recover from Seller the sum of $_____ in full and final liquidated damages of Buyer, said sum being a reasonable pre-estimate of Buyer's actual damages and not a penalty.*

> **Special Stipulation 39: Seller's Liability Limited to Return of Earnest Money and Reimbursement of Actual Expenses if Seller Cannot Convey Title at Closing**
>
> *Holder is presently holding $_____ in earnest money in this transaction. Buyer acknowledges that Seller has not yet acquired title to the Property. In the event Seller cannot convey good and marketable title to the Property at closing, Buyer's sole remedy shall be to receive all funds deposited with Holder, and Seller shall pay to Buyer all of Buyer's actual out-of-pocket expenses associated with this Agreement up to $_____, in full settlement of all claims of Buyer.*

The contract may be entered into conditionally upon the seller's ability to acquire title prior to closing. If the contract is not conditional, the seller will be liable in damages for breach of contract if she is unable to secure title to the property in time to make delivery of it at the closing.[612]

---

609 *Northington-Munger-Pratt Co. v. Farmers Gin & Warehouse Co.*, 119 Ga. 851, 47 S.E.200 (1904); *Williams v. Bell*, 126 Ga.App. 432, 190 S.E.2d 818 (1972).

610 *Northington-Munger-Pratt Co. v. Farmers Gin & Warehouse Co.*, 119 Ga. 851, 47 S.E.200 (1904); *Williams v. Bell*, 126 Ga.App. 432, 190 S.E.2d 818 (1972).

611 *Smith v. Hooker/Barnes, Inc.*, 253 Ga. 514, 322 S.E.2d 268 (1984).

612 *Northington-Munger-Pratt Co. v. Farmers Gin & Warehouse Co.*, 119 Ga. 851, 47 S.E.200 (1904); *Horn v. Wright*, 157 Ga.App. 408, 278 S.E.2d 66 (1981); *Williams v. Bell*, 126 Ga.App. 432, 190 S.E.2d 818 (1972).

Special Stipulation 40:   Contract Contingent Upon Seller Obtaining Title to Property

The parties hereto acknowledge that the Seller does not presently have good and marketable title to the Property. This Agreement is contingent upon the Seller obtaining good and marketable title to the Property prior to closing or any extension thereof. In the event the Seller is unable to timely obtain good and marketable title to the Property then, upon notice of the same being delivered by Seller to Buyer, this Agreement shall automatically terminate and Buyer shall be entitled to the return of all sums deposited with Holder without penalty.

In many of the cases cited in this chapter, the buyers could have protected themselves at the beginning of the contract period by conducting a title search on the property they were planning to purchase. The title search would have disclosed the identity of all legal owner(s) of the property and/or whether the contracting party had the authority to execute a contract for the conveyance of the property. In all situations where the buyer contracted with incorrect parties, the buyer could have raised title objections which the seller would have been obligated to remedy before closing. If the title objections were not remedied by closing, the buyer would then have a good claim for breach of contract against the individual who represented that she owned the property. Most buyers in Georgia do not take these steps to protect themselves, but a little work before entering a real estate contract could save a great deal of time and heartache later.

§ 3.13   UNMARRIED PERSONS OWNING PROPERTY

It is becoming increasingly common for persons who are not married to purchase property together. Typically this is done by couples who either cannot get married in Georgia or have chosen to live together without the benefit of marriage. As in any marriage, legal issues can arise if the relationship ends but the parties continue to own property together.

Oftentimes unmarried persons who purchase property together find that the laws surrounding property ownership are insufficient to protect their interest in commonly owned property. Although neither party may anticipate separating at the time the property is purchased, having a written agreement in place to address the rights of the respective parties in the event of dissolution of the relationship can avoid problems down the road. This type of agreement is often referred to as a tenancy agreement. In some sense, it is the real estate equivalent of the pre-nuptial agreement. Without an agreement specifically providing each party's respective rights in the property, the common law rules of tenancy in common will apply.[613]

This chapter discusses the most common issues that arise when two unmarried persons, whether in a relationship or not, own property together, and offers suggestions on how to deal with those issues. These issues include the interests of the parties in the property when purchased, a party's right to possess the property, the responsibility for taxes and assessments, the responsibilities for financing any improvements made to the property, the responsibility to account for profits received from the property, and the sale of the property. More specifically, each section discusses the issues that arise in the absence of an agreement defining each party's rights.

§ 3.13.1   Interest In Common Property

In Georgia, when an unmarried couple purchases property together, each person has an equal undivided interest in the property, unless there is an agreement that states otherwise.[614] Therefore, a conveyance of real property to an unmarried couple gives each person an equal fifty percent (50%) interest in what is known as a tenancy in common.[615]

---

613 O.C.G.A. § 44-6-120.

614 O.C.G.A. § 44-6-120.

615 O.C.G.A. § 44-6-120.

As such, an agreement to sell the property normally requires the consent of both parties. If one party wants to sell and the other does not, the party who wants to sell is left having to file a lawsuit seeking partition of the property. Since in most cases, the property cannot literally be divided in half, the court will normally order the property to be sold and for the proceeds to then be evenly divided between the two parties.[616]

If one of the parties has paid more of the purchase price than the other or otherwise put more money into the property, it is possible to establish unequal interests in common property without an agreement between the parties.[617] A court will often allow for the introduction of parol or verbal evidence of the transaction or the conduct of the parties to determine each party's interest.[618] The evidence must be clear and convincing and is ultimately a question for the jury.[619] Therefore, maintaining records showing a person's disproportionate financial contributions to the property is important for recovering such contributions.

For example, John and Jim are unmarried and purchase property together. There is no agreement between them providing their respective interests in the property. John pays a substantial down payment for the property and they verbally agree that Jim will make the monthly payments. Jim rarely makes the monthly payments and John ends up also making most of the mortgage payments on the property. Shortly thereafter, John and Jim part ways. The parties cannot agree on how to sell the property and split the proceeds because John thinks he should get more of the proceeds from the sale. John files a lawsuit seeking partition of the property. Generally, without an agreement stating otherwise, each party would have an equal interest and thus, John would only get 50% of the proceeds.[620] However, if John can present evidence that he disproportionately paid for the property, he could collect a greater proportion of the sale proceeds based upon the proportion of the costs he paid for the property.[621]

To provide for each party's interest in the commonly owned property, the following sample special stipulation may be used.

Special Stipulation 41: Ownership of the Property

Title to the Property is held in the names of John Smith and Jim Brown, as tenants in common. John Smith shall have an undivided eighty percent (80%) interest and Jim Brown shall have an undivided twenty percent (20%) interest in the Property, subject to the terms of this Agreement.

§ 3.13.2 Right To Possess Common Property

Another common issue that arises when unmarried persons own property together is each party's right to possess the common property. Most often, this issue comes to light when the couple separates and one party wants the other to move out. Under Georgia law, when two unmarried persons purchase property together, each person has an equal right to possess the property unless there is an agreement stating otherwise.[622] Therefore, in the absence of an agreement, each person has the right to use and possess the entire property, so long as that party's use and possession does not affect the rights of the other owner.[623]

---

616 O.C.G.A. § 44-6-120.

617 *Brown v. Leggitt*, 226 Ga. 366, 174 S.E.2d 889 (1970).

618 *Burt v. Skrzyniarz*, 272 Ga. 35, 526 S.E.2d 848 (2000).

619 *Burt v. Skrzyniarz*, 272 Ga. 35, 526 S.E.2d 848 (2000).

620 O.C.G.A. § 44-6-120.

621 *Estes v. Estes*, 205 Ga. 814, 55 S.E.2d 217 (1949).

622 O.C.G.A. § 44-6-121(a).

623 *Allstate Ins. Co.v. Ammons*, 163 Ga.App. 385, 294 S.E.2d 610 (1982).

Each owner has an equal right to possess the common property regardless of whether each party's respective interest in the property is equal.[624] Even if there is an agreement providing for unequal interests in the common property, the unequal interest will not give the person holding the greater interest a superior right to possess the property.[625] Moreover, the person holding the smaller interest does not have a lesser right to possess the property.[626] Therefore, even if the event the couple separates, each owner still has a right to possess the entire property.

If the parties want to establish equal rights to possess and use the common property, the unmarried couple should include the following provision in the tenancy agreement.

Special Stipulation 42: Possession

> *Subject to the terms of this Agreement, each party shall have equal rights of possession with respect to the Property. No other person shall be entitled to occupy the Property without the prior written consent of both parties.*

Oftentimes, parties may want to establish specific areas within a property that are exclusively for her possession. This situation is common when two (or more) friends or family members purchase property together and each person wants to exclusively occupy a particular bedroom in the house. In Georgia, one owner may not select a particular area within the property for her exclusive possession unless there is an agreement that gives the party that right.[627] Therefore, if the owners want to establish exclusive areas, the following provision should be included in the tenancy agreement.

Special Stipulation 43: Possession and Exclusive Area

> *Subject to the terms of this Agreement, each party shall have equal rights of possession with respect to the Property, provided, however, that John Smith shall have the exclusive right to occupy the master bedroom and its connecting bathroom on the second floor of the residence and John Brown shall have the exclusive right to occupy the bedroom and connecting bathroom on the first floor of the residence.*

In drafting a tenancy agreement, it is not uncommon to attach floor plans of the residence as an exhibit, in which areas that are exclusively assigned to one co-tenant or another are delineated. Neither owner has the right to exclude the other from possessing or using the common property that has not been exclusively assigned to one party or the other.[628] Moreover, a common owner's right to possession and use of a property does not change when the other owner moves out.[629] In other words, when an unmarried couple separates and one person moves out, that does not give the remaining person any greater right to use or possess the property than she had originally.[630] Therefore, if one owner moved out and thereafter decided to move back in, the remaining owner may not exclude that owner from doing so because each owner has an equal right to possess the common property.[631] If one owner excludes the other from the common property, that owner can be liable for damages to the owner who is being excluded.[632]

---

624 *Fountain v. Davis*, 71 Ga.App. 1, 29 S.E.2d 798 (1944).

625 O.C.G.A. § 44-6-120.

626 O.C.G.A. § 44-6-120.

627 *Haden v. Sims*, 127 Ga. 717, 56 S.E. 989 (1907).

628 *Whigby v. Burnham*, 135 Ga. 584, 69 S.E. 1114 (1911).

629 *Allstate Ins. Co.v. Ammons*, 163 Ga.App. 385, 294 S.E.2d 610 (1982).

630 *Allstate Ins. Co.v. Ammons*, 163 Ga.App. 385, 294 S.E.2d 610 (1982).

631 *Whigby v. Burnham*, 135 Ga. 584, 69 S.E. 1114 (1911).

632 O.C.G.A. § 44-6-121(b).

To avoid any issues regarding a party's right to possess the property in the event the couple separates, either a right of first refusal or a buy-sell provision is generally included in the tenant agreement. These provisions are discussed more in detail in § 3.13.5 (Right of First Refusal on the Sale of Common Property) and § 3.13.6 (Buy-Sell Agreements).

§ 3.13.3 Maintenance Of And Improvements To The Common Property

Oftentimes, issues arise over which owner is responsible for the payment of maintenance and any improvements made to the property. In Georgia, either person may maintain or improve the property without the other owner's permission.[633] However, unmarried persons who purchase property together are generally not required to split the cost of maintenance and improvements equally. Therefore, if one owner chooses to maintain or make valuable improvements to the property, the other owner does not have to share in the costs for the maintenance and/or improvements unless there is an agreement that states otherwise.

However, even in the absence of an agreement, an owner who has paid money to maintain a property may be reimbursed for such costs.[634] An owner who has improved the property may also be entitled to compensation for any improvements that increased the property's value.[635] Of course, not all improvements will result in a dollar for dollar increase in the property's value and in some cases will not increase the value of the property at all.

Generally, an agreement providing each party's responsibilities for maintenance and improvements will control the parties and a court will not interfere.[636] However, if the agreement provides a method of repayment that is incapable of being performed, a court will consider the expenditures made by the owner just as if there was no agreement.[637]

For example, four (4) friends purchase rental property together. The owners enter into an agreement to make valuable improvements to the property but only two owners will pay for the improvements. The parties agree that the owners paying for the improvements will be paid back out of the rents from the property, plus seven percent (7%) interest until the costs they spent on the improvements are fully repaid. The improvements end up costing substantially more than anticipated and the owners decide to sell the property before the improvements are completed. The owners who paid for the improvements have not yet been paid back any of their costs. The parties cannot agree on how to divide the proceeds from a sale of the property and file an action for partition of the property. In such a case, a court will consider the money spent by the two owners when dividing the proceeds from the sale because the method of repayment never allowed those owners to be repaid the debt from the improvements.[638]

If the parties want to provide for equal responsibility for the cost of maintenance and improvements to the common property, the following provision should be included in the tenancy agreement.

---

633 *Turnbull v. Foster*, 116 Ga. 765, 43 S.E.42 (1902).

634 *Clay v. Clay*, 269 Ga. 902, 506 S.E.2d 866 (1998).

635 *Helmken v. Meyer*, 138 Ga. 457, 75 S.E. 586 (1912).

636 *Turnbull v. Foster*, 116 Ga. 765, 43 S.E.42 (1902).

637 *Turnbull v. Foster*, 116 Ga. 765, 43 S.E.42 (1902).

638 *Turnbull v. Foster*, 116 Ga. 765, 43 S.E.42 (1902).

Special Stipulation 44:   Both Parties Responsible for Maintenance, Repairs and Improvements to the Property

The parties contemplate that they may invest additional sums in the future to pay for maintenance, renovations and improvements to the Property to facilitate the parties' use and enjoyment of the Property and to enhance the Property's resale value ("Additional Contributions"). Without limiting the foregoing, Additional Contributions shall include maintenance of the Property, all capital expenditures and expenses incurred in making alterations, additions or improvements to the Property, together with all capital repairs and replacements to the Property. For purposes hereof, such expenditures may include: repairs or replacements of equipment and appliances necessary or useful in the operation or enjoyment of the Property, including kitchen equipment, and similar items; structural improvements or additions to the Property; repairs or replacements of doors and windows and HVAC equipment; and any other payments which may qualify for basis treatment as capital expenditures under applicable federal income tax rules and regulations.

Subject to the terms of this Agreement, each party shall have equal responsibility for the repayment of Additional Contributions to pay for and defray the cost of capital improvements and expenditures contemplated by the provisions of this Paragraph ____.

Notwithstanding any contrary provisions of this Agreement, unless a proposed capital expenditure is required on an immediate basis to prevent damage to the Property or to maintain habitability as a residence, the consent of both parties shall be required for any project or expenditure [over $_____]. Consent by either party shall be unreasonably withheld or delayed. Further, in the event Additional Contributions are made by the Co-Tenants in unequal amounts, no breach or default shall arise under this Agreement, but rather the excess Additional Contribution shall be credited to the account of the Co-Tenant making such payment (to the extent of such excess) and shall be recovered by such Co-Tenant upon sale of the Property, as a payment from sales proceeds (to the extent available) that has priority over the payment of other sums due and owing to either Co-Tenant.

Some unmarried couples may want to provide that one person is solely responsible for maintaining, repairing and improving the commonly owned property. This situation often arises when one owner has a significantly higher interest in the property than the other owner. For example, John Smith and Jim Brown enter into a tenancy agreement and purchase property together. John Smith is providing almost all of the money for the purchase and sale of the property. The agreement states that John Smith has a ninety-eight percent (98%) interest in the property and Jim Brown has only a two percent (2%) interest in the property. In this case, both parties can agree that John Smith is solely responsible for any maintenance, repairs and improvements made to the property by providing a provision in the tenancy agreement.

If the parties want to provide for unequal responsibilities for financing maintenance and improvements, the information included in the provision will be different. Oftentimes, when one party is solely responsible for any maintenance and improvements, the parties will not want to require consent from both parties. If the parties want to establish unequal responsibility for these expenses, the following provision should be included in the tenancy agreement.

Special Stipulation 45:   Sole Responsibility for Maintenance, Repairs and Improvements to the Property

The parties contemplate that John Smith may invest additional sums in the future to pay for maintenance, renovations and improvements to the Property to facilitate the parties' use and enjoyment of the Property and to enhance the Property's resale value ("Additional Contributions"). Without limiting the foregoing, Additional Contributions shall include all capital expenditures and expenses incurred in making alternations, additions, maintenance or improvements to the Property, together with all capital repairs and replacements to the Property. For purposes hereof, such expenditures may include repairs and replacements of equipment and appliances necessary or useful in the operation or enjoyment of the Property, including kitchen and HVAC equipment, and similar items; structural improvements or additions to the Property; repairs or replacements or doors and windows; and any other payments which may qualify for basis treatment as capital expenditures under applicable defer income tax rules and regulations.

Subject to the terms of this Agreement, John Smith shall be solely responsible for the Additional Contributions to pay for and defray the cost of capital improvement and expenditures contemplated by the provisions of this Paragraph_____.

Notwithstanding any contrary provision of this Agreement, John Smith shall have the sole discretion to construct, develop, and complete related improvements on the Property. Further, in the event Additional Contributions are made to the Property, any and all profits, revenue or other income from the Property shall be divided by the parties in proportion to their respective interests in the Property.

§ 3.13.4   Right To Profits From The Property

One of the most common disputes that arise between unmarried couples or common owners is over profits received from the property.[639] Under Georgia law, unless there is an agreement that states otherwise, each common owner has the right to an equal share of any profits received from the property. Therefore, when the property is sold, each party will receive an equal fifty percent (50%) share of the profits unless there is an agreement providing for unequal shares. However, regardless of whether either party's rights to the profits are equal, the agreement between the parties should clearly state each party's respective rights to any profits received from the property.

Similarly, parties often have disputes over the collection of rents from the common property. The collection of rent or other proceeds by one owner is for the benefit of all the owners.[640] Under the Official Code of Georgia, if one owner receives any profit, rent or other proceeds from the property, that owner must give the other her equal share.[641] Any owner that withholds profits received from the property will be liable to the owner whose funds are being withheld.[642]

Common owners still have a duty to split profits from the property even if one common owner moves out.[643] In Georgia, common owners owe a fiduciary relationship to one another[644] and thus, have a heightened duty to give the other owner any profits received from the property. For example, John Smith and Jim Brown purchase property together and they do not have a tenancy agreement. Eventually, they separate and John moves out. Jim, the remaining owner, cannot afford

---

639 *White v. Lee*, 250 Ga. 688, 300 S.E.2d 517 (1983).

640 *Chambers v. Schall*, 209 Ga. 18, 70 S.E.2d 463 (1958).

641 *Hardin v. Council*, 200 Ga. 822, 38 S.E.2d 549 (1946).

642 O.C.G.A. § 44-6-121(b); *White v. Lee*, 250 Ga. 688, 300 S.E.2d 517 (1983).

643 *White v. Lee*, 250 Ga. 688, 300 S.E.2d 517 (1983).

644 *Fuller v. McBurrows*, 229 Ga. 422, 192 S.E.2d 144 (1972).

the mortgage payment of $900 so he also moves out and leases the property to Tom for $1,200 a month. Jim keeps the extra $300 each a month and never gives any of that profit to John. In this case, John is entitled to one half the profits Jim received while Tom was renting the house.[645]

However, one owner is not required to pay the other owner rent for staying in the property.[646] For instance, if one owner moves out of the property and the other remains, the remaining owner does not have to pay rent to the owner who left for staying in the property.[647] As long as the remaining owner is not withholding any profits received from the property, that owner does not have to account to the other owner.[648] As another example, John Smith and Jim Brown purchase property together and do not have a tenancy agreement. The couple separates and Jim moves out. Instead of renting the house to someone else, John stays and exclusively occupies the property. In this case, John would not have to pay any rent to Jim because Jim moved out leaving John the entire property by himself.[649]

Oftentimes, if the agreement provides for equal interests in the property, the parties will also want equal division of any rents or profits received from the property. In order for the parties to provide for equal rights to any profits received, the following provision should be included in the tenancy agreement.

Special Stipulation 46: Revenue

Any and all rents, profits, insurance proceeds, revenue or other income from the Property shall be shared by the parties equally.

It is not uncommon for owners with unequal interests to provide for an unequal division of any profits received from the property. A provision of this nature is often included at the request of the party with the greater interest. This type of unequal division is commonly based on each party's respective interest in the property. For example, John Smith and Jim Brown purchase property together. John has a 70% interest in the property and Jim has a 30% interest in the property. Both parties agree to split any rent or profits received from the property in proportion to their interests. Including a provision of this nature will avoid any issues that may later arise regarding the collection of rents or splitting the proceeds from the sale of the common property. To provide an unequal division of any profits received from the property based on the parties' respective interests, the following provision should be included in the tenant agreement.

Special Stipulation 47: Revenue

Any and all rents, profits, insurance proceeds, revenue or other income from the Property shall be shared by the parties in proportion to their respective undivided interest in the Property.

§ 3.13.4.1 Statute Of Limitations Claims For Excess Proceeds

Unmarried persons who purchase property together often have questions concerning the right to keep another owner's profits from the property after a certain period of time. Generally, the statute of limitations for keeping a co-owner's share of the profits is seven years from the date that the owner is aware of the profits.[650] Once that owner is put on notice, she must demand the funds back or risk losing them.[651] The burden will be on the owner retaining possession of the funds to prove that she has met the statutory requirements to possess the other owner's proceeds.[652]

---

645 *White v. Lee*, 250 Ga. 688, 300 S.E.2d 517 (1983).

646 O.C.G.A. § 44-6-121(a).

647 O.C.G.A. § 44-6-121(a); *White v. Lee*, 250 Ga. 688, 300 S.E.2d 517 (1983).

648 O.C.G.A. § 44-6-121(a).

649 O.C.G.A. § 44-6-121(a); *White v. Lee*, 250 Ga. 688, 300 S.E.2d 517 (1983).

650 *Chambers v. Schall*, 209 Ga. 18, 70 S.E.2d 463 (1958).

651 O.C.G.A. § 44-6-123.

652 *Erwin v. Miller*, 203 Ga. 58, 45 S.E.2d 192 (1947).

§ 3.13.5 Right Of First Refusal On The Sale of Common Property

Another common dispute that arises between unmarried persons who purchase property together is whether and when to sell the property. With commonly owned property, there is nothing which prevents either party from selling their respective interest in the property unless the parties agree otherwise in writing.[653] As a result, if one co-tenant sells her interest in the property, the other co-tenant could find himself or herself co-owning property with a stranger. One way to prevent this is for the parties to each grant to the other a right of first refusal. An example of this type of provision is set forth below.

Special Stipulation 48: Right of First Refusal

1) Right of Sale and First Refusal. If a Selling Tenant shall desire to transfer all, but not less than all, of its interest in the Property to another individual or entity, the Selling Tenant may consummate such transfer only if compliance has been made with the provisions and conditions of Sections 2 through 6. This provision shall remain in full force and effect until termination of this Agreement in accordance with Section _____ hereof.

2) Appraised Value. The Selling Tenant shall deliver to the Non selling Tenant a written notice stating its desire to transfer the interest of the Selling Tenant in the Property. The Selling Tenant and the Non-selling Tenant shall agree upon an appraiser to determine the appraised value of the Property within fifteen (15) days of the Non-selling Tenant's receipt of said notice. The appraised value as determined by such appraiser and set forth in her report and shall be binding on the parties. The Selling Tenant shall pay the fees and costs of the single appraiser, if applicable. If the Selling Tenant and the Non-selling Tenant cannot mutually agree upon a single appraiser to determine the appraised value of the Property, each of the Selling Tenant and the Non-selling Tenant shall appoint an appraiser. If the two appraisers agree upon the appraised value of the Property, they shall jointly render a single report stating that value and this shall be deemed the appraised value of the Property. If the two appraisers cannot agree upon the appraised value of the Property, they shall each render a separate written report and they shall jointly appoint a third appraiser, who shall determine the appraised value and shall render a written report of her opinion. The Selling Tenant shall pay the fees and other costs of the appraiser appointed by the Selling Tenant and one-half of the fees and costs of the appraiser appointed by the Non-selling Tenant, and the fees and other costs of the third appraiser shall be shared equally by Selling Tenant and the Non-selling Tenant. The appraised value contained in the written report of the third appraiser shall be deemed the appraised value of the Property; provided, however, if the appraised value of the Property contained in the appraisal report of the third appraiser is more than the higher of the first two appraisals, the higher of the first two appraisals shall govern, and provided, further, that if the appraised value of the Property contained in the appraisal report of the third appraiser is less than the lower of the first two appraisals, the lower of the first two appraisals shall govern.

3) Non Selling Tenant's Obligations. The Non selling Tenant shall either (i) allow the Selling Tenant to transfer the interest of the Selling Tenant in the Property for a price and upon terms as shall be acceptable to the Selling Tenant for a period of one hundred and twenty (120) days, or (ii) purchase the Selling Tenant's entire interest in the Property at the

---

653 *Glover v. Ware*, 236 Ga.App. 40, 510 S.E.2d 895 (1999).

price equal to the product of the appraised value of the Property determined in accordance with Section 2 and the undivided percentage interest of the Selling Tenant in the Property.

4) Notice of Election. The Non selling Tenant shall have a period of thirty (30) days after the date of the determination of the appraised value of the Property in accordance with Section 2 within which to serve upon the Selling Tenant a notice which shall specify whether the Non selling Tenant will permit a transfer to a prospective transferee, or whether the Non selling Tenant shall purchase the entire interest of the Selling Tenant as provided in Section 3. If the Non selling Tenant fails to respond within the allocated time, the Non selling Tenant shall be deemed to have elected and agreed to the transfer of the interest to such prospective transferee as the Selling Tenant deems appropriate, and the Non selling Tenant shall, if necessary, execute, acknowledge and deliver such documents, or cause the same to be done. If the Non selling Tenant shall have served upon the Selling Tenant the notice specifying that the Non-selling Tenant shall purchase the entire interest of the Selling Tenant, and if the Non selling Tenant shall thereafter fail or refuse to close such purchase as required by Section 5 or to execute, acknowledge and deliver documents as required by this Section 4, the Non selling Tenant shall thereupon be and become in default under this Agreement and the Selling Tenant shall be entitled to damages for such default, in addition to all other remedies available at law or in equity.

5) Closing. Any closing in respect to the transfer of the Selling Tenant's interest in the Property to the Non-selling Tenant shall be held within sixty (60) days after the notice sent by the Non selling Tenant as provided in Section 4 at such place in _____ and at such date and time as shall be designated by the Non-selling Tenant at least seven (7) days before the scheduled closing.

6) Transferee. In the event that a proposed transfer is completed for a price and upon terms acceptable to the Selling Tenant, the new Tenant shall be a Tenant under the terms and provisions of this Agreement with the deemed consent of the other Tenant, together with all of the rights, duties and obligations pertaining thereto, including, without limitation, the rights and restrictions contained in this Article with respect to transfers.

§ 3.13.6 Buy-Sell Agreements

Another approach to buy out a co-tenant is a buy-sell agreement. In some cases, such agreements will provide that the buy-sell option can only be exercised a certain number of years after the agreement has been signed. In a typical buy-sell agreement, the party interested in buying out the other makes an offer to buy the other party's interest in the property at a specific price. The other party can then either accept the offer and sell at that price or buy out the party who made the offer at the same price that she offered. So, for example, Jim notifies John that he is exercising the buy-sell portion of the tenancy agreement and offers to buy John out at $200,000. John can either accept the offer and sell to Jim for this amount or John can chose to buy Jim out for $200,000.

The theory behind this approach is similar to children cutting cake where the child who cuts the cake then has to let the other child decide which piece of cake to eat. By giving John the right to buy out Jim for the same price Jim offered to buy out John hopefully ensures that Jim will offer John a fair price for the property in the first instance. A sample buy-sell provision is set forth below.

Special Stipulation 49:   Buy-Sell Agreement

1) Deadlock. A deadlock shall be deemed to exist in either of the situations set forth below: (i) At any time after three (3) years from the date of this Operating Agreement, one Member wants to sell the Real Property and the other Member does not; or (ii) there is a disagreement over an acceptable sales price for the Real Property; or (iii) if there is any other deadlock on a material issue that could adversely affect the Company.

2) Definitions. For purposes of this Article _____, the following terms have the meanings indicated: (i) "Specified Value" means a Member's good faith estimate of the fair market value of all of the assets of the Company; (ii) "Purchase Price" means the distribution a Member would receive if the Company sold its assets at the Specified Value, satisfied all of its liabilities, and were liquidated in accordance with the terms of this Agreement.

3) Reciprocal Purchase Rights.

(A) If a deadlock occurs, either Member (hereinafter sometimes referred to as "Offering Member" or "A"), may offer to purchase the Membership Interests of the other Member, (hereinafter sometimes referred to as "Offeree Member" or "B") at the Purchase Price determined based upon the Specified Value of the Company.

(B) If A offers to purchase the Interest of B, then A's offer shall state that A wishes to apply the provisions of this Section 1 to purchase the entire (and not part of the) right, title, and interest of B in the Company and shall set forth the Specified Value of B's Membership Interests.

(C) Within fifteen (15) days after receipt of A's offer, B shall give written notice to A electing to do one (1) of the following: (i) purchase A's entire (and not part of the) Membership Interests at an amount equal to the Purchase Price of A's Membership Interests based upon the Specified Value designated by A in A's offer; or (ii) sell B's Membership Interests to A at an amount equal to the Purchase Price of its Membership Interests based upon the Specified value.

(D) If B exercises its right to purchase or sell, the closing of the sale shall take place pursuant to Section 3(E) below.

(E) If a sale pursuant to this Section 3 occurs, the closing shall take place at the office of the Company within the sixty (60) days following the expiration of the fifteen (15) day period set forth in Section 3(C), unless the parties otherwise agree. The purchaser shall pay the Purchase Price to the seller in immediately available funds. The purchaser shall execute and deliver to the seller a document (in form and substance reasonably satisfactory to the seller) indemnifying the seller from and against any and all personal liabilities and obligations of the seller with respect to debts of the Company. The purchaser and seller shall cause any loans made by the seller to the Company, or by the Company to the seller, together with interest accrued thereon, to be repaid in full. On due performance by the purchaser, the seller shall execute and deliver all deeds, assignments, and other instruments as may be reasonably required to vest in the purchaser the seller's entire Membership Interests, free and clear of all liens and encumbrances.

(F) If the purchaser fails to consummate the purchase, pay the Purchase Price, and perform all of the purchaser's other obligations in accordance with Section 3(E), the seller, in addition to and not by way of limitation of any other rights or remedies available at law or in equity, shall be the right to: (i) purchase the entire Membership Interests of the defaulting

purchaser at a price equal to eighty percent (80%) of the Purchase Price for the defaulting, purchaser's Membership Interests determined with reference to the Specified Value; or (ii) consider the issue with respect to which there was a deadlock to have been resolved in the seller's favor and cause the Company to act or decline to act accordingly.

(G) To elect the remedies set forth in either Sections 3(F), the seller shall give written notice to the defaulting purchaser within fifteen (15) days after the default. If the seller elects to exercise the right to purchase the Membership Interests of the defaulting purchaser, the closing of the purchase shall take place at the office of the Company on the date and at the time specified in the notice, which shall be not less than fifteen (15) or more than ninety (90) days after the date of the notice.

(H) Except as expressly set forth herein, no sale pursuant to this Section 3 shall relieve the seller or purchaser from any duty or obligation owed to the Company or the other Member which accrued prior to the date of the sale or shall constitute a waiver or release of claims with respect thereto.

§ 3.13.7   Statutory Partition Of Property

If there is no right of first refusal or buy-sell agreement, the parties can ask the court for a statutory or equitable partition of the property.[654] Every common owner has the right to ask the court to partition the property unless there is an agreement to the contrary.[655]

The Official Code of Georgia provides a judicial method to sell the property and divide the proceeds among the common owners.[656] Specifically, when a party applies for a statutory partition, that party must give the other owner at least twenty (20) days notice of her intention to file for partition.[657] When the partition is filed, the court will appoint three qualified persons to appraise the property.[658] Once the appraisal is complete, three commissioners will be appointed to conduct the sale of the property.[659] Thereafter, the proceeds will be returned to the court and the court will divide them among the common owners in proportion to each party's respective interests.[660] As stated above, absent an agreement to the contrary, each owner is presumed to have an equal undivided interest in the property.[661] Therefore, in a suit for a statutory partition, each owner will receive fifty percent (50%) of the profit based on their equal undivided interest.[662]

§ 3.13.8   Equitable Partition Of Property

A statutory partition of the property is not the only remedy available for unmarried persons who cannot voluntarily sell and divide the property. When a party files an application requesting a partition by the court, either party may request an equitable partition instead of a statutory partition.[663]

---

654 *Glover v. Ware, 236 Ga.App. 40, 510 S.E.2d 895 (1999).*

655 *Mansour Properties, L.L.C. v. I-85/GA. 20 Ventures, Inc.*, 277 Ga. 632, 592 S.E.2d 836 (2004).

656 O.C.G.A. § 44-6-160.

657 O.C.G.A. § 44-6-162.

658 O.C.G.A. § 44-6-166.1.

659 O.C.G.A. § 44-6-167.

660 O.C.G.A. § 44-6-168.

661 O.C.G.A. § 44-6-120.

662 O.C.G.A. § 44-6-120.

663 O.C.G.A. § 44-6-166.1.

An equitable partition of the property allows the court to consider additional evidence when dividing the proceeds of the sale between the parties.[664] Although an agreement providing a clear method of selling and dividing the property is the best option for an unmarried couple, in the absence of such an agreement, an equitable partition generally gives the court greater discretion to divide the property more fairly than a statutory partition. Specifically, in an equitable partition, each party is entitled to have her accounts and claims adjusted after the sale but before the distribution of the proceeds to reflect the amounts owed to each party.[665] For instance, the court will consider the expenditures of either party for improving or maintaining[666] the property, taxes[667] or insurance[668] paid, any income received by either party from renting the property, or any other applicable expenses, to adjust the proceeds received by the common owners.[669]

However, an equitable partition of the property is not available to every party who requests it.[670] This remedy is only available if a party can show that the remedies provided in a statutory partition will be insufficient or that particular circumstances exist that make this type of remedy more suitable and just.[671] An equitable partition of the property will be ordered at the sole discretion of the trial court.[672] Generally, a court will allow an equitable partition of the property in the following situations: (i) if a party presents evidence that she made improvements to the common property; (ii) a claim by one owner asking the other to account for profits received from the property[673]; or (iii) evidence that the value of the property will be depreciated by a statutory partition.[674] However, if the court determines that there is no special reason for an equitable partition, the parties will be required to resort to the remedies afforded by the Official Code of Georgia for a statutory partition.[675]

If the parties want to agree to waive the right to seek a partition of the property, the following provision should be included in the tenancy agreement.

Special Stipulation 50: Waiver of Partition

The parties agree to and do hereby waive the right of partition with respect to the Property, and agree that the provisions of this Agreement governing voluntary and involuntary sale are reasonable as a substitute for such right.

§ 3.13.9 The Limited Liability Company Alternative

Unmarried couples or persons who want to purchase property together are not limited to the sole option of entering into a tenancy agreement to purchase common property. The best alternative to a tenancy agreement is for the parties to create a limited liability company ("LLC") to purchase the property.

Oftentimes, this method is used by parties with a business relationship looking to purchase an investment property. This option is particularly attractive for purchasing an investment property due to the "flow through" tax treatment. In other words, once the limited liability company is formed, this entity does not have to pay a corporate tax for holding

---

664 *Baker v. Baker*, 242 Ga. 525, 250 S.E.2d 436 (1978).

665 *Baker v. Baker*, 242 Ga. 525, 250 S.E.2d 436 (1978).

666 *Clay v. Clay*, 269 Ga. 902, 506 S.E.2d 866 (1998).

667 *Evans v. Little*, 246 Ga. 219, 271 S.E.2d 138 (1980).

668 *Weeks v. Gay*, 243 Ga. 784, 256 S.E.2d 901 (1979).

669 *Baker v. Baker*, 242 Ga. 525, 250 S.E.2d 436 (1978).

670 *Burnham v. Lynn*, 235 Ga. 207, 219 S.E.2d 111 (1975).

671 O.C.G.A. § 44-6-140; *Burnham v. Lynn*, 235 Ga. 207, 219 S.E.2d 111 (1975).

672 *Gifford v. Courson*, 224 Ga. 840, 165 S.E.2d 133 (1968).

673 *Johnson v. Wilson*, 212 Ga. 264, 91 S.E.2d 758 (1956).

674 O.C.G.A. § 44-6-166.1.

675 *Gifford v. Courson*, 224 Ga. 840, 165 S.E.2d 133 (1968).

the property. Instead, any profits and losses sustained by the LLC "flow through" to the member's tax returns based on the percentage they own in the company. Any losses sustained by the LLC after purchasing the property are taxed at the owners' personal income rate. Therefore, the owners' will not sustain any greater tax disadvantage for owning property this way because any losses are based on their personal income rate.

An unmarried couple would generally not find this method of purchasing property desirable because owners who purchase property through a LLC do not enjoy the same tax advantages as owners who purchase property as tenants in common. For example, the limited liability company cannot file for a Homestead Exemption and cannot deduct mortgage interest from the taxes for the property. Regardless of whether the property is used for investment purposes or otherwise, forming a limited liability company to purchase property is available to all types of buyers.

Two (or more) parties who want to purchase a particular property together may do so by creating a LLC to purchase the property. To form a limited liability company, the parties simply need to file articles of organization with the Secretary of State and pay a minimal filing fee. Once those steps are completed, a LLC may be formed for any lawful purpose.[676] However, the parties may establish a limited purpose in the articles of organization or operating agreement.[677] Therefore, if the parties want to form a limited liability company solely to purchase a particular property, the parties should clearly state that limited purpose in the articles of organization or operating agreement.[678]

Title to property purchased by a limited liability company is held in the name of the company rather than in the name of any person individually.[679] As such, when two persons form a LLC to purchase property, those persons become the members of and hold interest in the company. The property rights for members of a limited liability company that purchases property are different from those of who purchase property as tenants in common. Any person holding interest in a limited liability company has no specific interest in the property purchased and instead the property is owned by the LLC.[680] Therefore, it is particularly important for the members of the LLC to define each party's respective rights to the company property to avoid any issues that may arise later between the members.

Most often, two or more persons who form a LLC to purchase property define each party's respective rights in an operating agreement. Although an operating agreement is not required when a limited liability company is formed,[681] this agreement is particularly useful when the LLC's sole purpose is to purchase property. Once an operating agreement is created, any rights and responsibilities contained therein will bind the limited liability company and its members.[682] Therefore, it is important for the operating agreement to be as thorough as possible to avoid any issues between the members over the property. Oftentimes, an operating agreement includes each party's rights in the event the company dissolves, becomes insolvent, or when one of the members wants to sell her interest in the company.

However, an operating agreement can also provide rights similar to those included in a tenancy agreement. For example, two unmarried persons form a LLC for the sole purpose of buying a property. Similar to the provisions included in a tenancy agreement, the operating agreement should provide each party's respective rights. These rights would most likely include each party's right to occupy the property, finance any improvements and maintenance required, and the right of either party in the event the property is sold or the company is dissolved. In addition, the operating agreement should specifically state that the company property is being used for the purpose of the unmarried persons' residence. In a sense,

---

676 O.C.G.A. § 14-11-201(a).

677 O.C.G.A. § 14-11-201(b).

678 O.C.G.A. § 14-11-201(b).

679 Pindar, 3 Ga. Real Estate Law & Procedure, § 26-17.2 (6th ed.).

680 O.C.G.A. § 14-11-501(a); *Word v. Stidham*, 271 Ga.App. 435, 609 S.E.2d 651 (2004).

681 O.C.G.A. § 14-11-101.

682 O.C.G.A. § 14-11-101.

the operating agreement would become the parties' tenancy agreement. Ultimately, it would be the best practice for the members to provide each party's respective rights in the operating agreement.

Some buyers who are looking to purchase property together find that using a limited liability company is an easy and flexible way to purchase property. Forming this type of entity in Georgia is a relatively quick and inexpensive process. Therefore, if the parties choose to form a LLC to purchase property, it is the best practice to define each party's respective rights in the operating agreement to avoid any issues that may arise in the future. However, if two unmarried persons are looking to purchase a property to use as their primary residence, the best option would be to enter into a tenancy agreement instead of forming a LLC to purchase the property.

The **RED BOOK**

CHAPTER 4

DESCRIBING THE PROPERTY

OVERVIEW

A real estate sales contract must include a clear description of the property being conveyed. The most precise description of a property is based on a survey prepared by a licensed Georgia surveyor which describes the property through metes and bounds and is attached and incorporated into the contract. This chapter will discuss the different ways property can be described in a contract and explain why some property descriptions have been upheld by Georgia courts while others have been struck down.

This chapter also includes a discussion of how to determine whether personal property is considered a fixture that must remain with the property, and when to use a bill of sale and a financing statement.

§ 4.1 IDENTIFYING REAL PROPERTY

§ 4.1.1 Land System In Georgia

The method of transferring title to land in Georgia traces its roots back to 1802, when the United States Government ceded the land to the State of Georgia. The State of Georgia in those early years used various methods for determining and passing title to land, including: lottery;[683] headrights (according to the number in a family); [684] bounties or pensions to soldiers, and as payment to citizens to encourage the development of business enterprises.[685] Counties created land courts to manage the conveyances and hired surveyors to lay out the survey of the lands being granted or sought. The coastal areas are made up of grants that are irregular in shape, and their legal descriptions are heavily dependent upon the use of natural landmarks. In other areas of the state, the land is divided into militia districts (or simply "districts"). In some counties, districts are further divided into sections, and then divided into land lots. It is these land lots to which most legal descriptions will refer.

§ 4.1.2 Description Must Clearly Identify Property

When preparing a contract for the sale of real property, it is necessary to include an accurate and definite description of the property to be sold. Many real estate sales contracts provide for an actual legal description to be attached to the contract as an exhibit. The GAR Contracts allow for the property to be described in a number of different ways, including: (a) using an actual legal description attached to the Agreement as an Exhibit; (b) using a description where the lot, block and district number of the property are filled in along with the book and page number of the recorded plat showing the property is recorded; or (c) referencing the deed book and page number where the actual legal description can be found.[686] Rather than describing the property in three different ways it is best to describe it correctly once since problems can arise if multiple legal descriptions conflict with one another. When an actual legal description is attached to a contract, the user should confirm that it was the same legal description used by the seller to acquire the property and that the seller has not either acquired additional property or disposed of some portion of the property in the interim.

There are limitations to describing the property in reference to a written legal description where there is not an accompanying survey identifying the boundary lines of the property. Without a survey, the buyer may know what property she is buying but not know where it is located. This means, for example, that if the property is smaller in size or in a different location than what the buyer thought, the buyer may not have a remedy unless the buyer is protected elsewhere in the contract. Therefore, it is recommended that a buyer in this situation obtain a survey of the property during a due diligence period.

---

683 Land Lottery Act of 1825; *Vickery v. Scott*, 20 Ga. 795 (1856).

684 *Vickery v. Scott,* 20 Ga. 795 (1856).

685 Pindar, 1 Ga. Real Estate Law & Procedure, § 13-57, N.2.

686 GAR Forms F20, F23, F27, F29, F33 and F34.

One way for the buyer to be protected against the property being smaller than what the buyer thought is for the seller to warrant the property as being at least a minimum specified size, and to give the buyer the right to terminate the contract if prior to closing the buyer has a survey done which reveals that the property is smaller than warranted. In this way, if the buyer discovers prior to closing that the property is smaller than the buyer had thought, the buyer can terminate the contract.[687] The GAR Contract also gives the buyer the right to request that the seller attach a survey to the contract.[688] If this is done, the buyer can then obtain a new survey prior to closing and terminate the contract if the new survey is materially different from the old survey.[689]

A property description must describe the location of the property intended to be sold by the seller with sufficient certainty so that it can be reasonably identified.[690] Even without a precise description, the property description will be valid as long as the contract contains a "key" which will "lead unerringly to the land in question."[691] This "key" allows the reader to consider something outside the terms of the contract to identify the property with certainty. If the description of property is sufficient to furnish a "key", parol evidence (evidence outside the terms of the contract), that does not add to, enlarge, or in any way change the description, is admissible to identify property intended to be conveyed.[692] The "key" relied upon must be sufficient to provide identification by reference to evidence which exists at the time that the contract is entered into by the parties."[693]

In one case, a reference to property in Chatham County, Georgia, known as 124, 126, 128, 130 East Waldburg Street being approximately 60 x 55 feet in size was sufficient to constitute a "key" by which the property could be identified.[694] This "key" allowed the parties to look outside of the terms of the contract (the addresses which were in place at that time in Chatham County, Georgia) to specifically identify the property referenced.

The "key" must help to identify the property with certainty. If the "key" does not do this, the property description will not be valid. In one case, the contract identified the property as "the premises situated at Howard [Road] and more particularly described as all that tract or parcel of land which comprises the 81.14+/-acres lying and being in Land Lots 1153-1154 of the Third District and First Section of Forsyth County, Georgia."[695] At the time of this case, the only tax parcel in Land Lots 1153-1154 was parcel no. 011-009. Moreover, there had been a recent tax appraisal for that parcel which listed the seller as the owner. The tax appraisal also mentioned a warranty deed which described the property by metes and bounds, and the warranty deed referenced a survey showing the property's precise location. Unfortunately, while the tax appraisal and the contract referred to a parcel of 81.14 acres located in land lots 1153 and 1154, the warranty deed and survey described the property as 93.45 acres of land situated in land lots 1153, 1154, and 1223. Since the deed and survey were inconsistent, the court decided that the contract did not contain a "key" that led "unerringly to the land in question."

Information not included in the contract cannot be used to aid in locating property described in vague and uncertain terms in the contract itself.[696] There must be some indication in the contract itself of the location of the property to be conveyed. While the courts will consider extrinsic evidence to clarify an ambiguous description, they will not refer to extrinsic evidence to supply a non-existent description.[697] If the property description in the contract fails to sufficiently

---

687 *See* Special Stipulation 28.

688 GAR Forms F20, F23, F27 and F29.

689 *See* discussion on surveys at § 4.1.12 (When Surveys Can Be Used To Supplement Description of Property).

690 *Wallace v. Adamson*, 129 Ga.App. 792, 201 S.E.2d 479 (1973), citing *Gainesville Midland Railroad v. Tyner*, 204 Ga. 535, 538, 50 S.E.2d 108, 110 (1948).

691 *Blumberg v. Nathan*, 190 Ga. 64, 66, 8 S.E.2d 374, 375 (1940).

692 *Gainesville Midland Railroad v. Tyner*, 204 Ga. 535, 50 S.E.2d 108 (1948).

693 *Royal v. Bland Properties*, 175 Ga.App. 250, 333 S.E.2d 145 (1985).

694 *Blumberg v. Nathan*, 190 Ga. 64, 8 S.E.2d 374 (1940).

695 *Makowski v. Waldrop*, 262 Ga.App. 130, 584 S.E.2d 714 (2003), *cert. denied*.

696 *Smith v. Wilkinson*, 208 Ga. 489, 67 S.E.2d 698 (1951).

697 *McClung v. Atlanta Real Estate Acquisitions, LLC*, 282 Ga.App. 759, 639 S.E.2d 331 (2006).

locate and identify a certain tract of land, evidence outside of the contract, such as discussions of the parties regarding the location of the property or what is included on the property, cannot be used to correct or clarify an otherwise invalid description. In such a case, the property description fails and the contract is void.[698] While a metes and bounds description based on a professional survey of the property is the best type of description and will generally control over other types of descriptions, many contracts contain far less detailed property descriptions.[699] Discussed below are several general types of property descriptions which are used either alone or in combination in real estate sales contracts, such as street addresses, tax plats, recorded and unrecorded plats, and surveys.

§ 4.1.3 Identifying Air Space

Most property is legally described by setting out the property's boundary lines. The property owner also owns the ground beneath and the air space above,[700] subject to the rights of flight.[701] However, it is possible to sell the air rights separately from the land and to create a metes and bounds legal description for air rights parcels. Such legal descriptions must not only describe the boundary lines but also the upper and lower elevation lines enclosing the air rights parcel. For example, an air rights parcel might describe the property through a normal boundary survey but then provide that it is all of that property above 715 feet from mean sea level and below 730 feet from mean sea level. Just because a property is described through an air rights parcel does not mean that the parcel cannot be improved. In some vertical mixed use developments that are not organized as condominiums, each vertical use within a building above ground level may be its own air rights parcel. An exception is in the case of condominiums where Georgia law provides that a description of a condominium unit is sufficient if it contains the unit number, condominium name, county, and the deed book and page number of the recorded declaration of condominium.[702]

If a person is buying an air rights parcel, it is important for there to be an agreement with the other owners in the vertical stack of shared property owners that requires all owners to maintain insurance against fire and other casualties and for there to be some common agreement on whether or not the property will be rebuilt in the event of fire. Obviously, an air rights parcel will be of little or no value if the structure below, that supports the structure, is destroyed by fire.

§ 4.1.4 Identifying Water

When a property's boundary lies within or is adjacent to a body of water, such as a stream, ocean or lake, the following rules apply when determining the exact boundary of the property unless the deed provides otherwise.

§ 4.1.4.1 Rivers And Streams

Property boundaries adjacent to streams are determined in two different ways, depending upon whether the stream is considered navigable. A stream is defined as navigable when it is capable of transporting boats loaded with goods in the regular course of trade, either for the whole or a part of the year. However, merely because timber can be rafted or wood transported in small boats on a stream does not make it navigable. [703] There are two key parts to this definition: "capable of transporting" and "in the regular course of trade." Under federal case law, a stream need not be actually used for such navigation, but need only be capable of such use to be considered a navigable stream.[704] And in one Georgia case, the passage of a small styrofoam and wood raft transporting a goat, a bale of cotton, and two passengers was argued to be

---

698 *Blumberg v. Nathan*, 190 Ga. 64, 8 S.E.2d 374 (1940).

699 *Johnson v. Willingham*, 212 Ga. 310, 92 S.E.2d 1 (1956); *Floyd v. Carswell*, 211 Ga. 36, 83 S.E.2d 586 (1954); *Carswell v. Sanders*, 182 Ga. 251, 185 S.E. 282 (1936).

700 O.C.G.A. § 44-1-2 provides that the property right of the owner of real estate extends downward indefinitely and upward indefinitely.

701 O.C.G.A. § 6-2-5, providing for right of flight over land unless interferes with reasonable use of the land, or conducted so as to be imminently dangerous to persons or property lawfully on the land.

702 *See* § 4.2 (Description of Condominium and Condominium Units).

703 O.C.G.A. § 44-8-5(a).

704 *U.S. v. State of Utah*, 283 Ga. 64, 51 S.Ct. 438 (1931).

similar to the transporting of freight that would have been done in the 19th Century, making the stream navigable. The court held that this was insufficient evidence to show the stream to be navigable "under current commercial standards."[705]

If the property boundary is to the edge of a stream that is navigable, the boundary line of the property extends to the low-water mark.[706] The state will own the streambed from the low-water mark, except where there is a state grant that includes the riverbed.

When the boundary line of a property is to the edge of a non-navigable stream, the exact boundary of the property is deemed to be where the streambed begins. The owner of the adjacent land owns the bed of the stream.

If the stream is a dividing line between two parcels of land, each owner's boundary extends to the center of the main current of the stream. If the current changes gradually over time, the boundary lines of the properties adjacent to the stream change along with the gradual changes to the current of the stream. However, if the stream suddenly changes its course or direction (as a result of a major storm, for example), the original boundary line, if identifiable, remains the boundary. Sediment on either side accrues to the owner of that side.[707]

In one case, a dispute arose between two adjoining landowners on where the property boundary should be. The property boundary was described in the deed as "commencing on the west bank of the Chattahoochee River at a corner … at or near a ford of said river, thence in an eastern direction across the river, thence in a northern direction up said river to a white oak near the bank of said river …".[708] The issue was whether the property boundary included the river bed. The court stated that when a deed establishes a non-navigable stream as a boundary line the owners on either side are entitled to the land running to the center of the main current. It also stated that where the line is described as running to the stream language which describes it as thereafter running "with," "along," "by," "on," "up," or "down" the stream will be construed to carry the title to the center unless contrary intention appears from the description.

§ 4.1.4.2 Tidewaters

Tidewaters are waters which fall and rise according to the tide, such as in bays and rivers. It does not apply to the open sea. Where property boundary is adjacent to or is covered by non-navigable tidewaters, the boundary of the property ends where the tidewater bed begins.[709] The owner of the adjacent land will own the beds of all non-navigable tidewaters. Where the property is adjacent to or is covered by navigable tidewaters, the boundary of the property extends to the low-water mark.[710]

A navigable tidewater is defined as any tidewater or any other bed of water where the tide regularly ebbs and flows which is used for navigation or is capable of transporting boats loaded with goods in the regular course of trade at mean low tide. The rafting of timber or passage of small boats on the waters, whether for the transportation of persons or freight, does not make the tidewaters navigable.

If the dividing line between two parcels of land lies within the non-navigable waters, each owner's boundary extends to the main thread or channel of the water. If the main thread or channel of the water changes gradually, the boundary line follows the changing thread or channel. If for any reason the water takes a new channel, the original line, if identifiable, remains the boundary. Sediment on either side accrues to the owner of that side.

---

705   *Givens v. Ichauway, Inc.*, 268 Ga. 710, 493 S.E.2d 148 (1997).

706   O.C.G.A. §44-8-5.

707   O.C.G.A. §44-8-2.

708   *Westmoreland v. Beutell*, 153 Ga.App. 558, 266 S.E.2d 260 (1980).

709   O.C.G.A. §44-8-6.

710   O.C.G.A. §44-8-7.

§ 4.1.4.3 Beaches And Open Seas

Generally, the boundary of private lots adjoining the seashore extends to the high water mark of the tide. The build-up of sediment on the shore accrues to the owner of the lot.[711] The property between the high-water mark and low-water mark (called the "foreshore") belongs to the government.

§ 4.1.4.4 Lakes

When the boundary line of a property lies next to a lake, the property boundary is deemed to extend to the low-water mark existing at the date of the execution of the deed.[712] However, this is only a general rule and will not be applied if the deed provides otherwise. An example is a case where the deed conveyed land which was covered by a pond, but stated that the pond was to be maintained at no more than a certain maximum height. The court held that the property boundary to be the line of water in the pond at such height.[713]

If lots are sold in reference to a recorded subdivision plat which identifies a lake as a recreational area, an easement across the whole lake will arise for the benefit of all of the lot owners in the subdivision. This is the case regardless of whether the property is subject to recorded restrictive covenants. Such an easement is considered an "express grant" and is an irrevocable property right. It is the recording of a subdivision plat showing the lake that is controlling here.[714]

However, in the case of a privately owned lake (which is not sold with reference to a subdivision plat), the owner of the lake has the exclusive right to the use of the waters above his boundary line and may exclude other lakebed owners and fence off his portion.[715] In one case, almost all the land in and around an 880-acre lake was owned by a fishing club, which tried to prevent a lot owner from fishing in the waters. The boundary of the lot owned by the lot owner extended to one-fourth acre below the high water mark of the lake. The lot owner argued that as owner of property adjoining a lake, he has rights over the entire surface waters as long as he does not interfere with the rights of other owners. Georgia law, however, is that the owner of a bed of a non-navigable lake has the exclusive right to the surface waters above the bed. A person who places a boat within that area without permission would be trespassing. For this reason, the court found that the lot owner, by fishing in waters beyond the boundary of his lot, was trespassing.

§ 4.1.5 Identifying Mineral Rights

In a legal sense, "minerals" includes many different types of valuable inert substances formed or deposited by natural processes in or under the soil of the earth. The term includes without limitation substances such as sand and gravel,[716] granite,[717] coal,[718] oil and natural gas,[719] kaolin and clay[720] and gold.[721] When such substances remain in the earth without being mined, they are part of the land and as such are considered realty rather than personal property. A conveyance of the land, therefore, includes a conveyance of all minerals located within the land, unless either (a) some specific mineral rights have been reserved by a previous owner of the land, or (b) the current grantor makes a specific reservation of some type of ownership interest in or usage rights to those minerals.[722] Consequently, once the substance has been removed

---

711 *Cherry v. Hopkins*, 254 Ga. 260, 328 S.E.2d 702 (1985).

712 *Boardman v. Scott*, 30 S.E. 982 (Ga. 1897).

713 *Prescott v. Herring*, 212 Ga. 571, 94 S.E.2d 417 (1956).

714 See § 4.1.9.3 (Identifying Common Areas on Subdivision Plat).

715 *Lanier v. Ocean Pond Fishing Club, Inc.*, 253 Ga. 549, 322 S.E.2d 494 (1984), citing *State Highway Department v. Noble*, 114 Ga.App. 3, 8, 150 S.E.2d 174 (1966).

716 *LaRowe v. McGee*, 171 Ga. 771, 156 S.E. 591 (1932).

717 *Northern Pacific Ry. Co. v. Soderberg*, 188 U.S. 526, 23 S.Ct. 365 (1903).

718 *Zugar v. Crystal Springs Bleachery*, 71 Ga.App. 821, 32 S.E.2d 414 (1944).

719 *Allgood Farm, LLC v. Johnson*, 275 Ga. 297, 565 S.E.2d 471 (2002).

720 *McCaw v. Nelson*, 165 Ga. 202, 147 S.E. 364 (1929).

721 *Brown v. Bowman*, 119 Ga. 153, 46 S.E. 410 (1903).

722 *Wright v. Martin*, 149 Ga. 777, 102 S.E. 156 (1920).

from the land, it takes on the character of personal property and is no longer considered a part of the real property.

A reservation or exception of mineral rights from a conveyance of real property needs to clearly and specifically state exactly what rights are being retained by the grantor, whether the reservation is with respect to specific minerals only or all mineral rights. Any reservation of such rights is considered an interest in the real property itself, and unless the conveyance specifies otherwise, carries with it an implied easement upon the surface for the purpose of mining or removing the minerals.[723]

If a property is zoned for residential use, no mining activities will typically be permitted without having the property rezoned to an industrial use. This has effectively made mineral rights of little value in most residential neighborhoods.

§ 4.1.6   Use Of Metes And Bounds Legal Description

A metes and bounds legal description, also known as courses and distances, is a means of describing the boundary lines of land as measured by distances and angles from designated landmarks and in relation to adjoining properties.[724] A metes and bounds description is prepared by a surveyor using both compass directions and distances to create a survey of the boundaries. The description begins at a definite point and follows the exterior boundary lines of the property until it returns to the point of beginning. These compass directions and distances are reduced to written "calls," which when taken together form the metes and bounds legal description.[725] The legal description created by listing the directions and distances can be attached to the contract and deed in order to fully describe the location and size of the property. A metes and bounds description taken from an accurate survey is usually the most complete and definitive means of describing property.

The exception is where the metes and bounds description is different from the boundaries set out by landmarks that have been in place for more than 30 years. In one case, the property boundary was marked by a fence which crossed an adjoining property for a certain distance.[726] The fence had been in place for more than 40 years and an affidavit stating that the fence line was the boundary was filed and recorded with the deed in a previous sale of the property. The court held that it was the fence line, and not the courses and distances in the deed, that defined the true property boundary.

§ 4.1.7   Use Of Street Address To Identify The Property

If the street address provides sufficient information to locate the property, it will generally be found to be an adequate description for a deed. A street address without any reference to the city, county, or state in which the property is located is generally considered to be too indefinite.[727]

§ 4.1.7.1   Examples Of Street Addresses Held To Be Inadequate

The following are examples of property descriptions containing street addresses which have been held to be inadequate:

(a) "4582 Club Drive" (no indication of the city, county, state, or country in which the property was located).[728]

(b) "Home on Pine Mountain Road" (no further identification included).[729]

(c) "The property and business (known as BP Food Mart) located at 199 Upper Riverdale Road, Jonesboro, GA 30236"

---

723 *Davison v. Reynolds*, 150 Ga. 182, 103 S.E. 248 (1920).

724 Black's Law Dictionary (8th ed. 2004).

725 Such "calls" often read as follows: "Beginning at an iron pin found on the northeasterly right-of-way of Vernon Springs Trail (50 foot right-of-way) 353.40 feet southerly from its intersection with the southerly right-of-way of Mount Vernon Highway (the POINT OF BEGINNING) and run north 75 degrees 14 minutes 30 seconds east 87.88 feet to an iron pin found . . ."

726 *Duncan v. Harcourt*, 267 Ga.App. 224, 599 S.E.2d 196 (2004).

727 *Molton v. Woodruff*, 175 Ga. 168, 165 S.E. 59 (1932); Murphy v. Morse, 96 Ga.App. 513, 100 S.E.2d 623 (1957).

728 *Murphy v. Morse*, 96 Ga.App. 513, 100 S.E.2d 623 (1957).

729 *Bell v. Babb*, 139 Ga.App. 695, 229 S.E.2d 511 (1976); *overruled on other grounds, Brack v. Brownlee*, 246 Ga. 818, 273 S.E.2d 390 (1980).

(no metes-and-bounds description to identify property with certainty).[730]

(d) "All that tract of land shown by the attached sketch showing boundaries and including eight-room brick house, fronting a distance on Victory Drive of 210 feet, and a depth as shown on the attached plat" (attached plat did not disclose location of property or dimensions).[731]

(e) "All that tract of land being 9 to 10+/- acres near Pendergrass in Jackson County, Georgia near U.S. Highway 129 on the south and Interstate I-85 on the west and being marked parcel 1 (60,000 s.f. Hotel Site) as per Exhibit 'A' attached and made a part of this contract on the attached survey, more particularly described in Exhibit 'B' ...."[732] Exhibit A was a portion of the master plan but did not contain a metes and bounds description. Exhibit B was not attached. The court held that the property description was insufficient.

(f) "All that tract of land lying and being in Land Lot 267 of the 12th District of Pulaski County, Georgia at Hwy 247, in Hawkinsville, Georgia, 31036...as recorded in Plat Book see, Page Ex. A..."[733] The court held that this description was insufficient because it did not sufficiently identify the quantity or the location of the property being sold.[734]

§ 4.1.7.2 Examples Of Street Addresses Held To Be Adequate

The following are examples of property descriptions containing street addresses, which have been held to be adequate:

(a) "Houses and lots on South Stevens Street in Thomasville, Thomas County, Georgia, fronting on the northeast side of said street and being designated by...[ten stated numbers]."[735]

(b) "[A]ll that tract of land and improvements thereon known as 344 Wilkerson Drive, S.E., Atlanta, Georgia (a complete legal description is to be attached hereto and become a part of this contract)."[736] In this case, the court concluded that the fact that the description failed to state whether the property was located in Fulton or DeKalb County was not a fatal omission that deprived the seller of an opportunity to prove the allegations of the amended complaint by extrinsic evidence. The better practice, however, is to always include a detailed address, including the city and county.

(c) "All that tract of land in Atlanta, Fulton County, Georgia, being improved property located at 126 Ashby Street, S.W., according to the present system of numbering houses in the City of Atlanta; being a 2-story, 14-room frame dwelling."[737]

(d) Property described as "3200 Clairmont Road" which was the address of the entire condominium complex was sufficient to furnish a "key" by which property could be identified as the individual unit at 3229 Clairmont Road.[738] Based on courts' analyses in more recent cases, it is unclear whether this property description would be deemed to be sufficient today. The Georgia Association of REALTORS® has a form exhibit to be used for a condominium property description.[739]

---

730 *Salim v. Solaiman*, 302 Ga.App. 607, 691 S.E.2d 389 (2010).

731 *Bryan v. Rusk*, 89 Ga.App. 125, 78 S.E.2d 853 (1953).

732 *White v. Plumbing Distributors, Inc.*, 262 Ga.App. 228, 585 S.E.2d 135 (2003).

733 *Oconee Land & Timber, LLC v. Buchanan*, 300 Ga.App. 853, 6868 S.E.2d 452 (2009).

734 *Oconee Land & Timber, LLC v. Buchanan*, 300 Ga.App. 853, 6868 S.E.2d 452 (2009).

735 *Silverman v. Alday*, 200 Ga. 711, 38 S.E.2d 419, 420 (1946).

736 *Essuon v. Raynor*, 231 Ga. 297, 201 S.E.2d 416 (1973).

737 *Greenspan v. Caison*, 101 Ga.App. 632, 114 S.E.2d 803 (1960).

738 *Romanik v. Buitrago*, 153 Ga.App. 886, 267 S.E.2d 301 (1980).

739 GAR Form F127, Condominium Legal Description Exhibit. See § 4.2 (Description of Condominium and Condominium Units) regarding legal description of a condominium.

(e) Property was described as "All that tract of land Wellington Square at Indian Trail-Lilburn and Dickens Road as more particularly described in Exhibit 'A'" (which was not attached).[740] The court decided that the contract contained several "keys". It identified the name of the property, "Wellington Square." It also contained a warranty by the seller in respect of the value and use of the property as a shopping center. Lastly, the contract required the seller to pay Georgia property transfer tax. These "keys" allowed the court to consider external evidence to identify the property. The court was exceptionally generous here and its decision does not mean that property descriptions are no longer important. An important fact was that the purchasers had admitted that they contracted to purchase the property in one of their court documents, where they had described the property as "that certain shopping center known as 'Wellington Square' located at the intersection of Indian Trail and Dickens Road, Lilburn, Georgia."

(f) "All that tract of land lying and being in Land Lot 294 & 295 of the 28th District, 3rd Section of Catoosa County, Georgia, and being known as Address as shown on Map 42, Parcel 24 in the Tax Assessor's Office."[741] The agreement also referred to the plat book and page number, which described the property in detail and referred to a survey plat. In addition, the agreement specified that the purchaser was to acquire the rear 1-acre of the above described property as shown on a survey to be conducted prior to closing. This legal description was legally sufficient to indicate which portion of the property was being sold.[742]

§ 4.1.7.3 When Street Address Is Insufficient To Describe Property

A street address is not a good way to describe property when: (a) it is unclear how much of the property at the address is being conveyed, or (b) the street address does not include all of the property intended to be transferred. An example is a case where a buyer contracted to purchase property described as "2003 Pinetree Trail, Gainesville, Georgia."[743] The buyers contended that the property also included one-half of the adjoining lot. When the transaction closed, the buyers received a deed describing only one lot in the subdivision. When the seller began constructing a house on the adjoining lot, the buyers discovered that they did not own all the property they thought they owned. The buyers sued to have the deed from the sellers reformed to include the disputed property.

The court concluded that the contract of sale merged[744] into the warranty deed from the sellers to the buyers and that there was no evidence that anyone made any misrepresentations to the buyer, practiced any fraud, or that there was any mutual mistake either in appropriation, delivery, or acceptance by the buyers of the deed sought to be reformed.[745] The court denied the request to reform the deed. When the actual property being sold is more or less than what might be revealed by a street address, it is best to use a metes and bounds property description or survey of the exact property to be transferred.

The situation may have had a different outcome if there had been mutual mistake (*i.e.* a mistake on the part of both the buyer and the seller), in which case it may be possible to reform the warranty deed. In another case, a contract for the sale of property described one lot.[746] At the closing of that contract, two adjoining lots with different street addresses were conveyed to the buyer. There was contradictory evidence as to whether it was the intent of the parties to convey one or two lots. The court concluded that the contract for sale did not merge into the deed where there was evidence of a mutual mistake. The court therefore allowed evidence outside of the contract to be considered in determining whether a mutual mistake had occurred.

---

740 *Nhan v. Wellington Square, LLC*, 263 Ga.App. 717, 589 S.E.2d 295 (2003).

741 *Kay v. W.B. Anderson Feed & Poultry Co., Inc.*, 278 Ga.App. 674, 629 S.E.2d 408 (2006).

742 *Kay v. W.B. Anderson Feed & Poultry Co., Inc.*, 278 Ga.App. 674, 629 S.E.2d 408 (2006).

743 *Fields v. Davies*, 235 Ga. 87, 218 S.E.2d 828 (1975).

744 The doctrine of merger generally provides that a real estate sales contract merges into or is swallowed up into the deed at closing and does not survive afterward except to the extent that the parties have provided in the contract for specific obligations or rights to survive the closing. *Anziano v. Appalachee Enterprises, Inc.*, 208 Ga.App. 760, 432 S.E.2d 117 (1993).

745 *Fields v. Davies*, 235 Ga. 87, 218 S.E.2d 828 (1975).

746 *Rasmussen v. Martin*, 236 Ga. 267, 223 S.E.2d 663 (1976).

§ 4.1.7.4 When Only The "Premises" Are Being Conveyed

In using street addresses, the parties must be clear in the contract about whether they intend to convey only the dwelling or the dwelling and the land surrounding the dwelling. In one case, the court concluded that a property description contained in an option and lease which stated "certain premises in state and county aforesaid known as 1310 Butler Avenue and located on Section 3 of Beach Lot 83, Savannah Beach, Chatham County, Georgia" included the entire lot and the building located on the lot and not merely the building alone.[747]

However, the term "premises" has varying meanings. When used in a lease of property without qualifying words, it has been held to mean land and buildings, land and tenements, land and appurtenances, etc.[748] In a case interpreting a will, the Georgia Supreme Court considered whether the phrase "house and land" included an adjacent lot.[749] In that case the, will identified: (a) the "house and lot" at 65 Temple Avenue, the City of Newnan; (b) the "house and land" at 70 Clark Street, Newnan, Georgia; and (c) the "house and lot" at 69 Temple Avenue. The court distinguished between the phrases "house and lot" and "house and land" and concluded that the reference to land meant that the adjacent vacant property, another lot, would be included within the property transferred through the will.

Given the various interpretations of the term "premises", it is important to specifically describe exactly what property is being conveyed. The following special stipulation may be used in cases of doubt.

> **Special Stipulation 51: Additions to Property Description**
>
> *As used herein the term "Property" means that property defined in paragraph 1 hereof, which is further defined as including_____.*
>
> **Special Stipulation 52: Subtraction from Property Description**
>
> *As used herein the term "Property" means that property defined in paragraph 1 hereof, but from which the following is specifically excluded:_____.*

§ 4.1.8 Use Of Tax Plats To Identify Property

A tax plat may be used to supplement the property description contained in the contract. A tax plat shows the general configuration of the property; however, it is not clear that a tax plat alone is adequate to locate the property. Generally an additional description, such as a reference to a prior deed describing the property by metes and bounds, an adequate street address, or some other means of specifically locating the property will be necessary to constitute a complete property description.[750]

§ 4.1.9 Use Of Other Plats To Identify Property

Reference in a contract to the deed book and page number of a recorded plat describing the property is sufficient as a legal description of property.[751] In fact, where a description of the property in a sales contract refers to a plat for a more complete description, the plat ordinarily will be considered part of the property description in the contract.[752] The GAR Contracts give the option to specifically reference and incorporate the plat by identifying the Plat Book and Page numbers.[753]

---

747 *Deich v. Reeves*, 203 Ga. 596, 48 S.E.2d 373 (1948).

748 *Deich v. Reeves*, 203 Ga. 596, 48 S.E.2d 373 (1948).

749 *Mathews v. Loftin*, 224 Ga. 98, 160 S.E.2d 399 (1968).

750 *Sackett v. Wilson*, 258 Ga. 612, 373 S.E.2d 10 (1988); *Johnson v. Sackett*, 256 Ga. 552, 350 S.E.2d 419 (1986) (tax plat attached to a contract supplemented the writing to make a legal description valid).

751 *Crooke v. Property Management Services, Inc.*, 215 Ga. 410, 110 S.E.2d 677 (1959).

752 *Kilby v. Sawtell*, 203 Ga. 256, 46 S.E.2d 117 (1948).

753 GAR Forms F20, F23, F27, F29, F33 and F34.

§ 4.1.9.1   Use Of Recorded Plats To Identify Property

Reference to a recorded plat in a property description can constitute a "key" by which property may be identified. In one case, a property description stated, in part, "The full legal description of said property Lot 3 and part of Lot 2 …. is the same as it is recorded with the Clerk of the Superior Court of the County in which the property is located and is made a part of this agreement by reference … Plat Book 33, Page 59, Fulton County, Office of Clerk of Superior Court …".[754] The court held that since the description provided a "key" (deeds and a recorded plat), which was incorporated by reference, the description was valid.

§ 4.1.9.2   Use Of Unrecorded Plats To Identify Property

Even if a plat is not recorded, it may be used as a "key" by which property may be identified. In one case, the court held that an unrecorded plat was incorporated into a contract's property description when the property was described as "… tract #3 located in Land Lots 422 & 453 of the 12th Land District of Brooks County, Georgia as by plat made by DeVane Associates, dated 6th December 1968."[755] The court noted that the plat showed the acreage of the tract and all of its boundaries – by compass calls and distances, land lot lines, roads, a water course, and boundaries of adjoining tracts and of lands of other named owners – and the plat stated that "acreage, bearings and distances are derived from deeds, aerial photographs and plats of record." The contract to purchase was a sufficient "key" by which the property description could be determined by review of extrinsic evidence such as the deeds, aerial photographs, and plats of record from which the plat was drawn.

§ 4.1.9.3   Identifying Common Areas On Subdivision Plat

If lots are sold in reference to a recorded subdivision plat which identifies an area for the common use and enjoyment of all the property owners in the subdivision, an easement to use those common areas will arise for the benefit of all of the lot owners. For example, when a lake is shown on a subdivision plat and lots are sold according to the plat, the lot owners will acquire an irrevocable easement to use the lake, even if the lake is not designated as a common area. The recording of a subdivision plat showing the adjoining lake is key. In such cases, the availability of the lake is a material part of the value of the property, and is "often the principal incentive for its purchase. The lake is in the same category as a recreational area or park shown on a subdivision plat, and the sale of lots by reference to the plat should be regarded as a dedication of the lake as a recreation area for the benefit of all adjoining owners."[756]

One case involved a beach subdivision fronting the Atlantic Ocean. All the land area was subdivided into lots and sold except for a few common areas, such as the beach area, a street and an open area between the beach and the street.[757] There were no reservations made for these common areas on the subdivision plat. The court held that where there was a sale of one or more lots referred to in recorded plat, each purchaser in the subdivision was conveyed an easement to use such common areas as a beach and as means of access to the ocean. The court also held that an easement acquired in such manner is considered an express grant and is an irrevocable property right.

However, a subdivision lot owner may not have a right to use the common areas if his warranty deed did not refer to the subdivision plat that sets out the common areas. In one case, the subdivision was developed as a "fly in" residential community where many residents owned airplanes and have hangers on their lots.[758] Many residents used the gravel roadway for vehicular traffic and taxiing airplanes to and from the airport. When the developers fenced the roadway off, a few of the owners sued the developer claiming that they had an easement over the roadway. The court held that

---

754   *Suttle v. Northside Realty Associates, Inc.*, 171 Ga.App. 928, 321 S.E.2d 424 (1984).

755   *Furney v. Dukes*, 226 Ga. 804, 177 S.E.2d 680 (1970).

756   *Patterson v. Powell*, 257 Ga.App. 336, 571 S.E.2d 400 (2002), cert denied; *Dillard v. Bishop Eddie Long Ministries, Inc.*, 258 Ga.App. 507, 574 S.E.2d 544 (2002).

757   *Smith v. Bruce*, 241 Ga. 133, 244 S.E.2d 559 (1978).

758   *Durham v. Mathis*, 258 Ga.App. 749, 575 S.E.2d 6 (2002).

the owner whose deed referred to the subdivision plat had the easement rights over the roadway, and denied easement rights to owners whose deeds did not refer to the subdivision plat.

§ 4.1.9.4   Use Of Plats To Clarify Metes And Bounds Description

A reference in a contract to a plat can be used to clarify a detailed metes and bounds description if there is an error in one or more of the calls of the metes and bounds description. A contract which contains such an error will be considered to have an accurate and valid property description if it refers to a plat of survey recorded in the county land records which contains a definite, certain, and adequate property description.[759]

§ 4.1.9.5   Insufficient Plat Does Not Cure Defective Property Description

If a reference to a plat is itself insufficient (fails to provide a "key", fails to show courses and distances, or has no fixed starting point), the person contending that the property description is adequate may not be able to demonstrate that the plat fulfilled the necessary requirements.[760] A map or plat attached and made a part of the contract will generally be considered indefinite and uncertain if it does not show the location of any other properties of the adjoining land owners, the distances or designation of any of the "points" on the plat to which it refers, contains no scale, and shows no directions. Such a plat does not materially aid in the description, will generally be considered to be indefinite and uncertain, and will not be considered in determining whether the property description in the contract is sufficient.[761]

§ 4.1.9.6   Reference To Lots On Plat May Be Insufficient Description

Reference to lots on a plat may not be an adequate description if the lots are not sufficiently identified in the contract. In one case, a contract referred to 36 lots of a group of 51 shown on a plat.[762] However, there was nothing to identify which specific 36 lots were the subject of the contract. The court held that the property description was inadequate.

§ 4.1.10   Surveys Generally

The word "survey" comes from the Anglo-French word "surveer" which literally means "to look over".[763] Most surveys will include a description of the exterior limits or boundaries of the property. This is normally done by first locating the property in space as being in one or more counties, districts, sections and land lots. These terms all describe commonly referenced points used in identifying the location of real property. Counties are obviously the largest of these descriptive reference points and land lots are the smallest.

A survey must begin somewhere and this point is referred to as a precise and specific "point of beginning." Surveys then measure a series of points along the property line with each point being either a straight or curved line. The distance from one point to the next on a survey is referred to as a "call." The description of the property should return to the point of beginning so that there is a line around the entirety of the property. If a description of a property on a survey does not return to a point of beginning, the survey is defective in that it lacks what is referred to as closure.

The course of a line between two points on a survey is measured based upon the bearings of a compass. The compass directions are based upon a 360 degree radius that is then broken down further into four 90 degree quadrants (northeast, northwest, southeast and southwest). Due north is at 0 degrees. Each quadrant then goes from 0 to 90 degrees with 90 degrees being due east and west in their respective quadrants (see Exhibit 1 below). Each degree is

---

759   *Barto v. Hicks*, 124 Ga.App. 472, 184 S.E.2d 188 (1971).

760   *Herrington v. Rose*, 225 Ga. 452, 169 S.E.2d 312 (1969).

761   *Smith v. Georgia Indus. Realty Co.*, 215 Ga. 431, 111 S.E.2d 37 (1959).

762   *Delfosse v. Coleman*, 211 Ga. 888, 89 S.E.2d 518 (1955).

763   Merriam-Webster Online Dictionary.

then further broken down into degrees and seconds. A line that is north 20 degrees (20°) 50 minutes (50'), 33 second (33") west or north 20°, 50' 33" west is a line that is in the north west quadrant that is 20 degrees west of due north.

Exhibit 1

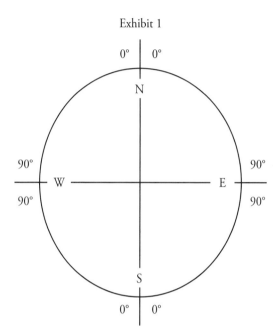

A metes and bounds legal description cannot be prepared without a survey.

§ 4.1.10.1   Benefits Of A Survey

Surveys can provide critical information to buyers of real property. First, they show where the property is located in space. While the general boundary lines of a property can sometimes be determined from walking the property, the location of landscaping, fences, driveways, and garages can often confuse a casual observer as to where the exact property lines are located.

Buyers who have not obtained a survey during a time period when they can terminate the agreement usually have little recourse if the property then turns out not to have the dimensions the buyer thought.[764] For example, a buyer and seller entered into a purchase and sale agreement which provided a description of the property to be purchased and included an attached survey. The attached survey showed the property to be purchased, but also included an adjoining tract of land (which was not included in the legal description). The agreement allowed the buyer to survey the property during the due diligence period and terminate the agreement for any reason whatsoever. The buyer did not conduct a survey and entered into the agreement under the belief that the adjoining tract of land was included in the sale. After the sale was completed, the buyer learned that the adjoining tract was not included in the agreement and brought suit against the seller for fraudulent misrepresentation. The court rejected the buyer's claim and held that the buyer is prohibited from claiming that he has been deceived by false representations when he could have learned the true boundary lines of the property by exercising due diligence.[765] In this case, a survey would have revealed that the adjoining land was not included in the sale.

---

764   *Gospel Tabernacle Deliverance Church, Inc. v. From the Heart Church Ministries, Inc.*, 312 Ga.App. 355, 718 S.E.2d 575 (2011).

765   *Gospel Tabernacle Deliverance Church, Inc. v. From the Heart Church Ministries, Inc.*, 312 Ga.App. 355, 718 S.E.2d 575 (2011).

Surveys also typically locate all easements affecting the property.[766] Therefore, a survey can reveal that the improvements are built over an easement, or that there are encroachments onto the property such as a neighbor's fence, driveway or improvements not intended to be located on the property.[767] The buyer will have no claim for fraud if the buyer could have protected himself or herself by obtaining a survey.[768]

Surveys also identify the size of the property being purchased. Whether the property is a large acreage tract or the sale of a small subdivision lot, buyers are never happy when the property turns out to be smaller than it was believed to be. Surveys also typically identify whether the property is located in a flood plan. Knowing where the property and the improvements located therein are in a flood plain can be critical both to a decision to purchase as well as whether to obtain flood insurance.

§ 4.1.11   Types Of Surveys

There are many different types of surveys used in residential, commercial and land/lot transactions. Some of these surveys are standard in any transaction and others are specific to either residential, commercial or land/lot deals. The most common surveys include boundary surveys, as-built surveys, lot consolidation plats, and topographical surveys. Other types of surveys, such as the FEMA Evaluation Certification and the ALTA/ACSM survey, are more specific depending on the property or type of transaction. These surveys are discussed in detail below.

§ 4.1.11.1   Boundary Surveys

A boundary survey (also referred to as a Georgia Minimum Standard) is the most basic type of survey for both residential and commercial properties. A boundary survey is traditionally provided at a closing and is attached to a purchase and sale agreement. When this type of survey is completed, a surveyor will visit the property and collect information regarding property lines, bearings and distances along such lines, and the total acreage of the property. A surveyor will also mark all the property corners and re-set any pins that are missing. Thereafter, a plat will be drawn to illustrate the property based on this collected information. This survey will show if there are any improvements that may exist, such as buildings, driveways or fences, as well as any encroachments on the property.

§ 4.1.11.2   As-Built Surveys

An as-built survey is generally conducted in new construction transactions when the construction project is completed in order for a property owner to obtain a Certificate of Occupancy. With this type of survey, the surveyor will locate all new improvements on the property and verify that the location and elevation of the new construction to determine if the work is in compliance with local building ordinances. In addition, a surveyor will verify if the plan was initially approved and permitted by the local governing authority.

§ 4.1.11.3   Lot Consolidation Plats

When two or more adjacent parcels of land are combined into one parcel, a lot consolidation plat will be completed. A survey will first need to perform a boundary survey to determine the exact dimensions and land boundaries of both parcels. Thereafter, the surveyor will create a plat indicating the original parcels and the new combined parcel of land. The final plat is then submitted to the governing authority for approval of the combination of the two parcels.

---

766 *Security Union Title Ins. Co. v. RC Acres, Inc.*, 269 Ga.App. 359, 604 S.E.2d 547 (2004).

767 Pindar's 3 <u>Ga. Real Estate Law & Procedure</u> § 26-8 (6th ed.). Survey can reveal any conflict between the possession lines and the deed lines, encroachments, visible easements, improvements erected near or on the boundary lines, available access, overlaps and disputed boundaries; <u>Ga. Real Estate Title Exam. And Closings</u> § 3-10.1 (3rd ed.). Surveyor locates all buildings and other improvements and trace around the property boundary to see that the improvements do not encroach onto an adjoining neighbor's property or upon easements located on the survey or encroach upon building setback lines or other no-build restrictions.

768 *Gospel Tabernacle Deliverance Church, Inc. v. From the Heart Church Ministries, Inc.*, 312 Ga.App. 355, 718 S.E.2d 575 (2011).

§ 4.1.11.4   FEMA Evaluation Certification

A FEMA Evaluation Certification is a lengthy and highly technical document used to determine whether a property is required to obtain flood insurance. This form is used for both residential and commercial transactions. The surveyor first determines if the property located on the Flood Insurance Rate Map (FIRM) which identifies the 100-year flood locations or if the property is located in certain flood insurance zones. If the property is located in either of those indicated areas, the surveyor will evaluate the house and the adjacent ground levels to determine the possibility of flood loss. Based on this evaluation, a specific property may or may not be required to obtain flood insurance.

§ 4.1.11.5   Topographical Surveys

A topographical survey is used to identify and map the contours of the ground of a property, including any existing features on or slightly above or below the property's surface. To complete this survey, a surveyor will establish horizontal and vertical control that will serve as the frame work for the survey. The surveyor will then determine enough horizontal location and evaluation of the ground points for plotting the property when a map is created. Thereafter, all natural and man-made features will be located and identified. Once all the information is collected, a topographic map will be created. These types of surveys are commonly attached to new construction contracts to serve as a base map for the design of a residence or commercial building.

A topographical survey is often obtained when a buyer to determine if portions of the property are in a floodplain or as part of the siting or grading of the improvements on the property. The GAR New Construction Contract does not specifically address topographical issues related to the property. To address grading issues, the buyer may require a topographical survey of the property to be provided at closing showing that the grade of that portion of the lot upon which the improvements are to be made will have an elevation of not less than a specified number of feet above sea level. The buyer may use the following special stipulation for this purpose.

> **Special Stipulation 53:   Specification on Elevation**
>
> *Seller and Buyer agree that the final grade of the front yard of the Lot upon which improvements are to be made shall be at an elevation of not less than ____ feet above sea level. Seller agrees to provide to Buyer an as-built topographical survey of the Property at closing.*

In other cases, the buyer may want to limit the grade of the lot to simply ensure that the main level of the dwelling will not be beneath the grade of the adjoining street. An example of this type of special stipulation follows.

> **Special Stipulation 54:   Grade Not to be Lower Than Grade of Street**
>
> *Buyer and Seller agree that the grade of the front yard of the lot between the street and the residence constructed on the lot shall not be any lower than the present grade of the street.*

Another topographical issue occurs when a builder or property owner changes the level of a property which results in damage to an adjacent property. Georgia law prohibits an owner from altering his property so as to increase or alter the flow of water on adjacent property, thereby damaging that property.[769] In one case, a neighbor brought a trespass and nuisance action against the homeowner, homebuilder, independent contractor, and subdivision alleging that construction on neighbors' property caused flooding.[770]

The Court of Appeals ruled that a property owner may be held liable for trespass and nuisance when construction on the owner's property causes an increase in water runoff onto neighboring property. In this case, a husband and wife hired a builder to build a home on their property in a subdivision. The builder (who was an independent contractor of

---

769 *Cox v. Martin*, 207 Ga. 442, 62 S.E.2d 164 (1950).

770 *Greenwald v. Kersh*, 265 Ga.App. 196, 593 S.E.2d 381 (2004).

the owners) apparently brought in dirt to level the lot. The dirt altered the flow of surface water, resulting in increased water runoff onto the neighbor's property and subsequent flooding. The owners for whom the house was built argued that they should not be held responsible for this damage because their builder was an independent contractor. They also argued that they had very little to do with the construction and had no control over what the contractors did. However, the court held that the owners were responsible because they moved into the property and therefore accepted the work of the contractor. The court also held that the owners knew about the problem and refused to do anything about it.

Therefore, to limit potential liability when the buyer acquires title to the property, the buyer may want assurance from the seller that the grade has not been altered so as to increase or alter the flow of water on adjacent property. The buyer may incorporate the following language in the contract to accomplish this.

> **Special Stipulation 55: Grade Change to Channel Water Run-off Prohibited**
>
> *Seller warrants to Buyer that Seller shall not change the grade of the property so as to channel, direct, or increase the flow of surface water runoff onto adjacent properties.*

§ 4.1.11.6 ALTA/ACSM Survey

An ALTA/ACSM survey is a comprehensive boundary survey used for completing land title surveys in commercial transactions. This survey sets forth detailed instructions and minimum standards for completing a survey and also addresses issues that are of concern to lenders and title companies.

To complete this survey, the survey will measure the boundaries of the property with a digital and/or laser measuring instrument, taking into account any boundary markers already in place. The surveyor will then indicate any buildings or improvements on the land, as well as the distance between such buildings and the boundary line. This is done to determine if the property complies with existing zoning restrictions. The surveyor will also locate any easements and determine whether there are any encroachments upon such easements or setback lines. A number of issues identified in an ALTA/ACSM survey are similar to those identified in a typical boundary survey, but others are not. For instance, this type of survey will also determine if the property is located in a flood zone, any water boundaries on the property, evidence of cemeteries and topographical information to determine the viability of the land for building.

Once this information is collected, a lender or title company will be able to evaluate the property for any potential risks. For this reason, lenders and title companies in commercial transactions generally require an ALTA/ACSM survey of a property. However, even if this type of survey is not required, using an ALTA/ACSM survey is recommended for commercial transactions to ensure no issues on a property are missed.

§ 4.1.12 When Surveys Can Be Used To Supplement Description Of Property

Surveys are often attached to contracts to supplement the property description set out in the contract. If the survey contains sufficient information, such as a metes and bounds description of the property that specifically identifies the property, it can serve as the property description on the condition that it is referenced and attached to the contract as an exhibit.

Surveys can also be used to ensure that the buyer has a clear idea of the property. A buyer and a seller can agree to have a survey done to determine the acreage of the property before the closing and also provided that the purchase price will depend on the acreage set out in the survey.[771] The buyer can also include a special stipulation that allows the buyer to terminate the purchase and sales agreement if a survey obtained after the binding agreement date and prior to closing reveals that the property is smaller than a particular size. An example of such a special stipulation follows.

---

771 GAR Form F138, Survey Resolution Exhibit.

Special Stipulation 56:   Buyer's Right to Terminate if Survey Shows Property to be Smaller or Larger

Notwithstanding any provision to the contrary contained herein, Buyer shall have the right to terminate this Agreement without penalty upon notice to Seller if survey performed by a licensed Georgia surveyor reveals that the Property is less than _____ acres or more than _____ acres.

If the parties leave the property description blank in a contract, but reference an intent to attach a survey at a later date to provide the description of the property, the contract will be void even if the survey is attached later and provides a clear and precise description of the property (unless the parties subsequently affirm the contract and survey in writing).

In one case, the seller and buyer agreed that the buyer would pay for a survey and incorporate the description of the property into the sales contract when the survey became available.[772] The seller was unable to meet his obligations under the contract and argued that the contract was void because it did not contain a legal description of the property to be sold. The buyer argued that the seller implicitly, if not expressly, contractually authorized the buyer to enter the legal description of the property after the contract was executed. The court concluded that the arguments made by the buyer might apply to a contract for services or personal property, but did not apply to a contract for the sale of real estate. The court stated, "A provision for subsequent survey will not cure a contract which at the time of execution contains no description of the land to be sold at all."

In another case, the buyer entered into a contract to purchase a "house and 10 acres of a 40-acre tract more or less that is now the property of H. C. Tysinger, Jr., on Martain Mill Road, Coweta County, GA".[773] The exact boundaries were to be determined by a survey. The court held that while the larger 40-acre tract may have been identifiable, the ten acres the description refers to were not identifiable and could not be more specifically identified by a survey prepared and attached after the execution of the contract.

Another example is a case where the parties agreed that the metes and bounds of the property, as well as the acreage, were to be determined by a survey to be conducted after the contract was executed.[774] The purchase contract itself did not contain a sufficient legal description of the property because it did not: (1) contain a metes and bounds description; (2) make any reference to the acreage of the tract; or (3) incorporate a plat of survey. It did identify the property as 4190 Cedar Ridge Trail located in Land Lot 192 of District 15 of DeKalb County and the preprinted language in the contract stated that the full legal description "is the same as is recorded by Clerk of the Superior Court of the county in which the property is located and is made a part of this agreement by reference." However, the warranty deed recorded in DeKalb County which contained a metes and bounds description referred the tract as located in Land Lots 191 and 192, whereas the sales contract states that the tract is located in Land Lot 192. The court found that the property description was inadequate and the parties cannot rely on a post-contract survey to provide the legal description. The court stated that because the "key" relied upon must be sufficient to provide identification of the property by reference to extrinsic evidence which exists at the time that the contract is entered into by the parties.

§ 4.1.12.1   Use Of Surveys In GAR Contract To Identify Property

The GAR Contract for residential property provides that if a survey of the property is attached to the contract it shall be a part of the contract.[775] The GAR Contract further provides that the buyer has the right to terminate the contract upon written notice to the seller if a new survey performed by a licensed surveyor is materially different from the attached survey. The term "materially different" does not apply to any improvements or repairs constructed by the

---

772   *McCumbers v. Trans-Columbia, Inc.*, 172 Ga.App. 275, 322 S.E.2d 516 (1984).

773   *McMichael Realty and Ins. Agency, Inc. v. Tysinger*, 155 Ga.App. 131, 270 S.E.2d 88 (1980).

774   *Gateway Family Worship Centers, Inc. v. H.O.P.E. Foundation Ministries, Inc.*, 244 Ga.App. 286, 535 S.E.2d 286 (2000).

775   GAR Forms F20, F23, F27, and F29.

seller in any agreed-upon locations. It is incumbent upon a buyer of property to ensure that the property described in the contract and the deed is the property that actually intends to purchase. It is useful to include a survey in the contract for this purpose to avoid mistakes as to the location of property.

In one case, the buyer was shown property in a subdivision.[776] He walked the property he wanted to purchase, which was identified as Lot 4 on the subdivision plat which the listing agent gave him. However, the plat was outdated and the recorded revised plat identified the property he walked as Lot 1 instead of Lot 4. The buyer subsequently purchased Lot 4, which was not the lot he had inspected with the listing agent. He soon began construction of a house on the lot he thought he owned. After he completed about 75% of the construction of the house, he received notice from the actual owner of the lot asserting ownership over the lot and stated that as actual owner, he was taking possession of the house and lot and that he would complete the construction of the house.

The buyer sued the listing agent and the actual owner of the lot. The court held that the buyer was not entitled to damages from the listing agent who had given him the incorrect plat and that the actual owner was allowed to keep the house without paying for any of the construction done prior to the notice. The reasoning of the court was that if the buyer had obtained a survey of the property he had contracted to purchase prior to closing and had reviewed it carefully, he could have discovered the error and the case would probably never have arisen.

Under the GAR Contract, even if the seller could attach a survey to a contract which shows certain title defects, such as an encroachment, the buyer can still raise defects shown on the survey as title defects. If the seller wants to limit the ability of the buyer to raise matters revealed on a survey as title defects, the seller can add the following special stipulation to the purchase and sale agreement.

> **Special Stipulation 57:   Matters Revealed on a Survey Attached to Contract Cannot be Raised as Title Defects**
>
> *Buyer and Seller acknowledge that a survey dated _____, 20____ is attached to the Purchase and Sale Agreement between the parties as an exhibit and is expressly incorporated herein (hereinafter "Survey"). Notwithstanding any provision to the contrary contained herein, Buyer agrees not to raise any matter revealed on the survey as a title objection and agrees to accept such conditions "as-is".*

In some cases, the precise location of the improvements will be critical to the buyer. The buyer may want to incorporate a provision requiring the seller to obtain written consent from the buyer before changing the location of improvements as shown on the survey. The following provision may be used for this purpose.

> **Special Stipulation 58:   Location of Footprint for Improvements**
>
> *Seller and Buyer agree that the footprint of the improvements shall be constructed by Seller in the location shown on the survey attached hereto as Exhibit "___."*
> *No material changes in the location of the footprint of the improvements shall be permitted without the written consent of Buyer.*

§ 4.1.13   Use Of Previous Deeds

One method of describing property is to incorporate any previous deed that conveyed the property to the seller into the contract by referring to the deed book and page number of that deed. Assuming that the property was properly and legally described in the seller's deed, this is a valid means of describing property in a contract. Alternatively, a copy of the seller's deed or the legal description from that deed could be attached as an exhibit to the contract.

---

776 *Dundee Land Co. v. Simmons*, 204 Ga. 248, 49 S.E.2d 488 (1948); *Reidling v. Holcomb*, 25 Ga.App. 229, 483 S.E.2d 624 (1997).

§ 4.1.14   "More Or Less" Descriptions May Be Insufficient

Descriptions of property which include statements such as "5 acres, more or less," or "running south 75 feet, more or less," or "25 acres +/-," can create problems but are not necessarily invalid. As long as the property description gives the precise location of the property, the property description will be deemed to be valid. If the description including the term "more or less" or "+/-" is not precise enough to locate the exact property in question, it will be invalid.[777] Again, the parties should strive to provide the most detailed property description possible.

§ 4.1.15   Attaching Property Description Or Later Survey To Contract After Execution

Contracts will sometimes provide that a "legal description [or survey] will be attached later." However, if the contract itself does not contain a sufficient property description to provide a "key" to the location of the property, a provision stating the intent of the parties to attach a property description or survey later will not be effective. The Court of Appeals of Georgia has aptly described this practice:

> [A]lthough it may be realized that it is the practice of real estate brokers to merely use this phrase 'legal description to be attached later' in order to avoid copying a lengthy legal description into the sales contract, and that many sales are consummated on sales contracts which read this way, it cannot be said that the courts can approve such a practice when neither the sales contract itself, nor the source of the 'legal description to be attached later' is definite enough to limit such description to any one tract of property.[778]

In another case, the parties' contract identified the property by street address, referred to its location in a certain Land Lot and District of the county, and referred to a full legal description recorded in the county records (which in fact was at odds with the partial description in the deed). The parties also intended to have a survey conducted after the contract was executed, which would provide the certainty required for the legal description. The court stated that although a valid contract with a valid legal description "may rely on a subsequent survey to determine the exact acreage, a post-contract survey cannot be used to provide the description itself." The contract failed for lack of an adequate legal description.[779]

Taking the time to have a survey of the property prepared prior to entering into a contract can obviously avoid problems later. If this is not possible, the parties should upon obtaining a proper legal description either amend the contract to incorporate it, or terminate the defective contract and enter into a new one.

§ 4.1.16   Use Of Preliminary Drawings Or Diagrams To Supplement Description

Preliminary drawings or diagrams are sometimes attached to a contract to supplement the property description set forth in the contract or to provide the property description when none is set out. The drawing or diagram must be sufficiently definite and precise to identify the property in order for it to constitute a valid property description. If the preliminary drawing or diagram is not sufficiently definite to locate the property, the contract will not be enforceable without some other adequate property description.

In one case, the seller agreed to sell a 32.6 acre tract "less and except for a 25,000 square foot lot, inclusive of Seller's current residence, said exact location to be determined by Purchaser."[780] The contract attached a document that designated the lot, but the buyer redesigned the lot configuration. The seller refused to go through with the contract

---

777   *Dangler v. Rutland*, 229 Ga. 439, 192 S.E.2d 156 (1972); Malone v. Klaer, 203 Ga. 291, 46 S.E.2d 495 (1948).

778   *Murphy v. Morse*, 96 Ga.App. 513, 100 S.E.2d 623, 625 (1957).

779   *Gateway Family Worship Centers, Inc. v. H.O.P.E. Foundation Ministries, Inc.*, 244 Ga.App. 286, 535 S.E.2d 286 (2000).

780   *Scheinfeld v. Murray*, 267 Ga. 622, 481 S.E.2d 194 (1997).

because, as a result of the buyer's redesign of the lot, the seller's home faced a street sideways and her driveway would have to bisect the front yard to reach the garage. The court concluded that the contract was void because it did not specifically describe the land to be sold, since the preliminary designation of lots did not accurately reflect the actual site on which the seller's home was to be located.

Similarly, it has been held that a contract describing property to be sold by reference to an attached diagram that did not disclose the location of the property or furnish a "key" to its description was unenforceable.[781]

§ 4.1.17 Occupancy Does Not Cure Defective Description

Even if the intent of the parties is clear, if the description of property in a contract is not adequate or sufficiently definite to allow it to be located, the contract is void. If the property is not adequately described in a contract, for example, the fact that a proposed buyer has occupied the actual property does not prevent the buyer from contesting the validity of the description of the property and does not cure a deficiency in the property description.[782]

§ 4.1.18 Acceptance Of A Counteroffer May Cure Defect In Property Description

If an offer to purchase property contains a defect in the property description, the buyer's acceptance and partial performance (*i.e.*, deposit of earnest money) of a counteroffer cures the defect if the counteroffer incorporates a complete property description. For example, a buyer executed a contract of sale offering to purchase property described as "Oakview Terrace Apartments, 1301 Oakview Road, Decatur, Georgia, as further described in Exhibit 'A' attached." The offer was transmitted without Exhibit "A" attached.[783] The seller signed the contract and attached the property description, which should have been a part of the original offer. When the buyer who neglected to incorporate Exhibit "A" put up a security deposit, that action was deemed to be an acceptance of the counteroffer, which incorporated the Exhibit "A" and the original defective property description issue was remedied. Likewise, if a contract does not contain a sufficient property description, the problem can be cured by a subsequent amendment to the contract signed by both parties.

§ 4.1.19 Use Of Owner's Name To Locate Property

As long as there is a sufficient "key" description such as "the Robinson Place," "the Humphrey Place," or "the Anderson Place" should be adequate. For example, if a contract describes property sold by name, the Anderson Place, and locates it specifically on a rural road 12 miles out of Augusta, Georgia, the description may be adequate.[784]

Similarly, a property description which identifies the county and the state in which the property is located, states that it is bounded on the north, east, south, and west by certain named owners and states the number of acres in the property, is sufficiently definite.[785]

§ 4.2 DESCRIPTION OF CONDOMINIUM AND CONDOMINIUM UNITS

A condominium is created when property is legally submitted to the condominium form of ownership in accordance with the Georgia Condominium Act (the "Act").[786] A condominium must contain units subject to individual ownership, and common elements owned and used collectively by the unit owners and occupants.[787] There may also be "limited common elements" that are assigned to one or more, but less than all of the units.[788]

---

781 *Bryan v. Rusk*, 89 Ga.App. 125, 78 S.E.2d 853 (1953).

782 *Fourteen West Realty, Inc. v. Wesson*, 167 Ga.App. 539, 307 S.E.2d 28 (1983).

783 *Uitdenbosch v. Gasarch*, 160 Ga.App. 85, 286 S.E.2d 63 (1981).

784 *Marsh v. Baird*, 203 Ga. 819, 48 S.E.2d 529 (1948).

785 *Deaton v. Swanson*, 196 Ga. 833, 28 S.E.2d 126 (1943).

786 O.C.G.A. § 44-3-70, *et seq.*

787 O.C.G.A. § 44-3-71.

788 O.C.G.A. § 44-3-71(19).

The boundaries of a condominium unit are typically described through intersecting vertical and horizontal planes making the unit itself something of a cube. Such a legal description would be particularly hard to describe through a traditional metes and bounds legal description. This is particularly the case since there are often indentations and protrusions from the "cube" for windows, doors, eaves, and other similar items. The Georgia Condominium Act solves this problem by allowing the units to be described in reference to the declaration of condominium.[789] The declaration of condominium is the document which creates the condominium.[790] It describes exactly what property is being submitted to the condominium form of ownership (the overall property), the boundaries of the individual units in the condominium, and what percentage ownership interest in the common elements is allocated to each unit. Most condominium contracts, including the GAR Condominium Resale Purchase and Sale Agreement, reference the declaration of condominium in the legal description of the property.

For a more complete treatment of various issues related to condominiums, please see Chapter 20 (Condominiums, Homeowner Associations and Other Forms of Common Interest Communities). Here we will address specific issues affecting the description of condominium units in the typical purchase and sale transaction.

§ 4.2.1   Description Of Property Which Is Part Of Condominium

In the typical transaction involving purchase and sale of a condominium unit, one area that often creates issues is determining just what property is included with the unit being purchased. In a condominium, the property which is made a part of the overall condominium project is required to be described in the declaration of condominium. This includes a description of the common elements and any limited common elements. When buyers purchase a condominium unit, they are taking title to the space encompassed by vertical and horizontal boundaries, plus an undivided percentage ownership interest in all common elements in the condominium and any "limited common elements" that are assigned to one or more, but less than all units.[791]

§ 4.2.1.1   Common Elements

The common elements in a condominium include all of the property that is not a part of the units.[792] This typically includes building exteriors, landscaped areas, roads and recreational facilities. Together, the collective group of all condominium unit owners own 100% of the common elements as tenants in common. Separately, the owners of an individual condominium unit own a certain percentage of the common elements.[793] Sometimes the percentage of common element ownership is the same for all unit owners in the condominium and sometimes it is weighted to correspond to the size of the unit (bigger units owning a larger percentage of the common elements than smaller units).[794] In most condominiums, the amount of assessments paid by the unit owner to the association corresponds to the percentage of ownership interest such owner has in the common elements of the condominium. However, this does not have to be the case. A condominium declaration can provide that all unit owners pay the same monthly assessment

---

789 O.C.G.A. § 44-3-73.

790 O.C.G.A. § 44-3-72.

791 O.C.G.A. § 44-3-71(19).

792 O.C.G.A. § 44-3-71(4).

793 See O.C.G.A § 44-3-78.

794 The size of the unit is usually based on heated square feet in the unit type. For example, the percentage of ownership interest in the common elements may be based strictly on the square footage of each individual unit. If there are 50 different size units, each unit has a different percentage of ownership in the common elements. However, in some condominiums there may be a number of units that are almost the same size and a number of units that are much bigger or smaller. Instead of dividing the percentage of ownership interest in the common elements by the square footage of each unit, the ownership percentages may be based on types of units. Basing ownership percentages on unit types allows the developer to assign all of the small units (i.e., studios and one bedrooms) the same percentage of ownership interest, all of the medium size units (i.e., two bedroom units) a higher percentage than the smaller units and all of the large units (i.e., three bedroom or penthouse units) an even greater percentage of ownership interest.

regardless of the size of their unit.[795] Notwithstanding the above discussion regarding percentage of ownership interest in the common elements, the collective owners of each unit usually have one equally-weighted vote.[796]

§ 4.2.1.2   Limited Common Elements

In a condominium there also can be "limited common elements." A limited common element is a portion of the common elements reserved for the exclusive use of those entitled to use one or more, but less than all, of the units.[797] Limited common elements usually consist of such things as balconies, patios, entrance stoops, or parking spaces.[798] To some degree, limited common elements are something of a legal fiction. They were created because certain property in a condominium (*i.e.*, a balcony or patio) is not truly part of a condominium unit, as defined by its horizontal and vertical boundaries, but not really a part of the common elements, because less than all of the unit owners have the exclusive right to use the area. In order to distinguish such property from the defined unit and from the common elements, the idea of a limited common element was created.

Limited common elements may be assigned to a unit in the initial declaration or may be assigned at a later time, as long as the declaration permits such later assignment.[799] In order to convert common element property to an assigned limited common element, the association, by and through its board of directors, must sign and record an amendment to the condominium declaration. Such amendment also must be executed by the unit owner(s) to whose unit the assignment is being made and such owners must pay all reasonable costs for the preparation, execution and recordation of the amendment.[800] A limited common element may not be taken away from an owner or reassigned without the consent of the owner to whom it was assigned.[801]

However, an owner whose unit is served by a limited common element may request that it be reassigned (*i.e.*, two unit owners switching parking spaces), so long as the declaration does not prohibit such reassignments.[802] In order to reassign a limited common element, the owners requesting the reassignment must consent to the assignment and submit a written application to the association. Thereafter, the association must sign and record an amendment to the condominium declaration. The amendment also must be executed by all of the unit owners affected by the reassignment and such owners must pay all reasonable costs for the preparation, execution and recordation of the amendment.[803] While there is no case law in Georgia on this point, it has long been assumed that an "affected unit owner" within the meaning of this code section is a party who is directly affected because the reassignment changes the limited common elements assigned to his/her unit.

---

795   In choosing which way to establish the assessment obligations, a developer should think about the realities of the budgeting process. The annual condominium budget will include line items for administration, management fees and insurance. Does an owner cause the association to incur more expenses in these areas because his/her unit is larger than other units? If not, is it fair to require the owner of the larger unit to pay more to the association in monthly assessments than the owner of the smaller unit? Juxtapose this with the budget line items for maintenance and reserve funds. For such expenses it probably does make sense to require the owners of larger units to pay more per month than the owners of smaller units. However, the budget is not divided up into those items that will be assessed equally among all of the units and those items that will be assessed based on the ownership percentage of the common elements assigned to each unit. When the condominium declaration is initially drafted, the developer of the condominium must decide how assessments will be allocated in that association. Changing such allocation later requires the consent of the unit owners and their mortgagees and is very difficult to accomplish.

796   There are condominiums that have weighted voting based on the unit's percentage of ownership of the common elements, but such situations are rare. Weighted voting creates logistical problems for the association during board elections and with respect to amending the condominium legal instruments. It is for this reason that most condominium declarations provide for one vote per unit, regardless of unit size or type.

797   O.C.G.A. § 44-3-71(19).

798   O.C.G.A. § 44-3-75(a)(5).

799   O.C.G.A. § 44-3-82(a).

800   O.C.G.A. § 44-3-82(c).

801   O.C.G.A. § 44-3-82(a).

802   O.C.G.A. § 44-3-82.

803   O.C.G.A. § 44-3-82(b).

§ 4.2.1.3 Development In Phases

A condominium development is often phased, meaning that it is being developed in separate steps or phases. Only the property included in the initial phase of the condominium is described in the declaration. Subsequent phases of the condominium are added by filing an amendment to the declaration in the office of land records.[804] Each amendment must describe the property included in that phase of the condominium.[805] Sometimes a condominium can appear to be larger than it truly is because not all of the physical property in the development has been submitted to or made a part of the condominium. For example, if there are twelve buildings in a development but only six have been submitted to the condominium regime, some purchasers might mistakenly believe that the condominium consists of all twelve buildings. However, since a description of the property which is a part of the condominium is a matter of public record, it is very difficult for a buyer to successfully sue a condominium developer for misrepresentation or fraud in relation to the property description of the unit.

This point was confirmed in a case where the buyer sued the listing agent and seller for misrepresenting the property submitted to the condominium.[806] When showing the property the agent told the buyers that some amenities, including the deck, barbecue area and some landscaped area, was included in the price. She also said that "you're going to enjoy being out here cooking, using this grill, cooking your fish, and you'll love that deck." The buyers were also given a "Fact Sheet" which listed the amenities. However, the condominium declaration and survey expressly excluded these amenities. The question posed to the court was whether the agent's misrepresentations could be relied upon without the buyers being required to prove that they could not have protected themselves through the exercise of due diligence. The court noted that the buyers did not survey the property or request a copy of the condominium declaration. They also did not make independent inquiries concerning the boundaries of the property. The court ruled that the buyers could not as a matter of law justifiably rely on the statements made by the real estate agent to support a claim of misrepresentation, and that the agent's statements did not cancel the buyers' duty to exercise due diligence.

§ 4.2.2 Description Of Condominium Units

In a conveyance of a single family detached home that is not subject to a condominium regime, the property being purchased is defined by the physical boundary lines of the property. These boundary lines are referenced by points or landmarks on the land itself. A condominium is different in that a condominium unit is defined with both vertical and horizontal boundaries.[807] Legal descriptions can therefore be more easily created for stacked residential flats in a multi-family building, where the boundaries of units could not otherwise be easily defined by references to points on the land.

Typical vertical boundaries of a residential condominium unit might be the centerline of the wall separating a unit from an adjoining unit and the midpoint of a wall between a hallway and a unit, or the unfinished surfaces of the interior walls (*i.e.*, the gypsum board or plaster behind the wallpaper). Horizontal boundaries refer to the upper and lower boundaries of a unit.[808] The upper horizontal boundary of a unit might include the unfinished surfaces of the gypsum board comprising the ceiling or it might extend to the underside of the roof materials. In some loft condominiums, the upper horizontal boundaries of the units include the roof joists and cross braces. The lower horizontal boundaries of a unit might be the unfinished surfaces of the interior flooring on the lowest floor of the unit (*i.e.*, the underside of the carpet or hardwood planks) or it may be the subflooring below the interior flooring.

---

804 O.C.G.A. § 44-3-89.

805 O.C.G.A. § 44-3-89.

806 *Brakebille v. Hicks*, 259 Ga. 849, 388 S.E.2d 695 (1990).

807 O.C.G.A.§ 44-3-75(a)

808 In certain situations, a unit may be defined to have no horizontal boundaries. In such a condominium, an owner would hold title to all of the ground underneath his/her unit and all of the air space above it. Townhome condominium units often have no upper or lower horizontal boundaries. This situation could only exist in a condominium, in which there are no units stacked one on top of the other.

The Georgia Condominium Act provides that a description of a condominium unit is sufficient if it contains the unit number, condominium name, county, and the deed book and page number where the declaration of condominium is recorded in the land record office.[809] This information will enable a buyer to easily make an independent inquiry regarding the boundaries of a condominium unit. This is because the declaration of condominium for the condominium sets out the vertical and horizontal boundaries of the unit and references the survey and floor plans of the condominium, which are also recorded. To comply with the Georgia Condominium Act, the floor plans of a condominium unit must contain the following information:

(a) Square footage or dimensions of the unit;

(b) Seal and signature of the preparing architect;

(c) A statement by the preparing architect indicating how measurements were made;

(d) The following statement printed on each floor plan:

These floor plans and the dimensions and square footage calculations shown hereon are only approximations. Any Unit Owner who is concerned about any representations regarding the floor plans should do his/her own investigation as to the dimensions, measurements and square footage of his/her Unit.

(e) Each limited common element ("LCE");

(f) Identification on the floor plans the name of the condominium; and

(g) Identification of the unit type and unit number on each floor plan.

§ 4.2.3 Master Condominiums

Developers are now often creating master planned communities that are themselves often set up as master condominiums. The Act defines a master condominium as "a condominium in which the condominium instruments permit one or more of the units to constitute a sub-condominium." For example, a twenty-story mixed used building may be subject to a master condominium declaration, and the overall property divided into six units. A unit could be an entire building, or just part of a building. Some units may be restricted for commercial use and some for residential use. The master condominium declaration provides that any of the units may be developed as sub-condominiums. The purchaser of a unit, which may be an entire building, is purchasing one unit in the master condominium and may choose to submit that unit to a sub-condominium declaration. The sub-condominium declaration establishes units within that sub-condominium, and creates its own common elements and use restrictions. In a purchase and sale transaction involving a unit of the sub-condominium, it is important for purchasers to carefully review both the master and the sub-condominium documents to determine just what they are buying. (For a more complete review of master and sub-condominiums, see § 20.1.10 (Master Condominium)).

§ 4.3 MEASUREMENT OF SQUARE FOOTAGE

Questions often arise concerning the measurement of the improvements on a property. Do you measure the square footage of a property from the interior walls or the exterior walls? If it is a residential property, do you include unheated square footage, such as the garage and basement, or just heated square footage in the calculation?

In Georgia, there is no common standard of measurement when calculating the square footage of the improvements on a property.[810] However, the real estate industry follows certain standards depending on the type of property being measured. For instance, the methods of calculating the square footage of a single-family dwelling and commercial property tend to be different.

809 O.C.G.A. § 44-3-73.

810 Ga. Landlord & Tenant Lease Forms & Clauses § 1:1 (3rd ed.).

For most types of commercial property, "square footage" normally refers only to heated space.[811] Heated space means the total space within the property that needs to be heated and cooled to provide effective temperature control.[812] This definition often involves measuring from the exterior surface of the walls to include the insulation space within the wall, rather than measuring from the interior surfaces within the property. For this reason, a buyer will often find the calculation of a property's square footage different from the actual space capable of being used. Most buyers would measure the square footage of a property from the interior walls because that is the amount of space they are able to use and occupy. However, the real estate industry customarily measures a property's square footage from the exterior walls of the property. Therefore, the number of square feet may be higher than what a buyer considers useable space.

In addition, unfinished spaces, such as garages, porches and basements are generally not included in the calculation of the property's square footage. These areas are normally not considered heated space and thus not included in calculation. Buyers, however, may include basements, garages and porches because again, these spaces are considered useable. If these areas were included in the calculation, the owner is going to think the square footage of the property is much higher than it actually is.

Differing methods of measurement often create exposure to claims for a seller, developer or building representing the square footage of a home. As a general practice, the method of calculation should always be included in a purchase and sale agreement along with a disclaimer that the actual square footage is an approximation only. A sample of such a stipulation is set forth below.

> **Special Stipulation 59:   Square Footage Calculation Disclaimer**
>
> *Buyer acknowledges that all references to square footage have been included herein only to give the Buyer the most general sense of the square footage of the improvements on the Property. Buyer further acknowledges that there are different ways to measure square footage and that each such method can result in different square footage calculations. In this transaction, Seller has ☐ or has not ☐ included only heated and cooled square footage in its calculations. Seller specifically disclaims the accuracy of the square footage of the improvements on the Property. If Buyer is concerned about determining the precise square footage of the improvements on the Property, Buyer agrees to hire an architect, surveyor or other professional to measure the same.*

In this way, if a buyer comes up with a different square footage for the property (because a surveyor used a different method of calculation), the seller or developer will be generally protected from liability for any alleged misrepresentation.

§ 4.3.1   Measurement For Single-Family Dwellings

As stated above, there is no required method of measurement to calculate the square footage of a residential dwelling. However, the standards created by the American National Standards Institute (ANSI) are customarily followed when calculating the square footage of a single-family residence. Since this method is not required, the square footage of a residence may vary slightly depending on the calculation method used.

Under the ANSI standard of measurement, only the finished areas of a house, including any additions,[813] are measured when calculating the square footage. A finished area is defined as an enclosed area in a house that is suitable for year-round use, embodying walls, floors and ceilings that are similar to the rest of the house. Unfinished areas are sections of the house which do not meet this criterion.

---

811 *Brock v. King*, 279 Ga.App. 335, 629 S.E.2d 829 (2006).

812 *McKnight v. Golden Isles Marina, Inc.*, 186 Ga.App. 228, 366 S.E.2d 830 (1988).

813 *Brock v. King*, 279 Ga.App. 335, 629 S.E.2d 829 (2006).

The finished areas are measured from the exterior surface of the exterior walls of the home. Two homes with the same layout may have slightly different square footage measurements if the exterior of the homes are built with different materials. Unfinished areas, such as garages, unfinished basements and porches, should be excluded from the calculation because they are not considered heated space. In addition, finished basements (referred to as a "below grade area") cannot be lumped in the square footage calculation of a home. Any below grade area must be calculated separately from the rest of the home. More information on the ANSI standard of measurement can be obtained by visiting the American National Standards Institute Website, available at http://webstore.ansi.org.

§ 4.3.2 Measurement For Condominiums

The customary industry method for calculating the square footage of a condominium is measured by the amount of heated space within the unit.[814] However, the exact measurements of a condominium unit should match the unit boundaries as described in the Declaration of Condominium. For example, if the unit's vertical boundaries are the outermost surface of the sheetrock enclosing the unit, this should also be the dimension from which square footage are calculated. Measuring the area of heated space in condominiums (or other structures that share a common wall) is accomplished by measuring from the exterior surface of the exterior walls to the center line of the common walls.[815] The measurable square footage does not stop at the surface of the interior wall.[816] Rather the insulation space within the walls that keeps the condo heated and cooled is also included in the calculation.[817] Including this extra space is necessary to determine the total area that needs to be heated and cooled to provide effective temperature control and to determine the size of heating and cooling equipment needed for an individual unit.[818]

This method of measurement may cause a buyer to think a condo is larger than it actually is because the square footage will be higher than the amount of usable space. For instance, a buyer who purchases a 1,420 square foot condo expects to be able to use all 1,420 square feet. However, if the property is measured using the custom industry method, the square footage capable of being inhabited is actually less than what is described. Measuring a condominium from the interior surfaces of the unit's interior walls is not the customary standard for determining a condominium's square footage.[819] Although this calculation may be a more accurate description of the accessible space available for a resident's use, it is not the standard of measurement customarily used.

§ 4.3.3 Measurement For Commercial Property

The industry standard for measuring the square footage in a commercial property is also based on the amount of heated space within property.[820] Since Georgia does not have a mandatory standard of measurement,[821] the same method used to calculate the square footage of a condominium could be used to calculate the square footage of a commercial property if that property shared a common wall. However, most commercial properties use the standards developed by the Building Owners' and Managers Association (BOMA).[822]

814 *McKnight v. Golden Isles Marina, Inc.*, 186 Ga.App. 228, 366 S.E.2d 830 (1988).

815 *McKnight v. Golden Isles Marina, Inc.*, 186 Ga.App. 228, 366 S.E.2d 830 (1988).

816 *McKnight v. Golden Isles Marina, Inc.*, 186 Ga.App. 228, 366 S.E.2d 830 (1988).

817 *McKnight v. Golden Isles Marina, Inc.*, 186 Ga.App. 228, 366 S.E.2d 830 (1988).

818 *McKnight v. Golden Isles Marina, Inc.*, 186 Ga.App. 228, 366 S.E.2d 830 (1988).

819 *McKnight v. Golden Isles Marina, Inc.*, 186 Ga.App. 228, 366 S.E.2d 830 (1988).

820 *Brock v. King*, 279 Ga.App. 335, 629 S.E.2d 829 (2007).

821 Ga. Landlord & Tenant Lease Forms & Clauses § 1:1 (3rd ed.).

822 Ga. Landlord & Tenant Lease Forms & Clauses § 1:1 (3rd ed.).

§ 4.4 BOUNDARY LINE DISPUTES

§ 4.4.1 Boundary Line Disputes And Fences

Fences and walls may or may not be indicative of the property line location. When a fence is constructed on the exact property line itself, each property owner is deemed to have a property interest in the fence and neither owner may obliterate the fence without the permission of the other owner,[823] and both owners are jointly responsible for maintenance of the fence or wall.

Some owners will intentionally construct a fence a couple of feet off of the boundary line for ease of maintenance to avoid questions regarding the ownership of the fence or to avoid disputes as to the exact location of the property line. Whether a fence is intended as a boundary line is normally a question of fact for a jury to decide.[824]

§ 4.4.2 Boundary Line Disputes And Trees Or Vines

Trees on or near boundary lines are often the subject of boundary line and other disputes between neighbors. In Georgia, the ownership of a tree is determined by the location of its trunk rather than its limbs,[825] and ownership of the tree includes ownership of its fruit or product.[826] The types of boundary issues that generally arise are either (1) the limbs of a tree on the land of one property owner overhang the property of an adjoining owner, (2) vines, or the roots of a tree, located on one property invade the property of another and cause damage, or (3) a tree is growing over a boundary line so that portions of the tree lie on either side of the boundary.

§ 4.4.2.1 Overhanging Limbs

In regard to liability for a defective tree, the ordinary rules of negligence apply. In other words, the owner of a tree is liable for injuries or property damage that result from either the tree or one of its limbs falling, only if he knew or reasonably should have known the tree was diseased, decayed or otherwise constituted a dangerous condition.[827] Therefore, if a landowner knows that a tree on his property is diseased and may fall and damage the property of his neighbor, the tree's owner is under a duty to eliminate the danger.

Branches of a tree which encroach onto another owner's property do not constitute a trespass onto the other owner's property. However, the adjoining property owner generally has the right to prune or trim back tree limbs overhanging her property.[828]

§ 4.4.2.2 Invasive Roots Or Vines

Roots from a tree which grown onto a neighbor's property are not thought of as trespassing onto a neighbor's property. However, the adjoining owner would have the right to remove or cut such roots. Nuisance claims have sometimes been brought by property owners against adjoining neighbors when they plant invasive vines that grow onto the neighbor's property. For example, if one neighbor planted kudzu along the property line, the other neighbor might be able to enjoin that owner from maintaining a nuisance which interferes with his quiet enjoyment of his property.

---

823 *Lyons v. Bassford*, 242 Ga. 466, 249 S.E.2d 255 (1978).

824 *Martin v. Patton*, 225 Ga.App. 157, 483 S.E.2d 614 (1997).

825 *Willis v. Maloof*, 184 Ga.App. 349, 361 S.E.2d 512 (1987).

826 Am. Law of Prop., § 19.15, note 11.

827 *Klein v. Weaver*, 265 Ga.App. 390, 593 S.E.2d 913 (2004).

828 Pindar, 1 Ga. Real Estate Law & Procedure § 9-21 (6th ed.).

§ 4.4.2.3   Trees Growing On Boundary Lines

If a tree is on the property line, it would be treated as co-owned by the two abutting property owners in much the same way as a party wall. Following the party wall analogy, neither owner would be entitled to damage that portion of the tree on their side of the property line. In fact, each owner has a duty to maintain the tree and take reasonable steps to guard against any hazardous condition the tree may pose.[829] If a tree on a boundary line becomes diseased and needs to be removed from the property, each owner would owe a duty to help pay for the removal of the diseased tree.

§ 4.4.3   Right To An Unobstructed View And Sunlight

Generally, a property owner does not have a right to an unobstructed view or a right for the free passage of sunlight onto her property.[830] In Georgia, when a property is purchased, the owner receives no protection against a neighboring owner's trees or other structures that may block the owner's scenic view or passage of light onto her property.[831] The reasoning behind this lack of protection is based on the common law principle that a property owner is entitled to use her property for any lawful purpose.[832]

In Georgia, a property owner's respective right to use a property for any lawful purpose is superior to a neighboring owner's right to an unobstructed view and the free passage of sunlight onto her property.[833] Based on this superior right, a property owner may in good faith plant trees and improve their property in a way that obstructs a neighboring property owner's view or passage of sunlight onto the property.[834] Absent an agreement providing otherwise, courts are reluctant to protect an owner's right to a scenic view or sunlight at a neighboring owner's expense by prohibiting her lawful use of the property.[835]

Although an owner may obstruct another owner's view or passage of light while lawfully using her property,[836] a court may interfere with this right in certain circumstances. A property owner only has a superior right to obstruct a neighboring owner's view or passage of light when the owner is using her property in good faith.[837] An owner will not be protected if it is determined that the owner is intentionally obstructing another owner's view.[838] For instance, if an owner intentionally plants trees solely for the purpose of interfering with a neighboring owner's scenic view, the obstructing property owner will not be protected[839] and a court may grant relief to the neighboring owner.[840] As soon as the owner creates an obstruction (in bad faith and) solely for the purpose of interfering with another owner, the neighboring owner can file suit for relief.[841]

If a property owner is concerned about the scenic views or passage of sunlight onto her property, two adjoining land owners may define each party's respective rights in an easement agreement. In this agreement, the adjoining property owner (grantor) would give the property owner whose view is blocked (grantee) the right to remove any obstructions from a specified area to ensure an unobstructed view from her property.[842] To preserve these rights, the following provision should be included in an easement agreement.

---

829   *Id.*

830   Pindar, 1 Ga. Real Estate Law & Procedure, § 14-7 (6th ed.).

831   Pindar, 1 Ga. Real Estate Law & Procedure, § 14-7 (6th ed.).

832   *Hornsby v. Smith*, 191 Ga. 491, 13 S.E.2d 20, 133 A.L.R. 684 (1941).

833   *S.A. Lynch Corp. v. Stone*, 211 Ga. 516, 87 S.E.2d 57 (1955).

834   *S.A. Lynch Corp. v. Stone*, 211 Ga. 516, 87 S.E.2d 57 (1955).

835   *S.A. Lynch Corp. v. Stone*, 211 Ga. 516, 87 S.E.2d 57 (1955).

836   *S.A. Lynch Corp. v. Stone*, 211 Ga. 516, 87 S.E.2d 57 (1955).

837   *Hornsby v. Smith*, 191 Ga. 491, 13 S.E.2d 20, 133 A.L.R. 684 (1941).

838   *Hornsby v. Smith*, 191 Ga. 491, 13 S.E.2d 20, 133 A.L.R. 684 (1941).

839   *Hornsby v. Smith*, 191 Ga. 491, 13 S.E.2d 20, 133 A.L.R. 684 (1941).

840   *Hornsby v. Smith*, 191 Ga. 491, 13 S.E.2d 20, 133 A.L.R. 684 (1941).

841   *Hornsby v. Smith*, 191 Ga. 491, 13 S.E.2d 20, 133 A.L.R. 684 (1941).

842   *Gulf House Ass'n, Inc. v. Town of Gulf Shores*, 484 So.2d 1061 (1985); *Noronha v. Stewart*, 199 Cal.App.3d 485 (1988).

Special Stipulation 60:   Unobstructed View

Grantor reserves, as and for an appurtenance to the real property particularly described and designated as "Parcel ," a perpetual easement of right to an unobstructed view over that portion of the real property described above, to the extent that view will be received and enjoyed by limiting any structure, fence, trees, or shrubs on the property described above, or any part, to a height not extending above a horizontal plane feet above the level of the sidewalk of Street, as the sidewalk level now exists at the junction of the [northern or southern] and [eastern or western] boundary lines of the property described above. Any obstruction of such view above the horizontal plane, except [specify existing obstructions and other desired exceptions, including any exceptions to be allowed for radio and television receiving devices, power and telephone poles and lines other than those required to be buried, and required flues or vents, as well as fixtures required under any building regulations], will be considered an unauthorized interference with such right or easement and will be removed on demand at the expense of [grantee], in the ownership of that real property described above or any part of the property.

Parcel, to which the perpetual easement of right to an unobstructed view is an appurtenance, is described as follows: _____

An implied easement for the free passage of light may be created in limited circumstances.[843] Under the Official Code of Georgia, when an owner sells a property and the light necessary for that property's reasonable enjoyment is obstructed from a neighboring property owned by the same owner (as the first property), the sold property will obtain an implied easement for the free passage of light.[844] This right exists only when a house is located on the sold property and the neighboring lot is vacant.[845] This statute is best illustrated with an example.

For example, John Smith owns a one-story house located on lot 30. John is looking to sell the lot but instead of selling the whole property, he divides the lot into two parcels; parcel A and parcel B. John's one-story house is located on parcel A and parcel B is a vacant lot. John sells parcel A to Jane. Jane's property enjoys ample sunlight because there is nothing on parcel B that is obstructing her light. John Smith then sells parcel B to Larry. Larry decides to build a three-story house on the property, ultimately blocking the passage of sunlight onto Jane's property. In this case, the statute would take effect and give Jane an implied easement for the passage of light through Larry's property onto her property.[846] Therefore, Larry would be restricted in the construction of his property to avoid intruding on Jane's implied easement for sunlight. This situation would be different if parcel B had a house on it at the time parcel A was sold to Jane. If there was a house located on parcel B when the original owner sold Jane the house on parcel A, parcel A would not have enjoyed an implied easement for the free passage of light through parcel B.[847] As stated above, this statute only applies if the adjoining lot was vacant at the time the new owner purchased the property.[848]

---

843   *Weinstock v. Novare Group, Inc.*, 309 Ga.App. 351, 710 S.E.2d 150 (2011).

844   O.C.G.A. § 44-9-2; *Weinstock v. Novare Group, Inc.*, 309 Ga.App. 351, 710 S.E.2d 150 (2011).

845   *Goddard v. Irby*, 255 Ga. 47, 335 S.E.2d 286 (1985).

846   *Goddard v. Irby*, 255 Ga. 47, 335 S.E.2d 286 (1985).

847   *Goddard v. Irby*, 255 Ga. 47, 335 S.E.2d 286 (1985).

848   *Goddard v. Irby*, 255 Ga. 47, 335 S.E.2d 286 (1985).

The enjoyment of this implied easement is based on necessity.[849] Therefore, when the necessity for the light ceases, so does the easement protecting the owner's right to the free passage of light through the neighbor's property.[850] It is not clear what constitutes necessity. Arguably, the definition of this term would depend on the facts and circumstances of each case. For this reason, it is important for property owners who are concerned about the free passage of light [or an unobstructed view] to expressly provide each party's respective rights in an express easement.

§ 4.4.3.1 Solar Easements

During the last twenty years, there has been an increasing interest in solar energy as an alternative source of power to reduce the nation's reliance on imported fuels.[851] In response to this interest, many states, including Georgia, are encouraging solar energy development.[852] However, in order for states to implement successful solar energy programs, a property owner using solar energy devices must have a protected right to access sunlight. Therefore, despite the general rule stating that a property owner does not have a right to the free passage of sunlight through a neighboring property, the state of Georgia recognizes an owner's right to negotiate an easement over a neighboring property for the use of solar energy devices.[853]

Under the Solar Easement Act of 1978, a property owner with solar energy devices may establish a solar easement to negotiate the right to continued access to sunlight.[854] To avoid any confusion, the Act does not create a solar easement; rather, it merely recognizes a specific type of easement that is created between two adjoining landowners. So what is the difference between creating a solar easement and an express easement for sunlight? In the state of Georgia, a solar easement must be obtained for the limited purpose of ensuring the unobstructed exposure of the solar energy device.[855] An easement obtained for any reason other than the limited purpose provided in the Act will not create a solar easement. Overall, creating a solar easement under the Act provides adjoining land owners a specific and recognized right to sunlight for the use of solar energy devices.

An easement obtained for the purpose of ensuring the exposure of an owner's solar energy device must be created in writing.[856] The written device creating and granting the easement must include (i) a definite and certain description of the airspace affected by such easement; and (ii) any terms or conditions under which the solar easement will be granted and terminated.[857] In most cases, solar easements also include the amount the solar device owner is paying the neighboring owner for the easement and any penalties in the event the use of such easement is interfered with. [858]

When creating a solar easement, the adjoining landowners may specify any particular restraints on trees, structures or other objects that may interfere with the solar device's access to sunlight.[859] Therefore, once a solar easement is created over a neighboring owner's property, the solar energy device owner may prevent a neighbor from building improvements or maintaining trees that interfere with the device's sunlight.[860] The parties should make the restrictions as specific and as clear as possible. Overall, parties should following the requirements under the Act when creating a solar easement to avoid any issues that may arise when enforcing the owner's right to access sunlight.

---

849 *S.A. Lynch Corp. v. Stone*, 211 Ga. 516, 87 S.E.2d 57 (1955).

850 *S.A. Lynch Corp. v. Stone*, 211 Ga. 516, 87 S.E.2d 57 (1955).

851 O.C.G.A. § 44-9-21.

852 O.C.G.A. § 44-9-21.

853 O.C.G.A. § 44-9-22.

854 O.C.G.A. § 44-9-21.

855 O.C.G.A. § 44-9-22.

856 O.C.G.A. § 44-9-22.

857 O.C.G.A. § 44-9-23.

858 3 Ga. Forms Legal & Bus. § 24:16.

859 3 Ga. Forms Legal & Bus. § 24:16.

860 3 Ga. Forms Legal & Bus. § 24:16.

§ 4.4.4 Public Restrictions On Tree Removal: Tree Preservation Ordinances

In response to growing concerns about the destruction of trees during rapid urbanization and development, many jurisdictions are enacting tree ordinances designed to protect existing trees and vegetation and require the replacement of trees when preservation is not possible.[861] Tree ordinances are rules and limitations implemented by each city and county designed to protect tress on public and private property. Oftentimes, tree ordinances will limit the property owner's right to remove a particular type of tree without the proper permit.

The purpose of these ordinances is to limit the removal of trees and specify when new trees are required to be planted.[862] Tree ordinances are implemented at the local level and will vary by city and county. For example, DeKalb County's Tree Protection Ordinance[863] imposes a requirement that any "specimen tree"[864] that is removed or cut down must be replaced with replacement trees with one and one half times the removed tree's diameter to offset the burden caused by the initial cutting of the tree. The replacement trees must also be a species of comparable size and quality when the tree has reached maturity.[865] Several jurisdictions in Georgia have enacted tree preservation or vegetation ordinances in recent years. The purpose of enacting these tree ordinances generally concerns environmental, aesthetic and urban design considerations. For example, the City of Atlanta Tree Ordinance states as that the purpose behind this ordinance is to ensure that the city will "continue to enjoy the benefits provided by its urban forest."[866] Moreover, Fulton County states that the purpose behind its tree ordinance is to improve control of soil erosion, moderate storm water runoff, reduce noise and glare, improve aesthetic and scenic amenities, etc.[867]

A common type of tree preservation ordinance requires owners to file an application for tree removal. For example, if a property owner living in Atlanta wants to remove a tree that is close to his property line so he can put up a fence to define the property boundary between his property and the neighbor's property. The owner may not remove the tree without filing an application for tree removal and obtaining a permit.[868] In Atlanta, an owner wanting to remove a tree from his property is required to submit an application for tree removal to the city for a determination if the proposed removal will result in a net loss of trees within the boundaries of the city.[869] According to this ordinance, a property owner is prohibited from moving, destroying or injuring any private tree on her property that is six inches in diameter breast height. Applicants may seek the removal of a diseased tree or one a tree impeding upon a building through the approval of a tree replacement plan.[870] Either way, approval from the city and a permit is required. These ordinances are enforced by the Atlanta Tree Conservation Commission and the failure to comply with such ordinances can result in a $500 penalty for the first offense and a $1,000 penalty for every offense thereafter.

It is important to check with the city or county in which the property is located to determine if any restrictions or requirements exist before removing trees located on the property owner's property.

§ 4.4.5 Private Restrictions On Tree Removal: Homeowners Associations

Even if a property owner complies with her local tree preservation ordinances, the owner may also be limited in removing or trimming trees and structures from her private property if the neighborhood in which the property is

---

861 Zeigler, Rathkopf's The Law of Zoning and Planning, § 20:1.

862 Zeigler, Rathkopf's The Law of Zoning and Planning, § 20:1.

863 DeKalb County, Ga., Ordinance § 14-39.

864 A "specimen tree" is a hardwood or pine tree larger than thirty inches measured "diameter at breast height," ("DBH") or a smaller tree such as a dogwood measuring ten or more inches DBH. DeKalb County, Ga., Ordinance § 14-39(g)(8)(b).

865 DeKalb County, Ga., Ordinance § 14-39.

866 City of Atlanta Ordinance, § 158-28.

867 Fulton County Ordinance, § 26-396.

868 Atlanta, Georgia Municipal Code 158-102.

869 Atlanta, Georgia Municipal Code 158-28.

870 Atlanta, Georgia Municipal Code 158-101(c)(2).

located is subject to recorded covenants restricting these activities (normally set out in what is known as a Declaration of Covenants, Conditions, Restrictions and Easements or CC&Rs). These types of restrictions often prevent the removal of a tree with a caliper of more than a certain number of inches without the approval of the community's architectural control committee. The purpose of these types of covenants is to prevent an owner from clear cutting her lot or removing trees that will alter the tree canopy in a neighborhood. Most of these covenants allow trees to be removed or if they are dead, diseased or if it can be established that the tree roots are clogging sewer lines or threatening the structure of a building.

In Georgia, two parties may contract away or extend their rights regarding the use of real property so long as public policy is not violated.[871] When the property owner purchases property in a neighborhood subject to covenants, the property generally agrees to any regulations and restrictions imposed by the association pertaining to the property. Moreover, courts favor the parties' right to contract freely; therefore, such covenants will only be invalidated if they are clearly contrary to public policy.[872] The restrictive covenants implemented by the homeowners association run with the title to the land and inure to the benefit of all property owners affected by them.[873] Therefore, a homeowners association may validly restrict the owner's removal of trees from her yard without first obtaining permission or approval. The Georgia courts have been consistent in upholding restrictive covenants imposed on property owners by homeowners associations. Homeowners associations are further discussed in § 20.2 (Homeowner Associations).

It is important for the homeowner to check with the city or county in which the property is located to determine the procedure for removing a tree on the property without incurring fines or penalties. Depending on the area, it is likely some type of permit or permission is required from the government. Moreover, if the property is located in a neighborhood regulated by a homeowners association, the property owner should identify any additional regulations regarding tree removal to ensure the appropriate permission is granted to remove the tree or vegetation on the property.

§ 4.5 FIXTURES AND PERSONAL PROPERTY

§ 4.5.1 What Is Considered A Fixture

A Georgia statute provides that anything permanently attached to land or to the buildings is part of the property.[874] It further provides that "anything which is intended to remain permanent in its place even if it is not actually attached to the land is a fixture which constitutes part of the realty and passes with it."[875] The term "fixture" includes all movable things, which, because they are annexed to the property, have the nature of both personalty and realty, regardless of whether they are removable.[876] Whether an item attached to property becomes a fixture depends on the circumstances under which the item was placed upon or attached to the property, the uses to which it is adapted, and the parties who are at issue.[877] However, if the seller wishes to keep a fixture that is normally considered attached to the property and not removable, she may indicate in the purchase agreement or deed that such fixture is to be considered personal property and its possession is to remain with the seller when the sale is consummated.[878] The fixture may be removed as long as the removal does not damage the property.[879] The seller has the ability to either remove the fixtures

---

871 *Godley Park Homeowners Ass'n, Inc. v. Bowen*, 286 Ga.App. 21, 649 S.E.2d 308 (2007).

872 *Bryan v. MBC Partners*, L.P., 246 Ga.App. 549, 541 S.E.2d 124 (2000).

873 *Godley Park Homeowners Ass'n, Inc. v. Bowen*, 286 Ga.App. 21, 649 S.E.2d 308 (2007).

874 O.C.G.A. § 44-1-2.

875 O.C.G.A. § 44-1-6.

876 *Burpee v. Athens Production Credit Ass'n*, 65 Ga.App. 102, 15 S.E.2d 526 (1941).

877 *Wolff v. Sampson*, 123 Ga. 400, 51 S.E. 335 (1905); *State v. Dyson*, 89 Ga.App. 791, 81S.E.2d 217 (1954).

878 *Farrell v. Atlanta Gas Light Co.*, 61 Ga.App. 18, 5 S.E.2d 607 (1939).

879 *Farrell v. Atlanta Gas Light Co.*, 61 Ga.App. 18, 5 S.E.2d 607 (1939).

before the sale or reserve them in an agreement or deed; however, if the seller does neither, the general rule in Georgia states that all fixtures actually or constructively attached to the realty will pass to the buyer in the sale.[880]

There is limited case law in Georgia to assist in determining whether an item is a fixture. This is likely because the cost of litigating whether an item is a fixture outweighs the cost of simply replacing an item which has been removed from the property. Georgia courts have held that whatever is placed in a building to carry out the purpose of the building, or to permanently increase its value for such purpose, and is not intended to be removed but to be permanently used, becomes part of the building.[881] Generally, items such as mailboxes, light fixtures, and ceiling fans are considered fixtures.[882] Georgia courts have said that sewer lines[883] and sheds[884] are fixtures, while mobile homes[885] are not. Courts in other states have found that furnaces[886] and garbage disposals[887] are fixtures, while stereo systems, gas grills, satellite dishes,[888] and track lighting[889] are not fixtures. While court decisions from other states may be looked to for guidance, they do not establish binding precedent in Georgia.

Trees, plants and shrubbery are considered fixtures and are thus part of the property.[890] The general rule in Georgia is that personal property actually or constructively attached to the real property is considered part of the real property.[891] However, it has been established in Georgia that all mature or immature "crops" are personal property, meaning that unless there is a special provision including them in the sale, the "crops" on the property will not be included.[892] In 2001, the definition of crops previously set forth in O.C.G.A. § 44-14-101 was deleted, thus there is no statutory definition of the word. However, the term "crops" has been assumed to include the fruits and products of all plants, trees and shrubs, both annual and perennial. Therefore, if the seller contracts to sell his property and the property contains an apple tree, the seller may remove the apples on the tree before the sale is consummated. The apples are crops because they are the product of the tree; thus, the seller may remove them without incurring liability.

Crops have been distinguished from trees, plants and shrubs located on the property. Trees, plants and shrubs growing in the soil of the property are not considered crops and will generally pass with the property when the sale is consummated.[893] For example, a seller has a large vegetable garden in the rear of her property. The seller contracts to sell the property and prior to closing she pulls all of the ripe and unripe vegetables off the plants. The buyer objects to the removal of the vegetable garden. Does the buyer have a legitimate claim? The answer to this question is usually "no" since the vegetables would likely be seen as crops. However, all other plants, trees and shrubs would be considered fixtures (since they are not crops) and would thus be a part of the property.

In another example, the seller contracts to sell her property to the buyer. The seller has planted and maintained rare flowers and trees on the property. The seller states in the purchase agreement which rare flowers and trees are not

880 *Wolff v. Sampson*, 123 Ga. 400, 51 S.E. 335 (1905).

881 *Waycross Opera-House Co. v. Sossman*, 94 Ga. 100, 20 S.E.252 (1894); *Brigham v. Overstreet*, 128 Ga. 447. 57 S.E. 484 (1907).

882 *Equibank v. U.S.*, 749 F.2d 1176 (5th Cir. 1985) (The court noted that any electrical unit detachable by pulling out a socket will generally be treated as personalty, but where the article is permanently connected to the building's wiring, it is a fixture). Using this analysis, a wired security system in a house would probably be considered a fixture.

883 *Adams v. City of Macon*, 204 Ga. 524, 505 S.E.2d 598 (1948).

884 *Hargrove v. Jenkins*, 192 Ga.App. 83, 383 S.E.2d 636 (1989). Since a playhouse is similar to a shed, it would also likely be considered a fixture.

885 *Homac, Inc. v. Fort Wayne Mtg. Corp.*, 577 F. Supp 1065 (N.D. Ga. 1983).

886 *Rose v. Marlowe's Cafe, Inc.*, 68 Ohio Misc. 2d 9, 646 N.E.2d 271 (1994).

887 *First Nat'l Bank in Dallas v. Whirlpool Corp.*, 517 S.W.2d 262 (Tex. 1974).

888 *Marshall v. Bostic*, 1995 WL 115971, Tenn. Ct. App. (Mar. 15, 1995).

889 *Rose v. Marlowe's Cafe, Inc.*, 68 Ohio Misc. 2d 9, 646 N.E.2d 271 (C.P. 1994). In Georgia, track lighting may be considered the same as any other light fixture; however, this issue has never been litigated before a Georgia appellate court.

890 *Adcock v. Berry*, 194 Ga. 243, 21 S.E.2d 605 (1942).

891 *In re Wright*, 128 B.R. 838 (Bankr. N.D. Ga. 1991).

892 *Chatham Chem. Co. v. Vidalia Chem. Co.*, 163 Ga. 276, 136 S.E. 62 (1926).

893 *Adcock v. Berry*, 194 Ga. 243, 21 S.E.2d 605 (1942).

included in the sale of the property and the buyer agrees. In this case, even though the plants and trees would normally be considered part of the property, the seller explicitly stated in the agreement that such items were not included in the sale. As stated above, the seller has the ability to remove fixtures that would normally be considered part of the property if such removal is stated in the purchase agreement or deed and no damage is done to the property by the removal.[894] In this example, the seller would be able to remove the specified rare flowers and trees without incurring liability.

In another case, a seller of land allegedly sold a shed to a third party after entering into a contract for the sale of the land on which the shed was located but before the closing of the sale of the land.[895] The purchaser of the shed did not remove the shed before the closing of the sale of the land. The buyer of the land contended that the shed was a fixture that could not be removed. The court did not determine who owned the shed as it sent the issue back to the trial court, but noted that it was within the power of the seller to detach fixtures before sale, or to reserve them by contract or deed. If the seller does not do so, the strict rule of the common law controls and all fixtures actually or constructively annexed to the land pass by conveyance of the property even though the contract may describe only the land. Therefore, unless there is some contractual agreement to the contrary, all items should be removed from the property prior to the closing.

The best way to eliminate a dispute over whether a beloved item, such as an heirloom chandelier, is a fixture is to remove the item before listing the property for sale. If this is not possible, it is important to be as specific as possible in the sales contract as to items the seller intends to remove or items that the buyer wants to ensure remain with the property. For example, in today's world of built-in refrigerators or stereo speakers as opposed to the more easily removable type, it is not at all clear whether such refrigerators or speakers would be considered fixtures or personal property. The following contract provision could be added.

> **Special Stipulation 61:   Credit for Removed Fixture at Closing**
>
> *Prior to closing Seller shall have the right to remove the following fixture from the Property:_____. The parties agree that the value of the fixture being removed is $_____. At closing, this amount shall be credited toward the purchase price of the Property.*

§ 4.5.2   The Right To Remove Fixtures

In Georgia, the general rule is all fixtures either actually or constructively attached to the property pass to the new owner with the sale of the property.[896] An owner does have the right to reserve the fixtures by removing them from the property before a sale, or explicitly reserving them in a purchase and sale agreement or property deed.[897] However, if the fixtures are not removed or reserved, the strict common law rule prevails and all fixtures attached to the property will pass to the new owner.[898] In addition, an owner's right to remove fixtures from the property is limited when the property is financed through a mortgage and offered as collateral to secure the repayment of the debt.[899] This section discusses an owner's right to remove fixtures from a mortgaged property in the event of a sale and foreclosure.

§ 4.5.2.1   Removing Fixtures From Mortgaged Property

When purchasing a home, most buyers obtain a mortgage to finance the property and enter into a security deed with the lender to secure the financing. Typically, the buyer secures the loan by granting the lender a security interest in the

---

894 *Wolff v. Sampson*, 123 Ga. 400, 51 S.E. 335 (1905).

895 *Hargrove v. Jenkins*, 192 Ga.App. 83, 383 S.E.2d 636 (1989).

896 *Wolff v. Sampson*, 123 Ga. 400, 51 S.E. 335 (1905); O.C.G.A. § 44-1-6.

897 *Power v. Garrison*, 141 Ga. 429, 81 S.E. 225 (1914).

898 *Wolff v. Sampson*, 123 Ga. 400, 51 S.E. 335 (1905); *Schrampfer v. Lindal Cedar Homes of Georgia, Inc.*, 118 Ga.App. 92, 162 S.E.2d 806 (1968).

899 *Cunningham v. Cureton*, 96 Ga. 489, 23 S.E. 420 (1895).

property.[900] Once the property is offered as collateral to secure the indebtedness, the lender acquires the same title to the property (and its fixtures) that any other buyer purchasing the property would have.[901] Therefore, the owner may not remove the fixtures from a property while there is an outstanding security deed or mortgage, absent an agreement to the contrary.[902] Of course, property owners regularly remove and replace fixtures in real estate all of the time. Lenders largely do not know or care except in situations in which they are foreclosing on the property and discover that the fixtures have been stripped from the property.

Most standard security deeds describe the specific property being offered to secure the loan. For example, the standard Fannie Mae/Freddie Mac Security Deed secures the owner's repayment of the loan by conveying and granting certain property to the lender. In this standard agreement, the property includes, "…all the improvements now or hereafter erected on the property, and all easements, appurtenances, and *fixtures* now or hereafter part of the property." Even if the property's fixtures are not specifically included as part of the collateral, the lender would still have an interest in the fixtures because a mortgage on the land generally gives a lender this right.[903] If the buyer wants to avoid including fixtures as collateral in the security deed, there should be a provision explicitly stating that the fixtures are not included and the owner reserves the right to remove them before the loan is repaid. Otherwise, the fixtures will be included as part of the collateral.

An owner may remove the fixtures from a mortgaged property when the loan from the lender is fully repaid.[904] Most commonly, a loan is repaid in a purchase and sale transaction in which the seller sells a property to a buyer for a price.[905] If a buyer purchases a property and the seller pays off the outstanding loan, the lender no longer holds the property's title[906] and the security interest in the collateral is terminated.[907] Therefore, a seller may reserve or remove the fixtures from the property using the methods mentioned above once the loan is fully repaid.[908]

§ 4.5.2.2   Removing Fixtures From Foreclosed Property

Generally, when a property is foreclosed on, the owner has no right to remove the property's fixtures because the lender has an outstanding security interest in the property.[909] As stated above, a property pledged in a security deed belongs to the lender[910] until the loan is repaid and their security interest is terminated.[911] When a property is foreclosed on due to the owner's inability to repay the mortgage (or loan), the lender has the right to use the collateral offered in the security deed to repay the outstanding debt. If the owner removes the fixtures from a foreclosed property, the owner will be liable to the lender[912] or new owner who purchases the property at a foreclosure sale.[913]

When an owner removes the property's fixtures prior to foreclosure, the lender or new owner may recover the fixtures.[914] The new owner may recover the fixtures because when the property is purchased at a foreclosure sale,

---

900 *Cunningham v. Cureton*, 96 Ga. 489, 23 S.E. 420 (1895).

901 *Cunningham v. Cureton*, 96 Ga. 489, 23 S.E. 420 (1895).

902 *Logan v. Greer*, 36 Ga.App. 200, 136 S.E. 165 (1926).

903 *Cunningham v. Cureton*, 96 Ga. 489, 23 S.E. 420 (1895).

904 O.C.G.A. § 44-14-60; *In re Georgia Steel, Inc.*, 71 B.R. 903 (M.D. Georgia) (1987).

905 *In re Georgia Steel, Inc.*, 71 B.R. 903 (M.D. Georgia) (1987).

906 O.C.G.A. § 44-14-60.

907 *In re Georgia Steel, Inc.*, 71 B.R. 903 (M.D. Georgia) (1987).

908 *In re Georgia Steel, Inc.*, 71 B.R. 903 (M.D. Georgia) (1987).

909 *Cunningham v. Cureton*, 96 Ga. 489, 23 S.E. 420 (1895).

910 *Cunningham v. Cureton*, 96 Ga. 489, 23 S.E. 420 (1895).

911 *In re Georgia Steel, Inc.*, 71 B.R. 903 (M.D. Georgia) (1987).

912 *Burpee v. Athens Production Credit Ass'n*, 65 Ga.App. 102, 15 S.E.2d 526 (1941).

913 *Logan v. Greer*, 36 Ga.App. 200, 136 S.E. 165 (1926).

914 *Logan v. Greer*, 36 Ga.App. 200, 136 S.E. 165 (1926).

the owner acquires the same interest in the property that the lender had under the security deed.[915] In one case, the Logans borrowed money from an insurance company and used their property as collateral in a security deed. At the time the security deed was executed, a windmill was located on the property. Shortly thereafter, the Logans defaulted on their loan and placed the windmill on another property in an attempt to keep the windmill from being sold. The insurance company foreclosed on the property to repay the debt and Greer bought the property at the foreclosure sale. Greer learned that a windmill was once located on the property and demanded it back. The Georgia Court of Appeals ordered the Logans to give the windmill back to Greer; holding that the fixture removed by the prior owner could be recovered by the new owner because the fixture was included in the security deed.[916]

Although an owner of a foreclosed property may not generally remove the fixtures, the owner may remove personal property.[917] Issues often arise over whether an item is a fixture or removable personal property. In a general sense, items that are considered personal property are easily removable, such as appliances. However, the determination will vary depending on the facts and circumstances of each case.[918] For example, the Smith family obtained a loan from a local bank to finance the construction of their new home and secured the loan by offering the property as collateral in a security deed. The security deed covered "all existing and future improvements, structures fixtures and replacements that may now, or at any time in the future, be part of the real estate." When the house was almost complete, a crystal chandelier was placed in the foyer of the home. Shortly thereafter, the Smiths filed bankruptcy and removed the chandelier from the foyer in an attempt to sell it and pay off other debts. Atlantic Southern Bank bought the property at the foreclosure sale. When the bank learned that the chandelier had been removed, they demanded it back arguing that it was a fixture that could not be removed by the prior owner. A U.S. Bankruptcy Court disagreed holding that the chandelier is personal property used for decorative purposes and not a fixture. Therefore, the Smiths had the right to remove the chandelier even if the property was foreclosed on.[919] More information on personal property is located in § 4.5 (Fixtures and Personal Property).

§ 4.5.3 What Is Removable Personal Property

Items such as removable appliances and window treatments are not generally regarded as fixtures, but rather are considered personal property. The seller may elect to include certain personal property such as the refrigerator, washer or dryer, or window treatments in the sale and those items should be identified in the sales contract. The seller also may wish to list items of personal property that could arguably be considered fixtures but that he does not want to remain with the property. One area that is increasingly the subject of disputes is the combination of wiring and separate plug-in receivers that power surround sound systems. The following special stipulations can be used to address this issue.

> **Special Stipulation 62:   Surround Sound System Will Remain with Property**
>
> *Notwithstanding any provision to the contrary contained herein, all portions of the surround sound system currently serving the property including but not limited to wiring, speakers receivers, speaker and receiver cabinetry and all other equipment needed to make the system operational shall remain with the property.*

---

915 *Logan v. Greer*, 36 Ga.App. 200, 136 S.E. 165 (1926).

916 *Logan v. Greer*, 36 Ga.App. 200, 136 S.E. 165 (1926).

917 *In re Smith*, 2008 WL 7390623, U.S. Bankr. Ct. (Oct. 24, 2008).

918 *In re Smith*, 2008 WL 7390623, U.S. Bankr. Ct. (Oct. 24, 2008).

919 *In re Smith*, 2008 WL 7390623, U.S. Bankr. Ct. (Oct. 24, 2008).

§ 4.5.4 Manufactured Homes – A Special Case

Manufactured homes are in a separate class of property because they can be considered either part of the real property, or a separate item of personal property. When manufactured housing is built, of course, it would be considered personal property because it is not permanently attached to land. Even when such housing is installed on a piece of land, it is relatively easy to relocate it. Georgia statutes have taken the special case of manufactured homes and created two statutory procedures; one in which such an item of personal property can be converted to become real property for all legal purposes,[920] and the other by which that manufactured home can again become personal property.

§ 4.5.4.1 Making Manufactured Housing Part Of The Real Property

If a manufactured home is installed on real property yet retains its initial classification as personal property (*i.e.*, a certificate of title is issued for the home as though it were an automobile), both the real property and the mobile home will have their own valuation for ad valorem tax purposes. It is often advantageous to have the mobile home considered part of the realty. When that happens, it will be taxed as part of the real property, and will be subject to the same encumbrances, tax liens, etc. as is the underlying realty.[921]

Any manufactured housing sold after July 1, 2006 will qualify for the conversion to real property if no certificate of title has yet been issued on the home, and if:

(a) the home is to be permanently affixed on real property, so long as at least one person with an ownership interest in the mobile home also has an ownership interest in the real property; and

(b) the owner of the home and all security interests therein file a Certificate of Permanent Location in the land records of the county in which the real property is located.[922]

The certificate must include the name and address of the owner of the home and of the owners of any security interest therein, must attach the manufacturer's original certificate of origin, and must include a description of the real estate on which it will be located (including name of the owner and deed book and page number referencing the chain of title). Once that certificate is properly filed with the Clerk, that manufactured home will thereafter be considered a part of the real property on which it is located.

§ 4.5.4.2 Converting Manufactured Housing From Real To Personal Property

Once manufactured housing has become a part of the real property upon which it is located, it will remain part of the real estate unless a second procedure is followed. This procedure would allow the mobile home to be removed from the property and require it to be registered in the manner of an automobile. The procedure is available if:

(a) the home is to be removed from the real property with the written consent of the owner of the real property and holders of any security interests therein; and

(b) the owner of the real property and holders of any security interests therein sign and file a Certificate of Removal from Permanent Location (setting forth in essence the same identifying information as set forth above, plus the title number formerly assigned to the home, if applicable).[923]

The Certificate must be filed both with the state revenue commissioner as well as with the land records in the county where the real property is located.[924] The home will thereafter be dealt with a personal property, subject to separate taxation, etc.

---

920 O.C.G.A. § 8-2-183.1.

921 O.C.G.A. § 8-2-183.1(c).

922 O.C.G.A. § 8-2-183.1(a).

923 O.C.G.A. § 8-2-183.1(b).

924 O.C.G.A. § 8-2-183.1(a)(2).

§ 4.5.5   Use Of Bills Of Sale And Financing Statements

If the contract between the parties includes the sale of personal property that would not be considered part of real property under the statutory definitions outlined above, the parties may want to have a bill of sale prepared. The bill of sale identifies the value of the personal property transferred from the seller to the buyer. If the buyer is not financing the purchase of the personal property the bill of sale is simply evidence of the value of the property transferred. The Georgia Association of REALTORS® has an exhibit in its forms to use when a bill of sale is needed.[925]

The sale of large amounts of personal property is common in the sale of vacation and second-home property. In such situations, sellers will often want to characterize the value of the personal property as being as high as possible to minimize the seller's gain on the sale of the property. However, the higher the value of the personal property, the more difficult it may be for the buyer to obtain mortgage financing, since such property is not normally viewed as being part of the security collateral.

In the event the seller is financing the sale of the personal property, the seller may want the buyer to execute a security agreement and UCC Financing Statement and file the same in the county records where the property is located. The UCC Financing Statement is used to document the lender's interest in that property.[926] An example of when such a statement would be useful is in the case of a seller who sells a furnished house and finances the entire transaction. A security agreement and properly filed UCC Financing Statement would secure the seller's interest in the furniture and appliances sold with the real estate. In the event the buyer defaults in making required payments, the seller could then bring an action to foreclose on the real property and recover the personal property covered by the security agreement.[927] Generally, institutional lenders do not file UCC Financing Statements in residential transactions. However, in commercial transactions, it is common for a lender to file a UCC Financing Statement for certain fixtures and personal property. It should also be noted that UCC Financing Statements have to be refiled at regular intervals to remain effective.

§ 4.5.6   Fixtures Checklist And Seller's Property Disclosure Statement

The GAR Seller's Property Disclosure Statement includes a fixtures checklist so that sellers can identify the fixtures and other personal property that will remain with the real estate.[928] The idea behind the checklist is to minimize disputes between buyers and sellers by having the seller clearly disclose to the buyer what fixtures and personal property will remain with the property prior to the parties entering into a contract. The GAR Contracts for residential property provide that the Seller's Property Disclosure Statement is attached to the contract and incorporated therein.[929]

If fixtures or other items identified on the Seller's Property Disclosure Statement checklist are not checked as remaining with the property, they can be removed. If the property contains a fixture or other item that is not on the fixtures checklist, the common law of fixtures would apply in determining whether the fixture may be removed from the property. As noted above, the common law provides that personal property can generally be removed while fixtures remain with the property.

If the property contains an item that is not listed on the GAR Property Disclosure Statement and it is unclear whether the item is a fixture or personal property, the seller wishing to retain the item should include language in the contract to exclude the item from the sale. The GAR Property Disclosure Statement provides a space where such items can be listed.

---

925   GAR Form F136, Personal Property Agreement.

926   O.C.G.A. § 11-9-502, *et seq.*

927   The seller also may include the personal property in the security deed to secure the seller's interest in the property transferred.

928   GAR Form F50, Seller' Property Disclosure Statement.

929   GAR Form F20.

While the GAR Contract states in paragraph 1 that the "Property" includes "all fixtures, landscaping, improvements and appurtenances," this is nothing more than a statement of the common law with respect to fixtures. While this provision is inconsistent with the fixtures checklist in the Seller's Property Disclosure Statements (since it allows the Seller to remove certain fixtures), the exhibit would control over the main body of the GAR Contracts.

§ 4.5.6.1 When There Is More Than One Of A Particular Type Of Fixture

If an item is checked on the fixtures checklist as remaining with the property, all items with that particular description remain. For example, if light fixtures are identified as staying with the property, all light fixtures stay. If "refrigerator" is identified as staying, all refrigerators stay.

The fixtures checklist includes two spaces where the seller can make modifications, additions or deletions to the checklist. So, for example, if a seller wants to remove one ceiling fan but leave the rest, the seller should indicate this in the appropriate space.

§ 4.5.6.2 Seller's Property Disclosure Statement Not Attached To Contract

The GAR Contract for residential property assumes that the Seller's Property Disclosure Statement is attached. What should the purchaser do if the Disclosure Statement is not available to be attached to an offer?

The preferred way of handling this would be for the buyer to contact the seller and request that a disclosure statement be provided before an offer is made. In practice, however, this may not always be an option. In such situations, the buyer should both (1) include a statement of what fixtures and other items he wants to remain with the property, and (2) use a special stipulation such as the one below.

> **Special Stipulation 63:   Additional Time to Attach Seller's Property Disclosure Statement**
>
> *The Seller's Property Disclosure Statement is not attached hereto. Seller shall have three days from the Binding Agreement Date to provide Buyer with a properly and fully completed Seller's Property Disclosure Statement. In the event that Seller fails to timely provide the Statement then Buyer may terminate this Agreement without penalty by providing written notice to Seller. The Due Diligence Period referenced herein shall commence on the date that the Seller's Property Disclosure Statement is delivered to Buyer.*

The special stipulation above does not give the buyer any recourse to terminate the contract should the buyer be dissatisfied with a condition revealed in the Seller's Property Disclosure Statement. A buyer who wishes to have some protection against such a possibility should only use the special stipulation above if the property is being sold subject to a right to terminate the contract.[930]

§ 4.5.7 Failure To Timely Remove A Fixture

Under common law all fixtures, whether actually or constructively attached to the property, pass to the purchaser upon the execution of the deed unless the contract provides otherwise.[931]

The fixtures checklist contained in the GAR Seller's Property Disclosure Statement provides that the seller must remove fixtures or other items that are not included in the sale of the property prior to closing or the transfer of possession of the property to the buyer, whichever is later. Sellers with a large item to remove, such as a play-set, must make their removal plans in advance or include a special stipulation in the contract allowing for the fixtures to be removed after closing. The following is an example of such a stipulation.

---

930   *See* Chapter 8 (Appraisals and Other Contingencies) regarding "free look" issues.

931   *Burpee v. Athens Production Credit Ass'n*, 65 Ga.App. 102, 15 S.E.2d 526 (1941).

Special Stipulation 64:   Allowing Seller Access to Remove Personal Property and Fixtures After Closing

Notwithstanding any provision to the contrary contained herein, Seller shall have the right within _____ days from the date of closing to enter upon the Property after notice to Buyer and remove the following fixture(s) and item(s): (describe). Buyer agrees to permit Seller to remove the above referenced fixture(s) and item(s) and specifically grants Seller the right to come onto the Property within the above time frame to do so. If any fixture or item Seller has a right to remove is located within any residential dwelling on the Property, Seller shall not enter any such dwelling without first notifying the Buyer and arranging a mutually convenient time for the item or fixture to the removed. If Seller has not removed the fixture(s) and item(s) in a timely manner (except where the failure to remove is due to the fault of the Buyer or an inability of the parties to arrange a mutually convenient time for the Seller to remove the item or fixture), Seller shall lose the right to thereafter remove said fixture(s) and item(s). In removing the above referenced fixture and/or item, Seller shall have no obligation to repair the specific area where the above-referenced fixture and/or item was attached to the Property. However, Seller agrees to indemnify and hold Buyer harmless from any damage caused in physically removing the above referenced fixture and/or item from the Property and any claims involving personal injury arising out of or related to the above referenced fixture and/or item from the Property. This provision shall specifically survive the closing.

In the absence of such a provision, the seller will lose the right to take the fixture or personal property after the closing or transfer of the property.

§ 4.5.8   Duty To Restore After The Removal Of A Fixture

What is the seller's obligation to restore or repair the property after the removal of a fixture? Under common law, the seller could remove fixtures so long as they did not materially injure the value of the real estate.[932]

The GAR Property Disclosure Statement provides that in removing fixtures the seller shall use reasonable care to prevent damage and, if necessary, to restore the property to its original condition. The GAR Contracts provide that the seller shall deliver the property clean and free of debris.[933] It is clear, therefore, that if the seller removes a light fixture and in the process pulls down a large portion of the ceiling, she must fix the damage. There can, however, still be room for disagreement between the buyer and the seller. If the seller removes a light fixture is she entitled to leave the wires and junction box exposed or must he patch the ceiling? Must the seller replace the light with another fixture? If so, must it be of a similar design or value of the one removed? These are questions that clearly should be addressed in the contract. The special stipulations below are examples of some of the different approaches which can be taken in this area.

Special Stipulation 65:   Seller Has No Obligation to Repair Damage While Removing Fixtures

Seller, in removing the _____ from the_____ is not required to replace the said item or fixture or to patch, paint or repair the area from which the item or fixture was removed. Notwithstanding the above, Seller shall use reasonable care to prevent damage to the Property in removing the item or fixture.

---

932 *Lasch v. Columbus Heating & Ventilating Co.*, 174 Ga. 618, 163 S.E. 486 (1932).

933 GAR Forms F20 & F23.

Special Stipulation 66:   Seller's Obligation to Replace Removed Fixtures

Seller shall have the right to remove the following item from the Property: _____ _____. Seller shall replace this item with an item paid for by Seller but selected by Buyer and available at _____, at least _____ days prior to the date of closing. Said item shall not exceed a cost of $_____, excluding the cost of any labor to install the same. In the event Buyer fails to close on the purchase of the Property due to no fault of Seller, Buyer agrees that the fixture or item selected by Buyer shall become the property of Seller and Buyer hereby relinquishes any interest in the same. The cost of labor, if any, to install the replacement fixture or item shall be paid for by the Seller.

Special Stipulation 67:   Increasing Seller's Obligation to Repair Damage While Removing Fixtures

Seller, in removing the _____ from the Property, shall prior to closing, patch, paint, or otherwise repair the portion of the Property to which the said item or fixture was attached in a good and workmanlike manner such that there is no obvious evidence that the said item or fixture was previously affixed to the Property. The repair work shall be performed by _____.

Special Stipulation 68:   Seller to use Reasonable Efforts to Patch or Repair Damage While Removing Fixtures

Seller, in removing the _____ from the Property, shall use reasonable care to patch, paint, or otherwise repair the portion of the Property to which the said item or fixture was attached. The parties acknowledge that the area in which the repair work shall be performed shall extend no further than _____ feet from where the fixture/item was physically attached to the Property and that Seller's obligations shall only be to use reasonable efforts to have the patch and repair work blend in with the existing improvements. The repair work shall be completed in a good and workmanlike manner prior to closing.

Special Stipulation 69:   Repairs Paid by Seller, Limit on Cost

Seller shall not be obligated to pay more than $_____ for the following repairs and replacements: _____ _____. Buyer shall be obligated to reimburse Seller at closing for any additional costs in excess of this amount. At or prior to closing, Seller shall provide Buyer with copies of paid invoices to verify that Seller has fulfilled Seller's obligations hereunder.

Special Stipulation 70:   Repair or Replace Named Items After Closing (Seller's Obligation Survives)

Seller warrants that the following item(s), which Buyer is unable to inspect, shall be in good working order and repair for a period of _____ days from the date of closing: _____ _____. If any of the above-referenced items are found not to be in good working order and repair, and notice of the same is given to Seller during the warranty period, Seller shall immediately repair and/or replace said items at Seller's sole cost and expense, so that said items are in good working order and repair. This provision shall survive the closing.

Special Stipulation 71:   Removal of Chandelier

Prior to Closing Seller shall have the right to remove the chandelier in the dining room of the Property. If Seller removes the chandelier Seller shall: (a) use its best efforts not to damage any portion of the ceiling or the supports to which the chandelier is attached, (b) provide Buyer with an allowance of $_____ to purchase a new chandelier or light fixture, and (c) cause the new chandelier to be attached to the ceiling of the dining room. Buyer shall be responsible for paying for any additional bracing supports necessary to properly support the new chandelier or light fixture and any upgrades, if any, to the electrical system needed for the new chandelier or light fixture to function properly. Any unused portion of the allowance shall be the property of the Seller.

Seller shall be responsible for repairing in a first-class professional manner any damage caused in either removing the old chandelier or installing the new chandelier or light fixture selected by Buyer. Buyer must select a new chandelier or light fixture, pay for the same, and provide it to the Seller at least 14 days prior to the date of Closing set forth in the Agreement or in any amendment thereto. If Buyer fails to provide a new chandelier or light fixture to Seller within the time frame set forth above, Seller shall have no obligation to install the new light fixture or chandelier. The amount Buyer paid for the new chandelier or light fixture, up to the amount of the allowance, shall be reimbursed to the Buyer by Seller at Closing, provided that Buyer produces a paid receipt for the chandelier or light fixture selected by Buyer.

The **RED BOOK**

CHAPTER 5

EARNEST
MONEY

OVERVIEW

This chapter will address the broker's duties in holding earnest money. In addition, this chapter discusses the mechanics of interpleader actions and the legal standard for when a real estate broker may interplead disputed earnest money funds.

§ 5.1 WHAT THE GAR CONTRACT PROVIDES

It is customary for a buyer to deposit a sum of money to show the buyer's commitment to purchasing the property. This is commonly referred to as earnest money. Some new construction contracts may refer to earnest money as a construction deposit.[934] The nature of the payment will be determined by the intent of the parties rather than how it is labeled. A contract to buy and sell property is enforceable even when it does not provide for payment of any deposit.

The GAR Contracts contemplate the payment of earnest money to a third party known as a "Holder." It also sets out the type of account into which the earnest money must be deposited, what the earnest money may be used for, when and how the Holder may disburse the earnest money, and what the Holder should do in the event of a dispute about the earnest money.

§ 5.2 PAYMENT OF EARNEST MONEY

The GAR Contract requires that the earnest money be deposited in an escrow account within five banking days from the Binding Agreement Date or the date it is actually received by the Holder. This requirement is based upon the broker's obligation to timely deposit all trust funds coming into its possession.[935] The earnest money may be paid by check, wire transfer, or cash.

§ 5.2.1 Payment By Check

The GAR Purchase and Sale Agreement provides that if the earnest money check is not honored for any reason, the Holder is required to immediately notify all parties, even if she believes that the bank has made a mistake. After the Holder's notification, the buyer then has three banking days to deliver good funds to the Holder. If the buyer does not timely deliver good funds, the seller has the right to terminate the agreement within seven days upon written notice to the buyer.[936] If the seller does terminate the agreement within that time, the seller's right to terminate the agreement will be waived. The GAR Contract does not allow a seller to sue a buyer for damages in the event an earnest money check is dishonored or not timely paid. This approach allows for greater efficiency and thus the seller's remedy is termination of the agreement. It should be noted that even without earnest money, the contract is still enforceable.[937] Therefore, the seller may choose to terminate or waive the earnest money requirement.

§ 5.2.1.1 Civil Remedies

Sellers using a non-GAR contract, however, may sue the writer of a bad check for damages by following the statutory procedure.[938] In Georgia, a person to whom the check was payable may file a civil suit against the party who issued the dishonored check.[939] Generally, this involves a seller suing a buyer because the seller is the party receiving the bad check.

---

934 *Magnum v. Jones*, 205 Ga. 661, 54 S.E.2d 603 (1949). A sales contract may be valid without the payment of earnest money, if the contract is based on mutual promises to buy and sell.

935 The Georgia Real Estate Commission requires licensees to "place all cash, checks or other items of value received by the licensee in a brokerage capacity into the custody of the broker holding the licensee's license as soon after receipt as is practicably possible." GREC. Sub. Reg. 520-1-08(1)(b). Additionally, "unless otherwise agreed to in writing by the party or parties at interest, the broker holding such cash or check shall promptly deposit said funds in a federally insured checking account designated by the bank as a trust account ...." GREC Sub. Reg. 520-1-.08(1)(d).

936 GAR Form F20.

937 *Brack v. Brownlee*, 246 Ga. 818, 273 7S.E.2d 390 (1980). The court held that an agreement is enforceable if it has sufficient consideration, which may be in the form of mutual promises or any other form, such as earnest money.

938 O.C.G.A. § 13-6-15.

939 O.C.G.A. § 13-6-15(a) and (c).

However, what if the bad check is made out to a real estate broker and held in trust for the benefit of the seller in the transaction? Based on the language of the statute, a real estate broker that received a bad check could sue the party who issued the dishonored check. However, the seller to whom the check was being held in trust for would most likely not be able to sue the buyer to recover the amount on the bad check because the check was not made out to them.

Once it is discovered that a check has been dishonored, the person receiving the check must first send the party who issued the bad check a written demand for payment.[940] The written demand for payment must be sent to the address printed on the check or the party's last known address by certified mail, overnight delivery, or first-class mail.[941] The party who issued the dishonored check then has ten (10) days from the date the demand was received to pay the full amount on the check to the payee.[942] If the party does not tender such payment within that time, the seller may pursue a civil claim for the double amount owed on the check, but no more than $500, plus any court costs incurred by taking such action.[943]

§ 5.2.1.2 Criminal Penalties

Any person who knowingly writes a bad check may also endure criminal penalties.[944] In Georgia, a person who draws, executes or delivers a check for payment knowing that it will not be honored commits the crime of deposit account fraud.[945] Under the Code, a person "knows" a check will not be honored if that person has no account with the bank listed on the bad check at the time it was made, or the check bounced for insufficient funds and that person failed to deliver the amount due to the bank within 10 days of receiving notice of the same.[946]

Deposit account fraud can be either a misdemeanor or a felony depending on the amount issued on the bad check.[947] A person will be guilty of a misdemeanor if the amount of the bad check is $1,499 or less.[948] If a person commits such a misdemeanor, she will be liable for a fine comparable to the amount issued on the bad check, or imprisonment up to 12 months, or both.[949] If the amount of the bad check is for $1,500 or more, the person will be guilty of a felony and shall receive a fine not less than $500 but not more than $5,000, imprisonment up to three years, or both.[950]

§ 5.2.2 Payment In Cash

While most earnest money is paid by check or wire transfer, there are circumstances when earnest money is paid in cash. The cash payment may be placed or held in the broker's escrow account instead of a separate designated account if the real estate broker is licensed in Georgia.[951] Although the Georgia Real Estate Commission allows cash as an acceptable form of earnest money, a broker can always establish the terms under which she will act as the escrow holder when holding this type of payment. If a broker is uncomfortable accepting a large amount of cash, the broker can simply announce that she is unwilling to act as the holder of the earnest money.[952] For obvious reasons, the broker

---

940 O.C.G.A. § 13-6-15(c).

941 O.C.G.A. § 13-6-15(c).

942 O.C.G.A. § 13-6-15(c).

943 O.C.G.A. § 13-6-15(a).

944 O.C.G.A. § 16-9-20(a).

945 O.C.G.A. § 16-9-20(a).

946 O.C.G.A. § 16-9-20(a).

947 O.C.G.A. § 16-9-20(b) and (c).

948 O.C.G.A. § 16-9-20(b)(1) and (2).

949 O.C.G.A. § 16-9-20(b)(1) and (2).

950 O.C.G.A. § 16-9-20(b)(3).

951 O.C.G.A. § 44-3-112(a).

952 *Fickling & Walker Company v. Giddens Construction Company*, 258 Ga. 891, 376 S.E.2d 655 (1989).

should not accept any cash without giving a written receipt for the funds and keeping a copy of the same for the record. Moreover, if the amount of earnest money exceeds $10,000, the Holder would have an obligation to report the same as discussed in § 5.15 (Law Against Money Laundering).

§ 5.2.3　Payment By Wire Transfer

If the earnest money has already been wired to the broker's escrow account at the time the contract is entered into, it effectively is the same thing as the Holder having received cash. Nevertheless, the Holder may want to add the following special stipulation to make it clear that the money on deposit is for the particular transaction at hand.

> **Special Stipulation 72:　Purpose of Wire-Transferred Funds**
>
> *Holder has received a wire transfer of $_____ from Buyer, which funds are presently in Holder's escrow account. Buyer acknowledges that these funds are to be held as earnest money in the transaction and disbursed under the terms and conditions of this Agreement.*

If the funds are to be wired after the Binding Agreement Date, the parties should include Special Stipulation 79: (Delayed delivery of earnest money).

§ 5.2.4　Payment By Money Order

Payment of earnest money may also be via money order. However, the GAR Contract does not specifically contemplate the Holder receiving earnest money by money order. Therefore, if a money order is going to be used to pay the earnest money, a stipulation should be added to this effect.

> **Special Stipulation 73:　Earnest Money Paid by Money Order**
>
> *All parties acknowledge and agree that the earnest money in this transaction of $ _____ has been paid by money order.*

Money orders are generally considered to be more reliable than personal checks, since the buyer must purchase the money order from some third party (*i.e.*, the United States Postal Service, food stores, convenience stores). However, unlike a personal check, there is no way to be certain as to the source of the funds used to purchase the money order. As a result, money orders can be a favorite vehicle for money laundering. Additionally, since money orders are not processed through the Federal Reserve System as are checks, it may take longer for any irregularities to be reported back to the Holder. Finally, while United States Postal Services money orders are considered to be difficult to counterfeit, the same cannot be said for money orders from food stores, convenience stores, and other non-governmental or non-quasi governmental issuers.

§ 5.2.5　Tangible Property Used As Earnest Money

If the buyer and seller are in agreement, there is nothing that prohibits tangible personal property from being used as the equivalent of earnest money in a real estate transaction. So, for example, a painting, piece of jewelry, sculpture, antique piece of furniture or any other tangible piece of property can all be used as the equivalent of earnest money in a real estate transaction. Reaching an agreement as to who is going to hold the property being treated as earnest money and where the property will be held can create other issues. There is no requirement that requirement that real estate licensees place such tangible personal property into an escrow account. Georgia license law only requires money belonging to others to be placed in an escrow account.[953] However, tangible personal property used as earnest money would still have to be deposited with the broker.[954] For example, if a piece of art is going to be held as earnest

---

[953]　*See* Generally, O.C.G.A. § 43-40-25(b)(3).

[954]　Georgia Real Estate Commission Substantitive Rule 520-1-08 which provides that "A license shall place all cash checks or other items of value received by the licensee in a brokerage capacity into the custody of the broker holding the licensee's license as receipt as is practicably possible."

money in the transaction, where is the art going to be held while it is serving as earnest money? If the buyer proceeds to closing, is the value of the work of art going to be applied to the purchase price of the property or not? If artwork is going to be used as earnest money in a real estate transaction, the following special stipulation can be used.

Special Stipulation 74:   Art as Earnest Money

Notwithstanding any provision to the contrary contained herein, all parties agree that the oil painting with the following dimensions _____ a photograph of which is attached hereto (hereinafter "Art") shall be held by Holder in lieu of monetary earned money. The Art shall be stored in a locked closet in Holder's office. Buyer and Seller acknowledge that no other special precaution shall be taken to secure the Art and it is therefore subject to being stolen in the unlikely event of a break-in. In the event Buyer proceeds with the purchase of the Property, the Art shall be returned to Buyer at the closing and its value shall not be deducted from the purchase price of the Property. In the event Buyer fails to close due to Buyer's default, all parties agree that Holder, upon a reasonable interpretation of the Purchase and Sale Agreement and notice to all parties as provided elsewhere herein, shall tender the Art to Seller as full and complete liquidated damages arising out of Buyer's breach it being agreed that the value of the Art is a reasonable pre-estimate of Seller's actual damages and is not a penalty.

§ 5.2.6   Construction Deposits And/Or Earnest Money

Although not a part of the GAR New Construction Contract, many builder contracts require the buyer to pay a construction deposit to be used by the seller to pay the initial costs of construction. This deposit may be in addition to,[955] or in lieu of, the payment of earnest money and is typically treated the same as earnest money upon a default of the buyer.

The main reason for a builder to collect a construction deposit is for assurance that the buyer intends to consummate the transaction. When building a custom home, the builder may wish to collect the builder's initial overhead or base costs to reduce the builder's out of pocket expenses if the contract later falls through. In such case, collecting the construction deposit is only the first condition to be fulfilled before a builder will commence construction. When building custom homes, most builders require a firm mortgage commitment and the release of all contractual contingencies, especially any financing contingency or any contingency regarding the buyer's sale of an existing home.

The GAR New Construction Contract does not provide for the payment of a construction deposit. If the builder wishes to collect a construction deposit, the following stipulation can be used.

Special Stipulation 75:   Payment of Construction Deposit

Provided that Seller is not in default of this Agreement, Buyer shall pay to Seller the following sums as a construction deposit:

$_____ on _____ [date];

$_____ on _____ [date]; and

$_____ on _____ [date].

Seller shall be authorized to immediately use said funds solely for the construction of the improvements on the Property. This construction deposit shall be non-refundable except where the Seller is in default of its obligations under this Agreement.

---

955 The HBA's New Home Purchase and Sale Agreement.

When a construction deposit is required, most contracts provide that the construction deposit is non-refundable and treat the deposit the same as earnest money upon a default of the buyer. More specifically, the contract will provide that the seller can retain any such construction deposit as liquidated damages upon the buyer's breach. The builder will also typically reserve the right to bring an action for specific performance or the right to pursue actual damages. A builder may also wish to limit the amount of damages that the buyer can claim in the event of the builder's breach. The following stipulation, which also provides for the payment of broker commissions upon the buyer's default, may be used to provide for these options.

> **Special Stipulation 76: Construction Deposit and Other Deposits as Liquidated Damages**
>
> *If Seller elects to terminate due to the default of Buyer, Seller may elect to retain all construction deposits and other payments made by Buyer hereunder as agreed upon liquidated damages, it being acknowledged that it is impossible to more precisely estimate the specific damages to be suffered by Seller, and that this is a reasonable estimate of such damages and the parties hereto expressly acknowledge and intend that this provision shall be a provision for the retention of the construction deposit and other sums paid hereunder as liquidated damages and not as a penalty pursuant to the provisions of O.C.G.A § 13 6 7, whereupon all rights, liabilities and obligations created under the terms and provisions of this Agreement shall be deemed null and void and of no further force and effect.*
>
> *Alternatively, Seller may elect to seek enforcement of this Agreement by specific performance. Upon default by Buyer prior to closing, Buyer shall, notwithstanding anything to the contrary herein, also immediately pay the full amount of the real estate commissions due hereunder. Listing Broker and Selling Broker may jointly or independently pursue Buyer for that portion of the commission which they would have otherwise received had this transaction closed. If prior to closing Seller defaults under this Agreement then Buyer as its sole and exclusive remedy shall be entitled to the following: (a) the return of Buyer's construction deposit and the other monies paid hereunder from Buyer to Seller, and (b) the sum of $250 as full and complete liquidated damages, it being agreed that it is impossible to precisely estimate the actual damages to be suffered by Buyer in the event of a default by Seller and that the same is a reasonable pre-estimate of Buyer's actual damages and is not intended as a penalty under O.C.G.A § 13-6-7. Thereafter, all further rights, obligations, and liabilities created hereunder shall be deemed terminated and of no further force and effect.*

§ 5.2.6.1 Protecting Buyer's Earnest Money And/Or Deposit

In many new home sales contracts, builders provide that the deposit money can be deposited into company accounts to pay construction costs or other expenses. There is a risk that the buyer will either have to wait a long time before receiving a refund in the event of a dispute or not get a refund at all if the builder has financial problems. To protect themselves, buyers should perform background checks on the builder, such as contacting the local homebuilder's association or Better Business Bureau to see if any complaints exist against the builder.

When substantial amounts of the buyer's money will be used for construction, some buyers may want to pay certain vendors directly for materials and supplies. Other buyers may want the money deposited with an escrow agent who disburses only in accordance with a specific construction draw schedule.

If the buyer is to provide substantial funds to the builder, the buyer may want to require the builder to execute a note and deed to secure debt on the property in favor of the buyer. Receipt of a promissory note and deed to secure debt will give the buyer a security interest in the property, and with it a right to accelerate and foreclose on the deed to secure debt if the seller defaults. Such a provision also includes a requirement that the buyer execute a quitclaim deed in favor of the builder to satisfy the deed to secure debt if the buyer defaults on the buyer's obligations. The quitclaim deed is generally held by the broker or the attorney representing the builder.

Although such a procedure may give the buyer some additional security, the security deed for the earnest money will generally be subordinate to the lender's construction loan or other loans and judgments against the property. For example, if there is a first priority construction loan of $200,000 on the property and the buyer has a security deed in an inferior position for $50,000, the buyer can still get wiped out if there is a foreclosure by the construction lender. To determine the priority of the security deed for earnest money or a construction deposit, it is recommended that a title search be performed before entering into such an agreement.

§ 5.2.7 Payment Of Earnest Money When Buyer Has A Right To Terminate

When the buyer has a due diligence period during which the buyer can terminate the agreement, some thought should be given to whether any special stipulation needs to be made for the handling of earnest money. If the payment of the earnest money is made by check, and the holder of the earnest money is a real estate licensee, Georgia license law provides that the broker shall not return the earnest money until the check has cleared.[956] If the buyer terminates the agreement shortly after it is entered into, the buyer may have to wait several weeks to get the earnest money back. If the buyer wants to ensure that all or a portion of the earnest money is repaid sooner, the buyer may want to provide in the purchase and sale agreement that the earnest money check will not be deposited until the due diligence period expires or is waived without the buyer terminating the Purchase and Sale Agreement. The special stipulation below is an example of this type of provision.

Special Stipulation 77: Delayed Deposit of Earnest Money

Buyer and Seller expressly agree that Buyer's earnest money check of $_____ paid pursuant to this Agreement shall be held by Holder and not deposited into Holder's trust account until after the Due Diligence Period referenced herein has expired without Buyer electing to terminate this Agreement. Upon the occurrence of this event, Holder shall deposit the earnest money check into Holder's trust account within three (3) business days thereafter. If Buyer elects to terminate this Agreement during the Due Diligence Period, Buyer shall be entitled to the return of Buyer's earnest money without penalty.

An approach that will likely be more acceptable to a seller is for a portion of the earnest money to be deposited and for the buyer to provide a check for the remainder of the earnest money to be deposited when the buyer's termination right has either been waived by the buyer or has expired. The following stipulation may be used for such situations.

Special Stipulation 78: Delayed Payment of Additional Earnest Money

In addition to the earnest money of $_____ held by Holder, Buyer shall deposit additional earnest money of $_____ by check with Holder no later than three (3) days from the date that the Due Diligence Period referenced herein expires. Holder shall deposit this check for additional earnest money in Holder's trust account within five (5) business days of the receipt of said check.

In addition, there are often situations in which the earnest money is not deposited with the holder thereof until some period of time after the parties have entered into a contract. The special stipulation below can be used in such situations.

956 GREC Sub. Reg. 520-1-08(3)(c).

Special Stipulation 79: Delayed Delivery of Earnest Money

All parties acknowledge and agree that Holder is not presently holding earnest money in this transaction. Buyer agrees to deposit with Holder earnest money of $_____ by [select one; the box not checked shall not be a part of this Agreement]: _____ check or _____ wire transfer of immediately available funds, within _____ days from the Binding Agreement Date. In the event Buyer fails to timely deposit the above-referenced earnest money with the Holder, Seller shall have the right within seven (7) days after being notified that the earnest money has not been received to terminate this Agreement upon notice to Buyer. In the event, Seller elects not to terminate this Agreement within the time frame specified above, the obligation of Buyer to deposit earnest money hereunder shall be waived and the Purchase and Sale Agreement shall proceed without earnest money.

§ 5.2.8 Payment Of Earnest Money By Third Party

On occasion, the earnest money will be paid on the buyer's behalf by someone other than the buyer. In such a situation, the earnest money should be handled and disbursed by the holder thereof in the same manner as if the buyer had deposited the earnest money with the holder. In other words, when the earnest money is paid by a third party instead of the buyer, it should be treated as a loan from the third party to the buyer. Consequently, if the buyer breaches the purchase contract and the earnest money is paid as liquidated damages to the seller, any claim by the third party for the loss of the earnest money should be brought against the buyer rather than against the broker.

While there is little case law on this point, the purpose of earnest money means that the buyer is put at risk if she does not perform under the contract. If the payment of the earnest money by a third party were to somehow give that party special rights regarding those funds, it would defeat the purpose of the earnest money.

One risk with earnest money paid by a third party is the potential for the third party to argue that the money was paid pursuant to a different transaction than the one for which the broker believes it is being held or that it was to simply be held by the holder without being applied to any transaction. To avoid this risk, the holder of the earnest money should try to get the third party to sign the following type of acknowledgement.

Payment of Earnest Money by Third Party

Re: Offer to Purchase Property dated _____, 20___ by and between _____ ("Buyer") and _____ ("Seller") for property located at the following address _____ _____ _____ _____. The undersigned hereby acknowledges that she is giving _____ ("Holder") a ☐ check or ☐ wire of $ _____ to be used as earnest money in the above referenced transaction. The undersigned acknowledges that: 1) the earnest money is at risk and may be paid to the Seller in the event the Buyer breaches the Purchase and Sale Agreement with the Seller; and 2) the undersigned shall in no event have no right to the return of the earnest money from Holder. In the event the real estate purchase and sale transaction is terminated and the Buyer is legally entitled to the earnest money, the undersigned shall solely look to the Buyer for the return of the same and 3) all earnest money, including all sums advanced by the undersigned shall be applied toward the purchase price of the Property at closing.

*The undersigned acknowledges that the monies being advanced as earnest money are a
loan or gift to the Buyer and that no contractual relationship exists between the Holder
and the undersigned nor does Holder owe any duties whatsoever to the undersigned.
The undersigned covenants not to sue Holder for either the recovery of the monies being
advanced to the Buyer or any decision of Holder regarding the disbursement of the
earnest money.*

By: _____

§ 5.2.9   Defining Banking Day In Earnest Money Section

The GAR Contract requires that the Holder deposit the earnest money into the Holder's escrow account within "five banking days" from the Binding Agreement Date. If for some reason the earnest money check is dishonored, the buyer has "three banking days" after notice to deliver good funds to the Holder.

How are these timeframes calculated? The meaning of "within" is "no later than"[957] and a day means an entire 24-hour day beginning immediately after midnight and ending 24 hours later. Therefore, if the Holder receives a check on the 2nd of January and must deposit the same within five banking days, the end of January 3rd would be the first banking day, the end of January 4th would be the second banking day and so on until five banking days have elapsed. The time starts to run midnight on January 2nd with 24 hours for each banking day.

What is meant by a banking day? A banking day is defined under Georgia law as "a part of a day on which a bank is open to the public for carrying on substantially all of its banking functions."[958] Therefore, what constitutes a banking day will vary from one financial institution to another. For most banks, Saturdays, Sundays, and holidays are not banking days because even if certain branches are open, the bank is not open to the public for carrying on substantially all of its banking functions. There are some banks, however, where Saturdays are banking days because they carry on substantially all of their banking functions. An officer of the bank should be able to answer questions regarding which days the bank treats as official banking days.[959]

The requirement in the GAR Contract to deposit the earnest money within five banking days is calculated based on the practices of the bank in which the Holder has established its escrow/trust account. For example, if Saturday were a day when substantially all of the bank's functions are performed, this day would count toward the requirement that the earnest money be deposited within five banking days.

What is unfortunately unclear is whether the practices of the buyer's bank or the Holder's bank would be used in counting the three banking days the buyer has to make good on a dishonored earnest money check. Since there is no Georgia case on this issue, sellers and real estate brokers are well advised to evaluate the banking practices of both banks and decide any variances between the two banks' practices in favor of the buyer. For example, if Saturday is not a banking day at the buyer's bank but is a banking day at the Holder's bank, the safe approach is to not count Saturday as a banking day for the purpose of determining a buyer's default. The following special stipulation can be used to clarify the buyer's obligation.

Special Stipulation 80: Definition of "Banking Day" for Replacing Dishonored Check

*In the event Buyer's earnest money check is dishonored for any reason whatsoever Buyer
shall have three banking days to provide good funds to the Holder. For purposes of this
special stipulation, a banking day is a day on which the bank upon which the check is
written carries on substantially all of its banking functions.*

---

957   *Wall v. Youmans*, 223 Ga. 191, 154 S.E.2d 191 (1967); Head v. Williams, 269 Ga. 894, 506 S.E.2d 863 (1998).

958   O.C.G.A. § 11-4-104(a)(3).

959   *See* Chapter 1 (Creating a Binding Contract), §1.6.3 and 1.6.4.

Sometimes the parties to a contract will request that a particular time period in a contract be measured in terms of banking days rather than business days. The following special stipulation can be used in this situation.

> **Special Stipulation 81:   Time Period Measured in Business Days**
>
> *All parties agree that the following time period in the Agreement shall be measured in business days from the Binding Agreement Date, rather than calendar days:*
>
> _____.

§ 5.3   PAYMENT OF EARNEST MONEY IN COMMERCIAL TRANSACTIONS

The earnest money paid in commercial transactions is often in significantly larger amounts than in most residential transactions. When this occurs it is not uncommon for earnest money to be held by a title insurance company rather than a real estate broker. Interest on the earnest money also often accrues to the benefit of one of the parties rather than the broker, even if the broker is functioning as the holder of the earnest money. An example of this type of provision is set forth below.

> **Special Stipulation 82:   Interest on Earnest Money Accrues to the Benefit of the Buyer**
>
> *The Earnest Money shall be deposited in an interest-bearing escrow account and the interest thereon shall accrue to the benefit of the Buyer and be applied at closing along with the Earnest Money toward the purchase price.*

If the real estate broker is holding earnest money, it is not unusual for the parties to agree to arbitrate any dispute relating to entitlement to earnest money instead of having the broker disburse based upon a reasonable inspection of the property. It is also fairly typical for the buyer to deposit additional earnest money upon the end of the due diligence period. The GAR Commercial Purchase and Sale Agreement[960] includes the following provision.

> **Special Stipulation 83:   Arbitration of Earnest Money Disputes**
>
> *Buyer and Seller agree that any earnest money dispute shall be settled by arbitration in accordance with the Commercial Arbitration Rules of the American Arbitration Association. Buyer and Seller agree to engage _____or another arbitrator mutually agreeable to the parties ("Arbitrator"), to settle the earnest money dispute. The award of the Arbitrator shall be final and binding upon the parties hereto, and Holder shall promptly disburse the earnest money in accordance with said award. The costs of any such arbitration shall be shared equally between the Buyer and Seller and shall be promptly paid directly to the Arbitrator. Notwithstanding any provisions to the contrary contained herein, if the parties have not selected an Arbitrator above and cannot agree on an Arbitrator to resolve any dispute within thirty (30) days from the beginning of the earnest money dispute, Holder shall have the right to interplead the earnest money in accordance with paragraph 5.D(1) above.*

§ 5.4   INTEREST ON THE EARNEST MONEY

License law governing real estate agents and brokers in Georgia does not permit the broker to keep the interest earned on an earnest money deposit absent the agreement of the parties to the transaction.[961] The GAR Contract authorizes the Holder to deposit the earnest money in an interest-bearing account and to retain the interest therefrom.

---

960 GAR Form CF2.

961 G.R.E.C. Sub. Reg. 520-1-.08.

On occasion, the earnest money will be a large amount and/or held for a long period of time. In such instances, the parties may negotiate for the earnest money to be applied toward the purchase price or divided between the buyer and seller. While the parties are free to negotiate who will receive the interest on the earnest money, there is nothing which requires a real estate broker to hold earnest money on terms unacceptable to the broker. Set forth below is a sample special stipulation regarding interest on earnest money.

> **Special Stipulation 84:   Interest on Earnest Money to be Applied to Purchase Price at Closing**
>
> *Buyer, Seller and Holder agree that the interest earned on the earnest money deposit shall accrue to and be the property of the Buyer, and shall be applied toward the purchase price of the Property at closing.*

§ 5.4.1   Lawyer Or Title Company Holding Earnest Money

Sometimes the parties will ask an attorney or a title company to hold the earnest money for a fee. This is fine, since anyone can act as the Holder of the funds. However, since an attorney or title company (or anyone else who is not the buyer, seller, or real estate broker to the transaction) will not generally be a signatory to the purchase and sale agreement, care must be taken to assure the terms upon which the attorney or title company is holding the funds.

One way to accomplish this is for an agent of the attorney or title company who is serving as the Holder to agree to sign the sales contract. In this case, the provisions normally included in an escrow agreement should be set out in the purchase and sale agreement. Such provisions would include the duties and responsibilities of the Holder, as well as some formula for protecting the escrow agent against disputes and related litigation costs.

In practice, however, many attorneys and title companies may be reluctant to sign sales contracts when they are neither the buyer nor seller. In such a case, the Holder will often sign the contract for the sole purpose of acknowledging the Holder's duties and responsibilities regarding the earnest money. In other cases, the Holder will charge a fee to serve as the Holder of the earnest money. The following special stipulation can be used if the Holder is planning to charge a fee for her services.

> **Special Stipulation 85:   Holder Agrees to Hold Earnest Money for a Fee**
>
> *The undersigned Holder is signing this Agreement solely for the purpose of agreeing to: 1) serve as the Holder of earnest money hereunder; and 2) perform all of the duties of Holder as set forth in this Agreement. In serving as the Holder of earnest money hereunder, Buyer and Seller consent to Holder deducting from the earnest money the sum of $ _____ as compensation for Holder performing the duties of Holder hereunder. This sum shall be shown on the settlement statement and paid to Holder out of the proceeds of the sale upon the closing of this transaction. In the event this transaction does not close, Holder shall perform its duties hereunder without charge and no compensation shall be deducted from earnest money.*

Alternatively, the attorney or title company, buyer, and seller should all sign a separate escrow agreement that spells out the terms upon which the funds are being held and upon which they can be released. Most escrow agreements also include a description of the funds received, the specific situations in which the funds will be released, the responsibilities of the Holder, the fee the attorney or title company is charging to hold and verify the earnest money, whether the earnest money is held in an interest-bearing account and if the earnest money is held in an interest-bearing account, which party is entitled to the interest upon disbursement.

Parties should be aware that normally the interest on funds deposited into an attorney's escrow account is not available to the parties, but rather, is automatically paid to the State Bar of Georgia through the IOLTA (Interest On Lawyer's Trust Account) program of the State Bar.[962] Lawyers are permitted in certain circumstances to deposit earnest money into a non-IOLTA account, but this should be discussed with the attorney prior to the deposit of the funds.

§ 5.5   PAYMENT OF EARNEST MONEY TO EXTEND CLOSING DATE

Many commercial purchase and sale agreements provide that the contract can be extended by the buyer upon the payment of additional earnest money. The following special stipulation is an example of such a provision.

> **Special Stipulation 86:   Buyer Can Extend Closing Date Upon the Payment of Additional Earnest Money**
>
> *Buyer shall have the right to extend the closing date for up to _____ days from the date of closing set forth herein upon Buyer: 1) giving notice of the same to Seller; and 2) paying Seller additional earnest money in the sum of $_____. In the event Buyer property exercises its right to extend the closing date, all earnest money paid by the Buyer thereafter shall be non-refundable, except if this Purchase and Sale Agreement fails to close due to the breach of this Agreement by the Seller. All earnest money shall be applied towards the purchase price of the property at closing.*

§ 5.6   CONTRACT MAY BE ENFORCEABLE EVEN IF BUYER FAILS TO PAY EARNEST MONEY

A contract may still be enforceable even if the earnest money referenced in the contract is not paid. Georgia courts have held that failure to make a down payment or pay escrow money does not make the contract void for lack of consideration.[963] In one case, a buyer and seller signed a contract for land. Although the contract required the buyer to deposit $3,000 as earnest money, the buyer failed to do so. The seller argued that the contract was invalid due to a failure of consideration. The court rejected this argument and stated that "the agreement on the part of one to sell for a stipulated amount is a good consideration for a promise of the other to buy."[964]

If a contract does not expressly allow the seller to terminate if the earnest money is not paid, the courts will not give the seller the right to do so. Instead the seller can sue the buyer to recover the earnest money contemplated by the contract.[965] As discussed below, in order to help avoid costly and timely litigation, the GAR Contract gives the seller an express right to terminate the contract within a specific period of time if the earnest money check is dishonored and the buyer does not make good the funds within three banking days after notice.

Another approach is to give the seller the right to immediately terminate the contract if the earnest money check is dishonored for any reason whatsoever. The special stipulation below is an example of such a provision.

> **Special Stipulation 87:   Right to Terminate Immediately if Earnest Money Check Bounces**
>
> *Buyer shall be in breach of this Agreement in the event Buyer's earnest money check is dishonored for any reason whatsoever. Holder shall notify the parties in the event Buyer's earnest money check is dishonored. Seller shall have _____ days from the receipt of said notice to terminate this Agreement upon notice to Buyer. Seller shall be deemed to have*

---

962 *See* State Bar of Georgia Rules and Regulations, Rule 1.15(II).

963 *Mangum v. Jones*, 205 Ga. 661, 54 S.E.2d 603 (1949); *Atlanta Six Flags Partnership v. Hughes*, 191 Ga.App. 404, 381 S.E.2d 605 (1989).

964 *Mangum v. Jones*, 205 Ga. 661, 666, 54 S.E.2d 603, 607 (1949).

965 *Stone Mountain Abstract Co. v. Valcovy Realty Co.*, 141 Ga.App. 875, 234 S.E.2d 705 (1977).

> *waived the breach in the event Seller does not terminate this Agreement within _____*
> *days of receiving notice that the earnest money check has been dishonored.*

Mutuality of obligation is generally required for a valid contract. Mutuality of obligation requires that unless both parties to a contract are bound, neither is bound. That is, if a contract provides that a contingency is wholly within the discretion of one party, the contract lacks mutuality.

Although earnest money is not required as consideration for a real estate sales contract, if a party pays some form of consideration (such as earnest money), then the contract will generally not lack mutuality. In evaluating mutuality, one court held that a financing contingency in a contract did not render the contract void for lack of mutuality because the exchange of earnest money and the buyer's showing of good faith and cooperation in trying to obtain a loan evidenced her "consideration."[966] Also, obtaining a loan is not usually in the sole discretion of one party to the contract because the buyer's lender is usually a third party making such a decision. Mutuality of obligation is further discussed in § 1.2.1 (Mutuality Requirement).

§ 5.7 SELLER HOLDING EARNEST MONEY

Most contracts for the sale of property, including the GAR Contract, allow the real estate broker or some other party to serve as the Holder of the earnest money. When the earnest money is held by the broker, it must always be deposited in an escrow/trust bank account. However, there is nothing that prohibits the seller from holding the earnest money if that is what the parties specify.[967] This is often the case where the seller is also the builder or developer, such as in new home sales.

If the parties elect to have the seller hold the earnest money, the GAR Earnest Money Held by Seller Exhibit should be used.[968] This form disclaims the broker's responsibility for the earnest money if it is held by the seller. The exhibit also includes a checkbox for the seller to disclose whether or not the earnest money will be deposited in a trust account. Typically, builders will elect to hold the earnest money in their general account and are authorized by the exhibit to use such funds without having to set them apart in any manner.

§ 5.7.1 Earnest Money On Condominium Sales

The Georgia Condominium Act requires that any payment of money in respect of the first sale of a residential condominium unit that is paid before the closing be held in escrow in a separate account designated for this purpose, or in a Georgia licensed real estate broker's account.[969] The funds must be held in the account until either: (1) the unit is delivered at closing, (2) the deposit is delivered to the person(s) entitled to receive it upon breach of the contract, or (3) a part of the earnest money deposit may be paid to the seller on certain conditions.

In order for any part of the deposit to be paid to the seller, the following conditions must be met:[970]

(a) the purchase price of the condominium is at least $150,000;

(b) construction of improvements has commenced; and

(c) the contract contains the following notice in large, boldfaced type on the first page of the contract: ANY PAYMENT IN EXCESS OF 1 PERCENT OF THE PURCHASE PRICE MADE TO THE SELLER PRIOR TO CLOSING PURSUANT TO THIS CONTRACT MAY BE USED FOR CONSTRUCTION PURPOSES BY THE SELLER.

---

966 *Brack v. Brownlee*, 246 Ga. 818, 273 S.E.2d 390 (1980); Koets, Inv. v. Benveniste, 169 Ga.App. 352, 312 S.E.2d 846 (1983), aff'd, 252 Ga.520, 314 S.E.2d 912 (1984).
967 *Williams v. Northside Realty Associates, Inc.*, 116 Ga.App. 253, 157 S.E.2d 166 (1967).
968 GAR Form F80.
969 O.C.G.A. § 44-3-112(a).
970 O.C.G.A. § 44-3-112(b).

The seller may use the funds for actual construction and development of the condominium property in which the unit is located. However, the funds may not be used for salaries, commissions, expenses of real estate licensees, or advertising purposes.[971]

§ 5.8 BUYER OR SELLER MODIFYING EARNEST MONEY PROVISION

On occasion, a buyer or seller will present an offer or counteroffer in which the rights of the Holder of the earnest money have been modified. Normally this is done to limit the ability of the Holder to recover its costs and attorneys fees in the event a dispute about the earnest money is litigated or to delete the Holder's ability to disburse the earnest money based upon a reasonable interpretation of the contract. The real estate broker is obligated to present such offers even when they contain modifications to the earnest money section which the Holder might find objectionable.[972] Of course, nothing requires the listing or selling broker to serve as the Holder of the earnest money if the terms of the escrow in the contract are not acceptable to such broker. In such situations, the real estate broker can simply decline to serve as the Holder of earnest money unless it is on terms acceptable to her.

§ 5.9 RIGHTS AND DUTIES OF ESCROW AGENT UNDER GAR CONTRACT

§ 5.9.1 Holder Of Earnest Money Is Agent For Both Parties

In Georgia, a party holding earnest money is considered an escrow agent.[973] As such, the Holder acts as a trustee of an express trust with duties to perform for each of the parties. If the earnest money is being held by the broker, the broker may specify the terms under which she will hold the earnest money. The broker's powers with regard to the earnest money are strictly limited to those set forth in that part of the contract (or other agreement) establishing the terms upon which the earnest money will be held. [974]

Even though the real estate broker may be representing the buyer or the seller in any given transaction, the broker serving as the Holder of earnest money owes duties to both parties. These duties are limited to the handling of earnest money and do not create a client relationship. For example, if the broker represents the buyer as a client, the broker's agreement to act as the Holder has no bearing upon whether the broker has a client relationship with the seller. Such relationship would need to be created by an express written agreement between the broker and the seller.[975]

§ 5.9.2 Broker Who Is Escrow Agent Must Account For And Remit Earnest Money

To establish a valid escrow with regard to earnest money, the following criteria must be met: (a) there must be a valid, lawful contract between the parties; (b) there must be an absolute deposit of the earnest money with the escrow agent (normally the real estate broker); and (c) the earnest money must pass beyond the control of the buyer to unilaterally withdraw.[976]

A licensee must account for and remit any money coming into the licensee's possession that belongs to others.[977] If a broker serving as an escrow agent fails to account for or remit the earnest money, the broker may lose her real estate license.[978] As soon as reasonably possible, the associate broker or licensee must place the earnest money in the custody

---

971 O.C.G.A. § 44-3-112(b).

972 O.C.G.A. § 43-40-25(b)(19).

973 *Carter v. Turbeville*, 90 Ga.App. 367, 83 S.E.2d 72 (1954).

974 *Fickling & Walker Co. v. Giddens Constr. Co., Inc.*, 258 Ga. 891, 376 S.E.2d 655 (1989).

975 O.C.G.A. § 10-6A-3(1).

976 O.C.G.A. § 44-5-42; *Brown v. Brown*, 192 Ga. 852, 16 S.E.2d 853 (1941).

977 O.C.G.A. § 43-40-25(b)(3).

978 *Clark v. Georgia Real Estate Commission*, 129 Ga.App. 741, 200 S.E.2d 926 (1973).

of the broker who must deposit the money in a trust or escrow account.[979] A broker cannot generally comingle the earnest money with the broker's own money.[980] Further, the broker must maintain and deposit in a separate, federally insured checking account all money received by the broker acting as escrow agent of the funds of others, unless all the parties having an interest in the money have agreed otherwise in writing.[981]

If the broker deposits funds into an interest-bearing account, the broker must obtain a written agreement of the parties indicating to whom the broker will pay any interest earned prior to depositing the funds into such an account.[982] The GAR Contract provides that the earnest money will be deposited in the Holder's escrow/trust account with the Holder retaining the interest if the account is interest-bearing.[983]

§ 5.9.3 When Holder Can Disburse Earnest Money

The GAR Contract obligates a Holder to disburse earnest money as follows:[984]

(a) at closing;

(b) upon a subsequent written agreement between the buyer and seller. The agreement must be separate from the contract directing the broker to hold the funds, which in most cases is the sales contract;

(c) upon order of a court or arbitrator[985] with jurisdiction over a dispute involving the earnest money; or

(d) upon the parties' failure to enter into a binding agreement (where there is no dispute over the formation or enforceability of the GAR Purchase and Sale Agreement).

The GAR Contract also allows the Holder to disburse the earnest money based upon a reasonable interpretation of the contract.[986] The Holder in these situations must give 10 days' notice stating to whom and why the disbursement of disputed earnest money will be made. This provision was included in the GAR Contract to give the parties an opportunity, within the 10-day period, to provide the Holder with any objections they may have to the disbursement, any disputed questions of fact or law to justify an interpleader action, or any additional facts or laws to support a proposed disbursement of the earnest money.

When the Holder wishes to disburse earnest money based upon a reasonable interpretation of the contract, the Holder first gives all parties 10 days' notice as to whom and why the disbursement will be made. Any party may object in writing to the proposed disbursement, provided the Holder receives the objection within the 10-day period. All objections not raised in a timely manner are waived. In the event a timely objection is made, the Holder must consider the objection and choose either to: (a) hold the earnest money for a reasonable period to allow the parties to resolve the dispute; (b) disburse the earnest money and notify all the parties; and/or (c) interplead the earnest money into the appropriate court. If the Holder changes her mind about the disbursement, the GAR Contract requires the Holder to send a new 10-day notice to the parties, including the rationale for the modification from the first 10-day notice and to whom the disbursement will now be made.

Even if the disbursement is based upon specific directions in the purchase and sale contract to return earnest money to the buyer immediately upon the happening of a particular event, the Holder is still required under the GAR Contract to send a 10 day notice if both parties do not sign a termination and release agreement. This is because under the GAR

---

979 O.C.G.A. § 43-40-20(h).

980 O.C.G.A. § 43-40-25(b)(4).

981 O.C.G.A. § 43-40-25(b)(5).

982 O.C.G.A. § 43-40-25(b)(30).

983 GAR Form F20.

984 GAR Form F20.

985 *See* § 13.6 of this book regarding arbitration. Arbitration is being used more and more frequently to resolve earnest money disputes.

986 The Georgia Real Estate Commission has similar provisions, *see* Rule 520-1.08(3)(b).

Contract, the agreement to disburse the earnest money must be a written agreement subsequent to the agreement directing the broker to hold the funds. For example, if the buyer terminates a GAR Contract during an agreed-upon Due Diligence Period and the seller refuses to sign a termination and release agreement, the Holder cannot disburse based upon a reasonable interpretation of the contract without first sending a 10 day letter. This would be the case even if the parties included a special stipulation stating that the Holder shall immediately return the earnest money to the buyer, in the event the buyer terminates the contract during the due diligence period.

An example is the provision in the GAR Contract in which the buyer has the right to terminate the agreement if a new survey is materially different from any survey attached to the contract, in which event the earnest money shall be returned. Even though the buyer may have validly terminated the contract on the basis of this provision, and even though the contract clearly states that the earnest money is to be refunded, the Holder is required under the GAR Contract to send a 10 day notice of the Holder's interpretation of the contract if all parties do not sign an agreement subsequent to the agreement creating the escrow, which means that she needs to comply with the GAR provision requiring 10 days and seller both sign a termination and release agreement permitting the funds to be returned to the buyer. If a real estate broker does not disburse the earnest money according to the provisions of the contract, the Georgia Real Estate Commission may consider that the broker has acted incompetently.[987]

§ 5.9.4   Interpreting The GAR Contract

To assist the Holder in deciding which party is entitled to the earnest money, the GAR Contract includes a section setting out when the buyer or the seller is entitled to the earnest money.[988]

The GAR Contract provides that the buyer is entitled to the earnest money upon the following events:

(a) failure of the parties to enter into a binding agreement;

(b) failure of any contingency or condition of the agreement

(c) termination of the agreement due to the default of seller;

(d) termination of the agreement according to a right to terminate contained in the agreement; or

(e) upon closing if other funds are used to pay the purchase price.

The GAR Contract also provides that the seller is entitled to the earnest money if the Agreement is terminated due to the default of buyer.

§ 5.9.5   Using The GAR "Unilateral Notice To Terminate; Agreement To Disburse Earnest Money" Form

As noted above, an earnest money deposit may be disbursed in accordance with a subsequent written agreement signed by all parties with an interest in the funds. One way to do this is to have the party sign the GAR "Unilateral Notice to Terminate; Mutual Agreement to Disburse Earnest Money" form.[989] The form may be used as a notice of unilateral termination by one party who has a legal right to do so and is signed by both the buyer and the seller.

For example, if a seller is unable to convey good and marketable title to the property after being put on notice of a title defect, the seller would be in breach of contract. The buyer could terminate the contract due to the seller's default by giving the seller unilateral notice of buyer's decision to do so. Alternatively, if the buyer wishes to terminate a contract during an agreed-upon Due Diligence Period in a GAR Contract, the buyer merely has to give unilateral notice of the buyer's decision. However, even when the buyer or seller can terminate unilaterally, the Holder of the earnest money cannot disburse the same unless both the buyer and seller sign the Unilateral Notice to Terminate Agreement; Mutual

---

987   Georgia Real Estate Commission Rule 520-1-.08(3)(a).

988   GAR Form F20.

989   GAR Form F83, Unilateral Notice to Terminate Agreement; Mutual Agreement to Disburse Earnest Money.

Agreement to Disburse Earnest Money form. This form also allows one party to a contract to request that the other party to the contract let her out of the agreement. This is done by the first party signing the top "Unilateral Notice to Terminate" section of the form and requesting that the other party do so as well.

§ 5.9.6   What Is A Reasonable Period For Broker To Hold Earnest Money

The Georgia Real Estate Commission and the courts have not defined a particular time as a "reasonable period" for the real estate broker to hold the earnest money in the event of a dispute between the parties. The intent of the provision in the GAR Contract was to give the real estate broker the time to do any or all of the following: (a) impose a "cooling off" period on the parties to an earnest money dispute; (b) have time to thoroughly investigate which party is entitled to receive the earnest money; or (c) otherwise attempt to resolve the dispute.

The time by which the earnest money must be disbursed by the Holder will likely depend on the facts in each case. The Holder should have the right to hold the earnest money if there is some realistic hope that the parties may resolve their earnest money dispute, or if the Holder is waiting on information which will make it possible to disburse, based upon a reasonable interpretation of the contract. The period of time that disputed earnest money can legitimately be held, however, is probably measured in weeks rather than months.

Earnest money should not be held for an extended period of time merely because the broker would rather not deal with the dispute. Brokers should also be aware that if the earnest money is a large sum and is placed in an interest-bearing account with the Holder, the longer it is kept the greater the likelihood the parties will claim the Holder is breaching her duty by retaining the earnest money for her own financial gain.

§ 5.9.7   Commencing An Interpleader Lawsuit

§ 5.9.7.1   What Is An Interpleader Action?

The Holder of earnest money may file what is known as an interpleader action when there are competing claims to the earnest money and the Holder is unsure how to disburse the funds. An interpleader is a lawsuit where the Holder deposits the earnest money into the registry of the court and asks the court to make a decision with regard to its disbursement.[990]

Many buyers and sellers do not realize that an interpleader action is a lawsuit in which the broker sues both the seller and the buyer. When the suit is filed, the broker deposits the earnest money into the registry of the court and requests the judge to make a judicial determination regarding who is entitled to the earnest money. The change in terminology may help educate buyers and sellers more clearly as to what they are getting themselves into when they encourage a broker to interplead the funds.

It is important to note, however, that in Georgia only a licensed attorney is authorized to represent a corporation in any proceeding in a court of record. This means that the qualifying broker of an incorporated real estate brokerage firm may not file an interpleader without retaining the services of a licensed attorney.[991]

§ 5.9.7.2   The Cost Of Interpleading

Brokers should also remind buyers and sellers that the GAR Contract provides that "The prevailing defendant in the interpleader lawsuit shall be entitled to collect her attorney's fees and court costs and the amount deducted by Holder from the non-prevailing defendant." In other words, if the attorney representing the brokerage firm charges the broker $1,500 to prepare and file the interpleader lawsuit, this amount can be assessed against the losing party in the interpleader lawsuit.

---

990   O.C.G.A. § 9-11-22.

991   *Eckles v. Atlanta Technology Group, Inc.*, 267 Ga. 801, 485 S.E.2d 22 (1997).

The GAR Contract gives the Holder the right to deduct from the funds interplead its costs and expenses, including reasonable attorney's fees. In addition, it provides that the prevailing party has a right to be reimbursed for any funds paid to the Holder from the losing party. This procedure, although untested in the appellate courts, gives the Holder the advantage of being reimbursed for the costs and expenses of the interpleader immediately rather than having to wait for a final determination by the court as to the dispute between the buyer and seller. Therefore, there is a monetary risk in insisting that disputed earnest money be interpleaded into court.

The idea that prevailing parties can recover their costs and attorneys fees is designed to encourage parties to be cautious in demanding that earnest money be interpleaded into court. The risk of additional costs and charges being assessed against a buyer or seller is often used as leverage to negotiate resolutions of earnest money disputes. A great many earnest money disputes involve sums in the $1,000 to $2,000 range. Disputes over sums in this range would normally be considered small by most litigation standards. While these disputes can be extremely contentious, they rarely justify the significant attorney's fees usually expended on the part of the buyer and seller and real estate broker to litigate. Like it or not, it is often in the parties best financial interest to reach a settlement rather than risk spending even larger amounts arguing over who is entitled to the earnest money.

§ 5.9.7.3 When Interpleader Is Appropriate

As a condition of interpleading, the funds into court the Holder must show that the conflicting claims create a reasonable doubt as to whom the funds belong such that the Holder "is or may be exposed to double or multiple liability."[992] A petition for interpleader will be denied if the escrow agent is in possession of all the facts and the questions of law are not intricate or debatable. In other words, an interpleader is not available if there is no bona fide controversy between the parties.

A broker who files an interpleader action inappropriately may incur liability, which is illustrated in the following case.[993] The earnest money provision in the contract stated: "If the sale, due to buyer's default, willful or otherwise, is not consummated, then said earnest money shall be refunded." The sale was not consummated and after a period of unsuccessful negotiations to save the deal, the buyers demanded return of the deposit. When the money was not returned to the buyers, they sued the escrow agent and the seller for conversion, claiming that the escrow agent had wrongfully refused to return the earnest money in accordance with the contract. The escrow agent responded by interpleading the earnest money into the registry of the court asserting that it was "in great doubt" as to whether the buyers or sellers were entitled to the funds.

After the interpleader was filed, the trial court and the parties agreed to have the earnest money returned to the buyers. The trial court also denied the buyers' claim against the escrow agent for wrongfully refusing to return the escrow before litigation ensued and judgment was entered in favor of the escrow agent on that issue. The buyers appealed the trial court's ruling on that issue, claiming they should be entitled to money damages from the escrow agent for all their expenses, costs, and attorney's fees in trying to get their earnest money back. The Court of Appeals agreed with the buyers and held that the escrow agent should not have been entitled to interplead the money in order to withhold the disposition of the funds, because the terms of the contract were clear. The Court of Appeals then returned the case to the trial court for a determination of the amount of damages the buyers were entitled to recover. The jury ultimately found against the escrow agent for general damages, punitive damages, and litigation expenses. Then the escrow agent appealed the jury award. The Court of Appeals concluded that evidence of the buyer's litigation expenses and attorney's fees could be heard by the jury because the escrow agent had no basis for withholding the earnest money in the first place (since the contract terms were clear). Additionally, the court authorized punitive damages and general damages even though the earnest money had been refunded with interest.

---

992 O.C.G.A. § 9-11-22.

993 *Panfel v. Boyd*, 187 Ga.App. 639, 371 S.E.2d 222 (1988); *Callahan v. Panfel*, 195 Ga.App. 891, 395 S.E.2d 80 (1990).

The case discussed above is different from a situation in which the broker gives the earnest money to a third party when there is a legitimate issue as to whether the earnest money is an unenforceable penalty. For example, the court in one case had to decide on a dispute over the allocation of earnest money where the seller sought, among other things, an award of punitive damages for breach of fiduciary duty, fraud, and conversion as a result of the escrow agent's refusal to agree to an unconditional release of the escrowed funds on seller's demand.[994] In this case, there were questions about the enforceability of the liquidated damages provision in the contract and the court ultimately concluded that punitive damages against the broker as escrow agent were not appropriate.

§ 5.9.7.4 Practical Advice On When To Interplead Or Disburse

While the courts in Georgia have clearly stated that it is inappropriate to interplead earnest money when there is no bona fide dispute between the parties, this does not mean that the real estate broker must sit as a judge and jury in all cases of disputed earnest money. Instead the courts merely require that there be a bona fide dispute before an interpleader action is brought. A bona fide dispute is more than a dispute where both sides claim the funds. To be a bona fide dispute, there must be some legitimate question of fact or law which makes it unclear to whom the earnest money should rightfully be disbursed. A bona fide dispute would exist when the contract was unclear as to when the Holder can disburse the earnest money, as illustrated in the following case.[995] The buyer had paid $5,000 earnest money to the broker as required under the contract. Subsequently, the buyer paid the seller an additional $60,000 earnest money to buy more time to complete an environmental report that the lender required before it would provide financing.

The contract provided that the $5,000 earnest money be refunded "upon the failure of any contingency or failure of either party to fulfill its obligations as set forth in this Agreement." When the buyer paid the $60,000 to the seller, the parties agreed in an addendum that the $60,000 is non-refundable except if the property becomes irreparably damaged and that the earnest money provisions in the original contract (1) shall remain in full force and effect and (2) apply to both broker and seller. The environmental report was unsatisfactory and the lender refused to finance the purchase. The buyer requested the refund of the earnest money on the basis of a failure in the financing contingency. The seller objected, presumably on the basis that he was entitled to keep the earnest money unless the property was destroyed.

Since the language of the contact was uncertain, the court stated that it was necessary to look at the agreement between the buyer and the seller as a whole to ascertain the intention of the parties. The contract stated that the earnest money could be disbursed only at (1) closing; (2) upon written agreement signed by all parties having an interest in the funds; (3) upon court order; (4) upon the failure of any contingency or failure of either party to fulfill its obligations under the contract; and (5) as otherwise may have been provided in the contract. In the event of a dispute, the broker was authorized to disburse the earnest money based upon a reasonable interpretation of the contract or, in the alternative, could interplead the disputed sum into the court.

The contract between the parties also contained a default provision stating that if the transaction did not close due to the buyer's default, the seller could retain the earnest money and vice versa. The seller warranted in the contract that the subject property was not used for the handling, storage or disposal of toxic chemicals creating an environmental hazard. Lastly, the purchaser's obligation to purchase the subject property was subject to an inspection of the property and the ability of the purchaser to obtain financing.

Taking these contractual provisions into consideration, the court held that the buyer did not waive, amend or modify the financing or the inspection contingencies provided in the original contract. These contingencies were required to be satisfied as a condition precedent to the contract, and the earnest money was nonrefundable only if these contingencies were met. Since the buyer could not obtain financing due to the environmental conditions revealed through an inspection of the property, these contingencies were not met. The buyer was therefore entitled to a refund

---

994 *Fickling & Walker Co. v. Giddens Constr. Co., Inc.*, 258 Ga. 891, 376 S.E.2d 655 (1989).

995 *Ali v. Aarabi*, 264 Ga.App. 64, 589 S.E.2d 827 (2003).

of the earnest money. The lesson in this case is to make the intention of the parties absolutely clear in the contract.

As a further example, a bona fide dispute would not exist in a situation where the buyer has been legitimately declined for a loan and the contract contains a loan contingency. If the seller wants the earnest money simply because she is angry that her house has been off the market, the Holder should disburse the money to the buyer upon a reasonable interpretation of the contract. If there is an issue about whether the buyer was declined for a loan because she failed to provide all necessary information to the lender, however, a factual question arises which could justify an interpleader action. Similarly, if the loan contingency fails because the buyer cannot obtain a loan with a 7% fixed interest rate and the buyer rejects the seller's offer to pay the amount necessary to buy the loan down to 7%, a question might arise as to whether the buyer must accept the seller's offer to buy down the interest rate. Such a question might justify interpleading disputed earnest money.

The Holder should take a close look at the whole contract and not rely solely on the earnest money provision when considering whether to file an interpleader action. In one case, the earnest money provision stated that "disbursement of earnest money held by Holder, escrow agent, can occur only as follows…upon failure of any contingency or failure by either party to fulfill his obligations contained in this Agreement."[996] The contract was contingent upon the buyer's ability to obtain a 75% mortgage loan. The buyers did not even apply for a loan and had clearly breached the contract. Since the buyer was clearly in breach, the Holder had correctly disbursed the $50,000 earnest money to the seller. The buyer then sued the seller for the $50,000 and the seller counterclaimed against the buyer for lost profits.

The brokerage provision of the contract stated: "Buyer shall forthwith pay Broker the full commission immediately; provided that Broker may apply one-half of the earnest money toward payment of, but not to exceed, the full commission and *may pay the balance thereof to Seller as liquidated damages to Seller, if Seller claims balance as Seller's liquidated damages in full settlement of any claim for damages.*" [*Emphasis added.*] The court held that since the seller had accepted the $50,000 as liquidated damages the seller was precluded from seeking additional liquidated damages. If the seller had wanted the earnest money but made it clear to the Holder that he was unwilling to accept the funds as liquidated damages, the Holder should file an interpleader action.

§ 5.9.8 Broker's Entitlement To Earnest Money As Commission

Georgia law provides that a broker is not entitled to any part of the earnest money, security deposit, trust funds or other money paid to the broker in connection with any real estate transaction, as part or all of the broker's commission or fee, until the transaction has been consummated or terminated.[997] Once the transaction has been consummated or terminated, the contract will determine the broker's entitlement to the earnest money. Otherwise, the Georgia Real Estate Commission prohibits a broker from taking any part or all of the earnest money as commission or a fee unless the broker has secured a written agreement to such an arrangement that is separate from the sales contract and signed by all parties having an interest in the transaction.[998]

Earlier versions of the GAR Contract provided that the Holder had the right to apply one-half of the earnest money to the payment of the broker's commission.[999] Newer versions of the GAR Contract eliminate the broker's entitlement to any portion of the earnest money as commission. Instead, a broker's commission is paid according to a separate brokerage engagement agreement that is specifically incorporated in the GAR Contract by reference. The rationale for this change is that if the broker is to serve in a disinterested role as escrow agent, removing the broker's interest in the escrow money will better ensure that the broker holding earnest money is not accused of disbursing the earnest money for financial gain.

996 *Hawkins v. GMAC Mortgage Corporation*, 241 Ga.App. 234, 526 S.E.2d 421 (1999).

997 O.C.G.A. § 43-40-20(e).

998 Georgia Real Estate Commission Rule 520-1.08(3)(d)4.

999 GAR Form F20, paragraph 3 (1995 Printing).

§ 5.9.9   Parties To Contract Cannot Sue Holder For Damages

The GAR Contract provides that all parties agree to indemnify the Holder against all claims, causes of action, suits and damages arising out of or related to the performance of the Holder's duties under the earnest money paragraph. The GAR Contract further provides that "the parties covenant and agree not to sue Holder for damages relating to the decision of Holder to disburse earnest money made in accordance with this Agreement".[1000] This provision gives the Holder of the earnest money a great deal of protection from claims made against her for decisions she makes regarding the disbursement of earnest money in accordance with the contract. However, it does not protect a Holder from claims against her for failing to perform in accordance with the express terms of the contract.

A broker who disburses trust funds from the broker's designated trust or escrow account contrary to the terms of a contract for the sale or rental of real estate, or other contract creating the escrow, or who fails to disburse trust funds according to the terms of any contract creating the escrow, may be considered by the Georgia Real Estate Commission to have demonstrated incompetence to act as a real estate broker in such manner as to safeguard the interest of the public.[1001]

§ 5.9.10   Broker's Liability For Failure To Timely Deposit Earnest Money

As discussed above, a real estate broker generally does not have liability for disbursing trust funds in accordance with the terms of the purchase and sale agreement. However, what happens if the broker, acting as the Holder, fails to collect and/or fails to timely deposit, the earnest money?

The GAR Contract[1002] allows for earnest money is to be paid as part of the offer or within an agreed upon number of days from the Binding Agreement Date. If the parties want to indicate a different due date, the parties may do so by placing that information on the blank line immediately below the other payment options. The GAR Contract further provides that the "earnest money shall be deposited in Holder's escrow/trust account …within 5 (five) banking days from the Binding Agreement Date." Finally, the GAR Contract provides that the Holder will immediately notify the parties if the earnest money is dishonored for any reason, at which point the buyer shall have 3 banking days in which to make the funds good or the seller may terminate the contract.

There are three potential areas of liability for the Holder of earnest money. These are: (1) not being in possession of the earnest money at the time the Holder signs the contract; (2) the failure of the Holder to timely deposit the funds; and (3) the failure of the Holder to timely notify the parties that earnest money had been dishonored. As demonstrated by the following examples, the Holder may have some degree of liability under each scenario.

§ 5.9.10.1   Failure Of The Holder To Collect Earnest Money

Example #1: Broker A signs a GAR Contract that reflects that Broker A is serving as the Holder of $5,000 earnest money. In reality, Broker A does not have any earnest money from the buyer. The buyer promised to deliver the funds because he left his checkbook in his other wallet (or some other similar excuse), but somehow the funds never materialize. Three days later Broker A tells the seller that he does not have the earnest money and the seller terminates the contract. Does Broker A have any liability to the seller and, if so, how much?

Answer: Broker A may have liability to the seller, but the amount of any such claim is questionable. Broker A would not appear to be liable to the seller for the $5,000, since the broker never actually was in possession of these funds. Furthermore, Broker A as Holder has not contractually agreed to be liable for the amount of the earnest money. The seller did not incur any expenses (such as buyer requested repairs) as a result of the failure of the Holder to collect the earnest money. The property was off the market for a total of 3 days (assuming its status in the Multiple Listing Service was changed from "active" to

---

1000   *Id.*

1001   Georgia Real Estate Commission Rule 520-1.08(3)(a).

1002   GAR Form F20.

"under contract." In theory, there is some negligible amount for which the Holder may be liable, which amount would need to be determined by a judge or jury. A more significant concern to the Holder in this case is that the Georgia Real Estate Commission could sanction the licensee for "being or becoming a party to any falsification of any portion of any contract…"[1003] *The real estate licensee is considered to have falsified a contract because the contract states that the Holder has earnest money when in fact the Holder does not have the earnest money.*

Example #2: Broker A signs a GAR Contract that reflects that Broker A is serving as the Holder of $5,000 earnest money. In reality, Broker A does not have any earnest money from the buyer. The buyer promised to deliver the funds because he left his checkbook in his other wallet (or some other similar excuse), but somehow the funds never materialize. In the meantime, the seller makes $2,000 worth of buyer requested upgrades and repairs to the property. Thirty days later, Broker A tells the seller that he does not have the earnest money and the seller terminates the contract. Does Broker A have any liability to the seller and, if so, how much?

Answer: Broker A may have liability to the seller in the amount of $2,000. The seller incurred $2,000 in buyer requested expenses that the seller presumably would not have incurred had she known that the buyer never paid any earnest money. Broker A can try to argue that his liability should be something less than the $2,000 because certain of the repairs would certainly have been requested by any purchaser, and therefore would have been expenses incurred by the seller under any circumstances. Broker A would not appear to be liable for the full $5,000 for the reasons stated in Example #1. Again, Broker A could be sanctioned by the Georgia Real Estate Commission for being or becoming a party to the falsification of a real estate contract.

Example #3: Broker A signs a GAR Contract that reflects that Broker A is serving as the Holder of $5,000 earnest money. In reality, Broker A does not have any earnest money from the buyer. The buyer promised to deliver the funds because he left his checkbook in his other wallet (or some other similar excuse), but somehow the funds never materialize. In the meantime, the seller makes $15,000 worth of buyer requested upgrades and repairs to the property. Thirty days later, Broker A tells the seller that he does not have the earnest money and the seller terminates the contract. Does Broker A have any liability to the seller and, if so, how much?

Answer: Broker A may have liability to the seller in the amount of at least $5,000. While the seller incurred $15,000 in buyer requested expenses, this exceeded the amount of earnest money the seller believed Broker A was holding. Therefore, Broker A can argue that the seller assumed that risk when he made repairs in an amount greater that the earnest money. The seller, however, may be able to argue that he only spent the $15,000 because he believed the buyer was truly interested in purchasing the property and that he would not have spent a dime on repairs if he knew there was no earnest money.

§ 5.9.10.2   Failure Of The Holder To Timely Deposit Earnest Money

Example #1: Broker A signs a GAR Contract that reflects that Broker A is serving as the Holder of $5,000 earnest money. Broker A has the buyer's earnest money check but forgets to deposit it for a month. When Broker A discovers the error he immediately deposits the check, which clears his account. Does Broker A have any liability to the seller and, if so, how much?

Answer: Broker A does not appear to have any civil liability under this scenario. While the funds were deposited late, they nonetheless cleared the broker's account. No harm, no foul. However, while the broker may escape civil liability she may still need to answer to the Georgia Real Estate Commission. Specifically, Broker A has GREC Substantive Rule 520-1-.08(b) which requires that "A licensee shall place all cash, checks, or other items of value received by the licensee in a brokerage capacity into the custody of the broker holding the licensee's license as soon after receipt as is practically possible."

Example #2: Broker A signs a GAR Contract that reflects that Broker A is serving as the Holder of $5,000 earnest money. Broker A has the buyer's earnest money check but forgets to deposit it for a month. When Broker A discovers

---

1003   O.C.G.A. § 43-40-25(b)(28).

the error, he immediately deposits the check, only to learn that the account has insufficient funds to cover the check (*i.e.*, it "bounces"). Does Broker A have any liability to the seller and, if so, how much?

Answer: It depends. If it can be shown that the account never had sufficient funds, so that even if the check had been timely deposited it still would not have cleared, then Broker A can make a good argument that she should not be liable to the seller because the funds would never have been any good. This is probably a winning argument, assuming that the seller has not incurred any other costs by virtue of the delayed deposit.

However, a different result could be reached if, during the month delay, the seller made $2,500 worth of buyer requested repairs. In that event, the seller may be able to show that had the check been timely deposited it would have been returned in time to alert them of the insufficient funds prior to incurring the expense of the repairs. As with the example of the broker failing to obtain the earnest money, the amount of the damages to the seller should be limited to the $2,500. If the repairs were $10,000, then the Holder will argue the seller assumed the risk in making repairs in excess of the amount of earnest money and the seller will counter that she would have made no repairs at all had she known sooner that the earnest money was no good. There is no definitive answer to which of these arguments will prevail. Again, if a complaint is filed against Broker A with the Georgia Real Estate Commission, Broker A will likely be sanctioned for failing to timely deposit the earnest money.[1004]

§ 5.9.10.3   Failure To Timely Notify The Seller The Buyer's Funds Did Not Clear

Example #1: Broker A signs a GAR Contract that reflects that Broker A is serving as the Holder of $5,000 earnest money. Broker A timely deposits the buyer's earnest money check but forgets to notify the seller that it was returned marked insufficient funds. A month later Broker A notifies the seller. Does Broker A have any liability to the seller and, if so, how much?

Answer: It depends. There may be no liability if the seller incurred no loss during the month delay. However, if, during the month delay, the seller made $2,500 worth of buyer requested repairs, the seller may be able to show that the repairs were made after Broker A knew the earnest money had been dishonored. The seller will argue that she would have made no repairs at all had she know about the returned check. As with the example of the broker failing to obtain the earnest money, the amount of the damages to the seller should be limited to the $2,500. If the repairs were $10,000, then the Holder will argue the seller assumed the risk in making repairs in excess of the amount of earnest money and the seller will counter that she would have made no repairs at all had she known sooner that the earnest money was no good. There is no definitive answer to which of these arguments will prevail.

§ 5.10   APPLICATION OF EARNEST MONEY WHEN CONTRACT BREACHED

If a buyer breaches a real estate sales contract, the existence of an earnest money provision in the contract will have one of three effects: (a) the money may be considered partial payment of any actual damages incurred by the seller if it can be proven that such damages resulted from buyer's breach; (b) the money can be applied as part payment of the purchase price of the property in a lawsuit against the buyer for specific performance of the contract; or (c) the money may be considered liquidated damages[1005] for the buyer's breach of the contract. However, under Georgia law, a provision for earnest money cannot be used for all three results.[1006] The effect of the earnest money will depend on the language used in the contract and the intent of the parties.[1007]

1004   GREC Substantive Rule 520-1-.08(b).

1005   A liquidated damages provision in a real estate contract is a specific sum of money that has been stipulated by the parties as the amount of damages to be suffered by either party for a breach of the contract.

1006   *Southeastern Land Fund, Inc. v. Real Estate World, Inc.*, 237 Ga. 227, 227 S.E.2d 340 (1976).

1007   *Everett Associates v. Gardner*, 162 Ga.App. 513, 291 S.E.2d 120 (1982).

As discussed below, the GAR Contracts provide that if the buyer is in default the Holder may pay the earnest money to the seller by check.[1008] If the seller cashes or deposits the check then the funds are deemed to be liquidated damages in full settlement of all claims. This same right to "retain" the earnest money upon a default by the buyer is given to the seller in the GAR Earnest Money Held by Seller Exhibit.[1009] The GAR Contracts also provide that if the seller rejects the tender of an earnest money from the Holder, the Holder may return the earnest money to the buyer and the seller will be able to pursue additional claims against the buyer.

§ 5.10.1 Partial Payment Of Actual Damages

If a buyer breaches the real estate sales contract, courts will look to the terms of the contract to determine how the earnest money should be applied. If the contract limits a seller's damages to the earnest money and if the seller does not terminate the contract because of the buyer's breach, the seller's recovery will be limited to the amount of the earnest money, even though the seller may have incurred additional expenses in preparing to sell the property.[1010] If the contract does not expressly limit the seller's remedy to the earnest money as liquidated damages, the seller may terminate the contract and sue the buyer for any actual damages incurred by the seller.[1011]

§ 5.10.2 Partial Payment In Suit For Specific Performance

Under the GAR Contracts, unless the contract limits the seller's recovery to the earnest money as liquidated damages, the seller may forego money damages and seek specific performance of the contract.[1012] In seeking specific performance, the seller asks the court to require that the buyer purchase the property. Even if the contract does not expressly say that the seller can seek specific performance, case law holds that a seller may seek this general remedy for a breach of contract.[1013] In one case, the court concluded that the following language did not prevent the seller from seeking specific performance of the contract: "If said sale is not consummated because of Purchaser's default, then the Seller shall be entitled to retain the Purchaser's earnest money for liquidated damages of such default by the Purchaser."[1014]

The GAR Contract provides that if the seller terminates the agreement due to the buyer's default, the Holder may pay the earnest money to the seller by check. If the seller accepts and deposits the check, the seller accepts the earnest money as liquidated damages and waives all other claims.[1015] Therefore, under the GAR Contract, the seller will not be entitled to specific performance if the earnest money is accepted.

The special stipulation below provides that the seller's sole remedy is to retain the earnest money in the event of a breach of the contract by the purchaser. The use of this type of special stipulation is increasingly common since more buyers than ever are ending up in default of their contracts due to last minute problems obtaining mortgage financing. Some buyers are even deleting the section of the GAR Contract obligating the defaulting party to pay the brokers the real estate commission they would have earned had the transaction closed.[1016] Deleting the paragraph does not mean that all claims of the brokers to a commission are extinguished. The broker representing the defaulting party still has whatever claims to a commission that exist under the brokerage engagement agreement with that party. If the parties want to limit remedies the following special stipulations can be used.

1008   GAR Form F20.

1009   GAR Form F80.

1010   *New York Ins. Co. v. Willett*, 183 Ga.App. 767, 360 S.E.2d 37 (1987).

1011   *New York Ins. Co. v. Willett*, 183 Ga.App. 767, 360 S.E.2d 37 (1987).

1012   *See* Chapter 14 (Disputes Arising from the Contract) for a more detailed discussion of specific performance; GAR Form F20 and F23.

1013   *Laseter v. Brown*, 251 Ga. 179, 304 S.E. 2d 72 (1983); *Southeastern Land Fund, Inc. v. Real Estate World, Inc.*, 237 Ga. 227, 227 S.E.2d 340 (1976).

1014   *Laseter v. Brown*, 251 Ga. 179, 304 S.E.2d 72 (1983).

1015   GAR Form F20.

1016   GAR Form F20.

Special Stipulation 88: Seller's Damages Limited to Earnest Money as Liquidated Damages

Notwithstanding any provision to the contrary contained herein, Buyer and Seller hereby agree that in the event of Buyer's breach of this Agreement, Seller's sole remedy shall be the receipt of the earnest money deposited by Buyer with Holder as liquidated damages, which is a reasonable pre-estimate of the Seller's damages and not a penalty. Seller shall not be entitled to actual damages or specific performance. The parties may also limit the buyer's remedies by providing a similar special stipulation. Some contracts provide that the buyer's sole remedy is limited to the return of earnest money plus a stipulated amount. If the parties want to limit the buyer's remedies, the following special stipulation may be used.

Special Stipulation 89: Buyer's Damages Limited to Return of Earnest Money Plus Payment of $ _____.

Notwithstanding any provision to the contrary contained herein, Buyer and Seller hereby agree that in the event of Seller's breach of this Agreement for any reason whatsoever, Buyer's sole remedy shall be the return of the earnest money deposited with Holder plus the payment by Seller to Buyer of $ _____ as liquidated damages, it being agreed that such damages are a reasonable pre-estimate of Buyer's actual damages and not a penalty. Buyer shall not have the right of specific performance or the right to pursue Seller for damages.

§ 5.10.3 Earnest Money Designated As Liquidated Damages Cannot Be Penalty

The GAR Contracts provide that if a buyer is in default, the earnest money may be paid to the seller. This means that if the seller has performed the seller's obligations but the buyer refuses to close the purchase of the property by the closing date, then the seller is entitled to keep the earnest money.[1017] Georgia courts, however, will not allow a seller to keep earnest money as liquidated damages for a buyer's breach of a real estate contract if the buyer can show that doing so would be a penalty. The distinction between an enforceable liquidated damages provision and an unenforceable penalty can be slight and, in many cases, there will be no clear distinction. The courts have, however, repeatedly cited a three-part test for the enforceability of liquidated damages. First, the injury caused by the breach must be difficult or impossible to accurately estimate. Second, the parties must intend to provide for damages rather than for a penalty. Third, the sum stipulated as liquidated damages must be a reasonable pre-estimate of the probable loss.[1018] The burden will be on the defaulting party to show that the liquidated damages provision is a penalty and therefore unenforceable.[1019]

The courts will look at the facts, the contract, and the intent of the parties in determining whether the liquidated damages provision is enforceable. In one case, the court reviewed whether a $10,000 earnest money payment on a contract of sale for a $111,000 condominium unit was intended as liquidated damages in the event of the buyer's default. The buyer argued that $10,000 was a penalty and since such penalties are not enforceable, recovery should be limited to the seller's actual damages shown. The court noted that it must decide whether to permit the $10,000 to serve as liquidated damages based on the three-part test referenced above. The court concluded that the amount of earnest

---

1017 *Henderson v. Millner Developments LLC*, 259 Ga.App. 709, 578 S.E.2d 289, (2003).In this case, the liquidated damages clause provided that the builder may retain the $250,000 earnest money deposit in the event of the buyer's breach only if the builder had performed all of its own obligations under the contract. Since, the seller had not performed all of its obligations, the liquidated damages clause was not applicable and the seller was not entitled to retain the earnest money.

1018 *Southeastern Land Fund, Inc. v. Real Estate World, Inc.*, 237 Ga. 227, 227 S.E.2d 340 (1976); citing Calamari & Perillo, <u>The Law of Contracts</u>, 367 (1970).

1019 *Liberty Life Ins. Co. v. Thomas B. Hartley Const. Co., Inc.*, 258 Ga. 808, 375 S.E.2d 222 (1989).

money demanded was a reasonable pre-estimate of the probable loss, especially in light of the seller's uncertainty of the real estate market in the early 1980's and the staggered payments called for in the earnest money provision.[1020]

On the other hand, the court in another case reviewed the payment of $50,000 as earnest money on an $800,000 purchase price. In correspondence, the president of the realty company had set out revised terms of payment and added that they would deposit the $50,000 non-refundable earnest money with the escrow agent which would apply in full against the purchase price. When the parties failed to close, the buyer demanded return of the earnest money. At trial, the real estate agent testified that "the $50,000 figure bore no relation to estimated damages; rather it was an arbitrary number -high enough to insure that the buyer would go through with the deal."[1021] The court concluded that at least two of the three factors required for a finding of liquidated damages were missing: the intention to provide for damages and the estimate of the probable loss. Therefore, the non-refundable earnest money was found to be an unreasonable and unenforceable penalty.[1022]

The label the parties place on the payment does not generally determine whether the liquidated damages are an unreasonable penalty.[1023] However, in one case, the court concluded that use of the term "forfeited" in the addendum to the sales contract showed an intent of the parties to impose an unenforceable penalty rather than a reasonable pre-estimate of the seller's probable loss should the buyer fail to close the transaction. Therefore, the seller was not entitled to the earnest money as liquidated damages.[1024] While there is no "magic" number that will ensure that a certain sum will be found to be valid liquidated damages rather than a penalty, the Georgia Supreme Court in one case found that a liquidated damages clause in the amount of ten percent (10%) of the purchase price is per *se* reasonable.[1025]

§ 5.10.3.1 Alternative Provisions

In some cases, the seller may want to specify an amount greater than the earnest money as the agreed upon liquidated damages upon a default of a buyer. Keep in mind that the same rules discussed above regarding the liquidated damages not being a "penalty" will apply so it is important that the amount be a "reasonable estimate" of the damage to the seller. The following stipulation may be used to provide the seller with this option.

> ### Special Stipulation 90: Liquidated Damages More Than Earnest Money
>
> *Seller and Buyer acknowledge that it would be extremely impractical and difficult to ascertain the actual damages that would be suffered by Seller if Buyer failed or refused to consummate the purchase of the Property for any reason other than Seller's inability, failure, or refusal to perform any of Seller's covenants herein. Seller and Buyer have considered carefully the loss to Seller as a consequence of the negotiation and execution of this Agreement; the personal expenses Seller has incurred in connection with the preparation of this Agreement; Seller's performance hereunder; and the other damages, general and special, which Seller and Buyer realize and recognize that Seller would sustain, but which Seller cannot calculate with absolute certainty. Based upon all these considerations, Seller and Buyer have agreed that the damage to Seller would reasonably be expected to be equal to the amount of $_____ .*

1020   *Everett Associates v. Garner*, 162 Ga.App. 513, 291 S.E.2d 120 (1982).

1021   *Budget-Luxury Inn of Dayton, Ltd. v. Kamash Enterprises, Inc.*, 194 Ga.App. 375, 390 S.E.2d 607 (1990).

1022   *Budget-Luxury Inn of Dayton, Ltd. v. Kamash Enterprises, Inc.*, 194 Ga.App. 375, 390 S.E.2d 607 (1990).

1023   *Martin v. Lott*, 144 Ga. 660, 87 S.E. 902 (1916).

1024   *Fickling & Walker Co. v. Giddens Constr. Co., Inc.*, 258 Ga. 891, 376 S.E.2d 665 (1989). The addendum to the contract read as follows: "It is expressly understood and agreed to by all parties that, if for any reason this sale is not consummated by November 30, 1985, the $1,000 earnest money and the $400 security deposit shall be forfeited as liquidated damages and the sale contract shall become null and void."

1025   *Oran v. Canada Life Assur. Co.*, 194 Ga.App. 518, 390 S.E.2d 879 (1990), citing *Liberty Life Ins. Co. v. Thomas B. Hartley Construction Company, Inc.*, 258 Ga. 808, 375 S.E.2d 222 (1989).

If Seller has performed Seller's covenants hereunder, but Buyer has failed or refused to consummate the purchase of the Property by the closing date, then Seller shall be entitled to retain the earnest money toward payment of said amount of liquidated damages and to recover from Buyer the balance of said amount of liquidated damages for such default of Buyer. Said amount of liquidated damages is intended not as a penalty, but as full liquidated damages pursuant to O.C.G.A § 13-6-7. In lieu of claiming said amount as full liquidated damages, Seller shall have the right to bring an action for specific performance of the terms of the Agreement or actual damages incurred by Seller as a result of Buyer's breach, including, but not limited to, all rents due, the cost of repairs and redecorating, continued insurance coverage, utility bills, maintenance costs, ad valorem taxes, loss of use of the proceeds of the sale and decrease in value.

If the buyer wants to limit his liability to the earnest money as liquidated damages and prohibit the seller from seeking specific performance or actual damages, she may use the following special stipulation.

Special Stipulation 91:   Seller's Damages Limited to Earnest Money as Liquidated Damages

Notwithstanding any provision to the contrary contained herein, Buyer and Seller hereby agree that in the event of Buyer's breach of this Agreement, Seller's sole remedy shall be to receive or retain the earnest money as liquidated damages, which is a reasonable pre-estimate of the Seller's actual damages and not a penalty. Seller shall not be entitled to actual damages or specific performance.

§ 5.11   DEDUCTIONS FROM EARNEST MONEY

In some instances, the seller and buyer may agree that the seller can use part of the earnest money paid for the buyer's benefit. In one case, the parties agreed that the seller would use the earnest money to prepare plans for building a home. The seller drew two sets of plans at the request of the buyer. The seller was also contractually obligated to initiate the loan process. When the loan process was not initiated timely, the buyers demanded return of their full earnest money. The court concluded that even though the seller breached the contract, the seller was entitled to retain the amounts that were spent for the buyer's benefit (*i.e.*, the expense of preparing the plans) with the balance refunded to the buyers.[1026] If the parties agree that the seller will use a portion of the earnest money to do work expressly authorized for and benefiting the buyer, the following language can be used.

Special Stipulation 92:   Seller May Deduct from Earnest Money Amount Spent on Work Done for Buyer's Benefit

If the sale is not consummated for reasons other than the default of Buyer, the total amount of earnest money paid to Holder, less amounts as may be expended on Buyer's request and for Buyer's benefit and account, shall be returned to Buyer.

Of course, the risk to the buyer of having difficulty in obtaining a refund of earnest money in the event of seller's breach may be greater if the seller, rather than a third party, holds the earnest money. A broker may therefore want to include the following language in a real estate sales contract if the seller will be holding the earnest money.

Special Stipulation 93:   Buyer's Acknowledgement of Risk in Seller Holding Earnest Money

Buyer recognizes and accepts the risk of depositing earnest money with Seller since the funds will not be held by neutral party without an interest in the funds. Buyer

---

1026   *Jeff Goolsby Homes Corp. v. Smith*, 168 Ga.App. 218, 308 S.E.2d 564 (1983).

> *acknowledges that Buyer has not relied upon the advice of Broker or Broker's affiliated*
> *licensees in deciding to pay such earnest money to Seller.*[1027]

§ 5.12   DISBURSEMENT OF EARNEST MONEY IF CONTRACT VOID

If a determination is made that a contract is void, the prospective buyer will be entitled to a return of the earnest money. In one case, a real estate contract included a special stipulation stating that the contract was conditioned upon getting the property rezoned.[1028] The contract was silent as to whose duty it was to have the property rezoned. The court refused to enforce the contract on such vague terms and concluded that since the contract was void for vagueness, the buyer's earnest money must be returned. The same principle should apply to any contract ultimately found to be unenforceable.

§ 5.13   MAKING EARNEST MONEY NON-REFUNDABLE

§ 5.13.1   Making Earnest Money Non-Refundable In A Contingent Contract

Most real estate sales contracts contain contingencies. When a real estate sales contract is subject to a contingency, it means that the condition must be satisfied before the contract becomes enforceable.[1029] In other words, the condition must be met, or the contingency waived, before the parties are bound to carry out their obligation to buy or sell the property.[1030] If earnest money had been paid with respect to a sale that is contingent upon a condition being fulfilled and the condition is not met, the earnest money would normally be refunded to the buyer unless the sale contract provides otherwise.

If a contract contains a contingency, it does not mean that a party to the contract is not bound until the contingency is removed or is fulfilled. The Georgia Court of Appeals has stated that a contingency does not defeat the existence of a valid contract.[1031] Every party to a contract has an implied duty to act in good faith and fair dealing in performing her obligation. For example, the seller cannot rescind the contract during the contingency period to sell the property to a third party who has offered a higher price. The Georgia Court of Appeals stated:

> *"[M]any real estate contracts contain…financing conditions. If a vendor could successfully*
> *utilize this contract term (which is unquestionably for the buyer's protection) to rescind*
> *the contract at any time prior to the occurrence of the condition (presumably whenever*
> *the vendor received a better offer), a purchaser would never be able to rely on the contract*
> *while he sought financing. Any vendor could rescind such a contract with impunity. This*
> *result would be intolerable and would destroy the good faith reliance among individuals*
> *which permits them to act in accordance with their agreements."*[1033]

Likewise, when the contract is subject to a financing contingency, the buyer has a duty to seek financing diligently. Some real estate contracts provide that all of a portion of the earnest money is non-refundable even when the contract is subject to a contingency. The question in these situations is whether this type of provision is enforceable. The answer to this question usually hinges upon whether the language in the contract is deemed to be an enforceable liquidated damages provision or an unenforceable penalty.

1027   *See* GAR Form F80, Earnest Money Held by Seller, for more complete disclaimer.

1028   *Hit v. Lord*, 194 Ga.App. 655, 391 S.E.2d 681 (1990).

1029   *Parker v. Averett*, 114 Ga.App. 401, 151 S.E. 2d 475 (1966).

1030   *Grier V. Brogdon*, 234 Ga.App. 79, 505 S.E. 2d 512 (1998).

1031   *Grier V. Brogdon*, 234 Ga.App. 79, 505 S.E. 2d 512 (1998).

1032   *Patel v. Burt Development Company*, 261 Ga.App. 436, 582 S.E.2d 495 (2003).

1033   *Brack v. Brownlee*, 246 Ga. 818, 273 S.E. 2d 390 (1980).

In most real estate contracts, earnest money is returned to the buyer if a contingency to which the contract is subject fails. Under the GAR Contracts, the seller is only entitled to the earnest money if the contract is breached by the buyer.

There are two theories which can be used to make earnest money non-refundable. The first is to characterize it as separate consideration paid by the buyer to the seller to keep the property off of the market while the buyer satisfies contingencies to which the contract is subject. A sample special stipulation for such situations follows.

Special Stipulation 94: Portion of Earnest Money is Non-Refundable

Buyer and Seller acknowledge and agree that in this transaction there is value to the Seller agreeing to enter into a contract subject to contingencies benefiting the Buyer, in that the Property is being kept off the market while Buyer seeks to satisfy these contingencies. Notwithstanding any provision to the contrary contained herein, Buyer agrees that $_____ of earnest money shall not be deposited with Holder but shall instead be paid by Buyer directly to Seller as separate consideration for Seller entering into a contract subject to contingencies. In this transaction the earnest money held by Holder shall be $_____. The earnest money paid to Seller shall immediately become the property of Seller and shall be non-refundable to Buyer. In the event Buyer closes on the purchase of the Property, all earnest money paid in this transaction, including the earnest money paid to Seller, shall be applied toward and credited against the purchase price of the Property.

A second approach is to treat the earnest money as liquidated damages in the event the buyer does not close. An example of this type of provision is set forth below.

Special Stipulation 95: Earnest Money Non-Refundable as Liquidated Damages in Contract with Contingencies

Buyer and Seller acknowledge and agree that while the parties have entered into a contingent contract for the benefit of the Buyer, if Buyer cannot satisfy the contingencies and close on the purchase of the Property, Seller will be substantially damaged because the Property will have effectively been kept off the market while Buyer attempted to satisfy the contingencies to which this Agreement is subject. Therefore, all parties agree that if Buyer fails to close upon the purchase of the Property for any reason whatsoever (other than the breach of this Agreement by Seller), the earnest money shall be paid to Seller as liquidated damages. All parties agree that the amount of the liquidated damages is a reasonable pre-estimate of Seller's actual damages and not a penalty.

§ 5.13.2 Making Earnest Money Non-Refundable In An "As Is" Contract

When a property is sold "as-is," some purchase and sale agreements provide that the earnest money deposit is non-refundable. An exception that is commonly provided, however, is in the event the agreement is terminated due to the seller's default. An example of this type of provision is set forth below.

Special Stipulation 96: Earnest Money Non-Refundable as Liquidated Damages in "As-Is" Contract

Notwithstanding any provision to the contrary contained herein, Buyer agrees to purchase the Property in "as-is, where-is" condition. Prior to entering into this Agreement, Buyer had the full opportunity to evaluate the Property to confirm its condition and fitness for Buyer's intended purposes. In the event, Buyer fails to close upon the purchase of the Property, all earnest money and other amounts paid by Buyer under this Agreement shall be paid to Seller as full and complete liquidated damages (except in the event the failure

of Buyer to close is caused by the breach of this Agreement by Seller). Seller and Buyer
agree that the amount of the liquidated damages is a reasonable pre-estimate of Seller's
actual damages and is not a penalty.

§ 5.14 BROKERAGE COMPANY NOT LIABLE FOR AGENT'S MISREPRESENTATIONS WITH REGARD TO EARNEST MONEY

The general practice in Georgia is that real estate licensees are independent contractors and not employees of the real estate brokerage firms for which they work. The court has upheld the independent contractor relationship between the broker and the licensee.[1034] This should be the case so long as the broker does not attempt to control the licensee's time, manner, or method of work but merely instructs the agent as to the desired outcome (*i.e.*, obtain listings and/or purchasers, etc.).[1035]

As an independent contractor, the broker and her real estate company cannot be held liable for the tortious acts of the licensee unless the broker takes an active role in the wrongful act or subsequently affirms the licensee's misdeed. In one case, the court reviewed a situation in which the real estate licensee falsely represented that he had received an earnest money check from the prospective buyer.[1036] The seller continued with the contract, keeping the property off the market and causing the seller harm when the transaction did not close. Because the seller did not have the earnest money as liquidated damages, the seller sued the real estate company as well as the agent. The court concluded that the realty company was not responsible for the tortious acts of its independent contractor affiliated licensee.

In at least one reported case, however, the broker went too far and was found to have created an employer/employee relationship with the licensee.[1037] In this case, the court described what it found to be the "more typical business arrangement" between a broker and agent as one in which the agent "clearly occupies the position of an independent contractor." The court described the brokers in such typical situations as follows:

> [G]reat care is taken by the [broker] to refrain from exercising control over the manner in which individual salespersons conduct their work. No particular working hours are set. The salespersons exercise personal initiative to obtain 'listings,' or the opportunity to sell existing houses, from individual owners. Duties that could be considered 'control' by the [broker], such as attending sales meetings or assisting in the broker's office, are clearly designated as 'optional.' Items such as form contracts, telephones, and office supplies are either paid for by the salesperson or provided as a convenience with no requirement that they be used.

In this case, "evidence was presented that [the agent] was by no means a 'typical' real estate salesperson." The agent was assigned by the broker to work in a new home subdivision as her sole and exclusive employment during certain specified business hours or "staff duty schedule." She was required to be on duty during these hours. She was required to use certain procedures when negotiating the sale of a lot in the subdivision. She was required to use standard forms. The agent was also subject to quarterly performance reviews. In light of the nature and degree of these controls, the court found that there was a true employer/employee relationship. The court found that as such the broker could be liable for the wrongful acts of her employee.

1034 *Ross v. Ninety-Two West, Ltd.*, 201 Ga.App. 887, 412 S.E.2d 876 (1991).

1035 *Caveat*: The broker still has supervisory duties of all licensees affiliated with the firm.

1036 *Ross v. Ninety-Two West, Ltd.*, 201 Ga.App. 887, 412 S.E.2d 876 (1991).

1037 *Mark Six Realty Associates, Inc. v. Drake*, 219 Ga.App. 57, 463 S.E.2d 917 (1995).

§ 5.15   LAW AGAINST MONEY LAUNDERING

Federal and state law requires financial institutions and other money service businesses to report transactions exceeding $10,000 and transactions deemed suspicious for any reason. The law also prohibits any party from structuring a transaction where the transaction is divided into two or more transactions which, if considered as a whole, would be reportable.[1038] Under federal law, property that is involved in a transaction or attempted transaction in violation of the money laundering statutes is subject to forfeiture to the government.[1039]

The court ordered forfeiture of a residence in one case where the mortgage on the property had been paid by checks drawn on three accounts funded by 33 cash deposits, each in an amount less than $10,000 and made over a period of two days in three financial institutions.[1040] The federal government argued that the property was involved in, facilitated, or represented proceeds of deposits structured to avoid the currency reporting requirements.

In another case, the court found that the property was involved in a transaction or attempted transaction in violation of federal reporting and structuring law when the $95,000 down payment on the property was made by way of ten cashier's checks ranging in amount from $7,500 to $10,000, and where the checks were obtained on five different dates and from five different banks. The court noted that the owners failed to prove that the property was not involved in the structuring or other violations.[1041]

1038   31 U.S.C.A. § 5313(a), 31 U.S.C.A. § 5324(a) and O.C.G.A. § 7-1-912.

1039   18 U.S.C.A. § 981(a)(1) and 18 U.S.C.A. § 982(a)(1).

1040   *United States v 5709 Hillingdon Rd.* (1996, WD NC); 919 F Supp 863.

1041   *United States v 874 Gartel Drive*, (1996, CA9 Cal) 79 F3d 918, 96 CDOS (1945).

The **RED BOOK**

CHAPTER 6

PURCHASE PRICE

OVERVIEW

This chapter on purchase price is short; nevertheless, understanding the implication of how a purchase price is stated is critical in real estate contracts. We will first discuss what the GAR contracts provide regarding the stating of the purchase price. We will also discuss the implications of determining purchase price based on acreage or on an appraisal. The consequences of failing to adequately define the purchase price will also be discussed.

The next chapter will discuss in detail the various ways that a buyer can finance the purchase of property and the buyer's obligations to pursue financing.

§ 6.1 WHAT THE GAR CONTRACTS PROVIDE

A contract for the sale of real property should always state the purchase price either (a) as a definite and specific amount, or (b) in a manner in which the purchase price can easily be determined.[1042] The GAR Contracts provide that the purchase price be a definite and specific amount which may be subject to certain financing contingencies. Other GAR Form agreements and stipulations discussed below allow the parties to state the purchase price in other ways. This is permissible provided the purchase price can be easily determined.

§ 6.2 PURCHASE PRICE BASED ON ACREAGE

In some transactions, the exact purchase price is determined after execution of the contract by the buyer and seller. In contracts for the purchase of raw land, for example, the purchase price is often stated as an amount to be paid per acre with the total acreage to be determined by a survey prepared at a future date. Courts in Georgia have held that so long as the property is clearly defined, such contracts are enforceable even though an exact dollar price for the property is not specified.[1043]

The GAR Lot Purchase and Sale Agreement[1044] and the GAR Land Purchase and Sale Agreement[1045] provide an option for a purchase price based on acreage as an alternative to a specific total dollar amount. If the purchase price is based on acreage, the buyer and seller agree to have a survey made of the property (at the buyer's expense) by a registered Georgia surveyor. The purchase price is then determined by multiplying the total number of acres, to the nearest one-hundredth of an acre, by a stipulated sum per acre. If the survey is not mutually acceptable, the parties agree to resolve that issue in accordance with the provisions of the GAR Survey Resolution Exhibit.[1046]

The GAR Survey Resolution Exhibit establishes a procedure to resolve differences between the buyer's survey and the seller's survey (if the seller elects to commission a survey after reviewing the buyer's survey.) If the seller and buyer are unable to agree upon a survey, then both the buyer and seller will cause their respective surveyors to name a third surveyor. If the two surveyors have not named a third surveyor within seven calendar days from the date they are requested to make an appointment, a superior court judge serving the county where the property is located may appoint a third surveyor. The third surveyor is employed by the buyer and seller to make a survey of the property, the cost of which is equally borne by the buyer and seller. The acreage on the survey by the third surveyor will be used in the formula to calculate the purchase price.

1042 *Carroll v. Jones*, 206 Ga. 332, 57 S.E.2d 173 (1950).

1043 *Bowles v. Babcock and Wilcox Co.*, 209 Ga. 858, 76 S.E.2d 703 (1953). It is important that even if the actual acreage is not known and is to be determined on the basis of a survey, the location of the property must be clearly defined. *See* Chapter 4 (Describing the Property) for a detailed discussion of the sufficiency of the property description.

1044 GAR Form F27.

1045 GAR Form F34.

1046 GAR Form F138.

If the purchase price is based on acreage, a contingency may also be included in the contract giving the buyer the right to terminate the contract if the property is more or less than a specified number of acres. An example of such a contingency is set out in Special Stipulation 56 ("Buyer's Right to Terminate If Survey Shows Property to be Smaller or Larger").

§ 6.3 PURCHASE PRICE BASED ON APPRAISAL

Contracts providing that the purchase price of the property will be based on an appraisal prepared by a licensed appraiser are generally recognized as being sufficiently definite, and, therefore, enforceable. In one case, a Georgia court held that an option contract was legally sufficient when the purchase price was "the appraised value of the property based on an MAI Appraisal" because the contract provided a "key" by which the purchase price could be determined.[1047]

On the other hand, the following phrase within an exclusive listing contract, which did not specify the method of appraisal or of determining the amount of consideration, resulted in an unenforceable contract: "w/option to accept appraised in 60 days."[1048] The court found that the phrase was not sufficiently certain to provide a "key" to determine the sale price, holding that the phrase was incomplete as to the manner in which the property was to be appraised. In another case, the parties agreed that the property would be sold at an appraised value. The court stated that "appraised value" was too indefinite to create a binding contract. In this case, the court did note that a price based on an appraised value might be enforceable if there is a "key" by which a definite price can be ascertained.[1049]

While selling a property based on a future appraisal of the property may be legal, it does not mean that doing so is a good business idea. Appraisals are opinions of value that can widely vary from appraiser or appraiser. Therefore, relying on one appraiser's opinion in setting the sales price of a property could result in the sales price being much higher or lower that what the parties anticipated.

If the parties agree to have the purchase price determined by an appraisal, the following provision may be incorporated in the contract. The risk of the appraisal coming in at either a very high or a very low valuation is addressed in the special stipulation by establishing a floor and ceiling for the appraised price above and below which the parties do not have to proceed with the purchase and sale.

> **Special Stipulation 97: Purchase Price Based on Appraisal**
>
> *The Purchase Price of the Property shall be determined by an appraisal of the Property prepared by the following appraiser (Name), who holds a certified residential or better designation from the Georgia Real Estate Appraiser's Board, no later than (number) days from the Binding Agreement Date. The appraisal shall be jointly arranged by the Buyer and Seller, and the parties agree to instruct the appraiser to immediately provide a copy of the appraisal to both parties upon its completion. Buyer and Seller shall each pay the following percentage of the costs of the appraisal: Buyer ___%, Seller _____%. If the Property appraises for more than $_____, then within ___ days of Buyer's receipt of the appraisal, Buyer may terminate this Agreement by written notice to Seller and all earnest money shall be promptly refunded to Buyer. If Buyer fails to timely exercise this termination right, it shall be deemed waived. If the Property appraises for less than $_____, then within ___ days of Seller's receipt of the appraisal, Seller may terminate this Agreement by written notice to Buyer and all earnest money shall be promptly refunded to Buyer. If Seller fails to timely exercise this termination right it shall be deemed waived.*

1047 *Miller v. McCullough*, 236 Ga. 666, 224 S.E.2d 916 (1976).

1048 *Wiley v. Tom Howell & Associates, Inc.*, 154 Ga.App. 235, 267 S.E.2d 816 (1980).

1049 *Pettigrew v. Collins*, 246 Ga.App. 207, 539 S.E.2d 214 (2000).

§ 6.4 EFFECT OF FAILURE TO STATE FULL PURCHASE PRICE

Parties to a contract should ensure that the full purchase price is stated in the written contract and should not rely on oral promises or side agreements of the buyer to pay additional amounts. When a written contract for the sale of property includes a merger clause[1050] (*i.e.*, provides that it is the sole and entire agreement of the parties) and makes no mention of additional sums due from the buyer, the buyer's alleged oral promise to pay an additional sum is generally unenforceable.

The effect of failure to state the full purchase price in the written contract is demonstrated in a case in which the buyer delivered a letter to the sellers agreeing to purchase the property for $135,000 plus an additional $5,000 if the buyer was able to sell all of the lots which were to be subdivided from the property within six months from the date of closing.[1051] The sellers accepted this proposal and entered into a contract for the sale of the property for $135,000 and did not make any reference to the payment of the additional $5,000 outlined in the letter. The contract also contained a provision that it constituted the sole and entire agreement between the parties (*i.e.*, a merger clause). The sellers sued the buyer when the buyer refused to pay the sellers the additional $5,000 after all of the subdivided lots was sold within six months from the closing date. The court concluded that because the contract stated that it was the sole and entire agreement, the parties expressly excluded the use of any evidence outside the contract to show the intent of the parties. Therefore, the buyer's promise to pay the additional $5,000 was unenforceable.

A court more recently concluded that a buyer's oral promise to pay an additional $24,740 to a seller was unenforceable.[1052] The seller argued that the buyers fraudulently induced her to enter the contract using an oral promise; however, the merger clause in the contract precluded the seller's recovery. The seller's alternative would have been to rescind the contract and sue for the alleged fraud and deceit. Such an action would need to be brought immediately upon the discovery of the fraud.[1053]

§ 6.5 PAYMENT OF PURCHASE PRICE IN ALL CASH

Most buyers obtain a mortgage from a lender to finance a purchase and sale transaction. However, some buyers have the means to purchase a property by paying all cash. The GAR Contract for residential property gives the buyer an option to specify that the purchase price will be paid in all cash or its equivalent at closing without a financing contingency. Even if a contract for the purchase and sale of property does not specify the method for paying the purchase price, it is presumed that the purchase price will be paid in full at closing.[1054]

If the contract provides for financing, the purchaser can waive the financing contingency in most cases. The general rule that the buyer may waive a financing contingency is based on the theory that the contingency is for the buyer's benefit.[1055] However, if the financing terms call for the seller to finance the transaction the financing contingency may also be for the seller's benefit, in which case the buyer may be precluded from waiving the financing contingency and paying all cash.[1056] Generally, a buyer in an all cash transaction pays the purchase price by either cashier's check or wire transfer. Cash is normally not used in this type of transaction because the amount of the purchase price being paid normally triggers the reporting requirements pursuant to federal and state money laundering statutes.[1057]

1050   GAR Forms F20, F23, F27 and CF2.

1051   *Kiser v. Godwin*, 90 Ga.App. 825, 84 S.E.2d 474 (1954).

1052   *Mitchell v. Head*, 195 Ga.App. 427, 394 S.E.2d 114 (1990).

1053   *See* Chapter 14 (Disputes Arising from the Contract) for a more detailed discussion on rescission.

1054   *Allen v. Home Service & Constr., Inc.*, 93 Ga.App. 438, 92 S.E.2d 36 (1956).

1055   *Edwards v. McTyre*, 246 Ga. 302, 271 S.E.2d 205 (1980); *Blanton v. Williams*, 209 Ga. 16, 70 S.E.2d 461 (1952).

1056   The possibility of such an outcome is hinted at in *Sikes v. Markham*, 74 Ga.App. 874, 41 S.E.2d 828 (1947). In this case the court referred to the fact that a lien holder "may not wish to surrender before the many respective monthly maturity dates" of payments due under a monthly installment loan. If the lien holder is the Seller, the financing contingency may actually be for the Seller's benefit. *See* § 7.1 of this work for a discussion of waiver of contingencies.

1057   31 U.S.C.A. § 5311 *et seq.* and O.C.G.A. §7-1-910 *et seq.*

§ 6.5.1 Payment Of Purchase Price By Cashier's Check

Only certain types of checks may be used in a purchase and sale transaction. Most purchase and sale agreements provide that cashier's checks are an acceptable form of payment in an all cash transaction. This type of check is a popular method of payment because it affords a certain level of security to the person receiving the check. The Official Code of Georgia defines a check as (i) a draft, other than a documentary draft, payable on demand and drawn on a bank; or (ii) a cashier's check, teller's check, or money order.[1058] However, only certain types of checks provide a secure payment to a seller. For instance, personal checks are not considered a secure form of payment because there is the possibility that the check may be dishonored or be made subject to a stop payment order and the seller would be left with no payment at all. Cashier's checks and certified checks, however, are generally considered acceptable forms of payment.

There is one major difference between a cashier's check and a certified check. A cashier's check is a check drawn on the *bank's* credit at the request of the account holder.[1059] A certified check is a check drawn on the *account holder's* credit at the request of the account holder.[1060] The distinction is subtle but it creates a significant difference in the type of checks preferred when paying the purchase price of a property.

Since a certified check is drawn on an account holder's credit, the account holder has the ability to stop payment on a certified check that has been issued to another person.[1061] In other words, after a person draws a certified check, she may instruct the bank to withhold the funds and refuse payment to whomever the check was issued to.[1062] The person drawing a cashier's check, however, may not thereafter instruct the bank to refuse payment because the check was drawn on the bank's credit.[1063] For this reason, sellers (or other persons receiving payment) often prefer payment by a cashier's check over a certified check because the seller is guaranteed payment by the issuing bank.[1064] By requiring a cashier's check, a seller will be provided a secure form of payment and potentially avoid the trouble of dealing with cancelled checks.

The GAR Purchase and Sale Agreement[1065] provides a cashier's check issued by a federally insured bank as an acceptable form of payment. Therefore, payment by certified check, personal check, or any other form not specifically provided therein would not be an acceptable method of payment in an all cash transaction.

Certified checks may be issued for any amount.[1066] With the growing resources in technology, however, many closing attorneys have encountered numerous problems with fraudulently issued certified checks. As a practical way of dealing with this issue, some closing attorneys have stopped accepting certified checks issued over a certain amount. Any payment above that limit would then need to be completed by wire transfer. Other closing attorneys have stopped accepting certified checks altogether and have exclusively turned to wire transfers to secure payment at closing.

§ 6.5.2 Payment Of Purchase Price By Wire Transfer

Payment by wire transfer has become increasingly popular in real estate transactions. This form of payment is attractive to both buyers and sellers because it is a relatively quick and secure method of payment in an all cash transaction.

1058   O.C.G.A. § 11-3-104.

1059   *Wright v. Trust Co. of Ga.*, 108 Ga.App. 783, 134 S.E.2d 457 (1963).

1060   *Wright v. Trust Co. of Ga.*, 108 Ga.App. 783, 134 S.E.2d 457 (1963).

1061   *Wright v. Trust Co. of Ga.*, 108 Ga.App. 783, 134 S.E.2d 457 (1963).

1062   *McIntire v. Raskin*, 173 Ga. 746, 161 S.E. 363 (1931).

1063   *David v. First Nat. Bank of Commerce*, 27 U.C.C. Rep. Serv. 2d 1321, 650 So. 2d 1227 (La. App. 1995).

1064   *David v. First Nat. Bank of Commerce*, 27 U.C.C. Rep. Serv. 2d 1321, 650 So. 2d 1227 (La. App. 1995).

1065   GAR Form F20.

1066   O.C.G.A. § 44-14-13(c)(1) and (4). Under Georgia law, a [personal] check or checks in an aggregate amount may not exceed $5,000 per loan closing.

To complete a wire transfer, the person making the payment sends a payment instruction to her bank which is instructed to pay, or cause another bank to pay, the recipient of the payment.[1067] Wire transfers require an individual bank to process the transaction. Therefore, a buyer who is purchasing a property would send payment instructions to her bank and instruct the bank to pay the seller. Once the seller's bank received the instruction from the buyer's bank, the seller's bank would process the transaction and place the money in the seller's account to complete the purchase and sale transaction.

Wire transfers are relatively a quick payment method of payment. When a buyer uses a wire transfer to pay the purchase price, the funds are transferred using a wire transfer network, automated clearing house, or other association of banks which allows a payment order by a bank to be transmitted to the recipient's bank.[1068] This system allows wire transfers to take place usually within minutes.[1069] However, a receiving bank may establish a cut-off time on a funds-transfer business day for the receipt and processing of payment orders.[1070] Different cut-off times may apply to senders generally, different payment orders or different categories of payment orders.[1071] If a payment order is not received by the cut-off time or at the end of the funds-transfer business day, the receiving bank may not process the payment order until the next funds-transfer business day.[1072] Therefore, before using a wire transfer, it is important for the buyer and seller to check with their banks to determine the respective cut-off times for the particular transaction. If the seller is expecting immediate payment, the parties should plan for the closing to take place with enough time for both banks to process the wire transfer to complete the transaction.

Buyers and sellers in real estate transactions favor using wire transfers to pay the purchase price in an all cash transaction due to the security this method of payment offers. Every bank that completes a wire transfer establishes security procedures to ensure each transaction is completed with accuracy.[1073] Most security procedures are implemented to detect any errors in the transmission, verify the identity of the customer, and confirm the amount of the payment order in each wire transfer request.[1074] Security procedures often prevent payment orders that are fraudulent or transmitted by mistake.[1075] Most often, there is less chance of fraud when completing a transaction through a wire transfer. For these reasons, most purchase and sale agreements, including the GAR Purchase and Sale Agreement,[1076] provides that a wire transfer is an acceptable form of payment when completing an all cash transaction.

§ 6.5.3 What Constitutes Good Funds

Georgia law places limitations on settlement agents for any real property closing in Georgia. No settlement agent may disburse settlement proceeds to the seller unless those proceeds are "collected funds."[1077] That means that the seller's payment of the purchase price (in an all-cash transaction) or the lender's payment of loan proceeds into the closing attorney's trust account must be actually collected by the bank, and not just deposited into the attorney's account.

1067   U.C.C. § 4A-104.

1068   O.C.G.A. § 11-4A-105.

1069   U.C.C. § 4A-104.

1070   O.C.G.A. § 11-4A-106.

1071   O.C.G.A. § 11-4A-106.

1072   O.C.G.A. § 11-4A-106.

1073   O.C.G.A. § 11-4A-201.

1074   O.C.G.A. § 11-4A-201.

1075   O.C.G.A. § 11-4A-201.

1076   GAR Form F20.

1077   O.C.G.A. § 44-14-13(c).

There are four exceptions to this rule. The closing attorney will be allowed to disburse proceeds after receipt of any of the following negotiable instruments, even if the funds are not yet actually collected funds:

(a) A cashier's check issued by a federally insured bank, savings bank, savings and loan association, or credit union, issued by a lender for a closing or loan transaction, provided that the funds are immediately available and the cashier's check cannot be dishonored or refused when negotiated or presented for payment;[1078]

(b) A check drawn on the escrow account of an attorney licensed to practice law in Georgia, or on the escrow account of a real estate broker licensed in Georgia, if the settlement agent has reasonable and prudent grounds to believe that the check will constitute collected funds within a reasonable period;[1079]

(c) A check issued by the federal government or any agency thereof, or by the Georgia state government or any agency or political subdivision of the State of Georgia;[1080] or

(d) A check or checks in an aggregate amount not to exceed $5,000 per loan closing.[1081] Older versions of the "good fund" statute specifically provided that a personal check or checks in the aggregate amount could not exceed $5,000 per loan closing.[1082] Although this language has been removed, the current statute is still interpreted to limit the amount of a personal check to $5,000 or less.

§ 6.5.4 When A Lender Closes Its Doors

In recent years, a number of mortgage lenders have either closed their doors or gotten out of the business of originating mortgage loans. As a result, O.C.G.A. § 44-14-13 has been amended to its current form (summarized above) and various exceptions that existed previously have been removed. The new version of the statute became effective on July 1, 2008. These changes were made in light of the aftermath of several mortgage lenders closing their doors or filing for bankruptcy protection after issuing their checks to closing attorneys for the funding of numerous real estate loans. When the transactions were closed, the closing attorneys paid the loan proceeds to sellers. Then when the mortgage lender did not honor their check, the closing attorneys had to make good the funds. Many closing attorneys are now accepting only wire transferred funds for closings.

The problem with lenders closing their doors has also left some buyers in the lurch when they have been fully approved for a loan but the mortgage lender cannot then fund the mortgage loan. For example, let's assume that a buyer has qualified for the loan specified in the GAR Purchase and Sale Agreement within the Financing Contingency Period. Three days prior to the scheduled closing the buyer is notified that the lender with whom he is qualified has filed for bankruptcy protection.

The GAR Purchase and Sale Agreement does provide that the parties may agree to extend the closing date. But what if one party does not agree? Either party can only extend the closing date unilaterally for a period of 7 days. That may be enough time for the buyer to obtain financing through another lender, but that's a tight spot for any buyer to be in. Until the mortgage lending business calms down a bit, selling brokers may want to consider the following special stipulation to further protect their clients from such event:

1078   O.C.G.A. § 44-14-13(c)(1).

1079   O.C.G.A. § 44-14-13(c)(2).

1080   O.C.G.A. § 44-14-13(c)(3).

1081   O.C.G.A. § 44-14-13(c)(4).

1082   O.C.G.A. § 44-14-13(c)(6) (2007); 2007 Georgia Senate Bill No. 355, Georgia One Hundred Forty-Ninth General Assembly-2007-2008 Regular Session.

Special Stipulation 98:   Lender's Failure to Fund Buyer's Loan

In the event the Buyer's mortgage lender ceases to originate mortgage loans, or fails to fund Buyer's mortgage loan after the Buyer has already been approved for said loan, Buyer may unilaterally extend the closing date for 21 days to give Buyer additional time to obtain mortgage financing from a different mortgage lender.

§ 6.6   ALLOCATION OF CLOSING COSTS IN ALL CASH TRANSACTIONS

There have been some disputes between buyers and sellers over what constitutes and who pays closing costs in transactions where a non-GAR contract is used. The following special stipulation can be used to try to allocate costs between the buyer and the seller in such a transaction.

Special Stipulation 99:   Allocating Closing Costs in all Cash Transactions

In this transaction, the following costs and charges shall be paid for by either the Buyer or Seller as indicated below:

1. Preparation of Survey   _____*Buyer* _____*Seller*

2. Preparation of Warranty Deed   _____*Buyer* _____*Seller*

3. Preparation of Seller's Affidavit   _____*Buyer* _____*Seller*

4. Preparation of Settlement Statement _____*Buyer* _____*Seller*

All other costs and charges necessary to close the transaction shall be paid for by the

_____.

The **RED BOOK**

CHAPTER 7

METHODS
OF PAYMENT
AND
FINANCING

OVERVIEW

This chapter discusses FHA and VA loans, commercial loans, financing contingencies, seller financing, loan assumptions, and tax-deferred exchanges. We will also address issues such as the requirement that the buyer have sufficient cash at closing, the seller's right to provide financing or buy down the interest rate on a loan on behalf of the buyer, whether the buyer can receive a credit for repairs at closing, and the effect of the buyer applying for a different loan than any which might be described in the contract.

§ 7.1 MORTGAGE FINANCING GENERALLY IN GEORGIA

In Georgia, loans received by real property are referred to as mortgages. However, a deed to secure debt is the correct legal name for such a loan.[1083] The borrower signs a promissory note promising to repay the loan in accordance with the terms of the note. The borrower also signs a deed to secure debt pledging the real property as collateral for the loan described in the promissory note.[1084] Technically, when a borrower signs a Deed to Secure Debt, the borrower is deeding the property to the lender to secure the loan.[1085] However, the borrower retains an equitable interest in the real property which gives the borrower the right to occupy the property.[1086] In the event the borrower defaults on the loan, the lender can either sue on the promissory note and/or foreclose on the property.[1087]

Georgia is known as a non-judicial foreclosure state. This means that the lender does not need to obtain the permission of a court prior to foreclosing against the property.[1088] Instead, the lender can foreclose based upon what is referred to as a power of sale set forth in the deed to secure debt.[1089] There are certain statutory requirements that must be met prior to foreclosing based on a power of sale, including sending a notice of default to the borrower and advertising the property for sale for four consecutive weeks prior to the week of the foreclosure in the official newspaper for the county.[1090] The foreclosure itself always takes place on the first Tuesday of the month on the courthouse steps of the county in which the property is located. The lender or her agent literally stands on the courthouse steps, reads aloud a variety of documents and sells the property at auction to the highest bidder. Most lenders will also bid on the property up to either the amount of their loan or a lesser amount that is what the lender believes is the fair market value of the property.

In Georgia, once the foreclosure has taken place, the borrower losses all of the her interest in the property. If the borrower does not move out of the property voluntarily, the lender has the right to evict the tenant from the property. Once the sale under power has occurred, the borrower has no right to redeem the property where the borrower can pay off the amount owed and re-claim the property.

§ 7.2 FINANCING PROVISIONS GENERALLY

It is an economic necessity for most buyers to obtain a mortgage loan in order to have sufficient funds to purchase a property. Buyers needing to obtain a mortgage loan will normally make the purchase and sale agreement contingent upon the buyer being approved for a specific loan.

1083   O.C.G.A. § 44-14-60. "Whenever a person in this state conveys any real property by deed to secure any debt to any person loaning or advancing the grantor any money or to secure any other debt and takes a bond for title back to the grantor upon the payment of the debt or debts or in like manner conveys any personal property by bill of sale and takes an obligation binding the person to whom the property is conveyed to reconvey the property upon the payment of the debt or debts, the conveyance of real or personal property shall pass the title of the property to the grantee until the debt or debts which the conveyance was made to secure shall be fully paid. Such conveyance shall be held by the courts to be an absolute conveyance, with the right reserved by the grantor to have the property reconveyed to her upon the payment of the debt or debts intended to be secured agreeably to the terms of the contract, and shall not be held to be a mortgage..."

1084   O.C.G.A. § 44-14-60.

1085   O.C.G.A. § 44-14-60.

1086   *In re Polo Club Apartments Associates Ltd. Partnership*, 150 B.R.840 (N.D. Ga. 1994) (applying Georgia law) citing O.C.G.A. § 44-14-60.

1087   *Bowen v. Tucker Federal Sav. & Loan Ass'n*, 210 Ga.App. 764, 438 S.E.2d 121 (1993).

1088   O.C.G.A. § 44-14-161(a).

1089   O.C.G.A. § 44-14-161(a).

1090   O.C.G.A. § 44-14-162(a).

In times when credit standards were lax and mortgage money was plentiful, mortgage loans were quick and easy to obtain with relative certainty. As such, many buyers chose not to include a separate financing contingency in their purchase and sale agreements but simply used the Due Diligence Period to confirm that the buyer could obtain a mortgage loan. As credit standards have tightened and mortgage loans have become harder to obtain, it is increasingly common to see buyers include financing contingencies in their purchase and sale agreements that do not expire until either the closing or shortly before the closing. This is because the ability to obtain mortgage financing has become sufficiently uncertain that even buyers with good credit cannot always be assured of getting a loan. Among the reasons for the uncertainty are a lack of mortgage loan products for all types of housing including some condominium developments, properties not appraising leaving the buyer with insufficient cash to make up the shortfall between the sales price and the amount of the available mortgage loan and negative re-evaluations of the credit worthiness of the borrower after the loan has been initially approved by the lender. As a result, buyers are trying to mitigate the risks they face in this area, some of which are beyond their control by increasing the length of the financing contingency period. Obviously, the extent to which buyers are able to achieve a loner financing contingency period is a matter of negotiation between the parties. Sellers generally want to have all contingencies removed from the purchase and sale agreement as quickly as possible. Many are reluctant to begin to pack up their belongings until they know that the financing contingency has been removed from the contract. As such, when sellers agree to a financing contingency period that expires on or near the date of closing, many sellers will insist on having a right to remain in the property for some period of time after closing to pack up and move.

There are two situations where buyers using the GAR Contracts should include a separate financing contingency exhibit. The first is when the buyer only has a short Due Diligence Period and thus may need a financing contingency which extends beyond the end of the Due Diligence Period. The second situation is when the buyer is purchasing the property subject to a GAR "Property Sold With Right To Request Repairs."[1091] In this situation, the buyer has no general right to terminate the contract if she cannot obtain financing, but instead can only terminate if the seller refuses to repair defects. As such, the need for a financing contingency becomes critical.

GAR now includes its financing contingency in a separate GAR Conventional Financing Contingency Exhibit. This exhibit basically gives the buyer a certain number of days from the Binding Agreement Date to determine if the buyer has the ability to obtain the specific loan described in the contingency or such other loan for which the buyer applied and was approved.

The seller has an interest in ensuring that any specific financing contingency not be used as a basis for invalidating the contract if the buyer becomes dissatisfied with the property for other reasons. Georgia courts require that the terms of the contract, including any financing contingency, be sufficiently definite so as to ascertain the intent of the parties.[1092] If the financing provision is vague and indefinite, the contract may be unenforceable.

§ 7.2.1 Pre-Qualification Letters

A seller will sometimes require the buyer to provide the seller with a letter from the buyer's mortgage lender indicating that the buyer is qualified to obtain a mortgage loan in a particular amount. While the buyer normally provides these letters to the seller prior to the buyer making an offer to purchase the property, they are sometimes required in the sales contract to be provided shortly after the binding agreement date.

Pre-qualification letters were originally intended to give the seller a sense of comfort that the buyer had the financial means to complete the purchase of the property. If there were two prospective buyers of a property, the buyer who provided a letter to the seller that she was qualified to buyer the property was seen as having a competitive advantage over the other prospective buyer. These letters have over time became less of an accurate prediction of whether the buyer had

1091   GAR Form F129.

1092   *Denton v. Hogge*, 208 Ga.App. 734, 431 S.E.2d 728 (1993).

the financial means to complete the transaction, because mortgage lenders tend to issue these letters relying on verbal information provided by the buyer rather than doing a credit check. As a result, the letters are not always reliable.

Pre-qualification letters would have far greater value if the lender did a full credit check of the buyer prior to issuing such a letter. An example of a special stipulation requiring the same is set forth below.

> **Special Stipulation 100: Pre-Qualification Letters**
>
> *Within _____ days from Binding Agreement Date, Buyer shall provide Seller with a letter from an institutional mortgage lender confirming that the Buyer is qualified to obtain a _____ type mortgage loan in the principal amount of _____ with an interest rate at par of not more than _____ to be repaid in monthly payments over a term of _____ years. The lender shall warrant in the letter that the lender: (1) has done a full credit check on and income verification of the Buyer and (2) understands that the letter may be relied upon by prospective sellers in deciding whether or not to sell their properties to Buyer.*

Of course, for the effort involved in issuing this type of letter, it may be easier for most lenders to simply issue a loan commitment.

§ 7.2.2 Contract For Deed

On rare occasions, a buyer or seller will inquire about doing a real estate transaction where the seller proposes to hold title to the property until the buyer has paid for the property. Usually the payments are made in installments over a period of years. This is also known as a bond for title or a bond for deed.[1093]

While legal title to the property remains with the seller until the buyer has paid the full amount for the property, the buyer (or holder of the bond for title) has an equitable interest in the property.[1094] Bonds for title were once common in Georgia. However, their use has now all but disappeared in favor of purchase money security deeds in which a power of sale is included.

Buyer needs to be particularly careful in paying for property in a contract for deed arrangement when there is an existing deed to secure debt on the property recorded prior to the contract for deed. Obviously, if the owner stops paying the mortgage and the lender forecloses on the property, the foreclosure wipes out the rights of the buyer to purchase the property.

§ 7.3 MECHANICS OF FINANCING

In a financed transaction, a buyer will execute a promissory note in favor of the lender in which the buyer promises to repay the lender the amount financed. The buyer also executes a deed to secure debt in which the buyer grants the lender a security interest in the property being sold to secure the amount of the note due to the lender. By executing the deed to secure debt, the buyer pledges the property being purchased to the lender as security or collateral for the loan.

§ 7.3.1 The Promissory Note

The promissory note is a contract between the buyer and lender in which the buyer "promises" to repay the lender the amount of the loan plus interest. It sets out the amount of the loan, maturity date, interest rate, payment terms, default provisions and pre-payment rights. As in the case with most other contracts, the promissory note must be in writing and be signed by all parties obligated under its terms. In addition to personally obligating the buyer to repay the loan, the note also outlines the terms and method of repayment.

1093 *Ingram v. Smith*, 62 Ga.App. 335, 7 S.E.2d 922 (1940).

1094 *Bell v. McDuffie*, 71 Ga. 264 (1884).

While a promissory note in a residential transaction is usually a straightforward repayment of the amount borrowed, a commercial loan is more complex. There may be special payment terms or even a sharing of the revenue from the property. The loan may also be disbursed incrementally, as is often the case with construction loans. Another issue in a commercial loan is whether the loan will be a recourse or non-recourse loan. With a non-recourse loan, the borrower is released from liability and the lender looks solely to the property or other collateral in the event of a loan default.

With an institutional lender, loan approval is conditioned on the buyer's acceptance of the terms outlined in the note, which will normally include a requirement that the note be secured by a deed to secure debt on the property. In a seller-financed transaction, however, it is important for the seller to include a requirement in the sales contract that the property being sold shall serve as security for the repayment of the indebtedness due under the note. If the contract provides only that the buyer is to execute a note and does not require that the note be secured by a deed to secure debt on the property, the loan will merely be a personal obligation of the buyer and the seller/lender will not have a security interest in the property.[1095] An example of such a special stipulation is set forth below.

> **Special Stipulation 101: Buyer to Execute Purchase Money Note and Security Deed in Favor of Seller**
>
> *Buyer agrees as a condition of Seller's financing of the purchase of the property described herein, to execute a Purchase Money Note and a Security Deed as customarily used in the State of Georgia at the time of closing. Buyer acknowledges that the property is the collateral that will be secured by Seller until such time as the repayment of the Purchase Money Note has been paid in full and cancelled. Said Security Deed is to be recorded in the county where the property is located in a first lien position. Buyer agrees that it will not create any additional security interest or encumbrance that will place the Seller's Security Deed in a subordinate interest prior to the recording of the Security Deed executed hereunder.*

Most notes also provide that if more than one buyer executes a note, each individual buyer will be jointly and severally liable for repayment of the debt. This means that if both a husband and wife sign a note, they are each individually liable for the entire debt and not just for their respective share. This remains the case even if the husband and wife later file for divorce. Any agreement between the ex-spouses as to who is responsible for the repayment of the note is not binding upon the lender.

§ 7.3.2 The Deed To Secure Debt

Different states have different laws regarding the use of security instruments. In Georgia, lenders obtain a security interest in the property being sold through execution of a deed to secure debt, which is also known as a security deed or mortgage deed. A buyer executing a deed to secure debt conveys legal title in the property to the lender; however, the buyer retains equitable title to the property. This means that the buyer retains the usual rights of ownership such as possession and use of the property as long as the buyer is not in default on the loan. The deed to secure debt, which is executed by the buyer in favor of the lender, is filed in the land records of the county in which the property is located.

Because the security deed transfers legal title to the lender, Georgia is known as a "title theory" state. Other states, such as Florida, are known as "lien theory" states. Lien theory means that the security instrument (usually a mortgage) acts as a lien on the property rather than actually transferring title.

The deed to secure debt is a separate and distinct document from the promissory note. While the note serves as evidence of the buyer's personal obligation for the debt, the deed to secure debt provides the lender with a mechanism

---

1095   *Rumph v. Rister*, 210 Ga. 679, 82 S.E.2d 508 (1954), *appealed on other grounds at* 211 Ga. 312, 85 S.E.2d 768 (1955) and 92 Ga.App. 29 (1955).

for recovering the property, which serves as collateral in the event that the note is not paid. The collateral or security provided under a deed to secure debt may include personal property as well as real property. A deed to secure debt without an underlying note, however, may be held to be unenforceable.[1096] Therefore, most lenders have the borrower execute both a promissory note and a deed to secure debt to protect their interests as much as possible.

For commercial loans, additional documents are often necessary either due to the nature of the transaction or the need for additional security. For example, it is usual to have a separate security agreement against inventory or accounts receivable. The lender may also require loan guarantees. In the case of a construction loan, the construction loan agreement will set out the terms of the loan, the conditions required before the bank advances any part of the loan and the lender's rights relating to the construction project.

§ 7.3.3 Power Of Sale In Deed To Secure Debt

In Georgia, most deeds to secure debt contain a "power of sale" clause. This clause entitles the lender upon default to accelerate and call due the entire outstanding loan balance. If the default continues, the lender may invoke the power of sale clause and sell the property in accordance with state foreclosure laws and apply the proceeds from the sale to the payment of the debt.[1097] For the most part, Georgia foreclosure laws are lender-friendly in that the lender does not have to initiate a lawsuit in order to foreclose on the property. Instead under Georgia law, if and when a default occurs, a lender may typically rely on what is referred to as "non-judicial foreclosure."[1098] A non-judicial foreclosure is a legal procedure in which the lender is authorized under the deed to secure debt to sell the property serving as collateral for the loan upon default and apply the proceeds to the debt. Such a sale must meet certain minimum standards. Specifically, the sale must be advertised in a newspaper considered an official paper for the county in which the property is located for four consecutive weeks prior to the week in which the property is sold on the courthouse steps. The day of sale is always on the first Tuesday of the month, except when it falls on a holiday. In the event the sale does not yield enough money to satisfy the debtor's outstanding balance to the lender, the lender must obtain judicial confirmation of the sale prior to initiating a lawsuit against the debtor seeking what is referred to as a "deficiency judgment."[1099] The lender's failure to obtain judicial confirmation of the sale is a bar to any later action against the borrower for a deficiency.

§ 7.4 TERMS OF LOAN MUST BE DEFINITE

If a real estate sales contract contains a financing contingency, it must be sufficiently certain and definite to create an enforceable contract.[1100]

At the time the buyer makes an offer to purchase, she may not know under what specific terms a loan will be available. The goal in preparing the Financing Contingency Exhibit is to set forth loan requirements which are acceptable to the buyer but which are not so restrictive so as to give the buyer an automatic or easy way out of the contract. If interest rates are on the rise, for example, it may be advisable to state an interest rate somewhat higher than the prevailing rate or give the seller the option of buying down the interest rate for the buyer.

§ 7.4.1 When Buyer Has "Ability To Obtain" Loan In The Financing Contingency Exhibit

The GAR Financing Contingency Exhibit defines the buyer's "ability to obtain" the loan as being qualified to obtain the loan(s) described in the exhibit based upon the lender's customary and standard underwriting criteria. If the buyer

---

1096   *Bramblett v. Bramblett*, 252 Ga. 21, 310 S.E.2d 897 (1984).

1097   *Smith v. Bukofzer*, 180 Ga. 209, 178 S.E. 641 (1935).

1098   O.C.G.A. § 44-14-160, *et seq.*

1099   O.C.G.A. § 44-14-161.

1100   *A.S. Reeves & Co., Inc. v. McMickle*, 270 Ga.App. 132, 605 S.E.2d 857 (2004).

is unable to qualify for the loan(s), the buyer must deliver to the seller, prior to the end of the Financing Contingency Period, a letter from the lender stating the reason for buyer's failure to qualify for the loan based upon the lender's customary and standard underwriting criteria. The loan denial letter may not be based upon one of the following, the buyer is deemed to have the ability to obtain the: (1) the buyer lacking sufficient cash to close, (2) the buyer needing to lease or sell other real property as a condition of obtaining the loan, or (3) the buyer did not timely provide the lender with information needed to evaluate whether buyer had the ability to obtain the loan including such things as loan documentation, Official Georgia Wood Infestation Reports, structural letters, well tests, septic system certifications, flood plain certifications and other similar information required by lender.

These two qualifiers are part of the definition of "ability to obtain" because the buyer warrants elsewhere in the GAR Contract that the buyer has sufficient cash to close the transaction and does not need to sell or lease other real property as a condition to obtaining a loan. By providing that the buyer is deemed to have the ability to obtain the loan if any one of these is the basis of the loan denial, the buyer cannot use any of these reasons as an excuse not to close.

§ 7.4.2   Amount And Type Of Loan

The amount of the loan to be obtained from a third party must be clearly stated in the financing section of the contract, or, in the alternative, the contract must provide a method by which the amount of the loan can be calculated. For example, it would be legally acceptable, and in fact it is often provided, that a contract will be contingent upon a buyer's ability to obtain a loan in an amount equal to 80% of the purchase price.[1101] Since the amount of the loan is directly tied to the purchase price, the amount of the loan is easily ascertainable.

In one case, a contract to purchase property for $36,900 was made contingent upon the buyer applying for and accepting, if available, "a 2/3 first mortgage loan …with interest at the current prevailing rate with principal and interest payable monthly for 20 years, and the balance in cash at closing."[1102] The buyer refused to accept a loan in the amount of $24,600 at 8% and terminated the contract. When the seller sued, the buyer argued that the contract was void because the financing provision was vague and uncertain. In ruling against the buyer, the court stated that the language in the contract which referenced a "2/3 first mortgage loan" obviously referred to 2/3 of the purchase price of $36,900, and the prevailing interest rate was readily ascertainable. The court concluded that the contract was neither vague nor uncertain as to the terms of purchase and sale.

§ 7.4.2.1   Applying For Different Loan Than Stated In Contract

Many real estate contracts require the buyer to apply for the specific loan described in the Contract or any other loan for which the Buyer may qualify more easily. For example, assume that the buyer agrees to apply for an adjustable rate mortgage with an initial interest rate of 5% and a loan term of 15 years. The buyer could fulfill the requirements of this contingency by applying for an adjustable rate mortgage with a 30-year term since it is easier for the buyer to qualify for such a loan. The buyer could not fulfill the requirement of the loan contingency by applying for a fixed rate mortgage with the same interest rate and term since it would be more difficult to qualify for such a loan.

If the buyer only applies for the loan(s) described in the contract and the loan(s) are not approved, the buyer is entitled to terminate the contract. Let's assume that a contract is conditioned upon the buyer's ability to obtain a fixed rate loan "in the principal amount of 80% of the purchase price listed, with an interest rate at par of not more than 5½% per annum on the unpaid balance." The mortgage lender informs the buyer that while she will not be approved for a fixed rate loan, she can be approved for an adjustable rate loan. In this situation, the buyer is still entitled to terminate the contract due to the failure of the financing contingency because the buyer has been denied the loan for which the buyer was obligated to apply and has not actually applied for a different loan. If the buyer applies for the adjustable rate loan, however, the buyer

---

1101   The purchase price, of course, must be clearly stated.

1102   *Barto v. Hicks*, 124 Ga.App. 472, 184 S.E.2d 188 (1971).

would then be obligated to accept that loan if the buyer is approved for the same. Of course, proving whether the buyer actually applied for a loan in this situation is sometimes difficult. The GAR Financing Contingency Exhibit also provides that if the buyer applies for any other type of loan (regardless of whether it is easier or more difficult to obtain than the loan described in the contract), and is approved for the same, the buyer must accept the loan.

§ 7.4.2.2   Requirement Of Sufficient Cash At Closing

As previously stated, the GAR Contract calls for an all cash transaction unless the Financing Contingency Exhibit is attached. However, that is not the case in all real estate contracts. Many contracts contain a provision wherein the buyer warrants that she will have sufficient cash at closing which, when combined with the amount of any loans, will allow the buyer to complete the transaction.[1103] In other words, the buyer is warranting that if she is approved for a loan, she will have the rest of the money needed to close. For example, if a lender requires a buyer to fund certain escrows at closing, this amount would be part of the funds needed to close that the buyer is warranting she will have. If the buyer does not have these funds, the buyer will be in default under the contract.

Assume that a buyer is required under the contract to obtain a loan equal to 80% of the purchase price at an interest rate of not more than 9% payable over 30 years. After making loan application, the buyer is approved for such a loan. If the buyer cannot then close the transaction because she does not have the funds to close (*i.e.*, the additional 20% of the purchase price plus closing costs, lender required escrow amounts, and any other fees or charges associated with the closing), the buyer would be in default of the contract. Since buyers may not be aware of how much cash they will need in order to close or obtain loan approval, it is prudent for the buyer to speak with a mortgage lender about these issues prior to entering into a sales contract.

§ 7.4.3   Interest Rate Should Be Specifically Identified

As a general rule, if a financing contingency is part of a contract the interest rate at which the loan is to be repaid must be specifically identified in the contract. For example, a contract which contained a provision that "[t]he within sale is contingent upon purchaser's ability to secure a conventional loan of $10,000 for ten (10) years" was held unenforceable because the contract failed to specify both the interest rate at which the loan was to be repaid and the terms of repayment.[1104]

In another case, the contract was contingent upon the buyer's ability to obtain a loan of 80% of the purchase price to be paid in monthly installments over a term of at least 30 years.[1105] The preprinted financing contingency contained a blank space where the interest rate on the loan could be filled in and another blank space in which a monthly payment amount could be written. Neither of these blanks was filled in. The Court of Appeals held that the contract was missing critical terms and was, therefore, unenforceable.

The court would rule the same way if the phrase "TBD" or "to be determined" was used instead of a specific interest rate. In 2009, the Georgia Court of Appeals held that the phrase "TBD" in the interest rate section of a financing contingency makes an agreement unenforceable.[1106] In Georgia, the courts have consistently held that a contract that does not list the loan amount or the interest rate on the loan is too vague and indefinite to be enforced.[1107] Therefore, indicating that the interest rate on the loan is "TBD" or "to be determined" at a later time is also too vague and indefinite to be enforced.[1108]

1103   GAR Forms F20, F23 and Form F27.

1104   *Scott v. Lewis*, 112 Ga.App. 195, 144 S.E.2d 460 (1965).

1105   *Homler v. Malas*, 229 Ga.App. 390, 494 S.E.2d 18 (1997).

1106   *Parks v. Thompson Builders, Inc.*, 296 Ga.App. 704, 675 S.E.2d 583 (2009).

1107   *Parks v. Thompson Builders, Inc.*, 296 Ga.App. 704, 675 S.E.2d 583 (2009).

1108   *Parks v. Thompson Builders, Inc.*, 296 Ga.App. 704, 675 S.E.2d 583 (2009).

Contracts that specify the type of loan should also identify whether the interest rate on the loan is a fixed rate, adjustable rate or interest only. The buyer should identify a maximum interest rate on the loan to protect against interest rates rising between the Binding Agreement Date and the date of closing.

Our courts have viewed the inclusion of a maximum rate of interest above which the buyer does not have to close as being for the protection and benefit of the buyer. In one case, a buyer entered into a contract contingent on the ability to obtain a fixed rate mortgage loan with an interest rate of not more than 10⅓% per annum on the unpaid principal balance.[1109] The contract provided (as does the GAR Financing Contingency Exhibit) that "ability to obtain" meant that the buyer was qualified to receive the loan described in the contract based on lender's customary and standard underwriting criteria. The contract also gave the buyer "at its option" the right to apply for a loan with different terms and conditions and close the transaction. There was nothing in the contract, however, which required the buyer to close if she applied for and was approved for a different loan. The buyer was approved for an adjustable rate mortgage with an initial rate of 9-7/8%. The court found that the buyer was required to close only if she was able to obtain a fixed rate loan with an interest rate of not more than 10⅓%.

It should be noted that this case would likely have had a different result had the GAR Financing Contingency Exhibit been used since it now requires the buyer to close if the buyer applies for and is approved for the Primary Loan or any other loan for which it is easier to qualify or any other loan for which the buyer has applied for and is approved, irrespective of whether it is easier to obtain than the Primary Loan.

§ 7.4.3.1 "Prevailing Rate" Exception

A contract contingent on the buyer being able to obtain a loan for a certain amount with interest payable "at the current prevailing rate" is generally enforceable. In an era of fluctuating interest rates, such a provision is common in general business usage and does not render a contract void for uncertainty.[1110] Therefore, once the buyer is approved for a loan with an interest rate at the then current prevailing rate, she is obligated to accept such a loan even if the interest rate exceeds her expectations. Purchasers should pay particular attention to agreeing to accept a loan at the "current prevailing rate" when there is a lengthy period of time between the date of contract and the date of closing since there is a greater risk of rising interest rates.

The other risk in defining the interest rate on the loan as the prevailing rate is that it can lead to disputes between buyers and sellers over what is meant by the term "prevailing rate" since there can be significant variations in the pricing of mortgage loans. A buyer could argue, for example, that she does not qualify for a loan at a prevailing interest rate of 4.75%, when at the same time the seller is arguing that the prevailing rate is 5.25%.

§ 7.4.3.2 Setting An Interest Rate Range

Another approach in this area is to define the interest rate which will be accepted by a buyer in terms of a range. The following special stipulations illustrate this type of provision.

> **Special Stipulation 102: Buyer to Accept Stipulated Interest Rate Plus Two Percentage Points**
>
> *With respect to the Primary Loan, Buyer agrees to accept an interest rate at par of _____ % (or less) or an interest rate at par of no more than two percentage points higher than the above-stated interest rate. All other terms of the Primary Loan shall remain the same.*

This type of provision is sometimes used by builders when the home closing is still many months away. In addition, the buyer may want to include a provision in the contract in which the buyer contemplates and accepts some increase

---

1109 *Carroll v. Harry Norman, Inc.*, 198 Ga.App. 614, 402 S.E.2d 357 (1991).

1110 *Barto v. Hicks*, 124 Ga.App. 472, 184 S.E.2d 188 (1971); *Southern Prestige Homes, Inc. v. Moscoso*, 243 Ga.App. 412, 532 S.E.2d 122 (2000).

in interest rates which might occur between the Binding Agreement Date and the date of closing. An example of this special stipulation is as follows.

Special Stipulation 103:   Interest Rate Fluctuations Prior to Closing

Buyer and Seller acknowledge and agree that interest rates on first mortgage loans may fluctuate between the date of this Agreement and the date of closing. Accordingly, Buyer agrees that, notwithstanding anything to the contrary contained herein, a loan with an interest rate not more than two percent (2%) higher than that interest rate set forth herein, shall be acceptable to Buyer and shall satisfy the new loan contingency.

If the buyer is unwilling to assume the risk of an increase in interest rates above the rate stated in the contract, the seller may want to incorporate the following special stipulation, which gives the seller the flexibility to buy down the loan to ensure that the contract closes.

Special Stipulation 104:   Seller's Right to Buy Down Interest Rate

Notwithstanding any provision in this Agreement to the contrary, Buyer and Seller agree that if Buyer is unable to obtain the Primary Loan, Seller shall have the right, but not the obligation, at Seller's sole expense (and in addition to any amounts Seller is contributing toward Buyer's costs to close) to buy down the loan for which Buyer has applied to the agreed-upon interest rate at par by paying additional discount points, provided that the loan otherwise conforms to the requirements set forth in this Agreement. Buyer shall notify Seller immediately if Buyer is unable to obtain the Primary Loan. If Seller intends to buy down the loan, Seller shall notify Buyer of the same no later than within one day of receiving notice from Buyer that Buyer was unable to obtain the Primary Loan.

Additionally, the special stipulation below can be used by the seller to require that her contribution to the closing costs and discount points first be applied to the payment of such discount points as are necessary to buy down the loan to the agreed-upon interest rate. Under this option, the seller will not pay any more at closing but will have somewhat greater protection against the financing contingency not being fulfilled.[1111]

Special Stipulation 105:   Seller's Contributions to be First Used to Purchase Discount Points

Notwithstanding any provision to the contrary contained in this Agreement, Seller shall pay at closing a sum not to exceed ($ amount) which shall first be used by Buyer to pay for any discount points necessary to buy down or reduce the interest rate on the loan to the highest rate at which the financing contingency will be fulfilled by Buyer. Any portion of the above amount not used for discount points shall be used at Buyer's discretion to pay for closing costs, survey costs, insurance relating to the Property or mortgage and, if allowed by lender, other costs to close, including escrows and prepaid items. Buyer shall pay any additional closing costs, insurance premiums, or escrow amounts to fulfill lender requirements or to otherwise close this transaction.

§ 7.4.3.3   Relationship Between Interest Rate And Discount Points And Meaning Of The Phrase "At Par"

While most form real estate contracts provide for identifying the maximum interest rate above which the buyer does not have to close, some are silent on whether the buyer is obligated to close on a purchase if a particular interest

---

1111   Fannie Mae guidelines will not permit a seller to contribute more than a certain percentage of the purchase price or appraised value of the property (whichever is less) toward closing costs (not to include pre-paids). Therefore, the buyer and seller should consult a mortgage loan officer when completing the above and below stipulations because they may be completed in such a manner to prohibit the buyer from obtaining loan approval.

rate can be obtained by paying discount points. A discount point is 1% of the amount of the loan. Therefore, on a $200,000 loan, one discount point would be $2,000. The GAR Financing Contingency Exhibit provides that the interest rate ceiling is calculated "at par" or without reference to discount points. This is the rate at which the mortgage broker does not have to pay a fee in order to "buy down" the loan. An interest rate lower than the par rate would cost the broker money; an interest rate higher than the par rate would pay the broker a commission. Therefore, if the buyer wants a loan at an interest rate which is lower than the par rate, the broker will have to "buy down the interest rate" at a cost which is passed on to the buyer in the form of discount points.

Under the GAR Financing Contingency Exhibit, the buyer is not obligated to close on the purchase unless the buyer can obtain a loan at the interest rate specified in the contract without the buyer having to buy down the interest rate on the loan by paying discount points.

For example, a buyer agrees to purchase a home contingent upon the buyer obtaining a loan of 80% of the purchase price of $100,000 for a term of 30 years, with an interest rate at par not to exceed 8%. The buyer applies for financing and is told that she can only get a 30-year fixed rate loan at 8% only by paying two discount points. In this example, the financing contingency has not been met because the buyer cannot obtain the 8% loan at par or without paying discount points. Therefore, the buyer does not have to accept the loan and purchase the property.

§ 7.4.3.4   Locking In An Interest Rate

Interest rates may fluctuate between the Binding Agreement Date and the date the buyer "locks in" a particular interest rate on a loan. Assume a contract provides that the buyer will not have to purchase the property if the buyer cannot obtain an adjustable rate mortgage with an initial interest rate of 5%, which is the then-prevailing market rate. The closing is set 90 days from Binding Agreement Date. The buyer, thinking that the rates are likely to decrease, does not do anything to assure that she can get the 5% rate (*i.e.*, the buyer does not "lock in" the rate). Ten days before the closing the market rate increases to 5.5%. Can the buyer terminate the contract on the basis that she is unable to obtain the specified financing? While arguments can be made on both sides of this issue, the answer is likely yes.

In times of rapidly changing rates, a seller may therefore want to require the buyer to "lock-in" an interest rate shortly after the Binding Agreement Date. In this way, a buyer cannot tie up the property while gambling that rates may go lower. An example of such a special stipulation is set forth below.

Special Stipulation 106:   Buyer Must Lock In Rate Early

Buyer agrees to "lock in" the interest rate on the Primary Loan within _____ days from Binding Agreement Date. The minimum "lock-in" period shall be through the date of closing referenced in this Agreement plus 7 additional days. The interest rate on the Primary Loan shall be the best available interest rate offered by the mortgage lender with whom Buyer has applied. Upon "locking in" the interest rate Buyer shall immediately give notice to Seller of having done so and the interest rate Buyer has "locked in."

§ 7.4.4   Term Of Loan Must Be Identified

The time period in which the loan will be repaid must be identified. The GAR Financing Contingency Exhibit, if properly completed, identifies the period over which the loan is to be repaid.

The effect of failing to describe when installments of principal and interest are due under a loan is demonstrated in the following case. A buyer entered into a contract conditioned upon the buyer obtaining a loan of $5,400.[1112] The court stated that the contract was deficient because it failed to set forth not only the amount of the interest rate of the loan to be obtained, but also when the installment payments of principal and interest would be due. Similarly, a court

---

[1112]   *Brown v. White*, 73 Ga.App. 524, 37 S.E.2d 213 (1946).

held that a contract which stated that $11,000 of the purchase price was to be paid in three equal installments was too vague and indefinite because it did not state when the installments were to be paid.[1113]

§ 7.4.5   Lender Authorization To Release Information To Seller And Broker

Lenders are not normally allowed to release information about the loan application process to third parties.[1114] As a result, for the lender to be able to release information about the loan application to the seller or the real estate licensees involved in the transaction, the buyer would need to authorize the release of such information. Many financing contingencies now contain such authorizations so that the seller and real estate licensees involved in the transaction can track the progress of the loan approval process.

§ 7.5   CONTINGENCIES AND OBLIGATIONS RELATED TO FINANCING

§ 7.5.1   Buyer's Duty To Deliver Evidence Of Ability To Close

§ 7.5.1.1   Seller's Right To Terminate If Source Of Funds Information Not Fully Or Timely Provided

Most sellers do not care what type of mortgage loan the buyer obtains, so long as she obtains some mortgage loan (if the buyer needs one) to purchase the property. The GAR Conventional Financing Contingency Exhibit[1115] now includes a section obligating the buyer to provide the seller with evidence confirming that the buyer has the funds or loan commitment to purchase the property.

This provision protects the seller in two important ways. First, most sellers do not want to begin the process of moving until they know that the seller has sufficient funds to close. While there are obviously no guarantees that any sale will ultimately close, having the buyer provide evidence to the seller that she has been approved for a mortgage loan or has sufficient cash to close without obtaining a loan is obviously a good predictor of this.

Second, these types of provisions normally give the seller the right to terminate the purchase and sale agreement if the buyer fails to provide the required information regarding the buyer's source of funds to the seller. The GAR financing contingency exhibits require the buyer to provide the seller evidence of the buyer's ability to purchase the property within an agreed upon number of days from the end of the Financing Contingency Period. The failure to do so gives the right to terminate the contract due to buyer's default under the contract. In such a situation, the seller could retain the buyer's earnest money as liquidated damages. Buyers need to be particularly mindful of this time deadline in transactions in which the buyer is making a large earnest money deposit. This is because in some transactions in which the seller has made a large earnest money deposit, the seller may have a financial incentive to terminate the contract due to the buyer's default and keep the earnest money. One way to address this risk when large amounts of earnest money are being deposited in a real estate transaction is to limit the liquidated damages that the seller gets to retain in the event of a breach of the contract to a monetary amount that is less than the amount of the earnest money. An example of such a special stipulation is set forth below.

> **Special Stipulation 107:   Damages Limited to Percentage of Earnest Money in the Event of Buyer Default**
>
> *Notwithstanding any provision to the contrary contained herein, in the event this transaction does not close due to the default of the Buyer, the parties agree that Seller's sole remedy for such a breach shall be to retain _____% of the earnest money as liquidated damages, it being agreed that the same is not a penalty and a reasonable pre-estimate of*

1113   *Cook v. Barfield*, 224 Ga. 355, 162 S.E.2d 417 (1968).

1114   15 U.S.C.A. § 6802.

1115   GAR Form F64.

> *Seller's actual damages. All sums being held by Holder in excess of this amount shall be returned without penalty to Buyer.*

Without the GAR Conventional Financing Contingency Exhibit,[1116] the seller has little practical recourse to terminate a contract in advance of the closing date if the buyer appears to have lost interest in consummating the purchase but has not breached the contract on an anticipatory basis. So, for example, a buyer puts up a nominal amount of earnest money and does not inspect the property during an agreed-upon Due Diligence Period. That the Closing date is 60 days from the Binding Agreement Date. While the seller may rightfully be anxious regarding the buyer's intentions to close on the purchase of the property, without the GAR Conventional Financing Contingency Exhibit, the seller the GAR Conventional Financing Contingency Exhibit must simply wait out the buyer. However, if the GAR Conventional Financing Contingency Exhibit is used and the buyer does not provide the seller with the detailed information regarding the source of the buyer's funds by the agreed-upon date, the buyer is in breach of contract.

§ 7.5.1.2 Evidence Of Funds

The GAR Source of Buyer's Funds Exhibit identifies the type of information the buyer must provide to the seller to satisfy the requirement to prove the buyer's source of funds. This evidence can be any one of the following: (a) a letter from a trust, stock brokerage firm, or other financial institution holding funds, stocks, bonds, or other assets on behalf of buyer; (b) an account statement from a trust, stock brokerage firm, or other financial institution confirming funds held on behalf of buyer; or (c) a loan commitment letter from the lender indicated on the Exhibit. If a letter is provided, it must be dated subsequent to the Binding Agreement Date. If a statement of account is provided, it must be for the regular time period that such statements are issued immediately preceding the Binding Agreement Date. The evidence submitted must verify to the seller that the amount or value of the funds or assets held on behalf of the buyer are sufficient, when combined with an approved loan, to allow buyer to complete the purchase.

§ 7.5.1.3 Loan Commitment

If the buyer is obtaining mortgage financing, the evidence of the loan commitment must meet certain conditions. The loan commitment must be dated after the Binding Agreement Date of the contract, and must:

(a) include the name of the borrower(s);

(b) include the type, amount, terms and conditions of the loan for which the buyer(s) have been approved;

(c) state that it is not subject to the receipt of additional information regarding the buyer's financial condition which has not yet been provided to the mortgage lender (other than such information required to be provided if the buyer's financial condition materially changes); (d)state that the loan commitment shall run through the date of closing set forth in the Agreement.

This section of the Buyer's Source of Funds Exhibit can also be used to require that the buyer obtain the letter of loan commitment from a particular lender or from a group of lenders. Of course, this does not necessarily obligate the buyer to ultimately obtain a mortgage loan from that particular lender, and the buyer could ultimately close with a mortgage loan from a different lender.

§ 7.5.2 Buyer's Good Faith Obligation To Pursue Loan Approval

Some purchase and sale agreements expressly provide that the buyer shall pursue "qualification for and approval of such loan diligently and in good faith."[1117] As a result if the buyer fails to provide the lender with necessary documents, the buyer can be found to have breached the contract for failing to diligently pursue financing.

1116   GAR Form F64.

1117   *Brack v. Brownlee*, 246 Ga. 818, 273 S.E.2d 390 (1980).

Some older case law attempted to distinguish between language in contracts which require the buyer's "obtaining a loan" versus having "the ability to obtain a loan," concluding that the former was invalid for lack of mutuality. Case law now indicates that the buyer's obligation to diligently pursue financing eliminates this distinction.[1118] However, to avoid any question about whether the financing contingency has been fulfilled, the GAR Financing Contingency Exhibit was changed to refer to the buyer's ability to obtain the loan(s) described in the Exhibit.

From the seller's perspective, the problems inherent in determining whether a buyer has diligently pursued financing in good faith are demonstrated in the following case. The contract had a financing contingency that obligated the buyer to "promptly make application and pursue said application with reasonable diligence to obtain said loan when it is available."[1119] The buyer applied for a loan, and it was granted with conditional approval of payment in full of an outstanding credit card account. The lender received information that the buyer had sufficient funds available in various bank accounts to pay off the debt, but the buyer refused to do so. The buyer stated that although her boyfriend was not named on the accounts or listed as a co-owner of the funds on the loan application, the monies in the account also belonged to him. The buyer also stated that her boyfriend had recently lost her job and might need the money. The trial court concluded that the buyer's actions were reasonable and exhibited the good faith and diligence implied in the contract.

§ 7.5.2.1 Must Buyer Apply For Loan To Satisfy Financing Contingency?

One frequently asked question is whether the buyer must actually apply for a loan even when the buyer has no hope of obtaining one or which is unavailable. While the safe answer to this question is yes, there is case law precedent for the opposite conclusion. In one case, a buyer orally inquired about a loan that would comply with the terms of the contract from two savings and loan associations, an insurance company and a bank.[1120] None of the lenders contacted offered any loan under the terms provided for in the contract. In allowing the buyer to recover earnest money paid under the contract, the court found that there was sufficient evidence produced at trial to authorize the finding that the buyer had sought in good faith to obtain a loan, which was required of her under the contract, even though she did not make a written application for the loan.

Questions of whether the buyer acted in good faith to satisfy the financing contingency are questions of fact rather than of law. Applying for a loan and receiving a written letter of loan denial helps to eliminate any factual disputes over whether the buyer fulfilled her contractual obligations.

In some situations, the seller may want information about whether the buyer is fulfilling her loan obligations. The following special stipulations can then be used.

> **Special Stipulation 108: Release of Loan Information to Seller**
>
> *Buyer hereby authorizes, directs and agrees to cause Buyer's mortgage lender to provide Seller, upon Seller's request, with verification of the amount and type of loan or loans for which Buyer has applied, the status of the application (including whether it is complete, whether it has been approved and, if it is not complete, the terms which remain outstanding,) and whether there is anything in Buyer's credit history and/or in other information provided to Buyer's mortgage lender as part of Buyer's loan application which could negatively affect Buyer's ability to be approved for the Primary Loan.*

1118 *Benveniste v. Koets*, 252 Ga. 520, 314 S.E.2d 912 (1984), *overruling F. & C. Inv. Co. v. Jones* 210 Ga. 635, 81 S.E.2d 828 (1954).

1119 *Century 21 Mary Carr & Associates, Inc. v. Jones*, 204 Ga.App. 96, 418 S.E.2d 435 (1992).

1120 *Carmichael v. Gonzales*, 111 Ga.App. 695, 143 S.E.2d 190 (1965).

§ 7.5.2.2 Buyer Deemed Approved For A Mortgage Loan Unless Buyer Gives Notice Of Disapproval

Some sellers have grown frustrated with the delays of either the buyer in applying for a loan or the lender in approving the loan. As a result, some sellers have shifted the burden to the buyer to provide notice of loan denial to the seller within a defined time frame. The GAR Financing Contingency Exhibit takes this approach. Failure by the buyer to provide the seller with a letter of loan denial within the required time frame is deemed an approval of the loan.

Another approach to this issue is to give the seller a right to terminate the contract unless the buyer fails to submit an amendment to the contract to remove the financing contingency within a defined period of time. The special stipulation below is an example of this type of provision.

> **Special Stipulation 109: Seller May Terminate Contract if Buyer Does Not Timely Remove Financing Contingency**
>
> *If Buyer does not present Seller within _____ days from the Binding Agreement Date an amendment signed by Buyer permanently removing any and all financing contingencies to which this Agreement is subject and agreeing to purchase the Property for all cash, Seller may but shall not be obligated to terminate this Agreement upon notice to Buyer. If Buyer presents the amendment in accordance with the above referenced requirements, Seller shall promptly sign the amendment and return a fully executed copy of the same to the Buyer.*
>
> *If Buyer does not timely present the amendment meeting all the above-referenced requirements, Seller shall have ten (10) days from the last date the amendment removing any and all financing contingencies was to have been delivered from Buyer to Seller to terminate the Agreement. If Seller does not terminate the Agreement in a timely manner, the obligation of Buyer to provide the above-mentioned amendment to Seller shall thereafter be deemed to be waived by the Seller and shall no longer be an obligation of the Buyer to perform under this Agreement. All other terms and conditions of the Agreement shall remain in full force and effect.*

§ 7.5.2.3 Financing Contingency Removed Unless Buyer Obtains Loan Denial Letter From Lender

Under the GAR Financing Contingency Exhibit, the buyer is given a certain number of days from the Binding Agreement Date (the Financing Contingency Period) in which to determine if the buyer has the ability to obtain the described loan(s). If the buyer discovers she is unable to obtain the loan, the buyer must obtain a letter from the lender denying the loan and deliver the letter to the seller. The letter must state the terms of the loan for which the buyer was not qualified, and the reasons for the denial. If the buyer does not provide the seller with such a letter before the end of the Financing Contingency Period, the buyer is deemed to have the ability to obtain the loan, and the agreement will no longer be subject to a financing contingency.

The same result applies even if the buyer does provide such a letter from the lender but the basis on which the buyer failed to obtain the loan was (a) insufficient cash to close, (b) the buyer is required to sell or lease other property as a condition of obtaining the loan, or (c) the buyer did not provide the lender with required information.

§ 7.5.3 Obligation To Apply For Loan With Second Lender

Appellate courts in Georgia have not addressed the question of whether the buyer's good faith obligation to pursue financing requires the buyer to apply for a loan with a different lender if the buyer's initial loan application is denied. Whether such a duty exists will likely depend on the facts and circumstances of the transaction. The chances that a buyer will be found not to have acted in good faith in diligently pursuing a loan are greater if (a) there was sufficient time between the initial loan denial and the closing date to apply for and be approved for a loan, and (b) the reasons for the initial loan denial were such that there was some reasonable likelihood the buyer would be approved for a loan the second time around.

Sellers may want to incorporate a special stipulation to address the buyer's obligations in pursuing a loan with a second mortgage lender if the initial lender denies the loan. Set forth below is an example of a contract provision that obligates the buyer to apply for a loan with a second lender if the buyer's initial loan application is denied.

> **Special Stipulation 110:   Buyer's Obligation in Pursuing Second Loan (if GAR Contract Not Used)**
>
> *Notwithstanding any provision to the contrary contained in this Agreement, in the event Buyer is notified that her loan is disapproved and more than ____ days remain until the scheduled date of closing in the Agreement, Buyer shall immediately notify Seller of such fact and shall be required to submit a loan application to another lender, to pursue said application diligently and in good faith, to execute all papers, to provide all documents, to perform all other actions necessary to obtain said loan, and to accept said loan if approved by lender. Upon written request by Seller, Buyer shall provide the name and telephone number of any such additional lender to whom Buyer has submitted a loan application.*

§ 7.5.4   Obligation To Accept Seller Financing Or Allow Seller To Buy Down Rate

The seller may offer to finance all or a portion of the sale if the buyer is unable to obtain a conventional loan. Alternatively, the Seller may agree to buy down the interest rate on the buyer's loan if it exceeds the rate called for in the contract. While some buyers might appreciate such offers, can the seller force these options on a reluctant purchaser?

Our appellate courts have not yet ruled on these issues. It is likely, however, that a seller could force the buyer to accept her offer to buy down the interest rate on the buyer's loan. This makes sense because, from the buyer's perspective, the loan will be on the exact terms for which she applied. In one example, the buyer applies for an 80% loan at 9% interest and is offered an 80% loan at 10% interest. If the seller agrees to buy down the loan by paying one point (*i.e.*, 1% of the loan), the net result to the buyer is an 80% loan at 9% interest. The buyer likely would have difficulty arguing that she was not obligated to accept such an offer. Any such offer by the seller would need to be in addition to any sums the seller already agreed in the contract to pay toward closing costs, discount points, etc. If the seller wanted to avoid any uncertainty she could use . (Seller's right to buy down interest rate).

It is far less clear whether the GAR Financing Contingency Exhibit requires the buyer to accept seller financing from the seller. The seller may argue that the buyer's good faith obligation to diligently pursue financing includes accepting an offer of seller financing (after the buyer's initial loan application has been denied) if the loan is on the same terms and conditions as are set forth in the financing contingency. The better argument, however, is that the buyer is only obligated to pursue or accept financing from an institutional lender. This is because the phrase "ability to obtain" as used in the GAR Financing Contingency Exhibit, is defined to mean a loan "based upon lender's customary and standard underwriting criteria." If the buyer was unable to obtain such a loan, the buyer can make a good argument that she did not have the "ability to obtain" the loan and that the financing contingency thereby fails. Moreover, the typical seller of residential property does not have any customary or standard loan underwriting criteria.[1121] The buyer may, therefore, argue that seller financing was not the intent of the parties. If the terms of a note or security deed proposed by the seller differ in any material respects from those used by the lender to whom the buyer initially applied, the buyer can additionally argue that she would not be in the same legal position as with an institutional loan.

The seller can use the following special stipulation in anticipation of this.

1121   GAR Forms F20, F23 and F27.

Special Stipulation 111:   Seller's Right to Provide Seller Financing

In the event Buyer is not able to obtain Primary Loan, then Seller, at Seller's option, may agree to make a loan to Buyer on terms identical to those contained herein and Buyer shall be obligated to accept the loan. Seller may elect this option by giving written notice to Buyer within three (3) days of Seller's receipt of notice from Buyer that Buyer's loan application was denied. Seller and Buyer agree to use a standard FNMA Note and Deed to Secure Debt to evidence Buyer's obligation in such a loan transaction.

Another issue is raised when the seller offers to finance a portion of the purchase price. Suppose the purchase price is $100,000 and the contract calls for a 90% loan. The property appraises for $90,000 and the lender is only willing to make a loan based upon the appraised value (*i.e.*, 90% of $90,000). Assuming that the contract is not contingent upon the property appraising for the purchase price, can the seller insist upon giving the buyer a $10,000 loan, thereby reducing the outstanding amount for which the buyer needs financing to $90,000? The answer should be no. This is because the buyer can again argue that the financing contingency was not fulfilled because the buyer was not able to obtain a loan based upon the lender's customary and standard underwriting criteria.

Additionally, the financing contingency in some real estate contracts specifies that the loan to be obtained by the buyer will be secured by a first lien security deed on the property. Since a second mortgage is not a first lien security deed, a good argument can be made that the express requirements of such a financing contingency were not fulfilled.

§ 7.5.5   Inability To Procure Or Have Ability To Procure Loan

§ 7.5.5.1   Involuntary Change In Financial Condition

Problems may arise when the contract contains a financing contingency, the buyer is approved for a loan, but prior to the closing the buyer's financial condition changes due to no fault of the buyer (such as the buyer losing her job due to a company downsizing). Loan approval by an institutional lender is generally subject to being withdrawn if the buyer's financial condition substantially changes before closing. If the buyer no longer has the ability to obtain a loan due to changed financial circumstances beyond her control and the financing contingency has not yet expired, the buyer would normally be relieved from performing her obligations under the contract and would be entitled to a return of her earnest money.

Similarly, if a lender will only approve a mortgage loan based on the combined income of a husband and wife, the death of a spouse resulting in the loan being disapproved would be an involuntary change in financial condition.

A buyer would probably not be relieved from her contractual obligations simply because her job transfer to an area in which she contracted to purchase a home is changed or canceled by her employer. If this is a possibility, the buyer should include a special stipulation in the contract allowing her to terminate the contract in the event this occurs.[1122]

Special Stipulation 112:   Buyer's Right to Terminate Due to Change of Employment

Seller recognizes that Buyer is being transferred to (City) by her employer. Should Buyer's transfer be changed or canceled by Buyer's employer, such that Buyer will no longer be moving to (City), then Buyer may terminate this Agreement by giving written notice to Seller. Buyer's right to terminate this Agreement under this special stipulation shall expire if not exercised prior to (Date).

1122   The buyer may still have an out, however, if as a result of the canceling of the job transfer the lender was no longer willing to make the loan because the property would no longer be the buyer's principal place of residence.

§ 7.5.5.2 Voluntary Change In Financial Condition

If a buyer intentionally changes her financial condition, the buyer may not be able to use failure of the financing contingency to avoid her obligations under the contract. The GAR Financing Contingency Exhibit provides that from the binding agreement date through the closing, the buyer shall not intentionally make any material changes to the buyer's financial condition that would adversely affect the buyer's ability to obtain a loan.[1123] If after signing a sales contract the buyer purchases an expensive new car on credit and, as a result, cannot obtain loan approval, the buyer will likely be deemed to have breached her duty not to make material changes in her financial condition which adversely affect the buyer's ability to obtain a loan. Similarly, if the buyer quits her job without having a new job at a similar salary in place, and the buyer loses her ability to obtain a mortgage loan, the buyer will likely have breached her obligation not to intentionally alter her financial condition. While the courts have yet to decide this issue, a deliberate discretionary change in financial condition may make it difficult for the buyer to prove that she pursued the loan in good faith. As noted above, whether the buyer acted in good faith is generally a question of fact rather than a question of law.

§ 7.5.6 Buyer May Waive Financing Contingency

Georgia courts have held that since the financing contingency is typically for the benefit of the buyer, the buyer may generally waive the contingency and pay the purchase price in all cash.[1124] However, the buyer must notify the seller that the buyer is waiving the financing contingency and that she is ready, willing, and able to pay for the property without financing.[1125]

The following case affirms the buyer's right to waive a financing contingency. The contract for the purchase of property provided that the purchase price was to be paid in all cash at the time of closing.[1126] The contract was also made contingent on the buyer applying for and being approved for an FHA-insured loan in the amount of $27,000 to be amortized in equal monthly payments over a 30-year period. The seller apparently changed her mind and called off the deal. At trial, the seller argued that the sales contract was too uncertain to be enforced because the terms of the loan were vague and indefinite. The court ruled that even if the terms of the loan to be obtained were uncertain, if the buyer actually had the purchase price in cash to pay the seller as required by the contract, then it should not make any difference to the seller how the cash is obtained. The court went on to say "since under the terms of the contract, the purchase price was stated to be all cash at time of closing, the provision as to the procurement of a loan was merely for the protection of the buyer and could be waived by him."[1127]

§ 7.5.7 Exceptions To Buyer Waiving Financing Contingency

The buyer may be precluded from waiving the financing contingency if the contingency is for the seller's benefit. For example, if the contract provides that the purchase price is to be paid to the seller in deferred payments, the seller may have incorporated this provision for tax reasons and the buyer may not be able to force the seller to accept payment of the entire purchase price in cash.[1128]

§ 7.5.8 Married Persons And Financing Contingencies

If both spouses sign a contract containing a financing contingency, then generally both will be obligated to apply for and pursue the loan in good faith. If only one spouse signs the contract containing a financing contingency clause and

---

1123   GAR Form F60.

1124   *Edwards v. McTyre*, 246 Ga. 302, 271 S.E.2d 205 (1980); *Blanton v. Williams*, 209 Ga. 16, 70 S.E.2d 461 (1952).

1125   *Covington v. Countryside Inv. Co., Inc.*, 263 Ga. 125, 428 S.E.2d 562 (1993).

1126   *Edwards v. McTyre*, 246 Ga. 302, 271 S.E.2d 205 (1980); *Blanton v. Williams*, 209 Ga. 16, 70 S.E.2d 461 (1952).

1127   *Edwards v. McTyre*, 246 Ga.302, 271 S.E.2d 205 (1980), citing *Blower v. Jones*, 226 Ga. 847, 178 S.E.2d 172 (1970).

1128   *Sikes v. Markham*, 74 Ga.App. 874, 41 S.E.2d 828 (1947).

that spouse fails to qualify for a loan, the spouse who did not execute the contract will not be obligated to apply for a loan. It is therefore generally in the seller's best interest to get both spouses to sign the contract.

§ 7.5.9   Loss Of Financing After End Of Due Diligence Period Or Expiration Of Financing Contingency Period

Buyers sometimes lose their ability to obtain financing after their right to terminate the sales contract for the same has expired. This sometimes creates hardships for the buyer by leaving the buyer in breach of the contract due to no fault of the buyer. However, the GAR Contracts recognize that an inability of the buyer to close on the purchase of the property can also work a hardship on the seller. This is particularly the case if the seller has packed up her belongings to move, bought another house, or kept her house off the market waiting for the buyer to close.

Under the GAR Contracts, the buyer's exposure in such a situation can be significant with the buyer facing a claim for the broker's commission and either a claim for damages or the loss of the buyer's earnest money. There are several special stipulations the buyer can consider to try to minimize this risk.

The first is a right on the part of the buyer to terminate the contract if the mortgage loan cannot be obtained as a result of some action or inaction of the mortgage lender (rather than on the part of the buyer). An example of this type of provision follows.

> **Special Stipulation 113:   Buyer May Terminate if Lender Fails to Perform its Obligations**
>
> *All parties acknowledge that Buyer has received a loan commitment to purchase the Property from the following mortgage lender: _____. In the event the lender is unable to fulfill the loan commitment due to no fault, delay, lack of cooperation or voluntary change in financial circumstances on the part of the Buyer, then Buyer may terminate this Agreement without penalty upon notice to Seller.*
>
> *Examples of situations where Buyer may terminate this Agreement hereunder include, without limitation, the following:*
>
> - *the lender going out of business, filing for bankruptcy protection, or losing its source of funds to originate mortgages;*
> - *the loan program that was the basis of the loan commitment to Buyer no longer being available or being subject to new conditions for which the Buyer can no longer qualify;*
> - *the lender failing to timely honor its letter of commitment.*
>
> *Notwithstanding any provision to the contrary contained herein, any subsequent review appraisal by the mortgage lender resulting in the Property not appraising for at least the purchase price [check one] ☐ shall OR ☐ shall not a basis for the Buyer terminating this Agreement hereunder.*

An alternative to this approach is to limit the Buyer's damages to the earnest money in the event the loan is not made due to circumstances purely under the control of the lender.

> **Special Stipulation 114:   Buyer's Damages Limited in the Event of Loss of Financing Caused by Mortgage Lender**
>
> *All parties acknowledge that Buyer has received a loan commitment to purchase the Property from the following mortgage lender: _____. In the event the lender is unable to fulfill the loan commitment due to no fault, delay, lack of cooperation or change*

in financial circumstances of the Buyer, and Buyer is unable to close on the purchase of the Property, then Seller's sole remedy for such a default shall be to retain Buyer's earnest money as full and complete liquidated damages, it being agreed that this amount is a reasonable pre-estimate of Seller's damages and not a penalty.

Examples of situations where Buyer may terminate this Agreement hereunder include, without limitation, the following:

- *the lender going out of business, filing for bankruptcy protection, or losing its source of funds to originate mortgages;*

- *the loan program that was the basis of the loan commitment to Buyer no longer being available or being subject to new conditions for which the Buyer can no longer qualify;*

- *the lender failing to timely honor its letter of commitment.*

Notwithstanding any provision to the contrary contained herein, any subsequent review appraisal by the mortgage lender resulting in the Property not appraising for at least the purchase price [check one] ☐ shall OR ☐ shall not be a basis for the Buyer terminating this Agreement hereunder.

Of course, the above stipulation does not eliminate the broker's claim to a commission even though the buyer's failure to close is not the fault of the buyer. Therefore, when this stipulation is used, the brokers may also want to strike the language in the Agency and Brokerage paragraph of the GAR Contract obligating the buyer to pay the broker's the commission they would have earned had the default not taken place.

§ 7.6   FHA LOANS

The Federal Housing Administration ("FHA") was created by the federal government to provide mortgage lenders with insurance against losses in the event a borrower defaults on a loan. The FHA is not a lending institution, but functions as an insurance company by insuring loans made by banks, mortgage companies, and savings and loan associations. Because FHA insures 100% of the loan amount, the lender's risk is eliminated. FHA's single-family programs are limited to owner-occupied principal residences. A principal residence is defined as a property that will be occupied by the borrower for a majority of the year.[1129]

§ 7.6.1 Maximum Loan Amount And Appraisal

The FHA establishes the maximum loan amount for which it will provide insurance coverage. The maximum mortgage loan limits vary by program and number of family units within a dwelling. The maximum insurable mortgage is generally the lesser of the statutory loan limit for the area (typically a county or metropolitan statistical area) or the applicable loan-to-value limit. The statutory limit for each program changes on a regular basis. In high cost areas, the maximum amount can be increased by the local FHA office to 95% of the median one-family house price in an area or 87% of the FHLMC limit, whichever is less.[1130] FHA mortgage limits for all areas can be obtained on the Internet at the HUD website. Since the maximum mortgage loan limits will change depending on the county in which the property is located, a mortgage loan officer or the U.S. Department of Housing and Urban Development should be contacted to determine the maximum FHA loan permitted in a given area in Georgia.

1129   Transmittal Handbook No: 4155.1, REV 5, CHG 1, § 1.2 (October 2003).

1130   Transmittal Handbook No: 4155.1, REV 5, CHG 1, §1 6 (October 2003),citing 203(b) of the National Housing Act, as updated by the U.S. Department of Housing and Urban Development Mortgagee Letter 2003 23, December 31, 2003.

In addition to the statutory loan limits, there are certain loan-to-value limits. These limits vary depending on occupancy status, value,[1131] and stage of construction. For the purpose of determining the loan-to-value limit for a particular property, all property will be considered either "proposed or existing construction" if it meets one of the following criteria:

(1) construction is completed more than one year prior to the borrower's application;

(2) the dwelling site, plans, and materials were approved before construction began by VA, eligible DE underwriter, or a builder under FHA's builder certification procedures or by an "early start" letter;

(3) the dwelling is covered by the builder's 10 year insured warranty which is acceptable to FHA; or

(4) the dwelling is being moved to a new location and has been approved for mortgage insurance.

For example, in one Georgia county at the time of this writing, the loan-to-value limit for owner-occupied principal residences for proposed and existing construction with values of $50,000 or less is 98.75%. The maximum loan-to-value limit for owner-occupied residences with values of more than $50,000 and up to $125,000 is 97.65%. The limit for properties with values of more than $125,000 is 97.15%. Owner-occupied residences under construction or less than one year old are limited to 90%, unless the property meets one of the above-listed criteria and can be considered a "proposed or existing construction" property. In that situation, the maximum loan-to-value rating will be greater than 90%.[1132]

Contributions and inducements to purchase from the seller, or repair and similar expenses to be borne by the buyer, may result in either an increase or decrease in the maximum loan amount. The following expenses result in a dollar for dollar reduction in the sale price before applying the appropriate loan-to-value ratio: decorating allowances, repair allowances, moving costs, and certain gift funds. Certain items of personal property may serve to reduce the appraised value of the property. Therefore, in computing the maximum loan amount available under an FHA loan, the value of any personal property items being conveyed from a seller to a buyer will be deducted from the sale price which will generally result in a reduction of the appraised value. Typically, under an FHA loan, personal property items such as cars, boats, riding lawn mowers, furniture, and televisions are not included as part of the sale price. Depending on local custom, FHA will not deduct some items of personal property such as refrigerators, stoves, dishwashers, washers, dryers, carpeting, and window treatments; provided, however, no cash allowance is given to the borrower.

In some cases, the maximum mortgage amount may be increased. This is generally permitted only when the appraised value exceeds the purchase price and only the amount that the value exceeds the purchase price may be added. For example, repairs and improvements required by the appraiser, which are essential for property eligibility and are to be paid by the borrower, may be included in the mortgage amount. If such repairs are not to be paid by the borrower, they cannot be included.

A buyer of property whose obligation to close is contingent on the buyer's ability to obtain an FHA loan may cancel the contract if the appraisal of the property is less than the amount set forth in the contract.[1133] The GAR FHA Loan exhibit allows the parties to identify a minimum appraised value.[1134] Presumably, the appraised value does not have to be the same as the purchase price. As a matter of practice, however, the minimum appraised value is generally identified as the purchase price.

1131 The applicable value is the lesser of the appraised value plus allowable closing costs or the adjusted sale price of the property in Transmittal Handbook No: 4155.1, REV 5, CHG 1, § 1 8F (October 2003).

1132 For more detail, refer to Transmittal Handbook No: 4155.1, REV 5, CHG 1, § 1 7 to 15 (October 2003).

1133 Purchasers not applying for FHA loans who wish to have this same protection may do so by using Special Stipulation 101 or 102.

1134 GAR Form F63, FHA Loan Exhibit.

§ 7.6.2 Limitation On Contributions To Closing Costs And Discount Points

Under a FHA loan, the seller may not pay more than 6% of the purchase price toward a buyer's actual closing costs, prepaid expenses, discount points, and other financing concessions.[1135] Included in the 6% limitation are interest rate buy-downs, payments of mortgage interest (but not principal), mortgage payment protection insurance, and payment of the up-front mortgage insurance premium. Items typically paid by the seller such as real estate commissions, pest inspections, and fees for the release of a deed to secure debt, are not considered contributions by the seller because they are customarily seller expenses. Since the FHA regulations do not allow the buyer to pay the underwriting, document preparation, and tax service fees, these fees are not included in the 6% limitation. Each dollar exceeding the 6% limitation is subtracted from the property's sale price before applying the appropriate loan-to-value ratio.

Recently, however, the FHA has announced its intention to revise the rules in favor of a lower percentage of allowable seller concessions. Although the current limit on seller concessions is no more than six percent (6%), the FHA plans to reduce that percentage down to three percent (3%). The rationale behind this proposed change is to protect the FHA and borrowers from the impacts of inflated appraisals. This reduction will also bring FHA-guaranteed loans in line with conventional loan requirements. If this change is implemented, the greatest impact will be to first-time homebuyers. These buyers often have good income streams but limited cash available and rely upon such concessions from sellers in order to get into a property.

The GAR FHA Loan[1136] exhibit also allows the parties to provide whether the buyer or the seller shall pay certain prepaid items including the following any repairs required in the FHA Commitment and the cost of connection to public water or public sewer system. Although the seller may pay these costs, the buyer generally pays them. If the seller pays the above-referenced costs they will be subtracted from the total amount seller has agreed to pay in the closing costs and discount point subparagraph of the contract and will count toward the 6% maximum contribution.

§ 7.6.3 Certain Lender Fees Cannot Be Paid By Buyer

FHA guidelines prohibit a buyer from paying certain lender fees: underwriting, document preparation, and tax service fees. The GAR FHA loan exhibit, however, expressly provides that the seller pays the tax service fees. The seller may indicate whether such fees are included or not included in the seller's contributions. If the seller wants to limit her obligation to the buyer for payment of costs associated with the buyer's loan, the parties may modify the GAR FHA loan exhibit to include underwriting, document preparation, and tax service fees in any closing costs the seller may have agreed to pay. If this paragraph is rewritten, the following special stipulation may be used.

> **Special Stipulation 115: Seller to Pay Stipulated Sum to be First Applied Toward FHA Fees That Buyer is Not Allowed to Pay**
>
> *Notwithstanding any other provision contained herein Seller agrees to pay at closing a sum not to exceed $_____ to be used by Buyer in obtaining an FHA loan, which sums shall be applied first toward the payment of any fees FHA prohibits Buyer from paying, including, but not limited to, any underwriting, document preparation, and tax service fees charged by lender in connection with any such FHA loan. The balance of the sum Seller agrees to pay may be used at Buyer's discretion to pay for other closing costs, loan discount points and survey costs. Buyer shall pay any additional closing costs, insurance premiums, or escrow amounts to fulfill lender requirements or to otherwise close this transaction.*

1135   Transmittal Handbook No: 4155.1, REV 5, CHG 1, § 1.7.A (October 2003).

1136   GAR Form F63.

It is essential for the buyer that the FHA loan exhibit is included as part of the contract in all transactions in which the buyer anticipates obtaining FHA financing. Even though FHA guidelines prohibit the buyer from paying the underwriting, document preparation, and tax service fees, the seller is not obligated to pay these fees unless she has contractually agreed to do so. The seller may elect to void the contract rather than pay fees that she is not contractually obligated to pay.

§ 7.6.4 Mortgage Insurance Premium

Because FHA loans typically do not require a large down payment, FHA charges a mortgage insurance premium to ensure against the higher risk of default, which is inherent when a low down payment is made. Recently, the FHA increased the up-front mortgage insurance premium paid by a homebuyer from 1.0% to 1.75% of the base loan amount.[1137] This applies to all homebuyers regardless of the amortization term or LTV ratio. This increase will be effective in all cases dated on or after April 9, 2012.[1138] However, the FHA has indicated its intent to increase the percentage again by fifty (50) basis points to 2.25%. Although this change is not currently in effect, it is expected to be implemented during 2012.

The GAR FHA Loan exhibit provides that the premium can be paid in its entirety by buyer at closing or may be financed by the buyer into the loan. The seller does not have the option to pay the up-front mortgage insurance premium percentage. The premium is collected in an amount based on a percentage of the loan amount. Under FHA guidelines, the seller may pay the up-front mortgage insurance premium, but if such an election is made, it will be counted toward the 6% maximum seller contribution. Further, the seller must pay the entire premium at the time of closing and not just a portion of the premium. If the parties desire to have the seller pay the up-front mortgage insurance premium, the following special stipulation may be used.

> **Special Stipulation 116:   Seller to Pay Part of Up-Front FHA Mortgage Insurance Premium**
>
> *The FHA up-front ___% mortgage insurance premium shall be paid by Seller in full at closing.*

In addition, an annual premium for mortgage insurance is charged and added to the buyer's monthly loan payment. The amount of the up-front mortgage insurance premium as well as the annual premium varies based on the term of the loan as well as the loan to value ratio. It should be noted that there is no FHA up-front mortgage insurance premium for condominiums.

§ 7.6.5 FHA Credit And Down Payment Requirements

Before approving a loan, a lender will analyze the borrower's past credit performance. The FHA will consider if a buyer has filed for bankruptcy in the past, has a history of late payments, allowed foreclosure of a property, and the existence of any delinquent federal debt, such as tax liens or student loans.[1139] Buyers who have filed for bankruptcy may still be eligible if enough time has elapsed since the discharge date of the bankruptcy and the buyer has started to re-establish good credit. Buyers who have a consistent history of making late payments, have delinquent tax liens or student loans, or whose prior property was foreclosed on generally do not qualify for an FHA loan. Only buyers with good credit and a strong history of timely payments will generally qualify for this type of loan.

1137   Transmittal Handbook No: 4155.2, REV 5, CHG-7, § 7.3.g (March 2011), as updated by the U.S. Department of Housing and Urban Development Mortgagee Letter 2012-4, March 6, 2012.

1138   Transmittal Handbook No: 4155.2, REV 5, CHG-7, § 7.3.g (March 2011), as updated by the U.S. Department of Housing and Urban Development Mortgagee Letter 2012-4, March 6, 2012.

1139   Transmittal Handbook No: 4155.1, REV-5, CHG-4, § 4.C.2.a (March 2011).

Borrowers with less than sterling credit may still qualify for an FHA loan but the amount will be limited depending on their credit score.[1140] These buyers, or buyers with less than a 20% down payment, frequently turn to FHA loans over conventional loans. The reasoning is likely attributed to the lower down payment percentage required to obtain an FHA loan.

The FHA currently requires homebuyers to have a down payment of 3.5% when purchasing a home.[1141] However, new policy changes require buyers to have a FICO score of at least 580 in order to qualify for the 3.5% down payment program.[1142] A 10% down payment will be required from borrowers with FICO scores below that threshold. This new requirement allows the FHA to continue providing access to FHA loans for those buyers who have historically performed well. However, just because the FHA requires a FICO score of at least 580 does not mean that a particular bank will be willing to issue a loan to buyers with that score. The FHA cannot force lenders to lower their minimum FICO score for loans. In fact, many participating FHA lenders still require a FICO score of at least 620 in order to qualify for an FHA loan.

§ 7.6.6 Prohibition Against Buyer Receiving Credit For Repairs At Closing

In FHA loan situations, a buyer may not receive a cash payment or credit at closing for repairs, renovations, and decorating allowances. Typically, if the necessary repairs are not completed prior to closing, a check will be cut out of the seller's proceeds and made payable to the contractor in an amount representing the estimated cost of repairs. In the alternative, a portion of the seller's proceeds may be put in escrow pending satisfactory completion of the repairs.[1143] Upon satisfactory evidence that the required repairs have been completed, a check in the amount of the repairs will generally be issued directly to the contractor. To the extent the amount due for the final repairs is less than the amount put in escrow, the seller is entitled to a refund. Under no circumstances can any portion of the funds that were escrowed for repairs be disbursed directly to the buyer.

§ 7.6.7 Assumption Of FHA Loan

Buyers could assume FHA loans prior to December 15, 1989, without having to qualify with the respective lender. All FHA loans closed since December 15, 1989, however, require that a buyer's creditworthiness be independently reviewed prior to assuming an FHA loan. Assumptions without credit approval are grounds for acceleration of the mortgage, if permitted by applicable state law and subject to HUD approval, unless the seller retains an ownership interest in the property or the transfer is by devise or descent.[1144]

In most instances, an individual may be eligible to receive only one FHA-insured loan at a time. If a seller wants to ensure that she remains eligible for a subsequent FHA loan, it may be necessary to make the contract contingent on the seller obtaining a release of liability from the lender. Even if the seller is not concerned about obtaining another FHA loan, it is in her best interest to obtain a release of liability so that the FHA cannot pursue her for repayment of any amounts due if the buyer later defaults. Set forth below is an example of a provision which makes the contract contingent on the seller being released from liability by the lender.

1140   Transmittal Handbook No: 4155.1, REV-5, CHG-4, § 4.A.1 (March 2011).

1141   Transmittal Handbook No: 4155.1, REV-5, CHG-2, § 2.A.2.a (March 2011).

1142   Transmittal Handbook No: 4155.1, REV-5, CHG- 4, § 4.A.1.c (March 2011) citing Mortgagee Letter 2010-29, September 3, 2010.

1143   Transmittal Handbook No: 4155.1, REV 5, CHG 1, §1.7(C)(1)(October 2003).

1144   Transmittal Handbook No: 4155.1, REV-5, CHG-4, § 2 (March 2011).

> ### Special Stipulation 117: Contract Contingent on Buyer's Assumption of Seller's FHA Loan
>
> *This Agreement is contingent on Buyer's ability to assume Seller's existing FHA loan and to assume Seller's liability for repayment of the FHA loan, and Seller being released from liability from repayment of said loan. Buyer agrees to immediately apply to FHA and submit any and all documents necessary for Buyer to qualify for loan approval. If Buyer fails to obtain loan approval from FHA within thirty (30) days from the Binding Agreement Date, or if Buyer fails to obtain approval to assume Seller's liability under the FHA loan, Buyer shall give Seller written notice of such denial within five days of its receipt. Seller may, at her option, terminate this Agreement within five days of receipt of Buyer's notice and all earnest money shall be immediately returned to Buyer. If Seller fails to timely exercise this termination right, it shall be deemed waived.*

§ 7.6.8   FHA Financing For Condominium Units

FHA will not insure a loan for the purchase of a condominium unit unless a certain percentage of the properties are owner-occupied as opposed to leased. The property must be at least 70% owner-occupied in order for FHA to insure loans in such a community.[1145] In the event a real estate contract contemplates that the buyer will obtain FHA-insured financing, the buyer may desire to terminate the contract if the community in which the property is located does not meet the permitted owner-occupied ratio and the buyer cannot obtain spot approval from FHA for her particular transaction. The following special stipulation can be used for such purpose.

> ### Special Stipulation 118: Contract Contingent on Property Approval by FHA
>
> *Seller acknowledges and agrees that if Buyer is unable to obtain an FHA-insured loan because the condominium in which the Property is located is not on the FHA approved property list, does not meet the permitted owner-occupied ratio, or the Buyer's lender cannot obtain spot approval from FHA for this transaction, Buyer may terminate this Agreement by written notice to Seller, in which case all earnest money shall be immediately returned to Buyer.*

§ 7.7   VA LOANS

The Veterans Administration ("VA") was formed shortly after World War II to provide housing, medical and educational assistance, and aid to veterans.[1146] The VA is an independent agency of the federal government and guarantees repayment of a portion of a loan made by a conventional lender such as a bank or mortgage company. The VA loan program was established to encourage traditional lenders to make mortgage loans to veterans.

§ 7.7.1   Eligibility Requirements And Entitlement

Certain active members of the armed services, discharged members of the armed services (so long as the discharge was not dishonorable), and certain members of the Selected Reserve or National Guard are eligible for VA loans.[1147] A veteran determines her eligibility by applying for a Certificate of Eligibility from the VA.[1148] Once obtained, the Certificate evidences the maximum entitlement that the veteran is qualified to receive.

1145   Transmittal Handbook No: 4265.1, REV-5, CHG-3, § 10.4 (July 1973).

1146   38 U.S.C.A. § 3701, *et seq.*

1147   Veteran's Administration Lender's Handbook Pamphlet 26-7, Chapter 2, § 5(a).

1148   Veteran's Administration Lender's Handbook Pamphlet 26-7, Chapter 2, § 5(a).

Home buyers using a VA loan do not need to be first-time home buyers in order to qualify. Unlike FHA loans, the VA loan benefit can be reused by the veteran.[1149] However, a veteran may only have one open VA loan at any time. In other words, a veteran who has used a VA loan for the purchase of one home must pay that loan in full (by refinancing with another lender, sale of the home to a third-party who arranges other financing, etc.) before the veteran may obtain another VA loan on a different home.

Before a VA loan can be used to purchase a home, a VA appraisal must be done by an approved VA appraiser. The maximum loan amount a qualified veteran may be eligible to receive changes frequently. The VA has no specified dollar amount for the maximum amount of the loan.[1150] A VA loan may permit a qualified veteran buyer to finance 100% of the purchase price of the property,[1151] but is not permitted to finance certain closing costs into a VA loan. Any closing costs payable in connection with a VA loan must be paid out-of-pocket at closing. Computing the maximum loan entitlement available to veterans under a VA guaranteed loan can be complicated and is beyond the scope of this book.

The VA guidelines provide that a buyer is not required to complete the purchase of the property or forfeit her earnest money if the contract purchase price exceeds the appraised value established by the Veterans Administration. This provision is somewhat different from the FHA provision, which allows the parties to establish the minimum appraised value. As with an FHA loan, however, the buyer has the option to proceed to close the transaction without regard to the appraised value.

§ 7.7.2 Funding Fee

Veterans are not required to purchase mortgage insurance under VA loans, even if they are making less than a 20% down payment. Subject to a few specific exceptions, however, a veteran must pay a VA funding fee at closing as a condition to obtaining a VA loan.[1152] The VA funding fee varies depending on the type of loan obtained and is a percentage of the loan amount. A funding fee exception is possible upon proper verification of disability.

The funding fee is intended to offset and replenish losses resulting from veterans who have previously defaulted on VA-guaranteed loans. Either buyer or seller may pay the funding fee in full at closing, or the buyer may finance the funding fee into the loan. If the funding fee is financed into the loan, it will be included in the total loan amount for purposes of determining the maximum amount a qualified veteran is entitled to borrow.

§ 7.7.3 Certain Lender Fees Cannot Be Paid By Buyer

VA guidelines, like FHA guidelines, prohibit a buyer from paying certain fees, including the following: underwriting, document preparation, and tax service fees.[1154] The GAR VA loan exhibit[1155] expressly provides that these costs are paid by the seller. (*See* § 7.6.3 above for implications, and Special Stipulation 115: (Seller to pay stipulated sum to be first applied toward FHA fees that buyer is not allowed to pay).

§ 7.7.4 Prohibition Against Buyer Receiving Credit For Repairs At Closing

As in the case of FHA loans, a buyer may not receive a cash payment or credit at closing for repairs, renovations, and decorating allowances.

1149   Veteran's Administration Lender's Handbook Pamphlet 26-7, Chapter 2, § 6(a).

1150   Veteran's Administration Lender's Handbook Pamphlet 26-7, Chapter 3,§ 1(a).

1151   Veteran's Administration Lender's Handbook Pamphlet 26-7, Chapter 3,§ 3(a).

1152   Veteran's Administration Lender's Handbook Pamphlet 26-7, Chapter 8, § 1(b). (VA Funding Fee Requirement).

1153   Veteran's Administration Lender's Handbook Pamphlet 26-7, Chapter 8,§ 1(b).

1154   Veteran's Administration Lender's Handbook Pamphlet 26-7, Chapter 8,§ 2(d).

1155   GAR Form F65, VA Loan Exhibit.

§ 7.7.5   Assumption Of VA Loan

A VA loan closed prior to March 1988 may be assumed without the buyer qualifying. On VA loans closed after March 1, 1988, the new buyer must qualify to assume the loan.[1156] When a VA loan is assumed by a buyer, the veteran selling the property may not be entitled to obtain another VA loan. Sellers with a VA loan will generally want to obtain a release of liability when she permits a buyer to assume their loan.[1157] Obtaining a release of liability serves two purposes. First, a release may enable the seller to have her VA loan guarantee entitlement restored, thereby allowing the seller to receive another VA loan.[1158] Second, a release will ensure that the VA cannot pursue the seller for repayment of any amounts due if the buyer later defaults. The Special Stipulation 117: (Contract contingent on buyer's assumption of seller's FHA loan) set forth above may also be used if the contract is contingent on the buyer obtaining a release of the seller's liability.

§ 7.8   SELLER FINANCING

There are benefits for both seller and buyer in a transaction that provides for seller financing. Seller financing may afford a motivated seller an opportunity to sell her property more quickly. A seller may also offer to finance the purchase of the property because she would prefer to receive payments over time rather than a lump sum. On the other hand, buyers who may not be able to qualify for a loan with a conventional lender often find seller financing attractive. Closing costs associated with a seller-financed transaction are also typically much lower than when a buyer secures financing from a traditional lender.

A seller will normally secure her loan by taking back a promissory note and deed to secure debt on the property. If there is no lender involved in the transaction, the deed to secure debt of the seller will normally be in a first priority position, which in real estate parlance is commonly referred to as a first mortgage. A seller may also agree to finance a portion of the purchase price by taking back a note and second priority deed to secure debt on the property. This is usually done when the down payment of the buyer plus the loan from an institutional lender do not add up to the purchase price. Keep in mind that this type of secondary financing must have the prior approval of the buyer's first mortgage lender.

Not every seller has the option of extending seller financing to a buyer. Although many states do not require a purchaser of residential mortgage loans to be licensed as a mortgage lender, Georgia is one of the few states that impose this requirement. For this reason, it is particularly important for sellers to recognize the limitations Georgia imposes on seller financing before offering this option to a buyer.

§ 7.8.1   Who Is Required To Be A Licensed Mortgage Lender?

Beginning in 2010, the Georgia Residential Mortgage Act[1159] ("Act") provided that all persons (including individuals, sole proprietorships, corporations, limited liability companies, partnerships, trusts or any other group of individuals, however organized[1160]) performing the acts of a mortgage lender are required obtain a license, unless an exemption applies.[1161]

1156   Veteran's Administration Lender's Handbook Pamphlet 26-7, Chapter 3, § 12(d).

1157   Veteran's Administration Lender's Handbook Pamphlet 26-7, Chapter 2, §2(a).

1158   Restoration of a previously-used entitlement may be applied for if the following conditions are met: (a) the property has been sold and the loan has been paid in full, or (b) a qualified veteran transferee has agreed to assume the outstanding balance on the loan, agrees to substitute her entitlement of the same amount of entitlement originally used for the loan, and the assuming veteran meets the occupancy, income, and credit requirements of the law. Veteran's Administration Lender's Handbook Pamphlet 26-7, Chapter 2, § 2(a).

1159   O.C.G.A. § 7-1-1000, *et seq.*

1160   O.C.G.A. § 7-1-1000(25).

1161   O.C.G.A. § 7-1-1002.

A mortgage lender is generally thought to be a person that makes loans. However, the Act defines a mortgage lender as "any person who directly or indirectly makes, originates, underwrites or purchases mortgage loans or who services mortgage loans."[1162] Therefore, a seller offering financing to a buyer for a real estate transaction is considered a mortgage lender under the Act and thus requires a license unless she qualifies for an exemption.

Even if the purchase took place outside the state of Georgia, the Act would still apply to a seller if the purchase was of a Georgia residential loan.

§ 7.8.2 Exemptions

Fortunately for sellers offering this type of financing, the Act provides a number of exemptions to the licensing requirement. If a seller qualifies for an exemption under the Act, a mortgage license will not be required to offer this type of financing to a buyer.[1163]

The first exemption applies if the seller financing is from a natural person (*i.e.*, a real live person) who makes 5 or fewer mortgage loans in any one calendar year.[1164] However, this exception does not apply if the seller is an entity such as a corporation or limited liability company.

The second exemption applies if the seller financing comes from a natural person who makes a purchase money mortgage for financing the sale of their own property.[1165] Again, however, this exception only applies to natural persons.

The third exemption applies if the seller financing is on a house that serves as the seller's individual residence.[1166] However, this exemption does not apply if the property is not the seller's residence.

There is also an exemption for loans made by the seller to an immediate family member, such as a spouse, child, sibling, parent, grandparent or grandchild.[1167] In other words, a parent can still make a loan to a child buying a house and take back a security deed on the property without obtaining a mortgage license.

While it may seem like all seller financing is permitted one way or another, this is actually not the case. For example, Mr. and Mrs. Smith are the sole members of a limited liability company that own a rental property they need to sell. They find a buyer but the buyer cannot purchase the property without getting seller financing. In this case, the sellers may not give the buyer the option of seller financing since the property is owned by a limited liability company. Moreover, it does not appear that any other exemptions allowing seller financing apply in this transaction. The sellers could try to avoid this problem by transferring the property to their individual names. Once they own the property personally, they should be able to extend seller financing to the buyer by qualifying for one of the exemptions applicable to natural persons. Alternatively, if the property becomes the sellers' residence, they can also offer seller financing based on a different exemption under the Act.

Most exemptions under the Act are not applicable to parties who purchase residential mortgage loans as a real estate investment strategy. One possible exemption that could apply is for "any person who purchases mortgage loans from a mortgage broker or mortgage lender solely as an investment property and who is not in the business of brokering, making, purchasing or servicing mortgage loans."[1168] While there is little guidance as to how many purchases put a company in the "business" of purchasing residential mortgage loans, it is likely that the Georgia Department of Banking and Finance ("GDBF"), which administers, interprets and enforces the Act, would look to the person's

---

1162   O.C.G.A. § 7-1-1000(20).

1163   O.C.G.A. § 7-1-1001.

1164   O.C.G.A. § 7-1-1001(16).

1165   O.C.G.A. § 7-1-1001(8).

1166   O.C.G.A. § 7-1-1001(10).

1167   O.C.G.A. § 7-1-1001(4).

1168   O.C.G.A. § 7-1-1000(a)(15).

general business activities and the frequency of transactions involving residential mortgage loans in determining whether or not a particular person is "in the business."

With these new restrictions in place, residential builders and developers are also limited in offering seller financing to buyers. Prior to this Act, it was not uncommon for builders to take back a 2nd mortgage and offer this type of financing to a buyer. However, to avoid violating the Act, builders and developers must adhere to the applicable limitations before offering this type of financing. Failure to comply with the Act can result in stiff penalties. Transacting business either directly or indirectly as a mortgage lender without a license of exception constitutes a felony, and upon conviction, is punishable by imprisonment for not less than one nor more five years or a fine of $10,000.[1169]

§ 7.8.3   Special Issues Regarding Seller Financing

A contract contemplating seller financing must set forth in specific detail the essential terms of the note and deed to secure debt, just as is required with institutional lenders. One contract was found to be vague and unenforceable when it referred to additional terms to be agreed upon at a later date.[1170] In seller-financed transactions, the contract should incorporate the provisions to be stated in the note and provide that it will be secured by a deed to secure debt on the property.[1171]

The GAR Seller Financing (First Mortgage) Exhibit[1172] includes the following protection for the seller: the obligation of the buyer to provide the seller with credit information; a due on sale clause; the right to impose a late charge; the obligation of the buyer to provide hazard insurance; and the obligation of the buyer to pay for any charge associated with the preparation of the note and deed to secure debt (if prepared by the buyer's attorney), the intangible tax, and the recording fee.[1173] The GAR form also provides certain protection for the buyer including a prepayment privilege and the right to cure a default.

The GAR Seller Financing (Second Mortgage) Exhibit[1174] also provides additional protection for the seller by including a cross-default clause which states that a default under the terms of the first priority deed to secure debt and note constitute a default under the terms of the second mortgage authorizing the seller to accelerate the entire indebtedness and foreclose on the property.

The Brokerage Relationships in Real Estate Transactions Act ("BRRETA") (codified at O.C.G.A. §10-6A-1 *et seq.*) also attempts to protect sellers offering purchase money financing or allowing loan assumptions by requiring the real estate broker representing the buyer as a client to "disclose to a prospective seller … all material adverse facts actually known by the broker concerning the buyer's financial ability to perform the terms of the sale, and in the case of a residential transaction, the buyer's intent to occupy the property as a principal residence."[1175]

§ 7.8.3.1   Satisfactory Credit Report

Seller financing should always be contingent on the buyer providing the seller with a satisfactory credit report, particularly if the buyer is making only a small down payment.

The GAR Seller Financing (First Mortgage) and (Second Mortgage)[1176] Exhibits give the seller the right to terminate the contract if the buyer's financial statement and past credit listings do not meet underwriting guidelines as

1169   O.C.G.A. § 7-1-845(b).

1170   *Rush v. Autry*, 210 Ga. 732, 82 S.E.2d 866 (1954).

1171   *Rumph v. Rister*, 211 Ga. 312, 85 S.E.2d 768 (1955).

1172   GAR Form F67, Seller Financing (First Mortgage) Exhibit.

1173   GAR Form F67, Seller Financing (First Mortgage) Exhibit.

1174   GAR Form F68, Seller Financing (Second Mortgage) Exhibit.

1175   O.C.G.A. § 10-6A-7(b).

1176   GAR Forms F67 and F68.

established by the Federal National Mortgage Association ("FNMA" or "Fanny Mae"). These exhibits also provide that the seller shall not unreasonably withhold the approval of a buyer's credit.

§ 7.8.3.2 Excessive Or Unlawful Interest Rates

A seller agreeing to provide financing must be careful to ensure that the rate of interest to be charged under the promissory note does not exceed the rate permitted by applicable law. The permissible rate of interest that can be charged on a loan is set by statute. Georgia law provides for civil and criminal liability for any lender, including an individual, who makes a loan with an excessive interest rate.[1177] Other restrictions on lender fees and charges are contained in the Georgia Fair Lending Act.[1178]

§ 7.8.3.3 Ability Of Buyer To Resell Or Transfer Interest In Property

The GAR forms include a due on sale clause to protect the seller who takes back a first or second deed to secure debt on a property.[1179] Under a due on sale clause the buyer is obligated to pay the entire principal balance outstanding on the note and deed to secure debt if the buyer transfers the property to a third party. Such a provision protects the seller against the buyer selling the property to an unreliable or unknown third party buyer who then assumes the loan.

If the seller desires for tax or other reasons to have the proceeds of the sale payable over an extended term, the seller may incorporate a provision that allows a qualified successor buyer to assume the loan. If the seller desires to offer a qualified assumable loan, the following language may be used.

> **Special Stipulation 119: Qualified Assumption by Subsequent Buyer of Seller-Financed Property**
>
> *Notwithstanding any other provision in this Agreement to the contrary, Buyer and Seller agree that the promissory note and deed to secure debt to be executed by Buyer in favor of Seller shall contain a provision that Buyer may sell the Property and have the subsequent purchaser assume the promissory note and deed to secure debt, provided that: (1) the subsequent purchaser is determined by the Seller to be creditworthy based upon the underwriting guidelines as established from time to time by the Federal National Mortgage Association ("FNMA"), and (2) the subsequent purchaser provides all information requested by Seller which is reasonably necessary to determine the creditworthiness of such purchaser.*
>
> *Seller agrees not to unreasonably withhold approval of credit to the intended transferee. In the event the subsequent purchaser is determined by Seller to be creditworthy and assumes all of Buyer's obligations and liabilities under the promissory note and deed to secure debt, Buyer shall thereafter immediately be relieved of any further obligations and liabilities under the note and deed referenced herein.*

1177   O.C.G.A. § 7-4-18(a) prohibits a lender from collecting any rate of interest greater than 5% per month.

1178   O.C.G.A. § 7-6A-1 *et seq.*

1179   GAR Form F67 and F68.

§ 7.8.3.4   Ability Of Buyer To Assign Rights

The seller and buyer may have different interests with regard to the ability of the buyer to assign her obligations under the contract, note, and deed to secure debt.

From the seller's perspective, the seller may want to limit the buyer's ability to assign her obligations because the seller's willingness to provide financing may be based on the seller's evaluation of the financial ability of the buyer to fulfill the terms of the financing obligation. The GAR Contract provides that there shall be no assignment of the contract unless signed by all parties. Therefore, the buyer will be unable to assign the contract unless the seller approves the assignment. The seller is not under any legal obligation to be reasonable in granting or denying approval for an assignment.[1180] The buyer contemplating a possible assignment of the contract may wish to use the following special stipulation.

> **Special Stipulation 120:   Seller's Consent to Assignment Cannot be Unreasonably Withheld**
>
> *Buyer may assign this Agreement to a third party with the consent of the Seller which consent shall not be unreasonably withheld.*

The buyer, of course, may want to have the absolute right to assign a contract to a third party. The following provision allows the buyer to assign the contract to a third party without the seller's consent.

> **Special Stipulation 121:   Buyer's Right to Assignment Without Seller Consent**
>
> *Notwithstanding any provision to the contrary, this Agreement and all obligations required hereunder, including but not limited to the obligation of Buyer to execute a promissory note and deed to secure debt in favor of Seller, may be assigned by Buyer without the consent of Seller, provided, however, that Buyer shall remain jointly and severally obligated with the assignee on the promissory note and deed to secure debt.*

§ 7.8.3.5   Personal Obligation For Tepayment

When a buyer executes a promissory note and a deed to secure debt, the promissory note generally becomes the personal obligation of the buyer. If the seller is forced to foreclose on the property and the proceeds from the sale are not adequate to satisfy the indebtedness, the buyer then remains personally obligated for the deficiency.[1181]

The buyer may attempt to include a provision in the contract to limit her personal liability by providing that the note and deed to secure debt shall contain what is commonly referred to as an exculpation clause.[1182] This means that the seller may look only to the real property to satisfy the debt and cannot hold the buyer personally responsible for its repayment. Such a clause eliminates the ability of the seller to proceed against the buyer on the personal obligation in lieu of foreclosing the seller's interest in the property. Set forth below is an example of an exculpation clause that relieves the buyer from personal obligation for the debt.

> **Special Stipulation 122:   Exculpation Clause Relieving Buyer from Personal Liability**
>
> *Buyer and Seller acknowledge and agree that the promissory note and deed to secure debt to be executed by Buyer in connection with this Agreement shall each contain an exculpation clause, which limits Buyer's responsibility for repayment of the secured indebtedness on the Property. Seller acknowledges and agrees that Buyer shall be fully*

1180   *Vaswani v. Wohletz*, 196 Ga.App. 676, 396 S.E.2d 593 (1990).

1181   Provided, however, that the seller has obtained judicial confirmation of the foreclosure so as to allow the seller to pursue the deficiency.

1182   Another way to describe such a situation is that the note and security deed are "non-recourse."

released from any and all personal liability for repayment of the indebtedness under the promissory note and deed to secure debt and that in the event of a default on the promissory note and deed to secure debt Seller's sole remedy shall be against the Property.

§ 7.8.3.6 Personal Property As Additional Collateral

In addition to obtaining a security interest in the real property being sold, the seller may be able to further protect her interest by obtaining a security interest in personal property owned by the buyer.

To obtain a valid security interest in personal property that is not considered a fixture, it is necessary for the buyer to execute a security agreement and a financing statement in accordance with the Uniform Commercial Code (UCC). The seller needs both a security agreement, in which the personal property is actually pledged as security, and a UCC Financing Statement, which gives notice of the security interest. It is possible for a single document to serve as both a security agreement and a UCC Financing Statement, so long as it contains the correct language.

The UCC Financing Statement is filed in the land records of the county where the property is located and identifies the personal property being pledged as additional collateral for the indebtedness.[1183] If the seller does not properly file a UCC Financing Statement, she may not be able to enforce her security interest in the personal property against a third-party purchaser who does not have knowledge of the security agreement. UCC Financing Statements must be refilled from time to time to remain in effect. Set forth below is an example of a contract provision which contemplates that the buyer will pledge personal property as additional collateral for the loan.

> ### Special Stipulation 123: Buyer Pledge of Personal Property as Additional Collateral for Seller Financing Loan
>
> *Buyer hereby agrees to execute any and all instruments and documents necessary to grant and perfect in favor of Seller a security interest in the following personal property owned by the Buyer which is not deemed to be a part of the real property (describe). During the term of Seller's loan to Buyer, Buyer shall be entitled, upon written notice to Seller and prior written approval by Seller, to substitute certain items of personalty for those items which secure the indebtedness.*

§ 7.8.3.7 Proof Of Payment Of Taxes

A seller's security interest can be jeopardized if the buyer fails to pay any *ad valorem* property taxes. Most institutional lenders reduce this risk by requiring the buyer to set up an escrow with the lender for payment of taxes. If the seller who agrees to accept a note and purchase money deed to secure debt does not require the buyer to escrow taxes, the seller may want to include provisions in the contract (as well as in the note and deed to secure debt) which require the buyer to provide to seller proof of payment of property taxes. An example of such a contract provision is set forth below.

> ### Special Stipulation 124: Buyer's Obligation to Provide Proof of Payment of Property Taxes to Seller
>
> *Buyer agrees that any promissory note and deed to secure debt to be executed in favor of Seller in connection with Seller agreeing to finance a portion of the purchase price of the Property shall contain the following provision: Each year as long as the indebtedness due to Seller remains unpaid, Buyer agrees to furnish a copy of a paid tax receipt evidencing that the ad valorem taxes for the Property securing the promissory note have been fully paid for the year in question.*

1183 O.C.G.A. § 11-9-501.

Buyer hereby further agrees to submit to Seller such fully paid receipt within thirty (30) days from the date that such taxes become fully due and payable. If Buyer fails to produce such fully paid receipt within the aforementioned time period, Buyer shall be deemed to be in default under the terms of the promissory note and deed to secure debt. Alternatively, Buyer, in her sole discretion, may pay any delinquent ad valorem taxes and the amount of such payments will be added to and become additional amounts due under the terms of the promissory note and deed to secure debt.

§ 7.8.3.8 Third Party Guarantee For Repayment Of Loan

In some instances, the seller may desire to have a third party execute a guarantee agreement. The person executing a guarantee agreement agrees to satisfy the debt of the buyer only if the buyer fails to repay the debt. The seller then has additional recourse if the buyer defaults on repayment of the loan. An example of such a contract provision is set forth below.

> **Special Stipulation 125:   Contract and Seller Financing Contingent on 3rd Party Guarantee**
>
> *Buyer agrees that _____ ("Guarantor") shall execute a Guarantee Agreement as consideration for Seller agreeing to accept a promissory note and deed to secure debt from Buyer. Guarantor, after receiving written notice from Seller, agrees to immediately satisfy the debt of Buyer if Buyer is deemed to be in default. If Guarantor fails to execute the Guarantee Agreement attached hereto as Exhibit "_____" and deliver the same to Seller at least ten days prior to the date of closing, Seller may terminate this Agreement upon written notice to Buyer.*

§ 7.8.4 Assignment Of Rents And Leases

The seller may want to have the buyer execute what is commonly referred to as an assignment of rents and leases. An assignment of rents and leases provides that if the buyer has leased all or any portion of the property to a third party, any rents received by the buyer are pledged to the seller as additional collateral for the debt. If the buyer is in default and the seller has obtained an assignment of rents and leases, then the seller may require the tenant under the lease to make rent payments directly to the seller and not to the buyer. The seller could then apply the rent proceeds to any indebtedness of the buyer that is currently outstanding and due. The following provision, which may be included in the contract as well as the note and deed to secure debt, requires the buyer to assign to the seller any rental income generated on the property being sold.

> **Special Stipulation 126:   Buyer's Assignment of all Rents to Seller/Holder**
>
> *Buyer and Seller hereby agree and acknowledge that the promissory note and deed to secure debt executed by Buyer in connection with this Agreement shall contain the following provision: Borrower (Buyer) hereby assigns to Lender (Seller) all of the rents of Property. Seller shall forebear from collecting such rents so long as Borrower is not in default in payments to Lender (Seller). All rents collected by Lender shall be applied first to the costs of management of the Property and then to sums secured by the promissory note and deed to secure debt.*

§ 7.8.5 Alterations To Property

Some form deeds to secure debt expressly prohibit the buyer from making any alterations to the property. Since it is not uncommon for a buyer to make improvements, the contract should expressly provide that the deed to secure debt shall permit the buyer to make alterations to the property without constituting default. Failure to include such a provision may result in unusual and unjust results. For example, in one case, a buyer executed a deed to secure debt that obligated the buyer to obtain permission from the seller prior to buyer making any improvements or alterations to the property. The buyer undertook a small amount of demolition and made improvements to the property without obtaining prior consent of the seller. The court held buyer to be in default under her deed to secure debt even though buyer was able to show that she had spent $50,000 in making such improvements.[1184] Set forth below is a contract provision that entitles the buyer to make repairs and improvements to property without triggering a default under the deed to secure debt.

> **Special Stipulation 127:   Buyer's Right to Renovate Without Seller Approval**
>
> *Buyer and Seller hereby expressly agree that the deed to secure debt to be executed by Buyer in favor of Seller in connection with this transaction shall include the following provision: Buyer shall not be required to obtain permission from Seller prior to undertaking any improvements, repairs, or demolition on the Property which serves as security for this Promissory Note so long as such improvements, repairs, or demolition do not reduce the value of the Property. Any such improvements, repairs, or demolition undertaken by Buyer shall not constitute a default under the terms of the Deed to Secure Debt.*

§ 7.8.6   Costs Associated With Preparing And Recording Documents

The GAR Seller Financing (First Mortgage) and Seller Financing (Second Mortgage) Exhibits require that the buyer pay any charge for preparation of the note and deed to secure debt as long as the buyer's attorney prepares them.[1185] These GAR exhibits also provide that if the seller chooses to have these documents prepared by seller's attorney (and the seller reserves the option to do so), then the seller shall bear the expense of such document preparation. There may be instances where the buyer and seller's interests diverge as to the language to be incorporated in the note and deed to secure debt. Since the seller has the greater risk because her money is at stake, the seller may therefore want her attorney to prepare the note and deed to secure debt in a way that favors him. If the parties agree, the buyer may pay the seller's expenses for having the note and deed to secure debt prepared. A special stipulation allowing the buyer to reimburse the seller for her expenses follows.

> **Special Stipulation 128:   Buyer Pays for Seller's Attorney to Prepare Promissory Note and Deed to Secure Debt**
>
> *Seller's attorney shall prepare the promissory note and deed to secure debt and Buyer shall reimburse Seller for the costs and expenses of such preparation.*

Under Georgia law, the holder of a long-term promissory note[1186] secured by real property is obligated to pay the intangible tax and any fee charged for recording the deed to secure debt.[1187] The GAR Seller Financing (First Mortgage) and Seller Financing (Second Mortgage) Exhibits both obligate the buyer to pay the intangible tax.[1188] If the GAR forms are not used and if the real estate contract is silent as to which party shall be responsible for the payment of taxes and recording fees, the seller, as holder of the note, will be obligated to pay these costs.

1184   *Tybrisa Co. v. Tybeeland, Inc.*, 220 Ga. 442, 139 S.E.2d 302 (1964). (The court noted that there was conflicting testimony as to whether the property altered, changed, or removed was an "improvement" or a "detriment" and that there was no question of failure of title.)

1185   GAR Forms F67 and F68.

1186   A long-term promissory note is defined as any note representing credits secured by mortgages, deeds to secure debt, purchase money deeds to secure debt, bonds of title, or other form of security instrument, when any part of the principal of a note falls due more than three years from the date of the note or from the date of any instrument executed to secure the note and conveying or creating a lien or encumbrance on the real estate. O.C.G.A. § 48-6-60(3).

1187   O.C.G.A. § 48-6-61.

1188   GAR Forms F67 and F68.

§ 7.8.7 Note And Deed To Secure Debt Made In Favor Of More Than One Seller

Problems and confusion may arise when a buyer executes a note and purchase money deed to secure debt in favor of more than one seller. Unless the contract provides otherwise a deed to secure debt must be canceled by all the sellers who are payees under the note and deed to secure debt. Various issues may arise when there is more than one seller to whom the buyer should make payments. For instance, what happens if all the sellers are unavailable to execute a cancellation of the note and deed to secure debt upon satisfaction of the same by the buyer? A contract provision that addresses some of the potential problems when there are multiple sellers is set forth below.

> **Special Stipulation 129: Note and Deed to Secure Debt Authorizes Named Payee to Accept Payment on Behalf of all Payees**
>
> *Buyer and Sellers hereby agree that the promissory note and deed to secure debt shall provide that any one of the named payees may accept payment on behalf of all payees. Buyer and Seller further agree that the promissory note and deed to secure debt shall provide that upon payment of the indebtedness under the note in full, any one of the named payees may execute a valid cancellation of the deed to secure debt on behalf of all named payees and such cancellation shall be binding and enforceable against all payees and serve as conclusive proof of payment in full of the debt by Buyer.*

§ 7.8.8 Additional Issues If Seller Takes Second Priority Security Interest

A seller who takes a second (or later) priority note and deed is not afforded the same degree of protection as the lender who holds the first priority interest. If the buyer defaults under the first priority deed to secure debt that lender would be able to foreclose on the property and extinguish the seller's second priority deed to secure debt.

If the buyer does not default on the first mortgage but defaults on the seller's second mortgage, the seller may be able to foreclose on the property serving as collateral for the loan. However, the seller will be responsible for making payments to the first priority holder. It is therefore important for a seller to consider the following issues when granting a second or other subordinate security interest.

§ 7.8.8.1 Default Under First Priority Deed To Secure Debt

The GAR Seller Financing (Second Mortgage) Exhibit includes a cross-default clause.[1189] This means that a default under the terms and conditions of the first position deed to secure debt or note constitutes a default under the terms and conditions of the second position deed to secure debt and note, and the seller may declare the entire indebtedness secured by the note due and payable at once (*i.e.*, the seller may accelerate the debt). Upon default of the buyer on the first mortgage, this provision allows the seller to foreclose on her deed to secure debt and thereby protect her interest by foreclosing and paying the first mortgage.

The holder of a first priority deed to secure debt is not required, however, to give junior lien holders notice of default. A seller who holds a second or other subordinate deed to secure debt may protect her interest by obligating the holder of a superior deed to secure debt to notify her of the default under the first priority deed. To legally obligate the first priority holder to provide the requisite notice, there must be an agreement between the first priority holder and the buyer. An example of a contract provision that affords the seller holding a second or other subordinate deed such added protection is set forth below.

1189   GAR Form F68.

Special Stipulation 130:   Contract Contingent on First Mortgage Holder Agreeing to Notify Seller of Buyer's Default

Buyer and Seller agree that this Agreement is contingent on the holder of the first priority promissory note and deed to secure debt incorporating a provision in its promissory note and deed to secure debt which legally obligates the first priority holder to provide written notice to Seller in the event of a default by Buyer under the first priority deed to secure debt. If the holder of the first position promissory note does not include such a provision in the first priority promissory note and deed to secure debt, Seller may terminate this Agreement upon written notice to Buyer.

The seller should also be aware that many priority security deeds include what is known as a cross-default provision, such that a default under the terms of seller's secondary security deed constitutes a default under the terms of the first deed. Under such a cross-default provision, the holder of a first priority mortgage could declare a default in the event the buyer defaults on the second mortgage. Once the holder of the first mortgage is notified that the buyer has defaulted on a second mortgage, the holder could initiate its own foreclosure proceeding that would extinguish the seller's second priority security deed.

§ 7.8.8.2   Payment To Reinstate First Priority Loan

The holder of the second priority security interest may want to include a provision in the contract that stipulates that any payments made by seller to cure a default under the first priority loan will be added to the debt secured under the second priority loan. An example of such provision follows.

Special Stipulation 131:   Seller May Cure Buyer's Default of First Priority Mortgage

Buyer and Seller hereby agree that the following provision will be included in the promissory note and deed to secure debt to be executed by Buyer in favor of Seller: Seller shall be entitled, at her sole discretion, to cure any default under Buyer's first priority Promissory Note and Deed to Secure Debt; however, Seller shall have no obligation whatsoever to do so. Any amounts expended by Seller to reinstate such first priority Promissory Note and Deed to Secure Debt shall be added to and become additional amounts due under the indebtedness secured by the second priority deed to secure debt held by Seller.

§ 7.8.8.3   Excess Proceeds To Second Priority Deed Holder

The seller who accepts the second priority note and deed to secure debt may want to provide that any excess proceeds paid under an insurance claim, condemnation award, or by virtue of foreclosure of the first priority deed to secure debt, go directly to the seller as the holder of the second priority deed. An example of such provision follows.

Special Stipulation 132:   Seller Entitled to Excess Proceeds from First Priority Mortgage Foreclosure/Condemnation/ Statement of Insurance Claim

Buyer and Seller agree that any promissory note and second priority deed to secure debt to be executed by the Buyer shall contain the following provision: In the event there are any excess proceeds remaining pursuant to a foreclosure of Buyer's first priority holder's Promissory Note and Deed to Secure Debt, condemnation award, or settlement of an insurance claim, then after the first priority holder has received payment in full of its debt, Seller, as the second priority holder, shall be entitled to the balance thereof prior to any distribution to Buyer.

§ 7.8.9 Wrap Mortgage

To further protect the seller who accepts the second priority note and deed to secure debt, the seller may consider a wrap mortgage. Under a wrap mortgage, the seller's first priority mortgage obligation remains in place. The seller accepts a note from the buyer in the amount of the combined balance owed to the seller's lender under the first priority note and deed to secure debt plus any additional amounts being loaned by the seller to the buyer. Under this arrangement, the buyer pays the seller, who in turn makes her regular payments to the holder of the first priority loan. This permits the buyer to purchase property when the buyer may not be able to obtain her own loan and the seller does not have sufficient cash to pay off the first mortgage.

Whether such an option is feasible depends on whether the seller's current loan contains a due on sale clause. If the seller's loan contains a due on sale clause, a wrap mortgage would be in violation of the terms of the seller's existing financing. However, if the seller's present loan does not have a due on sale clause (*i.e.*, the seller's present loan is assumable), or if the seller's lender so permits, a wrap mortgage may be possible. The buyer would be well advised to require that the seller produce written confirmation from her first mortgage holder that the wrap mortgage will not trigger a due on sale clause. The buyer may use the following stipulation.

> **Special Stipulation 133:   Buyer's Right to Terminate Contract if Seller Cannot Obtain Seller's Lender's Confirmation That Wrap Mortgage Will Not Trigger Due on Sale Clause or Constitute Default**
>
> *This Agreement is contingent upon Seller providing to Buyer written confirmation from Seller's first mortgage holder that a wrap mortgage will not trigger a due on sale clause or otherwise constitute a default under the terms of Seller's first mortgage. If Seller does not provide such confirmation to Buyer within thirty (30) days of the Binding Agreement Date, Buyer may terminate this Agreement upon written notice to Seller and Buyer's earnest money shall be immediately returned to Buyer.*

Although the seller is provided additional protection under a wrap note, the buyer has some risks if the seller collects the money from the buyer but fails to remit the amount due on the first mortgage. The GAR Seller Financing (Wrap Around Mortgage) exhibit outlines both the seller and buyer's obligations.[1190] The seller's obligations include the obligation to make payments of principal, interest, and escrow deposits to the present lender during the life of the wrap loan as long as (1) the buyer is not in default under the terms of the wrap loan and (2) no other default exists under the seller's present loan other than with respect to payments of principal, interest and escrow deposits. To provide additional protection to the buyer, the buyer may want to incorporate a provision in the contract and note that requires the holder of the seller's present loan to notify the buyer if there is a default on that loan.

> **Special Stipulation 134:   Seller's Right to Terminate if Unable to Obtain Notice of Default of Buyer's Loan**
>
> *Buyer and Seller agree that Seller shall obtain an agreement from the holder of Seller's present loan that Buyer shall be notified in the event of any default under said loan. If Seller does not provide a copy of this agreement to Buyer within thirty (30) days of the Binding Agreement Date, Buyer may terminate this Agreement upon written notice to Seller and Buyer's earnest money shall be immediately returned to Buyer.*

§ 7.9   THIRD PARTY ASSISTING WITH FINANCING

On occasion, a third party will help a buyer acquire property by helping the buyer with the cash, guaranteeing the mortgage loan, or by applying for the mortgage loan along with the buyer. Such third parties are usually a parent, relative

---

1190   GAR Form F70.

or significant other of the buyer. In many cases, the third party will sign the purchase contract and be a co-owner of the property. In others, the third party will merely lend her good name, and hopefully credit, to the mortgage application or help the buyer with the needed cash to close the transaction. These are times when a buyer will not want to warrant that the buyer has sufficient cash to close the transaction without getting a commitment from a third party that they will provide some portion of the necessary cash to close. The following special stipulation can help the buyer in this situation.

> **Special Stipulation 135:   Contract Contingent Upon Third Party Contributing Funds to Close**
>
> *This Agreement is contingent upon Buyer receiving from _____ the sum of $_____ within ____ days of the Binding Agreement Date which monies shall give Buyer the necessary funds to close (along with the proceeds of the mortgage loan for which Buyer has applied). If Buyer does not provide written evidence that these funds have been deposited into the following account of Buyer: Account #_____ with (name of financial institution], within___ days from the Binding Agreement Date, then this Agreement may thereafter be terminated by Seller.*

It is important that any loaned or gifted funds be reported by the buyer to her lender. Many lenders have limitations on the amount of gifted funds that the buyer can receive for the closing. If the third party is agreeing to guarantee a mortgage loan to be obtained by the buyer, the following special stipulation may be of benefit to the seller.

> **Special Stipulation 136:   Ability of Buyer to Obtain a Loan Based on Credit of Buyer and Third Party**
>
> *For all purposes hereunder, the Buyer's ability to obtain the mortgage loan described herein shall be based upon the financial ability of both the Buyer and (name) as co-borrowers to qualify for said loan.*

§ 7.10 ASSUMING OR TAKING SUBJECT TO EXISTING LOAN

Assuming an existing loan can be advantageous to the buyer because there are little or no closing costs and very few loan documents to execute. In some instances, a buyer may find this method of financing to be attractive because she may be able to assume a loan with a lower interest rate than the current prevailing rate. Although there remain some non-qualifying assumable loans, most lenders now require a new party assuming a loan to independently qualify for that loan. Some lenders also retain the right to adjust the interest rate upon assumption.

There is some distinction between taking subject to an outstanding loan and assuming an outstanding loan. A buyer is not generally personally liable for indebtedness under the deed to secure debt if the contract specifies that the property be sold "subject to" an existing deed to secure debt.[1191] This means that the lender may foreclose on the property if the buyer defaults but will not be able to obtain a personal judgment against the buyer. When a buyer takes the property "subject to" a loan without expressly agreeing to pay the seller's debt to the lender, the buyer pays the remaining loan payments as they come due, but the seller continues to be personally liable to the lender for the repayment of the loan in accordance with the terms of the original promissory note.

Most contracts provide that the buyer "assumes" the loan rather than takes "subject to" the loan. A buyer who assumes a loan will be personally liable for the payment of the mortgage debt.[1192] If there is a default and the amount realized on the sale of the property at the foreclosure sale does not equal the amount of the debt due under the loan, the lender will normally attempt to obtain a deficiency judgment against any party who is personally liable under the note. If there is no

---

1191   *Alsobrook v. Taylor*, 181 Ga. 10, 181 S.E. 182 (1935).

1192   *Smith v. Kingsley*, 178 Ga. 681, 173 S.E. 702 (1934).

express release of liability for the seller, the seller as the original party to the note and deed to secure debt will continue to be personally liable to the lender as well.[1193]

Buyers and sellers should also be mindful that the lender is generally not required to foreclose prior to attempting to obtain a money judgment. In some cases, such as where the value of the real estate has decreased substantially or the property is found to contain hazardous material, the lender will simply ignore the security deed and sue for monetary damages against the buyer under the terms of the promissory note. This may be a preferred option for a seller who has taken back a second mortgage on property in which there is very little or no equity. If the purchaser wishes to force the seller to foreclose prior to obtaining a monetary judgment she should use language such as the following in the contract.

> **Special Stipulation 137:   Holder of First Security Deed Must Proceed Against Property Before Pursuing Monetary Judgment Against Buyer**
>
> *Buyer and Seller agree that any promissory note and deed to secure debt to be executed by the Buyer shall contain the following provision: In the event of any default by the maker hereof, the holder must, prior to bringing any legal action against the maker for monetary damages, foreclose on the Property described herein by judicial, or if permitted by the terms hereof, non-judicial foreclosure, and obtain judicial confirmation of such foreclosure.*

§ 7.10.1   Identifying The Loan

The GAR Loan Assumption Exhibit[1194] and the GAR Loan Assumption (Cash to Control The Purchase Price) Exhibit[1195] provide that the parties identify the loan by the loan number, servicer, original date, original principal amount, term of the loan and monthly installments. If the GAR exhibits are used and fully completed, the loan will be adequately described. Failure to adequately describe the loan with specificity may render the contract unenforceable. The following cases address the enforceability of the contract based on specificity of the loan description.

In one case, the court held the contract to be enforceable even though it failed to state the date of maturity and the outstanding balance of the loan to be assumed.[1196] The contract in that case described the loan as being the "loan of $900 now outstanding against" the property purchased, "which loan bears eight per cent. interest, which matures in about eighteen months…." The court concluded that the contract offered a method for identifying the loan with definite terms contained therein through examination of the real estate records. In two other cases the court concluded that a loan description was inadequate and the contract was therefore unenforceable.[1197] In one such case the court held that a contract, which provided for the buyer to assume a loan of $9,500, was unenforceable because it failed to completely identify the specific loan to be assumed.[1198] In another case a contract recited that the purchase price was to be paid subject to terms of an existing loan "which is approximately $30,000" was held to be too indefinite to identify the loan referenced.[1199]

These cases indicate that if the loan description provides some sort of "key" for identifying the loan, the contract may be enforceable. Reference to the recorded loan and deed documents will generally be adequate since the recorded documents contain additional information to supplement the loan description in the contract. To avoid any question about the enforceability of a contract based on a loan description the parties should at a minimum include all the information set

---

1193   *Federal Land Bank of Columbia v. Conger*, 55 Ga.App. 11, 189 S.E. 567 (1936).

1194   GAR Form F61, Loan Assumption Exhibit.

1195   GAR Form F62, Loan Assumption (Cash to Control Purchase Price) Exhibit.

1196   *Massell Realty Co. v. Hanbury*, 165 Ga. 534, 141 S.E. 653 (1927).

1197   However, in both of the following cases, the loans were not against the property. Since there were no documents of public record, the terms of the loan could not be determined with reasonable specificity.

1198   *Trust Co. of Georgia v. Neal*, 161 Ga. 965, 132 S.E.2d 385 (1926).

1199   *Morgan v. Hemphill*, 214 Ga. 555, 105 S.E.2d 580 (1958).

forth in the GAR form.[1200] In addition to the information set forth in the GAR form, if the parties have a copy of the note and deed to secure debt being assumed, they should attach those documents to the contract as exhibits.

§ 7.10.2 The Purchase Price And Loan Assumptions

There are potential pitfalls that await an unwary draftsman when setting forth the purchase price of the property under a contract that provides for the property to be taken subject to an existing loan or under a loan assumption. Identification of the purchase price under such a contract is complicated by the fact that the balance of the loan to be assumed or taken subject to is constantly changing as payments are made by the seller. Consequently, the loan balance will generally change between the time the contract is entered into and the time the property is conveyed to the buyer on the date of closing.

If the purchase price is not properly expressed, there is a risk that the contract will be deemed void for uncertainty. In one case, a Georgia court held that a contract was not enforceable because it referred to the purchase price as $57,000 net with buyer paying $18,500 in cash and agreeing to assume a loan with the balance of approximately $39,000.[1201] The court determined the contract was unenforceable because it was too vague because the loan which was to be assumed actually had a balance of more than the $39,000 referenced in the contract. The court stated that the purchase price could not be increased without simultaneously decreasing the down payment, which would essentially require the court to write an entirely new contract.

As explained below, there are two commonly used methods to determine the purchase price when the buyer assumes the seller's loan.

§ 7.10.2.1 Purchase Price Set In Contract

The GAR Loan Assumption exhibit[1202] contemplates that the purchase price will be set forth in the contract and that the buyer will assume the seller's loan. This exhibit also provides that the balance of the purchase price in excess of the principal balance assumed at closing by the buyer, less the amount of interest accrued on the loan to the date of closing, will be paid by the buyer to the seller in cash at closing.[1203] This approach has the advantage of establishing the exact purchase price at the time the contract is entered into. The disadvantage to the buyer is the uncertainty as to the amount of cash that the buyer will have to provide at closing.

For example, buyer and seller enter into a contract in which the purchase price is $48,000 with the buyer to assume an existing loan on the property and pay the balance of the purchase price to the seller in cash at closing. The loan to be assumed has a balance of $35,250 on January 15, the Binding Agreement Date. The sale of the property occurs on March 15. If the closing was to have occurred at the same time the contract was entered into, the buyer would have had to bring $12,750 in cash ($48,000 - $35,250). However, if the balance of the loan is reduced by the February and March monthly payments made by the seller, then the buyer will have to bring more cash to closing to compensate seller for any reduction in the principal balance of the loan.

Under this example, if the balance of the loan as of the date of closing is $34,195, the buyer would have to bring a cash payment of $13,805 ($48,000 - $34,195), as opposed to the $12,750 she may have thought would be required when she executed the contract.

1200   GAR Form F61, Loan Assumption Exhibit.

1201   *Austin v. Willis*, 229 Ga. 193, 190 S.E.2d 532 (1972).

1202   GAR Form F61, Loan Assumption Exhibit.

1203   GAR Form F61, Loan Assumption Exhibit.

§ 7.10.2.2   Cash To Control Price

The alternative GAR Loan Assumption (Cash to Control Purchase Price) Exhibit[1204] contemplates that the buyer will pay an identified amount of cash at closing plus the seller's outstanding principal loan balance as of the date of closing.[1205] The total of these two amounts shall be the purchase price. Although the exact purchase price is not identified in the contract, the contract is enforceable because, like a contract which establishes purchase price based on cost per acre, this contract will establish purchase price based on a specified amount of cash plus the outstanding principal of the loan at closing (*i.e.*, the agreement provides a method for calculating the purchase price). Under this approach, the purchase price may actually decrease between the date the contract is entered into and the date of closing.

Assume that buyer and seller enter into a contract which provides that the buyer will pay $10,000 in cash to seller and assume the seller's loan balance as of the date of closing. If the loan balance were $35,250 on January 15, the Binding Agreement Date, then the total purchase price of the property would be $45,250 ($35,250 + $10,000). If by March 15, after the seller has made two more payments, the loan balance is $34,195, then the total purchase price of the property will be $44,195 ($34,195 + $10,000). Regardless of whether the loan balance changes between the time the contract is entered into and the date of closing, the buyer's cash at closing remains the same ($10,000).

§ 7.10.3   Special Issues Regarding Loan Assumptions

Many of the issues with regard to loan assumptions are the same as issues in any other type of financing. These provisions include, but are not limited to, due on sale clauses, prepayment penalties, and restrictions in the use of property. In addition, there are several special issues with regard to loan assumptions.

§ 7.10.3.1   Release Of Seller Liability On Loan

It is in the seller's best interest to obtain a release of liability from the lender by substituting the buyer's liability for that of the seller. When the original borrower, the seller in this case, is relieved of her personal obligation under the note and deed to secure debt, there has been what is commonly called a "novation" of the seller's liability, and the lender can look only to the buyer to repay the loan. Because the novation operates to absolve the seller from liability for the debt, the lender will generally require that the buyer qualify for the loan. In such instances, the seller will not be able to obtain a release of liability if the loan is a non-qualifying assumable loan. If the seller wants to make the contract contingent on the seller obtaining a release of liability the following special stipulation may be incorporated in the agreement.

> **Special Stipulation 138:   Agreement Contingent Upon Seller Being Released from Loan Liability**
>
> *This Agreement is contingent upon Seller obtaining a release of liability from the holder of the above-referenced promissory note and deed to secure debt. Buyer agrees to take any and all steps necessary to qualify for the loan herein. If Seller is unable to obtain the aforementioned release of liability, then Seller may, upon written notice to Buyer, terminate this Agreement, in which case all earnest money shall be immediately returned to Buyer.*

§ 7.10.3.2   Protection Of Seller Where There Is No Release of Liability

If the seller is unable to obtain a release of liability from the holder of the loan but elects to go forward with the sale, she may want to enter into an agreement with the buyer giving her a security interest in the property. For example, buyer and seller could execute a note and deed to secure debt for $500 which would be payable at a specified date in the future.

1204   GAR Form F62, Loan Assumption Cash to Control Purchase Price Exhibit.

1205   The seller's outstanding principal loan balance will be the last loan balance after the last payment from the seller plus any accrued interest up to the date of closing.

The note and deed to secure debt would also provide that a default on the loan assumed by the buyer would constitute default under the buyer's note and deed to secure debt and authorize the seller to foreclose on the property to protect her interest. In conjunction with this agreement the real estate sales contract could also be contingent on the holder of the loan being assumed agreeing to provide the seller with notice of any default by buyer. In the alternative, the agreement between the buyer and seller could provide that if payments to the holder of the loan being assumed remain current for a specified period of time, the seller's note and deed to secure debt would be canceled. Presumably, after the buyer has an adequate amount of equity in the property, the likelihood of a deficiency in the event of foreclosure would be reduced or eliminated. In either example described above the buyer would not have the right to pre-pay and satisfy the seller's note or deed to secure debt. An example of contract language using these means to protect the seller follows.

> **Special Stipulation 139: Cross-Default Provision in Secondary Seller Financing**
>
> *In addition to assuming the loan as provided for in this Agreement, Buyer and Seller agree that Buyer shall execute a promissory note and deed to secure debt in favor of Seller in the amount of $_____ which shall be payable in full on (date). (Buyer shall not have an option to pre-pay such amount to Seller unless such pre-payment is concurrent with Buyer's satisfaction and full repayment of the loan identified in this Agreement to be assumed by Buyer); provided, however, if there has been no default by Buyer under the terms of the loan identified in this Agreement to be assumed by Buyer on or before such date, Seller shall cancel her promissory note and deed to secure debt and Buyer shall not be obligated to pay Seller $_____. Seller's promissory note and deed to secure debt shall contain a cross-default provision and acceleration provision substantially in the form attached hereto as Exhibit "A."* [1206] *Buyer and Seller further agree that Buyer shall obtain from Lender an agreement that Lender shall notify Seller of any default under the loan identified in this Agreement to be assumed by Buyer. If Buyer is unable to obtain an agreement from Lender regarding the notice requirement set forth herein, Seller may terminate this Agreement upon written notice to Buyer, in which case all earnest money shall be immediately returned to Buyer.*

§ 7.10.3.3 Increase In Interest Rate On Loan Assumption

The note to be assumed may include a provision that entitles the holder to increase the interest rate when the property is sold without the loan being paid off. Both the GAR Loan Assumption Exhibit[1207] and the Loan Assumption Cash To Control Exhibit[1208] provide that if the loan is a qualifying loan, it will be contingent on the "ability to obtain" approval with an interest rate not to exceed a specified amount which is to be identified by the parties. If the underlying loan agreement authorizes the lender to increase the interest rate, it is in the seller's interest to set forth an interest rate as high as the lender may increase its rate. If the buyer has particular concerns about the total cost of the loan to her it may be in her interest to limit the increase in the interest rate to an amount acceptable to the buyer.

§ 7.10.3.4 Dragnet Or Open End Clauses

The deed to secure debt may contain what is called an open end or dragnet clause. Such a clause typically states that the deed to secure debt secures not only the debt referred to in the original note, but also secures any and all other present and future debts or liabilities of the original borrower to the lender.

1206   GAR Form F68, Seller Financing (Second Mortgage), contains cross default clause.

1207   GAR Form F61, Loan Assumption Exhibit.

1208   GAR Form F62, Loan Assumption (Cash to Control Purchase Price) Exhibit.

A case in Georgia serves to highlight how such an open end or dragnet clause can have particularly severe consequences for a buyer. In this case, a buyer purchased property subject to a loan in the amount of $1,000.[1209] The deed securing the loan contained a clause which stated that it was made to secure the debt of $1,000 and any other present or future indebtedness or liability of such borrower to the holder. The buyer subsequently decided to pay off the loan and submitted to the lender a check in the amount of $1,000 plus interest. The lender refused to accept the payment based on the fact that there was an additional $5,032.05 that was still outstanding on the open account that the original borrower owed at the time of the loan.

The court found in favor of the lender on the basis that the deed to secure debt secured not only the face amount of the loan which the buyer agreed to assume, but also any other present or future indebtedness or liability of the original borrower to the lender. If a dragnet clause is contained in a deed to secure debt of a loan being assumed by a buyer, the buyer may be able to reduce her risk by using the following special stipulation in the contract.

> **Special Stipulation 140:   Seller's Warranty that Loan Assumed by Buyer is Seller's Entire Debt to Lender**
>
> *Seller hereby warrants that as of the Binding Agreement Date, Seller's only outstanding indebtedness or liability to the holder of the debt identified in this Agreement to be assumed by Buyer equals $_____. Seller further agrees and warrants that on or after the Binding Agreement Date and continuing as long as the loan identified in this Agreement to be assumed by Buyer remains outstanding, Seller will not increase the balance of said loan by virtue of requesting or accepting any future advance, renewal, or extension of the aforementioned loan. Buyer and Seller agree that Seller shall obtain an executed agreement between Seller and Lender providing that Seller will not increase the balance of said loan and that Lender will not authorize any increase in the balance of said loan. If it is determined that as of the Binding Agreement Date, Seller's outstanding indebtedness or liability to the holder of Seller's promissory note and deed to secure debt exceeds the amount specified above or if Seller fails to obtain an agreement from Lender as described herein, Buyer may terminate this Agreement upon written notice to Seller, in which case all earnest money shall be immediately returned to Buyer.*

The buyer should have the seller's promissory note and security deed carefully reviewed to determine whether a dragnet clause is contained in these documents.

In another case, the court held that a future advance made to the original borrower after the property was sold to the buyer was still secured by the original deed to secure debt assumed by the buyer.[1210] If a future advance clause is contained in a deed to secure debt of a loan being assumed by the buyer, the buyer may be able to reduce the potential risk inherent in such a clause by including the following provision in the contract.

> **Special Stipulation 141:   Seller Agrees Not to Increase Loan Amount After Loan is Assumed by Buyer**
>
> *Seller hereby agrees that on or after the date of closing and continuing as long as the loan identified in this Agreement to be assumed by Buyer remains outstanding, Seller will not increase the balance of said loan by virtue of requesting or accepting any future advance, renewal, or extension of the aforementioned loan. Buyer and Seller agree that Seller shall obtain an executed agreement between Seller and Lender providing that Seller will not increase the balance of said loan and that Lender will not authorize any increase in the*

1209   , 210 Ga. 184, 78 S.E.2d 417 (1953).

1210   , 146 Ga. 741, 92 S.E. 214 (1917).

balance of said loan to Seller. If Seller fails to obtain such an agreement from Lender,
Buyer may terminate this Agreement upon written notice to Seller, in which case all
earnest money shall be immediately returned to Buyer.

§ 7.10.4 Costs Associated With Loan Assumption

In most cases, the holder of the seller's loan will require the payment of a loan transfer fee when a contract stipulates that the purchase price will be paid in part by the buyer assuming or taking subject to the seller's existing loan. It is also necessary to determine how reserves such as taxes and insurance that have previously been paid into an escrow account are to be treated. The GAR Loan Assumption and Loan Assumption (Cash to Control The Purchase Price) exhibits provide that the buyer will reimburse the seller in cash for any escrow deposit being assumed by the buyer that the seller has made to the holder and that seller will transfer the escrow deposit to the buyer. The buyer is generally responsible for purchasing the funds in the escrow account because she receives the benefit when future payments are made out of the account for taxes or insurance, which represent amounts owed during the period that the buyer owns the property.

If the buyer is concerned about the amount of up-front cash she will need at closing, the buyer may want to request that the seller transfer the escrow accounts to the buyer in lieu of prorating the taxes and insurance. Set forth below is an example of such a provision.

> **Special Stipulation 142: Seller's Obligation to Transfer Lender's Escrow Account to Buyer at Closing**
>
> *Notwithstanding any other provision to the contrary contained in this Agreement, Seller shall transfer the escrow account held by Seller's Lender to Buyer at closing at no additional cost to Buyer. This transfer shall occur in lieu of proration of taxes, hazard insurance, and private mortgage insurance, if applicable. In the event there is an escrow account deficit, the Seller shall be responsible for the payment of the deficit at closing. Any future escrow accrual shortage shall be the responsibility of Buyer. In the event there is an escrow account overage, Seller shall be entitled to the overage.*

§ 7.11 TAX-DEFERRED EXCHANGES

The Internal Revenue Service recognizes and sanctions the exchange of real property for other real property instead of cash. Specifically, Internal Revenue Code Section 1031, commonly referred to as the like-kind or tax-deferred exchange provision, provides as follows:

> No gain or loss shall be recognized on the exchange of property held for productive use in a trade or business or for investment purposes if such property is exchanged solely for property of like-kind which is to be held either for productive use in a trade or business or for investment.[1211]

An individual can use a tax-deferred exchange when the property being sold or purchased is investment or income-producing property such as rental property. The reason for using a tax-deferred exchange in such a situation is that federal and state laws will tax gains realized on the sale of income-producing or investment property differently from the gain realized on the sale of a personal residence.

The sale of real property is taxed as a capital gain. The amount of gain is calculated by taking the difference between the seller's "basis" in the property (usually what the seller paid for the property plus any capital improvements made during ownership) in the property and the amount the seller recognized on the sale of that property after deducting

---

1211 I.R.C. § 1031.

the sales expenses. In certain circumstances an individual may be exempt from the payment of capital gains taxes realized on the sale of her personal residence. An individual will generally not have to pay taxes on up to $250,000 of capital gain (or up to $500,000 of capital gain for a married couple) received from the sale of a personal residence as long as she has lived in the property for at least two of the last five years before the sale.[1212]

If an individual sells investment property, however, any profit or gain realized from that sale is usually subject to being taxed. By using a tax-deferred exchange, an individual can postpone or defer indefinitely the recognition of any gain realized on the sale of such investment or income-producing property.

There are many issues to be considered in structuring a tax-deferred exchange. While a number of the basic issues are discussed below, a fully detailed analysis of the tax issues involved in such an exchange is beyond the scope of this book.

§ 7.11.1   Sale Of Property Versus Exchange Of Property

A *sale* occurs when real property is exchanged for the payment of cash. As discussed above, if the property being sold is not the personal residence of the seller, the seller may have to pay taxes on any profit (cash) realized on the sale. A *tax-deferred exchange* occurs when one parcel of real property is traded for another parcel of real property. A properly conducted exchange may therefore be treated as a non-taxable event. Anyone considering a tax-deferred exchange should consult a CPA or tax attorney for advice specific to the facts and circumstances of the transaction.

§ 7.11.2   Property Being Acquired Must Be Exchanged For Property Of Like-Kind

To qualify as a tax-deferred exchange, the properties being exchanged must be considered of a "like- kind." What property is considered to be like-kind? A common misconception is that the properties being exchanged must be exactly the same type of property; for example, unimproved property would have to be exchanged for other unimproved property. This is simply not true. Under Internal Revenue Code Section 1031 an apartment building may be exchanged for a shopping center or even unimproved property.[1213] Like-kind does not refer to the type, nature, or character of the property, but instead refers to the owner's intended use of the property. Therefore, if the apartment building was acquired and held for business or investment purposes, it may be exchanged for a shopping center which will be held for the same purposes.

Even though the definition of like-kind is extremely broad, some property is clearly not considered to be like-kind. Some examples of properties which are not considered to be like-kind under the regulations are: (1) stocks, bonds, or notes; (2) interests in a partnership; (3) other property held primarily for sale; and (4) property not located within the United States.[1214]

A tax-deferred exchange must be structured so that an individual has an equal or greater amount of debt and equity in the property being acquired as in that of the property being exchanged. Failure to do so may result in the individual paying taxes on the portion of the property received in the exchange that is not considered to be "like-kind." Property received in an exchange which is not deemed to be like-kind, is commonly referred to as "boot." Therefore, to ensure the most favorable tax treatment, a tax-deferred exchange must be structured to reduce or eliminate "boot." An example of a tax-deferred exchange that eliminates taxable boot altogether is set forth below.

A seller exchanges an apartment building with a sale price of $200,000 for a shopping center that has a sale price of $250,000. There is a loan on the apartment building for $125,000 and a loan on the shopping center for $175,000. The seller has $75,000 of equity in the apartment building. After the exchange the seller will also have $75,000 of equity in the shopping center. In this case, the seller (who is known as the "exchanger") would not realize any taxable

---

1212   I.R.C. § 1034; O.C.G.A. § 48-7-27.

1213   I.R.C. § 1031; 26 U.S.C.A. § 1031.

1214   I.R.C. § 1031 (a)(2) and 1031(h)(1).

boot because not only does she have the same amount of equity in the properties being exchanged, she also has incurred a debt in the acquired property that is equal to or greater than the debt in the exchanged property.

§ 7.11.3   Exchange Of Properties Does Not Have To Occur Simultaneously

Prior to 1979, a tax-deferred exchange required that transfers of both properties being exchanged had to close on the same day. The Internal Revenue Service now recognizes that a "delayed" exchange also can be eligible for a tax deferral.[1215] In order for a delayed exchange to be recognized as valid, the property to be acquired must be identified in writing within 45 days and closed on within 180 days from the date of the existing property being sold. During this 45-day identification period, the exchanger can use several different methods to identify the replacement property to be acquired.[1216]

He can identify up to three properties, regardless of their value, and must then close on at least one of these three properties before the 180 day deadline. Alternatively, she can identify any number of properties so long as their combined value is no greater than 200% of the value of the exchanged property and again must close on at least one of those she has selected. Finally, she can identify an unlimited number of properties with a total value greater than 200% of the value of the exchanged property, but in this scenario she must then close on a combination of them sufficient to equal at least 95% of the total value of the properties she has selected. In any situation where multiple closings are necessary to purchase replacement properties for an exchange, all of the closings must be completed within the 180 day time limit for the exchange transaction.

§ 7.11.4   Use Of Qualified Intermediary In Tax-Deferred Exchanges

A person or company called a "Qualified Intermediary" is used in most tax-deferred exchange transactions. There are a number of local and national companies and accounting firms that regularly serve as qualified intermediaries. In selecting a qualified intermediary to assist with a transaction, it is important to note that there is minimal federal or state regulation of persons and companies acting as intermediaries. It is wise to choose to work with well established, experienced qualified intermediaries who carry sufficient errors and omissions liability insurance and are bonded to protect the exchange funds held in their escrow accounts. Certain individuals may not serve as qualified intermediaries. For example, close family members or individuals such as brokers who are considered agents of the seller are disqualified from functioning as intermediaries. The closing attorney handling the sale or purchase of property that is the subject of the exchange is also prohibited from serving as a qualified intermediary for the transaction.

§ 7.11.4.1   The Tax-Deferred Exchange Process

A tax-deferred exchange usually begins when a contract entered into by a buyer and seller for the purchase of real property is assigned to a qualified intermediary. Internal Revenue Service regulations require that a seller-exchanger give notice to the buyer and to all other parties under the sales contract on or before the date of transfer that the exchanger intends to assign the contract for the purpose of conducting a tax-deferred exchange. The exchanger enters into an Exchange Agreement with a qualified intermediary. Under this Exchange Agreement, the qualified intermediary will hold the proceeds received from the sale of the property until such time as the exchanger can locate suitable replacement property. Typically the property being sold is then conveyed to the buyer directly from the exchanger. In some cases, the exchanger may instead first convey the property to the qualified intermediary, who then transfers the property to the buyer. In both instances, the sales contract must be assigned to the qualified intermediary.

1215   , 602 F.2d 1341 (1979).

1216   I.R.C. § 1031(a)(3).

The exchanger will have 45 days from the date of the sale of the exchanged property to identify suitable replacement property. Once the replacement property has been identified, the exchanger then notifies the qualified intermediary by providing a written list of the properties she has selected. The exchanger then will enter into a contract or contracts to purchase some or all of the replacement property she has identified. The contract(s) will again be assigned to the qualified intermediary who may acquire title and then transfer title to the exchanger, or the exchanger may acquire title directly. As with the initial sale of the exchange property, the sales contract must be assigned to the qualified intermediary and the other respective parties must be notified of the intent to participate in a tax-deferred exchange.

Set forth below are two examples of contract provisions to be included in a sales contract when it is contemplated that a tax-deferred exchange may be utilized by either a buyer or seller or both.

Special Stipulation 143: Buyer Obligated to Cooperate in Seller's Tax-Deferred Exchange

In selling the Property, Seller may elect to utilize an I.R.C. Section 1031 tax deferred exchange where the proceeds from the sale of the Property are used by a qualified intermediary to purchase like-kind property, and the Property may be: (1) conveyed by Seller directly to Buyer, or (2) conveyed by Seller to the qualified intermediary who shall then transfer the Property to Buyer. In such event, Buyer agrees to cooperate with and assist Seller in connection with Seller's like-kind exchange and execute an assignment of this Agreement to the qualified intermediary, provided that Buyer shall not be obligated to incur any additional expense or liability in connection with Seller's exchange of property.

Special Stipulation 144: Seller Obligated to Cooperate in Buyer's Tax-Deferred Exchange

In purchasing the Property, Buyer may elect to utilize an I.R.C. Section 1031 tax deferred exchange by trading Property with a qualified intermediary. In such event, Seller agrees to cooperate with and assist Buyer in connection with Buyer's like-kind exchange and execute an assignment of this Agreement to the qualified intermediary, provided that Seller shall not be obligated to incur any additional expense or liability in connection with Buyer's exchange of property. In the event Buyer so elects to utilize I.R.C. Section 1031 if requested, Seller shall convey the Property to the qualified intermediary designated by Buyer.

It may be possible to eliminate the necessity of having either party consent to an assignment of the contract with respect to a contemplated exchange by including the following contract provision.

Special Stipulation 145: Assignment of Contract Limited to Qualified Intermediary for Tax-Deferred Exchange

This Agreement may not be assigned by either party hereto except in connection with an Assignment to a Qualified Intermediary in accordance with an I.R.C. Section 1031 tax-deferred exchange.

The **RED BOOK**

CHAPTER 8

APPRAISAL
AND OTHER
CONTINGENCIES

OVERVIEW

Many real estate contracts are subject to one or more contingencies which, if not fulfilled, will allow the buyer or seller not to have to perform his or her obligations under the contract. This chapter discusses the more common of these contingencies and distinguishes them from other legal rights.

§ 8.1   CONTINGENCIES IN GENERAL

A contingency is a clause in a contract making the enforceability of the agreement conditional upon the occurrence of some future event which is itself uncertain or questionable.[1217] Contingencies are distinguishable from options[1218] in that options create a unilateral right for a buyer to purchase "if he feels like it" whereas a contingency obligates the party to perform so long as the contingency has been met or waived.[1219]

A contingency that purports to allow a party to purchase or sell at their pleasure will render the contract void for lack of mutuality.[1220] For example, a contract made contingent upon the property being served by sewers at a cost which the buyer "considers to be reasonable" leaves the entire contract subject to the purchaser's whim and is not enforceable.[1221] However, if the contract recites the receipt of consideration for such a discretionary contingency the agreement will not fail. Rather, the consideration transforms the unilateral contingency into an enforceable option contract.[1222]

The presence of a contingency that requires some action by one of the parties carries with it an implied duty of good faith and fair dealing. So, for example, in the case of a financing contingency, there is an implied duty upon the purchaser to diligently seek financing that to comply with reasonable lender requests.[1223]

By their nature, contingencies run to the benefit of one party or the other. The party for whose benefit the contingency exists may waive the contingency, in which event the contract will proceed forward as if the contingency had never existed.[1224] Such a waiver can be express, in writing, or can be effectuated through actions. In one case the seller was obligated to provide a wood destroying organisms report (*i.e.*, a "termite letter") to the buyer prior to closing.[1225] The sellers did not produce the letter but the buyers proceeded to close anyway. The buyer subsequently discovered a termite infestation and filed suit against the seller. The court dismissed the buyer's claims, finding he waived the contingency by proceeding to the closing without the termite letter.[1226]

§ 8.2   APPRAISAL CONTINGENCIES GENERALLY

Appraisal contingencies in residential real estate sales contracts have become common as it becomes less clear whether particular properties will appraise for the purchase price. The simplest appraisal contingency gives the buyer a right to terminate the contract if the property does not appraise for at least the purchase price. Of course, even the simplest contingency in this area must address who will do the appraisal, when it must be done, who will select the appraiser, who will pay for the appraisal, and what obligations the buyer and seller each have if the property does not appraise at the desired value. A sample of this type of contingency is set forth below.

1217   Black's Law Dictionary, 5th Ed.

1218   *See* Chapter 18 (Special Types of Contracts) of this work.

1219   *Krogh v. PARGAR, LLC*, 277 Ga.App. 35, 625 S.E.2d 435 (2005).

1220   *Stone Mountain Properties, Ltd. v. Helmer*, 139 Ga.App. 865, 229 S.E.2d 779 (1976).

1221   *Stone Mountain Properties, Ltd. v. Helmer*, 139 Ga.App. 865, 229 S.E.2d 779 (1976).

1222   *Rowland v. Hunt*, 172 Ga.App. 895, 324 S.E.2d 826 (1984).

1223   *Patel v. Burt Development Co.*, 261 Ga.App. 436, 582 S.E.2d 495 (2003).

1224   *Giallanza Realty, Inc. v. Rosebud Properties, Inc.*, 209 Ga.App. 571, 434 S.E.2d 130 (1993).

1225   *Brock v. Allen*, 186 Ga.App. 769, 368 S.E.2d 536 (2002).

1226   *Brock v. Allen*, 368 S.E.2d 536 (2002).

Special Stipulation 146: Buyer May Terminate Contract if Property Does Not Appraise [Appraiser to be Selected by Buyer's Mortgage Lender]

Buyer and Seller acknowledge that the Property will be appraised one or more times by a licensed Georgia real estate appraiser(s) selected by or at the direction of Buyer's mortgage lender. In the event the opinion of the value of the Property in any of these appraisals is for an amount less than the purchase price of the Property, Buyer shall have the right at Buyer's option to terminate this Agreement without penalty upon notice to Seller. The notice shall include a full copy of the appraisal in which the opinion of value is less than the purchase price of the Property.

A sample of a contingency where the buyer selects the appraisal follows.

Special Stipulation 147: Buyer May Terminate Contract if Property Does Not Appraise [Appraiser to be Selected by Buyer]

Buyer shall have the right at Buyer's sole cost to have one appraisal done of the Property. The appraiser shall: (a) be selected by Buyer, (b) have a certified residential appraisal designation, and (c) be selected from the list of certified residential appraisers listed below:

_____

_____

_____

In the event the opinion of the value of the Property in the appraisal done pursuant to this special stipulation is for an amount less than the purchase price of the Property, Buyer shall have the right at Buyer's option to terminate this Agreement without penalty upon notice to Seller. The notice to Seller shall include a full copy of the appraisal in which the opinion of value is less than the purchase price.

§ 8.2.1 The Approach In The GAR Contract

The GAR Purchase and Sale Agreement does not provide an appraisal contingency for the buyer. However, an appraisal contingency is included in the GAR Conventional Financing Contingency Exhibit.[1227] With this exhibit, the buyer's lender obtains an appraisal of the property. If the appraisal is for less than the purchase price, the buyer has a right within an agreed upon number of days from the Binding Agreement Date to request that the seller reduce the sales price of the property to a price not less than the appraised price. This means that the buyer can ask the seller to agree to any price between the sales price reflected in the purchase and sale agreement and the appraised price. Of course, if the buyer asks for a reduction in the sales price to a price that is below the original sales price but above the appraised price, the buyer will likely have to come up with additional funds to close the transaction since most lenders will only make a loan based upon the appraised value of the property. The seller can then either agree or not agree to the reduction. If the seller does not agree to the reduction, the buyer may or may not terminate the purchase and sale agreement. With the appraisal contingency in the GAR Conventional Financing Contingency, the buyer must get the lender to perform the appraisal and request a reduction in the sales price within an agreed upon number of days from the Binding Agreement Date. If the buyer fails to meet the agreed upon time deadline, the buyer is deemed to have waived his or her right to request a reduction in the sales price. It should be noted that if the seller rejects the request to reduce the purchase price, there is no certain date by which the buyer must then state whether or not she will terminate the contract. If the seller wants to compose such a deadline, the following special stipulation can be used.

1227 GAR Form F64.

Special Stipulation 148:   Buyer Must Promptly Terminate the Contract if Seller Refuses to Reduce the Sales Price of the Property

Notwithstanding any provision to the contrary contained herein, in the event Seller does not agree to the Amendment to Reduce Sales Price, Buyer shall, within the earlier of: 1) _____ days from the date Buyer received notice of the same; or 2) the closing date, notify Seller whether or not Buyer is terminating this Agreement. In the event Buyer does not notify Seller of its decision to terminate this Agreement within this timeframe, Buyer shall have waived Buyer's right to terminate the Agreement for this reason.

The GAR Forms also includes a standalone appraisal contingency exhibit[1228] which follows the same general approach as the above-referenced appraisal contingency.

This exhibit does not give the buyer an automatic right to terminate the contract in the event the property does not appraise for at least the purchase price. Instead, the buyer must first ask for a reduction in the purchase price to an amount not less than the amount listed in the appraisal. In other words, if the sales price of the property is $300,000 and the appraisal price is $290,000, the buyer can ask for a reduction in the sales price to any amount between $290,000 and $300,000. If the buyer does not ask for a reduction within a specified time frame, the buyer loses his or her right to seek a reduction in the sales price and agrees to buy the property for the sales price. The rationale behind giving the buyer flexibility for the amount of the price reduction she may seek is that some buyers may not ask for a reduction in the sales price equal to the amount by which the property did not appraise, and may instead pay the difference out of their own pockets.

When asking for a price reduction, the buyer is required to submit an Amendment to Reduce Sales Price form to the seller along with a full copy of the appraisal in question. If the seller agrees to the reduction in the sales price, the seller signs the amendment and the buyer is then obligated to purchase the property for the appraised price. If the seller does not agree to the price reduction, the buyer then has the right to terminate the contract. The idea behind this approach is that if the buyer was willing to purchase the property at the original sales price, she should also be willing to purchase it at a lower appraised price.

One of the requirements of the appraisal performed pursuant to the GAR Appraisal Contingency Exhibit is that it be an "independent appraisal assignment." This means that in performing the appraisal the appraiser "would be perceived by third parties or the public as acting as a disinterested third party in rendering an unbiased analysis, opinion or conclusion relating to the nature, quality, value or utility of identified real estate."[1229]

§ 8.2.2   Types Of Appraiser Classifications

Anyone who appraises real property for a fee in Georgia must have an appraiser classification unless that person falls under the exceptions to the classification requirements. There are four types of real estate appraiser classifications in Georgia: state registered, state licensed, state certified residential or state certified general. An appraiser is only permitted to appraise what is within the scope of his or her classification. Therefore, before engaging an appraiser, it is important to know how the appraiser is classified and its restricted activity.

Registered appraisers are generally not permitted to appraise real property. Licensed appraisers are permitted to appraise residential property up to a certain value depending on whether it is a complex transaction, and commercial property or land of up to $250,000. Certified residential appraisers are permitted to appraise any residential property, and commercial property or land of up to $250,000 in value. Certified general appraisers are permitted to appraise all kinds of real estate. Detailed information about what type of classification is required for a particular appraisal can be obtained from the Georgia Board of Real Estate Appraisers.

1228   GAR Form F93.

1229   O.C.G.A. § 43-39A-2(13).

§ 8.2.3   Appraisal Arbitration

Some sellers strongly object to a low appraisal and demand a second opinion. While any number of additional appraisals can be performed if the parties so agree, they are unlikely to make everyone happy. An appraisal is an opinion of value. Different appraisers may well have different opinions of the value of the property.

However, obtaining a second appraisal is generally a better option than reviewing the first appraisal for errors. An appraisal review focuses only on whether there are any facts to support the original appraisal, which is less likely to produce an agreement between the parties than is a new, independent appraisal. A new appraisal may completely eliminate the dispute altogether. If a new appraisal is performed, there needs to be come finality in the process absent fraud. Therefore, the parties should make the second appraisal final.

When a dispute over the value of a property appraisal occurs, a buyer is essentially handed a "get out of the transaction for free" card if the contract is subject to an Appraisal Contingency Exhibit, unless the seller agrees to reduce the sales price to the lower appraised price. Oftentimes, parties will add an appraisal arbitration stipulation in the agreement in the event a dispute occurs of the appraised value of the property.

For example, after a low appraisal a property, the parties agree to a second appraisal which comes back substantially higher than the first. In this case, the seller and buyer may simply be trading places with regard to who is now unhappy. Because of this parties will on occasion agree to an appraisal arbitration provision, a sample of which is set forth below.

> **Special Stipulation 149:   Appraisal Arbitration**
>
> *Either the Buyer or Seller can challenge any appraisal performed pursuant to this Agreement ("Challenge") by giving notice of the same to the other party within two business days of the receipt of the appraisal. In the notice, the party filing the challenge shall provide the names, business addresses and business telephone numbers of at least three independent certified residential appraisers who are willing to do a new appraisal of the Property, along with each appraiser's estimate of the costs to perform the appraisal. Within two days of the receipt of the notice, the other party to the Agreement shall select one of the appraisers ("Selected Appraisers") on the list and provide notice of the selection to the party filing the challenge. The party filing the challenge shall immediately contact the Selected Appraiser, cause him or her to promptly commence a new appraisal of the Property, and communicate that the appraisal must certify in his/her appraisal report that: (1) he/she did not receive any Prohibited Information (as that term is defined below) and (2) the appraisal report was independent. All parties agree to cooperate fully with the Selected Appraiser in the performance of the new appraisal of the Property.*
>
> *The Selected Appraiser shall be provided with a copy of the purchase and sale agreement but shall not be provided with the following information ("Prohibited Information"):*
>
> 1. *A copy of the original appraisal; and*
>
> 2. *Any other opinion of the value of the Property.*
>
> *The Selected Appraiser shall certify in the appraisal report that she did not receive any Prohibited Information and, prior to performing the appraisal, did not know either of the parties or any real estate licensee working with either of the parties. The Selected Appraiser shall use his or her best efforts to deliver the new appraisal to all the parties or to the real estate licensees working with the parties at roughly the same time.*

The appraisal of the Selected Appraiser shall be binding upon all parties and shall for all purposes be treated as the appraisal contemplated by this Agreement. Buyer and Seller shall each pay half of the cost of the appraisal performed by the Selected Appraiser; provided, however that in the event the opinion of value of the Property in the appraisal performed by the Selected Appraiser is 95%-105% of the opinion of value set forth in the original appraisal, the entire cost of the appraisal performed by the Selected Appraiser shall be paid by the party initiating the Challenge.

In the event the new appraisal cannot be performed and delivered to all parties prior to the closing date in the Agreement, the closing date shall be automatically extended to the date that is three days subsequent to the new appraisal being delivered to all parties (or to the licensees working with the parties).

§ 8.2.4   Property Rarely Appraises Above Purchase Price

There are times when a buyer purchases a property at well below its true market value only to then find that it appraises at the price being paid by the buyer. This often makes the buyer feel like she did not get the deal on the property for which the buyer had hoped. Many buyers in this situation do not understand that the lower price being paid by the buyer usually establishes, at least for some period of time, the fair market value of the property. Moreover, when an appraisal is performed the appraiser is largely evaluating whether his or her opinion of the value of the property is consistent with the sales price. Appraisers have no need or incentive to value a property above the sales price. Instead, if the value can be supported, most appraisers will simply state that the property is worth the sales price. The appraiser is justified in stating that the contract price is the fair market value of the home.

Sellers may want to include the following special stipulation if there is concern that the receipt of such an appraisal during the Due Diligence Period will cause a buyer to terminate the contract.

> **Special Stipulation 150:   Property Not Likely to Appraise for More Than Purchase Price**
>
> *Buyer acknowledges that property will rarely appraise for more than its purchase price even when its purchase price is perceived by the buyer to be substantially less than its true value. Appraisers are normally evaluating whether the purchase price in the sales contract can be supported by the sale price of other comparable properties.*

§ 8.3   TERMINATION OF AGREEMENT IF PROPERTY DOES NOT APPRAISE FOR PURCHASE PRICE

The GAR Special Stipulations include language that contemplates that the contract can be subject to the property appraising for at least the purchase price. If the property does not appraise for at least the purchase price, the buyer has an option to terminate the contract. This means that a buyer can make the contract contingent on the property appraising for not less than the purchase price to avoid overpaying for the property. An example of such a contingency is set out below.

> **Special Stipulation 151:   Buyer Has Right to Terminate if Property Does Not Appraise for Contract Price**
>
> *This Agreement is contingent upon the Property appraising for an amount equal or greater than the purchase price of the Property. The appraisal shall be performed by a certified Georgia real estate appraiser holding a certified residential or better designation*

> *from the Georgia Real Estate Appraiser's Board selected by _____ and paid for by _____. The appraisal shall be performed on or before the closing date. In the event the appraisal is not performed in a timely manner, this contingency shall be deemed waived.*

An alternative to the above special stipulation is where the appraiser is selected by the buyer's mortgage lender as set forth below.

> **Special Stipulation 152: Buyer has Right to Terminate if Appraisal Performed by Buyer's Mortgage Lender is Less Than the Purchase Price**
>
> *Buyer at Buyer's option may terminate this Agreement without penalty and upon notice to Seller if an appraiser selected by Buyer's mortgage lender as part of the process of the lender deciding whether to make a specific mortgage loan to Buyer determines that the appraised value of the Property is less than the purchase price of the Property.*

Rather than incorporating the above type of special stipulation in a commercial real estate purchase and sale agreement, most buyers simply give themselves a sufficiently long due diligence period during which time the buyer can terminate the contract without cause. Buyers of residential real estate can also give themselves a sufficiently long "free look" period to determine whether and on what terms the property can be financed.

§ 8.4   SALE OR LEASE OF OTHER PROPERTY OWNED BY BUYER

Residential real estate contracts are often made contingent upon the sale or lease of property owned by the buyer. There are many questions that need to be answered when drafting this type of contingency, including:

(a) What obligation will the buyer have to market his or her property to maximize the likelihood of it selling or being leased?

(b) How long should the buyer be given to sell or lease his existing property?

(c) If another buyer makes an offer to purchase the property, should the seller have the right to require the buyer to remove all contingencies in the contract or risk losing the property?

(d) If another buyer makes an offer to purchase the seller's property, should the seller have the right to require the buyer to remove the sale of other property contingency or risk losing the property? If so, what procedure should be followed to accomplish the kick-out of the sale of other property contingency?

(e) If the buyer's existing property is under contract to be sold but the closing does not occur before the closing of the purchase of the property the buyer wants to buy, should the seller have a right to unilaterally extend the contract until the buyer has completed the sale of his or her property?

§ 8.4.1   Purchase Contingent On Sale Or Lease Of Buyer's Current Residence

A contract is often made contingent upon a buyer being able to sell or lease other property.[1230] Under the GAR Contracts, the buyer warrants that he does not need to sell or lease other real property to complete the purchase of seller's property. Accordingly, the buyer would be in breach of contract in the event the loan was denied solely because of a failure to sell or lease a current residence. If there are multiple reasons for the loan denial, however, such that they buyer would have been disapproved for the loan even if the buyer had sold or leased his current residence, the buyer would not likely be found to have breached his or her warranty.

1230   GAR Forms F20, F23 and F27.

If the buyer must sell other property to complete the transaction, the buyer should include a "sale of other property contingency" in the purchase contract.[1231] As an extra measure of protection, buyers may also wish to include a special stipulation similar to the one set forth below.

> **Special Stipulation 153:   Purchase Contingent on Sale of Buyer's Property**
>
> *Notwithstanding any provision to the contrary contained herein, the purchase of the Property is contingent upon the sale and closing of Buyer's property located at (Address) on or before the closing date (or any permitted extension thereof) in the Agreement. Buyer agrees to pursue and seek to complete the sale and closing of the above-referenced property diligently and in good faith. Buyer shall immediately notify Seller upon entering into any contract to sell the property and shall immediately provide Seller with a copy of the same. Buyer shall also keep Seller fully and immediately informed of any changes in the status of the contract and facts which could adversely affect the likelihood of the property being closed.*

§ 8.4.2   Purchase Contingent On Sale Or Lease Of Buyer's Property

A second approach is to make the sale of the property contingent upon the buyer either selling or leasing other property. An example of this approach is set forth below.

> **Special Stipulation 154:   Purchase Contingent on Sale or Lease of Buyer's Property**
>
> *Notwithstanding any provision to the contrary contained herein, this Agreement is contingent upon Buyer's ability, acting diligently and in good faith, to close the sale or to enter into a lease certain real property owned by Buyer and located at (address) on or before (date). In the event said property is not closed or leased by this date due to no fault of Buyer, this Agreement shall be null and void. For purposes of this Agreement, the term "leased" shall mean that the parties to the lease have executed the same whether or not the actual lease term has commenced. Buyer shall immediately notify Seller upon entering into any lease or contract to sell the property and shall immediately provide Seller with a copy of the same. Buyer shall also keep Seller fully and immediately informed of any (1) changes in the status of the lease or contract to sell and (2) facts which could adversely affect the likelihood of the property being sold or leased.*

§ 8.4.3   Seller Allowed To Continue Marketing Property For Sale

Another approach is to allow the seller to continue to market the property for sale while the buyer is attempting to sell or lease other property. If the seller receives an acceptable offer from another buyer, the seller must give written notice to the buyer. The buyer then has a specified number of hours to remove all contingencies including any financing contingency, thereby making the contract an "all cash" contract. This type of provision in real estate vernacular is referred to as a "kick-out" clause. Under this approach, the buyer may also be required to deposit additional earnest money with the Holder. An example of this type of provision is set forth below.

1231   GAR Form F90, Sale or Lease of Buyer's Property Contingency. If a buyer is using this GAR Form because his purchase of the seller's property is going to be contingent upon the sale (and not the lease) of his own property, the buyer should be careful to strike the "or lease" language from the form. If such language is not removed, the seller could conceivably agree to lease the buyer's property in order to force the buyer to close.

Special Stipulation 155: Purchase Contingent on Sale or Lease of Buyer's Property, with Kick-Out Right to Seller and Removal of All Contingencies

(1) This Agreement is contingent upon Buyer's ability, acting diligently and in good faith, to close the sale or enter into a lease certain real property owned by Buyer and located at (address), on or before (date). Seller shall have the right to continue to offer and actively market Seller's Property for sale. In the event that Seller receives another acceptable offer to purchase the property, Seller shall give written notice to Buyer or Selling Broker that Seller has received another acceptable offer. Seller shall ☐ or shall not ☐ be obligated to provide the terms or a copy of said offer to Buyer.

(2) Buyer shall then have (number) hours after receipt of Seller's notice to deliver to Seller an amendment to this Agreement signed by Buyer in which Buyer agrees to remove all contingencies set forth in this Agreement, including, without limitation, the contingency provided for in this Exhibit, any inspection contingency or Due Diligence Period to which this Agreement may be subject, and any financing contingency, thereby making this an "all cash" transaction, without any contingency whatsoever. Furthermore, Buyer shall deposit with Holder additional earnest money of $_____ and said earnest money to be delivered to Holder with the amendment. Upon Seller timely receiving the amendment signed by Buyer, Seller shall promptly sign the same and return a copy to Buyer.

(3) In the event Buyer does not timely provide the Seller with the above-referenced amendment to this Agreement, Seller may terminate this Agreement upon notice to Buyer.

(4) Nothing herein shall limit or void any of Seller's other obligations under this Agreement, including the obligation to deliver good and marketable title to the Property by warranty deed or to make any agreed-upon repairs.

The above provision refers to the Amendment, which is the GAR Amendment to Remove Contingency of Sale or Lease of Buyer's Property.[1232] If the buyer chooses this option, the buyer must complete this form, which sets out: (1) the additional earnest money payment, (2) the removal of all contingencies, and (3) the removal of the sale contingency.

If the buyer wishes to proceed with the purchase after receiving the seller's notice of another offer but to only waive the financing contingency, the buyer should use the following stipulation.

Special Stipulation 156: Purchase Contingent on Sale or Lease of Buyer's Property with Kick-Out Right to Seller and Removal of Financing Contingency

(1) This Agreement is contingent upon Buyer's ability, acting diligently and in good faith, to close the sale or enter into a lease certain real property owned by Buyer and located at (address), on or before (date). Seller shall have the right to continue to offer Seller's Property for sale. In the event that Seller receives an acceptable offer, Seller shall give written notice to Buyer or Selling Broker.

(2) Buyer shall then have (number) hours after receipt of Seller's Notice to deliver to Seller a signed written amendment to this Agreement signed by Buyer in which Buyer agrees to remove all contingencies set forth in this Agreement, including, without limitation, the contingency provided for in this Exhibit, any inspection contingency and any financing contingency, thereby making this an "all cash" transaction, without any contingency whatsoever. Furthermore, Buyer shall deposit with Holder additional earnest money of

---

1232   GAR Form F103.

*$____ and said earnest money to be delivered to Holder with the amendment. Upon
Seller timely receiving the amendment signed by Buyer, Seller shall promptly sign the
same and return a copy to Buyer.*

*(3) All notices hereunder shall be delivered to the parties or representatives of the parties
permitted to receive notice on their behalf in accordance with the notice requirements of
this Agreement.*

The GAR Sale or Lease of Property Contingency obligates the buyer to act diligently and in good faith to sell or lease
buyer's property. Some sellers may want to incorporate the following provision by which the parties agree to the listing
price of the buyer's property to be sold or leased.

> **Special Stipulation 157: Parties Agree as to Listing Price of Buyer's Property**
>
> *Seller and Buyer agree that Buyer shall list Buyer's property located at (address) for a
> price not to exceed $_____ and shall list the property with a real estate broker licensed in
> Georgia for a term of at least _____days.*

§ 8.4.4   The Approach In The GAR Forms

The GAR Forms include a Sale or Lease of Buyer's Property Contingency[1233] that is subject to being kicked out by the seller
if another offer is made which is acceptable to the seller. Under this contingency, upon the receipt of the other acceptable
offer the seller gives written notice of the same to the buyer. The buyer then has a negotiated period of time during which to
remove *all* contingencies from the contract, not just the contingency regarding the sale or lease of the buyer's other property.
If the buyer does not do so, the entire Agreement becomes null and void. This leaves the buyer in a position where she must
either go forward with the contract on an "as-is," "all cash" basis or risk losing the contract to the other prospective buyer.

Some buyers have requested more of a limited kick-out provision where the buyer only agrees to remove the particular
contingency to which the Exhibit applies, rather than all contingencies. An example of this type of provision, which
would be added to the Sale or Lease of Buyer's Property Contingency Exhibit, is set forth below.

> **Special Stipulation 158: Kick-Out Clause Only Affects Sale of Other Property by
> Buyer Contingency**
>
> ☐ *C. Contingency with Limited Kick-Out Provision*
>
> *Notwithstanding any other provision to the contrary contained herein, in the event Seller
> receives another acceptable offer on the Property, Seller shall give Buyer written notice of the
> same. Buyer shall then have _____ [hours/days] after receipt of Seller's notice to deliver to
> Seller an Amendment to this Agreement signed by the Buyer in which Buyer has removed
> from this Agreement the Sale or Lease of Buyer's Property Contingency. It is the express
> intent of this provision that any other contingency or Due Diligence Period to which this
> Agreement may be subject in favor of Buyer shall remain in full force and effect.*

§ 8.4.5   Specifying Listing Broker Or Listing Price For Buyer's Property

The above approach makes sense when the buyer's property is already under contract at the time the property the
buyer hopes to purchase is put under contract. However, if the buyer has not yet begun to try to sell or lease his or her
existing property, the seller may want to specify how the buyer will go about marketing the property. So, for example,
the seller may want to require that the buyer list his or her property with a particular real estate brokerage firm to help
ensure that it is properly marketed. An example of this type of special stipulation follows.

1233   GAR Form F90.

Special Stipulation 159: Buyer Must List Property Buyer Needs to Sell with Particular Broker

Notwithstanding any provision to the contrary contained herein, Buyer agrees to list the property referenced herein, which Buyer needs to [sell/lease] in order to allow the Buyer to complete the purchase of the Property, with the following real estate brokerage firm, or such other brokerage firm as may be approved in writing by Seller, for the entire time that the Sale or Lease of Buyer's Property Contingency Exhibit is a part of this Agreement: _____ [name of brokerage firm].

Of course, merely listing the buyer's property with a particular real estate brokerage firm does not ensure success in getting that property sold. The issue which is rarely addressed in contingencies where the buyer must sell other property is the price at which the other property will be sold. Certainly, the seller can require that the property be listed for a particular price. The seller could even add to such a stipulation the requirement that the buyer drop his or her listing price every 30 days. A sample of such a provisions is as follows.

Special Stipulation 160: Buyer Agrees to List Property Needing to be Sold for a Particular Price [*Optional*: and Requirement That Listing Price be Reduced Every 30 Days]

Notwithstanding any provision to the contrary contained herein, Buyer agrees to list the property referenced herein, which Buyer needs to [sell/lease] in order to complete the purchase of the Property, for a [sales price/monthly lease price] not to exceed $_____.

[OPTIONAL] If the Buyer has not entered into a contract to [sell/lease] Buyer's property within _____ days of the date it is listed, Buyer agrees to reduce the [listing/lease price] by _____% every _____ days thereafter until the Property is put under contract to be [purchased/ leased].

§ 8.4.6 Buyer's Delaying Of Closing Date On His Or Her Property

An issue which sometimes arises with the GAR Sale or Lease of Buyer's Property Contingency is that the buyers change their minds about buying the property and drag their feet in closing the sale of the other property. If the closing of the sale of buyer's property does not take place by the date the buyer is obligated to close on the purchase of the property, the contingency fails and the contract becomes null and void. One way to prevent this if the buyer's property is under contract but has not yet closed is to give the seller the unilateral right to extend the closing date in the Agreement. A sample of this additional language is set forth below.

Special Stipulation 161: Closing of Other Property Scheduled After Scheduled Closing Under This Agreement

Notwithstanding any other provision to the contrary contained herein, if the property which Buyer needs to sell in order to complete the transaction is under contract but not scheduled to close before the date that Buyer is supposed to close on the purchase of the Property, Seller may unilaterally extend the Closing date upon notice to Buyer to a date that is no more than 7 days from the date that the other property of Buyer is scheduled to close, provided that such date is no more than ____ days from the original date of Closing set forth herein.

The logic behind this provision is that if the buyer is asking the seller to be patient while the buyer sells his or her property, the buyer should be willing to allow the closing date of the primary agreement to be extended to allow the buyer to complete the sale of his other property.

§ 8.5 PURCHASE OF OTHER PROPERTY BY BUYER

In many real estate transactions, the purchase of property by the buyer is contingent upon the simultaneous acquisition of other property by the buyer. This type of contingency is normally used in transactions where the buyer is attempting to aggregate a series of smaller properties. An example of the type of provision that is used when multiple properties are to be acquired follows.

> **Special Stipulation 162:   Assemblage**
>
> *Seller acknowledges that Buyer is attempting to acquire all of the properties described in Exhibit "__." This Agreement is therefore contingent upon Buyer simultaneously closing on the purchase of the properties described in Exhibit "__." This contingency shall be for the benefit of Buyer and Buyer shall have the right to waive the contingency in whole or in part.*
>
> *Buyer shall keep Seller fully apprised of Buyer's efforts to purchase the other properties. In this regard, Buyer shall provide Seller with copies of any real estate purchase agreement entered into by Buyer to purchase any of the properties described in Exhibit "____" or any portion thereof, but Buyer shall be permitted, but not required, to cover up and not reveal the purchase price Buyer is paying for any of the other properties. The date of Closing shall be on any business date prior to _____, 20_____ selected by Buyer, provided that Buyer shall give Seller _____ days prior notice of the date, time and location of the Closing.*

Normally with provisions such as the one above, the Buyer has an extended period of time to put the other properties under contract and close upon their purchase. This often includes giving the Buyer the right to set the specific closing date provided that it is within a given time period.

With other stipulations of this type, the purchase may be contingent upon the purchase of only one other property which is already under contract to be purchased by the buyer. A sample of this stipulation is set forth below.

> **Special Stipulation 163:   This Agreement Voidable if the Simultaneous Purchase of Other Property by Buyer Does Not Occur**
>
> *This Agreement is contingent upon Buyer simultaneously closing upon the purchase of the property described and in accordance with the terms of the Purchase and Sale Agreement attached hereto as Exhibit "___" and incorporated herein (hereinafter "Contract to Buy Other Property"). In the event Buyer is unable to simultaneously close on the Contract to Buy Other Property due to no fault of Buyer, this Agreement shall be voidable by Buyer upon notice to Seller.*

In some cases, buyer's obligation to purchase a property is contingent upon the seller simultaneously purchasing the buyer's property. This type of provision is sometimes used by builders who purchase a buyer's house in order to allow the buyer to purchase the builder's house. A sample of this type of provision follows.

Special Stipulation 164:   This Agreement Void if Simultaneous Purchase of Other Property by Buyer Does Not Occur

This Agreement is contingent upon Seller simultaneously purchasing the property of the Buyer pursuant to that certain Purchase and Sale Agreement attached hereto as Exhibit "___" and incorporated herein. In the event Seller does not purchase Buyer's property in accordance with the Purchase and Sale Agreement attached hereto due to no fault of Buyer, this Agreement shall be null and void.

§ 8.6   BACK-UP CONTINGENCY

On occasion, a prospective buyer will so like a property that she is willing to put a back-up contract on it so that if the primary contract fails to close, she is automatically put in first position to buy the property. There are risks to both buyers and sellers with use of a back-up contract.

§ 8.6.1   Sellers And Back-Up Contracts

From the seller's perspective, if the language of the back-up contract is not written to protect the seller, it can leave the seller under contract to sell a property to two different buyers. The key issue for sellers is what triggers the back-up contract becoming a primary contract. For example, let's say that the primary contract is set to close on May 1. The seller and the buyer in the back-up position agree in their contract that if the primary contract does not close by May 1, the second contract becomes primary. If the buyer in the primary contract has a right to unilaterally extend the closing date for 7 days and exercises this right, the primary contract is still in effect, but the seller is now also obligated to sell the same property to the back-up buyer. Most well drafted back-up contingencies have a very clear triggering event to cause the back-up contract to become primary. Often times, the event will be in the control of the property owner such as the provision set forth below.

Special Stipulation 165:   Builder/Seller to Buy Buyer's Property

All parties acknowledge that this Agreement is a back-up agreement to that certain Purchase and Sale Agreement entered into between the Seller and _____ dated_____ for that certain real property located at the following address: _____ _____ (hereafter "Primary Agreement"). Buyer under this back-up agreement shall have no right to purchase the Property if Buyer and Seller close on the purchase and sale of the Property either pursuant to the terms and conditions of the Primary Agreement or as the same may be amended by the parties. In the event both parties mutually agree in writing to terminate the Primary Agreement, this Agreement shall become primary and the Buyer and Seller hereunder shall fulfill the terms of this Agreement. Moreover, if either the Buyer or Seller under the Primary Agreement gives the other party notice to terminate the Primary Agreement and the Seller notifies the Buyer that the Primary Agreement has been terminated, this Agreement shall become primary and the Buyer and Seller hereunder shall fulfill the terms of this Agreement.

§ 8.6.2   Buyers And Back-Up Contracts

A buyer in a back-up position will often continue to look for other suitable property while she waits to see if the primary contract is going to close. If the buyer in the meantime finds other property that is suitable to purchase, she must be careful not to put the second property under contract while there is still a possibility that the back-up contract on the first property could become primary. Buyers in a back-up position can protect themselves in several different ways.

The first is for the buyer to limit the duration of being in a back-up position to a relatively short period of time. In this way, if the buyer finds other acceptable property she will not have to wait too long to put it under contract. A sample of this type of special stipulation is set forth below.

> **Special Stipulation 166: Buyer Can Terminate if she Remains as a Back-Up Contract for Too Long**
>
> *Notwithstanding any other provision to the contrary contained herein in the event this Agreement remains in a back-up position to the primary contract for more than ___ days, Buyer may but shall not be obligated to terminate this Agreement upon notice to Seller.*

The second approach is for the buyer to include a right to terminate the back-up contract if the buyer finds other suitable property. For such a provision to be enforceable, the buyer should pay the seller a separate fee for this right to terminate. A sample of this type of provision is set forth below.

> **Special Stipulation 167: Buyer Can Pay Fee to Terminate Contract**
>
> *Notwithstanding any provision to the contrary contained herein, Buyer shall have a right to terminate this Agreement by giving notice to the Seller of Buyer's decision and paying Seller a termination fee of $_____. Other than the termination fee, all earnest money and other sums paid by Buyer to Seller pursuant to this Agreement shall be refunded to Buyer.*

§ 8.6.3 The GAR Approach

The GAR Back-Up Agreement Contingency Exhibit[1234] tries to protect the seller by not having the back-up contract become primary unless the primary agreement is terminated or becomes null and void and the seller or listing broker gives written notice of the same to the buyer in back-up position. When the primary agreement is terminated, the back-up agreement contingency becomes the primary agreement and the seller must close the transaction in accordance with the terms and conditions of the GAR Back-Up Agreement Contingency Exhibit.

§ 8.7 GENERAL KICK-OUT CONTINGENCIES

A kick-out clause can be applied to any number of contingencies. The sale of other property, a financing contingency, a due diligence period, and a traditional right to inspect and request the repair of defects can all be made subject to kick-out clauses. When agreeing to a kick-out clause, sellers accept a contract with a contingency that may take more time to satisfy than the seller might like. On the theory that a bird in the hand is worth two in the bush, the seller accepts the contract but then has the right to force the buyer to remove, or kick out, the contingency if another buyer comes along who is willing to buy the property without the contingency.

The GAR forms include a General Contingency Exhibit[1235] that can be used for this purpose. The approach taken in the GAR form is to allow the seller to notify the buyer when another acceptable offer is made, and for the buyer to then have a negotiated period of time to either agree to remove the contingency referenced in the General Contingency Exhibit or have the Agreement become null and void.

Some buyers have argued that giving the seller the right to invoke the kick-out clause whenever the seller decides that she has received a better offer gives the seller too much power. These buyers have argued that the seller should only be able to invoke the kick-out clause if the seller receives an offer that does not contain the same contingency as the one which the seller is now trying to kick-out. For example, if the seller has agreed to a purchase and sale contract subject to the sale of the buyer's property, should the seller have a right to kick-out this contingency because another buyer has offered to purchase the property under an agreement that is also subject to the sale of that buyer's property?

1234   GAR Form F91.

1235   GAR Form F92.

This can be addressed by adding a definition of the term "other acceptable offer" to the GAR General Contingency Agreement. A sample of this type of provision is set forth below.

Special Stipulation 168: Definition of "Other Acceptable Offer"

For all purposes herein the term "acceptable offer," the receipt of which will allow the seller to invoke the kick-out contingency, shall mean an offer which is not contingent upon the same contingency or contingencies which the Seller is seeking to remove, or kick-out, of this Agreement with Buyer.

§ 8.8 REZONING CONTINGENCIES

If the buyer must have the property rezoned in order to use it for its intended purpose, the parties should incorporate the Rezoning Contingency special stipulation providing that the agreement is contingent on the property being rezoned to a specified category of zoning by the appropriate governmental authorities by a specified date. A sample of such a special stipulation follows.

Special Stipulation 169: Rezoning Contingency

Buyer understands and agrees that Property is currently zoned _____. The Buyer's obligation to purchase the Property is conditioned upon the Property being rezoned to _____ zoning category, subject only to the conditions, if any, listed below:

_____ _____
_____ _____
_____ _____ by the
appropriate _____ *(City/County) authorities by the date of* _____. *(Buyer/Seller) shall diligently, and in good faith, apply for and pursue the rezoning of the Property and pay for all costs associated therewith. In the event that final rezoning is not obtained by the date referenced above, the Buyer shall have the right (but not the obligation) to terminate this Agreement without penalty. All rezoning applications shall be approved in advance of filing by Seller as to their conformance with this paragraph. All parties agree to cooperate with one another to obtain the above-referenced rezoning and, in keeping therewith, shall sign all necessary documentation related to the rezoning and generally support the same. For all purposes herein the term "final rezoning" shall mean thirty (30) days from the date the final government action is taken to approve the rezoning with no legal challenges or appeals to the rezoning having been filed during that time period.*

There are several key issues to remember when property is contracted to be sold subject to being rezoned.

§ 8.8.1 Appeals Period

First, the statute of limitations to challenge a rezoning approved by local government is 30 days from the date of the final governmental approval. As a result, most buyers will want the rezoning contingency to be triggered by the approval of the rezoning and no appeal being filed during the appeals period. Therefore, the term "final rezoning" in this special stipulation and in most real estate sales agreements is defined as 30 days from the date that the local government has approved the rezoning of the property.

§ 8.8.2 Court Challenges Of Zoning Requests

Second, sellers need to carefully think through the wisdom of giving their buyers an open-ended ability to challenge a denial of rezoning request in court. Court challenges can often take several years, particularly if the ruling of the trial court is appealed. Therefore, many sellers will want to include an outside date for the closing of the property (even if a lawsuit has been filed), after which the seller may, but is not obligated, to terminate the agreement.

§ 8.8.3 Denial Of Rezoning And Its Effect Upon Later Applications

Third, the seller must remember that if the rezoning is denied, the seller or the seller's representatives are normally prohibited from seeking any rezoning of the property for at least six months[1236] and, in some jurisdictions, up to two years. Therefore, the seller may want to check with the local planning and zoning department to determine the likelihood of the rezoning being approved before contractually agreeing to allow a buyer to seek to rezone the property on behalf of the seller. Sellers may also want to include an outside date for the closing of the property (even if a lawsuit has been filed), after which the seller may, but is not obligated, to terminate the agreement. A sample of such a provision follows.

> **Special Stipulation 170: Outside Closing Date**
>
> *Notwithstanding anything to the contrary contained herein, and for and in exchange of the sum $10 and other good and valuable consideration, in the event that this transaction has not closed on or before _____ (insert date) due to any then pending zoning application or appeal, Seller may, at Seller's option, elect to terminate this Agreement by giving notice to Buyer within twenty-one (21) days of said date. In the event that Seller does not give timely notice, then this option shall expire and be of no further effect.*

§ 8.8.4 Specificity Required

Fourth, the seller should avoid general rezoning contingencies such as "the property being rezoned to multi-family residential use." Instead, the rezoning contingency should state the specific zoning category being sought by the buyer and density of development which will cause the contingency to be fulfilled or to fail. The following sample stipulation is an example of a portion of a zoning provision where the zoning category and density are specifically defined.

> **Special Stipulation 171: Zoning Contingency**
>
> *This agreement is contingent upon Buyer rezoning the Property to an RM-8 multi-family residential zoning category at a density of eight (8) units per acre in accordance with the Zoning Ordinance of _____ County.*

§ 8.8.5 Conditions Imposed By Local Zoning Authority

Sellers should also avoid zoning contingencies in which the buyer has a right not to purchase the property if the local zoning authority imposes conditions upon the rezoning which are unacceptable to the buyer. There are two problems with this type of provision. The first is that the buyer is the sole judge of whether she is satisfied with zoning conditions and as such the agreement may be void for a lack of mutuality. Second, almost all rezonings approved by local government are subject to certain conditions. Therefore, including such a provision effectively gives the buyer an almost automatic ability to get out of the agreement.

§ 8.8.6 Purchase Price Tied To Rezoning Results

In some real estate land agreements, the purchase price of the land is tied to the results of the rezoning. For example, a residential developer may pay a certain price per single-family dwelling approved as part of a rezoning of the property. Another approach is for the seller to be paid extra depending on what range of density is achieved on the property. Examples of these types of provisions are set forth below.

1236   O.C.G.A. § 36-66-4.

Special Stipulation 172: Purchase Price of Land Will Increase Over Base Price if Certain Densities are Achieved Through Rezoning [*Number of Single-Family Homes Approved*]

The Base Price of the Property shall be $_____ per acre as determined in accordance with the Survey Resolution Exhibit attached hereto and incorporated herein. In the event the Property is rezoned to permit more than fifty (50) single-family residential dwelling units in total on the Property, Buyer shall be paid the additional sum of $_____ for each single-family residential dwelling unit in excess of fifty (50) approved as part of the final rezoning of the Property.

Of course, merely because the property is zoned for a particular number of units or lots does not always mean that the property can be laid out to achieve this density. Side, front and rear yard setback requirements, a stream running through the property, the need for a detention pond and the layout of roads can all affect the ultimate lot yield of a property. To accommodate this reality, the following special stipulation can be used.

Special Stipulation 173: Price of Land Will Increase Over Base Price if Certain Densities are Achieved Through Rezoning and the Platting Process

The purchase price of the Property shall be a base price of $_____ plus $_____ per lot for each lot owner _____ which is approved by local zoning officials to be developed on the Property. Buyer agrees to submit a preliminary subdivision plat along with Buyer's rezoning application showing the number of lots Buyer is seeking to develop on the Property if the rezoning is approved. Buyer agrees to additionally request that the maximum number of lots for which Buyer is seeking approval as shown on the subdivision plat be made a condition of rezoning. buyer shall then pay Seller at closing the purchase price of the Property which shall be equal to the base price of the Property plus $_____ for each lot over _____ for which the Property is rezoned.

Another approach is for the seller to be paid extra depending upon what range of density is achieved in the rezoning process, as shown in the following special stipulation.

Special Stipulation 174: Price of Land Will Increase Over Base Price if Certain Densities are Achieved Through Rezoning [Density Range]

The Base Price of the Property shall be $_____ per acre as determined in accordance with the Survey Resolution Exhibit attached hereto and incorporated herein. In the event the Property is rezoned to permit a density of more than _____ units per acre on the Property, Buyer shall be paid the additional sum of $_____.

When the desired rezoning is for commercial use, the following stipulation may be used.

Special Stipulation 175: Price of Land Will Increase Over Base Price if C-1 Zoning Granted Allowing More Than 100,000 Square Feet of Commercial Square Footage

Buyer shall pay Seller a Base Price of $_____ for the Property. Buyer is seeking to have the Property rezoned to a C-1 commercial zoning under the Zoning Ordinance for _____ County. In the event the Property is rezoned under a final rezoning to allow more than 100,000 square feet of commercial square footage on the Property, Buyer shall pay Seller an additional amount at Closing in accordance with the formula set forth below:

Commercial Sq. Footage Approved	Additional Payment
100,000 – 124,999 square feet	$ _____
125,000 – 149,999 square feet	$ _____
150,000 – 174,999 square feet	$ _____
175,000 square feet and above	$ _____

The additional payment referenced above shall be in addition to the Base Price of the Property and shall be paid at the Closing of the Property.

§ 8.8.7 Zoning Issues For Buyers

From the buyer's perspective, the buyer does not want to make a large investment of time in seeking to rezone the Property only to have the seller terminate the agreement because the rezoning process has taken longer than the buyer has anticipated. One way for the buyer to try to address this is for the buyer to include in the agreements the right to extend the time period to close in the event the vote on a rezoning application is delayed, by depositing additional earnest money with the seller. An example of such a provision follows.

> **Special Stipulation 176: Buyer May Extend Closing Date Due to Rezoning Delays by Depositing Additional Earnest Money**
>
> *Notwithstanding any provision to the contrary contained herein, in the event the Board of Commissioners of _____ County, at a meeting where Buyer's rezoning application is heard, decides to postpone or table the vote on such rezoning application, Buyer may unilaterally extend the Closing date for a period of time equal to the length of the postponement by: (a) depositing additional earnest money with Holder in the amount of $_____ within seven (7) days from the date that the meeting where the case was tabled was held; and (b) notifying Seller of Buyer's decision to so extend the Closing date because of a postponement in the application being voted upon.*
>
> *For the purposes of this Agreement the length of the postponement shall be deemed to be the number of days from the date that the Board of Commissioners tabled or postponed a vote on the Buyer's rezoning application until the case is brought back for a vote before and voted upon by the Board of Commissioners.*
>
> *Notwithstanding any provision to the contrary contained herein, for Buyer to be able to unilaterally extend the Closing date pursuant to this provision, Buyer may not initiate the request for the postponement of the vote on the application, but may consent to the same if the postponement is initiated by the Board of Commissioners.*

§ 8.9 OTHER CONTINGENCIES

There are many other contingencies which buyers and sellers use to protect themselves in real estate purchase and sale agreements. Examples of the most common are set forth below.

> **Special Stipulation 177: Sale Contingent Upon Job Transfer of Buyer Being Successfully Consummated**
>
> *The Buyers in this transaction are_____ and _____. One of the Buyers, _____, is currently employed by _____ ("Company") and is being transferred to _____ by the Company. In the event*

Company cancels or revokes the transfer Buyer may terminate this Agreement upon notice to Seller, provided that such notice is given at least 7 days prior to the date of Closing stated in this Agreement. If the notice is not given within this time frame, Buyer's right to terminate due to the transfer being revoked or cancelled shall expire and thereafter be of no force and effect.

This same type of provision can also be used by sellers who are being transferred. An example of a special stipulation that can be used in that circumstance follows.

Special Stipulation 178:   Sale Contingent Upon Job Transfer of Seller Being Successfully Consummated

The Sellers in this transaction are _____ and _____. One of the Sellers, _____, works for _____ ("Company") and is being transferred by Company to _____ as part of his or her employment. In the event the transfer is cancelled or revoked by Company Seller shall have the right to terminate this Agreement, provided that notice of the termination is given to Buyer at least 7 days prior to the date of Closing set forth herein. In the event notice of termination is not given within this time frame, Seller's right to terminate this Agreement shall lapse and be of no further force and effect.

The **RED BOOK**

CHAPTER 9

DISCLOSURES

OVERVIEW

The Seller's Property Disclosure Statement is a unique tool developed by GAR to help sellers disclose defects in their properties. A seller of residential property owes a duty to disclose defects in a property to prospective buyers which the seller knows of or should have known about and which could not be discovered upon a reasonably diligent inspection of the property by the buyer.[1237] While sellers owe a duty to disclose hidden or latent defects, there is no state law requirement that the disclosure be made using the GAR Seller's Property Disclosure Statement. By disclosing defects, the seller protects himself or herself against claims of misrepresentation or fraud.

Among other things, this chapter includes an explanation of why the GAR Seller's Property Disclosure Statement is incorporated into the GAR Contracts, the seller's obligation to disclose defects, the delayed delivery of the property disclosure statement, and the need for the statement to be complete and accurate as of the Binding Agreement Date.

§ 9.1 WHAT THE GAR CONTRACTS PROVIDE

§ 9.1.1 Seller's Property Disclosure Statement For GAR Contract

The Seller's Property Disclosure Statement[1238] referenced in the GAR Purchase and Sale Agreement is a list of questions relating to the physical condition of the property both historically and at the present time. The GAR Contracts reference and incorporate the Seller's Property Disclosure Statement into the Contract.[1239] The GAR Contract also assumes that the buyer has received a Seller's Property Disclosure Statement prior to making an offer to purchase a property. To avoid any disclosure issues, listing brokers and agents should encourage their sellers complete the Seller's Property Disclosure Statement as soon as possible (preferably at the time of listing). Copies should also be made available to potential buyers for them to review and attach to any purchase offer.

This disclosure statement includes directions on how sellers should fill out the statement. In completing the disclosure statement, the seller agrees to the following: (1) answer all questions in reference to the Property (which unless noted, shall include any improvements); (2) leave no questions unanswered; (3) answer all questions fully and accurately based upon the best knowledge and belief of all sellers in the purchase and sale agreement; (4) fully explain in the "additional explanations" paragraph any questions to which the answer is "yes" or "other" referencing the number of the question for which the additional explanation is being given; and (5) promptly revise the statement and provide a copy of the same to the buyer and any broker involved in the transaction if prior to closing there are any material changes in the answers to any of the questions.

The GAR Seller's Property Disclosure Statement also contains an extensive list of items and fixtures to be identified by the seller as either staying or remaining with the property.[1240] Care should be taken to be sure the list is fully completed and if there is more than one of a particular item, that it is clear which one or ones stay with the property. For example, if the seller indicates that the refrigerator is staying, but there are two refrigerators, the Disclosure Statement needs to specific which one, or both, remain.

1237   *Wilhite v. Mays*, 239 Ga. 31, 235 S.E.2d 532 (1977).

1238   GAR Form F50.

1239   GAR Form F20.

1240   GAR Form F50.

The GAR Seller's Property Disclosure Statement contains a section for the seller to disclose whether the property is within, partially within, or adjacent to any property zoned or identified on an approved county land use plan as agricultural or forestry use.[1241] This provision is included in the GAR form to comply with Georgia law[1242] which requires sellers to provide notice to purchasers that such zoning or permitted use could mean that the property is used for activities that cause discomfort and inconveniences, such as twenty-four hour use of heavy machinery, spraying of pesticides, smells, noise, dust, smoke, and storage of manure.[1243]

Finally, the disclosure statement also gives buyers advice on how to use the Seller's Property Disclosure Statement once they receive it. More specifically, it advises buyers that the disclosure statement should be the starting point for a buyer's investigation rather than the entire investigation. It also tries to explain to buyers that *caveat emptor* is still the law in Georgia and if an inspection reveals an issue or concern that would cause a reasonable buyer to investigate further, the buyer will likely be out of luck if the buyer chooses not to do so. The new disclosure statement language is as follows.

> *The answers of Seller below should not be a substitute for Buyer conducting a careful, independent evaluation of the Property. Caveat Emptor or buyer beware is the law in Georgia. Buyer is expected to use reasonable care to identify defects in the Property and satisfy herself or himself that the Property is suitable for Buyer's needs and purposes. If an independent evaluation of the Property reveals potential problems or areas of concern that would cause a reasonable buyer to investigate further, Buyer may not have legal recourse if Buyer fails to investigate further.*

§ 9.1.2 Seller's Property Disclosure Statement For GAR New Construction Contract

The GAR New Construction Purchase and Sale Agreement[1244] provides for the parties to complete and attach the GAR Seller's Property Disclosure Statement (New Construction).[1245] This exhibit contains information substantially similar to that found in the GAR disclosure exhibit for existing home sales but is tailored to apply to new construction. The exhibit contains disclosures regarding the present condition of the property, certain past repairs and the history of the property. More specifically, the disclosure statement includes information regarding the soil, trees, drainage, and boundaries of the property; termite treatment; any structural items located or moved from the property; plumbing related items; the existence of any toxic substances; and any other systems and components serving the property, such as heating and air conditioning systems.

§ 9.1.3 Seller's Property Disclosure Statement For GAR Lot Purchase And Sale Agreement

The GAR Lot Purchase and Sale Agreement[1246] also provides that a Seller's Property Disclosure Statement (Lot/Land) Exhibit[1247] is attached and incorporated into the agreement.[1248] The buyer should carefully review this disclosure statement to determine if it addresses all issues which are of concern to the buyer. The Seller's Property Disclosure Statement (Lot/Land) Exhibit includes information related to the acreage and current zoning of the property as well as information concerning whether any mineral, oil and timber rights are excluded or have been licensed to third parties. It also addresses whether there is or will be any fill dirt or landfill on the property. This disclosure should address the issue of whether the seller has buried trees or other construction debris on the property.

1241   GAR Form F50.

1242   O.C.G.A. § 44-1-17.

1243   12 Ga. St. U. L. Rev. 313 (1995).

1244   GAR Form F23.

1245   GAR Form F51.

1246   GAR Form F27.

1247   GAR Form F53.

1248   GAR Form F27.

§ 9.1.4 Seller's Property Disclosure Statement For GAR Condominium Resale Purchase And Sale Agreement

The GAR Seller's Property Disclosure Statement (Condominium) Exhibit[1249] is used if the sale involves a resale condominium and is specifically incorporated into the GAR Condominium Resale Purchase and Sale Agreement.[1250] This exhibit creates a similar distinction between the condominium unit and the common elements. Specifically, the disclosure statement specifically provides that for purposes of answering the questions in this statement, the term "unit" does not include the common elements in which the owner has an undivided interest. The use of the term "property" then refers to all property which is a part of the condominium. Some of the information included in this disclosure statement pertains to the following: occupancy; the roof, gutters and downspouts of the condominium; drainage, flooring and moisture; fees assessments and property management; parking and storage; and other related matters.

§ 9.2 INCORPORATING THE PROPERTY DISCLOSURE STATEMENT INTO THE CONTRACT

§ 9.2.1 Rationale For Property Disclosure Statement Being Part Of Contract

Prior to 1997, the GAR Contract did not incorporate the Seller's Property Disclosure Statement into the contract. Buyers were often confused on this point because the Seller's Property Disclosure Statement was usually attached to the contract and was therefore assumed by many to be a part of it. Since the Seller's Property Disclosure Statement was not actually a part of the contract buyers had difficulty asserting claims for breach of contract against sellers when sellers answered questions inaccurately on the Seller's Property Disclosure Statement.

In one case where the Seller's Property Disclosure Statement was not incorporated into the contract, the sellers did not disclose the rupture and subsequent repairs that they had made to the bottom of the swimming pool.[1251] The contract had a provision where the buyer acknowledged receipt of the property disclosure statement, but it did not contain a provision stating that it incorporated the property disclosure statement into the contract. The court stated that the provision was not sufficient to incorporate the statement into the contract. Since the false statement was made outside the contract and the contract contained an "entire agreement" clause, the buyers could not sue the sellers for fraud.

The solution of the Georgia Association of REALTORS® was to make the Seller's Property Disclosure Statement a part of the contract and to have sellers warrant that the information contained therein is accurate and complete to the best of the seller's knowledge as of the Binding Agreement Date. This way, buyers using the 1997 and later GAR Contracts should be able to bring successful claims against sellers for breach of contract or breach of warranty if sellers make material misrepresentations in the Seller's Property Disclosure Statements. With this new potential for liability, sellers should use care to accurately complete their Property Disclosure Statements and should provide buyers with additional written explanations about issues which might otherwise be unclear to buyers.

For example, in a case where the Seller's Property Disclosure Statement was incorporated into the contract, the sellers checked the "yes" box on the disclosure statement to the question on whether the septic tank had been professionally serviced.[1252] They also stated on the disclosure statement that they were not aware of any past or present leaks or problems relating to the plumbing or sewer system in the property. In fact, the sellers had the system repaired instead of merely serviced as indicated on the disclosure statement. The court held that the sellers were liable for fraud. A breach of contract claim brought by the buyer against the seller for answering questions inaccurately in a Seller's Property Disclosure Statement is often easier to prove than a claim for fraud and misrepresentation. This is because in order to prevail in a claim for fraud and misrepresentation the buyer must prove that she exercised due diligence to protect themselves against

1249   GAR Form F52.

1250   GAR Form F33.

1251   *Ainsworth v. Perreault*, 254 Ga.App. 470, 563 S.E.2d 135 (2002).

1252   *Hudson v. Pollock*, 267 Ga.App. 4, 598 S.E.2d 811 (2004).

the fraud. This normally requires buyers to show that they attempted to independently verify all of the representations made by the seller or seller's agent or broker instead of just blindly relying on the representations.[1253] This high standard often leaves buyers without an effective remedy to pursue sellers for failing to disclose defects in the property.

§ 9.2.2   Effect Of Property Disclosure Statement Being Part Of Contract

When a seller discloses a defect relating to the property in the Property Disclosure Statement, the buyer is put on notice of the same and cannot then bring a claim against the seller for failing to disclose the defect. A buyer should never blindly rely upon the seller's property disclosure statement but should instead independently inspect the property to determine if there are additional defects and to better understand the nature and extent of the defects being disclosed. This is because when the seller discloses a defect, the buyer is not only put on notice of the defect but also any other condition that the disclosure of the defect would normally lead a reasonably prudent person to examine.[1254] In this way, the Property Disclosure Statement protects sellers.

An example is the case where the sellers stated in the Property Disclosure Statement that the property's exterior contained untreated stucco.[1255] The sellers also provided a letter from a stucco inspector stating that the hard-coat stucco was in good condition. However, the letter referenced an earlier letter provided by the same inspector stating that the trim was made of synthetic stucco. The contract provided that the buyers had the right to void the contract if a stucco inspection revealed major defects in the property. However, the buyers did not conduct a separate stucco inspection or obtain a copy of the letter referred to in the stucco inspection letter provided to the buyers. The court held that the failure of the buyers to conduct such an inspection constituted a lack of due diligence and therefore a claim for fraud could not be maintained.

An "entire agreement clause" (also known as a merger clause) operates independently as a disclaimer in a real estate sales contract. If this clause is properly drafted, it establishes that the final written agreement between the parties represents the entire agreement of the parties and that the parties are only relying on what is written in the contract. Consequently, a properly drafted entire agreement or merger clause effectively bars a buyer from asserting reliance on alleged misrepresentations not contained in the written agreement.[1256] The Georgia Court of Appeals recently held that buyers could successfully sue the sellers for facts falsely stated in the Property Disclosure Statement even if the Statement was not made part of the contract if the sellers actively concealed the damage. In this case, the seller gave the buyers a property disclosure statement (which was not made a part of the contract) in which he stated that he was not aware of any damage due to termites or structural defects in the home.[1257] A few months after the closing, the buyers saw termites swarming in the house and called an inspector who found that putty and paint had been used to conceal holes and gaps in the wood caused by termite infestation. The buyer then sued the seller alleging that he was defrauded by the seller's active concealment of the damage. The court held that the seller was liable for fraudulently concealing the termite damage. This was the case even though the contract used in selling the property did not incorporate the seller's property disclosure statement into the contract (unlike the current GAR Purchase and Sale Agreement) and contained an "entire agreement" clause, stating that it "constitutes the sole and entire agreement between the parties" and no representation, promise, or inducement not in the Agreement shall be binding upon any party to the contract.

§ 9.2.3   Broker's Liability For False Statements In Property Disclosure Statement

In Georgia, a buyer has no claim against the listing broker for false statements made by the seller in the Seller's Disclosure Statement unless the listing broker knows the representations to be false.[1258] Neither can the buyer sue the seller's agent for

---

1253   *Copeland v. Home Savings of America, F.A.*, 209 Ga.App. 173, 433 S.E.2d 327 (1993).

1254   *Ben Farmer Realty Co. v. Woodard*, 212 Ga.App. 74, 441 S.E.2d 421 (1994).

1255   *Meyer v. Waite*, 270 Ga.App. 255, 606 S.E.2d 16 (2004).

1256   *Novare Group, Inc., v. Sarif*, 290 Ga. 186, 718 S.E.2d 304 (2011).

1257   *Browning v. Stocks*, 265 Ga.App. 803, 595 S.E.2d 642 (2004).

1258   O.C.G.A. §10-6A-5(b).

fraud when the seller fails to disclose concealed defects in the property.[1259] A good example is the following case where the buyers sued the sellers, the real estate agent, and the brokerage firm for fraud, conspiracy to defraud, breach of contract and breach of BRRETA.[1260]

The buyers and sellers had entered into a contract of sale which contained a disclaimer provision stating that they did not rely on any statements made by the broker. The contract also contained an "entire agreement clause" stating that the contract represented the entire agreement between the parties and any representations made that were not included in the contract would not be binding. Finally, the contract incorporated by reference the sellers' disclosure statement. Before the parties signed the contract, the sellers gave the buyers the Property Disclosure Statement which referred to past and present termite damage, but stated that the damage had been corrected. It also stated that there were problems with the walkways and water intrusion, but that there had been no water in the basement since 1989. Shortly after the closing the homeowners found termite and rodent infestation, water intrusion, and soil settlement problems.

The court held that with respect to the buyer's claims against the agent and the broker there was no evidence that the agent knew about the home's defects apart from what was stated in the Seller's Disclosure Statement. Therefore, the agent and the broker could not be held liable for the seller's false statement. When listing agents are asked questions regarding the condition of the property, it is always a good idea to answer them in reference to the Seller's Property Disclosure Statement. So, for example, let's say that a buyer asks if the roof on a particular property leaks. The Seller's Property Disclosure Statement provides that the roof does not leak. To avoid any claim against the listing broker, it is always better to say, "The seller indicates in his Seller's Property Disclosure Statement that the roof does not leak," rather than "The roof does not leak." The former statement makes it clear that the broker is merely repeating information provided by the seller. The latter statement could be misconstrued as a representation of the broker.

To help further avoid this issue, all GAR purchase and sale agreements protect brokers by requiring the seller and buyer to acknowledge that they have not relied on any representations of brokers related to certain information concerning the property. For example, under the GAR Contract, this disclaimer explicitly states that the broker has no duty to advise the buyer or seller on any matter relating to the property which could have been revealed through a survey, title search, Official Georgia Wood Infestation Report, inspection by a professional home inspector or construction expert, utility bill review, an appraisal, inspection by an environmental engineering inspector, consulting governmental officials or a review of purchase and sale agreement and transaction by an attorney, financial planner, mortgage consultant or tax planner.

The GAR New Construction Purchase and Sale Agreement also contains a disclaimer that states that the broker is not responsible to advise the parties on any matter including, but not limited to the following: building products and construction techniques; the necessity or cost of any repairs to the property; views from the property; mold; hazardous or toxic materials or substances; termites and other wood destroying organisms; the tax or legal consequences of the contract and transaction; the availability and cost of utilities or community amenities; the appraised or future value of the property; any conditions existing off property which may affect the property; the terms, conditions and availability of financing; and the uses and zoning of the property, whether permitted or proposed. Overall, incorporating this type of disclaimer into the purchase and sale agreement will help protect the broker from potential liability.

§ 9.3 COMMUNITY ASSOCIATION DISCLOSURE

As an ever larger number of residences are built in communities with either condominium or homeowners associations, buyers want to better understand what their obligations will be as members of the association. Moreover, they are often looking for the answers to their questions to be incorporated into the purchase and sale agreement as seller warranties.

1259   *RE/MAX North Atlanta v. Clark*, 244 Ga.App. 890, 537 S.E.2d 138 (2000).

1260   *Bircoll v. Rosenthal*, 267 Ga.App. 431, 600 S.E.2d 388 (2004).

The main questions buyers are focusing on include the following:

1. What kind of and how many associations will the buyer be a member of?

2. What fees will the buyer have to pay to the association?

3. Are there any initiation fees in addition to regular monthly assessments?

4. Are there any pending special assessments?

5. Is the community in which the buyer is purchasing a home age restricted?

6. What services will the owner receive as a member of the Association and are there any services available for which an extra fee must be charged?

§ 9.3.1 Type And Number Of Associations

It is increasingly common for buyers of residences in mixed-use developments and master planned communities to be members of more than one homeowners association. Typically, there may be some type of master condominium or master property owners association that is responsible for maintaining portions of the overall development such as entrance features, roads, common landscaping, recreational facilities and in the case of a master condominium, the exterior of buildings. A sub-association is then typically created in these developments that is responsible for the maintenance and lease operation of a smaller portion of the overall community. For example, let's say that a large master planned community includes a variety of housing types including one section with townhomes. The owners in the townhome section of the master planned community will also usually be subject to a townhome association (that is a sub-association within the master planned community) that will maintain the exteriors of the townhomes and that portion of the common areas only serving the townhomes themselves.

Almost all homeowners associations established today are now mandatory membership associations. This means that membership in the association is required for all property owners in the community based on recorded covenants running with the land. Membership in condominium associations is required pursuant to state law.[1261]

In some of the early homeowners associations created in Georgia, membership was voluntary rather than mandatory. These early communities tended to have very limited recreational facilities and other common areas. The theory was that these facilities could be supported by whatever group in the community volunteered to be a member of the association from year to year. In practice, this concept was flawed. As common areas and recreational facilities aged and money was needed to make more significant repairs and renovations in the community, membership in the voluntary homeowners associations tended to fall resulting in the association's downward spiral. With the realization that homeowners associations need a more consistent financial base to support their operations, few homeowners associations today are voluntary associations.

§ 9.4 THE GAR COMMUNITY ASSOCIATION DISCLOSURE EXHIBIT

The approach of the GAR Contracts is to aggregate all of the disclosures regarding community associations in one exhibit that is attached and incorporated into the Purchase and Sale Agreement. This exhibit is separate from the Seller's Property Disclosure Statement. However, there is a question in the Seller's Property Disclosure Statement in which sellers are asked to disclose whether the property is a party of a community association. If it is, the seller is then directed to fill out a separate community association disclosure.

1261   O.C.G.A. § 44-3-100.

§ 9.4.1 Seller Warranty Of Information Contained In The Community Association Disclosure Exhibit

The seller signing the GAR Community Association Disclosure exhibit now warrants that to the best of seller's knowledge and belief, the information in the exhibit is accurate and complete. Earlier versions of the exhibit did not contain this type of warranty. Instead, the seller indicated that while she thought the information contained therein was accurate and complete it was not warranted. This was changed because as between the buyer and the seller, it was decided that the seller was likely in the better position to obtain the information required to be in the Community Association Disclosure exhibit and warrant its accuracy and completeness.

§ 9.5 SELLER'S DUTY TO DISCLOSE WITHOUT PROVIDING PROPERTY DISCLOSURE STATEMENT

Sellers are not obligated by law to complete the GAR Seller's Property Disclosure Statement or any other written property disclosure statement. If the seller refuses to complete the Property Disclosure Statement, the section about the Property Disclosure Statement should be deleted from the contract that is executed by the parties. When deciding not to provide a Property Disclosure Statement sellers should be aware that since the use of a property disclosure statement is becoming increasingly customary in the real estate industry, buyers may be reluctant to purchase property for which no such document has been completed. Moreover, the failure to complete a disclosure statement does not relieve the seller from disclosing defects in the property of which the seller knows or should know and which are not discoverable by a prospective purchaser upon a reasonable inspection of the property.[1262] Answering "I don't know" to questions on the Seller's Property Disclosure Statement or simply leaving them blank would similarly not protect the seller from the above disclosure obligations. For example, if the seller checks "I don't know" about any roof damage, but in fact has knowledge that the roof leaks, the seller could be held liable for his failure to accurately and honestly disclose this information.

While *caveat emptor*, or buyer beware, is still generally the law in Georgia, there are three circumstances in which sellers of residential property can be held liable for failing to disclose defects in the property. The first is when the seller knowingly lies about the existence of a concealed defect. In one case, the buyer asked the seller about the septic system, and the seller replied that the system had been serviced and was in perfect working condition. The truth was that the septic system was repaired as opposed to being merely serviced and the system should have been replaced rather than repaired.[1263]

The second situation involves active concealment where the seller does not discuss the defect, but takes steps to prevent its discovery by the prospective buyer. A good example is the case where the seller concealed termite damage by filling holes with putty and fresh paint.[1264]

The third circumstance is passive concealment when the seller knows of a concealed material defect and does not attempt to hide the problem but simply keeps quiet and makes no disclosure of its existence. In such cases, the seller can also be liable if the seller fails to disclose special knowledge he has of a defect which would not be reasonably apparent to the buyer.[1265] An agent may be liable for passive concealment if the agent had actual knowledge of the defect but did not disclose it.[1266]

To date, the passive concealment exception to the law of *caveat emptor* has only been applied in a residential context. This is likely the case because the courts tend to view purchasers of nonresidential property as being more sophisticated than residential buyers, and thus more capable of protecting themselves. For example, in the case of *Condon v. Kunse*,[1267] buyers were purchasing land for the purpose of raising horses. The sellers knew that the grass in the pasture was infected

---

1262   *Wilhite v. Mays*, 140 Ga.App. 816, 232 S.E.2d 141 (1976), *aff'd*, 239 Ga. 31, 235 S.E.2d 532 (1977).

1263   *Hudson v. Pollock*, 267 Ga.App. 4, 598 S.E.2d 811 (2004).

1264   *Browning v. Stocks*, 265 Ga.App. 803, 595 S.E.2d 642 (2004).

1265   *Fincher v. Bergeron*, 193 Ga.App. 256, 387 S.E.2d 371 (1989).

1266   *Ikola v. Schoene*, 264 Ga.App. 338, 590 S.E.2d 750 (2003).

1267   *Condon v. Kunse*, 208 Ga.App. 856, 432 S.E.2d 266 (1993).

with a fungus which could damage the hooves of the horses. The fungus apparently caused the grass to turn an unusually deep shade of green. The sellers did not disclose what they knew about the fungus. The buyers purchased the land and thereafter the buyer's livestock became sick from the fungus. When the buyers learned that the sellers had some knowledge of the fungus, they sued the sellers for fraud for passively concealing the defect. In denying the claim, the Georgia Court of Appeals noted that the cases creating and interpreting the legal doctrine of passive concealment had clearly limited its application to controversies between residential homeowners and residential builders/sellers as an exception to the doctrine of *caveat emptor*, and refused to apply it to the sale of commercial farm land.

The Seller's Property Disclosure Statement by its own terms requires the Statement to be updated through the date of closing. If a Seller's Property Disclosure Statement is not used, it is unclear whether the seller has any duty to disclose latent defects which the seller learns of after a contract is entered into. The passive concealment exception to the doctrine *caveat emptor* of passive concealment is intended to prevent the buyer from being fraudulently induced into signing the purchase and sale agreement. If it can be clearly established that there was no fraud in the inducement in getting the buyer to sign the contract, there may well be no claim for passive concealment on issues arising after the parties have entered into a contract.

A great many disputes arise regarding items contained in the Seller's Property Disclosure Statement. Sellers should take the time necessary to fully and completely fill in the Disclosure Statement. Buyers should insist that they receive a fully completed Disclosure Statement and should ask any and all questions they have related thereto. This is oftentimes the buyer's only chance prior to closing to receive information concerning the property directly from the seller.

§ 9.6 DUTY OF A BROKER TO DISCLOSE DEFECTS MAY BE GREATER IN SOME SITUATIONS THAN THE DUTY OF THE SELLER

As discussed in the previous section, the passive concealment exception to the rule of *caveat emptor* may not apply in nonresidential contexts. Therefore, sellers of commercial property may not owe a duty to disclose latent defects in a property. While sellers may not owe the duty, a listing broker with knowledge of a latent defect representing the seller would still be obligated to disclose such defects. Licensees can be sanctioned up to and including the revocation of their licenses for making substantial misrepresentations. While the passive concealment of a defect is not an affirmative misrepresentation, the Georgia Real Estate Commission has tended to view the duty not to make substantial misrepresentations as generally obligating a licensee to disclose latent defects.

Interestingly, the duty not to make substantial misrepresentations appears to exist even when the party to whom the misrepresentation was made could have protected himself or herself through the exercise of due diligence.

Moreover, the Brokerage Relationships in Real Estate Transactions Act ("BRRETA") requires brokers to disclose material adverse facts pertaining to the physical condition of the property of which the broker has actual knowledge and which could not have been discovered upon a reasonable inspection of the property.[1268] This obligation is not qualified or limited in any way. Georgia law is also well settled that even when the property is sold "as is," the broker must also disclose latent defects of which the seller is aware.[1269]

So, how and when does the licensee make the required disclosure? The answer is in writing and preferably prior to the buyer and seller entering into the purchase and sale agreement. There is no special format for the licensee to use in making the disclosure. For example, a licensee is aware that the basement previously flooded. The licensee would simply disclose to the buyer the specifics of what the licensee actually knows. The following special stipulation may be used.

1268   O.C.G.A. § 10-6A-5(b)(1).

1269   *Ikola v. Schoene*, 264 Ga.App. 338, 590 S.E.2d 750 (2003).

Special Stipulation 179:   Water Disclosure

During an unusually heavy rainstorm in July of 2011, I was inspecting the property and saw a large puddle of water in the basement near the patio doors that was approximately 4 feet by 4 feet in size.

What if the broker didn't actually see the water in the basement but was told by a neighbor that water regularly ponds in the basement during heavy rains? Must the broker disclose in this situation? BRRETA ties the disclosure obligation to the knowledge of the broker. If the broker knows of the water in the basement, the broker must disclose. While a broker might argue that a neighbor having knowledge is not the same thing as the broker having knowledge, the safer approach is to disclose. This is because if the neighbor tells the broker about the water, the neighbor is likely also going to tell the new owner about the water. The last thing the broker wants is for the new owner to hear from the neighbor that she told the broker about the water and the broker didn't disclose it to the buyer. In this case, the type of the disclosure that the licensee should make is as follows.

Special Stipulation 180:   Water Disclosure from Neighbor's Statement to Broker

A neighbor informed me that he had seen water ponding in the basement of the property after a big rain. Since we have had little rain this summer, I have not seen the condition and do not know if it continues to exist or has been corrected.

This type of disclosure would put the buyer on notice of a potential problem and would cause a reasonable buyer to investigate the situation further. As such, it fulfills the broker's duties under state law. More information on a broker's requirements under BRRETA is discussed in Chapter 19 (The Georgia Brokerage Relationships in Real Estate Transactions Act ("BRRETA")).

§ 9.7 DISCLOSURE TO BE ACCURATE AND COMPLETE AS OF BINDING AGREEMENT DATE

The GAR Contract requires the seller to warrant that the information contained in the Seller's Property Disclosure Statement is accurate and complete as of the Binding Agreement Date. Before their clients enter into a contract, brokers may want to review the Seller's Property Disclosure Statement to make sure that all questions have been answered and inquire whether any information on the Seller's Property Disclosure Statement has changed since it was first completed. Obviously, if it has, the Seller's Property Disclosure Statement should be updated to ensure that the information is accurate and complete as of the Binding Agreement Date. To the extent the seller revises the Seller's Property Disclosure Statement after it is included as part of an offer to purchase, the revisions would constitute a counteroffer to which the buyer would need to agree.

Listing agents should also confirm that all questions on the Seller's Property Disclosure Statement have been answered to avoid a later claim for breach of warranty for incompleteness. Of course, listing agents should avoid answering any of the questions on the Seller's Property Disclosure Statement on behalf of the seller because: (1) it is the seller's statement to make, and (2) answering questions could expose the listing broker to significant legal liability. Agents should also avoid the temptation to ask the seller the questions and then fill in the blanks on the form on behalf of the seller. Even though the seller will ultimately sign the Disclosure Statement, the seller could still claim that the agent checked the wrong box, either intentionally (a fraud claim) or by mistake (a negligence claim).

The seller has an ongoing obligation to promptly update the GAR Disclosure Statement and provide any revised copy to the buyer. This is to help the buyer determine whether the property is in the same condition on the date of the closing as it was on the Binding Agreement Date.

While the GAR Contract contemplates that a property disclosure statement be attached, there is nothing which prevents builders or other sellers from using their own form disclosure statement so long as it has been completed in full and is accurate as of the Binding Agreement Date. For example, a builder using the GAR Contract could develop its own disclosure statement which either addresses fewer questions or has more specific questions than the GAR Seller's Property Disclosure Statement. Of course, if there is a house on the property for which an alternative property disclosure statement has been prepared and which was constructed prior to 1978, the listing broker should confirm that the property disclosure statement contains the disclosures and acknowledgments regarding lead-based paint.

§ 9.8   DELAYED DELIVERY OF SELLER'S PROPERTY DISCLOSURE STATEMENT

If the Seller's Property Disclosure Statement is unavailable at the time of contract, the buyer and seller can agree that it be provided after the contract is signed. If the buyer has purchased the property subject to a Due Diligence Period, delivering the Seller's Property Disclosure Statement a couple of days after the Binding Agreement Date is not significant because the buyer can terminate the contract if the buyer is not satisfied with the contents of the Statement. Samples of special stipulations dealing with this issue are set forth below.

> **Special Stipulation 181:   Buyer's Right to Terminate for Delayed Delivery of Property Disclosure Statement**
>
> *Seller shall provide Buyer with a complete and accurate Seller's Property Disclosure Statement on the GAR form within _____ days from Binding Agreement Date. If Buyer has not received the Seller's Property Disclosure Statement within such time period Buyer may terminate this Agreement without penalty provided that written notice of termination is delivered to Seller within ____ days from the Binding Agreement Date.*

Another approach to encourage the seller to timely deliver the Seller's Property Disclosure Statement is to provide that the Due Diligence Period is extended for every day the seller delays in delivering the Seller's Property Disclosure Statement. A sample of this type of provision is set forth below.

> **Special Stipulation 182:   Due Diligence Period Extended if Seller's Property Disclosure Statement is Delivered Late**
>
> *Seller shall provide Buyer with a Seller's Property Disclosure Statement on the GAR Form no later than _____ days from Binding Agreement Date. For each day thereafter that Seller fails to provide Buyer with the Seller's Property Disclosure Statement, the Due Diligence Period shall be extended for one day. IN the event, the Seller's Property Disclosure Statement is not provided to Buyer within _____ days of the Binding Agreement Date, Buyer may terminate this Agreement without penalty upon notice to Seller.*

It is also possible that the Disclosure Statement will be available at the time an offer is made, but that the buyer has questions regarding the seller's responses. The seller may indicate on the Disclosure Statement, for example, that she has knowledge of damage to the property from termites. Even though the Seller's Property Disclosure Statement provides that the seller is to give a detailed explanation of the damage, not all sellers will do so. A prudent purchaser may want to know more about the damage before binding himself to purchase the property. The buyer can always simply ask the seller to more fully complete the Disclosure Statement. Alternatively, the buyer could insert a special stipulation similar to the following.

> **Special Stipulation 183:   Explanation of Specific Items in Seller's Property Disclosure Statement**
>
> *Seller shall provide Buyer with a complete and accurate written statement, including all related and pertinent documents, regarding Seller's response to item(s) _____ in the Seller's*

Property Disclosure Statement within _____ days from Binding Agreement Date. If Buyer has not received the additional explanation such statement within such time period Buyer may terminate this Agreement provided that written notice of termination is delivered to Seller within _____ days from Binding Agreement Date. If the Property is being sold with the right to request repairs Buyer may request, in Buyer's inspection amendment, that Seller repair, among other things, any defects revealed in the statement.

§ 9.9 DISCLOSURE OF REPAIRS MADE TO GET A HOUSE READY TO SHOW

Most sellers do a number of tasks to get a house ready to sell without thinking about whether these repairs should be disclosed. These types of repairs are often suggested by the listing agent. The problem arises when what is considered as "normally cosmetic repairs" by many sellers and listing agents can be twisted into an attempt to actively conceal defects in the house by a talented plaintiff's lawyer.

This issue is better illustrated with an example. Let's say a 50-year old house has a variety of different settlement cracks in the sheetrock and some noticeably rotted wood around a couple of the interior window sills. At the listing agent's suggestion, the seller has the interior of the house repainted. The painter fills all of the settlement cracks with caulk, scrapes the rotted wood from the windows, fills them with wood fill, and then repaints the interior of the home with two coats of paint.

An argument can be made that all of these repairs are cosmetic in nature and do not require disclosure to the buyer. In most cases, this would be the right answer. However, although settlement cracks may disappear when the house is repainted, they will normally come back and be visible again within a year or so. In fact, this process could be turned into a claim for the active concealment of defects by a seller, with the knowledge and help of the listing broker. Problems would most likely arise if the house had some more significant structural issues, but they were missed by the buyer because the settlement cracks (which would have revealed the problem) had all been hidden when the house was repainted. Similarly, what if the rotted area on the window sill, which was filled in with wood fill, turns out to be termite damage. Suddenly an innocent act to make the house look better can turn into something that seems insidious and wrongful.

To minimize the risk of making cosmetic repairs before a sale, the following disclosures (applicable to the house being sold) should be included in the Seller's Property Disclosure Statement, the purchase and sale agreement, or both. These disclosures will protect a seller from being accused of concealing a defect.

The Seller has made certain repairs in order to get the house ready to sell. These include the following:

1. ***Interior House Painting:*** *Seller has hired a painter to clean interior walls, caulk or otherwise fill small holes and cracks, repair or replace any rotted wood and paint the walls, doors and trim with two coats of the following paint: _____.*

2. ***Exterior House Painting:*** *Seller has hired a painter to pressure wash the exterior of the house, replace or repair all rotted wood or other siding materials, re-caulk around windows and doors, and paint the exterior of the house with two coats of the following paint: _____.*

3. ***Exterior Walkways:*** *Seller hired a contractor to pressure wash the walkways leading to the house and fill any loose mortar on walkways.*

4. ***Exterior Deck:*** *Seller hired a contractor to pressure wash the deck, replace and repair and rotted wood and reseal the deck with the following sealer: _____.*

5. ***Carpet Cleaning:*** *Seller hired carpet cleaning company to professionally clean carpets to remove stains and eliminate pet odor.*

6. ***Brick Mortar:*** *Seller hired contractor to fill cracks in brick mortar with new mortar or caulk.*

§ 9.10   DISCLOSURE OF LEAD-BASED PAINT

The lead-based paint disclosure requirements apply in both lease transactions and purchase and sale transactions.[1270] The Residential Lead-Based Paint Hazardous Reduction Act of 1992[1271] requires a seller or landlord of a property to meet certain disclose obligations when selling or renting a residential property any portion of which was constructed prior to 1978. This is also known as a target home.

Under the lead-based paint disclosure, law real estate licensees, when selling target housing, must advise sellers of the seller's obligation to disclose their actual knowledge of lead-based paint or lead-based paint hazards in the property. Moreover, the law requires that real estate licensees ensure that the seller has performed all activities required of him under the law, or the licensee must personally ensure compliance on the seller's behalf. The law further provides that by informing sellers of their obligation to disclose the licensee will not be held liable for failing to disclose to a purchaser that lead-based paint and/or lead-based paint hazards exist on the property, when such hazards are known to the seller but were not disclosed to the licensee.

Determining whether the dwelling was constructed prior to 1978 and advising the seller of his disclosure obligations should be standard operating procedure on all listing calls. Licensees should require that the seller sign the "Disclosure of Information and Acknowledgment of Lead-Based Paint and/or Lead-Based Paint Hazards," prepared by the National Association of REALTORS,® in which sellers acknowledge being advised of their disclosure obligations.[1272]

§ 9.10.1   Sellers' Disclosure Obligations

Before a buyer executes a contract with a seller, the regulations require the seller of target housing to do the following:

(a) Disclose to the buyer or tenant and to each agent of the buyer or tenant, any actual knowledge she has regarding (i) the presence of known lead-based paint, (ii) the presence of any lead-based paint hazards, and (iii) any additional information concerning the lead-based paint and lead-based paint hazard in the property being sold.[1273] "Actual knowledge" means any information that the seller received through first-hand account.[1274] While a rumor is not actual knowledge, the law even requires a seller to disclose knowledge of the rumor to the buyer;

(b) Provide the buyer with copies of all available records or reports that relate to the presence of lead-based paint and/or lead-based paint hazards in the property being sold;[1275]

(c) Provide the buyer with a federally approved lead-based paint hazard information pamphlet entitled "Protect Your Family From Lead in Your Home;"[1276] and

(d) Provide the buyer with a period up to ten days (or some mutually agreed time period), prior to becoming obligated under the contract, during which time the buyer may conduct a risk assessment or inspection for the presence of lead-based paint and/or lead-based paint hazards (the buyer may agree to waive this testing opportunity).[1277]

In addition, the Act requires the inclusion or attachment of the following disclosure statement regarding the hazards of lead-based paint in every purchase and sale or lease agreement.[1278]

1270   42 U.S.C. §§ 4852d(a)(1).

1271   42 U.S.C. §§ 4851 to 4856.

1272   See GAR Form F54, Lead-Based Paint Exhibit, and Form F55, Lead-Based Paint Pamphlet.

1273   42 U.S.C. §§ 4852d(a)(1)(B).

1274   42 U.S.C. §§ 4852d(a)(1)(B).

1275   42 U.S.C. §§ 4852d(a)(1)(B).

1276   42 U.S.C. §§ 4852d(a)(1)(A).

1277   42 U.S.C. §§ 4852d(a)(1)(C).

1278   42 U.S.C. §§ 4852d(a)(3).

Special Stipulation 184: Lead Warning

*Every purchaser of any interest in residential real property on which a residential dwelling
was built prior to 1978 is notified that such property may present exposure to lead from
lead-based paint that may place young children at risk of developing lead poisoning. Lead
poisoning in young children may produce permanent neurological damage, including
learning disabilities, reduced intelligence quotient, behavioral problems, and impaired
memory. Lead poisoning also poses a particular risk to pregnant women. The seller of any
interest in residential real property is required to provide the buyer with any information
on lead-based paint hazards from risk assessments or inspections in the seller's possession and
notify the buyer of any known lead-based paint hazards. A risk assessment or inspection for
possible lead-based paint hazards is commended prior to purchase.*

The disclosure obligation does not extend to all prospective buyers or lessees, regardless of their degree of interest. Only
the actual buyer or lessee must receive information on target housing. The disclosure must be made before a purchaser
or lessor is obligated under any contract to purchase or lease target housing. Under the law, sellers are required to permit
buyers a ten-day period to have the property tested for lead-based paint or lead-based paint hazards unless a different
period of time is agreed to in writing, or the inspection period is waived in writing by the buyer.[1279] The ten-day
inspection period does not apply to lease transactions.[1280]

§ 9.10.2 The GAR Lead-Based Paint Exhibit

The GAR Lead-Based Paint Exhibit[1281] contains the Act's required lead warning disclosure and is incorporated by
reference into both the GAR Purchase and Sale Agreement and the GAR Lease For Residential Property if the property
was built prior to 1978.[1282] This disclosure exhibit allows the seller or lessor to indicate whether she has knowledge of
any lead-based paint hazards in the housing and whether any records pertaining to such hazards exist and have been
provided to the buyer or tenant. In addition, the disclosure exhibit gives the buyer an opportunity to conduct a risk
assessment or inspection for the presence of lead-based paint or lead-based paint hazard as required under the Act or
waive such opportunity.

§ 9.11 THE INTERSTATE LAND SALES FULL DISCLOSURE ACT

Developers selling certain lots and condominium units are required to make disclosures pursuant to the Interstate
Land Sales Full Disclosure Act[1283] ("ILSA"). The purpose of ILSA is essentially to insure that a buyer, prior to
purchasing certain kinds of real estate, is informed of facts which will enable her to make an informed decision about
purchasing a particular property.[1284] ILSA issues often arise in lot transactions, and thus developers should be aware of
their obligations under federal law.

The Interstate Land Sales Full Disclosure Act[1285] requires a statement of record to be prepared and filed with the
appropriate department.[1286] Prior to 2011, this record was required to be filed with the Secretary of Housing and Urban
Development. However, the enforcement of the ISLA shifted to the new Bureau of Consumer Financial Protection in
the Department of Treasury. As such, all statements of record must be filed with the Bureau of Consumer Financial

---

1279   42 U.S.C. §§ 4852d(a)(2).

1280   42 U.S.C. §§ 4852d(a)(2).

1281   GAR Form F54.

1282   GAR Form F20 and 40.

1283   15 U.S.C.A.§ 1701 and 15 U.S.C.A.§ 1720.

1284   *Venezia v. 12th & Div. Properties, LLC*, 685 F.Supp. 2d 752 (M.D.Tenn. 2010).

1285   15 U.S.C.A. § 1701 *et seq.*

1286   15 U.S.C.A. § 1706.

Protection.[1287] The Act requires developers to include certain environmental disclosures in the statement of record. For instance, certain environmental aspects of a subdivision, such as roads, water, sewage, drainage, soil, erosion, climate, and zoning restrictions must be disclosed for the protection of purchasers.[1288]

The developer must also furnish a printed property report to the purchaser before or at the closing.[1289] The property report must contain the same information contained in the statement of record and any other information required by the Bureau of Consumer Financial Protection.[1290] If such property statement is not provided, the purchaser may terminate the agreement.[1291]

Like many legislative programs passed by the federal government, compliance with ILSA is onerous, time consuming and expensive. Such compliance is beyond the scope of this book. Without knowledgeable legal counsel, navigating one's way through the required disclosures, contractual requirements and other stipulations of the Act can be hazardous to the developer.

§ 9.12   DISCLOSURES OF NEIGHBORHOOD CONDITIONS

As discussed in § 9.5 (Seller's Duty to Disclose Without Providing Property Disclosure Statement), Georgia generally applies the maxim *caveat emptor*, or "buyer beware," to the sale of real property in this state.[1292] As discussed in that section, there are three circumstances in which sellers of residential property can be held liable for failing to disclose defects in the property. One of these is where the seller passively conceals a latent defect which could not have been discovered by the buyer upon a reasonable inspection of the property. Passive concealment occurs when the seller knows of a concealed material defect and does not attempt to hide the problem but simply keeps quiet and makes no disclosure of its existence.[1293]

To date, Georgia courts have applied the doctrine of passive concealment only to physical defects in a property. It has not, as yet, been extended to apply to the disclosure of adverse neighborhood conditions of which a seller is aware. The Brokerage Relationships in Real Estate Transactions Act ("BRRETA") sets forth the broker's duty to disclose defects and neighborhood conditions. (See § 19.3 (Duties Owed to Clients by Brokers) of this book for a more complete discussion of a broker's responsibilities under BRRETA.) The GAR Contracts put the burden on the buyer to investigate the neighborhood.

§ 9.12.1   Disclosure Of Neighborhood Conditions

Under both the GAR Contract and the GAR New Construction Purchase and Sale Agreement, buyers acknowledge that they are responsible to familiarize themselves with the conditions in the neighborhood in which the subject property lies.[1294] The inspection should cover any conditions existing or proposed in the neighborhood that could affect the property, including land-fills, quarries, high-voltage power lines, cemeteries, airports, prisons, crime, stadiums, odor and/or noise producing land uses, schools, political jurisdictional maps, etc. Specifically, the GAR Contract includes the following provision:

1287   15 U.S.C.A. § 1706.

1288   *Flint Ridge Development Co. v. Scenic Rivers Ass'n of Oklahoma*, 426 U.S.776 (1976).

1289   15 U.S.C.A. § 1707 and 1703(b).

1290   15 U.S.C.A. § 1707.

1291   15 U.S.C.A. § 1703(c).

1292   *Cendant Mobility Financial Corp. v. Asuamah*, 285 Ga. 818, 684 S.E.2d 617 (2009).

1293   *Worthey v. Holmes*, 249 Ga. 104, 287 S.E.2d 9 (1982); *Wilhite v. Mays*, 239 Ga. 31, 235 S.E.2d 532 (1977).

1294   GAR Forms F20 and 23.

> *In every neighborhood there are conditions which different buyers may find objectionable.*
> *Buyer shall have the sole duty to become familiar with neighborhood conditions that*
> *could affect the Property such as landfills, quarries, power lines, air ports, cemeteries,*
> *prisons, stadiums, odor and noise producing activities, crime and school, land use,*
> *government and transportation maps and plans.*

Some builder contracts for new construction go further than the GAR Contract in obligating the buyer to become familiar with neighborhood conditions. A sample of this type of provision is set forth below.

Special Stipulation 185:   Buyer to Become Familiar with Neighborhood Conditions

> *Buyer shall be responsible to become fully acquainted with neighborhood and other*
> *off-site conditions affecting the Property by (1) diligently inspecting and (2) reviewing*
> *all reasonably available governmental records, maps and documents (examples of which*
> *are set forth in the Brokerage Relationships in Real Estate Transactions Act ("BRRETA")*
> *O.C.G.A. § 10-6A-1, et seq.) relating to the surrounding neighborhood.*

The parties can also include a provision such as one or more of the samples below, which give the buyer the right to terminate the contract on the basis of the discovery of specified neighborhood conditions.

Special Stipulation 186:   Buyer's Right to Terminate Because of School District

> *Notwithstanding any other provision in this Agreement to the contrary, Buyer shall have*
> *the right to terminate this Agreement upon written notice to Seller within _____ days*
> *from the Binding Agreement Date if it is determined by Buyer that the children living in*
> *the Property would attend [NAME] Elementary School, [NAME] Middle School, and*
> *[NAME] High School.*

Special Stipulation 187:   Buyer's Right to Terminate Because of Rezoning

> *Notwithstanding any other provision in this Agreement to the contrary, Buyer shall have*
> *the right to terminate this Agreement upon written notice to Seller within _____ days*
> *from the Binding Agreement Date if Buyer determines that the Property is within 300*
> *feet of any other property subject to a rezoning application to a more intensive land use*
> *which was filed prior to the Binding Agreement Date.*

Special Stipulation 188:   Buyer's Right to Terminate Because of Political Jurisdiction

> *Notwithstanding any other provision in this Agreement to the contrary, Buyer shall have*
> *the right to terminate this Agreement upon written notice to Seller within _____ days*
> *from the Binding Agreement Date if it is determined by Buyer that the Property is not*
> *located within the incorporated city limits of _____.*

Buyers should also ensure that the property they are planning to purchase does not contain any violations of any subdivision or condominium covenant. Buyers may want to add the following stipulation to their contract to ensure that if a covenant violation is found, the seller will agree to repair, remove, or abate the violation prior to closing.

Special Stipulation 189: Seller's Obligation if Covenant Violation Discovered on Property

Buyer shall have _____ days from the Binding Agreement Date to determine if a violation of a neighborhood or subdivision covenant exists on the Property. If it is determined that such a violation exists, Buyer shall present Seller with written notice of such violation, which notice shall also include the steps Seller shall take to repair or remove said violation. Seller shall comply with Buyer's written notice and repair or abate the violation prior to closing.

Special Stipulation 190: Buyer's Right to Terminate Due to Violation of Neighborhood or Subdivision Covenants

Notwithstanding any other provision in this Agreement to the contrary, Buyer shall have the right to terminate this Agreement upon written notice to Seller within _____ days from the Binding Agreement Date if it is determined by Buyer that a violation of a neighborhood or subdivision covenant exists on or with respect to the Property (other than which violation can be cured by the Seller at or before closing through the payment of money.)

§ 9.12.2 Presence Of A Registered Sex Offender Or Drug Laboratory In Neighborhood

There is no affirmative duty placed on homeowners or brokers to disclose whether a registered sex offender, a drug laboratory or dumpsite is located within the vicinity of the property for sale. Under both the GAR Purchase and Sale Agreement[1295] and GAR New Construction Purchase and Sale Agreement,[1296] a buyer has a duty to inspect the neighborhood for any objectionable conditions, including crime. Therefore, the buyer should research whether any registered sex offenders or reported drug laboratories or dumpsites are located near the property as part of their duty to inspect the neighborhood.

Georgia law requires all convicted sex offenders to register, among other things, their name, address and place of employment with the Georgia Bureau of Investigation and the county sheriff's office.[1297] Therefore, if a buyer is concerned about the possibility of registered sex offenders residing in a neighborhood in which the buyer is interested, the buyer should review the Georgia Violent Sex Offender Registry available on the Georgia Bureau of Investigation Website at www.gbi.georgia.gov.

Similarly, the U.S. Department of Justice provides a public website containing the locations where law enforcement agencies reported chemicals or other items that indicated the presence of either drug laboratories or dumpsites. This site contains the county, city and address of each reported drug lab or dumpsite. For example, if a law enforcement agency discovered that a property was used as a methamphetamine laboratory, the address of the property would be listed on this website. However, the department does not confirm the accuracy of these reports. Concerned buyers must verify the accuracy of the reported drug lab or dumpsite with the local law enforcement or health departments.

If the buyer is concerned about potential drug labs or dumpsites located within a neighborhood in which the buyer is interested, the buyer should review the reported locations available on the United States Drug Enforcement Administration Website at http://www.justice.gov/dea/seizures/index.html.

1295   GAR Form F20.

1296   GAR Form F23.

1297   O.C.G.A. § 42-1-12(e).

§ 9.13 GEORGIA'S STIGMATIZED PROPERTY STATUTE

Sometimes a property is "stigmatized" by the existence of various adverse circumstances which may affect a buyer's interest in a property, such as the occurrence of a murder or other violent crime, the suicide of a former occupant, or perhaps an infectious illness of a former occupant. Georgia has enacted a statute which protects sellers, brokers and licensees from any liability for failure to disclose certain facts about a property unless they are specifically asked about them. These include informing prospective buyers if the property was (a) the site of a homicide or other felony; (b) the site of a suicide; (c) the site of a death by other accidental or natural causes; or (d) occupied by a person who was infected with a virus or any other disease which has been determined by medical evidence as being highly unlikely to be transmitted through the occupancy of a dwelling place presently or previously occupied by such an infected person.[1298] Section (d) was included in the stigmatized property disclosure law at a time when there was fear that AIDS was potentially contagious through means other than the exchange of bodily fluids. Persons with AIDS are now considered disabled under the Fair Housing Act Amendments of 1988[1299] and thus it would be unlawful to inquire whether a person with AIDS resided in the property.

Note that if the seller, broker or licensee is asked specifically whether any of these conditions apply to a specific property, they are obligated to answer the questions truthfully to the best of that person's knowledge. However, the stigmatized property disclosure law provides that the broker is not required to answer any question if answering such question violates any federal or state law, including but not limited to the federal Fair Housing Act, or the state's fair housing laws set forth in O.C.G.A. §8-3-200 – §8-3-223.[1300] Therefore, if a listing broker were asked whether someone with AIDS resided in the property, the best answer would be to tell the person that asking such a question violates the Fair Housing Act[1301] and that the broker will not answer the question. See § 19.3 (Duties Owed to Clients by Brokers) of this work for a more complete discussion of the broker's responsibilities under the Brokerage Relationships in Real Estate Act.

§ 9.14 BUILDER DISCLOSURES FOR NEW CONSTRUCTION CONTRACT

An effective way for builders and developers to limit potential legal liability is to include disclaimers in their sales contracts. When a buyer is specifically told about a condition relating to the property, it is difficult for the buyer to then argue that she did not know about the condition or that the builder fraudulently concealed the condition.

In addition to the disclosures mentioned above and those already provided in the GAR New Construction Purchase and Sale Agreement, a builder may also want to consider including some or all of the following disclosures. While some of these disclosures may strike the reader as stating the obvious, each of the following was written in response to a claim asserted by a home buyer.

§ 9.14.1 Subdivision/Neighborhood Disclosures

(1) Buyer consents to the Seller changing, in its sole discretion, the subdivision name and the street names and addresses in the subdivision including the street address of the Property before or after closing.

(2) Buyer acknowledges that the sizes, architectural styles and prices of any future homes constructed in the subdivision may be significantly different than what will be or has been constructed on the Property.

(3) Buyer acknowledges that the construction of other homes and improvements in the area may create noise, odors, smoke and debris and agrees that none of these activities shall be considered to be a nuisance.

1298   O.C.G.A. § 44-1-16.

1299   42 U.S.C.A. § 3602.

1300   O.C.G.A. § 44-1-16(a)(2).

1301   *Support Ministries for Persons with AIDS, Inc. v. Village of Waterford, N.Y.*, 808 F.Supp. 120 (N.D. New York 1992).

(4) Buyer acknowledges that the Property is or will be subject to recorded protective covenants ("Covenants"), that Buyer has received a copy of the Covenants or substantially similar covenants, and that Buyer and the property shall be bound by the Covenants. Buyer agrees that Buyer has read and fully understands the Covenants, and that Buyer is fully and solely responsible for compliance with the Covenants. Furthermore, Buyer acknowledges that only Buyer, and not the developer, builder or sales agent, is fully responsible for Buyer's and the Property's adherence to the Covenants as they apply to both new construction on the Property and any exterior or other changes to the home and the Property after construction.

(5) Buyer acknowledges that current development plans for the neighborhood are subject to change without notice and no guarantees are made that any of the components presently proposed will be a part of the neighborhood, or that additional components will not be added to the neighborhood. If some or all of such components are provided, no guarantees are made as to the date of availability for use or that current plans will accurately reflect actual construction or location of such components.

§ 9.14.2 Environmental Disclosures

(1) Radon, Carbon Dioxide and Other Contaminates. The grading of the soil and other elements created by nature, as well as building materials developed by man, many times create unwanted and undesired gases and other contaminates in homes and residential buildings, both new and used. Also, since energy conservation has become a concern, there is a need to build homes and residential buildings that are more airtight. As a result, these homes and residential buildings trap unwanted gases in different degrees depending on how each person lives within their home or such residential building. To date, measurements of such unwanted gases are reported as parts of the air they occupy. Since the quality of air we breathe can affect our health, Seller recommends frequent airing of Buyer's home by simply opening windows to introduce fresh air uncontaminated with such gases.

(2) Mold and/or mildew can grow in any portion of the home that is exposed to elevated levels of moisture. Buyer acknowledges and agrees that it is necessary for Buyer to provide appropriate climate control in the home, keep the home clean, and take other measures to retard and prevent mold and mildew from accumulating in the home. Buyer agrees to clean and dust the home on a regular basis and to remove visible moisture accumulation, mold or mildew on windows, walls and other surfaces as soon as reasonably possible. Buyer agrees not to block or cover any of the heating, ventilation or air-conditioning ducts in the home.

(3) Buyer acknowledges that the home may contain toxic mold. Molds are a type of fungus. More than 1,000 different species have been found in the United States. Most molds are not harmful; however, over 100 mold species are believed to potentially cause infection in humans. In addition, several types of molds are considered by some to be "toxic," which means that they can produce toxic agents (metabolites) called mycotoxins, which may cause serious health problems. Seller is not an expert with regard to mold or the health effects of mold exposure. Accordingly, it is the sole responsibility of Buyer to retain appropriate professionals to inspect any property that the Buyer may purchase to determine the presence of any toxic mold.

(4) All power lines and electrical appliances that draw electric current have electromagnetic fields ("EMFs") around them. There are various types of studies currently being conducted by researchers to determine whether or not there are health risks associated with EMFs. The electric utility industry and local power companies monitor those research activities and work with their customers to explain what EMFs are and how people can find out more about them. Seller has no expertise regarding EMFs. As a result, Seller does not make representations or warranties of any kind, express or implied, or provide information about the presence or effect of EMFs on or in proximity to the Property. The local electric company servicing the property, the state or the local environmental, energy or health agencies, or the regional office of the EPA may provide such information about EMFs.

(5) All parties to this Agreement acknowledge that various substances used in the construction of the improvements on the Property or otherwise located on the property may now or in the future be determined to be toxic or hazardous and may need to be specially treated, handled and/or removed from the Property. Persons who have an interest in the Property may be required by law to undertake the cleanup of such substances. Buyer acknowledges (1) that Seller and Brokers have no expertise with respect to toxic wastes or hazardous substances; (2) that such substances can be extremely costly to correct and remove; (3) that Seller and Brokers have made no investigations or representations with respect to such substances; (4) that Seller and Brokers shall have no liability to Buyer regarding the presence of such substances on the Property; and (5) Buyer releases Seller and Brokers from any claim, rights of action or suits relating to the presence of such substances on the Property to the fullest extent permitted by law.

§ 9.14.3   Disclosures Related To The Home

(1) Buyer acknowledges that Seller may substitute construction materials, appliances, equipment and fixtures from those specified in the plans and construction specifications in Seller's reasonable discretion, provided that the substitutions are of equal or better quality materials, appliances, equipment and fixtures than those originally specified and provided. Buyer agrees that industry standards, as determined in the reasonable exercise of Seller's discretion, shall govern the acceptability of any particular variance. The variations, substitutions and deviations referenced above shall not be the basis of any claim by Buyer against Seller nor shall it be a basis for Buyer not to accept the Property or otherwise not fulfill Buyer's obligations under this Agreement.

(2) Buyer hereby acknowledges and agrees that any floor plans, advertising materials, brochures, renderings, drawings, and the like, furnished by Seller to Buyer which purport to depict the home to be constructed or any portion thereof, are merely approximations and do not necessarily reflect the actual as-built conditions of the same. Due to the unique nature of the construction process and site conditions, room dimensions, size and elevations may vary from home to home. Seller makes no representation as to the location of mailboxes, utility boxes, street lights, fire hydrants or storm drain inlets or basins. Buyer further acknowledges and agrees that the decorations, furniture, furnishings, wallpaper, appliances, fixtures, floor coverings and window treatments, landscaping, displays and promotional materials, and the like, contained in any model home are for marketing and demonstrative purposes only, and are not included in the Property which is the subject of this Agreement.

(3) Buyer acknowledges that the performance and methods and practices of operating heating and cooling systems can be directly affected by the orientation and location of a room or home in relation to the sun. Seller shall, therefore, have no obligation other than to install a heating and cooling system at the Property which has been sized and designed based on industry standards for the type and size of home to be constructed and which functions in accordance with industry standards.

(4) Condensation may appear on the interior portions of windows and glass surfaces, and fogging of windows and glass surfaces may occur due to temperature disparities between the interior and exterior portions of the windows and glass.

(5) Buyer acknowledges that small amounts of water may pond on sidewalks, driveways, patios and balconies.

(6) The cost of upgrades may not necessarily result in a commensurate increase in the value of the Property.

(7) No representations are made that any room, wall, ceiling or floor in any dwelling on the Property or any pipes located therein will be soundproof.

(8) No representations are made that the systems in the Property including, by way of example only, heating and air conditioning and electrical systems, will operate or perform at a level or standard greater than the minimum specifications of the manufacturer.

(9) Any alarm systems installed in the home shall only be installed on all first floor operable windows (lower windows only) and doors, including basement level windows (lower windows only) and doors.

(10) Lumber contains moisture when installed and will dry, shrink and settle after installation. As a result, nails pop from drywall locations, baseboards may move slightly and exposed wood may striate or crack. Doors made of wood may shrink, swell or warp. Swelling may affect the way a door fits in an opening and it may cause sticking. In some instances paint and/or drywall seams may slightly crack. These conditions are normal incidents of home ownership unless they occur in the extreme.

(11) Buyer is aware that certain materials used for fixtures in a new home (including, but not limited to, brass/chrome plumbing fixtures, brass/chrome bathroom accessories and brass/chrome light fixtures) are subject to discoloration and/or corrosion over time.

(12) Natural wood has considerable color variation due to its organic nature. There may be shades of white, red, black or even green in areas. In addition, mineral streaks may also be visible. Grain pattern or texture will vary from consistent to completely irregular; wood from different areas of the same tree can also have variations in pattern or texture. It is because of these variations that wood is in such high demand of aesthetic products. These variations in grain will in turn accept stain in varying amounts, which will show throughout the wood products from one door to the next, one panel to the next or one piece of wood to the next. Also, cabinet finishes (including gloss and/or matte finishes) will not be entirely consistent and some minor irregularities will be apparent. Additionally, wood and wood products may be subject to warping, splitting, swelling and/or delamination.

(13) Marble and granite are natural pieces of stone. Marble and granite veins and colors may vary drastically from piece to piece and are all different. Marble and granite also have chips and shattering veins which look like scratches. The thickness of the joints between marble, granite or other materials against which they have been laid will vary and there will be irregularities in surface smoothness. Marble and other stone finishes may be dangerously slippery and Seller assumes no responsibility for injuries sustained as a result of exposure to or use of such materials. Periodic use of professionally approved and applied sealant is needed to ensure proper maintenance of the marble and granite, and it is the Buyer's responsibility to properly maintain these materials. Marble, granite and other stone surfaces may scratch, chip or stain easily. Such substrates, as part of their desirable noise attenuating properties, may flex or move slightly in order to absorb impacts. Such movement may in turn cause grout to crack or loosen or cause some cracking in the stone flooring which may need to be repaired as part of normal home maintenance.

(14) Buyer is aware that it is impossible to avoid a certain amount of cracking in stucco and other cementitious materials. Cracks in Stucco, GFRC, GFRG and concrete, including, but not limited to, floors, foundations and building envelope, are to be expected due to normal curing, hot and cold weather, and general stress from movement. Stucco, GFRC and GFRG, like concrete, are cement-based products and are subject to cracking due to, among other reasons, settlement, lumber shrinkage and weather conditions. Cracking is customary at the corners of windows and doors. Concrete floors may not be perfectly flat when poured and some sloping and pooling are common.

§ 9.14.4 Disclosures Related To The Lot

(1) Since trees and landscaping existing on the Property prior to the commencement of construction thereon may be adversely affected or even killed by construction activities, Seller shall have no responsibility for the same. In particular, Buyer acknowledges that the underground root system of a tree often extends as much as its canopy and that the viability of the tree can be affected when the root system, or a particular portion thereof, is damaged through construction activities.

(2) While the drainage system for surface water runoff on the Property will be constructed in accordance with applicable governmental standards, the Property may still be subject to erosion and/or flooding during unusually intense or prolonged periods of rain.

§ 9.14.5 View Disclosures

(1) Future development and construction activities in the Community can and will modify the view from the property (including but not limited to the Property). Trees and other foliage may be added or removed from Lots or common areas of the community. Additional housing, high-rise buildings and other improvements will be added within the community. Because future development and construction activities in the community will modify views from the property, Seller does not warrant or guarantee any existing views will be maintained in the future relative to the property.

§ 9.14.6 Miscellaneous Disclosures

(1) Buyer acknowledges that the Property is located adjacent or near thoroughfares which may be improved or widened in the future and in an area where additional transportation improvements may be made.

(2) Buyer acknowledges that no representations are made regarding the zoning or use of adjacent property, or which schools now or in the future may serve the Property.

(3) Buyer hereby grants Seller the right to obtain and use photography of the Property for publication and advertising purposes.

(4) Buyer acknowledges that the views from the Property may change from time due to, among other things, additional development and the removal or addition of landscaping.

(5) Seller has no control over the installation and energizing of streetlights. Streetlights may not be in operation prior to Buyer's move in.

§ 9.15 USE OF BROCHURES TO LIMIT LIABILITY

Two of the most important forms in the GAR forms package are the Protect Yourself When Buying a Home[1302] brochure and the Protect Yourself When Selling A Home[1303] brochure. Both brochures provide useful information to the buyer and seller during the home buying and selling process. In addition, brochures that are incorporated into the purchase and sale agreement often prevent claims by a party against a REALTOR®.

§ 9.15.1 Protection Brochure For Buyers

The GAR Protect Yourself When Buying a Home[1304] brochure outlines reasonable steps all buyers should take to protect themselves when buying a home.

Overall, this brochure contains basic information that will protect buyers in the home buying process, as well as a series of recommendations when buying a home. The recommendations include: get a home inspection; get a termite inspection; familiarize yourself with the neighborhood; get a survey; buy title insurance; get a home warranty; read the purchase and sale agreement; and hire a REALTOR®. If a buyer follows all the steps in the brochure, she is less likely to miss a material defect in the property or overlook an adverse fact that may have affected the buyer's decision to purchase the property in the first place.

1302   GAR Form F13.

1303   GAR Form F16.

1304   GAR Form F13.

In addition, the brochure should also help protect real estate licensees against legal claims. The new GAR Purchase and Sale Agreement provides a checkbox in which buyers are asked to check whether or not they have received this brochure. If the buyer acknowledges receipt of the brochure, it is incorporated by reference into the purchase and sale agreement. On occasion, problems will arise in a real estate transaction because buyers have not, for example, obtained a survey, a home inspection or followed other advice in the brochure. If buyers try to blame their real estate licensee for not advising them with sound basic advice, licensees have a defense that they did not previously have. Specifically, they will now be able to say that they gave the buyer a brochure telling them the things they should do in the home buying process. The fact that the brochure is incorporated by reference into the agreement essentially makes the advice contained therein a part of the sales agreement.

§ 9.15.2 Protection Brochure For Sellers

Similarly, the GAR Protect Yourself When Selling A House[1305] brochure was created to help sellers through the process of selling a home.

This brochure contains the reasonable steps necessary for sellers to protect themselves through this process. Some of the steps include: guidelines for setting the sales price; disclosure obligations and use of the GAR Seller's Property Disclosure Statement exhibit[1306]; preparing the property for showing; reading the purchase and sale agreement; compliance with fair housing laws; and understanding the obligations to convey title to the property. The brochure also recommends that sellers chose a REALTOR® before beginning the house selling process. Sellers are encouraged to consult with experts of their own choosing to ensure they are protected when selling a house. Obtaining a REALTOR® can provide sellers with the names of attorneys, home inspectors, termite companies and persons providing other services relating to real estate transactions. Overall, if a seller follows the advice in the brochure, the seller is less likely to encounter problems in a real estate transaction.

This brochure is not specifically incorporated by reference in the GAR Purchase and Sale Agreement.[1307] The GAR Purchase and Sale Agreement provides a section at the back of the agreement where sellers may incorporate this brochure by reference as an exhibit. Once the brochure is incorporated, the advice therein becomes part of the purchase and sale agreement. Ultimately, the incorporation of this brochure will protect a real estate licensee from liability if the seller claims the real estate licensee failed to give certain advice. However, it is also sufficient if the seller acknowledges in some other way that she has received the brochure.

Unfortunately, a brochure is something of a double-edged sword. It offers great protection if it is given by the real estate licensee to all buyers and sellers. However, giving brochures will likely become a new standard in the industry that all licensees will quickly be expected to follow. Therefore, over time, there could be potential exposure to a licensee if they fail to provide buyers or sellers with the brochure. The best solution is to give buyers and sellers the brochure as a standard practice for all real estate licensees to follow.

1305   GAR Form F16.

1306   GAR Form F50.

1307   GAR Form F20.

CONSTRUCTION AND REPAIR ISSUES

OVERVIEW

Caveat emptor, or buyer beware, is still the law in Georgia.[1308] Buyers are expected to use ordinary and reasonable care to protect themselves when purchasing real estate. The best way for buyers to do this is to thoroughly inspect and evaluate any property they are considering buying. Most inspections take place after the property is put under contract with provisions included in the contract that the buyer can terminate for any reason whatsoever during a Due Diligence Period or inspection period.

In Georgia, inspection and repair issues are normally handled in one of three ways. The most common is for the buyer to have a Due Diligence Period during which the buyer can inspect the property for any condition of concern, request the repair of such conditions, and terminate the contract if the buyer is not satisfied with the condition of the property or with the seller's willingness to make repairs. The second is an "as is" provision where the buyer accepts the property in its present condition. The third is a limited right to inspect for and request the repair of defects. This last approach was for many years the primary method of addressing concerns arising out of inspections in the GAR Contracts. However, it eventually fell out of favor due to the large number of disputes arising out of whether a particular condition constituted a defect.

This chapter discusses the inspection issues generally addressed during a Due Diligence Period, including inspections for termites, lead-based paint, radon or asbestos or other environmental hazards, and the inspection of the neighborhood in which the property is located. Commonly asked questions, including who may inspect, and when, how and for what they may inspect, will be addressed. The mechanics of the inspection, the procedures for the negotiation and repair of defects, how to deal with a bad inspection report, making mistakes in completing the time periods in the inspection section of a contract, and inspecting seasonally-difficult items (such as swimming pools in the winter) are also discussed.

Numerous sample special stipulations are provided largely to give the buyer alternatives to the inspection approach set forth in the GAR Contract. Finally, hazardous conditions such as radon and lead-based paint are addressed in detail, including the specifics of the Georgia Lead Poisoning Prevention Act of 1994[1309] and the Childhood Lead Exposure Control Act.[1310]

In addition, while mortgage lenders rarely require the buyer to obtain an Official Georgia Wood Infestation Report (typically referred to as a "termite letter") covering a property prior to closing, it is strongly recommended that buyers do so. Termites are very active in Georgia and it is common for older houses to have some termite damage. In most cases, termite damage will not be a basis to cancel a purchase and sale agreement unless it is severe. However, since termite damage is often hidden from view or can be easily missed, buyers are encouraged to have a termite inspection by a qualified Georgia pest control operator to avoid what can otherwise be expensive surprises. This chapter will discuss various issues regarding the termite letter and how both buyers and sellers can protect themselves from legal issues in this arena.

§ 10.1 INSPECTION ISSUES

The inspection provision of the GAR Contracts give the buyer and/or buyer's representatives the right to inspect, examine, test, and survey the property at the buyer's expense. This inspection right also extends to all appliances and equipment remaining with the property. The inspection provision allows the buyer access to the property (including prior to closing) to confirm that fixtures have not been removed and all agreed upon repairs have been completed. The GAR Contracts now include a Due Diligence Period and provide that once the Due Diligence Period has expired,

1308 *Swiedler v. Ferguson*, 195 Ga.App. 364, 393 S.E.2d 456 (1990).

1309 O.C.G.A. § 31-41-1.

1310 O.C.G.A. § 32-41-10.

the buyer agrees to take the property in "as is" condition. If the seller is unwilling to give the buyer a Due Diligence Period, the length of the Due Diligence Period would simply be filled in with a zero (0).

§ 10.1.1 Buyer's Right To Inspect Generally

The GAR Contract gives the buyer the right to enter and to thoroughly inspect, examine, test, and survey the property. This right exists regardless of whether the property is being sold "as is," subject to a Due Diligence Period, with a right to request repair of defects. The right to inspect has to be exercised at reasonable times, and exists up to the time of closing. It also includes the right to inspect and test for lead-based paint and lead-based paint hazards for not less than ten days from the Binding Agreement Date. All such inspections are at the buyer's expense. The seller must ensure that all utility services and any pool, spa, and similar items are operational so that the buyer may complete all inspections. The buyer agrees to hold the seller and all brokers harmless from all claims, injuries, and damages arising out of or related to the exercise of these inspection rights. This means, for example, that if the buyer's inspector damages the property as part of inspecting it, the buyer would need to pay for the damages caused by the inspector.

If the buyer or buyer's inspector is injured on the property as the result of owner's failure to exercise ordinary care in keeping the property safe, the owner is liable in damages to the inspector for such injury and the indemnification provision will not shield the seller from liability.[1311] So, for example a seller is aware of a broken step leading to the basement. The stairwell is dark and it is hard to see the broken step. The owner knows about the perilous condition of the staircase but does not warn the inspector, who unfortunately falls on the broken stairs and is injured. Even though the buyer has agreed to indemnify the seller for all claims and injuries arising out of the buyer's inspection of the property, this obligation would likely not apply where the seller breached his duty to take ordinary care in keeping the premises safe for invitees.

An owner is only liable if she knew about a condition that may expose the invitees to a reasonable risk of harm and the invitee did not have such knowledge.[1312] For example, in one case, a meat inspector who slipped and fell on the floor of a break room provided by law for the exclusive use of meat inspectors could not claim for his injury because he was generally familiar with the break room by his "daily use" and had equal, if not superior, knowledge of the slippery condition of floor.[1313]

The right to inspect immediately prior to closing clearly gives the buyer the right to do a "walk-through" inspection prior to closing to confirm that repairs have been made in a good and workmanlike manner, to confirm that there have been no changes to the condition of the property, and to confirm that no fixtures have been improperly removed.

While the issue of what constitutes "reasonable times" to inspect has not been decided by the courts, it would likely be interpreted broadly to allow the buyer ample opportunity to visit the property. For example, if the buyer had conducted a very thorough inspection of the basement during dry weather but then wanted to return to the property during rainy weather to check for moisture in the basement, such an inspection would clearly be permissible. Similarly, it would generally be permissible if the buyer wanted to measure the property for the placement of furniture, measure the windows for window treatments, bring in contractors to give estimates for possible renovations or show the property to the parents of the buyer.

If the seller is concerned about loss of privacy resulting from giving the buyer a right to inspect, the seller may want to limit the right to inspect to specific days and hours. The following special stipulation is an example of such a limitation.

1311   O.C.G.A. § 51-3-1, § 51-3-2.

1312   *Kitchens v. Keadle Lumber Enterprises, Inc.*, 249 Ga.App. 831, 549 S.E.2d 781 (2001).

1313   *Pierce v. Fieldale Corp.*, 194 Ga.App. 303, 390 S.E.2d 298 (1990).

Special Stipulation 191:   Limiting the Time to Inspect

Notwithstanding any other provision in this Agreement to the contrary, Buyer and Buyer's representatives shall have no right to inspect, test, survey or otherwise enter or come onto the Property for any other purpose during the following times: (1) on Sundays; (2) on weekdays and Saturdays after 8:00 p.m. or before 8:00 a.m.; and (3) at any time without 24-hour advance notice to Seller.

§ 10.1.2 Buyer's Duty To Inspect

The buyer not only has a right to inspect the property, but under the doctrine of *caveat emptor*, or "buyer beware," also owes a duty to inspect. Under Georgia law, this means that the buyer is assumed to know about defects that are obvious and patent. In other words, the buyer is expected to make his own examination and draw his own conclusions as to the condition of the property.[1314] There is no confidential or fiduciary relationship between a buyer and seller simply because they are parties to a real estate transaction.

As part of the buyer's due diligence, the buyer should determine who resides at the property. If any resident is not a party to the contract, the buyer should inquire of all such persons (such as a tenant) what right or claim they have to the possession of the property.[1315] The buyer is charged with notice under the law of how such persons would have replied to the buyer's questions, even if the buyer never fulfills his obligation to speak with them.[1316]

A buyer should also carefully inspect the property for defects. The following cases illustrate the importance that the law places on the buyer carrying out independent investigation as to the condition of the property. In the first case, buyers sued the sellers for fraudulently concealing the presence of synthetic stucco trim in the property.[1317] The sellers had informed the buyers in the Property Disclosure Statement that the property contained untreated stucco cladding. The sellers also gave the buyers a letter from a stucco inspector which referenced a 1997 inspection. While the letter stated that the stucco was in good condition, the 1997 inspection indicated that there was synthetic stucco trimming. However, the buyers did not request for a copy of the 1997 inspection report, nor did they conduct a separate stucco inspection. The court stated that the underlying principle of law is that the buyer cannot claim that he has been deceived by false misrepresentations about defects that the buyer could have discovered. This case shows that the law requires that buyers exercise diligence before consummating a real estate contract, and courts will not give buyers relief when the buyer could have discovered by inspection the truth or falsity of a representation made by a seller or an agent. In other words, where a buyer could have learned the truth and avoided later damages, the law will not permit the buyer to claim he had been deceived by false misrepresentations.

In another case, the buyers of a house sued the seller for breach of contract and fraud because of problems with the sewage system the buyers discovered after moving into the house.[1318] The buyers claimed that the seller assured them that "the property was in reasonably satisfactory condition" and did not mention any problems with the sewage system. The contract expressly called for the buyer's prior inspection of the sewage and plumbing system, and although the buyers inspected portions of the property, the evidence was unclear as to how comprehensively they inspected it. Once the buyers moved into the house they discovered that the sewage "backed up" or "percolated" in the plumbing system.

1314   *Duval v. Kidder*, 191 Ga.App. 856, 383 S.E.2d 356 (1989); *Westbrook v. Beusse*, 79 Ga.App. 654, 54 S.E.2d 693 (1949), *cert. denied*.

1315   *Pierce v. Thomas*, 258 Ga. 469, 369 S.E.2d 742 (1988).

1316   *Yancey v. Montgomery & Young*, 173 Ga. 178, 159 S.E. 571 (1931).

1317   *Meyer v. Waite*, 270 Ga.App. 255, 606 S.E.2d 16 (2004).

1318   *Duval v. Kidder*, 191 Ga.App. 856, 383 S.E.2d 356 (1989).

The court found that the seller was not responsible for the malfunctions of the sewage system. First, the seller was not liable for breach of contract because it was the buyers who failed to fulfill their contractual obligation to inspect the sewage and plumbing system. The court further held that the seller was not responsible for fraud even if the seller represented that she had no problem with the sewage system. The buyers did not show any evidence that the seller had problems with the sewage system prior to the sale or that she should have discovered any problems.

The court found no reason why the buyers could not have discovered the problems with the sewage system "by simple observation upon a prudent inspection." Thus, the court held that even if the seller had misrepresented the facts, she was not liable for the sewage problems because the buyers: (1) failed to show that they were justified in relying on her representations, (2) that they exercised reasonable diligence required of everyone to discover misrepresentations, and (3) that they complied with their own duty to inspect or were excused from this duty for some reason.

§ 10.1.2.1   Duty To Investigate Further

If the discovery of a condition would cause a reasonably prudent buyer to investigate further, the buyer is under an obligation to investigate further. For example, if a buyer views a property and notices a large stain on the ceiling, the buyer should investigate the source of that stain to determine the cause of the stain. If the buyer does no such investigation and later determines that it was caused by a leaking roof, the buyer will likely have no recourse against the seller because the defect was in plain sight and a reasonably prudent buyer upon seeing the condition would have investigated further.[1319]

§ 10.1.2.2   Invasive Testing

The GAR Contract permits buyers to perform invasive testing on the property. Specifically, the GAR Contract would allow testing for lead-based paint, which may involve drilling holes in walls and removing paint samples from various rooms. Similarly, a buyer may remove some pieces of siding or synthetic stucco to check for rotten wood and structural damage, or even to open a sheetrock wall to see if termites may have damaged a wooden support joist.

Although the GAR Contract requires the buyer to repair any damage caused by his tests, the seller may want to address this issue in a special stipulation by requiring the buyer to post money, held by one of the brokers, to cover the cost of repairing any damage to the property caused by any invasive testing. The following special stipulation can be used in such a situation.

> **Special Stipulation 192:   Buyer Posting Funds with Listing Broker for Repairs Caused by Seller's Invasive Testing**
>
> *Should Buyer or Buyer's representatives desire to perform any invasive tests or inspections to the Property that involve the removal of siding, stucco, or paint or the drilling, boring, or sampling of the physical dwelling or soil, then Buyer shall notify Seller in writing of the exact nature and extent of the tests to be performed not less than three days in advance of said tests and shall post a sum of money with listing broker as set forth below to insure that the Property is repaired or restored to its original condition.*
>
> *Buyer shall provide Seller with a written estimate from a contractor to repair the Property according to the type and nature of tests and shall post one and one-half times the amount of the repair estimate with the listing broker. Listing broker shall be entitled to disburse said funds to repair all damage done by invasive testing and to refund any excess to Buyer. All decisions of listing broker with respect to repairing damage caused by invasive testing shall be final and binding upon all parties, and no claims shall be asserted against listing broker for any decisions made hereunder in good faith.*

1319   *Brown v. Rowe*, 178 Ga.App. 575, 344 S.E.2d 245 (1980).

§ 10.1.3   Home Inspection Report

The home inspector's report should describe the scope of the inspection, including both what was inspected and how it was inspected. Many professional home inspectors use standard checklists in conducting an inspection prepared by trade associations, such as the American Society of Home Inspectors. It is important to focus on the scope of the inspection so that buyers can decide what, if any, additional testing and evaluations should be done.

No assumption should be made that a professional home inspector's report is so comprehensive that no additional testing is needed. For example, a professional home inspector cannot inspect for termite infestation unless she is also a licensed Georgia Pest Control Operator. Therefore, most buyers will also have a separate termite inspection of the property. Similarly, many home inspectors will not inspect a swimming pool, so a separate inspection for this is often necessary. Some home inspectors focus on the energy efficiency of a home while others do not. A thorough inspection of a residential property by a professional home inspector will generally include an evaluation of all of the major systems and components in the residence, including the roof, gutters, whether rain water flows away from the house, the exterior surface of the residence, the windows and doors, garage, crawl space, the building structure, any fireplaces, and the electrical, plumbing, heating and cooling systems serving the property.

The report should identify any defects noted during the inspection. Defects in or with the property that are indicated in the report should be reviewed and discussed with the inspector so that a decision can be made on whether and what additional testing should be done and by whom. For example, if the home inspector has a question or concern about a structural condition on the property, the inspector may recommend a more thorough review of the condition by a structural engineer.

§ 10.1.3.1   Ownership And Disclosures Of Inspection Reports

In some cases, a seller will want to review all inspection reports prepared by the buyer's representatives. In other cases, particularly if the buyer is terminating the contract, the seller will not want to see any inspection reports. The theory behind this is that once the seller has knowledge of latent defects revealed in the report, the seller then has a duty to disclose these things to all future buyers. If the seller does not know about these things, the seller has no obligation to disclose.

The "tell me nothing" approach has its limitations. For example, a selling broker verbally tells the seller or the listing broker that the buyer is terminating the purchase and sale agreement because the inspector discovered that the roof supports are inadequate to hold the weight of a recently installed slate roof. In this instance, the listing broker would now be aware of the problem regardless of whether she received the inspector's report. As such, a disclosure obligation would thereafter exist with respect to the condition even though no written report was provided to the seller.

Some listing agents have argued that the inspection report belongs to the buyer who paid for the report and it is therefore not something that they as a representative of the seller have a right to give to subsequent buyers. Such reasoning is a quick path to a lawsuit and potentially to the loss of one's real estate license. This is because the disclosure obligation is created by the licensee's receipt of adverse material facts relating to the physical condition of the property. Once the licensee is aware of such facts, she thereafter has an affirmative duty to disclosure them. While there is no duty to provide a physical copy of the report, there is a duty to disclose the substance of the report.

If the seller does not want to receive any information regarding the property that may have been learned by a prospective buyer, the following special stipulation can be used.

> ### Special Stipulation 193:   Seller Not to Receive Buyer's Inspection Reports if Contract Terminated
>
> *In the event Buyer decides to terminate this Agreement for any reason whatsoever during the Due Diligence Period, Buyer agrees that neither Buyer nor Buyer's representatives shall provide Seller or Seller's representatives with any inspection reports, studies or*

*evaluations of the Property obtained by or for Buyer as part of the Buyer doing her due
diligence on the Property, nor will Buyer or Buyer's representative reveal the substance of
those reports, studies or evaluations to Seller or Seller's representatives.*

Of course, in many transactions, the seller will want to receive copies of all reports, studies and evaluations obtained by a buyer who elects not to proceed with the purchase of the property. There are two reasons for this. First, many sellers want to know if there is anything wrong with the property so that they can address areas of legitimate concern. The theory behind this approach is that most future inspectors will likely uncover the same problems with a property. Therefore, rather than postponing an inevitable discussion of how to address whatever problems may exist with the property, it is better to know about them early and go ahead and fix them.

Second, in many commercial transactions, the cost of studies, inspections, evaluations and surveys can be expensive. By obtaining this information from a buyer who elects not to proceed with the purchase of the property, it can save time and money for a subsequent purchaser. Sellers who want to receive such studies from a buyer who elect not to proceed with the purchase of the property can include the following special stipulation in their purchase and sale agreements.

Special Stipulation 194:   Buyer to Provide Seller with All Inspection Reports

*Notwithstanding any provision to the contrary contained herein, in the event Buyer elects
to terminate this Agreement for any reason whatsoever, Buyer shall immediately return
to Seller all copies of Due Diligence Materials provided by Seller to Buyer. In addition,
Buyer shall provide Seller with copies of all surveys, inspection reports, studies and
evaluations of the Property conducted by or for Buyer relative to the Property, including,
but not limited to, phase one environmental reports, marketing studies, engineering
reports and other construction evaluations.*

§ 10.1.3.2   Dealing With Bad Inspection Report

Sellers and listing brokers often inquire what their duty is to disclose a bad inspection report that has been provided to the seller (particularly one with which they disagree) to a subsequent prospective buyer. There is no statute or legislation governing the conduct of the seller in this instance. The listing broker must comply with the Brokerage Relationships in Real Estate Transactions Act ("BRRETA") as discussed below.[1320]

Georgia case law has long held that a seller has a duty to disclose defects in the property of which the seller knew or should have known and which would not have been observable by the buyer upon a reasonable inspection of the property.[1321] While a seller may not have a legal obligation to provide prospective buyers with prior inspection reports, the seller does owe a duty to reveal defects in the report which could not have been reasonably discovered by the buyer. The problem is that inspectors sometimes reach different conclusions regarding whether an item or condition is in fact a defect. Therefore, the risk to the seller is relying on the wrong inspector in deciding not to reveal disputed defects in an inspection report. If there are conflicting inspection reports or a disputed inspection report and the seller chooses not to disclose the defects in the report or reports, the seller may still be legally liable if a judge or jury later concludes that the defects could not otherwise have been reasonably discovered.

The listing broker may have a different obligation regarding disclosure. All real estate licensees in Georgia are required to comply with BRRETA, which also places certain duties of disclosure upon the seller's real estate agent. BRRETA requires agents of the seller to timely disclose all adverse material facts pertaining to the physical condition of the property and improvements located on the property which could not be discovered upon a reasonably diligent

---

1320   O.C.G.A. §§10-6A-1 - 10-6A-14.

1321   *Wilhite v. Mays*, 140 Ga.App. 816, 232 S.E.2d 141 (1976), aff'd, 239 Ga. 31, 235 S.E.2d 532 (1977); *Holmes v. Worthey*, 159 Ga.App. 262, 282 S.E.2d 919 (1981), aff'd, 249 Ga. 104, 287 S.E.2d 9 (1982).

inspection by the buyer.[1322] Listing brokers must timely disclose to all prospective buyers all material facts pertaining to existing adverse physical conditions in the immediate neighborhood within one mile of the property which are actually known to the broker and which could not be discovered by the buyer upon a diligent inspection.[1323]

The GAR Seller's Property Disclosure Statement[1324] includes the question, "Have there been any inspections of the Property in the past year?"[1325] Answering this question in the affirmative would not necessarily obligate the seller to provide prospective buyers with actual copies of the other inspection reports. Most buyers, however, will request the other inspection reports (if the seller indicates that other inspections have been performed) and not enter into a contract without first reviewing them.

In light of these legal requirements, the seller and the listing broker may take one of several courses of action in dealing with a bad inspection report. First, the seller can disclose the report to subsequent prospective buyers so that they cannot claim that latent defects were concealed from them. Under Georgia law, while hidden defects do not have to be repaired, they do have to be disclosed.

Second, the seller can fix all of the defects listed in the report.

Third, if the seller disputes the defects, the seller can hire another inspector and obtain a second report. The seller should then give both reports to a prospective buyer to minimize the negative impact of the first report. Obviously, this approach only makes sense if the second report contradicts the findings of the first.

Finally, if the bad inspection report was not prepared by an expert, the seller can hire an expert to refute the opinion of the first inspector. It is strongly recommended, however, that sellers and real estate brokers avoid providing buyers with only the expert's report. As discussed above, this is because if it turns out that the expert report is incorrect, the seller may be liable for fraud and the real estate broker may be found to have violated BRRETA.

BRRETA provides that a listing broker is not excused from his duties simply because the seller instructs him to perform in a manner that violates the law.[1326] Therefore, the listing broker must make an independent decision with respect to disclosure. BRRETA provides protection to the listing broker from liability to the seller if the listing broker discloses material adverse facts relating to the physical condition of the property even though the seller instructed him not to do so.[1327] If the listing broker and the seller cannot agree on what should be disclosed, the listing broker can either disclose to the buyer or can terminate his brokerage engagement with the seller.

§ 10.1.3.3 Only Latent Or Hidden Defects Need Be Disclosed By Seller

Georgia law only requires a seller to disclose latent, or hidden, defects. If the defect has been corrected such that it is no longer a defect, the seller arguably has no general duty under common law to disclose the fact that at one time the condition may have been defective. The leading case in this area is *Ainsworth v. Pererault*.[1328]

In that case, the property being sold had a swimming pool which had required major repairs the year before the sale took place. The sellers had completed the repairs and had no further problems with the pool during the intervening year, and did not disclose the past repairs to the buyers. The home inspector hired by the buyers concluded that the pool was in good condition prior to the closing. Several months after the closing the buyers learned from a landscape professional that the repairs had been done. Nearly two years after the closing, the buyers noticed that one corner of

---

1322   O.C.G.A. § 10-6A-5(b).

1323   O.C.G.A. § 10-6A-5(b).

1324   GAR Form F50, Seller's Property Disclosure Statement.

1325   GAR Form F50, Seller's Property Disclosure Statement.

1326   O.C.G.A. § 10-6A-5(b).

1327   O.C.G.A. § 10-6A-5(b).

1328   *Ainsworth v. Perreault*, 254 Ga.App. 470, 563 S.E.2d 135 (2002).

the pool was settling, and that a crack was developing in the pool. The buyers sued the sellers for fraud, claiming that the seller should have disclosed the previous repairs to the pool in the property disclosure statement on which buyers relied. The court held that "the law does not require sellers to disclose every past repair made to their homes; rather, they must inform potential buyers of current defects of which they are aware."[1329]

Of course, the disclosure of a condition that has been corrected eliminates the potential for a claim by an unhappy buyer who believes she should have been told about the condition.

§ 10.1.4 Duty To Hire A Professional Inspector

There is no legal duty for a buyer to hire a professional home inspector. However, the failure to retain a professional home inspector can be used as a defense against a purchaser who subsequently discovers damage to the property. The argument is that the buyer failed to exercise due diligence by not retaining a professional. The courts have not held that the failure to hire a professional inspector constitutes lack of due diligence as a matter of law, but have allowed that argument to be put to the jury.[1330]

§ 10.1.4.1 Seller Wants Buyer To Hire A Professional Home Inspector

Sometimes a seller is so unfamiliar with the condition of the property she makes a special disclosure of that fact and encourages the buyer to have the property professionally inspected. This may be the case where property is being sold by an estate, for example, where property has been used as a rental property for a significant period of time, or where the seller has only recently purchased the property. In such cases, encouraging the buyer to obtain a professional inspection is done in an effort to reduce the seller's exposure to a claim that the seller failed to disclose hidden defects that he knew, or should have known, about.

Obviously, if the seller discloses that her knowledge of the property is limited, the buyer will have a harder time providing that the seller should have known about the condition of the property to the same extent as if the seller had lived on the property for many years. Furthermore, by encouraging the buyer to have the property thoroughly inspected by a professional home inspector, the seller is putting the buyer on notice that she should scrutinize the property more carefully to ensure that nothing is missed.

A sample of this type of special stipulation is set forth below.

Special Stipulation 195:   Seller Not Familiar With Condition of Property

Buyer acknowledges that Seller is not as familiar with the condition of the Property as sellers of other properties might be because: [Check all which apply. The sections not checked shall not be a part of this Agreement.]'

_____ Seller has not resided on the Property

_____ Seller has used the Property as a rental property

_____ Seller has only owned the Property for a short period of time

Seller agrees to provide Buyer with a copy of the inspection reports Seller received when Seller purchased the Property no later than _____ days from the Binding Agreement Date.

Seller is not providing Buyer with a Seller's Property Disclosure Statement because of Seller's lack of familiarity with the condition of the Property. Seller makes no representations concerning the condition of the Property.

1329 *Id.*, p. 475.

1330 *Power v. Georgia Exterminators, Inc.*, 243 Ga.App. 355, 532 S.E.2d 475 (2000).

In light of Seller's lack of familiarity with the condition of the Property, Buyer agrees to accept the Property in "as is" condition.

While such a special stipulation should help protect the seller against claims, it does not relieve the seller from a duty to disclose latent defects of which the seller has knowledge.

§ 10.1.5   Inspection For And Damage From Termites And Other Pests

Under the GAR Contract and most form real estate contracts, the burden is on the buyer to inspect for termites and other wood destroying organisms. Most mortgage lenders no longer require the buyer to obtain an Official Georgia Wood Infestation Report as part of the buyer's due diligence of the property. However, termites are a major problem in Georgia and the authors strongly recommend that buyers always obtain such a report.

If the inspection reveals termite infestation or damage, the buyer can, depending on the terms of the contract, request that it be treated or repaired. So, for example, if the contract provides for a due diligence period, and termites are discovered, the buyer can seek to have the seller treat the property and repair any and all damage resulting from the inspection.

§ 10.1.5.1   Builder Contracts And Termites

Most new construction contracts, including the GAR New Construction Purchase and Sale Agreement[1331], includes a provision in which the builder discloses the type of system used to control termites and other wood destroying mechanisms. These include treating the soil for termites prior to constructing the improvements on the property, installing a termite baiting system, or using any other system meeting the standards of the Georgia Department of Agriculture to control termites. In the GAR New Construction Purchase and Sale Agreement, the builder is required to provide the buyer at closing with a letter or report from a licensed Georgia Pest Control Operator certifying that the property includes the agreed upon termite control system. Since the structures are new, the termites should not have had an opportunity to cause any damage.

§ 10.1.5.2   Limiting Seller's Obligation To Repair Termite Damage

If the seller agrees to be responsible for damage from termites or other wood-destroying organisms but wants to minimize this obligation, the following provision can be used.

> **Special Stipulation 196:   Seller Not Responsible to Repair Termite Damage**
>
> *Notwithstanding any other provision in this Agreement to the contrary, including Buyer's right to request repairs, Buyer may not request, and Seller shall not be obligated to make, any repairs of damage caused by termites and other wood-destroying organisms, the total cost of which exceed the sum of $_____. If Seller receives a written estimate from a third-party contractor that such repairs will exceed $_____, Seller shall immediately notify Buyer and provide Buyer with a copy of the estimate. Buyer shall have the right, within five (5) days from the delivery of such notice, to terminate this Agreement by written notice to Seller, in which case Buyer's earnest money shall be immediately refunded to Buyer. If Buyer elects not to terminate this Agreement Seller shall, in Buyer's sole discretion and upon notice from Buyer to Seller, either: (a) make the repairs up to the amount specified above prior to closing and provide written documentation to Buyer of the cost and nature of the repairs made by Seller for the above-specified sum, or (b) deduct the amount specified above from the purchase price with Buyer paying the balance at closing.*

1331   GAR Form F23.

Buyers should be mindful that most lenders, if they are aware that the property has structural damage from termites, will require such damage to be corrected prior to closing (except possibly where the loan already designates a portion of the loan proceeds to be used for the rehabilitation of the property). If the buyer is responsible for the repair of structural damage from termites, she may not be able to obtain approval for the loan or may be forced to repair the termite damage out of her own funds prior to closing.

§ 10.1.5.3   Seller To Provide Termite Report

In some cases, the buyer will request in the purchase contract that the seller provide an Official Georgia Wood Infestation Report to the buyer. The concern with this approach is that an unscrupulous seller might have a less than reputable licensed Georgia Pest Control Operator who may not conduct a thorough inspection. This risk is mitigated if the pest control operator is known and identified. Examples of such special stipulations are set forth below.

> **Special Stipulation 197:   Seller to Provide Termite Report by Closing**
>
> *Notwithstanding any provision to the contrary contained herein, Seller shall be responsible at Seller's expense to provide Buyer with an Official Georgia Wood Infestation Report ("Report") on the Property prepared by a licensed Georgia pest control operator which already is under contract with the Seller for termite control services under an assumable termite inspection and repairs bond. The Report shall confirm that the Property is free and clear of any evidence of active infestation by termites or other wood-destroying organisms. The Report shall be dated within 30 days of the date of the Closing. If any treatment or repairs are needed in order to obtain the Report, the same shall be the responsibility of Seller.*

§ 10.1.5.4   Broadening Seller's Obligation To Repair Termite Damage

Buyers may broaden the scope of the seller's repair obligations to include all improvements on the property by including a special stipulation such as the one following.

> **Special Stipulation 198:   Seller Responsible for Structural Termite Damage**
>
> *Notwithstanding any other provision in this Agreement to the contrary, Seller shall be obligated to correct all structural damage resulting from termites and other wood-destroying organisms and shall provide documentation at closing to the Buyer of the treatment of the infestation and the correction of all structural damage for the following improvements on the Property: [Examples: decks, fences, gazebos, outbuildings, carports, playhouses, trash enclosures, sheds, etc.]*

§ 10.1.5.5   Buyer Obtaining Termite Inspection And Report At Seller's Expense

Another approach on termites is for the buyer to obtain the termite inspection and report, but for the seller to pay for the report. The idea behind this provision is that if the buyer selects the termite company it can help prevent the seller from shopping for a company, which through incompetence or collusion, fails to identify termite infestation or damage.

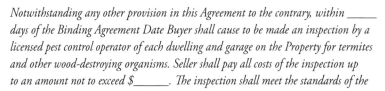

> **Special Stipulation 199:   Buyer to Obtain Termite Report**
>
> *Notwithstanding any other provision in this Agreement to the contrary, within _____ days of the Binding Agreement Date Buyer shall cause to be made an inspection by a licensed pest control operator of each dwelling and garage on the Property for termites and other wood-destroying organisms. Seller shall pay all costs of the inspection up to an amount not to exceed $_____. The inspection shall meet the standards of the*

Georgia Structural Pest Control Commission. If visible evidence of active or previous infestation is found, Seller agrees at his own expense, prior to the closing, to (a) treat the active infestation, correct all structural damage resulting from any infestation, and provide documentation to Buyer of the treatment of the infestation and the correction of the structural damage, or (b) provide documentation, satisfactory to the lender, if any, indicating that there is no structural damage resulting from any infestation. Seller shall provide at closing a standard letter from the licensed pest control operator selected by Buyer to perform the inspection (or such other inspector as may be acceptable to Buyer) meeting the requirements of the Georgia Structural Pest Control Commission stating that each dwelling and garage on the Property has been so inspected and found to be free from visible evidence of active infestation of termites and other wood-destroying organisms.

Some buyers may seek to have the seller repair both structural and cosmetic damage to the property resulting from termites and to ensure that the repairs match the existing property. The following is a special stipulation to the contract which would address this issue.

Special Stipulation 200: Seller Responsible for Structural and Cosmetic Termite Damage

If any repairs, renovations, or excavations to the Property are necessary due to infestation of the Property by termites and/or other wood-destroying organisms, Seller agrees at Seller's sole cost and expense to repair all damage to the Property regardless of whether the damage is structural or cosmetic. If there is damage to any wallpaper the Seller shall seek to replace the wallpaper with matching wallpaper if it can be readily obtained. If Seller does not have and cannot readily obtain such wallpaper, Seller shall replace the wallpaper in the entire room where it appears with wallpaper of equal or better quality and cost and in a design reasonably similar to the existing wallpaper. If there is damage to any wood paneling, Seller shall replace the damaged wood with the same type of wood and stain it to reasonably match the existing wood.

Regardless of who obtains or pays for the termite report, the buyer should coordinate the timing of the termite report with the timing of their property inspection to assure that the report is obtained prior to the expiration of the Due Diligence Period.

§ 10.1.5.6 Problems With Carpenter Ants

Buyers should be aware that the standards of the Georgia Structural Pest Control Commission do not apply to carpenter ants. Therefore, termite inspections and termite bonds do not cover inspection or treatment for carpenter ants even though carpenter ants can destroy wood. Carpenter ants tend to be more localized in their infestation than termites. They also tend to be easier to treat than termites. Nevertheless, because carpenter ants can cause damage, buyers may want to utilize the following special stipulation to require that the termite inspection include an inspection for carpenter ants and require the seller to repair any damage caused by carpenter ants.

Special Stipulation 201: Seller to Complete Inspection for Carpenter Ants

Within 30 days prior to closing the Seller shall cause to be made, at Seller's sole cost and expense, an inspection of each dwelling and garage on the Property for termites and other wood-destroying organisms, including but not limited to carpenter ants. The inspection shall meet the standards of the Georgia Structural Pest Control Commission. If visible evidence of active or previous infestation is found, including but not limited to infestation of carpenter ants, Seller agrees, prior to the closing, to treat the active infestation, correct all structural damage resulting from any infestation, and provide documentation to Buyer of the treatment of the infestation and the correction of the structural damage. Seller shall provide at closing a standard letter meeting the requirements of the Georgia Structural Pest Control Commission stating that each dwelling and garage has been so inspected and found to be free from visible evidence of active infestation of termites and other wood-destroying organisms, including but not limited to carpenter ants.

§ 10.1.5.7   Seller's Actual Knowledge Of Termite Damage Necessary For Fraud Claim

To successfully pursue a claim against a seller for termite damage after closing on the purchase of the property, the buyer must show that the seller had actual knowledge of the damage before the closing.[1332]

In one Georgia case, a buyer lost when he sued his seller for fraudulent concealment and misrepresentation of termite damage because the buyer could not prove that the seller had actual knowledge of the termite damage.[1333] In that case, the seller hired an exterminator to inspect and issue a termite clearance letter. The exterminator discovered and treated a minor infestation of subterranean termites but reported that the house was free of other wood-destroying insects or fungus, structural damage, or rotten timbers. The exterminator also conducted an inspection after the initial treatment and reported no active infestation or damage.

After the buyer moved into the house, he discovered termites in the kitchen and den. Upon investigation, the buyer's exterminator found termite infestation and damage to the den floor, the sub-flooring, and the frame and jambs of the entrance door. The buyer's exterminator also found that the den floor tiles had been patched and structural repairs had been made during the 33 years that the seller had lived in the house. While the inspector did not find evidence of repairs to termite damage or concealment, the buyer argued that the court should infer such knowledge from the structural repairs that were made during the years that the seller lived in the house. The court held that this alone was not enough to support an action for fraud.[1334]

The court may sometimes infer that the seller must have actual knowledge of the damage. This is illustrated in a recent case where a property owner had bought a home that he had completely rebuilt because it was almost entirely destroyed by a fire.[1335] The seller was the general contractor in the renovation and lived in the property for several years, and as such was very familiar with the condition of the property. A few months after the closing, the buyers saw termites swarming in the house and began to investigate further. The buyers hired a contractor to inspect the damaged area, who discovered extensive damage covered up with putty and fresh paint. They then called the inspector who had conducted the initial inspection back to re-inspect the property. He concluded that there was indeed extensive termite damage, and that he did not discover it earlier because of the concealment of holes and gaps in the wood caused by termite infestation. The buyers sued the seller for fraud based upon his concealment of the termite damage. Based on these facts, the court held that the jury was authorized to find that the seller must have known about the termite damage and was therefore liable for fraudulent concealment.

This is a significant case because the court also held that in cases of active fraudulent concealment, the buyers could use representations that were not a part of the contract to show a *pattern of deception* by the seller even where the contract itself specifically stated that the buyer was not relying on such representations. In this case, the seller had given the buyers a Seller's Property Disclosure Statement in which he stated that he was not aware of any damage due to termites or structural defects in the home. The contract contained an "entire agreement" clause stating that the

---

1332   O.C.G.A. § 51-6-2.

1333   *Webb v. Rushing*, 194 Ga.App. 732, 391 S.E.2d 709 (1990).

1334   *Webb v. Rushing*, 194 Ga.App. 732, 391 S.E.2d 709 (1990).

1335   *Browning v. Stocks*, 265 Ga.App. 803, 595 S.E.2d 642 (2004).

contract *"constitutes the sole and entire agreement between the parties"* and *"[n]o representation, promise, or inducement in the Agreement shall be binding upon any party thereto."* The contract did not make the Seller's Property Disclosure Statement a part of the contract, unlike the current GAR Purchase and Sale Agreement.

Under Georgia law when a buyer sues a seller for fraud and monetary damages but plans to keep the house, the buyer is said to "affirm" the purchase and sale contract. The buyer is normally bound by (or stuck with) any disclaimer in the contract which protects the seller. Previously the "entire agreement" clause would bar the introduction of any representations not included in the contract, *i.e.*, the buyer cannot be said to rely upon representations made outside the contract. The court distinguishes this situation as follows:

> The property disclosure statement was not made a part of the sales contract, so it was subject to the entire agreement clause in the contract and could not form the basis for a suit by the [buyers] that they were fraudulently induced to enter into the contract *by misrepresentations in the statement.* [Citations omitted.] Nevertheless, the statement was properly admitted… because it was relevant to the [buyers'] claim that [seller] fraudulently induced the sale by actively concealing the termite damage… Therefore, the jury could infer that it was *part of a pattern of deception…*"[1336]

The effect of this decision is that in cases of active fraudulent concealment, representations of sellers and real estate licensees may be used against them even if the representations are not written into the contract and if the contract specifically states that the contract reflects the entire agreement of the parties.

The court inferred actual knowledge in another case where the seller had constructed the den in which the buyer discovered termite infestation after the closing. The buyer sued the seller and the pest control company that had inspected the property. When the buyer moved in, he discovered a "soft spot" in the den's floor. Several months later he removed the baseboards around two walls, found six holes drilled through the carpet into the wood floor, and detected a chemical odor in the carpet at these locations. The buyer removed the carpet to find a linoleum floor and under the linoleum he found pieces of flooring, sub-flooring and floor joists. At the trial, the buyer showed evidence of the deteriorated condition of the lumber from the den floor and sub-floor and evidence that the lumber was highly infested with termites. The buyer's expert testified that it would have taken one to three years for the termites to accomplish this level of infestation. Based on this evidence, the court held that the seller could be liable for fraudulently concealing the termite damage from the buyer.[1337]

§ 10.1.5.8 Buyer Must Use Due Diligence To Protect Against Fraud

Buyers seeking to bring fraud claims against sellers for concealing termite damage must also show that they attempted to protect themselves against the fraud through the exercise of due diligence. In one case, the buyer sued the seller for fraud and negligent misrepresentation after moving into a house and discovering substantial termite damage.[1338] While the buyer was remodeling his kitchen, he discovered that portions of the house were propped up with wood, stacks of stones, bricks, and railroad ties. Before purchasing the property the buyer knew that some of the wood in the porch area was damaged and the buyer had been given a termite clearance letter reflecting that there had been previous infestations of termites and beetles. However, the buyer never independently investigated the property. The court held that the buyer could not recover against the seller for fraud because of the buyer's lack of diligence in inspecting the property himself.

1336   *Browning v. Stocks*, 265 Ga.App. 803, 804, 595 S.E.2d 642 (2004).

1337   *Allred v. Dobbs*, 137 Ga.App. 227, 223 S.E.2d 265 (1976).

1338   *Lester v. Bird*, 200 Ga.App. 335, 408 S.E.2d 147 (1991).

The general rule is that when purchasing property a buyer cannot claim that she has been deceived by false representations if the buyer could have learned the truth had she only exercised due diligence. Issues that frequently arise are whether the buyer could have discovered the truth via due diligence and whether the seller's alleged fraud prevented the buyer from exercising due diligence.

§ 10.1.5.9 Seller's Pest Control Inspector May Be Liable To Buyer For Negligent Inspection

If the buyer can show that visible evidence of termite damage or infestation was present at the time of the pre-closing inspection, the exterminator may be liable to the buyer for negligently inspecting and failing to report the damage.[1339] Pest control companies are generally required to make a thorough inspection of a home and make a qualified inspection report as to what wood-destroying organisms are visible in the home, and whether there are signs of wood-destroying organisms such as previous infestation or subsequent damage, including a graph showing where the problems are located.[1340] If these standards are not met the pest control company may be liable for negligence. Even though the seller hires the pest control company for the inspection (and there is no contract between the buyer and the pest control company), the buyer can sue the company for negligently inspecting the property.[1341]

In one case, a pest control company hired by the seller prepared an infestation report which was presented to the buyer at closing.[1342] The report stated that there had been no previous infestation of wood-destroying organisms. One month after closing, the buyers began remodeling the house and discovered extensive structural and other damage caused by infestations of wood-destroying organisms. At the trial of the case, the buyer's expert testified that the damage was present at the time of the inspection because the damage had been present for at least five years. Because the buyer's expert testified that damage was present when the seller's pest control company inspected the house, the court held that the seller's pest control company might be liable to the buyer for its negligent inspection.

In another case, the buyer discovered severe termite infestation in the floor and sub-flooring of his den several months after moving into the house.[1343] The exterminator hired by the seller had issued an inspection report prior to closing which certified that the company completed a comprehensive inspection of the property and found that it was completely clear of termite or beetle infestation. The court found that based on the exterminator's report the company could be liable to the buyer because it guaranteed that the entire property was completely clear of termites. If the termite inspection had been limited only to areas that were accessible to the termite company (as most inspections are), the company might not have been liable to the buyer for this infestation. The damage here was discovered in the lumber of the floor and sub-flooring in the den which was under both carpet and linoleum and was not accessible to the termite company for inspection.

In yet another case, the seller hired the pest control company that had treated the home for over 20 years to provide a termite clearance letter.[1344] The inspection report stated that there had been termite infestation in the past, but that there was no visible evidence of damage to the home. After the sale the buyers discovered that although there was no active infestation, their home had been severely and extensively damaged by earlier infestations of termites. Support jacks had been installed to shore up the structure, and the damage to the wooden beams had been concealed with black paint.

The court found that there was evidence of termite damage and that the exterminator knew of the prior infestation and damage, yet failed to probe the painted wood which would have revealed the extensive damage. Because the company had treated the house for over 20 years and knew of the previous infestation and extensive damage, it was responsible for knowing the contents of its records about the treatment of the house.

1339   *American Pest Control, Inc. v. Pritchett*, 201 Ga.App. 808, 412 S.E.2d 590 (1991); *Tabor v. Orkin Exterminating Co., Inc.*, 183 Ga.App. 807, 360 S.E.2d 34 (1987), *cert. denied.*

1340   *Getz Services, Inc. v. Perloe*, 173 Ga.App. 532, 327 S.E.2d 761 (1985).

1341   *Getz Services, Inc. v. Perloe*, 173 Ga.App. 532, 327 S.E.2d 761 (1985); *Allred v. Dobbs*, 137 Ga.App. 227, 223 S.E.2d 265 (1976).

1342   *American Pest Control, Inc. v. Pritchett*, 201 Ga.App. 808, 412 S.E.2d 590 (1991).

1343   *Allred v. Dobbs*, 137 Ga.App. 227, 223 S.E.2d 265 (1976).

1344   *WMI Urban Services, Inc. v. Erwin*, 215 Ga.App. 357, 450 S.E.2d 830 (1994), *cert. denied.*

§ 10.1.5.10 Pest Control Company May Be Liable For Fraudulently Concealing Termite Damage

In order for the pest control company to be liable for fraudulently concealing termite damage the buyer must show that the termite company had actual knowledge of the damage.[1345] The buyer must show that the company concealed its knowledge of the damage with the intent and purpose of deceiving the buyer.

For example, in one Georgia case the seller obtained a wood infestation inspection report in 1982 for his house which a buyer had contracted to purchase.[1346] The seller used the company which regularly treated the house for pest control. The company's report stated that the inspection was conducted by "a qualified inspector" who performed a "careful visual inspection of the readily accessible areas" of the house. The report indicated no active infestation of any sort but reported visible evidence of previous termite infestation and structural damage. After buying the house, the buyer assumed the seller's contract with the pest control company. In 1986 he contracted to sell the house and obtained a second wood infestation inspection report from the company. The 1986 report again indicated no active infestation, but the previous infestation and structural damage was reported to be far more extensive in the crawl space of the house than indicated in the 1982 report.

The buyer then learned that the damage reflected on the 1986 report had existed prior to the 1982 report and, in fact, had existed prior to 1952, all of which the pest control company knew. He also discovered that the inspector who issued the 1982 report was not a licensed termite technician and did not examine any of the crawl space under the house, as is essential for a proper inspection. Under these facts, the court held there was more than sufficient evidence to hold the pest control company liable for fraudulent concealment of the termite damage.

§ 10.1.5.11 Oral Promise To Provide Termite Letter At Closing Unenforceable

Most contracts, including the GAR Contract, specifically provide that only the terms written in the agreement are binding on the parties. This is also a general rule of contract construction and means oral representations, promises, or statements that are not included in the terms of the actual written contract will not bind either party. Additionally, a separate written agreement that is not referenced in the contract and that does not itself reference the contract will not generally be used by the court for purposes of interpreting the contract.

If the contract does not require the seller to provide a wood infestation inspection report or to warrant that the property is free and clear of wood-destroying organisms and/or damage caused by wood-destroying organisms, the seller will likely not be liable for any treatment or damage related to such organisms later discovered by the buyer, even if the seller made some related oral promise or representation to the buyer to the contrary.

One contract for the sale of a house included the statement that "Buyers waive termite inspection."[1347] However, at the closing the buyers asked the sellers for the termite certificate and the seller responded that he did not have it with him, but "there were definitely no termites on the property." When the buyers discovered termites, they sued the seller for damages. The court held that the seller was not liable for damages for the termite infestation because nothing in the contract required any information or action by the seller regarding termites.

Buyers should therefore confirm that the contract specifically requires the seller to provide a wood infestation inspection report, treat the infestation, and provide for the repair or negotiation of any resulting structural damage. Most lenders will require a wood infestation inspection report no matter what the terms of the contract state, so if the contract does not provide that the seller must obtain the report, the buyer will most likely have to obtain one at her own expense in order to meet the underwriting requirements for loan approval. It is a common misunderstanding that a termite letter is required by law. It is not. Rather, it is a requirement imposed by most lenders.

1345   *Tabor v. Orkin Exterminating Co., Inc.*, 183 Ga.App. 807, 360 S.E.2d 34 (1987), *cert. denied*.

1346   *Orkin Exterminating Co., Inc. v. Flowers*, 187 Ga.App. 270, 370 S.E.2d 29 (1988).

1347   *Hannah v. Shauck*, 131 Ga.App. 834, 207 S.E.2d 239 (1974).

§ 10.1.5.12   Inspection Standards Of Georgia Pest Control Commission

All structural pest control companies and operators must be licensed by the State of Georgia must comply with Georgia's Structural Pest Control Act[1348] ("Act") and the Rules of Georgia Structural Pest Control Commission[1349] ("Rules"). Georgia's Department of Agriculture oversees compliance with and enforcement of the Act and Rules.

The Rules require that pest control companies and operators must use the Official Georgia Wood Infestation Report ("Report") when certifying that a structure is apparently free from wood-destroying organisms in conjunction with the sale of real property.[1350] This Report provides that if visible evidence of active or previous infestation is reported, it should be assumed that some degree of damage is present. A diagram identifying the structure inspected and showing the location of the active or previous infestation must be attached to the Report. The disclosure that some degree of damage should be assumed to be present if there is visible evidence of active or previous infestation will likely result in more situations where buyers and lenders are concerned about termite damage.

The Report may be issued only by a pest control operator certified in wood-destroying organisms.[1351] The Report must carry a guarantee that if the Report certifies that a structure is apparently free from wood-destroying organisms and wood-destroying organisms are found in the structure within 90 days from the date of issuance, the infested structure will be treated by the pest control operator free of charge in accordance with the minimum adequate treatment prescribed by the Rules.[1352]

§ 10.1.5.13   Pest Control Contracts And Guarantees

Pest control companies must issue a separate written contract to the property owner each time they undertake to control wood-destroying organisms on the property.[1353] The contract must state: (1) the specific type of application to be performed; (2) the effective date and contract period; and (3) a diagram consisting of a reasonable depiction of the structure(s) to be treated, indicating the location of any visible active or previous infestation.[1354] Pest control companies are bound to treat the areas depicted on the contract diagram. One Georgia appellate court held that a pest control operator could be liable for breach of contract and fraud when it failed to treat a homeowner's carport where the carport was depicted on the contract diagram and the carport later became infested with termites.[1355]

If the pest control company tries to limit its liability for treatment of the property based on any modification or addition to a structure as it is depicted in the contract diagram, the contract must specifically state that the homeowner is obligated to notify the pest control company of any modifications or alterations to any structure on the property during the contract period.[1356] The pest control contract must also state the price of the contract.[1357] If the pest control company is going to perform repairs, replacement, or excavations on the property which are related to the control of wood-destroying organisms, the contract must give an estimate of such work.[1358]

1348   O.C.G.A. § 43-45-1, *et seq.*

1349   Rules of Georgia Structural Pest Control Commission ("Rules"), § 620-1-.01, *et seq.*

1350   Rules, § 620-6-.03(2).

1351   Rules, § 620-6-.03(1).

1352   Rules, § 620-6-.03(2).

1353   Rules, § 620-6-02(1).

1354   Rules, § 620-6-.02(a) to (c).

1355   *Woodall v. Orkin Exterminating Co., Inc.*, 175 Ga.App. 83, 332 S.E.2d 173 (1985).

1356   Rules, § 620-6-.03(g).

1357   Rules, § 620-6-.02(d).

1358   Rules, § 620-6-.02(d).

The contract must also provide for the specific terms of any guarantee or warranty and whether it applies to the re-treatment of the structure(s) under the contract and/or the repair of damages to the structure(s) under the contract.[1359] If the guarantee or warranty provides only for re-treatment, the type of re-treatment and the details of the re-treatment must be specified in the contract.[1360] Most guarantees or warranties in pest control contracts will cover only "new damage" to the structure, that is, damage caused by wood-destroying organisms after the date of the initial treatment by the company.[1361]

The Rules also require that the Inspection Report include a guarantee for the inspection. The guarantee required is that if the Report certifies that a structure is apparently free from wood-destroying organisms and wood-destroying organisms are found in the structure within 90 days from the date of issuance, the infested structure will be treated by the pest control operator free of charge. The treatment necessary is "the minimum adequate treatment prescribed by the Rules.[1362] Unless the buyer can prove negligence in the pest control operator's inspection, if the buyer finds infestation within the 90-day period and the inspector fulfills its obligations to retreat the structure in accordance with Georgia's minimum adequate treatment standards, the inspector will not be liable for further damages in accordance with the limitations of the Report's guarantee.[1363]

§ 10.1.5.14 Pest Control Bonds

Unlike the guarantee for treatment in a contract for treatment of wood-destroying organisms or the guarantee of proper inspection in the Report, pest control bonds guarantee actual performance of the extermination. Pest control bonds are written instruments issued by a bonding, surety, or insurance company guaranteeing the fulfillment of a contract between a pest control company and its customer. They are surety bonds issued by a third party insuring the performance of the pest control company. They do not include any warranty or guarantee between the pest control company and the customer.[1364]

Pest control companies are not required to maintain performance bonds. However, if a pest control company is bonded, the company must maintain a master or blanket bond in an amount equal to 5% of its previous year's gross sales or gross liability assumed during the previous year, whichever is higher, up to a maximum of $100,000, or it must provide a separate bond for each job.[1365] In order for a pest control company to advertise that it is bonded, the pest control company must state in writing to each customer that it is bonded as part of every proposal or contract, whether or not such proposal or contract is covered by the bond.[1366] The pest control company must also submit proof of the existence and type of bonding in force to the Georgia Structural Pest Control Commission.[1367]

Pest control companies themselves issue two types of bonds to their customers: repair bonds and treatment bonds. Repair bonds provide greater protection to an owner and guarantee treatment of the property for termite infestation and repair of any damage to the property caused by termites. Treatment bonds are limited to the guarantee of treatment of any termite infestation.

Buyers who purchase properties already under bond should consider renewing the seller's bond. In addition to the guaranteed treatment for infestation and/or repair of related damage, bonds provide other cost savings. If an owner

---

1359   Rules, § 620-6-.02(e).

1360   Rules, § 620-6-.03(e).

1361   *Parsells v. Orkin Exterminating Co., Inc.*, 178 Ga.App. 51, 342 S.E.2d 13 (1986).

1362   Rules, § 620-6-.03.

1363   *Holbrook v. Burrell*, 163 Ga.App. 529, 295 S.E.2d 201 (1982).

1364   Rules, § 620-2-.01.

1365   Rules, § 620-4-.01(3)(a).

1366   Rules, § 620-4-.01(3)(c).

1367   Rules, § 620-4-.01(3)(d).

decides to sell the property, the wood infestation inspection report will be much less expensive if the house is under bond. The annual renewal charge for bonds is also much less expensive than the cost of an annual inspection and repair for a property not under bond. Although a repair bond has more value than a treatment bond, an owner will save money with either type of bond.

Buyers can provide in the contract that if termites or wood-destroying organisms are discovered during the inspection or at the time the seller or buyer obtains the necessary closing letter, the seller shall obtain a treatment or repair bond from a pest control company of buyer's choosing. Then, when the buyer takes title to the property after closing, the buyer can assume the bond from the seller. Care must be taken to determine whether there is any cost associated with the transfer of a bond. Buyers should also be aware that some repair bonds convert to retreatment bonds upon transfer unless an additional fee is paid.

When the buyer makes an offer on a property, the offered contract could include a provision which would require the seller to obtain a bond from a certain pest control company if it is determined before closing that wood-destroying organisms are or were active on the property. The following special stipulation can be used for either of these two purposes.

> **Special Stipulation 202:   Seller to Obtain Termite Bond**
>
> *For purposes of obtaining the termite Report at closing, Seller agrees to use either ABC Pest Control Company or XYZ Pest Control Company to inspect for termites and other wood-destroying organisms and provide a termite letter regarding such inspection. If termites or other wood-destroying organisms are found, Seller agrees to purchase from the same pest control company chosen for the termite inspection and letter, a treatment/ damage bond (choose one) which will guarantee the property for at least one year and which shall be assumable by Buyer after the closing of this transaction without additional charge during the first year.*

When considering from whom and what type of termite bond to purchase, owners should choose a reputable pest control company which offers bonds with reasonable annual renewal charges. Many bonds exclude an obligation to retreat or repair termite infestation and/or damage which is a consequence of moisture. Since termites cannot live without moisture, such an exclusion can arguably be used to reject most, if not all, requests for termite repairs. One solution to this problem is to slightly modify this provision of the pest control contract. The following language should be added to a pest control contract which excludes retreatment or repairs caused by moisture.

> **Special Stipulation 203:   No Exclusion on Termite Bond [*Stipulation for Pest Control Contract*]**
>
> *Notwithstanding any provision to the contrary contained herein, the pest control operator shall not be permitted to limit its obligations to treat and, if applicable, repair and/or replace damage to structures resulting from termites and other wood-destroying organisms caused by excessive moisture in the area of the infestation and/or damage unless the pest control operator has previously identified in writing to Owner any areas with excessive moisture which could contribute to termite infestation and/or damage.*

§ 10.1.5.15   Amount Of Damages To Which Buyer May Be Entitled

Damages for injury to property generally equals the cost to restore the property to its condition at the time of the loss. If the seller or pest control inspector is liable to a buyer for damages caused by wood-destroying organisms, the buyer will usually be entitled to recover the costs necessary to restore the property to its condition immediately prior to the damage.[1368]

1368   *American Pest Control, Inc. v. Pritchett*, 201 Ga.App. 808, 412 S.E.2d 590 (1991); *Getz Services, Inc. v. Perloe*, 173 Ga.App. 532, 327 S.E.2d 761 (1985).

However, if the cost to restore the property to its original condition is much greater than the market value of the property prior to the damage, then the buyer's damages will be measured by the decrease of the property's market value from before the damage to after the damage, unless the property has historical or other intrinsic worth to the owner. If damaged property has historical or other intrinsic worth to the owner which is not reflected in the fair market value of the improved property, the proper measure of damages is the cost of repair, even though this may result in a recovery which far exceeds the fair market value of the improved property prior to the damage.

Depending on the circumstances, there may be more than one appropriate measure of damages for injury to improved property. For example, in one case the termite damage was so extensive that the repair costs were estimated to be twice the purchase price of the house. The court held that the jury could consider whether repairing the house was an absurd undertaking or whether the house had intrinsic value to the buyers and thus should be repaired despite the cost. The actual amount of damages to award in a case is usually a question of fact rather than of law.[1369]

§ 10.1.5.16 Emerging Pest Issues

A serious pest issue is emerging in the form of Formosan termites ("Formosans"). It is believed that Formosans were first introduced into the United States in the 1950's when they stowed away onboard ships returning from the Pacific after World War II.[1370] Formosans are a particularly hardy species of termite having a high tolerance to sunlight and air and extremely large colonies. Under the proper conditions, Formosans can establish secondary or tertiary nests in walls or the attic. They then proceed to destroy the house both from the ground up and the roof down. While a "normal" termite colony may contain several hundred thousand individuals, Formosan colonies can run into the millions. They aggressively forage for food and have been found as far as 300 yards away from the main nest. They will even repeatedly test chemical barriers and find ways to penetrate breaches in the treated soil.[1371] Although they feed mostly on wood, they will eat other cellulose-containing materials such as cardboard and paper. However, they are known to chew through foam insulation boards, thin lead and copper sheeting, plaster, asphalt, and some plastics. Formosan subterranean termites infest a wide variety of structures (including boats and high-rise condominiums).

Unfortunately, it appears that whatever natural predators or diseases help keep Formosans in check in the Pacific was not also imported to the United States. It is estimated that Formosan termites cause damage in the United States in the amount of $1 billion a year.[1372]

The United States Department of Agriculture's Agricultural Research Service has undertaken a comprehensive program to determine the Formosans' natural enemies and hopes to one day eradicate Formosans.[1373] In the meantime, Formosans have already become a serious problem in Louisiana, having costs hundreds of millions of dollars in damage.[1374] In the past few years Formosans have started to appear in Georgia. Most, if not all, repair bonds specifically exclude the repair and damage caused by Formosans.

§ 10.1.5.17 Bed Bugs

According to the U.S. Environmental Infestations Protection Agency, bed bugs infestations are on the rise due to more travel, increased resistance to pesticides and lack of knowledge about preventing infestations. Some buyers have begun to inspect the bedding in homes they are considered buying for evidence of bed bug infestation on the theory that the bed bugs, if not treated, will likely infest the bedding of the new homeowner.

1369   *American Pest Control, Inc. v. Pritchett*, 201 Ga.App. 808, 412 S.E.2d 590 (1991); *Getz Services, Inc. v. Perloe*, 173 Ga.App. 532, 327 S.E.2d 761 (1985).

1370   Southern Regional Research Center, Agricultural Research Service, USDA, New Orleans, La. 70179.

1371   Louisiana State University, Agricultural Center, report dated 04/05/05.

1372   Southern Regional Research Center, Agricultural Research Service, USDA, New Orleans, La. 70179.

1373   Southern Regional Research Center, Agricultural Research Service, USDA, New Orleans, La. 70179.

1374   In New Orleans alone it is estimated that Formosans infest as many as 30 percent of all trees. Southern Regional Research Center, Agricultural Research Service, USDA, New Orleans, La. 70179.

Other than bites on the skin, evidence of bed bug infestation include live bed bugs (which can be seen with the naked eye), rusty or reddish stains on bed sheets or mattresses caused by bed bugs being crushed, eggs and egg shells (which are tiny and white) and dark small spots on bedding which are bed bug excrement.

§ 10.1.6 Residential Lead-Based Paint Hazard Reduction Act Of 1992

On September 6, 1996, the Residential Lead-Based Paint Hazard Reduction Act of 1992[1375] ("Act") went into effect. (Owners with four or fewer dwelling units had until December 6, 1996, to comply with the new law.) The Act imposes lead-based paint disclosure requirements on sellers, real estate brokers, and landlords for all sales and rental transactions if the dwelling was built before 1978. (This book addresses the Act only as it relates to brokers, agents, sellers, and buyers of real property. The obligations of landlords and their agents in complying with the Act will not be discussed.)

Although the law was adopted in 1992, it did not go into effect until the fall of 1996 because the Department of Housing and Urban Development had to issue regulations to implement the new law. The regulations are referred to as The Requirements for Disclosure of Known Lead-Based Paint Hazards in Housing.

The legislation was passed to protect consumers, particularly children, who may suffer health problems because of inadvertent exposure to lead-based paint. For instance, children exposed to large amounts of lead may experience hearing loss, decreased bone and muscle growth, anemia, kidney damage, nervous system damage, speech problems, language impairment and behavioral problems. Adults exposed to large amounts of lead may experience digestive problems, loss of appetites, cataracts, anemia, nerve disorders and memory problems. The risk of exposure to lead-based paint is especially great if the paint is chipping or flaking. Sanding of lead-based paint occurring during renovation can also result in lead particles in the air.

The Act requires disclosure of lead-based paint in the purchase or lease of what is referred to as "target housing." The term "target housing" covers most forms of residential dwellings (or any portion thereof) constructed before 1978. Both the Environmental Protection Agency and the U.S. Dept. of Housing and Urban Development consider "target housing" to include housing for which a construction permit was obtained before January 1, 1978. (If no permit was obtained, housing in which construction was started before January 1, 2978 will be considered target housing.)[1376] In other words, if the house was started in December of 1977 and finished in March of 1978 it is still considered "target housing" and must comply with the Act. The types of properties classified as target housing are most single- and multi-family dwellings, including detached housing, apartments, condominiums, co ops, and townhouses. The law does not apply to commercial, office, or other properties used for nonresidential purposes.

The disclosure requirements are for homes built before 1978 because that was the year lead-based paint was banned from further use. The focus of the law is on disclosure rather than repair. If lead-based paint exists in a dwelling, the purpose of the law is to let consumers know about it when they buy the property. Owners of residential dwellings built after 1977 have no special obligations unless they know their property contains lead-based paint or lead-based hazards, in which case they must disclose this information. Even though lead-based paint was banned beginning in 1978, it was still used in some housing after that time. Therefore, if lead-based paint is a concern to prospective buyers, they may be well-advised to check houses built any time in the late 1970s.

§ 10.1.6.1 Pre 1978 Residential Properties Exempt From Act

Certain types of residential properties completed before January 1, 1978 are exempt from the Act. The exempt properties include the following:

1375   42 U.S.C.A.§ 4852, *et seq.*

1376   "Interpretive Guidance for The Real Estate Community on the Requirements for Disclosure of Information Concerning Lead-Based Paint in Housing," August 20, 1996, prepared jointly by U.S. EPA and HUD.

(a) Property sold at foreclosure (however, the Act applies when the property is later resold);[1377]

(b) Zero-bedroom dwellings where the sleeping area is not separated from the living area (such as studio apartments, efficiencies, dormitories, military barracks, and individual rooms rented in residential dwellings);[1378]

(c) Housing for the elderly or disabled, where children under the age of six are not expected to reside;[1379] and

(d) Unoccupied dwelling units that are to be demolished, and will remain unoccupied until the demolition.[1380]

§ 10.1.6.2 Seller's Right To Copy Of Buyer's Lead-Based Paint Test Results

If the buyer submits an amendment requesting repairs due to the existence of lead-based paint or any lead-based paint hazards, the buyer is obligated to give a copy of the lead-based paint test results to the seller along with the amendment. Absent this or some other specific contractual provision requiring that the report be provided to the seller, there is no obligation in the lead-based paint law requiring a buyer to give the report to a seller. If a buyer includes a special stipulation giving him an absolute right to terminate the contract if lead-based paint is found and the seller agrees to such a provision, the seller should require the buyer to give him all test reports involving lead-based paint.

§ 10.1.6.3 Record-Keeping Requirements

The real estate broker, agent, and the seller must sign and retain a completed copy of certain information contained in the National Association of REALTORS® "The Disclosure of Information and Acknowledgment Form," along with its accompanying documents.[1381] The information must be kept for three years from the date the sale of the property was completed. The form can be found in the National Association of REALTORS® publication, "Lead-Based Paint--A Guide to Complying with the New Federal EPA/HUD Disclosure Regulations."

§ 10.1.6.4 Penalties For Violating Act

The consequences for violating the federal regulations are severe. Sellers and licensees who knowingly violate the regulations may be subject to civil and criminal penalties. The civil penalties can range up to $10,000 per violation. Violators may also be liable for three times the damages incurred by the buyer. These damages often include costs of correcting lead-based paint hazards and medical costs related to lead-based paint. The criminal penalties are fines of $10,000 per violation and/or up to one-year imprisonment. Brokers and their affiliated licensees may face additional liability under the Brokerage Relationships in Real Estate Transactions Act ("BRRETA") if they knowingly fail to disclose any adverse material facts relating to lead-based paint in the dwelling.

§ 10.1.6.5 Level At Which Lead-Based Paint Becomes Hazardous

The existence of lead-based paint in a dwelling is not necessarily dangerous. Whether the lead-based paint is hazardous often depends on the condition of the structure or object covered with lead-based paint. For example, lead-based painted walls of a child's bedroom that are chipping pose a greater threat to the health of the occupants of the property than a non-chipping lead-based painted pipe under the kitchen sink. Buyers should be advised to seek expert advice about whether the existence of lead-based paint in a residential property is hazardous.

1377   40 C.F.R. § 743.101(a).

1378   40 C.F.R. § 743.103.

1379   40 C.F.R. § 743.103.

1380   24 C.F.R. § 35.115(a)(6).

1381   24 C.F.R. § 35.92.

§ 10.1.6.6   Right To Terminate If Lead-Based Paint Found

The literal language of the law gives the buyer only the opportunity to inspect and test for lead-based paint or lead-based paint hazards; it does not give the buyer a right to terminate a contract if lead-based paint is found in the property. Brokers and licensees representing buyers will therefore want to confirm that the contract protects their buyer clients in the event the testing for lead-based paint is positive.

The GAR Contract gives buyers the right to inspect the property during the due diligence period. During that time, the buyer may terminate the agreement for any reason, including an inspection revealing the existence of lead-based paint or any lead-based paint hazards. However, if the property is sold "as is" (with no due diligence period), the existence of lead-based paint would not give a buyer a right to terminate the agreement.

Some buyers will want the absolute right to terminate a purchase contract if the property is found to contain any lead-based paint. Buyers with this position may want to include the following special stipulation as a special stipulation to the contract to allow for such a contingency.

> **Special Stipulation 204:   Buyer's Right to Terminate Contract on Discovery of Lead-Based Paint**
>
> *Buyer shall have the right to terminate this Agreement upon written notice to Seller if it is determined within _____ days of the Binding Agreement Date that the Property contains lead-based paint or lead-based paint hazards. For the purposes herein, the term lead-based paint shall mean paint or other surface coatings that contain lead equal to or in excess of 1.0 milligram per square centimeter or 0.5 percent by weight.*

On the other hand, the parties may want to include the following special stipulation which provides more flexibility and allows the seller an opportunity to correct the problem to avoid terminating the contract.

> **Special Stipulation 205:   Lead-Based Paint Testing Contingency**
>
> *This Agreement is contingent upon a risk assessment or inspection of the Property for the presence of lead-based paint and/or lead-based paint hazards at Buyer's expense within _____ days of the Binding Agreement Date. This contingency will terminate at said predetermined deadline unless Buyer (or Buyer's agent) delivers to Seller (or Seller's agent) a written contract amendment listing the specific existing deficiencies and corrections needed, together with a copy of the inspection and/or risk assessment report. Seller may, at Seller's option, within _____ days after delivery of the addendum, elect in writing whether to correct the condition(s). If Seller decides to correct the condition, Seller shall furnish Buyer within _____ days after delivery of Buyer's addendum, a certification from a risk assessor or inspector demonstrating that the condition has been remedied. If Seller elects not to make the repairs, or if Seller makes a counteroffer, Buyer shall have _____ days to respond to the counteroffer or remove this contingency and take the Property in "as is" condition or this contract shall become void. Buyer may remove this contingency at any time without cause.*

§ 10.1.6.7   Renovation And Repairs Of Property With Lead-Based Paint

If an inspection reveals the existence of lead-based or lead-based paint hazards, some buyers may ask the seller to fix the problem during a Due Diligence Period. Repairing or renovating a house containing lead-based paint is subject to strict regulations.

Common renovations and repairs can create hazardous lead dust by disturbing the lead-based paint, which can be harmful to both children and adults. For this reason, the Environmental Protection Agency created the Renovation,

Repair and Painting Rule in 2008 ("Rule").[1382] This Rule provides that any persons performing renovation, repair and painting projects that disturb lead-based paint in homes created prior to 1978 are required to use certified renovators trained under EPA-approved training procedures.[1383] Theses renovators must follow specific safety practices[1384] and meet certain information distribution requirements.[1385]

The Rule applies to the renovation and repair of homes and rental units. Before beginning the renovations or repairs, the persons performing the projects must; (1) provide the owner of the house or adult living within the dwelling with the EPA Renovation Right pamphlet, and either (i) obtain, from that person, a written acknowledgement that they have received the pamphlet; or (ii) obtain a certificate of mailing at least 7 days prior to the renovation.[1386]

The rule imposes strict work practice standards to ensure the health and safety of both the occupants living in the home and the renovators performing the work. For example, the work area must be completely isolated so no dust or debris escapes while the renovation or repair is being performed.[1387] Any person not involved in the project must remain outside the work area until it is fully completed.[1388] If the renovations or repairs take place within the interior of the home, all objects within the work area, such as furniture, rugs, window coverings, etc., must be removed.[1389] In addition, all ducts opening in the work area must be closed and taped-down with plastic sheeting and the floor surface must be completely covered.[1390] Open-flame burning or torching of painted surfaces is prohibited, as well as the use of machines designed to remove paint or other surface coatings through high speed operation.[1391] Any waste from renovation activities must be contained to prevent releases of dust and debris before the waste is removed from the work area for storage or disposal.[1392]

Once the renovations are complete, the area is cleaned and inspected to ensure no dust, debris or residue is still present.[1393] Activities conducted after the post-renovation cleaning verification that do not disturb paint, such as applying paint to walls that have already been prepared, are not regulated by the Restoration, Repair and Paint Rule.

It is important to remember that no person may perform renovations or repairs on a target home unless the appropriate EPA certification is obtained.[1394] Failure or refusal to comply with this Rule is a violation of the Toxic Substances Control Act[1395] and can result in both civil and criminal sanctions.[1396]

§ 10.1.7   Other Environmental Issues: Radon And Asbestos

§ 10.1.7.1   Radon Testing

Buyers may be concerned about radon levels in the property they intend to purchase and may want to terminate the contract if radon levels exceed current acceptable levels. Radon is a radioactive gas that is colorless, odorless and tasteless. It comes from the natural decay of uranium that is found in nearly all soils. It typically moves up through the ground to

---

1382   40 C.F.R. § 745.80.

1383   40 C.F.R. § 745.82.

1384   40 C.F.R. § 745.82.

1385   40 C.F.R. § 745.84.

1386   40 C.F.R. § 745.84(a).

1387   40 C.F.R. § 745.85(a)(2).

1388   40 C.F.R. § 745.85(a)(1).

1389   40 C.F.R. § 745.85(a)(2)(i).

1390   40 C.F.R. § 745.85(a)(2)(i)(D).

1391   40 C.F.R. § 745.85(a)(3).

1392   40 C.F.R. § 745.85(a)(4).

1393   40 C.F.R. § 745.85(b).

1394   40 C.F.R. § 745.89.

1395   15 U.S.C. 2689.

1396   40 C.F.R. § 745.87.

the air above and into a house through cracks and holes in the foundation. Studies link high concentrations of radon in homes to an increased risk of lung cancer.

The U.S. Environmental Protection Agency publishes an excellent brochure entitled "A Citizen's Guide to Radon" that explains how to reduce radon levels in a home if levels of radon are found. According to the brochure, the average indoor radon level is estimated to be about 1.3 pCi/l. In the outside air, radon levels of 4 pCi/l are generally found. Houses testing at 4 pCi/l are considered to have high levels of radon and treatment is recommended in such cases to reduce the levels of radon within a house. Radon levels can normally be lowered without such difficulty through a combination of crawl space fans, ventilation and/or foundation pumps.

Alternatively, the buyer may want to give the seller the opportunity to lower the radon levels. The following stipulations can be used for these purposes.

Special Stipulation 206:   Radon Testing Contingency

This Agreement is contingent upon having the Property inspected for the presence of radon within _____ days from Binding Agreement Date at Buyer's discretion and expense. Said testing shall be conducted by a current National Environmental Health Association ("NEHA") Certified Measurement Provider using an EPA approved testing method and reporting format. Testing device shall be placed and retrieved by a current NEHA Certified Measurement Provider. This contingency shall terminate at said predetermined date unless Buyer or Buyer's agent deliver to Seller or Seller's agent a written amendment stating that said results reveal a radon level within the residential dwelling on the Property equal or higher than the level established by the EPA as being potentially hazardous to human beings. Seller may, at Seller's option and within _____ days of delivery of the amendment, elect in writing to remedy the condition at Seller's sole expense. If Seller decides to remedy the condition, Seller shall undertake all remedial measures necessary to reduce the radon level in the residential dwellings on the Property to a level within the recommended safe level established by the EPA and provide the Buyer with written re-test results performed by current NEHA Certified Measurement Provider confirming such reduction of radon. Said remediation may include the installation of fans which may increase utility costs to the buyer. If Seller elects not to remedy the condition, makes a counteroffer or does not respond within the time period in which Seller has to respond, Buyer shall have _____ days from the expiration of said time period to respond or remove this contingency or this contract shall become void. Buyer may waive this contingency at any time.

Some buyers may want an absolute right to terminate if the test results show a radon level equal or higher that the action level established by the EPA. The following special stipulation may then be used.

Special Stipulation 207:   Buyer's Right to Terminate if High Radon Level

Buyer shall have the right to have the Property inspected for the presence of radon within _____ days from Binding Agreement Date at Buyer's discretion and expense. Testing shall be conducted by a current National Environmental Health Association ("NEHA") Certified Measurement Provider using an EPA approved testing method and reporting format. Testing device shall be placed and retrieved by a current NEHA Certified Measurement Provider. If said radon testing reveal a radon level equal or higher than the level established by the EPA as being potentially dangerous to human beings in the Property, Buyer shall have the right to terminate this Agreement upon written notice to Seller within _____ days of the Binding Agreement Date.

§ 10.1.7.2 Right To Remove Asbestos

Buyers may be concerned about elevated levels of asbestos present in the property they intend to purchase. Asbestos is a mineral fiber. In the past, it was added to a variety of products to strengthen them and to provide heat insulation and fire resistance. Until the 1970's many types of building products and insulation materials used in homes contained asbestos. Homes built after this time generally do not have building products and insulation with asbestos.

Exposure to asbestos increases the risk of a variety of lung diseases including lung cancer, asbestosis and mesothelioma. In older homes, asbestos was most commonly found in roofing and siding shingles, insulation in homes built between 1940-1950, attic and wall insulation using vermiculite, or textured paint and patching compounds used on ceiling joints and walls.[1397]

Unless it is labeled, it is not possible to tell whether a material contains asbestos.[1398] Houses with asbestos can either be repaired (which normally involves covering or encapsulating the asbestos) or removed. Removal can be expensive because it poses the greatest risk of the release of asbestos fibers. As such, it should only be done by asbestos professionals.

If buyers have such concerns, they may want to include special stipulations requiring the seller to take steps to remove all asbestos. The following special stipulation can be used for these purposes.

> **Special Stipulation 208: Asbestos Removal**
>
> *During the inspection period, Buyer shall have the Property inspected for the presence of asbestos. If it is determined within _____ days of the Binding Agreement Date that asbestos is present in the Property, Seller shall remove the asbestos from the Property in a good and workmanlike manner and in accordance with all applicable laws and regulations prior to the closing.*

In the alternative, the parties could agree that the presence of asbestos is a defect pursuant to the contract. Adding a stipulation that such conditions constitute defects allows buyers to request that sellers repair the problem as part of the inspection contingency. The following provision can be used.

> **Special Stipulation 209: Asbestos Constitutes Defect**
>
> *During the inspection period Buyer shall have the property inspected for the presence of asbestos. Notwithstanding any other provision in this Agreement to the contrary, Buyer and Seller agree if the results of said inspection reveal the presence of asbestos in or on the Property, this shall constitute a defect pursuant to the provision of the Agreement entitled "Property Sold With Right to Request Repairs."*

Some buyers may prefer to have the right to terminate the contract if the property contains asbestos. In this event, the parties may include the following special stipulation in the contract.

> **Special Stipulation 210: Buyer's Right to Terminate if Asbestos Found**
>
> *Notwithstanding any other provision in this Agreement to the contrary Buyer shall have the right to terminate this Agreement upon written notice to Seller within _____ days of the Binding Agreement Date if an inspection for asbestos reveals that asbestos is present in or on the Property.*

1397 "Asbestos in Your Home," United States Environmental Protection Agency (2010).

1398 *Id.*

§ 10.1.7.3 Right To Terminate Due To Inability Or High Cost Of Obtaining Property Insurance

Buyers should note that the possibility of obtaining property insurance on the property she is contracting to purchase and its cost might depend on the number of claims that the previous owner filed on the property. Insurers have long used loss histories to underwrite and rate a homeowner's insurance. When a homebuyer approaches an insurance provider for homeowner's insurance regarding a prospective home purchase, the insurer may obtain information on the buyer's former home to check how responsible the person is as a homeowner. The insurer may also obtain information on the new home to check whether or not that home has had recurring problems that justify higher premiums. Water leaks, for instance, are treated with more caution because of the threat of mold.

An insurer can obtain the loss history of a property from databases, such as CLUE (Comprehensive Loss Underwriting Exchange). If a property has negative marks on its CLUE report, it may be more difficult for a buyer to purchase the property because the buyer may either have to pay a high property insurance premium or may not be able to obtain property insurance at all. Each insurer will use the CLUE report based on its own underwriting and rating criteria. Therefore, while one insurer may qualify a home prone to flooding as high risk, another insurer may refuse insurance altogether.

A buyer may wish to make the purchase contingent upon a satisfactory CLUE report. The following special stipulation can be used for these purposes.

> **Special Stipulation 211:   Buyer's Right to Terminate Due to Unsatisfactory CLUE or Other Claims Report**
>
> *Notwithstanding any other provision in this Agreement to the contrary, Buyer shall have the right to terminate this Agreement upon written notice to Seller within _____ days from the Binding Agreement Date if an insurance provider of Buyer's choice determines, based on the Property's CLUE (Comprehensive Loss Underwriting Exchange) report or any other report that (1) it cannot insure the Property or (2) it is able to insure the Property with limitations which is unacceptable to Buyer or (3) is able to provide property insurance at a higher premium than what the insurance provider would normally price.*

§ 10.2 REPAIR ISSUES

§ 10.2.1 Selling A Property "As Is"

Prior versions of the GAR Contract included an explicit "as is" clause giving a buyer the option to purchase a property without an inspection. Under the new GAR Contract, the parties may agree that the property is being sold "as is" by filing in "0" under the length of the Due Diligence Period. More specifically, the agreement provides that the "property is being sold subject to a Due Diligence Period of ___ days from the Binding Agreement Date."

Generally, a buyer will want to provide for a Due Diligence Period to inspect and examine the property. When the property is subject to the completion of a due diligence period, the buyer may terminate the agreement if the inspection, survey or evaluation is unsatisfactory. Some sellers, however, may want to sell the property "as is" without giving the buyer an option to terminate. If this is the case, the buyer must accept the property with all (known and unknown) defects and faults, including lead-based paint, lead-based paint hazards, radon hazards, and/or asbestos hazards. Furthermore, the seller will not be obligated to make any repairs to the property except as may be specially stipulated otherwise in the contract.

In one Georgia case, the buyer sued the seller and the seller's real estate agent to recover the cost of structural repairs necessitated when she discovered after purchasing a house that the attic had been damaged by fire. The house in this case was vacant and in a dilapidated condition, not suitable to be lived in. The buyer paid $25,000 for the house with the understanding that she would have to undertake substantial repairs. The buyer's agent drafted the contract which contained a special stipulation that the house was being purchased "as is" with no termite certification.[1399] After the closing, the buyer began to make repairs and the contractor installing the HVAC equipment in the attic discovered fire damage to the ceiling joists. The appellate court in ruling against the seller found that the buyer did not exercise reasonable care to discover the charred timber and thus could not maintain her fraud claim. The court also ruled that the buyer should have exercised a heightened degree of diligence in inspecting the house because she knew that it was in dilapidated condition with many major defects and was purchasing the house in "as is" condition.

A different result was reached in another Georgia case. The buyer purchased a house "as is" yet recovered damages from the seller who fraudulently concealed insect damage.[1400] In this case, a provision in the purchase agreement required the seller to give the buyer a termite certificate declaring the property free from termite infestation or damage. At the closing, the seller stated that he did not have such a certificate, and when the buyer refused to proceed with the closing, the seller promised to give the buyer a certificate in order to complete the sale. The seller's agent typed into the contract the words "The sale is as is condition."

After the buyer took possession of the house, she discovered wood beetle damage. She also discovered that more than two years before she bought the house the seller had hired an exterminator to treat an infestation. On this basis, the buyer sued the seller and his agent for fraud in the inducement of the contract and affirmative and willful nondisclosure of the insect damage.

The buyer settled her claim with the seller's agent, and a jury awarded her general damages and punitive damages against the seller. The seller argued that the words "as is" in the sales contract removed any question of fraud as to the condition of the property, on the ground that the acceptance of a contract with an "as is" clause forces the buyer to undertake an absolute duty of inspection. The court ruled against the seller and found that the "as is" provision does not protect a seller who willfully misrepresents the condition of the property to the buyer.

§ 10.2.1.1   Special Disclosure By Sellers Unfamiliar With Condition Of Property

Some sellers are unfamiliar with the condition of the property they sell. In such instances, sellers are well advised to add a special stipulation to the contract informing the buyer of this fact and encouraging them to do a more thorough inspection. Special Stipulation 195: ("Seller Not Familiar with Condition of Property") is an example of this type of provision.

§ 10.2.2   Negligent Repair Of Property

Most buyers prefer to purchase a home subject to a home inspection, rather than purchasing a home "as is." Without a home inspection, the doctrine of *caveat emptor* will generally bar a homebuyer's claims against a seller absent a showing of fraud.[1401] The Georgia Supreme Court, however, has carved out an exception to this rule holding that the application of *caveat emptor* will not bar a homebuyer's claim in a negligence suit against a builder/seller.[1402] More specifically, this exception will allow a homebuyer's negligence claim if the house is sold containing latent defects which the builder in the exercise of ordinary care knew or should have known and which the buyer could not have

1399   *Ben Farmer Realty Co. v. Woodard*, 212 Ga.App. 74, 441 S.E.2d 421 (1994), *cert. denied.*

1400   *Mulkey v. Waggoner*, 177 Ga.App. 165, 338 S.E.2d 755 (1985).

1401   *Reininger v. O'Neill*, 2012 WL 2434755.

1402   *Cendant Mobility Financial Corp. v. Asuamah*, 285 Ga. 818, 684 S.E.2d 617 (2009).

reasonably discovered the existence of ordinary care.[1403] This exception has a limited application and thus will continue to bar a homebuyer's negligence claim against a seller that did not build the home.

In one case, the homebuyers tried to argue that because the seller completed the negligent repairs to the home himself, the *caveat emptor* exception should allow the negligence claim against the seller. The court disagreed and refused to expand the exception holding that the negligent repair claim failed as a matter of law because the seller was not the builder of the home.[1404] In this case, the buyers purchased a 16-year old home from the seller who was the only owner. Prior to the sale, the seller noticed that the basement was leaking so he dug a retaining hole to collect the excess water when it rained and used sealant and cement to fix the problem area in the basement. The seller claimed that no further leakage occurred before the sale.

The agreement stated that the property was being sold "as is" and also contained a property disclosure statement from the seller. On the disclosure statement, the seller indicated that there had been water leakage in the past and repairs made to fix the water damage. The buyers still decided to purchase the property. Sometime after the transaction was complete, the basement started leaking again and a home inspection revealed the extent of the property's water damage. The buyers tried to rescind the contract based on the seller's negligent repair of the property but the court affirmed the general rule of *caveat emptor*.[1405] All parties understood that the property was being sold "as is" and regardless of whether the seller performed the repairs to the water damage himself, the exception to *caveat emptor* does not apply to a non-builder/seller.[1407]

§ 10.2.3 Property Sold With Right To Request Repair Of Defects

There are three separate time periods of which buyers should be aware if the property is being sold subject to a right to request repairs. The first is the inspection period during which the buyer can hire an inspector (or inspectors) to inspect the property to determine if it contains any defects. The second is a "Defect Resolution Period" during which the buyer and seller negotiate, through offers and counteroffers, the defects to be repaired and/or replaced by the seller. Finally, if the parties are not able to reach an agreement regarding the defects to be repaired and/or replaced during the Defect Resolution Period, there is then a one-day time period thereafter during which either party can accept the other's last offer of repairs. If neither party does this the contract then terminates automatically.

To seek the repair of defects the buyer must provide the seller with the following: (1) a copy of the inspection report prepared by an inspector detailing the defects which the buyer is seeking the seller to repair and/or replace, and (2) an Amendment to Remove Inspection Contingency form[1408] requesting that the seller repair and/or replace these defects.

The buyer must present the inspection report and the proposed amendment to the seller within a specified number of days from the Binding Agreement Date. If the buyer does not do this in a timely manner, the buyer is deemed to have accepted the property in "as is" condition. If the buyer timely submits the inspection report and the written amendment, the buyer and seller then have a specified number of days to negotiate, through written offers and counteroffers, the defects to be repaired and/or replaced by the seller. This time period is called the "Defect Resolution Period." If the buyer and seller agree on what is to be repaired and/or replaced they must sign a written amendment to reflect their agreement.

1403   *Cendant Mobility Financial Corp. v. Asuamah*, 285 Ga. 818, 684 S.E.2d 617 (2009).

1404   *Reininger v. O'Neill*, 2012 WL 2434755.

1405   *Cendant Mobility Financial Corp. v. Asuamah*, 285 Ga. 818, 684 S.E.2d 617 (2009).

1406   *Reininger v. O'Neill*, 2012 WL 2434755 citing *Cendant Mobility Financial Corp. v. Asuamah*, 285 Ga. 818, 684 S.E.2d 617 (2009).

1407   *Cendant Mobility Financial Corp. v. Asuamah*, 285 Ga. 818, 684 S.E.2d 617 (2009).

1408   GAR Form F100.

If the buyer and seller do not agree on the defects to be repaired and/or replaced by the expiration of the Defect Resolution Period, the buyer or seller may either accept the other party's last offer or counteroffer of repairs (if any) or the buyer may accept the property "as is." The party who accepts the offer or counteroffer must give notice of acceptance by providing to the other party a written agreement stating what is to be repaired and/or replaced. This has to be done within one day of the expiration of the Defect Resolution Period. If neither the buyer nor seller gives this notice in a timely manner, the contract then automatically terminates.

Once the parties agree on which defects the seller will repair and/or replace, the repairs and replacements must be completed in a good and workmanlike manner prior to closing. If the seller is willing to repair and/or replace all of the defects in the inspection amendment regardless of how numerous they may be, the buyer may not use the inspection contingency as a basis to terminate the contract.

§ 10.2.3.1 Counting Time Periods Correctly When Property Is Sold With Right To Request Repairs

When the property is sold subject to a right to request repair, the inspection period and the "Defect Resolution Period" are both measured from the original Binding Agreement Date. The Defect Resolution Period is not measured from the end of the inspection period.

There are two blanks in this section of the GAR Property Sold with the Right to Request Repairs[1409] exhibit, the first of which is to be filled in with the length of time the buyer has to do her inspection and the second of which is the length of the Defect Resolution Period. So for example, if the actual inspection period is 10 days and the Defect Resolution Period is intended to be 5 days thereafter, the first blank in this section of the GAR Contract would be filled in with the number "10" and the second blank would be filled in with the number "15." Again, this is because both time periods are measured from the Binding Agreement Date.

If the buyer and seller cannot come to an agreement within the Defect Resolution Period on the defects to be repaired, either party can then accept the other party's offer of repairs within one (1) day thereafter. Case law defines a day to mean an entire 24-hour day beginning immediately after midnight and ending 24 hours later.[1410]

If a buyer has a ten (10) day inspection period and the Binding Agreement Date is January 1st, the inspection period would end upon the conclusion of January 11th. This is because when a party counts days from a specific date, the day after the Binding Agreement Date is the first day and January 11th would be the tenth day from the Binding Agreement Date.[1411]

§ 10.2.3.2 Buyer Can Only Request Repairs To "Defects" Identified By Professional Inspector

Under the GAR Property Sold with the Right to Request Repairs exhibit, the right to request the repair and/or replacement of defects in the property applies only to defects which have been identified by buyer's inspector in a written report. Therefore, while the buyer is still entitled to have anyone inspect the property, the buyer can only ask the seller to repair and/or replace defects identified by a professional inspector.

The term "Inspector" means "a person or company with specific, professional expertise in property inspections or in an item, building product, or condition therein, for which the 'Inspector' is inspecting, examining, testing and/or surveying."

Georgia law provides for certain requirements with which home inspectors must comply. The law defines a "home inspector" as any person who for consideration inspects and reports on the condition of any home or single-family dwelling or the grounds, roof, exterior surface, garage or carport, structure, attic, basement, crawl space, electrical

---

1409   GAR Form F129.

1410   *Southern Trust Ins. Co. v. First Federal Sav. & Loan Ass'n of Summerville*, 168 Ga.App. 899, 310 S.E.2d 712 (1983).

1411   O.C.G.A. § 1-3-1(d)(3).

system, heating system, air-conditioning system, plumbing, on-site sewage disposal, pool, hot tub, fireplace, kitchen, appliances, or any combination of these for a prospective purchaser or seller.[1412]

Every home inspector must provide to the person on whose behalf he is inspecting a home or single-family dwelling a written document specifying the following information:

(a) the scope of the inspection, including the structural elements, systems, and subsystems to be inspected;

(b) that the inspection is a visual inspection; and

(c) that the home inspector will notify in writing the person on whose behalf the inspection is being made of any defects noted during the inspection, along with any recommendation that certain experts be retained to determine the extent and corrective action necessary for the defects.[1413]

Any person who violates any of these home inspector requirements is guilty of a misdemeanor criminal offense.[1414] Misdemeanor offenses generally carry a maximum penalty of a $1,000 fine and up to 12 months in jail.[1415]

The GAR Contracts does not require inspections to be done by home inspectors who are members of professional associations such as the American Society of Home Inspectors ("ASHI") for two reasons.[1416] First, inspectors with ASHI or other similar certification might not be available in every locale in Georgia. Second and more importantly, with many homes, specialized inspections of roofs, heating and air conditioning systems, swimming pools, and structural components are also needed. There may be the need for specialized inspections for mold, radon, asbestos and other toxic substances. Such inspections are often conducted by engineers or other professionals, who may not be members of a professional home inspection organization but are nevertheless experts in their respective areas. Limiting inspections to only members of ASHI would leave buyers without the legal ability to ask for repairs and/or replacement of defects identified by these experts.

On the other hand, buyers may engage less credible inspectors who make partial or inaccurate findings. In this case, sellers may want to limit the initial inspection of the property to a member of ASHI to ensure a fairly objective review of the property. If the seller wants to make such a requirement part of the contract, the following special stipulation can be used.

> **Special Stipulation 212:   Buyer Obligated to Employ Only an ASHI Certified Inspector**
>
> *Notwithstanding any provision to the contrary contained herein, Buyer shall employ only a member of the American Society of Home Inspectors to conduct the initial inspection of the property for defects and prepare the inspection report referenced in this Agreement. If the Inspector recommends that specific follow-up inspections or tests be done to the Property, such inspections do not have to be performed by a member of ASHI provided that such inspector(s) has expertise in the portion of the Property or condition or product therein being inspected or tested.*

In a new construction contracts, sellers may also want to restrict building inspections to be conducted only by certified building inspectors. If this is the case, the following stipulation may be added.

1412   O.C.G.A. § 8-3-330.

1413   O.C.G.A. § 8-3-331.

1414   O.C.G.A. § 8-3-332.

1415   O.C.G.A. § 17-10-3.

1416   ASHI is a professional organization of home inspectors. Each inspector belonging to ASHI must have a specific level of education and experience in the home inspection field.

Special Stipulation 213:   Inspector to be ASHI or GAHI Member

Any building inspection must be performed during normal business hours (Monday through Friday 9 a.m. – 5 p.m.) by an inspector (Inspector) with the following credentials:

(a) Inspector must be a current member of The American Society of Home Inspectors, Inc. or the Georgia Association of Home Inspectors, Inc. Prior to the inspection, the Inspector shall furnish to Seller a letter from the association of which it is a member identifying the Inspector as a member of such organization.

(b) Inspector shall present to Seller evidence of general liability insurance insuring the Inspector in an amount of not less than One Million Dollars.

(c) Inspector shall present a valid business license for the jurisdiction in which the Inspector is operating.

(d) The Inspector shall be CABO 1 and 2 certified Family Dwelling Code (International Residential Code) (or state other certification) and shall present evidence to Seller of such certification.

(e) Inspector shall sign an agreement prepared by Seller in which the Inspector agrees to indemnify and hold Seller harmless any loss, damage or injury to persons or property arising out of or related to the inspection of the Property.

Builder and developer contracts often require inspections to be done by qualified home inspectors. This normally occurs where the builder has had a bad experience with particular inspectors aggressively claiming that items in a property are defects when such claims are disputed by the builder. Some builders have gotten so frustrated with particular inspectors that they have limited a buyer's right to inspect to certain approved inspectors or provide that they will only pay closing costs if the buyer uses an inspector from an approved list. A detailed discussion of this issue is set out in § 10.2.3.6 (Right to request repairs limited to "defects") below.

§ 10.2.3.3 Inspectors Can Limit Their Liability

Before signing a contract with a home inspector, the buyer should carefully read the terms and conditions of the contract. Some inspection contracts may limit any loss for negligent inspection to the cost of the inspection. In one Georgia case the buyer of a condominium unit sued her inspector for $23,700 in damages allegedly resulting from the negligent inspection of her unit.[1417] The buyer signed a contract at the time of the inspection which provided that the inspector's liability was limited to the cost of the inspection. The buyer argued that a contract with this type of limitation against liability was void as against public policy. The Georgia Court of Appeals disagreed, holding that such a limitation of the inspector's liability was enforceable and the buyer could only recover the costs she paid for the inspection. This case also serves as the legal basis for the limitation against liability contained in the GAR listing and buyer brokerage agreements.

§ 10.2.3.4 Extending The Inspection And Defect Resolution Period

The GAR Property Sold With Right to Request Repairs Exhibit[1418] gives the buyer a right to extend the inspection period and Defect Resolution Period once for up to seven days in the event the inspector recommends any additional test, study, inspection or evaluation of any product, item or condition in the property. The recommendation of the

---

1417   *Brainard v. McKinney*, 220 Ga.App. 329, 469 S.E.2d 441 (1996).

1418   GAR Form F129.

inspector for a follow-up test must be contained in the inspector's written report. The buyer must provide the seller with the notice to extend the inspection and Defect Resolution Period, along with a copy of the inspector's report recommending the additional test, study or evaluation, prior to the end of the inspection period. In other words, the buyer cannot give notice to extend the inspection period once the Defect Resolution Period has commenced.

The date of closing is not automatically extended along with the inspection period and the Defect Resolution Period. Instead, it is only extended if the new Defect Resolution Period overlaps the original closing date. So, for example, let's assume that the date of closing is May 1st and the Defect Resolution Period is to end on April 15th. If the inspection period and Defect Resolution Period are properly extended by the buyer for 7 additional days, the new Defect Resolution Period would end on April 22nd, and since the new date does not overlap the date of closing the closing date would remain the same. However, if the Defect Resolution Period ends on April 25th and is extended for 7 additional days, it would overlap the original date of closing by 1 day. In such a case the closing date would then also be extended for 7 additional days until May 8th. There is a special GAR form which can be used to give notice to unilaterally extend the inspection period.[1419]

§ 10.2.3.5 Meaning Of "Last Offer Or Counteroffer"

When using the GAR Property Sold With Right to Request Repairs Exhibit[1420] the buyer or seller may, within one day after the end of the Defect Resolution Period, accept the other party's last offer or counteroffer. This may be done even if the offer or counteroffer has expired or has been rejected by the party to whom the offer was made. The GAR Contract specifically states that it is intended to override the common law which provides that once an offer has been rejected or has lapsed, it is no longer capable of being accepted. An offer or counteroffer expires when it specifies a time limit for acceptance and that period has passed. An offer or counteroffer is rejected when the receiving party rejects it outright or responds with a counteroffer. The following examples show how the GAR provision works.

Example #1: Buyer timely submits an amendment and a copy of the inspection report asking the seller to repair and/or replace ten defects. During the Defect Resolution Period, the seller submits a counteroffer agreeing to repair seven items. The Defect Resolution Period then expires. Under common law, if the counteroffer has expires there is no binding agreement. However, the GAR Contract will allow the buyer to accept the seller's offer to repair the seven items within one-day of the expiration of the Defect Resolution Period, even though the time limit on his counteroffer has already expired. Likewise, the seller can agree to the buyer's request to repair the ten defects even though the seller has responded with a counteroffer. The party who accepts the other's offer first creates a Binding Agreement. If neither party acts within the one-day period, the contract automatically terminates.

Example #2: Buyer timely submits an amendment to remove inspection contingency and a copy of the inspection report asking for ten defects to be repaired. During the Defect Resolution Period, seller submits a counteroffer agreeing to repair seven items. The buyer submits another counteroffer to the seller asking the seller to repair eight of the original ten items. The Defect Resolution Period expires. The buyer can either accept the property "as is," let the contract terminate or accept the seller's counter to repair seven items even though the buyer has rejected that offer by making another counteroffer asking the seller to fix eight items. Alternatively, the seller can agree to fix the eight defects identified in the buyer's last counteroffer.

Example #3: Buyer timely submits a repair amendment to remove inspection contingency and a copy of the inspection report asking the seller to repair and/or replace ten defects. During the Defect Resolution Period seller submits a counteroffer agreeing to repair four items. The buyer submits another counteroffer to the seller asking the seller to repair eight of the original ten items. The seller responds, again stating that they will only make four repairs.

1419   GAR Form F134, Notice to Unilaterally Extend Inspection Period.

1420   GAR Form F129.

The buyer makes no further counteroffers and the Defect Resolution Period ends. The seller may agree to fix the eight items and force the buyer to purchase the property. Similarly, the buyer may agree to have the seller repair only four items even though the Defect Resolution Period has ended.

If the buyer or seller is no longer anxious to complete the transaction, they may want to make their last offer of repairs less desirable than their previous offers. If the buyer originally requested the repair of 15 defects but through negotiations reduced this number to 10, the buyer may want to revert back to his original request of 15 items if he wants to discourage the seller from accepting his last offer of repairs.

§ 10.2.3.6   Right To Request Repairs Limited To "Defects"

If the property is being purchased subject to the GAR Property Sold With Right to Request Repairs Exhibit,[1421] the buyer is limited to asking the seller to repair "defects" identified by an inspector in a written report. The Property Sold With Right to Request Repairs Exhibit defines "defects" as any infestation by termites, insects or other wood destroying organisms or any condition, building product or item in the Property or portion thereof which:

(a) is in a condition which represents a significant health risk (including lead-based paint and\or lead-based paint hazards) or an imminent risk of injury or damage to persons or property;

(b) constitutes a violation of current laws, governmental codes or regulations except if it is "grandfathered" because it was initially installed or constructed prior to or in accordance with all applicable laws, codes or regulations; or

(c) is not at the present time in good working order and repair (including damage caused by termites, infiltrating pests, and any other wood destroying organisms), normal wear and tear excepted.

It is important to note that an item is considered a "defect" if it meets any one of the above definitions rather than all three. One of the admitted weaknesses of the definition is that it is very general and leaves room for the parties to debate whether an item or condition in the property is a defect. Unfortunately, with our housing stock in Georgia varying in age from brand new to over 300 years old, it is difficult in a few short sentences to come up with a "one-size fits all" definition of a defect.

The following are examples of what would be considered a defect under the GAR Property Sold With Right to Request Repairs Exhibit.

Situation #1: Buyer hires an inspector to examine a house he has just put under contract. The inspector reports that: (a) the roof is old but still in good repair; (b) the house has lead-based paint in it; and (c) the building code has been changed since the time the house was constructed to now require additional floor bracing. The house has not shown any signs of stress from the lack of bracing, and there is no requirement to retrofit the house with additional bracing. What right does the buyer have to request that these items be repaired?

Answer: Under the current GAR Property Sold With Right to Request Repairs Exhibit the buyer does not have a right to request that the roof be replaced. This is because the roof is simply old rather than defective. The same would likely apply to the floor bracing if the original method of construction is grandfathered and there is no present requirement to add the bracing. The buyer should be able to request that the lead-based paint be remedied.

Situation #2: The inspector discovers that the house has the following: (a) aluminum wiring which would not be permitted under today's building code but is grandfathered and does not need to be replaced, and (b) no ground fault interrupt outlets in the bathrooms. The inspector believes that the current condition of the aluminum wiring is such that a fire could occur if it is not repaired. He also believes that not having ground fault interrupt outlets is a safety hazard.

1421   GAR Form F129.

Answer: While the buyer has no right to have the aluminum wiring repaired as a code violation, he probably can have it repaired as a condition which represents an unreasonable risk of injury or damage to persons or property since this is what the inspector concluded. The same argument applies to the lack of ground fault interrupt outlets.

Under the GAR New Construction Contract,[1422] the term "defects" is defined as any portion of an item in the property which: (1) is not in good working order and repair, (2) constitutes a non-grandfathered violation of applicable laws or governmental codes or regulations; (3) has not been substantially completed or constructed in substantial accordance with the plans and specifications, if any, for the property; or (4) is a defect as that term is defined in any warranty provided by the seller. The seller agrees to correct the defects in a good and workmanlike manner prior to closing. This is a very broad definition of "defect" and is protective of the buyer.

It should be noted that not all contracts for new construction define defects in the same manner as the GAR New Construction Contract. Some contracts provide that the only criteria and standards that will be used in connection with an inspection are those set forth in the warranty described and, if there is no warranty, then customary and generally accepted local area building industry standards will be used. Although customary building standards may address the issues which would be commonly defined as "defects," they may not address work that has not been substantially completed in compliance with the plans and specifications for the property.

Some builders will allow the buyer to conduct inspections of the property prior to closing but do not obligate themselves to make any repairs identified by such inspection if the builder has been able to obtain a certificate of occupancy or final inspection certificate covering the property. The builder takes this position because it has limited the definition of defects to those constituting violations of applicable governmental codes and regulations, and claims it would not have been able to obtain any such certificate if the property did not fully comply with all applicable building or health codes.

If a builder wishes to limit a buyer's inspection to violations of applicable governmental codes or regulations, the following stipulation may be used.

Special Stipulation 214:   Standards for Inspection

Notwithstanding anything to the contrary contained herein, any inspection shall be limited and restricted to inspections of the Property for violations of applicable governmental codes and regulations. In the event of any dispute between a third-party inspector and Seller regarding the existence of an alleged code violation, such dispute shall be resolved by the applicable governmental code enforcement officer and that individual's final determination shall be binding on Buyer and Seller. Notwithstanding the foregoing, the issuance of a certificate of occupancy, temporary certificate of occupancy, or final inspection certificate covering the Property by the applicable governing authority shall be conclusive and determinative of such approval and compliance with applicable governmental codes and regulations thereby indicating substantial completion of the home and obligating Buyer to close hereunder. Buyer acknowledges and agrees that at the time of any inspection certain utility services and similar items may not be fully operational and Seller shall have no liability for Buyer's inspector failing or being unable to inspect same. Upon the completion of any inspection, examination or test, Buyer shall restore the Property to its former condition. Buyer agrees to indemnify and hold Seller harmless from any and all loss and expense (including, without limitation, attorney's fees) resulting from claims and damages caused by, arising out of or incurred in connection with the exercise by Buyer of Buyer's rights under this Section.

1422   GAR Form F23.

§ 10.2.3.7   Right To Terminate For Condition That Is Not A "Defect"

When the buyer is using the Property Sold With Right to Request Repairs Exhibit, the buyer may want to include a special stipulation to allow for termination of the contract upon discovery of certain conditions on the property or structures which are not considered "defects" under the terms of the contract but which might lower the property value or about which the buyer has special concern. For example, the buyer may not want to purchase the property if it is determined that a portion of the dwelling on the property lies in a flood plain. In this circumstance, the buyer may include the following special stipulation.

> ### Special Stipulation 215:   Flood Plain Termination
>
> *Notwithstanding any other provision in this Agreement to the contrary, Buyer shall have the right to terminate this Agreement without penalty upon written notice to Seller within _____ days of the Binding Agreement Date if it is determined that any portion of the residential dwelling or garage on the Property is located in a 100 year flood plain.*

§ 10.2.3.8   Accepting Certain Defects

In the alternative, the buyer and seller may also agree that the buyer will accept a certain defect present in or on the property if the purchase price of the property is lowered accordingly. The following provision contemplates such an agreement while reserving the buyer's right to request repairs for all other defects in or on the property.

> ### Special Stipulation 216:   Buyer Accepts Certain Defects "As Is"
>
> *Notwithstanding any other provision in this Agreement to the contrary, Buyer and Seller acknowledge that the agreed-upon purchase price of the Property contemplates that the Property contains the following defects_____; Buyer agrees to accept these defects in the Property in "as is" condition and will not request that the defects be repaired or replaced in any Amendment to Remove Inspection Contingency or Amendment to Address Concerns With Property submitted on the Property.*

§ 10.2.3.9   "Defects" Include Products Subject To Class Action Lawsuits

The GAR Property Sold With Right to Request Repairs Exhibit provides that all parties acknowledge that certain building products are or have been the subject of class action lawsuits and are generally considered by inspectors to be defective. Such a building material is termed as a "Defective Product" in the GAR Contract.

Just because a property contains a Defective Product does not necessarily give the buyer the right to request that it be repaired or replaced. A Defective Product is not considered to be a defect (which the buyer can request be repaired or replaced) if: (1) the Defective Product is disclosed in the Seller's Property Disclosure Statement; (2) the Seller's Property Disclosure Statement is provided to the buyer prior to the acceptance date of the purchase contract; and (3) the Defective Product is functioning according to the manufacturer's specifications and is reasonably fit for the purposes for which it was intended as of the time of the inspection.

If a Defective Product is properly disclosed and is not presently performing in accordance with the manufacturer's specifications, the buyer can request the seller to repair or replace only the currently defective portion of the Defective Product. In the event that either of the first two conditions are not met, the buyer can request the repair or replacement of the entire Defective Product, irrespective of whether it is currently failing or not. This is explained in the following example.

Situation: An inspector discovers that the house has certain siding that was the subject of class action lawsuit. The seller is unaware that his house has this defective siding and does not disclose it as a Defective Product the Seller's

Property Disclosure Statement. The siding on the southern exposure of the house is swelling and delaminating. The rest of the siding appears to be in good condition. Can the buyer seek to have all of the siding replaced or only those boards which are delaminating?

Answer: If the particular siding is a Defective Product and was not disclosed in the Seller's Property Disclosure Statement, the buyer could request the seller to repair and/or replace the entire siding. This would also be the case if the seller answered "don't know" to the question of whether the property contained any Defective Product. However, if the seller had disclosed this condition in the Seller's Property Disclosure Statement, the buyer would only be able to request the repair and/or replacement of those portions of the siding which are not functioning in accordance with the manufacturer's specifications.

§ 10.2.3.10   Resolving Disputes Over What Is "Defect"

As discussed above, the GAR Property Sold With Right to Request Repairs Exhibit does not allow the buyer to request that the seller repair items that are not defects. What happens when a buyer and the seller disagree on whether an item is a defect? Suppose, for example, that the buyer requests the seller to, among other things, replace as a defect an old-fashioned electrical circuit box with screw-in fuses because the inspector believes it is a fire hazard. The seller agrees to fix the other items on the buyer's inspection amendment but asserts that the circuit box is old but not defective in any way.

Another example is the buyer who requests that five windows in a ten-year-old house be replaced because the inspection reveals that the seals in these windows are broken, causing them to fog. The buyer maintains that since the inspector noted that the seals are "broken," they fall within the definition of a "defect" under the contract. The seller asserts that the windows are not defective in that the glass is not broken and they open and close properly. The seller takes the position that the fog in the windows is merely cosmetic, and that the alleged broken seals are merely normal wear and tear.

In all of these examples the buyer and seller can argue and even litigate over whether these items constitute defects. If the buyer terminates the contract on the basis that the parties could not agree upon the defects to be repaired, the seller may claim that the buyer wrongfully terminated the contract.

The above examples illustrate that that there may be no clear definition of the term "defect." While there is not yet case law interpreting the definition of the term "defect," courts will likely apply a reasonableness standard when it comes to whether a particular condition is or is not a defect. The courts will also likely place heavy reliance on the conclusions of a professional home inspector who at least in theory at least should be able to give more of an objective opinion on whether a particular item in the property is a defect.

Based upon this reasonableness approach, the inspector can conclude that the windows in the above example are not in good working order and repair if the broken seals are not providing the insulating value for which they were designed. Similarly, the inspector can find that the old electrical circuit box is defective if he reasonably believes it constitutes a fire hazard. If it can be scientifically proven, however, that the risk of fire is no greater with old fashioned versus more modern circuit breakers, the likelihood is that the condition would not constitute a defect as defined by the GAR Property Sold With Right to Request Repairs Exhibit.

There are steps the parties could have taken to prevent the disputes over the meaning of the term "defect" referenced in the above examples. First, buyers should always negotiate in the contract the specific repair of as many items as can be easily identified. For example, if the buyer's offer includes a requirement that the seller replace specific windows with broken seals or the old fashioned circuit breakers, and the offer is accepted, the potential for further disputes on these issues has likely been eliminated. If the seller's disclosure statement indicated synthetic stucco, this can be addressed in the initial offer. Cosmetic items, like dings in sheetrock, peeling wallpaper, chips in paint, or stains in the carpet are also items which can be easily identified by the buyer and negotiated at the time of the offer. The following special stipulation can be used in the buyer's initial offer to the seller.

Special Stipulation 217: Listing Items Which Seller Agrees to Repair Before Inspection

Notwithstanding any other provision in this Agreement to the contrary, Seller agrees prior to closing to repair or replace in a good and workmanlike manner the following items in the Property _____. Seller's obligation herein shall in no way limit Buyer from submitting an inspection amendment in accordance with the section of the Agreement entitled "Property Sold With Right to Request Repairs."

If it is unclear whether an item in the property is a defect, the parties can contractually agree in advance that an item is considered defective. For example, the parties could agree in the contract that a heating or air conditioning system with an efficiency rating below a certain level is a defect, or that the presence of polybutylene pipes in the plumbing system is a defect regardless of whether there has been any history of breakage of the pipes on the property. The following is a sample special stipulation which could be used in this situation.

Special Stipulation 218: Certain Items Deemed to be Defects

Notwithstanding any other provision in this Agreement to the contrary, Buyer and Seller agree that the following conditions or items if discovered in or on the Property during the inspection shall be deemed a "defect" pursuant to the terms and conditions of this Agreement: _____.

The parties may also want to include a special stipulation in the contract which provides that if the parties disagree as to whether an item is a "defect," a mutually agreed upon arbitrator would decide the issue. For example, the parties could decide in advance that should a dispute arise, they would contact the Georgia Chapter of the American Society of Home Inspectors ("ASHI") who would then randomly pick an ASHI-approved inspector to act as an arbitrator and to make a binding decision as to whether the disputed item constitutes a defect. The parties could agree to split the cost of this inspector's services. This would provide a quick and effective resolution to a potential problem. The following special stipulation can be used for this purpose.

Special Stipulation 219: Agreement to Hire ASHI Certified Inspector to Arbitrate Whether Item is a Defect

Notwithstanding any other provision in this Agreement to the contrary, if Buyer and Seller cannot agree as to whether a certain item is a "defect" as that term is defined in this Agreement, Buyer and Seller agree to immediately contact the American Society of Home Inspectors ("ASHI"), to request that it randomly pick an ASHI-approved inspector to determine whether such item is a "defect" pursuant to this Agreement. Buyer and Seller further agree that: (1) the decision of said inspector shall be binding upon all parties to this Agreement; (2) the cost of obtaining such a determination shall be evenly split between the parties; and (3) the Defect Resolution Period shall be extended until one day after the determination is made to allow the parties to consider the decision of the inspector.

§ 10.2.3.11 Seller Does Not Have To Replace Defect If It Can Be Repaired

The GAR Property Sold with the Right to Request Repairs Exhibit[1423] provides that the seller does not have to replace a defect if it can be repaired such that at closing it is reasonably fit for the purposes for which it is intended. This language was added to try to resolve one of the more common disputes between buyers and sellers. While the new language opens the door for buyers and sellers to argue over whether a defect can be repaired such that it is fit for the purposes for which it is intended, it should help give guidance that replacing a defect is not needed if it can be reasonably repaired.

1423 GAR Form F129.

§ 10.2.3.12   Walk Through

The GAR New Construction Contract provides for the buyer and seller prior to closing to inspect the property and execute a "walk through list" or "punch list" specifying all items that remain to be completed.[1424] While items previously identified during a buyer's inspection can be included on this list, the GAR New Construction Contract distinguishes between minor punch list items and "defects." Under the New Construction Contract, defects would have to be remedied prior to closing; however, minor repairs, touch-ups, or adjustments may be completed subsequent to closing. The buyer may not fail or refuse to close because any such repairs, touch-ups or adjustments are incomplete. The seller is only obligated to use its best efforts to complete all such items as soon as reasonably possible. In addition, there is to be no withholding of any of seller's proceeds at closing for any walk through items which may be completed after closing without the written approval of the seller.

Like the GAR New Construction Contract, most builder contracts provide that "punch list" items do not have to be corrected until after closing, and that none of the seller's proceeds can be withheld pending completion of these items provided that the builder is able to obtain a certificate of occupancy on the property. A sample of this type of provision is set forth below.

> **Special Stipulation 220:   Seller Can Correct Punch List Items After Closing if Builder Can Obtain Certificate of Occupancy**
>
> *Buyer and Seller agree that so long as Seller can obtain a certificate of occupancy on the Property, Seller shall not be obligated to repair "punch list" items until after the Closing has occurred. Seller shall use Seller's best efforts to complete all punch list items within 30 days of the date of Closing.*

This gives the builder greater flexibility as to when repairs are to be made. However, it can sometimes be a problem for buyers if after closing, the builder loses interest in completing the repairs. Buyers can attempt to avoid this by asking the builder/seller to commit to a designated deadline by which the repairs must be completed or requiring that the funds necessary to complete the repairs be held in escrow until the repairs are completed. The following special stipulations can be used for these situations.

> **Special Stipulation 221:   Completion of Walk Through Items**
>
> *Notwithstanding anything contained herein to the contrary, Buyer and Seller agree that all items on the Walk Through List shall be completed by Seller within _____ days of the closing date.*

> **Special Stipulation 222:   Completion of Walk Through Items and Escrow of Funds**
>
> *Notwithstanding anything contained herein to the contrary, in the event that items on the Walk Through List remain to be completed as of the closing date, then Seller shall deposit into a separate escrow account sufficient funds to cover the cost of completing the said items. In the event that Seller does not complete the items on the Walk Through List within ____ days of the closing date, then the funds (or so much of them as are necessary to complete the Walk Through List items) shall be immediately paid to Buyer.*

§ 10.2.4   Seller's Duty To Repair

The GAR Property Sold With Right to Request Repairs Exhibit states that the agreed-upon defects shall be repaired or replaced. The seller has the option of repairing or replacing the defective item himself, unless the parties specifically state

---

1424   GAR Form F23 and GAR Form F26, Walk Through List.

otherwise in the contract. Moreover, the contract does not specify the type or quality of materials to be used in making repairs to the property, the methods of repair, or whether the repairs will be warranted for any period of time. The contract does provide that all agreed-upon repairs shall be made in a good and workmanlike manner prior to closing.

There is implied, in every construction contract, the obligation to perform the work in a fit and workmanlike manner, which is breached when the contractor fails to exercise a reasonable degree of care, skill, and ability.[1425] In other words, repairs must be performed in a good and workmanlike manner whether or not this is stated in the contract. The standard of "good and workmanlike manner" means that the work is to be performed in accordance with industry standards and applicable building codes. It has also been held that inspection and repair provisions of an agreement will prevail over a closing date provision where the two are in conflict. In one case, the court determined that in such a situation the closing date will be automatically extended until the repairs are made in a workmanlike fashion.[1426]

The GAR Property Sold With Right to Request Repairs Exhibit specifically provides that the seller is not obligated to replace a defective item if it can be repaired such that at closing it is reasonably fit for the purposes for which it was intended. For example, if some shingles fall off a relatively new roof, the seller would not have to replace the entire rood if it can be adequately repaired by merely replacing the missing shingles. If the repair will not leave the repaired item reasonably fit for the purposes for which it was intended, the buyer could demand that the item be replaced.

§ 10.2.4.1   Deciding Who Should Make Repairs

Some buyers may want to require that repairs be performed by a particular contractor or with a higher level of skill than what might normally be used by a contractor. The special stipulations below can be used to address these concerns.

> **Special Stipulation 223:   Agreement to Hire Specific Company to Perform Repairs**
>
> *Seller agrees that all repairs and replacements of defects agreed to by the parties (excepting items the cost of which to repair or replace is less than $10) shall be performed by XYZ Contractor prior to closing. Prior to closing Seller shall present Buyer with a paid invoice from said contractor confirming that the agreed upon repairs have been performed.*

> **Special Stipulation 224:   Agreement to Hire Contractor with Experience**
>
> *Seller agrees that all agreed upon repairs to the Property shall be performed by a highly skilled contractor with at least _____ years of full-time experience in the area requiring repairs and who is licensed (where it is possible to obtain a license to perform the repair in question) to make the agreed upon repairs. Seller further agrees that all repairs shall be performed prior to closing in a first quality manner typical of a contractor with the level of expertise described above.*

§ 10.2.4.2   Deciding Who Should Pay For Repairs

The seller may be willing to hire a particular company to perform the work but may be concerned about the cost of the repairs. In this instance the seller can try to cap the seller's financial obligations to make repairs. The special stipulation below is an example of this type of provision.

1425   *Nulite Industries Co., LLC v. Horne*, 252 Ga.App. 378, 556 S.E.2d 255 (Ga.App.,2001)

1426   *Yargus v. Smith*, 254 Ga.App. 338, 562 S.E.2d 371 (2002).

Special Stipulation 225: Agreement to Hire Specific Company to Perform Repairs and Replacements with Cost Limitation

Seller shall hire XYZ Contractor to complete the following agreed-upon repairs and replacements:_____. However, Seller shall not be obligated to pay more than $_____ for said repairs and replacements based on the bid provided by Contractor attached hereto and incorporated herein. If the bid is higher than this amount, Buyer at his/her option may either terminate this Agreement upon notice to Seller and without penalty, or agree in writing to reimburse Seller for the additional amount at the Closing.

Buyers may also require the seller to assign to the buyer any warranty for such repairs or replacements, as in the following stipulation.

Special Stipulation 226: Seller Assigns Repair Warranties to Buyer

Notwithstanding any provision to the contrary contained herein, where the contractor who performs any agreed-upon repairs or replacement offers a warranty for the work performed by the contractor, Seller shall either provide that the warranty be issued in the name of the Buyer or assign his interest in the warranty to the Buyer at or before closing.

In the alternative, if the buyer is responsible for the cost of repairs, she may want to include an inspection stipulation for greater flexibility if the cost of repairs is too demanding. The parties could stipulate, for example, that the buyer will have the right to terminate the contract if the repair costs for the defects exceed a specified amount. The following sample provision may be used in this instance.

Special Stipulation 227: Buyer's Right to Terminate if Repair Costs Excessive

Notwithstanding any other provision in this Agreement to the contrary, Buyer shall have the right to terminate this Agreement upon written notice to Seller within _____ days of the Binding Agreement Date if after inspecting the Property the Inspector estimates that the cost of repairing and/or replacing any defects (as defined in this Agreement) discovered therein will cost more than $_____.

§ 10.2.4.3 Repairs With Guarantees

There are some repairs which buyers will likely want warranted or guaranteed in order to be comfortable closing on the purchase. This is particularly the case with recurring defects such as roof leaks or leaking basements. While the inspection amendment procedure in the GAR Contract does not give the buyer a right to demand a warranty or guarantee of repairs, such a right can be negotiated as part of an offer. The following is an example of such a provision.

Special Stipulation 228: Seller Required to Use Contractor that Provides Warranty for Recurring Defects

Should the Inspector's report reveal any roof leaks or moisture damage, flooding or water leakage problems affecting any portion of the residential dwelling or garage on the Property, then all agreed-to repairs shall be performed by a licensed Georgia contractor who has been continuously in the business for at least five (5) years and who will upon the completion of the work issue an assignable written guarantee against any defects in labor and materials used in this repair for a period of not less than one year from the date of the repair, which guarantee or warranty shall be assigned by Seller to Buyer at or before closing (if not issued in the Buyer's name).

§ 10.2.4.4 Specifications On How Repairs To Be Made

Some buyers may want more control over the repair process than to simply have the seller agree to make repairs in a good and workmanlike manner. An example of a special stipulation where the buyer controls the method of repairs is set forth below.

> **Special Stipulation 229:   Seller Must Make Repairs According to Inspector's Specifications**
>
> *Notwithstanding any other provision to the contrary contained in this Agreement, Buyer shall have the right to require Seller to cause all agreed-upon repairs and replacements of defects to be repaired and/or replaced in accordance with specifications prepared by Buyer's Inspector.*

Similarly, there may be occasions when the buyer wants a particular method of a repair. For example, damaged or discolored wood flooring may be present and the buyer desires to have a thorough repair performed rather than simply having the area sanded and/or refinished. The following is an example of a special stipulation that gives very specific instructions on how the repair of wood flooring is to be handled. The greater the precision in specifying how a repair is to be made, who is going to make it and when, the less the potential for disputes.

> **Special Stipulation 230:   Detailed Description of Repair Work to Wood Flooring**
>
> *Prior to Closing Seller shall cause a professional flooring contractor who specializes in the repair and installation of hardwood floors to repair the following area of the Property: [describe in detail; for example, the approximately two foot by two foot area in the living room where water has stained and discolored the hardwood floor].*
>
> *The contractor shall first determine if any part of the flooring material is soft or rotted and replace all soft or rotted flooring with new flooring (and, if necessary, sub-flooring). The new flooring shall be of the same type, width and length as the flooring currently in the room.*
>
> *Contractor shall then sand the damaged area to remove the water stains, stain the sanded floor area to substantially match the color to the color of the existing flooring in the room, and seal it with two coats of a polyurethane sealer.*
>
> *Buyer acknowledges that the contractor shall not have to sand the hardwood floor in the entire room where the repair is being made and shall only be responsible to use her best efforts to blend the appearance of the repaired area with the general appearance of the remainder of the floor in the room.*

For certain structural repairs the buyer may require that the seller obtain an engineer's opinion that structural defects on the property were properly corrected in accordance with accepted standards and practices of the construction industry. The special stipulation below is an example of this type of provision.

> **Special Stipulation 231:   Seller Required to Provide Engineer's Opinion for Structural Repairs**
>
> *Notwithstanding any provision to the contrary contained herein, for any agreed-upon repair of a structural defect, Seller shall at Seller's sole expense cause to be provided to Buyer at or prior to closing a written letter or report of a licensed Georgia structural engineer (which is signed by the engineer and has the engineer's seal affixed to the letter*

or report) that in the professional engineer's opinion, the structural defect described as follows: _____ was corrected in accordance with sound engineering practices and principles and all applicable building code requirements.

§ 10.2.4.5 Seasonal Inspections

In some circumstances, several months might be required in order for the buyer to obtain a complete inspection of a particular condition or structure in or on the property. For example, even though the GAR Contract requires the seller to have all utility services and any pool, spa, or similar item operational during the inspection period, in reality, if the property has a pool or outdoor spa and a contract is entered into in December, the pool or spa may not be open for inspection. Likewise, the air conditioning may not be properly tested during colder months and the heating system may not be tested in hot weather.

In these situations, the parties may agree that for a specified time period after closing the seller will warrant that such items are fully and properly operational. If the item is then not functioning properly when it is put back into service, the seller will agree to make any necessary repairs. The following special stipulation may be used for such an agreement.

> **Special Stipulation 232: Seller's Obligation to Fix Defects Not Found Before Closing Due to Seasonal Issues**
>
> *Buyer and Seller acknowledge and agree that the following item or items in or on the Property cannot be properly inspected due to seasonal weather or other conditions: _____. Seller therefore warrants that these items are in good working order and repair and free of defects as of the Binding Agreement Date. If, for a period of _____ days from the closing date of this Agreement, Buyer uses such items for the first time and finds that any of the above items are not in proper working order and repair or are defective, Seller shall be responsible at Seller's sole expense to reimburse Buyer for the cost of repairing or replacing said item(s). If Buyer does not use such item for the first time within the period specified above or if the defects of which the Buyer complains were caused by the Buyer or his guests, agents, or representatives, Seller's obligation to repair or replace the item shall be void. This provision shall survive the Closing.*

To protect the seller from having to spend a great deal of money to fix the defect after closing, the above special stipulation could also limit the amount of money the seller would be required to pay for this type of repair. For example, the seller could add the following language to the end of the above stipulation.

> **Special Stipulation 233: Seller's Obligation to Pay to Fix Defects is Capped**
>
> *Notwithstanding any provision to the contrary contained herein, Seller's financial obligation to make repairs and/or replacements shall not exceed the sum of $_____."*

§ 10.3 PROPERTY SOLD SUBJECT TO DUE DILIGENCE PERIOD

The GAR Contracts contain a Due Diligence Period provision which, if agreed to by the seller, gives the buyer a right to terminate the contract without penalty within a negotiated period of time. The right to terminate the contract is often referred by to by real estate agents as a "free look." Prior to the expiration of the Due Diligence Period the buyer may conduct whatever due diligence on the property the buyer deems appropriate, request that any item of concern to be buyer be addressed, and terminate the contract without obligation if that is the desire of the buyer. The contract also states that the buyer has paid the seller $10 as consideration for the seller granting the buyer a right to terminate.

§ 10.3.1 Due Diligence Period Intended To Create Option Contract

The Due Diligence Period is intended to give the buyer an option to purchase the property which is automatically exercised unless the buyer terminates the contract. An option contract is one of the few legal devices available to buyers to give them a discretionary right to buy or not buy property.

The Due Diligence Period includes a recital of $10 separate consideration being paid by the buyer to the seller for the seller granting this option to the buyer. One question which regularly arises when a GAR Due Diligence Period is included in a contract is whether the $10 consideration recited as payment for the option must actually be paid by the buyer to the seller. While there is little harm done in paying the $10, it should not have to be paid to the seller. This is because the Due Diligence Period includes an acknowledgment on the part of the seller that the $10 has been paid to and received by the seller, and is sufficient consideration for the seller allowing the buyer to have the Due Diligence Period.

When questions arise regarding whether an amount recited in the contract as having been paid has actually been paid, Georgia courts will interpret the contract in accordance with its terms. The Court will not allow the introduction of parol evidence or oral testimony unless there is an ambiguity in the contract itself.[1427] Since the GAR Contract plainly states that the $10 consideration has been paid, received, and is sufficient consideration for the grant of the rights contemplated in the Due Diligence paragraph, normally there should not be any reason for a court to look beyond the four corners of the contract to see if that amount was actually paid.

Some sellers have argued that the price paid by the buyer for a "free look" should be significantly more than $10 if a property is to be taken off the market for any period of time. A special stipulation where the money paid by the buyer for the "free look" is significantly more than $10 is set forth below.

> **Special Stipulation 234: Larger Payment by Buyer to Seller for Right to Terminate**
>
> *Notwithstanding any provisions to the contrary contained herein, the consideration for Seller granting Buyer the right to terminate as set forth herein shall be the payment by Buyer to Seller of the sum of $_____. This payment shall be made no later than within one (1) day from the Binding Agreement Date. In the event the payment is not timely made the Seller may, but shall not be required to, terminate this Agreement upon notice to Buyer. Since this payment is consideration of Seller granting Buyer the right to terminate this Agreement, it shall not be refundable to Buyer and shall not be applied to the purchase price of the Property.*

Another approach is for the buyer to give the seller a significant sum for the right to terminate the contract, but then provide that a portion of this payment is applied toward the purchase price of the property if the buyer closes upon the purchase of the property. The special stipulation set for below is an example of such a provision.

> **Special Stipulation 235: A Portion of Payment for Right to Terminate to be Applied Toward Purchase Price**
>
> *Notwithstanding any provision to the contrary contained herein, the consideration for the Seller granting Buyer the right to terminate as set forth herein shall be the payment by Buyer to Seller of the sum of $_____. This payment shall be made no later than within one (1) day from the Binding Agreement Date. In the event the payment is not timely made the Seller may, but shall not be required to, terminate this Agreement upon notice to Buyer. Since this payment is in consideration of Seller granting Buyer the right*

1427   See § 1.3.11.2 of this work for a more detailed discussion of the parol evidence rule prohibiting the admission of oral evidence to contradict the stated terms within a contract.

to terminate this Agreement it shall not be refundable to Buyer. However, if Buyer elects to close upon the purchase of the Property, _____% of the above-referenced amount shall be applied toward the purchase price of the Property at closing.

§ 10.3.2 Due Diligence Period In Commercial Transactions

§ 10.3.2.1 Length Of Due Diligence Period

The GAR Contracts allow the parties to indicate the length of the due diligence period. The parties may provide for any agreed upon length of time. For instance, the parties may agree to a "zero day" due diligence period (in which the property would be sold "as is") or a 120 day due diligence period. The due diligence period in residential transactions typically ranges anywhere from 5 days to 30 days, while the due diligence period in commercial transactions generally takes much longer. The due diligence period in land/lot transactions can vary depending on the different inspections conducted.

For two reasons, the due diligence period in commercial real estate transactions tends to be more comprehensive in scope and often time longer in length. First, the purchase price of commercial properties is often larger than residential properties. Therefore, buyers tend to be more careful in studying a commercial property than a residential one. Second, in Georgia, the passive concealment doctrine has not yet been extended to commercial real estate transactions.[1428]

The passive concealment doctrine is an exception to the general legal principle of *caveat emptor* (buyer beware).[1429] Under this exception, sellers are obligated to disclose latent or hidden defects in a property that would not normally be observable by a buyer under a routine inspection of the property.[1430] This doctrine prevents sellers of residential properties from sitting on their hands and saying nothing about hidden defects of which the seller is aware.[1431] With the passive concealment doctrine not yet applicable to commercial transactions, buyers are under a greater duty to protect themselves through a careful inspection of the property.

The theory in not extending the passive concealment doctrine to buyers of commercial properties is that buyers tend to be far more sophisticated than residential buyers and are thus better able to protect themselves. Therefore, buyers of commercial properties usually insist on longer due diligence periods so that they can fully evaluate the property.

It is not unusual for sellers of commercial properties to provide extensive due diligence materials to buyers in commercial real estate transactions. Often times these materials are provided under a confidentiality agreement in which the buyer agrees to return the due diligence materials to the seller if the buyer terminates the contract prior to the end of the due diligence. In other cases, the seller will also request that the buyer return any due diligence materials prepared on behalf of the buyer. So for example, if a buyer obtains a new survey during the due diligence period and then elects not to proceed with the purchase of the property, the buyer would be under a duty to provide all due diligence materials to the seller.

An example of a provision requiring the return of due diligence materials is as follows.

Special Stipulation 236: Return of Due Diligence Materials

In the event of termination of the contract after inspection, buyer will provide without fee or charge to the seller, a copy of any and all reports, studies and information obtained by the buyer during the due diligence period, including, but not limited to, zoning, sanitary and storm sewer, water, electricity, gas, and telephone service availability to the Property,

---

1428   *Savage v. KGE Associates Ltd. Partnership*, 260 Ga.App. 770, 580 S.E.2d 591 (2003).

1429   *Savage v. KGE Associates Ltd. Partnership*, 260 Ga.App. 770, 580 S.E.2d 591 (2003).

1430   *Deckert v. Foster*, 230 Ga.App. 164, 495 S.E.2d 656 (1998).

1431   *Deckert v. Foster*, 230 Ga.App. 164, 495 S.E.2d 656 (1998).

containment letters, governmental approvals submitted and/or obtained, surveys, plats, covenants, restrictions and easements affecting the Property, all title opinions, title insurance commitments and title insurance policies, agreements affecting the Property, inspection reports and studies (i.e. rock, environmental (Phase I-III), dam studies, radon, etc.).

It is also not uncommon for such buyers to request due diligence materials relating to the property or any business being operated on the property. Buyers will also often seek to have the seller make warranties regarding the due diligence materials, the property, and/or the business being operated thereon to help the buyer evaluate the property. The approach of the GAR Contracts to due diligence is to provide an exhibit to the purchase and sale agreement in which the user can check all those that apply to the transaction. The GAR Commercial Due Diligence Documents Exhibit[1432] is a checklist of the types of materials buyers might want to see in different types of transactions to help them evaluate the property.

For example, in most commercial real estate transactions it would not be unusual for the buyer to request copies of the following: the most recent survey of the property; *ad valorem* property tax bills; a title insurance policy; all inspection reports; a phase one environmental assessment of the property; copies of pending, threatened or existing litigation arising out of or related to the property; all notices or code and other violations of government regulations affecting the property; leases; insurances policies; service contracts; and financial records of any business run from the property.

§ 10.3.2.2 Seller's Representations And Warranties In Commercial Real Estate Transactions

It is common in commercial real estate transactions for the buyer and seller to each make warranties and representations in the purchase and sale contract for the benefit of the other party. Representations and warranties are promises that are incorporated into the contract. If they survive the closing, they can give a party greater legal protection from she would otherwise have because if the warranty later turns out to be incorrect, it creates a cause of action for breach of contract by the party who relied on the warranty.

Representations and warranties are also a way of getting the buyer and seller comfortable with each other and the transaction prior to investing what can often be a significant amount of time and money in due diligence.

In some cases, representations and warranties are as simple as a party saying that she has the authority to enter into the contract or the buyer, if it is a legal entity, warranting that the entity has been duly created. Other representations and warranties are designed to avoid unwelcome surprises coming out later in the transaction after a party is psychologically invested in the deal. If there are issues in the deal that may prevent a party from proceeding with the purchase or sale of the property, it is best to get them on the table early and try to get them resolved.

For example, a buyer requests that the seller warrant that she is unaware of any pending condemnation or eminent domain proceedings involving the property. If there is a pending condemnation action, this request will likely force a seller's hand and result in a more complete disclosure of the status of such a condemnation action.

Set forth below are examples of some of the most common representations and warranties in commercial transactions. Additional representations and warranties for commercial purchase and sale agreements can be found in the GAR Commercial Purchase and Sale Agreement Exhibit "D" Seller's Representations and Warranties.[1433]

(a) that seller has the right, power and authority to enter into the Agreement and to convey the property in accordance with the terms and conditions of the Agreement; and the persons executing the Agreement on behalf of the seller have been duly and validly authorized by the seller to execute and deliver the Agreement and have the right, power and authority to enter into the Agreement and bind the Seller;

1432   GAR Form CF4, Exhibit "B" to Commercial Purchase and Sale Agreement (Due Diligence Materials).

1433   GAR Form CF6.

(b) that seller represents and warrants that the seller is solvent and has not made a general assignment for the benefit of creditors or been adjudicated as bankrupt or insolvent, nor has a receiver, liquidator or trustee of the seller or any of its respective properties (including the property being sold) been appointed or a petition filed by or against the seller for bankruptcy, reorganization, arrangement or protection pursuant to the Federal Bankruptcy Act or similar federal or state statute, or any proceeding institutes for the dissolution or liquidation of the seller;

(c) that seller has not been notified that any condemnation or other taking by eminent domain of the property or any portion thereof has been instituted and, to the best of seller's knowledge, there are no pending or threatened condemnation or eminent domain proceedings (or proceedings in the nature or in lieu thereof) affecting the property or any portion thereof or its use;

(d) that the seller is not aware of any structural or other defects, latent or otherwise, in the improvements. The heating, ventilating, air conditioning, electrical, plumbing, water, storm drainage and sanitary sewer systems at or servicing the property, are to the best of the seller's knowledge, in good condition and working order and the seller is not aware of any material defects or deficiencies therein;

(e) that to the best of the seller's knowledge, there is no default, or any event in which the passage of time or notice, or both, would constitute a default or breach on the part of the seller under any declaration of easements and/or restrictive covenants affecting the property; and, to the best of the seller's knowledge, there is no default or claim of default or any event which the passage of time or notice, or both, would constitute a default or breach thereunder on the part of any party whose property is encumbered by or benefits from any declaration;

(f) that to the best of the seller's knowledge (a) no "hazardous substances," as the term is defined in the Comprehensive Environmental Response, Compensation, and Liability Act, and the rules and regulations promulgated pursuant thereto, or any other pollutants, toxic materials, or contaminants have been or shall prior to the closing be discharged, disbursed, released, stored, treated, generated, disposed of, or allowed to escape on the property in violation of applicable law; (b) no underground storage tanks are located on the property or were located on the property and subsequently removed or filed; (c) the property has not been previously used as a gas station, cemetery, landfill, or as a dump for garbage or refuse; and (d) the property has not previously been used and is not currently listed on the Georgia Environmental Protection Division Hazardous Site Inventory. Seller has not received any notice or demand from any governmental or regulatory agency or authority requiring the seller to remove any hazardous substances or contaminants or toxic materials from the property;

(g) that the rent roll which the seller has provided to the buyer is the complete and accurate rent toll for the property as of the date hereof setting forth the leases in effect relating to the property and setting forth with respect to each of the leases (a) the name of the tenant thereunder; (b) the commencement and termination dates of the term of each lease and information relating to renewals or extensions thereof; (c) the premises covered by each such lease; (d) the amount of rent, percentage rent and other charges payable thereunder and the date to which rent and other charges payable thereunder have been paid; and (e) the amount of the security deposit required under each said lease and held by the seller;

(h) that there are no actions, suits, or proceedings pending or, to the best of the seller's knowledge, threatened by any organization, person, individual, or governmental agency against the seller with respect to the property or against the property, or with respect thereto, nor does the seller know of any basis for such action. The seller also has no knowledge of any currently pending application for charges in the zoning applicable to the property or any portion thereof;

(i) that the seller has not been notified that there are any proceedings that could have the effect of impairing or restricting access between the property and adjacent public roads and, to the best of the seller's knowledge, no such proceedings are pending or threatened;

(j)   that to the best of the seller's knowledge, there are no violations of law, municipal or county ordinances, building codes or other legal requirements with respect to the property; the improvements comply with all applicable legal requirements (including applicable zoning ordinances) with respect to the use, occupancy, and construction thereof; and the conditions to the granting of the zoning of the property have been satisfied; and

(k)   that to the best of the seller's knowledge, no assessments (other than ad valorem taxes) have been made against the property that are unpaid whether or not they have become liens.

§ 10.3.3   Due Diligence In Lot/Land Transactions

The GAR Land Purchase and Sale Agreement,[1434] the GAR Lot Purchase and Sale Agreement[1435] and the GAR Purchase and Sale Agreement[1436] provide the same due diligence options for a buyer. A buyer can agree up front that to purchasing the property "as is" or it can elect to have a due diligence period. The due diligence period for this type of transaction varies because during this time, the buyer will conduct whatever inspections it deems necessary to determine if the property can be used by the buyer for its intended purpose.[1437]

In addition, unlike the other GAR Contracts, the GAR Land Purchase and Sale Agreement obligates the seller to provide the buyer with certain Due Diligence Materials affecting the property. The Due Diligence Materials include certain tax and title information, environmental reports and assessments, any leases affecting the property, and any permits, licenses and authorizations affecting the property.

The inclusion of a Due Diligence Period should be important to a buyer purchasing undeveloped land. The buyer will want to review matters such as governmental ordinances, environmental issues, zoning issues, whether the property can support a septic system of the size needed for the contemplated improvements on the property (commonly referred to as a percolation test), as well as utility service matters. For example, if utilities are not available at the lot line, the buyer's expense in bringing such utilities can significantly increase the cost of the property to the buyer.

In rural areas, for example, it was and is still common for trash and debris to be burned, buried or simply dumped in an inconspicuous spot on the property. In some cases, this included chemicals used in agriculture or in other home-based industries. Buyers coming upon dump sites or areas of trash on a property should consider having such areas tested to confirm that they are not buying an environmentally contaminated area that could require remediation.

A significant issue for buyers purchasing larger tracts of land should be potential hazardous waste being discovered on the property. The Federal Comprehensive Environmental Response, Compensation and Liability Act (CERCLA)[1438] addresses environmental contamination resulting from uncontrolled hazardous waste sites. CERCLA imposes liability on the current owner or operator of a facility as well as the owner or operator of the facility at the time of disposal. To address potential hazardous waste issues as part of the feasibility study, buyers may commission (and lenders will likely require) a Phase I Environmental Site Assessment to identify obvious or reasonably likely sources of hazardous or regulated materials that may be associated with the property.

§ 10.3.4   Buyer Contracting For Multiple Properties

The GAR Contracts once used a checkbox to indicate whether buyers had other properties under contract and whether or not they would have the right to put other properties under contract. This language was removed from the GAR Contract because it was extremely difficult to police whether or not a buyer had other property under contract. As a

---

1434   GAR Form F34.

1435   GAR Form F27.

1436   GAR Form F20.

1437   GAR Form 34.

1438   42 U.S.C.A. § 9601 to 42 U.S.C.A. § 9675.

practical matter, when a buyer has a Due Diligence Period with an absolute right to terminate the purchase and sale agreement for any reason whatsoever, the seller has little or no way to know or control the novations of a buyer for purchasing a property. Sellers wanting the buyer to warrant that they do not have other properties under contract and will not put other properties under contract while the purchase and sale agreement is subject to contingencies can use the following special stipulation.

> **Special Stipulation 237: Buyer Will Not Contract to Purchase Multiple Properties**
>
> *Buyer warrants that as of the Offer Date herein, the Buyer does not have other real estate under a pending contract to purchase (including an option contract). Buyer further agrees that Buyer will not enter into any other agreement to purchase or option to purchase real property while this Purchase and Sale Agreement is subject to any contingencies, Due Diligence Periods or conditions precedent in favor or Buyer. In the event Buyer breaches the above warranty, Seller may terminate this Agreement due to Buyer's breach.*

§ 10.3.5 Amendment To Address Concerns With Property

The Due Diligence Period in the GAR Contracts is the time for the buyer to inspect the property and decide whether or not to purchase it. All inspections and the negotiations regarding any concerns with the property must be completed prior to the end of the Due Diligence Period. The "free look" period is therefore similar to the buyer's due diligence period in the GAR Commercial Purchase and Sale Agreement.[1439]

Prior to the expiration of the Due Diligence Period, the buyer must notify the seller that she is not going forward with the purchase of the property. If the buyer does nothing and the Due Diligence Period expires, the buyer is obligated to purchase the property in "as-is" condition.

During the Due Diligence Period, the buyer may also propose an amendment to the contract to address any concerns the buyer may have with the property. Let's assume the buyer hires an inspector who indicates that the roof is old and will need to be replaced in the next couple of years. Can the buyer request that the seller replace the roof? The answer is yes. The buyer can submit an amendment requesting the seller to either replace the roof prior to closing or reduce the purchase price in an amount sufficient to allow the buyer to do the work after the closing. The amendment should be on the GAR Amendment to Address Concerns with Property form.[1440] When the buyer has a Due Diligence Period, he no longer has to prove that items of concern in the property are defective. Instead, the buyer can request the repair of any item in the property and propose any amendment to the Agreement the buyer desires. The seller, of course, can accept, reject or counter any proposed amendment of the buyer. The buyer can also elect to terminate the contract if the seller does not agree to any proposed amendment and the right to terminate has not expired.

The nature of the negotiations between buyers and sellers are more open-ended during a Due Diligence Period. Unlike the traditional inspection section where the negotiations are restricted to "defects," no such restrictions apply with a Due Diligence Period. So for example, nothing would prevent a buyer who realizes that she is paying too much for a property to simply go back to the seller and say that she will terminate the contract if the seller does not agree to an amendment reducing the purchase price of the property.

Similarly, it is also likely that buyers will ask for price concessions in lieu of repairs since there is nothing limiting buyers to request only the repair and/or replacement of defects. However, if the seller makes a financial concession without stating in the contract the defects or concerns the price concession is intended to address, the seller runs the risk that an unscrupulous buyer might later assert a claim against the seller for those very defects.

[1439] GAR Form CF2.

[1440] GAR Form F107.

This risk is particularly great if the buyer discovers after the closing that the cost of the repairs turns out to be greater than the price concession made by the seller. To avoid problems in this area sellers agreeing to reduce the purchase price instead of making repairs should state in the contract what repairs the reduction in price is intended to cover, or clearly state that the payment is being made in lieu of all repairs. The special stipulation below is typical of this kind of provisions.

> **Special Stipulation 238: Clarification of Repairs to be Addressed Through Price Concessions**
>
> *Buyer acknowledges that Seller is agreeing to reduce the purchase price of the Property by $_____ to reflect the fact that the Property contains certain problems, conditions and/or defects including the following:_____*
>
> *Buyer: (1) acknowledges that Buyer and Buyer's inspectors and/or other experts have had an ample opportunity to inspect and become thoroughly familiar with the above-referenced problems, conditions and/or defects; (2) agrees to accept the same "as-is;" and (3) covenants and agrees never to sue Seller with respect to the same or with respect to any other problems, conditions or defects that a thorough investigation of the above referenced problems, conditions and/or defects by Buyer and Buyer's inspectors and experts would have revealed.*

The GAR Amendment to Address Concerns with Property[1441] form on which amendments can be requested during the Due Diligence Period also provides a check-box in which the buyer and seller can agree whether the Due Diligence Period terminates or does not terminate if the seller accepts the Amendment to Address Concerns With Property.

§ 10.3.5.1 Using Amendment To Address Concerns With Property As Notice To Terminate

If the buyer is concerned about failing to timely give a notice to terminate when the buyer has a Due Diligence Period, the buyer can use the GAR Amendment to Address Concerns with Property form as a notice to terminate if the Amendment is not accepted. This can be done by adding the following special stipulation to the end of the GAR Amendment to Address Concerns with Property.

> **Special Stipulation 239: Using GAR Amendment to Address Concerns With Property as a Notice to Terminate**
>
> *In the event this Amendment to Address Concerns with Property is not accepted by Seller and delivered back to Buyer prior to the end of the Due Diligence Period, this Amendment to Address Concerns with Property shall serve as notice of Buyer's decision to terminate this Agreement.*

Of course, the problem with this type of provision is that if it is not accepted, the contract is automatically terminated.

§ 10.3.5.2 Right To Proceed Rather Than Right To Terminate

Another approach to a due diligence period is to provide that the contract automatically terminates unless prior to the end of the "free look" period the buyer gives a notice that she will proceed with the purchase of the property. With this approach, if no notice is given to the seller, or if notice is given late, the contract terminates. In this way the risk of the buyer being forced to buy a property that she does not want to buy is minimized. This approach is often used with commercial contracts. The special stipulation below is an example of this type of provision.

1441   GAR Form F107.

Special Stipulation 240: Free Look Where Notice to Proceed is Required

For and in consideration of ten ($10) dollars and other good and valuable consideration, the receipt and sufficiency of which is hereby acknowledged, Seller hereby grants to Buyer the option for _____ days from the Binding Agreement Date ("Option Period") to purchase the Property in accordance with the terms and conditions of this Agreement. If Buyer elects to purchase the Property, Buyer must give notice of Buyer's decision to proceed with the purchase of the Property prior to the expiration of the Option Period. If Buyer does not give Seller notice of his decision to proceed with the purchase of the Property prior to the expiration of the Option Period, this Agreement shall automatically terminate and Buyer shall be entitled to the return of his earnest money. During the Option Period, Buyer shall have the right to seek to amend the Agreement to address any concerns of Buyer with the Property.

§ 10.3.5.3 Including A Due Diligence Period But Agreeing Not To Ask For Repairs

Some real estate licensees want the purchase and sale agreement to include a Due Diligence Period with no right to request repairs. The theory behind such an approach is that the buyer is going to take the property in "as is" condition and not request repairs. However, the buyer wants a time period during which she can verify that there are no major problems with the property. While this approach works well in theory, it does not tend to work well in practice. If defects are discovered that are sufficient to cause the buyer to terminate the contract, the parties end up negotiating for the repair of the defects or for a price concession to reflect the existence of the defects. This makes the provision somewhat self-defeating and raises the question as to why not simply include a Due Diligence Period in the purchase and sale agreement to begin with.

Nevertheless, some licensees still use this type of provision as a practical way to eliminate the buyer from asking for the repair of minor defects in the property. Certainly, if a request is made for minor repairs, it gives the seller the moral high ground to remind the buyer that the agreement of the parties was that no repairs would be requested. A sample of this type of special stipulation is set forth below.

Special Stipulation 241: Due Diligence Period With No Right To Request Repairs

Buyer acknowledges that the Property may contain any number of minor defects or deficiencies which Buyer agrees to accept in "as-in" condition. Therefore, while Buyer shall retain the right to terminate this Agreement for any reason whatsoever during the Due Diligence Period, Buyer agrees that the Property is being accepted in "as-is" condition. Buyer agrees not to request any price concessions or repairs resulting from the discovery of defects or other adverse conditions in or relating to the Property.

§ 10.3.5.4 Combining Right To Terminate With Seller's Right To Continue Offering Property For Sale

The seller may want the right to continue marketing efforts while the buyer inspects the property. The special stipulation below is an example of this type of provision.

Special Stipulation 242: Due Diligence Period With Kick Out Provision

This Agreement is subject to a Due Diligence Period which ends on _____, 20_____. Seller shall have the right to continue to offer Seller's Property for sale. In the event Seller receives an acceptable offer, Seller shall give notice of having received such an offer to Buyer in accordance with the Agreement. Buyer shall then have _____ hours, after receipt of such notice to deliver a notice to Seller terminating and ending Buyer's Due Diligence Period. The removal and termination of the Due Diligence Period shall not, however, terminate or affect any other contingencies to which the Agreement may be subject. In the event Buyer does not deliver the required notice within the time period stated above, then the parties agree that this Agreement shall become null and void upon the expiration of said time period, and Buyer shall be entitled to a return of Buyer's earnest money.

§ 10.3.5.5 Buyer Exercising Right To Terminate During Due Diligence Period

If the buyer elects to terminate the contract during the Due Diligence Period set forth in the GAR Contracts, the buyer must give written notice of the buyer's decision prior to the expiration of the Due Diligence Period. There is now a GAR Form that can be used to give notice of such a termination.[1442] If the buyer fails to do this, buyer agrees to purchase the property in "as is" condition. This means that buyers must know when the Due Diligence Period ends, and ensure that any notice of termination is delivered to the seller or the broker representing the seller as a client prior to the expiration of the right to terminate.

Being in the middle of negotiations regarding items of concern will not stop or prevent the Due Diligence Period from expiring. For example, if the buyer has a remaining concern regarding the property and the seller is obtaining bids for its repair, the Due Diligence Period will still expire if the parties do not agree and sign off on the Amendment to Address Concerns With Property prior to the expiration of the right to terminate.

In such a situation, the buyer can give the seller a notice of the buyer's decision to terminate the contract pursuant to the right set forth in the Due Diligence Period provision, or get an amendment to the contract signed extending the right to terminate for some additional time period. An example of an amendment to extend the right to terminate period is set forth below.

> **Special Stipulation 243: Amendment to Extend Time to Exercise Right to Terminate**
>
> *For and inconsideration of the sum of $10, the receipt and sufficiency of which is hereby acknowledged, Buyer and Seller agree that the Due Diligence Period as set forth in the Agreement shall be extended for _____ additional days from the Binding Agreement Date. All other pro-visions in the Agreement shall remain the same.*

§ 10.3.5.6 End Of The Due Diligence Period

The end of the Due Diligence Period is normally when the buyer's earnest money becomes non-refundable. This is what is often referred to as the earnest money "going hard." Some purchase and sale agreements provide that the contract automatically terminates at the end of due diligence unless the buyer provides an affirmative notice to proceed with the agreement. A sample provision requiring notice to proceed is set forth below.

> **Special Stipulation 244: Due Diligence Period: Contract Terminates if no Notice to Proceed is Given**
>
> *Notwithstanding any other provision to the contrary contained herein, no later than the date of expiration of the Due Diligence Period, Buyer or its designee shall notify Seller in writing of Buyer's decision to proceed with the purchase of the Property (a "Notice to Proceed"). If Buyer has not delivered a Notice to Proceed by the expiration of the Due Diligence Period, this Agreement shall terminate automatically (with no need for Buyer to send any type of additional notice to Seller).*

1442   GAR Form F83, Notice to Terminate; Termination and Release Agreement.

The other approach is for the Due Diligence Period to automatically terminate if the buyer does not provide the seller with a notice to terminate the contract. A sample of this type of provision is set forth below.

> **Special Stipulation 245: Due Diligence Period: Due Diligence Period Ends if No Notice to Terminate is Given.**
>
> *Notwithstanding any other provision to the contrary contained herein, no later than the date of expiration of the Due Diligence Period, Buyer or its designee shall notify Seller in writing if the Buyer has decided not to proceed with the purchase of the Property (a "Notice of Termination"). Buyer shall have the right to make the decision not to proceed and to thus terminate the Agreement in its absolute and sole discretion for any reason or for no reason. If the Buyer has not delivered a Notice of Termination by the expiration of the Due Diligence Period, it shall be conclusively deemed that (i) Buyer is waiving its right to terminate this Agreement based upon Buyer's right to do so under the Due Diligence Period; (ii) Buyer has decided to proceed with the purchase of the Property; and (iii) the Due Diligence Period shall have expired and Buyer's rights thereunder are now terminated.*

The basic difference between the two approaches is that with the first approach, the contract terminates automatically if no notice is given. With the second approach, if no notice is given, the parties agree to move forward with the contract and the buyer's right to terminate for any reason ends.

§ 10.3.5.7   Expiration Of Right To Terminate Does Not Affect Other Contingencies In Contract

The GAR Contract specifically provides that the expiration of the right to terminate the contract based on the Due Diligence Period does not eliminate any other contingencies to which the contract is subject. So, for example, if the contract contains a financing contingency, the expiration of the Due Diligence Period does not eliminate the financing contingency.

If the seller grants the buyer a right to terminate for a particularly long period of time, the seller may want to provide that all contingencies in the contract are eliminated upon the expiration of the Due Diligence Period. The following is an example of such a special stipulation.

> **Special Stipulation 246:   All Contingencies in Contract Eliminated Upon Expiration of Right to Terminate**
>
> *Upon the expiration of the Due Diligence Period this Agreement as set forth herein, the parties agree that all other contingencies and conditions precedent favoring the Buyer to which this Agreement is subject shall also end. At that time, this Agreement shall no longer be subject to any contingencies.*

§ 10.4   SPECIAL TYPES OF DUE DILIGENCE

§ 10.4.1   Due Diligence In Purchasing A Lot

As part of the buyer's due diligence in buying a lot on which the buyer is planning to build a residence, the buyer should check with local government to determine whether the lot is properly zoned for the buyer's intended use, what building setback requirements are applicable to the lot, whether the buyer will have to pay impact fees to develop the property, and whether there are any special regulations or conditions (such as tree ordinances, flood plains, or historic preservation ordinances) or special setbacks from rivers and streams that may limit the development of the lot. If the lot is part of a larger subdivision of property, buyers should also determine whether the property was properly subdivided, and whether there are subdivision covenants that require house and development plans be approved by an architectural control committee, establish a minimum square footage requirement for dwellings, and/or regulate the type of building materials which can and cannot be used in construction.

Buyers will sometimes seek to condition the purchase of a lot on obtaining a building permit from the local governmental authority to construct the buyer's anticipated improvements. However, in most jurisdictions in Georgia, a building permit will not be issued until a complete set of construction plans has been approved by the local government. Therefore, unless such plans have already been prepared, such a contingency may make little sense.

In addition, buyers should determine whether water, sewer and other utilities are available to the property. If public utilities are not available, buyers should determine whether the soil conditions on the property permit the use of a septic system and if so, how large a system can be installed. If the source of water will be a private well, the water should be tested to see if it is potable. These issues are discussed in greater detail in the sections below.

§ 10.4.2 Size Of Septic Tank

If a residential property is served by a septic system, one question that frequently arises is whether the system is properly sized for the number of bedrooms in the property. For example, most health department regulations allow a 1,000 gallon septic system to be used in a house that has no more than four (4) bedrooms.[1443] However, the same regulations would normally require a septic system of 1,250 gallons or larger to be used in a house with five (5) or more bedrooms.[1444]

Some builders have tried to get around the requirement of having a larger septic system by trying to re-characterize a bedroom as something other than a bedroom. This can be done by either leaving a bedroom in an unfinished area within the home that can be converted into a bedroom at a later time or by replacing a closet with a framed opening and/or removing the door to the room in order to claim that the room is not a bedroom. Of course, while these changes may technically make the room no longer a bedroom, the changes can and are easily undone by the buyer. A subsequent owner of the property may not realize that the septic system is now undersized for the actual number of bedrooms in the house (until the system fails in some form or fashion).

Under the regulations of most departments of health in Georgia, the size of the required septic system is based on the number of bedrooms. Whether the system is ultimately adequate will depend on the intensity of use of the system by the residents of the home. A septic system that is generally inadequate under the health regulations in a five (5) bedroom home may still work fine if a smaller family is occupying the same house.

Buyers of homes with septic systems can normally check with the Department of Health in the county in which the property is located to determine the number of bedrooms that were approved on the property based on the size of the septic system.

§ 10.4.3 Septic Systems

In a lot transaction, if the lot is not served by public sewer, the buyer should confirm that the lot can accommodate a septic system. This can be determined by a soils engineer performing what is known as a percolation test, or "perc test."

Merely because a lot can accommodate a septic system does not mean that the buyer's due diligence in this area is at an end. If a lot only marginally passes the percolation test, it may only be able to accommodate a septic system with a limited capacity. As a result the governing authority may restrict the number of bedrooms in the house to prevent the system from being overwhelmed and failing. Buyers concerned about this issue can include the following stipulation in their contracts.

1443   Ga. Comp. R. & Regs. 290-5-26-.05(3).

1444   Ga. Comp. R. & Regs. 290-5-26-.05(3).

Special Stipulation 247:   Lot Can Accommodate Septic System

Buyer plans to erect a home and other improvements on the Lot in the location shown on the survey attached hereto as Exhibit _____. Notwithstanding any provision to the contrary contained herein, this Agreement is contingent upon a licensed Georgia soils engineer, selected and paid for by Buyer, determining that a septic system other than a drop emitter system can be installed on those portions of the Lot on which a septic system is permitted to be installed under local, state and federal law, excluding that area where the home and other improvements are to be constructed as shown on the attached Exhibit, and such that the Lot can accommodate a septic system which will allow the house to contain at least _____ bedrooms, _____ full bathrooms, _____ half bathrooms, and _____ garbage disposals designed for use with a septic system. In the event the soils engineer determines that the above-referenced standard cannot be met, Buyer may terminate this Agreement without penalty prior to closing upon notice to Seller.

It should be noted that the use of a garbage disposal in a home with a septic system can limit the capacity of the system for other uses.

§ 10.4.4   Utilities

Buyers purchasing lots in a land/lot transaction should ensure that they can be used for their intended purposes. There is no guarantee that a lot will be served by utilities. Some lots have utilities physically located on the lot itself or located on a public right of way adjacent to a lot. In other cases, utilities are located on adjacent property and can only be accessed if an easement is obtained from the owner of the neighboring land. With regard to sewer lines, buyers should not only check with the sewer provider to determine if sewer lines are located nearby, but also whether there is sufficient capacity to allow the buyer to tie into the sewer.

§ 10.4.5   Soil Conditions

Even if sewer is available to the lot in a lot transaction, buyers should still consider having the lot evaluated by a soils engineer to confirm that there are no sub-surface conditions which could impair the ability to develop the lot. If a lot has large amounts of underground rock, or an underground spring, it could make the development of the lot expensive if not impossible. In Georgia, the presence of large amounts of granite is often a good predictor of the presence of higher radon levels on a property. While radon can easily be controlled with blowers, buyers concerned about radon should take this into consideration. In other cases, the lot may contain uncompacted fill dirt or buried construction debris which will either need to be compacted or removed before construction can commence. The following special stipulation may be helpful to buyers concerned about this possibility.

Special Stipulation 248:   Warranty Regarding Construction Debris

Seller warrants that no construction debris has been buried on the Property including but not limited to tree trunks, stumps, concrete, plastic, brick, stone, wood or other organic or inorganic materials. This warranty shall survive till closing.

§ 10.4.6   Well Test

Another issue that commonly arises in a lot transaction is whether a property is served by well water. A buyer of property served by well water will likely want the well water tested to determine its suitability for drinking or any other use and such testing will most likely be required by any lender. An example of a special stipulation to use in such circumstances is set forth below.

Special Stipulation 249:   Well Clearance Letter, Allocation of Fees

*Notwithstanding any other provision to the contrary contained herein,
_____ shall pay the fee associated with obtaining any
lender-required well clearance letter meeting the requirements of the lender. Such letter
shall generally provide that the necessary bacteriological and/or organic tests of the well
have been conducted and shall provide the results of such tests.*

§ 10.4.7   Environmental Due Diligence

One of the more important parts of due diligence when purchasing commercial property is obtaining or performing an environmental inspection. Commercial lenders will almost always require such an inspection because if the property is contaminated, the buyer's mortgage lender could have liability for the clean-up in the event it ends up owning the property as the result of a foreclosure. There is a greater perceived risk of environmental contamination with commercial properties since in some cases they may have been used for activities that generated environmental hazards and contaminants.

The initial inspection by an environmental engineer is known as a Phase One environmental report in which the environmental engineer reviews the history of the property and surrounding properties to determine if they may have been used in a way that may cause the property to now be contaminated. The engineer also typically does soil studies and other basic evaluations to determine if environmental contaminants are present in the soil or ground water.

If the initial study produces any evidence of contamination, the lender will normally insist that a follow-up Phase Two study be undertaken. If the property is found to have serious environmental contamination, it will normally be difficult to obtain financing to purchase the property unless the site is remediated.

Since the cost of an environmental clean-up can be quite large, buyers and sellers often vigorously negotiate what representations and warranties the seller of the property will make regarding the presence of environmentally hazardous substances on the property. Sellers will normally not want to make warranties that the property is free of environmental contamination and will instead try to encourage the buyer to use her due diligence period to assess the environmental condition of the property. In cases where the seller has less negotiating leverage, the seller may warrant that she did not use the property in ways which contaminated the property or that the seller does not have any actual knowledge of environmental contamination on the property. An example of this type of provision is set forth below.

> *To the best of Seller's knowledge:*
>
> *(i) no "hazardous substances," as that term is defined in the Comprehensive Environmental Response, Compensation, and Liability Act, and the rules and regulations promulgated pursuant thereto, or any other pollutants, toxic materials, or contaminants have been or shall prior to Closing be discharged, dispersed, released, stored, treated, generated, disposed of, or allowed to escape on Property in violation of applicable law;*
>
> *(ii) no underground storage tanks are located on the Property or were located on the Property and subsequently removed or filled;*
>
> *(iii) Property has not previously been used as a gas station, cemetery, landfill, or as a dump for garbage or refuse; and*
>
> *(iv) Property has not previously been and is not currently listed on the Georgia Environmental Protection Division Hazardous Site Inventory.*
>
> *Seller has not received any notice or demand from any governmental or regulatory agency or authority requiring Seller to remove any hazardous substances or contaminants or toxic materials from Property.*

> *For the purposes of this warranty, the term "knowledge" shall be limited to the actual knowledge of directors, officers and managers of the selling entity and to no other person.*

In other cases, the buyer will seek an affirmative warranty that no environmental problems exist and an agreement on the part of the seller to indemnify against any problems.

> *With respect to the Property, (i) no Hazardous Materials are present or have been released in, on, under or around the Property or have migrated onto or from the Property; (ii) there are not and have not been any underground or aboveground storage tanks at, on, under or around the Property; (iii) the Property is not and has never been used as a dump or landfill, (iv) the Property is and has been in compliance with all applicable Environmental Laws; (v) there are no actions, suits, claims, proceedings, investigations or enforcement actions pending or, to Seller's knowledge, threatened under any Environmental Law with respect to the Property; and (vi) Seller has not received any notice, claim or demand from any governmental entity or other person regarding the presence of Hazardous Materials at, on, under or around the Property or alleging that the Property is in violation of any Environmental Laws.*

> *Seller agrees to indemnify, defend and hold harmless Purchaser and Purchaser's parents, subsidiaries, affiliates, officers, directors, employees, agents, successors and assigns from and against any and all claims, demands, notices, liabilities, causes of action, damages (including without limitation multiple and natural resources damages), fines, penalties, assessments, costs and expenses whatsoever (including without limitation reasonable attorneys' and consultants' fees and the reasonable cost of any Remedial Work) (collectively "Losses") arising out of or related directly or indirectly to: (i) the presence or suspected presence of any Environmental Condition in, on, under or around the Property or the improvements thereon on or prior to the date of Closing; (ii) any migration on, under or from the Property, before or after the date of Closing, of any Environment al Condition existing in, on, under or around the Property on or before the date of Closing; (iii) any actual or alleged violation of any Environmental Law with respect to the Property on or before the date of Closing;*

> *For the purposes of this Agreement:*

> *"Environmental condition" means any condition, contamination, constituent(s) or set of circumstances that requires any Remedial Work pursuant to any Environmental Law, or otherwise gives rise to liability under any Environmental Law, including without limitation the presence or Release, or threatened Release, or any Hazardous Material in, on or into the air, soil, surface water, groundwater or other media.*

> *"Environmental Laws" shall include, without limitation, any present and future local, state and federal laws, statutes, regulations, rules, ordinances and common law, and all judgments, decrees, orders, agreements or permits issued, promulgated, approved or entered thereunder by any governmental agency or authority, relating to the use, storage, handling or release of Hazardous Materials, protection of the environment and / or protection of human health and safety, including without limitation the Comprehensive Environmental Response, Compensation and Liability Act ("CERCLA"), 42 U.S.C. § 9601 et seq., as amended by the Superfund Amendments and Reauthorization Act of 1986 ("SARA").*

"Hazardous Materials" means any substance, waste or material that is regulated by, forms the basis of liability under, or is defined as hazardous, extremely hazardous or toxic under, any Environmental Law, including without limitation petroleum or any byproducts or fractions thereof, any form of natural gas, asbestos, polychlorinated biphenyls, radon or other radioactive substances, infectious, carcinogenic, mutagenic or etiologic agents, pesticides, defoliants, explosives, flammables, corrosives, urea formaldehyde, alcohols, chemical solvents, pollutants or contaminants.

"Release" means any spilling, leaking, pumping, pouring, emitting, emptying, discharging, injecting, escaping, leaching, migrating, dumping or disposing (including without limitation the abandonment or discarding of barrels, containers or other open or closed receptacles).

"Remedial Work" means any and all investigation, assessment, cleanup, containment, restoration, removal, monitoring, or other remedial or treatment, or post-remedial or post-treatment, work or services concerning Environmental Conditions.

§ 10.5 SELLER'S REPRESENTATIONS AND WARRANTIES IN COMMERCIAL REAL ESTATE TRANSACTIONS

It is common in commercial real estate transactions for the buyer and seller to each make warranties and representations in the purchase and sale contract for the benefit of the other party. Representations and warranties are promises that are incorporated into the contract. If they survive the closing, they can give a party greater legal protection from she would otherwise have because if the warranty later turns out to be incorrect, it creates a cause of action for breach of contract by the party who relied on the warranty.

Representations and warranties are also a way of getting the buyer and seller comfortable with each other and the transaction prior to investing what can often be a significant amount of time and money in due diligence.

In some cases, representations and warranties are as simple as a party saying that she has the authority to enter into the contract or the buyer, if it is a legal entity, warranting that the entity has been duly created. Other representations and warranties are designed to avoid unwelcome surprises coming out later in the transaction after a party is psychologically invested in the deal. If there are issues in the deal that may prevent a party from proceeding with the purchase or sale of the property, it is best to get them on the table early and try to get them resolved.

For example, the buyer requests the seller to warrant that she is unaware of any pending condemnation or eminent domain proceedings involving the property. If there is a pending condemnation action, this request will likely force a seller's hand and result in a more complete disclosure of the status of such a condemnation action.

Set forth below are examples of some of the most common representations and warranties in commercial transactions. Additional representations and warranties for commercial purchase and sale agreements can be found in the GAR Commercial Purchase and Sale Agreement Exhibit "D" Seller's Representations and Warranties.[1445]

(a) that seller has the right, power and authority to enter into the Agreement and to convey the property in accordance with the terms and conditions of the Agreement; and the persons executing the Agreement on behalf of the seller have been duly and validly authorized by the seller to execute and deliver the Agreement and have the right, power and authority to enter into the Agreement and bind the Seller;

(b) that seller represents and warrants that the seller is solvent and has not made a general assignment for the benefit of creditors or been adjudicated as bankrupt or insolvent, nor has a receiver, liquidator or trustee of the seller or

---

1445   GAR Form CF6.

any of its respective properties (including the property being sold) been appointed or a petition filed by or against the seller for bankruptcy, reorganization, arrangement or protection pursuant to the Federal Bankruptcy Act or similar federal or state statute, or any proceeding institutes for the dissolution or liquidation of the seller;

(c) that seller has not been notified that any condemnation or other taking by eminent domain of the property or any portion thereof has been instituted and, to the best of seller's knowledge, there are no pending or threatened condemnation or eminent domain proceedings (or proceedings in the nature or in lieu thereof) affecting the property or any portion thereof or its use;

(d) that the seller is not aware of any structural or other defects, latent or otherwise, in the improvements. The heating, ventilating, air conditioning, electrical, plumbing, water, storm drainage and sanitary sewer systems at or servicing the property, are to the best of the seller's knowledge, in good condition and working order and the seller is not aware of any material defects or deficiencies therein;

(e) that to the best of the seller's knowledge, there is no default, or any event in which the passage of time or notice, or both, would constitute a default or breach on the part of the seller under any declaration of easements and/or restrictive covenants affecting the property; and, to the best of the seller's knowledge, there is no default or claim of default or any event which the passage of time or notice, or both, would constitute a default or breach thereunder on the part of any party whose property is encumbered by or benefits from any declaration;

(f) that to the best of the seller's knowledge (a) no "hazardous substances," as the term is defined in the Comprehensive Environmental Response, Compensation, and Liability Act, and the rules and regulations promulgated pursuant thereto, or any other pollutants, toxic materials, or contaminants have been or shall prior to the closing be discharged, disbursed, released, stored, treated, generated, disposed of, or allowed to escape on the property in violation of applicable law; (b) no underground storage tanks are located on the property or were located on the property and subsequently removed or filed; (c) the property has not been previously used as a gas station, cemetery, landfill, or as a dump for garbage or refuse; and (d) the property has not previously been used and is not currently listed on the Georgia Environmental Protection Division Hazardous Site Inventory. Seller has not received any notice or demand from any governmental or regulatory agency or authority requiring the seller to remove any hazardous substances or contaminants or toxic materials from the property;

(g) that the rent roll which the seller has provided to the buyer is the complete and accurate rent toll for the property as of the date hereof setting forth the leases in effect relating to the property and setting forth with respect to each of the leases (a) the name of the tenant thereunder; (b) the commencement and termination dates of the term of each lease and information relating to renewals or extensions thereof; (c) the premises covered by each such lease; (d) the amount of rent, percentage rent and other charges payable thereunder and the date to which rent and other charges payable thereunder have been paid; and (e) the amount of the security deposit required under each said lease and held by the seller;

(h) that there are no actions, suits, or proceedings pending or, to the best of the seller's knowledge, threatened by any organization, person, individual, or governmental agency against the seller with respect to the property or against the property, or with respect thereto, nor does the seller know of any basis for such action. The seller also has no knowledge of any currently pending application for charges in the zoning applicable to the property or any portion thereof;

(i) that the seller has not been notified that there are any proceedings that could have the effect of impairing or restricting access between the property and adjacent public roads and, to the best of the seller's knowledge, no such proceedings are pending or threatened;

(j) that to the best of the seller's knowledge, there are no violations of law, municipal or county ordinances, building codes or other legal requirements with respect to the property; the improvements comply with all applicable legal requirements (including applicable zoning ordinances) with respect to the use, occupancy, and construction thereof; and the conditions to the granting of the zoning of the property have been satisfied; and

(k) that to the best of the seller's knowledge, no assessments (other than ad valorem taxes) have been made against the property that are unpaid whether or not they have become liens.

§ 10.6 HOME WARRANTY PROGRAMS

Many companies now offer home warranties programs to buyers of both new and existing homes. With regards to new homes, the warranties generally cover most defects in labor and materials for one to two years and then provide for a longer warranty on the structural components and/or major systems in the residence. Warranties on existing homes usually offer coverage for one (1) year against an appliance breaking, roof leaks or a problem with one of the systems serving the property such as electrical, heating and air conditioning and plumbing. The purpose of warranties on existing homes is to give buyers some peace of mind about purchasing a previously occupied home where the systems and appliances in the home may be older and their condition is unknown.

Buyers should read the terms and conditions of the program they select carefully to determine what items are actually covered and to determine all exclusions. Buyers should also determine any additional costs for service calls and deductibles.

Sellers of existing homes may offer to purchase a warranty for the buyer as an incentive to the buyer, and the cost of the warranty can be included in the contract. In other cases, the buyer may choose to purchase a warranty on her own. For the relatively modest cost of a home warranty, warranties are an increasingly popular marketing tool to help sell their properties and reassure buyers that they will have some protection against things breaking after closing.

With new construction, most builders typically provide a one-year warranty with the sale of the home or offer a warranty with longer coverage periods offered by a third party home warranty system. In the GAR New Construction Contract, the seller agrees to either warrant the property for a one-year period from the date of closing against all defects of labor and materials, normal wear and tear excepted or to provide a warranty with at least that coverage.[1446]

Buyers should carefully review the terms and conditions of such warranties. Some warranties require the buyer to pursue a warranty claim prior to being able to sue in court for damages. Others require arbitration in the event of a disagreement over the coverage of the warranty conducted by arbitrators selected by the home warranty company. Buyers should also be careful to follow exactly the notice requirements for filing claims in a builder's warranty. Many such warranties only provide coverage if notice is sent via certified mail to a specified address, etc. In addition, the systems in a newly constructed home may be under a manufacturer's warranty when the home is purchased by the buyer. An example of a warranty provision in which the seller pays for the home warranty is as follow.

> **Special Stipulation 250: Seller to Pay for Home Warranty**
>
> *At or before Closing, Seller agrees to reimburse Buyer for the actual cost of a home warranty of Buyer's choosing up to the following amount: $_____. If Buyer selects a home warranty which costs in excess of this sum, any overage shall be paid by Buyer.*

Real estate licensees should be extremely careful about accepting payment for performing services relative to the issuance of a home warranty. Such fees must be disclosed in writing to the licensee's customer and client.[1447] Additionally, unless the payment is carefully structured, it could be a RESPA violation to accept such a payment.[1448]

1446   GAR Form F23.

1447   O.C.G.A. § 43-40-25 (b)(6); GREC Rule 520-1-.10(6).

1448   FR Doc. 2010–15317.

§ 10.6.1 Limited Warranty

Many builders also include either an insured limited warranty or a builder's limited warranty with the home. These additional warranties are attached to and incorporated in the contract. With this approach, the buyer will have, at a minimum, a one-year workmanship warranty even if no warranty is attached to the contract. Although not specifically found in the GAR New Construction Contract, most builder contracts will contain language limiting a buyer's remedies to the particular warranty offered in the contract and requiring the buyer to waive any other available remedies. The following language can be used for this purpose.

> **Special Stipulation 251: Waiver of Additional Warranties/ Rights**
>
> *THERE ARE AND WILL BE NO OTHER OR FURTHER WARRANTIES OR REPRESENTATIONS ON THE PROPERTY AND IMPROVEMENTS (INCLUDING, WITHOUT LIMITATION, WARRANTIES OF MERCHANTABILITY, WORKMANLIKE QUALITY, HABITABILITY, SUITABILITY FOR RESIDENTIAL PURPOSES, OR FITNESS FOR A PARTICULAR PURPOSE, OR OTHERWISE), EITHER EXPRESS OR IMPLIED, WRITTEN, ORAL OR STATUTORY, MADE BY SELLER OTHER THAN AS EXPRESSED IN THE WARRANTY DESCRIBED HEREIN, AND ALL SUCH OTHER WARRANTIES ARE HEREBY EXPRESSLY EXCLUDED AND DISCLAIMED BY SELLER. THE WARRANTY PROVIDED HEREIN IS ALSO GIVEN BY SELLER AND ACCEPTED BY PURCHASER IN LIEU OF ALL OTHER RIGHTS OR REMEDIES THAT PURCHASER HAS OR MAY HAVE AT LAW OR IN EQUITY AGAINST SELLER RELATING TO THE PROPERTY, CONSTRUCTION ON THE PROPERTY, AND THE CONDITIONS OR CIRCUMSTANCES EXISTING ON THE PROPERTY, INCLUDING BUT NOT LIMITED TO, ANY RIGHTS OR REMEDIES BASED ON NEGLIGENT CONSTRUCTION, MISREPRESENTATION, ANY TORT, VIOLATION OF ANY CODE, STATUTE OR RULE, BREACH OF CONTRACT (EXPRESS OR IMPLIED) OR BREACH OF WARRANTY (OTHER THAN BASED ON THE TERMS OF THE WARRANTY HEREIN GIVEN), AND ALL SUCH OTHER RIGHTS OR REMEDIES ARE HEREBY EXPRESSLY WAIVED BY BUYER. BUYER ACKNOWLEDGES THAT BUYER HAS RECEIVED AND READ A COPY OF THE CURRENT WARRANTY AND CONSENTS TO THE TERMS THEREOF, INCLUDING, WITHOUT LIMITATION, THE MANDATORY BINDING ARBITRATION PROVISIONS CONTAINED HEREIN.*

Just because a builder's warranty has expired does not necessarily mean that the buyer is without recourse if a construction problem develops or is discovered in the property. Depending on the facts and circumstances of the case, other legal claims can sometimes be asserted for negligent construction, breach of contract, and/or fraud if the period of time in the relevant statute of limitations has not elapsed.

The **RED BOOK**

CHAPTER 11

NOTICE

OVERVIEW

This chapter explains what constitutes proper notice to a party in an agreement as well as the form requirements for such notice. This chapter also contains a discussion of who may receive notice, as well as the various methods used to deliver notice to another party. Sample stipulations are also provided to show how parties can include these different notice requirements and delivery methods in a purchase and sale agreement.

§ 11.1 NOTICE

§ 11.1.1 Notice Generally

Most real estate contracts require notices to be in writing since verbal notices raise evidentiary questions as to whether a particular notice was given. The Statute of Frauds requires that a contract for the sale of property or any interest in or concerning property is required to be in writing.[1449] Verbal notice of the acceptance of a purchase and sale agreement is also generally insufficient to create a binding agreement for the purchase and sale of real property.[1450] Any amendment or termination of a real estate purchase and sale agreement must also generally be in writing.[1451]

There are occasions where a court will find that the parties waived the requirement for written notice through their conduct. Verbal agreements to extend the date of closing or the date by which an offer could be accepted have been found to be a waiver when the parties ignore the contractual requirements and continue to deal with one another as if the contract is still in existence. So, for example, let's say that a buyer contracts to purchase the seller's property with a closing date scheduled for June 1, 2012. The purchase and sale agreement explicitly provides that any modification to the agreement must be in writing. Nonetheless, on May 31, the buyer informs the seller that he is still working with the lender to obtain financing for the transaction and the parties verbally agree to extend the closing date to July 1, 2012. Before, the rescheduled closing date, the parties continue to negotiate the terms of the agreement. On July 1, the buyer shows up at the closing only to learn that the seller refuses to close the transaction on the basis that the contract is expired for failure to properly extend the closing date. In this case, even though the contract contains a requirement that all modifications be in writing, the seller waived that requirement by his conduct.[1452] Since the seller acted in a manner as to lead the buyer to believe that the closing date would not be strictly enforced, the seller cannot then claim that the contract is expired because the closing did not take place on the original closing date and the rescheduled closing date was not extended pursuant the agreement.[1453]

Another example is when a buyer contracts to purchase the seller's property with the closing scheduled for January 5, 2012. The contract provides that any extension of the closing date in the agreement must be in writing. Regardless, when the buyer informs the seller that he cannot obtain financing by the closing date, the seller verbally agrees to reschedule the closing for March 1. The seller also informs the buyer that it is not necessary to change the closing date in the agreement. Before the rescheduled closing date, the seller accepts the buyer's escrow payment and the parties continue to negotiate the terms of the agreement. When the buyer shows up for the closing on March 1, the buyer is informed that the seller refuses to sell the property to the buyer because the contract is expired (as of January 5). Similar to the example above, the seller after the original closing date acted in such a manner as to lead the buyer to believe that strict compliance to the closing date was not necessary.[1454] As such, the seller will be deemed to have waived the writing requirement to extend the closing by his conduct and cannot now claim that the contract is expired.[1455]

1449 O.C.G.A. § 13-5-30.

1450 *Pate v. Newsome*, 167 Ga. 867, 147 S.E. 44 (1929).

1451 *RHL Properties, LLC v. Neese*, 293 Ga.App. 838, 668 S.E.2d 828 (2008); see also 7 Ga. Jur. Contracts § 4:3.

1452 *Miller v. Coleman*, 284 Ga.App. 300, 643 S.E.2d 797 (2007).

1453 *Miller v. Coleman*, 284 Ga.App. 300, 643 S.E.2d 797 (2007).

1454 *Frank v. Fleet Finance, Inc. of Georgia*, 227 Ga.App. 543, 489 S.E.2d 523 (1997).

1455 *Frank v. Fleet Finance, Inc. of Georgia*, 227 Ga.App. 543, 489 S.E.2d 523 (1997).

Parties are well advised to closely examine their contracts to determine if there are limitations as to when, where, or how notice may, or must, be given. This is because many real estate purchase and sale agreements, particularly in commercial real estate transactions, limit the means by which notice can be sent. If the parties wish to allow notices to be sent in a variety of different ways, the following special stipulation can be used.

Special Stipulation 252: Notice Requirements

All notices shall be in writing and shall be delivered either by personally delivering it by Federal Express or similar overnight courier service (provided that the service maintains a tracking log from which a written record of when the notice was delivered can be produced upon request) to the person to whom notice is directed, or by email, or by facsimile transmission, or by depositing it with the United States Postal Service, certified mail, return receipt requested, with adequate postage prepaid, addressed to the appropriate party (and marked to a particular individual's attention). Such notice shall be deemed delivered at the time of personal or email delivery or, if mailed, when it is deposited as provided above, but the time period in which a response to any such notice must be given or any action taken with respect thereto shall commence to run from the date it is personally delivered or, if mailed, the date of receipt of the notice by the addressee thereof, as evidenced by the return receipt. Notwithstanding the above, notice by facsimile transmission shall be deemed to have been given as of the date and time it is transmitted if the sending facsimile machine produces a written confirmation with the date and time the notice was sent and the telephone number to which the notice was sent. Rejection or other refusal by the addressee to accept the notice shall be deemed to be receipt of the notice. In addition, the inability to deliver the notice because of a change of address of the party of which no notice was given to the other party as provided below shall be deemed to be the receipt of the notice sent. The addresses of the parties to which notice is to be sent shall be those set forth below. Such addresses may be changed by either party by designating the change of address to the other party in writing. Notwithstanding anything to the contrary herein, in the event Seller requests Purchaser provide consent to any item related to this Agreement, the consent by Purchaser shall be deemed implied and consented to if Purchaser fails to submit a response to any written request for consent within fifteen (15) days after Purchaser receives notice of the requested consent.

§ 11.1.2 Notice Under The GAR Contract

The GAR Contracts provide that notice may only be delivered by one of the following methods: (a) in person; (b) by an overnight delivery service, prepaid; (c) by facsimile transmission (FAX); (d) by the United States Postal Service, postage prepaid, registered or certified return receipt requested; or (e) by email.[1456]

The GAR Contract[1457] provides that all notices, including but not limited to offers, counteroffers, acceptances, amendments, demands, notice of termination and all other notices permitted or required between the parties, must be in writing and be signed by the person giving the notice. The GAR Contract goes on to provide that it is the intent of the parties that the written notice requirement shall apply even prior to a contract having been created. While it is uncertain whether this will ultimately be upheld in court, this language was intended to force a party making an offer to provide written notice of any intent to withdraw or modify that offer prior to its acceptance by the other side. If the parties wish to require notices in this manner, the following special stipulation can be used.

1456   GAR Form F20.

1457   GAR Form F20.

Special Stipulation 253: Notices Must Be In Writing

All notices, including but not limited to offers, counteroffers, acceptances, amendments, demands, notices of termination and other notices, required or permitted hereunder shall be in writing, signed by the party giving the notice. It is the intent of the parties that the requirements of this Notice paragraph shall apply even prior to this Agreement becoming binding.

The written notice requirement was included in the GAR Contract to minimize disputes between the parties as to the substance of the notice and whether it was actually delivered. Giving notice verbally when the GAR Contract requires notice to be in writing creates a significant risk that the notice will be deemed to be ineffective. For example, an attempt to accept an offer in a manner inconsistent with the terms of the contract may result in the offer being deemed to be a counteroffer. In one Georgia case, the court held that an attempted verbal acceptance of an offer constituted a counteroffer because the verbal acceptance varied the terms of the offer which required the acceptance of the offer to be in writing.[1458] The GAR Contract also requires that notices be signed by the party giving the notice. This effectively prevents a real estate licensee from giving notice on behalf of a client unless the licensee first gets the notice signed by the licensee's client. In other words, under the GAR Contract, licensees can receive notice on behalf of a client but cannot normally send notice without it first being signed by the client.

In the event a client wanted to authorize a real estate licensee to send notice on behalf of the client, the following special stipulation could be used.

Special Stipulation 254: Licensee Can Send Notice on Behalf of Client

Notwithstanding any provision to the contrary contained herein, any notice signed and delivered by _____ (Licensee) on behalf of the [Buyer/Seller] in this transaction shall for all purposes herein be deemed to have been signed and delivered by the [Buyer/Seller] and shall for all purposes satisfy the notice requirements herein that notice be signed and delivered by [Buyer/Seller].

§ 11.1.3 Notice To Broker Or Agent Is Generally Notice To Broker's Or Agent's Client

The GAR Contract provides that notice to the broker shall be deemed to be notice to a party being represented by the broker as a client, except when the broker is acting in a designated agency capacity. Notice is also sufficient if delivered to the broker's employee or affiliated licensee who is acting on behalf of a client. However, notice to the broker is not notice to the broker's customer. Therefore, in determining whether notice to the broker or sales agent is sufficient, the parties must first determine whether the broker or agent have a client relationship with any of the parties to the transaction.

As discussed above, an exception to this rule is in cases where the broker is practicing designated agency. With designated agency (where the broker has a client relationship with both the buyer and seller and has designated one agent to represent the seller and another to represent the buyer) notice given to an agent will be deemed notice to the agent's client. However, notice to the broker will not be considered notice to either client.

For example, a buyer wants to notify the seller that she has decided to terminate the contract. If the seller is represented as a client by a listing broker, delivering notice to the listing broker, or the sales agent who is working for the seller, is the same thing as delivering it directly to the seller. The notice is deemed to be delivered to the seller as of the time it is received by the listing broker or agent, even though they have yet to deliver the notice to the seller. If, however, the seller is not being represented by a listing broker as a client, then the notice would have to be received directly by the seller to be considered good notice. If the same broker was representing both the buyer and seller in a designated agency, then notice to the agent who was designated to represent the seller would be valid notice to the seller.

1458   *Frey v. Friendly Motors, Inc.*, 129 Ga.App. 636, 200 S.E.2d 467 (1973).

If the parties wish to allow notice to the broker as notice to the broker's client, except in situations of designated agency, the following special stipulation may be used.

> **Special Stipulation 255:   When Notice to Broker is Notice to Broker's Client Except in Designated Agency Transactions**
>
> *Except in transactions in which the Broker is practicing designated agency, notice to the Broker, the Broker's employees or the affiliated licensee of Broker representing a party in the transaction shall for all purposes herein be deemed to be notice to that party and such persons are hereby authorized to act as agents of the party for the limited purpose of receiving notice. In any transaction in which the Broker is practicing designated agency, only notice to the affiliated licensee designated by Broker to represent the party in the transaction shall be notice to that party. Personal delivery of notice may only be delivered to the party intended to receive the same or that party's designated agent.*

§ 11.1.4   Notice To An Unrepresented Party

Under the GAR Contract, a real estate licensee working with an unrepresented customer cannot normally receive e-mail on behalf of the customer. The theory behind this approach is that absent a client relationship there may not be a significant enough relationship between the parties for the licensee to accept notices on behalf of the customer. In these situations, notice must be sent directly to the customer. To ensure that the other party in the transaction has an ability to give notice to the unrepresented party, the GAR Contract now requires the unrepresented party to provide an e-mail address and/or facsimile number at which the unrepresented party can receive notice.

Although a client relationship is generally required for sufficient notice, there may be situations when the buyer or seller is merely working with, but not represented by a broker or sales agent. If this is the case, the parties may wish to allow notice to the broker or agent to be considered valid notice to an unrepresented buyer or seller. If so, they may use Special Stipulation 02: Notice to broker working with customer is deemed notice to customer.

There may be situations in which a party wants allow a power of attorney, or attorney representing the party to accept notice on that party's behalf. If this is the case, the parties may use the following special stipulations.

> **Special Stipulation 256:   Notice to Power of Attorney Shall Be Notice to Person Giving Power of Attorney**
>
> *All parties agree that for all purposes under this Agreement, notice to a person acting as the power of attorney for a party shall be deemed notice to that party.*
>
> **Special Stipulation 257:   Notice to Attorney for Party Shall Be Notice to Party**
>
> *All parties acknowledge that _____ [Attorney] is representing _____ [Buyer/Seller] in this transaction in an attorney/client relationship and agree that notice to said attorney shall for all purposes under this Agreement be deemed to be notice to _____ [Buyer/Seller].*

§ 11.1.5   Notice Delivered In Person

The GAR Contracts permit notice to be delivered in person. On its face, this requires delivery to the person who is named in the contract or to the broker or agent representing that person in a client capacity. More specifically, the GAR Contract provides, "personal delivery of notice may only be delivered to the party intended to receive the same or that party's authorized agent."[1459]

If parties wish to allow for personal notice to be effective when delivered to someone other than one of the people named in the contract (*i.e.,* a spouse or person acting pursuant to a power of attorney), they can insert the following special stipulation.

> **Special Stipulation 258: Personal Delivery of Notice to Other Parties**
>
> *All parties agree that notice personally delivered to _____ will be deemed effective as if such notice had been personally delivered to [Seller / Buyer]. If the notice is delivered in person and a party is there to receive the notice, it is always good practice to have that party sign an acknowledgement that she received the notice along with the date and time of delivery. The acknowledgment can merely state, "I, the undersigned, do hereby acknowledge that I personally received a Notice of [state type of notice] on the _____ day of _____, 20____ from _____ with respect to the Purchase and Sale Agreement referenced below." If the notice is delivered in person to a broker's office, for example, and the licensee (or his or her broker) is not present to receive the notice, the party delivering the notice should get the receptionist or the agent on duty to acknowledge in writing the date and time of delivery. Unfortunately, notice in this situation is probably not considered received by the licensee on behalf of his or her client until it is actually received by the licensee.*
>
> *While the GAR Contracts permit notices to be delivered in person, there is no requirement that the person to whom the notice is given be present to receive the notice. Because proof of delivery can become an issue, if the addressee is not expected to be available the party giving the notice should have another person present (let's call them a witness) who can attest to the delivery of the notice. In all events, the party delivering the notice should create a record of the time, date and manner of the delivery of the notice.*

§ 11.1.6   Notice Delivered Via Overnight Delivery Service

The GAR Contracts permit notice to be delivered via overnight delivery service if the cost of delivery is pre-paid. The benefit of this type of delivery is that it is relatively quick (when compared to the U.S. Mail Service) and the delivery person acts as an independent third-party witness to the fact of the delivery. Many such services obtain a signature from the recipient and provide on-line tracking of delivery.

> **Special Stipulation 259:   Notice by Overnight Delivery**
>
> *All parties agree that notice may be delivered by overnight delivery prepaid provided that the delivery company maintains a tracking system from which a written record of the receipt and delivery of the notice can be generated upon request.*

An issue not addressed in the GAR Contract is whether notice sent via second day delivery (as opposed to overnight) is sufficient. To be safe, the parties can add the following special stipulation.

> **Special Stipulation 260:   Delivery Via Second Day Shipping**
>
> *All parties agree that notice may be delivered via second day shipment provided that notice is sent prepaid by a delivery service that also provides overnight delivery service.*

§ 11.1.7   Notice Delivered Via U.S. Mail

The GAR Contract permits notice to be sent via U.S. Mail, provided it is sent registered or certified, prepaid, return receipt requested. By including the registered or certified mail requirement the GAR Contract does not allow for notice to be sent via regular mail. While sending a letter via registered or certified mail does not always assure proof of delivery (sometimes the green return receipt cards are themselves lost in the mail) it is intended to provide more secure method of delivery than regular post. The GAR Contracts do not permit notice to be sent by regular first class mail because it is a less reliable means of sending notice and difficult to prove actual receipt. While the legal doctrine known as the "mailbox rule," discussed in § 11.1.10 (When Is Notice Received), applies to regular first class mail, it does not apply to notice sent by certified mail.

§ 11.1.8   Notice Delivered By Facsimile

Notice by facsimile is the preferred form of giving notice under the GAR Contracts. This is because under the Contract the notice is deemed received as soon as it is sent if the sender's facsimile machine generates a written confirmation sheet showing the facsimile number to which it was sent and the accurate date and time of the transmission. To be safe, a copy of the entire facsimile transmission should be saved. In this way, the sender can prove not only that a fax was sent, but proof of the nature of the fax as well.

What if a party sends a notice by facsimile but does not send it on a machine which produces a fax confirmation sheet, or sends it on a machine where the date and time are seriously miscalibrated? In such an instance, the fax notice would not be presumed to have been received when transmitted, but it can still constitute good notice if the sender can otherwise prove that it was received.

Under the GAR Contract, notice may be delivered by facsimile to the facsimile number, if any, of the broker or broker's affiliated licensee that is set forth on the signature page of the GAR Contract or subsequently provided by the broker or broker's affiliated licensee pursuant to the notice procedures in the agreement. Since notice to a broker or agent is not notice to their customers, the GAR Contract contains a blank space where an unrepresented buyer or seller can provide their facsimile number.

If no facsimile number is provided on the signature page (for brokers or agents or unrepresented buyers or sellers) or is subsequently provided by the broker or broker's affiliated licensee following the notice procedures, then notice via facsimile will not be deemed a valid form of delivery of notice to that party.

What if a party (or broker) initially does not provide a fax number but wants to add one later? It is permissible for anyone to add a facsimile number by providing notice of the number to all parties to the contract via one of the other acceptable forms of notice permitted therein (*i.e.*, in person, via overnight delivery, etc.). Thereafter, notice to the newly provided facsimile number will be deemed an acceptable form of delivery upon the person providing the facsimile number.

To avoid any uncertainty, the GAR Contract specifically provides that a faxed signature of a party shall constitute an original signature binding upon that party. Additionally, a party sending notice by fax is required to send the original signed notice if the receiving party so requests.

The GAR Contracts contain no restriction on the fax number an agent must use when providing a fax number. Therefore, an agent can fill in his or her home facsimile number instead of the broker's facsimile number on the signature page of the GAR Contracts. The best practice is to list the broker's main office facsimile number. This is because in all but the smallest brokerages someone should be able to receive the faxed transmission at the office even if the agent is out of town. However, in today's market many agents work from their home offices and only infrequently go to the broker's office. For this reason the GAR Forms Committee has permitted an agent to list their own home office facsimile (or any other number they wish).

Brokerages should carefully consider whether to permit agents to list their home facsimile numbers. As noted, an agent could be on vacation when a notice is sent via facsimile. If the notice goes to the agent's home office, they are not likely to receive it until they return. As discussed below,[1460] this can be particularly dangerous due to notice by facsimile often being deemed received at the time they are sent.

1460   *See* § 11.1.10 of this work.

A compromise that allows the agent the flexibility to have facsimiles sent to their home office but gives the brokerage the security of knowing that faxed notices will be timely received is to require that notices by facsimile be sent to both the broker's facsimile number and the agent's facsimile number. The special stipulation below is an example of this type of provision.

> **Special Stipulation 261:   Facsimile Notices Shall Be Sent to Two Facsimile Numbers**
>
> *All parties agree that all facsimile notices sent to Listing Agent/Selling Agent shall be sent to the following two facsimile telephone numbers _____ and _____. Such notice shall be deemed received in accordance with the other terms of this Agreement.*

Parties need to take great care to send notice to the facsimile number(s) specifically provided in the GAR Contract. This is because notice can only be delivered via facsimile if sent to the facsimile telephone number identified in the parties' contract. For example, the listing agent provides her home office facsimile number in a contract. The selling agent, who has worked with the listing agent before, has the listing agent's broker's facsimile number in speed dial. The selling agent faxes a Notice of Unilateral Termination to the listing agent. However, by mistake, the selling agent dials the broker's facsimile number rather than the listing agent's home office number. Since the notice was not delivered to the facsimile number identified in the contract, the notice is not valid, even though it went to the listing broker's main office.

The same result could occur if notice is sent via facsimile to a different number as a courtesy. Let's use the example above, only this time the listing agent is away on vacation. Before leaving she telephones the selling agent and gives him the facsimile number of the hotel where she is staying and asks if he will fax any notices to her at the hotel while she is away. The selling agent complies and sends the Unilateral Notice of Termination to the hotel. Unless the selling agent also sends the Notice to the listing agent's home facsimile telephone number (the one provided in the contract) the notice will be insufficient. This is because the hotel facsimile number is not identified in the contract and is not, therefore, a permissible method of delivery of facsimile notice. "But wait," one may ask, "why isn't the notice to the hotel facsimile sufficient since the listing agent gave that number to the selling agent?" Remember that the hotel facsimile number was provided in a telephone conversation. Additional or alternative facsimile numbers are only considered effective if they are provided by means of an otherwise permissible form of notice under the GAR Contract. Those methods do not include oral delivery.

§ 11.1.9 Notice Via E-Mail

Most real estate contracts now permit notices to be sent by e-mail. The GAR Contract goes further and provides that notices sent by e-mail are deemed received when and if the sender receives a "read receipt" notice indicating that the notice has been opened by the recipient. It should be noted that the "read receipt" function will not work on all computers depending on the operating system powering the computer. Therefore, it is quite possible for the recipient of an e-mail notice to open the e-mail where no "read receipt" notice is sent back to the sender of an e-mail. Therefore, the person giving a notice should continue to send important notices by facsimile as well as by e-mail. Of course, there are other ways to confirm the receipt of an e-mail. So, for example, if a party replies to an e-mail, the sender now has proof that it has been delivered. If a real estate contract does not provide that notice by e-mail is deemed received when a "read receipt" notice is sent back to the sender of the e-mail, the following special stipulation may be included in the purchase and sale agreement.

Special Stipulation 262:   Email Notice Effective When Email Opened

All parties agree that notice by email shall be deemed to be received when the email is opened at the computer address to which it was sent. In the event the opening of the e-mail triggers a computer generated notification to the sender of the email that the e-mail has been opened, the date and time the email was opened, shall be presumed to be the official date and time of such notification.

Under the GAR Contract, notice may be delivered by e-mail to the address, if any, of the broker or broker's affiliated licensee that is set forth on the signature page of the GAR Contract or subsequently provided by the broker or broker's affiliated licensee pursuant to the notice procedures in the purchase and sale agreement. Since notice to a broker or agent is not notice to the broker's customers, the GAR Contract contains a blank space where an unrepresented buyer or seller can provide his or her e-mail address.

If no e-mail address is provided on the signature page of the GAR Contract (for brokers or agents or unrepresented buyers or sellers) or subsequently provided following the notice procedures in the agreement, then notice via e-mail will not be deemed a valid form of delivery of notice to that party.

What if a party (or broker) initially does not provide an e-mail address but wants to add one later? It is permissible for anyone to add e-mail address by providing notice of the address to all parties to the contract via one of the other acceptable forms of notice permitted therein (*i.e.*, in person, facsimile, etc.). Thereafter, notice to the newly provided e-mail address will be deemed an acceptable form of delivery upon the person providing the address.

To avoid any uncertainty, the GAR Contract specifically provides that an e-mail signature of a party shall constitute an original signature binding upon that party. Additionally, a party sending notice by e-mail is required to send the original signed notice if the receiving party so requests.

Parties can provide for e-mail to be sent to multiple addresses as provided in the following special stipulation.

Special Stipulation 263:   E-mail Notices Shall be Sent to Multiple Addresses

All parties agree that all e-mail notices sent to _____ shall be sent to both of the following e-mail addresses _____ and _____. Provided that notice is sent to both e-mail addresses, notice shall be deemed given when it is first received at either of the above addresses.

As with notice delivered via facsimile, parties need to take great care to send notice to the e-mail address(es) specifically provided in the GAR Contract. This is because notice can only be delivered via e-mail if sent to the e-mail address identified in the parties' contract. So, for example, let's say the listing agent provides her personal e-mail address in a contract. The selling agent, who has worked with the listing agent before, has the listing agent's broker's e-mail address in her address book. The selling agent e-mails a Notice of Unilateral Termination to the listing agent. However, by mistake, the selling agent sends the notice to the broker's e-mail address rather than the listing agent's e-mail address. Since the notice was not delivered to the e-mail address identified in the contract, the notice is not valid, even though it went to the listing broker's e-mail address.

The same result could occur if notice is sent via e-mail to a different address as a courtesy. Let's use the example above, only this time the listing agent is on a cruise ship on vacation where she will have access to a special, temporary e-mail address provided by the cruise line, but not to her regular account. Before leaving, she telephones the selling agent and gives him the temporary cruise ship e-mail address and asks if he will e-mail any notices to her at that address while she is away. The selling agent complies and e-mails the Unilateral Notice of Termination to the cruise ship account. Unless the selling agent also e-mails the Notice to the listing agent's personal e-mail address (the one provided in the contract) the notice will be insufficient. This is because the cruise ship address is not identified in the contract and is not, therefore, a permissible method of delivery of e-mail notices. Remember that the cruise ship e-mail account was provided in a telephone conversation. Additional or alternative e-mail addresses are only considered effective if they are provided by means of an otherwise permissible form of notice under the GAR Contract. Those methods do not include oral delivery.

§ 11.1.10 When Is Notice Received?

With just one exception, notice is deemed received under the GAR Contract at the time it is actually received by the party to whom the notice was intended, or that person's authorized agent. This is in contrast to the so-called "mail box rule"[1461] in which notice sent by regular first class mail is deemed received as of the moment it is sent, irrespective of when the recipient actually receives it (if ever). Just because notice is properly delivered via e-mail, for example, it is not deemed received until the other party actually views it.

The sole exception regarding receipt of notice applies to notice sent via facsimile. If notice is sent via facsimile to a facsimile number provided in the contract, the notice is deemed to have been given as of the date and time it is transmitted, so long as the sending facsimile machine produces a written confirmation with the accurate date, time, and telephone number to which the notice was sent. In other words, the sending of a facsimile is the equivalent of receipt provided that the sending facsimile machine produces the required information and it is accurate.

§ 11.1.11 Limiting Form Of Notice

There are times when a party will only want notice given in one particular way, such as by facsimile. This is most often the case when there are time critical deadlines in a transaction and the parties want to know the specific means by which notice will be delivered. The special stipulation below can be used to limit the form of notice.

> **Special Stipulation 264:   Limited Form of Notice**
>
> *All parties agree that all notices hereunder shall be only given by facsimile and through no other means.*

The other situation where some parties using the GAR Contracts have been known to want to limit the method of receiving notice is when the broker is acting in a dual agency capacity and thus is representing both parties as clients. In this event, notice to the broker is instantly notice to both the buyer and seller, since notice to the broker constitutes notice to the broker's clients.

If a party does not want the broker to be able to receive notice on his or her behalf, the following special stipulation can be used.

> **Special Stipulation 265:   Broker Cannot Receive Notice on Behalf of Party**
>
> *Notwithstanding any other provision to the contrary, all parties agree that neither the Broker representing the _____ [Buyer/Seller] as a client nor the Broker's affiliated licensees shall be permitted to receive notice on behalf of _____ [Buyer/Seller].*

1461   *Carterosa, Ltd. v. General Star Indem. Co.*, 227 Ga.App. 246, 489 S.E.2d 83 (1997).

The **RED BOOK**

CHAPTER 12

CLOSING
AND
POSSESSION

OVERVIEW

This chapter discusses the closing and the transfer of possession of the property to the buyer. Among the issues which are addressed include how closings work generally, who pays for various charges at closing such as transfer tax and intangible tax, how items like property taxes are prorated, under what circumstances the closing date may be extended, and what happens when one party fails to close as required under the contract.

This chapter also discusses issues regarding possession of the property, such as buyers moving in early and sellers and tenants remaining in possession after closing. An explanation of what happens if the property is destroyed or damaged after the contract has been signed but prior to closing is also included.

§ 12.1 CLOSINGS GENERALLY

§ 12.1.1 Only Attorneys Can Conduct Closings

The closing of the sale of property in Georgia consists of the conveyance of title to the property from the seller to the buyer and payment of the purchase price for the property by the buyer to the seller. In Georgia, unlike some other states, only an attorney can conduct a closing of a real estate purchase and sale transaction.

The Georgia Supreme Court recently confirmed that anyone other than a Georgia licensed attorney who prepares or executes a deed of conveyance on behalf of another, or facilitates its signing, is engaged in the unauthorized practice of law.[1462] This includes witness-only closings in which a lawyer merely notarizes the deed but does not do so as someone who is practicing law.[1463] The court stated, "we have consistently held that it is the unauthorized practice of law for someone other than a duly-licensed Georgia attorney to close a real estate transaction or to prepare or facilitate the execution of such deed(s) for the benefit of a seller, borrower or lender." This confirms the approach taken in an earlier opinion where the court stated, "it would be ethically improper for a lawyer to aid non-lawyers to 'close real estate transactions' or for a lawyer to delegate to a non-lawyer the responsibility to close the real estate transaction without the participation of the attorney."[1464] Therefore, even a title company cannot close a real estate transaction without the participation of an attorney.

The court's reasoning is that the public is best protected when such work is limited to attorneys. Unlike a purely commercial enterprise, attorneys are trained to protect the rights of the party they represent. Further, attorneys are held accountable through a malpractice or bar disciplinary action.

In Georgia, the unauthorized practice of law is a criminal offense.[1465] Anyone other than an attorney licensed in Georgia who conducts any real estate closings, which include real estate transaction loan closings and "witness-only" closings, is engaging in the unauthorized practice of law and will be guilty of a misdemeanor.[1466] The punishment extends to every officer, trustee, director, agent, or employee of a corporation or voluntary association who directly or indirectly engages in the unauthorized practice of law.[1467]

1462 *In Re UPL Advisory Opinion 2003-2*, 277 Ga. 472, 588 S.E.2d 741 (2003).

1463 *In Re UPL Advisory Opinion #2003-2*, 277 Ga. 472, 588 S.E.2d 741 (2003). Witness-only closings occur when notaries, signing agents and other individuals who are not a party to the real estate closing preside "over the execution of the deeds of conveyance and other closing documents, but purport to do so merely as a witness or notary, not as someone who is practicing law."

1464 Formal Advisory Opinion 86-5.

1465 O.C.G.A. § 15-19-56.

1466 O.C.G.A. § 15-19-56.

1467 O.C.G.A. § 15-19-56.

§ 12.1.2 Closing Process

The closing is the final step in buying or selling property. It is during a closing when the seller signs the deed transferring title to the property and affidavits required for title purposes. If the buyer obtains a loan, it is also the time when the buyer will sign the promissory note, deed to secure debt, and other lender-required documents.

All costs and prorations provided for under the contract will be stated on a settlement or closing statement, using a form specified by the Department of Housing and Urban Development and often called a "HUD-1." This form has separate columns for the buyer and seller and itemizes each cost or credit showing the amount owed by the buyer and the net proceeds to be paid to the seller.

The closing attorney confirms receipt of wired funds from the lender and deposits the funds from the purchaser into the law firm's escrow account. If the purchaser must pay more than $5,000, Georgia law requires that such funds must be presented in the form of certified check(s), money orders, or wire transfers. The closing attorney also disburses checks from the escrow account to pay all the costs of the closing, including the net proceeds check to the seller and the commission to the real estate brokers. All special stipulations and other contract obligations should be fulfilled at the closing, unless the contract terms provide for a later date of completion and such provisions survive closing.

If the buyer is obtaining a mortgage loan on the property, the closing attorney will normally be representing the lender at the closing. If the closing is an all cash transaction, the closing attorney can represent either the buyer or the seller.

§ 12.2 BUYER OR SELLER UNAVAILABLE AT CLOSING

Generally, the buyer and seller complete the purchase and sale transaction in person at the closing. However, in some instances, either the seller or the buyer will be unable to physically attend the closing. If such an instance occurs, the absent party may complete the transaction by (i) appointing a power of attorney, or (ii) mailing the closing documents to the other party.

§ 12.2.1 Power Of Attorney

A power of attorney is a recordable document signed by the buyer or seller appointing another person to act as their "attorney-in-fact" to carry out the terms of the agreement.[1468] An individual who has been appointed as a power of attorney may sign an agreement on behalf of the absent party.[1469] In most situations, an absent party will use a power of attorney to sign the necessary documents at closing to complete the transaction.

If an absent party uses this method to complete the transaction, the buyer or seller should notify their agent that they have already signed a power of attorney that was prepared for them. REALTORS® should always have any power of attorney approved by the closing attorney before the closing date to eliminate any last minute issues.

Title companies and lenders often have specific requirements in order to insure a title based upon a power of attorney. For example, a seller and the buyer enter into a purchase and sale agreement in which the buyer will purchase the seller's property. The buyer is unable to attend the closing and is obtaining financing for the purchase of the property. In this scenario, the buyer wants to use a power of attorney to execute the transaction, but the lender must give permission for the documents to be signed by someone other than the buyer. Generally, a lender will allow a buyer to appoint his or her spouse to sign on their behalf using a power of attorney, but not an unrelated party. If an unrelated party is appointed to sign the documents on behalf of the absent buyer, the selling agent should contact the closing attorney in advance so permission can be obtained from the lender and the power of attorney can be prepared, sent and executed by the buyer. The original executed power of attorney, along with a copy of the buyer's identification,

---

1468   O.C.G.A. § 10-6-1.

1469   O.C.G.A. § 13-5-30(4).

must be brought to the closing. The selling agent should then follow up with the buyer and the closing attorney to ensure that the power of attorney has been approved. The precloser in the closing attorney's office will also ask for the executed power of attorney to be faxed back prior to the closing to make sure the document was properly witnessed, notarized and signed. There is usually a fee of approximately $75.00 for the preparation of the power of attorney.

However, not all power of attorneys are sufficient to appoint a person to execute documents on the absent party's behalf. The buyer or seller should be cautious about using and preparing power of attorney forms obtained by a legal forms service over the Internet. Often, these forms will not be approved by title companies for use in Georgia. Even military power of attorneys should also be reviewed by the closing attorney.

§ 12.2.1.1 Notarization And Equal Dignity Rule

Under the Statute of Frauds, an agreement for the purchase of land or property is required to be in writing.[1470] As such, under the equal dignity rule, the authority of an agent to execute an instrument required by the Statute of Frauds to be in writing must also be in writing.[1471]

In Georgia, a power of attorney giving someone the authority to execute a real estate transaction of an absent party's behalf must be both in writing[1472] and notarized by a public notary[1473] to be valid. The reasoning behind this requirement is that since a deed to convey land or property must be witnessed and notarized at the closing, the equal dignity rule requires that the power of attorney must also be witnessed and notarized to be valid.

§ 12.2.2 Mail-Away Closings

An absent buyer or seller may also complete the purchase and sale transaction through a "mail-away closing." Due to the risk of identity theft and mortgage fraud, this process is often more complex than it sounds. A loan package may not be e-mailed or mailed directly to the other party. In fact, most closing attorneys now require the absent party to make arrangements with an attorney or title company to receive their closing documents. Before the closing begins, the absent party must choose an attorney or title company and must provide the closing attorney with the name, phone number and address of the attorney or title company where the documents will be sent. The closing attorney will then send the loan package and all the closing documents to the designated attorney or title company. Once the documents are received, the absent party must schedule a time with the attorney or title company to sign the documents in front of a notary. It is the responsibility of the attorney or title company to obtain acceptable identification from the seller or buyer and have the documents properly signed, witnessed and notarized. The documents and the money (if the absent party is the buyer) will be sent back to the closing attorney to complete the transaction.

Generally, this process requires advance planning and proper timing to make sure the documents are signed and returned to the closing attorney to meet the closing date. There is also an additional expense associated with mail-away closings. The attorney or title company who handles the signing will usually charge a fee and the closing attorney will also charge a fee for the mail-away. REALTORS® who have a buyer or seller closing by mail need to make sure the agent and party on the other side are informed throughout this process.

§ 12.2.3 Seller Or Buyer Unavailable Due To Incarceration

In some instances, there may be a situation in which the seller or buyer is planning on attending a closing but is unavailable because she becomes incarcerated. The best solution in this case is to use a power of attorney to complete the purchase transaction. Hopefully, the seller or buyer has made arrangements for his or her affairs before

---

1470   O.C.G.A. § 13-5-30.

1471   O.C.G.A. § 10-6-2; *Turnipseed v. Jaje*, 267 Ga. 320, 477 S.E.2d 101 (1996).

1472   *Turnipseed v. Jaje*, 267 Ga. 320, 477 S.E.2d 101 (1996).

1473   O.C.G.A. § 10-6-142.

incarceration. However, let's say the seller did not anticipate going to jail but was locked up last Saturday night and is now in city or county jail. His or her criminal defense attorney along with a notary may go to the jail at any time to get a power of attorney signed and notarized to close the purchase and sale transaction. Anyone on the inmate's visitation list may also visit the jail at the proper visitation times. Considering that the power of attorney must be notarized,[1474] the best practice is to take a notary along for the visit. But remember, any person visiting the inmate must be on the visitation list so adding the appropriate people to execute the transaction is imperative. Some jails may have a notary available. The seller should inquire with the officer on duty if she wishes to use this notary and also inquire if there is a fee for the notary service.

Let's say the seller is in state or federal prison as opposed to a city or county jail. If this is the case, the process can be much more difficult. Only the attorney of record may visit the inmate, and everyone else must make an appointment through the Warden's office. If visitation is not possible, the power of attorney may be mailed to the inmate, and after the letter is opened and inspected, it will be passed to the inmate. The prisoner would then have to make arrangements with the Warden's office to get the power of attorney executed, witnessed and notarized and sent back to his or her attorney. This process could take several weeks and should be done in as far advance of closing as possible.

It is always the best practices for the buyer and seller, as well as the listing and selling agents, to attend the closing. REALTORS® should strongly encourage their clients to make the necessary arrangements to be present; however, if such presence is merely impractical or impossible, the above methods should be used to complete the transaction.

§ 12.3   PROPERTY CONDITION

§ 12.3.1   Risk Of Property Loss Before Closing On Buyer

The general rule of law in Georgia is that before the seller conveys title to the buyer, the risk of loss falls upon the buyer if a substantial part of the property is destroyed and neither party is at fault. However, the seller and buyer must have entered into a binding contract and the seller must be willing and able to consummate the sale.[1475]

This rule, established in England in 1801, is based on the principle that the buyer is, in fact and substance, the effective owner of the property (if the seller is prepared to convey clear title and is not in default) and the seller retains only the legal title to the property during the contract period in order to secure the purchase money. The exception to the general rule is when the parties agree that the seller will bear the risk of loss.

§ 12.3.2   Risk Of Loss Of Timber Or Crops In Land Sales Transactions

Under the common law principle, the risk of damage to a property rests with the buyer. In the GAR Land Purchase and Sale Agreement,[1476] however, the seller warrants that there will be no material adverse changes in the physical condition of the property, including acts of God, prior to the closing or the transfer of possession of the property, whichever is later. In the event material changes are caused by acts of God, the buyer may terminate the agreement without penalty. However, any improvements on the property containing defective conditions or in need of repairs will not give the buyer a right to terminate. The logic behind this approach is that any improvements to the property are of nominal value and that the property is being purchased for the value of the land.

If the land has substantial timber on it, or other crops of value, the buyer may want to add a special stipulation to protect against the risk of loss. One approach is to give the buyer a specific right to terminate the contract if substantial damage is done to the timber or other crops on the property. An example of this type of special stipulation follows.

1474   *Turnipseed v. Jaje*, 267 Ga. 320, 477 S.E.2d 101 (1996).

1475   *Bleckley v. Langston*, 112 Ga.App. 63, 143 S.E.2d 671 (1965); *Phillips v. Bacon*, 245 Ga. 814, 267 S.E.2d 249 (1980).

1476   GAR Form F34.

Special Stipulation 266: Risk of Destruction of Timber

All parties acknowledge and agree that the timber on the Property has substantial value. Seller warrants that prior to closing Seller will not cut or permit to be cut any of the timber located on the property. In the event that prior to closing the timber is materially damaged or destroyed as a result of fire, wind, storm, flood, or other natural calamity, Buyer shall have the right to terminate this Agreement without penalty upon notice to Seller.

[OPTIONAL: For the purposes of this Agreement, all parties agree that the term "materially damaged or destroyed" shall mean a partial or total loss to at least _____ % of the total merchantable timber located on the Property.]

Another approach is to provide for a reduction in the sales price based upon the damage to standing timber. An example of this type of special stipulation is set forth below.

Special Stipulation 267: Reduction in Sales Price if Timber is Destroyed

All parties acknowledge and agree that the timber on the Property has substantial value and is a basis for which Buyer is purchasing Property from Seller. All parties further agree that the timber cruise report attached hereto as Exhibit _____ and incorporated herein is a reasonable calculation of the merchantable timber presently located on the Property. If prior to closing the existing timber on the Property is materially damaged or destroyed as a result of fire, wind, storm, flood, or other natural calamity, Buyer shall have the right at his sole expense to have a new timber cruise report prepared on the Property. The report shall be prepared by the same person or company that prepared the original report. If for any reason the person or company is unavailable to do the second report, the timber cruise report shall be prepared by _____.

If the follow-up report reveals that more than 5% of the merchantable timber on the Property has been materially damaged or destroyed, all parties agree that the sales price for the Property shall be reduced by the amount of merchantable timber damaged or destroyed based upon a comparison of the two reports and using the prices for timber set forth in the original report. If the follow-up report reveals that 5% or less of merchantable timber on the Property has been materially damaged or destroyed, all parties agree that there shall be no reduction in the sales price of the Property and that the risk of this loss shall rest with the Buyer.

§ 12.3.3 Contract Provisions Alter General Rule On Risk Of Loss

The GAR Contract provides that if the property is destroyed or substantially damaged prior to closing the seller must promptly notify the buyer of the same and provide the buyer with whatever information the seller has regarding the availability of insurance and the disposition of any insurance claim.[1477] The GAR Contract also provides that either the buyer or the seller may terminate the contract by giving written notice to the other party not later than fourteen days from the seller's notice. Under older versions of the GAR Contract if the buyer or seller did not terminate the contract, the buyer received at closing the insurance proceeds which had not been spent to repair the damage. This provision was somewhat problematic for buyers because few mortgage lenders will lend money on seriously damaged property until the damage had been fixed.

1477   GAR Form F20.

The GAR Contract provides that if neither the seller nor the buyer chooses to terminate the contract, the seller shall restore the property to substantially the same condition it was in at the Binding Agreement Date. The new closing date will then be extended until the earlier of one (1) year from the original closing date or seven days from the date the property is restored to substantially the same condition as on the Binding Agreement Date and, if required, a new certificate of occupancy is issued.

Most preprinted form contracts include a provision to relieve the buyer of the obligation to purchase the property when the improvements thereon have been substantially destroyed. The reason for shifting the risk of loss to the seller is illustrated by a case decided by the Georgia Court of Appeals.[1478] A buyer entered into a contract with a seller for the sale of property for $120,000, which property included pecan trees. The contract did not contain any language shifting the risk of loss to the seller. An ice storm damaged all the pecan trees and the fair market value of the property decreased by at least $32,000. The buyer sought to terminate the contract and a lawsuit was filed. The court concluded that under the general rule the contract could not be terminated and the risk of the loss fell on the buyer.

The GAR Contract does not define how much damage is necessary before the property "has been destroyed or substantially damaged." In each case this is a question of fact, and the outcome will vary from case to case. Examples of the factors a court will consider in deciding whether property has been destroyed or substantially damaged include the condition of any improvements to the property before and after the loss,[1479] and any change in the fair market value of the property.[1480]

§ 12.3.4   Property Condition At Closing To Be Same As At Binding Agreement Date

The GAR Contract provides that the property and all items remaining with the property will be in substantially the same condition (including conditions disclosed in the Seller's Property Disclosure Statement) as on the Binding Agreement Date except for changes made to the condition of the property pursuant to a written agreement between the buyer and seller. This means that the seller is responsible for making any changes to the property that are needed to keep the property in substantially the same condition as it was on the Binding Agreement Date. Any concerns the buyer has with the condition of the property must be addressed during the Due Diligence Period. Thereafter, the buyer accepts the property "as is."

Previous versions of the GAR Contracts provided that the property did not have to be in substantially the same condition on the date of closing as it was on the Binding Agreement Date if the cause of the property not being in this condition was normal were and tear. This exception was eliminated from the GAR Contracts because it provided results that were not always equitable or consistent with the expectations of the parties. For example, a buyer purchases a residence with an older heating system. During the Due Diligence Period, the home inspector notes that the heating system is close to the end of its useful life but appears to be in good working order and repair. After the end of the Due Diligence Period but prior to the closing, the heating system breaks and a repair technician indicates that the system will need to be replaced.

If normal wear and tear is an exception to the seller's duty to ensure that the property is in the same condition on the date of closing as it was on the binding agreement, the seller could reasonably take the position that she is not going to replace the heating system because normal wear and tear means that older systems will break and need to be replaced. Therefore, the seller could choose to use space heaters until the closing and transfer the property to the buyer with a heating system that needs to be replaced in its entirety. Such a result, while likely legally correct, would be inconsistent with the expectations of most buyers who would assume that if the system breaks during the seller's ownership of the property, the seller will repair it.

1478   *Bleckley v. Langston*, 112 Ga.App. 63, 143 S.E.2d 671 (1965).

1479   *Bruce v. Jennings*, 190 Ga. 618, 10 S.E.2d 56 (1940).

1480   *Bleckley v. Langston*, 112 Ga.App. 63, 143 S.E.2d 671 (1965).

Another example of what could be considered wear and tear. Let's say that a house has an older railroad tie wall supporting a swimming pool in the rear yard of the property. After the end of the Due Diligence Period but prior to closing, a hurricane with torrential rains causes the wall to bow out. The seller hires a structural engineer who indicates that the wall is old and that the torrential rainstorm was the straw that broke the camel's back or in this case the wall's back. The engineer indicates that the wall is structurally unsound and that the cost to replace the wall will be $50,000. Most buyers in this situation would expect the wall to be replaced at the seller's expense because it occurred on the seller's watch. However, if the seller is excused from having to make repairs that are the result of normal wear and tear, the seller could reasonably take the position that the repair is the responsibility of the buyer. This is because things get older and, eventually, breaking is a part of normal wear and tear as is damage caused by acts of God.

The following section discusses in greater detail what constitutes normal wear and tear. If the seller wants his or her obligation to preserve the property in substantially the same condition to be qualified by a normal wear and tear standard, the seller can include the following special stipulation.

> **Special Stipulation 268: Seller Warrants That Property will be in the Same Condition, Normal Wear and Tear Excepted**
>
> *Seller warrants that the Property will be in substantially the same condition on the date of closing or the transfer of possession, whichever comes first, as it was in on the Binding Agreement Date, normal wear and tear excepted.*

§ 12.3.4.1 Property Being In Same Condition Includes Conditions Revealed In Seller's Property Disclosure Statement

The seller's warranty that at the time of closing, or upon the granting of possession if at a time other than at closing, the property will be in substantially the same condition as on the Binding Agreement Date includes conditions revealed by the seller in the Seller's Property Disclosure Statement. For example, a seller discloses in his Seller's Property Disclosure Statement that a portion of his property periodically floods during periods of heavy rain. This provision means, for example, that if on the Binding Agreement Date the property was not flooded but it was flooded on the date of closing, the buyer could not avoid his contractual obligations to close by arguing that the condition of the property had changed since the condition was revealed in the Seller's Property Disclosure Statement.

§ 12.3.4.2 What Is Normal Wear And Tear?

"Normal wear and tear" is also often referred to as "ordinary wear and tear," "fair wear and tear," or "reasonable wear and tear." Legally, "normal wear" means the deterioration caused by the reasonable use of the property. It does not include damage caused by negligence, carelessness, accident, or abuse.[1481] It means the deterioration caused by the ordinary operation of natural forces.[1482] Normal wear and tear also includes what are commonly referred to as "Acts of God." Georgia statute defines acts of God to mean accidents produced by physical causes which are irresistible or inevitable, such as lightning, storms, perils of the sea, earthquakes, inundations, sudden death, or illness, but excludes all causes due to human intervention.[1483] Therefore, if lightning strikes the house on a date after the Binding Agreement Date but before the date of closing, the damage would qualify as normal wear and tear because the cause was a natural force and the buyer would arguably have to bear the loss.

However, let's say that the damage was caused by a dead tree limb falling on the roof during a storm accompanied by high winds. If the tree was diseased and the seller knew or should have known about the condition of the tree, the

---

1481   By analogy to landlord and tenant law, O.C.G.A. § 44-7-34.

1482   Blacks Law Dictionary 8th edition (2004).

1483   O.C.G.A. § 1-3-3.

seller would arguably be negligent in not removing the tree or at least the dead tree limb. Since normal wear and tear does not include damage caused by negligence, the seller would be responsible for the damage to the house. The seller may also be responsible if the tree had dangerous characteristics (the species is known to have weak limbs) or if the danger was visible and apparent and the seller did not take any steps to remove the danger.

In earlier versions of the GAR Contract, the seller owned a duty to ensure that the property was in substantially the same condition on the closing data as it was on binding agreement date, normal wear and tear expected. As a practical matter, this meant that the buyer was assuming more risk regarding the condition of the property upon there being a binding agreement than most buyers (and their selling agents) realized they were assuming. As a result, beginning with the 2013 GAR Contract, the normal wear and tear exception was eliminated from the property condition section so that the seller is now obligated to ensure that the property is in substantially the same condition as the closing binding agreement date as it was on the binding agreement date. Of course, under the GAR Contract, if the property is substantially destroyed between the binding agreement date and the closing date, either party can terminate the contract.

One question which will likely arise is whether a seller can be held in breach of contract due to not being able to deliver the property in substantially the same condition it was in on the closing date as a result of an act of God. If the failure of the same condition is the result of the result of an act of God where it is impossible for the seller to perform, the seller would normally not be found to be in breach. The following example illustrates the effect of normal wear and tear provision in the GAR Contract. Assume that prior to the closing but after the Due Diligence Period has lapsed the dishwasher breaks, or the hot water heater springs a leak, or a leak develops in the roof. With each of these items the seller can no longer argue the she is not responsible for making repairs because the damage was caused by normal wear and tear. Instead, since the property is not in the same condition it was in on the Binding Agreement Date, the seller would have an obligation to make repairs. This result is more consistent with the expectation of many buyers that the seller will maintain the property right up until the day of closing.

§ 12.3.5   Risk Of Loss With A "Tear-Down" Home

Some buyers purchase property with the idea of tearing down the existing home and building a new one. In other words, the buyer is purchasing the property for the value of the land. In such cases the buyer would not want the seller to have the right to terminate the contract in the event the same is destroyed or substantially damaged prior to closing. The buyer would also not want the seller to repair or rebuild a damaged or destroyed property since the destruction of the improvements would likely expedite the process for the buyer of having the existing house torn down. Of course, some agreement would need to be reached as to who would receive any insurance proceeds and whether the seller would be obligated to remove the debris caused from the destruction of the improvements. These issues might be addressed by the following special stipulation.

> **Special Stipulation 269:   Seller Shall Not Repair in the Event of Casualty**
>
> *Buyer and Seller acknowledge that Buyer will tear down or substantially alter the house and other improvements on the Property after closing on the Property. Therefore, Seller shall not have a right under any circumstances to terminate this Agreement in the event the Property or any improvements located thereon are destroyed or substantially damaged prior to Closing.*
>
> *If the Property or the improvements located thereon are destroyed or substantially damaged prior to the closing of the Property so as to render the Property uninhabitable (and not capable of being lawfully occupied prior to the date of closing), then Seller agrees not to repair or rebuild the improvements which were destroyed or substantially damaged. Seller shall be entitled to keep all insurance proceeds, if any, received by Seller as a result of the casualty. However, Seller shall be obligated to the extent*

required by law to promptly remove from the Property, at the sole expense of Seller, all damaged or destroyed improvements and all other trash and debris on the Property resulting from the casualty or the clean-up thereof.

§ 12.3.6 Seller Has Right To Remove House Or Other Major Improvements

In some real estate contracts, the seller is given the right to remove a house or other improvements on the Property for a given period of time after the closing. This is normally done in commercial transactions and land transaction where the buyer is going to otherwise tear down the existing improvements or dwelling and redevelop the property. In most cases, the seller will not want to tear down the existing improvements or remove the dwelling until after the closing just in case the buyer does not actually close on the property purchase.

An example of a special stipulation addressing the seller's right to remove improvements located on the property after the closing is set forth below.

Special Stipulation 270: Seller May Remove Improvements After Closing

Within _____ days after the date of closing ("Removal Period") Seller shall have the right to come onto the Property and remove at its own expense the following improvements presently located on the Property (hereinafter collectively referred to as "Improvements"):

_____

_____

_____

Buyer acknowledges that Buyer is completely familiar with the Property and the Improvements and agrees to fully accept the risk of damage to the Improvements and of injuries to Buyer or to persons assisting Buyer in removing the Improvements. Buyer warrants that Buyer shall warn those persons helping Buyer remove the Improvements of any hazardous conditions on the Property that might not be readily observable to those persons. Buyer agrees to indemnify and hold Seller harmless from all claims, injuries, damages and suits arising out of or related to the exercise of these rights.

Buyer agrees to obtain all necessary licenses and permits required under applicable law to remove the Improvements on the Property.

In removing the Improvements Buyer shall not leave any area disturbed as a result of the removal of the Improvements in a condition where it represents a hazard or risk to persons coming onto the Property.

Any improvements remaining on the Property after the end of the Removal Period shall become the property of Seller and Buyer shall lose the right to remove the same. This special stipulation shall survive the Closing.

An example of a provision giving the seller the right to remove the entire dwelling after closing is set forth below.

Special Stipulation 271: Seller Shall Have the Right to Remove Dwelling After Closing

Subject to the terms and conditions of this paragraph, Seller and Seller's contractors and agents shall have the right to come onto the Property during the _____ day period after the date of the Closing to remove the single-family residence currently located on the Property. Seller shall be obligated to obtain all required governmental licenses and permits needed to remove a dwelling from a property. Seller shall also be responsible for confirming that all utilities have been turned off and disconnected from the meter.

Seller acknowledges that Seller is at least as familiar if not more familiar with the Property than Buyer, including with any hazardous or dangerous conditions located thereon, and agrees to warn Seller's contractors and agents who come onto the Property of any such conditions. Seller agrees to indemnify and hold Buyer harmless from and against any and all claims, causes of action, suits and damages, both to persons and property, arising out of or related to the work of removing the dwelling from the Property. Upon the removal of the dwelling from the Property, Seller shall not leave any sharp wooden or metal pipes, poles, stakes or supports protruding from the ground where the dwelling was located.

§ 12.3.7   Buyer's Obligation To Build On Lot

In some lot transactions, the developer of a subdivision will require that the buyer of a lot commence construction of a home on the lot within a certain number of days after the lot closing. This is normally done to ensure that the community appears as inviting and successful as possible. A sample of this type of provision is set forth below.

Special Stipulation 272:   Buyer's Obligation to Construct Residence

Buyer covenants and agrees to commence construction of a residential dwelling on the Lot in accordance with the terms and conditions of this special stipulation within _____ days of the Closing of the purchase of such Lot, and to thereafter continuously and expeditiously pursue the construction of the dwelling until it has been completed and a certificate of occupancy has been issued on the Property by _____ County.

All construction plans shall first be approved by the Architectural Control Committee established in the Declaration of Covenants, Conditions, Easements and Restrictions for _____ which covenants bind the Lot. For the purposes of this special stipulation, the term "continuously and expeditiously pursue the construction of a residential dwelling" shall mean that the Buyer shall engage a licensed Georgia general contractor to construct the residential dwelling and contractually obligate the contractor to employ a full construction crew consisting of at least _____ workers who shall all work in the construction of the dwelling until such time as it is dried-in and who shall each work at least 5 days a week, 8 hours a day, except on federal holidays, weekends, and inclement weather days. The obligations set forth herein shall expressly survive the Closing, be binding upon successors and assigns of the Buyer, and may in the discretion of Seller be recorded in the deed of conveyance to Buyer so as to run with the time to the Lot.

§ 12.3.7.1   Developed Lot Standards

When entering into a contract to purchase a lot in a new development, a buyer might want to incorporate a special stipulation that requires the lot to meet certain development standards before the buyer is obligated to purchase [and/or build on] the lot. If a buyer is required to build on a lot within a certain period of time after closing, or simply plans on purchasing an undeveloped lot to build on, a buyer should consider the standards in the following stipulation. The buyer can use some or all of the standards when incorporating this special stipulation into the purchase and sale agreement.

Special Stipulation 273:   Development Lot Standards

Notwithstanding anything to the contrary herein, Buyer shall not be obligated to close on the Property until the Property is a "Developed Lot." For purposes hereof, the Property shall be a "Developed Lot" when all of the following requirements are met (and Seller warrants that the Property shall satisfy the following requirements):

(a) the Property has been staked out accurately with iron pins and has been clearly marked at all corners;

(b) the final subdivision plat showing the Property has been approved by Buyer and by all applicable governmental entities and has been recorded;

(c) all roads providing access to the Property: (i) include asphalt paving and concrete curb and gutter; (ii) have been constructed in accordance with the standards of applicable governmental entities; (iii) have been dedicated to and accepted by such entities subject to normal maintenance bonds to be posted by Seller; and (iv) will be maintained by Seller until such governmental entities assume full maintenance responsibility therefore;

(d) storm water sewers for surface water drainage for all roads providing access to the Property and for the Property shall have been installed in accordance with plans approved by the applicable governmental authorities;

(e) underground telephone, electrical, gas and CATV lines necessary for the development of residential dwellings have been installed in the right-of-way adjacent to the Property and will be available to Buyer solely upon the payment by Buyer of tap-on fees and user charges imposed by the utility companies or governmental agencies supplying such services;

(f) water and sewer laterals are installed and ready to be immediately used for their intended purpose at the lot line of the Property and are available to Buyer solely upon the payment by Buyer of tap-on fees and user charges imposed by the entities supplying such services;

(g) all utilities have been marked as to location;

(h) no stump holes exist partially or wholly under the building site and all fill areas are compacted in accordance with industry standards as per standard Proctor test;

(i) no condition related to Seller's development of the Property will prevent (i) a building permit being issued immediately for the Property and (ii) upon completion of construction of the home on the Property, a certificate of occupancy being issued immediately;

(j) all impact fees levied by any governmental entity have been paid in full by Seller;

(k) the Seller shall have removed all stored fill dirt from the Property; and

(l) sidewalks shall have been installed at Seller's expense (or adequate provision to Buyer made therefore) where and to the extent required by any governmental entity having jurisdiction over the Property.

§ 12.3.8   Buyer Has Right To Do Work On Property Prior To Closing

In some rare instances, a buyer in a new construction contract may work on a property prior to the closing. Most new construction contracts prohibit the buyer or the buyer's contractor from doing any work on the property prior to the buyer closing on the purchase of the property. There are good reasons to do this, since it raises a whole new group of issues that must be addressed. With some homes, particularly more expensive homes, prohibiting the buyer's contractors from doing specialized work may be unrealistic. If such work is going to be allowed, the parties should address in the contract when the work will be done, who is responsible for any damage caused by the buyer's contractors, whether the buyer's contractors will be required to have liability insurance, and what happens if the buyer does not close on the purchase of the property. A sample of such a provision designed to generally protect the builder is set forth below.

> **Special Stipulation 274:   Buyer's Contractors to Install Items Prior to Closing**
>
> *Prior to Closing the Buyer shall have the right to have Buyer's contractors [describe work; for example: install window treatments and speakers in the Property] (hereinafter "the Work"). The Work shall only be performed at a time approved in advance by Seller. While Seller agrees not to unreasonably withhold its approval, Buyer acknowledges that the Work needs to be performed at a time when it does not unreasonably interfere with the work being performed by Seller. In the event Buyer does not close upon the purchase of the Property due to no fault of Seller, Buyer hereby agrees to abandon the Work performed by Buyer's contractors, relinquish legal title to the same, and covenants not to sue to recover the value of the Work. In so doing Buyer acknowledges that the cost of removing the Work and restoring the Property to the condition it was in prior to the Work being done is anticipated to exceed the value of the Work itself.*

§ 12.3.9   Cleanliness Of The Property At The Time Of Closing

In the GAR Contract, the Seller agrees to deliver the Property clean and free of trash and debris at the time of possession.[1484] This paragraph has been the source of much controversy between buyers and sellers, probably as a result of occasionally differing standards of cleanliness on their party. One solution to the problem is to include a more specific obligation on the part of the seller to clean the house. A sample of such a stipulation is set forth below.

> **Special Stipulation 275:   House to be Clean at Closing**
>
> *1. Seller to Thoroughly Clean House*
>
> *Seller agrees that as of the date of the transfer of possession of the Property, the Property shall have been thoroughly cleaned with all trash and debris removed from the Property, all tiled and hardwood floors having been swept and damp mopped, all carpets having been vacuumed, all cabinets, countertops, ledges, sills, ceiling fans and doors and door frames having been wiped down with a moist rag and cleaner, all appliances having been scrubbed free of dirt, grease and grime, all bathroom sinks, commodes and bathtubs having been scrubbed and cleaned with a bathroom cleaner and disinfected and all cobwebs and dust having been removed from around corners of the house and light fixtures. Seller shall not leave any personal property of Seller in the Property other than what is contemplated under this Agreement.*
>
> *2. Carpet Cleaning*
>
> *Seller shall have all carpeted areas in the house professionally cleaned not later than three days from the date of closing. Seller shall provide the receipt for said cleaning to Buyer at closing.*

Another issue which sometimes arises is that sellers will clean their houses but fail to remove debris from their yards. Since the seller's obligation is to remove debris from the entire property, it would include the obligation, for example, of removing a large pile of tree limbs.

1484   GAR Form F20.

Similarly, the issue of construction debris commonly arises in new construction contracts. Although, the GAR New Construction Purchase and Sale Agreement[1485] does not specifically address construction debris, the seller is still required to deliver the property clean and free of trash and debris at the time of possession. However, to ensure that construction debris is not buried on the property, the buyer may want to include the following special stipulation in the contract.

> **Special Stipulation 276: Disclosure of Buried Construction Debris, Stumps or Other Materials**
>
> *Seller shall not bury any construction debris, trees, stumps, or other organic materials on the Property without the written consent of Buyer. Seller warrants that to the best of Seller's knowledge and information no construction debris, trees, stumps or other organic materials were buried on the Property during the development of the Property. This warranty shall survive the closing.*

It is especially important to disclose construction debris in planned unit developments (PUDs) because many PUD covenants provide that fines will be levied against an owner if construction debris is left on the property. The buyer may want to incorporate a provision stipulating that all construction debris will be removed from the property prior to closing so that the buyer will not be subject to a fine when he takes title to the property. The following provision may be used for this purpose.

> **Special Stipulation 277: Seller to Remove All Construction Debris Before Closing**
>
> *Seller agrees that all construction debris shall be removed from the Property prior to the date of closing. Seller agrees that if all construction debris is not removed, Buyer may require that sufficient funds be placed in escrow at closing to cover the cost of removal.*

The other issue which arises in this area is when the seller leaves personal property in the house or garage. While most buyers appreciate the seller leaving extra paint, tile or roofing shingles that were used on the property, they do not typically want other property that the seller didn't have the time or inclination to move. The special stipulation below can be used by the buyers who want the extra building materials that can be used on the property without getting the junk.

> **Special Stipulation 278: Extras Building Materials Stay with Property**
>
> *Any usable paint, tile, tile grout, roof shingles, bricks, siding, moldings and other building materials or wallpaper that matches any presently used on or in the Property shall remain with the Property.*

§ 12.4 ALLOCATION OF COSTS ASSOCIATED WITH PURCHASE AND SALE

There are a number of costs associated with a purchase and sale transaction. Many of these charges are defined as closing costs. Other costs will be expenses of either the buyer or the seller. Although identified below as typically buyer or seller expenses, the parties may reallocate these expenses by an agreement between themselves.

§ 12.4.1 Closing Costs

A major component of the closing costs are the lender charges which include (but are not limited to) the following: the loan origination fee; the underwriting fee; the processing fee; courier fees; tax service fee; document preparation fees; escrow waiver fee, if applicable; mortgage broker fee; commitment fee; appraisal fee; appraisal review fee; credit report fee; flood certification fee; Georgia Residential Mortgage Loan Fee; and loan assumption fee, if applicable.

1485 GAR Form F23.

In addition to these lender fees, the following costs are customarily considered to be closing costs: the intangible tax; the title examination; the lender's title insurance; and attorneys' fees and costs, including miscellaneous fees such as courier fees, recording fees, and tax report fees.

§ 12.4.1.1 Seller's Contribution At Closing

Since the costs associated with closing a loan are for the benefit of the buyer, in the absence of an agreement to the contrary the buyer will be responsible for these costs. However, the GAR Contracts, as well as most other form contracts, include a section in which the seller can make some specified contribution toward the closing costs.

The GAR Contract provides that the seller's financial contribution may be used to pay any cost or expense of buyer related to the transaction.[1486] In addition, the seller is required to pay all costs, fees and charges necessary to clear title encumbrances and/or defects necessary to allow the seller to be able to convey good and marketable title to the property and any extra costs, fees and changes resulting from seller not being able to attend the closing in person. The buyer then pays all other costs or fees required to close the transaction. This provision eliminates the need for any interpretation or calculation as to the manner in which closing costs and discount points are to be allocated between the parties and provides the parties with greater certainty as to the amount of their respective cost obligations at closing. With the buyer having so much discretion to spend any contribution to closing costs made by the seller, the likelihood of the seller getting some type of refund of an unused portion of the contribution is remote. However, the buyer does acknowledge that the buyer's mortgage lender may not allow the seller's contribution to be used for some costs or expenses. If this is the case, any unused portion of the seller's contribution will remain the property of the seller. If the seller is contributing to the closing costs, the seller may wish to ensure that the buyer selects a reputable lender who can deliver the mortgage and provide the closing firm the information and funds in a timely manner, instead of a lender who quotes the lowest interest rate. The seller may include the following financing contingencies in the contract for this purpose.

> **Special Stipulation 279: Buyer to Seek Loan From List of Lenders**
>
> *Seller agrees to contribute at the time of closing the sum of $_____ which sum may be used by Buyer for any of the costs, fees and charges specified in Paragraph 2(c)(3) of the Agreement, provided that Buyer seeks a mortgage loan from only one of the following mortgage lenders:_____*
>
> *In specifying a list of approved mortgage lenders seller is making no representations or warranties regarding the qualifications or capabilities of any of these mortgage lenders. Seller is merely trying to ensure that Buyer obtains mortgage financing from a lender who is actively involved and well known in the mortgage lending industry.*

Provisions such as the above are often used in new construction contracts where the builder or seller agrees to pay certain closing costs if the buyer utilizes the seller's preferred lender.

Parties should be very careful when deciding the amount of the seller's contribution to closing costs because FHA, VA, and conventional loans will not be approved for a buyer if the seller is contributing too much money toward closing costs. An in-depth discussion about this as it relates to FHA loans appears in § 7.6.2 (Limitation on Contributions to Closing Costs and Discount Points) of this book.

As to conventional loans, Fannie Mae guidelines state that for property that will be occupied as a principal residence where the buyer is obtaining a loan for more than 90% of the purchase price, the seller cannot contribute more than

---

1486   GAR Form F20.

3% of the purchase price or appraised value of the property, whichever is less, toward closing costs. This limitation is raised to 6% if the buyer's loan will be 90% or less of the property purchase price.[1487]

The parties may wish to utilize the following special stipulation if there is any question regarding whether the lender will approve the amount of closing costs to be paid by the seller.

> **Special Stipulation 280:   Seller's Contribution to Closing Costs to be Reduced to Meet FHA/VA Rules**
>
> *The parties agree that the closing costs to be paid by Seller exceed the highest amount permitted to be paid by Seller by applicable FHA, VA or Fannie Mae rules and regulations (but not exceeding the original amount set forth in the Agreement), Seller's contribution shall be reduced to the maximum permitted amount.*

For commercial properties, what is paid by seller and buyer should be clearly set out in the contract. In the case of the GAR Commercial Contract, the parties are allowed to allocate who is to pay for the survey, title examination and title insurance premium.[1488]

§ 12.4.1.2   Seller's Contribution To Closing Costs Must Be Used For Specified Purposes

The seller's contributions at closing must first be used to pay for the preparation of the warranty deed and owner's affidavit by the closing attorney. The idea behind this provision was that if there is a separate charge for the deed and affidavit, it should be paid out of the seller's contribution to closing costs. The remainder of any contribution can then be used to pay for any cost or expense of buyer related to the transaction.

If there are excess funds from the seller's contribution after all the buyer has used the contribution for everything possible, the GAR Contracts provide that the excess funds remain the property of the seller. While in most transactions, the buyer will find some way to use the entire seller's contribution, there may be some situations where the contribution is so large it cannot be used in its entirety. In filling in form purchase and sale agreements, real estate licensees should be aware that in these types of situations it is normally better to reduce the sales price of the property and the seller's contribution rather than keeping both artificially high.

§ 12.4.1.3   Choice Of Closing Law Firm

The GAR Contract provides that if the specified law firm is listed on the lender's approved list and the buyer is given the choice of law firms on the list, the buyer agrees to select the closing law firm specified in the agreement. If the specified law firm is not on the lender's list and cannot be added in time to closing the transaction, the buyer may then select another closing attorney who is on the lender's approved list. This change was made to comply with the Georgia Fair Lending Act, which classifies a home loan as a high cost loan under a "points and fees" test.[1489]

The Georgia Fair Lending Act requires that if the lender wishes not to include attorneys' fees in the "points and fees" test, then the borrower must be given the right either to select an attorney to conduct the title search and closing from an approved list, or to select an attorney acceptable to the lender. This provision enables the buyer to make an informed choice by consulting with his or her real estate agent on selecting a capable closing attorney.

§ 12.4.2   Closing Costs In Commercial Transactions

In most commercial transactions, each party pays his or her own attorney's fees. The other costs to close the transaction are then usually specifically allocated between the buyer and the seller in the transaction. Since the transfer tax has

---

1487   Fannie Mae Seller Servicer Guide, Selling Part VI, Chapter 2, § 203.01.

1488   GAR Form CF2.

1489   O.C.G.A. § 7-6A-2(17)(b).

historically been paid for by the seller in commercial transactions most commercial contracts reflect this approach. The seller also usually pays for the cost to prepare and record the deed and clear title. The buyer usually pays for all costs associated with obtaining a loan to purchase the property, the cost of title insurance and the cost of any survey the buyer chooses to obtain of the property.

§ 12.4.3   Other Buyer And Seller Expenses

Unless otherwise provided in the contract, the following pre-paid items are typically considered to be the buyer's expense: insurance, including hazard insurance, flood insurance, if required, and mortgage insurance, if required; escrows for taxes and insurance; and prepaid interest. The owner's title insurance is a buyer's expense.

Unless otherwise provided in the contract, the following expenses are generally considered to be seller expenses: transfer tax; termite letter; the broker's commission; and if the seller is a nonresident, the withholding tax.

§ 12.4.3.1   Flood Insurance Issues

One of the costs usually associated with obtaining a mortgage loan is a fee for a flood certification. Lenders retain third-party providers to examine the Federal Emergency Management Administration ("FEMA") flood maps and determine whether the property that is to secure the lender's loan is located in a federally designated flood hazard area. If the flood certification provided to the lender discloses that the property is located within a flood hazard area, the lender will usually require the borrower to obtain a flood insurance policy naming the lender as a loss payee. Some of the GAR Contracts explicitly provide that the buyer may use the seller's financial contribution to pay any "insurance premiums (including flood insurance, if applicable).[1490] Other GAR Contracts,[1491] however, simply provide that the buyer may use the seller's contribution to pay any cost of expense related to the transaction, which would include any flood insurance premium.

Buyers should be aware that in some instances the flood certification obtained by the lender will indicate that the property is located in a flood hazard area, but a current survey of the property will disclose that either: (a) the property is not located within a flood hazard area, or (b) a portion of the property is located within a flood hazard area, but the improvements which have been constructed on the property are located outside the flood hazard area. The buyer may be able to convince a non-FHA lender to waive the flood insurance requirement based on this survey information. FHA will not insure a loan on a property on which construction is proposed, a property under construction, or a property with a dwelling less than one year old if any portion of the property is located in a flood plain.

Sellers should be cautious in making any representations regarding whether their properties are in a flood plain because flood maps can change over time. Likewise, the fact that a property is not shown to be in a flood hazard area on a FEMA map is no guarantee that the property does not flood. FEMA can take years to update its maps. The rapid pace of development in many parts of Georgia in recent years has resulted in a substantial increase in water runoff. As a result, many properties that do not appear on the current FEMA maps as being in flood hazard areas may be located in flood hazard areas once FEMA updates its maps.

Purchasers of property located adjacent to streams, creeks, or in close proximity to recently developed areas should be certain that their homeowner's insurance provides adequate coverage for flood damage even if the property is not located in a FEMA designated flood hazard area.

1490   Gar Form F23 and F27.

1491   GAR Form F20.

§ 12.4.3.2 Mortgage Insurance

Lenders may require the borrower to obtain private mortgage insurance (PMI) which protects the lender against losses due to borrower default or in the event of foreclosure. A lender will be able to sell a PMI-backed loan, which would otherwise be considered too risky, to third-party investors like the Federal National Mortgage Association (FNMA) and the Federal Home Loan Mortgage Corporation (FHLMC). It is common business practice for lenders to sell loans to these investors as a way to maintain their liquidity so that they may continue to provide new loans.

Usually a portion of the premium is paid up front at closing and the rest is paid as part of the monthly mortgage payment. The lender will usually collect 14 months premium at closing and pay twelve months of the premium to the PMI provider. The remaining two months is placed in the escrow account to start the collection for the next year. The lender then collects 1/12 of the renewal every month thereafter.

The mortgage insurance only covers the lender for a percentage that the lender will designate. This percentage is usually based on what the investors (often Fannie Mae or Freddie Mac) require. The insurance does not cover the whole loan. Instead, it covers only the difference between the loan amount and 80% value of the property. Generally, a lender will require the borrower to obtain private mortgage insurance unless the borrower is able to make a 20% down payment for the purchase of the home. By buying private mortgage insurance the buyer may need to only make a 3%-5% down payment.

The Homeowners Protection Act of 1998, which became effective in 1999, establishes rules for mortgage lenders to cancel PMI when certain criteria are met.[1492] These protections apply to certain home mortgages signed on or after July 29, 1999 for the purchase, initial construction, or refinance of a single-family home. These protections do not apply to government-insured FHA or VA loans or to loans with lender-paid PMI.

These rules provide for two cancellation options. The first option is known as automatic cancellation, which will occur when the loan-to-value (LTV) ratio reaches 78% based on the original market value of the home. This may take some time. For example, for a home mortgage signed on or after July 29, 1999, the PMI must be terminated automatically when the borrower accumulates 22% equity in the property based on the original property value.

The second option, called owner-initiated cancellation, occurs at 80% LTV. This option allows a lender and a borrower to agree to cancel PMI before automatic cancellation occurs at 78% LTV. The exceptions to the above provisions are: (1) the loan is "high-risk," (2) the mortgage payments have not been current within the year prior to the time for termination or cancellation, and (3) there are liens on the property.

The law does not provide for automatic cancellation for mortgages before July 29, 1999. Instead, the borrower must request for PMI cancellation once she has 20 percent equity in the property.

§ 12.4.3.3 Properties Serviced By Septic Systems And Wells

If the property that is being purchased has a septic system, the mortgage lender will usually require the buyer to provide a letter verifying that a visual inspection of the septic system site has been conducted and that the system appears to be in proper working order.

If there is a well on the property certain bacteriological and/or organic tests may be required by the buyer's lender to ensure the acceptability of this private water system. In some counties, a branch of the local government, usually the health department, conducts these inspections. If the local government does not provide this function the lender will usually require that a licensed plumber or qualified septic inspector make the inspection.

Any expense associated with a letter regarding the septic system or well is typically a buyer expense because the buyer's lender imposes the requirement. Under the GAR Contract, if this cost is not covered by the seller's contribution to

---

1492 12 U.S.C.A. § 4901.

closing costs, the buyer would normally pay the fee for this letter as part of the buyer's obligation to pay all other costs, fees and charges to close the transaction.[1493] To avoid any confusion on the point, however, the following special stipulation can be included in the contract for property containing a septic system.

> **Special Stipulation 281: Allocation of Fees for Septic System Clearance Letter**
>
> *Notwithstanding any provision to the contrary contained herein, _____ shall pay the fee associated with obtaining any Lender-required septic system clearance letter meeting the requirements of Lender. Such letter shall generally provide that a visual inspection of the septic system site has been conducted and shall provide the results of such visual inspection.*

The following special stipulation can be used in a contract for property on which a well is located.

> **Special Stipulation 282: Allocation of Fees for Well Clearance Letter**
>
> *Notwithstanding any other provision to the contrary contained herein, _____ shall pay the fee associated with obtaining any Lender-required well clearance letter meeting the requirements of the Lender. Such letter shall generally provide that the necessary bacteriological and/or organic tests of the well have been conducted and shall provide the results of such tests.*

It should be noted that under the FHA Loan Exhibit the seller is obligated to provide proper certification that the property is connected to and serviced by a public sewer system.[1494]

Buyers should keep in mind that these inspections are, in most instances, only visual inspections to verify that sewage is not escaping from the septic field and that the accompanying reports will not include any sort of warranty as to the soundness of the septic system. Buyers should therefore consider having a thorough inspection of the septic system performed by a licensed plumber as part of their inspection of the property. Buyers should also verify the condition of the septic system with the county health department even if a private clearance letter has been obtained. Unfortunately, some buyers have received private septic approval letters only to learn, too late, that the county health department had determined the system to be substandard.[1495]

§ 12.4.3.4   Credits At Closing

Buyers and sellers sometimes want to include contract stipulations that provide for the seller to give the buyer a credit at closing for items such as repairs, renovations, or decorating allowances. The GAR New Construction Exhibit allows the parties to identify monetary allowances for floor coverings, fixtures, wallpaper, landscaping, and appliances and provides for identifying the make, model, and color of appliances.[1496] If a buyer substantially exceeds an allowance amount, the seller has the option of collecting such additional amounts as a change order. If a buyer does not spend the full amount of an allowance, some builder contracts provide a credit to the buyer at closing for such unused amounts. The GAR New Construction Contract provides that if the buyer varies from the identified allowances, the final reconciliation will be handled at closing. This suggests that a buyer would be entitled to a credit if the buyer did not use all of a stated allowance amount. Other builder contracts provide that a buyer is not entitled to a refund for any unused allowance amount.

While this arrangement is frequently desirable to the parties in that it relieves the seller of making certain repairs or improvements requested by the buyer and provides the buyer with a source of funds to undertake the requested repairs

---

1493   GAR Forms F20, F23 and F27.

1494   GAR Form F63.

1495   *Georgia Real Estate Commission v. Peavy*, 229 Ga.App. 201, 493 S.E.2d. 602 (1997).

1496   GAR Form F24.

or improvements, it is generally not permitted by mortgage lenders due to Fannie Mae guidelines.[1497] The rationale for this lender prohibition is that these types of credits or concessions are actually just reductions in the purchase price and should be reflected as such. For example, a contract reflects a purchase price of $100,000 and includes a stipulation for a $3,000 repair credit to be given by the seller to the buyer and also includes a financing contingency providing for the buyer to obtain a loan of 90% of the purchase price. What the parties have actually done in providing for the $3,000 repair credit is to reduce the purchase price to $97,000, and the lender is now willing to lend only 90% of this amount, which is a smaller loan than was called for in the financing contingency.

Lenders will occasionally allow these types of credits with transactions in which there is a low loan-to-value ratio. If the above-referenced contract included a financing contingency providing for the buyer to obtain a loan of 60% of the purchase price, the lender may be willing to allow the repair credit to remain in the contract, since the loan of $60,000 would still be adequately secured by the collateral with an actual purchase price of $97,000.

The alternative to these types of credits or concessions which is preferred by lenders is to have the seller undertake any requested repairs prior to closing and have any invoices for this repair work paid either prior to closing or from the sale proceeds at the closing. In instances where the repairs cannot be completed prior to closing, the lender may authorize a portion of the sale proceeds to be held in escrow for a limited period of time following the closing and disbursed directly to a vendor upon the completion of any requested repairs.

As a practical matter, buyers should contact their mortgage lenders regarding any contract provisions concerning proposed credits, allowances, or repairs in order to resolve any potential loan underwriting issues.

§ 12.5 TAXES, UTILITIES, AND HOMEOWNERS ASSOCIATION DUES

§ 12.5.1 Proration Of Property Taxes

Since real estate taxes are a lien on property they must be paid at closing to convey clear title. Although property taxes are assessed on a calendar year basis and are based on the condition of the property on January 1st, they are not billed until later in the year and generally are not due until the third or fourth quarter of the year.

Each city or county in Georgia sets the due date for taxes for property located in its jurisdiction. Because the taxes are assessed for the calendar year, once billed they become a lien against the property regardless of the due date. Therefore, once the tax bill is issued it must be paid at closing in order for the seller to convey clear title to the property. The seller is responsible for payment of property taxes from January 1 up to the date of closing, and the buyer is responsible for the payment of property taxes from the date of closing through December 31.

While the proration of property taxes between a buyer and seller is customarily included in purchase and sale agreements, such proration is not required under Georgia law unless there is an agreement stating otherwise.[1498] Without an agreement, the seller is responsible for the full amount of taxes for that tax year regardless of whether the property was sold to a buyer.[1499] For example, John Smith owned certain real property on January 1, 2008. On March 7, 2008, Jim Brown purchased the property. On September 10, 2009, the county tax commissioner filed suit against John Smith for the unpaid 2008 real estate taxes on the property. John claimed that he should only be responsible for a portion of the 2008 taxes since Jim bought the property in March. The court disagreed holding that the owner of the property on January 1, 2008 was responsible for all the 2008 taxes even if the title to the property was transferred, unless there was an agreement stating otherwise.[1500]

1497   Fannie Mae Seller Servicer Guidelines, Part VI, Chapter 2, § 203.01.

1498   *Dehco, Inc. v. Fulton County Tax Com'r*, 2012 WL 1432522.

1499   *Dehco, Inc. v. Fulton County Tax Com'r*, 2012 WL 1432522.

1500   *Dehco, Inc. v. Fulton County Tax Com'r*, 2012 WL 1432522.

Generally, the allocation of property taxes between the seller and the buyer will be determined by the contract. Most contracts, including the GAR Contract, provide that *ad valorem* property[1501] taxes will be prorated as of the date of closing. If the closing takes place before the tax bills have been issued, however, the proration is normally based on the prior year's taxes. Most settlement statements provide that the parties agree to account to one another for any differences between what is charged based on an estimate from the previous year's bill and what is actually billed. In addition, the GAR Contracts now provide that in the event real estate taxes are paid at closing based upon an estimated tax bill or tax bill under appeal, the buyer and seller will make any financial adjustments between themselves as are necessary to correctly prorate the tax bill upon the issuance of the actual tax bill or the appeal being resolved.[1502]

If the buyer knows that property taxes will be based on an estimate and wants to incorporate a provision in the contract to address adjustments when actual bills are issued, the following special stipulation may be used.

> ### Special Stipulation 283: Proration of Taxes After Closing and Assignment of Right to Appeal Tax Assessments
>
> *Buyer and Seller understand that the allocation of ad valorem property taxes is based on last year's actual taxes because the tax bill(s) for the current year have not been issued. If the actual bill is greater or less than the estimated amount allocated at closing, Buyer and Seller agree to prorate the taxes among themselves. Further, Seller does hereby agree to assign to Buyer any rights Seller may have to appeal the tax assessment effective as of the date of closing.*

If the seller wants to eliminate responsibility for paying additional funds for taxes, the following special stipulation may be incorporated in the contract.

> ### Special Stipulation 284: No Further Proration of Taxes After Closing and Assignment of Right to Appeal Tax Assessments
>
> *Buyer and Seller understand that the allocation of taxes is based on last year's actual taxes because the tax bill(s) for the current year have not been issued. Buyer and Seller agree that neither party shall have any obligation to the other in the event that actual taxes are greater or less than paid at closing; provided, however, that Seller agrees to assign any rights Seller may have to Buyer to appeal the tax assessment effective as of the date of closing.*

A problem that occasionally arises in the new construction context is when the taxes for the prior year are based upon the unimproved value of the property, but the taxes for the year in which the sale occurs are based upon the improved value of the property. For example, assume that as of January 1, 2011, (the date upon which the property is valued for the 2011 taxes) the property is unimproved and is taxed at a value of $25,000. A house is subsequently built on the property and, as a result, the property is valued at $150,000 as of January 1, 2012. The property is sold on March 15, 2012. The 2012 tax assessments and bills are not yet available and the 2011 assessment will substantially understate the year 2012 taxes. In this instance the parties may wish to make a "best guess" estimate of what the new taxes will be and set the tax proration accordingly. Additionally, the parties may wish to have funds held in escrow to cover anticipated tax increases.

> ### Special Stipulation 285: Proration of Taxes After Closing with Seller Depositing Funds Into Escrow
>
> *Buyer and Seller recognize that the ad valorem property taxes for the Property for the year in which this transaction is scheduled to close may not be available as of the Closing Date.*

1501   See Chapter 25 (Ad Valorem Tax on Real Property) for further discussion on *ad valorem* property taxes.

1502   GAR Form F20.

The parties agree that in this event the ad valorem taxes will be prorated at closing based upon the prior year's ad valorem taxes and Seller shall deposit the sum $_____ with the closing attorney. The funds shall be held in escrow until such time as the ad valorem property taxes are available, at which time the funds shall be disbursed based upon the actual tax bill. Any overage shall be paid to the Seller. In the event the escrowed funds are insufficient to pay Seller's prorated portion of the taxes then Seller shall pay any remaining difference to Buyer.

§ 12.5.2   Selling Property During Pending Tax Appeal

A buyer will sometimes contract to purchase property that is subject to a tax appeal. The most common way to deal with this issue is for the parties to prorate the taxes at closing based on the tax bill under appeal. When the appeal is finally resolved, the parties will make any necessary adjustments to reflect the proration of the actual tax bill.

Most purchase and sale agreements, including the GAR Contract, provide this method to deal with properties sold during a pending tax appeal and properties sold before the issuance of the tax bill for that tax year. The GAR Contract provides that in the event the real estate taxes paid at the closing are based on an estimated amount or tax bill under appeal, the buyer and seller will make any financial adjustments between themselves as are necessary to correctly prorate the tax bill upon the issuance of the actual tax bill or the appeal being resolved.[1503] Any pending tax appeal is deemed assigned to the buyer as of the date of closing. Furthermore, the GAR Contract also now provides that if there are any tax savings resulting from a tax appeal, any third party costs to handle the appeal may be deducted from the savings before re-prorating. The idea behind this provision is that if a party with an obligation to re-prorate incurs substantial expenses in appealing the ad valorem property taxes, the cost of the appeal should be borne by both the seller and the buyer. The deduction of these expenses is only permitted if there are tax savings.

If the property is sold during a pending tax appeal or before the tax bill has been issued, the following special stipulation may be used.

Special Stipulation 286:   Proration of Taxes

Seller and Buyer agree to prorate as of the date of closing, ad valorem property taxes, community association fees, if any, and solid waste and other utility bills for which service cannot be terminated as of the date of closing. In the event ad valorem property taxes are based upon an estimated bill or tax bill under appeal, Buyer and Seller shall, upon the issuance of the actual tax bill or the appeal being resolved, promptly make such financial adjustments between themselves as are necessary to correctly prorate the tax bill. In the event there are tax savings resulting from a tax appeal, any third party costs to handle the appeal may be deducted from the savings for that tax year before re-prorating.

Another (less common) option for the parties to deal with this issue is to specifically address in the agreement whether the appeal will continue after the property is sold, who will be responsible for handling the appeal, and who will receive any tax refund. The following stipulations may be used to address such a situation.

Special Stipulation 287:   Proration of Taxes in a Pending Tax Appeal

Buyer and Seller acknowledge that the Property is currently the subject of an appeal of ad valorem property taxes for the following tax years: _____. Seller hereby assigns to Buyer upon the closing of the Property all of Seller's right, title and interest in said appeal. Buyer shall have the right to proceed with said appeal either in Buyer's own name or in the

---

1503   GAR Form F20.

name of Seller. Upon the closing of the Property Seller does hereby authorize Buyer to act as Seller's attorney-in-fact with respect to said appeal.

Seller agrees to provide Buyer will a copy of all written materials pertaining to the tax appeal and to answer any of Buyer's questions regarding the appeal so that Buyer may pursue the appeal through to its conclusion.

Special Stipulation 288: Seller Shall Have No Further Responsibility for Ad Valorem Taxes

Upon the closing of the Property, Seller shall have no further responsibility for any ad valorem property taxes on the Property and Buyer hereby agrees to indemnify Seller from and against any and all claims arising out of or relating to the same.

Special Stipulation 289: Seller May Continue with Tax Appeal After Closing

Buyer and Seller acknowledge that the Property is currently the subject of an appeal of ad valorem property taxes for the following tax years: _____. Seller shall have the right to continue with the appeal after the closing of the Property and to retain any tax refund resulting therefrom. Seller agrees to be fully responsible for the payment of any additional taxes owing as a result of the appeal for the tax years referenced above and agrees to indemnify and hold Buyer harmless arising out of or relating to the same.

§ 12.5.3   Payment Of Transfer Tax

A real estate transfer tax is not a property tax. It is an excise tax levied by statute on the sale of property for the privilege of selling that particular property to another person.[1504] Under the old GAR Contract, this tax was customarily paid by the seller. However, the GAR Contract now provides that the transfer tax is paid by the buyer, but the Seller may elect to pay the transfer tax by including a special stipulation in the agreement.

This change was prompted because sellers using the GAR Contract often misunderstood the amount they were required to pay in a purchase and sale transaction. Under older versions of the GAR Contract, a seller would indicate the percentage she was willing to contribute towards closing costs, while under the impression that this contribution was their only financial obligation. When closing came, many sellers would become upset when they discovered they were also required to pay the transfer tax. In most cases, this knowledge would have affected the amount a seller was willing to contribute towards closing. To avoid this issue, the new GAR Contract provides that the responsibility to pay the transfer tax falls on the buyer.

If the parties want to provide that the seller will be responsible for the payment of the transfer tax, the following special stipulation should be included in the agreement.

Special Stipulation 290: Payment of Transfer Tax

Notwithstanding any other provision contained herein, the Seller shall be solely responsible for the payment of the transfer tax.

The amount of the transfer tax is based on the sale price of the property.[1505] Georgia law provides that the transfer tax is calculated as follows:

> $1 for the first $1,000 or fractional part of $1,000 and at the rate of $.10 for each additional $100 or fractional part of $100 on each deed, instrument, or other

---

1504   O.C.G.A. § 48-6-1.

1505   *City of Columbus v. Ronald A. Edwards Constr. Co.*, 155 Ga.App. 502, 271 S.E.2d 643 (1980).

writing by which any lands, tenements, or other realty sold is granted, assigned, transferred, or otherwise conveyed to or vested in the purchaser or purchasers, or any other person or persons by his or their direction, when the consideration or value of the interest or property conveyed (exclusive of the value of any lien or encumbrances existing prior to the sale and not removed by the sale) exceeds $100.[1506]

For example, the transfer tax on property sold for $100,000 would be $100. However, if the buyer assumed a loan already securing the property in the principal amount of $65,000, then the value of the loan is subtracted from the purchase price and the transfer tax owed would be $35.

The tax must be paid to the clerk of the superior court of the county where the property is located. The clerk certifies the amount and the date of payment on the face of the recorded deed or other instrument. This tax must be paid as a pre-requisite to recording the deed, and no deed is to be recorded without payment of the transfer tax.

Recording of the following do not require payment of a transfer tax:[1507]

(a) any deed to secure debt;

(b) any deed of gift;

(c) any deed, instrument, or other writing to which any of the following is a party: the United States, Georgia, any agency, board, commission, department, or political subdivision of either the United States or Georgia, any public authority, or any nonprofit public corporation;

(d) any lease of lands, tenements, standing timber, or any realty or any lease of any estate, interest, or usufruct in any of the foregoing;

(e) any transfer of real estate between husband and wife in connection with a divorce case;

(f) any order for year's support awarding an interest in real property;

(g) any deed in lieu of foreclosure for a purchase money deed to secure debt in existence and properly executed and recorded for a period of 12 months;

(h) any deed from the debtor to the first transferee at a foreclosure sale;

(i) any transfer of property which is acquired for transportation purposes;

(j) any deed of assent or distribution by an executor, administrator, guardian, trustee, or custodian or other instrument carrying out the exercise of a power of appointment and any other instrument transferring real estate to affirm a fiduciary (this exemption applies only if the transfer is without valuable consideration); and

(k) any deed which effects a division of real property among joint tenants or tenants in common if there is no consideration other than the division of the property.

§ 12.5.4 Payment Of Intangible Tax

Georgia law provides that every holder of a long-term note secured by real estate must, within 90 days from the date the instrument is executed, record the security instrument in the county where the property is located and pay an intangible recording tax at the rate of $1.50 for each $500 or fraction thereof of the face amount of the note. The maximum amount of any intangible tax payable on a single note is $25,000.[1508]

1506   O.C.G.A. § 48-6-1.

1507   O.C.G.A. § 48-6-2.

1508   O.C.G.A. § 48-6-61.

A long-term note secured by real estate is defined as any note representing credits secured by mortgages, deeds to secure debt, purchase money deeds to secure debt, bonds of title, or other form of security instrument, when any part of the principal of a note falls due more than three years from the date of the note or from the date of any instrument executed to secure the note and conveying or creating a lien or encumbrance on the real estate.[1509] For example, a buyer obtains a 30-year loan evidenced by a note and security deed which will be recorded in the county land records. Since payment is not required in less than three years, intangible tax must be paid upon the recording of the security deed.

A short-term note is defined as a note secured by real estate where the whole of the principal of the note falls due within three years from the date of the note or from the date of any instrument executed to secure the note.[1510] For example, a seller grants a short-term loan payable in 30 months to a buyer as evidenced by a note and security deed. Since payment is due within three years, no intangible tax is due upon recording the security deed. This would be true regardless of the number of years over which the payments are amortized. The only factor considered is whether or not the note matures within three years.

As with the transfer tax, payment of the intangible recording tax is a prerequisite to the recording of the security instrument. The collecting official (the tax commissioner or, in counties of 50,000 or more, the clerk of the superior court) must determine the amount of intangible tax owed and collect the tax before the security instrument is recorded.

Georgia law also provides that no intangible tax shall be collected on that part of the face amount of a new instrument securing a long term note secured by real estate which represents a refinancing by the original lender of unpaid principal on a previous instrument securing a long term note if all intangible recording tax due on the previous instrument had been paid or was exempt from intangible recording tax.

As a prerequisite, either the new instrument must contain a statement of what part of its face amount represents a refund of the unpaid principal on the previous instrument, or the holder of the new instrument must submit an affidavit identifying what part of the face amount of the new instrument represents a refinancing of unpaid principal on the previous instrument.[1511]

For example, if a buyer refinances a 30-year fixed rate $100,000 loan with the same lender for a new $100,000 loan at a better interest rate, no additional intangible tax would need to be paid since the new loan is for the same or a lesser principal amount. If the new loan is for $110,000 then intangible tax is owed on only the additional $10,000 in principal. Note that this only applies when the same lender is involved in both loans.

§ 12.5.5 Water Bills, Utility Bills, And Sanitation Bills

An unpaid or delinquent water bill is not a lien against the property unless a lien is filed in the county records by the water supplier. However, by statute, a public or private water supplier cannot file a lien for unpaid water bills against property unless the owner is the person who incurred the charges.[1512] The same is true for gas, sewer, or electricity.[1513]

By a law which became effective in April 1994, a water supplier cannot refuse to supply water to a single or multi-family residential property with separate meters for each unit upon application of an owner or tenant because of a delinquent bill of a prior owner, occupant, or tenant.[1514] Even though these statutory protections now exist, the best practice is to verify prior to closing that the water bill has been paid through the date of closing. To further protect the buyer, the contract should include a provision regarding prorating all utility bills after final bills are received.

1509   O.C.G.A. § 48-6-60(3).

1510   O.C.G.A. § 48-6-60(4).

1511   O.C.G.A. § 48-6-65(b)(2)(B).

1512   O.C.G.A. § 36-60-17(c).

1513   O.C.G.A. § 36-60-17(d).

1514   O.C.G.A. § 36-60-17(a).

Most cities and counties include a sanitation tax as part of the property tax bill. In a few counties and cities, however, separate bills or periodic bills (*i.e.*, quarterly) are sent to owners of property for sanitation (garbage pickup) services. At closing any outstanding sanitation bills should be paid and prorated between the seller and buyer.

§ 12.5.6   Changes In Prorations After Final Bills Received

Changes in prorations must be addressed by contract. Most form real estate contracts, including the GAR Contract, provide that the seller and the buyer agree to prorate between themselves as of the date of closing or the date of possession of property by the buyer, whichever is later, all utility bills which are issued after closing. This would apply only to utility bills that include service for any period of time the property was owned or occupied by the seller or any other person prior to the buyer.

§ 12.5.7   Withholding Tax On Sale Of Georgia Property

§ 12.5.7.1   Requirements Under Georgia Law

Georgia law requires withholding of up to 3% of the purchase price on any sale or transfer of real property and related tangible personal property located in Georgia from nonresidents of the state of Georgia.[1515] The burden to withhold and remit this tax to the Commissioner is placed on the buyer. The buyer must file the required return and remit payment on or before the last day of the month after the month in which the sale has occurred.[1516] If the tax payable is more than the sale proceeds, the buyer must withhold the entire sale proceeds.

Any buyer who fails to withhold the 3% when required is personally liable for this tax, and the state revenue commissioner may collect any unpaid withholding tax in the same manner as all other withholding taxes are collected.[1517] This means the commissioner may file a lien for any unpaid withholding tax which lien attaches to the entire buyer's property.[1518] For purposes of this statute, the seller or transferor of property will not be considered a nonresident of Georgia if he executes an affidavit affirming that all of the following conditions have been met:[1519]

(a)   the seller or transferor has filed Georgia income tax returns or appropriate extensions have been received for the two income tax years immediately preceding the year of sale;

(b)   the seller or transferor is in business in Georgia and will continue substantially in the same business in Georgia after the sale or the seller or transferor has real property remaining in the state at the time of closing equal to or greater in value than the withholding tax liability as measured by 100% property tax assessment of such remaining property;

(c)   the seller or transferor will report the sale on a Georgia income tax return for the current year and file it by its due date; and

(d)   if the seller or transferor is a corporation or limited partnership, it is registered to do business in Georgia.[1520]

(e)   The withholding requirement does not apply to the following types of transactions: sale or transfer of principal residences, deeds in lieu of foreclosure with no additional consideration, or when the transferor or transferee is an agency or authority of the United States, the state of Georgia, the Federal National Mortgage Association (Fannie Mae) or Federal Home Loan Mortgage Corporation (Freddie Mac) or the Government National Mortgage Association (Ginny Mae), or a private mortgage insurance (PMI) company.[1521]

1515   O.C.G.A. § 48-7-128.

1516   O.C.G.A. § 48-7-128(b)(1) and (f).

1517   O.C.G.A. § 48-7-128(b)(1).

1518   O.C.G.A. § 48-7-128(b).

1519   O.C.G.A. § 48-7-128(a).

1520   O.C.G.A. § 48-7-128(a).

1521   O.C.G.A. § 40-7-128(d).

If the seller is a partnership, S corporation or unincorporated entity, and there are nonresident owners of such entity, the buyer is not required to withhold if the entity certifies to the buyer that a composite return is being filed on behalf of the nonresident owners and that the entity will remit the tax on behalf of the nonresident owners.[1522]

§ 12.5.7.2   Requirements Under Federal Law

The Federal Investment in Real Property Tax Act ("FIRPTA") is similar to the Georgia legislation described above. When the seller of an interest in real property located in the United States is a foreign person or business entity, FIRPTA requires buyers to withhold a tax equal to 10% of the amount realized on the disposition that real property interest.[1523] The exemptions are:

(a) seller provides to buyer an affidavit by the transferor stating, under penalty of perjury, the seller's United States taxpayer identification number and that the transferor is not a foreign person;[1524]

(b) if the seller is a privately held U.S. corporation, it provides to the buyer an affidavit stating, under penalty of perjury, that it is not and has not been a United States real property holding corporation or as of the date of the sale, the interests in such corporation are not United States real property interests;[1525]

(c) buyer receives a statement by the Secretary of State that the seller has reached agreement with the Secretary for the payment of any tax imposed by the law on any gain recognized by the transferor on the disposition of the United States real property interest, or is exempt from any such tax and either the buyer or seller has satisfied any of the seller's unsatisfied withholding liability or has provided adequate security to cover such liability;[1526]

(d) the property is acquired by the buyer for use by him or her as a residence and the sale proceeds do not exceed $300,000[1527]; or

(e) the sale of the real property interest comprise of a share of a class of stock that is regularly traded on an established securities market.[1528]

The federal regulations in this area are substantial and detailed, and beyond the scope of this book. In any situation involving a foreign seller of real property, REALTORS® should advise their clients to seek specialized advice from their tax advisor. In the event the withholding requirement applies to a transaction and the buyer does not withhold the required amount, the buyer then becomes liable for the taxes due.[1529]

§ 12.5.8   Condominium And Homeowner Association Dues

When property is located in a condominium or mandatory membership homeowners or property owners association, the dues owed to the association must be prorated at closing and any past due amount paid by the seller, absent a contract provision to the contrary.

The closing attorney should contact the board of directors or the manager of the association and obtain a written statement of all past due assessments and related charges on the property.[1530] Since the closing attorney does not

---

1522   O.C.G.A. § 48-7-128(e)(1).

1523   26 U.S.C.A. § 1445(a).

1524   26 U.S.C.A. § 1445(b)(2).

1525   26 U.S.C.A. § 1445(b)(3).

1526   26 U.S.C.A. § 1445(b)(4).

1527   26 U.S.C.A. § 1445(b)(5).

1528   26 U.S.C.A. § 1445(b)(6).

1529   26 U.S.C.A. § 1460; *Del Commercial Properties, Inc. v. C.I.R.*, 251 F.3d 210 (2001).

1530   The charges include the prorated liability insurance and casualty insurance policy for all structures within the condominium, which the association was required to obtain under the Georgia Condominium Act (O.C.G.A. § 44-3-107).

normally represent the buyer, the buyer would be well advised to independently confirm whether there are any outstanding assessments and other charges due against the property.

The seller generally pays all assessments owed to the date of closing and the dues are prorated for the month (or other time period applicable) between the parties. If a special assessment has been adopted which is being paid in increments, then confirmation must be obtained from the association as to whether the assessment is structured as a one-time assessment with periodic payments or is split and due only on the periodic payment dates. This will determine whether the full amount is due at closing and whether or not it is all owed by the seller. See Chapter 2 on Title for a discussion of liens created by unpaid association dues.

§ 12.6   CLOSING DATE AND POSSESSION

§ 12.6.1   What The GAR Contract Provides

The GAR Contracts provide for the closing to be on a stipulated date or on such other date as the parties may agree to in writing.[1531] This was added to prevent the closing date from being extended orally.

§ 12.6.2   Effect Of Time Of Essence Clause On Closing Date

Many real estate contracts, including the GAR Contract, specifically provide that time is of the essence. Such a provision serves to require that actions to be taken by a certain date or within a certain time period must be performed in a timely manner.

If the sale does not close on the date specified in the contract as a result of the acts or omissions of one of the parties and the contract contains a "time is of the essence" clause, the non-breaching party can terminate the contract due to the breach of the other party and seek to recover his or her damages.[1532]

§ 12.6.2.1   Absent Contract Provision, Time Not Of Essence

If a contract does not have a time is of the essence provision, then the general rule is that time is not of the essence in a contract of sale and merely providing a certain time within which the transaction will be closed does not require tender of the purchase price within that time.[1533] However, delay must not be willful, must not be unreasonably long, and must not result in damages that cannot be compensated. If there has been a failure to comply within the time stipulated the other party may, by notice, assign a reasonable time for completing the contract and may require the defaulting party to perform within the time specified.[1534]

§ 12.6.2.2   Timely Performance When Time Is Of The Essence

Georgia courts have held that if the contract specifies that time is of the essence the court will require timely performance. The facts in the following lease purchase case are illustrative.

The buyer brought an action against the seller for specific performance of a contract.[1535] After hearing the evidence, the trial court concluded that the buyer had not tendered the contract price before the date specified in the contract. The court also implicitly found that there was not sufficient evidence to prevent enforcement of the time requirement in the contract.

1531   GAR Form F20, F23, F27, and F34.

1532   See § 1.6 of this book for an explanation of contract terms relating to time; see Chapter 10, § 10.3 regarding effect of "time is of the essence" provision on buyer's notification to seller of defects in title prior to closing; and Chapter 18 with respect to time as it relates to option contracts.

1533   It should be noted that the rule with reference to options is the reverse. An option "is peculiarly an agreement of which time is of the essence. *Piedmont Center 15, LLC v. Aquent, Inc.*, 286 Ga.App. 673, 649 S.E.2d 733 (2007), citing *Larned v. Wentworth*, 114 Ga. 208, 39 S.E. 855 (1901).

1534   *Gulf Oil Corp. v. Willcoxon*, 211 Ga. 462, 86 S.E.2d 507 (1955).

1535   *Dulock v. Shiver*, 239 Ga. 604, 238 S.E.2d 397 (1977).

The contract provided that a down payment was to be made November 10, 1975 and the balance of the purchase price paid on or before November 10, 1976. The buyer paid rent in the interim. The buyer was to assume the seller's loan and pay for the equity in the property in cash. On November 10, 1976, the buyer tendered a check for the equity in the property and informed seller's counsel that due to a misunderstanding, the loan assumption had been disapproved but that the assumption would be approved in a few days. On November 15, 1976, counsel for the seller returned the uncashed check for the equity and refunded a fee for title and deed services not performed. The seller took the position that the contract expired and the buyer was required to vacate the property. The buyer argued that time was not of the essence; however, the preprinted portion of the form contract stated that time was of the essence. The court concluded that with time being of the essence, the seller was justified in returning the down payment and refusing to close at a subsequent date.

In another case, the buyer failed to provide the purchase money by the closing date. Five days later, the buyer sent the closing attorney the payment to buy the property. The seller refused to accept the money and the buyer sued for specific performance. The Georgia Supreme Court stated that when a contract provides that time is of the essence and the buyer failed to close, the buyer could not then apply for specific performance.[1536]

The parties through their conduct may waive the requirement of timely performance before or after the date of closing. In one case, the seller, who was also the mortgage lender, prepared and processed a loan application for the buyers after the closing date had passed. The court stated that the seller should not after the time of closing act in a manner as to lead the buyer to believe that it will not insist upon the date set for closing.[1537]

§ 12.6.2.3 Contract Does Not Automatically Terminate When Closing Date Passes

In Georgia, real estate sales contracts do not automatically expire if the transaction fails to close.[1538] This is the case even if there is a "time of the essence" clause in a contract.[1539] The injured party must serve a notice of termination to the other party. If written notice of termination is not given, the contract does not actually terminate.

The GAR Contract, like the contract in the above-referenced case, contains a clause stipulating that time is of the essence and it does not expressly provide that the contract expires if not closed by the date specified or the date of any authorized extensions. Therefore, if the sale is not closed by the date specified or by the date of any authorized extension, the non-breaching party may terminate the contract by giving written notice to the breaching party, and the non-breaching party has a cause of action for breach of contract.

If the parties wish to provide for automatic termination of the contract following the closing date set forth in the contract, the following alternative language may be used.

> **Special Stipulation 291:   Automatic Termination of Contract Following Closing Date**
>
> *In the event the closing does not occur on or before the date set forth in this Agreement, including any permitted extensions, then this Agreement shall automatically terminate and the non-defaulting party shall have the right to pursue all available claims at law or in equity against the defaulting party.*

1536   *Benedict v. Snead*, 253 Ga.App. 749, 560 S.E.2d 278, 2 FCDR 437, (2002).

1537   *Frank v. Fleet Finance, Inc.*, 227 Ga.App. 543, 489 S.E.2d 523 (1998).

1538   *Peachstate Developers, LLC v. Greyfield Resources, Inc.*, 284 Ga.App. 501, 644 S.E.2d 324 (2007).

1539   *Separk v. Caswell Builders, Inc.*, 209 Ga.App. 713, 434 S.E.2d 502 (1993).

§ 12.6.3 Timing Of Date Of Closing And Possession

Some contracts for the sale of land may provide that parties may have "until" a certain date to close, or that closing will take place "on or before," "within" or "by" a specified date. Such language may raise an issue as to whether the buyer can unilaterally demand that the closing take place before the specified date, thereby forcing the seller to vacate the property before the anticipated outside closing date. It also creates ambiguity as to the exact date of the closing.

For example, use of the word "until" has resulted in a number of lawsuits, even though Georgia statute states that when "until" is used with reference to a certain day, it includes all of that day.[1540] This meaning of "until" was applied in one case where the court stated that the word "until" includes such day, term or time.[1541]

In another case, the court held that a statutory meaning given to a word should be applied to contracts unless there is a good reason not to.[1542] In other cases, the courts have looked at the context in which the word was used in the contract and the intention of the parties. Based on this approach, the court in one case decided that "until December 1993" meant up to "midnight, November 30" instead of up to December 31.[1543]

To prevent any uncertainty it is best to avoid using ambiguous words. Instead, parties should state an exact closing date. For example, the GAR Contract provides that closing will be on a specified date "or on such earlier date as may be agreed to by the parties in writing."[1544]

As with the date of closing, time of possession will be dictated by the contract. The GAR contract provides for the seller to remain in possession either until the closing, for a specified number of hours after the closing, or until a specified time a specified number of days after the closing.[1545]

§ 12.6.3.1 Indefinite Closing Date Generally Construed As Reasonable Date

Even if a contract is missing a provision identifying time of performance, a reasonable time for performance will be implied.[1546] Therefore, if the closing date is specified as 15 days after completion of construction, the contract will not necessarily be void for indefiniteness. Failure to include a time for performance should not be a violation of the rule against perpetuities,[1547] because a reasonable time will be implied.

§ 12.6.3.2 Date Of Closing Can Be Extended By Oral Agreement

Even when the contract states that time is of the essence, this provision can be waived. Conduct by a party either before or after the deadline may show waiver. As stated by the Georgia Court of Appeals, "[t]imely performance may be waived orally when acted upon by one or both of the parties."[1548]

The following case illustrates how an oral agreement may waive timely performance. The buyer entered a contract which expressly stipulated that time was of the essence and included a financing contingency for the buyer's benefit.[1549] Before obtaining financing, the buyer told the seller that financing was not a problem and that the seller was to

---

1540   O.C.G.A. § 1-3-3

1541   *Rogers v. Cherokee Iron and Railway Company*, 70 Ga. 717, 1883 WL 3058 (1883).

1542   *Brooks v. Hicks*, 230 Ga. 500, 197 S.E.2d 711 (1973).

1543   *Burns v. Reeves*, 217 Ga.App. 316, 457 S.E.2d 178 (1995).

1544   GAR Form F20.

1545   GAR Form F20.

1546   *Read v. GHDC, Inc.*, 254 Ga. 706, 334 S.E.2d 165 (1985), citing *Whitley v. Patrick*, 226 Ga. 87, 172 S.E.2d 692 (1970); *Brown v. McInvale*, 18 Ga.App. 375, 163 S.E.2d 854 (1968).

1547   The rule against perpetuities is a legal principle that a property interest is void unless it vests within 21 years of a life in being plus gestation period.

1548   *Edwards v. McTyre*, 246 Ga. 302, 271 S.E.2d 205, 206 (1980). In this case, the court concluded that an issue of fact remained as to whether or not timely performance was waived. *Frank v. Fleet Finance, Inc.*, 227 Ga.App. 543, 489 S.E.2d 523(1998).

1549   *Koets v. Benveniste*, 169 Ga.App. 352, 312 S.E.2d 846 (1983).

proceed with customizing work on the home. The seller proceeded with the work. Approximately three weeks after the stipulated closing date, the buyer notified the seller that the transaction would not close and demanded full return of the earnest money. The court concluded that there was a question of fact for jury determination on whether the buyer waived the financing contingency before or after the date specified, thereby precluding the buyer from having a right to a full refund of the earnest money as a matter of law. The court also noted that a contract provision requiring all modifications to the contract to be in writing does not preclude waiver of the financing contingency or its timely expiration.

In another case, the Georgia Court of Appeals concluded that evidence that the fact that one of the parties expressly agreed to an extension of the closing date, and both parties continued to make arrangements for closing after the originally scheduled closing date, would authorize the jury to conclude that strict compliance with the time provisions of the contract were waived.[1550]

The result is that even where a contract provides that amendments must be in writing and that time is of the essence, the conduct of the parties may be sufficient to waive a time requirement. Parties to a contract must be careful not to conduct themselves in a manner that could be interpreted as waiving the timeliness of performance of obligations under the contract.

§ 12.6.3.3 Closing On A Sunday

When preparing a contract, the parties may elect to close on a particular date without considering the day of the week on which it falls. If the contract states a closing date which falls on a Sunday or a legal holiday, Georgia law provides that the closing will extend to the following business day, even if time is of the essence.[1551] If the contract does not state that closing shall take place on a specific date but it is to take place either "by" or "on or before" a certain date and that date falls on a Sunday or legal holiday, closing will extended to the next business day.[1552]

A similar conclusion would likely be reached when an act of God interferes with performance of the contract terms. Under Georgia law, an "act of God" is an accident caused by physical forces that are irresistible or inevitable, such as lightning, earthquakes, and sudden death.[1553] Similarly, the bad ice storms which periodically paralyze Georgia would be considered acts of God. Such an event protects a person against responsibility for non-performance of a contract.[1554] Where an act of God does not destroy the property, but interferes with the closing, equity would allow the parties to reset the closing to a different date.

§ 12.6.3.4 Extending Closing Date Unilaterally

Although parties by their conduct can waive their right to require timely performance of contract terms, courts have held that one party cannot unilaterally modify the terms of the contract for reasons other than the default of a party. Addressing termination of a contract the Georgia Court of Appeals held one party cannot unilaterally terminate a contract where there is no evidence of a mutual decision to terminate.[1555] In that case, the court also cited a case in support of the general rule that an oral agreement to modify a written contract for the sale of land is unenforceable.[1556]

1550   *Ferris v. Hill*, 172 Ga.App. 599, 323 S.E.2d 895 (1984); *Edwards v. McTyre*, 246 Ga. 302, 271 S.E.2d 205 (1980).

1551   *Brooks v. Hicks*, 230 Ga. 500, 197 S.E.2d 711 (1973).

1552   *Target Properties, Inc. v. Gilbert*, 192 Ga.App. 161, 384 S.E.2d 188 (1989).

1553   O.C.G.A. § 1-3-3(3).

1554   *Sampson v. General Electric Supply Corp.*, 78 Ga.App. 2, 50 S.E.2d 169 (1948).

1555   *Atlanta Six Flags Partnership v. Hughes*, 191 Ga.App. 404, 381 S.E.2d 605 (1989).

1556   *Sanders v. Vaughn*, 223 Ga. 274, 154 S.E.2d 616 (1967).

§ 12.6.3.5   Contract May Authorize Party To Extend Closing Date

The GAR Contract allows either the buyer or seller to unilaterally extend the closing date for a period of seven days so long as notice is given to the other party before or on the original closing date. However, the closing date may only be unilaterally extended if: (1) the seller cannot satisfy valid title objections (excluding title objections that either: (a) can be satisfied through the payment of money or by bonding off the same; or (b) do not prevent Seller from conveying good and marketable title to the property; or (2) the buyer's mortgage lender, if any, (including in "all cash" transactions) or the closing attorney cannot fulfill their respective obligations by the date of closing, provided that: (a) the delay is not caused by the buyer; and (b) if the buyer is obtaining a mortgage loan, the buyer has already obtained a loan commitment.[1557]

Based on the above language, there are several situations when the buyer or seller cannot unilaterally extend the closing date. The first is if there is a title problem that can be satisfied through the payment of money or by bonding off the lien. So, for example, the closing attorney in doing a title search in preparation for closing discovers a materialmen's lien against the property for $2,000. The closing attorney brings the lien to the seller's attention and the seller acknowledges that he withheld final payment in re-roofing the property due to poor workmanship on the part of the roofer. In this instance, neither the seller nor the buyer could unilaterally extend the closing date for seven (7) days because while the lien is a title objection, it can be satisfied though the payment of money or by bonding off the lien. Of course, the buyer and seller could mutually agree to amend the purchase and sale agreement to extend the closing date for any period of time agreeable to both parties to give the seller more time to resolve the dispute. However, if the parties do not agree to amend the purchase and sale agreement and the seller does not pay or bond off the lien, the seller would be in breach of the contract.

Another example of when neither the buyer not seller can unilaterally extend the closing date is in situations where there is a title defect but it does not rise to the level of preventing the title insurance company from issuing a title policy at its regular rates subject only to standard exceptions. For example, the buyer has a survey done of the property and discovers that there is a small encroachment of the neighbor's fence onto the property. The buyer wants the seller to get the fence encroachment issue resolved before closing and send the seller a unilateral notice to extend the closing date for seven (7) days to allow this to occur. The seller already has title insurance on the property and the title insurance company has already assumed this risk of the minor encroachment. The title insurance company is willing to insure over the minor encroachment at the regular rates and without the fence encroachment being listed on an exception to coverage. In this instance, the buyer would not have the right to unilaterally extend the closing date because while there is a technical title defect, it does not prevent the seller from conveying good and marketable title to the property (which is defined in the GAR Contract as title which a title insurance company licensed to do business in Georgia will insure at the regular rates, subject only to standard exceptions[1558]).

The GAR Contract also requires that the need for a unilateral delay in the date of closing not be due to the fault of the buyer. The rationale for this change is that the buyer should not be able to extend the date of closing when the need for the delay is within the control of the buyer. So, for example, the closing cannot take place as scheduled because the buyer repeatedly fails to provide the lender with needed information. If this can be proved, the buyer would not be able to extend the closing date for this reason.

In addition, for either the buyer or seller to be able to unilaterally extend the closing date for seven (7) days because of a delay on the part of the mortgage lender, the buyer needs to have already obtained a mortgage loan commitment at the time of the unilateral extension. In other words, the GAR Contract assumes that the buyer is not going to be using the extension of the closing date to get preliminary loan approvals that should have been obtained before closing.

1557   GAR Form F20.

1558   GAR Form F20.

Other than the above, the provision allowing for the closing date to be extended unilaterally is broadly written to allow for any reasonable delay on the part of the mortgage lender or the closing attorney to close the transaction. This would likely include everything from the closing attorney having a personal emergency to the mortgage underwriter taking a particularly long time to approve the loan.

To unilaterally extend the GAR Contract, notice of the same must be received on or before the closing date.[1559] The notice must also contain the reason for the delay. GAR has a notification form which may be use to provide such notice.[1560] The same provisions are included in the GAR New Construction Purchase and Sale Agreement.[1561]

In one recent case, a Georgia court gave effect to such a provision and allowed the buyers to extend the closing date.[1562] The standard form contract provided for a closing on April 20, 2000. The contract also contained a standard unilateral extension of the closing for seven days to remedy either (1) that the mortgage cannot close before the closing date, or (2) that the seller fails to satisfy a valid title objection prior to the closing date. Otherwise, the contract provided that all the parties in writing must agree to any extension of the closing date. The buyers could not complete the loan documents prior to April 20 which allowed them to unilaterally extend the closing date.

The GAR Contract also provides that if either the buyer or seller unilaterally extends the closing date once, the right to thereafter extend the closing date is thereafter terminated. For example, if the buyer unilaterally extends the closing date for seven (7) days because of a delay in getting the mortgage loan package to the closing attorney, the seller cannot thereafter extend the closing date for seven (7) days to cure a title problem with the property. Once either party unilaterally extends the closing date, the right to thereafter extend the closing date is terminated.

If either the buyer or seller wants to limit the unilateral ability of either party to extend the closing date, the following alternative language may be used.

Special Stipulation 292:   No Right to Unilaterally Extend Contract

This transaction shall be closed on _____, 20___ or such earlier date as may be agreed to by the parties in writing. Notwithstanding any other provisions of this Agreement, neither party shall have the right to unilaterally extend the closing and no further extensions of the closing date shall be authorized except as may be agreed to in a separate writing by the Seller and Buyer.

§ 12.6.3.6   Closing Date Extended Due To Construction Delays

In new construction transactions, it is not uncommon for the closing date to be extended due to construction or other delays out of the builder's control. For this reason, most new construction contracts (including the GAR New Construction Exhibit[1563]) provide that the property is deemed ready to close upon the issuance of a certificate of occupancy or final inspection certificate. This means that even if the parties agree on a closing date, the closing will not take place until the certificate of occupancy or final inspection certificate is issued.

User of the GAR New Construction Contract[1564] often use the GAR New Construction Exhibit[1565] to protect the builder in the event of unavoidable delays in construction due to strikes, acts of God or nature, sewer or other governmental moratoriums or delays directly caused by the buyer's change orders and/or selection of materials. In such

---

1559   GAR Form F20.

1560   GAR Form F133, Notice to Unilaterally Extend Closing Date For Seven Days.

1561   GAR Form F23.

1562   *Yargus v. Smith*, 254 Ga.App. 338, 562 S.E.2d 371 (2002).

1563   GAR Form F24.

1564   GAR Form F23.

1565   GAR Form F24.

events the builder may extend the closing for up to 30 calendar days in its sole discretion. The seller is obligated to notify all parties immediately of the cause of delay and the new closing date.[1566]

The GAR New Construction Exhibit does not cover other contingencies that may cause delays in construction. Examples of such contingencies are inadequate or delay in the provision of utility services or shortage in construction materials. Builders may wish to include the following stipulation to take into account a broader range of contingencies and to provide that the builder has the right to extend the closing for the period of such delay.

> **Special Stipulation 293:   Extension of Closing Date Due to Construction Delays**
>
> *Seller shall not be responsible for delays in construction caused by strikes, acts of God or nature, poor weather, failure or unavailability of adequate sewer, water, electricity, gas, fire protection or other utility service, material and labor shortages, theft, unanticipated soil conditions, sink holes, underground springs, sewer or other governmental moratoriums, delays in government approvals for land development and construction, and delays caused by buyer's change orders or selections. The Closing Date shall be extended for a period of time equal to such delays.*

This type of provision is often referred to as a *force majeure* provision, which in Latin literally means "superior force." It is used to describe situations where there are delays due to circumstances beyond the control of the builder.

Alternatively, builders may wish to select a closing date depending on the anticipated completion date, and to provide for automatic extensions to take into account construction delays. The following stipulation may be used.

> **Special Stipulation 294:   Automatic Extensions for Construction Delays**
>
> *The closing of this transaction shall be during normal business hours on a date and time selected in the discretion of Seller upon substantial completion of the improvements on the Property ("Closing"). Such date shall be on or before (in the discretion of Seller) _____, 20___ ("Final Closing Date"). Substantial completion shall be deemed to occur when a certificate of occupancy, temporary certificate of occupancy or final inspection certificate covering the Property has been issued by the applicable governmental agency. Should the closing date change from the above date, Seller shall give Buyer advance notice of the date and time of the closing. Seller shall have the right (and in addition to all other rights therein) upon notice to Buyer to extend Final Closing Date unilaterally for two (2) periods of thirty (30) days each OR two (2) extension periods of up to sixty (60) days for each extension period [CHOOSE ONE].*

§ 12.6.3.7   Closing Date Extended If Due Diligence Period Extends Beyond Closing Date

In one case, the Due Diligence Period did not end until after the original contract closing date. The Court of Appeals resolved this conflict by not only extending the closing date to after the Due Diligence Period, but also to a reasonable time period thereafter during which the seller could complete the repairs in a good and workmanlike manner.[1567] The court ruled that to do otherwise would frustrate the intent of the parties to have a time frame of a specific duration during which the parties could agree on the defects to be repaired and the seller could then complete the repairs.

The obvious lesson of this case is to insure that the closing date is after the Due Diligence Periods have lapsed.

1566   GAR Form F24.

1567   *Yargus v. Smith*, 254 Ga.App. 338, 562 S.E.2d 371 (2002).

§ 12.6.3.8   Damages For Failing To Close

The measure of damages is the difference between the contract price and the market value of the property at the time of the breach.

The Georgia Court of Appeals ruled on such a case. A seller who was a builder brought an action against a buyer, claiming that the buyer breached a contract to purchase a house and lot.[1568] The seller contracted to construct a house and after completion of the house to sell the house and lot to the buyer. The contract provided that time was of the essence. There were various modifications of the contract including increasing the price and extending the closing date. However, the closing did not take place as specified in the modified contract, and the parties did not agree to further extend the contract. The buyer refused a demand to close on a certain date, and the seller sold the house to a third party.

Subsequently, the seller sued the buyer for damages in an amount constituting the difference between the price the buyer agreed to pay and the price for which the house ultimately sold. The buyer argued that such a measure of damages was contrary to law because there was no contract between the parties. The buyer based his contention on the theory that when there is a time of the essence clause, the contract terminates when the sale does not close on the date specified. The court concluded that this argument was without merit because there was no expiration date in the contract and no clause imposing a condition of closing by the date specified. Rather, the contract provisions merely bound the parties to perform certain actions by the dates specified or the contract would be breached. The court also noted that the measure of damages in a breach of contract case is the difference between the contract price and the market value of the property on the date of the breach. In this case, since testimony established a range of damages in excess of the amount awarded, the damages were within the range authorized.

§ 12.7   TRANSFER OF WARRANTIES AND SELLER WARRANTIES IN NEW CONSTRUCTION CONTRACTS

Contracts for the sale of property should address transfer of the seller's interest in any manufacturers' warranties, service contracts, termite treatment guarantees, and/or repair guarantee and/or other similar warranties which by their terms may be transferable to the buyer. In the GAR New Construction Contract, as in most other builder contracts, the seller agrees to transfer seller's interest in any existing manufacturers' warranties and service contracts which are transferable to buyer. Some builder contracts provide that the buyer is responsible for any costs associated with any such transfer of warranties. The GAR Contract also provides that the seller agrees to transfer to the buyer at closing, subject to the buyer's acceptance thereof, the seller's interest in any of the above-referenced warranties. The "subject to the buyer's acceptance thereof" language was added to ensure that buyers are not forced to accept undesirable service contracts. Since warranties are generally of a personal nature, they will not transfer without an express agreement to do so.

The GAR Contract provides that if there are any costs associated with transferring a warranty, such costs shall be paid for solely by the buyer. This change was made because some security companies are now charging a fee to transfer security systems and some termite companies are charging a fee to transfer a termite bond. The GAR New Construction Purchase and Sale Agreement[1569] also requires the seller to provide a home warranty to the buyer. The warranty can be one of two types. First, it can be a direct seller warranty against defects in either labor or materials for a one (1) year period from the date of closing. Alternatively, it can be a warranty provided by an independent third party that is in the business of regularly issuing home warranties that covers the property against defects in labor and materials for at least one (1) year from the date of closing.

1568   *Separk v. Caswell Builders, Inc.*, 209 Ga.App. 713, 434 S.E.2d 502 (1993).

1569   GAR Form F23.

§ 12.8 SELLER REMAINING IN POSSESSION AFTER CLOSING

On many occasions, the seller will want to retain possession of real estate for a short period of time after the closing. This allows the seller time to pack up and move after the seller knows for sure that the sale has closed. It is important that the provisions regarding the seller remaining on the property be certain and definite. A contract provision that the seller would be allowed to remain in a house for rent not to exceed $300 per month "as long as necessary until seller finds a new home," was found to be uncertain by its terms so as to render the entire contract unenforceable.[1570]

To best protect the buyer, the parties should enter into a temporary occupancy agreement. Most standard deeds to secure debt and standard FNMA and FHLMC requirements provide that the buyer must occupy the property as her principal residence on or before 60 days from the date of closing. In addition to identifying the period of occupancy, the occupancy agreement should specify that the seller will leave the property in the same or better condition than at the date of closing and that the seller will be responsible for any damage to the property. If the buyer wants additional protection, the buyer may require that the seller pay a security deposit to the buyer which will be refunded if the property is turned over in the same condition as existed on the date of closing. The occupancy agreement may also provide that the seller will continue to pay utilities until occupancy is terminated. As owner of the property, the buyer will maintain insurance on the structure; therefore, the occupancy agreement should also provide that the seller is responsible for the seller's personal property. The buyer may also want to specify that the seller is responsible for any costs of legal action necessary to enforce the occupancy agreement.[1571]

The GAR Temporary Occupancy Agreement For Seller After Closing[1572] provides the buyer protection and gives the Seller a right to occupy the property until the date specified in the Agreement ("Temporary Occupancy Period"). This Agreement also recently added a new provision to address a mortgage financing issue. More specifically, the GAR Temporary Occupancy Agreement For Seller After Closing provides that the form should be used only if the seller is occupying the property after the closing for 30 days or less. This new thirty-day language was added because if the buyer is going to immediately lease the property for more than thirty (30) days, the buyer is technically ineligible to receive mortgage financing as an owner occupant of the property (and instead must apply for more expensive investor financing). If the occupancy is going to be for more than thirty (30) days, it is probably best to use a full lease agreement.

This Agreement also addresses the common issues that arise during temporary occupancy. For instance, the agreement provides that the seller will continue to maintain all utilities and bills in the seller's name and pay the bills when they become due during the Temporary Occupancy Period. The seller is prohibited from making any improvements or modifications to the property during that time. If the property is damaged, the seller will be liable for any expenses incurred while repairing such damage. In addition, if the property is destroyed by fire or other occurrence, the seller bears the risk of the loss to his or her property, not the buyer.

Unlike the GAR Temporary Occupancy Agreement for Buyer Prior to Closing,[1573] this temporary occupancy agreement provides that any occupancy of the property by the seller after the closing date is free of charge. The form allows the seller to occupy the property free of charge because the rent for the Temporary Occupancy Period is normally paid by the seller to the buyer at the closing. Some mortgage lenders will not allow the seller to give the buyer back money at the closing or will treat such payments as a seller concession (and thus impose limits on how much the seller can contribute). However, if the buyer wants the seller to pay rent, the best way to try to accomplish this is for the sales price to be increased to reflect what would otherwise be rental payments. Of course, the property may not always appraise in such situations resulting in the seller truly occupying the property rent free.

1570   *Farmer v. Argenta*, 174 Ga.App. 682, 331 S.E.2d 60 (1985).

1571   GAR Form F140, Temporary Occupancy Agreement for Seller After Closing.

1572   GAR Form 140.

1573   GAR Form F139.

Under the GAR Temporary Occupancy Agreement For Seller After Closing, if the seller does not vacate the property by the end of the Temporary Occupancy Period, she becomes a tenant at sufferance and must start paying rent to the buyer at the daily rate specified in the agreement for every day the seller resides in the property after the Temporary Occupancy Period. Since it may take up to two to three months to dispossess the seller/tenant who refuses to voluntarily move, it is recommended that this daily rental amount be set as high as possible to encourage the temporary occupant to move at the end of the temporary occupancy period. This amount of the hold over rent can also be sought as part of any eviction proceeding.

When the seller remains in the property after closing pursuant to a temporary occupancy agreement, it is important that the seller check with his or her insurance carrier to determine whether the seller's homeowner's policy will cover any damage or loss to the property resulting from a casualty or whether a new insurance policy will need to be obtained.

The Agreement further provides that the occupant will be liable for the cost of any action instituted by the buyer to enforce the terms of the Agreement. The buyer should not, however, use "self-help" or forcibly remove or lockout the seller. Such action could lead to claims by the seller for wrongful eviction. Georgia law requires a landlord to obtain a writ of dispossession before the landlord is entitled to dispossess a tenant. Essentially, this means filing a lawsuit to remove the temporary occupant from the property.

§ 12.9 BUYER OBTAINING POSSESSION BEFORE CLOSING

In some cases, a buyer may want to move in to the property in advance of the closing. This may happen, for example, if a buyer is currently renting other property and the lease expires a few weeks prior to the scheduled closing date.

Many sellers are reluctant to allow a buyer to move in prior to closing out of fear she will discover something undesirable about the house or neighborhood and refuse to close the sale. The terms of any occupancy agreement allowing the buyer to occupy the property before closing should be definite and certain. Many of the same issues identified in the previous section should be addressed. In addition, the seller may want to provide that the buyer may not make any alterations to the property without the seller's prior written consent and, if changes are permitted, the buyer will be responsible for their cost without reimbursement if the sale does not close. If the buyer makes alterations and does not pay the contractors performing the work a lien may be placed on the seller's property. Therefore, it is important to specify that the buyer will be responsible for the cost of improvements and will indemnify the seller for any damages arising from modifications or alterations to the property. If the seller has concerns about the condition of the property during the buyer's occupancy, the seller may require a security deposit. Since the seller is the owner of the property the seller will maintain property insurance on the structure, and the buyer should be responsible for insuring personal property.

The GAR Temporary Occupancy Agreement For Buyer Prior To Closing[1574] form can be used to address these concerns.[1575] Unlike the GAR Temporary Occupancy Agreement For Seller After Closing, this form gives the buyer the right to occupy the property before the closing in exchange for a specified daily or monthly rate payable to the seller. No part of the buyer's rental payment is applied towards the purchase price of the property when the sale is eventually consummated. To provide the seller with further protection, the Agreement provides that the buyer is required to pay a security deposit which is returnable when the sale is completed. However, the seller is entitled to keep the security deposit if the sale is not consummated due to the buyer's default.

The GAR Temporary Occupancy Agreement For Buyer Prior To Closing also prohibits the buyer from making any alterations, repairs or improvements to the property without the seller's prior written consent. Even if the seller gives his or her consent, the buyer will not be entitled to reimbursement for any expenses. In the event the sale is not

---

1574   GAR Form F139.

1575   GAR Form F139.

completed (for any reason), any changes to the property are the sole property of the seller. Furthermore, under the Agreement, the buyer not only waives any right to file a lien against the property, but also indemnifies the seller for any losses or claims arising out of the alternations, repairs or improvements.

Although the Agreement is for temporary occupancy, if the sale is not consummated or is terminated and the buyer remains in the property, a landlord-tenant relationship will likely be found to exist by the courts. In one case, the purchaser took occupancy in advance of closing pursuant to a temporary occupancy agreement.[1576] While in possession, he discovered a termite infestation and announced he was not going to close. Curiously, he also announced that he was not going to vacate the property either. The seller filed a dispossessory action against the purchaser, seeking to have him removed from the property as a tenant holding over beyond the term of his lease. The buyer argued that pursuant to the temporary occupancy agreement he could not be considered a tenant, but was a buyer in possession and that normal landlord-tenant law did not apply to him.

The court ruled in favor of the seller and ordered the buyer out. The court observed that while the buyer had a contract to purchase the property, he never became the owner. Rather, the seller, who was the true owner, granted the buyer the right to live in the house before ownership was transferred. Pursuant to Georgia law,[1577] when the owner of real estate grants to another person, who accepts such grant, the right simply to possess and enjoy the use of such real estate either for a fixed time or at the will of the grantor, a landlord-tenant relationship is created.[1578]

For this reason, the GAR Temporary Occupancy Agreement for Buyer Prior to Closing explicitly provides that the buyer will be considered a tenant at sufferance if the sale is not consummated and the buyer remains in the property. As noted above, this will allow the seller to dispossess the buyer in a matter of weeks rather than having to bring a much more time-consuming action for eviction.

§ 12.10   TENANT REMAINING IN PROPERTY AFTER CLOSING

If there is a tenant in the property prior to closing, the buyer should request a copy of the lease agreement. If the lease agreement does not provide for early termination by the lessor, the buyer will be bound to allow the tenant to remain on the property for the balance of the lease term. If the lease is on a month-to-month basis, the landlord must give the tenant sixty (60) days notice to terminate the lease. If the buyer wants possession as close to the closing date as possible, the buyer may include the following provision in the contract requiring the seller to give the required sixty (60) day notice.

> **Special Stipulation 295:   Termination of Seller's Lease**
>
> *Seller agrees that within 5 days of the Binding Agreement Date, Seller shall notify in writing Seller's tenant in the Property, by U.S. mail, certified, return receipt requested, that his or her lease agreement shall be terminated sixty days from the date of the notice. Seller's notice to tenant shall inform tenant that if tenant remains in possession of the Premises after expiration or earlier termination of the lease without buyer's agreement, tenant shall be a tenant at sufferance and commencing on the date following the date of such expiration or termination, the monthly rental payable by tenant shall be twice the monthly rental for each month or fraction thereof during which tenant so remains in possession of the premises.*

The law requires the sixty-day provision and the parties should not reduce this time period unless a shorter period is provided under the terms of the lease. Of course, the risk to the seller in agreeing to such a provision is that if the transaction does not close, the seller may not have a tenant after the sixty days pass.

1576   *Hallisy v. Snyder*, 219 Ga.App. 128, 464 S.E.2d 219 (1995).

1577   O.C.G.A. § 44-7-1.

1578   *Hallisy v. Snyder*, 219 Ga.App. 128, 464 S.E.2d 219 (1995).

§ 12.10.1   Tenant Remaining In Foreclosed Property

The minimum time period for evicting a tenant is longer when the eviction involves a foreclosure property.[1579] In 2009, Congress passed the Protecting Tenants at Foreclosure Act which provides longer eviction periods to tenants residing in foreclosed properties. Prior to the adoption of the Act, tenants of foreclosure properties often found that they were required to vacate their homes on short notice, even after they paid rent and security deposits to their landlords.

Under the Act, the new owner of a foreclosure property must provide the existing tenant at least ninety (90) days notice to vacate the property,[1580] instead of the sixty days required under Georgia law.[1581] Even if the tenant's lease is month-to-month or terminable at will, the tenant must still receive at least ninety (90) days notice to vacate.[1582] A tenant may, however, be entitled to more than ninety (90) days depending on the lease. If the tenant leased a property pursuant to a formal rental agreement, the tenant will be entitled to stay in the property until the end of the remaining term or for a period of ninety (90) days, whichever is longer.[1583] As such, if the lease involved has a significant portion of the term remaining, the eviction process could be substantial in length. However, if the new owner intends to use the property as his or her primary residence, the tenant may only remain in the property for ninety (90) additional days.[1584]

This Act only applies to "bona fide" tenants or leases. A tenant or lease will be considered bona fide if (i) the borrower, or the child, spouse or parent of the borrower of a foreclosed mortgage is not the tenant; (ii) the lease or tenancy was the result of an arms-length transaction; and (iii) the lease or tenancy requires the receipt of rent that is not substantially less than the fair market value of the property.[1585]

Originally, the Act was set to be in effect for only 3 ½ years, with a termination date of December 31, 2012. Congress, however, has extended the length of the Act, which now provides a termination date of December 31, 2014.[1586]

1579   Pub. L. No. 111-22, div. A, titl. VII, §§ 701-704 (enacted May 2009).

1580   Pub. L. No. 111-22, div. A, titl. VII, § 702(a).

1581   O.C.G.A. § 44-7-7.

1582   Pub. L. No. 111-22, div. A, titl. VII, § 702(a)(2)(B).

1583   Pub. L. No. 111-22, div. A, titl. VII, § 702(a)(2)(A).

1584   Pub. L. No. 111-22, div. A, titl. VII, § 702(a)(2)(B).

1585   Pub. L. No. 111-22, div. A, titl. VII, § 702(b).

1586   Pub. L. No. 111-22, div. A, titl. VII, § 704.

The **RED BOOK**

CHAPTER 13

REAL
ESTATE
COMMISSIONS

OVERVIEW

This chapter discusses the broker's right to claim a commission contractually and under the doctrines of procuring cause and *quantum meruit*. It also discusses how the GAR Contract and other form contracts provide for the broker's commission.

§ 13.1 WHAT THE GAR CONTRACT PROVIDES ABOUT COMMISSIONS

§ 13.1.1 Commission To Be Set Out In A Separate Agreement

The GAR Contract does not contain a blank in which the amount of the commission to be paid to the broker can be filled in. The commission blank was removed from the GAR Contract because the commission should be included in the brokerage engagement agreement between the broker and the party paying the commission. Including a blank in the purchase and sale agreement often incorrectly caused buyers and sellers to think that the commission remained an item that had not yet been agreed upon when in fact a binding agreement on the commission already existed. The GAR Contract simply provides that the brokers are to be paid a commission pursuant to a separate brokerage engagement agreement.[1587] This typically refers to a listing agreement or buyer's brokerage agreement, but there is no requirement for a specific form of agreement to be used. What is important, however, is that the amount of the commission actually be set out in at least one document.

This is critical due to the language in the GAR Contract referencing the commission being set pursuant to a separate agreement. The Georgia Court of Appeals addressed this issue in a case where a listing broker did not use a listing agreement, but rather, utilized a somewhat less than detailed listing sheet.[1588] Unfortunately, the listing sheet did not state the actual amount of the commission to be paid. The Court reviewed the GAR Contract and noted that it referenced that the amount of the commission was to be stated in a separate agreement or agreements. The Court then scrutinized the listing sheet and several other documents submitted by the broker, but could not find the amount of the commission spelled out in any of these documents. The Court denied the broker's claim to a commission.

A similar situation could arise if an unrepresented owner lists property for sale and the buyer's broker does not obtain confirmation from the seller as to the amount of commission that will be paid in the event the broker procures a buyer who purchases the property. This confirmation is usually set forth in the GAR Authorization to Show Unlisted Property[1589] form.

Brokers should use the GAR Authorization to Show Unlisted Property form[1590] in these situations.

§ 13.1.2 Including The Commission In The Purchase And Agreement

If all parties are in agreement as to the commissions to be paid in the transaction, there is no problem including a provision in the purchase and sale agreement stating the commissions that will be paid in the transaction. This should only be done in cases where the brokers are not concerned that either the buyer or seller will use the purchase and sale agreement to attempt to re-negotiate the broker's commissions. There is actually an advantage in including a commission provision in the purchase and sale agreement in that if the party obligated to pay the commission does not then do so, she is in breach of the purchase and sale agreement. This type of provision also gives the closing attorney leverage to refuse to close the transaction if the party obligated to pay the commission attempts not to do so.

If a broker wants to include the commission in the sales contract, the following special stipulation can be included.

1587   GAR Form F20. Brokers may use the appropriate brokerage contracts, such as GAR forms F1-F10.

1588   *Mitchell Realty Group, LLC. v. Holt*, 266 Ga.App. 217, 596 S.E.2d 625 (2004).

1589   GAR Form F3.

1590   GAR Form F3.

Special Stipulation 296: Commission in Sales Contract

At the Closing of this transaction Seller agrees to a total real estate commission equal to
_____ % of the sales price of the Property. This commission shall be divided between
the listing broker and the selling broker as follows: _____ % to the listing broker, and
_____ % to the selling broker.

The closing attorney is instructed to directly pay the brokers their respective shares of the commission at the Closing. The commission obligation set forth herein merely confirms the already existing contractual obligation on the part of the Seller to pay a real estate commission and as such, the amount of the commission set forth herein is not negotiable.

§ 13.1.3 Selling Broker Sharing Listing Broker's Commission

The GAR Contract provides for the seller to pay a commission to the listing broker, which is the custom in Georgia. It goes on to state that the selling broker will receive a portion of the listings broker's commission pursuant to a cooperative brokerage agreement.[1591] Typically the cooperative brokerage agreement arises by virtue of the selling brokers' participation in the same multiple listing service ("MLS") as the listing broker.

If the broker working with the buyer is not a member of the MLS in which the listing broker has listed the property, there is no obligation of the listing broker under MLS rules to share the listing broker's commission with the selling broker. In these situations, the broker from outside of the MLS should contact the listing broker and attempt to reach an agreement on whether the listing broker will pay a commission and if so, how much the commission will be. This should be done before showing the listing broker's property. if the listing broker agrees to pay a commission in a particular amount, this should be confirmed in a written agreement between the parties. An example of such an agreement is set forth below.

Agreement to Pay Commission

Re: Property located at the following address:

_____

_____

_____

For and in consideration of the undersigned Selling Broker agreeing to show the
prospective buyer identified below the above referenced Property, the undersigned Listing
Broker agrees to pay the undersigned Selling Broker a commission equal to _____%
of the purchase price of the above referenced Property in the event the prospective buyer,
whose name is _____ (or any family member of the above
person or any company in which the above person or family member of such person owns
any interest) contracts to purchase the above referenced Property within two (2) years
from the date hereof and thereafter closes on the purchase of the Property.

Listing Broker

_____

By Its: _____

Selling Broker

_____

By Its: _____

1591   GAR Form F20.

The rules of the MLS provide that when a property is listed, the listing broker must state the amount of its commission it will pay to another member broker if they procure a buyer who purchases the property. It is permissible for a listing broker to pay the selling broker a commission which does not equal the commission being paid to the listing broker. For example, a listing broker could provide that the listing broker is only entitled to receive a commission equal to 1% of the purchase price of the property while the listing broker is paid a commission equal to 5% of the purchase price of the property. However, the GAR Exclusive Seller Listing Agreement and the NAR Code of Ethics[1592] require disclosure to the seller of how the listing broker's commission will be shared with another broker.

§ 13.1.3.1 Variable Commissions

Some listing brokers will seek to pay a selling broker a variable commission depending on the amount of work performed by the selling broker or based on whether the listing broker has to reduce her commission in order to get the transaction closed.

While there is no case law either upholding or striking down variable commissions in Georgia, as a matter of general principal, there should be no reason why a listing broker should not be allowed to offer any commission she is wishes to offer a selling broker provided that it does not violate a specific state or federal law.

For example, while an offer of compensation by the listing broker of 3 chickens, 2 goats and a lottery ticket might not induce many selling brokers to show the property, there is no law of which the authors are aware that this approach violates. However, if the listing broker were to only offer to pay a commission to selling brokers who are or are not members of the Georgia Association of REALTORS®, such an approach would create potential anti-trust problems.

While listing brokers are free to offer variable commissions to selling brokers depending on the amount of work they do, such an approach may miss the mark considering that the primary function of any broker is to procure a buyer ready willing and able to purchase the property.

§ 13.1.3.2 Negotiating A Change In The Commission Paid To A Selling Broker

A selling broker may negotiate with the listing broker regarding the amount of the commission to be paid to the selling broker. However, if the selling broker attempts to negotiate the amount of her commission directly with the seller, this would be a violation of the Georgia license law governing real estate agents and brokers. This is because the license law prohibits anyone from inducing any person to alter, modify or change another licensee's fee or commission for real estate brokerage services without that licensee's prior written consent.[1593]

For example, a listing broker negotiates a 5% commission with a seller and agrees to pay half of that to the selling broker. The selling broker speaks to the seller and says that his buyer will not purchase the property unless the selling broker is paid an additional bonus equal to 1% of the sales price of the property. The broker working with the buyer might argue that he was not altering the total commission to be paid in the transaction since the listing broker was getting the same commission he would otherwise have received from the seller. However, the Georgia Real Estate Commission takes the position that the entire commission belongs to the listing broker and thus any changes to that commission must first be approved in writing by the listing broker.

Similarly, let's say that the broker working with the buyer approaches the seller and says that he is okay with a 5% commission being paid to the seller, but that he wants to be paid 80% of that commission. Since the overall commission being paid to the listing broker is not changing, it can be argued that no violation of license law has occurred. However, the Georgia Real Estate Commission takes the view that any change affecting either the gross commission paid on the transaction or the net paid to the listing broker can only be negotiated with the listing broker and not with the seller.

1592   Standard of Practice 1-12 of the Code of Ethics and Standards of Practice of National Association of REALTORS® (2012).

1593   O.C.G.A. § 43-40-25(b)(34).

A selling broker cannot ask a third party to negotiate directly with the seller regarding the commission to be paid to the selling broker. For example, if a buyer were to include language in a real estate sales contract at the request of the selling broker that the broker representing the buyer will be paid a larger real estate commission than what the listing broker agrees to pay the selling broker, this would also violate license law. This is because license law also prohibits a broker from inducing any person to seek a change in another broker's commission.

The safest approach for a selling broker to seek a change in a commission is for the selling broker to negotiate the change directly with the listing broker. Alternatively, the listing broker can give the selling broker prior written consent to negotiate a change in the commission directly with the seller.

§ 13.1.4   Payment Of Commission At Closing

The GAR Contract instructs the closing attorney to pay the commission of the Broker(s) at closing out of the proceeds of the sale. If the sale proceeds are insufficient to pay the full commission, the party owing the commission (usually the seller) must pay any shortfall at closing. If more than one broker is involved in the transaction, the closing attorney is directed to pay each broker their respective portions of said commission.

§ 13.1.4.1   Commission Confirmation Agreement, Instructions To Closing Attorney

Since the GAR Contracts do not include a place for the commission to be paid in the transaction to be listed or provide for how that commission is to be divided between the listing and selling brokers, GAR created a Commission Confirmation Agreement/Instructions to Closing Attorney form for that purpose.[1594] The parties to the agreement are the two brokers rather than the buyer and seller. Although there is no requirement that commission agreements between brokers be written, using this form protects brokers' commissions by serving as written evidence of their agreement. The form is also beneficial because closing attorneys needed direction on the total amount of the commission to be paid in the transaction and how it was to be divided between the listing and selling brokers since this information is no longer set out in the GAR Contracts. This GAR Commission Confirmation Agreement/Instructions to Closing Attorney[1595] form contains blanks for the listing broker and the selling broker to write in their respective share of the commission for a specific transaction both as a percentage of the purchase price and a dollar amount. The form allows the selling broker to accept a split that differs from that set out in the listing agreement or to accept a different amount of commission from that set out in the listing agreement. The agreement also specifically supersedes any prior agreement the brokers may have entered into. The agreement also provides that neither broker shall have a claim against the other broker in the event the closing does not occur.

§ 13.1.4.2   Commission Confirmation Agreement And Listing Agreement Should Be Sent To The Closing Attorney

If the real estate commission is not referenced in the purchase and sale agreement (as is the case with the GAR Contracts), the listing broker should notify the closing attorney of the total amount of the commission to be paid at closing. The listing or selling broker should also send a copy of the commission confirmation agreement to the closing attorney so that she knows how to divide the commission between the listing and selling brokers.

§ 13.1.4.3   Problems And Disputes Arising From Commission Confirmation Agreements

The GAR Commission Confirmation Agreement/Instructions to Closing Attorney[1596] form does not prohibit a listing or selling broker from challenging the commission that was either paid to a cooperating broker or received by a selling broker.

1594   GAR Form F32.

1595   GAR Form F32.

1596   GAR Form F32.

An issue that frequently arises with the use of the GAR Commission Confirmation Agreement/Instructions to Closing Attorney is whether a broker can seek to arbitrate a disputed commission after she has signed a Commission Confirmation Agreement. The answer to this question is yes. The GAR Commission Confirmation Agreement/ Instructions to Closing Attorney form specifically provides that nothing in the Agreement limits or waives the right of a broker after the closing to challenge either the entitlement to a commission or the amount of any commission paid or not paid, or to assert any claim or seek arbitration regarding the same. The idea behind this provision is to encourage brokers to put the best interests of their clients first by postponing commission disputes that might otherwise threaten the real estate transaction.

If the goal of the brokers is to waive their right to arbitrate any dispute regarding the commission at a later time, the language in the following special stipulation should be added to the Commission Confirmation Agreement.

> **Special Stipulation 297:** **Brokers Waive Right to Arbitrate Commission**
>
> *Notwithstanding any provision to the contrary contained herein, the Brokers agree that the commission split between the Listing Broker and the Selling Broker as stated in this Agreement reflects a full and final settlement of disputed commission claims between the Listing Broker and the Selling Broker. In reaching this settlement the Brokers do hereby agree to waive all rights to seek to arbitrate the commission reflected in this Commission Confirmation Agreement.*

The GAR Commission Confirmation Agreement/Instructions to Closing Attorney[1597] also provides that the agreement does not limit or waive a broker's right to assert any claim regarding her entitlement to a commission or amount of any commission paid or not paid. As such, the commission paid or received (or lack thereof) can be challenged in a judicial proceeding. Of course, brokers who are REALTORS® are required to arbitrate their commission disputes as a condition of being a REALTOR®. The theory behind allowing a broker to dispute the commission paid or received after the transaction has closed is that this puts the interests of the buyer and seller ahead of the interests of the brokers and prevents transactions from being held hostage to commission disputes.

In the alternative, if a broker is seeking the GAR Commission Confirmation Agreement/Instructions to Closing Attorney form to be the final and binding agreement on the commission between the parties the following special stipulation can be added to the commission confirmation agreement.

> **Special Stipulation 298:** **Commission to be Final Between Brokers**
>
> *Notwithstanding any provision to the contrary contained herein, Listing Broker and Selling Broker agree that the commission payments reflected in the Commission Confirmation Agreement/Instructions to Closing Attorney shall be final and binding and each of them waives and releases any and all of their rights to challenge the payments at a later time either through an arbitration or in a judicial proceeding. Selling Broker hereby releases Listing Broker from any and all claims to a commission in excess of the amount to be paid to the Selling Broker in the Commission Confirmation Agreement/Instructions to Closing Attorney form. Listing Broker hereby releases Selling Broker from any against any and all claims to recover any portion of the commission which Selling Broker is to be paid pursuant to the Commission Confirmation Agreement/Instructions to Closing Attorney form.*

In many situations, the real estate brokers will mutually agree to reduce a commission to get a deal done. Before a broker agrees to such a reduction, it is important to get the other broker's written consent to the reduction to avoid disputes regarding whether the commission reduction should come out of the share of only one broker, or should be shared on a pro rata basis by both brokers.

1597   GAR Form F32.

Some real estate brokers take the position that they should always be entitled to the commission reflected in the MLS listing sheet. This position is not always accurate. There are some cases where the listing broker is promised a particular commission only to have the seller then come back and seek a commission concession. If the listing broker unilaterally agrees to such a concession, the commission should appropriately be paid only out of the listing broker's side of the commission. However, if the listing broker presents the request for a commission concession and they both agree to the same, they should both pay their pro rata share of the commission concession. The problem with this approach is that sometimes the selling broker consents to the concession only to then argue that her consent was given merely to get the deal done and that the selling brokers had every intention to arbitrate the commission after the closing. Using the above referenced special stipulation is a good way to avoid this potential problem.

§ 13.1.5   Payment Of Commission Prior To Closing

In recent years, there has been a small but important change in the Georgia license laws regarding when and what form a real estate commission may be paid to the licensee. The law now provides that "a broker may not be paid any portion of the earnest money, security deposit or other trust funds paid to the broker in connection with the real estate transaction as part of the broker's commission or fee until the transaction has been completed or cancelled."[1598] This means that the broker may not be paid any portion of her commission from trust funds before the closing of the transaction or before the transaction is cancelled. Previously, the law was not limited just to trust funds so the broker had to wait until the transaction was completed to be paid a commission. This lead to disputes regarding when a transaction was completed.

§ 13.1.5.1   Flat Up-Front Fees

Brokers may now be paid up-front fees and/or commissions provided that the funds for the same are not being paid from the trust funds. For example, a broker wants to get paid a retainer fee for showing a buyer several properties. If the buyer writes a check to the broker for the retainer fee and the retainer fee agreement provides that this money immediately belongs to the broker, there is no problem with the broker keeping the money. However, if the retainer fee agreement provides that the retainer fee will be put into the broker's escrow account and paid seven (7) days later, this could be problematic.

Earlier versions of this law were applicable to *all* monies paid to the broker in connection with the real estate transaction, including flat fees paid to the broker to perform specific services rather than being paid to the broker in "trust." The newly added "trust language" gives brokers more flexibility to receive commissions. The term "trust funds" refers to money or other things of value belonging to others received by the broker for the benefit of others. The new language of the statute now makes a distinction between funds that are paid to the broker for the benefit of another and flat up-front fees. Fees that are not for the benefit of any other person do not need to be treated as trust funds. For example, if a broker charges a flat up-front fee for listing a property in a multiple listing service, where the fee is earned upon entering into this listing agreement, the fee is not money belonging to others and the broker is therefore not required to hold the funds in her escrow account until the transaction has been completed or cancelled. However, as stated above, if a broker wishes to charge a flat up-front fee, the broker should explicitly state in the agreement that the broker's fee is earned upon the parties entering into the listing agreement.

Similarly, if a broker is paid a fee for property management services, that fee can be paid directly to the broker and does not have to be deposited into the broker's escrow account. This money is not for the benefit of any other person; therefore, it does not have to be treated as trust funds. However, let's say a property manager employed by a property owner collects rent on behalf of the owner and the checks are made payable to the manager. In this instance, the

---

1598   O.C.G.A, § 43-40-20(e).

funds received by the broker are clearly funds the broker receives for the benefit of others, thus they would need to be deposited into the broker's escrow account. However, the broker and property owner can agree that the broker has the right to withhold her fee from the monthly rent checks before sending the remaining balance to the owner. As long as the agreement explicitly states what portion the broker may deduct as the broker's fee, that portion may be paid out of the trust account directly to the broker before the balance of the funds are paid to the owner.

§ 13.1.5.2   Commissions In Lease/Purchase Transactions

Brokers often have questions regarding when they can be paid their commissions in lease/purchase transactions where two commissions are paid (one for leasing and one for selling the property). Often brokers want to collect a leasing commission upon the commencement of the lease portion of the lease/purchase transaction, and then a sales commission for the purchase portion. The general rule with regard to the payment of commissions in lease purchase transactions when the commission is to be paid from trust funds is set forth in GREC Sub. Reg. 520-1-.08(3)(d) (4). This section provides that "a broker who claims any part of earnest money or other money paid to the broker in connection with any real estate transaction shall be deemed to have complied with O.C.G.A. § 43-40-20(e) if...(4) the broker has secured a written agreement, separate from the sales contract or lease agreement, signed by all parties having an interest in the transaction, who have agreed that the broker is entitled to any commission."[1599]

Based upon this provision, if the commission in a lease purchase transaction is to be paid from trust funds, the broker must have a commission agreement that is separate from the lease or purchase and sale agreement. The agreement must be signed by all parties having an interest in the transaction who have agreed that the broker is entitled to any commission. While it is not clear whether this is referring to the tenant/buyer and the landlord/seller or just the landlord/seller, the safer answer is that it requires everyone's consent.

With the newly added language in license law allowing a commission to be paid in advance of the consummation of the transaction if the commission is not paid with trust funds, a broker may receive a partial commission before the consummation of the transaction if the parties agree to the partial commission in writing. For example, if a seller paid the broker a partial sales commission upon the commencement of a lease and the parties agreed in writing that such commission was earned by the broker at the time and was non-refundable to the seller even if the sales transaction did not close, and the commission funds were not trust funds, the broker could be paid the partial commission without violation of the rules of the Georgia Real Estate Commission.

§ 13.1.5.3   Retainer Fees

Another area where an issue on payment of commissions has arisen is in the new Retainer Fee section of the GAR Exclusive Buyer Brokerage Agreement.[1600] There has been much confusion whether brokers can pay themselves the retainer fee upon entering into a GAR Exclusive Buyer Brokerage Agreement. The Georgia Real Estate Commission has informally interpreted retainer fees to be trust funds, or other people's money due to the possibility that it might be returned to the buyer if the buyer purchases a property. Therefore, the broker should treat the retainer as "trust funds" and refrain from paying himself or herself before the consummation of the transaction. REALTORS® wanting access to the retainer fee right away should include the following language as a substitute to the present retainer fee language in the GAR Exclusive Buyer Brokerage Agreement. However, to avoid any question regarding whether or not a fee is considered trust funds because it might not be returned to the buyer if the buyer purchases property, the safest approach is to make the fee non-refundable from the beginning of the transaction and not apply it to the purchase price of the property.

1599   Georgia Real Estate Commission Rule 520-1-.08(3)(d)(4).

1600   GAR Form F4.

RETAINER FEE. In entering into this Agreement Buyer has paid Broker a retainer fee of $_____. This fee shall be deemed to be earned by Broker at the time it is paid and shall thereafter be the property of Broker, shall not be refundable to Buyer, and shall not be considered trust funds under any circumstances.

In the event Buyer purchases real property in a transaction in which Broker is paid a commission, no portion of the fee shall be rebated to Buyer or applied toward the purchase price of the Property at closing.

§ 13.1.6 Commissions Owing When Buyer Or Seller Breaches The GAR Contract

The GAR Contract provides that in the event the sale is not closed because of the failure or refusal of the buyer or seller to perform any of their respective obligations, the defaulting party shall immediately pay the broker the full commission the broker would have been entitled to had the sale closed. As noted in § 13.1.1 Monetary Damages, it will be necessary for the broker to introduce into evidence a copy of an agreement or agreements setting forth the amount of the commission they would have received had the buyer or seller not breached.

An argument is sometimes raised by defaulting buyers that they should not have to pay a commission based upon the amount reflected in a listing agreement. Their argument is that they were not a party to the listing agreement and did not have knowledge of its terms. Accordingly, defaulting buyers sometimes argue that they should not be bound by whatever commission is recited therein. There is not yet any definitive case law directly on point, although at least once case that could add clarity to this area of the law was pending on appeal as this book went to print.[1601] In an effort to strengthen brokers' claims for commissions, the GAR Contract provides that the buyer and seller affirm that they are familiar with the commission amount to be paid to the brokers. In so doing it should be harder for buyers to argue that they did not know about the commission arrangement between the seller and the listing broker.

Another argument that has been raised by defaulting parties is that there must be a breach of the separate agreement in which the commission amount is stated (*i.e.*, the listing agreement) in order for a broker to pursue a commission. The GAR Contract also provides that a breach of the GAR Contract is, on its own, a sufficient basis for a broker to sue for a commission.

The GAR Contract provides that the seller will pay a commission to the listing broker, which will then split its commission with the selling broker. It is not necessary, however, for the listing broker to pursue a claim for the entire amount of commission that would be due to both brokers. The GAR Contract provides that the listing broker and the selling broker may jointly or independently pursue a defaulting party for their respective portion of the commission. Each broker can make an independent business decision as to whether to file suit for his commission in a given situation. The following example explains the value of such a provision.

Example: The listing agreement provides that the total commission to be paid is 7% of the purchase price of the property, with the selling broker to receive 50% of the total commission and the listing broker to receive the other 50%. The buyer gets cold feet, refuses to close on the purchase of the home, and thereby defaults under the contract. The buyer tells the selling broker that he has enjoyed working with him and wants his help in locating another home. In such a situation, the selling broker may not want to pursue his commission under this contract because he wants to continue to work with this buyer. The listing broker, however, may wish to pursue his commission and may do so under the language of the GAR Contract.

1601   *Pargar, LLC v. Jackson*, A08A1046 (Ga.App. 2008).

§ 13.1.7   Terms Of Sales Contract Can Control Over Listing Agreement

If the broker signs a sales contract which recites a reduced commission amount, a court would probably interpret this as a concession by the broker to be paid the lower amount and would preclude any action on the listing agreement for the higher commission amount. This is because the terms of the sales contract typically being the most recent agreement of the parties regarding the payment of the commission will generally control over the listing agreement as to the commission rights, assuming the real estate broker has signed the contract.[1602] The broker should therefore be careful to review the sales contract and confirm that the parties have not inserted any reduced commission amount into the contract.

The broker who is faced with a sales contract that includes a reduction in commission can take the position that the commission is non-negotiable. If that does not resolve the matter, the broker may decide not to sign the contract or to sign the contract but include a written caveat that the broker is not agreeing to any reduction in commission contained therein. Absent the broker signing a contract that has been modified to reflect a lower or reduced commission, the seller will be obligated to pay the commission amount set forth in the listing agreement.[1603]

§ 13.2   WHAT THE GAR EXCLUSIVE SELLER LISTING AGREEMENT PROVIDES ABOUT COMMISSIONS

§ 13.2.1   Amount Of Commission And Commission Split

The GAR Exclusive Seller Listing Agreement[1604] sets forth the amount of commission the seller agrees to pay to the listing broker. This is reflected as either a fixed dollar amount, a percentage of the sales price, or both. Some real estate brokerage firms now charge commissions that have both a flat fee and percentage components. So, for example, the seller may agree to pay the listing broker a flat fee commission of $195 plus a percentage of the sales price of the property.

The GAR Exclusive Seller Listing Agreement also states the portion of the total commission that it will share with a cooperating broker, if any, who procures the buyer of the property. This language was included to be sure the seller knows what commission split is being offered to cooperating brokers and because it is required to be disclosed to the seller under the Code of Ethics of the National Association of REALTORS®.[1605] A seller may want to know this because the amount of commission being shared may impact the marketability of the property. For example, assume two similar homes, in similar price ranges, are on the market at the same time. One listing reflects a 3% commission split while the other offers only 1.5%. A buyer's broker may well be inclined to show their buyers just the property with the higher percentage commission split.

§ 13.2.2   When Is Commission Earned?

The GAR Exclusive Seller Listing Agreement provides that the broker's commission is earned in the event that during the term of the agreement the broker procures a buyer ready, willing, and able to purchase the seller's property at the listed price or any other price acceptable to Seller. The broker is also owed a commission if, during the term of the listing, the seller enters into any contract for the sale or exchange of the property with any buyer, whether through the efforts of the broker or not. This commission is then due upon the closing of the transaction.

For example, a broker enters into a GAR Exclusive Seller Listing Agreement with a seller. During the term of the listing, the seller tells a friend at work that her house is for sale. The friend remembers the house from a party she attended at the house and asks to see it. In this transaction, if the friend decides to make an offer to purchase the

---

1602   *Parr Realty Co. v. Carroll*, 131 Ga.App. 549, 206 S.E.2d 550 (1974); *Blount v. Freeman*, 94 Ga.App. 110, 93 S.E.2d 820 (1956).

1603   *Jones v. Trail Cities Realty, Inc.*, 160 Ga.App. 533, 287 S.E.2d 588 (1981).

1604   GAR Form F1.

1605   Code of Ethics of the National Association of REALTORS®, Article 1, Standard of Practice 1-13.

property, it would be hard to argue that the listing broker is the procuring cause of the sale. Nevertheless, in such a transaction, the listing broker would still be entitled to a real estate commission because the GAR Exclusive Seller Listing Agreement specifically provides for the seller to pay the same.

§ 13.2.3 Protected Period After Expiration Or Termination

Sellers sometimes try to avoid their obligations to pay a brokerage commission by waiting until after the listing expired and to then sell the property to a buyer who was already identified during the term of the listing. In an effort to counter this, the GAR Exclusive Seller Listing Agreement provides certain commission rights after the Agreement has expired or been terminated. The Listing Agreement defines the term "Protected Period" to mean a negotiated period of time following the earlier of (a) the expiration of the listing agreement or (b) the date the agreement is mutually terminated by the parties in writing. In the event the seller breaches the agreement by attempting to unilaterally terminate the listing agreement, then the Protective Period is increased to include the period between the date of the breach and when the agreement would otherwise have expired.

For example, a listing broker and a seller enter into a 180 day listing agreement using the GAR Exclusive Seller Listing Agreement. After 90 days, the seller unilaterally terminates the listing agreement. The listing agreement contained a 90 day Protected Period. On the 91st day after the termination of the listing agreement, the seller enters into a purchase and sale agreement with a buyer who was introduced to the property during the term of the listing. Is the listing broker entitled to collect a commission in this situation? The answer to this question is yes, if the seller signs the GAR Exclusive Seller Listing Agreement. This is because when the seller unilaterally terminated the listing agreement, the Protected Period was increased by the length of the remaining term of the listing agreement prior to it being prematurely terminated by the seller. Since the remaining term of the listing agreement was 90 days and the original Protected Period was also 90 days, the new term of the Protected Period is now 180 days. Since the sale took place on the 91st day, it took placed during the Protected Period and the listing broker is entitled to her commission.

If during the Protected Period the seller sells, or contracts to sell, the property to any buyer who made an offer, was introduced[1606] to, visited, received information on, inquired about, or otherwise learned of the property during the term of the listing,[1607] then the seller will owe a commission to the broker. The term "buyer" is defined to include all members of the buyer's immediate family, any legal entity in which buyer or any member of buyer's immediately family owns or controls, directly or indirectly, more than 10% of the shares or interests therein, and any third party who is acting under the direction or control of any of the above parties. This language is, of course, intended to thwart the efforts of crafty sellers looking to avoid their commission obligations.

The only exception to the above is that the seller will not be obligated to pay the broker a commission during the Protection Period if: (a) the listing expired or was mutually terminated and (b) the Property is sold or contracted to be sold to a prospective buyer by or through another licensed broker with whom Seller has signed an exclusive right to sell listing agreement. The reason for this exception is the recognition that the seller was seemingly not trying to avoid paying a real estate commission, since they have paid it to another broker. Of course, the seller can avoid paying a large commission by allowing the listing agreement to expire and hiring a new listing broker during the Protected Period who agrees to list the property for a substantially reduced commission.

1606   The term "introduced" has been held to mean when the broker initially told the buyer about the property, provided the buyer with information about the property, or showed the buyer the property. *Snipes v. Marcene P. Powell & Assoc.*, 273 Ga.App. 814, 616 S.E.2d 152 (2005).

1607   This language was specifically added to the GAR Listing Agreement in response to *Roberts v. Coldwell Banker Kinard Realty*, 286 Ga.App. 7, 648 S.E.2d 442 (2007) in which a commission was denied because the buyer was first introduced to the property prior to the listing agreement by someone other than the broker or the broker's affiliated licensee. The current language in the GAR Listing Agreement should avoid this result in future cases.

§ 13.2.3.1 Difference Between Mutually Agreeing To Terminate A Listing Agreement And Having Seller Unilaterally Terminate The Same

There is a significant difference in the effect of terminating the GAR Exclusive Seller Listing Agreement depending on whether it is unilaterally terminated by the seller or with the mutual consent of the seller and the listing broker. If the listing broker and the seller agree to mutually terminate the listing agreement, the broker's Protected Period runs from the date the agreement is terminated. Moreover, the listing broker has no claim to a commission if the property is listed with another broker and sold during the Protected Period to a person who learned of the property during the first broker's listing term.

If the listing agreement is unilaterally terminated by the seller, the Protected Period is longer because it includes the period from the date of termination through the date the agreement would otherwise have expired. More importantly, the listing broker can claim a commission if the property is sold during the Protected Period to a person who was introduced, visited, received information about, or learned of the property during the term of the agreement even if the property was subsequently listed with another broker. This can leave the seller in a position where the seller owes two commissions. The rationale behind this approach is that unilateral termination by the seller should be discouraged.

The GAR Exclusive Seller Listing Agreement tries to prevent a mutual termination of the listing agreement arising by implication or through an oral agreement of the parties. Instead, the listing agreement requires the listing broker to give her express written consent to a mutual termination of the listing agreement. The listing agreement even goes so far as to state that the broker removing her signs or discontinuing the provision of brokerage services at the direction of the seller is not evidence of the listing broker's mutually agreeing to terminate the listing agreement.

§ 13.2.3.2 Extension Of The Listing Agreement While Property Is Under Contract

The GAR Exclusive Seller Listing Agreement provides that the term of the agreement is automatically extended for any period of time the property is under contract where the contract is not consummated. Let's assume that the property is listed for a 180 day term commencing January 1st. On the 30th day of the listing period, on January 30th, the seller and a buyer enter into a binding agreement. The property is under contract for 60 days until April 1st, after which time the contract is terminated due to the breach of the buyer. If the listing agreement would have originally expired at the end of June, the agreement is now automatically extended for an additional two months.

The rationale behind this provision is that since the broker is somewhat limited in her ability to sell the property while it is under contract, the broker should have an additional time period equal to the length of time the property was under contract to try to sell the property if that contract falls through.

§ 13.3 THE GAR EXCLUSIVE BUYER BROKERAGE AGREEMENT

The GAR Exclusive Buyer Brokerage Agreement[1608] is used by real estate brokers representing buyers as clients.[1609] The GAR Exclusive Buyer Brokerage Agreement provides that while it is not required, the custom in Georgia is for the selling broker to seek payment of a commission from the listing broker or from the seller in any transaction. As such, the percentage of the sale price or fee specified in the GAR Exclusive Buyer Brokerage Agreement will be paid to the selling broker by the listing broker or seller. In the event that neither the seller nor listing broker pays a commission to the selling broker, the buyer will not be liable to the selling broker for her commission. However, if neither the listing broker nor the seller pays the selling broker her full commission, the selling broker and the buyer may indicate in the GAR Exclusive Buyer Brokerage Agreement that the buyer will be responsible to pay the selling broker any difference in commission.[1610]

1608   GAR Form F4.

1609   See Chapter 19 on the types of agency relationships under BRRETA.

1610   GAR Form F4.

Since the GAR Purchase and Sale Agreement also provides for the selling broker's commission to be paid by the listing broker, a buyer will generally not be liable for the commission. The courts will, however, enforce provisions in the sales contract or other agreements stating that the buyer has agreed to be liable for the payment of the broker's commission.[1611]

For example, a non-GAR buyer brokerage agreement may state that the buyer will pay the broker representing the buyer a commission equal to 3% of the purchase price if the broker is not otherwise paid a commission. The broker for the buyer finds a property for the buyer where the commission due to the broker for the buyer equals 2.5% of the purchase price of the property. Once the broker for the buyer has accepted the commission from the listing broker, no further commission is owed. This remains the case even though the broker received a commission smaller than the 3% of the purchase price commission. However, the GAR Exclusive Buyer Brokerage Agreement now includes language in which the buyer can agree to pay the buyer broker the difference between a stated commission amount the selling broker normally expects to be paid and the commission the selling broker is actually paid.

For example, let's assume that this option is selected and the stated selling commission is 3% of the purchase price. The actual commission paid to the selling broker in the transaction is 2.5% of the selling price. In this case, the buyer would be obligated to pay the seller the difference of .5% of the purchase price.

There are pros and cons to having the buyer pay the difference between a stated commission the selling broker expects to receive in the transaction and the commission the selling broker actually receives. On the positive side for the selling broker it is a way to ensure that the selling broker is compensated fairly for her efforts and in accordance with terms agreed upon in advance. On the negative side, it can result in the buyer becoming a bit too focused on the selling broker's commission. Since the buyer is obligated to pay the difference between what the selling broker states she would like to receive in the transaction and what the selling broker actually receives, some buyers will ask for the selling broker's commission will be with respect to each piece of property looked at by the buyer and the selling broker.

The GAR Exclusive Buyer Broker Agreement also provides for a Protection Period of a negotiated number of days following the termination or expiration of the agreement. If, during the Protection Period the buyer purchases, contracts to purchase or exchange, leases or lease purchases any property identified or shown to the buyer by the broker or for which the broker provided information about to the buyer during the term of the agreement, then the buyer will owe the broker a commission. Unlike the GAR Exclusive Seller Listing Agreement[1612], the GAR Exclusive Buyer Broker Agreement[1613] does not contain an exception if the buyer uses the services of another broker. As a result, buyers must be very careful to avoid "shopping" brokers as they may otherwise be obligated to pay more than one commission in the transaction.

§ 13.4 DEFERRED PAYMENT OF REAL ESTATE COMMISSION

On occasion, brokers are forced to accept a deferred payment of a real estate commission. This tends to occur when there is little equity in the property and the seller is not receiving any profits from the sale. When this occurs, brokers should always get a promissory note signed by the seller and, if possible, have it secured with a deed to secure debt on some other property owned by the seller.

1611   *Milton v. Austin*, 124 Ga.App. 657, 185 S.E.2d 551 (1971); *Harling v. Tift*, 43 Ga.App. 94, 157 S.E. 914 (1931).

1612   GAR Form F1.

1613   GAR Form F4.

§ 13.5   OTHER METHODS OF CLAIMING A COMMISSION

In certain circumstances brokers may be entitled to a commission even if there is no written brokerage agreement. Since this issue is currently the subject of much litigation in our courts, the safe approach should always be to get a written commission signed with a party. The law continues to recognize a broker's claim for a commission if the broker can show that she is the procuring cause of the sale if the claim is justified based on the principle of *quantum meruit.*

The Georgia Supreme Court confirmed this in the case of a broker who sued for commission when the broker did not enter into a written brokerage agreement with the client.[1614] The client had purchased a substantial piece of property. Instead of a written brokerage agreement, the broker claimed that there was an understanding that the broker would be paid "an amount not less than seven percent (7%) of the value…for the transaction." When the sale closed, the client refused to pay and the broker sued for the commission.

The broker claimed that it was entitled to a commission because it acted as the buyer's real estate agent, pursued the transaction, undertook a feasibility study of the purchase, and performed other significant professional services. The buyer argued that since state law requires a broker and her client to have a written brokerage agreement, the broker was not entitled to a commission in a transaction in which there was no written agreement. This argument was based on a provision under BRRETA which defines "brokerage engagement" to mean a written contract.[1615] Therefore, the buyer argued, since there was no written contract there was no brokerage relationship, and no commission was owed.

The Georgia Court of Appeals and Supreme Court disagreed with the client's argument and stated that BRRETA does not regulate the payment of commissions. The primary purpose of BRRETA is to set out the duties and standards of skill owed by a broker. The court ruled that there is nothing in BRRETA which prevents a broker from suing for breach of an oral contract. Neither does BRRETA eliminate the legal principles of procuring cause and *quantum meruit* that would allow a broker to state a claim for payment for services rendered. The court held that the broker could sue for its commission even without a written brokerage agreement.

§ 13.5.1   Procuring Cause

When a contract expressly provided for how and under what terms real estate commissions are to be paid, the contract controls.[1616] However, in the absence of an express contract governing the conditions under which a commission is to be paid, the real estate broker may pursue a claim as the procuring cause of the sale.[1617] The "procuring cause doctrine"[1618] entitles a broker to a commission as soon as she is able to find a buyer who is ready, able and willing to purchase the property on the terms specified by the seller with no contingencies.

There are also situations where a contract exists, but does not spell out all the terms by which a commission will be paid. This could happen, for example, under an open listing where the owner generally indicates a willingness to sell but does not have an exclusive listing arrangement with any broker. There are also situations where the broker and seller sign a general commission agreement that sets forth the amount of the commission, but which is silent as to the circumstances upon which the commission will be deemed earned. Under these circumstances, a real estate broker would have difficulty establishing a claim for his commission on a breach of contract theory due to the missing contractual terms. The procuring cause doctrine may be used in this instance to fill in those terms.

1614   *Killearn Partners, Inc. v. Southeast Properties, Inc.*, 266 Ga.App. 508, 597 S.E.2d 578 (2004), *aff'd.*, 279 Ga. 144, 611 S.E.2d 26, *overturned on other grounds by Amend v. 485 Properties*, 280 Ga. 327, 627 S.E.2d 565. *Killearn* held, among other things, that a broker did not have to prove she was the procuring cause of a sale in order to receive a commission under the theory of *quantum meruit*. The case of *Amend v. 485 Properties* overturned the ruling by finding that being the procuring cause of the sale was a required element of the theory of *quantum meruit* as it relates to real estate commissions.

1615   O.C.G.A. § 10-6A-4.

1616   *D.R. Horton, Inc.-Torrey v. Tausch*, 271 Ga.App. 511, 610 S.E.2d 151 (2005).

1617   *B&B Realty, Inc. v. Carroll*, 245 Ga.App. 44, 537 S.E.2d 183 (2000).

1618   O.C.G.A. § 10-6-32.

Merely locating a prospective purchaser and attempting to make a sale, without more, is generally insufficient to entitle a broker to a commission under a procuring cause theory of recovery.[1619] This is true even if the broker locates the ultimate purchaser of the property. In one case, for example, a broker who procured the ultimate buyers of a property was denied a commission. The broker's oral agreement with the seller was that he would obtain a commission if he sold the property on certain terms, and if the buyer would pay the commission. Although the broker initially introduced the ultimate buyers to the property, the offer he made on their behalf was rejected by the seller. Several months later, with no further contact by the broker, the buyers made another offer which was accepted, and which did not include payment of any commission. The attorney for the buyers handled all negotiations, and the buyers never had any contractual relationship with the broker. The court found that the broker had abandoned its efforts to effect a sale between the parties, and that no party to the sale was bound by contract to utilize the services of the REALTOR®.[1620]

In determining whether a real estate broker is the procuring cause of a sale where there is no exclusive listing to sell, the broker must prove that there were negotiations still pending between the broker and the prospective purchaser and that the owner was aware that negotiations were still pending at the time he consummated the sale.[1621] However, where the owner knowingly interferes with the negotiations between the buyer and the broker, it becomes unnecessary to show that negotiations were pending when the sale was consummated. The broker can make out a *prima facie* case by showing that negotiations were set on foot through his efforts, that he performed every service required by his employment which it was possible to perform, and that the failure on his part to personally consummated the sale was due to the interference of the owner.[1622]

In one case, the owners agreed they would pay the broker a 10% commission if the broker negotiated a sale to the United States Postal Service.[1623] The Postal Service conditioned its purchase on several contingencies, including the removal of an old house and the rezoning of the property. The seller satisfied both contingencies. Due to intervening budget cuts, the Postal Service could no longer purchase the property. The sellers, apparently tired of negotiating with the Postal Service, instructed the broker to cease negotiations. Several years later, the Postal Service contacted the owner directly and purchased the property. The broker learned of the sale and demanded a commission. Affirming a jury award in favor of the broker, the Court of Appeals found that the broker was responsible for bringing the buyer and seller together, that the broker was an active participant in the initial negotiations, that the budget problems that previously prevented the sale were merely a "temporary setback," that the broker performed every service he could, and that the only reason he was not part of the consummation of the sale was because the owners told him to cease any involvement.

In another case, the buyer started negotiations directly with the seller.[1624] The buyer, mistakenly thinking that broker #1 had acquired the exclusive right to sell the property, ceased direct communications with the seller and began negotiating through broker #1. After his initial negotiations failed, the buyer learned that broker #1 had only an open listing on the property. The buyer later saw a sign on the property indicating that broker #2 had the exclusive right to sell the property. The buyer started negotiations through broker #2, which led to the purchase of the property. The court found that broker #1 was not the procuring cause of the sale because he did not introduce the buyer to the property and there was no evidence that the seller colluded with the buyer to prevent broker #1 from claiming a commission.

1619   *Christopher Inv. Properties, Inc. v. Cox*, 219 Ga.App. 440, 465 S.E.2d 680 (1996).

1620   *Fields Realty & Insurance Co. v. Teper*, 165 Ga.App. 28, 299 S.E.2d 74 (1983).

1621   *Christopher Inv. Properties, Inc. v. Cox*, 219 Ga.App. 440, 465 S.E.2d 680 (1996), *overruled on other grounds by Amend v. 485 Properties*, 280 Ga. 327, 627 S.E.2d 565 (2006).

1622   *Center Pointe Investments, Inc. v. Frank M. Darby Company*, 249 Ga.App. 782, 549 S.E.2d 435 (2001).

1623   *Green v. Bowers*, 229 Ga.App. 324, 493 S.E.2d 709 (1998).

1624   *Cartel Realty, Inc. v. Southern Bearings & Parts Company*, 243 Ga.App. 653, 534 S.E.2d 119 (2000).

§ 13.5.2 *Quantum Meruit*

In cases where there is no express contract for a commission, a broker may still assert a claim under the theory of *quantum meruit*.[1625] "Ordinarily, when one renders services or transfers property which is valuable to another, which the latter knowingly accepts, a promise is implied to pay the reasonable value thereof."[1626] "A real estate broker may bring a claim for commission based upon an implied obligation to pay where the broker's services have been rendered and accepted by the beneficiary thereof."[1627]

In order to prevail on a claim based on *quantum meruit* in Georgia, a real estate broker must show: (a) his performance as agent of services valuable to the defendant; (b) the services were performed at the request of the defendant or knowingly accepted by the defendant; (c) the defendant's receipt of those valuable services without compensating the broker would be unjust; (d) the broker's expectation of compensation at the time of the rendition of the services; and (e) that he was the procuring cause of the completed transaction.[1628] This last element, procuring cause, is presumably just a reference to the need for the transaction to have been consummated by or through the efforts of the broker. It seems logical that it must be something different from the statutory procuring cause doctrine discussed in § 13.5.1 (Procuring Cause). Otherwise, the doctrine of procuring cause would be entirely subsumed by the doctrine of *quantum meruit*. Unfortunately, the Georgia appellate courts have often used the same term to describe different things. As a result, this area of the law is somewhat muddied.

Under a *quantum meruit* theory the amount of the commission claim will be the reasonable value of the brokers services as measured by the recipient of those services. This may or may not be the same as the amount of commission the broker expected to receive.[1629]

In one case, a broker, acting without a commission agreement, introduced the tenant and landlord, assisted with lease negotiations, and was told by the landlord that it would "be protected" with regards to its commission.[1630] The owner and tenant thereafter finalized lease negotiations between themselves. The broker submitted an invoice for service rendered to the landlord, which it refused to pay. The court found that the landlord knew the broker was rendering a valuable service, that the broker expected to be paid, and that the landlord reassured the broker that it would be paid. Under these circumstances the court held that it would be unjust to allow the landlord to escape paying the fair value of the services that it knowingly accepted.

§ 13.6 ONLY A BROKER MAY PURSUE A COMMISSION

Irrespective of the legal theory (contract, *quantum meruit*, or procuring cause used to claim a commission), only a licensed real estate broker has standing to bring a claim for a commission.[1631] Georgia law provides that anyone pursuing a real estate commission in court must prove they were duly licensed as a Georgia broker at the time they rendered services giving rise to the commission claim. Additionally, the broker must establish that any person acting on the broker's behalf in the transaction giving rise to the commission claim was duly licensed in Georgia.[1632]

1625   *United Controls, Inc. v. Alpha Systems, Inc.*, 195 Ga.App. 331, 393 S.E.2d 694 (1990). (There can be no recovery on *quantum meruit* when the action is based on an express contract.)

1626   O.C.G.A. § 9-2-7.

1627   *Atlanta Apartment Investments, Inc. v. New York Life Insurance Company*, 220 Ga.App. 595, 469 S.E.2d 831 (1996).

1628   *Amend v. 485 Properties*, 280 Ga. 327, 627 S.E.2d 565 (2006).

1629   *Centre Pointe Investments, Inc. v. Frank M. Darby Company*, 249 Ga.App. 782, 549 S.E.2d 435 (2001).

1630   *Centre Pointe Investments, Inc. v. Frank M. Darby Company*, 249 Ga.App. 782, 549 S.E.2d 435 (2001).

1631   O.C.G.A. § 43-40-24; *Dixon v. Rollins*, 120 Ga.App. 557, 171 S.E.2d 646 (1969).

1632   *Id.*

§ 13.7 BROKERAGE COMMISSIONS IN COMMERCIAL REAL ESTATE TRANSACTIONS

Georgia law does not give a residential real estate broker the right to file a lien on a property to recover the payment of a commission[1633] unless expressly provided in an agreement.[1634] The broker in a commercial transaction, however, may file a lien on the property to recover a commission in certain circumstances.

§ 13.7.1 What Constitutes Commercial Real Estate?

The definition of "commercial real estate" under the Commercial Real Estate Broker Lien Act[1635] is unfortunately poorly written. This creates the potential for differing interpretations of when a commercial real estate broker's lien can be filed and therefore puts the lien rights of brokers at risk. It also gives property owners the ability to threaten brokers who have filed commercial real estate broker liens with slander of title claims if they do not dismiss their liens.

The definition of commercial real estate as set forth in the statute is as follows:

> "Commercial real estate means any real estate other than real estate containing one to four residential units; real estate on which no buildings or structures are located and which is not zoned for nor available for commercial, multifamily, or retail use; or real estate classified as agricultural for tax assessment purposes. Commercial real estate shall not include single-family residential units such as condominiums, townhomes, mobile homes or homes in a subdivision when sold, leased, or otherwise conveyed on a unit by unit basis even though these units may be part of a larger building or parcel of real estate containing more than four residential units."[1636]

A possible, but what we believe is an ultimately incorrect way to interpret this definition is to argue that commercial real estate upon which a lien may be filed includes: (i) any real estate other than real estate containing 1-4 residential units; (ii) real estate on which no buildings or structures are located and which is not zoned for nor available for commercial multifamily or retail use; or (iii) real estate classified as agricultural for tax assessment purposes. So, for example, under this interpretation of the statute, a commercial real estate broker's lien could be filed against agricultural land. While this interpretation would appear to be one way to interpret the definition, such an interpretation would lead to illogical results. This is because the first definition of commercial real estate being any real estate other than real estate containing 1-4 residential units is so encompassing, there would be no need for the other two definitions.

The only way such an interpretation should make logical sense is if the second two definitions of commercial real estate somehow modified the first definition. Since there is no such modification language in the definition, it can only be assumed that this is not what was intended in the statute.

The second and more logical way to interpret the definition of "commercial real estate" is to put an imaginary colon after "any real estate other than" and for everything which comes after this phrase to be an exception to when a commercial broker's lien can be filed. Interpreting the definition this way, it would then mean that commercial real estate is any real estate other than" (i) real estate containing one to four residential units; (ii) real estate on which no buildings or structures are located and which is not zoned for nor available for commercial multifamily or retail uses; or (iii) real estate classified as agricultural for tax assessment purposes.

1633   2 Ga. Real Estate Sales Contracts § 10:17 (6th ed.).

1634   2 Ga. Real Estate Law & Procedure § 18-50 (6th ed.).

1635   O.C.G.A. § 44-14-600 *et seq.*

1636   O.C.G.A. § 44-14-601(3).

While this interpretation of the definition would create a rationale for including all three exceptions, it is not completely clear that this is how a court would interpret the term "commercial real estate." The definition is a great example of how the lack of clarity in drafting state laws can lead to legal disputes.

Assuming that the second interpretation of commercial real estate is the correct interpretation, a commercial broker's lien cannot be filed if the real estate contains one to four residential units. Similarly, if land is zoned for agricultural purposes, a commercial broker's lien cannot be filed against the property. Finally, if the land has both no buildings or structures on it and is not zoned for or available for commercial multifamily or retail uses, then a lien cannot be filed against the property. This last exclusion is also less than completely clear. To better understand this exclusion, let's look at the example below.

A landowner is selling property zoned industrial use. Can a commercial broker's lien be filed against the property? The answer to this question is "yes" because the exclusion only applies to land on which there are both no buildings or structures and which is not zoned or available for retail, commercial or multi-family use. In this case, while the property is not zoned or available for industrial purposes, there is a building on the property.

However, let's say that the land is unimproved land zoned for industrial purposes. In this case, it would appear that no broker's lien can be filed because while the land is unimproved, it is not zoned or available for commercial, multi-family or retail purposes. (Why the statute would have excluded unimproved industrial land from the real estate upon which a commercial broker's lien can be filed is unknown.)

Similarly, let's say that a large acreage tract is zoned for single-family purposes and does not contain any improvements on it. Can a broker file a commercial broker's lien against the property in this situation? The answer to this question should be no. This is because a lien cannot be filed in cases where the land has no building or structures on it and is not zoned or available for multi-family, retail or commercial use.

Let's change the facts slightly in the above example. If a large acreage tract that is being sold is zoned for single-family residential use and on which there sits an old barn, can a commercial broker's lien be filed in this instance? While there is no case law on this point and while this may not have been what was intended by the drafters of the law, the answer to this question would appear to be yes. This is because while the land is not zoned for multi-family, commercial or retail purposes, the property does contain a building or structure taking it out of the scope of the exception.

The other problem with the definition of commercial property is that it does not define when a property is to be characterized as commercial property. For example, let's say that a broker lists agricultural property for sale subject to it being rezoned to a multi-family zoning category. Agricultural land is not subject to the commercial broker's lien law. However, multi-family zoned land is subject to the commercial broker's lien law. If the property is rezoned to multifamily use prior to closing and the property owner fails to pay a commission, does this then mean that a commercial broker's lien can now be filed? While a good argument can be made that this is a proper interpretation of the statute, there is no case law on this point.

Similarly, what if an owner is selling land that has a barn on it subject to it being rezoned from a multi-family zoning category to a commercial zoning. In such an instance, either zoning category for the land would normally bring the property under the scope of when a lien can be filed. However, no lien should be able to be filed since the land contains a barn. As discussed above, the broker's lien statute can only be filed if the land is zoned or available for commercial retail or multi-family purposes and if the land does not have any buildings or structures on it. In the example above, what if prior to closing, the seller of the property removes the barn and the seller then does not pay the brokers their commissions. In this situation, an argument can again be made that by removing the building or the property, a commercial broker's lien can now be filed.

§ 13.7.2   Right To File Lien To Enforce Payment Of Commission

The Georgia Commercial Real Estate Broker Lien Act[1637] provides that a real estate broker may file a lien in the amount of compensation agreed upon by the broker and the landlord or seller or other client or customer of the broker upon commercial real estate or any interest in commercial real estate in one of the following three circumstances:[1638]

The first is where the commission claim arises out of a listing agreement or any other agreement for the management, sale or lease of or otherwise conveying any interest in commercial real estate as evidenced by a writing signed by the owner or its expressly authorized agent and with written notice of the party whose property may be liened, if different, from the parties to the agreement;[1639]

The second is where the commission claim arises from the broker or broker's employees or independent contractors having provided licensed services that result in the procuring of a person or entity ready, willing or able to enter and who actually enters into a purchase or lease or otherwise accepts a conveyance of commercial real estate or any interest in the commercial real estate upon terms acceptable to the owner as evidenced by an agreement or conveyance signed by the owner or its expressly authorized agent and with written notice to the party whose property may be liened, if different from the parties to the agreement.[1640]

The third is where the commission claim arises from a broker, having a written agreement with a prospective buyer or tenant to represent the buyer or tenant as to the purchase, lease or other conveyance of commercial real estate becomes entitled to compensation and with written notice to the party whose property may be liened, if different from the parties to the agreement.[1641]

§ 13.7.2.1   When A Lien Can Be Filed

Under the Commercial Real Estate Broker Lien Act,[1642] the broker must file the lien within certain time frames depending on the method of payment and type of transaction.

In a lease transaction, if the payment to a broker is due in one lump sum and the sum is not paid, the lien must be recorded within 90 days after the tenant takes possession of the leased premises or the date the transaction procured by the broker is closed.[1643]

In a purchase and sale transaction, if the payment to the broker is due in installments, all or a portion of which is due only after the conveyance of the commercial real estate, any claim for lien for those payments due after the conveyance may be recorded at any time after the conveyance, so long as the claim for lien is recorded within 90 days of the date the payment was due and not paid.[1644]

If the broker has a written brokerage engagement agreement with a client, the lien will automatically attach to the client's interest when the client purchases, leases or otherwise accepts a conveyance of the commercial property and the recording of a notice of lien within 90 days after the later of the purchase, lease or other conveyance or transfer to the buyer or tenant; or the failure of the buyer or tenant to compensate the broker; or compensate the broker pursuant to their brokerage engagement agreement.[1645]

1637   O.C.G.A. § 44-14-600 *et seq.*

1638   O.C.G.A. § 44-14-602(a).

1639   O.C.G.A. § 44-14-602(a)(1).

1640   O.C.G.A. § 44-14-602(a)(2).

1641   O.C.G.A. § 44-14-602(a)(3).

1642   O.C.G.A. § 44-14-600 *et seq.*

1643   O.C.G.A. § 44-14-602(c).

1644   O.C.G.A. § 44-14-602(d).

1645   O.C.G.A. § 44-14-602(e).

If the broker has a written management agreement for an improved property, then the claim for lien must be recorded within 90 days of the termination of the agreement.[1646]

Lastly, if the broker's lien claim is based on an option to purchase or lease, the lien must be filed within 90 days of the date of the transaction for which a commission or other fee is due or within 90 days of the date of the transaction for sale, lease, or other conveyance is closed, whichever is later.[1647]

§ 13.7.2.2 How To File A Lien

To file a lien, a commercial broker must record a notice of lien in the county land records of the superior court of the county in which the commercial property or interest in such property is located.[1648] The notice of lien must also be sent to the owner of the commercial real estate by certified mail.[1649] Once the notice of lien is filed with the appropriate county, the lien will attach to the commercial real estate or any interest in such real estate to enforce the commission owed to the broker.[1650] Only prior recorded liens and liens for *ad valorem* taxes will have priority over a broker's lien.[1651]

§ 13.7.2.3 What The Lien Must Provide; Notice Of Lien

The lien notice must contain the following: the name of the claimant; the name of the owner; a description of the property upon which the lien is being claimed; the amount for which the lien is claimed; and the real estate license number of the broker.[1652] The notice of lien must also recite that the information contained in the notice is true and accurate to the knowledge of the signatory.[1653] In addition, the lien notice must recite that the broker has disclosed to all parties that a lien might be claimed under O.C.G.A. § 44-602(h).[1654] The notice of lien must be signed by the broker or by a person expressly authorized to sign on behalf of the broker and must be verified.[1655]

§ 13.7.2.4 Civil Suits To Collect On The Lien

The commercial broker may also file a civil suit to enforce the lien within one year after the lien is recorded.[1656] However, if the claim is not filed within one year after recording the lien, the lien will be extinguished.[1657] In an option to purchase or lease transaction, a broker claiming a lien must commence proceedings against the buyer or tenant by filing a complaint within six (6) months after the transfer or conveyance of the commercial property.[1658] Failure to commence proceedings within this time will extinguish the lien.[1659]

The civil complaint must contain the following information: a brief statement of the contract on which the lien is founded; the date when the contract was made; a description of the services performed; the amount due and unpaid; a description of the property that is subject to the lien; and any other facts necessary to state a claim for payment of a commission, fee or other compensation owed by the buyer or tenant to the broker.[1660]

1646   O.C.G.A. § 44-14-602(f).

1647   O.C.G.A. § 44-14-602(g).

1648   O.C.G.A. § 44-14-602(b).

1649   O.C.G.A. § 44-14-602(i).

1650   O.C.G.A. § 44-14-602(b).

1651   O.C.G.A. § 44-14-603.

1652   O.C.G.A. § 44-14-602(h).

1653   O.C.G.A. § 44-14-602(h).

1654   O.C.G.A. § 44-14-602(h).

1655   O.C.G.A. § 44-14-602(h).

1656   O.C.G.A. § 44-14-602(j)(1).

1657   O.C.G.A. § 44-14-602(j)(1).

1658   O.C.G.A. § 44-14-602(j)(1).

1659   O.C.G.A. § 44-14-602(j)(1).

1660   O.C.G.A. § 44-14-602(j)(3).

§ 13.7.2.5 Who Is Responsible For The Costs And Expenses Of The Proceedings?

All costs and expenses of any proceeding, whether a claim for a lien or civil claim to enforce the payment of a lien, must be paid by the nonprevailing party.[1661] These costs and expenses include reasonable attorney's fees actually incurred, costs and prejudgment interests due to the winning party.[1662] If more than one party is responsible for the costs and expenses of any claim for lien or civil suit, the court will equitably apportion such costs among those responsible parties.[1663]

§ 13.7.3 Dissolving The Broker's Lien

A broker's right to file a notice of a lien will be dissolved if the owner, purchasers from the owner, lender providing a loan secured by commercial real estate or other holder of the lienable interest in a commercial transaction shows the following:[1664]

(i) the lien has been waived in writing by the lien claimant or its expressly authorized agent; or[1665]

(ii) the owner or a person at whose instance the brokerage or management services were provided has given a sworn written statement that all such compensation due or to become due has been paid or has been waived in writing by the potential lien claimant; and[1666]

(iii) at the time the sworn written statement was obtained or given as part of a bona fide sale or loan secured by the commercial real estate, the lien of record had not been previously cancelled, dissolved or expired.[1667]

It is most common for the brokers identified in a commercial purchase and sale agreement to receive a specific commission and agree to release any lien claims they may have against the property. This is normally accomplished by each broker signing a separate lien waiver. A sample of such a provision is set forth below.

Special Stipulation 299: Broker's Release of Lien Law

The undersigned Broker, in consideration and receipt of $_____, which is the entire amount due for all services rendered by Broker with respect to the Transaction, does hereby waive and release to the aforesaid Seller, aforesaid purchaser and owners and mortgagees of aforesaid real property, any and all liens, claims, or rights to liens upon said land, or upon the improvements now or hereafter thereon, or upon the monies or other considerations due or to become due to the Seller in respect of the Transaction, which may arise as a result of the Commercial Real Estate Lien Act (O.C.G.A. § 44-14-600, et. seq.).

It is also common for brokers in commercial transactions to be identified and for the buyer and seller to warrant that no other brokers were involved in the transaction and to indemnify each other from any and all claims, cause of action and suits resulting from the warranty being inaccurate. A sample of such a provision is set forth below.

Special Stipulation 300: No Other Broker Involved in the Transaction

Purchaser and Seller represent and warrant to the other that each party has not dealt with any broker, agent, or finder in connection with this transaction and Purchaser and Seller covenant and agree, each to the other, to indemnify and hold each other harmless from any and all losses, damages, costs and expenses including, but not limited to, attorneys fees and court costs that may be incurred or suffered as a result of any claim for any fee, commission, or similar compensation

1661 O.C.G.A. § 44-14-602(k).

1662 O.C.G.A. § 44-14-602(k).

1663 O.C.G.A. § 44-14-602(k).

1664 O.C.G.A. § 44-14-605(d).

1665 O.C.G.A. § 44-14-605(d)(1).

1666 O.C.G.A. § 44-14-605(d)(2).

1667 O.C.G.A. § 44-14-605(d)(3).

with respect to this transaction made by any person or entity and arising through the actions of the indemnifying party, whether or not such claim for any fee, commission, or similar compensation with respect to this transaction made by any person or entity is meritorious.

§ 13.8 BROKERAGE COMMISSIONS IN LEASE TRANSACTIONS

Owners of a rental property generally hire real estate brokers to place tenants in the landlord's rental property. When a broker finds a tenant and a lease is consummated, the landlord pays the broker a commission just as the broker would receive in a purchase and sale transaction. This is often accomplished pursuant to a brokerage commission agreement which is entered into by both parties before the lease is consummated. Oftentimes, particularly in commercial real estate transactions, the ownership of a rental property will change during or after the broker has found tenants to lease the property. If this is the case, the successor owner of the rental property may still be required to continue paying the real estate broker a commission pursuant to the brokerage commission agreement between the original landlord/owner and the broker.[1668]

Under Georgia law, a residential and commercial[1669] broker's commission will be protected even if the ownership of the rental property transfers to a new owner, so long as certain conditions are met.[1670] When a written brokerage commission agreement is created, it can be made a binding agreement not only for the original landlord who is named personally in the agreement, grantees, successors, and assigns of the original landlord.[1671] In such a case, even if a rental property is sold, transferred, or assigned, the broker may still be entitled to her commission.[1672] Under state law, this can occur even if a property is sold for the enforcement of any mortgage lien, deed to secure debt, or any other security instrument.[1673]

The successor landlord is only obligated to pay the broker for any services rendered in connection with the consummation of a lease of the rental property if:[1674]

(i)   The written brokerage commission agreement between the original landlord and the broker is incorporated into the lease;

(ii) (1) The real estate broker recorded a notice of commission rights in the deed records in the office of the clerk of the superior court in the county in which the real property or leasehold interest is located within 30 days of the execution of the lease incorporating the written brokerage commission agreement; and (2) such notice was filed before the conveyance of the property, and was be signed by the broker or by a person expressly authorized to sign on behalf of the broker, and must follow the form provided in O.C.G.A. § 44-7-21(b).[1675]

(iii) The successing landlord assumes the benefits of the tenancy, rental amount, and the terms of the lease; and

(iv) The written brokerage commission agreement has not been waived in writing by the broker.

If all of these conditions are met, the successor landlord will be bound to all the obligations contained in the written brokerage commission agreement, including the payment of commission to the real estate broker.[1676] While this language is very beneficial to real estate brokers, property owners normally have greater bargaining power in commission negotiations and will rarely agree to the inclusion of the language referenced above.

1668   O.C.G.A. § 44-7-21(a).

1669   O.C.G.A. § 44-7-21(d).

1670   O.C.G.A. § 44-7-21(a).

1671   O.C.G.A. § 44-7-21(a).

1672   O.C.G.A. § 44-7-21(a).

1673   O.C.G.A. § 44-7-21(a).

1674   O.C.G.A. § 44-7-21(a).

1675   O.C.G.A. § 44-7-21(a) and (b).

1676   O.C.G.A. § 44-7-21(a).

CHAPTER 14

DISPUTES ARISING FROM THE CONTRACT

OVERVIEW

A variety of problems and disputes arise in residential real estate transactions. Buyers sometimes get cold feet and do not want to go through with their purchases. Sellers occasionally get better offers and look for ways to avoid their obligations. Buyers and sellers often disagree over what personal property stays with the real estate. Other disputes arise when the buyer discovers hidden defects in the property after the closing and accuses the seller or listing broker of knowing about the defects and not disclosing the same. With newly constructed homes, buyers may assert claims against the builder for negligent construction, breach of warranty or breach of contract.

Parties are often able to resolve such disputes by themselves either with the help of their brokers or through mediation. Parties who do not resolve their differences often end up suing each other, and sometimes suing the real estate broker or brokers involved in the transaction as well. The two most common legal claims arising out of real estate sales contracts are for: (a) breach of contract when a party does not close and/or refuses or fails to comply with the terms of the contract, and (b) fraud where the buyer alleges that the seller and/or the seller's broker knew about hidden defects in the property but failed to disclose to the buyer or concealed them in order to encourage the buyer to purchase the property.

This chapter discusses disputes between the parties including the kinds of claims that are asserted, the relevant statute of limitation periods, and the damages available to parties. This chapter also discusses contractual defenses to claims and alternatives to going to court, including arbitration and mediation.

§ 14.1 BREACH OF CONTRACT PRIOR TO CLOSING

The parties to a contract owe a duty of good faith and fair dealing in performing their obligations under the contract.[1677] When a party breaches a contract, courts have the power to order the breaching party to perform as agreed in the contract or pay for the damages caused by the breach.[1678] The most common breach alleged prior to closing is an anticipatory breach. The possible remedies will depend on the facts and circumstances of the dispute. Although the law may afford a party multiple remedies when there has been a breach of contract, the contract itself may limit what remedies are available. The remedies for breach of contract prior to closing generally include claims for monetary damage and/or rescission (cancellation) or specific performance (enforcement) of the contract. These different remedies are discussed in detail below.

§ 14.1.1 Anticipatory Breach

When a party refuses to perform his or her contractual obligations prior to the time performance is required, an anticipatory breach of contract has occurred.[1679] Georgia law generally allows a non-breaching party to treat an anticipatory breach as a breach of contract in certain circumstances.[1680] The type of breach which will form the basis for a claim of anticipatory breach is an unqualified repudiation of the entire agreement before the time of performance.[1681] In other words, the party must absolutely refuse to perform before his or her performance is required.[1682] For example, on April 1, the seller contracts to sell her property to the buyer, with the closing scheduled on June 1. On May 1, the seller tells the buyer that she is not going to close with the buyer because she got a better offer. The seller's statement is an unqualified repudiation of the entire agreement because the agreement stated she would sell her house to the buyer and now she is refusing to do so. As such, the buyer would have a basis for an anticipatory breach claim against the seller.

1677   *Brack v. Brownlee*, 246 Ga. 818, 273 S.E.2d 390 (Ga., 1980), citing Restatement, Second, Contracts, § 231.

1678   *Baker v. Jellibeans, Inc.*, 252 Ga. 458, 314 S.E.2d 874 (1984).

1679   *Clark v. Cox*, 179 Ga. App. 437, 347 S.E.2d 4 (1986).

1680   *CCE Federal Credit Union v. Chesser*, 150 Ga. App. 328, 258 S.E.2d 2 (1979).

1681   *Textile Rubbwe & Chemical Co., Inc. v. Thermo-Flex Technologies, Inc.*, 301 Ga.App. 491, 687 S.E.2d 919 (2009).

1682   *J.M. Clayton Co. v. Martin*, 177 Ga.App. 228, 339 S.E.2d 280 (1985).

A party simply requesting that the other party agree to different terms than those set forth in the agreement does not amount to an anticipatory breach.[1683] Moreover, a party's refusal of the proposed terms give neither party the right to terminate the purchase and sale agreement.[1684] For example, let's say a buyer sends the seller an amendment to the purchase and sale agreement before the closing. The amendment proposes to reduce the sales price but the buyer indicates that he agrees to remain bound by the terms of the current agreement if the proposal is not acceptable to the seller. This proposal is not an anticipatory breach because it is not an absolute refusal to perform before the closing.[1685] In addition, if the seller refuses the proposed terms, neither party would have a basis to terminate the contract because the buyer is still agreeing to be bound by the current terms.

The refusal to perform one or two essential obligations in an agreement, such as a material covenant or special stipulation,[1686] could be considered a breach of the whole agreement and thus form a basis for an anticipatory breach claim.[1687] Whether the obligation is essential to the entire agreement will likely depend on the facts and circumstances of each case. For example, let's say a seller and buyer contract for the sale of a piece of property. The seller provides a special stipulation in the agreement that the property is zoned for apartments. Thereafter, the buyer discovers that the property is not zoned for such use, but instead zoned for residential use. In this case, the buyer may refuse to close and terminate the agreement because the seller's nonperformance of the special stipulation constituted an anticipatory breach.[1688] The buyer was planning on using the land to build apartments and when the seller made this special stipulation, this was, in effect, a covenant that the property was already zoned for such use.[1689] Since the property was not zoned for apartments at the time the stipulation was made, the nonperformance of this stipulation allowed the buyer to terminate the agreement.[1690]

§ 14.1.1.1 Anticipatory Breach By Affirmative Statement

A party may commit an anticipatory breach by affirmatively stating she will not perform, or taking an action that renders the obligation unable or apparently unable to be performed without committing a breach.[1691]

In order to commit an anticipatory breach by an affirmative statement, the breaching party must inform the nonbreaching party that she will not perform or breach.[1692] For example, on April 1, the seller contracts to sell her property to the buyer, with the closing scheduled for July 1. However, on May 1 the seller tells the buyer that she is not going to sell the property to the buyer. The seller's refusal to perform is an anticipatory breach by affirmative statement and gives the buyer a basis an anticipatory breach claim against the seller.

A party merely indicating an expression of doubt as to his or her willingness or ability to perform would not constitute an anticipatory breach.[1693] As stated above, the breaching party must absolutely refuse to perform to constitute an anticipatory breach.[1694] For example, let's say on April 1 the seller contracts to sell his property to the buyer, with the closing scheduled for July 1. However, on May 1, the seller tells the buyer, "I am not sure that I can perform and I'm not going to unless I am legally obligated to." This scenario is similar to the example above where the buyer proposed

---

1683   *Jones v. Solomon*, 207 Ga. App. 592, 428 S.E.2d 637 (1993).

1684   *J.M. Clayton Co. v. Martin*, 177 Ga.App. 228, 339 S.E.2d 280 (1985).

1685   *J.M. Clayton Co. v. Martin*, 177 Ga.App. 228, 339 S.E.2d 280 (1985).

1686   *McLeod v. McLatcher*, 201 Ga. App. 17, 410 S.E.2d 144 (1991).

1687   *Textile Rubbwe & Chemical Co., Inc. v. Thermo-Flex Technologies, Inc.*, 301 Ga.App. 491, 687 S.E.2d 919 (2009).

1688   *Sachs v. Swartz*, 233 Ga. 99, 209 S.E.2d 642 (1974).

1689   *Sachs v. Swartz*, 233 Ga. 99, 209 S.E.2d 642 (1974).

1690   *Sachs v. Swartz*, 233 Ga. 99, 209 S.E.2d 642 (1974).

1691   *Alabama v. North Carolina*, 130 S.Ct. 2295 (2010).

1692   *Alabama v. North Carolina*, 130 S.Ct. 2295 (2010).

1693   *Coffee Butler Service, Inc. v. Sacha*, 258 Ga. 192, 366 S.E.2d 672 (1988). An anticipatory repudiation of a contract occurs when one party absolutely refuses to perform either by act or word.

1694   *J.M. Clayton Co. v. Martin*, 177 Ga.App. 228, 339 S.E.2d 280 (1985).

new terms to the seller. In both examples, the party making the statement is still agreeing to be bound to the terms of agreement. As such, the seller's statement is not an absolute refusal to perform, and thus it is not an anticipatory breach.[1695]

§ 14.1.1.2   Anticipatory Breach By Action

It is not necessary for the breaching party to indicate his or her intention of nonperformance by an affirmative statement.[1696] The breaching party may also commit an anticipatory breach by his or her actions.[1697] To constitute an anticipatory breach by action, the breaching party's act must be both voluntary and affirmative, and must make the obligation unable or apparently unable to be performed without a breach.[1698] The following scenarios evidence action constituting an anticipatory breach.

Example 1: On April 1, the seller contracts to sell his property to the buyer and the closing is scheduled for July 1. The seller doesn't say anything to the buyer about selling the property to someone else, but on May 1, the seller contracts to sell his property to a different buyer. The seller's making of the contract with the different buyer would constitute an anticipatory breach evidenced by action, thus giving the first buyer a basis for suit against the seller.

Example 2: On April 1, the seller contracts to sell his property to the buyer and the closing is scheduled for July 1. Without saying anything to the buyer, the seller mortgages his property to another buyer or company as security for a loan which is not payable until one year later. The seller's mortgaging the property also constitutes an anticipatory breach evidenced by action, giving the first buyer a basis for suit against the seller.

Example 3: On April 1, the seller contracts to sell his property to the buyer with the closing scheduled for July 1. Shortly after April 1, the buyer conducts a pre-closing inspection which reveals several significant problems with the house. The seller and buyer agree that the seller will fix the buyer's list of repairs before the closing date. However, when the buyer re-inspects the property the day before the closing, he finds that none of the repairs have been completed. The seller's nonperformance of the repairs would likely constitute an anticipatory breach because it would be impossible for the seller to complete the repairs before the next day. In this case, the seller's failure to fix the repairs would constitute an anticipatory breach by action, thus giving the buyer a basis for suit against the seller.

Example 4: On April 1, the seller and buyer contract for the sale of the seller's property with the closing scheduled for July 1. The seller promises to transfer possession of the property immediately upon closing. However, when the buyer conducts a pre-closing inspection the day before the closing, he discovers that all of the seller's possessions are still in the house. The seller's failure to remove his possessions would likely constitute an anticipatory breach because it appears the seller would be unable to remove all of those items before the closing.

There is no bright line distinction between what constitutes a proper anticipatory repudiation based on action and what does not. It is a case by case inquiry of whether the breaching party is unable or apparently unable to perform the obligation without committing a breach.[1699] However, in Example 4, if the buyer discovered that all the possessions were still located in the house a week before the closing, the buyer would most likely not be able to repudiate the contract or refuse to close because the seller would be able to remove them before the closing date. Furthermore, once the buyer repudiates the agreement, the seller is no longer obligated to remove the possessions from the property before closing.[1700] Therefore, if the buyer refused to close based on this discovery, and as a result, the seller is relieved of his obligated to remove them, the buyer could not thereafter rely upon the seller's nonperformance as justification for his refusing to close.[1701]

1695   *J.M. Clayton Co. v. Martin*, 177 Ga.App. 228, 339 S.E.2d 280 (1985).

1696   *J & E Builders, Inc. v. R C Development, Inc.*, 285 Ga.App. 457, 646 S.E.2d 299 (2007).

1697   *J & E Builders, Inc. v. R C Development, Inc.*, 285 Ga.App. 457, 646 S.E.2d 299 (2007).

1698   *Alabama v. North Carolina*, 130 S.Ct. 2295 (2010).

1699   *Jones v. Solomon*, 207 Ga.App. 592, 428 S.E.2d 637 (1993).

1700   *Clark v. Cox*, 179 Ga. App. 437, 347 S.E.2d 4 (1986).

1701   *Clark v. Cox*, 179 Ga. App. 437, 347 S.E.2d 4 (1986).

§ 14.1.1.3   Innocent Party Requirement With Terminating Due To Anticipatory Breach

A party's right to terminate an agreement for anticipatory breach depends on whether that party has breached the agreement himself.[1702] The party may only terminate the agreement for anticipatory breach if that party is free from substantial default.[1703] For example, the seller contracts to sell his property to the buyer, but before the closing, the seller tells the buyer that he is not going to sell his property to the buyer or show up at the closing. The seller's statement constitutes an anticipatory breach, but the buyer may only treat it as such if the buyer is not at that time in default of the agreement.[1704] Let's say that before the anticipatory breach occurred, the buyer breached the structural inspection provision of the agreement by failing to address any structural problems his inspection revealed in the manner required by the agreement. In this case, the buyer would have no right to rescind the agreement for the seller's anticipatory breach because the buyer has committed a substantial breach himself.[1705]

§ 14.1.1.4   Effect Of Anticipatory Breach

Merely because a party breaches a contract does not mean that the contract automatically terminates. If an anticipatory breach has occurred, the nonbreaching party is entitled to the following options: (i) treat the anticipatory repudiation as a breach, (ii) rescind the contract, or (iii) leave the contract in existence and wait for performance.[1706] If the nonbreaching party treats the anticipatory repudiation as a breach, termination will not take place unless the nonbreaching party sends a notice of termination due to the default of the breaching party. So, for example, if a buyer breaches a purchase agreement by failing to close, and the seller wants to re-list the property for sale, the seller should first terminate the contract due to the buyer's default. This can be done by using GAR's Unilateral Notice to Terminate form.[1707] If the seller terminates the contract due to a breach of the contract by the buyer, the seller can still pursue a damage claim against the buyer or, under the GAR Contract, retain the earnest money as liquidated damages. However, as discussed in greater detail in § 14.1.3 (Specific Performance) regarding specific performance, the seller should not terminate for anticipatory breach or any other breach if the seller wants to pursue the buyer for specific performance of the contract.

§ 14.1.1.5   Curing The Anticipatory Breach

Generally, if the breaching party commits an anticipatory breach, the innocent party is relieved from fulfilling his or her obligations and would have the basis for a claim against the breaching party for anticipatory breach.[1708] However, a retraction by the breaching party will nullify the effect of an anticipatory breach if the retraction is made before the nonbreaching party either changes his or her position in reliance on the breach or communicates that she considers the repudiation to be final.[1709]

For example, on April 1, the seller contracts to sell his property to the buyer with the closing scheduled for July 1. On May 1, the seller communicates to the buyer his decision not to sell the property to the buyer because the seller has received a higher offer from another person. This action would normally constitute an anticipatory breach. However, if the seller retracts the anticipatory breach by communicating his desire to complete the sale with the buyer before the buyer takes any action in response to the seller's refusal to sell the property, the anticipatory breach will be cured.[1710]

1702   *Martin v. Rollins, Inc.*, 138 Ga.App. 649, 226 S.E.2d 771 (1976).

1703   *Martin v. Rollins, Inc.*, 138 Ga.App. 649, 226 S.E.2d 771 (1976).

1704   *Martin v. Rollins, Inc.*, 138 Ga.App. 649, 226 S.E.2d 771 (1976).

1705   *McLeod v. McLatcher*, 201 Ga.App. 17, 410 S.E.2d 144 (1991).

1706   *Wilson v. Milam*, 156 Ga. App. 328, 274 S.E.2d 720 (1980).

1707   GAR Form F83.

1708   *J & E Builders, Inc. v. R C Development, Inc.*, 285 Ga.App. 457, 646 S.E.2d 299 (2007).

1709   *Mobil Oil Exploration and Producing Southeast, Inc., v. U.S.*, 530 U.S. 604, 120 S. Ct. 2423 (2000) (citing Restatement (Second) of Contracts § 256).

1710   *Nikas v. Hindley*, 98 Ga.App. 437, 106 S.E.2d 335 (1958).

Moreover, once the seller cures the anticipatory breach, the buyer will no longer have a claim for anticipatory breach against the seller and the buyer will again be required to perform his obligations under the agreement.[1711] However, if the seller gave the buyer notice that he was not going to sell the buyer the property and in response, the buyer contracted to purchase another property or notified the seller that he was cancelling their contract before the seller retracted his anticipatory breach, the buyer would have a basis to sue the seller for anticipatory breach.[1712]

§ 14.1.2 Monetary Damages

If a party to the contract refuses to complete the sale (*i.e.*, breaches the contract), the other party may choose to sue for monetary damages for the breach.[1713] The rules applicable to general breach of contract claims also apply to anticipatory breach claims.[1714] An obvious precondition to a claim for breach of contract requires that the contract be binding and valid in the first place.[1715] Also, the party seeking to recover must not himself be in breach, as this might excuse the other party's non-performance.

The general rule for the measure of damages for breach of a contract to purchase or sell real estate is the difference between the contract price and the fair market value of the property at the time of the breach.[1716] Questions of value are typically questions of fact and must be decided by a judge or jury.[1717] Additional damages (that is, damages other than general damages) recoverable for breach of contract are only those that arise naturally from the breach. They must also be expenses or costs contemplated by the parties when the contract was made and must be the probable result of a breach.[1718]

Recoverable monetary damages for breach of a contract to purchase or sell real estate are frequently far less than the parties to the contract imagine. Most purchasers will not knowingly contract to pay more for property than its fair market value. Similarly, most sellers will not knowingly contract to sell their property for significantly less than it is worth. It is, therefore, somewhat common for there to be no meaningful differences (*i.e.*, damages) between the contract price and the fair market value of the property at the time of the breach.

For example, if the contract purchase price was $100,000, and the property was worth $103,000 on the date of a seller's breach, a non-defaulting buyer would be entitled to $3,000 in damages (*i.e.*, the difference between the $100,000 contract price and the $103,000 fair market value of the property). However, if the buyer is in breach the non-defaulting seller would have no damages since he still owns the real estate which is worth $3,000 more than the contractual sales price.

The opposite result is obtained when the property decreases in value from the contract date. If the purchase price was $100,000, but the property was worth only $95,000 as of the date of breach, the non-defaulting buyer might have no damages because the property was worth less than he was paying for it. The non-defaulting seller would presumably have a $5,000 damage claim, since the contracted price exceeded the fair market value of the property.

While owning real estate is obviously not the same thing as cash in hand, the formula for calculating damages looks only to the cash value of the real estate. As a result, parties are most likely to have damages of significance only: (1) where one party struck a particularly good bargain; (2) in rapidly moving markets where prices are quickly moving

---

1711 *J & E Builders, Inc. v. R C Development, Inc.*, 285 Ga.App. 457, 646 S.E.2d 299 (2007).

1712 *Mobil Oil Exploration and Producing Southeast, Inc., v. U.S.*, 530 U.S. 604, 120 S. Ct. 2423 (2000) (citing Restatement (Second) of Contracts § 256).

1713 O.C.G.A. § 13-6-1.

1714 *Redman Development Corporation v. Piedmont Heating & Air Conditioning, Inc.*, 128 Ga. App. 447, 197 S.E.2d 167 (1973).

1715 *Covington v. Countryside Inv. Co., Inc.*, 263 Ga. 125, 428 S.E.2d 562 (1993; *McMichael Realty & Ins. Agency, Inc. v. Tysinger*, 155 Ga.App. 131, 270 S.E.2d 88 (1980).

1716 *Mills v. Parker*, 267 Ga.App. 334. 599 S.E.2d 301 (2004); *Quigley v. Jones*, 255 Ga. 33, 334 S.E.2d 664 (1985), *aff'd*; *SePark v. Caswell Builders, Inc.*, 209 Ga.App. 713, 434 S.E.2d 502 (1993), *cert. denied, Cameron v. Frazier*, 172 Ga.App. 794, 324 S.E.2d 773 (1984).

1717 *Croft v. Kamens*, 171 Ga.App. 105, 318 S.E.2d 809 (1984).

1718 O.C.G.A. § 13-6-2; *Quigley v. Jones*, 255 Ga. 33, 334 S.E.2d 664 (1985).

upward or downward; and (3) where there is an exceptionally long time between the contract date and the closing date, to allow greater time for market swings.

In general, incidental damages (costs and expenses beyond the difference between the contract price and the fair market value of the property at the time of breach) are not recoverable. Unless the language of the contract expressly authorizes it, the non-breaching party may not recover damages such as: utility bills; insurance coverage; *ad valorem* taxes; repair and maintenance costs; "lost opportunity" costs (such as the non-breaching seller's loss of another house which was contingent upon the sale of his current home, or the non-breaching purchaser's need to rent an apartment because he already sold his prior home); travel expenses; lost interest on earnest money; moving costs; lost income; long distance telephone charges; etc.[1719]

The parties may be able to recover incidental damages if they are specifically contemplated in the contract. One court, for example, allowed a buyer to recover increased interest costs when the closing was delayed because the seller failed to comply with the contract.[1720] In this particular case, the parties had discussed the concern about rising interest rates and the effect a delayed closing would have. Since the increased interest costs were contemplated by the parties, the court allowed them as damages.

§ 14.1.3 Specific Performance

The non-defaulting party to a contract may sue for specific performance in order to compel the defaulting party to purchase or sell, as the case may be, the property as agreed in the contract.[1721] In order for a party to be entitled to specific performance the contract must be clear and definite in its terms and entered into without fraud.[1722] The contract must have provided the seller with an adequate price for the real estate[1723] which the buyer typically must have already tendered for the property.[1724] The non-defaulting party must have fully performed as required by the contract and must have waived or satisfied any contractual contingencies or conditions.[1725] This is why buyers often send written notice to reluctant sellers declaring that they are "ready, willing, and able to perform" and go to closing even if they believe the sellers will not show up.

In one case, the sellers of property in Dalton, Georgia, contracted to sell their house to a couple who planned to move to Dalton from West Virginia but who changed their plans and failed to close on the property.[1726] The sellers sued the buyers for specific performance. At trial, the court found that the contract had been signed by all parties and had been complied with by the sellers who were "ready, willing and able to perform." The court ordered the buyers to complete the sale. On appeal by the buyers, the Georgia Supreme Court upheld the trial court's ruling that "[s]o long as the contract for the sale of land is in writing, signed by the other necessary parties, is certain and fair, for adequate consideration, and capable of being performed," the court can order that it be specifically performed. The buyers were compelled to comply with the terms of the contract and purchase the house.

In another case, the Georgia Court of Appeals converted a decree of specific performance requiring a buyer to purchase the seller's property into a monetary judgment when the buyer refused to buy to purchase the property.[1727] Hampton

1719 *Quigley v. Jones*, 255 Ga. 33, 334 S.E.2d 664 (1985); *Baker v. Jellibeans, Inc.*, 252 Ga. 458, 314 S.E.2d 874 (1984); *Mills v. Parker*, 267 Ga.App. 334, 599 S.E.2d 301 (2004).

1720 *Executive Constr., Inc. v. Geduldig*, 170 Ga.App. 560, 317 S.E.2d 564 (1984).

1721 *Baker v. Jellibeans, Inc.*, 252 Ga. 458, 314 S.E.2d 874 (1984).

1722 *Pridgen v. Saville*, 237 Ga. 49, 226 S.E.2d 905 (1976) (terms of payment not stated); *Fourteen West Realty, Inc. v. Wesson*, 167 Ga.App. 539, 307 S.E.2d 28 (1983) (property description inadequate); *McMichael Realty & Ins. Agency, Inc. v. Tysinger*, 155 Ga.App. 131, 270 S.E.2d 88 (1980)

1723 *Baker v. Jellibeans, Inc.*, 252 Ga. 458, 314 S.E.2d 874 (1984) (holding that court will grant specific performance only if contract price is "fair, just and not against good conscience," *Baker* at 461, 314 S.E.2d at 877); *Walker v. Bush*, 234 Ga. 366, 216 S.E.2d 285 (1975).

1724 *Covington v. Countryside Inv. Co., Inc.*, 263 Ga. 125, 428 S.E.2d 562 (1993); *Gallogly v. Bradco, Inc.*, 260 Ga. 311, 392 S.E.2d 529 (1990).

1725 *Stribling v. Ailion*, 223 Ga. 662, 157 S.E.2d 427 (1967).

1726 *Golden v. Frazier*, 244 Ga. 685, 261 S.E.2d 703 (1979).

1727 *Hampton Island, LLC v. HAOP, LLC*, 306 Ga.App. 542, 702 S.E.2d 770 (2010).

Island LLC contracted to purchase some land from the seller but failed to follow through and close the transaction. The sellers sued for specific performance and the court ordered Hampton Island to fulfill its contractual obligations and purchase the seller's property. After the decree was entered, Hampton Island informed the sellers that it was still not going to purchase the property and the sellers filed a motion for contempt. The court granted the motion for contempt and converted the decree of specific performance into a monetary judgment for the principal amount owed under the contract due to the refusal to perform. Hampton Island appealed claiming that its failure to comply with the decree was a result of limited financial resources and was not, therefore, willful to warrant the monetary judgment. The court rejected this argument because Hampton Island failed to show that it did not have the financial resources to perform its contractual obligations. As such, the court affirmed converting the decree into a monetary judgment for the principal amount owed to the seller under the contract plus interest.[1728]

While the above cases involve a successful specific performance claim by a seller against a buyer, sellers rarely file such claims. The seller must keep the property off the market and remain "ready, willing, and able to sell" the property while the suit, including any appeals, is pending. This can take years. Even if the seller eventually wins the suit, a judgment ordering the buyer to purchase the property or pay the amount owed under the contract does little good if the buyer lacks sufficient cash with which to close or satisfy the judgment. Lenders may be unlikely to lend to someone who does not want the property and who explains they are only purchasing the property because a court ordered them to do so. In another case the trial court refused to order the specific performance of a contract to sell land where the terms were too indefinite.[1729] That contract provided that the buyer would pay 29% of the price by August 1, but the contract did not provide for how the balance of the purchase price was to be paid. The Georgia Supreme Court affirmed the trial court's ruling that the payment terms were not definite or specific. The court reasoned that the terms of a real estate contract must be such that neither party can misunderstand them. The court stated that it would be inequitable to carry a contract into effect where the court is forced to guess the intent of the parties, because it might erroneously decree what the parties never intended or contemplated.

When a buyer sues for specific performance, the buyer will also normally want to file a *lis pendens* against the property to put others on notice that there is a pending claim involving the property. This is particularly important if there is any risk that the seller may sell the property to another buyer.[1730]

§ 14.1.4 Rescission Or Cancellation

Another option for a non-defaulting party is to simply cancel or rescind the sales contract. As with other remedies, the non-defaulting party must not himself be in breach.[1731] Rescission, or cancellation, of the contract is a remedy in which neither party is held liable for damages for breach of the contract.[1732] Rather, the contract is treated as no longer binding between the parties and the court proceeds to restore the *status quo ante* (putting the parties in the positions they were in prior to entering into the contract).[1733] The parties may cancel the contract by simple agreement through conduct, writing, or words.[1734] All earnest money should be returned to the buyer and the seller should be compensated for any extraordinary costs (*e.g.*, the cost of removable upgrades made at the buyer's insistence).

1728 *Hampton Island, LLC v. HAOP, LLC*, 306 Ga.App. 542, 702 S.E.2d 770 (2010).

1729 *Pridgen v. Saville*, 237 Ga. 49, 226 S.E.2d 905 (1976).

1730 See § 14.6.1, *et seq.*, for a more complete discussion of the use of a *lis pendens*.

1731 *Suleiman v. Marinello*, 217 Ga.App. 319, 457 S.E.2d 251 (1995); *McLeod v. McLatcher*, 201 Ga.App. 17, 410 S.E.2d 144 (1991).

1732 Once a contract has been rescinded, there is no liability for a breach of that contract. As is discussed in the next section, however, a party may still be liable for fraud arising out of the transaction.

1733 *Martin v. Rollins, Inc.*, 238 Ga. 119, 231 S.E.2d 751 (1977); *Ardex, Ltd. v. Brighton Homes, Inc.*, 206 Ga.App. 606, 426 S.E.2d 200 (1992), *cert. denied*.

1734 *Hennessy v. Woodruff*, 210 Ga. 742, 82 S.E.2d 859 (1954); *Shoup v. Elliott*, 192 Ga. 858, 16 S.E.2d 857 (1941); *Seaboard Coast Line R.R. Co. v. Metzger*, 126 Ga.App. 178, 190 S.E.2d 156 (1972).

Rescission can be based upon the mutual agreement of the parties where they both effectively conclude that they simply want to "call the deal off." Rescission can also be based upon a mutual mistake of a material fact. For example, the parties are both under the mistaken belief that the property is zoned for residential use. They are surprised when they discover that the property is actually zoned for light commercial use. The seller does not want to sell because he thinks the property might be worth more that the contracted for purchase price. The buyer does not want to purchase because he is interested in building a residence, not a commercial building.

Rescission can also be based upon a unilateral mistake as to a material fact, but only if the other party was aware of the mistake, knew it was a material condition to the sale, and the truth could not have been discovered by the exercise of due diligence.[1735]

In one Georgia case, a builder entered a contract with a buyer for the purchase and sale of a house and lot in Fulton County, Georgia. The buyer paid $5,000 earnest money. The house was to be completed by June 30, and the parties agreed to close on July 1. On June 30, the buyer and an inspector went to the house and found 40 items that needed attending to by the builder, and the builder agreed to address 35 of the items. A disagreement arose as to the date of closing. The builder wanted to close immediately, while the buyer wanted to wait until the house was totally completed. The builder advised the buyer that they could either close on the house or the buyer could take back his earnest money because the builder had the house ready and he wanted to close. The buyer's attorney called the builder to tell him that the deal was off and the buyer wanted his earnest money back. The builder then offered to compromise, but the buyer wanted to accept the earnest money and rescind the contract. The builder then put the house up for sale and returned the earnest money.

The house later sold for $4,450 less than the original contract and the builder had to pay points and additional interest on his construction loan. The builder also had to incur considerable painting and redecorating expenses in order to sell the house and pay for utilities, maintenance, and upkeep. The builder sued the original buyer to recover these expenses. The buyer counterclaimed for expenses the buyer had incurred because of the builder's refusal to complete the house as required by the contract. The trial court ruled against both parties and did not award either party any damages. The court found that the parties canceled the contract by mutual consent. Once the builder offered to return the buyer's earnest money and the buyer accepted this offer, the parties effectively rescinded the contract, thereby barring any recovery by either party.[1736]

§ 14.1.5 The GAR Contract

The GAR Contract does not limit the rights of either buyer or seller to pursue any claim against the other for an alleged breach of the contract. If one party breaches the contract, the other can sue for specific performance, monetary damages, rescission, or any other remedy provided by law.

The GAR Contract does contain an optional "liquidated damages" provision[1737] whereby the seller's monetary damages are limited to the earnest money if the seller accepts and deposits the earnest money from the Holder. This means that the seller could not then pursue other claims against the buyer.[1738] If the seller wants to avoid this limitation, he should decline to deposit the earnest money check from the Holder. If the seller does not accept the earnest money from the Holder the seller may pursue any other legal remedies against the buyer.

1735 *Lester v. Bird*, 200 Ga.App. 335, 408 S.E.2d 147 (1991).

1736 *Johnson Ventures, Inc. v. Barkin*, 141 Ga.App. 810, 234 S.E.2d 340 (1977), *cert. denied*.

1737 GAR Form F20.

1738 *Everett Assoc. v. Garner*, 162 Ga.App. 513, 291 S.E.2d 120 (1982), *cert. denied*.

§ 14.2 BREACH OF CONTRACT AFTER CLOSING

The remedies for breach of contract after the closing generally include claims for monetary damage and/or specific performance (enforcement) of some unfulfilled provision of the contract.

§ 14.2.1 Monetary Damages

The measure of damages for breach of contract after the sale has closed is the difference between the value of the property as contacted for and the value of the property as delivered. Damages may also be proven by showing the cost to repair or restore the property to the condition in which it was supposed to be delivered.[1739]

Typically, post-closing breach of contract claims involve allegations that the property was not in the condition in which it was warranted to be (*i.e.*, claims against a builder for failing to deliver the property in a good and workmanlike manner, claims against a seller for failing to have the roof properly repaired, etc.). In the case of new construction, such claims may be covered under the builder's warranty. In that event, the terms of the warranty should be followed.[1740]

§ 14.2.2 Specific Performance

As with pre-closing breaches of contract, specific performance is an available remedy for breach of contract after closing. Since the property would have already been conveyed, such claims would involve compelling the breaching party to perform some other act contracted for. For example, a buyer might bring a specific performance claim if the seller contracted to leave certain furniture in the house but failed to do so.

§ 14.2.3 The GAR Contract

The GAR Contract makes no specific references with regard to post-closing breach of contract claims. It does, however, contain a "survival clause" as follows: "The following shall survive the closing of this Agreement: (1) the obligation of a party to pay a real estate commission; (2) any warranty of title; (3) all representations of Seller regarding the Property set forth herein as a Special Stipulation; and (4) any obligations which the parties herein agree shall survive the closing or may be performed or fulfilled after the closing."[1741] The parties, therefore, need to be certain that any conditions or stipulations are fulfilled at the closing or that a new agreement is created to address any unfulfilled matters. The following example illustrates this point.

Assume that the sales contract contains a special stipulation that "seller shall replace the loose roof shingles identified on the attached inspection report, will replace the water heater, and, within 5 days after closing shall cause the rusty swing set to be removed from the back yard." The parties appear for closing and the seller presents an invoice from a roofer indicating that the shingles have been replaced. The seller does not provide any proof that the water heater has been replaced or that the swing set has been removed. After the closing the buyer discovers that neither of these matters have been addressed by the seller. Under the GAR Contract, the buyer can still maintain an action against the seller for the cost to remove the rusty swing set. This is because the sales contract clearly specified the parties' intent that the swing would be removed after closing. However, since the parties did not agree that the seller's obligation to replace the water heater would remain after the closing, this requirement is likely waived and the buyer could not successfully maintain an action against the seller.

The following special stipulation can be used to address matters that the parties wish to have survive the closing.

1739   *Ryland Group v. Daley*, 245 Ga.App. 496, 537 S.E.2d 732 (2000); *Rose Mill Homes, Inc. v. Michell*, 155 Ga.App. 808, 273 S.E.2d 211, (1980).

1740   *See* Chapter 15 regarding New Construction contracts and Chapter 14 regarding Georgia's Right to Repair Act.

1741   GAR Form F20.

Special Stipulation 301: Survival of Conditions

Notwithstanding anything else contained herein to the contrary, the parties specifically intend and agree that the following conditions and stipulations shall survive the closing until such time as said conditions or stipulations are performed or fulfilled:

_____.

What happens if the parties discover at the closing that certain obligations or conditions have not been met? Using the example above, what if the buyer learned at the closing that the seller had not replaced the water heater? In that event, the buyer has three options.

First, she can simply refuse to complete the closing on the basis that the seller has failed to fulfill the terms of the sales contract. Obviously, a buyer may be reluctant to do this if for no other reason than she may have no place to live if he can't move into the subject property.

A second option is for the buyer and seller to amend the contract or enter into a side agreement, whereby additional time is given during which to complete the unfulfilled contractual obligations. Such an agreement may look like the following.

Special Stipulation 302: Unfulfilled Conditions Discovered at Closing

The attached Purchase and Sale Agreement requires that the (Seller/Buyer) complete the following prior to closing: _____
___. For and in exchange of ten dollars and other good and valuable consideration, the receipt and sufficiency of which is hereby acknowledged, it is agreed that these items may be completed within _____ days after the closing. It is the intent of the parties that these items shall survive the closing until such time as said conditions or stipulations are performed or fulfilled

A third option is for the buyer and seller to enter into an amendment extending the closing date until the required obligation or condition is met.

§ 14.3 FRAUD

Many times a party to a contract believes that the other party had knowledge of a defect or unfavorable condition related to the property, which knowledge they lied about, did not share, or actively concealed. These circumstances can give rise to claims of fraud. As a practical matter, most fraud claims in real estate sales transactions are brought by the buyer and typically include claims against the seller and/or real estate broker(s).

§ 14.3.1 Elements Of Fraud

There are two general types of fraud recognized by our courts in Georgia: active fraud and passive fraud.

Active fraud requires proof that:

(a) the offending party lied or actively concealed a defect by taking steps to prevent the buyer from discovering the defect;

(b) the offending party intended to lie or was reckless as to the truth of the matter asserted;

(c) the lie was told to induce the buyer or seller to act (or not act, as the case may be);

(d) the buyer or seller justifiably relied on the misrepresentation; in other words, the buyer or seller could not have protected himself or herself against the fraud through the exercise of due diligence; and

(e) the lie was the proximate cause of the buyer or seller being damaged.[1742]

1742   *Gaultney v. Windham*, 99 Ga.App. 800, 109 S.E.2d 914 (1959); *Romedy v. Willett Lincoln Mercury, Inc.*, 136 Ga.App. 67, 220 S.E.2d 74 (1975); C.P.D. *Kim Co. v. National Car Rental Sys.*, 148 Ga.App. 756, 252 S.E. 665 (1979).

In most cases, it is difficult to prove all five of the elements of fraud. It is particularly difficult for buyers to show that the seller or broker had actual knowledge of the material fact.[1743] Another area of difficulty is that buyers must prove that they justifiably relied on the seller or real estate broker.[1744] Buyers are required to prove that they exercised "ordinary and reasonable care" or "due diligence" to protect themselves in order to be able to recover for fraud. Generally, this means that if the buyer could have discovered the problem if he had inspected the property or neighborhood, or noticed signs of the problem, and the seller did not prevent the inspection, then the buyer cannot recover.[1745]

With passive fraud, the party committing the fraud does not affirmatively tell a lie or actively conceal a defect. Instead, she simply possesses knowledge of a hidden or latent defect in the property and does not reveal what she knows.[1746]

§ 14.3.1.1 Cases Where Buyers' Fraud Claims Denied

The legal requirement that buyers first prove they exercised "due diligence" or "ordinary and reasonable care" to protect themselves against the fraud before they can succeed in an action for fraud is a difficult burden for many buyers to meet and thus prevents fraud claims against sellers and their real estate brokers. Courts will not allow buyers to merely rely on what they are told about the condition of the property; instead, buyers must independently investigate problems and defects of which they are aware. Cases where fraud claims were denied are discussed below.

In one Georgia case, a buyer sued the real estate agent with whom she was working (although the agent was representing the seller) for fraud, alleging that the agent concealed that the house was subject to flooding.[1747] The buyer inspected the house several times before closing and noticed a creek adjacent to the property. She also noticed that the basement was dank and smelled musty. The buyer asked the agent whether the property had flooding problems. The agent allegedly denied that there had been previous flooding. Moreover, the surveyor reported that the property was not in a flood hazard area. The trial court ruled in favor of the agent because the buyer could not prove that she justifiably relied on any representations. The buyer appealed, and the court held that the buyer was unable to establish the five elements necessary to maintain an action for fraud. The court noted that the buyer neglected to adequately investigate the risk of flooding, in spite of her many inspections of the property and her ability to check with the county records or her homeowner's insurance agent. Without such an investigation, the court did not believe the buyer could establish the fourth element of fraud, that her reliance on alleged false representations was justifiable. The court emphasized that the law does not offer relief to buyers who make no attempt to ascertain the condition of the property.

A buyer in another case raised similar issues of fraud where the buyer purchased a dilapidated, vacant, residential property for $25,000.[1748] The buyer inspected the property twice with a real estate licensee working with her but representing the seller, and understood that she needed to make substantial repairs. The sales contract, which was prepared by the licensee, stated that the house was being sold "as is," without a termite inspection, and that purchaser did not rely on any representations made by seller or his agents. During her inspections the buyer made no attempt to inspect the attic. After the closing, she discovered structural damage in the attic caused by a fire which had occurred prior to the sale. She stated that, using a flashlight, she could see the damage through the access hole to the attic. The buyer sued the seller and the listing and selling agents, claiming they fraudulently induced her to enter the sales

---

1743 *Lively v. Garnick*, 160 Ga.App. 591, 287 S.E.2d 553 (1981), *cert. denied*; *Wilhite v. Mays*, 140 Ga.App. 816, 232 S.E.2d 141 (1976), *aff'd*, 239 Ga. 31, 235 S.E.2d 532 (1977); *Ainsworth v. Perreault*, 254 Ga.App. 470, 563 S.E. 2d 135 (2002); *Bircoll v. Rosenthal*, 267 Ga.App. 431, 600 S.E.2d 388 (2004); *Resnick v. Meybohm Realty Inc.*, 269 Ga.App. 486, 604 S.E.2d 536 (2004); *Ikola v. Schoene*, 264 Ga.App. 338, 590 S.E.2d 750.

1744 *Real Estate Int'l, Inc. v. Buggay*, 220 Ga.App. 449, 469 S.E.2d 242 (1996), *cert. denied*; *Hill v. Century 21 Max Stancil Realty*, 187 Ga.App. 754, 371 S.E.2d 217 (1988).

1745 A buyer may be able to recover if it can be shown that the seller had "special knowledge" about the alleged defect that would require disclosure. *Brookshire v. Digby*, 224 Ga.App. 512, 481 S.E.2d 250 (1997).

1746 *Fincher v. Bergeron*, 193 Ga.App. 256, 387 S.E.2d 371 (1989), *cert. denied*; *Wilhite v. Mays*, 140 Ga.App. 816, 232 S.E.2d 141 (1976), *aff'd*, 239 Ga. 31, 235 S.E.2d 532 (1977).

1747 *Copeland v. Home Sav. of America, F.A.*, 209 Ga.App. 173, 433 S.E.2d 327 (1993).

1748 *Ben Farmer Realty Co. v. Woodard*, 212 Ga.App. 74, 441 S.E.2d 421 (1994), *cert. denied*.

contract by passively concealing the fire damage. The agents claimed they had no knowledge of the fire damage. The court held that in cases of passive concealment the buyer must prove that the concealment of the defect was fraudulent or deceitful, including evidence that the defect could not be discovered by the due diligence of the buyer and that the seller or agent was aware of the defect and did not disclose it. Since the buyer had failed to use due diligence to discover the fire damage, her claim for fraud was barred.

In another case, the buyers sued the sellers, the sellers' agent and the broker for fraud, conspiracy to defraud, breach of contract and violation of BRRETA.[1749] The buyers and sellers had entered into a contract of sale which contained a disclaimer provision and an "entire agreement" clause. The contract also incorporated by reference the seller's disclosure statement. The buyers knew that the house they were contracting for had a synthetic stucco exterior and that such houses were more likely to attract termites. Before the parties signed the sales contract the sellers gave the buyers a Seller's Disclosure Statement. The Statement referred to past and present termite damage, but stated that the damage had been taken care of. It also stated that there were problems with the walkways and water intrusion, but that there had been no water in the basement since 1989. After the parties signed the contract, the sellers' agent sent a detailed termite treatment history report to the buyers' agent. The report stated that existing conditions of the property might lead to future infestation. The buyers also conducted a professional visual inspection, which revealed possible water intrusion and stucco repairs. However, the buyers did not conduct a stucco or termite inspection. Just before the closing, the sellers obtained a detailed infestation report, which the buyers signed at closing.

The court held that the buyers' claim against the sellers for misrepresentation must fail because the buyers had affirmed the contract and were therefore bound by the disclaimer and merger clause. As for the claim against the agent and the broker, the court ruled that there was no evidence that the agent knew about the home's defects apart from what was stated in the Seller's Disclosure Statement. As for the claim against the seller, the court found no evidence that the sellers knew of any current problems with the property. Although the buyers' inspection listed problems with the stucco exterior and water intrusion, the buyers did not conduct a separate stucco or termite inspection. Therefore, the buyers could not claim justifiable reliance on the property disclosure statement.

In yet another case, the buyer sued claiming the property had been advertised as being 1.5 acres but was actually only 0.8 acres.[1750] The court ruled that even though the seller misstated the true acreage, this did not relieve the buyer of his obligation to independently confirm the size of the property. This could have been accomplished, for example, by looking at a plat or survey. In still another case, the buyers contracted to purchase a new home in a subdivision that was "the same house on Lot 74 as on Lot 65," which was the model home. However, the different lot size allowed a smaller foundation, which caused some design changes and a reduction in area. The buyers were informed of that the foundations were different and the rooms had to be redesigned. However, they did not take any steps to discover the change in area. In their claim against the broker for fraud in failing to disclose the reduced area, the court stated that since the buyers knew about the differences, the buyers were required to exercise due diligence to determine area of their redesigned property before relying on the representations of the broker.

In a case involving an "as is" clause, the Court of Appeals defined the scope of a broker's liability in the sale of a house with substantial defects. The case involved a buyer who decided to purchase a house "as is," despite the fact that he had knowledge that the roof was leaking, water was running down the walls, the carpet was mildewed, the fireplace had moisture all over it, and the house was in general disrepair. Prior to closing the buyer hired a home inspector to inspect the house. The home inspector's report found that the house was built on a sloping lot with inadequate grade and that there was water in the crawl space. While the inspector recommended that a drainage specialist examine the property, the buyer did not heed the inspector's advice. The listing agent allegedly informed the buyer that the water under the house was run-off from a hill in the backyard, the drainage problems could be repaired, and the house was structurally

---

1749   *Bircoll v. Rosenthal*, 267 Ga.App. 431, 600 S.E.2d 388 (2004).

1750   *Simmons v. Pilkenton*, 230 Ga.App. 900, 497 S.E.2d 613 (1998).

sound. However, the buyer was aware that prior repairs by the sellers had not been successful in correcting the drainage problems. At closing, the buyer was told that the termite inspection was not completed because the termite inspector could not get into the crawl space due to flooding. The house eventually closed but the buyer later discovered that the water problems stemmed from an underground spring beneath the house. The buyer sued all parties to the transaction for fraud and negligent misrepresentation.[1751]

The Court of Appeals determined that the buyer's reliance upon the alleged misrepresentations regarding the water problems was not justified as a matter of law, stating that the buyer failed to exercise due diligence to protect himself in light of evidence that would have caused most people to investigate further. The court emphasized that the law does not afford relief to one who does not use ordinary means of information to protect himself. It should be noted that under the 2000 revisions to BRRETA, the agent could also avoid liability by disclosing to the buyer the source of their information, which in this case was the seller.[1752] The GAR Broker's Information Disclosure form[1753] should be used whenever the broker has been asked to research or investigate information on behalf of his client. The Disclosure form provides a statement of the question asked, the answer, and the source of the information. So long as the source of the information is disclosed and the broker did not know that the information was incorrect at the time it was given, there will be no liability.

A recent decision by the Georgia Supreme Court suggests that the inclusion of an entire agreement clause or merger clause in a contract severely limits the ability of a plaintiff buyer to assert a fraud claim against a seller.[1754] In that case, the buyers of condominiums brought an action against the developers and brokers alleging, among other things, fraud and negligent misrepresentation. The buyers claimed that they purchased their units based on the developer's advertisements promising "spectacular city views" and statements by the brokers that any future development surrounding the building would be low-rise to mid-rise office buildings. However, at the time the buyers purchased their units, the developers had already undertaken plans to build a 46-story high-rise across the street. The crux of the buyer's argument was that they should not be bound by the terms of their agreements because the brokers and developers promised them spectacular city views. Nevertheless, each purchaser signed an agreement containing the following: (i) "the views from and the natural light available to the Unit may change over time due to, among other circumstances, additional development and the removal or addition of landscaping"; (ii) "oral representations cannot be relied upon as correctly stating the representations of seller"; (iii) "neither party has relied upon any representation or warranty not set forth in the Agreement"; (iv) and a comprehensive entire agreement or merger clause stating:

> "24. ENTIRE AGREEMENT: This agreement contains the entire agreement between the parties hereto. No agent, representation, salesman, or officer of the parties hereto has authority to make, or has made, any statements, agreements, or representations, either oral or in writing, in connection herewith, modifying, adding to, or changing the terms and conditions hereof and neither party has relied upon any representations or warranty not set forth in this Agreement. No dealings between the parties or customs shall be permitted to contradict, vary, add to, or modify the terms hereof."[1755]

The Georgia Supreme Court held that the statements relied upon by the buyers directly contradicted the terms of the written agreement and such statements could not form the basis of a fraud claim for the purposes of cancelling or rescinding a contract.[1756] The Court explained that in any case alleging fraud, the buyers are required to prove that

---

1751   *Real Estate Int'l, Inc. v. Buggay*, 220 Ga.App. 449, 469 S.E.2d 242 (1996).

1752   O.C.G.A. § 10-6A-5; O.C.G.A. § 10-6A-7.

1753   GAR Form F57.

1754   *Novare Group, Inc. v. Sarif*, 290 Ga. 186, 718 S.E.2d 304 (2011).

1755   *Novare Group, Inc. v. Sarif*, 290 Ga. 186, 718 S.E.2d 304 (2011).

1756   *Novare Group, Inc. v. Sarif*, 290 Ga. 186, 718 S.E.2d 304 (2011).

their reliance on any fraudulent representations were justified or reasonable. If an agreement contains a valid merger or entire agreement clause, the reliance on any statement outside the agreement cannot be reasonable because it directly contradicts the express terms of the agreement.[1757] Ultimately, the purchasers were not entitled to rescission as a remedy because the written terms of the agreement expressly contradicted the oral representations relied on to bring the claim.

As such, when a purchaser affirms an agreement that contains a properly drafted entire agreement or merger clause, she is prohibited from asserting reliance on representations that are not part of the agreement, except in cases where there was fraud in procuring a party's signature to the agreement.[1758]

Fraud that allegedly prevented a party from reading the contract to procure his or her signature would allow a buyer to rescind an agreement.[1759] For example, if the buyers in the present case alleged that the brokers or developers tried to prevent them from reading the terms of the agreement before they signed them and thus the buyers relied only on the broker's and developer's oral representations about the spectacular views, the buyers would be able to rescind the agreement.[1760]

This case is an important decision for sellers, developers and real estate brokers because had the case been decided in favor of the buyers, it would have opened the door to endless claims by buyers alleging that they relied on verbal or oral representations contrary to the written terms of the agreement. Fortunately, the Georgia Supreme Court reaffirmed its long standing position on disputes of this type. The entire agreement clause is discussed further in § 14.3.2: Remedies for Fraud Claims Against Seller.

Here is a quick reference to other cases where the buyers' fraud claims were denied: buyers could not claim fraud based on misrepresentations that the recreational amenities were included in planned community when they did not attempt to independently verify the boundaries of the property;[1761] buyer who made no attempt to discover the boundaries of the property could not justifiably rely on a misrepresentation by the seller regarding those boundaries;[1762] buyer could not claim against a broker for misrepresentations regarding financing on an assumed loan because the buyer failed to exercise ordinary and reasonable care to independently confirm the accuracy of the information;[1763] buyer could not assert claim against seller/broker for misrepresentations regarding zoning because buyer failed to exercise ordinary and reasonable care by inquiring about zoning himself;[1764] buyer's failure to examine title barred fraud claim for portion of property previously sold to Department of Transportation.[1765]

§ 14.3.1.2 Cases Where Sellers Found Liable For Fraud

The seller will be liable for fraud if the buyer is able to prove the five requisite elements. One case involved a four-year old house equipped with an inadequate septic tank that overflowed during rainy weather.[1766] Whenever it rained heavily, surface water would collect under the house, which caused it to deteriorate. The septic tank and drainage lines were inadequate, resulting in an overflow of raw sewage from the septic tank into the front yard of the home after a heavy rain. The court held that the buyer could not have discovered these defects by the exercise of due diligence at any time except after a heavy rain. The seller, however, was aware of the defects and failed to disclose them. The court held that the seller is obligated to disclose situations where he has special knowledge not apparent to the buyer and

---

1757   *Novare Group, Inc. v. Sarif*, 290 Ga. 186, 718 S.E.2d 304 (2011).

1758   *Novare Group, Inc. v. Sarif*, 290 Ga. 186, 718 S.E.2d 304 (2011).

1759   *Novare Group, Inc. v. Sarif*, 290 Ga. 186, 718 S.E.2d 304 (2011).

1760   *Novare Group, Inc. v. Sarif*, 290 Ga. 186, 718 S.E.2d 304 (2011).

1761   *Brakebill v. Hicks*, 259 Ga. 849, 388 S.E.2d 695 (1990).

1762   *Crawford v. Williams*, 258 Ga. 806, 375 S.E.2d 223 (1989).

1763   *Bennett v. Clark*, 192 Ga.App. 698, 385 S.E.2d 780 (1989.)

1764   *Hill v. Century 21 Max Stancil Realty*, 187 Ga.App. 754, 371 S.E.2d 217 (1988).

1765   *Jim Royer Realty v. Moreira*, 184 Ga.App. 848, 363 S.E.2d 10, *cert. denied.*

1766   *Wilhite v. Mays*, 140 Ga.App. 816, 232 S.E.2d 141 (1976), *aff'd*, 239 Ga. 31, 235 S.E.2d 532 (1977).

is aware that the buyer is acting under a misapprehension as to facts which would be important and would probably affect his decision in the purchase of the property. Therefore, the court found that the seller was liable to the buyer for fraud by "passively concealing" defects.

In another passive concealment case, the court held that the seller was liable for failing to inform the buyers of several concealed defects in the house which were not noticeable upon a reasonable inspection.[1767] The buyer's inspection could not have revealed the defects, which existed in the utility systems and the structural integrity of the dwelling house and pool house. The seller had actual knowledge of all of the defects and supervised a major renovation project on the main house. Moreover, the defects in the property were not the result of typical wear and tear, and none were noticeable on a visual examination.

Another seller was found responsible for fraudulently concealing numerous structural and hidden defects in a house which he built and in which he had lived for 12 years.[1768] In that case, the seller failed to reveal that the house had an unusual framing and roof structure which was concealed by a drop ceiling. The seller urged the buyer to go look at other houses he was currently building to see the framing and type of work, quality of materials, and workmanship present in the house the buyer was purchasing. However, none of the houses to which he referred the buyer were constructed in the same way. The seller also lied about the age of the well pump and about previous termite infestation and damage. The court found that the seller acted with the intention of misleading the buyer and that the buyer could not have discovered the defects by exercising due diligence.

An example of an active fraud case involved a house which was infested with termites.[1769] The seller had completely rebuilt the property because it was destroyed by a fire. The seller acted as a general contractor in the renovation, and the property was his personal residence for several years, so the seller was very familiar with the condition of the property. The seller gave the buyers a Seller's Property Disclosure Statement in which he stated that he was not aware of any damage due to termites or structural defects in the home. The buyers' inspection did not reveal any termite damage. A few months after the closing, the buyers saw termites swarming in the house and began to investigate further. They called the inspector who had conducted the initial inspection back to the property for another inspection. He found putty and paint that had been used to conceal holes and gaps in the wood caused by termite infestation. The court held that the seller was liable for fraud by concealing the termite-damaged wood.

§ 14.3.2 Remedies For Fraud Claims Against Seller

When a buyer alleges fraud against a seller and/or real estate broker, the buyer has various options to address the wrong. However, the buyer must choose which legal tool to use. This choice is referred to as an "election of remedies."[1770] First, the buyer may rescind the contract upon the discovery of fraud and, after offering to restore any benefits received under the contract, sue in tort for recovery of the purchase price and any additional damages resulting from the fraud.[1771]

If a party chooses to rescind the contract, she must tender notice of rescission prior to filing a lawsuit.[1772] The rationale behind this requirement is that the party who allegedly committed the fraud should have the opportunity to redress the wrong before they are served with a suit for rescission by the buyer.[1773] For example, if a buyer bought a condominium under the impression that it was going to have "spectacular views" but later found out that the views

---

1767 *Fincher v. Bergeron*, 193 Ga.App. 256, 387 S.E.2d 371 (1989), *cert. denied*.

1768 *Brookshire v. Digby*, 224 Ga.App. 512, 481 S.E.2d 250, 97 FCDR 453 (1997).

1769 *Browning v. Stocks*, 265 Ga.App. 803, 595 S.E.2d 642 (2004).

1770 *Hightower v. Century 21 Farish Realty*, 214 Ga.App. 522, 448 S.E.2d 271 (1994)

1771 *Ben Farmer Realty Co. v. Woodard*, 212 Ga.App. 74, 441 S.E.2d 421 (1994) *cert. denied*; *Price v. Mitchell*, 154 Ga.App. 523, 268 S.E.2d 743 (1980), *cert. denied*.

1772 *Novare Group, Inc. v. Sarif*, 290 Ga. 186, 718 S.E.2d 304 (2011).

1773 *Novare Group, Inc. v. Sarif*, 290 Ga. 186, 718 S.E.2d 304 (2011).

were going to be blocked by a high-rise building, the buyer would need to try to rescind the agreement before filing suit. The notice of rescission may not be offer simultaneously with a notice of filing suit.[1774] A party who fails to give notice of rescission will be deemed to have affirmed the contract and any fraud claim will be barred.[1775]

A buyer seeking rescission must also offer to restore to the seller any benefits received by virtue of the contract.[1776] This normally means that the buyer must offer to deed the property back to the seller. However, the buyer must also offer to restore any other benefits received under the contract. For example, if the buyer received a new television as part of the purchase of the property, the buyer would need to offer to return this as well.

In addition, upon learning of the fraud, the buyer is prohibited from making any improvements to the property before offering the property back to the seller. Therefore, if a buyer is seeking to rescind his or her purchase of a single-family home due to some alleged fraud of the seller, the buyer should not paint a bedroom a different color, add wallpaper, plant addition trees in the yard or making any other improvements or modifications to the property. Such actions would reflect the buyer's intention to keep the property and may be a basis for a court to deny the claim for rescission.

The buyer's other remedy is to affirm the contract upon discovery of the fraud and to sue for damages resulting from the fraud.[1777] Unlike the first remedy, this remedy allows the buyer to keep the "fruits" of the contract.[1778] The buyer's damages would be "the difference in the value of the property as sold to him and its value if the property had been the same as it was represented to be."[1779]

§ 14.3.2.1 Merger (Or Entire Agreement) Clause

If the buyer elects to affirm the contract, the buyer will generally be bound by the terms of the contract, including any "merger" (or entire agreement) clause. This type of provision is contained in most real estate agreements. An entire agreement or merger clause operates as a defense for the party being sued by preventing the other party from relying on representations not contained the written agreement as the basis of their fraud claim.[1780] However, even if this clause is contained in an agreement, it does not prevent a party from bringing a fraud claim arising from representations explicitly stated in the contract.[1781] Typically this clause provides that the purchase and sale agreement is the entire agreement of the parties and that no representations outside those contained in the written contract are being relied upon by any party. The GAR Contract includes a merger clause which provides that:

> This Agreement constitutes the sole and entire agreement between all of the parties, supersedes all of their prior written and verbal agreements and shall be binding upon the parties and their successors, heirs and permitted assigns. No representation, promise or inducement not included in this Agreement shall be binding upon any party hereto.[1782]

The effect of this clause is to merge all agreements between the parties during negotiations into the single written contract. It also excludes any "representation, promise, or inducement" that the seller or broker may have made during the contract negotiations that are not expressly written into the contract.[1783] A properly drafted entire agreement

---

1774   *Novare Group, Inc. v. Sarif*, 290 Ga. 186, 718 S.E.2d 304 (2011).

1775   *Ben Farmer Realty Co. v. Woodard*, 212 Ga.App. 74, 441 S.E.2d 421 (1994) *cert. denied.*

1776   *Novare Group, Inc. v. Sarif*, 290 Ga. 186, 718 S.E.2d 304 (2011).

1777   *Ben Farmer Realty Co. v. Woodard*, 212 Ga.App. 74, 441 S.E.2d 421 (1994) *cert. denied; Price v. Mitchell*, 154 Ga.App. 523, 268 S.E.2d 743 (1980), *cert. denied; Weaver v. ABC Bus, Inc.*, 191 Ga.App. 614, 382 S.E.2d 380 (1989), *cert. denied.*

1778   *Tuttle v. Stovall*, 134 Ga. 325, 67 S.E. 806 (1910); *Carpenter v. Curtis*, 196 Ga.App. 234, 395 S.E.2d 653 (1990).

1779   *Ben Farmer Realty Co. v. Woodard*, 212 Ga.App. 74, 441 S.E.2d 421 (1994), *cert. denied.*

1780   *Novare Group, Inc. v. Sarif*, 290 Ga. 186, 718 S.E.2d 304 (2011).

1781   *Novare Group, Inc. v. Sarif*, 290 Ga. 186, 718 S.E.2d 304 (2011).

1782   GAR Form F20.

1783   *American Demolition, Inc. v. Hapeville Hotel Ltd. Partnership*, 202 Ga.App. 107, 413 S.E.2d 749 (1991), *cert. denied; Carpenter v. Curtis*, 196 Ga.App. 234, 395 S.E.2d 653 (1990).

or merger clause will bar an action of fraud on the basis that this clause prohibits the plaintiff from relying on representations made not contained in the parties' final written agreement.

In a case where the contract did not incorporate the seller's property disclosure statement, the court held that the "entire agreement" clause in the contract precluded the statements made by the sellers on the property disclosure statement.[1784] The GAR Contract specifically incorporates the Seller's Property Disclosure Statement.

A clarification to the rule regarding rescission and merger clauses should be made to avoid any confusion. The Georgia Court of Appeals has held that affirming a contract that contains an "entire agreement" clause will not necessarily bar a fraud claim based upon active or passive[1785] concealment. When a buyer affirms a fraudulently induced contract claiming that the seller actively or passively concealed damage or defects in the purchased property, the seller may not use the existence of an entire agreement clause in the contract as a defense to the suit.[1786] In one case, the seller actively covered up extensive termite damage with wood putty and paint. No seller's disclosure statement was incorporated into the sales contact, which contained an entire agreement clause.[1787] The seller argued, unsuccessfully, that the presence of the clause barred the buyer's fraud claim because the buyer failed to rescind the contract. The court disagreed holding that the seller was liable to the buyer based on his affirmative acts of fraud, and the merger language in the contract did not act as a bar to such a claim.[1788]

§ 14.3.3 Remedies For Fraud Claims Against Brokers And Agents

Georgia courts have made it clear that the "entire agreement" clause applies in a malpractice claim against the broker in the same way it does in a fraud action to exclude any representations made outside the contract. If the buyer elects to affirm rather than rescind a contract containing a merger clause, the buyer will generally not be able to rely on any statement that the broker or agent has made as a basis for a malpractice claim.

This is illustrated in a case where the buyers brought a professional malpractice action against a real estate agent who represented the seller after they discovered that their house was infested with bats.[1789] The buyers argued that the seller and the listing broker knew about the problem and failed to disclose it to the buyers. There was evidence that the broker knew something about a bat problem, although he apparently did not know how severe the problem was. The buyers argued that they were suing for malpractice and all they had to prove was that (1) the listing broker had a duty to disclose, (2) the listing broker breached the duty by failing to carry out the duty according to the required standard of care and (3) the breach caused injury to the buyers.

The Georgia Court of Appeals stated that in a fraud claim the buyer has an election of remedies: to rescind the contract or affirm the contract and sue for damages resulting from the fraud. A fraud claim would be barred if the buyer affirmed the contract. The reason was because the buyer needed to prove that he relied on the misrepresentations, which would be impossible since the "entire agreement" clause provided that the buyer had not relied on any representations not in the contract. The buyer argued that reliance is not an element required to prove a malpractice claim and the presence of the merger clause should not bar a malpractice claim. The court rejected this argument, holding that a malpractice claim was the same thing as a fraud claim and required the same proof as a claim for fraud.

This rationale was followed in a case where the buyer brought a breach of duty claim against her own agent. Like the previous case, the Court of Appeals held that the "entire agreement" clause prevented the buyer from proving that she relied on misrepresentations made outside the contract and therefore barred her claim of breach of professional duty.[1790]

1784   *Ainsworth v. Perreault*, 254 Ga.App. 470, 563 S.E.2d. 135 (2002).

1785   *Reininger v. O'Neill*, WL 2434755 (June 2012).

1786   *Reininger v. O'Neill*, WL 2434755 (June 2012).

1787   *Browning v. Stocks*, 265 Ga.App. 803, 595 S.E.2d 642 (2004).

1788   *Browning v. Stocks*, 265 Ga.App. 803, 595 S.E.2d 642 (2004).

1789   *Pennington v. Braxley*, 224 Ga.App. 344, 480 S.E.2d 357 (1997), *cert. denied*.

1790   *Resnick v. Meybohm Realty Inc.*, 269 Ga.App. 486, 604 S.E.2d 536 (2004).

In another case, buyers brought a malpractice claim against their own agent and the sellers for fraudulently concealing a water problem in the property.[1791] The buyer had noticed a sump pump in the basement when she first saw the property. Her agent allegedly told her that she would never have to worry about flooding because of the pump, urged the buyer to accept the property "as-is," and discouraged her from conducting a professional inspection. The agent allegedly had also been given a Seller's Property Disclosure Statement indicating a prior water leak, but the agent did not provide this document to her client.

The Court of Appeals held that the "entire agreement" clause in the contract did not bar the buyer's breach of duty claim against her agent. Notably this case was decided based upon the pre-2000 revisions to BRRETA.[1792] As amended, BRRETA provides that no broker or agent will be held liable for failures to disclose without proof that the broker or agent committed fraud.

§ 14.4 LIMITING LIABILITY OF BROKERS

§ 14.4.1 Disclaimers In General

Exculpatory clauses, also called disclaimer provisions, provide that one party to a contract is relieved from liability for his own actions, even if the other party suffers harm as a result of those actions. With certain exceptions, disclaimer clauses are generally valid and binding and parties can usually limit their liability through carefully worded contracts.[1793]

It is general law in Georgia that parties are free to contract about any subject matter, on any terms, unless prohibited by statute, public policy, or if injury to the public interest clearly appears.[1794] As a result, exculpatory clauses in contracts in Georgia are generally valid and binding for matters involving breach of contract and negligence. However, public policy will not permit one to avoid the consequences of willful or wanton misconduct such as claims of fraud or gross negligence.[1795]

§ 14.4.2 How Disclaimer Language In GAR Contracts Protects Brokers

The disclaimer language in the GAR Contracts helps protect brokers against many types of claims, including breach of contract, negligence, fraud and misrepresentation, and claims under BRRETA.[1796] This protection is accomplished in several ways.

First, the disclaimer identifies areas in which the broker lacks expertise. This is a fairly inclusive list and includes "any matter which could have been revealed through a survey, title search, Official Georgia Wood Infestation Report, inspection by a professional home inspector or construction expert, utility bill review, an appraisal, inspection by an environmental engineering inspector, consulting governmental officials or a review of this Agreement and transaction by an attorney, financial planner, mortgage consultant or tax planner. This language would make it difficult, for example, for a disgruntled buyer who bought a house that turns out to be infested with termites to argue that the brokers involved in the transaction were negligent in not finding the termite infestation since the contract provides that this information could have been revealed through an Official Georgia Wood Infestation Report.

Second, the GAR disclaimer language provides that the buyer and seller should seek independent expert advice regarding any matter of concern to them relative to the property and the purchase and sale agreement. This would include any of the listed items about which the broker is not an expert. This language was developed to comply with

---

1791 *Ikola v. Schoene*, 264 Ga.App. 338, 590 S.E. 2d 750 (2003).

1792 O.C.G.A. § 10-6A-1 *et seq.*

1793 *West Side Loan Ofc. v. Electro-Protective Corp.*, 167 Ga.App. 520, 306 S.E.2d 686 (1983).

1794 *Hall v. Gardens Services, Inc.*, 174 Ga.App. 856, 332 S.E.2d 3 (1985)

1795 *Id.*

1796 A full discussion of the law on BRRETA is set out in Chapter 19 of this book.

the real estate broker's obligations under BRRETA to advise buyers and sellers "to obtain expert advice as to material matters which are beyond the expertise of the broker."[1797] Each of the items listed in the disclaimer are within the expertise of a professional other than the broker, be it a real estate attorney, surveyor, accountant, appraiser, engineer, or loan officer.

Finally, the GAR disclaimer provision has proven to be particularly effective at defeating claims against brokers. For example, in order to sue a broker for fraud or misrepresentation a party must show, among other things, that she relied upon some misrepresentation of the broker and was justified in doing so. The disclaimer language makes it more difficult to prove justifiable reliance, since the parties are acknowledging in the contract that they have not relied upon any advice or representations of the broker beyond what is included in the agreement. Brokers have successfully made this specific argument in Georgia courts to defend against claims of fraud and misrepresentation.[1798]

In addition to claims for fraud and misrepresentation, buyers and sellers can also bring claims against real estate brokers based on BRRETA. Specifically, BRRETA provides that brokers timely disclose the following: (a) all adverse material facts pertaining to the physical condition of the property and improvements excluding facts which could have been discovered by the party upon a reasonably diligent inspection of the property, and (b) and all material facts pertaining to existing adverse physical conditions in the immediate neighborhood within one mile from the property.[1799] BRRETA also states that the law "may serve as a basis for private rights of action and defenses by sellers, buyers, landlords, tenants, and real estate brokers."[1800] The acknowledgment by buyers and sellers in the GAR Contract that they are not relying on any statements of the brokers provides the broker with additional protection against claims filed under the above sections of BRRETA. It would be difficult for parties to argue that they were damaged by false statements upon which they contractually acknowledged they have not relied.[1801]

In a 1994 case, the Georgia Court of Appeals relied on the disclaimer language in a GAR Contract when it affirmed a trial court decision in favor of a listing broker against a buyer's claim for fraud and misrepresentation involving information provided to the buyer about a road widening project.[1802]

In this case, a selling agent was working with Florida residents in the purchase of a home in metro Atlanta. The buyers became interested in a house on a lot which backed up to Medlock Bridge Road. The buyers asked the selling agent to inquire with the proper highway authority as to whether the road behind the house was going to be widened. The buyers, one of whom was a licensed real estate agent, specifically asked their selling agent not to rely on the subdivision agents for this information.

The selling agent informed the buyers that she made the appropriate inquiries and that the road behind the subdivision was not going to be widened. The selling agent did not tell the buyers that she obtained this information from the subdivision agents and not the Department of Transportation. The buyers bought the house, and the road behind the house was subsequently widened. The buyers discovered that this information was available prior to the time they contracted to buy the house. The buyers sued the selling broker for, among other things, fraud and misrepresentation.

The Georgia Court of Appeals found that the buyers' fraud claim failed because the disclaimer language in the sales contract provided that the buyers had not relied upon the advice or representations by their broker or its salespersons relative to, among other things, the purchase and ownership of the property. Therefore, the buyers could not show that they justifiably relied upon their broker's statement either.

1797   O.C.G.A. §§ 10-6A-7, 10-6A-5.

1798   *Hanlon v. Thornton*, 218 Ga.App. 500, 462 S.E.2d 154 (1995); *Allen v. RE/MAX North Atlanta, Inc.*, 213 Ga.App. 644, 445 S.E.2d 774 (1994).

1799   O.C.G.A. § 10-6A-5; O.C.G.A. § 10-6A-7.

1800   O.C.G.A. § 10-6A-2.

1801   *See*, however, § 14.1.4 on rescission.

1802   *Allen v. RE/MAX North Atlanta, Inc.*, 213 Ga.App. 644, 445 S.E.2d 774 (1994).

§ 14.4.3 Limitation On Duties And Liability Of Brokers

In addition to the disclaimer language, there is language in the agency section of the GAR Contract which provides that the brokers owe no duties other than what is contained in BRRETA and their brokerage engagements. The GAR Exclusive Seller Listing Agreement and the Exclusive Buyer Brokerage Agreement provide further protection.[1803] Specifically, these documents limit the broker's liability, in the case of breach of contract or negligence, to the amount of commission actually received by the broker less any amount retained or paid to any other broker. While this type of provision has not yet been tested in any appellate court involving real estate brokers, it should withstand scrutiny absent fraud since similar provisions in architect's contracts[1804] and property inspector's contracts have been upheld.[1805] The Georgia Association of REALTORS® recently developed a new form agreement for brokers working with a customer for the first time. The GAR Agreement To Work With Buyer As A Customer[1806] form includes an exculpatory clause limiting the liability of the broker working with the buyer as a customer to the commission the broker is actually paid in a transaction, or if no commission is paid, then to a sum of $100.[1807]

This form is an alternative to the notice to buyers that already appears in the GAR Customer Acknowledgement[1808] form that can be used to disclose that the selling broker is working with the buyer as a customer and is not representing the buyer.[1809] This GAR form does not include such language because it is a unilateral notice rather than an agreement between the parties.

The new GAR Agreement To Work With Buyer As A Customer form gives much greater protection to selling brokers than the previous notice and should be used whenever possible.

§ 14.4.4 When Disclaimer Is Deleted Or Modified

There is probably little that real estate brokers can do to prevent a buyer or seller from deleting all or a portion of the disclaimer language from the GAR Contract. The buyer and seller are free to include in their contract any provision they desire with respect to the purchase and sale of property. Real estate brokers are obligated to timely present all offers to buy and sell property even when they include provisions that are not to their liking.[1810]

If all or part of the disclaimer language has been deleted from the contract, the broker should inquire why the particular language was struck. If there is a representation a party is relying upon and the broker has in fact made such a representation, the party and the broker may agree to allow the specific representation to be included in the contract as a special stipulation and otherwise preserve the language of the disclaimer. If a party is insistent on striking the entire disclaimer section, the broker can protect herself somewhat by providing the party with a written statement disclaiming the areas in which she lacks special expertise and stating that she has not made any representations upon which she intended the party to rely. Alternatively, the broker can simply refuse to participate in the transaction or sign the contract.

§ 14.5 LIMITING LIABILITY OF BUILDERS

While exculpatory provisions or disclaimers are generally enforceable in Georgia courts,[1811] there are certain types of exculpatory provisions that are specifically prohibited under state law. Builders, for example, are prevented

---

1803 GAR Forms F1 and F4.

1804 *Precision Planning, Inc. v. Richmark Communities, Inc.*, 298 Ga.App. 78, 679 S.E.2d 43 (2009).

1805 *Brainard v. McKinney*, 220 Ga.App. 329, 469 S.E.2d 441 (1996).

1806 GAR Form F15.

1807 GAR Form F15.

1808 GAR Form F6.

1809 GAR Form F6.

1810 O.C.G.A. § 43-40-25(b)(19).

1811 *Lanier At McEver, L.P. v. Planners And Engineers Collaborative, Inc.*, 284 GA. 204, 663 S.E.2d 240 (2008).

from limiting their liability in construction contracts in certain situations. Builders have a legal duty to complete construction in a good and work like manner. For this reason, builders cannot, by contract, exculpate themselves from potential liability for shoddy work, building code violations, negligent construction or other liabilities arising out of unfinished products.[1812] On this point, the Official Code of Georgia provides that:

> "A covenant, promise, agreement or understanding in or in connection with or collateral to a agreement or agreement relative to the construction, alteration, repair, or maintenance of a building structure, appurtenances, and appliances, including moving, demolition, and excavating connected therewith, purporting to require that one party to such contract or agreement shall indemnify, hold harmless, insure or defend the other party to the contract or other named indemnitee, including its, his or her officers, agents, or employees, against liability or claims for damages, losses, or expenses, including attorney fees, arising out of bodily injury to persons, death or damage to property caused by or resulting from the sole negligence of the indemnitee, or its, his or her officers, agents, or employees, is against public policy and void and unenforceable."[1813]

Therefore, not only does this provision limit the use of an exculpatory clause or disclaimer in residential homebuilding contracts, it also limits the use of such a provision in a contract to construct, repair, alter or maintain any type of building structure. This prohibition has been interpreted to prevent a building contractor, subcontractor or owner from contracting away legal liability for accidents caused solely by that person's negligence.[1814]

To protect themselves, builders may use one of three approaches. The first is to try to ensure against the risk of construction defect claims by providing the buyer with some type of third-party home warranty. HBW's 2-10 warranty is an example of this type of warranty. While this approach does not eliminate the builder's potential risk, it does give a buyer another deep pocket to pursue in the event of a claim.

The second approach is to create realistic expectations in the purchase and sale agreement as to the quality of construction the buyer will be getting for the money she is paying. Plaintiff's lawyers are quick to try to characterize less expensive building products and systems when they do not perform as well as expensive building products and materials as examples of negligent construction. So, for example, let's say that a builder uses an inexpensive siding that has a much shorter life expectancy than a more expensive siding. When the siding performs as expected and does not last as long as the more expensive siding, this is not negligence. It is most likely the result of using less expensive materials in the construction of a home. If the builder clearly contracts with the buyer to use less expensive materials (and no applicable building code is violated), a claim of negligent construction should not stand. However, by saying nothing in the contract, it creates an opportunity for a plaintiff's lawyer to argue that the more rapid deterioration of the siding is the result of negligent construction.

The third approach is to include disclaimers in the purchase and sale agreement to help eliminate potential fraud claims by unhappy buyers. Buyers sometimes argue that the builder/seller passively committed fraud by failing to disclose alleged defects in the property. For example, many air conditioning systems tend not to cool a house uniformly. Sometimes, the second floor of a home is warmer than the ground floor. In other cases, the siting of the residence relative to the sun may affect how well the system cools. If no disclosure is made on this subject, a buyer who is unfamiliar with air conditioning systems might argue that the failure to affirmatively disclose this condition constitutes fraud on the part of the builder/seller. However, this information is disclosed to the buyer in the purchase

---

1812   *Lanier At McEver, L.P. v. Planners And Engineers Collaborative, Inc.*, 284 GA. 204, 663 S.E.2d 240 (2008).

1813   O.C.G.A. § 13-8-2(b).

1814   *Lanier At McEver, L.P. v. Planners And Engineers Collaborative, Inc.*, 284 GA. 204, 663 S.E.2d 240 (2008).

and sale agreement in the form of a disclosure, the buyer can no longer argue that she was unaware of the situation or that the seller intentionally concealed this information. For a more in depth discussion of disclaimers, see § 14.4.1 (Disclaimers in General).

§ 14.6   COURT ACTION

§ 14.6.1   Use Of *Lis Pendens*

Under some circumstances, a notice of *lis pendens* may be filed in conjunction with a lawsuit. *Lis pendens* was a doctrine of common law and is recognized by statute in Georgia.[1815] It is a legal doctrine which describes the power or control which courts acquire over property involved in a lawsuit pending the outcome of the case and until final judgment is entered.[1816] The purpose of the doctrine of *lis pendens* is to keep any property which is the subject of litigation within the power of the court until the judgment is entered so that the court can ensure itself that it can enforce its judgment.[1817] A notice of *lis pendens* is a notice that an action is pending in which someone claims an interest in the subject real estate. This notice is filed in the court public records and would reveal the pending litigation to any potential buyer or lender. The doctrine also has the effect of protecting innocent purchasers of property involved in pending litigation.[1818]

§ 14.6.1.1   *Lis Pendens* Notice

The *lis pendens* Act requires that for any action seeking legal and/or equitable relief as to any property in Georgia, a notice must be recorded in the *lis pendens* docket in the office of the superior court clerk of the county where the property is located.[1819] The notice must contain the names of the parties to the pending suit,[1820] the date that the legal action commenced, the name of the court in which it is pending, a description of the real property involved, and a statement of the relief sought regarding the property.[1821]

A *lis pendens* notice is required only for property that is actually and directly brought into litigation by the pleadings in a pending lawsuit and as to which some relief is sought in the lawsuit respecting that particular property.[1822] *Lis pendens* notices apply only to actions which affect title to property and are not properly filed where the underlying litigation seeks only a money judgment.[1823] For example, it would not be proper for a broker seeking a real estate commission in a residential real estate transaction to file a notice of *lis pendens*.[1824] If a notice of a claim of lien on the property is properly and timely filed and recorded, a notice of *lis pendens* is neither necessary nor applicable.[1825]

§ 14.6.1.2   Effect Of *Lis Pendens* On Sale

A *lis pendens* does not prevent the sale of property and it does not constitute a lien.[1826] However, buyers should be extremely cautious before purchasing property as to which a *lis pendens* notice has been filed and recorded. The *lis*

1815   O.C.G.A. § 44-14-610.

1816   *Coleman v. Law*, 170 Ga. 906, 154 S.E. 445 (1930).

1817   *Carmicheal Tile Co. v. Yaarab Temple Bldg. Co.*, 177 Ga. 318, 170 S.E. 294 (1933).

1818   *Patent Scaffolding Co. v. Byers*, 220 Ga. 426, 139 S.E.2d 332 (1964).

1819   O.C.G.A. § 44-14-610, O.C.G.A. § 44-14-611.

1820   *Federal Deposit Ins. Corp. v. McCloud*, 478 F. Supp. 47 (N.D. Ga. 1979).

1821   O.C.G.A. § 44-14-610.

1822   *Hill v. L-A Management Corp.*, 234 Ga. 341, 216 S.E.2d 97 (1975); *Evans v. Fulton Nat'l Mortgage Corp.*, 168 Ga.App. 600, 309 S.E.2d 884 (1983).

1823   *Alcovy Properties, Inc. v. MTW Inv. Co.*, 212 Ga.App. 102, 441 S.E.2d 288 (1994); *South River Farms v. Bearden*, 210 Ga.App. 156, 435 S.E.2d 516 (1993) (stating that classic example of suit requiring *lis pendens* is one which seeks to have a prior conveyance of the property set aside or declared null and void); *Evans v. Fulton Nat'l Mortgage Corp.*, 168 Ga.App. 600, 309 S.E.2d 884 (1983).

1824   *See* Chapter 13 (Real Estate Commissions).

1825   *Grand Atlanta Corp. v. Chenggis*, 142 Ga.App. 375, 235 S.E.2d 779 (1977).

1826   *Bell v. King, Phipps & Assoc.*, 176 Ga.App. 702, 337 S.E.2d 364 (1985), *cert. denied*, citing *Lankford v. Milhollin*, 203 Ga. 491 (47 SE2d 70) (1948).

pendens puts the buyer on notice of the underlying lawsuit. Therefore, the buyer will be bound by any judgment entered and will be required to comply therewith.[1827] Also, title companies will in all likelihood not insure title to properties on which a *lis pendens* notice has been filed and recorded. As a practical matter, institutional mortgage lenders will not lend money secured by the real estate if the lender is unable to obtain lender's title insurance. Even if the title examiner does not find a *lis pendens* notice recorded for a property a buyer intends to purchase, as an added precaution the buyer may ask the seller to swear by affidavit that there are no suits pending against him as to the property. This is done by the seller signing an owner's affidavit which usually includes certifications regarding loan deeds, work done by contractors, labor and supplies, suits and bankruptcies, taxes, assessments, and other liens against the property.

§ 14.6.1.3   Duration Of Notice

A valid notice of *lis pendens* remains effective as notice to prospective purchasers of land until a final judgment has been entered in the pending litigation and the time for appeal of the case has expired.[1828] *Lis pendens* notices need not be canceled so long as the underlying lawsuit is satisfactorily terminated.

§ 14.6.2   Time Limit For Filing Suit

Parties should be aware that any claim arising out of or related to a real estate contract must be brought within a legally prescribed time period called the statute of limitations. If a claim is not filed in the appropriate court within the required time frame, the court may dismiss the claim. The applicable statute of limitations for a claim depends on the specific type of claim involved. Parties who believe they may have a claim arising out of or related to a real estate transaction should seek legal advice to determine the applicable statute of limitations for their claim in order to ensure that suit is timely filed, otherwise the claim may be lost.

Typically, a suit for breach of a real estate contract must be brought within six years after the time required for performance.[1829] Parties may contract to a lesser time limit within which an action may be brought so long as the period fixed is not unreasonable, as to raise a presumption of undue advantage.[1830]

The statute of limitations for breach of contract begins to run from the time that the contract is broken, not from the time the actual damage results or is ascertained.[1831] For example, if a buyer sues a builder for breach of contract for design defects in the construction of a home, the statute of limitations for the action commences when the defective construction is substantially complete and not when the defects become apparent.[1832]

In some circumstances, certain factors may "toll" or stop the calculation of the period of limitation. If there is fraud by the breaching party which prevents the non-breaching party from filing a lawsuit, the statute of limitations may be tolled and the right of action may not begin to run until the time the fraud is or should have been discovered.[1833] Promises by the breaching party to remedy the problem will not toll the statute of limitations.[1834] However, the parties can enter into a written tolling agreement in which they contractually agree that a statute of limitations will not run for some period of time.

1827   *Wilson v. Blake Perry Realty Co.*, 219 Ga. 57, 131 S.E.2d 555 (1963); *Walker v. Houston*, 176 Ga. 878, 169 S.E. 107 (1933).

1828   *Vance v. Lomas Mortgage USA, Inc.*, 263 Ga. 33, 426 S.E.2d 873 (1993).

1829   O.C.G.A. § 9-3-24. However, if the contract was executed under seal (the body of the instrument contains a recital that it is given under seal and there is a seal affixed to the instrument after the signatures of the parties), the suit may be brought within 20 years after the right of action has accrued. No instrument is considered "under seal" unless. O.C.G.A. § 9-3-23. *Chastain v. L. Moss Music Co.*, 83 Ga.App. 570, 64 S.E.2d 205 (1951).

1830   *Rabey Elec. Co. v. Housing Auth.*, 190 Ga.App. 89, 378 S.E.2d 169 (1989); *General Elec. Credit Corp. v. Home Indem. Co.*, 168 Ga.App. 344, 309 S.E.2d 152 (1983), *cert. denied.*

1831   *Mobley v. Murray County*, 178 Ga. 388, 173 S.E. 680 (1934); *R.L. Sanders Roofing Co. v. Miller*, 153 Ga.App. 225, 264 S.E.2d 731 (1980).

1832   *Space Leasing Assoc. v. Atlantic Bldg. Sys.*, 144 Ga.App. 320, 241 S.E.2d 438 (1977), *cert. denied.*

1833   O.C.G.A. § 9-3-96.

1834   *Mullins v. Wheatley Grading Contractors*, 184 Ga.App. 119, 361 S.E.2d 10 (1987).

An action for fraud and misrepresentation in inducing the purchase of property, which is an action in tort, must be brought within four years after the right of action accrucs.[1835] Generally in a tort action, the statute of limitations begins to run when the damage from the tortious act is actually sustained.[1836] For example, if a buyer sues a builder in tort for damages for negligent construction involving a defective roof, the claim must normally be brought within four years from the date that the roof was constructed. This is because the legal injury resulting from negligent construction occurs at the time of the construction, since the building itself is damaged at that time.[1837]

The Georgia Legislature carved out an exception to this rule in the 2000 session. It amended the Georgia Code to provide that the recovery of damages to a "dwelling due to the manufacture of or the negligent design or installation of synthetic exterior siding shall accrue when the damage to the dwelling is discovered or, in the exercise of reasonable diligence, should have been discovered."[1838]

If a seller, builder, or broker fraudulently conceals a defect in a house or fraudulently misrepresents information about a house which the buyer cannot discover because of the fraud, it is possible for a court to extend the statute of limitations for an additional limited time to allow the injured party to assert his claim.[1839]

For example, one buyer sued a builder for damages in tort for negligently constructing a house with a substandard foundation and fraudulently misrepresenting that the foundation was built in accordance with current home-building standards. The buyer did not file his lawsuit within the statutory limit (in this case, four years after the house was built); however, the court held that because of the builder's alleged fraud, the buyer could file his lawsuit within four years from the date that he discovered that the house's foundation was not constructed as the builder represented.[1840]

Where the cause of action is for fraudulent inducement in the execution of the contract, the period of limitation begins to run from the date of the execution of the contract.[1841]

§ 14.6.3   Action To Take Upon Breach Of Contract

What should you do when you learn that the other party to the contract has or is going to breach the contract? The answer is going to depend upon the specific facts of any given situation. There are several broad rules of thumb.

§ 14.6.3.1   Notice Of Breach

Usually the first action the non-breaching party should take is to give the breaching party notice of his actual breach or anticipated breach. Giving such notice provides the breaching party the opportunity to return to a position of compliance with the terms of the contract. This also gives the other party an opportunity to clarify any misperception in the event there has been no actual breach. The best practice is to give notice of breach in writing. If time is a critical factor, the notice may, as a practical matter, need to be given orally. This should be followed by a written confirmation of the notice.

1835   O.C.G.A. § 9-3-31; *Kerce v. Bent Tree Corp.*, 166 Ga.App. 728, 305 S.E.2d 462 (1983); *Phipps v. Wright*, 28 Ga.App. 164, 100 S.E. 511 (1922).

1836   *Hunt v. Star Photo Finishing Co.*, 115 Ga.App. 1, 153 S.E.2d 602 (1967).

1837   *U-Haul Co. of Western Georgia v. Abreu & Robeson, Inc.*, 247 Ga. 565, 277 S.E.2d 497 (1981). If a party has a cause of action (1) for any deficiency in a survey or plat, planning, design, specifications, supervision or observation of construction, or construction of an improvement to real property; (2) for any injury to property, real or personal, arising out of any such deficiency; or (3) for injury to the person or for wrongful death arising out of any such deficiency, the lawsuit to recover damages must be filed against the person performing or furnishing the survey or plat, design, planning, supervision or observation of construction, or construction of such an improvement within eight years after substantial completion of such an improvement. O.C.G.A. § 9-3-51(a) In the case of such an injury to property or the person or such an injury causing wrongful death, which injury occurred during the seventh or eighth year after such substantial completion, an action in tort to recover damages for such an injury or wrongful death may be brought within two years after the date on which such injury occurred, irrespective of the date of death, but in no event may such an action be brought more than ten years after the substantial completion of construction of such an improvement. O.C.G.A. § 9-3-51(b).

1838   O.C.G.A. § 9-3-30.

1839   *Hahne v. Wylly*, 199 Ga.App. 811, 406 S.E.2d 94 (1991).

1840   O.C.G.A. § 9-3-96; *Gilmore v. Bell*, 223 Ga.App. 513, 478 S.E.2d 609 (1996), *cert. denied*; *Ramey v. Leisure, Ltd.*, 205 Ga.App. 128, 421 S.E.2d 555 (1992), *cert. denied* (statute of limitation tolled until buyer's discovery of defect in footing).

1841   *Kerce v. Bent Tree Corp.*, 166 Ga.App. 728, 305 S.E.2d 462 (1983).

§ 14.6.3.2   Attending The Closing

Must the non-breaching party attend the closing in order to preserve his rights? Not always.[1842] The safest course of action is for the non-breaching party to be present at the closing, ready, willing and able to hold up his or her end of the bargain.

In one case, the buyer informed the seller that he would not purchase the property because the seller had not repaired certain structural defects.[1843] As a result, no closing was scheduled and the seller did not obtain a termite letter as required by the contract. The seller subsequently sued the buyer for breach of contract. The buyer argued that he had no liability because the seller failed to provide a termite letter at the closing (which was never scheduled). The court noted that the contract required the termite letter to be provided at closing and that it was therefore not due until well after the buyer's repudiation of the contract. The court went on to state that because the buyer repudiated the contract prior to the time the seller was obligated to perform, the seller was relieved of his responsibilities under the contract.

The risk a party runs by not attending the closing is demonstrated in the following case. The seller was required to make numerous repairs to the property prior to the time of the closing.[1844] The buyer inspected the property the afternoon before closing and found that not only were the repairs not made, but the yard was overgrown and a "pigsty," the carpeting was soiled, and there was water in the basement and on the main floor. The buyer declared that there was "no way that the items could be remedied" in time and, accordingly, he (the buyer) would not appear for the closing. The seller subsequently sued the buyer for breach of contract. The buyer argued that he did not need to appear for closing since the seller could not possibly have lived up to his end of the deal. The court, however, disagreed. The court held that the buyer's declaration that he would not attend the closing actually acted as a repudiation by the buyer, and that this relieved the seller of his obligation to make to repairs prior to the time of the scheduled closing. As demonstrated here, and as noted above, it is almost always best for the non-breaching party to attend the closing.

§ 14.7   ALTERNATIVES TO LITIGATION

Parties should be aware that going to court in litigation to resolve a dispute can be a very time-consuming and expensive process. Some litigation can take years to resolve, particularly if a party appeals the initial ruling in the case. Attorney's fees can mount and the expenses of suing can be very high. Many people find that protracted litigation is also emotionally draining. For these reasons, parties who have disputes which they cannot settle among themselves, but for which they do not want to go to court, may want to utilize alternative methods to settle their dispute. Alternative dispute resolution ("ADR") procedures are available to parties in this event. ADR has become increasingly common as individuals look for more cost-effective, time-efficient ways to resolve disputes rather than going to court.

§ 14.7.1   ADR Procedure For Residential Construction Disputes

Before a residential homebuyer can file a claim for a construction defect against a "contractor", the buyer must comply with the ADR procedure set out in the Resolution of Construction Defects Act[1845] ("Right to Repair Act"). Its purpose is to resolve residential construction disputes, thereby avoiding legal proceedings. If a claimant files a legal action (lawsuit or arbitration) "without first complying with the requirements" of the Repair Act, the court or arbitrator is required, if requested by the contractor or other party to the action, to stay the action (put it on hold) until the claimant has complied.

1842   *A.G. Nikas v. W.F. Hindley*, 98 Ga.App. 437, 106 S.E.2d 335 (1958) (if one party has clearly breached or repudiated the contract, the non-breaching party is excused from the necessity or performing or being ready to perform on his own part unless the repudiating party withdraws his repudiation).

1843   *McLeod v. McLatcher*, 201 Ga.App. 17, 410 S.E.2d 144 (1991).

1844   *Clark v. Cox*, 179 Ga.App. 437, 347 S.E.2d 4 (1986).

1845   O.C.G.A. §§ 8-2-36 through 8-2-43.

The Act requires that a sales contract between a residential homebuyer and a "contractor" contain the following notice:[1846]

> CONTRACTOR DISPUTES DISCLOSURE. GEORGIA LAW
> CONTAINS IMPORTANT REQUIREMENTS YOU MUST FOLLOW
> BEFORE YOU MAY FILE A LAWSUIT OR OTHER ACTION FOR
> DEFECTIVE CONSTRUCTION AGAINST THE CONTRACTOR WHO
> CONSTRUCTED, IMPROVED, OR REPAIRED YOUR HOME. NINETY
> DAYS BEFORE YOU FILE YOUR LAWSUIT OR OTHER ACTION, YOU
> MUST SERVE ON THE CONTRACTOR A WRITTEN NOTICE OF ANY
> CONSTRUCTION CONDITIONS YOU ALLEGE ARE DEFECTIVE.
> UNDER THE LAW, A CONTRACTOR HAS THE OPPORTUNITY TO MAKE
> AN OFFER TO REPAIR OR PAY FOR THE DEFECTS OR BOTH. YOU ARE
> NOT OBLIGATED TO ACCEPT ANY OFFER MADE BY A CONTRACTOR.
> THERE ARE STRICT DEADLINES AND PROCEDURES UNDER STATE
> LAW, AND FAILURE TO FOLLOW THEM MAY AFFECT YOUR ABILITY
> TO FILE A LAWSUIT OR OTHER ACTION.

Therefore, a residential sales contract where the seller qualifies as a "contractor" as defined under the Act must contain the notice set out above. The statutory definition of "contractor" includes any person or firm engaging in designing, developing, constructing or selling dwellings or common areas of developments, or altering or adding to existing dwellings or common areas.[1847] This definition is quite broad. However, the 2007 amendments to the Repair Act restricted its applicability to contractors and subcontractors and clarifies that the Act does not apply to anyone who is "not required to be licensed" in Georgia.[1848]

The Repair Act set forth a litany of notices, demands, and evidentiary disclosures that must be complied with on a timely basis. As such, it is important review the portions of this Act applicable to each respective transaction to ensure compliance.

§ 14.7.2   What The GAR Contracts Provide

§ 14.7.2.1   Alternative Dispute Resolution Between Buyers And Sellers In The GAR Purchase And Sale Agreement

Previous versions of the GAR Contract[1849] advised buyers and sellers that arbitration and mediation are available to them to resolve disputes. However, since most people are now familiar with ADR, the current GAR Contract does not reference the availability of these procedures. If parties to the GAR Contract wish to agree to arbitrate or mediate any disputes, they may use the GAR Arbitration/Mediation Agreement form.[1850]

The GAR Arbitration/Mediation Agreement[1851] may be attached to or incorporated in any purchase and sale agreement. When using this form, the parties may choose to submit their dispute to one of three options. The first option is binding arbitration in which the parties submit their dispute to one or more impartial persons for a final and binding decision. The second is mediation and settlement which involves an attempt by the parties to resolve their dispute with the aid of a neutral third party. The mediator offers suggestions, but the ultimate resolution of the

---

1846   O.C.G.A. § 8-2-41

1847   O.C.G.A. § 8-2-26(6)

1848   O.C.G.A. § 8-2-43(d).

1849   GAR Form F20.

1850   GAR Form F121.

1851   GAR Form 121.

dispute rests with the parties themselves. The last option is mediation-arbitration which combines the voluntary techniques of persuasion and discussion, as in mediation, but allows the third party to issues a final and binding decision when necessary.

Alternatively, if the parties are using a non-GAR contract and want to require arbitration, the following provision can be added to the contract.

> **Special Stipulation 303:   Agreement to Arbitrate**
>
> *Buyer and Seller agree that any unresolved claim arising out of or relating to this Agreement, or the breach thereof, shall be settled by arbitration in accordance with the Commercial Arbitration Rules of the American Arbitration Association. The decision of the arbitrator shall be final and the arbitrator shall have authority to award attorneys' fees and allocate the costs of arbitration as part of any final award. The arbitration shall be conducted in accordance with O.C.G.A § 9 1 1, et seq., and with the rules and procedures of the arbitrator.*
>
> _____/_____ [Buyer Initials] _____/_____ [Seller Initials]

If parties want to arbitrate disputes only as to certain matters, they can include the following special stipulation and specify which matters must be submitted to arbitration.

> **Special Stipulation 304:   Agreement to Arbitrate Particular Dispute**
>
> *Buyer and Seller agree that any unresolved claim arising out of or relating to_____ regarding this Agreement shall be settled by arbitration in accordance with the Commercial Arbitration Rules of the American Arbitration Association. The decision of the arbitrator shall be final and may be enforced by any court having jurisdiction thereof. The arbitration shall be conducted in accordance with O.C.G.A § 9-1-1, et seq., and with the rules and procedures of the arbitrator. Notwithstanding the above, Buyer and Seller are not obligated to arbitrate any dispute involving _____, and Buyer and Seller may pursue any and all available legal and/or equitable remedies as to such disputes.*
>
> _____/_____ [Buyer Initials] _____/_____ [Seller Initials]

§ 14.7.2.2   Alternative Dispute Resolution Between Builder And Buyers In The GAR New Construction Purchase And Sale Agreement

Unlike the GAR Purchase and Sale Agreement which does not specifically address alternative dispute resolution options in the body of the agreement, the GAR New Construction Contract[1852] includes a provision to which the buyer and seller may stipulate requiring the parties to settle any disputes they may have through arbitration. Builders will frequently insist on an agreement to arbitrate disputes because arbitration generally resolves disputes more quickly than court proceedings.

If the buyer and seller agree to this provision and initial it on the contract, all disputes between the parties must be submitted to arbitration, including disputes over construction as well as disputes regarding earnest money or other provisions of the contract. If the arbitration provision is not initialed by both parties, it will not be enforceable. The GAR New Construction Contract arbitration provision takes into account the new mediation procedure required by state law. It also takes into consideration any requirements for dispute resolution contained in a warranty given by the seller.

1852   GAR Form F23.

"Buyer and Seller agree that any construction defect claim not resolved after following the procedure described in O.C.G.A § 8-2-38 and all other claims between the parties shall be settled by arbitration through the services of an arbitrator mutually agreed upon by the parties. The decision of the arbitrator shall be final and may be enforced by any court having jurisdiction thereof. The arbitration shall be conducted in accordance with O.C.G.A. § 9-9-1 *et seq*. Notwithstanding the provisions of this subparagraph, if Buyer is claiming under a warranty provided by Seller, the terms and procedures of that warranty shall first apply to the resolution of the claim. In order for this paragraph to be a part of this Agreement, it must be initialed by Buyer and Seller; if not initialed it shall be void and unenforceable."[1853]

§ 14.7.2.3   GAR Brokerage Engagement Agreements

The GAR brokerage engagement agreements[1854] require arbitration for all claims between the broker and his or her client arising out of or relating to the agreement and alleged acts or omissions of any or all parties to the agreement. Any other claim, such as a claim regarding the handling and disbursement of earnest money or a claim of the broker regarding the entitlement to or non-payment of a commission, does not need to be resolved by arbitration. The arbitration must be conducted in accordance with the Federal Arbitration Act[1855] and the rules and procedures of the arbitration company selected to administer the arbitration.

Users of this form agree to work together to select a mutually acceptable arbitration company with offices in Georgia to administer and conduct the arbitration. If the parties can't agree on an arbitration company, the company will be selected by each party simultaneously exchanging with the other party a list of three acceptable arbitration companies with offices in Georgia. If there is one arbitration company that is common to both lists, that company will be chosen to administer and conduct the arbitration. If there is more than one arbitration company that is common to both lists, the parties will either mutually agree as to which company will be selected or flip a coin. If there is not initially one arbitration company that is common to both list, the parties will repeat the process by expanding their lists by two companies at a time until there is a common name on the lists selected by the parties. Once arbitration has begun, the arbitrator's decision will be final. The arbitrator also has the authority to award attorney's fees and allocate the costs of arbitration as part of any final award.

Neither class action suits nor any other form representative proceedings may be brought before the arbitrator under these GAR forms. As such, a party may not go to arbitration as member of a class in any purported class action or other representative proceeding. The GAR brokerage engagement forms explicitly state that any claim brought before the arbitrator must be brought by a party in his or her individual capacity. In addition, the arbitrator may not consolidate more than one person's claims and may not preside over any form of a representative or class action proceeding.

§ 14.7.3   Limiting The Disputes Which Can Be Arbitrated

In many cases, builders will want to limit the disputes that can be arbitrated to only those which exist after the closing has occurred. This is done to avoid having the closing delayed (which can result in increased carrying costs to the builder) while the parties arbitrate their dispute. A sample of this type of arbitration clause is set out below.

1853   GAR Form F23.

1854   GAR Form F1 and F4.

1855   9 U.S.C.A. §1 *et seq*.

Special Stipulation 305:   Agreement to Only Arbitrate Disputes Unresolved After Closing

Buyer and Seller agree that any claim arising out of or related to this Agreement which remains unresolved after the closing shall be settled by arbitration conducted by _____. The arbitration shall be conducted in accordance with O.C.G.A. § 9-1-1, et seq., and with the rules and procedures of the arbitrator. The decision of the arbitrator shall be final and binding upon the parties thereto and may be enforced by any court having jurisdiction thereof.

_____ *[Buyer's Initials]*   _____ *[Seller's Initials]*

§ 14.7.4   Agreement To Arbitrate Must Be Initialed

In order for a binding arbitration taking place under the Georgia statute to be enforceable, the parties must initial it on the contract. If both parties do not initial the provision, it will be void and unenforceable.[1856] The purpose of this requirement is to ensure that purchasers of residential property do not give up their common law right of access to the courts unless they specifically acknowledge their intent to do so by initialing the arbitration provision.

Therefore, if a buyer and seller desire to arbitrate any disputes which may arise between them, it is critically important that their agreement to arbitrate be initialed on the sales contract.

§ 14.7.5   Right To Insist On Arbitration May Be Waived

Parties should be aware that an agreement between them to arbitrate a dispute is waived by any action of a party which is inconsistent with the right of arbitration.[1857] This means that even if parties have entered into a valid arbitration agreement, by certain conduct they can waive their right to insist on arbitration as the means to settle a dispute. For example, if a party files a lawsuit despite the existence of an arbitration agreement, the opposing party must formally ask the court by written motion to order arbitration rather than participate in the litigation.[1858]

In one Georgia case, a builder waived his right to enforce an arbitration agreement with the buyers of a house he built.[1859] The buyers filed a lawsuit against the builder for breach of warranty asserting certain construction defects. The warranty agreement contained an arbitration provision specifying that any dispute arising out of the warranty would be settled by binding arbitration. After the buyers filed the lawsuit for breach of warranty, the builder responded to the lawsuit and asserted that any dispute as to the warranty must be settled by arbitration. However, the builder never filed a formal motion with the court to compel arbitration and the court heard the case and entered a judgment for the buyers. The Georgia Court of Appeals held that the builder waived his right to enforce the arbitration agreement because rather than filing a motion to compel arbitration he participated in the litigation.

§ 14.7.6   Arbitration Versus Mediation

Arbitration is the most traditional form of ADR and can be either binding or nonbinding. Binding arbitration is a process in which the parties choose a neutral person or persons to hear their dispute and to render a final and binding decision or award after hearing the evidence. Nonbinding arbitration uses the same process as binding arbitration except that the decision by the arbitrator is advisory only. If either of the parties is dissatisfied with the decision they are not bound by it and may resort to litigation.

1856   *Pinnacle Constr. Co., Inc. v. Osborne*, 218 Ga.App. 366, 460 S.E.2d 880 (1995).

1857   *Tillman Group, Inc. v. Keith*, 201 Ga.App. 680, 411 S.E.2d 794 (1991); *McCormick-Morgan, Inc. v. Whitehead Elec. Co.*, 179 Ga.App. 10, 345 S.E.2d 53 (1986), cert. denied.

1858   O.C.G.A. § 9-9-6(a); *Tillman Group, Inc. v. Keith*, 201 Ga.App. 680, 411 S.E.2d 794 (1991).

1859   O.C.G.A. § 9-9-6(a); *Tillman Group, Inc. v. Keith*, 201 Ga.App. 680, 411 S.E.2d 794 (1991).

An arbitration can be arranged in a variety of different ways. In its simplest form, the parties can agree to have any neutral party hear both sides of the dispute and render a decision. One of the challenges of arbitration in disputes involving residential real estate is that the cost of arbitration can quickly exceed the amount in dispute. As a result, more parties are turning to non-traditional arbitrators to resolve disputes involving lesser amounts. Arbitrations can also be arranged through dispute resolution organizations, such as the American Arbitration Association. There are both nonprofit and for-profit organizations that provide alternative dispute resolution services. Nonbinding arbitrations are also sometimes ordered by a court, as will be explained below.

Mediation is a process in which a neutral party tries to help the parties resolve their dispute. The mediator does not have authority to make a decision or impose a settlement. The mediator guides discussions and clarifies issues with the intent of producing settlement proposals which are nonbinding and which may help bring the parties closer together. The purpose of mediation is to help the parties work together to come to a mutually agreeable resolution. The most significant difference between mediation and arbitration is that the arbitrator decides for one side or another with respect to the dispute and the mediator facilitates discussion but does not render a decision.

§ 14.7.7 Selecting Arbitrator

The parties' agreement to arbitrate may provide for a method of selecting an arbitrator. If it does not a court may appoint an arbitrator pursuant to the Georgia Arbitration Code.[1860] The arbitration provision of the GAR New Construction Purchase and Sale Agreement[1861] provides that the arbitration must be settled by an arbitrator mutually agreed upon by the parties.

Typically, the parties are given a list of names and resumes of potential arbitrators. The potential arbitrators usually have some experience in the matter about which the parties have a dispute. For example, if the parties have a dispute about construction defects, it would not be surprising to see that most of the potential arbitrators have some type of construction background. The parties can mutually agree on an arbitrator to hear the matter, or an arbitrator will be appointed from the list they have been given. If the parties do not mutually agree on an arbitrator, each party must strike from the list the names of the arbitrators to which they object.

The rules of the organization conducting the arbitration will govern how many names each party can strike from the list of arbitrators. Once these lists are returned to the organization, it will assign an arbitrator to the case whose name was not struck from the list by either party. Some agreements between parties can require arbitration to be conducted by three arbitrators. Usually, in that circumstance, each party selects one arbitrator and then the two arbitrators select the third.

Buyers should be aware that contracts used by builders may contain an arbitration provision which requires that the arbitration of any disputes be conducted by a specific arbitrator or arbitration company which regularly arbitrates disputes between builders and buyers. Buyers should review all arbitration provisions carefully to determine the terms and conditions of the provision and should pay particular attention to the requirement that a particular arbitrator or arbitration company be named at the execution of the agreement.

§ 14.7.8 The Arbitration Process

The procedures for private arbitration are also controlled by written rules and regulations of the organization conducting the arbitration. Normally, the procedure is similar to a shortened and less formal version of what would happen if the parties litigated their dispute in court.

A hearing is usually scheduled at the office of the arbitrator or at the office of the organization conducting the arbitration. At the hearing, each party has an opportunity to present evidence supporting his side of the story.

1860   O.C.G.A § 9-9-7.

1861   GAR Form F23, New Construction Purchase and Sale Agreement.

While formal rules of evidence are not necessarily followed, each party can usually make an opening statement, present and cross-examine witnesses, and make a closing statement. If the arbitrator is experienced in the subject matter of the dispute, he may know as much as or more than the witnesses and may play an active role in asking questions about the dispute. Ultimately, the arbitrator will issue a ruling according to his own interpretation of the law and findings of fact.

§ 14.7.9 The Mediation Process

In the case of mediation, the process is that of negotiation with the assistance of a neutral facilitator. The mediator tries to help the parties communicate more clearly with one another rather than to focus on their "positions." The goal of mediation is to clarify the issues so as to enable parties to resolve their own differences. The mediator will usually do this by meeting with the parties together and separately to help them find some common ground.

If a mediation results in a successful resolution of the dispute, the parties should not leave the room until the terms of the resolution have been reduced to writing and signed by all involved. This creates a binding settlement agreement, which is itself a contract capable of being enforced by the courts. While the parties may wish to correct some of the language or otherwise "clean up" a settlement agreement at a later date, all the critical terms should be included in the document prepared on the day of settlement. This avoids parties attempting to renegotiate the terms of their settlement after they have had a day to reconsider their positions.

§ 14.7.10 Advantages Of ADR Procedures

The most commonly cited advantages of settling disputes through ADR rather than in court include the following:

(a) Resolving a dispute through ADR is often less time-consuming and costly than if the dispute were resolved through the traditional court system. Some arbitration companies have expedited procedures which can resolve the dispute from start to finish in as few as 45 days.

(b) Private ADR allows the parties to select the person or persons who will arbitrate or mediate their dispute. This allows the parties to select persons who are experienced in the field.

(c) Private ADR may also be scheduled at the convenience of the parties rather than at the convenience of the court.

(d) Private ADR is, as its name implies, generally private and confidential. Many parties find this aspect of ADR an appealing alternative to litigation, which makes the dispute a matter of public record.

(e) ADR is more likely than litigation to result in relationships being preserved. In many cases, the less formal procedures create a less hostile environment.

(f) Mediation allows the parties to reach a mutually agreeable resolution instead of having a third party decide the case.

§ 14.7.11 Disadvantages Of ADR Procedures

Although there are many advantages of ADR, in some cases ADR may not be desired.

(a) Arbitration, more so than mediation, can become an expensive and time-consuming process. If the ADR method is nonbinding and the parties do not resolve their dispute, the process can actually become more expensive and time-consuming, because the expense and time of ADR is then added to the resulting litigation.

(b) There may be cases where one of the parties would prefer to have the case heard by a jury. For example, a buyer with fraud claims for serious hidden defects may want to have the case heard by a jury which may be more sympathetic to the emotional nature of the claims than an arbitrator.

(c) A decision rendered in binding arbitration is not subject to review, except in limited circumstances.[1862] The finality of the process can be seen as an advantage or disadvantage. The successful party may see it as a speedy way to resolve a dispute with finality. The losing party may honestly believe that the award was inequitable and want "another bite at the apple." Our traditional justice system allows for such appeals.

§ 14.7.12 Enforcement Of Binding Arbitration

If a party refuses to comply with a binding arbitration award, a court must still be called upon to enforce the award. Fortunately, if a party has to resort to the courts to enforce an award, the judicial process is limited to confirming the order of the arbitrator and does not involve a retrial of the dispute.

§ 14.7.13 Court-Ordered ADR

After the filing of a lawsuit, the courts in Georgia may refer cases to nonbinding processes of either arbitration or mediation, depending upon the county of venue. A number of counties in Georgia already have various procedures for what they refer to as "court-annexed ADR," and others that do not currently have such programs are planning to institute them. These programs are being developed to try to resolve as many cases as possible outside of the traditional litigation process. Court-ordered ADR does not usually prevent the parties from continuing on with their lawsuit and having their day in court if they are unable to resolve the dispute.

§ 14.7.14 When ADR Is Recommended

Whether a party will want to try to resolve a dispute through litigation, arbitration, or mediation will depend on the facts and circumstances of the case and the objectives of the party. As a result, many individuals will want to wait until a dispute arises before committing to a particular method for resolving the dispute.

Real estate brokers should be comfortable explaining how ADR works in a general sense. However, they should be extremely cautious in advising clients to seek one legal method of resolving a dispute over another. Under BRRETA, brokers have a duty to advise their clients to obtain expert advice on matters which are beyond the expertise of the broker and which they are not licensed to provide. Unless a licensee has legal training, he will probably want to avoid potential liability for giving potentially bad advice concerning ADR. Rather, he should refer the client to an attorney to help make the decision on how best to resolve the dispute.

1862 An application to a court to vacate an arbitration award must be made within three months after the delivery of a copy of the award to the applicant. O.C.G.A. § 9-9-13(a). The court may vacate an award only if it finds that the rights of the petitioning party were prejudiced by "(1) corruption, fraud, or misconduct in procuring the award; (2) partiality of an arbitrator appointed as a neutral; (3) an overstepping by the arbitrators of their authority or such imperfect execution of it that a final and definite award upon the subject matter submitted was not made; (4) a failure to follow the procedure of [the Georgia Arbitration Code], unless the party applying to vacate the award continued with the arbitration with notice of this failure and without objection; or (5) the arbitrator's manifest disregard of the law." O.C.G.A. § 9-9-13(b).

The **RED BOOK**

CHAPTER 15

RISK ALLOCATION IN REAL ESTATE CONTRACTS

OVERVIEW

The following goals should be achieved in a well-written real estate purchase and sale contract: (i) the entire business agreement of the parties should be set out in writing; (ii) the areas of likely risk in the transaction (both before and after closing) should be identified and allocated in the contract between the buyer and seller in a manner that is acceptable to all parties; and (iii) the contract should meet all of the legal requirements to create an enforceable contract.

This chapter will discuss the special types of risks that commonly arise in different types of real estate transactions and how to eliminate or minimize those risks. In addition, several risk allocation charts are provided as a quick reference to spot certain risks relating to the condition of the property, financing and/or the economy, any life changing circumstances, and neighborhood conditions.

§ 15.1 SPECIAL RISKS IN REAL ESTATE TRANSACTIONS

There are literally hundreds of things that can go wrong in a real estate transaction. Some risks are more likely to occur than others. For example, the risk of there being defects in the property is so great that almost every contract gives the buyer the opportunity to inspect for defects and request that the seller repair any defects that are found. Some risks rarely arise. The general rule is that in the absence of a provision to the contrary in a real estate agreement, any risk of loss falls on the purchaser following the execution of the contract.[1863] Therefore, every real estate agreement should contemplate the risks that are likely to arise in that transaction and which of the parties is in a better position to demand that the other party bear certain risks by virtue of the strength of that party's negotiating position.

When a serious problem arises in the transaction, the parties usually consult their purchase and sale contracts to see if the risk was contemplated and addressed in the contract. Sometimes parties agree to assume remote risks only to get burned when the risk actually occurs. In other transactions, a serious problem will arise and the contract is altogether silent on the risk. In these situations, common law principles will sometimes provide guidance on who bears the risk. In other cases, the parties are left either to negotiate the allocation of a risk after it has already occurred or seek the guidance of a court to either interpret, enforce and in some cases, declare a contract unenforceable because it failed to address a material issue that is now at hand. When a contract is silent on an issue that has arisen in the transaction, it can create significant problems for the buyer and seller.

Four important goals are accomplished when real estate licensees and their clients think about contracts in risk allocation terms. First, it helps the client understand that risk is inherent in real estate transactions and there is never a guarantee that any particular real estate transaction will close. Second, when the client sees that both parties are assuming risk in the transaction, it makes some clients more reasonable in agreeing to compromises that allow a transaction to move forward. Third, viewing a contract in risk allocation terms helps clients prioritize which risks they can accept and which ones are deal breakers. For example, with REO contracts (*i.e.* – real estate owned by a bank), the one risk most buyers usually want to be protected against is the risk of the seller deciding to sell the property to someone else. Therefore, while there are numerous potential changes, most buyers wish they could make to a REO contract (since they tend to be so one-sided in protecting the seller), the one critical change that most buyers will insist on (knowing that the seller is not inclined to agree to any changes) is being given the remedy of specific performance of the contract. Finally, discussing contracts in risk allocation terms helps the real estate licensee representing the client understand the client's tolerance for risk. Some clients are risk averse. Other clients thrive on risk. Knowing how the client thinks about risk helps the licensee better serve the client's interests.

The challenge with risk allocation is that the more risks are addressed in the contract, the longer the contract becomes. It is generally much better to have a longer contract in which commonly occurring risks are addressed than a shorter

---

1863 Pindar's, 2 Ga. Real Estate Law & Procedure § 18-24 (6th ed.).

contract in which such risks are left unaddressed. However, at some point, the benefits of addressing risks can be outweighed by the sheer length of the contract. A contract addressing every imaginable risk that can arise in a real estate contract could easily run hundreds of pages in length. In fact, some complex commercial real estate purchase and sale agreements are this long and are often heavily negotiated by attorneys representing each of the parties in the transaction. However, in residential real estate transactions few people have the time, money or inclination to try to address every imaginable risk that might arise.

Knowing that it is impractical in most transactions to try to address all risks in a contract, how does the preparer of a contract decide which risks to address and which to ignore? There are two good answers to this question. First, the person preparing the contract should ask her client whether there are any special issues of concern that she would like to make sure are addressed in the contract. Some clients have particular hot button issues that are not shared by large numbers of other buyers. For example, some buyers would not ever consider living in a house in which a murder took place. This type of buyer would obviously benefit from a provision giving the buyer the right to terminate the contract if the buyer discovers that a murder took place on the property. Other buyers would never consider buying a property the numerical address of which they consider unlucky. If this buyer is purchasing a newly constructed home, she might want the right to terminate the contract if the street address number changes before closing. For some buyers, being in a particular school district is critically important and the discovery that a property is not in the desired district can be a deal breaker. Asking buyers about issues that are of particular concern to them is the only way to know about their unique concerns. Second, the preparer of the contract should use her experience with real estate transactions to identify those risks that are most likely to occur in that type of transaction. For example, the unique issues that arise in the purchase of a resale condominium unit are different than buying a lot in the north Georgia mountains. Similarly, buying a home with a septic system or served by well water raises different issues than a property in a historic district.

The sections below will discuss the special risks that can arise in different types of real estate transactions and how best to address these risks from the perspective of the buyer or seller.

§ 15.1.1   Property Being Purchased Is Served By Septic System

Risk #1: The septic system was approved for fewer bedrooms than currently exist on property.

Solution: Buyers should check with Department of Health in the county in which the property is located to see how many bedrooms the septic system was designed to serve. The following special stipulation may be included in the purchase and sale agreement to address this risk.

> #### Special Stipulation 306:   Buyer Can Terminate if Septic System is Undersized
>
> *Seller acknowledges that there are _____ bedrooms in the main dwelling on the Property. In the event, Buyer determines prior to closing that the septic system serving the Property was approved by the local Department of Health in the county in which the Property is located for less than the above-referenced number of bedrooms, Buyer may terminate this Agreement without penalty upon notice to Seller.*

Risk #2: A septic system may not be able to be installed on the Property and public sewer is not available.

Solution: The buyer could add the following special stipulation to the contract to protect against this risk.

> #### Special Stipulation 307:   Buyer Can Terminate if Septic System Cannot be Installed
>
> *Seller acknowledges that Buyer intends to construct a residence on the Property with _____ number of bedrooms. If prior to closing, Buyer determines that for whatever reason it is not possible to install a standard septic system on the Property (excluding a drip emitter system) to serve a residence with this number of bedrooms, Buyer may terminate this Agreement without penalty upon notice to Seller.*

§ 15.1.2 The Property Is On A Lake

Risk #1: The boat dock serving the Property is not on the Property and may be removed by the Seller on or before closing.

Solution: The buyer can add the following special stipulation to guard against this risk.

> ### Special Stipulation 308: Boat Dock Remains with Property
>
> *Seller warrants that the boat dock serving the Property (and generally located as shown on the survey attached hereto) is owned free and clear (or all liens and encumbrances by Seller is being threatened as part of the Property) and shall remain with the Property and become the property of Buyer upon the closing of this transaction. At closing, Seller shall provide Buyer with a bill of sale for the boat dock. This warranty shall survive the closing of this transaction.*

Risk #2: The boat dock serving the Property is a shared dock and may be used by more persons than just the buyer.

Solution: The buyer can add the following special stipulation to guard against this risk.

> ### Special Stipulation 309: Boat Dock Not Shared With Any Other Property
>
> *Seller warrants that: (1) the boat dock is serving the Property (and generally located as shown on the survey attached hereto) is for the exclusive use of the owner of the Property; and (2) no other person or entity has any right to either the temporary or permanent use of the boat dock for any purpose whatsoever. This warranty shall survive the closing of this transaction.*

Risk #3: The seller does not have a permit to maintain the boat dock on the lake.

Solution: The buyer can add the following special stipulation.

> ### Special Stipulation 310: Seller Has Permit to Boat Dock
>
> *Seller warrants that Seller has obtained all required permits to maintain the boat dock serving the Property in its present location (which is generally shown in the location identified on the survey attached as Exhibit # _____ and incorporated herein) on the lake. To the extent that the permit(s) are assignable, Seller agrees to assign such permits to Buyer at closing. This paragraph shall survive the closing of this transaction.*

Risk #4: Buyer does not own shoreline along the lake or there is an easement restricting buyer's use of the area around the shoreline.

Discussion: There are many lakes in Georgia in which the owners of lake lot do not own the shoreline or the owners' right to use the shoreline is restricted. Disclosing this condition is normally the best way to eliminate the risk of a claim.

Solution: The following is an example of such a disclosure.

> ### Special Stipulation 311: Disclosure that Lot Does Not Extend to the Lake
>
> *Buyer acknowledges that the boundary lines of Property do not extend to the water's edge of the lake. Upon the closing of this transaction Buyer shall not own any part of the lake's shoreline. Buyer right to use the area between the Property boundary line and the lake is based upon ☐ an easement; ☐ a license; **OR** ☐ a lease. Buyer should obtain a survey and title report to better understand Buyer's rights and limitations to use the area between the Property and the lake.*

Risk #5: The property is not served by year round water.

Discussion: There can be a significant difference in the value of a lake lot depending on whether or not it is served by year round water. In some cases, the drawdown of the lake will leave some lake lots high and dry while others will continue to have access to the water. On many lakes, the water is drawn down in the winter to allow owners to make repairs to the shoreline or for power generation. On other lakes, the lake level rises and falls with differing weather conditions. Sellers are advised to disclose if the lake lot is not served by year round water to avoid claims by buyers. Buyers are encouraged to get a seller warranty that the lake lot is served by year round water if that is how the property is being sold.

Solution: The seller can add the following stipulation if the lake lot is not served by year round water.

> ### Special Stipulation 312: Lake Lot Not Served by Year Round Water
>
> *Buyer acknowledges that the Property is not served by year round water and that the lake is normally drawn down during the following time period: _____. During the time period when the lake has been drawn down, it is not possible to access the lake or launch a boat from the Property.*

The buyer can add the following special stipulation if the property is being sold as having year round water.

> ### Special Stipulation 313: Lake Lot Served by Year Round Water
>
> *Seller warrants that during the tenure of the Seller's ownership of the Property there was always sufficient water in the lake even when the lake level was down to access the lake from the Property and that the dock serving the Property always had water beneath it of at least _____ feet at all times during the year. This warranty shall survive the closing.*

If the level of the lake fluctuates significantly due to weather conditions, the following special stipulation can help protect the seller against claim.

> ### Special Stipulation 314: Lake Level Fluctuates with Weather Conditions
>
> *Buyer acknowledges that the level of the lake serving the Property rises and falls with weather conditions and that during times of drought the dock serving the Property may not have water beneath it to launch a boat from the dock.*

§ 15.1.3   The Property Being Purchased Is A Short Sale

Risk #1: The closing may be delayed while the Seller's mortgage lender approves the short sale.

Solution: The following special stipulation can be used to protect the buyer in this situation.

> ### Special Stipulation 315: Buyer Can Terminate Contract or Extend Closing Date if Mortgage Lender Has Not Approved Short Sale
>
> *In the event the Seller's mortgage lender(s) have not approved or disapproved the short sale contingency set forth in this Agreement by the date of closing, Buyer shall have the option to either: 1) terminate the Agreement without penalty upon notice to Seller; or 2) unilaterally extend the closing date for successive periods of _____ days upon notice to Seller until the short sale contingency is either approved or disapproved by Seller's mortgage lender(s). If Seller's mortgage lender(s) condition the approval of a short sale on the Buyer and Seller agreeing to certain amendments to the Purchase and Sale Agreement for the benefit of the mortgage lender(s), Buyer shall have the right to terminate this Agreement without penalty and upon notice to Seller if the proposed amendments are not acceptable to Buyer.*

§ 15.1.4   The Property Being Purchased Is On A Stream

Risk #1: Buyer purchases lot near a stream and cannot build because of required stream buffers.

Discussion: State law provides that buyers cannot build within 25 feet of the centerline of a stream.[1864] This requirement applies to both sides of the stream. While this requirement does not apply to ephemeral streams which do not run all year, buyers should be aware of this risk and plan accordingly.

> **Special Stipulation 316:   Buyer Can Terminate if Stream Buffer Requirements Apply**
>
> *Buyer and Seller acknowledge that there is a small creek or drainage ditch that runs across or on a portion of the Property and Seller has indicated that it does not run year round. In the event Buyer determines prior to closing from a governmental official that the creek or drainage ditch is in fact considered a year-round stream and that stream buffer requirements will apply to all new construction on the Property, Buyer may terminate this Agreement without penalty upon written notice to Seller.*

§ 15.1.5 The Property Is Served By Well Water

Risk #1: Well water is unsafe to drink.

Solution: Buyers who are relying on well water as their source of drinking water should always have the well water tested to ensure that it is safe to drink. This is particularly the case in the event that there are no nearby public water lines. The following special stipulation can be used to help provide buyers some protection in this situation.

> **Special Stipulation 317:   Buyer Can Terminate if Well Water Unsafe to Drink**
>
> *Buyer shall have the right prior to closing to have the well water serving the Property tested by an independent laboratory. In the event the test reveals that drinking the water is unsafe for human consumption, Buyer may terminate this Agreement without penalty upon written notice to Seller.*

§ 15.1.6 The Property Being Purchased Is Older Or Historic

Risk #1: The property contains a nonconforming zoning use.

Discussion: Many properties with older improvements on them were built prior to the adoption of a zoning ordinance in the jurisdiction in which the property is located. As such, the present use or uses of the property may no longer be permitted under the current zoning ordinance. Such a nonconforming use is normally grandfathered so long as the property has been continuously used for the nonconforming purpose. For example, a large single-family residence contains a separate carriage house that has always been rented as an apartment. Even if the property is zoned for single-family use, the property can normally continue to be used for two residences so long as the use began before the zoning ordinance was adopted and the use is continuous. However, if the nonconforming use was started after the adoption of the zoning ordinance, or if the use was abandoned for a period of time set forth in the local zoning ordinance[1865], the use would then be considered an illegal non-conforming use and would be subject to being cited as being in violation of the zoning ordinance.

Solution: A sample special stipulation for this type of use is set forth below.

> **Special Stipulation 318:   Buyer Can Terminate if Uses Violate Zoning**
>
> *Buyer acknowledges that the Property is currently zoned only for _____ _____ use. However, the Property has*

1864   O.C.G.A. § 12-7-6(b)(15)(A).

1865   Many local zoning ordinances provide that if a non-conforming use is discontinued for more than one (1) year, the non-conforming use loses its grandfathered status.

been continuously used for _____

_____

___ *use since before the adoption of the zoning ordinance in the jurisdiction in which the Property is located. Seller warrants that the nonconforming use of the Property is a lawful, non-conforming use under the zoning ordinance of the jurisdiction in which the Property is located. In the event Buyer determines prior to closing from local zoning enforcement officials that the nonconforming use is not a grandfathered use, Buyer may terminate this Agreement without penalty upon notice to Seller.*

Risk #2: Property is in a historic district and the exterior cannot be changed.

Discussion: Many older homes are located in historic districts and exterior modifications are either not permitted or are only permitted with permission from the Historic Preservation Commission.

Solution: If the buyer does not want to purchase the property if the exterior cannot be changed, the following special stipulation can be used.

> **Special Stipulation 319: Buyer Can Terminate if Property is in an Historic District**
>
> *Seller warrants that the Property is not located in a historic district, is not a certified historic structure, and that there are no local government restrictions preventing or limiting the modification of the exterior appearance of the improvements on the Property other than applicable setback and building code requirements and zoning requirements unrelated to historic property districts. In the event Buyer discovers prior to closing that there are other governmental restrictions on Buyer's ability to make exterior modifications to the improvements on the Property, or that Buyer cannot make exterior modifications without the approval of a historic preservation committee or its equivalent, Buyer may terminate this Agreement without penalty upon notice to Seller.*

§ 15.1.7 The Property Being Purchased Is An Existing Condominium Unit

Risk #1: Buyer cannot lease the unit.

Discussion: Most condominium developments have some type of restriction on the percentage of units that can be leased to help ensure that mortgages originated in the development can be sold in the secondary mortgage market. As a result, buyers purchasing units to lease should check to determine if the leasing of units will be permitted. The following special stipulation can be used to give the buyer a right to terminate the contract if the buyer cannot lease the property.

Solution: The following special stipulation may be included.

> **Special Stipulation 320: Buyer Can Terminate if Condominium Unit Cannot be Leased**
>
> *Seller warrants that leasing is permitted in the _____ Condominium and that any limit on the percentage of the condominium units in the community that can be leased has not yet been reached. If prior to closing, Buyer determines from the condominium association or its manager that Buyer will not be able to lease the Unit upon it being purchased, Buyer shall have the right to terminate this Agreement without penalty upon notice to Seller.*

Risk # 2: The number of units already leased in the condominium is so large that it is not possible for a buyer to obtain mortgage financing.

Discussion: If more than a certain percentage of units in a condominium are leased, it is often difficult to obtain mortgage financing.

Solution: The following type of special stipulation can protect a buyer in this situation.

> **Special Stipulation 321:   Buyer Can Terminate if Condominium Financing Falls Through Because of Number of Leased Units**
>
> *Notwithstanding any provision to the contrary contained herein, in the event Buyer is notified by the mortgage lender with whom Buyer has applied for mortgage financing that Buyer is ineligible to receive the mortgage loan for which Buyer applied because of the percentage of units already being leased in the condominium, Buyer may terminate this Agreement without penalty upon notice to Seller.*

Risk #3: The percentage of owners in the condominium who are delinquent in paying their assessments is so high that it is not possible for the buyer to obtain mortgage financing.

Discussion: If more than a certain percentage of units in the condominium are delinquent in paying their assessments, it is often difficult to obtain mortgage financing.

Solution: A stipulation like the one set forth below can help the buyer in this situation.

> **Special Stipulation 322:   Buyer Can Terminate if Condominium Financing Falls Through Because of Delinquencies**
>
> *Notwithstanding any provision to the contrary contained herein, in the event Buyer is turned down for a mortgage loan because of the percentage of owners delinquent in paying assessments to the condominium association is too high, Buyer may terminate this Agreement without penalty upon written notice to Seller.*

Risk #4: There is a pending or proposed special assessment which seller did not disclose.

Discussion: If a large special assessment is planned or pending, some unscrupulous sellers will try to quickly sell their condominium units to avoid having to pay the special assessment. The following special stipulation can help protect against this possibility.

> **Special Stipulation 323:   No Pending Special Assessment**
>
> *Seller warrants that to the best of Seller's knowledge there are no special assessments either pending, being considered or which have been approved by the condominium association or Board of Directors that would be in excess of $_____ against the Property for calendar year _____ . In the event Buyer determines prior to closing that a special assessment greater than the above stated amount is being considered, is pending or has been approved, Buyer can terminate this Agreement without penalty upon notice to Seller.*

§ 15.1.8   The Property Being Purchased Is A New Construction Home

Risk #1: The builder goes out of business before the home is completed.

Solution: There are several ways to mitigate this risk. First, and most obvious, buyers should try to work with a builder who is financially stable and unlikely to go out of business. Second, to the extent possible, buyers should try to avoid advancing large sums of money directly to the builder. This may be difficult to do since most builders want as much earnest money as possible and will likely only perform upgrades if the builder is paid for them in advance. However, the buyer can propose that earnest money be held by the brokerage firm representing the buyer rather than the builder or by some other more neutral party. Similarly, the buyer can hold off on upgrades until after the closing where there is no longer a risk of the builder losing the property to foreclosure.

Risk #2: The house is not built in accordance with the plans and specifications.

Discussion: The most important part of any new home construction contract is the section that specifies what the builder is going to build. Many construction disputes arise because of a lack of specificity in the construction plans and specifications attached to the agreement. This lack of specificity can lead to different expectations on the part of the builder and homebuyer as to the size, type and quality of the home to be constructed by the builder.

Solution: The more detailed the plans and specifications the less the likelihood for disputes. The plans should preferably be an exhibit and incorporated into the contract where there is no question as to what the builder is obligated to build. The plans and specifications should be carefully reviewed by the buyer since the builder's obligations are generally limited to those things shown on the plans. If there are written construction specifications attached to the contract, they should be easy to understand. If the specifications are unclear, the buyer should have them rewritten so that a third party, such as a judge can read them and know what the intent was of the parties. The plans and specifications should not only address how the residence on the property will be built but also cover where the improvements will be built on the lot, the grade of the main floor of the residence relative to the grade of the street and how the other improvements on the lot besides a residence such as driveways, walkways, outbuildings, swimming pools, patios, and walls will be constructed.

In addition, the plans and specifications should be carefully finalized to limit the number of change orders. Change orders are agreed-upon deviations from the approved building plans and specifications. Oftentimes, change orders occur because buyers change their mind, mistakes are made by architects or draftsmen, previously unknown site conditions or building peculiarities are discovered, shortages or price increases in particular materials necessitate a change in a chosen building product or other reason unforeseen at the time the plans and specifications are created. Since change orders are practically inevitable, each change order should be as detailed as possible to reflect each change to the plans and specifications and the costs associated with those changes. Each change order should also be signed off and paid for before all of the work is complete.

Risk #3: The development in which the property is located not being completed.

Solution: In this last recession, the biggest risk buyers faced in buying homes in new subdivisions was being one of only a few houses actually built in the subdivision where the remainder of the subdivision were essentially pipe farms of vacant lots with stubbed out plumbing lines sticking out of concrete slabs. While many of these subdivisions were eventually developed, they were often developed with much less expensive homes. As a result, the value of the early homes built in these subdivisions decreased significantly. Being the first to buy in a subdivision carries risks that buyers need to understand. Oftentimes, builders will offer introductory pricing as a way to mitigate that risk. Just as a buyer should evaluate the financial strength of the builder, the same should be done with the developer as well if the developer is someone other than the builder. Of course, if the developer makes a sizable investment in the community's amenities, roads and entrance features, it is a good indicator that the developer is well capitalized. Some of the risks in this area are difficult to eliminate. In such cases, buyers should take the time to understand the risks so that they have realistic expectations in the event of a problem.

Risk #4: The house is not completed on time.

Solution: New homes are sometimes not completed on time. In some cases, the delays are because of factors beyond the control of the builder such as long periods of inclement weather, governmental moratoriums or the shortages of particular building materials. In other cases, the problem is human error or a lack of organization or effort. Almost every new home construction contract includes what is known as a force majeure provision that excuses the builder from delays caused by circumstances beyond the control of the builder. One way to limit extensions of time resulting from a claim of force majeure is to require the builder to notify the buyer within the same month of any delay that slows the progress of the work. An example of such a provision is set forth below.

Special Stipulation 324:   Builder Must Give Timely Notice of Delays

Notwithstanding any provision to the contrary contained herein, in order for Seller to avail itself of the force majeure provision set forth herein, Seller must notify the Buyer within the same month (or in the event of force majeure delays during the last week of the month or the first seven (7) days of the following month) that any delay occurs stating the date or dates on which there was a delay and the act or circumstance beyond the control of the Seller which occasioned the delay. Seller agrees that only delays causing work not to be performed for an entire day may be counted as a delay for which the force majeure provision may be applied. In the event Seller fails to notify buyer of such delays within time periods specified herein, Seller shall waive any right to contractually claim a legally valid excuse for such delay.

Another approach to builder delays in completing the house is to provide that if the residence is not completed by the date of closing, the Seller will reduce the sales price by a specified amount for every day thereafter that the residence is not complete. Sometimes, the builder will be given the unilateral right to extend the closing date for a certain period of time without reducing the sales price and any reductions in sales price only kick in after that date. An example of such a provision is set forth below.

Special Stipulation 325:   Sales Price Reduced if Builder Does Not Finish On Time

Seller shall have the right to unilaterally extend the closing date for up to thirty (30) days from the date set forth herein upon at least ten (10) days prior written notice to Buyer from the original closing date to allow for unanticipated delays beyond the control of Seller. Notwithstanding any provision to the contrary contained herein, in the event the improvements on the Property remain incomplete after the thirty (30) day extension, the sales price of the Property shall thereafter be reduced by $_____ per day for each day thereafter that the improvements remain incomplete. For the purposes of this Agreement the term "incomplete" shall mean that: 1) the improvements on the Property have not been constructed in substantial accordance with the Plans and Specifications attached hereto as an exhibit; and 2) the local governing authority has not issued a certificate of occupancy for such improvements. All parties agree that the reduction in the sales price shall be liquidated damages and reflect a reasonable pre-estimate of buyer's actual damages rather than being a penalty.

§ 15.1.9   The Seller Is Unfamiliar With The Property

Risk #1: The improvements on the property may be in poor condition with many unknown items needing to be repaired and/or replaced.

Solution: There are circumstances in which the seller of a property will not be particularly familiar with its condition and will want to sell the property in "as-is" condition. Many sellers mistakenly believe that selling the property "as-is" will eliminate the need to disclose latent or hidden defects of which the seller is aware. This is not the case as is discussed in greater detail in Chapter 9 (Disclosures). Sellers looking to disclaim knowledge of a property's condition should consider using the following special stipulation.

Special Stipulation 326: Seller Disclaims Condition of Property

Buyer acknowledges that Seller is not familiar with the condition of the Property. The Property is therefore being sold in "as-is" condition. The Property contains numerous conditions that are in need of repair or replacement. While Seller is unaware of latent or hidden defects in the Property, Seller has not examined the Property in search of latent or hidden defects. Buyer agrees to have the Property inspected by a professional home inspector, engineer and / or other construction experts to ensure that Buyer is familiar with the condition of the Property. Buyer covenants not to sue Seller for any matter arising out of or relating to the condition of the Property.

§ 15.1.10 The Property Being Purchased Is Leased

Risk #1: The written lease has unknowingly been amended or the provisions therein have been waived.

Solution: The following type of provision can help protect the buyer against this risk.

Special Stipulation 327: Seller Warrants That Lease Has Not Been Modified

Seller warrants that: 1) the lease attached hereto as an exhibit to this Agreement is complete, accurate and in full force and effect as of the Binding Agreement Date and has not been modified, amended or waived by Seller or Tenant; and 2) the Tenant under the Lease is not in default of any provisions under the Lease. This warranty shall survive the closing.

In commercial real estate transactions, the buyer will often require the seller to provide what are known as estoppel certificates in which the existing tenants certify that the lease has not been changed, is in full force and effect and that the tenant thereunder is not in breach of the agreement. Such estoppel certificates help prevent the tenant from coming back later and claiming that the lease agreement had been amended.

Risk #2: The property is being leased illegally.

Discussion: There are some single family home developments and many condominium associations where the leasing of property is prohibited or severely limited. The best way to protect against this risk is to carefully review the covenants or condominium documents applicable to the property during the Due Diligence Period. However, if the property is being sold with a lease in place, the buyer can also get the seller to warrant that the property is not being leased illegally.

Solution: The following special stipulation can help protect the buyer against this risk.

Special Stipulation 328: Property is Not Being Leased Illegally

Buyer and Seller acknowledge that the Property is being sold subject to an existing lease. Seller warrants that to the best of Seller's knowledge and belief, there are no covenants or other legal restrictions that prohibit leasing on which the present lease violates.

§ 15.1.11 The Property Being Purchased Is Leased For Agricultural Cultivation

Risk: The property is subject to an agricultural lease with a term that extends past the closing date.

Discussion: This is a common issue in the sale of farm land and large acreage tracts. Most sellers in this situation will add a special stipulation that the property is leased for agricultural cultivation and the term of any such lease.

Solution: The following special stipulation may be used to protect against this risk.

Special Stipulation 329: Property Subject to an Agricultural Lease

The Property is presently leased to _____ for agricultural cultivation until the date of _____. The rent ☐ includes Farm Service Agency (FSA) OR

☐ *does not include FSA payments as a part of the rent. Any prepaid rent and/or FSA payments* ☐ *will OR* ☐ *will not be prorated at closing. Any rent and/or FSA payments due for the current crop year* ☐ *will OR* ☐ *will not be prorated at closing. A copy of the lease* ☐ *is OR* ☐ *is not attached.*

§ 15.1.12   The Property Being Purchased Is Leased For Hunting

Risk: The property is subject to a lease for hunting rights with a term that extends past the closing.

Discussion: This is another common issue in the sale of large acreage tracts. The Hunting Rights special stipulation in the GAR Special Stipulations identifies any lease of hunting rights on the property as well as the term for such lease. It also provides for the parties to identify whether prepaid payments or payments due for the year of closing will be prorated at closing.

Solution: The following special stipulation may be used to protect against this risk.

> ### Special Stipulation 330:   Property Subject to Lease for Hunting
>
> *The Property is presently leased to _____ for hunting rights until the date of _____. Prepaid payments* ☐ *will OR* ☐ *will not be prorated at closing. Payments due for the current year* ☐ *will OR* ☐ *will not be prorated at closing. A copy of the lease* ☐ *is OR* ☐ *is not attached.*

§ 15.1.13   The Property Being Purchased Is Condemned After The Purchase And Sale Agreement Becomes Binding But Before Closing

Risk #1: The property is condemned after a contract has been signed but before the closing.

Discussion: While the possibility of condemnation is generally thought to be more of a risk in commercial transactions, it also occurs in residential transactions.

Solution: Most buyers will add a provision giving them the right to either: (i) terminate the purchase and sale agreement if a condemnation action is commenced; or (ii) close on the purchase and receive the proceeds from the condemnation. A sample special provision is set for the below.

> ### Special Stipulation 331:   Buyer Can Terminate if Condemnation Proceeding Commenced Against Property or Close and Receive Condemnation Proceeds
>
> *If, after the Binding Agreement Date and prior to Closing, Seller receives notice of the commencement or threatened commencement of condemnation or other similar proceedings against the Property or any portion thereof, Seller shall immediately notify Buyer in writing of the same. Within ten (10) days of receipt of such notice Buyer shall elect to either (a) terminate the Agreement without penalty by delivering written notice of such decision to Seller; or (b) close the transaction contemplated herein in accordance with its terms, but subject to such condemnation proceedings, in which event the Purchase Price shall remain the same but Seller shall transfer and assign to Buyer at Closing the right to receive all condemnation proceeds. In the event all or a portion of the condemnation proceeds have already been paid to Seller, the purchase price of the Property shall be reduced by the amount of the condemnation proceeds paid to Seller. If Buyer elects to purchase the Property after the receipt of such a notice, all actions taken by Seller with regard to such eminent domain proceedings, including, but not limited to, negotiations, litigation, settlement, appraisals and appeals, shall be subject to the approval*

of Buyer. If Buyer does not notify Seller at all after receiving the above-referenced notice by Seller, Buyer shall be deemed to have elected to close the transaction contemplated hereby in accordance with clause (b) of this Section.

§ 15.2   RISK ALLOCATION IN REAL ESTATE CHECKLISTS

Knowing what can go wrong in different types of real estate transactions is often learned through the school of hard knocks. One a real estate licensee is involved in a particular type of transaction in which something may or goes wrong, the licensee will normally either advise the licensee's client of the risk and/or include some provision in the contract to try to prevent the same problem from occurring again as a result of the risk. This next section identifies many of the risks that exist in real estate transactions and offers some guidance on how those risks are normally addressed.

§ 15.2.1   Risks Relating To The Condition Of The Property

RISK	HOW TO MITIGATE RISK
1. The Property not being the acreage the buyer thought.	1. Get a survey done during the Due Diligence Period to determine the exact acreage of the property.
2. The improvements on the Property being smaller than what the buyer thought.	2. Have an architect measure the square footage of the improvements on the property.
3. The boundary lines of the property not being where the buyer thought they were.	3. Get a survey done during the Due Diligence Period and have surveyor mark the exact location of the boundary lines.
4. The property having hidden or latent defects.	4. Have the property inspected by a professional home inspector or engineer.
5. The property having patent or obvious defects.	5. Have the property inspected by a professional home inspector or engineer.
6. The property having conditions that violate existing building code (but are grandfathered).	6. Have the property inspected by a professional home inspector or engineer.
7. The property having conditions that violate existing building code and are not grandfathered.	7. Have the property inspected by a professional home inspector or engineer. Call the local code enforcement to see if they have a record of uncorrected code violations.
8. The location of the improvements on the property violating building setback requirements.	8. Get a survey done during the Due Diligence Period to identify the exact building setback requirements and whether there are setback violations.
9. The property being a lawful nonconforming use under zoning.	9. Check with local zoning officials to determining if the property as it is being used is a lawful, non-conforming use.
10. The property being an illegal nonconforming use under zoning.	10. Check with local zoning officials to see if the use of the property is an illegal, non-conforming use.
11. A murder having taken place on the property.	11. Ask the owner if anyone was murdered on the property. Do a computer search of the property address to see if there are any news stories about the property and check with neighbors.
12. The house having been used as a meth lab.	12. Check the website of properties that were used for drug labs – http://www.justice.gov/dea/seizures/indes.html on page 353. Check with local police officials.

RISK	HOW TO MITIGATE RISK
13. The property (but not the house) being in a flood plain.	**13.** Have a survey done during the Due Diligence Period that identifies the location of flood plains.
14. The improvements on the property being in a flood plain.	**14.** Have a survey done during the Due Diligence Period showing the location of the flood plain. Include a stipulation giving the buyer the right to terminate the contract if the improvements are in a flood plain.
15. The improvements being built on a sewer or drainage line.	**15.** Get survey done which shows the location of all easements.
16. The property having termites, powder post beetles, carpenter ants, bed bugs, fleas, etc.	**16.** Have a licensed Georgia pest control operator inspect the property for termites and other wood destroying organisms.
17. The property having mold.	**17.** Have the property inspected by a professional property inspector. Be alert for dank smells in basements and other parts of the improvements on the property below grade.
18. The carpet in the house being stained and smelling of pet urine.	**18.** Be alert to perfumed houses with pets living in them. Have the home inspector pull back carpeted areas for signs of staining from pet urine.
19. The buyer thinking the property is served by sewer when it is really served by septic system.	**19.** Check with the local sewer department to see if the property is served by sewer.
20. Trees on the property being diseased.	**20.** Inspect the trees for disease. Have an arborist or tree service inspect suspicious looking trees.
21. Trees on the property being dead.	**21.** Look for dead trees. Have an arborist or tree service inspect the trees.
22. The property being destroyed by fire or other casualty before closing.	**22.** Confirm that the purchase and sale contract can be terminated without penalty in the event of a fire prior to closing.
23. An appliance in the house breaking before closing.	**23.** Provide in the purchase and sale agreement that all appliances will be in good working order and repair as of the date of closing. Have a professional home inspector inspect the appliances.
24. A system in the property (HVAC) breaking before closing.	**24.** Have all systems in the property inspected by a professional property inspector. Provide in the contract that all systems will be in good working order and repair as of the date of closing.
25. A storm destroying a beautiful, large specimen tree on the property.	**25.** Provide in the purchase and sale agreement that the buyer can terminate the contract prior to closing if the property is not in substantially the same condition on the closing date as it was in on the binding agreement date.
26. The condition of the property changing between the date of contract and the date of closing.	**26.** Provide in the purchase and sale agreement that the buyer can terminate the contract prior to closing if the property is not in substantially the same condition on the closing date as it was in on the binding agreement date.
27. The property being condemned prior to closing.	**27.** Provide in the purchase and sale agreement that the buyer can terminate the contract if the seller receives a notice of condemnation or if there is an ongoing condemnation proceeding involving the property.

RISK	HOW TO MITIGATE RISK
28. The house having high levels of radon.	**28.** Have the house tested for radon during the Due Diligence Period.
29. The house having lead based paint.	**29.** Have an older home (built before 1978) tested for lead-based paint.
30. The house having asbestos.	**30.** Have an older house tested for asbestos.
31. The house having synthetic stucco.	**31.** Have the house inspected by a professional home inspector. If there is synthetic stucco, have the stucco tested for moisture being trapped behind the stucco which can rot wood support structure and cause mold.
32. The house having defective siding.	**32.** Have the house inspected by a professional home inspector.
33. The house having double-paned windows whose seals have been broken.	**33.** Look for signs of condensation or a film between the two panes. Have the house inspected by a professional home inspector.
34. The house having aluminum wiring which can create a greater risk of fire.	**34.** Have the house inspected by a professional home inspector.
35. The basement leaking or periodically flooding.	**35.** Have the house inspected by a professional home inspector. Look for signs of water staining on basement walls and look for signs of wood rot at the bottom of basement doors. Look to see if there is positive site drainage away from the house. Look to see if downspouts direct water away from the property. Look for a basement sump pump and check with neighbors.
36. The property has windows that leak.	**36.** Have the property inspected by a professional property inspector. Look for evidence of water staining or wood rot on interior window frames. Look to see if windows close and properly seal.
37. The property has leaks from siding, roof or interior plumbing.	**37.** Have the property inspected by a professional home inspector. Look for evidence of water stains on interior walls, floors and ceilings. Look beneath floor rugs for evidence of staining.
38. The property has gutters that need to be replaced or adjusted.	**38.** Have the property inspected by a professional property inspector. Look for evidence of clogged gutters, gutters having pulled away from house, rotted fascia behind gutter, and rusted gutters.
39. The house has squirrels or possums in the attic.	**39.** Have the property inspected by a professional property inspector. Look for evidence of holes or openings in roof soffits, fascia or siding near the attic.
40. The house has damaged hardwood flooring.	**40.** Have the property inspected by a professional property inspector. Look for evidence of wood rot or termite damage to hardwood floors. Look for scratches or gouges in floors particularly near heavy furniture, chairs and beneath rugs. Look beneath any potted plant or pet food bowls for evidence of water damage to the hardwood floors.
41. The seller not owning personal property being sold to the buyer.	**41.** Have a UCC search done to see if the property is being subject to a UCC filing.
42. The house not having GFI outlets in bathrooms and the kitchen.	**42.** Have the property inspected by a professional property inspector. Look for outlets without trip and reset buttons.

RISK	HOW TO MITIGATE RISK
43. The electrical service on the property being undersized.	**43.** Have the property inspected by a professional property inspector. Look for small or older electrical panels.
44. The house not having high efficiency, low flow toilets.	**44.** Have the property inspected by a professional property inspector. Open to toilet lid to see if it indicates how many gallons per flush it uses.
45. The house having older water lines which may need to be replaced.	**45.** Have the property inspected by a professional property inspector. Turn on faucets to see if the water is initially rusty.
46. The house having inadequate water pressure.	**46.** Have the property inspected by a professional property inspector. Turn on showers and faucets to observe water pressure.
47. The property having settlement problems.	**47.** Have the property inspected by a professional property inspector or engineer. Look for cracks in the building exterior. Look for cracks in sheetrock. Look for doors that no longer can be closed. Look for sloping floors. Look for doors and windows that look out of plumb or out of kilter. Look for large trees planted too close to the house which could cause upheaval of the foundation.
48. The property having older, energy inefficient windows.	**48.** Have the property inspected by a professional property inspector. Look for older, single-pane windows. Look for windows that have been painted shut or no longer can be opened or closed.
49. The property lacking attic insulation.	**49.** Look at the amount of attic insulation. Have the property inspected by a professional property inspector.
50. The chimney having settled.	**50.** Look for signs of the chimney having pulled away from the house or cracked. Have the chimney inspected by a professional home inspector.
51. The chimney having creosote buildup.	**51.** Have the property inspected by a professional property inspector. Ask for reports showing that the chimney has been cleaned.
52. The house having an old, energy inefficient heating and air conditioning system.	**52.** Have the property inspected by a professional home inspector. Look for a date of manufacture of the system.
53. The house having an old hot water heater.	**53.** Have the property inspected by a professional property inspector. Check for a date of manufacture of the hot water heater.
54. The property having an older, leaking roof.	**54.** Have the property inspected by a professional property inspector. Look for cracked, broken our buckling roof shingles. Look for mold or algae growth on the shingles which can shorten its useful life.
55. The house having a leaking shower or tub.	**55.** Have the house inspected by a professional property inspector. Look to see if tile or tile grout is missing or cracked. Look to see if tub surrounds are properly caulked.
56. The house having leaking toilets.	**56.** Have the property inspected by a professional property inspector. Look to see if the toilet is firmly bolted to the floor. Look for evidence of wood rot or stains from leaking toilets around the base of the toilet.

RISK	HOW TO MITIGATE RISK
57. The house having leaking faucets.	**57.** Have the property inspected by a professional property inspector. Turn on faucets for evidence of leaks.
58. The property other than the house having settlement problems.	**58.** Have the property inspected by a professional property inspector. Look for cracked and unusually sloped sidewalks and driveways. Look for evidence of entrance or exit stairs having cracked, pulled away from the house, sloping at an unusual angle or having extremely large caulk joints where previous settlement has been fixed. Look for upheaval of sidewalks where there are tripping hazards.
59. The property having a burial pit or sinkholes.	**59.** Have the property inspected by a professional property inspector. Have the pit tested by a soil engineer. Look for evidence of unusual depressions in the soil.
60. The property having retaining walls that are not structurally sound.	**60.** Have retaining walls inspected by a structural engineer. Look for evidence of walls cracking or bowing. Look for evidence of wood rot on walls made of treated timbers. Look for evidence of sinkholes along the top of walls. Look for evidence on larger retaining walls that the walls lack drainage or weep holes to relieve hydrostatic pressure.
61. The property having erosion problems.	**61.** Have the property inspected by a professional property inspector. Look for steep slopes with little or no landscaping or ground cover. Look for evidence of soil erosion.
62. The property having site drainage problems.	**62.** Have the property inspected by a professional property inspector. Look for areas that receive and pond water runoff.
63. The property having a faulty septic system.	**63.** Have the septic system inspected by a company specializing in such inspections. Look for wet, mushy areas near septic fields. Look for areas with septic smell. Determine from Department of Health how many bedrooms the system was designed to serve.
64. The property having a broken irrigation system.	**64.** Have the irrigation system inspected by a reputable irrigation company.
65. The property having a leaking or broken swimming pool.	**65.** Have the pool inspected by an engineer or swimming pool company.
66. The property having insufficient or broken exterior lighting.	**66.** Have the exterior lighting tested by a professional property inspector.

§ 15.2.2 Risks Involving Financing And/Or The Economy The Buyer Faces When He Or She Signs A Contract

RISK	HOW TO MITIGATE RISK
1. The Property not appraising.	**1.** Make the purchase and sale agreement subject to the property appraising for at least the purchase price.
2. The buyer's mortgage lender going out of business.	**2.** Give the purchaser the right to extend the closing date in the purchase and sale agreement for 30 days if the lender goes out of business. Work with a reputable lender.
3. The lender not approving the loan.	**3.** Make the purchase and sale agreement subject to a financing contingency.

RISK	HOW TO MITIGATE RISK
4. The lender approving the loan and then disapproving the loan.	**4.** Make the purchase and sale agreement subject to a financing contingency that is as long as possible.
5. Interest rates increasing.	**5.** Lock in an interest rate early. Make the purchase and sale agreement subject to a financing contingency tied to a maximum interest rate.
6. A special loan program disappearing.	**6.** Include in the purchase and sale agreement as long a financing contingency as possible.
7. The housing market crashing.	**7.** Limit the amount of the earnest money and limit the seller's damages to the retention of the earnest money. Tie the purchase to an appraisal contingency.
8. The lender not being ready to close on the date of closing.	**8.** Include a right to unilaterally extend the closing date if the lender is not ready to close.
9. The closing attorney not being ready to close on the date of closing.	**9.** Include a right to unilaterally extend the closing date if the attorney is not ready to close.
10. The buyer or the buyer's spouse losing their job.	**10.** Have as long a financing contingency as possible.
11. The buyer needing to rent existing property in order to qualify for a loan.	**11.** Make the purchase subject to the lease for existing property. Have as long a financing contingency as possible.
12. The buyer needing to sell existing property in order to be able to buy a new property.	**12.** From the buyer's perspective, make the contract contingent upon the sale of the other property at a particular price by a specific date. Have as long a financing contingency as possible. Have a delayed closing to accommodate the need to sell the property. Offer to list the other property to be sold to maximize the likelihood of it selling.
13. The buyer needs a guarantor on her loan.	**13.** Have as long a financing contingency as possible. (From the seller's perspective, this risk is mitigated by having the guarantor be a co-buyer of the property).

§ 15.2.3 Risks Relating To Changing Life Circumstances The Buyer Faces In Signing A Purchase And Sale Contract

RISK	HOW TO MITIGATE RISK
1. The buyer dying.	**1.** Include a provision not making the purchase and sale agreement binding on the heirs of the buyer.
2. The buyer losing her job and not being able to afford to buyer the property.	**2.** Include a financing contingency in the purchase and sale agreement for a long as possible.
3. The buyer being transferred to another city and not wanting to buy the property.	**3.** Include a special stipulation giving the buyer the right to terminate the purchase and sale agreement without penalty in the event the buyer is transferred to another city.
4. The buyer being diagnosed with a fatal disease and not wanting to buy the property.	**4.** Limit the earnest money paid in the transaction and limit the seller's damages to retaining the earnest money.

RISK	HOW TO MITIGATE RISK
5. The buyer getting divorced before they close and not wanting to buy the property.	5. Limit the earnest money paid in the transaction and limit the seller's damages to retaining the earnest money.
6. The seller dying.	6. Make the contract binding upon the heirs of the seller and be willing to wait in that eventuality.
7. The seller refusing to close.	7. Include a right of specific performance in the contract.
8. The seller trying to change the deal.	8. Have a well-drafted contract that does not give the seller an ability to get out of her obligations.
9. The seller refusing to move.	9. Have the seller transfer possession of the property at closing. Check to see if the seller has moved right before closing.
10. The seller removing a fixture from the property.	10. Be clear in the purchase and sale agreement as to what can and cannot be removed from the property. Inspect the property right before closing.
11. The seller damaging the property when moving out.	11. Inspect the property right before closing. Get a security deposit if the seller is remaining in the property after closing.
12. The seller being foreclosed on before the closing.	12. Have the seller warrant that she is not subject to any foreclosure action. Contact the lender immediately if you learn of a foreclosure to determine if the lender will sell the property.
13. The seller is holding earnest money and will not return it.	13. Have the broker hold the earnest money.

§ 15.2.4 Risks Relating To Neighborhood Conditions The Buyer Faces When He or She Buys A House

RISK	HOW TO MITIGATE RISK
1. The Property turning out not to be in the city or county buyer thinks it is.	1. Carefully study a map to confirm where the property is located.
2. The Property turning out not to be in the homeowners association that the buyer thinks it is.	2. Review the property that is subject to being in the homeowners association during the Due Diligence Period. Check with the homeowners association.
3. The Property turning out not to be in the school district that the buyer thinks it is.	3. Check with the school district on school boundary lines and plans to change the same.
4. The Property having an objectionable land use near the Property (quarry, landfill, chicken rendering plant, high-tension power lines, airport).	4. Do a computer search of maps based on satellite photographs to determine nearby uses. Inspect the neighborhood using all of your senses.
5. There being an objectionable planned use near the Property (road widening, new development, etc.).	5. Check with local transportation officials and planners.
6. There being a registered sex offender in the neighborhood.	6. Review the sex offender list. www.gbi.georgia.gov Speak with neighbors.
7. There being excessive crime in the neighborhood.	7. Check with the local police department regarding crime in the neighborhood. Speak with neighbors.

RISK	HOW TO MITIGATE RISK
8. The schools in the neighborhood having bad test scores.	8. Check with the local Board of Education to determine test scores.
9. Property values are declining near the property.	9. Check trends in comparable home sales.
10. The buyer having a neighbor who does not take care of her property.	10. Carefully inspect nearby properties to learn whether neighbors have similar standards.

§ 15.2.5 Risks The Buyer Faces Relative To The Title Of The Property

RISK	HOW TO MITIGATE RISK
1. The seller does not own the property.	1. Get a title search done of the property. Buy title insurance.
2. Not all sellers sign the deed.	2. Get a title search done to determine who owns the property. Buy title insurance.
3. A seller's signature is forged on the deed.	3. Have the sellers sing the deed in the presence of the closing attorney. Buy title insurance.
4. There is a lien or mortgage on the property that is not discovered until after the closing.	4. Have a title search done of the property. Buy title insurance.
5. *Ad valorem* property taxes are owed on the property.	5. Have the closing attorney get a tax report on the property.
6. A neighbor's improvements encroach on the property.	6. Get a boundary survey prepared of the property. Buy title insurance. Buy an enhanced title insurance policy.
7. Part of your improvements encroach on a neighbor's property.	7. Get a survey and buy title insurance.
8. There is an unrecorded easement across the property.	8. Buy title insurance. Inspect the property for evidence of unrecorded easements.
9. There is a recorded easement across the property.	9. Get a title search done. Have a survey prepared showing the location of easements. Buy title insurance.
10. There are covenants affecting the property.	10. Get a title search done. Get copies of all recorded covenants during the Due Diligence Period.
11. There is a federal tax lien on the property.	11. Get a title search done.
12. The improvements built over a setback line.	12. Get a survey done which marks the setback lines and the location of improvements. Discuss violations with local planning staff.

The **RED BOOK**

CHAPTER 16

SHORT SALES AND REO PROPERTIES

OVERVIEW

This chapter addresses issues created when buyers and sellers experience financial difficulties. The first is the "short sale," which occurs when a property is sold for an amount insufficient to pay the mortgage encumbrance on the property and the mortgage holder agrees to accept a "short" payment in full satisfaction of the obligation. The second is the filing of a bankruptcy petition by sellers, buyers, builders, or lenders. Finally, this chapter will address the purchase and sale of "REO" (real estate owned) property being sold by the financial institution that foreclosed on a mortgage.

§ 16.1   SHORT SALES

A "short sale" occurs when the value of the property being sold is less than the total of the outstanding liens against the property. In order for the sale to happen at all, the lender(s) must agree to accept less than the full amount owed (a "short" payoff). Lenders are sometimes willing to do so in order to avoid dealing with a foreclosure. The lender accepts a "short" payment on the outstanding mortgage rather than deal with the delays, costs, and frustrations of a foreclosure when the owner/seller can no longer afford to keep up the payments.

§ 16.1.1   Preparing The Seller

Sellers need to understand that no short sale can occur without the lender's full agreement. In order to obtain that agreement, sellers need to go through something of a "reverse mortgage application" process. They will need to submit proof that they are unable to afford making payments on the loan(s) and have limited assets. Having a financial hardship which results in the owner no longer being able to afford the mortgage is the key to being approved for a short sale. Not wanting to pay on a mortgage which now exceeds the value of the property is almost never a basis to approve a short sale if the owner can still afford to make mortgage payments. Lenders usually request documentation similar to a typical loan application: pay stubs, bank statements, verification of savings accounts or investments, liquid 401K assets, etc. Sellers will also need a complete and up-to-date listing of all liens against the property: secondary mortgages, tax liens, etc. The documentation should be submitted to the lender with a "hardship letter" outlining the sources of the sellers' financial difficulties. This information typically has to be updated every 30 days. The challenge for listing agents with the short sale process is how to keep the seller sufficiently motivated to continue to provide the lender with needed information. Reminding sellers that a short sale generally has far less of an adverse effect on a person's credit score than a foreclosure is a good motivation.

§ 16.1.1.1   Tax Consequences

There may be negative tax consequences to a short sale. Specifically, unless the seller qualifies for an exception, the amount of debt forgiven on the mortgage is likely to be considered the equivalent of taxable income. For example, a mortgage on a property has an outstanding balance of $290,000 and the home is sold for $260,000. After deduction of commission and costs of sale the mortgage holder receives $245,000 in full payment of the mortgage, forgiving the $45,000 remaining amount. Unlike the borrower whose debt was forgiven qualifies for an exemption, it is likely that sellers would have to claim the $45,000 debt forgiveness as income and be prepared to pay taxes on that amount.

The general rule is that any forgiveness of mortgage debt on a person's residence is taxable income to the borrower unless the borrower qualifies for an exemption.[1866] The most common exemptions are set forth in the Mortgage Forgiveness Debt Relief Act of 2007.[1867] Under this federal law, up to $2 million in forgiven debt does not have to be counted as income on your federal tax return.[1868] However, this only applies to a person's primary residence.[1869]

1866   26 U.S.C.A. § 108(a).

1867   PL 110-142, 121 Stat 1803 (December 20, 2007) ("Mortgage Forgiveness Debt Relief Act of 2007").

1868   26 U.S.C.A. § 108(h)(2).

1869   26 U.S.C.A. § 108(h)(2).

Forgiveness of debt on investment property and second homes does not qualify for the exemption.[1870] Home equity loans used to pay off credit card debt or make other purchases also do not qualify for this exemption.[1871]

The debt cancelled by the lender must have been used "to buy, build or substantially improve your principal residence."[1872] Therefore, if the seller's need for a short sale is the result of the seller having obtained a home equity loan that was used for other things, the seller may not be entitled to the relief the seller was thinking she would obtain. The federal law also contains a sunset provision where the tax benefit to owners selling in a short sale expires at the end of 2012.[1873] It is unclear whether the law will be extended.

Sellers should be advised to consult their accountant or tax attorney for details relative to their specific situation.

§ 16.1.1.2 Mortgage Fraud Issues

Sellers also need to review how they reported the state of their financial affairs at the time they obtained the loan. Did they "fudge" a little (or outright lie) on their initial loan application to make it appear they were qualified to obtain the loan? If so, providing an accurate picture on the backend is likely to reveal their earlier untruthfulness and may potentially result in accusations of mortgage fraud.[1874] For example, if someone reported owning several automobiles, a boat, and a vacation home on their initial loan application, but does not show these assets when attempting to negotiate a short sale, the lender may well inquire as to their disposition. If the borrower cannot explain what became of them, this could be a problem.

§ 16.1.2 Role Of Real Estate Licensee In The Short Sale Process

State law limits what real estate licensee can do to assist a seller in obtaining short sale approval from the lender. The Georgia Residential Mortgage Act (GRMA) requires anyone who "directly or indirectly solicits, processes, places or negotiates mortgage loans for others" to be licensed as a mortgage broker.[1875] The Georgia Department of Banking and Finance has interpreted this definition broadly to mean that real estate licensees are not permitted to negotiate with a mortgage lender over reducing the amount of a mortgage loan to accommodate a short sale transaction. Specifically, the Georgia Department of Banking and Finance has states that "negotiating terms of any loan and/or modifying the current loan terms for a client with a lender would require a Mortgage Loan Originator License.[1876]

One of the exemptions from GRMA is for "a real estate broker or real estate sales person not actively engaged in the business of negotiating mortgage loans; however, a real estate broker or real estate sales person who directly or indirectly negotiates, places or funds a mortgage for others shall not be exempt from the provisions of this article.[1877] Based upon this exemption, the Georgia Department of Banking and Finance has indicated that a real estate licensee can "provide facts and information regarding the subject property to a lender"[1878] such as conducting a market analysis, recommending a list price or presenting offers to the lender.

1870   26 U.S.C.A. § 121(a). "Gross income shall not include gain from the sale or exchange of property if, during the 5 year period ending on the date of the sale or exchange, such property has been owed and used by the tax payer as the taxpayer's principal residence for periods aggregating two years or more." Any period less than this would not make the home a principal residence.

1871   26 U.S.C.A. § 163(h)(3). Exemption does not apply to the discharge of a loan if the discharge is on account of services performed for the lender or any other factor not directly related to the decline in the value of the residence or to the financial condition of the tax payer.

1872   26 U.S.C.A. § 163(h)(3).

1873   26 U.S.C.A. § 163(e)(1).

1874   See Chapter 21 for a detailed analysis of mortgage fraud.

1875   O.C.G.A. § 7-1-1000(19).

1876   See Georgia Department of Bank and Finance Q&A- GRMA and Safe Act Applicability to Real Estate Brokers.

1877   O.C.G.A. § 7-1-1001(a)(6).

1878   See Georgia Department of Bank and Finance Q&A- GRMA and Safe Act Applicability to Real Estate Brokers.

The position the Georgia Department of Banking and Finance appears to be that real estate licensee can provide factual information relative to the property but cannot be involved in filling out a short sale application or providing financial information about the borrower to the mortgage lender. However, the Georgia Department of Banking and Finance is currently reviewing its position on this issue since so many lenders are requesting that real estate licensees help in getting them the information they need to make a decision on the short sale. The Georgia Association of REALTORS® has been meeting with the Georgia Department of Banking and Finance to try to bring more clarity as to the permitted role of real estate licensees in the short sale process.

§ 16.1.3 Preparing For Listing And Sale

Once it becomes clear that a short sale will be necessary, sellers should be encouraged to have a title search done so that the full extent of the liens and encumbrances against the property can be determined. When doing the math, the existing liens (including the estimated interest that will accumulate from the time of the listing to the time of actual sale), the commission, and closing costs as necessary, should be subtracted from the likely sale price to determine just how short the sale needs to be. Keep in mind that many lenders will require all closing costs to be paid by the buyer.

§ 16.1.3.1 Second Mortgages And Short Sales

Second mortgage lenders are usually as meticulous as the first mortgagee in verifying the financial hardship of the seller. If there are any second mortgages on the property a short sale may not be possible. This is because holders of the first mortgage are unlikely to discount their loan unless the holder of a second mortgage releases its interest without payment. Under the federal HAFA program, if the first mortgage approves the short sale, then a fixed amount of $6,000 is available to the second mortgage lender if they agree to forgive the remainder of the second mortgage.[1879] Some second mortgage lenders will agree to accept this payment and others will not.

It is also increasingly common for second mortgage holders to ask the seller to sign a promissory note for the amount that the second mortgagee is owed. Most second mortgage holders know that they will be wiped out in the event the property is foreclosed upon by the holder of the first mortgage. However, many second mortgage holders are increasingly willing to note the amount due on larger second mortgages where they will have a large loss, even with a HAFA payment because they know that sellers want to avoid foreclosure if possible.

§ 16.1.3.2 Work Out Packet

Sellers who need to pursue a short sale need to contact the lender and ask for a "work out packet." These can usually be obtained from a department which may be designated as a loss mitigation department, work-out department, loan modification department, etc. The packet will tell sellers specifically what documentation and procedures their particular lender requires. It should generally include the following: cover letter with a checklist of items enclosed and a brief synopsis; completed financial disclosure (provided by the lender); handwritten hardship letter; purchase contract; net sheet or HUD-1 Form prepared by a closing attorney; proof of income for the past 2 pay periods; copies of last 2 bank statements; copies of last 2 years' full tax returns with W-2s and 1099s; and third party authorization form.

The following items are optional, but recommended if possible: deferred maintenance photo pages with captions; comparative market analysis; itemized cost breakdown and total estimated cost of repairs; statistics of foreclosures in the neighborhood (DataQuick Foreclosure Finder); proof of active listings in the area that are lower and not selling; and a copy of MLS printout if property has been on the market for a long time.

1879   Making Home Affordable Program Handbook v3.3, Chapter IV, Section 6.2.4.2 (2011).

§ 16.1.4   Listing And Sale Of The Property

§ 16.1.4.1   Information To Include In Multiple Listing

When listing any property where it is anticipated that the seller will need to do a short sale, any multiple listing service information will need to include clear details about the commission arrangement. For example, stating that "commission amount to be approved by lender" is one way to disclose that lender approval of the commission is required. The listing should also include information about where the seller is in the short sale process; *i.e.*, "lender has agreed to short sale" or "short sale packet has been submitted to lender for approval."

Lenders in short sale transactions will generally not accept a purchase and sale agreement that only comes into existence if the short sale is approved by the lender. Instead, most lenders want to see that there is an existing purchase and sale agreement with a Binding Agreement Date. Of course, the purchase and sale agreement should be subject to a short sale contingency in which the lender must approve the short sale.

Prospective buyers may want to consider having the property inspected before submitting any offer, since the property will likely be sold "as is." Buyers should not expect a short sale lender to pay for repairs to the property, Official Georgia Infestation Reports, home warranties, etc. While in some cases, the seller may be willing to pay for some repairs, in most transactions the seller does not have the financial wherewithal to do this. In fact, most lenders will insist that the transaction be "as-is-where-is."

§ 16.1.4.2   Short Sale Contingencies

Sellers facing a short sale situation need to protect themselves in case the lender does not accept the proposed deal. They need to include language making their contract contingent upon lender approval. Without such a contingency, they could find themselves in the position of needing to bring cash to the closing, if the lender does not approve the short sale, or being in breach of contract with the purchaser if they cannot clear title. Additionally, the parties should base contractual deadlines upon lender approval. For example, the buyer may want to have her due diligence period end "5 days after lender's approval is obtained."

Many real estate licensees now include entire exhibits to a standard purchase and sale agreement that address some of the issues that can arise out of a short sale transaction in one document. A sample of such an exhibit is set forth below:

EXHIBIT _____

SHORT SALE ISSUES AND DISCLOSURES

This exhibit is part of that certain Purchase and Sale Agreement between _____ *("Buyer") and* _____ *("Seller") with an Offer Date of* _____, *20____ for real property located at:*

_____

_____

_____ *("Property").*

1.   **<u>Short Sale Contingency.</u>** *Buyer acknowledges that the sale of the Property will not generate sufficient cash to pay off the mortgages and other title encumbrances on the Property and the other obligations of Seller with respect to this purchase and sale transaction. This Agreement is therefore contingent upon Seller's mortgage lender(s) agreeing to: 1) take a reduced pay off on its mortgage(s) in an amount sufficient such that the purchase price of the Property pays off the reduced amount of the mortgage(s), any other liens, judgments and other encumbrances on the Property, the real estate commission(s) owing to the Broker(s) and the other costs and expenses of sale for which*

Seller is obligated under this Agreement without Seller having to pay any additional sums; and 2) release Seller from any claim, cause of action, suit or judgment for the amount of the reduction in the payoff on said mortgage(s). In the event, the mortgage lender(s) do not agree to such reductions at least _____ days prior to closing, either Seller or Buyer may terminate this Agreement without penalty upon notice to the other party.

2. <u>**No Guarantee of Lender Approval.**</u> *Buyer acknowledges there is no guarantee that the mortgage lender(s) on the Property will: (a) accept less than the full amount Seller owes on the mortgage; or (b) decide within the time frame set forth herein whether or not to reduce the amounts owed on the mortgage(s) to facilitate the closing of this Agreement.*

Since this Agreement is subject to the approval by the mortgage lender(s) of the short sale reflected herein, and such approval is within the complete discretion of the mortgage lender(s) Buyer and is largely outside of the control of Buyer and Seller. Buyer and Seller further acknowledge that in the event the short sale is disapproved by the mortgage lenders, there is a likelihood that a mortgage lender will foreclose on the Property eliminating Buyer's contractual rights to purchase the same. Buyer and Seller therefore acknowledge the risk that they may expend significant time and financial resources to consummate the transaction only to have it ultimately disapproved by the mortgage lender(s).

3. <u>**Real Estate Brokers May Not Negotiate With Mortgage Lender(s).**</u> *Buyer and Seller acknowledge that, neither the Listing Broker nor the Selling Broker are licensed mortgage lenders. As such the Brokers are prohibited under state law from negotiating or re-negotiating any reduction in the amount of the mortgage(s) applicable to the Property, or any other condition, term or provision in the mortgage(s). The Broker's role in the short sale transaction is limited to providing the mortgage lender(s) with information requested by the mortgage lender(s) about the Property.*

4. <u>**Property Sold in "As-Is" Condition.**</u> *Buyer acknowledges that Seller lacks the funds to make any repairs to the Property. Therefore, Buyer agrees to accept the Property in "as-is" condition with any and all defects. Buyer is encouraged to hire a professional home inspector and/or other experts to fully evaluate the condition of the Property.*

5. <u>**Tax, Credit and Legal Consequences of a Short Sale.**</u> *Seller acknowledges that a short sale will likely have negative consequences to Seller's credit, may result in Seller owing taxes on any mortgage debt forgiven by the mortgage lender(s) and/or may leave the Seller obligated to repay the mortgage lender(s) the amount of any reduction in the mortgage(s) approved by the mortgage lender(s). Listing and Selling Brokers disclaim any expertise on these matters and recommend that Seller seek advice from an attorney, accountant, financial advisor and/or other professionals of Seller's choosing to obtain advice on the consequences of a short sale.*

6. <u>**Binding Agreement Date.**</u> *The Binding Agreement Date in this transaction is the date set forth elsewhere in this Agreement. Notwithstanding any provision to the contrary contained herein, the time periods by which Buyer or Seller must take an action or exercise a right reflected in this Agreement shall not be measured from the Binding Agreement Date but shall instead commence from the date that Buyer receives notice from Seller that mortgage lender(s) have approved this short sale transaction in writing and provided a copy of the same to Buyer.*

> 7. ***Closing Date.*** *In the event Seller has not obtained the approval of the mortgage lender(s) on the Property of the short sale of the Property as reflected in this Agreement, within _____ days prior to the date of closing, Buyer may either 1) terminate this Agreement without penalty upon notice to Seller, or 2) unilaterally extend the closing date for _____ additional days to give the mortgage lender(s) additional time to approve or disapprove the same.*
>
> *Buyer's Initials: _____/_____   Seller's Initials: _____/_____*

§ 16.1.5   Obtain The Lender's Approval

Most short sale lenders want to see a conformed or clean copy of the purchase and sale agreement signed by the buyer and seller. Some lenders will not accept a purchase and sale agreement signed by just the buyer and a counteroffer form signed by the buyer and seller. While having a GAR Counteroffer Form signed by the buyer along with a GAR Purchase and Sale Agreement signed by the buyer or seller clearly creates an enforceable contract in Georgia, it may fall outside the box of some lender's standard procedures for acceptable documentation of a real estate contract. In addition, many lenders in short sale transactions will not accept electronic signatures of the type offered by some companies to create a secure electronic signature. Many short sale lenders want what is referred to as a "wet signature" (*i.e.*, written by hand with a pen) on a purchase and sale agreement. However, once a contract has been signed, most lenders will accept a faxed or e-mailed copy of such a contract.

When a fully executed Purchase and Sale Agreement and any necessary special stipulations have been executed, they are submitted to the lender for approval, along with the seller's financial information, hardship letter, and any other items specified in the lender's work-out packet. This is the time to remember that patience is a virtue. The process of approving a short sale normally takes a matter of months rather than weeks. Generally, the lender will need about two months to give its approval. However, lenders may ignore deadlines in contracts requiring them to respond by a certain date, often preferring to wait and compare the current proposal with any other offer that may be submitted on the property. If there is a backup offer at a higher price, most lenders will only consider it after they have first decided whether or not they can accept the offer that has been presented to them. If the first contract falls apart and a new buyer steps in to purchase the property on the same or similar terms, a buyer should not expect the approval process to be expedited. For many lenders, the introduction of a new buyer will cause the approval process to be started over. The best way to shorten the approval process is to send the lender all of the documents the lender needs at one time. If the lender withholds approval, there can be no short sale. If approval is granted, the closing should be scheduled as quickly as possible.

§ 16.1.6   Commission Issues

The amount of commission paid by a short sale lender will vary from lender to lender. While many larger lenders are now willing to pay a commission equal to 6% of the purchase price, some lenders will only pay a 5% commission. Lenders agreeing to a short sale will often insist that the listing broker reduce her commission. The argument most lenders make to support this position is that if the lender has to take a hit on the mortgage, others should share in the pain as well. This can create problems for the listing broker if she has already committed to pay a cooperating selling broker a commission based upon a percentage of the sales price. If the listing broker cannot get the selling broker to agree to a voluntary reduction in the selling broker's commission, the listing broker is left in the unenviable position of having to choose between either killing a deal that the broker may have worked very hard to put together, or having the commission reduction come solely out of the listing broker's side of the commission. Determining the lender's position on payment of commissions is the best way for real estate licensees to avoid being disappointed.

§ 16.1.7   Closing Date

In setting a closing date for a short sale transaction, it is best to allow for at least 60 days for short sale approval. Including a provision in the contract to allow the contract to be unilaterally extended for an additional 30 days is also a good idea. A sample of such a provision is set forth below.

> **Special Stipulation 332:   Unilateral Right to Extend Closing**
>
> *Buyer shall have the unilateral right (but not the obligation) to extend the date of closing once for up to thirty (30) days upon notice to Seller if the mortgage lender(s) who are responsible for approving the short sale to which this Agreement is subject have not either approved or disapproved the short sale at least seven (7) days in advance of the date of closing.*

§ 16.1.8   Short Sale Purchase Addendums

It is common for mortgage lenders to require the buyer and seller to sign an amendment to the purchase and sale agreement as a condition of approving a short sale. Most of these addendums are written to ensure that the seller not benefit in any way from the sale of the property as a short sale. Common provisions that try to accomplish this goal include the following:

Example 1: "The Parties acknowledge and agree that none of the parties shall receive any proceeds from this transaction."

Example 2: "The Parties acknowledge and agree that neither the Buyers nor the Sellers nor their respective Brokers/ Agents have any agreements written or oral that will permit the Seller of the Seller's family member to remain in the property as renters or regain ownership of said property at any time after the execution of the Short Sale transaction. This includes if the seller is retaining a direct or indirect ownership or possessory interest in the property and / or has a formal or informal option to obtain such as interest in the future."

Example 3: "The Parties acknowledge and agree that the Subject Property must be sold through an "Arm's-Length" Transaction. "Arm's-Length" means two unrelated parties characterized by a selling price and other terms and conditions that would prevail in a typical real estate sales transaction. No party to this contract is a family member, related by blood or marriage, business associate or shares a business interest with the mortgagor (Sellers)."

§ 16.1.9   Short Sale Licensee Certifications

Many lenders now require the listing and selling agents involved in short sale transactions to also sign a certification confirming that they presented all offers to the seller, tried to get the maximum price for the property are not receiving anything of value other than what is listed on the HUD and are not engaged in either flipping or appraisal fraud. Examples of such certifications are below.

(i) Licensee representing Seller acknowledges and agrees that, in her professional opinion, Property has been listed on the appropriate local Multiple Listing Service at a listing price intended to generate open market competitive offers to purchase Property and not at an artificially low or high listing price. Licensee representing Seller further acknowledges and agrees that her marketing efforts were in fact and "in spirit" aimed toward maximizing the selling price of Property from a ready, willing and able buyer. Licensee has not engaged in any conduct that restricts or limits offers from buyers, including but not limited to requiring cash offers, using disparaging language regarding the property or tenants, or unreasonably restricting access.

(ii) Licensee representing Seller acknowledges that she has made Seller aware of all offers to purchase Property that Licensee received during the listing period and that she has not coerced, harassed or improperly influenced Seller in selecting a buyer for Property or in agreeing to the terms and conditions of the purchase contract.

(iii) Licensee acknowledges and agrees that Licensee is not engaging in appraisal fraud, flipping (a predatory lending practice whereby a recently acquired property is resold for a considerable profit with an artificially inflated value within a short period of time, as defined by the Federal Bureau of Investigation, identity theft and/or straw buying). Licensee has disclosed all agreements or understandings relating to the current sale or subsequent sale of Property of which Licensee is aware or should be aware. Licensee is not aware of any other agreements or understandings that call for the subsequent sale of the Property within 30 days of the current sale, the assignment of the property to the Seller or the option for the Seller to purchase.

(iv) Licensee acknowledges and agrees that she is not receiving any compensation, remuneration or benefit from the completion of this Residential Purchase Agreement other than what has been disclosed in the preliminary and certified HUD-1 closing settlement statements. Licensee is not aware of any arrangement for compensation or other remuneration to Seller, Buyer, Licensees or other lien holders, either directly or indirectly related to the purchase agreement, that has been or will be paid outside the official terms of closing as presented in the purchase contract and the preliminary and certified HUD-1 closing settlement statements.

(v) Licensee acknowledges and agrees that she has disclosed to Lender any known relationship to Buyer or ownership interest in Buyer's company, and Licensee representing Seller further acknowledges that she has no existing business relationship with Buyer and / or Seller other than the purchase of Property according to the terms and conditions of the purchase contract.

Licensees should carefully review these certifications before signing them to ensure that they are not creating potential liability for themselves if their certifications are inaccurate. Most of these certifications highlight the importance of an accurate certification by reminding licensees that any misrepresentation or omission of a material fact may subject the responsible party to civil and /or criminal liability.

§ 16.1.10   Short Sale Indemnity Agreements

Some lenders have instituted policies where all persons involved in short sale transactions, including the buyer, seller, listing agent, selling agent and closing attorney are required to indemnify the lender against negligent or intentional misrepresentations in short sale transactions. The indemnity obligation includes the payment to the lender of any reduced payoff to the seller's mortgage resulting from any misrepresentation. In many cases, these indemnity obligations are included in affidavits that must be signed and notarized by the parties as a condition of closing. Some parties signing these indemnity agreements have clarified the indemnity agreement by limiting it only to their own representations and not to the representations of any other party to the agreement. A sample of this type of limitation is set forth below.

> **Special Stipulation 333:   Limitation of Short Sale Affidavit**
>
> *Notwithstanding the above, _____ warrants only to the lender, loan servicer and Freddie Mac that it has made no knowing or intentional misrepresentations and that _____ makes no warranty or indemnity relative to any other signatory to this Addendum.*

§ 16.1.11   Short Sale Scams

There are several short sale scams designed to ensure that the lender not recover as high a percentage of the loan as would otherwise been possible. These include the buyer and seller with the possible involvement of the broker agreeing to a lower price for the property that the buyer might have otherwise paid in an arm's-length transaction.

The buyer then pays the seller a portion of the savings under the table (and in some cases the broker).

Another scam is for a relative of the seller to purchase the property at a low price and eventually sell the property back to the original owner.

A third approach is for the listing broker to contract to purchase the property at a low price with a delayed closing and the right to market the property for sale to a new buyer at a higher price. The listing broker then markets the property for sale but is now representing himself or herself rather than the seller. If a buyer comes along and is willing to pay a higher price for the property, the listing broker pockets the difference rather than this money going to pay down the mortgage. Most short sale contract addendums contain additional provisions trying to prohibit these types of transactions. They include the following:

Example 1: "The Parties acknowledge and agree the purchase contract cannot have any provisions for Assignment / Assignee and / or Option to purchase. Lender will NOT approve with these sales contract provisions and any such provisions are expressly deemed unapproved."

Example 2: "Buyer agrees that property cannot be sold or otherwise transferred within 30 days of closing."

Some lenders are beginning to rethink their strategies of prohibiting owners from leasing the property as tenants after a short sale. In part, such decisions are being driven by investors who are willing to buy multiple short sale properties if they can then be leased back to the current tenants.

§ 16.1.12 Advertising Short Sale

There is some debate as to whether a listing broker who knows that the property is being sold as a short sale must affirmatively disclose this fact to buyers interested in the property. There is no case law on this point in Georgia. However, Georgia License Law prohibits "any advertising that is misleading or inaccurate in any material fact or in any may misrepresents any property, terms, values, services or policies…"[1880]

However, BRRETA[1881] provides that a listing broker representing a seller shall "keep all confidential information received by the broker during the course of the engagement which is made confidential by an express requirement or instruction from the seller" unless, among other things, "such disclosure is required by law."[1882]

Based on the above two provisions, if the seller directs the listing broker not to disclose the seller's need for short sale, the listing broker should be able to keep this information confidential. This is because just like a pending divorce, this information could potentially harm the negotiating position of the seller and there is no other clear statutory duty to disclose. The buyer while possibly inconvenienced as a result of not knowing this information, will not likely be harmed because the buyer will almost certainly learn of the short sale prior to the purchase and sale agreement becoming binding since the seller will need to include a short sale contingency in that agreement.

While there is no clear answer on this issue, the good news is that any negative stigma associated with short sales has largely disappeared making sellers less reluctant to disclose this information. Additionally, listing brokers generally recommend disclosure since it tends to increase the interest of potential buyers in the property.

§ 16.2 WHAT IS A REO?

REO stands for Real Estate Owned. It refers to a property that has been foreclosed on by the lender. Most lenders have a REO department. Often lenders refer to departments as their special assets divisions or "SAD" for short. When a property goes to foreclosure, the person selling the property on the court house steps on the first Tuesday of the month

---

1880   Georgia Real Estate Commission Rule 520-1-.09.

1881   O.C.G.A. § 10-6A-1 *et seq.*

1882   O.C.G.A. § 10-6A-5.

after the property has been correctly advertised for sale. Essentially, a foreclosure involves an auction of the property to the highest bidder with the starting or opening bid set by the lender. The opening bid is normally either the amount owed on the mortgage or some lesser amount that the lender has established. It is essentially the price below which the lender will end up owning the property if no one else bids on a higher amount. If no one bids on the property or the lender outbids them, then the property is 'sold back' to the lender. The property is now a REO. If a third-party purchaser buys the property at a foreclosure sale on the courthouse steps, then it is not an actual REO. Sometimes, a junior lien holder will buy a property being sold by the first mortgage holder to prevent its lien from being wiped out. This would still typically be considered a REO property since it is owned by a lender.

§ 16.2.1   Offer And Counter Offer

When a prospective purchaser is interested in making an offer on a REO property, she must execute a purchase and sale agreement that is either provided by the lender or if not, to which the REO seller has attached a REO addendum protecting the lender's interests.

A REO addendum will typically including language confirming that the addendum controls over the purchase and sale agreement to which it is attached, and will then modify the contract in many respects. Most significantly, the REO seller will normally be selling the property in "as-is-where-is" condition.

§ 16.2.2   Condition Of Property

Purchasers often have very limited room to negotiate with a REO seller when it comes to the condition of the property. There is often a very short due diligence period and the REO seller is typically unwilling to agree to make many repairs.

§ 16.2.2.1   Sold "As Is/Where Is"

REO properties are normally sold "as is/where is." The buyer can always ask for repairs, but typically they are not going to get them. The addendums may go so far as to disclaim warranties related to hidden, known or unknown defects.

§ 16.2.2.2   Seller's Disclosure

Since the properties are being sold "as is/where is" and the seller obtained title through foreclosure, they generally have no knowledge about the physical condition of the property, any alterations or additions which may have been made to the property, or any other information which is contained on seller's property disclosure statements. The addendums, therefore, usually provide that no disclosure statement is being given and include language where the buyer waives all claims related thereto.

The inclusion of disclosures in a sales contract does not guarantee that a lender will be shielded from claims relating to or arising from the REO sale; however, disclosures can certainly help communicate matters that are known to the lender, but are not necessarily known to the purchasers, as such they can play a beneficial role in avoiding legal disputes in purchase and sale transactions. Most lenders already require that certain corporate disclosures be incorporated into the sales contract. Some of the disclosures and acknowledgements that a lender should consider include the following:

(i)   A disclosure that lender/seller (i) acquired the property through foreclosure, deed-in-lieu of foreclosure, loan liquidation, or other means; (ii) has not occupied the property and has not made, and does make ant warranty or representation, express or implied, regarding the quality, condition, merchantability, habitability, suitability of the property or fitness for a particular purpose, its soil conditions or release or hazardous materials; and (iii) is selling the property on an "as is" and "where is" basis.

(ii) An acknowledgement by purchaser that (i) purchaser has been encouraged to and has had the opportunity to thoroughly inspect the property and to hire professional home inspectors to assist in such inspections and confirm that the property (and all improvements located thereon, as applicable) is complete; (ii) the property located thereon meets the purchaser's needs, and that everything on the property, including fixtures, appliances, and systems included in the sale and in good working order and repair; (iii) lender/seller shall have no obligation to make any further improvements or repairs to the property subsequent to entering into the sales contract; (iv) to the extent permitted by applicable law, purchaser waives all warranties, representations or guaranties or any kind or character, express or implied, oral or written, past, present or future, with respect to the quality, design, condition or value of the property or any fixtures or personal property thereon or therein, or the compliance of such property, fixtures or personal property with any plans or specifications or any applicable laws, including but not limited to any implied warranties of quality, habitability, workmanlike construction, freedom from defects, merchantability, suitability of the property, or fitness for a particular purpose.

(iii) A disclosure regarding mold, mildew, spores and other microscopic organisms, particularly if the property being sold has been improved and may have been vacant or not maintained for an extended period of time.

Depending on the type of REO asset, there are a host of other disclosures and acknowledgements by purchaser that may be applicable.

§ 16.2.2.3 Duty Of Real Estate Licensee To Disclosure Adverse Material Facts Pertaining To Physical Condition Of The Property

Real estate licensees listing REO properties often have a greater knowledge of the condition of these properties than their lender clients. Even when the REO seller is making no disclosures, the real estate licensee still owes a duty to disclose adverse material facts pertaining to the physical condition of the property of which the licensee is aware and which would not be readily observable upon a reasonable inspection of the property.[1883] The failure to do so can result in civil liability[1884] and the licensee being sanctioned by the Georgia Real Estate Commission.[1885] There is no particular format that such disclosures should take and they do not necessarily need to be included in the purchase and sale agreement. However, they should be in writing and the licensee should be able to prove that they were provided to the buyer prior to the purchase and sale agreement becoming binding.

§ 16.2.2.4 Buyer's Right To Inspect

The GAR Contract allows for the option of the property being sold subject to a due diligence period. The GAR Contract allows for the buyer to terminate the contract during this time provided proper notice is given timely. Since there is often no due diligence period contained in REO counter proposals, the buyer has a more limited time to inspect the property and does not typically have another 'free out.'

The sale of REO commercial properties often requires a lender to provide a purchaser with reports (such as environmental, zoning and engineering reports), information, or other documents (such as surveys, floor plans and site plans) pertaining to the property so that a purchaser has an opportunity to conduct due diligence as to the property. However, as much as a lender might desire to provide such materials, it is often the case that a lender has very limited or perhaps no access to such documents due to the circumstances in which the lender acquired title to the property. If a sales contract requires a lender to provide purchaser with such due diligence materials, the lender should ensure that its obligation to provide such materials is limited to those documents that are in lender's physical possession and were obtained by the lender after the date on which the lender became the fee owner of the property. By incorporating such limitations, a lender can then defend against a possible termination of the sales contract by the purchaser over lender's failure or inability to provide due diligence materials.

1883   O.C.G.A. § 10-6A-5(b)(1).

1884   O.C.G.A. § 10-6A-2(c).

1885   O.C.G.A. § 43-40-25(b)(21).

§ 16.2.3 Type Of Transaction

The current GAR Contract is not contingent upon the buyer's ability to obtain financing. However, if the purchase has attached a financing contingency exhibit, they need to carefully check the REO addendum, which may limit the effect of any such financing contingency.

§ 16.2.3.1 Cash Transactions

In cash purchase transactions, the buyer must provide the REO seller with proof of funds when they return the executed addendum or the seller will often not accept the contract. Once any inspection period ends, the buyer often has only five days until the earnest money becomes non-refundable. If the closing doesn't occur on time for any reason, then the seller can terminate and retain the earnest money. Some REO addendums even include a provision that execution of the addendum is the only release needed to release the earnest money to the seller.

§ 16.2.3.2 Financed Transactions

Most REO addendums require the buyer to apply for financing within 72 hours of the binding agreement. The buyer is then required to provide the seller with an unconditional loan commitment within a fixed period of time.

§ 16.2.4 Seller Concessions

While the GAR Contract lists a wide range of closing costs that the seller can pay on behalf of the buyer, some REO addendums will limit the use of seller paid closing costs to specific items. Some will even go so far as to limit which lender fees, such as an origination or discount fee, will be paid by the seller. REO sellers usually consider all credits to buyers a concession. As discussed below, this is very important for its effect on real estate commissions.

§ 16.2.5 Commission

On REO transactions, commissions are typically paid on the Net Sales Price. The Net Sales Price is determined by taking the purchase price less all seller concessions. For example, if the purchase price is $100,000, the seller pays closings costs of $3,000 and there is a termite clearance letter that cost $50, then the net sales price is $96,950. The commission is then based upon the lower $96,950 price rather than the initial $100,000 figure.

§ 16.2.6 Special Conditions

The REO seller will list special conditions which can affect their ability to sell the property. There are three common exceptions that the seller provides in the addendums to allow it to terminate a contract through no fault of the buyer without penalty to the seller. These are: approval by the Private Mortgage Insurer; repurchase of the property by the prior mortgage servicer or insurer; or the ability of the seller to clear title as required by the contract.

§ 16.2.7 Settlement And Closing

There are a number of provisions in REO addendums which effect the settlement and closing. Some of these effect the where and when while others effect the what if and cost appropriation.

§ 16.2.7.1 Where Is The Closing?

Most REO addendums require that the transaction be closed in the offices of the seller's attorney or agent or at a place designated and approved by the seller. This is typically non-negotiable.

§ 16.2.7.2 When Is The Closing?

Unlike the GAR unilateral 7 day extension, most REO Addendums provide no automatic or unilateral right for the buyer to extend the closing. Rather, all extensions must be approved in writing by the seller. Even if a REO seller agrees to a closing extension, there is often a per diem charge (usually $100 per day) to the buyer for every day the closing is extended. This fee is to compensate the seller for its carrying costs and loss of marketability while the house is under contract and therefore off the market. Some REO sellers will also require an additional non-refundable earnest money deposit for the extension to be approved.

§ 16.2.7.3 Prorations At Closing

REO sellers do not re-prorate taxes, or any other costs for that matter. They will pay all assessments levied as of the time of the sale, but not those that are pending. For example, special assessments paid in installments are prorated as of the date of closing.

§ 16.2.7.4 Type Of Deed Transfer

The typical REO seller will transfer title by special or limited warranty deed or a quitclaim deed rather than by a general warranty deed. This is due to the fact that the seller took title on the day of foreclosure, and does not want to warrant anything that may have happened prior to that time.

§ 16.2.7.5 Title Policies

Most REO sellers will pay for the owner's title insurance if the buyer closes with the seller's attorney. They will not be responsible for any "gap" period on the title insurance. Furthermore, the seller often has the right to terminate, not the buyer, when the seller cannot provide insurable title.

§ 16.2.7.6 Additional Alterations

As a general rule in REO transactions buyers may not move in early nor may they assign the contract.

§ 16.2.8 Seller's Right To Terminate

The REO addendums, not surprisingly, are written to protect the REO sellers. There are multiple provisions that allow the seller to terminate without any additional liability other than returning the earnest money to the purchaser.

§ 16.2.8.1 Closing Date Has Passed

If the closing does not occur on time, then the seller reserves the right to either charge per diem or to terminate the contract. Furthermore, if they decide to terminate the contract, the seller can retain the earnest money and pursue other remedies against the buyer.

§ 16.2.8.2 Negative Proceeds

The seller reserves the right to cancel the contract and return the earnest money to the buyer in the event that the seller has negative proceeds. This would be due to unforeseen judgments and other financial obligations on the property such as a tax sale. Since this usually cannot be determined until a HUD-1 Settlement Statement is prepared, this may not be known until shortly before the closing.

§ 16.2.8.3 Lender Required Repairs

If certain repairs are required by the purchaser's lender, then the seller can choose to comply with the request or can terminate the contract. The REO addendum will typically list an amount that can be used for repairs and anything over that amount becomes the buyer's responsibility. However, most REO sellers do not pay for repairs and then only if they are structural in nature.

The **RED BOOK**

CHAPTER 17

LEASING

OVERVIEW

If a property cannot be sold, the owner will often lease it as a way to generate some cash flow from the property. Leasing is an area that is subject to numerous state statutes. While most leases are written to protect the landlord, many of the state statutes in the landlord/tenant area are written to protect the tenant. The failure to comply with state law can have significant negative consequences to the landlord in leasing transactions including in certain cases not being able to deduct the cost of repairing damage from the security deposit or being liable to the tenant for three times the amount of the security deposit. This chapter will provide an overview of some of the more significant issues in leasing real property.

§ 17.1 THE RENTAL APPLICATION

Most landlords will have the tenant fill out a rental application so that the landlord can better evaluate whether the tenant's request to lease the property should be approved or denied. A well-written rental application can benefit the landlord in many ways.

First, it provides the landlord with information about whether the tenant has the ability to pay rent to the landlord. More than any other factor, the landlord is looking to confirm that the tenant has a source of regular income from which she can pay rent.

Second, the rental application should include an authorization by the prospective tenant to do a credit and criminal background check to determine the credit worthiness of the prospective tenant. Such authorization is required under the Fair Credit Reporting Act.[1886] Many landlords charge a non-refundable fee to process the rental application. This can be both a source of revenue to the landlord and a deterrent to prospective tenants who know their rental application will likely be disapproved.

Third, the rental application should provide the landlord with a history of where the tenant has lived and worked and phone numbers of references for the landlord to call to verify the accuracy of the information provided by the tenant. Checking the rental history of a tenant can tell the landlord whether the tenant has been late in the past or skipped from a property. It should never be assumed that the phone numbers provided by prospective tenants are accurate and, whenever possible, the landlord should independently verify the phone numbers of previous residences and current places of employment.

Fourth, the rental application provides the landlord with valuable information about the tenant in the event the tenant later defaults on the lease. Knowing where the tenant works and banks and the tenant's social security number and driver's license number, can make it easier to collect on a judgment for unpaid rent against the tenant.

§ 17.2 DENIAL OF THE RENTAL APPLICATION

If the landlord denies the prospective tenant's rental application because of poor credit, the landlord is required, under federal law, to provide a special notification to the prospective tenant that among other things provide the applicant with the name, address and telephone number of the credit reporting agency, informing the applicant that the credit reporting agency did not make the adverse action and is unable to provide the applicant with the specific reasons why the adverse action was taken and gives the tenant the right to obtain a free copy of her credit report from the credit reporting agency to dispute the accuracy or completeness of the credit report.[1887] This type of notice must also be given if the landlord charges the tenant an extra amount as a result of having bad credit (such as an additional security deposit or extra rent[1888]). The notice does not need to state the specific information in the credit report that was of concern to the landlord.[1889] Instead, it merely needs to state that information in the credit report was a basis for the

[1886] 15 USC § 1681 *et. seq.*
[1887] 15 U.S.C.A. 1681(m)(a).
[1888] 15 U.S.C.A. 1681(m)(a).
[1889] 15 U.S.C.A. 1681(m)(a).

denial of the rental application. Credit denial letters are widely available on the Internet and the samples are available from the credit reporting companies themselves. A sample credit denial letter is set forth below:

Denial of Credit Letter

Dear _____ :

Unfortunately, the following adverse action was taken with respect to the rental application you filed with _____ .

_____ Your rental application was denied as a result of the following:

_____ .

_____ Your rental application can only be approved if it is co-signed by a creditworthy co-signor.

_____ An additional security deposit of $_____ will be needed to approve your rental application bringing the total amount of your security deposit to $_____ .

_____ You will be required to pay additional rent of $_____ per month in order to approve your rental application bringing your total rent to $_____ per month.

The above-referenced adverse action was taken based solely or partly on information in a consumer report.

The consumer report was supplied by the following credit reporting company.

Name of Credit Reporting Agency: _____

Address: _____

_____

Toll-free Telephone Number: _____

The credit reporting agency that supplied the report did not make the decision to take the adverse action described above and thus cannot give specific reasons for it.

Under the Fair Credit Reporting Act, you have a right to obtain a free copy of your consumer report from the above-referenced credit reporting agency. To obtain a copy of your consumer report, you must request it within 60 days of your receipt of this letter. If you believe your report is inaccurate or incomplete, you also have a right to dispute the accuracy or completeness of any of the information furnished by the credit reporting agency. This must also be done within 60 days of your receipt of this letter by contacting the credit reporting agency.

You may have additional rights under the credit reporting or consumer protection laws of your state. Contact your state or local consumer protection agency or a state Attorney General's office.

Sincerely

_____

Landlord/Agent

With most of these letters, the landlord also states the specific reason why the rental application was denied such as a recent eviction from another property, inadequate or undocumented income, a very low credit score or a felony conviction.

Property managers will often run credit and criminal background checks on behalf of a landlord. In so doing, it is a good idea to disclaim in the property management agreement the accuracy and completeness of any background check to avoid claims if the tenant turns out to be less reputable than was thought. A sample of this type of disclaimer is set for the below.

Special Stipulation 334: Manager Not Responsible for Background Checks.

Manager may run credit, criminal, reference and/or other background checks on prospective tenants on behalf of Landlord. Such reports and background checks involve reviewing information from credit reporting agencies and other persons. Such reports and background checks may contain errors and may not be complete or accurate. Landlord hereby agrees to indemnify and hold Manager harmless from any claim, cause of action, suite or damage arising out of or relating to Manager performing or obtaining any credit, criminal, reference or other background check of prospective tenants on behalf of Landlord.

§ 17.3 FAIR HOUSING ISSUES IN THE RENTAL OF RESIDENTIAL REAL ESTATE LEASING

Much of the testing that takes place for violations of our fair housing laws occurs in residential leasing transactions. For example, advertising a property for lease with a "no pet" provision may trigger a testing call to see if the property owner will unlawfully prohibit a service dog needed by a handicapped tenant.[1890] Landlords who tell prospective tenant with large families that a property has just been leased may get tested to see if the property is also unavailable to a childless couple. While landlords cannot discriminate on the basis of familial status, reasonable occupancy restrictions such as two (2) persons per bedroom are generally permissible.[1891]

Property owners who know that it is unlawful to discriminate on the basis of race, color, religion or national origin[1892] are sometimes unaware that discrimination is also prohibited on the basis of sex, familial status and handicap.[1893] Reviewing fair housing laws with landlords who do not regularly lease property is a good way to ensure that compliance with both the spirit and letter of the law in this area.

§ 17.3.1 Section 8 Tenants

Choosing not to rent to "Section 8" tenants has become increasingly common over the past decade. However, there is no federal law or Georgia law prohibiting a landlord from refusing to rent housing to a person receiving subsidized rental aid from the government. Tenants receiving such aid are commonly referred to as "Section 8" tenants.

Section 8 of the federal Housing Act of 1937[1894] provides assistance to lower-income tenants or families for the purpose of obtaining decent living and promoting economically mixed housing.[1895] In order to qualify for the Section 8 program, a prospective tenant must have an income within the Department of Housing and Urban Development's (HUD's) specified limits. Once accepted into the program, the tenant will lease an "assisted unit," paying the landlord a portion of the rent which is generally 30% of the tenant's monthly adjusted income or 10% of the tenant's monthly

1890   O.C.G.A. § 8-3-202(a)(7)(B).
1891   O.C.G.A. § 8-3-205(b)(2).
1892   O.C.G.A. § 8-3-202(a)(1).
1893   O.C.G.A. § 8-3-202(a)(1) and (7).
1894   42 U.S.C.A. § 1437 *et seq.*
1895   42 U.S.C.A. § 1437f(a).

income, whichever is greater.[1896] The amount of rent a tenant will pay will vary depending on whether the housing selected is public or private, whether the tenant is receiving other welfare assistance, as well as a variety of other factors.[1897] The rest of the rent owed to the landlord is paid by HUD as a form of assistance. HUD makes these rental payments monthly and directly to the landlord.[1898]

Landlords who want to rent apartments and homes to federally-subsidized tenants may do so by obtaining approval from their local public housing authority.[1899] However, as stated above, landlords of privately owned apartments or homes are not required to offer housing to low-income Section 8 tenants. A person's low-income or financial status does not subject them to the protections of the Fair Housing Act, which prohibits discrimination against certain protected classes.[1900] As such, landlords may refuse to rent to Section 8 tenants based on their low-income status without violating the Housing Act of 1937[1901], the federal Fair Housing Act[1902] or any other federal or Georgia law.

§ 17.4 MOVE-IN INSPECTION

Unless the landlord is exempt,[1903] state law requires that the tenant, prior to tendering a security deposit, be presented with a comprehensive list of any existing damages to the premises.[1904] This state law requirement is not always complied with by landlords some of whom collect the first month's rent and security deposit and then inspect the premises for damage prior to the tenant moving in. Some landlords have tried to comply with this section of the law by characterizing the security deposit as a refundable lease administration or application fee that is then converted into a security deposit upon the completion of the move in inspection. Whether temporarily giving the security deposit a different name alters its character is unclear and has yet to be ruled on by an appellate court.

Unless the landlord is exempt,[1905] state law also requires that: 1) the tenant has the right to inspect the premises to determine the accuracy of the list of damages to the property; 2) the landlord and tenant sign the list of damages; and 3) the tenant be given a copy of the list of damages for the tenant's records.[1906] Once the landlord and tenant sign the list, it is conclusive evidence as to the accuracy of the list of obvious damage to the premises.[1907]

In addition to the list, some landlords will also take photographs or a video of the premises at the time of occupancy to visually confirm the condition of the premises. On the theory that a picture is worth a thousand words, such pictures or videos can be useful evidence in any later legal dispute over damage to the premises. Photographs or a video should be marked with a date, time and the person taking the video or photograph. The person taking the photographs or video should be someone who can later testify as a witness as to when the video or photographs were taken.

1896   42 U.S.C.A. § 1437a.

1897   42 U.S.C.A. § 1437a.

1898   24 C.F.R. § 880.101(a).

1899   24 C.F.R. § 811.104(a).

1900   42 U.S.C.A. §3604. A person may not refuse to sell or rent or refuse to negotiate for the sale or rental of a dwelling to any person because of race, color, religion, sex, familial status, national origin or handicap.

1901   42 U.S.C.A. § 1437 *et seq.*

1902   42 U.S.C.A. §3601 *et seq.*

1903   A landlord is exempt if the landlord is a natural person, the property is not managed by a third party management company and the landlord and the landlord's spouse and minor children collectively own 10 or fewer rental units. O.C.G.A. § 44-7-36.

1904   O.C.G.A. § 44-7-33.

1905   A landlord is exempt if the landlord is a natural person, the property is not managed by a third party management company and the landlord and the landlord's spouse and minor children own 10 or fewer rental units. O.C.G.A. § 44-7-36.

1906   O.C.G.A. § 44-7-33(a).

1907   O.C.G.A. § 44-733(a).

Unless the landlord is exempt, state law also provides that the landlord may not generally withhold a portion of the security deposit or bring an action against the tenant for damages to the property if the landlord has not provided the damage list to the list in accordance with state law requirements.[1908]

It should be noted that landlords who are exempt from having to prepare a written move inspection report and have not done so and are at a significant disadvantage in being able to prove that damages done to the premises were caused by the tenant. If the tenant denies having caused the damage, the landlord and tenant often end up in a swearing contest over whether the damage was done before or after the commencement of the lease. Since the burden is on the landlord to prove that the damage was done by the tenant, the landlord is often unable to meet its legal burden in court. Moreover, judges tend to be unsympathetic to the landlord in this situation since the landlord could have protected himself or herself and chose not to do so.

§ 17.5 MOVE-OUT INSPECTION

Unless the landlord qualifies for an exemption,[1909] the landlord or her agent is required to do a move out inspection within three business days after the date of the termination of occupancy.[1910] So, for example, if the lease ends on Friday, July 7th, the move out inspection would need to be done by Wednesday, July 12th since the weekend would be excluded from the definition of a business day. The move out inspection is to compile a comprehensive list of any damage done to the premises which is a basis for any charge by the landlord against the security deposit. The tenant shall then have the right within five (5) business days after the date of the termination of occupancy to inspect the premises in order to ascertain the accuracy of the list.[1911] In preparing the list of damages, no security deposit may be retained to cover ordinary wear and tear.[1912]

Ordinary wear and tear includes any usual deterioration from use of the premises during the lease period.[1913] In determining whether the deterioration is chargeable to the tenant, a court will consider what the parties understood as the intended use of the property at the time the lease was entered into.[1914] Whether the deterioration is excusable as ordinary wear and tear depends on the facts and circumstances of each case and is a question for the jury.[1915] Ordinary wear and tear does not include deterioration resulting from a tenant's willful, negligent, or accidental acts.[1916]

Typically, the landlord will inspect the premises with the tenant upon the conclusion of the lease term. This is because state law requires the landlord and tenant to both sign the move out inspection.[1917] If the tenant disagrees with the damages listed on the move out inspection, the tenant is not required to sign the list but is required to state specifically in writing the items on the list with which the tenant disagrees and sign that list.[1918] If the tenant does not comply with this requirement the tenant is barred from suing the landlord for wrongfully withholding a portion of the security

---

1908   O.C.G.A. § 44-7-35(b).

1909   O.C.G.A. § 44-7-36. A landlord is exempt if the landlord is a natural person, the property is not managed by a third party management company and the landlord and the landlord's spouse and minor children own 10 or fewer rental units.

1910   O.C.G.A. § 44-7-33(b).

1911   O.C.G.A. § 44-7-33(b).

1912   O.C.G.A. § 44-7-34(a).

1913   *Raybestos-Manhattan, Inc. v. Friedman*, 156 Ga.App. 880, 275 S.E.2d 817 (1981) citing *Zeeman Mfg. Co. v. L.R. Sams Co.*, 123 Ga.App. 99,179 S.E.2d 552 (1970).

1914   *Raybestos-Manhattan, Inc. v. Friedman*, 156 Ga.App. 880, 275 S.E.2d 817 (1981). Court allowed evidence for the purpose of showing what reasonable anticipated use would be, and what reasonable depreciation might be expected on items repair of which was chargeable to the tenant, as well as evidence introduced for the purpose of demonstrating what reasonably could be expected depreciation from ordinary wear and tear.

1915   *Raybestos-Manhattan, Inc. v. Friedman*, 156 Ga.App. 880, 275 S.E.2d 817 (1981) citing *Kann v. Brooks*, 54 Ind.App. 625, 101 N.E. 513 (1913). Court held that where the intended use of the building was for the operation of a mill, beams which decayed not due to the negligence of the tenant but to its normal use as a mill were not damages for which the lessor could recover from the tenant.

1916   *Raybestos-Manhattan, Inc. v. Friedman*, 156 Ga.App. 880, 275 S.E.2d 817 (1981).

1917   O.C.G.A. § 44-7-33(b).

1918   O.C.G.A. § 44-7-33(b).

deposit for damages to the premises unless the move out inspection form does not include a written notice of the tenant's duty to sign or dissent to the list.[1919] If the tenant terminates occupancy without notifying the landlord, the landlord may make a final inspection within a reasonable time after discovering the termination of occupancy.[1920]

§ 17.6 SECURITY DEPOSITS IN LEASE TRANSACTIONS

If a real estate licensee is holding a security deposit, the funds must be deposited into a trust account under the supervision of the broker with whom the licensee is affiliated.[1921] This is the case even if the property being leased is owned by the licensee.[1922] If the security deposit is being held by the landlord, it needs to be held in a trust account established for that purpose in any bank or lending institution subject to regulation by the state of Georgia or any agency of the United States unless the landlord is exempt from this regulation. Exempt landlords are those who own 10 or fewer properties (either by themselves or in the name of their spouse or minor children) are natural persons where the property is not being managed by a third party.[1923] So, for example, if a landlord owns only 2 properties but the properties are owned by a limited liability company rather than a natural person, the exemption would not apply and the landlord would be required to deposit the money in a trust account. Similarly, if the property is managed by a third party property management company, any security deposit held by the landlord would need to be placed in an escrow account.

Where Georgia license law is not altogether clear is where the real estate licensee is a member of a legal entity that owns a rental property. Obviously, since the real estate licensee is not a natural person, the security deposit needs to be placed in an escrow account.[1924] However, does the escrow account need to be under the supervision of the licensee's broker? Our rule of thumb is that if the company is owned entirely by the licensee, the licensee should place the security deposit in an escrow account under the supervision of the broker. Similarly, if the licensee is managing the property for the company, we recommend that the security deposit be placed in an escrow account under the supervision of the broker. However, if the licensee does not control the company and does not manage its affairs, we believe the licensee is probably safe in depositing the security deposit in an escrow account not under the supervision of the licensee's broker.

The security deposit must be returned to the tenant within one month after the later of either (i) termination of the residential lease; or (ii) the surrender and acceptance of the premises.[1925] If the security deposit or a portion thereof, is retained to cover damage to the premises, the damages must be listed in the move out inspection.[1926] Of course, the security deposit can also be retained for nonpayment of rent, nonpayment of utility charges, repair work, cleaning, unpaid pet fees or other fees and charges relating to the tenant's breach of the lease.[1927]

The portion of the security deposit being returned to the tenant along with the statement explaining any deductions to the security deposit may be mailed to the last known address of the tenant via first class mail.[1928] If the letter

---

1919   O.C.G.A. § 44-7-33(c).

1920   O.C.G.A. § 44-7-33(b).

1921   O.C.G.A. § 43-40-25(b)(3); Georgia Real Estate Commission Rule 520-1-.08(c) which states that a licensee shall place all cash, checks, or other items of value received by the licensee when the licensee is acting in the capacity of principal in the sale of interest in real estate owned by such licensee and all security deposits it received on property owned by the licensee into the custody of the broker holding the licensee's license or in a trust account approved by that broker as soon after receipt as is practically possible.

1922   *Id.*

1923   O.C.G.A. § 44-7-36.

1924   *Id.*

1925   O.C.G.A. § 44-7-34.

1926   O.C.G.A. § 44-7-34.

1927   O.C.G.A. § 44-7-34.

1928   O.C.G.A. § 44-7-34(a).

is returned to the landlord undelivered and the landlord is unable to locate the tenant after reasonable effort, the payment becomes the property of the landlord 90 days from the date that the payment was mailed.[1929]

It should be emphasized that if the landlord fails to return any part of a security deposit which is required to be returned to a tenant, the landlord is liable to the tenant for three times the sum improperly withheld plus reasonable attorney's fees.[1930] However, if the landlord can show by a preponderance of the evidence that the withholding was not intentional and resulted from a bona fide error, the landlord is only responsible for the amount actually withheld.[1931] The burden of proof in this type of case, however, is on the landlord to show that the security deposit was withheld by mistake.

§ 17.7   REPAIR AND MAINTENANCE

Georgia law provides that "[t]he landlord must keep the premises in repair. He shall be liable for all substantial improvements placed upon the premises by his consent."[1932] This provision of Georgia law creates an affirmative obligation on the part of the landlord that cannot be waived in the lease.[1933]

Landlords have tried to distinguish the duty to maintain from the duty to repair. In Georgia, the duty to maintain requires a tenant to preserve a property in as good a condition as when it was received.[1934] Any repairs or improvements outside of this duty are the responsibility of the landlord.[1935] As a result, it is not uncommon for landlords to obligate the tenant to perform certain maintenance responsibilities such as cutting the grass, replacing light bulbs, replacing batteries in smoke alarms, changing filters and the like.

The duty to repair, on the other hand, refers to the upkeep or replacement of a component part of the property necessary to preserve the property in the same condition as it was at the time of the lease.[1936] This obligation includes the repair of any structural issues or the completion of capital improvements to the property.[1937] If a lease fails to address the repair obligation altogether, a landlord will be required to repair as well as maintain the property.[1938]

Some landlords try to make the tenant responsible for paying some portion of the repair costs. For example, the lease may require the tenant to pay the first hundred dollars of any service call by a person performing repairs. Such provisions likely do not comply with state law since the landlord has an absolute duty to perform repairs.

§ 17.7.1   Property In Need Of Repair

A landlord is not required to inspect a rented property to keep informed about its condition.[1939] If a property is in need of repair, a tenant must give the landlord notice of the property's defective condition and need for repairs.[1940] If a landlord fails to make certain repairs to a property within a reasonable time after the landlord has knowledge or notice that the property is in need of repair, the tenant may (1) make the repairs himself or herself and ask the landlord for

---

1929   O.C.G.A. § 44-7-34(a).

1930   O.C.G.A. § 44-7-35(c).

1931   O.C.G.A. § 44-7-35(c).

1932   O.C.G.A. § 44-7-13. *Paulk v. Ellis Street Realty Corporation*, 79 Ga.App. 36, 52 S.E.2d 625 (1949).

1933   O.C.G.A. § 44-7-2(b)(1).

1934   *Jacobi v. Timmers Chevrolet, Inc.*, 164 Ga.App. 198, 296 S.E.2d 777 (1982).

1935   *Jacobi v. Timmers Chevrolet, Inc.*, 164 Ga.App. 198, 296 S.E.2d 777 (1982). Court held that even if the lease agreement provided a duty for the tenant to maintain the property, such duty did not obligate the tenant to repair water damage to the roof of the property.

1936   *Sadler v. Winn-Dixie Stores, Inc.*, 152 Ga.App. 763, 264 S.E.2d 291 (1979).

1937   *Jacobi v. Timmers Chevrolet, Inc.*, 164 Ga.App. 198, 296 S.E.2d 777 (1982).

1938   O.C.G.A. § 44-7-13.

1939   *Adams v. Klasing*, 20 Ga.App. 203, 92 S.E. 960 (1917).

1940   *Valdes Hotel Co. v. Ferrell*, 17 Ga.App. 93, 86 S.E.333 (1915).

reimbursement[1941] or deduct the expenses from rental payments,[1942] (2) occupy the property without repair and sue the landlord for damages,[1943] or (3) in limited cases, vacate the property and withhold rent (*i.e.* constructive eviction).

Constructive eviction allows a tenant to vacate a property and suspend rental payments when a landlord whose duty is to keep the property in a proper state or repair allows the property to become uninhabitable.[1944] Constructive eviction is very difficult to prove in Georgia. The tenant must show (1) that the property has deteriorated to an uninhabitable condition, not merely an uncomfortable condition,[1945] and (2) the property cannot be restored to a fit condition by ordinary repairs without unreasonable interruption of the tenant's inhabitance.[1946] Both elements as well as the tenant being forced to move from the property must be present to allow a tenant to withhold rental payments.[1947]

In Georgia, there are limited cases demonstrating a successful constructive eviction by a tenant in a residential lease. Showing that a residential property is uninhabitable due to a landlord's failure to make certain repairs is difficult. In one case, evidence showing that the landlord failed to repair a leaky roof that was causing water to enter the property was held to be insufficient to establish an unfit place to live.[1948]

In another case, evidence that a property's air conditioning system failed to remove heavy cigarette smoke and odors from the air was also held to be insufficient to establish an uninhabitable residence.[1949] Since the heating and air conditioning system was not in need of repair and was operating as intended, the landlord did not have a duty to provide the tenant with a more advanced air conditioning system to remove the smells of which the tenant complained.[1950] Even a landlord's deprivation of a tenant's water supply for six days did not amount to an act which would constitute constructive eviction.[1951] This court was looking for evidence of some "grave act" of a permanent character done by the landlord with the intention of depriving the tenant of the enjoyment of the residence.[1952] Since there was no such evidence, the tenant's constructive eviction defense failed.[1953]

Strangely enough, a landlord's failure to fix a heating unit and cooking stove was sufficient to establish that a residence was uninhabitable.[1954] Unfortunately, there appears to be no set guidelines as to what constitutes an uninhabitable residence. The determination of whether a property is uninhabitable to support a constructive eviction claim will likely depend on the facts and circumstances of each case.

1941 *Borochoff Properties, Inc. v. Creative Printing Enterprises, Inc.*, 233 Ga. 279, 210 S.E.2d 809 (1974) citing *Valdes Hotel Co. v. Ferrell*, 17 Ga.App. 93, 86 S.E.333 (1915).

1942 *Shehane v. Eberhart*, 30 Ga.App. 265, 117 S.E. 675 (1923); *Abrams v. Joel*, 108 Ga.App. 662, 134 S.E.2d 480 (1963). The court held that tenant could not deduct cost of repairs from payments of rent because the lease agreement explicitly prohibited tenant from doing so if landlord failed to make necessary repairs. Once the tenant waives his right to set off the costs of necessary repairs from rental payments, the tenant must use another source of remedy.

1943 *Borochoff Properties, Inc. v. Creative Printing Enterprises, Inc.*, 233 Ga. 279, 210 S.E.2d 809 (1974).

1944 *Jenkins v. Brice*, 231 Ga.App. 843, 499 S.E.2d 734 (1998).

1945 *Jenkins v. Brice*, 231 Ga.App. 843, 499 S.E.2d 734 (1998). Court held that evidence that the property's roof was leaking, standing alone, is not evidence that the house was uninhabitable to warrant a defense of constructive eviction.

1946 *Snipes v. Halpern Enterprises, Inc.*, 160 Ga.App. 207, 286 S.E.2d 511 (1981).

1947 *Wellbaum v. Murphy*, 122 Ga.App. 654, 178 S.E.2d 690 (1970).

1948 *Hightower v. Daniel*, 143 Ga.App. 217, 237 S.E.2d 688 (1977).

1949 *Mullinax v. Doughtie*, 196 Ga.App. 747, 396 S.E.2d 919 (1990).

1950 *Mullinax v. Doughtie*, 196 Ga.App. 747, 396 S.E.2d 919 (1990).

1951 *Delta Cleaner Supply Co. v. Mendel Drive Associates*, 286 Ga.App. 227, 648 S.E.2d 651 (2007).

1952 *Delta Cleaner Supply Co. v. Mendel Drive Associates*, 286 Ga.App. 227, 648 S.E.2d 651 (2007).

1953 *Delta Cleaner Supply Co. v. Mendel Drive Associates*, 286 Ga.App. 227, 648 S.E.2d 651 (2007).

1954 *Wellbaum v. Murphy*, 122 Ga.App. 654, 178 S.E.2d 690 (1970).

§ 17.8   ADVERTISING THE PROPERTY FOR LEASE OR FOR SALE DURING THE TERM OF THE LEASE

When a landlord signs a lease, she parts with possession of the property.[1955] Therefore, unless the landlord reserves the right to place signage on and show the property to prospective tenants or buyers, the landlord does not have this right. Some landlords will limit their rights to show the property until three months before the lease terminates. If the landlord is seeking to sell the property while it is leased, a broad right to show the property is normally reserved to the landlord. An example of such a broad provision is set forth below.

> **Special Stipulation 335:   Landlord's Right to Market Property for Sale During Lease.**
>
> *Tenant acknowledges that Landlord shall have the right to market the property for sale during the term of his lease. Tenant expressly agrees to Landlord and Landlord's agents: 1) placing a standard sized real estate "for sale" sign and lockbox on the property during the term of the lease; and 2) showing the property to prospective buyers during the term of the lease by appointment. Upon receiving notice that the property will be shown to a prospective buyer, Landlord or Landlord's agent shall attempt to call tenant to notify Tenant of the showing. However, the failure to reach Tenant shall not prevent landlord or landlord's agents from showing the property. Since the property will be shown to the prospective buyers during the term of this lease, Tenant agrees to keep the premises in extra neat and clean condition with beds made, no dirty dishes left in the sink or outside of the dish washer, no dirty clothes on the floor, trash regularly taken outside and sinks, toilets, bathtubs and showers regularly cleaned, carpets vacuumed, floors swept and cleaned, and pillows on furniture neatly arranged. Tenant agrees to store jewelry, medicines, money, keys, checkbooks and other valuables in a secure location recognizing that there is a risk of loss in having strangers viewing the property. Tenant agrees to indemnify and hold Landlord and Landlord's agents harmless from and against any, claims, causes of action, suits and damage arising out of or relating to property of tenant going missing or being damaged as a result of the property being shown to prospective buyers during the term of the lease.*

§ 17.9   USUFRUCTS, ESTATE FOR YEARS, TENANCIES AT WILL, TENANCIES AT SUFFERANCE, AND VERBAL LEASES

These are a variety of legal terms used to describe the different types of leases.

§ 17.9.1   Usufructs

The most common type of lease is referred to as a usufruct in which the landlord grants and the tenant accepts the right to possess, enjoy and use the real estate of the landlord for a fixed period of time.[1956] All leases for a period of time of less than five (5) years are treated as usufructs unless the parties have agreed otherwise in the lease.[1957]

1955   O.C.G.A. § 44-7-1.

1956   O.C.G.A. § 44-7-1(a).

1957   O.C.G.A. § 44-7-1(b).

§ 17.9.2 Estate For Years

An estate for years as used to describe long time leases in which a legal interest or estate in the property is transferred to the tenant. Normally, 99 year leases and other long term leases are treated as estates for years. This type of lease is the only one that will normally subject the lessee to paying ad valorem property taxes on the leasehold estate.[1958]

§ 17.9.3 Tenancies At Sufferance

In all cases where a tenant continues to remain in possession of the property after the term of the lease has ended or after the tenant fails to pay rent when it is due, the tenant is treated as a tenant at sufferance[1959] and is subject to being evicted.

§ 17.9.4 Tenancies At Will

A tenancy at will is a lease where no time is specified for the termination of the lease.[1960] A month-to-month lease is the best example of a tenancy at will. A written lease where the term expires, the tenant continues to pay rent and the landlord accepts it would also be considered at tenancy at will. In order to terminate a month-to-month lease, the tenant must give the landlord thirty (30) days notice.[1961] While there is no requirement that the notice be in writing, it obviously limits dispute when the notice has been given in writing. There is also no requirement that the notice be a month in advance of the lease termination. Therefore for example, if the tenant gives thirty (30) days advance notice to the landlord of the termination of a verbal lease on September 15, the lease would terminate 30 days later.

§ 17.9.5 Verbal Leases

Unlike other types of real estate contracts, a verbal lease in Georgia is enforceable for a term not exceeding one year.[1962] Therefore, if a tenant were to claim the right to occupy the property by virtue of a three (3) year verbal lease, the court would not enforce the lease for more than one (1) year.[1963] However, if the tenant remains in possession of the property with the consent of the landlord after one (1) year, the lease would be treated as a month-to-month lease.

§ 17.10 DISPOSSESSING A TENANT

As a general rule, a tenant who does not pay rent under the lease is in breach of the lease and may be dispossessed by the landlord. Georgia law has no statutorily recognized grace period for the payment of rent although such a period may be provided for in the lease agreement. However, in residential rental agreements, if the tenant pays all back rent and the cost of the dispossessory warrant within seven (7) days of the day the tenant was served with the summons notifying the tenant of the lawsuit, the payment is a complete defense to the dispossessory action.[1964] However, the tenant can only avail itself of this defense once in any 12 month period.[1965] State law is written to obligate the tenant to pay all rents owed. As a result of this wording, most leases define late fees and other charges as "additional rent" so that it is clear that the tenant is obligated to pay all of these amounts to the landlord.

1958   *Eastern Air Lines, Inc. v. Joint City-County Bd. of Tax Assessors*, 253 Ga. 18, 315 S.E.2d 890 (1984).

1959   O.C.G.A. § 44-7-50(a).

1960   O.C.G.A. § 44-7-6.

1961   O.C.G.A. § 44-7-7.

1962   O.C.G.A. § 44-7-2.

1963   *Carl v. Hansbury*, 67 Ga.App. 830, 21 S.E.2d 302 (1942). The court held that a verbal lease for five years is invalid and will not create a tenancy for longer than one year, in the absence of part performance (such as a tenant making improvements to the property) to make the statute of frauds inapplicable.

1964   O.C.G.A. § 44-7-52(a).

1965   O.C.G.A. § 44-7-52(a).

§ 17.10.1   Commencing The Dispossession

In order to commence a dispossession, the landlord or her agent must first demand possession of the property from the tenant.[1966] Normally, this notice is in writing and is delivered in accordance with the notice requirements of the lease. The typical demand for possession notifies the tenant how she has breached the lease, that the landlord is terminating the lease and demands immediate possession of the property. If possession is not immediately delivered, the landlord or her agent may ask a judge or clerk of court in the county in which the property is located and make an affidavit under oath as to the breach of the lease by the tenant.[1967] The judge or clerk then issues a summons to the sheriff which, along with the affidavit is served upon the defendant.[1968]

§ 17.11   SERVICE OF THE SUMMONS AND AFFIDAVIT

State law requires the summons and a copy of the affidavit of the breach of the lease be personally served upon the defendant.[1969] However, if the sheriff is unable to serve the defendant personally, service may be had by delivering the summons and affidavit to any person residing in the property.[1970] If no person can be found, the sheriff is permitted to post a copy of the summons and affidavit on the door of the premises and on the same day mail a copy of the same to the defendant at her last known address.[1971] This last form of service is known as 'tack and mail" or "nail and mail". While this type of service is sufficient to dispossess the tenant from the property, it is insufficient for the purpose of obtaining a money judgment against the tenant.[1972] However, if the tenant answers the lawsuit or makes a court appearance, then notice is no longer an issue and the court has jurisdiction both to dispossess the tenant and issue a money judgment against the defendant.[1973]

In the event of service by tack and mail where the tenant does not answer, the landlord can file a separate action to collect a money judgment. However, this would need to be personally served on the defendant.

§ 17.12   ANSWERING THE SUMMONS OR LAWSUIT

Once the summons or lawsuit and affidavit are served, the tenant has to answer the same either verbally or in writing within seven (7) days from the date of actual service.[1974] If the answer date falls on a Saturday, Sunday or a legal holiday in Georgia, the answer can be made on the next day.[1975]

If the tenant fails to timely answer the lawsuit, the landlord is entitled to the writ of dispossession being sought by the landlord.[1976] If the tenant answers the lawsuit, a trial is then scheduled on the matter.[1977] The defendant is allowed to remain in possession of the premises pending the final outcome of the litigation; provided, that at the time the tenant answers the lawsuit the tenant pays into the registry of the trial court all rent admittedly owed prior to the issuance of the summons.[1978] If the amount of rent owed is in dispute, the court determines the amount of rent to be paid into

---

1966   O.C.G.A. § 44-7-50(a).
1967   O.C.G.A. § 44-7-50(a).
1968   O.C.G.A. § 44-7-51(a).
1969   O.C.G.A. § 44-7-51(a).
1970   O.C.G.A. § 44-7-51(a).
1971   O.C.G.A. § 44-7-51(a).
1972   *Housing Auth. v. Sterlin*, 250 Ga. 95, 295 S.E. 2d 564 (1982).
1973   *Housing Auth. v. Sterlin*, 250 GA. 95, 295 S.E. 2d 564 (1982). *Housing Auth. v. Hudson*, 250 Ga. 190, 296 S.E. 2d 558 (1982).
1974   O.C.G.A. § 44-7-51(b).
1975   O.C.G.A. § 44-7-51(b).
1976   O.C.G.A. § 44-7-53(a).
1977   O.C.G.A. § 44-7-53(b).
1978   O.C.G.A. § 44-7-75(a).

court.[1979] The tenant is also required to pay into the registry of the trial court all rent which becomes due after the issuance of the summons.[1980] If the tenant docs not pay the past due rent into court as she is required to do, the tenant is not allowed to retain possession of the property.[1981]

§ 17.13 WRIT OF POSSESSION

If the landlord is successful in obtaining a judgment, the court will issue a writ of possession. As a general rule, the wri is effective seven (7) days after the judgment is entered.

The writ of possession authorizes the removal of the tenant and her personal property as approved by the sheriff executing the writ of possession.[1982] Typically, the sheriff will require that the landlord hire a team of movers to remove the property of the tenant. State law specifically provides that the landlord is not responsible for the personal property after it is removed from the apartment.[1983]

§ 17.14 CUTTING OFF UTILITIES TO A TENANT IN BREACH OF HER LEASE

Georgia law specifically provides that it is unlawful for any landlord to knowingly and willfully to suspend the furnishing of utilities to a tenant until after the final disposition of any dispossessory proceeding.[1984] Any person who violates this law may be assessed a fine not to exceed $500.

§ 17.14.1 A Word On Magistrate Courts

Almost all residential leasing disputes are handled by magistrate's courts in Georgia. Magistrate courts are the lowest level of courts in Georgia. The parties making appearance in a magistrate's court are often not represented by attorneys and the court is what most people think of as small claims court. The focus of some of the judges in magistrate's court is as much on achieving what the judge believes is a fair and just result as on strictly complying with the technical requirements of applicable state statutes. As a result, there are instances where a magistrate court judge will not award a landlord the total sums she is seeking or will give the tenant every opportunity to remain in the property.

Decisions of magistrate courts can be appealed by either party to state court within thirty (30) days of the court's order.[1985] When such an appeal is filed, the case is then heard by the state court on a de novo basis.[1986] This means that the state court is not bound by the magistrate court's finding of fact or conclusions of law. Essentially, the state court starts over in hearing the dispute.

§ 17.15 MILITARY ACTIVATION OF TENANTS

Georgia law gives a service member[1987] the right to terminate her leases upon at least 30 days prior written notice to the landlord in certain circumstances.[1988]

(i) The service member is required, pursuant to a permanent change of station orders, to move 35 miles or more from the location of the rental premises;

1979 O.C.G.A. § 44-7-75(a).

1980 O.C.G.A. § 44-7-75(b).

1981 O.C.G.A. § 44-7-75.

1982 O.C.G.A. § 44-7-55(a).

1983 O.C.G.A. § 44-7-55(c).

1984 O.C.G.A. § 44-7-14.1.

1985 O.C.G.A. § 15-10-41; O.C.G.A. § 5-3-20.

1986 O.C.G.A. § 5-3-29.

1987 Under O.C.G.A. § 44-7-22, the term "service member" means an active duty member of the regular or reserve component of the United States armed forces, the United States Coast Guard, the Georgia National Guard, or the Georgia Air National Guard on ordered federal duty for a period of 90 days or longer.

1988 O.C.G.A. § 44-7-22.

ii) The service member is released from active duty or state active duty after having leased the rental premises while on active duty status and the rental premises is 35 miles or more from the service member's home of record prior to entering active duty;

iii) After entering into a rental agreement, the service member receives military orders requiring him or her to move into government quarters;

iv) After entering into a rental agreement, the service member becomes eligible to live in government quarters and the failure to move into government quarters will result in a forfeiture of the service member's basic allowance for housing;

v) The service member receives temporary duty orders, temporary change of station orders, or state active duty orders to an area 35 miles or more from the location of the rental premises, provided such orders are for a period exceeding 60 days; or

vi) The service member has leased the property but prior to taking possession of the rental premises receives a change of orders to an area that is 35 miles or more from the location of the rental premises.[1989]

The notice given by the service member to the landlord must be accompanied by either a copy of the official military orders or a written verification signed by the service member's commanding officer.[1990] Upon the termination of the lease, the service member is liable for the rent due under the rental agreement prorated to the effective date of the termination payable at such time as would have otherwise been required by the terms of the rental agreement.[1991] However, the tenant is not liable for any other rent or damages due to the early termination of the lease.[1992] In addition to the above, in the event a service member dies during active duty, an adult member of her immediate family may terminate the service member's residential lease agreement by providing the landlord with a written notice of termination to be effective on the date stated in the notice that is at least 30 days after the landlord's receipt of the notice. The notice to the landlord must be accompanied by either a copy of the official military orders showing the service member was on active duty or a written verification signed by the service member's commanding officer and a copy of the service member's death certificate.[1993]

§ 17.15.1 The Servicemembers Civil Relief Act

Federal law also gives an active service member the right to terminate a residential lease under certain circumstances without penalty.[1994] However, the Georgia laws are slightly more favorable to the service member on terms of how much notice is required for termination. Under the Servicemembers Civil Relief Act[1995], a service member may terminate her lease under the following circumstances:

(i) A service member may terminate her lease at any time if during the term of such lease, the service member enters into the military service;[1996] or

(ii) A service member, while in military service, may terminate her lease on the date of the service member's military orders[1997] for a permanent change of station, or to deploy with a military unit, or as an individual support of a military operation, for a period of at least ninety (90) days.[1998]

1989 *Id.*
1990 *Id.*
1991 *Id.*
1992 *Id.*
1993 *Id.*
1994 50 U.S.C.A. app. § 535.
1995 50 U.S.C.A. app. § 501 *et seq.*
1996 50 U.S.C.A. app. § 535(a)(1).
1997 50 U.S.C.A. app. § 535(a)(1).
1998 50 U.S.C.A. app. § 535(b)(1)(B).

Similar to the Georgia laws, a service member must give written notice of termination to the landlord,[1999] accompanied with copy of the service member's military orders.[2000] Such notice may be delivered by hand, private business carrier (such as FedEx or UPS) or by United States mail with return receipt requested.[2001] Notice may be given to the landlord or the landlord's agent.[2002] The landlord may not charge an early termination fee, but the service member is responsible for any unpaid rent prorated up to the effective date of the lease termination.[2003]

If the lease provides for monthly rental payments (as do most leases), the effective termination date of the lease is 30 days after the first date on which the next rental payment is due.[2004] In other words, if the service member gives his landlord notice of termination on July 20 and rent is normally due on the 1st of each month, his lease would be terminated as of August 31. For any other lease, termination is effective on the last day of the month following the month in which notice is delivered to the landlord.[2005] Therefore, if the service member gives his landlord notice of termination on July 1, his lease would terminate on August 31. These effective termination dates are where the federal and Georgia laws differ. As stated above, under Georgia law, once the service member gives his landlord notice, the lease will terminate thirty days from the date of the notice. So, if the service member gives his landlord notice of termination on July 20, then the lease is effectively terminated on August 20, as opposed to a termination date of August 31 under the federal law. Although the difference is slight, the Georgia laws provide a shorter termination date than the federal laws.

To avoid any confusion, military service members are not afforded protection from discrimination under the federal Fair Housing Act.[2006] Therefore, a landlord may refuse to rent housing to a military service member without violating the FHA. To deal with this issue, many states have provided additional protection to service members in their state specific Fair Housing Acts by making military service members a protected class.[2007] In these states, it would be unlawful for a landlord to refuse to rent to (or discriminate against) a person based on her military status.[2008] Georgia, however, does not afford such additional protection.[2009] As such, a landlord may refuse to rent to an active military service member if the landlord is concerned about the service member terminating her lease early without violating any (federal or state) laws. A more detailed discussion on the Fair Housing Act is located in Chapter 25 (Fair Housing Act and Americans with Disabilities Act).

§ 17.16 DISCLOSURES OF PROPENSITY TOWARDS FLOODING

State law provides that when the owner of real property, either directly or through an agent, seeks to lease the property for residential occupancy, the owner shall, prior to entering a written agreement for the leasehold of that property, notify the prospective tenant in writing of the property's propensity of flooding if flooding has damaged any portion of the living space covered by the lease at least three times during the five-year period immediately preceding the date of the lease.[2010] An owner failing to give such notice shall be liable in tort to the tenant and the tenant's family residing on the leased premises for damages to the personal property of the lessee or a resident relative of the lessee which is proximately caused by flooding which occurs during the term of the lease.[2011]

1999 50 U.S.C.A. app. § 535(c).

2000 50 U.S.C.A. app. § 535(c)(1).

2001 50 U.S.C.A. app. § 535(c)(2).

2002 50 U.S.C.A. app. § 535(c)(2).

2003 50 U.S.C.A. app. § 535(e)(1).

2004 50 U.S.C.A. app. § 535(d).

2005 50 U.S.C.A. app. § 535(d).

2006 42 U.S.C.A. § 3601 *et seq.*

2007 McKinney's Executive Law § 296(2-a).

2008 McKinney's Executive Law § 296(2-a).

2009 O.C.G.A. § 8-3-200 *et seq.*

2010 O.C.G.A. § 44-7-20.

2011 *Id.*

§ 17.17   DISCLOSURES OF AGENTS AND OWNER

State law provides that the landlord or the landlord's agent shall at or before the commencement of the lease, disclose to the tenant in writing the names and addresses of the following persons:

(i)   The owner of record of the premises or a person authorized to act for and on behalf of the owner for the purposes of serving of process and receiving and receipting for demands and notice; and

(ii) The person authorized to manage the premises.[2012]

In the event there is a change to the above-information, the landlord is required to advise each tenant of the change either in writing or by posting a notice of the change in a conspicuous place.[2013] Notice is often posted in the leasing office of an apartment complex and is usually mailed to tenants residing in single-family homes.

§ 17.18   ATTORNEY'S FEES PROVISIONS IN LEASING TRANSACTIONS

Most leases contain a provision that in the event of litigation between the parties, the prevailing party in the litigation will be entitled to recover its attorney's fees. Since most leases are written to protect the landlord, a person unfamiliar with leasing transactions might expect such an attorney's fee provision only to state that the landlord may recover its attorney's fees in the event it needs to sue the tenant. However, Georgia law provides that such attorney's fees provisions in leases are unenforceable unless they are reciprocal.[2014]

§ 17.19   COMMENCEMENT AND ENDING DATE OF LEASES

There is sometimes confusion over the ending date of the lease. Ideally, it is always good to provide that the lease ends "on and through" or "until and through" a particular date. Simply writing "until" or even "on" has lead to disputes over whether the date referenced is or is not included in the term of the lease. While such matters are sometimes the subject of debates between landlords and tenants, the use of "until" or "on" a particular date includes that date.[2015] In some instances, the landlord due to no fault of her part, will not be able to deliver the premises to the tenant at the beginning of the lease term. Usually, this is because the previous tenant has not moved out of the premises. Most leases provide that if the landlord is unable to deliver possession of the property by the commencement date: 1) that commencement of the lease is automatically extended until possession can be delivered; and 2) the landlord has no liability for any delay in delivering possession to the property to the tenant. Tenants will sometimes want the right to terminate the lease if possession cannot be delivered within a certain time frame. An example of such a special stipulation is set forth below:

> **Special Stipulation 336:   Tenant May Terminate Lease if Landlord Cannot Deliver Possession of Property.**
>
> *Notwithstanding any provision to the contrary contained herein, if Landlord cannot, for whatever reason, deliver possession of the property to Tenant within seven (7) days from the date that Tenant was originally going to receive possession hereunder, Tenant shall have the right but not the obligation to terminate this lease without penalty. The right to terminate set forth herein shall expire upon Tenant occupying the property without having terminated the lease.*

2012   O.C.G.A. § 44-7-33.

2013   O.C.G.A. § 44-7-33.

2014   O.C.G.A. § 44-7-2.

2015   *Brooks v. Hicks*, 230 Ga. 500, 197 S.E.2d 711 (1973).

The **RED BOOK**

CHAPTER 18

SPECIAL
TYPES OF
CONTRACTS

OVERVIEW

There are many specialized contracts used to purchase and sell real property. Many of these contracts are discussed in preceding chapters. This chapter will focus on some specialized contracts including lease/purchase contracts, option contracts and auction contracts. In addition, this chapter will discuss confidentiality agreements and rights of first refusal.

Contracts to purchase and sell real property can take a number of forms, many of which are discussed in detail in other chapters of this book. Generally, the most common contract type is the traditional purchase and sale agreement, in which there is a negotiated price and a closing at which time title is transferred from the seller to the purchaser. These may include residential purchase and sale contracts, new construction contracts, lot purchase agreements, condominium purchase agreements, land purchase agreements, and the commercial contracts.

Additionally, parties may enter into: option contracts in which the seller is obligated to sell the property but the buyer has the right, but not the obligation to purchase[2016] and lease-purchase agreements in which the buyer leases the property for a fixed period of time prior to being required to purchase.[2017] The parties may also enter into auction real estate purchase contracts in which a property is sold at a written or live auction and confidentiality agreements to prevent the disclosure of sensitive information. These special contracts are discussed below.

§ 18.1 OPTION CONTRACTS

§ 18.1.1 In General

An option contract is an agreement in which the owner is obligated to sell, and the purchaser has acquired the right, at her choice, to purchase property for a set price and on set terms.[2018] As with other real estate contracts, an option must include a sufficient description of the property, the purchase price, and the identity of the parties.[2019] Usually the best way to do this is for a purchase and sale agreement setting forth the terms and conditions of the transaction to be made an exhibit to the option agreement. Of course some conditions, such as the closing date, will not normally be known in advance of exercising the option. Therefore, it is common for a provision to be added to the option agreement specifying that the closing date will be within a certain number of days from the exercise of the option as may be determined by one of the parties upon notice to the other. Since options are often for extended periods of time, the most difficult term in the agreement to negotiate in advance may be the purchase price.

Option agreements have generally been held or recognized to be sufficiently definite as to price to justify their enforcement if either a specific price is provided for in the agreement or a practicable mode is provided by which the price can be determined by the court without any new expression by the parties themselves.[2020]

When drafting options that provide for a purchase price to be determined in the future, great care must be taken to assure that nothing has been left for the court to construe. For example, in one case a landlord granted an option to a tenant to renew the lease where the following was set as the rental rate:

> [T]he rental rate for the renewal term shall be the fair market rental with fair market escalations. Fair market rental rate and fair market escalations being that rate and escalation found within comparable premises in comparable properties within the Northwest office submarket, taking into account any concessions being offered at that time.[2021]

2016   GAR Form F31, Option Agreement.

2017   GAR Forms F29, Lease/Purchase Agreement and F30, Lease for Lease/Purchase Agreement Exhibit.

2018   *Bowles v. Babcock & Wilcox Company*, 209 Ga. 858, 76 S.E.2d 703 (1953); *Mattox v. West*, 194 Ga. 310, 21 S.E.2d 428 (1942).

2019   *Jakel v. Fountainhead Development Corp., Inc.*, 243 Ga.App. 844, 534 S.E.2d 199 (2000). *see* Chapter 1 (Creating a Binding Contract).

2020   *Pettigrew v. Collins*, 246 Ga.App. 207, 539 S.E.2d 214 (2000).

2021   *Insurance Industry Consultants, Inc. v. Essex Inv., Inc.*, 249 Ga.App. 837, 549 S.E.2d 788 (2001).

The court held that this did not set forth a specific rental rate because the fair market value would have to be determined by an undesignated party. The provision did not define an objective method of ascertaining the fair market rental rate, comparable premises, comparable properties, nor the Northwest office submarket. The rent was an essential part of the contract upon which there must be a meeting of the minds and even though the negotiations showed a complete willingness or determination to agree in the future upon such term, there was no binding contract. The court stated that unless all the terms and conditions are agreed on, and nothing is left to further negotiations, an agreement to reach an agreement in the future is of no effect.[2022]

The court in another case upheld an option contract to purchase improved real property in five years for "the appraised value of the property at time of purchase based on an MAI Appraisal." The court found this agreement to be valid because the contract defined an objective method by which the value could be ascertained.[2023] By comparison, however, an option which provided that the property would be purchased "for its appraised value" was held to be unenforceable because there was no provision for whom would perform the appraisal.[2024]

§ 18.1.2   The Owner Must Be Obligated To Sell

An agreement in which the buyer has the right to purchase, or not, and in which the seller has the right to sell, or not, is not a contract at all since neither side is obligated to perform. Such an illusory agreement is not capable of judicial enforcement.[2025] Rather, to be enforceable, an option must provide that the seller[2026] is absolutely bound to sell upon the election of the buyer to purchase.[2027] It is the binding of one party, coupled with the discretionary obligation of the other, than makes for an option contract.[2028]

§ 18.1.3   Expiration Date

Real estate sales contracts generally include a fixed date on which the transaction must be closed. In the absence of a set closing date, the court will set the date for a reasonable time.[2029] An option contract, however, is peculiarly a contract of which time is of the essence. Because of the singular one-sidedness of an option contract in creating, for a stated time period, an irrevocable offer to purchase the property, the law requires that option contracts have fixed expiration dates after which they are no longer capable of being exercised.[2030]

One possible exception to this is when the option is coupled with a lease. In the absence of a specified date for exercising the option, the court may construe it as being open until the end of the lease term.[2031]

Note, however, that while the option must contain a fixed date by which it must be exercised, the actual closing date for the transfer of title to the underlying property is not a critical term.

2022   *Insurance Industry Consultants, Inc. v. Essex Inv., Inc.*, 249 Ga.App. 837, 549 S.E.2d 788 (2001).

2023   *Miller v. McCullough*, 236 Ga. 666, 224 S.E.2d 916 (1976).

2024   *Pettigrew v. Collins*, 246 Ga.App. 207, 539 S.E.2d 214 (2000).

2025   *Billings Cottonseed, Inc. v. Albany Oil Mill, Inc.*, 173 Ga.App. 825, 328 S.E.2d 426, (1985).

2026   At least in theory a seller could have the option to sell while the buyer has the absolute obligation to purchase upon the seller's election. It is difficult, however, to imagine this occurring with any frequency in practice.

2027   *Swinks v. O'Hara*, 98 Ga.App. 542, 106 S.E.2d 186 (1958).

2028   *Swinks v. O'Hara*, 98 Ga.App. 542, 106 S.E.2d 186 (1958) (The obligation by which one binds himself to sell, and leaves it discretionary with the other party to buy, is what is termed, in law an 'option,' which is simply a contract by which the owner of property agrees with another person that he shall have a right to buy the property at a fixed price within a certain time.)

2029   *Moog v. Palmour*, 115 Ga.App. 602, 155 S.E.2d 692, (1967).

2030   *Jakel v. Fountainhead Development Corp., Inc.*, 243 Ga.App. 844, 534 S.E.2d 199 (2000).

2031   *McKown v. Heery*, 200 Ga. 819, 38 S.E.2d 425 (1946).

§ 18.1.4 Consideration Is Necessary

As with other contracts, consideration is a requirement for an option contract.[2032] In a sales contract, the payment of earnest money is one form of consideration.[2033] The consideration paid for the option will vary with the strength of the real estate market. In a market where real estate is selling quickly or in periods of high inflation, the price of the option will normally be higher because there is a greater likelihood that the value of the real estate will increase during the option period. In markets where property is selling more slowly or in deflationary times where property values are stable or decreasing, the price of an option will normally be lower or even a nominal amount.

To assure that consideration exists for an option, it is recommended that the option language include at least a recitation that it is "for and in exchange of the sum $10 and other good and valuable consideration." Such a recitation of even nominal consideration is sufficient.[2034]

§ 18.1.5 Exercise Of Option

The acceptance or exercise of an option must be effectively communicated to the seller, and must be unconditional. In the absence of contrary provisions in the option agreement, actual receipt by the vendor of the notice of acceptance is necessary to complete the exercise of an option.[2035] Otherwise, hearing nothing from the grantee of an option by the last day for its exercise, a grantor might well make other disposition of her property.[2036]

As with other notice provision contained in contracts, care must be taken to exercise an option according to the terms of the option agreement. In one case the court found that notice sent via regular mail was insufficient to exercise an option when the agreement required that notice be sent via certified mail.[2037]

Once an option contract is accepted, the acceptance converts the option contract into a bilateral contract for the sale of property which the purchaser may enforce against the seller.[2038]

§ 18.1.6 GAR Option Contracts

§ 18.1.6.1 Option

The GAR Option Agreement[2039] recites a negotiated amount to be paid by the buyer directly to the seller for the option. This amount is in addition to whatever earnest money may have been paid. The Option Agreement also contains blanks for the parties, the property, and the expiration date to be indicated.

The GAR Option Agreement is not incorporated by reference into the GAR Purchase and Sale Agreement. As such, to incorporate this option, users of the GAR Option Agreement must include the following in their GAR Purchase And Sale Agreement Special Stipulations section:

> *"This Purchase and Sale Agreement shall become binding upon the parties only when the Buyer exercises Buyer's option to purchase under the Option Agreement entered into by the parties simultaneously with the execution of this Purchase and Sale Agreement."*

2032   *Osborne v. Martin*, 136 Ga.App. 86, 220 S.E.2d 19 (1975).

2033   *Grier v. Brogdon*, 234 Ga.App. 79, 505 S.E.2d 512 (1998).

2034   *Goodman v. Spurlin*, 131 Ga. 588, 62 S.E. 1029 (1908); *Smith v. Wheeler*, 233 Ga. 166, 210 S.E.2d 702 (1974).

2035   *Musgrove v. Long*, 248 Ga. 902, 287 S.E.2d 23 (1982).

2036   *Musgrove v. Long*, 248 Ga. 902, 287 S.E.2d 23 (1982).

2037   *Atkinson v. Cook*, 271 Ga. 57, 518 S.E.2d 413 (1999).

2038   *Jakel v. Fountainhead Development Corp., Inc.*, 243 Ga.App. 844, 534 S.E.2d 199 (2000).

2039   GAR Form F31.

The GAR Option Agreement to Purchase Leased Property Exhibit[2040] is similar to the GAR Option Agreement but is tailored to situations in which the owner grants the tenant an option to purchase the leased property. For a more detailed discussion of the GAR Option Agreement to Purchase Leased Property Exhibit, see § 18.2.4 (Lease With An Option To Purchase).

§ 18.1.7   Purchase And Sale Agreement

The GAR Purchase and Sale Agreement[2041] contains a Due Diligence Period during which the buyer has a negotiated period of time during which to inspect the property and determine, in her sole discretion, whether or not to proceed with the purchase the property. The intent of this provision is to convert the GAR Purchase and Sale Agreement into an option contract.[2042] The option is not considered a true sales contact until the Due Diligence Period has expired without the buyer terminating the contract. The GAR Purchase and Sale Agreement's due diligence period includes a recital of $10 separate consideration being paid by the buyer to the seller for the seller granting this option to the buyer. Some real estate licensees have asked whether this consideration really needs to be paid or whether the mere recital of consideration in the agreement is sufficient. While the seller has every right to ask for the consideration, a recital of consideration in an option contract, even if the consideration has not been paid, will be sufficient.[2043]

Some sellers have argued that the price paid by the buyer for the "free look" afforded by the due diligence period should be significantly more than $10 if a property is to be taken off the market for any period of time. A special stipulation where the money paid by the buyer for the "free look" is significantly more than $10 is set forth below.

> **Special Stipulation 337:   Larger Payment by Buyer to Seller for Right to Terminate**
>
> *Notwithstanding any provisions to the contrary contained herein, the consideration for Seller granting Buyer an option to terminate this Agreement during the Due Diligence Period shall be the payment by Buyer to Seller of the sum of $_____. This payment shall be made no later than within one (1) day from the Binding Agreement Date. In the event the payment is not timely made the Seller may, but shall not be required to, terminate this Agreement upon notice to Buyer. Since this payment is consideration of Seller granting Buyer the right to terminate this Agreement, it shall not be refundable to Buyer and shall not be applied to the purchase price of the Property.*

Another approach is for the buyer to give the seller a significant sum for the right to terminate the contract, but then provide that a portion of this payment is applied toward the purchase price of the property if the buyer closes upon the purchase of the property. The special stipulation set for below is an example of such a provision.

> **Special Stipulation 338:   A Portion of Payment for Right to Terminate to be Applied Toward Purchase Price**
>
> *Notwithstanding any provision to the contrary contained herein, the consideration for the Seller granting Buyer the right to terminate as set forth herein shall be the payment by Buyer to Seller of the sum of $_____. This payment shall be made no later than within one (1) day from the Binding Agreement Date. In the event the payment is not timely made the Seller may, but shall not be required to, terminate this Agreement upon notice to Buyer. Since this payment is in consideration of Seller granting Buyer*

2040   GAR Form F36.

2041   GAR Form F20.

2042   *Kent v. Graham Commercial Realty, Inc.*, 279 Ga.App. 537, 631 S.E.2d 753 (2006).

2043   *Blount v. Lynch*, 24 Ga.App. 217, 100 S.E. 644 (1919). The court held that the fact that consideration named in an option contract for the sale of land had not been paid would not necessarily render the agreement unenforceable.

> *the right to terminate this Agreement it shall not be refundable to Buyer. However, if*
> *Buyer elects to close upon the purchase of the Property, _____% of the above-referenced*
> *amount shall be applied toward the purchase price of the Property at closing.*

§ 18.1.8   Right Of First Refusal

A close cousin to an option agreement is a right of first refusal. Similar to an option, a right of first refusal allows the purchaser the choice of purchasing the property, or not, at her whim. The difference, however, is that the purchaser is not at liberty to exercise the right whenever she likes.[2044]

Instead, the seller is required to notify the buyer of the terms of a third-party offer to purchase the property. The buyer then has a fixed time during which to match the terms of the third-party offer. If the buyer exercises the option, the seller must sell to her on the same terms as the third-party offer. If the purchaser declines to match the third-party offer, the seller is free to convey the property to the third party, thereby extinguishing the purchaser's right of first refusal.[2045] Rights of first refusal are sometimes granted to long-term lessees. In other cases, a buyer already owning of a portion of a seller's property (*i.e.*, common owners) will get a right of first refusal from the seller for the remainder of the property. While rights of first refusal usually involve a matching of the terms of the third party's offer, it may be possible for the right of refusal to pre-set a specified contractual price. The risk in doing so, however, is that the right could be set aside as a restraint on alienability if the price is set too low.[2046] As discussed by the Georgia Supreme Court, "in reaching the question of whether such a right [of first refusal] is an unlawful restraint on alienation the method of setting the price is critical. If the holder of the preemption right is merely entitled to meet the offer of an open market purchaser, there is little clog on alienability. But if he has a right to purchase at a fixed price, or at a reduced price from that offered in the market, it is likely to involve a sacrifice by the owner in order to alienate the property. Hence it becomes a far more serious interference with alienability."[2047]

Since a right of first refusal does not prevent the owner from seeking to sell the property on the open market, there is support for the notion that it can be perpetual in duration (whereas an option must have a fixed expiration date).[2048] The safer course, however, is to include a fixed end-date for the right of first refusal.

Normally, as with other option contracts, one must negotiate for a right of first refusal. There is an exception, however, in the case of a condominium conversion when a condominium is created from an existing apartment.[2049] In this instance, the tenant must be offered the option to purchase the newly converted unit within 60 days.[2050] If the tenant does not accept the sale offer presented to them during the first 60 days, they retain a right of first refusal to match any other contract accepted during the next 60 days.[2051] This is discussed further in § 20.1.8 (Conversion Condominiums).

Further, as discussed in Chapter 20: (Condominiums, Homeowner Associations and Other Forms of Common Interest Communities), a right of first refusal set forth in a Declaration of Condominium must meet certain requirements to be lawful.

2044   *Pearson v. Horne*, 139 Ga. 453, 77 S.E. 387 (1913).

2045   *Pearson v. Horne*, 139 Ga. 453, 77 S.E. 387 (1913).

2046   *Shiver v. Benton*, 251 Ga. 284, 304 S.E.2d 903 (1983).

2047   *Shiver v. Benton*, 251 Ga. 284, 304 S.E.2d 903 (1983).

2048   *CS-Lakeview at Gwinnett, Inc. v. Simon Property Group*, 283 Ga.App. 686, 642 S.E.2d 393 (2007).

2049   O.C.G.A. § 44-3-71(10).

2050   O.C.G.A. § 44-3-87(b).

2051   O.C.G.A. § 44-3-87(b).

§ 18.1.8.1   Form Of Right Of First Refusal

Typically, a right of first refusal is in writing and recorded in the land records office of the county in which the property is located to put the world on notice of its existence. As such, it is ideally witnessed and notarized so that it can be recorded. A sample of a right of first refusal is set for the below.

Upon recording return to: *Reference:* _____

_____   *Deed:* _____

_____   *Page Number:* _____

Grant of Right of First Refusal

For and in consideration of Ten Dollars ($10) and other good and valuable consideration, the receipt and sufficiency of which is hereby acknowledged, the undersigned ("Owner") does hereby grant to _____ ("Grantee") a right of first refusal to purchase the real property described in Exhibit A attached hereto and incorporated herein or any portion thereof which Seller might not decide to sell on the terms and conditions set forth herein.

1. The Right of First Refusal shall commence on _____, 20__ and end on _____, 20__ ("Term"). If Owner decides to list the Property or any portion of the same for sale, Owner shall notify Grantee of Owner's decision to list the Property, or any portion thereof prior to it being listed. The notice shall be sent to the address of Grantee set forth below or at such other address as Grantee may provide Owner from time to time in writing:

Address of Grantee:

_____

_____

_____

2. If during the Term of this Right of First Refusal, Owner either offers or receives an offer to sell, exchange, transfer or convey the Property or any portion thereof, on terms and conditions that are acceptable to the Owner, Owner shall only enter into a binding agreement if it is in writing and expressly made subject to this Right of First Refusal. Any such binding agreement shall be referred to as "Accepted Offer." Owner shall promptly notify Grantee of the Accepted Offer and shall provide Grantee with complete executed copy of the same. The notice of the Accepted Offer shall be sent to the Grantee's address for receiving notice referenced herein. Grantee shall then have a fourteen (14) day period from the date of delivery of the Accepted Offer to exercise Grantee's right of first refusal and notify Owner that Grantee will purchase the Property that is the subject of the Accepted Offer on the same terms and conditions as are set forth in the Accepted Offer.

3. If Grantee exercises the right of first refusal to purchase the Property, Grantee shall acquire the Property on the same terms and conditions as are set forth in the Accepted Offer, except that the Binding Agreement Date of the Agreement ("New Agreement") shall be the date that Grantee delivers notice to Owner of Grantee's decision to purchase the Property on the same terms and conditions as are set forth in the Accepted Offer.

Moreover, if a specific calendar date to close the transaction is included in the Accepted Offer, the closing date of the sale of the Property to Grantee shall be extended by the number of days that the Binding Agreement Date in the Accepted Offer was extended in the New Agreement.

4. If Grantee fails to timely notify Owner of Grantee's decision to exercise Grantee's Right of First Refusal or fails to notify Owner that Grantee is waiving its right to purchase the Property, or portion thereof, Grantee shall be deemed to have waived it's right to purchase the Property pursuant to this Right of First Refusal.

5. The waiver of the Right of First Refusal by Grantee with respect to any Accepted Offer shall not extinguish the Right of First Refusal with respect to any portion of the Property that was not included in the Accepted Offer. Moreover, if the buyer under the Accepted Offer does not close on the purchase of the Property or any portion thereof described in the Accepted Offer, said Property or portion thereof shall again be subject to this Right of First Refusal set forth herein.

6. Notwithstanding any provision to the contrary contained herein, Owner shall not sell, exchange, transfer, convey or gift the Property or any portion thereof, without first giving Grantee a Right of First Refusal to purchase the Property or portion thereof, on the same terms and conditions as are offered by Owner and agreed to be the person or entity to whom the Property, or portion thereof is sold, exchanged, transferred or gifted.

7. Time is of the essence herein. It shall be expressly permissible to record this Right of First refusal in the office of land records of the county in which the Property is located so that it is a matter of public record and shall run with the title to the Property.

IN WITNESS WHEREOF, the undersigned Owner does hereby set her hand to this Agreement this _____ day of _____, 20_____.

Sworn and subscribed before   *Owner:*

me this _____ day of _____.   _____

_____   _____

NOTARY PUBLIC
(Notary Seal)

Sworn and subscribed before   *Owner:*

me this _____ day of _____.   _____

_____   _____

NOTARY PUBLIC
(Notary Seal)

Sworn and subscribed before   *Grantee of Right of First Refusal:*

me this _____ day of _____.   _____

_____   _____

NOTARY PUBLIC
(Notary Seal)

Sworn and subscribed before	*Grantee of Right of First Refusal:*
me this _____ *day of* _____ .	_____
_____	_____
NOTARY PUBLIC	
(Notary Seal)	

§ 18.1.8.2 Verbal Rights Of First Refusal May Be Enforceable

There may be instances when a verbal right of first refusal is enforceable.[2052] In one case, a tenant who was granted an oral right of first refusal from the owner was entitled to specific performance even though the property was under contract with another buyer.[2053] Since the owner admitted granting the right of first refusal to the tenant and the evidence showed that the other buyer had notice of this right before entering into her written agreement to purchase the property, the tenant's oral right of first refusal was enforceable.[2054]

In this case, the tenant and her family leased the owner's property for over 30 years. During that time, the owner granted the tenant a verbal right of first refusal to purchase the property if it was ever sold. This verbal right was for an unspecified duration, without specific terms and without any consideration. Thereafter, the owner signed a listing agreement to sell her property and informed her broker of the tenant's right of first refusal. In response to the listing, a buyer expressed interest in the property and signed an option agreement with the owner to purchase the same. The option agreement did not disclose the tenant's right of first refusal, but the evidence presented showed that the owner verbally informed the buyer of this right in a meeting. During negotiations with the buyer, the owner notified the tenant of the potential sale, the tenant exercised her right of first refusal and the parties proceeded to closing. At the same time, the buyer tried to exercise her option to purchase the property but the owner refused. In response, the buyer filed suit for specific performance claiming that her written option contract was superior to the tenant's verbal right of first refusal to purchase the property.

The court disagreed and granted specific performance to the tenant because the owner admitted that the verbal right of first refusal existed.[2055] This ruling was based on O.C.G.A. § 23-2-131(a) which allows specific performance of a verbal contract for land when the owner admits that a verbal right of first refusal existed with the tenant.[2056]

Although a court may find verbal rights of first refusal enforceable in certain rare situations, it is the best to explicitly provide for a right of first refusal in a written (preferably recorded) agreement between the parties.

§ 18.2 LEASE/PURCHASE AGREEMENT

A buyer may enter into a lease/purchase agreement when the buyer does not have enough money to purchase the property but anticipates that she will be able to purchase the property within some defined period of time. The GAR Lease/Purchase Agreement[2057] is not an option to purchase. Like most lease/purchase agreements, the GAR Lease/Purchase Agreement is a lease with an obligation on the part of the tenant to buy the property at the end of the lease term. In other words, the buyer and seller agree to close on a specified date or such earlier date as may be agreed to by the parties. Many of the provisions in the GAR Lease/Purchase Agreement relating to the purchase of the property are the same as are set forth in the GAR Purchase and Sale Contract; however, there are some differences.

2052   *Shivers v. Webster*, 224 Ga.App. 254, 480 S.E.2d 304 (1997).

2053   *Shivers v. Webster*, 224 Ga.App. 254, 480 S.E.2d 304 (1997).

2054   *Shivers v. Webster*, 224 Ga.App. 254, 480 S.E.2d 304 (1997).

2055   *Shivers v. Webster*, 224 Ga.App. 254, 480 S.E.2d 304 (1997) citing O.C.G.A. § 23-2-131(a).

2056   *Shivers v. Webster*, 224 Ga.App. 254, 480 S.E.2d 304 (1997) citing O.C.G.A. § 23-2-131(a).

2057   GAR Form F29.

§ 18.2.1   Earnest Money

The earnest money provisions in the GAR Lease/Purchase Agreement and the GAR Purchase and Sale Agreement are virtually the same. The GAR Lease/Purchase Agreement provides that a third party ("Holder") will hold the earnest money. The GAR Lease/Purchase Agreement also provides that the Holder shall return the earnest money to the buyer only: (1) if the parties do not enter into a binding lease/purchase agreement; (2) upon failure of either party to perform any contingencies or conditions which the agreement is subject; (3) if the agreement is terminated due to the default of the seller; (4) upon written agreement signed by the parties; (5) if the agreement is terminated in accordance with a specified right to terminate; or (6) upon an order of a court or arbitrator having jurisdiction over the earnest money. The earnest money provisions allow the seller to retain the earnest money as liquidated damages if the seller terminates the agreement due to the buyer's default. If the seller accepts and deposits the earnest money from the Holder, then the earnest money is deemed to have been claimed by the seller as liquidated damages and the seller will be precluded from pursuing the buyer for specific performance or actual damages.

The earnest money in a lease purchase transaction should not be confused with the security deposit in the lease portion of the transaction. If a seller has to choose between requesting more earnest money or a larger security deposit, most sellers will choose more earnest money. This is because the earnest money is surrendered to the seller in the event the buyer fails to consummate the purchase part of the transaction. Some lease purchase agreements will include a stipulation allow for a portion of each month's rent to become additional earnest money. This creates a financial incentive for the tenant to complete the purchase portion of the lease purchase transaction. Of course, the entire sum is surrendered to the seller if the tenant does not purchase the property.

§ 18.2.2   Lease Compensation

The GAR Lease for Lease/Purchase Agreement[2058] provides that the parties agree that lease payments made in accordance with the lease attached as an exhibit to the agreement are not to be applied to the purchase price of the property unless otherwise stipulated.[2059] If the parties desire that a portion of the lease payment is applied to the purchase price, the following special stipulation may be used.

> **Special Stipulation 339:   Credit Toward Purchase Price for Rent**
>
> *Buyer and Seller agree that at closing, Buyer shall receive a credit toward the purchase price in the amount of ___% of the rent payments, excluding any late charges. This credit shall only be given if Buyer completes the purchase of the Property. In the event Buyer fails to close on the purchase of the Property, the entire amount of the credit shall be treated as rent belonging to the Seller.*

§ 18.2.3   Lease For Lease/Purchase Agreement

When entering a lease/purchase agreement, it is important for the seller to ensure that the termination date of the lease is the same as the proposed closing date. The GAR Lease for Lease/Purchase Agreement Exhibit provides that the term shall end at the closing of the purchase of the property pursuant to the Lease/Purchase Agreement.[2060] The lease also provides that the landlord has the right to deduct from the security deposit any unpaid rent.[2061]

2058   GAR Form F30.

2059   GAR Form F30.

2060   GAR Form F30, Lease for Lease/Purchase Agreement Exhibit.

2061   GAR Form F30.

The lessee has the same obligations under the GAR Lease for Lease/Purchase and the standard GAR Lease.[2062] The buyer/tenant performs the inspection under the Lease for Lease/Purchase Agreement before the security deposit is paid. During the inspection, the tenant will itemize any existing damages to the property and promptly notify the landlord of any dangerous conditions or need for maintenance existing in the property. Upon the receipt of this notice, the landlord must, within a reasonable time, repair the identified defects and to the extent required by state law, any other defects which, if not corrected, would leave the property in a state of disrepair.

Thereafter, the GAR Lease for Lease/Purchase provides that the tenant is responsible for maintaining the Property in the neat, sanitary and clean condition, free of trash and debris, reasonable wear and tear excepted. The parties may indicate who will be responsible for any lawn and exterior maintenance to the property and pest control. In addition to any indicated obligations in the agreement, the tenant is responsible for maintaining the smoke detectors, mold and mildew on the property, and freezing of the pipes (in the event the temperature outside falls below 32°F).[2063] Prior versions of the GAR Lease for Lease/Purchase Agreement provided that the tenant was solely responsible for all minor repairs and/or maintenance on the property from the date of occupancy to the date of closing or termination of the agreement, as further consideration for entering the Lease/Purchase Agreement. This obligation was removed, however, to align the parties' obligations with the owner's responsibilities to repair the leased property under Georgia landlord-tenant law.[2064]

The GAR Lease for Lease/Purchase prohibits the tenant from making any alterations, modifications, or improvements to the property (including painting) without first obtaining prior written consent of the landlord. If the landlord consents, any improvements, alterations or modifications will be deemed to be for the sole benefit of the tenant. As such the tenant expressly waives all rights to recover the cost or value of the same. Any improvements, alterations or modifications of the property made by the tenant without the approval of the landlord will be considered damage done to the property by the tenant. The GAR Lease for Lease/Purchase also authorizes the tenant or landlord to terminate the lease if flood, fire, storm, mold, other environmental hazards that pose a risk to the tenant's health, other casualty or Act of God destroys the property or substantially damages the property as to make the property uninhabitable.[2065] The party electing to terminate the lease must do so by written notice within thirty (30) days of the date of such destruction. The tenant may not terminate the lease if the damage or destruction of the property, whether total or partial, is the result of the negligence of the tenant or tenant's guests, invitees or licensees. If the tenant elects to cancel the lease, the tenant must either cancel the lease/purchase agreement or consummate the lease/purchase agreement pursuant to its terms which are the same as set forth in the GAR Purchase and Sale Agreement for condition of property.[2066]

If the tenant fails to close on the date specified in the GAR Lease/Purchase Agreement, the GAR Lease for Lease/Purchase Agreement terminates and the tenant must vacate the property. Although the tenant's failure to close is not considered a breach under the GAR Lease for Lease/Purchase Agreement, the tenant has no right to remain in the property after the closing date specified in the GAR Lease/Purchase Agreement. The GAR Lease/Purchase Agreement explicitly provides that the closing date is the same date that the lease terminates. As such, if the landlord wants to continue to allow the tenant to remain in and lease the property, the parties should enter into a normal lease agreement using the GAR Lease for Residential Property (Not to Be Used for Lease/Purchase Transactions) form.[2067]

2062   GAR Form F40.

2063   GAR Form F30.

2064   O.C.G.A. § 44-7-13. The landlord must keep the premises in repair. He shall be liable for all substantial improvements placed upon the premises by her consent.

2065   GAR Form F30.

2066   GAR Form F29, Lease/Purchase Agreement.

2067   GAR Form F40.

§ 18.2.4 Lease With An Option To Purchase

Many property owners are willing to grant the tenant the option to purchase the property during the lease term. The GAR Option Agreement to Purchase Leased Property Exhibit[2068] ("Option to Purchase contract") is intended to be used as an exhibit to a lease in situations in which the owner of the property is willing to grant the tenant an option to purchase. From the tenant's perspective, this approach can be beneficial because the tenant has the right but not the obligation to purchase the property. However, granting the tenant this right creates a number of risks to the seller discussed below.

§ 18.2.4.1 Consideration For Option To Purchase

Normally, the longer the term of the option, the more it will cost. With an option, the price at which the property can be purchased is set at the time the option is granted. In a normal real estate market, the longer the term of the option, the greater the likelihood that the value of the property will increase during the term of the option. Therefore, the buyer normally pays more to have an option of a longer duration because the buyer is getting the benefit of any increases in the value of the property over the lease term without owning the property. There should be stated consideration for the option that is separate from the consideration to lease the property since the right to buy the property is separate from the right to lease it.

The GAR Option Agreement to Purchase Leased Property Exhibit[2069] allows the parties to indicate the amount of consideration to be paid (referred to as the "option payment") by the tenant to the landlord for the option to purchase the leased premises. The option payment is nonrefundable regardless of whether the option is exercised. Even if the option is exercised, the option payment will also not be credited towards the purchase price or used to offset any other sum owed to the landlord.

§ 18.2.4.2 When Tenant Can Exercise Option To Purchase

In most cases, an option to buy the property can be exercised by the tenant at any time during the lease term. If such a broad right to exercise the option is granted, the option agreement should contemplate the possibility of the option being exercised at the end of the lease term. In such an instance, the tenant may need to stay in possession of the property as a renter after the regular term of the lease has ended but before the closing has occurred. An example of such a special stipulation is set forth below.

> **Special Stipulation 340: Tenant Can Extend Lease Term if Tenant Exercises Option to Purchase Property**
>
> *Tenant shall have the right to extend the lease term for up to an additional sixty (60) days on the same terms and conditions as in the original lease if Tenant exercises Tenant's option to purchase during the last thirty (30) days of the Lease and needs additional time to close.*

In some cases, the landlord will only give the tenant a limited window of time during which the option can be exercised. The stipulation below is an example of such a provision.

> **Special Stipulation 341: Option May Only be Exercised at Specific Time**
>
> *In the event Tenant is not in default of the Lease on the date _____ days from the commencement of the Lease, Tenant shall have the right during the seven (7) day period thereafter to exercise tenant's option to purchase the property for the price and on*

2068   GAR Form F36.

2069   GAR Form F36.

the terms set forth herein. In the event tenant does not exercise the option to purchase the property during this seven (7) day period, the option to purchase the Property shall expire and may no longer be exercised by the Tenant.

Most options to purchase also provide that the option can only be exercised if the tenant is not in default of the lease at the time the option is exercised. The theory behind this type of provision is that if the tenant cannot perform on the terms of the lease, the tenant will be unlikely to perform on the purchase of the property. An example of this type of stipulation is set forth below.

Special Stipulation 342:   Tenant Can Only Exercise Option to Buy if Tenant is Not in Default of the Lease

This Option can only be exercised by the Tenant if at the time it is exercised, the Tenant has paid all rents and other monies owed under the Lease to Landlord and Tenant is not in default of any other material terms and conditions under the Lease.

The GAR Option Agreement to Purchase Leased Property Exhibit[2070] allows a tenant to exercise this option to purchase only if the tenant is not in default under the lease at the time the option is exercised and if the option is exercised no later than the date specified in the agreement. If the option is not exercised by that date, the option will expire. More specifically, the GAR form provides:

Tenant shall only have the right to exercise Tenant's Option to purchase the Property if: (a) Tenant is not in default under the Lease at the time the Option is exercised, and (b) the Option is exercised in accordance with the terms of this Agreement not later than _____ days prior to the date that the term of the Lease expires. If the Option is not timely exercised by Tenant it shall lapse and be of no further legal force or effect. Notice of Tenant's decision to exercise the Option to purchase the Property shall be given by Tenant to Landlord in accordance with the Notice paragraph below. The date upon which the Landlord receives such notice shall be referred to as the Exercise of Option Date.

§ 18.2.4.3   Terms Of Purchase Should Be Specified In Option Agreement

The terms under which the tenant can purchase the property should be clearly spelled out in the option agreement. This avoids disputes over what the agreement of the parties is relative to the sale of the property.

While many terms of the purchase and sale agreement can be provided for the option agreement, others by definition must be left open. For example, the closing date is not normally provided at the time the option is granted since the option to purchase can typically be exercised by the tenant at any time over the duration of the lease. When there are terms which by their nature cannot be specified, the option contract should at least specify which of the parties gets to select the closing date and provide an outside date by which the closing must occur. The following special stipulation is an example of such a provision.

Special Stipulation 343:   Closing Must Occur Within Days of the Exercise of the Option

The closing of the purchase of the Property shall occur within _____ days from the Tenant exercising its option to purchase hereunder. The date of closing shall be selected by the Buyer and the Buyer shall provide the Seller _____ days notice of the same.

The GAR Option Agreement to Purchase Leased Property Exhibit contains a similar special stipulation. The buyer must choose a closing date and notify the seller of the same within a specified number of days from the Exercise of

---

2070   GAR Form F36.

Option Date. The parties also agree that the closing will occur between 14 and 45 days from the Exercise of Option Date, during normal business hours Monday through Friday and not on a federal holiday. Similar to the GAR Purchase and Sale Agreement, either party may unilaterally extend the closing date for a period of 7 days if (i) the seller cannot satisfy valid title objections or (ii) the buyer's mortgage lender or closing attorney cannot fulfill their respective obligations by the date of closing due to no fault of the buyer.

Typically, an option agreement granting a tenant the right to purchase the property will not contain as many terms as a purchase and sale agreement where the buyer is not in possession of the property. For example, an option agreement will not normally contain an inspection contingency or an appraisal contingency. The GAR Option Agreement to Purchase Leased Property also does contain an inspection contingency. Instead, the exhibit provides that the property is sold "as is," with all faults including but not limited to damage from termites and other wood destroying organisms and lead-based paint hazards. The duty also has no right to request that the seller make any repairs or replacements to the property during any type of due diligence period. The theory behind this is that the tenant is already in possession of the property and is familiar with its condition or can easily determine its condition before exercising the option. With regard to financing and an appraisal, the tenant also typically arranges for these things prior to exercising the option. To avoid disputes over the terms of the sale of the leased property, the GAR Option Agreement to Purchase Leased Property Exhibit contains many of the same terms provided in the GAR Purchase and Sale Agreement.[2071] Some of the terms included in this exhibit relate to the purchase price and method of payment, legal description of the property, earnest money, closing costs and other settlement expenses, title, agency and brokerage and notice. The goal behind including these terms is to provide the parties with a complete and comprehensive agreement in the event the buyer exercises the option to purchase the leased property.

§ 18.3 AUCTION REAL ESTATE PURCHASE CONTRACTS

It is increasingly common for real estate to be sold in either a written or live auction. Since a contract to sell real estate must be in writing, the winning bidder in a live auction typically fills out a written contract after the auction has taken place to create a binding contract. Normally, any copy of the contract the buyer is required to sign is provided to all bidders before the auction. Auction contracts are different than regular purchase and sale agreements in several ways. First, there are typically no financing or other contingencies in the auction contract. Auction contracts are normally all cash transactions. The contract is also typically "as-is-where-is" condition where the auctioneer disclaims any knowledge of the condition of the property. The auction contract often includes a reference to a buyer's premium. This is an amount that is paid by the buyer above and beyond the high bid price and is typically paid to the auctioneer as a fee.

In addition to the buyer's premium, it is not uncommon for the seller to pay a separate real estate commission to the listing broker who then shares the commission with any selling broker who is the procuring cause of the sale. Typically, when the buyer registers to bid at a live auction, the buyer is required to identify any selling broker at that time in order for the selling broker to be entitled to a commission.

In some auctions, the property is sold subject to a reserve. This means that if the bidding does not reach a minimum price for the property, the seller has the option not to sell the property. In some cases, the reserve price of a property is announced. In most cases, however, the reserve price is not announced. Therefore, the buyer who is the highest bidder sometimes thinks she won at the auction at a great price only to discover afterwards that the seller is not willing to sell the property to the buyer at that price. In other cases, the auction is an absolute auction without reserve. In this type of auction, the property is sold at whatever price the property brings.

---

§ 18.3.1 Auctioneer Of Real Property Must Be A Real Estate Licensee

In Georgia, an auctioneer who is auctioning real property must be licensed as a real estate broker, associate broker or salesperson.[2072] The auctioning of real property is also defined as real estate brokerage activity under real estate licensee law in Georgia.[2073]

In some auctions, the auctioneer who conducts the sale of the real property is affiliated with a different real estate broker than the real estate broker who is serving as the listing broker in the transaction.

§ 18.3.2 No Liens Permissible With Absolute Auctions

State auctioneering laws provide that no auction shall be advertised as an "absolute" auction except in certain limited circumstances. Specifically, among other things, there must either be:

(i) no liens or encumbrances on the property (except current tax obligations, easements, or restrictions of record, in favor of any person, firm, or corporation other than the seller, or unless each and every holder of each and every lien and encumbrance, by execution of the auction listing contract, or otherwise furnishing to the auctioneer written evidence f a binding commitment therefore, shall have agreed to the unqualified acceptance of the highest bid for the property, without regard to the amount of the highest bind or the identity of the high bidder); or

(ii) a financially responsible person, firm, or corporation, that, by execution of the auction listing contract or by otherwise furnishing to the auctioneer written evidence of a binding commitment therefore, shall have absolutely guaranteed the discharge and satisfaction of any and all liens and encumbrances immediately after the sale or at the closing, without regard to the amount of the highest bid received.

§ 18.3.3 Separate Agreements To Bid

In many cases, there is a separate agreement that bidders must sign to participate in the auction. In many of these agreements, the bidder agrees to deposit a certain monetary sum with the auctioneer as a precondition to participating in the auction. If the bidder has the winning bind and does not then either execute the purchase and sale agreement (provided by the auctioneer at the time the bidder registers for the auction) or close on the transaction, the auctioneer often has the right to retain all or most of the deposit as liquidated damages. This type of provision creates a financial disincentive for the winning bidder not to follow through and sign a contract to purchase the property.

§ 18.3.4 Auction Of Condominium Units

Auctioning previously unsold condominium units can be tricky because the buyer has a 7 day right to rescind the purchase and sale agreement[2074] if the contract is a covered contract.[2075] The seven (7) day rescission period begins from the point where the buyer has signed a purchase and sale agreement and received certain documents from the seller known as a condominium disclosure package.[2076]

As a result, a high bidder of a previously unsold condominium unit at an auction cannot normally be bound to her bid until seven (7) days after the bidder has signed the covered contract and received the other information required to be provided to the buyer under state law. Whether the seller of new condominium units in an auction can obligate the high bidder to surrender all or a portion of an auction registration fee if the high bidder does not execute the

---

2072   O.C.G.A. § 43-6-9.

2073   O.C.G.A. § 43-40-2(F).

2074   O.C.G.A. § 44-3-111(c).

2075   A covered contract refers to the "first bona fide sale of each residential condominium unit for residential occupancy by the buyer, any member of the buyer's family or any employee of the buyer" regardless of whether the seller is the declarant, the association or any other person" O.C.G.A. § 44-3-111(a)

2076   O.C.G.A. § 44-3-111(c).

purchase and sale agreement provided by the auctioneer is also unclear. This is because the Georgia Condominium Act specifically gives buyers the right to sue to recover damages if they have paid "anything of value toward the purchase of a condominium unit" without first having received the information required to be provided to buyers.[2077]

§ 18.4 CONFIDENTIALITY AGREEMENTS IN COMMERCIAL REAL ESTATE TRANSACTIONS

It is common in commercial real estate transactions for a prospective buyer to sign a confidentiality agreement prior to being given access to financial information about a property that is being offered for sale. Confidentiality agreements are intended to prevent the disclosure of information that could help the competitors of the seller or otherwise be embarrassing to the seller if it were widely distributed. There are several issues in drafting confidentiality agreements that are discussed below.

§ 18.4.1 Information To Be Kept Confidential

Normally a Confidentiality Agreement will clearly identify the materials that are being made confidential. In many cases, the confidential information is set forth in a package that is available online for review by the prospective buyer after she has consented in the form of a mouse click to keep the information confidential. Rather than making all information about the real estate confidential, it is normally best only to make truly sensitive information confidential (such as financial information about the operation of a property). If information is made confidential that is readily available elsewhere, it creates a potential defense that the owner waived the confidentiality agreement by disseminating the information to others on a non-confidential basis.

§ 18.4.2 Required Information To Be Kept Confidential

Most buyers of commercial property being legal entities rather than natural persons. One question that frequently arises is how the seller ensures that a company preserves confidential information when multiple people within the company are reviewing the confidential information. Typically, the person signing the confidentiality agreement on behalf of a company agrees to limit the dissemination of the confidential information only to those people within the company who need to see it in order to evaluate the purchase of the property. Additionally, the person signing the confidentiality agreement further agrees to cause those people reviewing the confidential information to preserve the confidentiality of the information to the same extent as the person signing the agreement on behalf of the company.

§ 18.4.3 Enforcing A Confidentiality Agreement

Enforcing a confidentiality agreement is difficult for two reasons. First, if the confidential information has been disseminated to a number of prospective buyers and many of those buyers are legal entities that have further disseminated the information within their companies it is often difficult to determine who leaked the confidential information. Second, even if the source of the lead can be determined, it is often difficult to prove that damages resulting from the breach of a confidentiality agreement. Some confidentiality agreements include liquidated damages provisions in which the party revealing the confidential information agrees pays a pre-determined monetary amount in the event the party breaches the agreement. However, such provisions can be off-putting to the person receiving the confidential information and are often resisted in a negotiation over the content of a confidentiality agreement. A sample of such a special stipulation is set forth below.

2077   O.C.G.A. § 44-3-111(i).

Special Stipulation 344:   Liquidated Damages for Breach of Confidentiality

Buyer acknowledges that the Seller will be significantly damaged in the event the Confidential Information being provided to Buyer herein is disclosed or disseminated by Buyer to competitors of Seller. For the purposes of this confidentiality Agreement, the term "Buyer" shall mean _____ and its officers, directors, managers, employees, attorneys and accountants and engineers who need to review the Confidential Information in order to assess whether to purchase the above-referenced Property. The term "Competitors of Seller" shall mean any natural person, company or business that owns real property of a similar type or classification to the Property subject to this Confidentiality Agreement. In the event, Seller can establish that the Confidential Information contained herein, or any portion of it, was distributed or disseminated by Buyer to any Competitor of Seller, Buyer agrees to pay Seller liquidated damages of $_____, it being acknowledged that the same is a reasonable pre-estimate of Seller's actual damages and is not a penalty.

The **RED BOOK**

CHAPTER 19

THE GEORGIA BROKERAGE RELATIONSHIPS IN REAL ESTATE TRANSACTIONS ACT

OVERVIEW

The Brokerage Relationships in Real Estate Transactions Act ("BRRETA")[2078] was enacted by the Georgia legislature in 1994 and was substantially revised effective July 1, 2000. The purpose of BRRETA is to define and to regulate the relationships between real estate brokers and the public through state statute rather than through the traditional common law rules of agency.

This chapter discusses the different types of brokerage relationships that are permitted in Georgia, the duties of brokers acting in each type of brokerage relationship, limitations on brokers' liability to customers and clients, brokers' disclosure obligations, handling the change from one type of brokerage relationship to another, and terminating the brokerage relationship. Also included are discussions of the GAR Brokerage Engagements and how they can be used by brokers to comply with BRRETA, as well a section on choosing the appropriate form of agency for different situations.

§ 19.1 AUTHORITY FOR LICENSEES TO COMPLETE LISTING OR SALES CONTRACTS

Although not actually a part of BRRETA, it is important to note here that Georgia law specifically authorizes real estate brokers and licensees to complete listing agreements, sales contracts or leases without concern that they will be charged with practicing law without a license, so long as the contracts have been prepared by legal counsel.[2079] The same code section specifies that whenever a licensee completes such documents the licensee must include (a) a description of the property involved, (b) the method of payment, (c) any special stipulations or addenda required, and (d) such date as may be required to determine whether the parties to the agreement have acted timely in meeting their responsibilities under the document.

§ 19.2 TYPES OF BROKERAGE RELATIONSHIPS

BRRETA divides brokerage relationships into two different groups: (1) broker-client relationships, in which the broker is representing the party with whom the broker is working as a client and (2) broker-customer relationships, in which the broker is not representing the party with whom the broker is working. As discussed below, brokers are allowed to perform more services and owe greater duties to clients than to customers.

§ 19.2.1 The Broker-Client Relationship

In a broker-client relationship the broker represents the client and is permitted to perform a variety of services for her. BRRETA imposes a few requirements on establishing a broker-client relationship, but also substantially limits the duties owed from the broker to the client as compared with the traditional common law rules of agency.

§ 19.2.2 Written Agreement Required For Client Relationship

BRRETA was revised effective July 1, 2000, to provide that a client relationship can only be formed by a written agreement between the broker and the party being represented as a client.[2080] The written agreement is referred to as the "brokerage engagement."[2081]

Prior to July 1, 2000, a client relationship could be formed through an express agreement of the parties. The express agreement could be either oral or written. The current requirement for a written agreement protects consumers and real estate brokers because written agreements tend to minimize the likelihood of disputes between the parties. This

---

2078   O.C.G.A. § 10-6A-1, *et seq.*

2079   O.C.G.A. § 43-40-25.1.

2080   O.C.G.A. § 10-6A-3(4), (6).

2081   O.C.G.A. § 10-6A-3(4).

requirement is consistent with the rules of the Georgia Real Estate Commission, which have long held that "exclusive brokerage agreements must be in writing and must fully set forth its terms and have a definite expiration date."[2082]

§ 19.2.3 Contents Of The Brokerage Engagement

BRRETA requires that the brokerage engagement must do the following things:

§ 19.2.3.1 Identify The Types Of Agency Relationships Available Through The Broker[2083]

To satisfy this requirement, the brokerage agreement must disclose to the prospective client which of the agency relationships permitted in Georgia (*i.e.*, seller agency, buyer agency, designated agency and dual agency, landlord agency, and tenant agency) are practiced by the brokerage firm.[2084] BRRETA also specifically requires the brokerage engagement to state whether the broker practices or rejects dual agency.[2085] If the firm does not offer dual agency, it is not sufficient for the firm to list only those forms of representation that the firm offers without mentioning dual agency. Rather, the firm must affirmatively state that it does not practice dual agency. Since transaction brokerage (discussed in § 19.5.2.3 (Transaction brokerage) hereof) is not an agency relationship,[2086] it does not need to be referenced in the broker's agency policy. Below are three sample agency policies:

> (i) <u>Single Agency Policy:</u> It is the policy of _____ Realty Company to only represent buyers as clients in real estate transactions. Other than buyer brokerage, _____ Realty Company does not offer its clients other agency relationships and does not practice dual agency.

> (ii) <u>Multiple Agency Policy:</u> It is the policy of _____ Realty Company to offer buyer agency, seller agency, dual agency, designated agency, landlord agency, and tenant agency.

> (iii) <u>Multiple Agency Policy:</u> It is the policy of _____ Realty Company to offer buyer agency, seller agency, designated agency, landlord agency and tenant agency. Company does not practice designated agency and does not offer that relationship to any client of Company.

§ 19.2.3.2 Conflicts Of Interest

Brokers must also notify their prospective clients of any existing brokerage relationships held by the broker with customers or clients that would conflict with any interests of the prospective client that are actually known to the broker.[2087]

It is clear that the broker does not have to make a blanket disclosure that he may be representing other sellers, landlords and tenants in selling or leasing property or other buyers in purchasing property.[2088] BRRETA does not give any other guidance on the types of brokerage relationships held by the broker that might be in conflict with the interests of the client and would therefore need to be disclosed to a prospective client. However, since the statute requires the broker to disclose conflicting agency relationships the broker has "with other parties," the provision does not appear to require disclosure of how one agency relationship might conflict generally with another agency

---

2082   Georgia Real Estate Commission Substantive Regulations 520-1-.06.

2083   O.C.G.A. § 10-6A-10(1).

2084   O.C.G.A. § 10-6A-10(1).

2085   O.C.G.A. § 10-6A-12(f).

2086   O.C.G.A. § 10-6A-3(14).

2087   O.C.G.A. § 10-6A-10(2).

2088   O.C.G.A. § 10-6A-10(2).

relationship. Instead, this portion of the statute requires only the disclosure of specific conflicts between individuals both of whom are represented by the same broker. The problem below gives an example of such a conflict.

Problem: A large corporation plans to expand its corporate headquarters into a surrounding neighborhood of single-family homes. The corporation knows that when its plans become public the prices of the homes will skyrocket. The corporation hires a local brokerage firm to quietly assemble as many homes in the neighborhood as possible at low prices. An owner of one of the homes in the neighborhood approaches the same brokerage firm. He says that he is thinking about hiring the firm to sell his home, but wants the firm's opinion as to whether holding onto the property would be a good investment. Would the firm have to disclose its agency relationship with the large corporation before listing the property?

Answer: The logical answer to this question would be yes. This is a case where the broker holds a specific agency relationship with one client that conflicts with, or is substantially likely to conflict with, the interests of another client. Because the price of real estate in the neighborhood is about to rise dramatically as a result of confidential information known to the broker, the brokerage firm cannot answer the seller's question regarding the investment potential for his property without jeopardizing the interests of an existing client. Similarly, failing to disclose the plans of the large corporation could potentially harm the interests of the seller. The best solution to this potential conflict is to decline to represent the seller as a client and to allow the seller to be represented by another broker.

§ 19.2.3.3   The Broker's Compensation

To satisfy this statutory requirement, the brokerage engagement must state the terms under which the broker will receive a commission.[2089] The law also requires that the brokerage engagement state whether the broker will share the commission with other cooperating brokers. The law does not require that the amount of compensation to be paid to a cooperating broker be revealed, but only whether the commission will or will not be shared. However, the GAR Exclusive Seller Listing Agreement[2090] includes a place for the listing broker to fill in the amount of the commission to be offered to cooperating brokers. This provision was included because REALTORS® are required to disclose to their sellers in listing a property how the commission will be split with a selling broker under the NAR Code of Ethics[2091] to insure that sellers were aware of the commission splits being offered by their listing brokers.[2092]

§ 19.2.3.4   The Broker's Legal Obligation To Keep Information Confidential

BRRETA requires that the broker's duty to keep information confidential also be explained in the brokerage engagement.[2093] All of the GAR Brokerage Engagement forms include an explanation of the broker's duties to keep confidences in dual agency transactions, and an explanation that brokers representing clients may not reveal any information they receive during the term of the brokerage agreement unless the client either allows the disclosure or the disclosure is required by law. The client may permit disclosure of confidential information by either words or conduct. BRRETA specifically states that a broker does not violate the duty of confidentiality by disclosing confidential information to any of the broker's affiliated licensees who are assisting the broker in the representation of the client,[2094] except in transactions where the brokerage firm is practicing designated agency. (Refer to § 19.3.5 (Confidential Information), *infra*, for a complete discussion of the duty of confidentiality under BRRETA.)

2089   O.C.G.A. § 10-6A-10(3).

2090   GAR Form F1.

2091   Standard of Practice 1-12 of The Code of Ethics and Standards of Practice of National Association of REALTORS® (2012).

2092   Cooperating brokers may be reluctant to show the property to prospective purchasers if the commission split is too low.

2093   O.C.G.A. § 10-6A-10(4).

2094   O.C.G.A. § 10-6A-5(a)(5), O.C.G.A. § 10-6A-6(a)(5), O.C.G.A. § 10-6A-7(a)(5), O.C.G.A. § 10-6A-8(a)(5).

§ 19.2.4   Broker Can Work With Customer Without Written Brokerage Agreement

A written agreement is not needed to establish a broker-customer relationship in Georgia.[2095] For example, a broker can show a buyer property without establishing a client relationship. In such cases the broker can perform only ministerial acts on behalf of the party being shown the property.[2096] Similarly, a broker can also have an oral, non-client, non-exclusive agreement with a seller in which the seller agrees to pay the broker a commission if the broker procures a buyer to purchase the property (*i.e.*, an "open listing"). Of course, the broker should not represent the seller as a client in such a transaction without a written agreement. Unlike when dealing with a client relationship, BRRETA does not require that agency be explained or offered to customers.

§ 19.2.5   Sales Agreement Is Not A Brokerage Engagement

Buyer customers often get to a point in the transaction where they ask the broker with whom they are working to represent them as clients. Before undertaking such representation the broker must be careful to enter into a written brokerage agreement meeting the requirements of BRRETA. The GAR Contract cannot serve as the written brokerage agreement because it does not contain all of the four items required by law to be included in a brokerage engagement. (*See* § 19.2.3 (Contents of The Brokerage Engagement)) Therefore, the broker should use a GAR Exclusive Buyer Brokerage Agreement[2097] as the written agreement to establish the client relationship.

§ 19.2.6   Different Brokerage Agreements Needed To Sell And Buy Property

It is not uncommon for buyers who have engaged a broker to represent them in purchasing a property to want to have the same broker list a property they may be selling or need to sell to consummate the first transaction. Similarly, sellers will often turn to their listing brokers to help them purchase other real property. Brokers representing the same client as both buyer and seller should enter into separate brokerage engagement agreements for each type of representation. This is because these transactions, while sometimes related, are essentially separate transactions where the duties owed as a listing broker are different from the duties owed as a buyer broker.

§ 19.2.7   Representing A Client Without Written Agreement

What happens if a broker enters into an agreement to represent a party as a client without reducing the agreement to writing as required by BRRETA? BRRETA provides no specific sanction for the failure to have a client relationship reduced to writing. However, the Georgia Court of Appeals has held that no broker-client relationship is created in the absence of a written engagement.[2098] Presumably, the would-be client could terminate the relationship on the basis that contracts made in violation of state law are subject to being challenged as unenforceable.[2099] The broker could also face potential sanctions from the Georgia Real Estate Commission, although a violation of its regulations will not render a contract unenforceable.[2100]

2095   O.C.G.A. § 10-6A-3(8).

2096   O.C.G.A. § 10-6A-3(8).

2097   GAR Form F4.

2098   *Harrouk v. Fierman*, 2008 WL 2280690 (Ga.App.).

2099   *Bowers v. Howell*, 203 Ga.App. 636, 637, 417 S.E. 2d 392, 393 (1992); *Harris v. Auto Finance Corporation*, 135 Ga.App. 267, 268, 218 S.E. 2d 83, 84 (1975); O.C.G.A. § 13-8-2. (A contract which is against the policy of the law cannot be enforced.)

2100   *Silver Pigeon Properties, LLC v. Fickling & Co., Inc.*, EL 2104164 (June 2012) citing *Johnson Realty, Inc. v. Hand*, 189 Ga.App. 706, 377 S.E. 2d 176 (1988). The Court, quoting the decision in *Johnson Realty, Inc. v. Hand*, held that unlike the Georgia Supreme Court, the Georgia Real Estate Commission has no inherent power over the real estate profession in Georgia, and unlike the Public Service Commission, the Georgia legislature has not delegated the Georgia Real Estate Commission plenary quasi-legislative power over the general conduct of the real estate business. Even assuming an agreement violates the GREC regulations, that does not render the agreement unenforceable.

What is clear is that the failure to reduce the terms of a client relationship to writing will not deprive the broker of its right to pursue a claim for its commission. The Georgia Supreme Court has expressly held that compliance with BRRETA has no bearing upon the broker's right to pursue its commission.[2101]

§ 19.2.8   Types Of Broker-Client Relationships

Prior to the enactment of BRRETA in 1994, brokers in Georgia almost exclusively practiced sub-agency in which the broker working with the buyer in the transaction was the sub-agent of the listing agent (if the two brokers worked for different firms). Under this arrangement, all of the brokers represented the seller, and the buyer did not have representation. Brokers referred to the buyers with whom they worked (but did not represent) as "customers." Sellers were referred to by their brokers as "clients" because an agency relationship existed between the parties. To differentiate between the two, the broker who was working directly with the seller was called the "listing" broker and the broker who was working with the buyer, but actually representing the seller, was called a "selling" broker.

Now, after BRRETA's adoption, there are multiple agency choices available to brokers and sub-agency has almost completely disappeared in Georgia. Unfortunately, the "listing" and "selling" broker designations have remained. This often leads to confusion since one may think that a "selling" broker represents the seller, when in reality the selling broker usually now represents the buyer. The following sections discuss these newer forms of agency.

BRRETA permits a variety of broker-client relationships. One category of client relationship is single agency representation in which the broker represents only a single party as a client in the transaction. There are two kinds of single agency representation: seller agency and buyer agency. BRRETA also permits brokers to offer designated agency and dual agency to clients. When these two agency relationships are used, the broker represents two parties in the transaction (*e.g.*, buyer and seller or landlord and tenant) as clients at the same time.

§ 19.2.8.1   Single Agency Representation

(a) Seller agency

With seller agency, sometimes called listing agency, the broker represents only the seller in the transaction. Neither the broker nor the broker's affiliated licensees have a client relationship with the buyer. In the GAR Exclusive Seller Listing Agreement,[2102] the duties of the listing broker are to use her best efforts to find a buyer ready, willing and able to purchase the seller's property at a price agreed to by the seller, and to assist, to the extent requested by the seller, in filling out a pre-printed real estate sales contract.

(b) Buyer agency

Buyer agency, also known as buyer brokerage, is the other form of single agency representation. In buyer agency, the broker represents only the buyer as a client in the transaction. Since the enactment of BRRETA, it has become common for buyers to have brokers representing them in real estate transactions. The broker working for the buyer is called the "selling broker" (not to be confused with the broker working for the seller, who is known as the "listing broker"). With a buyer agency, the broker works for the buyer-client in locating property for the buyer and, to the extent requested by the client, assisting with negotiations for the purchase of the property and completing form contracts. In most buyer brokerage agreements, including the GAR Exclusive Buyer Brokerage Agreement, the broker representing the buyer receives a portion of the listing broker's commission under a cooperative brokerage arrangement even though the broker is not representing the seller as a client. Thus, except in a few situations, the seller ultimately pays the entire commission. In Georgia, the broker can be paid a commission by one party yet represent another party.

2101   *Killearn Partners, Inc. v. Southeast Properties, Inc.*, 279 Ga. 144, 611 S.E.2d 26 (2005).

2102   GAR Form F1.

BRRETA specifically provides that "[t]he payment or promise of payment of compensation to a broker by a seller, landlord, buyer or tenant shall not determine whether a brokerage relationship has been created between any broker and a seller, landlord, buyer or tenant."[2103]

§ 19.2.8.2 Dual Agency

Dual agency is the brokerage practice in which one real estate broker simultaneously represents both parties in the same transaction as clients[2104] (*i.e.*, buyer and seller, or landlord and tenant) and where individual licensees affiliated with the broker have not been designated to exclusively represent each side of the transaction (*i.e.*, designated agency). In other words, the buyer and seller or landlord and tenant are both clients of the same real estate broker and neither client has a designated agent exclusively representing their interests. A broker may act as a dual agent only with the written consent of all clients.[2105] While dual agency is permissible under Georgia law, it is inherently risky and is recommended only when (1) no other form of agency is practical and (2) both clients are sophisticated and can appreciate potential for the broker to find himself or herself in a conflict role.

Because of the risks associated with dual agency, BRRETA requires every broker to develop and to enforce a policy regarding whether the broker practices dual agency or rejects dual agency.[2106] This brokerage policy must be included in the brokerage engagement agreement used by the broker.[2107] As a practical matter, dual agency occurs most frequently when the listing agent representing the seller as a client sells her own listing to a buyer client.

(a) What is considered the "same transaction?"

BRRETA does not define what is meant by the term "same transaction" in determining whether a dual agency relationship has been created. The dictionary roughly translates these words to mean the "identical business deal." For example, if a broker is representing both the buyer and seller as clients in the purchase and sale of a house, it is clearly the same transaction and a dual agency exists. There are other situations where it is not as clear whether the broker is dealing with the same or different transactions and therefore whether a dual agency exists. One such example is set forth below.

Example #1: A broker has a listing on property owned by Mrs. Jones. Mr. Smith, a buyer, visits the home during an open house and puts it under contract. Mr. Smith is not working with another real estate broker. The contract is conditioned upon a number of things, including the sale of Mr. Smith's present home. If the buyer now asks the broker to list his home for sale, can the broker do so without being considered a dual agent with respect to the sale of Mrs. Jones' home?

Answer: There is no case law on this point. The correct answer, however, should be that this is not a dual agency situation. While the sale of Mrs. Jones' home and the sale of Mr. Smith's home are related transactions, they are not the same transaction. Certainly, if the purpose of the dual agency warning is to protect the buyer and seller in situations where the broker is representing them in negotiating the purchase and sale of a specific property, that situation does not exist here because the broker is representing the parties in the purchase and sale of different properties.

Until there is judicial clarification on this point, the broker should disclose to the seller client that he is now listing the buyer's house for sale and has a client relationship with the buyer for purposes of that transaction.[2108] The disclosure should be made in writing so that there is written evidence that the disclosure was made. A broker representing the seller client has a duty to disclose material facts to the seller client which the broker has actual knowledge of concerning the transaction. A material

---

2103   O.C.G.A. § 10-6A-11.

2104   O.C.G.A. § 10-6A-3(10).

2105   O.C.G.A. § 10-6A-12(a).

2106   O.C.G.A. § 10-6A-12(f).

2107   O.C.G.A. § 10-6A-12(f).

2108   O.C.G.A. § 10-6A-5(a)(2)(c).

fact is defined as "facts that a party does not know, could not necessarily discover and would reasonably want to know." [2109] *Since most sellers could reasonably want to know that their broker is not representing the buyer in another transaction, the disclosure should be made.*

(b) Special written consent of all parties required for dual agency.

BRRETA only allows dual agency to be practiced by brokers with the written consent of both parties. [2110] There are no exceptions to this rule. Georgia real estate licensing law provides that a broker can be sanctioned (including the loss of the broker's license) by the Georgia Real Estate Commission if the broker represents more than one party in a transaction without the "express written consent of all parties to the transaction." [2111]

BRRETA mandates that the written consent to dual agency include:

(1) a description of the transactions or types of transactions in which the broker will serve as a dual agent;

(2) a statement that, in serving as a dual agent, the broker represents two clients whose interests are or at times could be different or even adverse;

(3) a statement that a dual agent will disclose all adverse material facts relevant to the transaction and actually known to the dual agent to all parties in the transaction except for information made confidential by request or instructions from another client which information is neither allowed to be disclosed nor required to be disclosed by BRRETA;

(4) a statement that the broker or the broker's affiliated licensees will timely disclose to each client in a real estate transaction the nature of any material relationship the broker and the broker's affiliated licensees have with the other clients in the transaction other than that incidental to the transaction. For the purposes of this Code section, a material relationship shall mean any actually known personal, familial, or business relationship between the broker or the broker's affiliated licensees and a client which would impair the ability of the broker or affiliated licensees to exercise fair and independent judgment relative to another client;

(5) a statement that the client does not have to consent to the dual agency; and

(6) a statement that the consent of the client has been given voluntarily and that the engagement has been read and understood. [2112]

(c) Written consent, which includes dual agency warnings, is "conclusively deemed to have been given and informed."

When the client signs a written consent that includes the dual agency disclosures discussed above, the consent of the client is conclusively deemed to have been given and informed." [2113] This means that after clients have signed a dual agency agreement they are barred statutorily from arguing that they did not give their consent or that their consent was not informed. Prior to this statutory protection a party could file a lawsuit against the broker and argue that she did not understand or give informed consent to the dual agency. [2114]

2109   O.C.G.A. § 10-6A-3(11).

2110   O.C.G.A. § 10-6A-12(a).

2111   O.C.G.A. § 43-40-25(a)(22).

2112   O.C.G.A. § 10-6A-12(a).

2113   O.C.G.A. § 10-6A-12(b).

2114   Prior to the adoption of BRRETA, Georgia law did not preclude dual agency provided that there was meaningful disclosure and the consent of the seller and buyer. *See Spratlin, Harrington & Thomas, Inc. v. Hawn*, 116 Ga.App. 175, 156 S.E. 2d 402, 406 (1967). Unfortunately, Georgia case law did not clearly define the level of understanding and consent that was necessary to proceed safely in a dual agency relationship. In a New Jersey case, the Supreme Court of that state applying general principles of agency stated, "Full disclosure requires… an explanation of the pitfalls that may arise in the course of the transaction which would make it desirable that the buyer" be independently represented. The full significance of the representation of conflicting interests should be disclosed to the client so that he may make an intelligent decision before giving his consent. The court went on to say that it would "not tolerate consents which are less than knowing, intelligent and voluntary. Consents must be obtained in such a way as to insure that the client has had adequate time… to reflect upon the choice, and must not be forced upon the client … " *See Matter of Dolan*, 76 N.J. 1, 384 A. 2d 1076 (N.J. 1978). Although the *Dolan* case was from another jurisdiction, the reasoning of the court was consistent with the *Spratlin* case above. Therefore, prior to having a state statute creating a conclusive presumption of consent, parties could argue that their consent was not informed and should not bar them from asserting a claim arising from the broker acting in a dual agency capacity.

(d) Written consent must be obtained prior to acting as a dual agent.

The consent to dual agency discussed above must be obtained before the licensee acts as a dual agent (*e.g.*, before the licensee performs anything more than ministerial services for a party with regard to a property in which the licensee will serve as a dual agent). Because the dual agency disclosure is contained in the GAR Contract, some real estate brokers have assumed that consent to dual agency is not necessary until the time the parties signed the purchase contract. This is not correct. BRRETA provides that "a broker may act as a dual agent only with the written consent of all clients."[2115] This language mandates that the consent be obtained from all the clients before the real estate agent acts in a dual agency capacity. By the time the parties are negotiating the terms of a purchase contract, it is most likely too late, as the broker will probably have already acted in a dual agency capacity.

To help licensees comply with the requirement of obtaining prior written consent, the dual agency disclosure is contained in the GAR Buyer Brokerage Engagement forms and the GAR Seller Listing forms, as well as in the various GAR Purchase and Sale Agreements. It is critical to include the dual agency consent in any brokerage agreement to avoid a later claim that the parties did not give informed consent to the dual agency. It should be noted that the disclosure in the brokerage engagement forms is not a statement that the broker will definitely be acting in a dual agency capacity. Rather, it is the client's consent to the possibility that the broker may act in a dual agency capacity. Then, at the point at which the broker actually shows a buyer client property in which the broker is also representing the seller as a client (and in which the broker is not acting in a designated agency capacity), the broker must disclose that in showing this particular property the broker will be acting as a dual agent. This disclosure is necessary because BRRETA requires a broker with an existing brokerage relationship to disclose whenever the broker's agency relationship changes.[2116]

In the event that a broker finds herself in a potential dual agency situation in which one of the clients does not consent to dual agency, BRRETA allows the broker to withdraw from representing that client.[2117] In such a case, the broker is permitted to continue to represent the client who gave his consent.[2118] When a broker withdraws from the representation of one client for this reason, BRRETA permits the broker to refer that client to another broker in another real estate brokerage company. The broker may receive a fee for such a referral.[2119] It is important to note, however, that in such a situation the Georgia licensing law requires that the broker obtain the client's agreement to the referral and to inform the client whether the broker will receive any consideration for the referral.[2120]

(e) Broker's duty to disclose adverse material facts to both clients in a dual agency transaction.

A broker acting in a dual agency capacity owes a duty to disclose adverse material facts known to the dual agent to both clients in the transaction. The only exception to this rule is if either party in the transaction instructs the dual agent to keep specific information confidential and the broker is permitted by law to keep that information confidential. The following examples illustrate this principle.

Example: Seller mentions to her listing broker that a neighbor's child is mentally impaired and very aggressive toward other children in the neighborhood. Seller explains that this is one of the reasons she is moving. Seller instructs the listing broker to keep this information confidential. If the listing broker becomes a dual agent, is she obligated to disclose this information to her buyer-client?

2115 O.C.G.A. § 10-6A-12(a).

2116 O.C.G.A. § 10-6A-(4)(b).

2117 O.C.G.A. § 10-6A-12(e).

2118 O.C.G.A. § 10-6A-12(e).

2119 O.C.G.A. § 10-6A-12(e).

2120 O.C.G.A. § 43-40-25(a)(36).

Answer: By virtue of the dual agency, the broker is generally obligated to disclose to her buyer-client all adverse material facts regarding the transaction.[2121] However, this duty is then qualified to exclude information made confidential by request or instructions from another client. The duty to keep certain information confidential is further limited by requiring the broker to disclose certain information required to be disclosed by state law regardless of whether or not a client has instructed the information to be kept confidential.[2122] While it is reasonable to view this as a potentially adverse material fact, the broker is obligated to keep this information confidential because of the client's instructions to do so. There is no overriding provision of state law that would require disclosure of this information.

The problem with dual agency, as reflected in the above example, is that regardless of whether the disclosure is or is not made one of the broker's clients is benefited and another is potentially harmed by the broker disclosing or not disclosing the adverse material facts. If disclosure is made, the seller's ability to sell the house may be impaired. If disclosure is not made, the buyer's children may be put in harm's way. At the very least if disclosure is not made and the buyer later learns that the broker knew this sensitive information but chose not to disclose it, the buyer will likely be extremely dissatisfied with the broker and may not speak well of him or her to friends and neighbors in the community. This creates something of a "no win" situation for the broker and underscores the conflicts which can arise when the broker tries to represent two parties at the same time.

In response to concerns about preserving client confidences, the GAR Contract and the various GAR Brokerage Engagements contain directives from both the buyer and seller to the dual agent to keep all information confidential which could affect the negotiating position of either party.

Example: A subdivision agent is aware that her builder client is experiencing serious financial problems and needs to contract to sell a half-completed home being built on a speculative basis quickly. If the subdivision agent becomes a dual agent, what are the agent's obligations to divulge this information to the buyer-client? What should the agent do or say if the builder asks to hold significant amounts of unrestricted earnest money?

Answer: If the parties have signed GAR Brokerage Engagement Agreements, the dual agent would be barred from revealing the builder's financial difficulties to a buyer because those engagements contain directions to keep all information confidential which could affect the negotiating position of the parties. The seller's precarious financial condition is something the buyer would want to know because it potentially affects the builder's ability to complete the house and puts the buyer's earnest money at risk. However, the information about the builder's financial condition is something that the broker is required to disclose under some other provision of state law or BRRETA. As such, it must be kept confidential to the potential detriment of the buyer. Again, this shows how dual agency can put the broker in a terribly awkward no-win situation.

If the dual agent discloses the damaging information about the builder's situation, she may be further jeopardizing the builder's financial status. If the dual agent fails to disclose the information, the buyer may be at risk of losing her earnest money. While some real estate agents believe that being silent in these situations is a way of staying neutral, the reality is that silence hurts the buyer and helps the builder. Additionally, if the buyer loses her earnest money and then finds out that the dual agent knew of the builder's financial predicament, the buyer may feel that the agent has not adequately represented him in the transaction.

Example: Seller tells the Listing Broker that he does not want it revealed that the exterior of his property is constructed with synthetic stucco. If listing broker becomes a dual agent, must this information be revealed to his buyer client?

Answer: BRRETA requires the disclosure of all adverse material facts to all parties in a dual agency transaction except those specific facts which either of the parties instructs be kept confidential and which are not otherwise required by law to be disclosed. In this case, the seller has specifically asked that the information about the synthetic stucco be kept confidential. However, BRRETA requires the disclosure of all material facts relating to the physical condition of the property which could

---

2121   O.C.G.A. § 10-6A-12(a)(3).

2122   O.C.G.A. § 10-6A-12(a)(3).

not be observed upon a reasonably diligent inspection of the property. While it can be argued that the synthetic stucco could be discovered upon a reasonably diligent inspection of the property, the better answer is that the synthetic stucco is a material adverse fact regarding the physical condition of the property and that the duty to disclose is superior to the duty to keep the information confidential.

§ 19.2.8.3 Designated Agency

Designated agency is a type of brokerage practice in which a broker appoints one or more licensees within the broker's firm to exclusively represent different clients (buyer and seller or landlord and tenant) in the same transaction.[2123] This situation most frequently arises when a real estate licensee has a client who desires to view a property that is listed by another licensee in the same brokerage firm.

(a) Designated agency differs from dual agency

Prior to the 2000 amendments to BRRETA, the situation in which there were two different licensees affiliated with the same brokerage firm, each of whom was exclusively representing their own client in the same transaction, was defined to be a form of dual agency. However, the 2000 BRRETA revisions changed the law by separating designated agency from dual agency and by establishing regulations to control designated agency.[2124] Although designated agency is inconsistent with traditional common law principles of agency since the same broker is still representing both the buyer and seller as clients, the legislature has the power to enact statutes in derogation of the common law and has done so in this case. BRRETA explicitly states that in designated agency situations "neither the broker, the broker's licensees, nor the real estate brokerage firm" are to be considered dual agents.[2125]

One issue which has not been completely settled is whether a special written consent of the buyer and the seller is needed to practice designated agency. BRRETA only requires that the buyer and the seller give a special written consent prior to practicing dual agency.[2126] However, Georgia license law still provides that a licensee can be sanctioned for "acting for more than one party in a transaction without the express written consent of all parties to the transaction."[2127] Since a broker is representing both the buyer and the seller in designated agency transactions, it would appear that license law requires the broker to obtain the express written consent of the parties prior to practicing designated agency. In light of this provision, the GAR brokerage engagements were modified to include not only a consent to dual agency but also to designated agency.

The most readily apparent consequence of carving designated agency out of dual agency is that a licensee can act in a designated agency capacity without having to provide the clients with a lengthy, written, dual agency consent. Designated agency is a much safer form of brokerage practice than dual agency because each client is exclusively represented by a licensee looking out for the client's interests. In a designated agency transaction each licensee functions as if she was acting in a single agency capacity (or as if the licensee for the other client was affiliated with a different real estate brokerage firm). Thus, each agent owes his client the same duties as he would if it were single agency representation.

(b) Designated agency and the duty to keep confidences

In a designated agency transaction, each designated agent is prohibited from disclosing to anyone except his broker any information which the client has requested to be kept confidential, unless such disclosure is required by law. This prohibition means that designated agents cannot reveal any confidential information to any other agent in the firm,

---

including the designated agent for the other party in the transaction. In addition, if the designated agent for one party had previously represented the other party in the transaction, the designated agent would be required to maintain previously learned confidences from the former client unless the confidences are waived through subsequent word or conduct, or the information is required by law to be disclosed.[2128] The problem below illustrates how this would work.

Problem: Agent A is representing buyer as a client. During the course of the representation, Agent A learns many things about buyer. Buyer becomes interested in a property on which Agent A is the listing agent. To avoid a dual agency, Agent A suggests that Agent B represent buyer, to which buyer agrees. What are Agent A's duties to keep confidential and not reveal to the seller the information Agent A has previously learned about buyer?

Answer: Agent A would not be permitted to disclose any information made confidential by the Buyer unless the Buyer permits such disclosure by subsequent word of conduct, or the disclosure is required by law.

In a designated agency transaction, the broker still acts in a supervisory and managerial capacity with respect to each of the designated agents; however, the broker must act as a wall preventing the flow of information between the buyer's designated agent and the seller's designated agent. In a designated agency transaction, BRRETA prohibits the broker from revealing any information made confidential by the client's request which he receives from a designated agent or that agent's client to the other designated agent or the other client unless the information is required by law to be disclosed. The statute defines confidential information for the purposes of designated agency to be any information that could harm the client's negotiating position which information the client has not consented to be disclosed.[2129]

BRRETA's limitations on the disclosure of confidential information by brokers and designated agents provides protection for licensees by eliminating the conflicting duties that are inherent in a dual agency setting. Thus, designated agency allows a brokerage firm to represent both sides of a transaction without as many risks as are associated with dual agency. Designated agency is also preferable from both the buyer and seller's standpoint because the licensee for each client does not represent the other client in the transaction.

(c) Assigning designated agents

In order to act as a designated agent, the broker must assign each licensee to act in that role.[2130] There are several ways in which brokers can accomplish this. A broker may directly assign designated agents on a case-by-case basis whenever a licensee in the firm representing the buyer as a client shows the buyer property which is listed by another licensee in the firm who is representing the seller. Such case by case assignments may be less practical in larger firms because licensees would constantly be calling their broker for permission to act in a designated agency capacity whenever they were showing their clients their own company's listings. BRRETA allows the broker to delegate to other management level personnel the responsibility for assigning designated agents through the adoption of company policy.[2131] In addition, the law also permits a brokerage firm to adopt firm-wide policies allowing for the automatic assignment of designated agents. However, the assignment of designated agents through the adoption of a company policy must be done in a way "reasonably calculated to ensure that each client is represented properly under that law."[2132] Adopting a policy which merely states that the firm's licensees will be designated agents in all situations where different licensees in the firm are representing the buyer and seller may create risks for the brokerage firm. Specifically, brokerage firms should evaluate whether they are comfortable allowing for the automatic assignment of designated agents in following situations:

(1) one licensee spouse is representing the seller and the other licensee spouse is representing the buyer or where a parent is representing the seller and a child is representing the buyer (or vice versa);

2128   O.C.G.A. § 10-6A-13(d).

2129   O.C.G.A. § 10-6A-13(c).

2130   O.C.G.A. § 10-6A-3(9).

2131   O.C.G.A. § 10-6A-13(a).

2132   O.C.G.A. § 10-6A-13(a).

(2) one member of a real estate team is representing the buyer and another team member is representing the seller;

(3) a licensed real estate assistant is representing the seller and the licensee for whom she works is representing the buyer (or vice versa); or

(4) a licensee asks another licensee in the company to act as a designated agent but limits the fee being paid to the designated agent to a nominal amount.

While the broker may not want to prohibit licensees from acting in a designated agency capacity in the above situations, it would probably be a good idea for the broker to insist that the licensee obtain permission from the broker on a case-by-case basis in such situations. An example of a sample policy is set forth below:

> Sample brokerage policy on assigning designated agents
>
> It is the policy of ABC Brokers that whenever one licensee in our company is representing the buyer as a client and another licensee in our company is representing the seller as a client in the same real estate transaction, ABC Brokers does hereby automatically assign each of the licensees to act in a designated agency capacity in the transaction except in the following situations:
>
> (1) Where the licensees representing the parties are husband and wife, or parent and child;
>
> (2) Where the licensees representing the parties are a licensee and the licensed assistant of said licensee; and
>
> (3) Where the licensees are part of the same real estate team.
>
> In the above three situations, the licensees may not act as designated agents without the express permission of the managing broker of the office in which the licensees work.

(d) Broker acting as one of the designated agents

BRRETA defines a "designated agent" as "one or more licensees affiliated with broker who are assigned by the broker to represent solely one client to the exclusion of all other clients in the same transaction and to the exclusion of all other licensees affiliated with the broker."[2133] Since the definition of a designated agent is limited to "a licensee affiliated with the broker" rather than the broker himself, the broker cannot act as one of the designated agents in the transaction.

BRRETA was specifically written to limit brokers from acting as one of the designated agents out of a concern that both parties would not be fairly represented in a transaction where the broker was supervising one of the designated agents, and thus privy to the confidential information in possession of the agent, but was also acting as the designated agent in the transaction.

§ 19.2.8.4 Sub-Agency

While sub-agency is rarely practiced anymore in Georgia, there is nothing that prohibits this form of agency. With sub-agency, the listing broker in one brokerage firm represents the seller. The selling broker in a different brokerage firm working with the buyers but is also representing the seller. Sub-agency is fraught with the potential for conflicts of interest. This is because when sub-agency was practiced, the selling broker often had little or no relationship with the seller the selling broker was representing.

The sub-agency relationship was established through the listing broker. Selling brokers also tended to have a strong connection or relationship with the buyers they were helping find properties. The natural loyalty that selling brokers often felt toward buyers sometimes made it difficult for selling brokers to act in the best interests of their seller clients.

2133 O.C.G.A. § 10-6A-3(9).

While sub-agency is still permitted in Georgia, a client relationship with a client can only now be established through a written brokerage engagement agreement between the broker and the client.[2134] Therefore, it is unlikely that the selling broker can represent the seller as a listing broker without having a direct brokerage engagement agreement with the seller.

§ 19.3   DUTIES OWED TO CLIENTS BY BROKERS

BRRETA sets forth the duties which a licensee owes to her client. Unless the parties expressly agree in a brokerage engagement agreement to different or additional duties which the licensee owes to her client, the licensee owes no duties other than those set forth in BRRETA.[2135] Any agreement that alters the duties owed to the client must be in writing and signed by both parties.[2136]

BRRETA contains separate sections devoted to the duties owed by brokers in client relationships with sellers, landlords, buyers, and tenants.[2137] The duties owed by brokers to each of these types of clients are very similar. Consequently, the discussion that follows analyzes these duties together. Any difference in duties owed to different kinds of clients is noted. Also, since designated agents must function as if they were acting in a single agency capacity, the following discussion is applicable to designated agency as well. BRRETA mandates that a broker owes her client the duties set forth below.

§ 19.3.1   Broker Must Perform Terms Of Brokerage Engagement Agreement

Brokers must look to the written brokerage engagement, either the listing agreement or the buyer brokerage engagement, to determine precisely what services they must perform for their clients. As discussed previously, the duties imposed upon the broker under BRRETA can be altered, increased, or even eliminated by a written brokerage engagement.[2138] While the GAR Brokerage Agreements all require compliance with BRRETA, the duties of the broker to the client are drafted very narrowly to limit the potential legal liability of the broker.

§ 19.3.2   Broker Must Promote Interests Of Client

§ 19.3.2.1   The Broker Must Seek A Price And Terms Acceptable To The Client

This requirement imposes a duty on the broker representing a seller/landlord to attempt to negotiate a sale or lease at the price established in the listing/leasing agreement or at a price that is acceptable to the seller/landlord. BRRETA specifically states that a listing agent is not obligated to continue to seek additional offers on the property for the seller or landlord client while the property is under a contract for sale or subject to a lease (or letter of intent to lease) unless the brokerage engagement agreement imposes this obligation.

A broker representing a buyer or tenant is required to attempt to find a property at the price and terms acceptable to the buyer or tenant. However, the broker is not required to search for other properties for the client while the buyer or tenant is a party to a contract to purchase or a party to a lease (or letter of intent to lease) unless the brokerage agreement imposes this duty of the agent.

§ 19.3.2.2   The Broker Must Timely Present All Offers To And From The Client

Regardless of whether they are representing seller, landlords, buyers or tenants, brokers must present all offers to their clients in a timely fashion. This requirement is consistent with the Georgia real estate licensing laws which also require

---

2134   O.C.G.A. § 10-6A-3(4).

2135   O.C.G.A. § 10-6A-4(a).

2136   O.C.G.A. § 10-6A-4(a).

2137   O.C.G.A. § 10-6A-5, O.C.G.A. § 10-6A-6, O.C.G.A. § 10-6A-7, O.C.G.A. § 10-6A-8.

2138   O.C.G.A. § 10-6A-4(a).

licensees to "deliver within a reasonable time" all offers to buy or sell and completed purchase agreements.[2139] Brokers must also present to the other party all offers which their client desires to submit. This is the case even when the broker disagrees with some of the provisions in the offer. For example, if an offer is presented which includes a lower commission than the seller and listing agent have agreed to in their listing agreement, the listing broker must still present this offer to the seller. Of course, the listing broker is not obligated to accept the reduction in the commission. To protect her rights the broker can write in a note on the offer which states that the broker does not agree to the reduction in her commission.

When a seller's or landlord's property is under a contract to sell or lease, the broker must submit additional offers to the broker's client, even if the offer comes from a different buyer. Likewise, a broker representing a buyer or tenant must submit to the buyer any offers or counteroffers which the client wishes to make even if the buyer or tenant is a party to a sales contract or to a lease (or letter of intent to lease). Interestingly, the obligation to timely submit all offers likely extends to oral offers, even though contracts for the purchase of real estate must generally be in writing to be enforceable.

§ 19.3.2.3   Adverse Material Facts

Brokers must disclose to the client adverse material facts regarding the transaction of which the licensee has actual knowledge. Whenever a broker learns of facts regarding the transaction that are unfavorable to his client, he must disclose those facts if they are "material." BRRETA defines the term "material facts" to be those "facts that a party does not know, could not reasonably discover, and would reasonably want to know."[2140] Because the definition of the term "material fact" is limited to those facts which the client "could not reasonably discover," the broker's duty of disclosure has been greatly narrowed by the statute from the common law duty which brokers would otherwise owe to their clients. Whether a disclosure must be made under this provision requires a case-by-case determination as the examples below illustrate.

Example #1: A broker in a large city enters into a listing agreement with a seller whom he has just met. During the listing period another broker shows the house to a prospective buyer. As it turns out, the buyer is a close friend or relative of the listing broker. Should the listing broker disclose this fact to the seller?

Answer: Yes. The listing broker should disclose this fact to his seller client for two reasons: (1) this relationship is one about which the seller would reasonably want to know since it may affect the negotiations, and (2) this relationship is one which the seller could not reasonably discover in a large metropolitan area. However, in a very small, rural community this same relationship may not have to be disclosed to the seller if the facts are such that the prospective buyer lives in the same small community with the seller and the buyer is a person who is widely known throughout the community to be a friend or relative of the broker.

Example #2: Two agents are working within a subdivision representing the builder/seller. A prospective buyer comes in and asks one of the agents to represent him as a buyer in the purchase of a home in the subdivision. Does the agent, who will now represent the buyer, have to make any disclosures to that buyer?

Answer: Yes. Under BRRETA, the agent representing the buyer would have to disclose to the buyer that in other transactions within that subdivision she has represented the builder. Again, this is because the relationship between the agent and the builder might impact the negotiations between the buyer and the builder. Of course, if the builder instructed the licensee now represented the buyer to keep confidential all information learned about the builder or subdivision while the licensee was representing the builder, the licensee would now be limited as to what she could disclose to things that are required to be disclosed under state law (such as latent defects in the property). To avoid confusion on the part of the buyer, the licensee

---

2139   O.C.G.A. § 43-40-25(19).

2140   O.C.G.A. § 10-6A-3(11).

should tell the buyer that the licensee is under directions from the licensee's former seller client to keep all information confidential learned during the course of that representation. In that way, the buyer will have reasonable expectations as to what the licensee can tell them.

Example #3: A broker representing a buyer shows his client a home in which a murder took place several years before. The broker knows this fact. Does the murder have to be disclosed?

Answer: No. While this would normally be considered an adverse fact which the buyer-agent would have to disclose to his client, Georgia's "Stigmatized Property Statute" protects real estate agents from liability for not disclosing that the seller's property was the site of a homicide, felony or suicide.[2141] Of course, real estate agents are required to answer truthfully to the best of their knowledge any questions regarding homicides, felonies or suicides on the property and are not protected from liability if they lie about the same.[2142]

§ 19.3.2.4 Obtaining Expert Advice

The broker must advise the client to obtain expert advice regarding any material matters which are beyond the expertise of the broker. Whenever the broker feels that an issue is arising in a transaction which is outside of the scope of the broker's expertise, the broker should inform the client of this and advise the client to seek the advice of an expert in the area involved. The GAR Contracts contain a disclaimer listing the areas in which the broker does not owe a special duty or have expertise. More specifically, the GAR Purchase and Sale Agreement states that the broker has no duty to advise the buyer or seller on any matter relating to the property which could have been revealed through a survey, title search, Official Georgia Wood Infestation Report, inspection by a professional home inspector or constriction expert, utility bill review, an appraisal, inspection by an environmental engineering inspector, consulting governmental officials or a review of the agreement and transaction by an attorney, financial planner, mortgage consultant or tax planner. (This paragraph is discussed in detail in § 14.4.2 (How Disclaimer Language In GAR Contracts Protects Brokers) of this work.) Nevertheless, oral disclosures regarding a broker's lack of expertise even in these areas are encouraged to ensure that the client understands the broker's limitations.

§ 19.3.2.5 Accounting For Funds Received

The broker must timely account for all monies and property received by the licensee in which the client has, or may have, an interest. This section of BRRETA merely codifies long-standing rules and regulations of the Georgia Real Estate Commission.[2143] Brokers must timely account for all money and property in their possession in which their client has an interest.

§ 19.3.3 Ordinary Skill And Care Required

The broker must exercise ordinary skill and care in performing duties under BRRETA, and any other duties agreed upon between the parties set forth in the brokerage engagement. In addition to narrowing the scope of substantive duties owed to clients to only those duties set forth in BRRETA and in the written brokerage agreement, BRRETA has altered the legal standard of care with which brokers must perform when representing their clients. In common law agency situations the agent is said to have a fiduciary relationship with the principal, *i.e.*, the person who has appointed him as agent.[2144] In such a fiduciary relationship, the agent owes the highest degree of loyalty to the principal and must perform his duties for the principal with the utmost degree of care. BRRETA, by contrast,

---

2141   O.C.G.A. § 44-1-16.

2142   O.C.G.A. § 44-1-16.

2143   *See* O.C.G.A. § 43-40-20.

2144   *See Rayborn v. Long*, 243 Ga.App. 128, 532 S.E.2d 433 (2000). It is interesting to note that the Court of Appeals appeared to reach its conclusions in this case without considering or citing BRRETA. The precedential value of this case would therefore appear to be extremely limited.

specifically states that unless the parties agree otherwise in a signed writing, a real estate broker is not in a fiduciary relationship with either a customer or a client.[2145]

In its original enactment, BRRETA lowered the standard of care from that of a fiduciary to a standard which required the broker to perform his duties with "reasonable" care. Under this standard, suits were still brought claiming that the broker did not carry out his duties in a manner consistent with the level of care that any broker, acting reasonably, would have used. The broker's liability therefore often hinged on the testimony of experts. After the 2000 amendments to BRRETA, brokers must only exercise "ordinary care" in the performance of the duties listed in BRRETA and those duties to which they agree to in the written brokerage agreement.[2146] This means that in performing the duties listed in BRRETA and in the written brokerage agreement, brokers owe no greater duty of care to their clients than they would to any other person who is not a client. The example below explains these legal standards in greater detail.

Example: A buyer purchases an older home with the help of his selling broker. The buyer does not ask for an inspection and the seller does not provide a Seller's Property Disclosure Statement. After moving in, the buyer discovers defects in the roof which cause the roof to leak. The buyer sues the broker claiming that the broker was negligent and failed to perform his duties with reasonable care by not advising the buyer to have the property inspected. Will the broker be held liable for not recommending that an inspection be performed?

Answer: Prior to the 2000 revisions of BRRETA, if the buyer's expert witness testified that any reasonable, prudent selling broker would have recommended that the buyer have an inspection done on the house, the broker may be found to have not acted reasonably and may thus be liable to the buyer. However, the 2000 revisions to BRRETA afforded brokers additional protection by further lowering the standard of care with which brokers must perform to exercising "ordinary care" in the performance of those duties agreed to by the broker in her brokerage engagement. Since in the GAR Buyer Brokerage Agreement the broker has no duty to advise the buyer to get an inspection, a good argument can be made that the broker should not have any liability to the buyer. See § 19.8.1 (Protections Against Liability in the GAR Brokerage Engagements) for a discussion of how GAR's Brokerage Agreements further reduce broker's liability by setting out the "sole duties of the broker."

§ 19.3.4 Broker Must Comply With All Applicable Laws And Regulations

This requirement means that the broker must comply with all applicable laws and regulations, including the Federal Fair Housing Act,[2147] the Georgia Fair Housing Act,[2148] and all state and federal civil rights statutes and regulations.

§ 19.3.5 Confidential Information

The broker must keep confidential all information received by the broker during the term of the brokerage engagement if the information has been made confidential the express request of or instruction from the client. If, while the broker is representing the client, the broker receives information from any source and the client expressly requests or instructs the broker to not reveal that information, BRRETA places a duty upon the broker to keep the information confidential. The statute provides that disclosing confidential information to other licensees within the same firm, except in a designated agency situation, does not violate the duty of confidentiality.[2149] If the client requests that information not be disclosed the broker can only reveal the information if (1) the client subsequently permits the disclosure or, (2) disclosure of the information is required by law. BRRETA provides that the client's permission can be given by "word or conduct."

2145   O.C.G.A. § 10-6A-4(a).

2146   O.C.G.A. § 10-6A-5(a)(3), O.C.G.A. § 10-6A-6(a)(3), O.C.G.A. § 10-6A-7(a)(3), O.C.G.A. § 10-6A-8(a)(3).

2147   42 USCA § 3602 *et seq.*

2148   O.C.G.A. § 8-3-206 *et seq.*

2149   O.C.G.A. § 10-6A-5(a)(5), O.C.G.A. § 10-6A-6(a)(5), O.C.G.A. § 10-6A-7(a)(5), O.C.G.A. § 10-6A-8(a)(5).

Example: A seller asks his listing broker to not mention that the seller and his wife are getting divorced. Later the seller passes a prospective buyer and his agent in the doorway as the seller is leaving. The seller calls over his shoulder to his teenage son that he is hurrying to a meeting with his divorce lawyer. Must the listing agent now continue to treat this information as confidential?

Answer: The answer to this question should be no, at least with respect to this buyer. The seller's conduct appears to indicate that his divorce is no longer confidential. However, in the event that the broker believes that the client has given his permission by conduct, the better approach is for the broker to verify with the client that the client's actions were meant to be interpreted as permission to disclose the information.

§ 19.3.5.1   Knowledge Is Not Imputed To The Broker In Designated Agency Or Dual Agency Situation

In some relationships, the law automatically deems that knowledge or responsibility is transferred from one party to another merely by virtue of the relationship, even though only one party has actual knowledge. This is known as implied knowledge. If that were the case in dual agency and designated agency situations it would not be possible for designated agents, dual agents, or their brokers to fulfill their duty of confidentiality to their clients. To prevent this automatic charging of knowledge held by one party to another, BRRETA defines both designated agency and dual agency such that the knowledge and information known to one party is not automatically considered to be in the possession of another party.[2150]

BRRETA specifically states that in a designated agency situation, the designated agents are considered to have only "actual knowledge" and that "there shall be no imputation of knowledge or information between and among the broker, designated agents, and the clients."[2151] This means that when an agent, broker or client is in possession of information, the other parties to the transaction, including the designated agent's client and broker, are not automatically deemed to have that information in their possession merely because they are also involved in the transaction. In other words, until a piece of information is, in fact, known to a party in a designated agency situation, the party is not charged with knowledge of that information.

Similarly, in a dual agency situation, BRRETA states that "each client and broker and their respective licensees possess only actual knowledge and information" and that there is no "imputation of knowledge or information among or between the clients, brokers, or affiliated licensees.[2152]

§ 19.3.5.2   Confidentiality After Termination Of Brokerage Engagement

The duty of confidentiality also exists after the brokerage agreement has expired, has been terminated, or the broker withdraws from representing the client, unless the client permits the disclosure, the disclosure is required by law, or the information becomes public from "a source other than the broker."[2153]

Example #1: Agent A is working with a buyer as a client. The buyer asks to see a house on which his agent is the listing agent. To avoid a dual agency situation Agent A refers the buyer to Agent B, who is in Agent A's firm. Does Agent A, who is now acting as the designated agent of the seller, still have to keep the buyer's secrets confidential?

Answer: Yes. Even though the buyer is no longer a client of Agent A, the agent must continue to preserve the buyer's confidences unless the disclosure is required by law, the information becomes public from a source other than Agent A, or the buyer permits disclosure.

2150   *Wall v. Century 21 Winnersvile Realty, Inc.*, 244 Ga.App. 762, 536 S.E.2d 798 (2000).

2151   O.C.G.A. § 10-6A-13(c).

2152   O.C.G.A. § 10-6A-12(d).

2153   O.C.G.A. § 10-6A-9(b)(2)(C).

Example #2: A client has asked that his listing agent not reveal that he and his wife may be getting a divorce. After the listing agreement expires, the seller actually files suit for divorce. Does the agent still have to preserve the seller's secret?

Answer: What is meant by information becoming "public" through a source other than the broker is not defined in either BRRETA or in case law. Courts will likely apply a reasonableness test in making decisions in this area. The more widely the information has been disseminated, the more likely it is that the broker may treat the information as no longer confidential. In this case, the filing of divorce papers with the court may not be wide enough distribution of the information to allow the broker to treat the information as public. If, on the other hand, an article about the divorce is published in the local newspaper, the broker would be much safer in assuming that the information has been made public by a source other than himself.

§ 19.3.6   Conflicting Duties

BRRETA imposes a duty on brokers to not give false information to customers. (See discussion in § 19.4.1.8 (Duty not to knowingly give false information)). BRRETA provides that in the event of a conflict between the duty to keep client confidences and the duty not to give customers false information, the duty not to give customers false information shall control and that a broker shall not be liable for disclosing information in this situation.[2154] Assume, for example, that in the course of listing a property the seller tells his broker that he believes the kitchen and dining area of the house are much too small and are out of proportion with the rest of the house. He says he explored the possibility of adding on to the existing kitchen and eating area, but he discovered that even a small expansion would violate state regulations requiring a buffer and setback requirement for a river that flows by the back lot line. He asks the broker to not reveal this information to any prospective buyers or their agents.

If at a subsequent time a buyer's agent asks if it is possible to add on to the kitchen, a conflict has been created between the broker's duty to preserve the client's confidences and the broker's duty to not give customers false information. Under BRRETA the duty to not give false information controls this situation. Thus, even though the broker is not required by law to disclose this information and the client has expressly asked that the information not be revealed, the broker must break the seller's confidence and tell the buyer's agent about the setback requirements to avoid telling a lie.

In other circumstances, the broker may be able to avoid disclosing the confidential information without giving false information. Consider the situation in which a seller tells his listing agent that he and his wife are getting a divorce and asks the agent to not mention this to anyone. A prospective buyer later asks whether the sellers are getting divorced since they've only owned the house for a short period of time and neither the husband nor the wife is ever around. The listing broker can say that he has been asked by his clients not to discuss their personal situation. Taking this approach allows the broker to preserve this client's confidence without giving the buyer false information.

§ 19.4   DUTY OF CARE TO CUSTOMERS

As discussed below, BRRETA imposes comparatively minor duties upon brokers relative to customers (*i.e.*, people with whom the broker does not have a client relationship).

§ 19.4.1   Duties Owed By Listing Broker To Prospective Buyers Or Tenants

BRRETA imposes the following duties on brokers representing client sellers or landlords toward buyers and tenants whom the broker does not represent: (1) the duty to disclose adverse material facts regarding the physical condition of the property, (2) the duty to disclose materials facts relating to certain adverse off-site conditions, and (3) the duty to not knowingly give false information. Each of these conditions is discussed below.

2154   O.C.G.A. § 10-6A-9(c).

§ 19.4.1.1   On-Site And Off-Site Disclosure Obligations Are Exclusive

With regard to both adverse on-site conditions and adverse off-site conditions, BRRETA provides that brokers representing sellers or landlords shall not be liable for the failure to disclose to purchaser or tenant clients any matters other than those specified in the statute,[2155] discussed below. This means that brokers are not responsible for disclosing to customer buyers or tenants anything except conditions described in the statute. The failure to disclose any other matter should therefore not be legitimate grounds for a claim against a broker.

§ 19.4.1.2   Duty To Disclose Adverse Conditions On Property

BRRETA requires brokers representing a seller or landlord to disclose to client buyers or tenants all "adverse material facts" regarding the physical condition of the property and improvements located on the property which are "actually known to the broker and which could not be discovered by a *reasonably diligent inspection* of the property by the buyer or tenant."[2156] As previously discussed, the term "material facts" specifically includes "those facts that a party does not know, could not reasonably discover, and would reasonably want to know."[2157] The statute lists three examples of physical conditions which must be disclosed: (1) material defects in the property, (2) environmental contamination, and (3) facts required by statute or regulation to be disclosed (the presence of lead-based paint is an example of this third type of condition required to be disclosed). Although the statute specifically says that the physical conditions required to be disclosed are not limited to these examples, the duties of brokers representing sellers and landlords to disclose adverse property conditions to customer buyers and tenants has been narrowed considerably by this provision from what these duties might otherwise be in the absence of BRRETA.

§ 19.4.1.3   No Duty For Broker To Discover Adverse On-Site Conditions

As discussed above, brokers representing sellers and landlords are required to disclose to customers adverse on-site conditions which are actually known to the broker. The statute specifically provides that brokers are under no legal obligation to initiate an investigation or to seek to discover any adverse on-site conditions. This means that the broker does not have to conduct an inspection of the property searching for unknown adverse conditions. Nor does the broker have to order an inspection by a professional inspector. The law only requires the broker to disclose those adverse matters relating to the physical condition of the property of which the broker is aware or becomes aware of during the course of listing the property and which could not be discovered by the buyer upon a reasonably diligent inspection of the property.

It is important to note, however, that if the broker suspects or believes that there is a reasonable likelihood that an adverse condition exists on the property or its improvements, that suspicion or belief may be sufficient knowledge to trigger a duty on the part of the broker to investigate the suspicion and to determine whether an adverse material condition does in fact exist on the property. For example, let's say that the roof on a property is in an obvious state of disrepair with water stains on the ceiling. Even if the seller indicates that the roof is not leaking, the listing agent would be well advised to point out these items to prospective buyers to avoid a claim that the listing broker had knowledge, but chose not to disclose. Since these conditions should also be observable by the buyer upon a reasonably diligent inspection of the property, the broker should be able to successfully defend any claim which is asserted.

§ 19.4.1.4   When Disclosure Of On-Site Conditions Is Required

Disclosure of on-site conditions is required only if the condition could not be discovered by a reasonably diligent inspection by the buyer.[2158] Many conditions may be discoverable by a buyer upon a reasonably diligent inspection of

---

2155   O.C.G.A. § 10-6A-5(b)(2), 10-6A-6(b)(2).

2156   O.C.G.A. § 10-6A-5(b)(1), 10-6A-6(b)(1).

2157   O.C.G.A. § 10-6A-3(11).

2158   O.C.G.A. § 10-6A-5(b)(1).

the property. While such conditions are not legally required to be disclosed, the safest approach is to always disclose the condition even if the broker believes that the buyer could discover the information for himself. Otherwise, the broker may find that he is defending a lawsuit about whether the buyer should have discovered the condition upon a reasonable inspection of the property.

The question of whether a buyer has conducted a diligent inspection of a property is often a fact question for the jury. What constitutes a diligent inspection varies with the facts of each case. A reasonably diligent inspection may require the buyer to hire an inspector, surveyor, or other specialist. In one case, a buyer sued the brokers and agents in a purchase and sale transaction for fraud claiming that the brokers breached their disclosure duties under BRRETA by failing to disclose previous flood damage to the property.[2159] The buyer's fraud claim failed because there were reasonably available government documents, records and maps that revealed that the property was in a flood zone.[2160] In addition, a thorough inspection of the property would have revealed such damage.[2161] Since the buyer failed to act diligently, she is unable to recover from the brokers and agents based on any alleged failure on their part to disclose information.[2162]

Moreover, although a purchaser may be found to have exercised due diligence even though he did not hire a professional inspector,[2163] the failure of the buyer who has notice of a potential problem to either inspect a problem further themselves or to hire an inspector or other specialist may be sufficient grounds for a court to find that the buyer did not exercise due diligence.[2164] For example, a reasonably diligent inspection by a buyer should arguably include a survey of the property to determine, among other things, if the property is in a flood plain. Similarly, problems with synthetic stucco could probably be discovered by a diligent inspection by a home inspector employed by the buyer. However, in both these cases it is advisable to be cautious on such matters and disclose them. The GAR Seller's Property Disclosure Statement, supplied by the seller, should put prospective buyers on notice of conditions that need to be investigated further by the buyer.[2165]

§ 19.4.1.5 Disclosure Of Adverse On-Site Conditions Shields Broker From Liability

BRRETA provides that brokers cannot be held liable for complying with the statutory requirement to disclose adverse material facts relating to physical conditions on the property.[2166] Thus, even though BRRETA has narrowed brokers' liability, if there is any doubt about whether a condition on the property should be disclosed to a prospective buyer or tenant the broker should err on the side of disclosure. It is better to defend a lawsuit complaining that the broker disclosed too much, rather than not enough.

If a seller is uncertain whether an adverse condition identified in an inspection report is a material fact or merely the incorrect opinion of the inspector, the broker would be well advised to treat the report as material and factual in nature rather than merely the inspector's erroneous opinion. This is true because under the GAR Contract brokers disclaim any expertise with regard to the physical condition of the property. Therefore, choosing not to provide the report could be construed as an exercise of the very expertise that brokers have specifically disclaimed that they have. The safe answer is not to substitute your judgment for that of the buyer, and to treat all such reports as factual. The following example illustrates this principal.

2159 *Shaw v. Robertson*, 307 Ga.App. 337, 705 S.E.2d 210 (2010).

2160 *Shaw v. Robertson*, 307 Ga.App. 337, 705 S.E.2d 210 (2010).

2161 *Shaw v. Robertson*, 307 Ga.App. 337, 705 S.E.2d 210 (2010).

2162 *Shaw v. Robertson*, 307 Ga.App. 337, 705 S.E.2d 210 (2010).

2163 *Aikens v. Couch*, 271 Ga. 276, 278, 518 S.E. 2d 674, 676 (1999).

2164 *Real Estate International v. Buggay*, 220 Ga.App. 449, 451, 469 S.E. 2d 242, 245 (1996); *Delk v. Tom Peterson Realtors*, 220 Ga.App. 576, 577, 469 S.E. 2d 741,742 (1996).

2165 *See* Chapter 8, *supra*, Property Disclosure Statement.

2166 O.C.G.A. § 10-6A-5(b)(2), O.C.G.A. § 10-6A-6(b)(2).

Two lots shared a common well. The owners of both lots used their property primarily as vacation homes. The owner of lot 1 put her property on the market with a broker. The owner of lot 2 paid a visit to the broker and told her that the shared well did not produce enough water to support both lots, and that they had to coordinate vacation schedules with the owner of lot 1 to avoid overtaxing the well. The owner of lot 1 denied this and explained that the owner of lot 2 was unhappy because he recently discovered that the well was actually located on lot 1, and not lot 2 as he previously believed. The broker already distrusted the owner of lot 2 because of some disparaging racial remarks he made several years earlier.

The broker took the position that her client, the owner of lot 1, was certainly in a position to know whether the well ran dry. She also assumed that the owner of lot 2 was just trying to chill any sale because he wanted to purchase lot 1 for a discount, thereby obtain ownership of the shared well. Based upon this, the broker did not disclose the claims of the owner of lot 2 to the ultimate purchaser.

Of course, it turned out that the owner of lot 2 was not exaggerating his claims about the well. The purchaser of lot 1 moved into the property on a full-time basis and soon discovered that the well ran dry whenever the owner of lot 2 was also in town. When the purchaser spoke to the owner of lot 2 he was quick to tell her that he had disclosed the information about the well to the broker and warned the broker that she needed to let any prospective purchaser know about the well. Suit soon followed.

The broker argued that she had no liability to the purchaser based upon the GAR Contract's disclaimers and that she did not have actual knowledge regarding the well, just the word of a neighbor whom she thought had ulterior motives. The broker won the case on summary judgment.

This point of this example is that the broker could have avoided the suit altogether (and thereby saved herself considerable time and money) by disclosing to prospective purchasers that there was some question about the capacity of the shared well. She could have then attempted to explain away the claims of the owner of lot 2 by also stating that the owner of lot 1 denied any problems. If the owner of lot 1 was adamant that no such disclosure and explanation be given, the broker could have insisted that the owner of lot 1 have a well flow test performed and provide that information to prospective purchasers. Here, the broker made the subjective determination that the owner of lot 2 was not telling the truth. This judgment call of whether to believe the owner of lot 2 is probably best left to the prospective purchaser.

§ 19.4.1.6 Sellers And Landlords Not Relieved Of Disclosure Duties For Adverse On Site Conditions

Sellers and landlords do not receive the benefit of the statutory protections that limit brokers' disclosure obligations. BRRETA does not in any way limit the obligation of a seller or landlord under any applicable law to disclose adverse material facts concerning the physical condition of the property.[2167] These obligations include: the obligation of a landlord to disclose of whether the property has a propensity to flood;[2168] certain disclosure obligations regarding lead-based paint;[2169] and the duty to disclose in situations where the seller has special knowledge not apparent to the buyer and is aware that the buyer is acting under a misapprehension as to facts which would be important to the buyer and which would probably affect her decision to purchase (*i.e.*, passive concealment).[2170]

§ 19.4.1.7 Duty To Disclose Adverse, Off-Site Conditions Under BRRETA

Prior to the revisions made to BRRETA in calendar year 2000, the law in Georgia was unclear regarding a broker's duty to investigate and disclose adverse off-site neighborhood conditions to prospective buyer or tenant customers. Fraud claims had long been brought against brokers alleging that they failed to disclose latent defects in property.

2167   O.C.G.A. § 10-6A-5(b)(2), O.C.G.A. § 10-6A-6(b)(2).
2168   O.C.G.A. § 44-7-20.
2169   42 U.S.C.A. § 4852(d).
2170   *Deckert v. Foster*, 230 Ga.App. 164, 495 S.E.2d 656 (1998).

Fraud claims have also been asserted with regard to the broker's failure to disclose or correctly represent adverse off-site conditions. While there have been few appellate decisions regarding the scope of a broker's duty in this area, it is clear that such claims can be maintained.[2171] Brokers wanting to avoid claims in this area found it difficult to come up with clear rules on how to avoid trouble. Questions for which there were no clear answers prior to the revisions made to BRRETA in calendar year 2000 included the following:

(a) How far away from a property does a broker need to go to identify adverse off-site conditions?

This question has been difficult to answer because some conditions (such as a paper mill or chicken rendering plant) might be 5-10 miles away yet still impact the property. Does this mean that to be safe the broker should look for adverse conditions many miles away from the property?

(b) What kinds of objectionable neighborhood conditions should the broker be looking for?

This question has also been hard to answer because things which are offensive or objectionable to some buyers or tenants might not bother other buyers or tenants at all. For example, a new grocery store at the entrance of a subdivision might be an objectionable condition to half of the neighborhood and a wonderful amenity to the other half of the neighborhood. When trying to define what is an adverse off-site condition, personal opinions can vary widely and there is much room for disagreement. To some extent the broker wishing to avoid a claim in this area had to either be a mind reader or ask extensive questions of buyers to learn of their concerns so that the broker could then evaluate whether the neighborhood contained the type of adverse conditions it was necessary to disclose.

(c) Is there potential legal exposure in every transaction since, if you go far enough away from any property, you will eventually run into some objectionable condition?

This question is rhetorical. However, it points out the difficulties in this area. The 2000 revisions to BRRETA limit the duty of brokers to disclose adverse off-site conditions. The law provides that brokers representing sellers and landlords have a duty to disclose the following to prospective buyers and tenants with whom the broker is working as customers:

> All material facts pertaining to existing adverse physical conditions in the immediate neighborhood within one mile of the property which are actually known to the broker and which could not be discovered by the buyer upon a diligent inspection of the neighborhood or thorough review of reasonably available governmental regulations, documents, records, maps, and statistics. Examples of reasonably available governmental regulations, documents, records, maps, and statistics shall include without limitation: land use maps and plans; zoning ordinances; recorded plats and surveys; transportation maps and plans; maps of flood plains; tax maps; school district boundary maps; and maps showing the boundary lines of governmental jurisdictions…[2172]

The subsections below break down this statutory language into its component parts and explain how this part of the statute operates.

(1) Disclosure required only if the condition is within one mile of the property

This requirement places a geographical boundary around the property in the transaction. Objectionable conditions within the one mile limit must be disclosed even if the property is separated from the condition by a physical barrier, such as a river or freeway, or by a political border such as a city-county boundary line. The statute does not describe how the one-mile boundary is to be measured. Presumably, the distance would be a one mile radius from any point in the property. However, some brokers may try to defend a failure to disclose by arguing that the standard should not

---

2171 *Hanlon v. Thornton*, 218 Ga.App. 500, 462 S.E. 2d 154 (1995); *Allen v. RE/MAX North Atlanta, Inc.*, 213 Ga.App. 644, 445 S.E. 2d 774 (1994).

2172 O.C.G.A. § 10-6A-5(b)(2), O.C.G.A. § 10-6A-6(b)(2).

be measured as the crow flies, but rather should be measured along major roads from the property. Such an argument would most likely not be successful.

The one mile radius boundary should also be thought of in three dimensions to include one mile of air space above the property and one mile into the ground.

Example: A broker has a listing on a home in a suburb on the edge of a rapidly growing city. Three miles to the east there is a paper mill which has been there for many years. The prevailing winds at the home are from the west. However, the wind periodically shifts and blows from the east, bringing a sulfurous odor from the paper mill to the home. A prospective buyer and his agent visit the property several times without smelling the odor before placing an offer on the property. Shortly after closing on the property the buyers notice the odor. Can the buyer maintain a cause of action against the listing agent for failing to disclose the existence of the paper mill?

Answer: The broker representing the seller or landlord does not owe a duty to disclose to a customer buyer or tenant any material facts regarding adverse conditions that are more than one mile from the property, even if the broker is aware of the condition. While a disgruntled customer buyer might argue that the odor itself is within one mile of the property and that therefore a disclosure obligation exists, such an interpretation was certainly not intended and would render the statutory one-mile limitation on disclosing adverse conditions meaningless. This is because all adverse off-site conditions beyond one-mile from the property would obviously not be adverse unless they affected the property in some tangible way.

(2) Disclosure required only if the condition is an existing condition

This limitation was included in BRRETA to try to minimize arguments that brokers were required to disclose potential, rather than existing, conditions. Arguments may arise regarding when a condition actually "exists" and is no longer a future or potential condition. For example, if a quarry operator purchases property and places heavy digging equipment on the land, does the quarry exist at that point in time, thus requiring disclosure? Although a case can be made that the quarry exists at that time, the better view is that the mere presence of machinery does not mean that the quarry is in existence. Moreover, even if it could be argued that the presence of the equipment signals the beginning of the quarry's existence, the better argument is that the equipment is not yet an adverse condition and thus does not have to be disclosed until the quarrying operation has actually begun.

Example: A broker has a listing in an in-town neighborhood which is within one mile of, but not adjoining, a two-lane thoroughfare. The broker is aware of the fact that the city transportation planning documents indicate that in the future the city will widen this road to four lanes to accommodate increasing traffic. However, the broker does not tell the prospective buyer or the selling agent about the city's plans. Shortly after the buyer moves into the home the city begins condemnation proceedings to widen the road. Has the broker violated BRRETA by not disclosing the city's plans?

Answer: No. Under BRRETA the broker is shielded from liability because the broker is only required to disclose existing adverse off-site conditions within one mile of the property. Potential or future conditions, such as possible road widenings or property rezonings, are not required to be disclosed even though the condition is within one mile of the property and even though the broker is aware of the future land use.

(3) Disclosure required only if the condition is actually known to the broker

This limitation is intended to protect brokers against claims that the broker "should have known" about an objectionable condition.

Example: A broker takes a listing on a friend's property in an area of town where the broker has never worked and with which he is unfamiliar. Within one mile of the property a telecommunications company has recently located a cellular phone tower on the rear of a commercial lot. After closing on the house the buyer discovers the presence of the tower in the neighborhood. Can the buyer win a claim against the broker for nondisclosure?

Answer: The answer to this question should be no. The broker would not be liable to the buyer because the disclosure requirement only applies to those existing, adverse, physical conditions which are actually known to the broker. Furthermore, this section of BRRETA specifically provides that there is no duty on the part of a broker to discover or seek to discover either adverse material facts about the physical condition of the property or existing adverse neighborhood conditions.[2173]

(4) Disclosure only required if the condition is a physical condition

BRRETA specifically limits the disclosure duty of brokers to those adverse off-site conditions that are physical in nature.

Example: While a broker is walking with the seller in the yard of a listing with the broker, a middle aged man walks up the street talking to himself and yelling obscenities. The seller mentions to the broker that the man lives several houses down from this property and that he has recently been released from a mental hospital. Does the broker have to disclose this fact to potential client purchasers?

Answer: The answer to this question should be no. Under BRRETA, a seller's or landlord's broker only has a duty to disclose existing physical offsite conditions within one mile of the property. Non-physical conditions, such as the behavior or criminal record of the neighbors, are not be required to be disclosed to a customer buyer or tenant. For instance, in 1996, Georgia enacted a sex offender registration law which requires some convicted sex offenders to register, among other things, their name, address and place of employment with the Georgia Bureau of Investigation and the county sheriff's office.[2174] *Under BRRETA brokers are not required to disclose such nonphysical conditions, nor are they required to investigate the neighborhood for the presence of such non-physical conditions. Although it may be possible to argue that people are physical conditions, the better view is that while people may exist physically, they are not "physical conditions" in relation to the property being purchased as contemplated by the statute.*

(5) Disclosure required only if buyer could not discover the condition upon a diligent inspection of the neighborhood

This limitation on disclosure offers listing brokers fairly extensive protection from liability for nondisclosure of adverse neighborhood conditions. It effectively places on the buyer the responsibility to conduct an investigation of the neighborhood. Furthermore, BRRETA states that the disclosure requirements placed on brokers under the Act do not limit the obligation of prospective buyers and tenants to familiarize themselves with potentially adverse conditions related to the physical condition of the property, any improvements located on the property, and the surrounding neighborhood.[2175]

It is important to note that although buyers have a duty to conduct a diligent inspection of the neighborhood, brokers do not have any duty to discover or investigate the neighborhood for adverse off-site conditions. Unless it can be proven that the broker had actual knowledge of an adverse off-site condition, a buyer will have a difficult time maintaining a claim against the broker who has no duty to inspect, especially since the buyer has an affirmative duty under the law to conduct a diligent inspection.

Example: After moving into a new home during the summer, the buyers realize in the fall that they can hear athletic events from a nearby high school. Was the listing agent required to disclose this fact?

Answer: The answer to this question should be no. The high school and its athletic fields should have been discovered by the buyers had they conducted a thorough investigation of the neighborhood. While the buyers may not have seen the athletic fields in use, it should be foreseeable to buyers that such fields will be used and generate noise during the school year.

(6) Disclosure required only if buyer could not discover the condition through the review of reasonably available governmental regulations, documents, records, map and statistics

---

2173   O.C.G.A. § 10-6A-5(b)(2), O.C.G.A. § 10-6A-6(b)(2).

2174   O.C.G.A. § 42-1-12(e).

2175   O.C.G.A. § 10-6A-5(b)(2), O.C.G.A. § 10-6A-6(b)(2).

This limitation on disclosure requires that a prospective buyer go beyond a physical inspection of the neighborhood. Rather, buyers are required to examine reasonably available governmental documents that may reveal the existence of an adverse off-site condition. BRRETA lists examples of documents that are considered to be reasonably available, including "land use maps and plans; zoning ordinances; recorded plat and surveys; transportation maps and plans; maps of flood plains; tax maps; school district boundary maps; and maps showing the boundary lines of existing governmental jurisdictions."[2176] BRRETA states that this is not an exhaustive list of all documents that a buyer must consult in order to fulfill his duty of a diligent inspection. The buyer must interpret this provision as broadly as possible and must thoroughly investigate any relevant documents.[2177]

Example: After closing on a property near the edge of a subdivision, the buyer discovers that the property across the street is zoned for commercial uses. He believes that this will lower his resale value. Did the listing agent violate BRRETA by not disclosing this information?

Answer: The answer to this question should be no. Even though this information is not apparent from a physical examination of the neighborhood, BRRETA protects the listing agent from liability in this case because the zoning ordinances are one of the specific examples of a governmental document readily available to the buyer. The buyer is obligated to conduct an investigation of such governmental records to discover adverse material facts in the neighborhood surrounding the property being bought.

§ 19.4.1.8   Duty Not To Knowingly Give False Information

BRRETA requires brokers representing sellers and landlords not to give information to prospective buyers or tenants which information they know to be false. Thus, a broker has a duty not to knowingly provide false information to a prospective buyer or tenant.

BRRETA protects brokers against liability in the event they unknowingly give parties false information. A broker has no liability for providing information that turns out to be incorrect if: (1) the broker does not have actual knowledge that the information is false; and (2) the broker discloses the source of the information to the party.[2178] The rationale behind this portion of BRRETA is that the broker may be gathering information for the benefit of the buyer or seller, but he is only the messenger and not a guarantor. If the buyer or seller knows the source of the information then he can, and should, use his own judgment to determine whether the source is reliable or whether he wants to investigate the matter further.

GAR has created an information disclosure form[2179] to help remind brokers doing research on behalf of a party to memorialize in writing the question being researched, the answer to the question, and the source of the information they obtain. This form should be used by brokers and a copy of it kept in the broker's file to help prove that proper disclosures were made in the event that a party later claims that the broker gave him false information and did not disclose its source. The broker should also try to get the party for whom the research was done to acknowledge receipt of the disclosure form wherever possible. While this provision should help prevent "shoot-the-messenger" type claims against real estate brokers, the safest approach in this area is to encourage parties to do their own research when questions of importance arise.

Example: A prospective buyer asks the listing broker if the seller has ever had any problems with termites at the house. After reviewing the Seller's Property Disclosure Statement, the broker calls the seller to verify the information in the disclosure statement. The seller answers that he has had no such problems and has made no termite damage related repairs. The broker leaves a voice mail for the prospective buyer saying that she rechecked the Property Disclosure Statement and confirmed with the seller that there were no termite problems since the seller purchased the house.

2176   O.C.G.A. § 10-6A-5(b)(2); O.C.G.A. § 10-6A-6(b)(2).

2177   O.C.G.A. § 10-6A-5(b)(2); O.C.G.A. § 10-6A-6(b)(2).

2178   O.C.G.A. § 10-6A-5(b)(2); O.C.G.A. § 10-6A-6(b)(2); O.C.G.A. § 10-6A-7(b); O.C.G.A. § 10-6A-(8)(b).

2179   GAR Form F57, Broker's Information Disclosure.

The termite clearance letter provided at the closing states that there are no visible signs of active termite infestation. After closing the transaction, when the buyer removes the carpet in the den to put down hardwood flooring, he discovers that a wooden patch has been put down in one corner of the floor concealing a soft spot and discovers that there are active termites in the sub-flooring underneath the patch. The buyer believes that the seller lied on the disclosure statement and that he tried to hide the termites with the patch and carpet. Is the broker liable under BRRETA for giving false information?

Answer: The answer to this question should be no, provided that the broker identified the source of his information. If the broker did not actually know that the information provided by the seller was false, the broker would not be able to be held liable for misrepresentation or passive concealment since the broker disclosed the source of her information. Even if the buyer can show that he could not have discovered the defect with a diligent inspection, the buyer should not be able to recover against the broker. Confirming the source of the broker's information in writing greatly reduces the likelihood of claims in this area.

§ 19.4.1.9   Elements Of Fraud Must Be Proven

Since the initial passage of BRRETA in 1994 there has been some argument that the statute only requires a showing that a broker misrepresented a material fact in order for a client to maintain a claim against a broker for failure to disclose. The 2000 revisions to BRRETA make it clear that BRRETA does not create an independent, statutory cause of action against brokers. All the elements of fraud, including the requirement that the plaintiff prove that she exercised due diligence to discover and protect against the alleged fraud, must be shown in order to hold a broker liable for failing to disclose an adverse material property condition or an adverse neighborhood condition.[2180] (Section 13.3 of this book discusses the elements which a plaintiff must prove to maintain a claim for fraud.)

Example: A prospective buyer asks if there have been any septic system problems on a particular property. The listing broker knows that there were past problems with the septic system but mistakenly answers no because the seller indicated that the problems had been corrected. Can the buyer maintain a claim against the listing broker for violating BRRETA without proving that the broker committed fraud?

Answer: No. BRRETA states that brokers are not liable for a failure to disclose an adverse material fact relating to the physical condition of the property or adverse material fact relating to the surrounding neighborhood unless there is a finding of fraud. The misrepresentation by the broker in and of itself does not give the buyer a claim against the broker absent a showing of fraud. Therefore, the buyer would have to show, among other things, that she could not have discovered the septic system problems upon a reasonably diligent inspection of the property.

§ 19.4.2   Duties Owed By Buyer's Or Tenant's Agent To Seller Or Landlord

BRRETA imposes several duties on the part of brokers who are representing tenants and buyers as clients. These duties include: (1) disclosing certain adverse facts concerning the buyer/tenants financial status, and (2) not knowingly giving false information. Each of these duties is discussed below.

§ 19.4.2.1   Financial Status Of Buyer Or Tenant

If a broker representing a buyer client is working with a seller in a transaction which will be financed either through partial or complete seller financing or through the assumption of a loan, BRRETA requires that the broker representing the buyer disclose to the seller "all material adverse facts actually known by the broker" regarding the buyer's "financial ability to perform the terms of the sale."[2181]

2180   O.C.G.A. § 10-6A-5(b)(2); O.C.G.A. § 10-6A-6(b)(2), O.C.G.A. § 10-6A-7(b); O.C.G.A. § 10-6A-8(b).

2181   O.C.G.A. § 10-6A-7(b).

If it is a residential transaction and the seller is providing financing, the broker representing the buyer must inform the seller of the buyer's intent to occupy the property as his/her principal residence.[2182] These disclosures serve to offer some protection to a seller when she will be acting as a lender in the transaction.

Similarly, brokers engaged by tenants are required to disclose to prospective landlords all adverse material facts "actually known" to the broker regarding the "tenant's financial ability to perform the terms of the lease or letter of intent to lease or intent to occupy the property."[2183]

Brokers representing buyers or tenants cannot be held liable for failure to disclose any matter other than those specifically listed in BRRETA. Furthermore, BRRETA prohibits causes of action against brokers representing buyers or tenants for complying with these disclosure requirements.[2184]

§ 19.4.2.2   Buyer/Tenant Not Relieved Of Duty To Disclose To Seller/Landlord

BRRETA specifically states that it does not in any way limit the obligation of prospective buyers "under any applicable law to disclose all adverse material facts actually known" to the buyer regarding the buyer's financial ability to perform the terms of the sale and in the case of a residential transaction, the buyer's intent to occupy the property as a principal residence.[2185]

Similarly, the statute does not limit the duty, under any applicable law, of prospective tenants to disclose to prospective landlords "all adverse material facts actually known by the tenant" regarding the tenant's financial ability to perform the terms of the lease or the letter of intent to lease or intent to occupy the property.[2186]

§ 19.4.2.3   Broker's Duty To Not Knowingly Give False Information

As with brokers representing sellers and landlords as clients, BRRETA mandates that brokers representing buyers and tenants as clients not give information to prospective sellers and landlords which they know to be false.[2187] Brokers have no liability for providing information that turns out to be incorrect provided they did not know of its falsity and disclosed the source of the information. (See § 19.4.1.8 (Duty not to knowingly give false information) for discussion.)

§ 19.5   BROKER-CUSTOMER RELATIONSHIPS

A broker-customer relationship is one in which the broker does not represent the individual in an agency capacity but for whom the broker may perform ministerial acts pursuant to either an oral or written agreement.[2188] In other words, the broker does not represent the individual in a legal sense, but may carry out a limited range of administrative tasks for the customer.

§ 19.5.1   Ministerial Services May Be Performed For Customers

Whenever a broker is in a broker-customer relationship, he may assist the customer in the transaction by performing limited brokerage services for the customer. These administrative services, known as "ministerial acts," are defined by BRRETA to be those acts which do not require the exercise of the broker's "professional judgment or skill."[2189] Prior to the 2000 revisions, BRRETA did not provide much guidance on what services would be considered ministerial

---

2182   O.C.G.A. § 10-6A-8(b).

2183   O.C.G.A. § 10-6A-8(b).

2184   O.C.G.A. § 10-6A-7(b), O.C.G.A. § 10-6A-8(b).

2185   O.C.G.A. § 10-6A-7(b).

2186   O.C.G.A. § 10-6A-8(b).

2187   O.C.G.A. § 10-6A-7(b), O.C.G.A. § 10-6A-8(b).

2188   O.C.G.A. § 10-6A-3(8).

2189   O.C.G.A. § 10-6A-3(12).

acts that could be performed for customers. The 2000 revisions provided guidance in this area by listing the following examples of ministerial acts:

(a) identifying property;

(b) providing real estate statistics and information regarding property;

(c) providing preprinted real estate form contracts;

(d) acting as a scribe in the preparation of form contracts;

(e) assisting in the location and identification of relevant professionals, such as architects, engineers, surveyors, inspectors, lenders, insurance agents, and attorneys; and

(f) identifying facilities and neighborhood amenities such as schools, shopping centers, and places of worship.[2190]

While this list is not exhaustive, it does give guidance to brokers on the broad range of services that can be performed for a customer. When in doubt, the rule of thumb should be that when working with a customer the broker can act as the customer's arms and legs but not as the customer's brains. In other words, the broker can perform administrative tasks for the customer at the customer's direction, such as those listed in the statute, but the broker cannot give advice to the customer requiring a high degree of professional judgment and skill.

§ 19.5.1.1 Ministerial Services Must Be Performed With Ordinary Care

BRRETA does not set out a standard of care with which a broker must perform ministerial acts for customers. However, Georgia case law holds that brokers must use reasonable and ordinary care when undertaking brokerage services for a customer.[2191] Although this is not a high threshold for performance, if a broker does choose to perform administrative tasks for a customer in a transaction the broker must carry through with ordinary care. It is interesting to note that the standard of care required of brokers in their performance toward clients has been lowered by BRRETA to virtually the same level of care required when a broker performs administrative tasks for customers.

§ 19.5.2 Types Of Broker-Customer Relationships

A broker-customer relationship can arise in several situations. For example: (1) prior to entering a written brokerage agreement forming a broker-client relationship, the individual with whom the broker is working is a customer; (2) when a broker represents one party to a transaction as a client the broker may, but is not required to, treat other parties to the transaction as customers; and (3) when a broker does not enter into a broker-client relationship with any party to a transaction, the broker is acting as a transaction broker. Transaction brokers have a customer relationship with all of the parties to the transaction.

§ 19.5.2.1 Customer Relationship Exists Before Entering Into Written Brokerage Agreement

Prior to forming a broker-client relationship by entering into a written brokerage agreement containing the specific items listed in § 19.2.3 (Contents of the brokerage engagement), the individual with whom the broker is working is a customer.

§ 19.5.2.2 Broker Representing Client In A Transaction May Perform Ministerial Acts For Other Party To The Transaction

When a broker represents one party to a transaction as a client the broker may, but is not required to, treat other parties to the transaction as customers. § 19.4 (Duty of Care to Customers) above discusses the duties which a broker representing one party as a client in a transaction owes to the other parties whom they do not represent in the transaction.

2190   O.C.G.A. § 10-6A-14(a).

2191   *Stelts v. Epperson*, 201 Ga.App. 405, 411 S.E. 2d 281 (1991).

In addition to those duties, the broker is permitted to treat the other parties to the transaction as customers and thus the broker may perform ministerial acts for those other parties. BRRETA specifically states that assisting the other parties is not a violation of the broker's duty to his client.[2192] Furthermore, BRRETA states that the performance of such ministerial acts for the other parties to a transaction does not create a client relationship between the broker and the other parties.[2193]

§ 19.5.2.3 Transaction Brokerage

Transaction brokerage is the practice in which a broker does not enter into a client relationship with any of the parties to a contract, performs only ministerial acts for one or more of the parties, and gets paid a valuable consideration for the performance of those services pursuant to an oral or written agreement.[2194] In other words, a transaction broker does not represent any of the parties as clients, but may treat the parties as customers by assisting them in administrative tasks.

As originally enacted BRRETA did not address transaction brokerage at all because this form of brokerage practice was essentially unheard of at that time in Georgia. Since 2000, however, transaction brokerage has become common practice in Georgia as more and more brokers are working with prospective buyers without entering into a client relationship.

§ 19.5.2.4 Duties Of Transaction Brokers To All Parties In Transaction

BRRETA allows a transaction broker to perform ministerial acts for the customers in a transaction. In addition to those forms of assistance that transaction brokers may provide, BRRETA specifically mandates that transaction brokers must fulfill the following duties:

(a) timely presenting all offers to and from the parties;

(b) timely accounting for all money and property received by the broker on behalf of any party to the transaction; and

(c) timely disclosure to buyers and tenants with whom the broker is working all adverse material facts about the physical condition of the property, improvements on the property, and all material facts pertaining to existing adverse physical conditions in the neighborhood within one mile of the property that are known to the broker.[2195]

BRRETA provides that transaction brokers cannot be held liable for disclosing information in compliance with this provision of the law.[2196] Transaction brokers can only be held liable for failing to disclose those matters specifically listed in the statute and cannot be held liable for failing to disclose any other matter.[2197] Finally, transaction brokers have no duty to familiarize themselves with the property or the surrounding neighborhood.

§ 19.5.2.5 Disclosure Of Parties To The Transaction Not Affected By Disclosure Duties Of Transaction Broker

BRRETA provides that the disclosure duties of the transaction broker do not reduce or in any way affect any duty of sellers to disclose to prospective buyers all adverse material facts known to the seller relating to the physical condition of the property.[2198] The duty of disclosure placed on transaction brokers does not affect the duty of buyers to familiarize him/herself with the surrounding neighborhood.[2199]

2192   O.C.G.A. § 10-6A-5(c), O.C.G.A. § 10-6A-6(c), O.C.G.A. § 10-6A-7(c), O.C.G.A. § 10-6A-8(c).

2193   O.C.G.A. § 10-6A-5(c), O.C.G.A. § 10-6A-6(c), O.C.G.A. § 10-6A-7(c), O.C.G.A. § 10-6A-8(c).

2194   O.C.G.A. § 10-6A-3(14).

2195   O.C.G.A. § 10-6A-14(b).

2196   O.C.G.A. § 10-6A-14(c).

2197   O.C.G.A. § 10-6A-14(c).

2198   O.C.G.A. § 10-6A-14(c).

2199   O.C.G.A. § 10-6A-14(c).

§ 19.5.2.6 Transaction Broker's Duty Not To Knowingly Give False Information

BRRETA provides that transaction brokers must not knowingly give false information to any party. Transaction brokers must treat all of the parties to a transaction honestly. This is the same requirement discussed in § 19.4.1.8 (Duty to not knowingly give false information), regarding a broker's duty not to give false information to the other party in a transaction when the broker is representing one side of the transaction as a client.

§ 19.5.3 Transaction Brokers' Liability For Providing False Information Limited By BRRETA

BRRETA protects transaction brokers, in the event that they unknowingly give any party to a transaction false information, by providing that the broker is not liable for giving a party false information if: (1) the broker does not have actual knowledge that the information is false, and (2) the broker discloses the source of the information to the customer.[2200] GAR has designed a form[2201] that can be given to the parties for their signature when a broker provides answers to a party's questions. This form should be used by brokers and a copy of it kept in the broker's files.

§ 19.5.4 The GAR Agreement To Work With Buyer As A Customer Form

In response to the growing concerns surrounding a broker's liability when representing a customer, the Georgia Association of REALTORS® created the GAR Agreement To Work With Buyer As A Customer[2202] form. This form describes the broker's responsibilities to a buyer in a customer relationship, when the broker is entitled to a commission, dispute resolution procedures in the event of a claim against either party, and an explicit provision limiting the broker's liability. This form was designed to help brokers avoid many of the common issues that arise out of a broker-customer relationship.

§ 19.5.4.1 Agreement To Work With Buyer As Customer

As stated above, the broker in a broker-customer relationship performs administrative ministerial tasks for the customer pursuant to a written or oral agreement.[2203] As such, the GAR Agreement To Work With Buyer As A Customer form provides that the buyer and broker agree to work together to locate real property to purchase that is suitable to the buyer's needs. The form also contains an explicit statement that the broker is not representing the buyer as a client, but only as a customer. To avoid any further confusion, the form states that, as a customer, the broker cannot represent or advise the buyer, but can only perform ministerial tasks on behalf of the buyer. In addition, either the buyer or broker may terminate the agreement at any time by written or electronic notice (such as an e-mail) to the other party.

§ 19.5.4.2 Customer Acknowledgement Regarding Commission To Broker

Under the GAR Agreement To Work With Buyer As A Customer, the broker is entitled to share in the commission being paid to the listing broker on any property purchased by the buyer if the broker is the procuring cause of the sale. The broker is also entitled to a commission if the broker would have been the procuring cause of the sale but for the customer's abandonment in the transaction.

§ 19.5.4.3 Arbitration

Users of this GAR form agree that all claims arising out of or relating to the agreement and the alleged acts or commission of any or all the parties to the agreement will be resolved by arbitration. The arbitration will be conducted in accordance with the Federal Arbitration Act[2204] and the rules and procedures of the arbitration company selected to

---

2200   O.C.G.A. § 10-6A-14(c).

2201   GAR Form F57, Broker's Information Disclosure.

2202   GAR Form F15.

2203   O.C.G.A. § 10-6A-3(8).

2204   9 U.S.C.A. § 1 *et seq.*

administer the arbitration. Although the arbitration provision applies to most claims, arbitration is not required for any claim regarding the handling and disbursement of earnest money or any claim by the broker regarding her entitled to the payment or non-payment of a commission in this agreement.

Under the GAR Agreement To Work With Buyer As A Customer[2205] form, the parties agree to work together to select a mutually acceptable arbitration company with offices in Georgia to administer and conduct the arbitration. If the parties can't agree on an arbitration company, the company will be selected by each party simultaneously exchanging with the other party a list of three acceptable arbitration companies with offices in Georgia. If there is one arbitration company that is common to both lists, that company will be chosen to administer and conduct the arbitration. If there is more than one arbitration company that is common to both lists, the parties will either mutually agree as to which company will be selected or flip a coin. If there is not initially one arbitration company that is common to both list, the parties will repeat the process by expanding their lists by two companies at a time until there is a common name on the lists selected by the parties. Once arbitration has begun, the arbitrator's decision will be final. The arbitrator also has the authority to award attorney's fees and allocate the costs of arbitration as part of any final award.

Neither class action suits nor any other form representative proceedings may be brought before the arbitrator under this GAR form. As such, a party may not go to arbitration as member of a class in any purported class action or other representative proceeding. The GAR form explicitly states that any claim brought before the arbitrator must be brought by a party in her individual capacity. In addition, the arbitrator may not consolidate more than one person's claims and may not preside over any form of a representative or class action proceeding.

§ 19.5.4.4 Limitation Against Liability

The GAR Agreement To Work With Buyer As A Customer[2206] form contains an important provision limiting a broker's liability under the agreement. More specifically, the form includes the following provision.

> **Limitation Against Liability.** *Broker shall, under no circumstances, have any liability to Customer greater than the amount of the real estate commission paid hereunder to Broker (excluding any commission amount paid to a cooperating real estate broker, if any) or, if no real estate commission is paid to the broker, than a sum not to exceed one hundred dollars.*

The inclusion of this language severely limits the amount of any claims brought against the broker. In the worst case scenario, the broker looses the amount of her commission or a maximum sum of one hundred dollars. Either way, the broker is not subjected to a limitless damages claim.

§ 19.6 CHANGING THE BROKERAGE RELATIONSHIP

When a brokerage relationship changes, brokers must give notice of the change to all parties involved in the transaction. BRRETA requires that whenever a broker with an existing brokerage relationship with a customer or client enters into a new brokerage relationship with the customer or client, the broker must "timely disclose that fact and the new brokerage relationship to all brokers, customers, or clients involved in the contemplated transaction."[2207] The purpose of this requirement is to notify all involved parties of changes in the broker's role and duties in the transaction. This disclosure requirement can come into play at various times during the course of a brokerage relationship including, for example, when the relationship changes from customer to client and vice versa, when a buyer agent or listing agent becomes a designated agent, and when a broker becomes a single-agent dual agent. The statute does not specify a time period within which this disclosure must be made, nor does it state whether the disclosure must be written. It would be advisable, however, for the broker to make the disclosure as soon as possible

---

2205   GAR Form F15.

2206   GAR Form F15.

2207   O.C.G.A. § 10-6A-4(b).

after the brokerage engagement has been signed and, when convenient, for the disclosure to be in writing. If it is not possible to fax or mail the notice due to time constraints, a viable option would be to make the disclosure orally and to then follow the conversation with a written confirmation sent to the parties. At the very least the broker should put a written memo or note in her file stating that she made the required disclosure and giving the date of the disclosure to protect against claims that the broker did not comply with the statutory disclosure requirement. The following examples illustrate the application of this statutory requirement.

Example #1: A broker has shown a house listed with another real estate brokerage firm several times to a prospective buyer who has not signed a buyer brokerage engagement and who is thus a customer of the broker rather than a client. Upon deciding to make an offer on the property, the buyer asks the broker to represent him in the negotiations. The broker explains to the buyer that he cannot represent him as his legal agent unless the buyer becomes the broker's client by entering into a written brokerage engagement. When the buyer and broker sign the brokerage agreement, their brokerage relationship changes from a broker-customer relationship to a broker–client relationship. BRRETA requires that this change be disclosed in a timely fashion to the listing broker and the seller, as well as to any other customer, client or broker who might be involved in the transaction.

Example #2: A real estate licensee working with a prospective buyer-client under a buyer's brokerage engagement shows the client several houses listed by different real estate firms. The buyer then decides that he wants to see a listing in which the licensee is acting as the listing agent. Showing this property will involve a change of brokerage relationship to either designated agency or dual agency. This change must be disclosed to all other parties in the transaction.

Failure to make prompt notice that a relationship has changed would likely result in a lawsuit alleging a broker's failure to fulfill statutory duties required in certain types of broker relationships. In one case, for example, a broker acted as dual agent representing both the buyers and the sellers in a purchase and sale transaction.[2208] The purchase and sale agreement was contingent upon the property being appraised for at least the purchase price of $195,000.[2209] When the appraised value did not satisfy the contingency, the buyers terminated the purchase and sale agreement and their agreement with the broker. The buyers then hired a new agent and attempted to negotiate the sale of the same home with the seller who was still working with the first broker (who previously acted as a dual agent). The second purchase and sale agreement also fell through. The parties then started negotiating a third agreement but during that time, the first broker successfully negotiated and closed the sale of the property with another buyer. The buyers then sued the first broker alleging that the broker breached his fiduciary duties owed to them as "clients" under BRRETA.[2210] The court disagreed holding that any broker-client relationship that may have existed in the first agreement when the broker was acting as a dual agent was terminated when the transaction failed.[2211] The buyers' new relationship with the first broker is that of a broker-customer which does not impose the same heightened duties.[2212] As such, the claim against the broker failed.[2213] However, a simple notice to the buyers that the relationship changed from broker-client to broker-customer could have avoided this suit in its entirety.

Giving prompt notice of changed relationships is critically important if the relationship changes after a GAR Contract has been signed. This is because the notice requirements under the GAR Contract vary depending upon whether a client or customer relationship exits. Under the GAR Contract, notice to a broker is notice to that broker's client, but not notice to that broker's customer.

2208 *Jones v. Bill Garlen Real Estate*, 311 Ga.App. 372, 715 S.E.2d 777 (2011).

2209 *Jones v. Bill Garlen Real Estate*, 311 Ga.App. 372, 715 S.E.2d 777 (2011).

2210 *Jones v. Bill Garlen Real Estate*, 311 Ga.App. 372, 715 S.E.2d 777 (2011).

2211 *Jones v. Bill Garlen Real Estate*, 311 Ga.App. 372, 715 S.E.2d 777 (2011).

2212 *Jones v. Bill Garlen Real Estate*, 311 Ga.App. 372, 715 S.E.2d 777 (2011).

2213 *Jones v. Bill Garlen Real Estate*, 311 Ga.App. 372, 715 S.E.2d 777 (2011).

§ 19.7   TERMINATION OF BROKERAGE RELATIONSHIP

The duties imposed on a broker by law begin at the time the client engages the broker. These duties are owed until either the engagement is completed, or until the first one of the following events takes place: (a) the expiration date in the brokerage agreement passes, (b) the parties terminate the agreement in a manner agreed upon in the brokerage engagement, (c) if no expiration is provided for and no termination has occurred, then one year after the initiation of the engagement.[2214]

§ 19.7.1   When Broker Can Terminate Brokerage Relationship

There are several instances in which a broker may desire to terminate her relationship with a client. If the broker and client have difficulty getting along with each other or difficulty communicating with each other to such extent that the broker feels she cannot adequately represent the client, it may be advisable for the broker to terminate the relationship. Similarly, if a broker wants to avoid a dual agency situation that would arise by showing a buyer-client one of the broker's own listings, the broker can withdraw from representing the buyer, thus ending her client relationship with the buyer. The GAR Buyer Brokerage Engagement forms permit either party to terminate the client relationship without the consent of the other party upon giving written notice to that party.

§ 19.7.2   Duties Of Broker Upon Termination Of Brokerage Relationship

After the brokerage relationship has terminated or expired, the broker owes no further duty to the client, with two exceptions. First, the broker must account for all moneys and property relating to the engagement.[2215] Second, after the brokerage engagement has ended the broker must continue to keep confidential any information which the broker received during the term of the engagement and which the client requested to be kept confidential. Even though a brokerage relationship no longer exists, any such confidential information can only be revealed by the broker under the following circumstances: (a) the client permits the disclosure by subsequent word or conduct, (b) disclosure is required by law, or (c) the information becomes public from a source other than the broker.[2216]

The same duties to account for money and property and to maintain confidences also arises when the brokerage relationship has changed such that the broker is no longer representing the individual as a client and broker-client relationship has technically ended.

§ 19.7.3   When Client Can Terminate Brokerage Relationship

Clients can terminate brokerage relationships whenever permitted in their contracts or in the event of a material breach of contract by the broker. However, Georgia case law is clear that in the absence of an express early termination provision or material breach, clients cannot unilaterally terminate listing agreements or buyer brokerage agreements.[2217]

§ 19.8   BRRETA AND GAR'S BROKERAGE ENGAGEMENTS

GAR's Listing Agreements and Buyer Brokerage Agreements have been designed to ensure that the broker-client relationship is formed in compliance with BRRETA. For example, all of the GAR form Brokerage Agreements include a bold face disclosure at the beginning of the form explaining that state law prohibits brokers from representing parties as clients without a written brokerage agreement. GAR's form Listing Agreements and Buyer Engagement Agreements include the four necessary elements of a brokerage engagement required under BRRETA discussed in § 19.2.3 (Contents of the brokerage engagement). These forms also set out specifically what other duties the broker has toward

---

2214   O.C.G.A. § 10-6A-9(a).

2215   O.C.G.A. § 10-6A-9(b)(1).

2216   O.C.G.A. § 10-6A-9(b)(1).

2217   *Ben Farmer Realty, Inc. v. Owens*, 286 Ga.App. 678, 649 S.E.2d 771 (2007).

the client. The forms assume that the brokerage firm is offering the complete range of agency relationships: seller agency, buyer agency, dual agency, designated agency, landlord agency, and tenant agency. Therefore, if a brokerage firm is not offering one or more of these agency relationships, the relationship or relationships not being offered would need to be specifically identified in the contract. The forms also include the disclosures that must be made if a firm practices dual agency.

§ 19.8.1   Protections Against Liability In The GAR Brokerage Engagements

The GAR form Brokerage Engagements limit the potential legal liability of brokers in two important ways.

First, the Brokerage Agreements provide that the maximum liability of the broker is the greater of (i) the amount of the real estate commission paid to the broker or (ii) $100.00. Excluded from the amount of commission paid is that portion of the commission paid to any cooperating broker or retained by the listing broker. The case of *Brainard v. McKinney*[2218] established the legal precedent for enforcing such a limitation on liability. In the *Brainard* case, the Georgia Court of Appeals upheld a home inspection contract that included a clause limiting the inspector's liability to the cost of the inspection. A later companion case, *Tanner v. Redding*,[2219] clarified the law further by holding that such a contractual limitation is enforceable only if the agreement is prepared and signed prior to the inspection. Thus, the GAR Brokerage Engagement forms not only ensure that the broker complies with BRRETA in the formation of the client relationship, but they also operate to cap the brokers' liability and to substantially reduce their legal exposure.

Second, the GAR Brokerage Agreements limit the duties owed by the real estate broker. BRRETA states that a broker only owes customers and clients the duties set forth in BRRETA unless the parties expressly agree in a signed writing to other duties.[2220] (Section 19.3 discusses in detail the duties owed by brokers to their clients under BRRETA.) Each kind of GAR Brokerage Engagement form sets out the specific duties owed to the client. For example, the GAR Exclusive Buyer Brokerage Agreement[2221] provides as follows:

> Broker's sole duties to Seller are to: (a) make all disclosures required by law;
> (b) attempt to locate property suitable to Buyer for purchase; (c) comply with
> all applicable laws in performing its duties hereunder including the Brokerage
> Relationships in Real Estate Transactions Act, O.C.G.A. § 10-6A-1 *et seq.* and (d)
> assist to the extent requested by Buyer in negotiating the terms and filling out a
> pre-printed real estate purchase and sale agreement.

BRRETA, in combination with the GAR Brokerage Engagement forms, significantly reduces the potential legal liability of a broker by narrowing the duties owed by a broker in her brokerage engagement and by limiting the potential damages in the event of an inadvertent breach of such duties.

§ 19.8.2   Getting Buyer-Clients To Sign Written Brokerage Agreement

Although it has never been difficult to get sellers to sign brokerage agreements (*i.e.*, listing agreements), some buyers have been reluctant to sign written brokerage agreements. The reason for this reluctance seems to be two-fold: (1) fear of having to pay a real estate commission (even though the commission is normally paid by the seller), and (2) general anxiety regarding committing themselves contractually to one particular broker.

There are several possible actions which brokers can take to alleviate the fear on the part of some buyers to sign written brokerage agreements. First, brokers should explain to their buyer-clients that under the form GAR Brokerage

---

2218   *Brainard v. McKinney*, 220 Ga.App. 329, 469 S.E. 2d 441 (1996).

2219   *Tanner v. Redding*, 231 Ga.App. 250, 498 S.E. 2d 156 (1998).

2220   O.C.G.A. § 10-6A-4(a).

2221   GAR Form F4.

agreements, both the client as well as the broker can terminate the agreement with or without cause upon written notice to the other. If the buyer no longer wants to work with the broker, all she has to do is send a letter of termination.

Second, there is nothing which requires a brokerage engagement to be of any particular duration. The broker can offer to make the initial term of the brokerage engagement extremely short. For example, the brokerage agreement can be for one weekend or even one day. Of course, once the initial term of the agreement has ended the broker should seek to make the renewal term substantially longer.

Third, if the buyer is concerned about the possibility of having to pay a real estate commission, the broker can explain that if the following basic rules are followed, the buyer will not have to pay a real estate commission:

a) The broker can agree to only show the buyer property listed in a multiple listing service where the seller is paying the commission. This can even be written into the GAR Buyer Brokerage Agreements as a special stipulation. In listing property in a multiple listing service ("MLS"), the seller is agreeing to pay a commission that may be shared with a cooperating broker who is the procuring cause of the sale. Therefore, if a broker explains to the buyer that if she only sees property with that broker, and if the broker agrees to only show the buyer property listed with the MLS in which the seller is paying the commission, the risk of the buyer having to pay a commission is significantly reduced.

b) The broker can agree that he not show the buyer a property that is for sale by owner without first working out an arrangement with the seller to be paid a commission. In this way, the buyer will not have any unpleasant surprises.

c) The buyer should be reminded to only see property with the broker if the buyer has signed an exclusive buyer brokerage agreement. This rule insures that the buyer broker will be the procuring cause of the sale in all transactions involving the buyer. This helps to avoid disputes regarding this issue with listing brokers. If the buyer is still uncomfortable, a special stipulation can be included in the Buyer Brokerage Agreement of the type similar to the one following.

> **Special Stipulation 345:   Broker to Show Property Without Written Brokerage Engagement**
>
> *Broker agrees to show Buyer only property which is listed in a multiple listing service in which the seller is agreeing to pay a commission. Broker will not show Buyer a property offered For Sale By Owner without first working out a written commission agreement with the seller or notifying Buyer that in viewing the Property, the Buyer will be paying a commission of _____% of the purchase price.*

19.8.3   Commission Claims And The GAR Brokerage Engagements

The GAR Contract no longer provides a space for the broker to fill in the amount of the commission or the split of the commission with any cooperating broker.[2222] The amount of the commission and any offer to split the commission is handled through separate agreements. This raises the question of how brokers can protect their right to a commission.

A selling broker would historically contact the listing broker and ask whether the listing broker was willing to split his commission. With the advent of the MLS and FMLS, the listing of a property in the systems indicates the amount of the split being offered. The rules of the FMLS or MLS require that brokers listing property with the services agree to cooperate with other members of the service. The GAR form Buyer and Seller Engagement Agreements and the GAR Contract discussed below help to further protect brokers' commissions.

---

222   GAR Form F20.

§ 19.8.3.1 The Exclusive Buyer Brokerage Agreement

(a) The commission obligation generally

The GAR Exclusive Buyer Brokerage Agreement provides that the buyer's real estate broker will seek to be paid its commission from the seller or listing broker pursuant to a cooperative brokerage arrangement. In the event neither of these parties pays a commission to the selling broker, then the commission may be paid by the buyer if such obligation is indicated in the brokerage agreement, regardless of whether or not the property is one which the broker identified for the buyer.

The GAR Exclusive Buyer Brokerage Agreement contains a blank to be filled in with the amount of the commission or percentage of the sales price in which the broker is entitled for completing the transaction. As stated above, it is generally the seller's obligation to pay the commissions of the real estate brokers. Previous versions of this agreement provided that in the event the seller or listing broker does not pay the buyer's broker a commission, the responsibility for paying the broker's full commission fell on the buyer. The current version of the GAR Exclusive Buyer Brokerage Agreement, however, does not place this payment responsibility on the buyer unless it is explicitly indicated in the brokerage agreement. More specifically, the Exclusive Buyer Brokerage Agreement provides that "in the event Seller does not pay the Broker the full amount of Commission, Buyer ☐ shall or ☐ shall not pay Broker the difference at closing between Broker's Commission and the commission actually paid to the Broker." As such, unless the buyer agrees to this payment obligation, any difference in the amount of commission owed to the buyer's broker will not fall on the buyer.

An issue may arise when the seller or listing broker agrees to pay a lesser commission than what has been designated by the buyer in the Exclusive Buyer Brokerage Agreement. In such situations, the buyer's broker cannot ask the buyer to pay the difference unless the buyer agrees to such payment obligation in the brokerage agreement. Below is an example of this situation.

Example: REALTOR® A enters into an exclusive buyer brokerage agreement using the GAR form in which the buyer agrees that in the event the seller or listing broker does not pay the selling broker a commission in accordance with a cooperative brokerage arrangement, the buyer will pay his broker the difference to ensure his broker receives a commission of 3 ½% of the purchase price of the property. The buyer purchases a property he viewed with his broker. The listing agreement and the MLS listing indicate that the commission to be paid to any cooperating real estate broker will be 2 ½%. Can the selling broker require the buyer to pay him any additional commission?

Answer: No. The selling broker is entitled to only 2 ½% commission as set out in the listing agreement and the MLS listing. By indicating such payment responsibility, the buyer only agrees to pay the difference in commission if the buyer's broker is paid a commission less than what is specified in the Exclusive Buyer Brokerage Agreement. The selling broker may not pursue the buyer for the difference to receive a commission that is higher than what is specified in the listing agreement and MLS listing.. The GAR Exclusive Buyer Brokerage Agreement specifically states that the commission is to be paid on all property which the buyer purchases during the term of this agreement whether or not it has been identified to the buyer by the real estate broker. This provision contractually modifies the general common law rule that the broker is only entitled to a commission if she is the procuring cause of the sale (i.e., the broker's efforts resulted in an uninterrupted series of events that resulted in the sale). However, under Georgia law, the parties to a contract are free to agree on whatever terms and about any subject matters in which they have an interest in the absence of a violation of public policy or law.[2223]

(b) Entitlement to commission after expiration or termination of Buyer Brokerage Agreement

The GAR Exclusive Buyer Brokerage Agreement provides that the broker is entitled to a commission if the buyer purchases or contracts to purchase, for a period of time after the termination or expiration of the brokerage agreement

---

2223   *Brainard v. McKinney*, 220 Ga.App. 329, S.E. 2d 441, 442 (1996); *First Capital Institutional Real Estate Ltd v. Pennington*, 1986 Ga.App. 617, 386 S.E. 2d 165, 166 (1988).

a property identified or shown to the buyer by the broker or for which the broker provided information about to the buyer during the brokerage agreement. While the terms "identified" and "shown" are not defined, the terms were intended to protect brokers in situations where the buyer learned of the property through the efforts of the broker. The language allowing a broker to collect a commission if the buyer purchased property due to information the broker provided to the buyer accomplishes the same goal. As such, it is not required that the broker actually show the property to the buyer provided that the broker has taken other reasonable steps to make the buyer aware of the property. The following three examples help explain this point.

Example #1: During the term of an exclusive brokerage engagement agreement (entered into on the GAR form) the broker faxes MLS information sheets to the buyer on six (6) properties the broker believes the buyer would be interested in purchasing. The buyer thanks the broker for the information, but terminates the brokerage agreement a few days later without explanation and without seeing the property. Two months later, the broker learns that the buyer purchased one of the six properties identified to the buyer by the broker. Should the broker be protected for a commission?

Answer: The answer to this question should be yes, assuming that the buyer entered into the purchase contract during the period of time after the termination of the contract in which the broker was protected for a commission. This is because while the broker did not actually show the buyer the property, the broker did identify the property to the buyer and cause the buyer to learn of its existence during the brokerage engagement. The broker's commission claim in this example would be against the buyer directly rather than the seller or listing broker of the property purchased by the buyer.

The amount of the commission and the number of days for which the broker is protected are shown in blanks on the GAR Exclusive Buyer Brokerage Engagement and must be filled in by the parties. Obviously, the greater the number of days specified, the greater the protection. If the parties fail to write into the agreement the amount of the commission or the number of days for which the broker's commission is protected, the broker would not be entitled to a commission if, after the termination of the agreement, the buyer purchases or contracts to purchase a property identified to the buyer by the broker. Below are several examples of how this process works.

Example #2: Broker shows buyer a property during the term of a buyer brokerage engagement. The agreement provides that the broker is protected for a commission for 120 days after the termination of the agreement. One hundred and ten days after the brokerage agreement terminates, the buyer enters into a contract to purchase the property shown to the buyer during the brokerage agreement. The closing is set for 45 days later, which is after the end of the broker's protected period. Can the broker recover a commission in this instance?

Answer: Yes. In order for the broker's commission protection provision to be effective, the buyer need only enter into a contract to purchase, during the protected time period, a property identified to the buyer during the brokerage agreement. The sale does not have to actually close within the protected time period. In this case, while the closing of the property takes place after the end of the protected time period, the buyer did enter into a contract to purchase the property during the protected time period thus entitling the broker to a commission in accordance with the brokerage agreement. The broker must carefully document the properties identified to the buyer to take advantage of this protection. Although this sounds difficult and tedious, it can be easily accomplished. Whenever the buyer brokerage agreement either expires or is terminated by one of the parties, the broker should send the buyer a letter specifically listing all the properties which the broker introduced to the buyer. This step lays the groundwork for the broker's claim to a commission in the event the buyer later contracts to buy a house identified by the broker.

Example #3: A buyer enters into an exclusive buyer brokerage agreement for a term of thirty (30) days with Broker No. 1. The agreement protects the broker's commission in the event the buyer within 90 days after the termination of the brokerage agreement, purchases or contracts to purchase a property identified to the buyer by the broker during the term of the buyer brokerage agreement. The broker shows the buyer numerous homes; however, the buyer does not submit an offer on any of the homes. After the term of the brokerage agreement expires, the buyer immediately enters into another exclusive buyer brokerage agreement with Broker No. 2. Within the 90 day protected period under the brokerage agreement with Broker No. 1, Broker No. 2 shows the buyer one of the same houses that Broker No. 1 had shown him earlier and the buyer enters a contract to buy this house. Is Broker No. 1 entitled to a commission?

Answer: The answer to this question should be yes. This is because the buyer, within the protected time period, contracted to buy a house which Broker No. 1 had shown him during the term of their brokerage agreement. At closing the buyer would owe Broker No. 1 a commission on the sale. Broker No. 1's claim to a commission would be directly against the buyer. Broker No. 2 should also be entitled to a commission. Assuming that Broker No. 2 and the buyer entered into a GAR Exclusive Buyer Brokerage Engagement, Broker No. 2 would be owed a commission either from the seller or listing broker, or, if no such commission was paid, from the buyer.

This is the same result from the parallel situation under an exclusive listing agreement. The GAR Exclusive Listing Agreement provides that if, after the termination of the listing agreement, the seller lists the property with a different broker and a buyer purchases the property who first saw the property during the initial listing, the first broker is entitled to a commission if the property was sold during the specified Protected Period.

(c)   GAR Exclusive Buyer Brokerage Agreement can reduce disputes over procuring cause between competing brokers

The growth of buyer brokerage in Georgia in recent years has created many disputes over whether the buyer broker is the procuring cause of the sale and thus entitled to share in the listing broker's commission. The term "procuring cause" is difficult to define, but refers to the general common law principal that a broker who is unable to finalize a sale of property can still claim a commission if she can show that her efforts triggered a key series of events which, without significant interruption, resulted in the sale of the property.[2224] A variety of factors influence whether a broker is the procuring cause of a sale, including whether the broker initiated the series of events leading to the sale, whether there was a break in negotiations, and the reason for any break in the negotiations.[2225]

The common law doctrine of procuring cause is inapplicable when an express contract addresses what constitutes the "procuring cause" of the sale.[2226] In one case, a seller entered into an exclusive listing agreement with a broker but the broker was unsuccessful in finding a buyer. During the term of the listing agreement, however, the broker gave Martin, the seller's neighbor, a flyer notifying him that the property was for sale. At the time, Martin was not interested in purchasing the property. After the first listing agreement expired, the seller hired a new listing broker. The exclusive listing agreement provided that the broker was entitled to an eight percent commission if: (i) the broker procured a purchaser during the term of the agreement; (ii) the property was withdrawn from sale, the seller's authorization was revoked during the term of the agreement, or if the seller otherwise prevented the performance of the agreement by the broker; or (iii) the sale was made within six (6) months after the termination of the agreement with person with whom the broker negotiated during the term and whose names the broker submitted in writing to the seller within ten (10) days after the termination of the agreement.

The second broker also failed to find a buyer to purchase the seller's property. However, shortly after the exclusive listing agreement expired, Martin purchased the seller's property and no commission was paid to the broker. The broker then brought suit against the seller for a commission on the basis of procuring cause. The court rejected the broker's claim because the broker failed to present evidence that he was entitled to a commission as the procuring cause of the sale under the express terms of the agreement.[2227]

Non-exclusive buyer brokerage agreements and open listing agreements can also create a situation in which a broker's right to a commission depends on whether he was the procuring cause of the sale.[2228] The use of the GAR Exclusive Buyer Brokerage Agreement can eliminate the need for the broker to prove that she was the procuring cause and thus can eliminate many disputes between competing agents. First, this agreement clearly establishes an exclusive agency in which the buyer specifically agrees not to work with any other broker or real estate licensee for a specified period

---

2224   *Georgia Real Estate Properties, Inc. v. Lindwall*, 303 Ga.App. 12, 692 S.E.2d 690 (2010).

2225   *See* Section 13.5.1 (Procuring Cause) of this work.

2226   *Georgia Real Estate Properties, Inc.v. Lindwall*, 303 Ga.App. 12, 692 S.E.2d 690 (2010).

2227   *Georgia Real Estate Properties, Inc.v. Lindwall*, 303 Ga.App. 12, 692 S.E.2d 690 (2010).

2228   *Cartel Realty, Inc. v. Southern Bearings and Parts Co., Inc.*, 243 Ga.App. 653, 534 S.E.2d 119 (2000).

of time. This means that during the term of the agreement the buyer is contractually prohibited from establishing an agency relationship with another broker without terminating the buyer brokerage agreement with the first broker. If the buyer does purchase a property using another broker during the term of the agreement, the first broker is still entitled to his commission, even if the property purchased is one which the first broker never identified to the buyer. Furthermore, even if the buyer (or broker) terminates the brokerage agreement, the broker is still entitled to a commission if, within an agreed-upon time after termination, the buyer purchases or contracts to purchase any property identified to the buyer by the broker during the term of the brokerage agreement. For identified properties bought or contracted for during this protected time period, the broker can claim a commission without proving that he was the procuring cause of the sale.

§ 19.8.3.2 The Non-Exclusive Buyer Brokerage Agreement

The GAR Non-Exclusive Buyer Brokerage Agreement is similar to the GAR Exclusive Buyer Brokerage Agreement discussed in the previous section in that the broker agrees to look to the seller or listing broker for his commission. However, there is a critical difference between the two agreements. With the Non-Exclusive Buyer Brokerage Agreement the broker can only recover a commission from the buyer if the buyer purchases property identified to the buyer by the broker during the term of the agreement. This is in contrast to the Exclusive Brokerage Agreement under which the buyer's broker can claim a commission for sales made during the term of the agreement whether or not the property was identified to the buyer by the broker.

§ 19.8.3.3 The Exclusive Seller Listing Agreement

The GAR Exclusive Seller Listing Agreement sets the amount of commission or the percentage of the sales price which the seller will pay upon a sale of the property. The Agreement states that this commission will be due to the Broker if during the term of the Agreement, Broker either (1) procures a person "ready, willing and able" to purchase the property at a price agreeable to the seller, or (2) the seller enters into a contract to sell or exchange the property with any buyer. The agreement also contains blanks which the parties fill in to establish what commission split the broker will pay to any cooperating broker who procures a buyer. The Agreement specifically makes cooperating brokers third-party beneficiaries to the agreement. This allows cooperating brokers who are not directly in contract with the seller to nonetheless pursue claims against defaulting sellers for their commission. It is critical that brokers fill in these blanks to protect their commission since the GAR Purchase and Sale Agreement no longer contains a place for the parties to write in the commission split for cooperating brokers.

Example: A seller enters into a GAR Exclusive Listing Agreement with a broker in which the seller agrees to pay the listing broker 7% of the purchase price. The listing broker fills in the blank in the listing agreement indicating that he will offer 50% of his commission to cooperating brokers. The listing broker enters the property into a multiple listing service at a commission of 7% with a 50/50 split on the commission. Later, the seller and listing broker orally agree to reduce the commission to 6%, but they do not amend the listing agreement, modify the information contained in the multiple listing system, or tell the selling broker of the commission reduction. Is the selling broker's commission limited to 3% (half of 6%)?

Answer: The answer to the question should be no. This is because when the listing broker offers to pay a selling broker a specific commission amount and the selling broker accepts the offer of the listing broker by producing a buyer ready, willing and able to purchase the property, a contract is created which should be capable of being enforced. Because the listing agreement specifically makes cooperating brokers third-party beneficiaries to the listing agreement, the selling broker should be able to sue the seller for breaching the listing agreement, even though the selling broker is not a party to that contract.

§ 19.8.3.4 The GAR Contract

The GAR Contract provides that a defaulting buyer or seller that does not have a brokerage engagement agreement with the broker, shall be responsible for the payment of a commission as liquidated damages to every broker involved in the transaction. The broker will be entitled to an amount equal to the share of commission the broker would have received if the transaction closed. Any written offer(s) of compensation or other written agreements establishing a broker's commission are incorporated by reference into the GAR Contract for the purposes of determining the amount of liquidated damages owed to the broker. However, if the broker has a brokerage agreement or other written agreement for the payment of a commission with a defaulting party, the broker's remedies will be provided according to such agreement.[2229]

§ 19.9 MAKING SMART CHOICES ABOUT AGENCY

Prior to the adoption of BRRETA in 1994, agency was relatively easy to understand. For the most part, all brokers represented sellers and practiced sub-agency when working with other brokerage firms. The introduction of buyer brokerage changed all of that. Suddenly brokers were representing buyers, sellers, buyers and sellers at the same time in the same transaction, and various other combinations. Most brokers have learned the different types of agency relationships which they can offer. If there has been confusion it has tended to be in learning how to choose the right agency relationship for different situations. This section will discuss an approach on how to make smart choices when it comes to agency.

§ 19.9.1 Rule #1. Only Offer Agency To A Party If You Do Not Already Have A Client In The Transaction

Many real estate brokers were incorrectly taught that they had to explain and offer agency at the first meaningful opportunity to all prospective clients and customers. In fact, the agency relationships offered by a real estate brokerage firm only have to be explained prior to entering into a client relationship. If agency is offered or explained to every party with whom the broker comes into contact, the effect is that the broker will needlessly end up acting in the high risk role of dual agent far more often than is wise. This is because most buyers, once they understand that being represented does not necessarily mean they have to pay a commission, will choose to be represented. Single-agent dual agency is the agency relationship with the greatest risk and should be avoided wherever possible. Following the above rule will help avoid this problem.

For example, a buyer walks into an open house on a Sunday afternoon, should the listing agent offer or explain agency to the buyer? The answer is no, because the broker already has a client in the transaction (*i.e.*, the seller). The same would be the case if an unrepresented buyer approaches a subdivision agent to see a new home. However, if the buyer walks into the broker's office on a Saturday morning and asks for the broker's help in buying a new home it is fine to offer the buyer agency because the broker does not have a client relationship with the owner of any specifically identified real estate.

Not offering agency does not mean the broker cannot work with or help buyer as a customer and perform ministerial acts on her behalf. The listing broker does not have to let a good customer slip away. Another example is if the broker meets an unrepresented buyer at an open house the broker is holding one afternoon. The broker does not offer agency to the buyer but instead treats the buyer as a customer. The buyer indicates that she is not interested in the listing. However, in speaking with her, it is obvious to the broker that she is a ready, willing and able buyer. Should the broker let this hot prospect slip through the cracks because she is not your client?

2229   GAR Form F20.

The answer to this question is clearly no. If the buyer is not interested in the listing, the listing agent should first determine if she has other listings which might meet the buyer's needs. If the listing agent has other suitable listings, the listing agent should offer to show the buyer those listings without offering or explaining agency to the customer. If the buyer rejects those listings, the broker should then offer to represent the buyer as a client in finding the buyer suitable property. By following this approach the listing agent should be able to avoid acting in a high risk single-agent dual agent capacity. This is because when the broker shows the buyer the listings of other brokerage firms, the broker will be acting as a buyer agent. When the broker shows the buyer the listings of other agents in her own brokerage firm, the broker should be acting in a designated agency capacity.

§ 19.9.2   Rule #2. Timely Disclose Who You Represent But Do Not Be Overly Legalistic

While real estate brokers are not required to offer or explain agency to everyone they meet, they are obligated to timely disclose to all parties in the transaction whom they are representing.[2230] This disclosure does not have to be made in an overly legalistic fashion. For example, if a buyer walks into a subdivision the listing broker can merely say something like the following: "Hello. Welcome to Tall Pines Subdivision. My name is _____. As you probably know, I've been hired by AAA Developers to sell these lovely homes. May I show them to you?"

If the broker makes an overly legalistic disclosure, it may lead the buyer to view the transaction the same way and heighten her concerns regarding the role of the listing broker.

§ 19.9.3   Rule #3. Practice Registration, Not Representation

The reason that most listing agents offer to represent buyers is to ensure that they get paid the entire commission in the transaction. While this motivation is understandable, it is not necessarily smart business because of the high risks associated with practicing single-agent dual agency. The better solution is to treat buyers as customers and register, rather than represent, them. In this way, the broker significantly increases the likelihood of being considered the procuring cause of the sale in the event a dispute arises over the commission at a later time.

Buyers are entitled to be represented by their own broker at any time they please. However, the listing broker is not obligated to share her commission with a selling broker unless the selling broker is the procuring cause of the sale. Listing brokers lose a significant portion of their real estate commissions by not preserving evidence that they, rather than another agent, were the procuring cause of the sale.

Questions of entitlement to a real estate commission are normally arbitrated at a Board of REALTORS® or litigated in court. Oftentimes, there is conflicting testimony by the listing broker, the selling broker and the buyer over when the selling broker first became involved with the buyer and the role of the selling broker in finding the buyer of the property. Such disputes may be quickly resolved if the listing broker has preserved the correct evidence regarding procuring cause.

Properly registering the buyer does not have to be done in a coldly technical fashion. Getting the buyer to answer in writing the following two basic questions is usually enough to protect the listing broker:

    (1) I am _____ or am not _____ working with another real estate agent or broker.

    (2) I found the property at _____ in the following
         way [check all of those which are applicable]:

        _____ a.   I saw the "For Sale" sign on the property.

        _____ b.   I saw an advertisement for the property in a newspaper or magazine.

        _____ c.   I found the property over the Internet.

2230   O.C.G.A. § 43-40-25(a)(31).

     _____ d.   A friend told me about the property.

     _____ e.   Another real estate agent or broker found or told me about the property.

By having buyers provide this information, listing brokers can better ensure that they are entitled to the entire commission when a buyer is not working with her own agent at the time the buyer first identifies the property.

§ 19.9.4   Rule #4. Avoid Transaction Brokerage

A real estate broker can only perform ministerial acts on behalf of a party when acting in a transaction brokerage capacity. This essentially means that the broker can be the "arms and legs of the parties, but not the brains." The problem with transaction brokerage is that most brokers have an extremely difficult time limiting their role to performing only ministerial acts. Real estate brokers by their nature want to help the people with whom they work. Giving advice is second nature to most real estate brokers. As a result, some real estate brokers who call themselves transaction brokers end up crossing the line and start to represent one party or another in the real estate transaction as a client. This arguably is an undisclosed agency relationship and can subject the broker to being sanctioned by the Georgia Real Estate Commission.[2231] This can also lead to uncertainty as to whether the broker is entitled to pursue a breach of contract claim for his commission.[2232]

§ 19.9.5   Rule #5. Avoid Dual Agency Whenever Possible

Dual agency is the highest risk form of agency because of the potential for the dual agent to find himself or herself in the middle of conflicts between buyers and sellers. What are the alternatives to dual agency? First, the agent can treat the buyer as a customer and not offer to represent her. Second, the agent can get the buyer to sign an agreement that the agent will represent the buyer as a client except in situations where the agent is showing the buyer her own listing. Third, to avoid dual agency, the agent can refer one client to another agent in her brokerage firm. In doing so, each agent would be acting in a designated agency capacity.

Many real estate agents are reluctant to refer a client to another agent in their brokerage firm for fear that they will then be obligated to pay the other agent the entire selling side of the commission. However, the amount of commission shared between the designated agents is a matter between the agents and their real estate broker and can be any amount agreed to between the parties. To avoid acting as a dual agent, the licensee could occasionally refer clients to another agent in her firm with the understanding that they would be paid only a nominal fee to represent the client and with the further understanding that the other agent would reciprocate and also occasionally refer clients to avoid being a dual agent. In this way, each agent should earn the same amount of commissions without having to act in a high risk, dual agency role.

2231   O.C.G.A. § 43-40-25(a)(31).

2232   *See* Chapter 13 (Real Estate Commissions).

CHAPTER 20

CONDOMINIUMS, HOMEOWNER ASSOCIATIONS AND OTHER FORMS OF COMMON INTEREST COMMUNITIES

OVERVIEW

This chapter discusses some of the more complex forms of property ownership involving common ownership or management of property. These include condominiums, homeowner associations, cooperatives and timeshares. These forms of property ownership are becoming increasingly complex and varied, especially with the growth of mixed-use developments. This chapter discusses the practical and legal issues relevant to different forms of property ownership, particularly to condominiums and homeowner associations.

§ 20.1 CONDOMINIUMS

§ 20.1.1 What Is A Condominium?

A condominium is a form of property ownership in which owners own their individual units in fee simple, together with an undivided (or shared) ownership interest in the common elements.[2233] The condominium form of ownership can exist in all types of housing, including single-family detached houses, town homes, mid-rise buildings, and high-rise buildings. However, it is best suited to dividing real property horizontally where the resulting units have both horizontal and vertical boundaries. The condominium form of ownership can also be applied to office and commercial space and to such facilities as parking lots, garages, marinas, and hotels. A condominium is normally created through the filing of a declaration of condominium in which property is submitted to a condominium regime. The common elements in a condominium typically include the grounds and recreational facilities for the common benefit of all owners, which they own jointly as tenants-in-common. Limited common elements are common elements that are reserved for the exclusive use of one or more, but less than all, of the units (*i.e.*, the balcony or patio attached to a unit). A more detailed discussion on common and limited elements is located in § 4.2 (Description of Condominium and Condominium Units).

§ 20.1.2 Creating A Condominium

New condominiums in Georgia must be created in accordance with the Georgia Condominium Act ("GCA").[2234] The GCA sets forth detailed requirements for the legal documents and disclosures required for the creation of a condominium. Condominiums are created by recording a declaration of condominium, a plat of survey, and floor plans in the land records in the county in which the property is located.[2235]

The declaration also includes the bylaws of the association. A condominium association must be incorporated, and may either be a non-profit or a for-profit corporation.[2236] Georgia law requires that all corporations file articles of incorporation with the Georgia Secretary of State. Additionally, all corporations must operate pursuant to a set of bylaws. The bylaws are not required to be recorded with the Secretary of State or with the county land records with the condominium declaration. However, it has become common practice for the developer to record the bylaws as an exhibit to the condominium declaration.

The declaration of condominium sets out details about the condominium, which include the metes and bounds legal description of the unit, the allocation of votes in the association, the sharing of maintenance costs, the maintenance responsibilities of the association and the unit owners, and the association's rights and restrictions.[2237] The declaration also contains numerous covenants which are binding on all owners. The covenants include the obligation to pay assessments to the association and use restrictions defining what the owners may or may not do at the condominium.

2233   O.C.G.A. § 44-3-71(4). Common elements are defined as all portions of the condominium other than the units.

2234   O.C.G.A. § 44-3-70, *et seq.*

2235   O.C.G.A. § 44-3-72.

2236   O.C.G.A. § 44-3-100(a).

2237   O.C.G.A. § 44-3-77 lists the information required for the declaration.

In a residential condominium, these use restrictions generally limit or regulate such things such as parking, pets, leasing, architectural changes to the exterior of units, buildings and grounds, and the extent to which the units can be used for conducting a business.

The declaration may contain other provisions, including granting the developer specific easement rights, procedures for amending the condominium documents, assigning and reassigning limited common elements, or reducing the size of or terminating the condominium.

§ 20.1.3   Disclosure Package

The Georgia Condominium Act requires that specific documents and disclosures (Disclosure Package) be provided to the first bona fide sale of each residential condominium unit for residential occupancy by the buyer, any member of the buyer's family, or any employee of the buyer.[2238] These requirements do not apply to subsequent sales, such as a resale condominium purchase and sale transaction. The documents required by the GCA include, but are not limited to, a copy of the floor plan, declaration, the articles of incorporation and bylaws of the association, a copy of every management, maintenance and other contract for the management and operation of the condominium, and the estimated or actual operating budget for the condominium. The documents must be contained in a bound, single package with an index sheet on the cover which lists each item required and shows that the item is attached or does not exist. The nature of disclosures made will change depending on the type of condominium unit being sold. For example, the disclosures in a unit that is part of a condominium conversion are different from the disclosures for a newly-constructed condominium unit.

The Georgia Condominium Act is silent on whether a buyer who was not given a current condominium disclosure package can rescind after they have closed on the purchase of their unit. However, it is likely that they can.

The seller may require a non-refundable deposit not in excess of $25 from the recipient of the Disclosure Package.[2239] That deposit must be applied to the purchase price in the event that the recipient purchases the unit. A dated written acknowledgment of receipt of all items required to be provided, executed by the recipient, is evidence that the items were delivered on the acknowledgment date.[2240]

A contract for the first initial sale to a person intending to occupy the same for residential purposes is referred to in the GCA is a "covered contract."[2241] Any covered contract is voidable by the buyer until at least seven days after the seller has furnished to the prospective buyer the documents required by the GCA. The seven-day period does not begin to run until the buyer has signed a contract and acknowledged in writing the receipt of the condominium sales contract. This requirement cannot be waived.[2242] However, the requirement only applies to persons of units who intend to occupy them for residential purposes. The right of rescission does not apply to persons who are purchasing for investment purposes. Within the text of the contract, the following information must be in boldface type or capital letters no smaller than the largest type in the text:

> THIS CONTRACT IS VOIDABLE BY PURCHASER UNTIL AT LEAST SEVEN (7) DAYS AFTER ALL OF THE ITEMS REQUIRED UNDER CODE SECTION 44-3-111 OF THE "GEORGIA CONDOMINIUM ACT," TO BE DELIVERED TO PURCHASER, HAVE BEEN RECEIVED BY PURCHASER. THE ITEMS SO REQUIRED ARE: (1) A FLOOR PLAN OF THE UNIT, (2) THE DECLARATION AND AMENDMENTS THERETO, (3) THE ASSOCIATION'S ARTICLES OF

2238   O.C.G.A. § 44-3-111.

2239   O.C.G.A. § 44-3-111.

2240   O.C.G.A. § 44-3-111(d).

2241   O.C.G.A. § 44-3-111(a).

2242   O.C.G.A. § 44-3-111(c)(1).

> INCORPORATION AND BYLAWS AND AMENDMENTS THERETO, (4) ANY
> GROUND LEASE, (5) ANY MANAGEMENT CONTRACT HAVING A TERM
> IN EXCESS OF ONE (1) YEAR, (6) THE ESTIMATED OR ACTUAL BUDGET
> FOR THE CONDOMINIUM, (7) ANY LEASE OF RECREATIONAL OR
> OTHER FACILITIES THAT WILL BE USED ONLY BY THE UNIT OWNERS,
> (8) ANY LEASE OF RECREATIONAL OR OTHER FACILITIES THAT WILL OR
> MAY BE USED BY THE UNIT OWNERS WITH OTHERS, (9) A STATEMENT
> SETTING FORTH THE EXTENT OF THE SELLER'S COMMITMENT TO
> BUILD OR SUBMIT ADDITIONAL UNITS, ADDITIONAL RECREATIONAL
> OR OTHER FACILITIES, OR ADDITIONAL PROPERTY, AND (10) IF THIS
> CONTRACT APPLIES TO A CONDOMINIUM UNIT WHICH IS PART OF
> A CONVERSION CONDOMINIUM, A STATEMENT DESCRIBING THE
> CONDITION OF CERTAIN COMPONENTS AND SYSTEMS, A STATEMENT
> REGARDING THE EXPECTED USEFUL LIFE OF CERTAIN COMPONENTS
> AND SYSTEMS, AND CERTAIN INFORMATION REGARDING ANY
> NOTICES OF VIOLATIONS OF COUNTY OR MUNICIPAL REGULATIONS.
> A DATED, WRITTEN ACKNOWLEDGEMENT OF RECEIPT OF ALL SAID
> ITEMS SIGNED BY PURCHASER SHALL BE PRIMA-FACIE EVIDENCE OF
> THE DATE OF DELIVERY OF SAID ITEMS.[2243]

A covered contract must also contain the following provision in boldface type or capital letters no smaller than the largest type on the first page of the contract:

> ORAL REPRESENTATIONS CANNOT BE RELIED UPON AS CORRECTLY
> STATING THE REPRESENTATIONS OF SELLER. FOR CORRECT
> REPRESENTATIONS, REFERENCE SHOULD BE MADE TO THIS
> CONTRACT AND THE DOCUMENTS REQUIRED BY CODE SECTION
> 44-3-111 OF THE "GEORGIA CONDOMINIUM ACT" TO BE FURNISHED
> BY A SELLER TO A BUYER.[2244]

If the covered contract applies to a condominium unit which includes a leasehold estate or estate for years in property such as a ground lease and if upon the expiration of such leasehold or estate, the unit will be deemed to have been withdrawn in accordance with the GCA or the condominium will be terminated, the contract shall contain the following text in boldface type or capital letters:

> THIS CONTRACT IS FOR THE TRANSFER OF A CONDOMINIUM
> UNIT SUBJECT TO A LEASE THAT EXPIRES [DATE], AND THE LESSEE'S
> INTEREST WILL TERMINATE UPON EXPIRATION OF THE LEASE.[2245]

If the covered contract applies to a condominium unit that is subject to a lien for rent payable under a lease of a recreational facility or common use facility, the contract shall contain the following text in boldface type or capital letters:

> THIS CONTRACT IS FOR THE TRANSFER OF A CONDOMINIUM UNIT
> THAT IS SUBJECT TO A LIEN FOR RENT PAYABLE UNDER A LEASE OF
> A RECREATIONAL FACILITY, AND FAILURE TO PAY THIS RENT MAY
> RESULT IN FORECLOSURE OF THE LIEN.[2246]

2243   O.C.G.A. § 44-3-111(c).

2244   O.C.G.A. § 44-3-111(e)(1).

2245   O.C.G.A. § 44-3-111(e)(3).

2246   O.C.G.A. § 44-3-111(e)(4).

It should be noted that long-term leases of recreational facilities in a condominium entered into between the condominium developer and the developer-controlled condominium association are uncommon because: (a) they have been attacked as being illegal tying arrangements in violation of the Sherman Antitrust Act, and (b) such contracts can be statutorily terminated by the condominium unit owners during the first year the unit owners take control of the condominium association from the developer in accordance with a procedure set forth in the Georgia Condominium Act.[2247]

If the condominium is in a jurisdiction which requires the issuance of a certificate of occupancy by any governmental entity, the covered contract must contain an express obligation by the seller to furnish the buyer at or prior to closing a true, correct, and complete copy of a certificate of occupancy covering the unit. In 2007, the Georgia legislature created an exception to this requirement. A seller is now not required to make the obligation to obtain a certificate of occupancy prior to closing if the buyer executes a separate agreement setting forth that the covered contract applies to a unit for which the seller is not obligated to obtain a certificate of occupancy and such agreement contains the following statement in at least 14-point boldface type or capital letters:

> THE SELLER IS NOT OBLIGATED TO OBTAIN A CERTIFICATE OF OCCUPANCY BEFORE CONVEYANCE OF THE UNIT TO THE BUYER. THE LACK OF A CERTIFICATE OF OCCUPANCY SHALL NOT EXCUSE THE BUYER FROM ANY OBLIGATION TO PAY ASSESSMENTS TO THE ASSOCIATION.

This provision is intended to permit a developer to sell a unit in shell condition to a buyer who desires to complete and finish the interior of the unit with the buyer's own contractors and designers. If a condominium unit is offered for sale before construction or remodeling of that unit is complete, the seller must make available to each buyer for inspection at a place convenient to the site, a copy of the existing plans or specifications for the construction or remodeling of that unit and of the improvements which will be part of the common elements.[2248]

§ 20.1.4 Advertising And Sales Brochure Requirements

The Georgia Condominium Act also imposes certain requirements on sellers with regard to the content of sales brochures and advertisements dealing with the first bona fide sale of a condominium unit. These requirements also do not apply to subsequent sales.[2249] Any sales brochure describing such a condominium unit must include a description and location of the recreational facilities proposed to be provided by the seller, the parking facilities, and other commonly used facilities together with a statement providing "which of the facilities will be owned by the unit owners as part of the common elements and which of the facilities will be owned by others; [and] with respect to each such facility, whether the seller will be obligated to complete the facility;" and limitations or conditions, if any, on the seller's obligation to complete the facilities.[2250]

On the inside front cover of a sales brochure or on the first page containing text in a sales brochure the following text must appear in boldface type or capital letters:

> ORAL REPRESENTATIONS CANNOT BE RELIED UPON AS CORRECTLY STATING REPRESENTATIONS OF THE SELLER. FOR CORRECT REPRESENTATIONS, REFERENCE SHOULD BE MADE TO THIS BROCHURE AND TO THE DOCUMENTS REQUIRED BY CODE SECTION 44 3 111 OF THE 'GEORGIA CONDOMINIUM ACT' TO BE FURNISHED BY THE SELLER TO A BUYER.[2251]

2247   O.C.G.A. § 44-3-101(b).

2248   O.C.G.A. § 44-3-111(f).

2249   O.C.G.A. § 44-3-111(a).

2250   O.C.G.A. § 44-3-111(g).

2251   O.C.G.A. § 44-3-111(g).

If the condominium unit or units are sold subject to a lease, then all written or printed advertising must contain the following statement in boldface type or capital letters:

> **THESE CONDOMINIUM UNITS WILL BE TRANSFERRED SUBJECT TO A LEASE.**[2252]

§ 20.1.5 Insurance In A Condominium

Unlike in a single-family home, the Georgia Condominium Act requires the condominium association to insure the structures constituting the condominium against certain kinds of insurable risks, including fire and extended coverage. The GCA was re-written in 2008 to more clearly define the nature of this obligation.[2253]

The new section requires condominium associations to carry fire and extended coverage insurance for the full insurable replacement cost, less deductibles, of all structures within the condominium. All common elements, limited common elements, foundations, roofs, roof structures and exterior walls (including windows, doors and framing therefore) must be insured, and all convertible space within the condominium, without reference to the actual boundaries of the condominium units.

Further, certain items must be insured by the condominium association regardless of who is responsible for their maintenance under the condominium documents, including the HVAC system serving a unit, and all sheetrock and plaster board comprising the walls and ceilings within a unit. Other items within a unit must also be insured "of the type and quality initially installed": floors and subfloors; wall, ceiling and floor coverings; plumbing and electrical lines and fixtures; built-in cabinetry and fixtures; and appliances used for refrigeration, cooking, dishwashing and laundry. If the unit is sold as an unfinished shell, these items are to be insured by the condominium unit owner rather than by the condominium association.

Finally, the condominium association must obtain a commercial general liability policy providing coverage for bodily injury and property damage in an amount not less than $1 million for a single occurrence and $2 million aggregate, covering the association, the board of directors, the officers of the association, all agents and employees of the association, and all unit owners and occupants with respect to claims arising out of use, ownership or maintenance of common elements.

This means that with condominium sales, the mortgage lender will be looking to the buyer to obtain a certificate of insurance from the condominium association confirming that the association has insurance in place on the condominium units in the event of fire or other casualty. This does not mean, however, that the unit owners should not purchase their own insurance. Instead, the insurance purchased by the owner normally covers the owner's personal property, improvements and betterments made to the unit which were not a part of how the unit was originally constructed, and insurable risks not covered under the master policy.

§ 20.1.6 Developer Control

Well-written condominium documents should try to balance the interests of individual owners and the interests of the condominium as a whole. The documents that attempt this balancing act are the declaration of condominium and the bylaws of the condominium association, which set forth an owner's rights and obligations as a member of the condominium community. The condominium association is the governing body that operates the condominium and enforces rules and restrictions designed to protect all unit owners.

2252   O.C.G.A. § 44-3-111(h).
2253   O.C.G.A. § 44-3-107.

§ 20.1.6.1   Members Of A Condominium Association

The members of a condominium association are all the unit owners. When a person buys a condominium unit, she automatically becomes a mandatory member of the association and is bound by the declaration of condominium, the articles of incorporation, bylaws, and other legal instruments of the association.[2254] The association works as a mini-government for the condominium and operates through an elected board of directors.

§ 20.1.6.2   Powers Of The Condominium Association

In order to carry out their duties condominium associations generally are given, by the condominium documents, a variety of quasi-governmental powers, including the power to tax unit owners in the form of annual and special assessments, adopt reasonable rules and regulations regarding use of the units and common elements, fine owners for violation of the covenants or rules or regulations of the association, institute legal action to enforce the obligations set forth in the legal documents, and approve changes or alterations to the exterior of units or to the common elements. It is not unusual for covenants contained in a set of condominium documents to regulate such things as parking, pets, leasing of units, architectural changes to the exterior of units, buildings, grounds, and the extent to which units may be used for conducting a business.

§ 20.1.6.3   What "Developer Control" Means And How Long It Continues

The developer, during the period in which she is developing the condominium, may reserve the right to control the operation of the association by being able to appoint or remove the directors and officers of the association. In most condominiums, the developer's right to control the association in this manner, however, cannot extend beyond any of the following dates:

(a) The date on which units to which eighty (80%) percent of the undivided ownership interest in the common elements pertain have been conveyed by the developer (unless the developer has an unexpired option to add additional property);[2255] or

(b) Three years after the recording of the declaration in the case of any other type of condominium.[2256]

In an expandable condominium, the developer's right to appoint and remove board members and officers cannot extend beyond either of the following:

(1) unless the developer still has the right to submit additional phases to the condominium, the date on which units to which eighty percent (80%) of the undivided interests in the common elements have been sold by the developer; or

(2) seven years after the recording of the declaration in the county land records.[2257]

By appointing the board members and directors, the developer exerts substantial control over the affairs of the association, including decisions relating to assessment amounts, the physical appearance and maintenance of the property, and enforcement of the association's rules and regulations against owners and occupants. However, there are legal restrictions to limit developers from abusing this authority. In carrying out their duties, the developer appointed-board members and officers are held to the same standard of conduct and duty of care as board members elected by the unit owners.

2254   O.C.G.A. § 44-3-100(a).

2255   O.C.G.A. § 44-3-101(a)(2).

2256   O.C.G.A. § 44-3-101(a)(3).

2257   O.C.G.A. § 44-3-101(a)(3).

Just like the developer-appointed board members are held to the same standard of conduct and duty of care as owner-elected board members, the developer-appointed board members have the same authority and latitude given to owner-elected board members. For instance, developer-appointed board members can determine how much association funds should be used for landscaping the front entrance to the community, even if the owners think the amount is too high and the decision is motivated by the developer's desire to create strong curb appeal.

The developer-appointed members and officers must discharge their duties in a manner they believe "in good faith to be in the best interest" of the association "[w]ith the care an ordinary prudent person in a like position would exercise under similar circumstances."[2258] This means that the developer-appointed board members and officers cannot act in a manner that unjustly favors the developer at the expense of the unit owners. For example, the developer-appointed board members cannot purchase supplies from a company affiliated with the developer at prices substantially above market price for such supplies. However, because it benefits the association, the developer-appointed board members can purchase supplies at a discounted price from a developer's affiliated company.

The GCA does not require that the developer appoint a minimum number of directors. A developer will often appoint a single person to serve as the association's sole director and officer. One reason for limiting the number of director appointed board members and offers is to reduce the number of persons who may be subjected to claims by disgruntled owners against the individual developer-appointed board members and officers.

§ 20.1.7 Remedies And Statutes Of Limitation

A buyer who pays anything of value toward the purchase of a condominium unit that is the first bona fide sale of the unit in reasonable reliance upon any false or misleading material or any statement published by or under the authority of the seller in advertising and promotional materials, including brochures and newspaper advertising, or who has not been given the information required to be furnished by law as listed above, is entitled to bring an action against the seller for damages.

This lawsuit must be brought prior to one year after the last of the following events: (1) closing of the transaction; (2) first issuance of a certificate of occupancy for the building containing the unit (or if no certificates of occupancy are issued, evidence of the date that lawful occupancy may first be allowed); (3) completion of the common elements and any recreational facilities, whether or not common elements, which the seller is obligated to complete or provide under the terms of the written contract for sale of the unit; (4) if the claim relates to the common elements and other portions of the condominium that are the responsibility of the association to maintain, the date upon which the declarant's right to control the association terminates under the GCA; or (5) if there is no written contract for the sale of the unit, the date of completion of the common elements and such recreational facilities the seller would be obligated to complete, whether or not the same are common elements.[2259] The outside limit for bringing a claim under this provision of state law is five years after the closing of the transaction.[2260]

The GCA also provides that a buyer who has a right of action for damages under the GCA also has the additional right to rescind any contract for the purchase of a unit at any time prior to the closing of the transaction.[2261] This right to rescind only applies to the first bona fide sale of a residential condominium unit[2262] and exists regardless of whether the right is included in the contract.[2263]

2258 O.C.G.A. § 14-2-830(1) -842(1).

2259 O.C.G.A. § 44-3-111(i).

2260 O.C.G.A. § 44-3-111(i).

2261 O.C.G.A. § 44-3-111(j).

2262 O.C.G.A. § 44-3-111(a).

2263 O.C.G.A. § 44-3-111(j).

§ 20.1.8   Conversion Condominiums

A condominium may be created from existing apartments or from new construction. Conversion condominiums are typically existing apartments or warehouses converted to the condominium form of ownership. The GCA defines a conversion condominium as "a condominium all or part of which may be used for residential purposes, which condominium contains any building… that… was occupied wholly or partially by persons other than persons who, at the time of the recording [of the condominium documents], had contractual rights to acquire one or more units within the condominium."[2264] In conversion condominiums, existing tenants are required to receive a notice of conversion at least 120 days before the tenant is required to vacate the apartment.[2265]

The GCA also requires that a sale offer first be made to each existing tenant for the initial 60 days of sales[2266] which sale offer must be made at least 120 days before the tenant is required to vacate the unit.[2267] If the tenants do not accept the sale offer presented to them during the first 60 days, they retain a right of first refusal to match any other contract accepted during the next 60 days.[2268]

The disclosure package for the first bona fide sale in a conversion condominium must include a statement describing the condition of certain components and systems, a statement regarding the expected useful life of certain components and systems, and certain information regarding any notices of violations of county or municipal regulations. The covered contract must also contain the following text in boldface type or capital letters:

> THIS CONTRACT APPLIES TO A CONDOMINIUM UNIT THAT IS PART
> OF A CONVERSION CONDOMINIUM.[2269]

§ 20.1.9   Expandable Condominiums

A developer has the right to develop a condominium in phases.[2270] In order to submit additional phases to the declaration of condominium, the initial declaration must explicitly reserve an option to expand the condominium and include a legal description by metes and bounds of the additional property which may be submitted.[2271] A developer's right to expand the condominium by adding additional phases cannot exceed seven years from the recording of the declaration except in very limited circumstances where unit owners other than the developer approve such expansion.[2272]

The disclosure package for the first bona fide sale in an expandable condominium must contain the following text in boldface type or capital letters:

> THIS CONTRACT APPLIES TO A CONDOMINIUM UNIT THAT IS PART
> OF AN EXPANDABLE CONDOMINIUM.[2273]

§ 20.1.10   Master Condominium

The Georgia Condominium Act now allows for both master and sub-condominiums.[2274] These are usually found in combination with one another in mixed use developments where each major use in a development may be a unit in

---

2264   O.C.G.A. § 44-3-71(10).

2265   O.C.G.A. § 44-3-87(a).

2266   O.C.G.A. § 44-3-87(b).

2267   O.C.G.A. § 44-3-87(a).

2268   O.C.G.A. § 44-3-87(b).

2269   O.C.G.A. § 44-3-111(e)(6).

2270   O.C.G.A. § 44-3-77(b).

2271   O.C.G.A. § 44-3-77(b)(1).

2272   O.C.G.A. § 44-3-77(b)(2).

2273   O.C.G.A. § 44-3-111(e)(2).

2274   O.C.G.A. § 44-3-71.

the master condominium, and may itself be a sub-condominium that is further divided into sub-units.

For example, the office, hotel, retail and multi-family residential components of a mixed use development may each be their own units in a master condominium association. These units may or may not additionally be part of a sub-condominium. If they are, then in effect there is a condominium within a condominium.

§ 20.1.11   Bank-Owned New Condominium Units

Many brand new, never previously sold bank-owned condominium units are now on the market for sale. A question which is increasingly being asked about such units is whether the bank must comply with the consumer protection requirements of the Georgia Condominium Act when selling these units. The answer to this question is yes.

Georgia law requires that consumers be given certain special protections in "the first bona fide sale of each residential condominium unit for residential occupancy by the buyer, any member of the buyer's family, or any employee of the buyer."[2275] Since these types of condominium units have not previously been sold, the disclosure and advertisement requirements, as well as the right to rescission apply to the sale of bank-owned condominium units. However, if the buyer is an investor (*i.e.*, the property is not being purchased for residential occupancy by the owner) the protections do not have to be given. The consumer protections apply to "any such sale regardless of whether the seller is the declarant, the association, or any other person."[2276]

Banks selling new condominium units should not simply use the condominium disclosure package prepared by the original developer or "declarant." The Georgia Condominium Act requires that the disclosure package be current. The foreclosure will often result in a new declarant and this must be reflected in the disclosure packet. The passage of time will normally result in the condominium association's budget being out of date. Additionally, if the bank merely banks out the original disclosure package, it runs the risk of being legally liable for any misstatements or out of date statements, of the original declarant. At a minimum, the bank should carefully review the condominium disclosure package which is being used to be certain it is current, accurate and complete.

§ 20.1.12   Resale Condominiums

The disclosure and advertisement requirements, as well as a buyer's right to rescind a condominium sale agreement do not apply to resale condominium transactions. These requirements only exist for the "first bona fide sale of each residential condominium residential for the occupancy by the buyer, any member of the buyer's family, or any employee of the buyer."[2277] What constitutes a "first bona fide sale" has been the subject of some debate over the years. Essentially, this language means that the requirements provided in O.C.G.A. § 44-3-111 only apply to new condominiums sold for residential purposes.

For example, let's assume that a buyer who is unrelated to the seller purchases a condominium unit, lives in it for two years, and then the unit is foreclosed on. The sale of this unit would be a resale condominium and would not be subject to the disclosure and advertisement requirements or the right of rescission afforded to a new condominium purchaser. On the other hand, if a construction lender forecloses on a group of unsold units in a condominium and then decides to sell them at auction, these units have not previously been sold, the lender/seller would be obligated to follow all the requirements for a new condominium sale.

Since condominium resales are a type of transaction sufficiently different from other condominium purchase and sale transactions, the Georgia Association of REALTORS® created the GAR Condominium Resale Purchase and

---

2275   O.C.G.A. § 44-3-111.

2276   O.C.G.A. § 44-3-111(a).

2277   O.C.G.A. § 44-3-111.

Sale Agreement.[2278] This agreement should not be used for the sale of new condominium units because the required disclosures under the GCA for the initial sale of a condominium unit are not included in this resale agreement.[2279] The GAR Condominium Resale Purchase and Sale Agreement[2280] is largely the same as the GAR Purchase and Sale Agreement[2281] except that some provisions are applicable to the unit including the common elements and other provisions are applicable to the unit excluding the owner's interest in the common elements.

§ 20.1.12.1   Common Expense Assessments

The GAR Condominium Resale Purchase and Sale Agreement provides that condominium assessments will be prorated as of the date of closing and includes a blank line where any required capital reserve contribution is disclosed. Any required contribution to the working capital or reserve fund will be paid by the buyer to the condominium association or to the seller for reimbursement of any previous contributions made by the seller. After the closing, the buyer agrees to pay all common expenses assessed against the unit.

§ 20.1.12.2   Property Condition

The GAR Condominium Resale Purchase and Sale Agreement provides that the unit (excluding the common elements of the condominium) will be in the same condition on the date of closing as on the Binding Agreement Date.[2282] This provision was limited to the unit (excluding the common elements) because if the entire condominium complex had to be in the same condition on the date of closing as on the binding agreement date it would give too many buyers an opportunity to avoid their contractual obligations due to circumstances beyond the control of the individual condominium owner selling her unit. Otherwise, every time the condominium association altered or changed the common elements after the binding agreement date, the buyer could terminate the agreement arguing that the common elements were no longer the same as on the binding agreement date.

§ 20.1.12.3   Common Elements Sold "As Is"

In the GAR Condominium Resale Purchase and Sale Agreement, the common elements, including any limited elements assigned to the unit, are sold "as is" with all faults, including but not limited to lead-based paint, lead-based paint hazards and damage from termites and other wood-destroying organisms. This is because (as stated in the agreement) the seller cannot normally repair and/or replace defects in the common elements of the condominium. Instead the common elements are normally maintained by the condominium association, which presumably will have some ongoing program for maintaining and repairing the common elements. If the condominium unit is being sold subject to a traditional right to request repairs, the buyer may only ask for the repair of defects in the unit itself rather than in the common elements.

§ 20.1.12.4   Copies Of Condominium Legal And Financial Documents

Resale sellers of condominium units are not legally required to provide potential purchasers with a Disclosure Package as is required under the GCA in the sale of new condominium units.[2283] Therefore, real estate brokers representing buyers should ensure that the buyer receives a copy of the association's legal instruments and financial documents prior to entering into a sales agreement. Otherwise, the buyer's real estate broker should condition the agreement upon receipt and approval of such documents.

2278   GAR Form F33.

2279   *See* Chapter 20 (Condominiums, Homeowner Associations and Other Forms of Common Interest Communities) for a more complete discussion of the nature of condominiums, and the purchase and sale of new condominium units.

2280   GAR Form F33.

2281   GAR Form F20.

2282   GAR Form F33.

2283   *See* § 20.1.3 (Disclosure Package).

The buyer's broker should take care to craft a special stipulation that requires the seller (and not the community association) to provide such legal documents because the buyer cannot enforce a special stipulation against the association, as the association is not a party to the sales agreement. To protect the buyer, the real estate broker should consider the following provision.

Special Stipulation 346:   Condominium documents to be provided by Seller

Seller shall provide Buyer with copies of all legal and general financial documents for _____ Condominium Association, Inc.(including but not limited to the declaration, bylaws, articles of incorporation, budget, profit and loss statement, rules and regulations, and all amendments to these documents) within _____ days of the Binding Agreement Date. Buyer may terminate this Agreement and receive back all earnest money paid to Seller within _____ days of the Binding Agreement Date upon notice to Seller if Seller does not provide all such documents to Buyer, or if Buyer does not find such documents satisfactory for any reason.

§ 20.2   HOMEOWNER ASSOCIATIONS

§ 20.2.1   What Is A Homeowner Association?

In a homeowner association (HOA), the owner holds title to her lot, which means that she owns the land beneath and typically around the building. All lot owners are normally automatic members of the HOA. There are common areas typically owned by the homeowner association, such as recreational amenities, greenbelts, and entrance facilities. Ownership of the common areas by the HOA differs from a condominium where the common areas are owned by the collective unit owners as tenants in common.

HOAs are commonly found in a townhouse development or a single-family detached development. A townhome development is comprised of attached dwellings, commonly referred to as the "fee-simple townhome." However, the term is misleading as it is often interpreted to mean a townhome which is not part of a mandatory membership homeowner association. Legally, the term fee-simple refers to a freehold interest, as opposed to a leasehold interest.

Each lot owner normally has an easement to use and enjoy common areas for as long as she owns the property.

§ 20.2.2   Creating A Homeowner Association

A homeowner association and the use and other restrictions on land in the respective subdivision are created by filing a declaration of covenants, often similar in length and scope to a declaration of condominium. However, the restrictive covenants and HOAs are not "creatures of statute" as are condominium restrictions and associations. Rather, the structure and organization of HOAs have developed over time according to the common law of real property. Hence there are substantially fewer procedural requirements for the forming of an HOA, or for imposing restrictive covenants (CC&Rs) on real property.

Homeowner associations are typically formed as non-profit corporations. The association is usually responsible for maintaining the common areas and operates through an elected board of directors.

§ 20.2.2.1   Homeowner Associations Created Under The Georgia Property Owners' Association Act

As of July 1, 1994, a homeowner association may (but is not required to) be created under or submit to a statutory scheme of development known as the Georgia Property Owners' Association Act ("POA").[2284] The Act applies to all

---

2284   O.C.G.A. § 44-3-220, *et seq.*

properties created under or submitted to the POA.[2285] Homeowners associations created under or submitted to the POA have collection and enforcement powers similar to those in condominiums and have a statutory automatic lien for unpaid assessments.[2286] Overall, the Act provides a comprehensive set of rules for the governance of property owner associations, including but not limited to, the assessment of expenses and liability for unpaid assessments,[2287] the powers and duties of the association,[2288] and a statutory method for imposing liens against property owners for unpaid assessments.[2289]

Under the POA, a developer may create a property owners development by recording a declaration of covenants, conditions, and restrictions expressly subjecting the property to the POA.[2290] If the property was not originally submitted to the POA, the owners in the community may subject the community to the terms of the POA by amending their declaration according to the amendment procedure set forth in such declaration.[2291] Covenants in an instrument submitted to the POA continue for perpetual duration unless terminated by agreement of the lot owners.[2292]

Property owners who are subjected to the POA must comply with all the rules and regulations contained in the Act.[2293] Failure to do so will subject the property owner to injunctions for prohibited activities or uses, or any other remedy available in law or equity.[2294] Homeowners associations under the POA may also impose and assess fines, temporarily suspend voting rights and restrict the home owner's use of certain common areas within the community.[2295] However, regardless of the measures a homeowners association created under the POA may use to enforce any recorded covenants, the HOA may not deny any property owner or occupant's access to the owner's property.[2296]

§ 20.2.2.2   Common Law Homeowner Associations

Homeowners associations that are not formed under the POA may also restrict a property owner's use of her property.[2297] These homeowners associations are often referred to as "common law HOAs." Common law HOAs are formed by recording a declaration of covenants with the appropriate county when the development is created.[2298] A developer is required to record a declaration of covenants at the time the community is developed.[2299]

Common law homeowners associations may choose to have mandatory or voluntary membership. However, most HOAs have mandatory membership. As such, once the covenants are recorded, any buyer who purchases property in a neighborhood governed by a recorded declaration is bound by all the obligations and restrictions contained therein.[2300] Moreover, since the recorded covenants run with the title to the land,[2301] any subsequent buyer is also bound by the covenants.[2302] Regardless of whether or not an owner receives a copy of the declaration of covenants when the property

---

2285   O.C.G.A. § 44-3-222.

2286   O.C.G.A. § 44-3-109 and O.C.G.A. § 44-3-232. Since the lien is automatic, it does not have to be recorded in the county land records. Title examiners in addition to doing their normal search of the land records must also check with the association to determine the existence of any automatic liens.

2287   O.C.G.A. § 44-3-232.

2288   O.C.G.A. § 44-3-231.

2289   O.C.G.A. § 44-3-232.

2290   O.C.G.A. § 44-3-222.

2291   O.C.G.A. § 44-3-226.

2292   O.C.G.A. § 44-5-60 and O.C.G.A. § 44-3 234.

2293   O.C.G.A. § 44-3-223.

2294   O.C.G.A. § 44-3-223.

2295   O.C.G.A. § 44-3-223.

2296   O.C.G.A. § 44-3-223.

2297   *Godley Park Homeowners Ass'n, Inc. v. Bowen*, 286 Ga.App. 21, 649 S.E.2d 308 (2007).

2298   O.C.G.A. § 44-3-222

2299   O.C.G.A. § 44-3-222.

2300   *County Greens Village One Owner's Ass'n, Inc. v. Meyers*, 158 Ga.App. 609, 281 S.E.2d 346 (1981).

2301   *Godley Park Homeowners Ass'n, Inc. v. Bowen*, 286 Ga.App. 21, 649 S.E.2d 308 (2007).

2302   *King v. Baker*, 214 Ga.App. 229, 447 S.E.2d 129 (1994).

is purchased or is merely unaware of their existence, the owner is considered to have legal notice because the covenants are recorded.[2303]

A property owner's failure to comply with the restrictions contained in the recorded declaration will be subject to liability by the homeowners association. Oftentimes, homeowner's associations ensure a property owners adherence by assessing monetary fines and filing liens on the property if the covenants are not followed.

§ 20.2.3 Restrictive Covenants

Although a property owner has the right to use her property for any lawful purpose,[2304] a property owner's use of a property may be restricted if a recorded declaration of covenants exist.[2305] However, the restrictions contained in the declaration must be clearly established.[2306] Any ambiguity in the application of the covenant restricting the home owner's use will be construed against the HOA.[2307]

Generally, covenants imposed by homeowners associations restricting a property owner's use will be upheld. In Georgia, it is well established that two parties may contract away or extend the rights regarding the use of real property, as long as public policy is not violated.[2308] As such, courts are reluctant to hold restrictive covenants void for violating public policy unless the violation is clearly against the public interest.[2309] Since there is a presumption in favor of restrictive covenants, buyers looking to purchase property in a neighborhood governed by a recorded declaration should be aware of potential use restrictions.

Oftentimes, the focus of most covenants contained in recorded declarations is to create a community with minimal conflict and prohibit objectionable uses of the properties located within the neighborhood. The type of covenants that frequently appear in recorded declarations include limitations on pets or certain dog breeds, restrictions prohibiting residents from playing loud music or drinking alcohol at the community pool, or restrictions prohibiting residents from using their property for business purposes.

§ 20.2.3.1 Homeowners Association Ability To Restrict Use Of Signs

Generally, by accepting the deed to a property governed by a recorded declaration, the home owner accepts and is bound by all of the covenants contained therein.[2310] This includes the common, yet controversial, restriction prohibiting a homeowner from placing signs on her property without the permission of the HOA.

A homeowners association may limit a property owner's ability to place a "For Sale" sign in her front yard unless prior written consent from the HOA is obtained.[2311] As stated above, once the restriction is recorded, an owner will be bound so long as public policy is not clearly violated.[2312]

In one case, a homeowner bought a property in a neighborhood regulated by a recorded declaration of covenants. The declaration prohibited any owner from placing a "For Sale" sign in the front yard of a property without first obtaining the prior written consent of the architectural review committee. One owner wanted to sell his property, so he hired a real estate agent and placed the property on the market. Without obtaining the required consent from the committee,

2303 *King v. Baker*, 214 Ga.App. 229, 447 S.E.2d 129 (1994).

2304 *Licker v. Harkleroad*, 252 Ga.App. 872, 558 S.E.2d 31 (2001).

2305 *Godley Park Homeowners Ass'n, Inc. v. Bowen*, 286 Ga.App. 21, 649 S.E.2d 308 (2007).

2306 *Licker v. Harkleroad*, 252 Ga.App. 872, 558 S.E.2d 31 (2001).

2307 *Licker v. Harkleroad*, 252 Ga.App. 872, 558 S.E.2d 31 (2001).

2308 *Godley Park Homeowners Ass'n, Inc. v. Bowen*, 286 Ga.App. 21, 649 S.E.2d 308 (2007).

2309 *Universal Mgmt. Concepts v. Noferi*, 270 Ga.App. 212, 605 S.E.2d 899 (2004).

2310 *Bryan v. MBC Partners, L.P.*, 246 Ga.App. 549, 541 S.E.2d 124 (2000).

2311 *Godley Park Homeowners Ass'n, Inc. v. Bowen*, 286 Ga.App. 21, 649 S.E.2d 308 (2007).

2312 *Godley Park Homeowners Ass'n, Inc. v. Bowen*, 286 Ga.App. 21, 649 S.E.2d 308 (2007).

the owner and his real estate agent placed a "For Sale" sign in the front yard. Shortly thereafter, the HOA demanded that the sign be removed because the proper consent was not obtained. When the owner refused, the HOA filed an injunction. The owner argued that the covenant restricted his ability to sell his property; therefore, the restriction was a restraint on trade contrary to public policy and thus unenforceable. The court disagreed, holding that since the covenant did not directly prohibit the owner from selling his property, the restriction was not a restraint on trade.[2313] The covenant merely required the prior written consent of the architectural review committee before the "For Sale" sign could be placed in the owner's front yard. Therefore, the HOA's restriction was upheld because it was not clearly against public policy.[2314]

This type of restriction typically makes it harder for an owner to sell a property since most buyers don't know whether a house is for sale without a "For Sale" sign in the front yard. The current real estate market has also intensified this struggle between owners and their HOAs. For instance, multiple property owners may want to sell their properties in a neighborhood but the HOA may want to restrict the placement of "For Sale" signs in the yards to keep the neighborhood from looking distressed. As illustrated by the case above, homeowners associations have a large amount of discretion when enacting covenants that restrict a homeowner's use of her property.

A homeowners association can also restrict the placement of other types of signs in a homeowner's yard.[2315] In this case, a home owner bought a vacant lot from a developer in a neighborhood regulated by a recorded declaration of covenants. The declaration contained a restriction prohibiting owners from placing any signs on their lots without the prior written permission of the architectural control committee. The owner hired a builder affiliated with the development to complete certain repairs to his home. When the work was complete, the owner was dissatisfied so he hung a sign from the front of his house, approximately seven feet by three feet, reading, "Before You Buy a Home in Here, PLEASE See US." The owner did not obtain the written consent of the committee before the sign was placed in his front yard. The HOA demanded that the sign be removed but the owner refused. In response, the HOA filed a temporary injunction. The homeowner argued that the restriction was contrary to public policy because it violated his right to free speech. The court disagreed holding that the homeowner waived his constitutional rights to place a sign on his property in this manner when he accepted the deed containing this restrictive covenant.[2316]

The notion that owners can be required to give up a certain amounts of freedom for the benefit of the community as a whole is widely accepted in the Georgia courts. Therefore, when a property owner purchases property in a neighborhood regulated by a recorded declaration, the owner should exercise caution and pay particular attention to any restrictions limiting the use of a property.

§ 20.2.4 Waiver Of Compliance

Generally, a homeowners association may file suit against a property owner for a breach of covenant or for an owner's failure to pay assessments or fines required in a recorded declaration. However, if a homeowners association fails to enforce a violation of a recorded declaration within the time allocated by the statute of limitations, the HOA will lose its ability to enforce the covenant.[2317] The statute of limitation barring a homeowners association's action is different depending on the alleged violation.

2313   *Godley Park Homeowners Ass'n, Inc. v. Bowen*, 286 Ga.App. 21, 649 S.E.2d 308 (2007).

2314   *Godley Park Homeowners Ass'n, Inc. v. Bowen*, 286 Ga.App. 21, 649 S.E.2d 308 (2007).

2315   *Bryan v. MBC Partners, L.P.*, 246 Ga.App. 549, 541 S.E.2d 124 (2000).

2316   *Bryan v. MBC Partners, L.P.*, 246 Ga.App. 549, 541 S.E.2d 124 (2000).

2317   O.C.G.A. § 9-3-29(a).

§ 20.2.4.1   Claims For Breach Of Covenant

If an owner breaches a covenant contained in a recorded declaration, the HOA must file suit for enforcement within two (2) years of the violation.[2318] Once the statute of limitations has passed, however, the HOA will be deemed to have waived its right to enforcement and cannot demand that the owner stop violating the covenant.[2319]

The time period for the statute of limitations begins to run immediately upon the home owner's violation.[2320] A mere threat to breach a covenant contained in the declaration will not form the proper basis to start this two year time period.[2321] In addition, the homeowners association must have knowledge of the violation.[2322] The HOA will not be deemed to have waived their right to enforce a covenant unless they had knowledge of the owner's breach.[2323] Generally, most homeowners associations have knowledge of a breach by complaints of an alleged violation by other home owners in the community.[2324] Therefore, a waiver could occur if the HOA received complaints of a violation from other home owners but did nothing in response to correct the violation for a period of two years or more.[2325]

Generally, once the homeowners' association has knowledge of an owner's violation, the HOA will issue a fine, demand letter, injunction or other similar tool to enforce the restrictive covenant.[2326] A HOA will not be deemed to have waived its right to enforce a violation so long as some action is taken to correct the owner's breach. For example, in one case, a recorded declaration of covenants contained a restriction prohibiting owners from constructing above-ground swimming pools on their properties without the written authorization of the architectural review committee.[2327] Despite the restriction, a home owner built an above-ground swimming pool in his back yard without the required authorization. When the HOA found out that the home owner was in violation of the covenant, three demand letters were issued requesting the removal of the pool. The owner refused and when the HOA brought suit, the owner argued that the HOA's claim was barred because it was not filed until two years after the violation occurred.[2328] The court rejected this argument because the HOA issued enforcement letters demanding the home owner's correction of his violation.[2329]

§ 20.2.4.2   Claims For Unpaid Assessments Or Fees

The statute of limitations for a claim alleging a home owner's failure to pay assessments or fines is longer than the allocated time for a general violation of a recorded declaration.[2330] If the home owner's violation is for her failure to pay assessments or fees required by the recorded declaration, the homeowners' association has four (4) years to file suit, rather than two years.[2331] If the HOA fails to enforce an owner's violation within that four year time limit, the HOA will be barred from enforcing the restriction.[2332]

2318   O.C.G.A. § 9-3-29(a).

2319   *Glisson v. IRHA of Loganville, Inc.*, 289 Ga.App. 311, 656 S.E.2d 924 (2008).

2320   O.C.G.A. § 9-3-29(c); *Lesser v. Doughtie*, 300 Ga.App. 805, 686 S.E.2d 416 (2009).

2321   *Lesser v. Doughtie*, 300 Ga.App. 805, 686 S.E.2d 416 (2009).

2322   *Devins v. Leafmore Forest Condominium Ass'n of Owners*, 200 Ga.App. 158, 407 S.E.2d 76 (1991).

2323   *Devins v. Leafmore Forest Condominium Ass'n of Owners*, 200 Ga.App. 158, 407 S.E.2d 76 (1991).

2324   *Glisson v. IRHA of Loganville, Inc.*, 289 Ga.App. 311, 656 S.E.2d 924 (2008).

2325   *Glisson v. IRHA of Loganville, Inc.*, 289 Ga.App. 311, 656 S.E.2d 924 (2008).

2326   *Hech v. Summit Oaks Owners Ass'n, Inc.*, 275 Ga.App. 265, 620 S.E.2d 490 (2005).

2327   *Hech v. Summit Oaks Owners Ass'n, Inc.*, 275 Ga.App. 265, 620 S.E.2d 490 (2005).

2328   *Hech v. Summit Oaks Owners Ass'n, Inc.*, 275 Ga.App. 265, 620 S.E.2d 490 (2005).

2329   *Hech v. Summit Oaks Owners Ass'n, Inc.*, 275 Ga.App. 265, 620 S.E.2d 490 (2005).

2330   O.C.G.A. § 9-3-29(b).

2331   O.C.G.A. § 9-3-29(b).

2332   *Heard v. Whitehall Forest East Homeowners Ass'n, Inc.*, 230 Ga.App. 61, 495 S.E.2d 318 (1997).

However, this four (4) year statute of limitation does not apply to all assessment covenants.[2333] Older communities with homeowners associations may still be bound to the two year statute of limitation requirement even if the violation concerns assessments or fines.[2334] In 1995, the Official Code of Georgia extended the two year statute of limitation for breach of covenant actions to four years if the actions resulted from a home owner's failure to pay assessments or fines.[2335] When enacted, the legislature intended to apply this new limitation prospectively.[2336] Therefore, any breach of covenant claim by a HOA, including claims for assessments, accruing before July 1, 1995 would still be bound to the two year statute of limitation to bar enforcement.[2337] Any claim for assessments accruing after that date would apply the new four year statute of limitations.[2338] Today, however, it is unlikely that this distinction in the application of the statute would cause issues since the statute was changed over a decade ago. However, it is important to recognize that if a HOA failed to enforce an owner's violation of an assessment covenant prior to July 1, 1995, the shorter two-year statute of limitation would apply to any attempted enforcement.[2339]

§ 20.2.5   Amending Declaration Of Covenants After Buyer Purchases Property

In Georgia, once a home owner accepts the deed to a property regulated by the CC&Rs of a homeowners association, the owner accepts and is bound by the covenants contained in the declaration.[2340] However, even if a buyer concludes that the covenants are acceptable at the time she purchases the property, there is no guarantee that the covenants will not change during the course of ownership. In fact, most declarations include an amendment procedure that allows the members of the community to change the covenants in the future to address new issues and meet changing conditions. Under both the Georgia Condominium Act[2341] and the Georgia Property Owners' Association Act,[2342] the owners holding at least two-thirds of the votes of the total association membership may amend the covenants contained in the recorded declaration. Consequently, when a property owner is bound to either of the above-mentioned Acts, it is not possible to include a provision in the purchase agreement limiting amendments.

Homeowners associations that are not bound by either the Georgia Condominium Act or the Georgia Property Owner's Association Act must obtain the approval of all the property owners for an amendment absent a provision in the declaration stating otherwise. More specifically, an amendment that prohibits or materially restricts the use of, occupancy of, or behavior within, individually owned lots within the community, or an amendment which changes the basis for allocating voting rights or assessments among community members, requires the unanimous approval of all property owners within the community.[2343] However, a declaration of covenants may expressly provide for less than a unanimous vote for any amendments after the initial declaration is recorded.[2344] If the declaration contains an amendment provision, all owners within the community are governed by the amendment procedures contained therein.[2345]

2333   *Heard v. Whitehall Forest East Homeowners Ass'n, Inc.*, 230 Ga.App. 61, 495 S.E.2d 318 (1997).

2334   *Heard v. Whitehall Forest East Homeowners Ass'n, Inc.*, 230 Ga.App. 61, 495 S.E.2d 318 (1997).

2335   *Heard v. Whitehall Forest East Homeowners Ass'n, Inc.*, 230 Ga.App. 61, 495 S.E.2d 318 (1997).

2336   *Heard v. Whitehall Forest East Homeowners Ass'n, Inc.*, 230 Ga.App. 61, 495 S.E.2d 318 (1997).

2337   *Heard v. Whitehall Forest East Homeowners Ass'n, Inc.*, 230 Ga.App. 61, 495 S.E.2d 318 (1997).

2338   *Heard v. Whitehall Forest East Homeowners Ass'n, Inc.*, 230 Ga.App. 61, 495 S.E.2d 318 (1997).

2339   *Heard v. Whitehall Forest East Homeowners Ass'n, Inc.*, 230 Ga.App. 61, 495 S.E.2d 318 (1997).

2340   *Bryan v. MBC Partners, L.P.*, 246 Ga.App. 549, 541 S.E.2d 124 (2000).

2341   O.C.G.A. § 44-3-93.

2342   O.C.G.A. § 44-3-226.

2343   *Brockway v. Harkleroad*, 273 Ga.App. 339, 615 S.E.2d 182 (2005).

2344   *Brockway v. Harkleroad*, 273 Ga.App. 339, 615 S.E.2d 182 (2005).

2345   *Brockway v. Harkleroad*, 273 Ga.App. 339, 615 S.E.2d 182 (2005).

Any amendment of a covenant may not impose a greater restriction on the use or development of the land unless the owner of the affected property agrees in writing at the time the change is made.[2346] Without the affected property owner's consent, any amendment imposing a greater restriction on her use of the property is void.[2347]

This requirement was recently interpreted by the Georgia Court of Appeals. In this case, the property owner purchased a home in a neighborhood governed by a recorded declaration of covenants. When she purchased the property, the applicable covenant provided that property owners within the community may lease their property for residential purposes. As such, the property owner leased her residence to four (4) college students. While her property was still being leased, the HOA amended the declaration to prohibit any owner from leasing their property, unless the owner is a "grandfathered owner" or the owner who is not a "grandfathered owner" has received a hardship permit from the board. The property owner was not a "grandfathered owner" and did not obtain a hardship permit but continued to lease her property. As a result, the HOA assessed several fines for violating the covenant. The owner brought suit against the HOA arguing that the amendment imposed a greater restriction on her use of the property which she did not consent to and thus, the amendment was void. In response, the HOA argued that the amendment does not impose a greater restriction on the land; rather, it merely imposed an occupancy restriction. The court disagreed with the HOA and held that the amendment prohibited a specific use of the property (residential leasing), which was within the owner's rights when she purchased the property. Therefore, without her consent, the amendment was inapplicable and void.[2348]

Buyers should be aware that amendments can affect fundamental property rights. Prior to the Fair Housing Amendments Act of 1988[2349] (which limited all-adult communities except in certain circumstances), the Georgia Supreme Court upheld the right of the members of a condominium association with a recorded declaration to amend the declaration to restrict the age of occupants.[2350] In that case, a man rented an apartment advertised as an adult only community. When the apartments were converted to condominiums, he bought a unit there. Subsequently, the association voted to restrict residents to persons over the age of 16 years. A few years, later his wife gave birth to a child. The court upheld the amendment to the condominium covenants, and prohibited the child from living in the community.

Buyers should also be wary of amendment procedures requiring either the consent of the developer for so long as the developer owns any property in the subdivision, or the approval of a very high percentage of the owners. Such provisions can make it difficult to pass needed changes to the declaration in the future. Buyers should also confirm that the covenants contain an amendment procedure. Otherwise, the likelihood is that the covenants can be amended only by a vote of all the owners, making it almost impossible to update the covenants in the future.

§ 20.2.5.1 Requirement For Uniformity

A buyer who purchases property in a community governed by a recorded declaration expects that the restrictions will be applied to everyone living within that community. As such, when buyers purchase property in this type of community, each buyer obtains a protected interest in the uniform scheme set forth in the declarations.[2351] In other words, each buyer has an interest in the HOA applying the restrictions equally to all residents.

Any amendment that is inconsistent with that uniform scheme may impair the protected interests of the owners who do not consent to that amendment, even if the amendment is enacted in accordance with the procedures set forth in the declaration.[2352] Therefore, unless there is a provision stating otherwise, amendments imposing different restrictions

---

2346   O.C.GA. § 44-5-60.

2347   *Charter Club on River Home Owners Ass'n v. Walker*, 301 Ga.App. 898, 689 S.E.2d 344 (2009).

2348   *Charter Club on River Home Owners Ass'n v. Walker*, 301 Ga.App. 898, 689 S.E.2d 344 (2009).

2349   42 U.S.C.A. 3601, *et seq.*

2350   *Hill v. Fontaine Condominium Ass'n, Inc.*, 255 Ga. 24, 334 S.E.2d 690 (1985).

2351   *Brockway v. Harkleroad*, 273 Ga.App. 339, 615 S.E.2d 182 (2005).

2352   *Brockway v. Harkleroad*, 273 Ga.App. 339, 615 S.E.2d 182 (2005).

on owners in the same community will not be enforceable unless the approval of the owners whose interests would be adversely affected is obtained.[2353] In other words, if an amendment removes a restrictive covenant from only a couple property owners, instead of all the owners in the community, that amendment will not be valid without the consent of the owners who are still adversely affected by the restriction.[2354]

For example, a buyer purchases property in a community governed by a recorded declaration of covenants. The declaration provides that any restrictions may be amended with ninety percent (90%) vote of the property owners. Ninety percent (90%) of the property owners attempted to amend a restrictive covenant that required only residential use of the properties within the community. The proposed amendment would allow the voting property owners' to use their properties for commercial purposes, while the remaining property owners could continue to use their properties for residential use. Ten property owners disagreed with the amendments and thus would not give their approval. The voting property owners argued that since the declaration required ninety percent (90%) approval and ninety percent (90%) of the owners approved, the amendment was valid. However, the court disagreed, holding that since the amendment did not have a uniform application to all properties within the community, the approval of the dissenting property owners was required.[2355] As such, since this approval was not obtained, the amendment is void and unenforceable.[2356]

However, if the declaration expressly provides that nonuniform amendments may be enacted, such amendments will be valid so long as they are enacted according to the procedures in the declaration.[2357] If the declaration expressly puts owners on notice that nonuniform amendments may be enacted, the court will generally uphold those amendments.[2358] Therefore, it is important for buyers purchasing property in this type of community to pay particular attention to the amendment provisions contained in a recorded declaration of covenants.

§ 20.2.6 Rules and Regulations Enacted Without Voting

While the declaration of covenants is viewed as a community's constitution, the rules and regulations are created to address the day-to-day issues that often arise in the community. Oftentimes, rules and regulations are implemented to manage or carry out the covenants explicitly provided in the recorded declaration.[2359] Unlike the declaration which is filed in the applicable county's land records,[2360] the rules and regulations do not need to be recorded.

A board or committee within a homeowners association may adopt reasonable[2361] rules and regulations without any voting by the property owners in certain circumstances.[2362] However, a board does not have the inherent power to adopt rules or regulations unless such authority is explicitly provided in the declaration of covenants.[2363] Therefore, HOAs created under the Georgia Condominium Act, Property Owners' Association Act, and common law HOAs should explicitly provide in the recorded declaration that a board has the authority to create rules and regulations for the community.

Furthermore, the provision providing such authority should clearly establish the scope of the rules and regulations capable of being adopted to avoid any issues when the rules and regulations are implemented. Oftentimes, a declaration will provide that a homeowners association may only grant the board authority to create reasonable

2353 *Brockway v. Harkleroad*, 273 Ga.App. 339, 615 S.E.2d 182 (2005).
2354 *Licker v. Harkleroad*, 252 Ga.App. 872, 558 S.E.2d 31 (2001).
2355 *Licker v. Harkleroad*, 252 Ga.App. 872, 558 S.E.2d 31 (2001).
2356 *Licker v. Harkleroad*, 252 Ga.App. 872, 558 S.E.2d 31 (2001).
2357 *Licker v. Harkleroad*, 252 Ga.App. 872, 558 S.E.2d 31 (2001).
2358 *Licker v. Harkleroad*, 252 Ga.App. 872, 558 S.E.2d 31 (2001).
2359 O.C.G.A. § 44-3-100(a).
2360 O.C.G.A. § 44-3-100(a).
2361 O.C.G.A. § 44-3-223.
2362 O.C.G.A. § 44-3-100(a).
2363 O.C.G.A. § 44-3-100; O.C.G.A. § 44-3-223.

ules and regulations with regard to the use and maintenance of the association common areas. Therefore, since the authority is limited to the common areas, a board would not have the authority to enact a rule regulation the use of an owner's property. Overall, a board may not adopt any rule outside the scope provided in the recorded declaration without a formal amendment to the declaration of covenants.[2364]

Every property owner governed by a recorded declaration must also comply with the rules and regulations adopted by a board or committee.[2365] However, rules and regulations are secondary in priority to the restrictions contained in the recorded declaration. Therefore, the rules and regulations adopted by a board or committee cannot expand or change any obligation of an owner beyond what is contained in the recorded declaration of covenants.[2366] In other words, the rule or regulation cannot have the effect of amending a covenant that would otherwise need the required vote pursuant to the declaration. Let's look at some examples.

Example 1: The declaration required all dogs and cats to be restrained by a leash. A rule was implemented by the board restricting the length of the leash to no more than 20-feet. This rule was valid and did not need a formal amendment to be implemented because it merely clarified the definition of a "leash."

Example 2: The declaration provided that no animals could be maintained by an owner without approval by the board. A rule was implemented that prohibited all owners from keeping new dogs after a specified date. This rule was valid because it clarified which dogs could be kept with the approval of the board.

Example 3: The declaration required that an owner obtain the written approval of the board before making any structural improvements to her house. A rule was implemented that required an owner to obtain a building permit before commencing any work on the house. This rule was valid because it did not expand an obligation in the declarations because the owner was already required to obtain a building permit pursuant to a city ordinance.

Example 4: The declaration provided that the board could assign parking spaces on a uniform, non-preferential basis. A rule was implemented that allowed the board to assign 78 of the 94 parking spaces to owners who did not have garages. This rule was invalid because the declaration allowed the assignment of spaces only on a non-preferential basis and this rule exceeded the express authority given to the board. To implement this rule, the board would need to amend the declaration.

Generally, rules and regulations adopted by a board are held to stricter scrutiny by a court than covenants contained in the declaration because the property owners do not typically vote on rules and regulations. If the board does not have the authority to implement the restriction through a rule or regulation, a formal amendment to the declaration is required.[2367] It is important for property owners to pay particular attention to any rules and regulations adopted by the board to ensure that the restriction is within the scope provided in the declaration of covenants and a formal amendment is not required.

§ 20.2.7   Copies Of Homeowner Association Covenants And Financial Documents

Whether a homeowners association is or is not submitted to the POA, Georgia law does not require any special disclosures or other consumer protections to be included in the real estate contract, except as provided by the Interstate Land Sales Disclosure Act and Georgia's related statutes. Neither the developer nor a resale seller is obligated to provide a potential buyer with a Disclosure Package or with copies of the association's legal and/or financial documents. However, real estate brokers representing buyers should be aware of whether covenants exist and if so, ensure that the buyer receives a copy of the recorded covenants and general financial documents prior to entering into a sales contract.

2364   *Crawford v. Dammann*, 277 Ga.App. 442, 626 S.E.2d 632 (2006).

2365   *County Greens Village One Owner's Ass'n, Inc. v. Meyers*, 158 Ga.App. 609, 281 S.E.2d 346 (1981).

2366   O.C.G.A. § 44-3-100(a).

2367   *Crawford v. Dammann*, 277 Ga.App. 442, 626 S.E.2d 632 (2006).

Otherwise, the buyer's real estate broker should condition the contract upon receipt and/or approval of any such documents. Some of the special stipulations mentioned in § 20.1.12.4 (Copies of condominium legal and financial documents) and in the sections below may be helpful in protecting buyers who may not be given the covenants or financial documents.

§ 20.2.8   Contract Issues To Consider Regarding Homeowners Association

§ 20.2.8.1   Mandatory Membership, Voluntary Association, Or No Association

Most new subdivisions are being developed with entry features, recreational facilities, and other amenities that require ongoing maintenance. Buyers should determine how those expenses will be paid by reviewing the covenants to see if there are provisions requiring membership in an owners association and the payment of assessments.[2368] If the covenants do not require the payment of assessments or if membership in the association is voluntary, there is no assurance that sufficient owners will join the association to pay the operational expenses. Additionally, many communities that were created with voluntary membership associations are converting to mandatory membership. Depending on which phase of the conversion process the community is in at the Binding Agreement Date and at the time of closing, the buyer may have a substantial initiation fee if she wants to submit the home to the mandatory membership category in order to use the recreational facilities. To avoid confusion or surprise, the buyer should consider the following provision.

> **Special Stipulation 347:   Seller's Warranty on HOA Membership Type**
>
> *Seller warrants:*
>
> ___*membership in an owners association is mandatory*
>
> ___*membership in an owners association is voluntary*
>
> ___*membership in an owners association is in the process of converting from voluntary to mandatory*
>
> ___*the duty to pay assessments shall be mandatory as of the Closing Date*
>
> ___*membership in a mandatory membership owners association and the duty to pay assessments will be conditioned on the payment of an initiation fee of $_____, which the seller shall be obligated to pay at Closing or which the buyer may choose to pay after Closing directly to the association*
>
> ___*the duty to pay assessments is mandatory as of the Binding Agreement Date*
>
> ___*the common areas, including but not limited to the recreational facilities, are or will be owned by the owners association*
>
> ___*the common areas, including but not limited to the recreational facilities, will not be owned by the owners association*

§ 20.2.8.2   Developer's Obligations To Build And Turn Over Recreational Facilities

In many subdivisions, the recreational facilities are constructed prior to the sale of any lots. In others, the developer promises to build the facilities at a later time. If the declaration does not specify the size, type, number, quality, location, and construction time frame for the facilities to be constructed, this should be set out as specifically as possible in the purchase contract.

2368   O.C.G.A. § 44-3-100(a) and 44-2-221. Owners of property in a condominium or subdivision subject to the Georgia Property Owners' Association Act are automatic members of the owners' association and obligated to pay assessments.

> **Special Stipulation 348:   Seller's Warranty on Construction of Recreational Facilities**
>
> *Seller warrants that the recreational facilities, including but not limited to the following: (i.e., a junior Olympic size swimming pool, six lighted tennis courts, a clubhouse, a jogging trail, nature areas) as shown on the plans attached hereto as Exhibit "A" shall be completed in a good and workmanlike manner by _____ (date) and transferred to the_____ Homeowners Association, free and clear of any liens and other title encumbrances.*

Some developers build recreational facilities on the front end of the development but then attempt to either transfer them to the owners subject to a loan or attempt to sell the facilities to the owners at the end of the development process. Generally, the value of the recreational facilities is factored into the sale price of the homes. Therefore, there should be no additional cost to the buyers for their recreational facilities. The declaration should require that specified recreational facilities and common areas be conveyed free and clear of all liens and encumbrances to the homeowners association by a specified time. If the declaration is silent on these issues, the buyer may want to specifically address them in the purchase contract.

> **Special Stipulation 349:   Seller's Warranty on Facilities Transferred to HOA**
>
> *Seller warrants the recreational facilities of _____ subdivision consisting of: [describe]_____ shall be deeded to _____ Homeowners Association, Inc., at no cost and free of any liens or other title encumbrances, no later than _____.*

§ 20.2.8.3   Buyers' Assurances That Other Homes In Community Will Be Of Same Standards And Equal Value

Many homeowners become upset when a developer constructs homes in later phases of a development that are substantially smaller or less expensive than the homes which were initially developed. The concern is that values of the larger, more expensive homes in the community will drop. Most developers want to preserve as much flexibility as possible and therefore place few restrictions in the covenants on the type, price, or size of the homes in later phases of the subdivision. The absence of such restrictions can leave buyers vulnerable to changing market conditions, or the developer may sell out to another developer to complete the development, and the successor developer may have a different vision of what will be built in the community.

If the covenants contain limited restrictions on development and the community is just beginning to be developed, the buyer may propose a contract provision such as the following to protect her interests.

> **Special Stipulation 350:   Seller's Warranty on Standard of Construction of Future Property**
>
> *Seller warrants on behalf of itself and successors and its assigns in title that future residences constructed on lots subject to the Declaration of Covenants, Conditions, and Restrictions for_____ ("Declaration") will consist of at least _____ square feet of heated floor area and will be substantially similar in size, quality of construction including building materials used, architectural design, and cost to construct (calculated in present dollars) as the residences on the lots which are presently subject to the Declaration, and that the future lots submitted to the Declaration shall be of equal or larger size to the existing lots subject to the Declaration.*

While this special stipulation may provide a remedy to a buyer against the seller for its breach, it will not provide the buyer with a remedy against builders or other third parties who purchase without notice of this restriction from the seller or who foreclose on the property. Such protections could be achieved by adding the following language to the above special stipulation, or by amending the declaration to incorporate the obligation and having all construction lenders consent to its terms.

> **Special Stipulation 351: Addition of Standard of Construction in Future Contracts [*Optional Additional Language for Special Stipulation 267*]**
>
> *Seller warrants and agrees that the provisions of this special stipulation shall be incorporated and included in all future purchase and sale agreements with other builders and third parties for lots in this subdivision.*

Similarly, such a provision obligates the developer only if the property is, or may become, subject to the declaration for the association. Unless the developer is obligated to formally incorporate future phases of the subdivision into the association, she can also get around such an obligation by developing the future phases as a different subdivision.

§ 20.2.8.4 Approval Of House Plans By Association

Most covenants require the written approval of the association before a home may be constructed or modified. The owner is required to submit plans and specifications to an architectural control committee for approval. In new construction, the developer typically retains control of the committee until all lots are sold or until a certain date, so that approval of the purchase agreement generally is an acceptance of the building plans. After that date, or if a purchaser wants to modify an existing structure, the purchaser must receive approval from the association board of directors or a committee of the board organized for this purpose. There is no guarantee that the board or the committee will approve the plans.

If architectural approval of new construction is not vested in the developer, or if the buyer intends to modify the dwelling to be purchased and such modification requires approval of the architectural control committee, the following provision in the contract will protect the buyer.

> **Special Stipulation 352: Approval of House Plans by Association**
>
> *Notwithstanding anything herein to the contrary, this Agreement shall not become binding until the Board of Directors or Architectural Control Committee or Architectural Review Committee, as appropriate, of _____ Association has approved Buyer's request for architectural approval of the following improvements [or changes and modifications], a copy of which is attached hereto as Exhibit "_____" and incorporated herein, and written notice of such approval has been delivered to Buyer.*

§ 20.3 COOPERATIVES

A housing cooperative is different from a homeowners association or condominium in that a cooperative corporation holds legal title to all of the property in the community, including the units. Members of the cooperative corporation receive membership certificates or shares which entitle them to lease a specific apartment, as long as they comply with certain provisions set forth in a lease agreement, typically called an occupancy agreement. A blanket mortgage often exists for the entire property. All of the rent payments made by the members of the cooperative, typically called carrying charges, are pooled by the cooperative association to pay the mortgage, taxes, and other operating expenses.

Most housing cooperatives in Atlanta were developed to provide affordable housing for low and moderate income people. However, the Atlanta area has recently witnessed cooperative developments as an upscale, higher priced housing alternative, as has been successful in New York and other major cities. As in the case of condominiums, cooperatives may be created from existing apartment properties or through new construction.

20.3.1 Creating A Cooperative

Unlike condominiums, the creation of cooperatives is not regulated by state statute, but is governed by general principals of corporate and landlord and tenant law. The legal documents to organize a cooperative development are articles of incorporation, bylaws, subscription agreements, occupancy agreements, rules and regulations, and sometimes regulatory agreements with federal or other agencies providing financing or subsidies. Members execute the subscription agreements to purchase shares of stock or membership in the cooperative association. The members then execute a lease or occupancy agreement defining the terms of each member's occupancy of a unit and requiring compliance with the rules and regulations of the cooperative. In cooperatives where funding or loan guarantees are obtained from mandatory agencies such as the Department of Housing and Urban Development, a regulatory agreement is prepared and executed between the cooperative and the regulatory agency.

Unlike condominium unit owners, the members in a cooperative generally are not responsible for maintenance and repair of the units. Cooperatives also differ from condominiums in that cooperative memberships may be terminated and members may be dispossessed for non-payment of carrying charges, but non-payment of condominium assessments does not automatically authorize termination of membership in the condominium association or eviction of a unit owner.

Cooperatives differ from condominium and homeowner associations in another substantial way. The board of directors of a cooperative has the right to approve or deny the potential purchasers of a cooperative unit. Any denial must be based on criteria that do not violate the Fair Housing Act. For example, a cooperative board can deny a potential owner because she does not have a high enough credit score, but such denial cannot be based on the potential owner's race, religion, color, national origin, sex, familial status or handicap status.

§ 20.4 TIME-SHARES

There is an increasing interest in various time-sharing forms of property ownership including time-shares, quarter-shares, fractional ownership, and undivided ownership in real property. In Georgia, a time-share estate means an ownership or leasehold interest in real property divided into measurable chronological periods.[2369] Each time-share estate constitutes a separate estate or interest in property.[2370]

To create a time-share estate, certain legal documents meeting specified requirements must be recorded in the superior court of the county in which the project is located.[2371] These documents must set forth, among other things, reasonable arrangements for the management and operation of the time-share program through the establishment of an association of time-share estate owners and collection of assessments from owners to help defray the expenses of management of the time-share program and the maintenance of the units.[2372]

The legal description of the time-share estate must be sufficient to identify the property.[2373] The time periods into which the property is then divided must be described by letter, name, number, or a combination thereof.[2374]

Developers of time-share projects are required to provide consumers with a public offering statement[2375] and a sales contract containing certain consumer disclosures, giving buyers a right of rescission and meeting other statutory requirements.[2376]

2369   O.C.G.A. § 44-3-162(21).

2370   O.C.G.A. § 44-3-163(c).

2371   O.C.G.A. § 44-3-166.

2372   O.C.G.A. § 44-3-167.

2373   O.C.G.A. § 44-3-166(a)(2).

2374   O.C.G.A. § 44-3-166(a)(3).

2375   O.C.G.A. § 44-3-172.

2376   O.C.G.A. § 44-3-174.

§ 20.5   MIXED-USE DEVELOPMENTS

The various forms of ownership discussed in this chapter are increasingly being used in combination to create master planned communities. For example, a developer may take a large piece of property and subject it to the terms of a declaration of covenants which create a master association responsible for commonly used roadways, green belts and recreational amenities. The developer may then create a series of sub-associations within the community. The sub-associations may consist of homeowner associations, condominiums, office developments, country clubs and the like. Each sub-association may be subject to a declaration of condominium or a declaration of covenants which applies just to the real property in that sub-association. In addition, members of the sub-association are also bound by the declaration of covenants for the master association. The process of layering covenants in a community is being increasingly used as a means to regulate and control the large scale development of real property. The relationship between the sub-associations and the master association is often similar to that of city and county governments, with each performing defined tasks within the same or partially overlapping jurisdictions.

Such developments are often characterized by people living in close proximity to one another in housing designed to encourage social interaction. Cars are de-emphasized and commercial and office land uses are located in close proximity to residential uses. A legal framework has to be created that can preserve the aesthetic appearance of such communities, resolve land use conflicts, accommodate some degree of individuality and freedom of expression, and provide for the short- and long-term operation of the community. The legal structure must also be sensitive to the unique realities of many new mixed use communities.

§ 20.6   COMMUNITY ASSOCIATIONS AND CLOSING LETTERS

Pursuant to the GCA,[2377] the POA,[2378] and most mandatory membership HOA covenants, the community association has automatic statutory lien rights, or the right to file a lien in the county land records, against an owner who does not pay mandatory assessments, special assessments, fines, late fees, interest, and/or costs of collection. The costs of collection could include attorneys' fees actually incurred by the association in the collection process. In order to confirm that no lien exists against a particular property, or to get a payoff of an existing lien, closing attorneys must obtain a closing payoff or estoppel letter from the association.

A condominium and a POA are not permitted to collect more than $10 for such a letter.[2379] However, many mandatory membership associations are professionally managed by licensed brokerage companies and no such limitation exists under Georgia law on the fees the management company can charge for providing such letters on behalf of the community. Therefore, most Georgia management companies charge substantially higher fees to provide the closing payoff/estoppel letter and to transfer the account from the seller to the buyer's name.[2380]

Remember that if a property is part of a mixed use community, the closing attorney may need to obtain more than one closing payoff/estoppel letter: one letter from the master and additional letter(s) from the sub-association(s) to which the property is subject. Sometimes that means more than one management company is involved and most of the time there will be more than one processing fee and more than one transfer fee.

2377   O.C.G.A. § 44-3-109.

2378   O.C.G.A. § 44-3-232.

2379   O.C.G.A. § 44-3-109; O.C.G.A. § 44-3-232.

2380   Although no Georgia statute or case law exists and the GAR Contracts are silent regarding which party pays these fees, closing attorneys typically charge the letter processing fee to the seller and the transfer fees to the buyer, and collect both on the closing settlement statement.

The **RED BOOK**

CHAPTER 21

MORTGAGE

FRAUD

OVERVIEW

Mortgage fraud is of concern for three reasons. First, mortgage fraud is a crime that can land the participants and those who aid and abet them in jail. It can also cost real estate professionals their licenses. The participants in mortgage fraud often include mortgage brokers, real estate appraisers, phony buyers, complicit sellers, closing attorneys, real estate agents, and dishonest, or greedy, employees of end lenders.

Some parties end up participating in mortgage fraud unknowingly due to a lack of understanding of how these schemes work or because they do not realize that their actions are unlawful. In other cases, participants may know or suspect certain transactions to be fraudulent but turn a blind eye because they are either: (1) unsure that they are really dealing with mortgage fraud, or (2) worried that they might be breaching a duty to their clients if they "blow the whistle" and cause a sale to fall apart.

Second, if real estate professionals end up being indicted in any significant numbers for mortgage fraud, confidence in these professions and industries could be seriously undermined. Such a "black eye" could, in addition to hurting professionals in their pocketbooks, also lead to greater regulation.

Finally, mortgage fraud can have a destabilizing effect on our housing and financial market. In some subdivisions and condominiums in which there have been numerous cases of mortgage fraud, the number of foreclosed properties has increased dramatically as the persons committing the fraud immediately stop making mortgage payments on "flipped" properties. The crooks will also sometimes allow unsavory characters to live in these properties until they are eventually evicted by the foreclosing mortgage lender. There have been reports of gun battles, drug dealing, prostitution and other criminal activity involving these occupants in neighborhoods previously unaccustomed to such events. Interestingly, at the same time that the market value of homes is being driven down as a result of foreclosures and increased crime, property taxes in these communities often increase as illegal property flips create a false impression that property values are actually increasing. Affected developments are not restricted to one geographic locale, housing type or particular price range of house. As a result, the damage which can be done as a result of mortgage fraud can be far-reaching.

The effect of mortgage fraud is not limited to neighborhoods where the fraud occurs. Indeed, world-wide financial markets have tumbled as otherwise seemingly reputable Wall Street companies have declared billions of dollars in losses due to sham mortgage backed securities. Additionally, fraudulent loans have been bundled and sold as securities, contributing to the crisis in financial markets in 2008.

In response to skyrocketing losses, the Georgia Legislature passed the Residential Mortgage Fraud Act ("RMFA" or "Act"),[2381] which established tough state-law based criminal penalties for mortgage fraud. The Act will hopefully have the desired effect of cutting down on the numerous instances of mortgage fraud in Georgia. However, the Act is written so broadly that some practices once thought of as "creative" now constitute crimes. Given the heightened scrutiny of transactions for mortgage fraud and the far-reaching effect of RMFA, it is critical that real estate professionals have a thorough understanding of the Act and of fact patterns that may suggest fraud.

§ 21.1 WHAT IS MORTGAGE FRAUD – GENERALLY

It is difficult to be comprehensive in describing mortgage fraud because the schemes used to perpetrate these frauds vary widely and new schemes are constantly appearing. Mortgage fraud generally falls into two categories: (1) fraud for housing, and (2) fraud for profit. Fraud for housing is most commonly committed by a borrower who makes minor misrepresentations in their goal of achieving the American Dream- owning a home. Generally this fraud is committed with the coaching assistance of a lender, mortgage broker or real estate agent. It is mistakenly thought of being the kinder, gentler fraud that harms no one. Fraud for profit schemes are the most costly type of fraud. This type of fraud is for pure financial gain. The schemes often involve groups of people, generally industry insiders (*i.e.*,

---

2381 O.C.G.A. § 16-8-100 *et seq.*

real estate agents, lenders, appraisers, underwriters, rehab contractors and closing attorneys) and are based on gross misrepresentation with the goal of reaping financial gain. The initiators often receive the greater portion of the profits from the scheme and the co-conspirators receive payment for their role.

In its broadest sense, mortgage fraud occurs when there is something about the transaction that is not known to the actual, final lender that, if known, would cause the lender to either not make the loan or not make the loan on the same terms and conditions. Typically, this involves one or more parties misrepresenting facts in a real estate transaction to obtain mortgage financing.

Normally, the financing allows the borrower to fraudulently "cash out" phantom or non-existent equity in a property. Mortgage fraud usually falls into one or both of two categories: (1) information and/or documents are falsified to make the property look more valuable than it really is in order to trick the lender into loaning too much money on an overvalued property, and (2) information and/or documents are falsified to get a loan application approved for a buyer who would not otherwise be qualified for a loan.

In addition to constituting a crime under the RMFA, persons committing mortgage fraud can be charged with any number of other state and federal crimes. At a state level, the more obvious crimes include criminal fraud, theft by taking, forgery, identity theft, criminal solicitation, criminal conspiracy and racketeering. At a federal level, persons committing mortgage fraud can, among other things, be charged with wire fraud, mail fraud, use of false identification documents, use of false social security numbers, conspiracy to defraud the United States government and racketeering.

Finally, and perhaps the least of their worries, real estate professionals participating in mortgage fraud put their licenses as risk. For example, real estate agents and brokers who participate in mortgage fraud can be sanctioned by the Georgia Real Estate Commission, up to and including the revocation of their licenses, for engaging in any number of unfair business practices including the following:

(a) making substantial misrepresentations;

(b) being or becoming a party to any falsification of any portion of any contract or other document involved in any real estate transaction;

(c) failing to keep for a period of three (3) years a true and correct copy of all sales contracts, closing statements, or other documents relating to real estate closings; and

(d) having demonstrated incompetency to act as a real estate licensee in such manner as to safeguard the interest of the public or any other conduct … which constitutes dishonest dealing.

Even if no specific charges are brought by the Georgia Real Estate Commission against a licensee for violating any of the above license law provisions, if a licensee is convicted of a state or federal crime involving mortgage fraud, they can also lose their real estate license as a result of the criminal conviction. Licensees are required to immediately report to the Georgia Real Estate Commission any felony conviction or any crime involving moral turpitude. The term "conviction" means a guilty finding, a verdict or plea, a sentencing to first offender treatment without a determination of guilt or a plea of *nolo contendere*. Upon such a conviction, the licensee's license is automatically revoked 60 days after the conviction unless the licensee timely requests a hearing to determine whether the licensee remains fit to hold a real estate license.

§ 21.2 WHAT IS MORTGAGE FRAUD – RMFA

As discussed above, mortgage fraud generally involves a scheme to extract funds from a lender through falsified information or documentation related to the property or the borrower. The Act certainly encompasses these activities within its provisions. However, the RMFA's definition of mortgage fraud is a good deal broader than the common, general, understanding of mortgage fraud. In a general sense, the RMFA covers fraudulent activity in any part of the residential mortgage loan process, from loan solicitation all the way through the closing and funding the loan. The law applies to tangible documents involved in the process including, without limitation, the uniform residential loan application, appraisal report, HUD-1 statement, W-2 forms submitted, income statements, employment letters, tax returns and pay stubs. More specifically, the Act contains two key underlying definitions that must be understood in order to appreciate the acts prohibited by it.

The first definition is "residential mortgage loan." This means a loan or agreement to extend credit, which is secured by a security deed, mortgage or similar document upon any interest in one-to-four family residential property located in Georgia.[2382] It includes a renewal or refinancing of such a loan. The Act only applies to residential mortgage loans.[2383] For example, if the loan is made in Georgia but the secured property is located in South Carolina, the Georgia statute does not apply. However, if a buyer is getting a mortgage on an office building or retail center located in the state, the Georgia law does apply.

The second key definition under the Act is "mortgage lending process." This means the process through which a person seeks or obtains a residential mortgage loan.[2384] It includes loan solicitation, application, origination, negotiation on terms, underwriting, signing, closing, and funding of the loan. Third-party provider services, such as appraisals, title examinations and title insurance are also covered. Such term also includes the execution of deeds under power of sale that are required to be recorded pursuant to O.C.G.A. § 44-14-160 and the execution of assignments that are required to be recorded pursuant to O.C.G.A. § 44-14-162(b).[2385] Documents involved in the mortgage lending process include, but are not limited to, loan applications, appraisal reports, settlement statements and credit documentation.

§ 21.2.1 What Constitutes Residential Mortgage Fraud?

Under the RMFA, a person commits the offense of residential mortgage fraud when, with the intent to defraud, such person:

(1) Knowingly makes any deliberate misstatement, misrepresentation, or omission during the mortgage lending process with the intention that it be relied on by a mortgage lender, borrower, or any other party to the mortgage lending process;[2386]

(2) Knowingly uses or facilitates the use of any deliberate misstatement, misrepresentation, or omission, knowing the same to contain a misstatement, misrepresentation, or omission, during the mortgage lending process with the intention that it be relied on by a mortgage lender, borrower, or any other party to the mortgage lending process;[2387]

(3) Receives any proceeds or any other funds in connection with a residential mortgage closing that such person knew resulted from a violation of paragraph (1) or (2) above;[2388]

(4) Conspires to violate any of the provisions of paragraph (1), (2), or (3) above;[2389] or

(5) Files or causes to be filed with the official registrar of deeds of any county of this state any document such person knows to contain a deliberate misstatement, misrepresentation, or omission.[2390]

2382   O.C.G.A. § 16-8-101.

2383   O.C.G.A. § 16-8-100 *et seq.*

2384   O.C.G.A. § 16-8-101.

2385   O.C.G.A. § 16-8-101.

2386   O.C.G.A. § 16-8-102(1).

2387   O.C.G.A. § 16-8-102(2).

2388   O.C.G.A. § 16-8-102(3).

2389   O.C.G.A. § 16-8-102(4).

2390   O.C.G.A. § 16-8-102(5).

§ 21.2.1.1 Conspiracy To Commit Mortgage Fraud

A person commits the crime of conspiracy (subparagraph (4) above) when that person, together with one or more other persons, conspires to commit any of the listed criminal acts and does any overt act to put such plan into effect.[2391] A prosecutor need not prove any express agreement between the parties, but need only prove that the persons came into a mutual understanding (even tacit) to accomplish or pursue a criminal objective.[2392] In other words, even if a real estate licensee does not actively participate in a deception, it is a crime for the licensee to knowingly receive funds from a mortgage loan closing which the licensee knows were obtained by making a false statement, or by omission, or by using a false document.[2393]

§ 21.2.1.2 Aiding Another To Commit Mortgage Fraud

Recently, the Georgia Court of Appeals held that the person(s) aiding fraudulently qualified buyers in their misrepresentation to the lender will also be liable for mortgage fraud.[2394] In 2009, the Residential Mortgage Loan Act was tested in court and established a starting point for the interpretations of the RMFA. The most significant case in this area is *Gilford v. State*, 295 Ga.App. 651 (2009).

In *Gilford*, the borrower submitted a loan application to Countrywide Home Loans but was denied because she had insufficient funds to close. The borrower then submitted another loan application to New Century Mortgage Corporation. The money for the down payment for this loan was given to the borrower by Gilford, a mortgage loan officer from Countrywide Home Loans, prior to the closing. The borrower falsely stated that none of the $13,000 down payment she provided at the closing was borrowed making the borrower liable for mortgage fraud.[2395] Although Gilford did not work for New Century Mortgage, the paralegal who worked for the law firm which closed the borrower's loan testified that she talked with Gilford "in coordinating some parts of the closing."[2396] Investigators discovered that the $13,000 had been withdrawn from Gilford's account on March 28, 2006. The next day, three different deposits were made at three separate bank branches into the borrower's account.

After being convicted of mortgage fraud by the trial court, Gilford appealed the conviction to the Georgia Court of Appeals.[2397] She argued that there was no evidence she knowingly made any deliberate misstatement or misrepresentation during the loan application process to cause her to be liable for mortgage fraud. While she may have assisted the borrower in defrauding the lender, Gilford's argument appeared to be that she could not be guilty because she was not the one making the direct misstatements to the lender.[2398] The Georgia Court of Appeals rejected that argument and found Gilford guilty of making deliberate misstatements and misrepresentations to the lender because "she was a party to the crime."[2399] To support this conclusion, the Georgia Court of Appeals cited O.C.G.A. § 16-2-20, which provides:

(a) Every person concerned in the commission of a crime is a party thereto and may be charged with and convicted of commission of a crime; or

(b) A person is concerned in the commission of a crime only if he…(3) intentionally aids or abets in the commission of the crime; or (4) intentionally advises, encourages, hires, counsels, or procures another to commit the crime.[2400]

2391   O.C.G.A. § 16-4-8.

2392   *Williamson v. State*, 300 Ga.App. 538, 685 S.E.2d 784 (2009).

2393   O.C.G.A. § 16-8-102.

2394   *Gilford v. State*, 295 Ga.App. 651, 673 S.E.2d 40 (2009).

2395   *Gilford v. State*, 295 Ga.App. 651, 673 S.E.2d 40 (2009).

2396   *Gilford v. State*, 295 Ga.App. 651, 673 S.E.2d 40 (2009).

2397   *Gilford v. State*, 295 Ga.App. 651, 673 S.E.2d 40 (2009).

2398   *Gilford v. State*, 295 Ga.App. 651, 673 S.E.2d 40 (2009).

2399   *Gilford v. State*, 295 Ga.App. 651, 673 S.E.2d 40 (2009).

2400   O.C.G.A. § 16-2-20.

Based on the broad interpretation in this case, any participation in deceiving a residential mortgage lender will put that party at risk. It does not matter if the party helping the person commit mortgage fraud does not directly represent or misrepresent anything to the mortgage lender. Aiding and abetting, advising, encouraging or counseling a person committing the fraud is enough to cause the helper to also be convicted of mortgage fraud.[2401]

In another example, a buyer tells his REALTOR® that he just quit his job and is worried about whether this could affect his ability to get a mortgage to close on the purchase of the home the following week. If the REALTOR® advises the buyer not to reveal this information to the mortgage lender, it would certainly appear that the REALTOR® was aiding and abetting in the commission of a crime. Even if the REALTOR® advises the buyer to disclose his job status to the lender and the buyer does not, the REALTOR® should be cautious about receiving commissions out of this transaction. While there is not yet a case on this point, the mortgage fraud statute prohibits a REALTOR® from receiving "any proceeds or any other funds in connection with a residential mortgage closing that such person knew resulted from a deliberate misrepresentation or omission."[2402] Therefore, based upon this section of the statute, the REALTOR® would be well advised not to take a commission in this situation since the commission could arguably be seen as being paid with the proceeds of a fraudulent mortgage loan.

§ 21.3 STRICTER APPRAISAL STANDARDS IN PLACE

In yet another regulatory rule sparked by the housing market decline and mortgage fraud, in March 2008, Fannie Mae and Freddie Mac announced an agreement to stricter appraisal standards for home mortgages. The independence of the appraiser is essential to maintaining the integrity of the mortgage industry.

The agreement was a result of an ongoing industry investigation of fraud by New York Attorney General Andrew Cuomo. The agreement is intended to discourage inflated appraisals, one of several major problems behind the sub-prime collapse and general housing slump. The price declines under way around the country are partly the result of systemic, intentional over valuations on home appraisals, much at the behest of loan officers illegally influencing or threatening appraisers to "hit the number" needed to close the deal.

Fannie Mae and Freddie Mac are the government-sponsored entities that provide mortgage market liquidity and funding for mortgage loans. The two companies buy about 60% of all home loans originated in the country. The federal regulatory arm with oversight of Fannie Mae and Freddie Mac is the Office of Federal Housing Enterprise Oversight (OFHEO). With this agreement, Fannie Mae and Freddie Mac will buy only those loans from banks that meet strict standards of independent, reliable appraisals. The code of conduct took effect in May of 2009.

The agreement first established the "Home Valuation Code of Conduct," which in part included several key components:

- Lenders and their representatives are prohibited from influencing or attempting to influence the development, result or review of an appraisal. Pressure from these sources cause appraisers to supply inflated estimates of property values. Appraisers are encouraged to succumb to such pressure: without appraisal values that allow loans to be extended, the appraisers risk losing business.

- Lender must have absolute independence between the appraisal function and the loan production. A lender's loan production staff is prohibited from being involved in the selection of the appraiser, or having any substantive communications with an appraiser or appraisal management company about valuation.

- A lender, in connection with the loan being originated, may accept an appraisal report prepared by an appraiser for a different lender, provided that the lender obtains written assurances from the other lender that it has adopted the Code and determines that such appraisal conforms to the appraisal requirements and is otherwise acceptable.

2401   *Gilford v. State*, 295 Ga.App. 651, 673 S.E.2d 40 (2009).

2402   O.C.G.A. § 16-8-102.

- Lenders are required to quality control test a randomly selected 10% (or other bona fide statistically significant percentage) sample of appraisal reports or valuations used by the lender, and report any adverse findings, including non-compliance of the Code, to Freddie Mac with respect to loans sold to Freddie Mac.

- The lender's appraisal functions are either annually audited by an external auditor or are subject to federal or regulatory examination, and the lender must provide Freddie Mac with any adverse audit findings indicating non-compliance with this Code.

In 2010, the "Appraiser Independence Requirements" ("AIR") were developed to replace the Home Valuation Code of Conduct ("HVCC"). The Appraiser Independence Requirements maintain the same intent of the HVCC by continuing to provide protections for mortgage investors, home buyers and the housing market in general. Overall, the AIR do not pose significant changes to the core principles of the HVCC. Instead, these new requirements clarify many questions that arose from the implementation of the Home Valuation Code of Conduct. The AIR took effect in October 2010 and now applies to any appraisal completed on or after that date. Several of the AIR's key components are listed below:

- No employee, director, officer or agent of the seller, or any other third party acting as joint venture partner, independent contractor, appraisal company, appraisal management company, or partner on behalf of the seller, shall influence or attempt to influence the development, reporting, result or review of an appraisal through coercion, extortion, collusion, compensation, inducement, intimidation, bribery, or in any other manner.

- The seller shall ensure that the borrower is provided a copy of any appraisal report concerning the borrower's subject property promptly upon completion at no additional cost to the borrower, and in any event no less than three days prior to the closing of the mortgage.

- The seller or any third party specifically authorized by the seller shall be responsible for selecting, retaining and providing for payment of all compensation to the appraiser. The seller will not accept any appraisal report completed by an appraiser selected, retained or compensation in any manner by any other third party (including mortgage brokers and real estate agents).

- There must be separation of a seller's sale or mortgage production functions and appraisal functions. An employee of the seller in the sales or mortgage production function shall have no involvement in the operations of the appraisal function.

- Sellers must adopt written policies and procedures implementing these Appraiser Independence Requirements, including, but not limited to, adequate training and disciplinary rules on appraiser independence. Additionally, sellers must ensure that any third parties, such as appraisal management companies or correspondent lenders, used in conjunction with the sale and delivery of a mortgage to Freddie Mae are also in compliance with these Appraiser Independence Requirements.

More information on the Appraiser Independence Requirements can be obtained by visiting the Appraisal Resources on the Fannie Mae and Freddie Mac website, available at https://www.efanniemae.com/sf/guides/ssg/relatedsellinginfo/appcode/.

§ 21.3.1   Inflated Appraisals

Appraisals are usually required by lenders before home loans are extended. The purpose of an appraisal is to provide a reliable estimate of the property's value. REALTORS® or brokers could find themselves facing charges for mortgage fraud for misstating or inflating property appraisals. For example, a builder tells his REALTOR® that he wants to show the sales price of the new home at $1,250,000 and then provide a credit to the buyer of $250,000 after the sale is completed. The builder's reasoning behind providing this credit is to create the appearance that this house and the other houses in the neighborhood are valued at a higher price.

of the REALTOR® or broker participated in this inflation, he would be liable for mortgage fraud. Even though no mortgage is being originated as part of the proposed transaction, the REALTOR® should be concerned with the builder's suggestion because this "credit" would make appraisals throughout the neighborhood higher than the properties' actual value. Therefore, the loan amount from the lender would be in excess of what the buyer actually needs to purchase the property. The seller and the listing broker working together to make the comparables higher than the actual value of the homes is a clear example of mortgage fraud. Similarly, if a REALTOR® recommends to a buyer that the sales price of the property be increased to reflect the value of the personal property being left with the property (where the personal property is then given a zero value), this misstatement could also potentially be seen a mortgage fraud.

Inflated appraisals can encourage bigger loans than necessary. This can hurt the borrower in their monthly payments and when home prices fall, it can also expose the lenders to losses. Some experts contend that appraisals nationwide are inflated at least 10 percent. However, if the legal settlement and new Code have its intended effect, the appraisal system will be changed radically in the coming years.

§ 21.4   EXAMPLES AND CASE STUDIES

As with all types of fraud, certain aspects of mortgage fraud are inherently difficult to prove. Probably the best way to gain an appreciation for the nuances of mortgage fraud is to examine a number of fact patters and discuss whether mortgage fraud may be involved.

§ 21.4.1   Inflated Property Values

Perhaps the best-known example of mortgage fraud is known as "property flipping." Flipping is a form of fraud that involves the purchase and quick resale of a property for more than its true value. Some property flips are perfectly legal and involve sophisticated buyers who purchase real estate that is simply undervalued. Because values in real estate can increase quickly due to legitimate market forces, it is sometimes difficult to know whether a transaction involves fraud or merely savvy business. An example of such a situation is discussed below.

Example: Joe Smith learns confidentially that a major new shopping center will be built at a particular location. An owner of a single-family home across the street from where the center will be located is selling his home on five acres of land and is unaware of the plans for the shopping center. Joe puts the property under contract for the $327,000 asking price. Joe then approaches the shopping center developer who agrees to purchase the same property for $750,000. Does the sale of the property to the developer constitute mortgage fraud if the developer obtains a mortgage to purchase the property?

Answer: The answer to this question is no. Joe capitalized on an opportunity by recognizing that the property would be worth significantly more to some buyers as a result of a major shopping center being located next door to the property. An increase in the value of property in anticipation of a major change in land use in an area is part of the normal workings of the market. While there is no mortgage fraud involved in this situation, it might appear that way to an outside observer without knowledge observing the second part of this transaction.

Let's compare the example above, however, with the example below.

Example: Sarah Smith, a former bank robber, enters into a contract to buy a property for $200,000. After the contract is signed, an accomplice of Sarah's enters into a contract to purchase the property from her for $450,000. The buyer is actually a person for whom a false identity has been created. The real estate appraiser is bribed to appraise the property for the contract amount. Do Sarah's actions in the transaction constitute mortgage fraud?

Answer: The answer to this question is obviously yes. Interestingly, however, the entire transaction may not be fraudulent. The initial sale of the property to Sarah is probably lawful if she pays the fair market value of the property based upon her own identity and her own true financial strength as a buyer. The fraud is occurring in the second part of the transaction because it *involves both a phony buyer and a false appraisal. The result of the fraud is that Sarah will pocket ill-gotten gains of roughly $250,000. The problem, however, is that someone who is involved in just the first part of the transaction would likely have no reason to suspect mortgage fraud.*

Let's look at the example below to see a variation on this crooked theme.

Example: Sarah Smith enters into a contract to purchase a single-family home for $200,000. She does this under a false identity. She then approaches the seller and tells him that she would like to increase the amount of the sales price on the contract by $100,000 so that the cost of certain improvements she would like to make to the property can be included in the purchase price. Sarah promises the seller that he will net the same amount he would have had the property been sold at the original contract price. With the seller's assistance, the contract is redrafted to reflect the higher sales price. The closing statement reflects that at closing $100,000 will be paid to a third-party contractor to perform certain remedial work. Is Sarah guilty of mortgage fraud?

Answer: The obvious answer to this question is again yes. The likelihood is that the contractor is working in cahoots with Sarah and will divide the $100,000 with her. While there are mortgage programs which allow an owner to make improvements to a property and to then include those amounts in a permanent mortgage on a property, it would be highly unusual that any legitimate transaction would involve increasing the sales price of the property to include the amount needed for repairs. Therefore, anyone participating in such transactions should be aware that there is a great likelihood that they are fraudulent.

There are multiple variations of the scheme described in the above example. The first is where the contract is assigned to a down and out buyer who gets paid a fee to impersonate a credit-worthy, fictitious buyer. Closing attorneys are now being encouraged by lenders and title insurance companies to be on the lookout for buyers whose appearance or attire does not match with the properties they are buying. When the closing attorneys encounter such a buyer, they are being asked to stop the closing until it can be confirmed that the buyers are who they say they are. For example, if an inarticulate man with no front teeth and soiled clothes shows up to purchase a million dollar home, it would be a red flag to the most closing attorneys that something may not be quite right with the buyer and hence the transaction.

In another variation of the flipping scheme, the con artist contracts to purchase property at a discounted rate and then looks for unsophisticated individuals with good credit who are interested in owning "investment property." The contract price for the buyer is greatly inflated over the price at which the crook will purchase the property. The crook may tell the unsuspecting buyer that the investment property can be purchased with no down payment or that the buyer will be paid several thousand dollars for each property that he purchases. In some cases, the crook says that he will pay the mortgage for the buyer or that he will provide a tenant who will pay the carrying costs for the property. The crook, often with the help of a co-conspirator who is a mortgage broker, creates fictitious mortgage packages to secure the loans for the buyer and has the buyer sign the loan documents.

As in the previous examples, the con artist either works with a dishonest appraiser to produce fraudulent appraisals supporting the inflated price as previously described, or in a fairly new development in this form of fraud, the con artist may steal the names and license numbers of appraisers in order to produce the fraudulent appraisal himself. The crook schedules the closing for his purchase of the property immediately before the closing on his resale to the buyer. The crook nets a large profit from his resale and then does not find tenants for the property, maintain the property, or pay the mortgage on the property. The buyer soon discovers that she owns a greatly over-valued property that has no tenants and is in a state of disrepair. Frequently, in this situation, the property goes into foreclosure because buyers duped by this kind of scam often could not have qualified for a loan to purchase the property without the manipulation of the system by the crook.

In thinking about how crooks get away with mortgage fraud, it should be apparent that for most of these schemes to work, crooks have to work in concert with one another or with settlement service providers who will at least look the other way when this type of criminal activity occurs. In other words, the crime of mortgage fraud is often a team sport.

For example, the crook may need to enlist the help of a dishonest mortgage broker who will hire the "right" appraiser for a property that is being flipped or to help get a phony buyer or buyer who is not credit worthy qualified.

Similarly, the crook may also need the help of a shady closing attorney who will not ask questions about suspect transactions or who is willing to actually participate in the mortgage fraud. In one extreme case, it was reported that the closing attorney allowed the buyer to refinance a property at a grossly inflated price before the buyer actually purchased the property so that the buyer essentially purchased the property from the proceeds of the refinance. The paperwork was then recorded in a different order to make it look like the sale of the property took place before the refinance. The HUD Settlement Statement is the important tool of the crooks because it is the only way money is paid out of any closing transaction.

Of course, con artists are considered "artists" because some of them are quite good at their "jobs." Sometimes a real estate professional can be duped into unknowingly participating in mortgage fraud. For example, the scam artists will often pick subdivisions where the prices of the homes vary widely because it is more likely that even an honest appraiser will incorrectly value a property in such situations. Let's look at the example below to see how this can happen.

Example: Monte Carlo is an upscale community where homes sell from between $400,000 to $1,400,000 dollars. A crook enters into a contract to flip a property for which he paid $400,000 for $725,000. The appraiser assigned to appraise the property is given the contract with the sales price written in of $725,000. Not suspecting mortgage fraud, the appraiser looks for recent home sales and finds several in this price range. Miraculously, the home is appraised at this higher price. Mortgage fraud?

Answer: This one is more difficult to call. The act of selecting appropriate comparables sales is part science and part art. It could be that objective factors are determinative. For instance, one comparable could have three bedrooms while the appraisal shows it as having five. Absent such relatively easy objective criteria, whether an appraiser should or should not have used any specific comparable to reach the $725,000 valuation will likely be a matter of expert opinion.

§ 21.4.2 Fraudulently Qualified Buyers

A wide variety of fraudulent practices can be used to make an unqualified borrower appear to be qualified for the loan for which he is applying. For instance, borrowers can lie about their income, job, or credit history by falsifying their pay stubs, forging their income tax returns, or falsifying their credit reports. The easy availability of do-it yourself income tax software make it easier than ever to produce falsified documents that are very authentic-looking. Some of these buyers commit identity theft to obtain other people's personal information, such as social security numbers, in order to qualify for a loan. Another common form of fraud for unqualified borrowers is the "stated income/stated asset" scam. This is commonly done by a borrower when they cannot qualify for a loan using actual income and assets, so they convert their application into a stated income/stated asset program (few of which programs are still in existence). The result is that borrowers "lie" about income and assets, receive loans they cannot afford, and eventually lose their homes by foreclosure when they cannot pay.

In some cases, the crook not only steals the identity of a person, but also steals her property. The following example illustrates how this crime occurs.

Example: Paul and Mary Martin are an elderly retired couple who live part of the year in St. Simons and part of the year in the mountains of North Carolina. Shortly after leaving for North Carolina, a crook has the locks changed on the Martins' house, puts the property up for sale at an attractive price, has two accomplices impersonate Mr. and Mrs. Martin, and creates false identification for them in the name of the Martins. The house is put under contract to legitimate buyers and the "fake" Martins appear at the closing and sell the property. When the real Martins return several months later, they find someone new living in their house and the equity in their home, as well as their furniture, literally stolen right out from under them.

Answer: While the real Martins should in time be able to get the property restored to them since it was sold pursuant to a forged deed, this will likely not occur quickly or without litigation. While these types of scenarios are hard to believe, they usually involve elderly sellers who may be more vulnerable to being taken advantage of by con artists.

§ 21.4.3 Inflating The Sales Price

Another example of mortgage fraud involves the artificial inflation of the sales price of the property.

Example: Jane Doe finds the house of her dreams but doesn't have a sufficient down payment. She has a well paying, stable job and can otherwise afford to purchase the property. Jane's real estate agent and mortgage broker suggest to Jane and the seller that the price of the house be increased by $25,000 and that the seller take a note for this amount. The plan is for the note to be torn up after closing. By doing this, Jane is able to effectively include the amount of the down payment into her mortgage. Does this constitute mortgage fraud?

Answer: The answer to this question is yes. Jane will be providing false information to her lender in order to procure mortgage financing. Moreover, the mortgage will be underwritten not based on the true, selling price of the property but instead on an artificially inflated price. At the time of closing, Jane has no equity of her own in the property which would also normally affect whether or not the loan was approved. Not only will Jane and the seller be guilty of mortgage fraud, but so will the real estate agent and mortgage broker who knowingly facilitated and/ or conspired with them.

Example: Desperate Developer is having trouble selling his homes in the current market. Based on market conditions, Developer reluctantly lowers the price of his home by $50,000. Angel Buyer and her real estate agent pounce on the deal, but request the Developer to raise the price again to the original asking price and pay the $50,000 difference as a consulting fee to Devil Designs. Devil Designs is a shell company and the end result is for Angel and her agent to split the $50,000.

Discussion: Although the Developer may not have had any original intent to commit mortgage fraud, he has become a willing participant to cooperate with the fraudsters who are diverting the price of $50,000 into their pockets as profits. This transaction is a prime example of the level of cooperation and participation needed by multiple parties.

§ 21.4.4 Short Sales

A rising area of fraud involves the short sale scams. For a discussion of short sale scams, see § 16.1.11 (Short Sales Scams).

§ 21.4.5 Fake Leases

Yet another example of mortgage fraud is the buyer who wants to close on a new house before his current residence is sold and who cannot qualify for a loan until his first house has sold. The buyer creates a fake lease under which a "friend" is said to be leasing the house and making the payments on the old mortgage so that the buyer appears to be making more money than he really does.

§ 21.4.6 Primary Residence Games

Probably one of the most frequent forms of mortgage fraud involves the buyer's misrepresentation about her intention to occupy the property as a primary residence. Many lenders charge higher rates of interest for investment loans than for owner occupied primary residence loans. A buyer who wants to purchase investment property but cannot afford (or doesn't want to pay) the higher interest rate normally charged for such loans may falsely indicates that the property will be her primary residence when in fact this is not the case. This constitutes mortgage fraud under the Act.

§ 21.4.7   End Lender Lack Of Diligence

Lest anyone come away with the belief that mortgage fraud always has a victim, in many cases the end lender itself could have easily avoided the mortgage fraud by simply exercising due diligence, following up on obvious "red flags" or even simply following its own underwriting guidelines and criteria.

Additionally, while many end lenders pay lip service to having anti-fraud measures in place, many still have not addressed their own best line of defense. Loan originators, who facilitate the gathering of information for the loan underwriters, are in many cases paid on a commission basis. This means their livelihood is determined by the number of loans that close. It is only human nature that some may want to look the other way or pretend they did not hear about a condition that should be reported to underwriting. However, if the information was known to the underwriter, the transaction would not be funded and they would not be paid.

Example: The seller and buyer agree that in lieu of the seller making repairs to the property he will pay the buyer $5,000 cash. The parties include this provision in an amendment to the sales contract. The lender's underwriter, however, rejects the loan application based upon the payment of cash from the seller to the buyer. The parties still want the sale to go forward so, either with or without the knowledge or assistance of a real estate agent, mortgage broker, or the lender's own loan originator, they remove the amendment page from the contract and re-submit the paperwork to the underwriter. Since the transaction now does not appear to contain any cash back from the seller to the buyer, the loan is approved. Of course, the buyer and seller have not really changed the terms of the transaction. Rather, they have simply held back the amendment from the underwriter. The seller plans to give the buyer a $5,000 check after the closing.

Discussion: This, of course, constitutes a prime example of mortgage fraud. The parties have concealed information from the end lender which if known would cause the lender to not fund the transaction. Now comes the interesting part. During the closing the closing attorney overhears the seller and buyer discussing the $5,000 payment. The closing attorney inquires, and is told that in fact the parties are exchanging the funds "under the table." Since the closing attorney represents the end lender, she dutifully telephones the loan originator, who is typically her only contact for the lender, and reports the payment. The loan originator, who is an employee of the lender, tells her not to worry about it, just be sure there is no record of the payment in any of the paperwork and close the transaction.

If the attorney complies with the direction of the loan originator, then she becomes a party to mortgage fraud. She has now facilitated the use of a misrepresentation during the lending process and/or conspired with others to do so. It is of no consequence that the loan originator was "in" on the deal. He is simply a co-conspirator.

Example: During the mortgage lending process, the mortgage loan officer tells the REALTOR® that he does not want to see the GAR Amendment to Address Concerns with Property[2403] form signed by the buyer and seller. The REALTOR® representing the buyer asks whether the buyer is obligated to provide all amendments to the purchase and sale agreement to the mortgage lender. The mortgage loan officer tells the REALTOR® that he can do whatever he wants but providing the amendment might create issues in underwriting and cause the lender not to make the mortgage loan on the property. The REALTOR® decides not to provide the amendments to the purchase and sale agreement to the mortgage lender.

Discussion: This one is difficult. If a mortgage loan officer asks a REALTOR® not to provide the loan underwriter with an amendment to the real estate agreement that is required to be provided to the mortgage lender, the REALTOR® should be asking, "why does the mortgage loan officer not want me to do this?" If the answer is that the loan officer wants to hide the amendment because giving it to the loan underwriter may cause the loan to be denied, the REALTOR® should provide the amendment to the underwriter or risk being convicted of mortgage fraud. This is because if the REALTOR® intentionally works with the loan officer so that the loan underwriter does not get information required by the lender in the mortgage loan

---

2403   GAR Form F107.

application, it could be viewed as facilitating "the use of any deliberate…omission…during the mortgage lending process with the intention that it be relied on by a mortgage lender…"[2404] *It also appears as though the mortgage loan officer and the REALTOR® are conspiring together to violate the Georgia mortgage fraud laws.*

Some REALTORS® argue that so long as the initial contract between the parties is provided to the lender, there is no need to provide amendments to the lender. Other REALTORS® provide the base contract, plus any exhibits or amendments. The best answer in this type of situation is determine what information the borrower is required to provide to the lender, and if the REALTOR® is helping obtain this information, ensure that the required information in the REALTOR®'s possession is given to the lender. Therefore, if the loan application requires the borrower to provide the lender with the entire purchase and sale agreement, the entire purchase and sale agreement, including all exhibits, should be provided. Similarly, if the loan application requires the borrower to update all required loan information, this would mean that all amendments to the purchase and sale agreement should be provided to the lender. With the law criminalizing material omissions, any other answer is fraught with legal risk.

It should be noted, however, that some REALTORS® may be getting their borrowers into trouble by providing information to the mortgage lender that is requested. For example, most mortgage lenders do not require a copy of the inspection report of the property unless it's a part of the purchase and sale agreement. However, lenders usually require a copy of all amendments to the agreement. Therefore, if the inspection report is made part of an exhibit to the GAR Amendment to Address Concerns with Property[2405] and, thus made part of the purchase and sales agreement, the report would have to be provided to the lender. While the report may not have been required, once the lender has it, the lender will likely consider it. In so doing, this may create problems for the borrower that might have been avoided had the report not been made a part of the agreement.

Therefore, if the lender does not require a copy of the property inspection report, the buyer should simply ask for specific repairs to the property without incorporating the inspection report into the GAR Amendment to Address Concerns with Property.[2406] This way, the report is not a part of the purchase and sale agreement and does not have to be provided to the lender. Of course, the inspection report can still be provided to the seller if the seller wishes to see it. However, it can simply be sent to the seller rather than making it part of an exhibit to an amendment to the contract.

§ 21.5 TIPS FOR RECOGNIZING MORTGAGE FRAUD

There are a number of potential warning signs that will help in the identification of possible mortgage fraud. A non-exhaustive list of "red flags" follows. It should be noted, of course, that while the answer "yes" to one or more of these questions may be a cause for concern, it does not necessarily mean that mortgage fraud is taking place.

(1) Does the earnest money check come from someone other than the buyer?

(2) Does the appraisal appear to be excessively high for the specific property or higher than seems warranted for the neighborhood?

(3) After the buyer and seller have settled on a price, does the buyer ask the seller to increase the sales price and to take back a second mortgage that will be repaid at closing?

(4) Does the buyer or the mortgage broker ask that at closing a significant portion of the seller's check be made payable to a third party for repairs, decoration of the house, etc.?

(5) Is a prospective buyer offering the seller a deal that seems too good to be true, such as an offer at or above the listing price, an offer by the buyer to pay the transfer tax and all closing costs, or an offer by the buyer to take the property as it is without any repairs even though the property obviously needs repairs?

2404   O.C.G.A. § 16-8-102(2).

2405   GAR Form F107.

2406   GAR Form F107.

(6) Is the title insurance commitment for the lender at a higher amount than the purchase price of the property?

(7) Is the same property involved in several rapid sales with a large unexplained increase in purchase price in the subsequent sale(s)?

(8) Does the buyer's dress, demeanor, knowledge of real estate, and/or hygiene appear out of whack with what you would expect of the buyer?

(9) Does the HUD-1 Settlement Statement match the true and correct financial realities of the transaction or are there any parts of the deal that do not appear on the settlement documents?

(10) Does the sales contract contain all of the terms of the transaction or are there any handshake or side deals?

§ 21.6 THE GAR AGREEMENTS

When real estate agents suspect that mortgage fraud is afoot in a transaction, they often do not know what steps to take. Some agents have expressed fear that if they report the suspicious activity, they will violate their duties to their client. Below is an example of this situation.

Example: A broker lists a seller's property for $120,000. Several months pass and there are no offers on the property. Then a buyer offers the full asking price for the property which the seller accepts. Several days later, the buyer asks to amend the contract to increase the sales price to $160,000 and asks that at closing, the difference between the original price and the amended price be paid to a third-party contractor whom the buyer says is going to perform renovation work on the property. Anxious to sell the property in a slow market, the seller wants to accept the amended contract price. The broker suspects that the buyer may be in the process of defrauding the lender, but is afraid that reporting the suspicious activity will be a violation of his duty to the client and will cause the deal to fall through, creating potential liability for the broker. What should the broker do in this situation?

Answer: If the broker is fairly certain that there is mortgage fraud involved in the transaction, he should alert the client to the potential scam. He should advise the client of the illegality of mortgage fraud and advise the client not to go through with the deal. If the client insists on accepting the amendment with the higher price, the broker should consider giving up the listing rather than risk being accused of being involved in criminal activity and losing his real estate license.

Obviously, the broker in this example is in a bind. If the broker reports the suspicious activity and the deal falls through, a claim could later be asserted against the broker if it turns out that the broker was incorrect in his assessment that mortgage fraud was occurring. On the other hand, if the broker does nothing, and mortgage fraud is actually occurring, the broker could be implicated in the scheme and could be dragged into a criminal investigation. Some broker have found themselves in a similar dilemma when they learn that their leg of a transaction, while legitimate, is part of a larger transaction involving mortgage fraud.

The GAR Agreements have tried to address this problem by adding language to all GAR form listing agreements[2407] and buyer brokerage agreements[2408] giving the brokers clear authority to report suspicious mortgage circumstances to the appropriate authorities. The language in the listing agreements reads as follows:

> Disclosure of Potentially Fraudulent Mortgage Activities
>
> (a) To help prevent fraud in real estate transactions, Seller does hereby give Broker permission to report any suspicious, unusual and/or potentially illegal or fraudulent activity (including but not limited to mortgage fraud) to: (1) governmental officials, agencies and/or authorities and/or (2) any mortgage

---

2407   GAR Forms F1, F2 and F7.

2408   GAR Forms F4 and F5.

lender, mortgage insurer, mortgage investor and/or title insurance company which could potentially be harmed if the activity was in fact fraudulent or illegal.

(b) Seller acknowledges that Broker does not have special expertise with respect to detecting fraud in real estate transaction. Therefore, Seller acknowledges that: (1) activities which are fraudulent or illegal may be undetected by Broker, and (2) activities which are lawful and/or routine may be may be reported by Broker as being suspicious, unusual or potentially illegal or fraudulent.[2409]

Similar language is contained in the GAR Exclusive Buyer Brokerage Agreement.[2410] The idea behind placing this language in the brokerage engagement agreements is that it allows the broker to get the client's permission to report suspicious activities at the outset of the broker-client relationship, before the client might be tempted by the lure of making easy money on a transaction (regardless of whether it is legal or illegal to do so).

Overall, this language is designed to allow the broker to report potential fraud even though the broker is not completely sure that fraud is occurring. It attempts to protect the broker in the event that he is wrong in her assessment that fraud of any type is occurring. In addition, these provisions help REALTORS® report mortgage fraud without fearing whether reporting suspicious activity will violate some duty to their clients if it causes the transaction to fall apart and create potential liability to them. The objection to this language by a potential client should send up warning signals to the broker and the broker should consider refusing to represent the potential client.

§ 21.7 HOW TO REPORT MORTGAGE FRAUD

If you suspect mortgage fraud is occurring, you can contact the District Attorney's office for your county, the Georgia Attorney General's Office at (404) 656-3300, or the Assistant United States Attorney in Atlanta at (404) 581-6000. Additionally, you may contact the Georgia Department of Banking and Finance, Legal and Consumer Affairs Division at (770) 986-1657 or (770) 986-1029, the State Bar of Georgia at (404) 527-8700, and the Georgia Real Estate Commission and Appraisers Board at (404) 656-3916. Other contacts can be accessed by visiting www.stopmortgagefraud.com, a website developed by the Mortgage Bankers Association and www.grefpac.org, the home page of the Georgia Real Estate Fraud Prevention and Awareness Coalition.

§ 21.8 CONSEQUENCES OF COMMITTING MORTGAGE FRAUD

Persons committing mortgage fraud can be charged with any number of state and federal crimes. At a state level, the more obvious crimes include criminal fraud, theft by taking, forgery, identity theft, criminal solicitation, criminal conspiracy and racketeering. At a federal level persons committing mortgage fraud can, among other things, be charged with wire fraud, mail fraud, use of false identification documents, use of false Social Security numbers, conspiracy to defraud the United States government, and racketeering.

Under the RMFA, mortgage fraud is a felony and carries both monetary fines and prison term penalties. A single incident may result in a fine up to $5,000 and a term of imprisonment between one (1) and ten (10) years.[2411] Multiple counts increase those penalties significantly. Participating in a pattern of mortgage fraud will result in a term of imprisonment between three (3) years and twenty (20) years, a fine up to $100,000 or both.[2412] Each instance of mortgage fraud is viewed as a separate violation.[2413]

2409   GAR Form F1.

2410   GAR Form F4.

2411   O.C.G.A. § 16-8-105(a).

2412   O.C.G.A. § 16-8-105(b).

2413   O.C.G.A. § 16-8-105(c).

For example, a Georgia real estate agent named Joseph Jetton was convicted on several criminal counts, including conspiracy, bank fraud, wire fraud and money laundering. Jetton was sentenced to fourteen (14) years in federal prison, followed by five (5) years of supervised release for his role in orchestrating a multi-million dollar mortgage fraud scheme. Jetton was also ordered to pay $11.1 million dollars in restitution. More than eleven other people were also sentenced to federal prison for their involvement in this mortgage fraud scheme. One closing attorney involved was sentenced to three (3) years in federal prison, while the loan broker was sentenced to five (5) years, followed by four (4) years of supervised release, and ordered to pay over $7.5 million in restitution.

Jetton's mortgage fraud scheme involved millions of dollars in fraudulently inflated mortgage loans provided to unqualified straw borrowers from late 2004 to 2006. The borrowers were paid as much as $600,000 per property from the loan proceeds. The funds were usually paid through shell companies set up for the scheme. Jetton, as the real estate agent involved, used his specialized knowledge of real estate transactions and mortgage lending practices to prepare the sales agreements, and personally derived more than $1 million in commissions from the fraudulent activities.

The Georgia legislature has also amended the state's Racketeer Influenced and Corrupt Organizations Act ("RICO") to include mortgage fraud as a potential racketeering offense.[2414] RICO offenses are felonies and persons convicted of such crimes are subject to imprisonment for up to twenty (20) years.[2415] The monetary penalties for RICO violations are also substantial. The fines imposed can be $25,000 per offense or three times the amount of any pecuniary value gained from the violation, whichever is greater.[2416]

Mortgage fraud is in the same category of crimes as murder, assault, and bank robbery. The RMFA criminalizes even the slightest deception and puts anyone who either knew of or participated in the deception at great risk. To protect the real estate industry as a whole, REALTORS® must use extreme care to comply with the law.

§ 21.9 CONSEQUENCES FOR REAL ESTATE LICENSEES

In addition to the penalties under state and federal law, real estate agents and brokers who participate in mortgage fraud can also be sanctioned by the Georgia Real Estate Commission, up to and including the revocation of their licenses, for engaging in any number of unfair business practices including the following:

(a) making substantial misrepresentations;[2417]

(b) having demonstrated incompetence to act as a real estate licensee in such manner as to safeguard the interest of the public or any other conduct … which constitutes dishonest dealing;[2418]

(c) failing to keep for a period of three (3) years a true and correct copy of all sales contracts, closing statements, or other documents relating to real estate closings;[2419] and

(d) being or becoming a party to any falsification of any portion of any contract or other document involved in any real estate transaction.[2420]

Even if no specific charges are brought by the Georgia Real Estate Commission against a licensee for violating any of the above license law provisions, if a licensee is convicted of a state or federal crime involving mortgage fraud they can also lose their real estate license as a result of the criminal conviction. Licensees are required to immediately report to the Georgia Real Estate Commission any felony conviction or any crime involving moral turpitude. The term

---

2414   O.C.G.A. § 16-14-3(9)(A).

2415   O.C.G.A. § 16-14-5(a).

2416   O.C.G.A. § 16-14-5(b).

2417   O.C.G.A. § 43-40-25(b)(21).

2418   O.C.G.A. § 43-40-25(b)(25).

2419   O.C.G.A. § 43-40-25(b)(27).

2420   O.C.G.A. § 43-40-25(b)(28).

"conviction" means a finding, verdict or plea of guilty, to a felony or any other crime involving moral turpitude, a sentencing to first offender treatment without a determination of guilt for a felony charge or any other crime involving moral turpitude, or a plea of *nolo contendere* to a felony charge or any other crime involving moral turpitude.[2421] Upon such a conviction, the licensee's license is automatically revoked 60 days after the conviction unless the licensee timely requests a hearing to determine whether the licensee remains fit to hold a real estate license.[2422]

§ 21.9.1 Brokers' Liability For The Fraud Of Their Agents

Brokers may also have exposure to sanctions before the Georgia Real Estate Commission for mortgage fraud committed by their licensees if the Commission determines that the broker did not properly supervise her licensees. This may be the case even though the broker may not even be aware of the licensee's fraud. The Georgia real estate licensing law specifically provides that the broker or qualifying broker is responsible for any licensee whose license is affiliated with the broker's firm unless the broker can prove all of the following:

(a) the broker had reasonable procedures in place for the supervision of the licensee's actions;[2423]

(b) the broker did not participate in the violation;[2424] and

(c) the broker did not ratify the violation.[2425]

As stated above, in order to avoid a sanction, the broker must also show that she had reasonable procedures in place to supervise the agent's actions.[2426] Georgia license law sets out numerous substantive areas in which brokers are required to establish and implement procedures to supervise affiliated licensees. Specifically, the law requires brokers to establish and implement procedures for reviewing "all listing contracts, leases, sales contracts, management agreements, and offers to buy, sell, lease or exchange real property secured or negotiated by the firm's associates" for compliance with the License Law and Regulations.[2427] This review must be performed within thirty (30) days of the date of the offer or the contract.[2428]

To fulfill the duties to supervise affiliated licensees, brokers should look deeper into the transactions of licensees whom they supervise. During the review of each document the broker should keep in mind other transactions in which the affiliated licensee has been involved. Brokers need to be on the lookout for patterns of quick re-sales of the same property, and if a property is involved in a rapid resale, the broker should ask the licensee about the circumstances surrounding the transaction including the parties to the sale, the loan, and the appraisal, until the broker is satisfied that the transaction is legitimate. Brokers should also be sure that their office procedures manual includes a discussion of mortgage fraud and the consequences for licensees who participate in or abet mortgage fraud.

2421   O.C.G.A. § 43-40-15(b)(1).

2422   O.C.G.A. § 43-40-15(b)(2)(i).

2423   O.C.G.A. § 43-40-18(b)(1).

2424   O.C.G.A. § 43-40-18(b)(2).

2425   O.C.G.A. § 43-40-18(b)(3).

2426   O.C.G.A. § 43-40-18(b)(1).

2427   O.C.G.A. § 43-40-18(c)(3).

2428   O.C.G.A. § 43-40-18(c)(3).

The **RED BOOK**

CHAPTER 22

MECHANICS' AND MATERIALMEN'S LIENS

OVERVIEW

Mechanics' and Materialmen's liens arise in a variety of contexts.[2429] They can become a significant factor in the sale, lease, or foreclosure of real estate. They can arise on any size project and can range from new construction projects to simple repairs. Georgia's mechanics' and materialmen's lien laws are a not a product of traditional common law. Rather, they were created by the legislature. As a result, they are exactingly construed and one wishing to take advantage of them must strictly comply with the letter of the law.[2430]

Lien laws attempt to provide mechanics and materialmen a claim upon the owner's property if the owner fails to receive assurances from his general contractor that all materialmen and mechanics have been paid.[2431] Lien laws attempt to balance the competing interests of (1) contractors and materialmen, who have rendered services or delivered material used for the improvement of real estate and want to be paid for their services and (2) the owners of the property, who may hire a contractor to do the work, but usually have no idea which subcontractors or suppliers are actually involved in the project.

The legislature's attempt to balance these interests has, unfortunately, resulted in a tangled knot of intertwined and seemingly arbitrary deadlines and filing and notice requirements that very much constitute a trap for the unwary.

§ 22.1   THE GEORGIA LIEN STATUTE

§ 22.1.1 Definitions

The Georgia Lien Statute[2432] (the "Act") contains a number of definitions that are used through its provisions. One must understand these and other terms to make sense of the provisions of the Act.[2433]

(1) "**Contractor**" means a contractor having privity of contract with the owner of the real estate.[2434] In other words, a contractor is someone who has a direct contract, either written or oral, with the owner of the real estate. This is in contradiction to subcontractors or sub-subcontractors (defined below) who do not have any direct contract with the owner.

(2) "**Land surveyor**" means an individual who is qualified to engage in the practice of land surveying and who possesses a current certificate of registration as a land surveyor issued by the board.[2435]

(3) "**Materials**" means tools, appliances, machinery or equipment used in making improvements to the real estate, to the extent of the reasonable value or the contracted rental price, whichever is greater, of such tools, appliances, machinery or equipment.[2436] Materials also includes things that go into and becomes a part of a finished structure, such as lumber, nails, glass, hardware, appliances, machinery, tools, or equipment which is necessary to the completion of the improvements to the land.[2437] Material does not include such items as scaffolding or rental

---

2429 Please note that this Chapter does not discuss other liens, such as those arising from a brokerage engagement or those provided for in the Georgia Condominium Act.

2430 *Trench Shoring Services of Atlanta, Inc. v Westchester Fire Ins. Co.*, 274 Ga.App. 850, 619 S.E.2d 361 (2005).

2431 *Cutler-Hammer, Inc. v. Wayne*, 101 F.2d 823 (1939); *Mullins v. Noland Co.*, 406 F.Supp. 206 (1975). (In Georgia general contractors have a substantial obligation to insure that all subcontractors and their materialmen are paid and the owner may withhold payment to the general contractor so long as subcontractors and materialmen remain unpaid.)

2432 O.C.G.A. § 44-14-360 *et seq.*

2433 O.C.G.A. § 44-14-360.

2434 O.C.G.A. § 44-14-360(1) .

2435 O.C.G.A. § 44-14-360(2) citing O.C.G.A. § 43-15-2(7).

2436 O.C.G.A. § 44-14-360(3).

2437 *Trench Shoring Services of Atlanta, Inc. v Westchester Fire Ins. Co.*, 274 Ga.App. 850, 619 S.E.2d 361 (2005).

equipment, which is not incorporated into the finished structure.[2438] Such non-permanent items cannot be converted into "material" by designating them in contracts as material or items subject to lien, since lien rights arise from the Act, not the contract between the parties.[2439]

(4) "**Materialmen**" means all persons furnishing the materials, tools, appliances, machinery, or equipment included in the definition of materials in paragraph (c) above.[2440]

(5) "**Mechanic**" is not defined by the Act, but has been held to constitute "an artisan, artificer, one who practices any mechanical art, one skilled or employed in shaping and uniting materials, as wood, metal, etc., into any kind of structure, machine or other objects, requiring the use of tools, or other instruments."[2441]

(6) "**Professional engineer**" means an individual who is qualified, by reason of knowledge of mathematics, the physical sciences, and the principles by which mechanical properties of matter are made useful to man in structures and machines, acquired by professional education and practical experience, to engage in the practice of professional engineering and who possesses a current certificate of registration as a professional engineer.[2442]

(7) "**Registered forester**" means a person who has registered with the State Board of Registration for Foresters and qualified to engage in professional forestry practices.[2443]

(8) "**Registered land surveyors**" and "**registered professional engineers**" mean land surveyors or professional engineers who are registered as land surveyors or professional engineers at the time of performing, rendering, or furnishing services.[2444]

(9) "**Residential property**" means single-family and two-family, three-family, and four-family residential real estate.[2445]

(10) "**Subcontractor**" means, but is not limited to, subcontractors having privity of contract with the contractor.[2446] This term also means a person who, pursuant to a contract with the prime contractor or in a direct chain of contracts leading to the prime contractor, performs services or procures another to perform services in furtherance of the goals of the prime contractor.[2447]

(11) "**Sub-subcontractor**" is not a term specifically defined by the Act. However, as used in practice, a sub-subcontractor is someone who may have privity of contract with a subcontractor, but who does not have privity of contract with the property owner or the contractor.[2448]

(12) "**Business day**" means any day that is not a Saturday, Sunday, or legal holiday.[2449]

(13) "**Lien action**" means a lawsuit, proof of claim in a bankruptcy case, or a binding arbitration.[2450]

2438   *Sears Roebuck & Co. v. Superior Rigging & Erecting Co.*, 120 Ga.App. 412, 170 S.E.2d 721 (1969); H.D. *Overmyer Warehouse Co. v. W.C. Caye & Co.*, 116 Ga.App. 128, 157 S.E.2d 68 (1967).

2439   *H.D. Overmyer Warehouse Co. v. W.C. Caye & Co.*, 116 Ga.App. 128, 157 S.E.2d 68 (1967).

2440   O.C.G.A. § 44-14-360(4).

2441   *Wager v. Carrollton Bank*, 156 Ga. 783, 120 S.E. 116, (1923).

2442   O.C.G.A. § 43-15-2(10).

2443   O.C.G.A. § 44-14-360(6) citing O.C.G.A. § 12-6-41(3).

2444   O.C.G.A. § 44-14-360(7).

2445   O.C.G.A. § 44-14-360(8).

2446   O.C.G.A. § 44-14-360(9).

2447   *Tonn & Blank, Inc. v. D.M. Asphalt, Inc.*, 187 Ga.App. 272, 370 S.E.2d 30 (1988).

2448   *Benning Const. Co. v. Dykes Paving & Const. Co., Inc.*, 204 Ga.App. 73, 418 S.E.2d 620 (1992).

2449   O.C.G.A. § 44-14-360(.1).

2450   O.C.G.A. § 44-14-360(2.1).

§ 22.1.2 Who Can File A Lien?

The following persons are permitted by the Act to file a lien on the real estate, factories, railroads, or other property for which they furnish labor, services, or materials:[2451]

(a) All mechanics who have taken no personal security for work done and material furnished in building, repairing, or improving any real estate of their employers;[2452]

(b) All contractors, all subcontractors and all materialmen furnishing material to subcontractors, and all laborers furnishing labor to subcontractors, materialmen, and persons furnishing material for the improvement of real estate;[2453]

(c) All registered architects furnishing plans, drawings, designs, or other architectural services on or with respect to any real estate;[2454]

(d) All registered foresters performing or furnishing services on or with respect to any real estate;[2455]

(e) All registered land surveyors and registered professional engineers performing or furnishing services on or with respect to any real estate;[2456]

(f) All contractors, all subcontractors and materialmen furnishing material to subcontractors, and all laborers furnishing labor for subcontractors for building factories, furnishing material for factories, or furnishing machinery for factories;[2457]

(g) All machinists and manufacturers of machinery, including corporations engaged in such business, who may furnish or put up any mill or other machinery in any county or who may repair the same;[2458]

(h) All contractors to build railroads; and[2459]

(i) All suppliers furnishing rental tools, appliances, machinery, or equipment for the improvement of real estate.[2460]

§ 22.1.3 To What Property May A Lien Attach?

The liens created by the Act may be filed against the real estate of the owner for which the labor, services, or materials are furnished if they were furnished at the instance of the owner, contractor, or some other person acting for the owner or contractor.[2461]

Mechanics can, of course, testify that they performed work on the property of the owner. Materialmen, however, must prove that materials were delivered, and that they were used in the improvement of, the owner's property.[2462] There is a presumption under the law that materials delivered to a jobsite for use at the site, were actually used thereon. The burden then shifts to the property owner to show that any such materials were not used for the improvement of the owner's property.[2463]

2451 O.C.G.A. § 44-14-361(a).
2452 O.C.G.A. § 44-14-361(a)(1).
2453 O.C.G.A. § 44-14-361(a)(2).
2454 O.C.G.A. § 44-14-361(a)(3).
2455 O.C.G.A. § 44-14-361(a)(4).
2456 O.C.G.A. § 44-14-361(a)(5).
2457 O.C.G.A. § 44-14-361(a)(6).
2458 O.C.G.A. § 44-14-361(a)(7).
2459 O.C.G.A. § 44-14-361(a)(8).
2460 O.C.G.A. § 44-14-361(9).
2461 O.C.G.A. § 44-14-361(b).
2462 *Bankston v. Smith*, 236 Ga. 92, 222, S.E.2d 375 (1976).
2463 *Bankston v. Smith*, 236 Ga. 92, 222, S.E.2d 375 (1976).

In addition to work or material performed to the property of the owner, the liens under the Act also extend to work done and materials furnished in any easement or public right of way adjoining real estate of the owner if the work done or materials furnished in the easement or public right of way is for the benefit of the owner's real estate and is within the scope of the owner's contract for improvements to the real estate.[2464] In such an instance, the lien attaches to the owner's property, and not the public right of way. This is because liens under the Act cannot be filed against public property.[2465]

§ 22.1.4 Exclusive Remedy As To Owner

A contractor who is in direct contractual privity with the owner may assert a claim against the owner under a theory of breach of contract, on a general account, and/or to establish and perfect a lien pursuant to the Act against the owner's property. However, any materialman or mechanic who is not in direct contractual privity with the owner cannot enforce any claim as to the owner or owner's property other than through the Act. For example, a subcontractor who does not have a contract with the owner is precluded from filing suit against the owner for payment or unjust enrichment. Rather, the subcontractor's sole remedy as to the owner or owner's property is through the lien provisions of the Act.[2466]

§ 22.1.5 Trouble With Tenants

As discussed in § 22.1.3 (To What Property May A Lien Attach), liens may attach to the property of the owner if the owner, or someone on his behalf, requested the work or material. This often creates problems for lien claimants who have provided work or material at the request of a tenant, rather than the true owner. The question is whether the tenant requested the work solely for their own benefit and on their own behalf or on behalf of the owner.[2467] If the work was not requested on behalf of the owner, then the claimant has no lien rights against the owner's property.

Whether a tenant's request for work is really made on behalf of the owner is a fact sensitive analysis that must be evaluated on a case-by-case basis. This may not always be an easy determination. In one case, the court found there was no evidence the owner requested work be done even though the owner was aware that the work was being done, that the work resulted in improvements to the owner's property, and that the owner would retain the improvements once the lease ended.[2468] In another case, the court disallowed a lien on the basis that the lease between the landlord and tenant provided that improvements to the property were to be made at the expense of the tenant.[2469]

§ 22.1.6 Creation Of Liens

In order to create a lien, the lien claimant must strictly company with all of the following conditions:[2470]

§ 22.1.6.1 Substantial Compliance By Lien Claimant

The lien clamant must substantially comply with her contract for building, repairing, or improving; for architectural services furnished; for registered forester services furnished or performed; for registered land surveying or registered professional engineering services furnished or performed; or for materials or machinery furnished or set up.[2471]

2464   O.C.G.A. § 44-14-361(b).

2465   *DeKalb County v. J & A Pipeline Co., Inc.*, 263 Ga. 645, 437 S.E.2d 327 (1993).

2466   *MCC Powers v. Ford Motor Co.*, 184 Ga.App. 487, 361 S.E.2d 716 (1987).

2467   *Capital Mechanical, Ltd. v. Dobbs Houses, Inc.*, 151 Ga.App. 142, 259 S.E.2d 147 (1979).

2468   *F.S. Associates, Ltd. v. McMichael's Const. Co.*, Inc., 197 Ga.App. 705, 399 S.E.2d 479 (1990).

2469   *Seckinger v. Silvers*, 104 Ga.App. 396, 121 S.E.2d 922 (1961).

2470   O.C.G.A. § 44-14-361.1.

2471   O.C.G.A. § 44-14-361.1(a)(1).

What constitutes substantial compliance is a question of fact that will be different for each case. However, it is a precondition to filing a lien for the claimant to have substantially fulfilled the obligations for which their services were retained.[2472]

§ 22.1.6.2   Timely Recording And Notice

The claim of lien must be filed of record in the Superior Court of the county in which the real estate is located within 90 days after the completion of the work or the material or machinery is furnished.[2473] The purpose in limiting the time during which the claim of lien can be filed is to provide certainty to the parties, by way of a cut-off date, whether a lien may be claimed.[2474]

The lien must include a statement regarding its expiration[2475] and a notice to the owner of the property that such owner has the right to contest the lien. The claim of lien must in the following general form:

> A.B., a mechanic, contractor, subcontractor, materialman, machinist, manufacturer, registered architect, registered forester, registered land surveyor, registered professional engineer, or other person (as the case may be) claims a lien in the amount of (specify the amount claimed) on the house, factory, mill, machinery, or railroad (as the case may be) and the premises or real estate on which it is erected or built, of C.D. (describing the houses, premises, real estate, or railroad), for satisfaction of a claim which became due on (specify the date the claim was due, which is the same as the last date the labor, services, or materials were supplied to the premises) for building, repairing, improving, or furnishing material (or whatever the claim may be).[2476]

No later than two business days after the date the claim of lien is filed of record, the lien claimant must send a true and accurate copy of the claim of lien by registered or certified mail or statutory overnight delivery to the owner of the property.[2477] Notice sent by any other means (*i.e.*, via facsimile) is not effective.[2478]

If the owner's mailing address cannot be found, the claim of lien can be sent to the contractor as the agent of the owner.[2479] If the property owner is an entity registered with the Georgia Secretary of State's Corporations Division (*i.e.*, corporation, limited liability company, limited partnership, etc.), it is sufficient to send a copy of the claim of lien to the entity's address or the registered agent's address as listed with the Secretary of State.[2480]

§ 22.1.6.3   Additional Notice If Notice Of Commencement Filed

If a notice of commencement[2481] has been filed with the clerk of the Superior Court, the lien claimant must also send a copy of the claim of lien by registered or certified mail or statutory overnight delivery to the contractor at the address shown on the notice of commencement.[2482]

2472   O.C.G.A. § 44-14-361.1.

2473   O.C.G.A. § 44-14-361.1(a)(2).

2474   *Womack Industries, Inc. v. B & A Equipment Co.*, 199 Ga.App. 660, 405 S.E.2d 880 (1991).

2475   O.C.G.A. § 44-14-367.

2476   O.C.G.A. § 44-14-361.1(a)(2).

2477   O.C.G.A. § 44-14-361.1(a)(2).

2478   *Phillips, Inc. v. Historic Properties of America*, LLC, 260 Ga.App. 886, 581 S.E.2d 389 (2003).

2479   O.C.G.A. § 44-14-361.1(a)(2).

2480   O.C.G.A. § 44-14-361.1.

2481   O.C.G.A. § 44-14-361.5; *see § 22.1.13* (Notice of Commencement; Notice to Contractor) in this Chapter.

2482   O.C.G.A. § 44-14-361.1.

§ 22.1.7 Perfecting The Lien

Assuming that the filing and notice requirements discussed in § 22.1.6 (Creation of Liens), above, have been timely met, the lien claimant must do all of the following to enforce the lien:[2483]

§ 22.1.7.1 Timely Commence A Lien Action Against Whomever Owes The Money

A lien action (lawsuit, proof of claim in a bankruptcy case, or a binding arbitration)[2484] must be commenced for the recovery of the amount of the party's claim[2485] within 365 days from the date of filing for record of the claim of lien.[2486]

If the lien claimant is the contractor, his suit will be directly against the owner. In all other cases, the lien claimant must usually file suit against whomever owes him money (the "Debtor") (*i.e.*, the general contractor or a subcontractor), seeking both a judgment for the amount owed and seeking to perfect his lien rights pursuant to the Act.[2487] A lien action against the Debtor based only upon an open account or promissory note, which does not seek to establish or perfect a lien under the Act, will not suffice, and such a failure precludes any subsequent action to enforce the lien against the property of the owner.[2488]

The owner of the improved property may be named in the lien action with the Debtor or can be named later in a separate action once judgment against the Debtor has been obtained.[2489] However, obtaining a judgment against the Debtor is a pre-condition to foreclosure of the lien against the owner's property. This is because in most cases the lien claimant will not be in direct privity of contract with the owner. Indeed, the owner often has no idea who the claimant is or that she provided material or services to the property. The owner should not be called on to pay a debt he did not contract, and for which his property is liable only by force of a statute, until the lien claimant has established by judgment, in a proceeding against the Debtor, that he is actually owed the amount for which he is seeking to assert his lien.[2490]

§ 22.1.7.2 Notice Of Commencement Of Lien Action

Within 30 days after commencing the lien action, the party claiming the lien must file a notice with the clerk of the Superior Court of the county in which the claim of lien was filed.[2491] The purpose of requiring the lien claimant to file a notice of commencement of the lien action against the Debtor is to provide constructive notice to potential purchasers of the property that the claimant has, in fact, initiated the process to perfect its claim of lien.[2492] Having been put on constructive notice, the prospective purchaser's title will be subject to the lien, once perfected.[2493]

The notice must contain a caption identifying the name of the then owner of the property against which the lien was filed and make reference to a deed or other recorded instrument in the chain of title of the affected property.[2494]

2483   O.C.G.A. § 44-14-361.1.

2484   O.C.G.A. § 44-14-360.

2485   The sum total of all liens claimed under the Act cannot exceed the contract price of the improvements made or services performed to the property. Further, if the contractor abandons the contract, the owner may have it completed and may deduct any cost of completion from the contract price for fixing the maximum amount of all liens. *Spirides v. Victory Lumber Co.*, 76 Ga.App. 78, 45 S.E.2d 65 (1947).

2486   O.C.G.A. § 44-14-361.1.

2487   O.C.G.A. § 44-14-361.1; *Chambers Lumber Co. v. Gilmer*, 60 Ga.App. 832, 5 S.E.2d 84 (1939).

2488   *Ben O'Callaghan Co. v. Schmincke*, 376 F.Supp. 1361 (1974).

2489   *Allied Asphalt Co. v. Cumbie*, 134 Ga.App. 960, 216 S.E.2d 659 (1975); *Chambers Lumber Co. v. Gilmer*, 60 Ga.App. 832, 5 S.E.2d 84 (1939).

2490   *Chambers Lumber Co. v. Gilmer*, 60 Ga.App. 832, 5 S.E.2d 84 (1939).

2491   O.C.G.A. § 44-14-361.1(3).

2492   *Gwinnett-Club Associates, L.P. v. Southern Electrical Supply, Co., Inc.*, 242 Ga.App. 507, 529 S.E.2d 636 (2000).

2493   *Home Mart Bldg. Centers, Inc. v. Wallace*, 144 Ga.App. 19, 240 S.E.2d 582 (1977).

2494   O.C.G.A. § 44-14-361.1(3).

The notice must be signed, under oath, by the party claiming the lien or by their attorney.[2495] While most provisions of the Act require strict compliance, the failure to sign the notice under oath is be an amendable defect that can usually be cured in advance of trial.[2496]

The notice must identify the court or arbitration venue where the lien action is brought; the style and number, if any, of the lien action, including the names of all parties thereto; the date of the filing of the lien action; and the book and page number of the records of the county where the lien is recorded.[2497]

§ 22.1.7.3 Exemption From Lien Action When Contractor Is Dead, Disappeared, Or Bankrupt

The law should not require one to undertake a futile act.[2498] In this regard, there are circumstances in which pursuing a lien action against a contractor or subcontractor does not make any sense.

The Act provides that a claimant need not file a lien action against the contractor or subcontract if:[2499]

(a) the contractor or subcontractor absconds, dies, or leaves the state during the required time period for filing a lien action, so that personal jurisdiction cannot be obtained on them;

(b) the contractor or subcontractor files for bankruptcy;

(c) after the filing of a lien action, no final judgment can be obtained against the contractor or subcontractor because they are dead or have filed for bankruptcy; or

(d) the contract between the lien claimant and the contractor or subcontractor includes a provision preventing payment to the lien claimant until after the contractor or the subcontractor has received payment.[2500]

In any of the events described above, the lien claimant does not need to commence (or in the case of number (3), continue) a lien action or obtain judgment against the contractor or subcontractor as a prerequisite to enforcing their lien against the owner's property.[2501]

Rather, in these circumstances, the lien claimant may proceed directly to enforce the lien against the property in a lien action against the property owner. The lien claimant must commence such a direct action within the time period permitted for the filing of a lien action (*i.e.*, 365 days from the filing of the claim of lien) and must thereafter timely file a notice of commencement (*i.e.*, 30 days from the commencement of the direct action). Any judgment obtained in such a proceeding will be *in rem* (against the property only), and will not create any personal liability upon the owner of the property.[2502]

While the lien claimant is relieved of the necessity to pursue a lien action against a contractor who has filed for bankruptcy, the lien claimant may, nevertheless, proceed against the bankrupt contractor by filing a proof of claim in the bankruptcy. However, by doing so the lien claimant waives the right to pursue a direct action against the owner of the property until all the normal requirements have been met. For example, if a lien claimant files a proof of claim (a lien action) against a contractor who is in bankruptcy, but does not timely file a notice of commencement, he will not be in compliance with the Act and his lien rights vanish.[2503]

2495 O.C.G.A. § 44-14-361.1(3).

2496 O.C.G.A. § 44-14-361.1.

2497 O.C.G.A. § 44-14-361.1.

2498 *BDI Distributors, Inc. v. Beaver Computer Corp.*, 232 Ga.App. 316, 317, 501 S.E.2d 839, 841 (1998). (Parties are not required to "whistle in the wind" or otherwise take useless and futile action.)

2499 O.C.G.A. § 44-14-361.1(4).

2500 O.C.G.A. § 44-14-361.1.

2501 O.C.G.A. § 44-14-361.1; *Reid v. Harbin Lumber Co. of Royston, Inc.*, 172 Ga.App. 615, 323 S.E.2d 845 (1984).

2502 O.C.G.A. § 44-14-361.1.

2503 *Action Concrete v. Portrait Homes-Little Suwanee Point, LLC*, 285 Ga.App. 650, 647 S.E.2d 353 (2007).

§ 22.1.8   Priority Of Liens

As between themselves, the liens created by the Act generally rank according to the date filed.[2504] However, all liens for repairs, building, or furnishing materials or services, upon the same property, shall, as to each other, be deemed to be of the same date when declared and filed for record within 90 days after the work is done or before that time.[2505]

The liens created by the Act are inferior to liens for taxes, to the general and special liens of laborers,[2506] to the general lien of landlords of rent when a distress warrant is issued out and levied,[2507] to claims for purchase money due persons who have only given bonds for titles,[2508] and to other general liens when actual notice of the general lien of landlords and others has been communicated before the work was done or materials or services furnished. The liens provided for by the Act are superior to all other liens.[2509]

Provided that the liens under the Act are properly created and that notice is properly given, they are deemed to have attached to the owner's property as of the time the work was commenced and the material became a part of the realty.[2510] Once such a lien has been established, it relates back and takes priority over title acquired by anyone who had actual notice of the claim of lien, even if the title is transferred to that person prior to the claim of lien being recorded.[2511]

§ 22.1.9   Dissolving Liens

The liens created by the Act are automatically dissolved under two circumstances. These are:

(a) If the owner, purchaser from the owner, or lender providing construction, purchase money, or any other loan secured by the real estate shows that the lien has been waived in writing by the lien claimant;[2512] or

(b) If the owner, purchaser from the owner, or lender providing construction, purchase money, or any other loan secured by the real estate shows that they have obtained a sworn written statement from the contractor or person other than the owner (but not a subcontractor) at whose instance the labor, services, or materials were furnished, or from the owner when conveying title in a bona fide sale or loan transaction, stating that the agreed price or reasonable value of the labor, services, or materials has been paid or waived in writing by the lien claimant.[2513] Additionally, if the sworn written statement was obtained or given as a part of a transaction involving: (i) a conveyance of title in a bona fide sale; (ii) a loan in which the real estate is to secure repayment of the loan; or (iii) where final disbursement of the contract price is made by the owner to the contractor, it must be shown there was not of record, at the time of the settlement of the transaction a valid preliminary notice or claim of lien which had not been previously canceled, dissolved, or expired.[2514]

The phrase, "final disbursement" of the contract price means payment of the agreed price between the owner and contractor for the improvements made upon the real estate or the reasonable value of the labor, services, and materials

---

2504   O.C.G.A. § 44-14-361.1.

2505   O.C.G.A. § 44-14-361.1.

2506   O.C.G.A. § 44-14-381.

2507   O.C.G.A. §§ 44-7-70 *et seq.*, 44-14-340 *et seq.*

2508   O.C.G.A. § 44-14-321.

2509   O.C.G.A. § 44-14-361.1.

2510   *Home Mart Bldg. Centers, Inc. v. Wallace*, 144 Ga.App. 19, 240 S.E.2d 582 (1977).

2511   *Home Mart Bldg. Centers, Inc. v. Wallace*, 144 Ga.App. 19, 240 S.E.2d 582 (1977).

2512   O.C.G.A. § 44-14-361.2(a)(1).

2513   O.C.G.A. § 44-14-361.2(a)(2)(A).

2514   O.C.G.A. § 44-14-361.2(a)(2)(B).

incorporated in the improvements upon the real estate and includes payment of the balance of the contract price to an escrow agent.[2515]

Interestingly, the owner can cause a lien to dissolve by obtaining an affidavit from the general contractor which facially comports with the requirements of section (b) above, even if the affidavit is false.[2516]

§ 22.1.10 Preliminary Notice Of Lien Rights

Prior to filing a claim of lien, a person having a lien under the Act may, but is not required to, file a preliminary notice of lien rights.[2517] The primary purpose for filing a preliminary notice of lien rights would be to prevent otherwise innocent third parties from cutting off unperfected potential liens.

The rights of a purchaser against the holder of a materialmen's lien depend upon whether the purchaser, at the time of the purchase, has notice of any preexisting, unperfected lien. Such an instance could arise if, for example, the Owner contracts for improvements to real estate on March 1st. On March 15th, prior to the work being completed and prior to any claim of lien being filed, the Owner sells the property to Buyer. Since there was no claim of lien filed, the Buyer would not have constructive notice of the potential lien. If Buyer did not have actual notice of the potential claim of lien, then he would take his title free and clear of any subsequently filed lien. If, however, a materialman filed a preliminary notice, this would put the Buyer on notice, thereby putting the materialmen's lien ahead of the Buyer's interest in the property.[2518]

§ 22.1.10.1 The Preliminary Notice Of Lien Rights Must:

(a) Be filed with the clerk of superior court of the county in which the real estate is located within 30 days after the date the claimant delivered any materials or provided any labor or services for which a lien may be claimed;[2519]

(b) State the name, address, and telephone number of the potential lien claimant;[2520]

(c) State the name and address of the contractor or other person at whose instance the labor, services, or materials were furnished;[2521]

(d) State the name of the owner of the real estate and include a description sufficient to identify the real estate against which the lien is or may be claimed;[2522]

(e) Include a general description of the labor, services, or materials furnished or to be furnished;[2523] and

(f) Anyone filing a preliminary notice of lien rights except a contractor must, within seven days of filing the notice, send by registered or certified mail or statutory overnight delivery a copy of the notice to the contractor on the property named in the notice or to the owner of the property. The lien claimant may rely on the building permit issued on the property for the name of the contractor.[2524]

2515 O.C.G.A. § 44-14-361.2(b)(2).

2516 *DeKalb County v. J & A Pipeline Co., Inc.*, 263 Ga. 645, 437 S.E.2d 327 (1993).

2517 O.C.G.A. § 44-14-361.3; *In re American Building Consultants, Inc.*, 138 B.R. 1015 (1992).

2518 *In re WWG Industries, Inc.*, 772 F.2d 810 (1985).

2519 O.C.G.A. § 44-14-361.3(a)(1).

2520 O.C.G.A. § 44-14-361.3(a)(2).

2521 O.C.G.A. § 44-14-361.3(a)(3).

2522 O.C.G.A. § 44-14-361.3(a)(4).

2523 O.C.G.A. § 44-14-361.3(a)(5).

2524 O.C.G.A. § 44-14-361.3(b).

§ 22.1.11   Dissolving Preliminary Notice Of Lien / Demand For Filing Claim Of Lien

A preliminary notice of lien rights is considered to be dissolved if it is canceled of record.[2525] Additionally, a preliminary notice also expires and is dissolved under any of the following conditions:

(a) The lien has been waived in writing by the lien claimant;[2526]

(b) The time has expired for filing a claim of lien with no such filing;[2527]

(c) On residential property, a demand for filing of a claim of lien has been sent by registered or certified mail or statutory overnight delivery to the potential lien claimant at the address specified in the preliminary notice of lien rights and at least 10 days have elapsed since the date of such mailing without the filing of a claim of lien;[2528] or

(d) On all property except residential property, a demand for filing of a claim of lien has been sent by registered or certified mail or statutory overnight delivery to the potential lien claimant at the address specified in the preliminary notice of lien rights and at least 10 days have elapsed since the date of such mailing without the filing of a claim of lien; provided, however, the demand for filing of a claim of lien shall not be sent until the contractor's contract is substantially complete or until the potential lien claimant's contract has been terminated or the potential lien claimant has abandoned the contract.[2529]

A demand for filing of claim of lien must contain the same information required to be contained in the preliminary notice of lien rights and must contain the following statement addressed to the potential lien claimant:

> This demand was mailed to you on _____ pursuant to Code Section 44-14-361.4.
> You are notified that unless you file a claim of lien with respect to this claim on
> or before the tenth day after said date of mailing your right to claim a lien will
> be dissolved.[2530]

If a demand for filing of a claim of lien is mailed and no claim of lien is timely filed, the preliminary notice of lien rights may be canceled. In order to obtain cancellation, the person who mailed the demand or his attorney must file with the clerk of superior court a copy of the demand and an affidavit that the demand was mailed and that 10 days have elapsed since said date of mailing without the filing of a claim of lien by the potential lien claimant. Upon such filing, the clerk of the superior court is required to cancel of record the preliminary notice of lien rights.[2531]

§ 22.1.12   Cancellation Of Preliminary Notice Of Lien Rights

Upon final payment after all labor, services, or materials have been furnished, a person who has filed a preliminary notice of lien rights is required to either deliver a cancellation of the preliminary notice of lien rights at the time of final payment or cause the notice to be canceled of record within 10 days after final payment.[2532] Any person who fails to cancel a preliminary notice is liable to the owner for all actual damages, costs, and reasonable attorney's fees incurred by the owner in having the preliminary notice canceled.[2533]

2525   O.C.G.A. § 44-14-361.4.

2526   O.C.G.A. § 44-14-361.4(a)(1).

2527   O.C.G.A. § 44-14-361.4(a)(2).

2528   O.C.G.A. § 44-14-361.4(a)(3).

2529   O.C.G.A. § 44-14-361.4(a)(4).

2530   O.C.G.A. § 44-14-361.4(b).

2531   O.C.G.A. § 44-14-361.4.

2532   O.C.G.A. § 44-14-362.

2533   O.C.G.A. § 44-14-362.

The form for the cancellation of a Preliminary Notice of Lien is as follows:

Clerk, Superior Court

of _____ County

You are authorized and directed to cancel of record the preliminary notice of lien rights which we filed on the property owned by (state name of owner) on (give date) and recorded by you in Book _____, Page _____, of preliminary notices kept by you.

This _____ day of _____, _____.[2534]

_____

Lien claimant or attorney

§ 22.1.13   Notice Of Commencement; Notice To Contractor

§ 22.1.13.1   Notice Of Commencement

Not later than 15 days after a contractor physically commences work on the property, a notice of commencement may be filed by the owner, the agent of the owner, or by the contractor, with the clerk of the superior court in the county in which the property is located.[2535] A copy of the notice of commencement must be posted on the project site. The notice of commencement must include the following information:

(a) The name, address, and telephone number of the contractor;[2536]

(b) The name and location of the project being constructed and the legal description of the property upon which the improvements are being made;[2537]

(c) The name and address of the true owner of the property;[2538]

(d) The name and address of the person other than the owner at whose instance the improvements are being made, if not the true owner of the property;[2539]

(e) The name and the address of the surety for the performance and payment bonds, if any;[2540] and

(f) The name and address of the construction lender, if any.[2541]

The failure to file a notice of commencement results in the waiver of the protections afford by the notice.[2542] Further, the contractor is required to give a copy of the notice of commencement to any subcontractor, materialman, or person who makes a written request of the contractor. The failure of the contractor to give a copy of the notice of commencement within 10 calendar days of receipt of the written request from the subcontractor, materialman, or person results in the waiver of the protections afforded by the Notice as to the subcontractor, materialman, or person making the request.[2543]

2534   O.C.G.A. § 44-14-362(b).

2535   O.C.G.A. § 44-14-361.5.

2536   O.C.G.A. § 44-14-361.5(b)(1).

2537   O.C.G.A. § 44-14-361.5(b)(2).

2538   O.C.G.A. § 44-14-361.5(b)(3).

2539   O.C.G.A. § 44-14-361.5(b)(4).

2540   O.C.G.A. § 44-14-361.5(b)(5).

2541   O.C.G.A. § 44-14-361.5(b)(6).

2542   O.C.G.A. § 44-14-361.5.

2543   O.C.G.A. § 44-14-361.5.

§ 22.1.14 Notice To Contractor

If a notice of commencement has been properly filed, then anyone having a right to a lien who does not have privity of contract with the contractor and is providing labor, services, or materials for the improvement of property must, within 30 days from the filing of the notice of commencement or 30 days following the first delivery of labor, services, or materials to the property, whichever is later, give a written notice to contractor to the owner or the agent of the owner and to the contractor.[2544]

A notice to contractor must be sent by registered or certified mail or statutory overnight delivery and must include:[2545]

(a) the name, address, and telephone number of the person providing labor, services, or materials;[2546]

(b) the name and address of each person at whose instance the labor, services, or materials are being furnished;[2547]

(c) the name of the project and location of the project set forth in the notice of commencement;[2548]

(d) a description of the labor, services, or materials being provided;[2549] and

(e) if known, the contract price or anticipated value of the labor, services, or materials to be provided or the amount claimed to be due, if any.[2550]

§ 22.1.15 Discharge Of Lien By Filing Bond

When anyone files a claim of lien under the Act, the owner of the real estate or the contractor may discharge the lien by filing a bond in the office of that clerk of the superior court in which the claim of lien is filed.[2551] The bond must be conditioned to pay to the lien claimant the sum that may be found to be due upon the trial of any lien action filed pursuant to the Act.

The bond must be in double the amount claimed under the lien and must be either a bond with good security approved by the clerk of the court or a cash bond, except in cases involving a lien against the owner's residential property, in which event the bond must be in the amount claimed under the lien.[2552]

Upon the filing of the bond, the real estate is discharged from the lien. This is because the bond is effectively substituted as collateral for the lien.[2553] Since the notice of commencement provisions of the Act are designed to protect prospective future purchasers from unknowingly buying property encumbered by a lien, the lien claimant need not file a notice of commencement in a lien action in which the lien has been discharged by a bond.[2554] However, the lien claimant is not relieved of any of the other requirements for a lien action, and remains subject to any defenses that could otherwise be raised to a lien action.[2555]

2544   O.C.G.A. § 44-14-361.5(a).

2545   O.C.G.A. § 44-14-361.5(c).

2546   O.C.G.A. § 44-14-361.5(c)(1).

2547   O.C.G.A. § 44-14-361.5(c)(2).

2548   O.C.G.A. § 44-14-361.5(c)(3).

2549   O.C.G.A. § 44-14-361.5(c)(4).

2550   O.C.G.A. § 44-14-361.5(c)(4).

2551   O.C.G.A. § 44-14-364.

2552   O.C.G.A. § 44-14-364(a).

2553   *Burgess v. Travelers Indem. Co.*, 185 Ga.App. 82, 363 S.E.2d 308, (1987).

2554   *Washington Intern. Ins. Co. v. Hughes Supply, Inc.*, 271 Ga.App. 50, 609 S.E.2d 99 (2004); *Burgess v. Travelers Indem. Co.*, 185 Ga.App. 82, 363 S.E.2d 308, (1987).

2555   *M. Shapiro & Son, Inc. v. Yates Construction Co. of Southeast*, 140 Ga.App. 675, 231 S.E.2d 497 (1976).

Within seven days of filing a bond, the party filing the bond must send a notice of the filing, including a copy of the bond, by registered or certified mail or statutory overnight delivery to the lien claimant at the address stated on the lien. If no such address is shown for the lien claimant, to the person shown as having filed such lien on behalf of the claimant at the indicated address of such person or, if the bond is filed by a contractor, to the owner of the property.[2556]

Whenever the lien claimant or the owner is an entity on file with the Georgia Secretary of State's Corporations Division (*i.e.*, corporation, LLC, etc.), the notice may be sent to the company's address or the registered agent's address on file with the Secretary of State.[2557] Curiously, the Act provides that the failure to send notice of the filing of the bond does not invalidate the bond.[2558] Presumably, the failure to timely provide notice of the filing of the bond may leave the person filing the bond subject to claims for any damages incurred as a result of the lack of notice of the filing.

§ 22.1.16   Waiver And Release Of Lien And Bond Rights

§ 22.1.16.1   Liens May Not Be Waived In Advance

A right to claim a lien or to claim upon a bond may not be waived in advance of furnishing of labor, services, or materials.[2559] Any purported waiver or release made in advance of furnishing of labor, services, or materials is null, void, and unenforceable.[2560]

§ 22.1.16.2   Requirements For Waiver

No oral or written statement by the claimant purporting to waive, release, impair, or otherwise adversely affect a lien or bond claim is enforceable or creates an estoppel or impairment of claim of lien or claim upon a bond unless it is pursuant to an appropriate waiver and release of lien that has been executed by the claimant and the lien claimant has received payment.[2561]

Payment is conclusively deemed received by the claimant upon the earliest to occur of:[2562]

(a)   actual receipt of funds;[2563]

(b)   execution by the claimant of a separate written acknowledgment of payment in full;[2564] or

(c)   sixty days after the date of the execution of the waiver and release, unless prior to the expiration of said 60 day period the claimant files a claim of lien or files in the county in which the property is located an affidavit of nonpayment, using substantially the following form in boldface capital letters in at least 12 point font:[2565]

2556   O.C.G.A. § 44-14-364(b).

2557   O.C.G.A. § 44-14-364.

2558   O.C.G.A. § 44-14-364.

2559   O.C.G.A. § 44-14-366(a).

2560   O.C.G.A. § 44-14-366(a).

2561   O.C.G.A. § 44-14-366(b).

2562   O.C.G.A. § 44-14-366(f)(1).

2563   O.C.G.A. § 44-14-366(f)(2)(A).

2564   O.C.G.A. § 44-14-366(f)(2)(B).

2565   O.C.G.A. § 44-14-366(f)(2)(C).

AFFIDAVIT OF NONPAYMENT UNDER

O.C.G.A. § 44-14-366

STATE OF GEORGIA

COUNTY OF _____

THE UNDERSIGNED MECHANIC AND/OR MATERIALMAN HAS BEEN EMPLOYED BY _____ (NAME OF CONTRACTOR) TO FURNISH _____ (DESCRIBE MATERIALS AND/OR LABOR) FOR THE CONSTRUCTION OF IMPROVEMENTS KNOWN AS _____ (TITLE OF THE PROJECT OR BUILDING) WHICH IS LOCATED IN THE CITY OF _____, COUNTY OF _____, AND IS OWNED BY _____ (NAME OF OWNER) AND MORE PARTICULARLY DESCRIBED AS FOLLOWS:

_____

_____

_____

(DESCRIBE THE PROPERTY UPON WHICH THE IMPROVEMENTS WERE MADE BY USING EITHER A METES AND BOUNDS DESCRIPTION, THE LAND LOT DISTRICT, BLOCK AND LOT NUMBER, OR STREET ADDRESS OF THE PROJECT.)

PURSUANT TO O.C.G.A. SECTION 44-14-366 THE UNDERSIGNED EXECUTED A LIEN WAIVER AND RELEASE WITH RESPECT TO THIS PROPERTY DATED _____, ____. THE AMOUNT SET FORTH IN SAID WAIVER AND RELEASE ($_____) HAS NOT BEEN PAID, AND THE UNDERSIGNED HEREBY GIVES NOTICE OF SUCH NONPAYMENT.

THE ABOVE FACTS ARE SWORN TRUE AND CORRECT BY THE UNDERSIGNED, THIS _____ DAY OF _____, ____.

_____(SEAL)

CLAIMANT'S SIGNATURE

SWORN TO AND EXECUTED

IN THE PRESENCE OF:

_____

WITNESS

_____

NOTARY PUBLIC

WITHIN SEVEN DAYS OF FILING THIS AFFIDAVIT OF NONPAYMENT, THE FILING PARTY SHALL SEND A COPY OF THE AFFIDAVIT BY REGISTERED OR CERTIFIED MAIL OR STATUTORY OVERNIGHT DELIVERY TO THE OWNER OF THE PROPERTY. IF THE FILING PARTY IS NOT IN PRIVITY OF CONTRACT WITH THE PROPERTY OWNER AND A NOTICE OF COMMENCEMENT IS FILED FOR THE

IMPROVEMENT ON THE PROPERTY FOR WHICH THE FILING PARTY'S LABOR, SERVICES, OR MATERIALS WERE FURNISHED, A COPY OF THE AFFIDAVIT SHALL BE SENT TO THE CONTRACTOR AT THE ADDRESS SHOWN ON THE NOTICE OF COMMENCEMENT. WHENEVER THE OWNER OF THE PROPERTY IS AN ENTITY ON FILE WITH THE SECRETARY OF STATE'S CORPORATIONS DIVISION, SENDING A COPY OF THE LIEN TO THE COMPANY'S ADDRESS OR THE REGISTERED AGENT'S ADDRESS ON FILE WITH THE SECRETARY OF STATE SHALL BE DEEMED SUFFICIENT.[2566]

If a claimant files an affidavit of nonpayment and is subsequently paid in full, he must upon request execute an affidavit acknowledging the receipt of payment in full.[2567] Upon the filing of the affidavit of receipt of funds, the affidavit of nonpayment is considered void.[2568]

§ 22.1.16.3   Interim Waiver

It is typical for many contractors to receive payment, and correspondingly to make payments to others, based upon a draw schedule. When this happens the owner or contractor will typically request that whomever has been paid execute an interim waiver, and release, acknowledging payment for work through a certain date.

Once an interim wavier has been signed and the claimant paid, the priority of his lien for future labor or material begins to run on the day after the date specified in the interim waiver. The failure to correctly complete any of the blank spaces in the form does not invalidate the release, so long as the subject matter of the release can reasonably be determined.[2569] An interim waiver and release must substantially follow the following form, in boldface capital letters in at least 12 point font.[2570]

INTERIM WAIVER AND RELEASE UPON PAYMENT

STATE OF GEORGIA

COUNTY OF _____

THE UNDERSIGNED MECHANIC AND/OR MATERIALMAN HAS BEEN EMPLOYED BY _____ (NAME OF CONTRACTOR) TO FURNISH _____ (DESCRIBE MATERIALS AND/ OR LABOR) FOR THE CONSTRUCTION OF IMPROVEMENTS KNOWN AS _____ (TITLE OF THE PROJECT OR BUILDING) WHICH IS LOCATED IN THE CITY OF _____, COUNTY OF _____, AND IS OWNED BY _____ (NAME OF OWNER) AND MORE PARTICULARLY DESCRIBED AS FOLLOWS:

_____

_____

_____

2566   O.C.G.A. § 44-14-366(f).

2567   O.C.G.A. § 44-14-366.

2568   O.C.G.A. § 44-14-366.

2569   O.C.G.A. § 44-14-366.

2570   O.C.G.A. § 44-14-366(c).

(DESCRIBE THE PROPERTY UPON WHICH THE IMPROVEMENTS WERE MADE BY USING EITHER A METES AND BOUNDS DESCRIPTION, THE LAND LOT DISTRICT, BLOCK AND LOT NUMBER, OR STREET ADDRESS OF THE PROJECT.)

UPON THE RECEIPT OF THE SUM OF $_____, THE MECHANIC AND/OR MATERIALMAN WAIVES AND RELEASES ANY AND ALL LIENS OR CLAIMS OF LIENS IT HAS UPON THE FOREGOING DESCRIBED PROPERTY OR ANY RIGHTS AGAINST ANY LABOR AND/OR MATERIAL BOND THROUGH THE DATE OF _____ (DATE) AND EXCEPTING THOSE RIGHTS AND LIENS THAT THE MECHANIC AND/OR MATERIALMAN MIGHT HAVE IN ANY RETAINED AMOUNTS, ON ACCOUNT OF LABOR OR MATERIALS, OR BOTH, FURNISHED BY THE UNDERSIGNED TO OR ON ACCOUNT OF SAID CONTRACTOR FOR SAID BUILDING OR PREMISES.

GIVEN UNDER HAND AND SEAL THIS _____ DAY OF _____, _____.

_____ (SEAL)

_____

_____

(WITNESS)

_____

(ADDRESS)

NOTICE: WHEN YOU EXECUTE AND SUBMIT THIS DOCUMENT, YOU SHALL BE CONCLUSIVELY DEEMED TO HAVE BEEN PAID IN FULL THE AMOUNT STATED ABOVE, EVEN IF YOU HAVE NOT ACTUALLY RECEIVED SUCH PAYMENT, 60 DAYS AFTER THE DATE STATED ABOVE UNLESS YOU FILE EITHER AN AFFIDAVIT OF NONPAYMENT OR A CLAIM OF LIEN PRIOR TO THE EXPIRATION OF SUCH 60 DAY PERIOD. THE FAILURE TO INCLUDE THIS NOTICE LANGUAGE ON THE FACE OF THE FORM SHALL RENDER THE FORM UNENFORCEABLE AND INVALID AS A WAIVER AND RELEASE UNDER O.C.G.A. SECTION 44-14-366.[2571]

§ 22.1.16.4   Final Waiver And Release

The following form must be substantially followed when a claimant is requested to execute a waiver and release in exchange for or in order to induce making of final payment. As with interim waivers, the failure to correctly complete any of the blank spaces in the form does not invalidate the release, so long as the subject matter of the release can reasonably be determined.[2572] The form must be in boldface capital letters in at least 12 point font.[2573]

2571   O.C.G.A. § 44-14-366(c).

2572   O.C.G.A. § 44-14-366(d).

2573   O.C.G.A. § 44-14-366.

WAIVER AND RELEASE UPON FINAL PAYMENT

STATE OF GEORGIA

COUNTY OF _____

THE UNDERSIGNED MECHANIC AND/OR MATERIALMAN HAS BEEN
EMPLOYED BY _____ (NAME OF CONTRACTOR)
TO FURNISH _____ (DESCRIBE MATERIALS AND/
OR LABOR) FOR THE CONSTRUCTION OF IMPROVEMENTS
KNOWN AS _____ (TITLE OF THE PROJECT OR
BUILDING) WHICH IS LOCATED IN THE CITY OF _____,
COUNTY OF _____, AND IS OWNED
BY _____ (NAME OF OWNER) AND MORE
PARTICULARLY DESCRIBED AS FOLLOWS:

_____

_____

_____

(DESCRIBE THE PROPERTY UPON WHICH THE IMPROVEMENTS
WERE MADE BY USING EITHER A METES AND BOUNDS
DESCRIPTION, THE LAND LOT DISTRICT, BLOCK AND LOT NUMBER,
OR STREET ADDRESS OF THE PROJECT.)

UPON THE RECEIPT OF THE SUM OF $_____, THE
MECHANIC AND/OR MATERIALMAN WAIVES AND RELEASES ANY
AND ALL LIENS OR CLAIMS OF LIENS IT HAS UPON THE FOREGOING
DESCRIBED PROPERTY OR ANY RIGHTS AGAINST ANY LABOR AND/
OR MATERIAL BOND ON ACCOUNT OF LABOR OR MATERIALS, OR
BOTH, FURNISHED BY THE UNDERSIGNED TO OR ON ACCOUNT OF
SAID CONTRACTOR FOR SAID PROPERTY.

GIVEN UNDER HAND AND SEAL THIS _____ DAY OF _____,
____.

_____ (SEAL)

_____

(WITNESS)

_____

(ADDRESS)

NOTICE: WHEN YOU EXECUTE AND SUBMIT THIS DOCUMENT,
YOU SHALL BE CONCLUSIVELY DEEMED TO HAVE BEEN PAID
IN FULL THE AMOUNT STATED ABOVE, EVEN IF YOU HAVE NOT
ACTUALLY RECEIVED SUCH PAYMENT, 60 DAYS AFTER THE DATE
STATED ABOVE UNLESS YOU FILE EITHER AN AFFIDAVIT OF
NONPAYMENT OR A CLAIM OF LIEN PRIOR TO THE EXPIRATION
OF SUCH 60 DAY PERIOD. THE FAILURE TO INCLUDE THIS NOTICE

LANGUAGE ON THE FACE OF THE FORM SHALL RENDER THE FORM
UNENFORCEABLE AND INVALID AS A WAIVER AND RELEASE UNDER
O.C.G.A. SECTION 44-14-366.[2574]

§ 22.1.17 Voiding Recorded Lines Which Have Not Been Perfected

§ 22.1.17.1 By Operation Of Law Due To Passage Of Time

If a lien claimant fails to commence a lien action to collect the amount of his claim within 365 days from the date the lien is filed, or fails to timely[2575] file a notice of commencement of lien action in the county where the property is located, the lien becomes unenforceable.[2576] This happens automatically. No action needs to be taken for the lien to be considered void as a matter of law.[2577]

Any lien filed after March 31, 2009, must include on its face the following statement in at least 12 point bold font: "**This claim of lien expires and is void 365 days from the date of filing of the claim of lien if no notice of commencement of lien action is filed in that time period.**"[2578] Failure to include such language results in the lien being invalid and the clerk of court will not permit it to be filed.[2579]

§ 22.1.17.2 By Notice Of Contest

An owner or contractor may not want to wait the full 365 days from the filing of a notice of claim to determine if a lien action will be filed or the additional 30 days to determine if a notice of commencement will be filed. In this event, the owner, contractor, or their agent or attorney, may shorten these time periods by filing a contest of lien in the superior court in which the notice of claim is filed.[2580]

The contest of lien must be in boldface capital letters in at least 12 point font, along with proof of delivery upon the lien claimant in substantially the following form:

NOTICE OF CONTEST OF LIEN

TO: [NAME AND ADDRESS OF LIEN CLAIMANT]

YOU ARE NOTIFIED THAT THE UNDERSIGNED CONTESTS THE CLAIM OF LIEN FILED BY YOU ON _____ 20____, AND RECORDED IN _____ BOOK _____, PAGE _____ OF THE PUBLIC RECORDS OF_____ COUNTY, GEORGIA, AGAINST PROPERTY OWNED BY _____, AND THAT THE TIME WITHIN WHICH YOU MAY COMMENCE A LIEN ACTION TO ENFORCE YOUR LIEN IS LIMITED TO 60 DAYS FROM RECEIPT OF THIS NOTICE. THIS _____ DAY OF_____, 20__.

2574 O.C.G.A. § 44-14-366(d).
2575 395 days from the date the claim of lien was filed (30 days from the 365 day time to commence a lien action).
2576 O.C.G.A. § 44-14-367.
2577 O.C.G.A. § 44-14-367.
2578 O.C.G.A. § 44-14-367.
2579 O.C.G.A. § 44-14-367.
2580 O.C.G.A. § 44-14-367.

THIS ABOVE-REFERENCED LIEN WILL EXPIRE AND BE VOID IF YOU DO NOT: (1) COMMENCE A LIEN ACTION FOR RECOVERY OF THE AMOUNT OF THE LIEN CLAIM PURSUANT TO O.C.G.A. SECTION 44-14-361.1 WITHIN 60 DAYS FROM RECEIPT OF THIS NOTICE; AND (2) FILE A NOTICE OF COMMENCEMENT OF LIEN ACTION WITHIN 30 DAYS OF FILING THE ABOVE-REFERENCED LIEN ACTION.

SIGNED:_____

(OWNER, CONTRACTOR, AGENT OR ATTORNEY)[2581]

The owner or her agent or attorney, or the contractor or her agent or attorney, must send a copy of the notice of contest of lien within seven days of filing by registered or certified mail or statutory overnight delivery to the lien claimant at the address noted on the face of the lien. Service is to be deemed complete upon mailing.[2582]

The lien is extinguished by operation of law 90 days after the filing of the notice of contest of lien if no notice of commencement of lien action is filed in that time period.[2583] No release or voiding of the liens is required.[2584]

§ 22.1.18 Computation Of Time

For the purposes of the Act, when counting days during which some action must be taken, the first day is not counted, but the last day is counted.[2585] If the last day falls on a Saturday, Sunday or a public and legal holiday, the party has until the next business day in which to complete the act.[2586]

2581   O.C.G.A. § 44-14-368(a).

2582   O.C.G.A. § 44-14-367(b).

2583   O.C.G.A. § 44-14-367(c).

2584   O.C.G.A. § 44-14-367(c).

2585   O.C.G.A. §§ 1-3-1 and 44-14-369.

2586   O.C.G.A. §§ 1-3-1 and 44-14-369.

The **RED BOOK**

CHAPTER 23

AD VALOREM
TAX ON REAL
PROPERTY

OVERVIEW

An *ad valorem* tax is a tax on property which is based on its valuation. Literally, *ad valorem* is Latin for "by its value." All property in Georgia, both personal property and real property, is subject to an *ad valorem* tax. However, this work will only focus on the *ad valorem* taxes which are imposed upon real property. All real property in the state of Georgia is subject to this taxation unless specifically exempted by statute. While the owner of the property is generally responsible for the payment of these taxes, the taxes can also be owed by the property itself.[2587] The former is known as an *in personam* tax (directed to a particular person), while the latter is referred to an *in rem* tax (attaching to the thing itself). Some jurisdictions will issue taxes both *in personam* and *in rem*. However, most jurisdictions will issue these taxes *in personam*, and will only issue them *in rem* if the owner of the property is unknown.[2588] The county assesses the taxes on property to finance a number of local government expenses as well as costs for the betterment of the community.[2589] This chapter will discuss how such taxes are calculated and billed, and what happens when *ad valorem* taxes are not paid.

§ 23.1 HOW PROPERTY TAXES ARE CALCULATED AND BILLED

§ 23.1.1 What Real Property Is Subject To The *Ad Valorem* Tax?

All real property lying within the boundaries of the State of Georgia is subject to property taxation by the State or its various subdivisions.[2590] This includes property of any title character, including a leasehold or something less than the full fee, or whether the property is owned by an individual or a corporation, a state resident or nonresident.[2591] All property owned by the Federal Government or any of its agencies are also subject to property taxes and are to be assessed at the same rate as all other property owners unless there is a specific provision in the United States Constitution or other Federal Law prohibiting the taxation.[2592]

§ 23.1.2 Identifying The Players

The valuation and assessment of an owner's property is performed by the board of assessors for the county in which the property lies. In the event a property is located in more than one county, either (a) one county can tax for the entire property, remitting to the other counties the portion owed to them, or (b) both counties can tax for the portions of the property that lie within their jurisdiction.[2593] While assessments for taxes are made by the board of assessors, county and state *ad valorem* property taxes are usually collected by the county's tax commissioner. In some cities, property taxes may be collected by a local revenue collector. However, other cities have agreements with the county tax commissioner's office that it will bill and collect for both county and city taxes and remit the portion of taxes due to the city back to the municipality.

§ 23.1.3 Assessment Of The Property For Taxes

Property is required to be assessed at its "fair market value" which is defined as "the amount that a knowledgeable buyer would pay for the property and a willing seller would accept for the property at an arm's length bona fide sale."[2594]

2587 O.C.G.A. § 48-5-9.

2588 O.C.G.A. § 48-5-9.

2589 O.C.G.A. § 48-5-220 (listing 22 discrete purposes for which a county may levy and collect taxes).

2590 O.C.G.A. § 48-5-3.

2591 *Id.*

2592 O.C.G.A. § 48-5-4.

2593 O.C.G.A. § 48-4-237.

2594 O.C.G.A. § 48-5-2.

Recently, however, the Georgia General Assembly made a significant change in the process for determining the fair market value of a property. The county in which the property is located must now apply foreclosures, REO sales, short sales, and auction sales when using comparables to determine the fair market value of the property.[2595]

This has both helped and hurt property owners. On the positive side, it has reduced the tax liability of property owners. However, on the negative side, some homeowners in areas with high foreclosures have argued that this new requirement has further reduced the market value of their homes leaving them even more upside down on their mortgages than they were before and making it even harder to sell their properties.

The board of assessors usually has staff appraisers who are charged with periodically reviewing property and assessing a monetary value of the property. Very generally speaking the assessors take the appraised value and multiply it by 40% to reach the assessed value. The assessed value is then multiplied by the millage rate for the tax district in which the property lies. The local government will break the county into individual districts and assign various millage rates to each district. This is the base amount of the *ad valorem* property taxes.

§ 23.1.4 Possible Deductions/Exemptions

The Georgia Constitution provides that all property is to be taxed at a uniform rate.[2596] However, the law does provide for several exemptions for *ad valorem* taxation on the grounds of public policy.[2597] O.C.G.A. § 48-5-41 creates a number of exemptions for lands owned by the government, churches or church-owned property, non-profit charities, non-profit hospitals open to the general public, public schools, public libraries, public art galleries, and nonprofit cemeteries.[2598] Other exemptions include property awarded by a probate court as year's support of a surviving spouse for one year.[2599]

§ 23.1.4.1 The Homestead Exemption

The most common exemption in Georgia is the homestead exemption. This exemption allows any Georgia resident actually occupying the property as their primary residence to receive an exemption not to exceed $2,000 of valuation from the taxation,[2600] or up to $4,000 for owners over 65 years of age.[2601] Other exemptions may exist for residents over 62 years of age, households with an income under $30,000,[2602] disabled veterans,[2603] senior citizens,[2604] or surviving spouses of policemen or firemen killed in the line of duty.[2605] It is important to note, however, that each county sets its own tax exemption amount.

In order to qualify for the homestead exemption, a resident must have occupied the property as of January 1 of that year. The most important thing to note, however, is that with the limited exception of some government-owned property, no exemptions are applied automatically. Rather, the exemption must be applied for and granted.

2595   O.C.G.A. § 48-5-2(3)(B).

2596   Ga. Const. Art. 7, § 1, P III; *Buckler v. DeKalb County Bd. of Tax Assessors*, 263 Ga.App. 305, 587 S.E.2d 797 (2003).

2597   O.C.G.A. § 53-3-4.

2598   O.C.G.A. § 48-5-41(a)(1).

2599   O.C.G.A. § 53-3-4.

2600   O.C.G.A. § 48-5-44.

2601   O.C.G.A. § 48-5-47.

2602   O.C.G.A. § 48-5-47.1.

2603   O.C.G.A. § 48-5-48.

2604   O.C.G.A. § 48-5-48.3.

2605   O.C.G.A. § 48-5-48.3.

Generally, homeowners can apply for their homestead tax exemptions at any time during the year. However, each county has specific procedures and deadlines by which to apply for the current taxable year to receive this exemption. For example, a homeowner in DeKalb County can apply by mail, in person, or online all year-round but the homeowner must apply by April 1 (and must have been the owner of the property on January 1) to receive this tax benefit in the current year.[2606] If that deadline is missed, the exemption will apply the following year and every year thereafter that the property remains the homeowner's legal residence.

To learn the specifics about each county's homestead exemptions, visit the website for the county in which the property is located or contact the county's tax office.

§ 23.1.5   Making A Property Tax Return

Every property in the state which is subject to taxation must complete a tax every year.[2607] In most counties, the property owner is expected to file the return on or before April 1 of each year.[2608] However, some counties require that the returns be filed by March 1 of each year.[2609] The return must be submitted to the tax assessor or tax commissioner for the county in which the property is located.[2610] The return states what the owner attests is the fair market value of the property. If a property owner fails to file a property tax return, the owner is deemed to have returned the same property it returned the previous year with the same claimed exemptions and values.[2611]

§ 23.1.6   Payment Of Taxes

Most counties and municipalities throughout the state will send out their property tax bills in the spring or summer. Each jurisdiction sets its own dates for payment. Counties are allowed to accept payments in installments,[2612] or one lump sum. Georgia law makes the payment of property taxes the responsibility of the property owner. While a property owner's mortgage lender may collect money from the owner and escrow that money for taxes, such an arrangement does not relieve the property owner from ensuring that taxes are paid. It is also the owner's responsibility to provide the taxing authority with its correct mailing address. Failure to receive a bill is not an excuse for non-payment. Additionally, if a co-tenant pays the entirety of the property taxes without contribution from the other co-tenants, he is deemed to have made the payment on behalf of the other co-tenants and is entitled to a lien against the co-tenants for that amount.[2613]

§ 23.1.7   Appealing Valuation Of Property Taxes

The Board of Tax Assessors review the returns submitted by the tax payers, and if they determine that the property should be assessed at a different value than appears on the return, they will send the owner a notice of assessment change.[2614] Irrespective of whether the owner filed a real property tax return, each county Board of Tax Assessors is required to send out annual assessment notices to every owner of taxable property in the county.[2615] Each notice is required to state, among other things: 1) the amount of the previous assessment; 2) the amount of the current assessment; 3) the year for which the new assessment is applicable; and 4) the fair market value of the property broker down into real and personal property classifications.

2606   DeKalb County Tax Commissioner: Homestead Exemption. (http://web.co.dekalb.ga.us/TaxCommissioner/homesteadGen.html#applications)

2607   O.C.G.A. § 48-5-15(a).

2608   O.C.G.A. § 48-5-18.

2609   O.C.G.A. § 48-5-18.

2610   O.C.G.A. § 48-5-15.

2611   O.C.G.A. § 48-5-20.

2612   O.C.G.A. § 48-5-24.

2613   *Bank of Tupelo v. Collier*, 191 Ga. 852, 14 S.E.2d 59 (1941).

2614   O.C.G.A. § 48-5-306.

2615   O.C.G.A. § 48-5-306(a).

§ 23.1.7.1 Who Has The Right To Appeal?

Every property owner has the right to appeal the government's valuation of its property,[2616] so long as she was the owner of the property by the appeal deadline of that year.[2617] Property owners do not have to file a property tax return in order to preserve their appeal rights.[2618] Every annual assessment notice is appealable to the county Board of Assessors regardless of whether the value remained the same from the prior year's assessment.

§ 23.1.7.2 Who Are Appeals Made To? When Must Appeals Be Filed?

Assessment appeals are initially made to the county's Board of Tax Assessors.[2619] Each Board adopts its own internal procedures for conducting the appeal process, so the intricacies of the process may vary county to county.[2620] Due to relatively recent changes in the law, the appeal time is now uniform across the state with the owner having to file their appeal of the assessment with the Board of Assessors within 45 days of the sending of the notice of tax assessment.[2621] The appeal notice must identify the property, contain the tax identification number of the property and state the grounds of the appeal.[2622]

§ 23.1.7.3 Appeal Decision

The Board of Assessors must make a written decision to the appeal which may be to make no change to the assessment, to change the assessment to the amount claimed by the owner, or make an altogether separate change.[2623] In the event the Board of Assessors makes the change requested by the owner, the appeal is over. If the Board of Assessors decides to not make a change to assessment, they must send written notice to the property owner and the county's Board of Equalization containing the reason for the denial.[2624] This notice constitutes the owner's appeal to the Board of Equalization without the necessity of the owner filing a separate appeal.[2625] However, if the tax payer and the Board of Tax Assessors execute a signed agreement as to valuation, the appeal is over as of the date of the agreement.[2626] If the Board of Assessors makes an altogether different decision (often a compromise between the new assessed value which appeared on the notice and the amount requested by the owner), the owner may accept the decision of the Board or file an appeal of this decision with the Board of Equalization in writing within 30 days.[2627]

If the county fails to respond to the appeal within 180 days, the appeal will automatically be referred to the Board of Equalization.[2628] Within 15 days of receipt of the notice of appeal, the Board of Equalization is supposed to set a hearing within 20-30 days from the date of the notice of hearing.[2629] Hearings on contiguous properties owned by the same owner may be consolidated at the request of the owner.[2630] At the hearing, the Board of Equalization will inquire into

---

2616   O.C.G.A. § 48-5-311(e).

2617   O.C.G.A. § 48-5-311(e)(1)(A).

2618   O.C.G.A. § 48-5-311(e).

2619   O.C.G.A. § 48-5-311(d)(1).

2620   O.C.G.A. § 48-5-311(d)(3).

2621   O.C.G.A. § 48-5-311(e)(2)(A).

2622   O.C.G.A. § 48-5-311(e)(2)(A).

2623   O.C.G.A. § 48-5-311(e)(2)(A).

2624   O.C.G.A. § 48-5-311(e)(2)(B) and (D).

2625   O.C.G.A. § 48-5-311(e)(2)(B).

2626   O.C.G.A. § 48-5-311(e)(2)(B).

2627   O.C.G.A. § 48-5-311(e)(2)(C).

2628   O.C.G.A. § 48-5-311(e)(3).

2629   O.C.G.A. § 48-5-311(e)(6)(A)-(B).

2630   O.C.G.A. § 48-5-311(e)(6)(C).

the uniformity of the assessment with comparable properties and render its decision.[2631] The decision of the Board of Equalization must be issued in writing stating the grounds of the decision.[2632] If the Board of Equalization grants the owner's appeal, any monies paid by the owner will be refunded to the owner with interest not to exceed $150.[2633]

§ 23.1.7.4 Arbitration Alternative

The owner may instead elect to refer the appeal to arbitration if it wishes to forego the hearing before the Board of Equalization.[2634] However, a recent change to the law has modified the process of arbitration. Before an arbitrator is appointed, the tax payer must now present a certified appraisal of the property to the Board of Assessors.[2635] The Board of Assessors has 45 days to accept or reject the owner's appraisal.[2636] This new legislation provides further protection to the owner from inordinate delay by the county. If the county fails to accept or reject the owner's appraisal within 45 days, the value set by the owner's appraisal becomes final.[2637] Additionally, the arbitrator's decision is now considered final as to issues of fair market value and uniformity.[2638] In other words, an arbitrator's decision on value can no longer be appealed to the county superior court. However, the owner, county or hearing officer may still appeal any legal issues separate from fair market value and uniformity within 30 days of the decision.[2639]

§ 23.1.7.5 Properties Valued Over $1,000,000

One of the most significant changes in regard to appealing property tax assessments has been the creation of a streamlined hearing process for properties valued over $1,000,000. In cases involving non-homestead properties valued over $1,000,000, the appeal may be heard in front of a designated hearing officer.[2640] Under the new provisions, hearing officers will be a certified appraiser approved by the county who has undergone a significant amount of training on Georgia law, appraisal techniques and evidentiary issues.[2641] The hearing officer may be chosen by the county and the property owner agreeing on one from a designated list, or alternatively will be selected by the superior clerk of court.[2642] Any decisions made by the hearing officer will be appealable to the county superior court.[2643]

§ 23.1.8 Claim For Refund Of Taxes Paid

Separate from appealing the valuation assessed to the property by the Board of Tax Assessors, a property owner can also seek a refund of taxes paid in error on property. This most frequently comes up in the context of someone who has overpaid their taxes, paid taxes on property which she mistakenly believed she owned, where tax payments were allocated to the wrong parcel, tax exempt property was erroneously assessed, or otherwise were erroneously or illegally assessed by the county.[2644] Where a taxpayer does not pursue a timely appeal of a property tax assessment, the statutory refund procedure is available to challenge issues of valuation, equalization, or uniformity only if the taxpayer alleges that the

---

2631   O.C.G.A. § 48-5-311(e)(6)(D)(i).

2632   O.C.G.A. § 48-5-311(e)(6)(D)(i).

2633   O.C.G.A. § 48-5-311(e)(6)(D)(iii)(II).

2634   O.C.G.A. § 48-5-311(f).

2635   O.C.G.A. § 48-5-311(f)(3)(A).

2636   O.C.G.A. § 48-5-311(f)(3)(A).

2637   O.C.G.A. § 48-5-311(f)(3)(A).

2638   O.C.G.A. § 48-5-311(f)(3)(B).

2639   O.C.G.A. § 48-5-311(g).

2640   O.C.G.A. § 48-5-311(e).

2641   O.C.G.A. § 48-5-311(e.1)(2).

2642   O.C.G.A. § 48-5-311(e.1)(6).

2643   O.C.G.A. § 48-5-311(e.1)(7).

2644   *National Health Network, Inc. v. Fulton County*, 270 Ga. 724, 514 S.E.2d 422 (1999).

assessment is based on matters of fact in the record which are inaccurate, or that the assessment was reached by the use of illegal procedures.[2645] Taxpayer may raise issues of valuation, uniformity, and equalization in action seeking refund of *ad valorem* real property taxes so long as claim is based on assertion of illegality in the assessment procedure used or on factual inaccuracy in the record; thus, under such circumstances, tax appeal process is not the exclusive method of challenging assessments.[2646]

To pursue a claim for a property tax refund, the tax payer must file a written claim with the county within three years of the payment of the tax.[2647] As each county is free to make its own rules as to what the claim must contain, the tax payer should check with the county tax commissioner to determine what information must be provided in the tax refund claim. If the tax payer wants a hearing on the matter, the written notice must indicate that. If the county denies the request or fails to rule on it within one year from the filing of the request for the refund, the tax payer can file suit for the refund in the superior court where the county lies.[2648] The tax payer will not have standing to bring the suit until it has filed the claim with the county and the county has denied the claim or at least one year has passed. However, in the event of a denial by the county, suit must be brought within one year unless the tax payer and the county agree in writing to extend that time period.[2649] If at any period the county grants the taxpayer's request or the court makes an award for refund, the county must pay those funds within 60 days.[2650] If a court renders a judgment in favor of the tax payer, the tax payer is entitled to prejudgment interest running from the date it made a written demand for the refund.[2651]

§ 23.2 PROPERTY TAX ABATEMENTS AND PREFERENTIAL ASSESSMENTS

§ 23.2.1 State-Wide Tax Abatement Programs

Property tax abatement programs are economic incentives offered by the state and local governments to encourage new development in economically depressed areas, encourage preservation of historically significant properties and expand access to affordable housing through offering preferential tax treatments for qualifying properties. While each program will differ in their particularities, they all generally operate by reducing the burden of higher taxes in neighborhoods targeted for development and/or preservation.

State-wide abatement programs typically require a state agency to certify the property as eligible for the program, and then the property owner submits the certification to its local county taxing official to receive the abatement. Some of the state-wide abatement programs are included below.

§ 23.2.1.1 Landmark Historic Property Tax Abatement Program

This program allows the owner of an income-producing building, which is listed on the National or Georgia Register of Historic Places and has been designated by the City of Atlanta as a Landmark Building or a contributing building in a Landmark District to obtain preferential property tax treatment.[2652] The building must be in standard repair or already have undergone rehabilitation. For purposes of tax assessment for City of Atlanta taxes, excluding bonded indebtedness, the fair market values of the building and up to two acres of land surrounding it, is frozen for eight years at the level existing at the time of application and certification. In the ninth year, the fair market value is fixed at one-half the

---

2645   *International Auto Processing, Inc. v. Glynn County*, 287 Ga.App. 431, 651 S.E.2d 535 (2007).

2646   *Gwinnett County v. Gwinnett I Ltd. Partnership*, 265 Ga. 645, 458 S.E.2d 632 (1995).

2647   O.C.G.A. § 48-5-380(b).

2648   O.C.G.A. § 48-5-380(c).

2649   *Id.*

2650   O.C.G.A. § 48-5-380(d).

2651   *Eastern Airlines, Inc. v. Fulton County*, 183 Ga.App. 891, 360 S.E.2d 425 (1987).

2652   O.C.G.A. § 48-5-7.3.

difference between the frozen value and the current fair market value. The application for this tax freeze must be filed by December 31st of the year before the freeze will go into effect.

§ 23.2.1.2 Rehabilitated Historic Property Tax Abatement Program

This program allows the owner of a building, which qualifies for listing on the Georgia Register of Historic Places and has undergone a major rehabilitation initiated after January 1, 1989, to obtain preferential property tax treatment.[2653] For purposes of tax assessment for City of Atlanta taxes, excluding bonded indebtedness, the fair market value is frozen at the pre-rehabilitation level for a period of eight years. In the ninth year, the fair market value is fixed at one-half the difference between the frozen value and the current fair market value. Qualifying rehabilitations must meet the standards promulgated by the Department of Natural Resources and must have increased the fair market value of the building by not less than 50% for owner-occupied residential real property, or not less than 100% for income-producing real property. The application for this tax freeze must be filed by December 31st of the year before the freeze will go into effect.

§ 23.2.2 Local Government Tax Abatement Programs

Some cities offer their own economic tax-based incentives to spur development or investment in particular properties or areas within the city or to preserve the historic character of some neighborhoods including Atlanta, Augusta, Savannah and others. By way of illustration, in 1996 the City of Atlanta passed an ordinance enacting a local abatement program which is outlined below.

§ 23.2.2.1 Urban Enterprise Zone Tax Abatement Program (UEZ)

The purpose of the UEZ program[2654] is to encourage private development and redevelopment in areas of the City or on sites which otherwise would unlikely be developed due to the existence of certain characteristics of the area or site. The economic advantages may include the abatement of a substantial portion of the *ad valorem* property taxes by the City of Atlanta and Fulton County during the first ten years of the life of the project, as well as the waiver of the payment of development impact fees by the City. There are currently almost 100 active UEZs throughout the city for a variety of purposes, including housing, industrial and mixed-use development.

The UEZ program does not have pre-existing designated urban enterprise zones. Rather, anyone who is interested in obtaining UEZ designation for a particular property must have a specific development proposal for that property, and must submit a detailed UEZ application to the Department to request that a UEZ be created for that property. The UEZ program requires that each UEZ be designated on the basis of a specific development proposal, thus it does not allow the designation of a UEZ for purely speculative real estate purposes. A UEZ property does not have to be of any minimum size. The decision to create a new enterprise zone is based on the specific plans proposed by a developer, and the suitability of the location when measured against a defined set of criteria for determining the eligibility of the program.

A particular property may become eligible for UEZ designation if the subject property meets <u>three</u> of the <u>four</u> following criteria:

(1) Evidence of Pervasive Poverty, defined as greater than 20 percent of residents within the census block group in which the subject property is located;

(2) Unemployment, defined as either (i) at least 10 % higher than the state average in the census tract in which the subject property is located; or (ii) significant job loss occurring either on the subject property or within the immediate vicinity;

2653   O.C.G.A. § 48-5-7.2.

2654   *See generally*, <u>City of Atlanta Code of Ordinances</u>, § 146-51, § 146-52 and § 146-53.

(3) General Distress, defined as either a crime rate greater than 20% for the police beat in which the subject property is located, or (ii) the presence of existing abandoned and/or dilapidated structures within one block of the project, or (iii) deteriorated infrastructure;

(4) Underdevelopment of the project area, defined as greater than 20% of the development activity occurring within the City. For mixed-use residential/commercial enterprise zones, this criterion may be satisfied by using either the residential or commercial City building permit data.

There are additional requirements for approval, such as the completed subdivision or replatting of the proposed property, completed site plans and surveys for the project, and compliance with all applicable zoning and land use plans. Mixed-use projects also have time restrictions for completion (within 4 years), and all approved uses must be built as planned. For residential projects, thirty percent (30%) of the housing units must be completed within the first year of the UEZ designation, and twenty percent (20%) of the total housing units for sale or rent must be available as affordable housing subject to specific income and price limits set out in the city code.

After the first year of UEZ designation, tax abatements occur via a sliding scale of reduced percentages over an eleven-year period, as follows:

Years of UEZ Designation	Maximum % of Property Tax Abatement
1-5 years	100%
6-7 years	80%
8 years	60%
9 years	40%
10 years	20%
11 years	0%

The tax abatement may or may not begin at the 100% level. The only time when property owners receive 100 percent tax abatements within the first five years of enterprise zone designation is when (for housing enterprise zones) the value of the improvements exceed the value of the land by a factor of eight times or more. For nonresidential zones, the value of improvements must exceed the value of the land by a factor of three times or more. If a project meets those qualifications, then for years one through five of the UEZ designation, the full 100% abatement applies.

While a complete discussion of both state sponsored and city sponsored tax abatements is outside the scope of this work, real estate professionals should be aware that some properties in a UEZ may qualify for the abatement, and thus buyers will not be required to pay the full property tax assessed on the parcel. Even if a project has met all of the requirements for a UEZ, the approved tax abatements may not necessarily include all of the elements that make up a property tax bill, such as school taxes, bonds, and state property taxes, so participation in the program does not mean that annual tax payments are reduced to zero. Using tax abatements and reduced fees can make some projects and purchases financially possible in depressed areas.

§ 23.3   WHAT HAPPENS WHEN TAXES ARE NOT PAID IN A TIMELY FASHION

§ 23.3.1   Late Payment Notices And Issuance Of A *Fiere Facias*, Or "*Fi Fa*"

After the last day for the payment of taxes has passed, the tax collector or tax commissioner must notify the taxpayer in writing of the fact that the taxes have not been paid and that, unless paid, an execution shall be issued.[2655] Thirty days after

---

2655   O.C.G.A. § 48-3-3(c).

that notice is sent, if payment of the taxes has still not been made, the tax commissioner may issue an execution for the collection of the taxes including any accrued penalty, interest, or collection costs due to the state.[2656] The execution (or "*fi fa*") is directed to "all and singular sheriffs of this state or to the commissioner or his authorized representatives and shall command them to levy upon the goods, chattels, lands, and tenements of the taxpayer, provided that the commissioner may transmit such executions electronically."[2657] The *fi fa*s bear interest at a rate of one percent per month,[2658] are recorded in the general execution or lien docket of the county, and remain collectable for seven years[2659] unless the *fi fa* is for an amount less than $5.[2660] If that is the case, the *fi fa* remains collectable for only one year.[2661] However, the *fi fa* can be renewed by making what is referred to as a nulla bona entry, by submitting the *fi fa* to the clerk for re-recording, which will serve to toll the statute of limitations on the *fi fa*'s dormancy and restart the seven year clock.[2662]

§ 23.3.2   Transfer Of Tax *Fi Fa*s To A Third Party

Whenever any person other than the person against whom a *fi fa* has been issued pays the tax on which the *fi fa* has been issued, the tax commissioner may transfer (or assign) the *fi fa* to the party volunteering payment.[2663] However, under no circumstances is the tax commissioner required to accept payment from a third party or transfer the *fi fa* to them. Instead, it is a matter of pure discretion by the tax commissioner.[2664] If the *fi fa* is transferred, the transferee has the same rights to enforce the *fi fa* and the same priority of payment as did the tax commissioner provided that the transferee record the *fi fa*. The transferee must, within 30 days of the transfer, have the assignment of the *fi fa* entered on the general execution or lien docket of the superior court of the county in which the *fi fa* was issued. If the transfer of the *fi fa* is not entered, the transferee risks losing its lien upon property to any bona fide purchaser who took in good faith, so long as they paid a valuable consideration for the property before the entry of the transfer and without notice of the existence of the *fi fa*.[2665]

Within 60 days following the transfer, the transferee must send out notice to the delinquent taxpayer of the transfer of the tax execution by first-class mail.[2666] The notice must provide the name, mailing address, and telephone number for the transferee's business office; the amount necessary to satisfy such execution; and any other information as deemed appropriate by the transferee.[2667] No pre-transfer notice is required to be sent to the tax payer since the 2006 revisions were made to this statute. However, in the event that the 60 day notice is returned undelivered, the transferee is required to perform due diligence in an effort to obtain the delinquent taxpayer's correct address or any new owner's correct address and resend the notice by first-class mail.[2668] Thereafter, the transferee has a continuing annual notice requirement as well. Until the execution is paid in full or satisfied, on or before November 15 of each year, the transferee must send notice by regular mail to the delinquent taxpayer and the record owner of the property advising that the tax execution is still outstanding.[2669] The notice must provide the transferee's most updated contact information, including mailing address and telephone number.[2670]

2656   O.C.G.A. § 48-3-1.

2657   *Id.*

2658   O.C.G.A. § 48-2-40.

2659   O.C.G.A. § 48-3-21.

2660   O.C.G.A. § 48-3-21.1.

2661   O.C.G.A. § 48-3-21.1.

2662   O.C.G.A. § 48-3-23.

2663   O.C.G.A. § 48-3-19.

2664   O.C.G.A. § 48-3-19(b)(1).

2665   *Id.*

2666   O.C.G.A. § 48-3-19(c)(1).

2667   O.C.G.A. § 48-3-19(c)(1).

2668   O.C.G.A. § 48-3-19(c)(2).

2669   O.C.G.A. § 48-3-19(f).

2670   O.C.G.A. § 48-3-19(f).

A transferred *fi fa* bears interest from the date of transfer just as *fi fa*s held by the tax commissioner do, *i.e.*, one percent per month, that interest amount being accrued upon the amount paid by the transferee to the tax collector.[2671] In addition, the transferee may charge and collect recording fees actually expended in recording the transferred execution on the general execution docket of any county in which the transfer is recorded. The transferee cannot submit the execution to the appropriate levying officer until 12 months after the date of the transfer or 24 months after the tax giving rise to the execution was originally due, whichever is earlier.[2672] A transferee cannot advertise and sell property under a tax execution; that is a matter which is left solely to a statutorily-appointed levying officer.[2673] Nonetheless, a transferee with multiple outstanding executions against the same property can submit all the executions it holds so long as at least one meets the referenced time requirements.[2674]

Lastly, any transferee that pays the tax official more than two million dollars in any calendar year for the transfer of tax *fi fa*s must maintain a reasonably accessible office within 50 miles of the superior court of the county wherein the transferred *fi fa*s were issued.[2675] The office must be open to the public for at least eight hours per day for five days a week, official state holidays excepted.[2676]

This current discretionary system of tax *fi fa* transfers has only been in place since replacement legislation on July 1, 2006. Since that time, only minor changes have been made to the legislation. Very different schemes existed prior to 2006 and many were fraught with problems.[2677] Any tax *fi fa*s transferred prior to that time should be regarded in light of the law enacted at the time. Accordingly, a property tax specialist familiar with the legislative history of this area should be consulted.

§ 23.4 THE LEVY AND SALE OF TAX *FI FA*S

There are two types of levies and sales resulting from non-payment of property taxes. The less frequently employed method is called the tax foreclosure and is also known as a judicial *in rem* tax sale. Tax foreclosures will be discussed in their entirety in the beginning of this section. Thereafter this section will discuss the levy and sale of taxes through a 'regular' or 'non-judicial' tax sale. All subsequent sections of this chapter will deal solely with said regular tax sales.

§ 23.4.1 Tax Foreclosures

Since 1995, the General Assembly has created a process by which local counties and municipalities can foreclose taxes through judicial means in a manner which is quicker and results in greater certainty of title than a regular tax sale.[2678] In order to utilize this procedure, the county or municipality must first pass enacting legislation adopting the tax foreclosure proceeding.[2679] However, the tax foreclosure procedure can only be utilized by government agencies and cannot be used by tax execution transferees.[2680]

Anytime after twelve months from when taxes originally become delinquent, the tax commissioner or other tax collector may file a petition for a tax foreclosure in the superior court of the county in the property lies.[2681] Although, if the tax

---

2671   O.C.G.A. § 48-3-20 and O.C.G.A. § 48-3-19(d).

2672   O.C.G.A. § 48-3-19(e)(1).

2673   O.C.G.A. § 48-3-19(e)(1).

2674   O.C.G.A. § 48-3-19(e)(2).

2675   O.C.G.A. § 48-3-19(g).

2676   O.C.G.A. § 48-3-19(g).

2677   *See, e.g., E-Lane Pine Hills, LLC v. Ferdinand*, 277 Ga.App. 566, 627 S.E.2d 44 (2005).

2678   O.C.G.A. § 48-4-75, *et seq.*

2679   O.C.G.A. § 48-4-76.

2680   O.C.G.A. § 48-4-76(c).

2681   O.C.G.A. § 48-4-78(a).

commissioner holds more than one *fi fa*, she may submit all of them to this proceeding so long as at least one is at least twelve months old.[2682] The petition for tax foreclosure will state the owner, the property address, a description of the property, the tax identification number, the taxes being foreclosed (including whether they are county or city taxes, the tax years, and the principal amount of the delinquent taxes including accrued interest and penalties), that the taxes remain unpaid, a listing of the interested parties, and that the relief requested is that the property be sold at public outcry.[2683]

Simultaneous with filing the petition, the tax commissioner must file a notice in the *lis pendens* docket.[2684] In addition, within thirty (30) days from filing the petition, the tax commissioner must run a notice in the county's legal organ on two separate dates,[2685] send notice to all the interested parties by certified mail or statutory overnight mail,[2686] send notice to the occupant of the property by regular mail,[2687] and post a notice on the property.[2688] In other words, despite the fact that this is civil litigation, no personal service on any named defendant is required. Anytime after thirty days from filing the petition the tax commissioner may request a hearing at which all parties may be heard.[2689] If the court finds that the allegations of the petition are correct, it will render a decree affirming that the taxes are delinquent and ordering the property to be sold at public sale.[2690]

Any interested party may redeem the property from the tax foreclosure prior to the sale.[2691] The redemption amount includes the taxes plus any accrued interest and penalties and the tax commissioner's collection costs.[2692] In the event the owner of the property tenders the redemption, the foreclosure action is dismissed and it is as if no action had been taken.[2693] However, if a lien holder redeems the property the action is still dismissed, but the lien holder is given a lien against the property for the redemption amount on an equal priority level as property taxes.[2694]

The sale of the property shall be advertised and conducted on the date, time, place, and manner which are required by law of sheriffs' sales although it shall not occur earlier than 45 days following the date of issuance of the order of the court.[2695] The tax commissioner cries the property out starting with a minimum bid price comprised of the amount of taxes owed with all accrued interests and penalties, and the costs incurred by the Tax Commissioner in collecting the taxes, including, but not limited to the title examination and publication costs.[2696] If the property is not redeemed prior to the sale, the sale is conducted at public outcry until it is sold to the highest bidder.[2697] The sale is final and binding, subject only to the right of the owner of the property to redeem the property from the sale upon payment into the registry of the superior court of the full amount of the minimum bid price of the sale within 60 days from the date of the sale.[2698] If the owner redeems the property within the 60 days after the sale, the tax commissioner must dismiss the foreclosure action and

---

2682   *Id.*

2683   O.C.G.A. § 48-4-78(c) and (g).

2684   O.C.G.A. § 48-4-78(e).

2685   O.C.G.A. § 48-4-78(f).

2686   O.C.G.A. § 48-4-78(d).

2687   *Id.*

2688   *Id.*

2689   O.C.G.A. § 48-4-79.

2690   O.C.G.A. § 48-4-79(a).

2691   O.C.G.A. § 48-4-80(a).

2692   O.C.G.A. § 48-4-77.

2693   O.C.G.A. § 48-4-80.

2694   *Id.*

2695   O.C.G.A. § 48-4-81(a).

2696   O.C.G.A. § 48-4-77(2).

2697   O.C.G.A. § 48-4-81(b).

2698   O.C.G.A. § 48-4-81(c).

refund the purchase price to the successful bidder at the sale.[2699] If the property is not redeemed by the owner within the 60 day period, then within 90 days of the date of the sale the tax commissioner must execute and deliver to the purchaser at the foreclosure a deed for the property, together with any required real estate transfer tax declaration forms.[2700] Also within the 90 day period, the tax commissioner must file a report of the sale with the superior court, which report must identify whether a sale took place, the foreclosure sale price, and the identity of the purchaser.[2701] If the foreclosure sale price exceeds the minimum bid amount at the foreclosure sale, the petitioner must deposit into the registry of the superior court the surplus to be distributed by the superior court to the interested parties, including the owner, as their interests appear and in the order of priority in which their interests exist.[2702]

Upon issuance of the deed from a tax foreclosure, title vests absolutely in the purchaser. Unlike regular tax sales, there are no open rights of redemption or title marketability issues. Because the tax foreclosure can vest title absolutely, many bidders will be willing to bid a higher amount than they would at a regular tax sale. However, because tax foreclosures require much more hands-on involvement from the tax commissioner whose staff may be ill-equipped to handle the sale procedures, more counties will perform regular tax sales. This shifts the burden of clearing title to the purchaser at the tax sale and is discussed below.

§ 23.4.2 Non-Judicial "Regular" Tax Sales

The conduct of a regular tax sale is technically done in two separate steps: the levy on the *fi fa*, or execution, and the sale of the property. While both are collectively referred to as the tax sale process, they are in fact two distinct steps and this discussion will treat them as such.

§ 23.4.2.1 The Levy On The Tax *Fi Fa*

Typically a tax commissioner or sheriff will be the officer conducting the sale and levy. Either the defendant in *fi fa* or the levying officer may choose what property of the defendant in *fi fa* that lies within the jurisdiction will be the subject to the levy.[2703] Practically speaking, the property against which the taxes were assessed is usually the selected property. However, the levy must not be considered excessive.[2704] Thus if the property can be subdivided and the execution can be satisfied out of a subdivided parcel, the subdivision must occur. To do otherwise will render the tax deed void.[2705] Additionally, if multiple executions are presented for levy, they may be aggregated and all made subject of the same sale.[2706]

In the case of executions which have been transferred to third parties, the transferee may present them to the sheriff for levy no sooner than one year after the transfer or two years from when the tax became due, whichever comes first.[2707] However, if the transferee holds multiple tax executions, it may present all of them for levy as soon as one of them meets one of those requirements.[2708] The sheriff then has 90 days to complete the sale and remit the collected tax.[2709] If the *fi fa* is valid on its face, the sheriff must levy. The sheriff cannot refuse to levy on the basis that she does not believe the *fi fa*

2699 O.C.G.A. § 48-4-81(c)(1).

2700 O.C.G.A. § 48-4-81(d).

2701 O.C.G.A. § 48-4-81(e).

2702 O.C.G.A. § 48-4-81(f).

2703 O.C.G.A. § 48-3-4.

2704 *West v. McBride*, 207 Ga. 261, 61 S.E.2d 133 (1950).

2705 *Id.*

2706 O.C.G.A. § 48-3-6.

2707 O.C.G.A. § 48-3-19(e)(1).

2708 *Id.*

2709 O.C.G.A. § 48-4-3.

s valid. This is because the determination of the validity of a *fi fa* calls for judicial interpretation, and the sheriff is not a member of the judiciary.[2710]

Once executions have been presented to the levying officer, it must send a notice to owner of the property and the holder of any security deed alerting them of the intent to sell the property.[2711] The notice must be sent twenty days prior to proceeding with sale preparations, including prior to running the legal notice of the sale in the county organ, and may be sent by certified mail or through personal delivery. or a security deed holder to be entitled to receive the 20-day letter, its name and mailing address must appear on the face of the security deed or subsequent assignment.[2712] The notice shall contain a description of the land levied upon, the name of the owner of the land, the year(s) for which the taxes were assessed, and a statement of the amount of the taxes due, together with the accrued costs.[2713]

The levy is also accomplished by making a physical entry on the *fi fa* which is the basis of the sale.[2714] If the levying officer omits this step, a constructive levy is nonetheless accomplished by physically posting the notice of levy on the subject property.[2715]

§ 23.4.2.2 Pre-Sale Requirements

If *fi fas* have been presented to an officer for levy, the levying officer has very specific guidelines for conducting the sale. The sale is generally conducted in the manner of judicial sales.[2716] This includes posting a notice on the property, running notice in the legal organ of the county, and providing notice to various interested parties.[2717] The notice is permitted to describe the property with a street address and tax parcel identification number, with a reference to a deed with a full description of the property.[2718] In other words, a full legal description of the property is not required. The levying officer is also required to send out a notice letter to the defendant in *fi fa* ten days prior to the sale by certified mail or statutory overnight mail.[2719] This is an additional required notice separate from the 20 day levy notice previously described.

§ 23.4.2.3 Day Of The Sale

The tax sale will be conducted by the levying officer on the first Tuesday of the month on the courthouse steps, between the hours of 10:00 a.m. to 4:00 p.m. (eastern standard time), continuing day to day until the property is sold.[2720] The sale starts with the levying officer crying out the notice of the sale, stating the opening bid and soliciting public bids much in the way of an auction. Just about anyone can bid at the sale, including the county itself.[2721] The only parties who are prohibited from bidding at the tax sale are the underlying owner[2722] and the tax commissioner and certain of its employees.[2723] The opening bid is comprised of the amount of the taxes owed including interest and penalties, plus the levying officer's costs of sale.

2710   *Vesta Holdings, LLC v. Freeman*, 280 Ga. 608, 632 S.E.2d 87 (2006).

2711   O.C.G.A. § 48-3-9(a).

2712   O.C.G.A. § 48-3-9(b).

2713   O.C.G.A. § 48-3-9(a), O.C.G.A. § 48-3-10.

2714   O.C.G.A. § 9-13-12.

2715   *Tharp v. Harpagon Co.*, 278 Ga. 654, 604 S.E.2d 156, (2004).

2716   O.C.G.A. § 48-4-1.

2717   *See generally*, O.C.G.A. § 9-13-140, *et seq.*

2718   O.C.G.A. § 48-4-1(d).

2719   O.C.G.A. § 48-4-1(a).

2720   O.C.G.A. § 9-13-160 through O.C.G.A. § 9-13-162.

2721   O.C.G.A. § 48-4-20.

2722   O.C.G.A. § 48-4-4.

2723   O.C.G.A. § 48-4-23.

Once a successful bidder is established, the bidder must tender its bid in either cash or certified funds at the conclusion of the sale.[2724] If the bidder does not submit its tender at that time, the levying officer may elect to go after the bidder for the funds bid or re-cry the property for sale.[2725] Upon the tax sale bidder's proper tender of the bid amount, the levying officer must issue a tax sale deed to the bidder within a reasonable time. However, it is the tax deed holder's responsibility to ensure the tax sale deed is properly recorded in the deed index of the county.

§ 23.5 DEFECTIVE AND PROBLEMATIC TAX SALES

§ 23.5.1 Levying Officer's Right To Rescind And The Court's Right To Set Aside A Sale

The levying officer holds with its sale powers the ability to rescind the sale if certain procedures are followed. This rescission must happen within thirty days and prior to the issuance of the tax sale deed.[2726] If the levying officer rescinds the sale, it must return the tax deed purchaser's full bid amount within five days.[2727] If the reason for the rescission is that the sale was inadvertently made in violation of the automatic bankruptcy stay created by the defendant in *fi fa*'s filing for bankruptcy protection, the tax deed purchaser is only entitled to the return of his bid amount.[2728] However, if the levying officer rescinds the sale because either the sale was not completed according to the statutory requirements, the taxes were paid prior to the sale, or that the plaintiff in *fi fa* and defendant in *fi fa* had agreed prior to the sale to cancel the sale, then the tax deed purchaser is also entitled to receive interest at the rate of eighteen percent per annum, calculated daily, as damages.[2729]

§ 23.5.2 Court's Authority To Set Aside A Tax Deed

After the thirty day window and upon the issuance of the tax deed, the levying officer no longer has any statutory right to cancel a sale. Nonetheless, a court of competent jurisdiction will maintain the authority to do so, but only if is proven that the sale process was infected with fraud, irregularity, or error to the injury of either party.[2730] In the event a court sets aside the tax deed, pre-judgment interest is not generally added to the amount the tax deed purchaser paid at the sale.[2731] However, if upon learning of the invalidity of the sale the tax deed holder made a demand for the return of the funds and the levying officer refuses to return the money, in the absence of fraud the tax deed holder will be entitled to pre-judgment interest running from the date of the demand.[2732]

§ 23.5.3 Common Defects Rendering A Tax Deed Void Or Voidable

Tax deeds which appear regular on their face are deemed valid, and evidence that the taxes were owed and that the sale was performed according to the statutory requirements.[2733] Tax deeds are nonetheless subject to being set aside as are any sales of real property if there is a defect in the sale of the property. The more common defects in a tax sale are set out below, although this is certainly not an exhaustive list:

2724   O.C.G.A. § 9-13-166.

2725   O.C.G.A. § 9-13-170.

2726   O.C.G.A. § 9-13-172.1.

2727   O.C.G.A. § 9-13-172.1(b).

2728   O.C.G.A. § 9-13-172.1(c).

2729   O.C.G.A. § 9-13-172.1(d).

2730   O.C.G.A. § 9-13-172.

2731   *West v. McBride*, 207 Ga. 261, 61 S.E.2d 133 (1950), *Canoeside Properties, Inc. v. Livsey*, 277 Ga. 425, 589 S.E.2d 116 (2003); *Clarence L. Martin, P.C. v. Wallace*, 248 Ga.App. 284, 546 S.E.2d 55 (2001).

2732   *Harpagon Co., LLC v. Freeman*, 281 Ga. 531, 640 S.E.2d 268 (2007).

2733   *Livingston v. Hudson*, 85 Ga. 835, 838, 12 S.E. 17 (1890).

(5) (a)   If the defendant in *fi fa* has filed for bankruptcy protection, any sale of the defendant's property is considered to be in violation of the automatic stay of the bankruptcy proceedings and is therefore void.[2734]

(6) (b)   "The excessive levy problem": If the property can be sub-divided and the outstanding executions can be satisfied by one of the smaller sub-divided parcels, then the subdivision must take place. If the property is not subdivided, the levy is considered excessive and more property has been seized than is warranted by the execution.[2735]

(7) (c)   If the levying officer cries or advertises the sale as being the lands of someone who is not the true owner, the sale will be void.[2736] The reason for this is that the levying officer cannot sell more than he has, and to sell the property in the name of a stranger to title would in effect convey nothing.

(8) (d)   As with any sale of real property, if the legal description in the deed is so vague that the property cannot be particularly identified, the deed is voidable. However, so long as the tax deed provides a key to which the property might be identified (such as a reference to a prior deed with a complete legal description), the description will suffice.[2737]

(9) (e)   Naturally, if property is sold for non-payment of taxes which were never owed, then that undermines the very nature of the sale and would thus so infect the proceedings with fraud that the sale would be void.

(10) (f)   If the levying officer were to improperly levy on the property prior to the sale, the sale voidable and subject to being set aside.[2738]

A common misperception should be dispelled at this point. The levying officer's failure to provide the owner of the property of the tax sale will not render a tax sale void and strip the tax deed holder of its title.[2739] Rather, this will merely serve to give the defendant in *fi fa* a claim of damages against the levying officer.[2740] The only exception to this rule is if the defendant in *fi fa* can prove that the levying officer and tax deed holder colluded to fraudulently deprive the defendant in *fi fa* of notice of the sale.[2741]

§ 23.6 POST TAX SALE ISSUES FOR THE TAX DEED PURCHASER IN THE FIRST YEAR

§ 23.6.1 Buyer's Title

Upon receiving a tax sale deed, the tax deed holder is not the owner of the property. It has a "defeasible fee interest" in the underlying property. That means that it holds a title interest in the property, but that the interest is subject to being stripped away (or defeased) by a party's redemption of the property from the tax sale. For the first year, those redemption rights are irrevocable and the tax deed holder can take no action to impair them or otherwise interfere with the owner's use of the land. However, any time after a year from the tax sale, the tax deed holder may take affirmative steps to terminate the rights of redemption. A more complete discussion of the methods to terminate redemption rights appears later in this chapter.

§ 23.6.2 Buyer's Rights To The Property

Since rights of redemption in interested parties are irrevocable for the first year, a tax deed holder's rights to the property are severely limited with respect to the property. The tax deed holder cannot enter into possession of the property. To do

---

2734   *Edwards v. Heartwood 11, Inc.*, 264 Ga.App. 354, 590 S.E.2d 734 (2003).

2735   *West v. McBride*, 207 Ga. 261, 61 S.E.2d 133 (1950).

2736   *Canoeside Properties, Inc. v. Livsey*, 277 Ga. 425, 589 S.E.2d 116 (2003); *Clarence L. Martin, P.C. v. Wallace*, 248 Ga.App. 284, 546 S.E.2d 55 (2001).

2737   *GE Capital Mortg. Services, Inc. v. Clack*, 271 Ga. 82, 515 S.E.2d 619 (1999).

2738   *Powers v. CDSaxton Properties, LLC*, 285 Ga. 303, 676 S.E.2d 186 (2009).

2739   *Harper v. Foxworthy, Inc.*, 254 Ga.App. 495, 562 S.E.2d 736, (2002).

2740   *GE Capital Mortg. Services, Inc. v. Clack*, 271 Ga. 82, 515 S.E.2d 619 (1999).

2741   *GE Capital Mortg. Services, Inc. v. Clack*, 271 Ga. 82, 515 S.E.2d 619 (1999).

so would result in a trespass. In tandem with that, the tax deed holder cannot evict tenants or squatters from the property. Any such action would be deemed an interference with interested parties' rights to the property without first terminating their right to redeem. However, because of the prohibition against entry onto the property, most municipalities agree that the tax deed holder cannot be compelled to enter the property to bring it into code compliance.

§ 23.6.3 Buyer's Responsibilities

Even though prior to the termination of equitable rights of redemption the tax deed holder's title and rights to the property are severely limited, the tax deed holder is nonetheless saddled with several obligations with respect to the land. It is responsible for any and all dues and assessments from the subdivision's homeowners' association which properly accrue after the date of the tax sale.[2742] Additionally, the Georgia Supreme Court in *National Tax Funding v. Harpagon*,[2743] noted that a tax deed delivers to the tax deed holder a "taxable fee," which many believe makes the tax deed holder responsible for any property taxes which accrue after the tax sale.

§ 23.7 SURPLUS FUNDS GENERATED BY THE TAX SALE

§ 23.7.1 How Surplus Funds Are Calculated And What Happens To Them

As mentioned previously, the bidding at a tax sale starts off with an opening bid that is calculated by the levying officer which includes the base amount of the taxes, accrued interest and penalties, and the levying officer's costs of running the sale. After the opening bid is announced, bids are made much in the manner of an auction with bidding continuing until the highest bidder out-bids all others on the courthouse steps. Any amounts collected by the levying officer which are in excess of the opening bid are deemed "surplus funds." After the tax sale has been concluded and the levying officer has collected the bid amount from the tax deed purchaser, the levying officer pays out the amount necessary to satisfy the tax executions which were the subject of the tax sale. The tax deed holder has no obligation to ensure that the levying officer performs this duty and will suffer no liability for the levying officer's failure to satisfy the executions upon which the sale was based.[2744] The levying officer holds the surplus funds as a fiduciary until such time that they are claimed by an eligible party.[2745]

§ 23.7.2 Levying Officer's Notice Of Surplus

Within thirty days after the tax sale, the levying officer must send out notices to anyone with a record interest in the subject property.[2746] The notice may be sent by first class mail and must contain the following information: a description of the land sold, the date of the sale, the name and address of the tax deed purchaser, the sale price, and the amount of the surplus retained by the levying officer.[2747] The notice shall alert all the recipients that they may apply to take down the surplus funds as their interests may appear and in the priority in which their liens exist.

§ 23.7.3 Process For Claiming Surplus Funds

Any party with a record interest in the property may apply to take down the surplus funds. However, the funds can only be paid out in accordance with rules of priority.[2748] In other words, a second mortgage holder may not take down surplus

---

2742   *Croft v. Fairfield Plantation Property Owners Ass'n, Inc.*, 276 Ga.App. 311, 623 S.E.2d 531 (2005).

2743   *National Tax Funding, L.P. v. Harpagon Company, LLC.*, 277 Ga. 41, 586 S.E.2d 235 (2003).

2744   O.C.G.A. § 9-13-168.

2745   *Scott v. Vesta Holdings, I, LLC*, 275 Ga.App. 196, 620 S.E.2d 447 (2005).

2746   O.C.G.A. § 48-4-6(a).

2747   *Id.*

2748   *Id.*

unds, if a first mortgage is still a lien against the property. The underlying owner cannot take down any funds while valid liens against the property still exist. Outstanding taxes may also be satisfied out of the surplus funds.[2749] Also, if a party with an interest in the property or creditor of the defendant in *fi fa* redeems the property and receives a statutorily compliant redemption quitclaim deed, this redeemer is deemed to have a superlien against the property[2750] which also entitles that redeemer to a first priority claim against the surplus funds.[2751] Regardless of the nature of the applicant's claim, the levying officer can require the surplus funds applicant to provide a certified title exam as evidence of the applicant's entitlement to the surplus funds. The amount of paperwork a surplus fund applicant must fill out varies greatly among the different counties within Georgia, so any prospective applicant should contact the levying officer to determine the procedures for submitting an application in that jurisdiction.

Any party may assign their rights to take down the surplus funds to a third party as a matter of contract. It was once believed by some that the execution of a deed by the defendant in *fi fa* would release the defendant in *fi fa*'s claim to the surplus funds to the grantee in the deed. However, the Georgia Court of Appeals has rejected that contention.[2752] Rather, a deed to property which is sold at a tax sale executed by the defendant in *fi fa* will only transfer her interest in the underlying property – namely the right to redeem the property from the tax sale. The Court hinted that the assignment of rights to the surplus funds may be accomplished by a specific recital in the deed releasing the rights to the surplus funds, but that the preferred mechanism would be by a separate assignment.[2753] However, that was not the specific question before the court and therefore is not the rule of the case.

The redeeming party must make its claim to the surplus within five years from the date of the tax sale. At the end of the five year term, the levying officer must turn any unclaimed surplus funds over to the Department of Revenue, unless there is an interpleader action or claim to the fund pending.[2754] Failure to act within the five years will thereafter require the filing of an interpleader action against the Department of Revenue.[2755]

§ 23.7.4 Interpleader Action For Surplus Funds

Occasionally, the levying officer may have competing claims for the surplus funds or the title to the property is in such disarray that the officer cannot reasonably ascertain to whom the surplus funds should be paid. In such instances, the levying officer can interplead the surplus funds into the registry of the superior court in the county wherein the property lies.[2756] This action permits competing claimants to argue their entitlement to the funds to the court, which will then make a legal determination as to the entitlement to the funds and instruct the clerk of court to pay out the funds to the appropriate parties. The levying officer can deduct its costs and attorneys fees associated with the interpleader action from the surplus funds.[2757]

§ 23.7.5 Compelling The Disbursement Of Surplus Funds By Filing A Money Rule Action

If the levying officer, either through inaction or willful refusal does not disburse surplus funds in a timely manner after a proper party has applied for the funds' disbursal, an applicant may seek to have the levying officer judicially compelled to disburse the funds. This is an action brought in the superior court of the county in which the levying officer operates and

---

2749   *Scott v. Vesta Holdings, I, LLC*, 275 Ga.App. 196, 620 S.E.2d 447 (2005); *Alexander Inv. Group, Inc. v. Jarvis*, 263 Ga. 489, 435 S.E.2d 609 (1993).

2750   O.C.G.A. § 48-4-43.

2751   *Wester v. United Capital Financial of Atlanta, LLC*, 282 Ga.App. 392, 638 S.E.2d 779 (2006).

2752   *Georgia Lien Services, Inc. v. Barrett*, 272 Ga.App. 656, 613 S.E.2d 180 (2005). *See in comparison, Barrett v. Marathon Inv. Corp.*, 268 Ga.App. 196, 601 S.E.2d 516 (2004).

2753   *Id.*

2754   O.C.G.A. § 48-4-5(c).

2755   *Id.*

2756   *Id.*

2757   *Id.*

is commonly called a money rule action.[2758] In the event the applicant properly made the demand to the levying officer for the release of the surplus funds, and no good cause can be shown for the court's refusal, the court must award twenty percent per annum in interest on the funds as damages against the levying officer.[2759] In certain circumstances, a court may even award attorneys fees and costs associated with bringing a money rule action.[2760]

§ 23.8   RIGHTS OF REDEMPTION FOLLOWING TAX SALES

§ 23.8.1   Who May Redeem

A tax deed holder holds title to property subject to any interested parties right to redeem the property from the tax sale. Only unless and until the equitable rights of the defendant in *fi fa* and all other parties with an interest in the property to redeem the property from the tax sale have been terminated will the tax deed holder then have clear title. A discussion of how interested parties' rights to redeem may be terminated will be discussed in greater detail later within this chapter. The defendant in *fi fa* or delinquent taxpayer is not the only party who may come forward and redeem the property from a tax sale. In addition to the defendant in *fi fa*, any party with an interest in the property can redeem.[2761] This may include holders of other tax liens which were not part of the original levy, a mortgage holder, unsecured creditors of the defendant in *fi fa*, to name a few. A party is still entitled to redeem even if their interest is acquired after the tax sale.[2762] Also, an heir or heirs of the defendant in *fi fa* may come forward to redeem, either individually or together, and if done individually the redeeming party is deemed to have done so on behalf of its other co-tenants.[2763]

Holders of additional tax executions which were not the basis of the tax sale also have a right to redeem. However, if a person submits some but not all of the executions they hold for levy at a tax sale, they must choose to either satisfy their remaining executions out of the excess funds or redeem the property from the tax sale.[2764] Under the current legislative scheme, a tax execution transferee can no longer assert its liens by attempting to sell the remaining executions at successive tax sales.[2765] To allow otherwise could potentially subject a property to an endless stream of tax sales.

§ 23.8.2   The Tax Deed Holder's Obligations To Allow Tender

If a person qualified to redeem the property approaches the tax deed holder to redeem the property from the tax sale, the holder must permit the redemption if the rights to redeem have not already been terminated. A tax deed holder may not obstruct a party's rightful exercise of their statutory right to redeem the property and to do so may put the holder at risk of significant liability. However, a tax deed purchaser may deny a redemption demand made by someone who is a stranger to the property if it requests the that the party requesting redemption prove that it is a party entitled to redeem under O.C.G.A. § 48-4-40 and the party requesting redemption cannot allege that it is entitled to redeem.

2758   O.C.G.A. § 15-13-1, *et seq.*

2759   O.C.G.A. § 15-13-3(a); *Scott v. Vesta Holdings, I, LLC*, 275 Ga.App. 196, 620 S.E.2d 447 (2005).

2760   *Barrett v. Marathon Inv. Corp.*, 268 Ga.App. 196, 601 S.E.2d 516 (2004).

2761   O.C.G.A. § 48-4-40.

2762   *Leathers v. McClain*, 255 Ga. 378, 338 S.E.2d 666 (1986).

2763   *Andrews v. Walden*, 208 Ga. 340, 66 S.E.2d 801 (1951); *Miles v. Blanton*, 211 Ga. 754, 88 S.E.2d 273 (1955); *see also, Bank of Tupelo v. Collier*, 191 Ga. 852, 14 S.E.2d 59 (1941); *Johnson v. Washington*, 152 Ga. 635, 110 S.E. 889 (1922).

2764   *National Tax Funding, L.P. v. Harpagon Company, LLC.*, 277 Ga. 41, 586 S.E.2d 235 (2003).

2765   *DRST Holdings, Ltd. v. AGIO Corp.*, 282 Ga. 903, 655 S.E.2d 586 (2008).

§ 23.8.3   How To Exercise The Right To Redeem

§ 23.8.3.1   Inquiry Addressed To Tax Deed Holder

If a party is interested in redeeming, they must request that the tax deed holder specify the amount necessary to redeem. A common misperception is that the sheriff or tax commissioner provides that information, but that is incorrect. The tax deed holder is frequently the only party with sufficient information necessary to properly calculate that amount. However, the officer conducting the tax sale can provide the contact information for the tax deed holder upon request. A more detailed discussion of the calculation of the redemption amount appears later in this chapter.

Upon request the tax deed holder must provide the amount necessary to redeem the property from the tax sale. There is no statutory time limit requiring that the tax deed holder issue the redemption calculation within a certain time period; nor is there a case directly on that point. However, inordinate delays may expose the tax deed holder to a claim that they are thwarting the redeeming party's equitable redemption rights.

If a tax deed holder has either failed or refused to provide an amount necessary to redeem the property from the tax sale, the redeeming party may desire to tender an estimated redemption to the tax deed holder to preserve its claim to redeem the property from sale. In fact, it is an absolute pre-requisite to tender the estimated redemption amount prior to filing a lawsuit to challenge the tax deed.[2766] That tender must be made prior to the institution of litigation and must be a continuous tender, unless the tender has been waived by the tax deed holder.[2767]

Only two statutory exceptions and one case law exception to this pre-litigation tender rule exist. The first statutory exception is when it is obvious that the taxes upon which the tax sale were in fact based were never owed.[2768] The second exception is when no notice of the foreclosure of the right of redemption has been given under O.C.G.A. § 48-4-40, *et seq*.[2769] Georgia courts have recognized a third exception to this rule when the party attempting to redeem can prove that the redemption tender would have been refused by the tax deed holder.[2770]

§ 23.8.3.2   Calculation Of Redemption

For all tax sales conducted after July 1, 2002, tax deed holders are limited in what amounts they can charge to redeem a property from a tax sale.[2771] The tax deed holder is entitled to take as a base the principal amount it paid for the property at the tax sale and add to it any additional taxes or special assessments it has paid on the property.[2772] On that base principal, it can charge a twenty percent premium for the first year or fraction of a year that has elapsed since the tax sale date.[2773] If the property remains unredeemed after the first year (as calculated from the tax sale date), an additional ten percent premium can be added for each year or fraction of a year that elapses between then and the time the redemption amount is actually paid.[2774] If a redeeming party pays the redemption amount more than thirty days after the notice to foreclose the right of redemption has been given, a tax deed holder can add to the costs of sheriff service and publication service to the amount necessary to redeem.[2775]

2766   O.C.G.A. § 48-4-47.

2767   *Durham v. Crawford*, 196 Ga. 381, 26 S.E.2d 778 (1943); *Machen v. Wolande Management Group, Inc.*, 271 Ga. 163, 517 S.E.2d 58 (1999).

2768   *Id.*

2769   *Id.*

2770   *B-X Corp. v. Jeter*, 210 Ga. 250, 78 S.E.2d 790 (1953).

2771   O.C.G.A. § 48-4-42.

2772   O.C.G.A. § 48-4-42.

2773   O.C.G.A. § 48-4-42.

2774   *Id.*

2775   *Id.*

The amount necessary to redeem the property from the tax sale needs to be paid in "lawful money of the United States."[2776] In other words, a tax deed holder may not require that redemption amounts be paid in certified funds and must accept a personal check if presented by the redeeming party. However, the type of funds tendered to the tax deed purchaser will affect how quickly the tax deed holder must issue a redemption quitclaim deed.[2777]

It should be emphasized that this statute is very strictly construed and any fees added to the redemption amount other than those expressly authorized by statute are forbidden. Attorneys' fees for conducting the notice of the foreclosure of the right of redemption are not recoverable. Also forbidden are costs of clean up of the property, a fee for preparation of the redemption quitclaim deed, payment of homeowners' association fees, etc.

Also it is important to note that the calculation scheme discussed in this section and in the current version of O.C.G.A. § 48-4-42 apply only to tax deeds generated from tax sales conducted after July 1, 2002. Prior to 2002, this statute was revised frequently and premium amounts and fees chargeable to the redeeming party varied widely over the years. Therefore, a tax deed specialist should be contacted with any questions related to redeeming a tax deed prior to July 1, 2002.

§ 23.8.3.3 Issuance And Form Of Redemption Quitclaim Deed

Upon tender of the proper redemption amount by the redeeming party, it is the tax deed holder's duty to issue and execute the redemption quitclaim deed[2778] within seven days.[2779] However, if the redeeming party tenders the redemption amount in certified funds and presents a redemption quitclaim deed to tax deed holder and brings a notary and unofficial witness to witness the execution of the redemption quitclaim deed, the tax deed holder must execute the redemption quitclaim deed on the spot.[2780]

The redemption quitclaim deed differs in its form from a regular quitclaim deed in a number of ways and must contain specific recitals. First, it is important to note that the effect of a tax sale redemption is not to transfer title into the redeeming party. Rather, it is to put title back into the state it was prior to the tax sale – as if the tax sale never happened.[2781] Therefore, the grantee on a redemption quitclaim deed is not necessarily the redeeming party, but the defendant in *fi fa*. This is true even if the defendant in *fi fa* no longer holds an interest in the subject property. Principles of merger, however, would allow the title from the redemption quitclaim deed to pass to the third party from the defendant in *fi fa* without a subsequent conveyance being necessary. Additionally, the redemption quitclaim deed should recite who the redeeming party is and the amount that the party paid for the redemption.[2782] This is necessary because the redeeming party acquires a "super-lien" against the property by virtue of the redemption.[2783]

In a departure from the general rule that it is a grantee's responsibility to record its own deed and put the world on notice of her claim to real property, it is actually the tax deed holder's responsibility to record the redemption quitclaim deed for the redeeming party.[2784] The tax deed holder must present the deed for recording to the clerk of superior court of the county in which the property lies within ten days of being presented with the amount necessary to redeem the property.[2785] The tax deed holder must bear the cost of recording the deed with the clerk's office and must return the deed to the redeeming party upon its recording in the county land records.[2786]

2776   *Id.*

2777   *See* § 23.8.3.3 (Insurance and form of redemption quitclaim deed) of this work.

2778   O.C.G.A. § 48-4-44(a).

2779   O.C.G.A. § 48-4-44(d).

2780   O.C.G.A. § 48-4-44(c).

2781   O.C.G.A. § 48-4-43.

2782   O.C.G.A. § 48-4-44(a) (1)-(2).

2783   *See* § 23.8.4 (Effect Of Redemption).

2784   O.C.G.A. § 48-4-44(e).

2785   *Id.*

2786   *Id.*

§ 23.8.4   Effect Of Redemption

Once a party entitled to redeem a property from a tax sale has tendered the redemption amount and the tax deed holder has issued and recorded the redemption quitclaim deed, the tax sale and tax sale deed are considered a nullity.[2787] The redemption quitclaim deed has put title back into the defendant in *fi fa*, subject to all outstanding liens at the time of the sale. A defendant in *fi fa* cannot, however obtain any greater title than it already had at the time of the tax sale by virtue of redeeming the property from the sale.[2788] Any liens, easements or other restrictions or encumbrances that existed against the defendant in *fi fa*'s title survive the tax deed upon redemption by the defendant in *fi fa*.

If the property is redeemed by a creditor of the defendant in *fi fa* who is a creditor at the time of her redemption,[2789] the title to the property still reverts to the defendant in *fi fa*. However, the redeeming creditor receives a "super-lien" against the property.[2790] The super-lien means that the lien shall have a first priority position over all other liens including liens for other taxes, mortgages, etc.[2791] Additionally, a super-lien holder may judicially foreclose on its lien[2792] and seek partial payment of its lien through application for the surplus funds generated by the tax sale, if any, as discussed previously herein.

§ 23.9   FORECLOSING THE RIGHTS OF REDEMPTION

As mentioned previously in this chapter, a tax deed confers a defeasible interest in the property. That is, the tax deed holder is the holder of title to the property, subject to divestment by any interested party's exercise of her equitable right to redeem the property from the tax sale. If the tax deed purchaser wants to convert its defeasible fee into fee simple title, it must take steps to terminate the rights of parties to redeem the property from the tax sale. The Georgia General Assembly has created by statute two methods by which a tax deed holder may terminate redemption rights and each method will be discussed in greater detail below. However, it is important to know that both require affirmative action by the tax deed holder. Since July 1, 1989, a tax deed can no longer convert into fee simple title by sheer passage of time.[2793]

There currently exists no statute or case which obligates a tax deed holder to attempt to cut off the right of redemption. Unless and until the tax deed holder completes one of the two methods to terminate the right of redemption, those rights remain open indefinitely under any and all tax deeds issued since July 1, 1989.

§ 23.9.1   Procedure To Foreclose The Equitable Right Of Redemption

The first of the two methods to terminate a defendant in *fi fa*, or any other party's, right to redeem a property from a tax sale is an administrative, non-judicial, procedure called the foreclosure of the equitable right of redemption. This is more commonly referred to as the barment proceeding. A barment proceeding involves sending out statutory notices to a class of individuals or entities alerting them that they may have a right to redeem the property from the tax sale, and that the right will be terminated if they do not exercise that right within a certain period of time. The barment process is likely the more common method employed by tax deed purchasers to terminate redemption rights as it can be employed as soon as a year after the tax sale.[2794] A more detailed discussion of that process is outlined below.

2787   O.C.G.A. § 48-4-43.

2788   *Elrod v. Owensboro Wagon Co.*, 128 Ga. 361, 57 S.E. 712 (1907).

2789   *DRST Holdings, Ltd. v. Brown*, 290 Ga. 317, 720 S.E.2d 626 (2012).

2790   O.C.G.A. § 48-4-43, O.C.G.A. § 48-4-41.

2791   *National Tax Funding, L.P. v. Harpagon Company, LLC.*, 277 Ga. 41, 586 S.E.2d 235 (2003).

2792   *Id.*

2793   *Moultrie v. Wright*, 266 Ga. 30, 464 S.E.2d 194 (1995); *Patterson v. Florida Realty & Finance Corp.*, 212 Ga. 440, 93 S.E.2d 571 (1956); *Community Renewal and Redemption, LLC v. Nix*, 279 Ga. 840, 621 S.E.2d 722 (2005).

2794   O.C.G.A. § 48-4-45.

§ 23.9.1.1   Determination Of Who Is Entitled To Notice And Form Of The Notice

The notices of the barment must be served upon the defendant in *fi fa*, the current record title holder of the property (who may or may not be the defendant shown on the underlying *fi fa* that was the basis of the tax sale), the occupant of the property, and any other parties having a record interest in the subject property.[2795] Any heirs of a deceased landowner are entitled to receipt of notice of the barment proceeding as well. This necessarily requires that the tax deed holder conduct a thorough examination of the public records maintained by the county in which the land lies. Anyone and everyone who has a recorded interest in the subject property has a right to be served notice of the barment proceeding. If no notice of the barment was sent to a party with a recorded interest, the barment will be ineffective as to the party who was not sent notice.

The notice must contain certain information, and may be substantially in the following form:

Take notice that:

The right to redeem the following described property, to wit:

_____ will expire and be forever foreclosed and barred on and after the _____ day of _____, _____. The tax deed to which this notice relates is dated the _____ day of _____, _____, and is recorded in the office of the Clerk of the Superior Court of _____ County, Georgia, in Deed Book _____ at page _____.

The property may be redeemed at any time before the _____ day of _____, _____, by payment of the redemption price as fixed and provided by law to the undersigned at the following address: _____

_____.

Please be governed accordingly.

_____ [2796]

§ 23.9.1.2   Sending Out Notice

Once the tax deed holder has identified the parties entitled to receive notice of the redemption and has prepared the notices, it must serve those notices in a very specific manner. All entities and individual residing within the county in which the property lies must be served by personal service by the sheriff.[2797] In the event that the subject property is vacant property, the "occupant" should be served by posting the notice on the property. The notices to be served by the sheriff should be delivered to the sheriff's office no less than 45 days prior to the redemption expiration date that is provided on the notices.[2798] This is because every party is entitled to receive notice of the barment proceeding thirty days prior to the barment expiration date, and the sheriff must be allowed fifteen days to effect service on the parties. The sheriff is to leave a copy of the notice with the party served and may do so by leaving notice at their residence.[2799] However, the sheriff is to make the entry of service on the original notice and return it to the tax deed holder.[2800]

All entities and individuals who reside outside the county, including those out of state, must be sent the notice by certified mail or statutory overnight mail.[2801] These notices must be sent out provided that the address is reasonably

---

2795   *Id.*

2796   O.C.G.A. § 48-4-46(a).

2797   O.C.G.A. § 48-4-45(a)(1).

2798   O.C.G.A. § 48-4-46(b).

2799   *Id.*

2800   O.C.G.A. § 48-4-46(d).

2801   O.C.G.A. § 48-4-45(a)(2).

ascertainable.[2802] Additionally, the notice must be published in the legal organ of the county in which the property lies for four consecutive weeks any time within the six months preceding the barment expiration date, provided that the sale occurred after July 1, 1989.[2803] No party who claims an interest in the property that does not appear of record is entitled with notice of the tax sale,[2804] therefore, they receive their notice through publication in the legal organ.

As part of sending out the statutory notices to the parties entitled to receive the barment notices, the tax deed holder must performs some basic steps to locate the parties entitled to notice. This is perhaps the part of the barment proceeding that is most fraught with peril for the tax deed holder. Nowhere does the law require the party entitled to notice of the barment proceeding actually and physically receive the notice. However, the extinguishment of rights in real property is governed by the due process clauses of the state and federal constitutions.[2805] Therefore, a tax deed holder must be careful not to infringe on a property owner's right to receive due process notice regarding that owner's rights to property. Accordingly, the courts require that the tax deed holder perform "reasonable diligence" in its effort to locate the parties entitled to notice of the barment proceeding.[2806]

There are few judicial interpretations of what is "reasonable diligence" for a tax deed holder when attempting to locate people to serve with the barment notice. Of course, many would argue that this obligation by the tax deed holder should be balanced by the corresponding duty of the taxpayer/property owner to provide their accurate contact information to the county tax commissioner. According to the *Hamilton v. Renewed Hope, Inc.* case merely looking at the records of the county tax commissioner and the deed records alone is not enough.[2807] In that case, the defendant in *fi fa* was listed in the local phone book which the court determined was included in the minimal effort a tax deed holder must undertake to locate the parties. What further efforts may be required by the Georgia Courts is a matter which will have to be clarified in later opinions. For now, the tax deed purchaser should take steps (and document those steps) to find parties in the event of a subsequent challenge on the sufficiency of service of its barment notices.

§ 23.9.1.3   Passage Of The Barment Expiration Date

Once the tax deed holder has sent out all the statutory barment notices, it waits for the barment expiration date to pass. It must make itself available for and diligently respond to any requests for redemption payoff figures and for the receipt of the redemption tender. If a party properly tenders the redemption payoff, it is the tax deed purchaser's responsibility to execute the redemption quitclaim deed, as discussed previously in this chapter. If however, the barment expiration date passes and no party has come forward to redeem, the right to redeem has been properly foreclosed.

§ 23.9.2   Ripening By Prescription Under O.C.G.A. § 48-4-48

The second form by which a tax deed holder may terminate a party's right to redeem a property from a tax sale is by taking steps to ripen its title by prescription. This is where the tax deed holder enters onto the property and adversely possesses it for a term of years.[2808] Having done this, the tax deed holder's title is deemed to have "ripened" from a defeasible fee into fee simple title. The underlying theory to this method of terminating redemption rights is that if the tax deed holder's possession of the property is uninterrupted during that period, interested parties are deemed to have acquiesced to the tax deed purchaser's dominion and control of the property to the extent that it thereby allows the tax deed purchaser's defeasible fee to ripen into clear title.

2802   *Funderburke v. Kellet*, 257 Ga. 822, 364 S.E.2d 845 (1988); *Mennonite Board of Missions v. Adams*, 462 U.S. 791, 103 S.Ct. 2706 (1983).

2803   O.C.G.A. § 48-4-45(a)(3).

2804   O.C.G.A. § 48-4-45(b).

2805   *Mennonite Board of Missions v. Adams*, 462 U.S. 791, 103 S.Ct. 2706, 77 L.Ed.2d 180 (1983).

2806   *Hamilton v. Renewed Hope, Inc.*, 277 Ga. 465, 589 S.E.2d 81 (2003).

2807   *Hamilton v. Renewed Hope, Inc.*, 277 Ga. 465, 589 S.E.2d 81 (2003).

2808   O.C.G.A. § 48-4-48.

Since the revision of O.C.G.A. § 48-4-48 in 1989, tax deeds can no longer ripen into fee simple title by sheer passage of time.[2809] The tax deed purchaser must actually enter into possession of the property and meet all the requirements of adverse possession as defined by the Georgia Code.[2810] The time required of adverse possession for a tax deed to ripen in fee simple title is dictated by O.C.G.A. § 48-4-48. That statute gives various requirements depending upon when the tax sale was performed. Tax deeds resulting from tax sales conducted prior to July 1, 1989 require seven years adverse possession by the tax deed holder before her title can ripen by prescription.[2811] That time period shall run from the date of the execution of the tax deed. Tax deeds resulting from sales after July 1, 1989 but prior to July 1, 1996 shall require four years of adverse possession running from the date of the execution of the tax deed.[2812] Finally, all tax deeds executed after July 1, 1996 shall still require four years of adverse possession, but that time shall run from the date the tax deed was recorded in the county real estate records.[2813]

When a tax deed holder is in possession of the subject property, if a defendant in *fi fa* or any other interested party wishes to exercise its right to redeem within the four year period, it must do so.[2814] Merely asserting that the party holds the equitable right of redemption is not enough.[2815] This is because redemption is considered a self-help remedy and failure to exercise it will result in the remedy's foreclosure.[2816]

§ 23.9.3   State Of Title Upon Termination Of The Equitable Right Of Redemption

Once the tax deed holder has successfully completed one of the two previously described methods to cut off interested parties' rights to redeem the property from the tax sale, the tax deed holder should record an affidavit in the deed records to put the world on notice that the barment or adverse possession process has been completed. While this is not a legal requirement found in any statute, the Georgia Supreme Court has determined that failure to record such an affidavit would open up the right of redemption in future bona fide purchasers of the property who took their interest without notice that the right to redeem has been foreclosed.[2817]

But what is the status of the tax deed holder's title to the property at this point? Georgia law says the tax deed holder is the fee simple owner of the property, upon completion of either of those statutory methods, subject only to any easements, right of ways, covenants and restrictions of record, and any claims which accrued after the tax sale. However, practically speaking, no title insurance company in the state of Georgia will issue an owners or lenders title insurance policy on the property. Therefore, while under the law, the tax deed holder may have fee simple title, it does not have insurable title. These days most real estate transactions involve a lenders or owners title policy, or both. Accordingly, insurable title for most practical purposes means marketable title.

To obtain insurable title, a tax deed holder will have to undergo a suit to quiet title in order to obtain a judicial confirmation of its title. A full discussion of suits to quiet title is outside the scope of this work. However, a real estate litigation professional should be consulted in connection with filing such an action. As quiet title actions take additional time and resources, a tax deed holder who wishes to sell the property should carefully consider her

---

2809   *Moultrie v. Wright*, 266 Ga. 30, 464 S.E.2d 194 (1995); *Community Renewal and Redemption, LLC v. Nix*, 279 Ga. 840, 621 S.E.2d 722 (2005), but *see also, B-X Corp. v. Hickory Hill 1185, LLC*, 285 Ga. 5, 673 S.E.2d 205 (2009) (holding that those tax deeds under the previous statutory scheme which had not yet ripened by passage of time by the time of the enactment of the 1989 revisions to O.C.G.A. § 48-4-48 are impacted by this revision, thereby making those tax deeds entered into between 1982 and 1989 subject to the same prescriptive requirement).

2810   O.C.G.A. § 44-5-161, *et seq.*

2811   O.C.G.A. § 48-4-48(a).

2812   O.C.G.A. § 48-4-48(b).

2813   *Id.*

2814   *Blizzard v. Moniz*, 271 Ga. 50, 518 S.E.2d 407 (1999).

2815   *Machen v. Wolande Management Group, Inc.*, 271 Ga. 163, 517 S.E.2d 58 (1999).

2816   *Forrester v. Lowe*, 192 Ga. 469, 15 S.E.2d 719 (1941).

2817   *Washington v. McKibbon Hotel Group, Inc.*, 284 Ga. 262, 664 S.E.2d 201 (2008).

obligations under the contract in regards to what kind of title she must deliver to the buyer. While fee simple title may be accomplished by the simple termination of the rights of redemption, insurable or marketable title may obligate the tax deed holder to complete a quiet title action. Similarly, a buyer must be aware of what kind of title it wants the seller to deliver if buying property at a tax sale. If the contract calls only for fee simple title, the seller may deliver title to the buyer, but the buyer may still be unable to obtain an owner's title policy at closing, or worse, their lender will refuse financing if a lender's policy is unavailable.

The **RED BOOK**

CHAPTER 24

WATER RIGHTS

OVERVIEW

Georgia has over 190 miles of coastland and more than 70,000 miles of streams and waterways within its boundaries. Some understanding of the law of water rights is therefore important when discussing real property law. Water is not itself real property, of course, since it is subject to flowing, evaporation, percolation through the ground, etc. and cannot be absolutely owned. Yet a significant and often confusing body of law has developed around water rights. Some matters are controlled by federal law, others by state law. The laws will vary according to whether the water is still or moving, whether it touches upon or flows through the property of more than one owner, and if flowing water, whether it is navigable or not.

This chapter will explain how those laws control water rights in Georgia. We will discuss the law relative to both nonnavigable and navigable waters, both Georgia and applicable federal law, and issues both of ownership of adjoining or underlying land and water usage.

§ 24.1 NONNAVIGABLE WATERS

§ 24.1.1 Definition

Georgia's definition of a navigable waterway is more specific than the broad federal definition. In Georgia, a navigable stream is one which is "capable of transporting boats loaded with freight in the regular course of trade either for the whole or part of the year. The mere rafting of lumber or the transportation of wood in small boats shall not make a stream navigable."[2818] If a stream is not capable of such transportation of freight, it is not deemed navigable and subject to the rules set out below.

The phrase "in the regular course of trade" limits the type of navigation that will be sufficient to consider a watercourse navigable under the statute. In one case, the floating of a Styrofoam and wood raft 4' x 16' loaded with two passengers, a goat and a bale of cotton did not render a creek navigable.[2819] The court found that such a craft was not sufficient to support freight traffic "in the usual course of trade." Since the stream involved was found to be nonnavigable, the public did not have a blanket right of passage over the waters and the owner was entitled to restrain canoers from traveling the creek through his land.

§ 24.1.2 Ownership Of Land Beneath Nonnavigable Waters

The beds of nonnavigable streams belong to the owner of the underlying or adjacent lands.[2820] If a stream is the dividing line between two parcels, each owner's boundary extends to the center of the main current of the water. Currents can gradually change, however, and if that happens the boundary line will follow the current. If for some reason a stream takes an entirely new channel, the original boundary line (if identifiable) will remain the boundary between the lands. Any gradual accretion of land on either side of the stream will belong to the owner of that side.[2821]

§ 24.1.3 Riparian Rights In General

The word "riparian" refers to the banks of a river or stream. The term "riparian rights" refers to the rights of the owner of land on the bank of a river or stream to use water from the waterway flowing through her land. The upper riparian owner is the owner of the land upstream; the lower riparian owner is the owner of the land downstream. Common usage of the phrase "riparian" has expanded its meaning to include land bordering on a lake or on coastal waters or tidelands, not just rivers and streams.

2818   O.C.G.A. § 44-8-5.

2819   *Givens v. Ichauway, Inc.*, 268 Ga. 710, 493 S.E.2d 148 (1997); *see also Georgia Canoeing Association v. Henry*, 267 Ga. 814, 482 S.E.2d 298 (1997).

2820   O.C.G.A. § 44-8-1 and O.C.G.A. § 44-8-2.

2821   O.C.G.A. § 44-8-2

Georgia law specifies that running water "belongs" to the owner of the land on which it runs, subject to certain limitations. The upper riparian owner has the right to pass water along to the next owner without obstruction. Similarly, the lower riparian owner has the right to receive the natural flow of water from the upper riparian owner. Owners have no right to divert the water from its usual channel nor adulterate it in any way that would interfere with the enjoyment of the water by another owner, or to create a nuisance (such as flooding) to any other owner.

§ 24.1.4   Usage Of Water In Nonnavigable Streams

§ 24.1.4.1   Possession And Fishing Rights

The owner of riparian land has the same exclusive right to possession of a stream flowing over the land as she has to any other part of the land.[2822] Where tidal waters are not involved, ownership of the bed of a stream generally carries with it exclusive rights of fishery in the stream.[2823] Fish in a watercourse are not literally the property of the riparian landowner, any more than is the water flowing in the watercourse. However, the owner of the bed of a nonnavigable stream has the exclusive right to remove fish from the water upon her land[2824] and may prohibit trespassing by others who wish to fish in those waters.

When the land is sold, the grantors have the right to reserve to themselves and their heirs boating and fishing privileges to the water on that land.[2825] Fishing rights can also be obtained by prescription. The right to fish in nonnavigable waters on private land can be acquired by "exclusive occupation adverse to land owner for 20 years."[2826]

§ 24.1.4.2   Irrigation

Every riparian owner is entitled to a reasonable use of the water flowing through her land.[2827] The use of water for agricultural purposes was recognized as a reasonable use (along with domestic use) in the first reported Georgia case on riparian rights.[2828] Use of the water for agricultural purposes specifically includes irrigation, even though irrigation is accomplished by diverting water from its natural flow.[2829] Although irrigation is allowed, it remains a question of fact whether such diversion substantially alters or diminishes the flow of the stream.

§ 24.1.4.3   Diversion, Detention Or Pollution Of Water

Owners of land through which water naturally flows are entitled to receive the "natural and usual flow" of that water, subject to the reasonable use of the water by other owners.[2830] That use may include reasonable detention or diminution for purposes of irrigation, as described above. One Georgia statute specifies that riparian owners have the right to divert nonnavigable watercourses through their own lands.[2831] This right is subject to the overriding restriction against changing the ultimate channel of a watercourse, such that if a stream is diverted through an owner's lands it must be returned to its usual course by the time it leaves their land and flows to the next owner's property. Although there are no cases directly on

---

2822   O.C.G.A. § 44-8-1.

2823   *West v. Baumgartner*, 124 Ga.App. 318, 184 S.E.2d 213 (1971); *see* § 24.5.4 (Fishing Rights in Tidewaters).

2824   *Thompson v. Tennyson*, 148 Ga. 701, 98 S.E. 353 (1919).

2825   *Bosworth v. Nelson*, 170 Ga. 279, 152 S.E. 575 (1930).

2826   *Bosworth v. Nelson*, 170 Ga. 279, 152 S.E. 575 (1930).

2827   *Price v. High Shoals Mfg. Co.*, 132 Ga. 246, 64 S.E. 87 (1909).

2828   *Hendrick v. Cook*, 4 Ga. 241 (1848).

2829   *Pyle v. Gilbert*, 245 Ga. 403, 265 S.E.2d 584.

2830   O.C.G.A. § 51-9-7.

2831   O.C.G.A. § 44-8-9.

point, it appears that a diversion for the purpose of creating a pond on one's property may be considered "reasonable," so long as the diversion is temporary and that the natural and usual flow of water will thereafter be restored.[2832]

Permanently diverting the flow of a nonnavigable watercourse, or obstructing it so as to impede the flow or to cause overflow onto another's property, or polluting of the water, is deemed a trespass on the property of other affected riparian owners.[2833]

§ 24.1.4.4 Construction Or Removal Of Dams

As discussed in § 24.1.3 (Riparian Rights in General) above, riparian owners may choose to build a dam on a nonnavigable waterway in order to create a pond on their property, whether for fishing, development of water power, or merely for aesthetics. (In that section, we discussed a situation where multiple owners agreed to build a dam to create a pond for their mutual recreational use.) If title to both sides of the waterway is in the same person or entity, Georgia statues allow the building of a dam by the owner.[2834] However, the right to build the dam does not relieve the property owner from responsibilities to other riparian owners. For example, if the dam were to cause flooding on the property of an owner upstream, or to significantly reduce the eventual flow of water onto property downstream, the owner building the dam could be liable to those owners for damages.

Before deciding to build a dam for any purpose, the property owner must obtain any necessary permits or licenses. She must also anticipate any interference with the volume of water that will flow downstream (whether increase or decrease), and would be well-advised to reach some type of agreement with the downstream property owner(s) before construction begins. The possibility of any overflow on property upstream must also be considered. If such a consequence is expected, the owner should seek to obtain flowage easements over any land expected to receive overflow. The details of such arrangements are beyond the scope of this work, and the owner should seek competent legal counsel before proceeding.

The removal of an existing dam carries the same considerations as construction. Permits may be required, depending upon the local jurisdiction, and the effects of the dam's removal upon upper and lower riparian owners must be considered. Again, competent legal counsel should be sought before demolition begins. It should be noted that nothing in the law requires a downstream landowner to remove a naturally occurring beaver-constructed dam in order to preserve the water flow for landowners further downstream, or to prevent overflow on land upstream.[2835]

§ 24.2 NAVIGABLE WATERS

§ 24.2.1 Federal Preemption Regarding Water Rights

The United States Constitution gives Congress power over admiralty and maritime matters[2836] and regulation of commerce.[2837] Because of this, Congress has paramount authority to control all public *navigable* waters. By statute, however, the federal government has limited its control over navigable waters to the right to regulate or improve navigation, flood control, or power production upon navigable waters.[2838] On these issues federal law will control. Other issues, such as title to the lands beneath navigable waters and the natural resources within such lands and waters, are left to the several states to determine. State laws will control in these areas.

2832   *See Brown v. Tomlinson*, 246 Ga. 513, 272 S.E.2d 258 (1980), wherein the *draining* of a pond was permitted "since the pond was only being temporarily drained."

2833   O.C.G.A. § 51-9-7.

2834   O.C.G.A. § 44-8-4.

2835   *Bracey v. King*, 199 Ga.App. 831, 406 S.E.2d 265 (1991).

2836   U.S. Const., Art. III, § 2, cl. 1.

2837   U.S. Const., Art. I, § 8, cl. 3; *In re Builders Supply Co.*, 278 F.Supp. 254 (D.C. Iowa, 1968).

2838   43 U.S.C.A. 1311.

It is the federal definition of navigable waters which defines and limits the jurisdiction of Congress. The federal definition of "navigable waters" under the Clean Water Act[2839] is broadly defined as "the waters of the United States, including the territorial seas."[2840] Determining the scope of this broad definition has been a heavily-litigated issue over the past decade.[2841] In 2006, the United States Supreme Court held that "the waters of the United States" includes only relatively permanent, standing or flowing bodies of water, not intermittent or ephemeral flows of water, and only those wetlands with a continuous surface connection to bodies that are waters of the United States.[2842] At the time this book was published, new regulations have not been implemented to further clarify the federal definition of "navigable waters" or "waters of the United States" in light of the 2006 Supreme Court decision.

However, it has been well established that in order for a stream to be considered navigable it must be "generally and commonly useful to some purpose of trade or agriculture."[2843] Mere pleasure fishing does not mean that a stream is navigable "when it has always been susceptible for use only for this purpose."[2844] If a particular watercourse does not qualify as "navigable" under federal law, then the laws of the state through which the water flows will control.

§ 24.2.2   Definition In Georgia Law

Georgia's definition of a navigable waterway is more specific than the federal definition. A navigable stream is one which is "capable of transporting boats loaded with freight in the regular course of trade either for the whole or part of the year. The mere rafting of lumber or the transportation of wood in small boats shall not make a stream navigable."[2845]

§ 24.2.3   Ownership Of Land Adjoining Navigable Waters

With waters that are navigable, the "centerline" rule of ownership does not apply. The owner of land adjacent to a navigable waterway owns the land to the low water mark in the bed of the stream.[2846] The bed of the stream is reserved to the state, in much the same way as a public highway, subject to the rights of the federal government in navigable waters. The state of Georgia has also long recognized the public right of passage over navigable waters, regardless of the ownership of the land through which they pass.[2847]

§ 24.2.4   Usage Of Water

§ 24.2.4.1   Areas Of Federal Control

As stated earlier, the federal government retains the right to control navigable waters with regard to regulating or improving navigation, flood control, or power production.[2848] This means that the federal government can dredge or widen a watercourse in order to facilitate navigation or control flooding, or to increase the ability of a watercourse to produce power. Basically, the federal government can take whatever steps it deems necessary to protect the public good in these areas. The Army Corps of Engineers is responsible for supervising and maintaining all navigable rivers and harbors, and should be consulted regarding its plans before buying any property which borders on such waterways.

2839   43 U.S.C.A. 1251 *et seq.*

2840   *Rapanos v. U.S.*, 547 U.S. 715 (2006).

2841   For a comprehensive time line detailing the evolution of the term "navigable waters," *see Rapanos v. United States*, 547 U.S. 715 (2006).

2842   *Rapanos v. U.S.*, 547 U.S. 715, 126 S.Ct. 2208 (2006).

2843   *U.S. v. Ross*, 74 F.Supp. 6 (D.C.Mo. 1947).

2844   *George v. Beavark, Inc.*, 402 F.2d 977 (C.A.Ark, 1968).

2845   O.C.G.A. § 44-8-5.

2846   O.C.G.A. § 44-8-5(b).

2847   *Charleston and Savannah Railway v. Johnson*, 73 Ga. 306 (1884).

2848   § 24.2.1 (Federal Preemption Regarding Water Rights); 43 U.S.C.A. 1311.

§ 24.2.4.2 Rights To Passage Upon The Waterway And Fishing Rights

The public has a right to free navigation on a navigable watercourse.[2849] If a navigable stream is obstructed by the owner of land through which it passes (by the building of a low bridge over it, for example), the obstruction will be considered a public nuisance and the courts can order its removal, plus the payment of damages to others affected by the nuisance.[2850]

The owner of land adjacent to a navigable stream has no "right to possession" of the water as it flows through his land, nor any exclusive right to fish in those waters. Fishing rights inure to the public's benefit, just as the right to passage. The owner of lands adjacent to navigable waters, therefore, may not restrain the public from either passage thereon or from fishing therein.

§ 24.2.4.3 Irrigation, Diversion Or Detention Of Navigable Waters

Georgia statutes provide that running water "belongs" to the owner of the land on which it runs, subject to certain limitations.[2851] The statute does not restrict its applicability only to nonnavigable waters, even though the cases interpreting it have all involved nonnavigable waters. Those cases have held that a diversion of some of the water for purposes of irrigation is acceptable.[2852]

When dealing with navigable streams, federal law must also be considered. Whatever use a riparian owner makes of the waters in a navigable stream are subject to the overriding interest of the public in navigation and fishing rights. The federal government has the right to "take all needed measures to preserve the navigability of the navigable water courses of the country...."[2853] Therefore, if sufficient water were diverted for irrigation so as to affect the navigability of the waterway, that irrigation would be considered a public nuisance and could be enjoined. The same rule applies to any other sort of diversion or detention of navigable waters. If it negatively impacts areas over which the government has jurisdiction (navigability, flood control or power production), the diversion or detention may be stopped by the courts.

§ 24.3 APPLICABLE TO BOTH NAVIGABLE AND NONNAVIGABLE STREAMS

Owners of land adjacent to waterways, both navigable and nonnavigable, are authorized to ditch or embank their lands to protect it from freshets and overflows from the watercourse, provided that doing so does not divert the water from its ordinary channel.[2854]

Ownership of land adjacent to a watercourse (whether navigable or nonnavigable) carries with it the right to build a bridge or to establish a ferry for private use across the watercourse.[2855] The right is not absolute, however, and if on navigable waters is subject to the overriding interest of the public in navigation, flood control and power production, which rights must not be interfered with by such bridge or ferry. Establishing and operating a public bridge or ferry is a franchise which can only be granted by the state.

§ 24.4 LAKES AND PONDS

The "centerline rule" applicable to non-navigable streams does not apply to lakes and ponds in Georgia. The irregular size and shape of such bodies of water make it extremely impracticable to try to divide ownership of the lakebed in such a fashion, since there is no clear and true "centerline." The ownership of land bordering on *natural* lakes and ponds is much

---

2849   *Charleston and Savannah Railway v. Johnson*, 73 Ga. 306 (1884).

2850   O.C.G.A. § 41-1-2 and O.C.G.A. § 41-1-3.

2851   O.C.G.A. § 44-8-1.

2852   *Pyle v. Gilbert*, 245 Ga. 403, 265 S.E.2d 584 (1980).

2853   *United States v. Rio Grande Dam & Irrigation Co.*, 174 U.S. 690, 19 S.Ct. 770 (1988).

2854   O.C.G.A. § 44-8-9.

2855   O.C.G.A. § 44-8-10.

the same as that of land bordering on navigable waters: ownership of the land ends at the low-water mark of the water.[2856] This rule is only a presumption, however, and a deed specifying another boundary will be honored.[2857]

If the lake or pond is man-made, however, the law gives us a less clear-cut approach. Man-made lakes or ponds are considered temporary, since they may be drained at any time via changes to, removal or destruction of the dam which created them. In *Boardman v. Scott*,[2858] the foundational case in Georgia on such questions, the Court discussed the difference between natural and artificial lakes/ponds this way:

> [W]here an artificial pond is raised by a dam swelling a stream over its banks, it would be natural to presume that a grant of land bounding upon such pond would extend to the thread of the stream upon which it is raised…[2859]

In other words, if a lake or pond is created on a stream by the erecting of a dam, the centerline of the stream will still be the boundary of adjacent land. The presence of a current would be one indicator that the body of water should be treated as a stream, rather than a lake. However, the court recognized the difficulties inherent in trying to find a current, no matter how weak it may be, in a body of water, and using that to determine ownership of the underlying land. It set out a more practical, case-by-case approach:

> [I]f the prominent, tangible characteristics of the thing… taken as a whole, are those of a lake or pond, and not those of a stream, and it is commonly known and designated as a certain lake or pond, and it has been in existence in this condition long enough to have become what may be termed a permanent body of water, with well-defined boundaries, the law applicable to lakes and ponds [*i.e., ownership to the low-water mark only*] should be applied to it, even though there may be some evidence of a current in it.[2860]

In the *Boardman* case, the body of water involved had been in existence for nearly 60 years. The court ruled that it had, in effect, become a permanent body of water with developed well-defined boundaries. Even though there was occasionally (at times of low water) evidence of a current running through the pond, that was not sufficient to warrant applying the centerline rule.

§ 24.4.1   Implied Easements For Lakefront Lots

Developers are now often creating subdivisions around artificial lakes, and selling lots with reference to a subdivision plat which depicts the lake area. When a developer sells such lots according to a subdivision plat, the purchasers of the lots obtain an irrevocable easement over the lake or pond in addition to title to their individual lot to the low-water mark of the lake. In one case, for example, a developer sold lots in a subdivision adjoining a lake. The lots were shown on a subdivision plat which also showed the lake area. The developer sold one of the lakefront lots to an individual to whom he also sold the lake itself. That owner attempted to build a fence around the entire lake to keep trespassers from using her lake. Other lot owners adjoining the lake objected, and the Georgia Supreme Court agreed with their position.[2861] When land is bounded by a lake or pond, the water constitutes one of the advantages of its location, is a material part of its value, and is often the biggest factor in purchasing that particular property. Even though the lake was thereafter sold to

---

2856   *Boardman v. Scott*, 102 Ga. 404, 30 S.E. 982 (1897).

2857   *Prescott v. Herring*, 212 Ga. 571, 94 S.E.2d 417 (1956). (A deed expressly conveying "all of the land… covered by Bradford Mill Pond…" was upheld as granting ownership of the entire tract of land underneath the Pond, not just land to the low-water mark.)

2858   *Boardman v. Scott*, 102 Ga. 404, 30 S.E. 982 (1897).

2859   *Boardman v. Scott*, 102 Ga. 404, 30 S.E. 982 (1897).

2860   *Boardman v. Scott*, 102 Ga. 404, 30 S.E. 982 (1897).

2861   *Higgins v. Odom*, 246 Ga. 309, 271 S.E.2d 211 (1980).

one individual, the easement over the lake obtained by other lot owners was irrevocable, and the lake's owner could not enjoin their use of the lake.

§ 24.5 TIDEWATERS AND TIDELANDS

§ 24.5.1 Definitions

The term "tidewaters," as used in Georgia statutes and cases, refers to the sea and all rivers and arms of the sea that are affected by the ebb and flow of tides, *and* which are capable of being used for fishing, passage, navigation, commerce, or transportation.[2862] "Tidelands," therefore, refers to the lands along the seacoast, including beaches, marshes, bays, harbors, islands, and the land under the open sea itself within Georgia's territorial boundaries.

§ 24.5.2 Ownership Of Land Including Nonnavigable Tidewaters

Nonnavigable tidewaters are handled in much the same way as nonnavigable streams.[2863] That is, if such waters are the dividing line between two parcels, the centerline of the waterway is the boundary, and the boundary will change if the channel of the water gradually changes. If for any reason the water takes a completely new channel, the old centerline, if identifiable, will remain the boundary.[2864]

§ 24.5.3 Ownership Of Land Abutting Navigable Tidewaters

By English common law, the ownership of lands abutting the sea extends only to the high-water mark, while the land between the high-water and low-water marks (called the "foreshore") belonged to the Crown.[2865] The State of Georgia became the owner of the beds of all tidewaters within the state as successor to the Crown of England.[2866] This means that beach area above the normal high-water mark remains the private property of the owner of the land.

§ 24.5.4 Fishing Rights In Tidewaters

As with navigable streams, the public has a general right to fish in navigable tidewaters.[2867] A series of cases and statutory law have amplified this approach with respect to certain rights. Specifically, owners of land abutting navigable tidewaters have the exclusive right to the clams and oysters (but not other fish) in the beds of those waters.[2868]

2862   O.C.G.A. § 51-1-3(4).

2863   *See* § 24.1.2 (Ownership Of Land Beneath Nonnavigable Waters) of this work.

2864   O.C.G.A. § 44-8-6.

2865   *Johnson v. State*, 114 Ga. 790, 40 S.E. 807 (1902).

2866   O.C.G.A. § 51-1-2; *Coastal Marshlands Protection Committee v. Center for a Sustainable Coast*, 286 Ga.App. 518, 649 S.E.2d 619 (2007).

2867   *West v. Baumgartner*, 12 Ga.App. 318, 184 S.E.2d 213 (1971), *rev'd on other grounds at* 228 Ga. 671, 187 S.E.2d 665 (1972).

2868   *Johnson v. State*, 114 Ga. 790, 40 S.E. 807 (1902); Constitution of the State of Georgia (1945); *State v. Ashmore*, 236 Ga. 401, 224 S.E.2d 334 (1976); O.C.G.A. § 44-8-7(b).

CHAPTER 25

FAIR HOUSING ACT AND AMERICANS WITH DISABILITIES ACT

OVERVIEW

Title VIII of the Civil Rights Act of 1968 is known as the Fair Housing Act (the "Act").[2869] The Act was enacted to protect a person's right to own, sell, purchase, or rent housing of her choice without fear of unlawful discrimination and to allow everyone equal access to housing. There is also a Georgia fair housing law[2870] that is almost identical to the Federal Act.

The U.S. Department of Housing and Urban Development ("HUD") is charged with the authority to enforce the Federal Act while the Georgia Commission on Equal Opportunity enforces the Georgia fair housing law.[2871] However, in many cases, HUD enlists the assistance of the Georgia Department of Equal Opportunity to investigate and make recommendations relative to the Act. Given the similarities between the Federal and State Acts they are discussed collectively in this chapter.

This chapter also contains a brief discussion of the Americans With Disabilities Act, in ("ADA") and its potential impact upon condominium and homeowners associations in discrimination claims.

§ 25.1 TO WHOM DOES THE ACT APPLY?

The Act applies to virtually all housing with the primary exemption being for a single-family house sold or rented by the owner.[2872] Even then, the exemption only applies if: (a) the individual owner does not own, or have any interest in the proceeds of, more than 3 single-family houses at any one time; (b) if the owner does not live in the property being sold, or was not the most recent resident of the house prior to the sale, the exemption only applies to one such sale within a 24 month period; (c) the owner does not use the services or facilities, in any way, of any real estate broker, agent, salesman or other person *in the business of selling or renting dwellings*; and (d) the owner does not publish, post or mail any advertisement that is otherwise in violation of the Act.[2873]

The phrase "in the business of selling or renting dwellings" means any person who: (1) has, within the preceding twelve months, participated as principal in three or more transactions involving the sale or rental of any dwelling or any interest therein, or (2) has, within the preceding twelve months, participated as agent, other than in the sale of his own personal residence in providing sales or rental facilities or sales or rental services in two or more transactions involving the sale or rental of any dwelling or any interest therein, or (3) is the owner of any dwelling designed or intended for occupancy by, or occupied by, five or more families.[2874]

The only other exception to the Act is for the rental or sale of rooms or units in dwellings containing living quarters occupied or intended to be occupied by no more than four families living independently of each other, if the owner actually maintains and occupies one of the living quarters as his residence.[2875]

Since the Act is a Federal law, it supersedes all contrary State and local laws, codes and ordinances as well as contradictory covenants, bylaws and declarations.[2876]

2869 42 U.S.C.A. § 3601 - 42 U.S.C.A. § 3619.

2870 O.C.G.A. § 8-3-200, *et seq.*

2871 O.C.G.A. § 8-3-206.

2872 42 U.S.C.A. § 3603.

2873 42 U.S.C.A. § 3603.

2874 42 U.S.C.A. § 3603.

2875 42 U.S.C.A. § 3603.

2876 The Act's preemption provision, which is codified at 42 U.S.C. § 3615, provides that "any law of a State, a political subdivision, or other such jurisdiction that purports to require or permit any action that would be a discriminatory housing practice under [the Act] shall to that extent be invalid."⁸ 42 U.S.C. § 3615.

§ 25.2   WHAT DOES THE FAIR HOUSING ACT PROHIBIT?

As originally enacted, the Act prohibits discrimination in any respect regarding the sale, rental or financing of dwellings[2877] or in the provision of brokerage services or facilities in connection with the sale or rental of a dwelling because of race, color, religion, sex or national origin.[2878] In 1988, the Act was amended to include prohibitions against discrimination in any activities related to the sale or rental of dwellings, in the availability of residential real estate-related transactions or the in provision of services and facilities in connection therewith on the basis of familial status and handicap.[2879]

Specifically, the Act provides that it is illegal:

(a)   To refuse to sell or rent after the making of a bona fide offer, or to refuse to negotiate for the sale or rental of, or otherwise make unavailable or deny, a dwelling to any person because of race, color, religion, sex, familial status, or national origin.

(b)   To discriminate against any person in the terms, conditions, or privileges of sale or rental of a dwelling, or in the provision of services or facilities in connection therewith, because of race, color, religion, sex, familial status, or national origin.

(c)   To make, print, or publish, or cause to be made, printed, or published any notice, statement, or advertisement, with respect to the sale or rental of a dwelling that indicates any preference, limitation, or discrimination based on race, color, religion, sex, handicap, familial status, or national origin, or an intention to make any such preference, limitation, or discrimination.

(d)   To represent to any person because of race, color, religion, sex, handicap, familial status, or national origin that any dwelling is not available for inspection, sale, or rental when such dwelling is in fact so available.

(e)   For profit, to induce or attempt to induce any person to sell or rent any dwelling by representations regarding the entry or prospective entry into the neighborhood of a person or persons of a particular race, color, religion, sex, handicap, familial status, or national origin.

(f)   To discriminate in the sale or rental, or to otherwise make unavailable or deny, a dwelling to any buyer or renter because of a handicap of: that buyer or renter; a person residing in or intending to reside in that dwelling after it is so sold, rented, or made available; or any person associated with that buyer or renter.

(g)   To discriminate against any person in the terms, conditions, or privileges of sale or rental of a dwelling, or in the provision of services or facilities in connection with such dwelling, because of a handicap of: that person; a person residing in or intending to reside in that dwelling after it is so sold, rented, or made available; or any person associated with that person. This includes a refusal to permit, at the expense of the handicapped person, reasonable modifications of existing premises occupied or to be occupied by such person if such modifications may be necessary to afford such person full enjoyment of the premises, except that, in the case of a rental, the landlord may where it is reasonable to do so condition permission for a modification on the renter agreeing to restore the interior of the premises to the condition that existed before the modification, reasonable wear and tear excepted; a refusal to make reasonable accommodations in rules, policies, practices, or services, when such accommodations may be necessary to afford such person equal opportunity to use and enjoy a dwelling; or in connection with the design and construction of covered multifamily dwellings … , a failure to design and construct those dwelling in such a manner that: the public use and common use portions of such dwellings are readily accessible to and usable by handicapped persons; all the doors designed to allow passage into and within all premises within such dwellings are sufficiently wide to

---

2877   42 U.S.C.A. § 3605(a).

2878   42 U.S.C.A. § 3604(b). Note that "age" is not a protected class. As will be discussed in greater detail below, familial status is protected but this protection applies to adults living with children under the age of 18. There is no state or federal law protecting people over the age of 18 who do not live with a child under the age of 18.

2879   42 U.S.C.A. § 3604

allow passage by handicapped persons in wheelchairs; and all premises within such dwellings contain the following features of adaptive design: an accessible route into and through the dwelling; light switches, electrical outlets, thermostats, and other environmental controls in accessible locations; reinforcements in bathroom walls to allow later installation of grab bars; and usable kitchens and bathrooms such that an individual in a wheelchair can maneuver about the space.

(h) For anyone engaged in residential real estate-related transactions, including lenders, real estate brokers, and appraisers, to discriminate against any person in making available such a transaction, or in the terms or conditions of such a transaction, because of race, color, religion, sex, handicap, familial status, or national origin.

(i) To deny any person access to or membership or participation in any multiple-listing service, real estate brokers' organization or other service, organization, or facility relating to the business of selling or renting dwellings, or to discriminate against him in the terms or conditions of such access, membership, or participation, on account of race, color, religion, sex, handicap, familial status, or national origin.[2880]

§ 25.2.1   Claims Of Discrimination Based On Disability

Currently, the most common housing discrimination complaints filed with HUD are based on disability. Some of the complaints alleging discrimination against persons with disabilities may come from a lack of understanding on the part of housing providers as to their duty to make reasonable accommodations to meet the needs of persons with disabilities.

§ 25.2.1.1   Refusal To Rent Or Sell

Under the Act, it is unlawful to discriminate in the sale or rental of a dwelling, or otherwise to make a dwelling unavailable because of a handicap of the buyer or renter, or a person residing in or intending to reside in the unit after it is purchased or rented, or any person associated with the buyer or renter. It is also unlawful to discriminate in the terms, condition, or privileges of sale or rental of a dwelling, or in the provision of services or facilities in connection with the dwelling, because of a handicap.[2881] Handicap means "a physical or mental impairment which substantially limits one or more of such person's major life activities; a record of having such an impairment; or being regarded as having such an impairment." The term does not, however, include current, illegal use of or additional to, controlled substances.[2882]

A "physical or mental impairment" includes: psychological disorder, cosmetic disfigurement, loss of any major body systems or mental or physical disorder such as retardation, cerebral palsy, autism, muscular dystrophy, multiple sclerosis, alcoholism, and drug addiction (so long as it relates to an addiction based upon prior drug use and not the current illegal use of a controlled substance).[2883] A "major life activity" includes: walking, seeing, hearing, speaking, breathing, learning and working.[2884]

The Act's prohibition against discrimination based on handicap also prohibits housing providers from asking certain questions during the application process. The law forbids asking applicants whether they or their associates have a handicap or inquiring into the nature or severity of a handicap.[2885] A housing provider is also prohibited from inquiring into the ability of applicants and tenants to meet their medical, hygiene, and other personal needs, except to the extent necessary to determine tenancy qualifications.[2886]

2880   42 U.S.C.A. § 3604, 42 U.S.C.A. § 3605 and 42 U.S.C.A. § 3606.

2881   42 U.S.C.A. § 3604(f)(1) and 42 U.S.C.A. § 3604(f)(2).

2882   42 U.S.C.A. § 3602.

2883   24 C.F.R. § 100.201(a).

2884   24 C.F.R. § 100.201(b).

2885   24 C.F.R. § 100.202(c).

2886   *Niederhausaur v. Independence Square Housing*, P-H; Fair Housing – Fair Lending Rptr. § 16,306 (N.D. Cal. 1998).

The HUD regulations permit 5 types of inquiries of all applicants.[2887] Those inquiries are: (1) inquiries into an applicants' ability to meet requirements of ownership or tenancy; (2) inquiry to determine whether an applicant is qualified for a dwelling available only to persons with handicap or to persons with a particular handicap; (3) inquiry to determine whether an applicant for a dwelling is qualified for a priority available to persons with handicaps to person with a particular type of handicap; (4) inquiring whether an applicant for a dwelling is a current illegal abuser or addict of a controlled substance; and (5) inquiring whether an applicant has been convicted of the illegal manufacture or distribution of a controlled substance. Landlords can ask questions concerning an applicants' income, references and other rental history so long as they are asked of all other applicants.

The Act, despite its protection of handicapped persons, does not require a landlord or owner make a dwelling available to an individual whose tenancy would constitute a direct threat to the health or safety of other individuals or whose tenancy would result in substantial physical damage to the property of owners.[2888] In determining whether a condition constitutes a direct threat to health or safety, one must look to the actual facts and issues, not prejudices or stereotypes. In one case, a tenant sought to rent a unit in a residential hotel.[2889] The tenant suffered from bipolar disorder. The on-site property manager and the owners of the property refused to rent the unit to the tenant. In the suit that followed, the Court awarded $30,000 for emotional damage, an $8,000 civil penalty, and costs.

§ 25.2.1.2   Reasonable Accommodations – Physical Modifications

In addition to outlawing discrimination of handicapped persons based on physical or mental impairment, the Act makes it illegal to refuse to permit persons with disabilities to make reasonable modifications to existing dwellings. Any such modifications must be made at the handicapped person's expense and is only required to be permitted if the modifications are necessary to afford the handicapped person full enjoyment of the premises.[2890] The obligation to permit reasonable accommodations not only applies to landlords but to condominium and homeowners associations with regard to the use of common areas and facilities.

"Premises" is defined to mean the interior or exterior spaces, parts, components or elements of a building, including individual dwelling units and the public common and use areas of a building. An individual with handicaps is permitted, at her expense, to make reasonable accommodations to lobbies, main entrances of buildings, laundry rooms and other common and public use areas if necessary for the full enjoyment of the premises.[2891]

The person wishing to make the modification "must seek the owner's approval before making the modification."[2892] The owner (*i.e.*, landlord, or board of directors of a condominium) may condition permission for a modification on receipt of a reasonable description of the proposed modification as well as reasonable assurances the work will be done in a workman like manner and that any required building permits will be obtained.[2893]

Permission may be further conditioned in some instances on the requestor agreeing to restore the premises to their prior condition. However, the obligation to restore the property is not absolute. It does not apply to reasonable wear and tear and it only applies to modifications made to the interior areas of the individual unit and does not require that modifications made to public or common areas be restored.[2894]

2887   24 C.F.R. § 100.202(c)(1)(5).

2888   24 C.F.R. § 100.202(d); 54 Fed.Reg. 3247 (Jan. 23, 1989).

2889   *HUD v. Flowers*, (HUD ALJ 09-99-0004-8, January 22, 2001).

2890   42 U.S.C.A. § 3604(f)(3)(A).

2891   24 C.F.R. § 100.203(a)(c).

2892   24 C.F.R. Ch. 1, subch. A at II and III.

2893   24 C.F.R. § 100.203(b).

2894   24 C.F.R. § 100.203(a).

Not all modifications made to the interior of the unit must be removed. Modifications that will not interfere with the use and enjoyment of the unit by future occupants can remain. For example, if a renter reinforces a wall by adding sheathing to enable the installation of grab bars, the tenant may be required to remove the grab bars upon vacating the unit but will not be required to return the wall to its previous condition since the addition of the sheathing does not impair its future use, where leaving the grab bar in place may impede the future use by a future tenant.[2895]

Landlords are prohibited from collecting an additional security deposit to ensure the modifications will be made.[2896] A landlord may, where it is reasonable to do so, condition permission for a modification on the tenant making payments into an interest bearing escrow account to ensure that funds will be available to pay for the restoration. The requirement must be reasonable which requires a case by case determination. Given the uncertainty this entails, the authors strongly caution against a landlord's insistence on such a requirement.

In one case, a tenant of an apartment community used a motorized wheelchair for mobility.[2897] The tenant lived in the apartment complex for over eighteen years. The tenant orally requested permission from the owners of the apartment complex to install a ramp leading to his apartment so that he could enter and exit his apartment in his wheelchair. Four other residents of the complex who were handicapped made similar requests for the installation of ramps. The landlord sent a letter approving the installation of the ramp with the sentence, "We are not responsible for any liability for this ramp should anything occur." The landlord took the position, "no insurance, no ramp." The landlord also required that the ramps be removed at the end of the tenancy. HUD filed a complaint alleging discrimination in the terms and conditions of the tenancy and failure to make reasonable accommodations for the tenants. The issue decided by the Court was whether the landlord's action was a condition on approval of installation of the ramps and, if so, were the conditions reasonable. The Court analyzed whether the installation of the ramps and potential liability that could occur imposed a substantial burden or undue hardship on the landlord. The Court held that it did not. The Court further held that requiring wheelchair-bound residents to carry renters insurance, without requiring non-handicapped tenants to also carry liability insurance was a violation of the Fair Housing Act based on a theory of disparate impact.[2898] The Court imposed a civil fine of $15,000 and civil damages of $40,000 to one resident and $75,000 to another resident.

§ 25.2.1.3   Reasonable Accommodations - Rules, Policies, Practices Or Services

In addition to the physical modifications required by the Act, housing providers must also make reasonable accommodations in their rules, policies, practices or services if they are necessary to afford a person with a handicap equal opportunity to use and enjoy a dwelling.[2899] For example, where a building has a "no pet" policy and a blind applicant with a seeing eye dog wants to live in the unit, the "no pet" provision cannot be enforced against that person.[2900]

The law requiring a housing provider to make reasonable accommodations in its rules and regulation to permit a handicap person full use and enjoyment of the property has arisen mostly in cases where a handicapped person asked a landlord or a condominium or homeowners association to assign a parking space convenient to the handicapped persons residence. For example, the owners of an apartment complex refused to assign a parking space close to the building for a tenant with multiple sclerosis.[2901] Parking at the complex was on a first-come, first-serve basis and it was difficult for the handicapped person to consistently park in a space near the building. Management refused to provide a reserved space

---

2895   24 C.F.R. § 100.203(a).

2896   24 C.F.R. § 100.203(a).

2897   *HUD v. Twin Brook Village Apartment*, P-H: Fair Housing – Fair Lending Rptr. § 2517 (HUD ALJ 2001).

2898   *HUD v. Twin Brook Village Apartment*, P-H: Fair Housing – Fair Lending Rptr. § 2517 (HUD ALJ 2001).

2899   42 U.S.C.A. § 3604(F)(3)(B).

2900   24 C.F.R. § 100.204.

2901   *Jankowski Lee & Associates v. HUD*, 91 F.3d 891 (7th Cir. 1996).

close to the building but increased the number of handicapped parking spaces from six to eight. Twenty-seven tenants had handicap sticker or tags for their vehicles. The Court held that the addition of the two additional handicapped spaces was not a "reasonable accommodation" under the Act.

In another case, the owner of a condominium unit was handicapped and requested the exclusive use of a parking space on the common elements close to his unit.[2902] The Board refused the request based on the condominium Declarations which provided that parking spaces constitute common elements for the non-exclusive use of unit owners. The Board took the position they could not grant the request without an amendment to the Declaration which required the approval of two-thirds of the members of the Association. The Board presented such an amendment to the membership, but it was not adopted.

The Court recognized that the issue was complicated by the fact that the parking spaces were owned by the condominium unit owners as tenants in common. The Court agreed that the Declaration provided that the parking spaces were part of the common elements for the non-exclusive use of all of the unit owners. Nevertheless, the Court held that, under the Act, the Board had a duty to avoid enforcing the Declaration in a manner that would result in discriminatory effects and also had the duty to regulate the use of the common elements so as to comply with the Act. The Court based its findings on the grounds that to the extent the Declaration contained provisions that either on their face or as applied, violate the Act, they cannot be enforced as written.

Discrimination can also arise on the basis of fees. One owner who lived in a mobile home park and had a respiratory disease that required the supervision of home healthcare aides.[2903] The park had a policy of charging $1.50 per day for the presence of long-term guests and $25 per month for guest parking. The park refused to waive the fees for the healthcare aid. The park argued that its obligation to make reasonable accommodations should not extend to financial matters. The Court held that in some instances, providers of residential housing must bear the cost related to the reasonable accommodation requirement of the Act. The Court also held that the fact that the fees were applicable to all residents and were facially neutral would not protect the park from a Fair Housing claim because they had an unequal impact on handicapped tenants. The Court emphasized that whether a provider must pay the cost for a reasonable accommodation is to be determined on a case by case basis considering whether "it may be necessary to afford [a handicap] person equal opportunity to use and enjoy a dwelling."

Housing providers are also required to accommodate support pets. In one case, a tenant sought to rent a single-family home.[2904] When she visited the property, she explained to the owner that her 9-year-old daughter suffered from epilepsy and required a service dog to control her seizures. The owner allegedly told her that he would not rent the house to her if the service animal was going to be on the premises.

Since the tenant needed to get her daughter settled before school began, she placed the service dog with another family and signed a one-year lease with the owner. A few months later the tenant noticed that her daughter was having more frequent and severe seizures. She took her daughter to the doctor, who concluded that the increase in seizures was due to the loss of the service animal and recommended that she get her daughter a "therapy dog." During the months that followed, the tenant repeatedly attempted to give the owner a copy of a letter from the doctor explaining that her daughter required a service dog, but the owner allegedly continued to refuse to permit a service animal on the property.

When the lease expired the owner allegedly refused to renew the lease, but permitted the tenant to stay on a month-to-month basis until she found alternative housing. However, the owner allegedly stated that he would not allow a dog on the property under any circumstances. The tenant filed a complaint with HUD which pressed numerous charges against the owner.

2902   *Gittleman v. Woodhaven Condominium Association, Inc.*, 972 F.Supp. 892 (D.NJ 1997).

2903   *United States v. California Mobile Home Park Management Company*, 29 F.3d 1413 (9th Cir. 1994).

2904   HUD Case No. 07-097.

§ 25.2.1.4   New Construction

All new construction must include accessibility enhancing features in the design and construction of "all covered multi-family dwellings."[2905] The accessibility requirements only apply to "covered multi-family dwellings" which are defined as a building with at least 1 elevator that has 4 or more units and, also, "ground floor" units in buildings without elevators consisting of 4 or more units.[2906] "Ground floor" is any floor of a building with a entrance on an accessible route.[2907] "Accessible route" is a continuous unobstructed pass connecting accessible elements and spaces in a building that can be negotiated by a person with severe disability using a wheelchair and it is also safe and usable by people with other disabilities.[2908]

The Act requires that all covered multi-family dwellings be designed and constructed to have at least one building entrance on an accessible route unless it is impractical to do so because of the terrain or unusual characteristics of the site. The burden of proving impracticability is on the person or persons who design or construct the building.[2909]

All covered family dwellings must be designed and constructed in such a manner that (1) the public use and common use portions of such dwellings are readily accessible to and usable by handicap persons; (2) all doors must be designed to allow passage into and within all premises within such dwelling and are sufficiently wide to allow passage by handicap person in a wheelchair; and (3) all premises within such dwellings contain the following features of adaptive design light switches, electrical outlets, thermostats and other environmental controls must be placed in accessible locations; reinforcement in bathroom walls to allow later installation of grab bars; and usable kitchens and bathrooms such that an individual in a wheelchair can maneuver about the space.[2910]

In one case, an owner sued the builder of a condominium alleging that the units were not wheelchair accessible.[2911] The site work on the property was done before the Act came into effect, but the property was not first occupied until after the effective date. The Court held that even though the builder did not design the buildings, he was subject to the Act. The Acts' requirement that the buildings be designed and constructed are not meant to be conjunctive, but are to be real broadly. Housing providers can be forced to retrofit buildings to bring them into compliance with the Act.

The Act provides that compliance with the appropriate provision of the American National Standards Institute for buildings and facilities providing accessibility and usability for physical handicap people satisfy the requirements of adaptive design.[2912] HUD also has issued a detailed set of Fair Housing and Accessibility Guidelines to assist builders and developers in complying with accessibility requirements of the Act.[2913]

§ 25.2.2   Discrimination Based Upon Familial Status

The Act prohibits discrimination on the basis of familial status. "Familial status" is defined by the Act as one or more individuals under the age of 18 living with a parent, a person having legal custody of such an individual(s), or the designee or such parent or legal guardian. It also includes a person who is pregnant, someone who is about to secure legal custody of someone under the age of 18, single parent families, foster families, adopted families, and restrictions on the use of facilities by children.[2914] HUD recently expanded the definition of "family" to include actual or perceived sexual orientation and gender identity.[2915]

2905   42 U.S.C.A. § 3604(f)(3)(c). *See also* 24 C.F.R. § 100.205 for detailed regulations and commentaries on these requirement.
2906   42 U.S.C.A. § 3604(f)(7).
2907   24 C.F.R. § 100.201.
2908   24 C.F.R. § 100.205.
2909   24 C.F.R. § 100.205.
2910   42 U.S.C.A. § 3604(f)(3)(C)(iii)(IV).
2911   *Baltimore Sleighborhoods, Inc. v. Romel Builders*, 40 F.Supp. 2d 700 (D.C. Md. 1999).
2912   ANSI A 117.1.
2913   56 Fed. Reg. 9472 (Mar. 6, 1991). *See also* 24 C.F.R. Ch. 1, subch. A at II and III.
2914   42 U.S.C.A. § 3602(k), 42 U.S.C.A. § 3604(a)-and (e), 42 U.S.C.A. § 3604, 42 U.S.C.A. § 3606, 42 U.S.C.A.§ 3617, 42 U.S.C.A. § 3631.
2915   24 CFR 5.403.

The familial status provisions of the Act primarily affect rental housing, condominium associations and homeowner associations. Restrictions imposed by landlords or contained in condominium or homeowner association documents restricting occupancy of families with children under the age of 18 or restricting or limiting a child under the age of eighteen's use of the facilities in a community are a violations of the Act, unless it can be shown that the regulation is both reasonable and designed to protect the health, safety, and welfare of the child.

Examples of familial status discrimination include: a landlord's advertisement for rental of an apartment limiting occupancy to no more than one child and one pet per household or no more than two children;[2916] a landlord's advertisement preferring "mature persons";[2917] an advertisement that a property was "perfect for single or couple";[2918] a condominium association's declaration prohibiting occupancy by families with children under 14;[2919] a mobile home parks' adoption of a $75 surcharge for each occupant over 2 persons per trailer.[2920]

In contrast, it was permissible for a landlord to ask tenants to move because of the conduct of their young child where the landlord showed the 4 year old was often left unsupervised in the common areas and engaged in a pattern of behavior that disturbed other tenants and neighbors.[2921] This was found to be acceptable because nothing in the Act prevents a landlord from evicting a family so long as the criteria being applied would also be used to judge non-familial tenants.

§ 25.2.2.1 Use Restrictions

Housing providers are entitled to develop, implement and enforce reasonable health and safety rules regulating the use of recreational and other facilities. Many communities have rules regulating use of the common areas that establish a priority for use in favor of adults by setting aside times when only adults may use the equipment or facility or by restricting use by children under a certain age or by requiring children to be accompanied by a parent or guardian.

While housing providers are entitled to develop, implement and enforce reasonable health and safety rules, rules that specifically target children or that generalize that all children are risks when using the facilities or are too noisy and will negatively affect adult use of the facilities will generally be found to violate the Act. The burden of proof is on the housing provider to show that the rule was enacted to protect the health, safety and welfare of the children.

The line between valid health and safety restrictions and illegal discrimination against children can be hard to draw. In one case, a homeowners association of single family detached houses posted a sign at the entrance to the community advertising it as an "Adult Community" and adopted rules which restricted the use of the swimming pool by prohibiting children under five (5) years old from using the pool at any time and limiting pool hours for children between 5 and 16 years old to the hours of 11 a.m. and 2 p.m. daily.[2922] The Association attempted to justify the prohibition of children under the age of 5 by arguing that children under 5 posed an inherent danger for drowning and posed a health risk because of the possible presence of fecal material in the pool from leaking diapers. The association attempted to justify the time limitation for children between the age of 5 and 16 by arguing that children are noisy and rowdy and disturbed other residents and that setting aside an exclusive time for young people to use the pool was reasonable to give them the opportunity to enjoy the pool [in a noisy and rowdy way]. The Court held there was no evidence to justify the ban on children under the age of 5 or limiting the time of use for 5-16 year olds. The Court rejected the argument that the rule was designed to protect residents [children] from drowning. The Court held

2916 *HUD v. Edelstein*, P-H, Fair Housing – Fair Lending Rptr. § 25825.018 (HUD ALJ 1991).

2917 *Janick v. HUD*, 44 F.3d 553 (7th Cir. 1995).

2918 *Guider v. Bauer*, 865 F.Supp. 492 (N.D. Ill. 1994).

2919 *HUD v. Schuster*, P-H: Fair Housing – Fair Lending Rptr. § 25091 (HUD ALJ 1995).

2920 *HUD v. Melody Lake Country Club Estates*, P-H: Fair Housing – Fair Lending Rptr. § 15974 (HUD ALJ 1994).

2921 *HUD v. Ludwid*, P-H: Fair Housing – Fair Lending Rptr. § 18130 (HUD ALJ 1997).

2922 *HUD v. Paradise Gardens*, P-H: Fair Housing – Fair Lending Rptr. § 25037 (HUD ALJ 1992).

hat the time limitation was overly broad, was not designed to protect the health, safety or welfare of the children and was to provide a "quiet" environment for the older residents. Finally, the Court also held that as a general rule, safety judgments are for informed parents to make, not landlords.

However, in another case, a condominium association's pool rule stating that children under the age of 14 had to be accompanied by an adult was held to serve a legitimate purpose for maintaining the health, safety and welfare of the child.[2923]

§ 25.2.2.2   Occupancy Restrictions

The Act allows housing providers to limit the number of occupants in a unit if the provider adheres to "any reasonable local, State or Federal restrictions regarding the maximum number of occupants permitted to occupy a dwelling."[2924] The exemption was intended to allow governmental authorities to continue to limit the number of occupants per unit based on square footage or the number of bedrooms in a unit as long they are reasonable and not applied in a discriminatory manner. The United States Supreme Court clarified that this exemption may only be based upon the actual number of occupants, and may not be based upon the familial relationship between them.[2925]

The HUD regulations also indicate that private housing providers may develop and implement reasonable occupancy limitations even in the absence of governmental occupancy restrictions.[2926] Reasonableness of private occupancy restrictions will be judged on the number and size of sleeping areas or bedrooms and the overall size of the dwelling unit. In one case a rental policy that limited occupancy to a number of persons equal to the number of bedrooms in a unit plus one was held to have an illegal impact on families with children.[2927] The policy must reasonably take into consideration the size of the unit as well as the number of bedrooms.

In 1998, HUD adopted a policy on occupancy standards known as the "Keating Memo."[2928] The Keating Memo states that HUD "believes that an occupancy policy of two persons in a bedroom, as a general rule, is reasonable under the Fair Housing Act."[2929] However, the reasonableness of any occupancy policy is rebuttable and HUD will carefully examine all non-governmental occupancy restrictions to determine whether they operate unreasonably to limit or exclude families with children from certain housing facilities.[2930] The policy also states that in reviewing such occupancy cases, the size and number of bedrooms and other special circumstances will be taken into consideration.[2931]

The special circumstances addressed in the policy include the following: (1) age of the children; (2) configuration of the dwelling in question; (3) other physical limitations of the housing, for instance the capacity of the septic, sewer and other building systems; and (4) whether the housing provider made discriminatory statements, adopted discriminatory rules regarding use of the common facilities, took steps to discourage families with children from living in their housing development or enforced its occupancy policies only against families with children.[2932]

2923   *HUD v. Murphy*, P-H: Fair Housing – Fair Lending Rptr. § 25002 (HUD ALJ 1990).

2924   42 U.S.C.A. § 3607(b)(1).

2925   *City of Edmonds v. Oxford House*, 514 U.S. 725 (1995).

2926   *See* HUD Preamble II, 24 C.F.R. Ch. 1, subch. 4, App. I, 54 Fed. Reg. 3237 (January 23, 1989).

2927   *Snyder v. Barry Realty, Inc.*, 953 F.Supp. 217 (N.D. Ill. 1996).

2928   63 Fed. Reg. 70256 (Friday, December 18, 1998).

2929   *Id.*

2930   *See id.* at 70257.

2931   *Id.*

2932   *Id.*

§ 25.2.2.3 Exemption For Housing For Older Persons

Prohibitions against familial status discrimination do not apply to "housing for older persons."[2933] Two separate categories of housing qualify as housing for older persons. To qualify, the housing must be provided under a State or Federal program that HUD determines is specifically designed and operated to assist elderly persons[2934] and which is either: (1) "intended for and solely occupied by persons 62 years of age or older;[2935] or (2) "intended and operated for occupancy by persons 55 years of age or older."[2936]

§ 25.2.2.4 62 And Over Housing

To qualify under this exemption, all residents of the housing development must be at least 62 years old. A development can lose the exemption if any unit is occupied by any person less than 62 years of age. The only exception to this rule is that units in a development may be occupied by employees less than 62 years of age and their families so long as those employees "perform substantial duties directly related to the management or maintenance of the housing."[2937]

§ 25.2.2.5 55 And Over Housing

Housing which is intended and operated for occupancy by persons 55 years of age or older is exempt from the Acts' prohibition against familial status discrimination if: (1) at least 80% of the occupied units are occupied by at least 1 person who is 55 years of age or older; (2) the housing facility or community publishes and adheres to policies and procedures that demonstrate the intent required and (3) the housing facility or community complies with rules by the Secretary of HUD for verification of occupancy.[2938]

§ 25.2.2.6 Age Verification Techniques And Formal Policies

Housing providers must develop procedures for routinely determining the occupancy of a unit. The procedures must provide for regular updates through surveys and must take place at least once every two years.

HUD adopted a rule that implements this requirement.[2939] HUD has stated the following documents are considered reliable documentation of the age of the occupants of the housing facility or community:

(a) Driver's license;

(b) Birth certificate;

(c) Passport;

(d) Immigration card;

(e) Military identification;

(f) Any other state, local national, or international official documents containing a birth date of comparable reliability; or

(g) A certification in a lease, application, affidavit, or other document signed by an adult member of the household asserting that at least one person in the unit is 55 years of age or older.

2933   42 U.S.C.A. § 3607(b)(1)-(3).

2934   42 U.S.C.A. § 3607(b)(2)(A).

2935   42 U.S.C.A. § 3607(b)(2)(B).

2936   42 U.S.C.A. § 3607(b)(2)(C).

2937   24 C.F.R. § 100.303(a)(3).

2938   42 U.S.C.A. § 3607(b)(2)(C)(iii).

2939   62 Fed. Reg. 2000 (Jan. 14, 1997).

of the occupants of a particular dwelling unit refuse to comply with the age verification procedures, the housing facility or community may, if it has sufficient evidence, consider the unit to be occupied by at least one person 55 years of age or older. Such evidence may include:

(1) Government records or documents, such as a census;

(2) Prior forms or applications; or

(3) A statement from an individual who has personal knowledge of the age of the occupants. The individual's statement must set forth the basis for such knowledge.

§ 25.2.2.7   Requirement Of Policies And Procedures

Housing for 55 and older residents must hold itself out as such to the public. Any such development has a duty to publish and adhere to policies and procedures which demonstrate an intent to provide housing for persons 55 years of age or older. HUD has issued regulations that identify factors relevant to determining whether certain policies and procedures satisfy that requirement, including, but not limited to, the way the housing is described in advertisements to prospective residents, the age verifications procedures, other written rules and regulations designed to insure that housing is occupied by persons 55 and older.

§ 25.2.3   Race And Color Discrimination

A frequent complaint filed with HUD is for discrimination on the basis of race or color.

In one case, the Secretary of HUD initiated an investigation of Iberville Parish, LA, to determine whether the Parish violated the Fair Housing Act when the Parish Council adopted a resolution that prohibited the Federal Emergency Management Agency ("FEMA") from placing trailer parks in 17 specific site locations within the Parish. The resolution was generated in response to 4,972 evacuee households residing in hotels and other forms of emergency housing who had requested transitional housing in Iberville Parish. HUD investigated the matter in order to determine whether or not race might have played a role in the Parish adopting the resolution.

HUD filed a Secretary-initiated complaint against Iberville Parish which ultimately resulted in a conciliation agreement. As part of the agreement, the Parish agreed that mobile home park owners of commercial sites operating within the unincorporated areas of Iberville Parish could place FEMA mobile homes or trailers on their properties.

This investigation shows that HUD is concerned not only with overt acts of racial discrimination, but also with actions that may disproportionately affect racial minorities in depriving them of equal housing opportunities.

The case of *HUD v. James Crockett Henry and Henry, LLC of Virginia Beach*[2940] involves allegations of a more overt form of racial discrimination. In that case, a tenant and her minor grandson, both of whom are African American, moved into the 15 ½ Street Apartments in Virginia Beach, VA.

Shortly after she moved in, the owner began imposing strict rules on her tenancy and monitoring the visits of her family. One month after the tenant moved in, the owner allegedly came to her apartment and told her he did not want her family visiting the property because "no one wants to see them." He advised her that her family should remain inside the apartment when they come to visit. Furthermore, the owner allegedly told the tenant that she was not permitted to have visitors when she was not at home and threatened to have her daughter, the mother of her live-in grandson, arrested if her daughter visited the property while the tenant was not at home. One day the tenant was not at home when her daughter came to visit her grandson and the owner carried out his threat, called the police and had the daughter removed from the property. The owner later terminated the tenant's lease for allegedly having visitors when she was not present.

2940   *HUD v. Henry*, FHEO No. 03-07-0004-8.

Moreover, the owner allegedly required the tenant to abide by his "quiet time" policy. The "quiet time" policy required tenants to remain in their units and engage only in "quiet" activities after 10:00 p.m.

The tenant filed a housing discrimination complaint with HUD alleging that the owner was discriminating against her because of her race. Later, HUD received four additional complaints from other African American tenants alleging that they were subject to similar treatment.

During the investigation, HUD found that the owner did not harass the visitors of white tenants, nor did he prohibit white tenants from having visitors while they were not at home. Furthermore, the investigation found that the owner did not impose his "quiet time" policy on white tenants. HUD charged the owner with violating the Fair Housing Act by discriminating against tenants based on their race.

The case of *Virginia Fair Housing Board v. Roy Lineberry*[2941] is another fair housing case alleging racial discrimination. The facts in this case are as follows.

The tenant was looking for a house to rent for herself, her husband, and her four children. She learned that a co-worker was moving out of the home that she rented and that it may be available. The tenant met with the owner, who told her that he had planned to do some repairs on the home so that it would not be available for several months. Shortly before the scheduled completion date of the repairs, the owner and tenant signed a 12 month lease that was to start the following month. A few days later the owner learned that the tenant, who was white, was married to someone who was African American.

Several days after that, the owner arranged a meeting with the tenant. He told her the repairs may take a considerably longer time than expected, that he needed to raise the rent above what was stated in the signed lease due to the cost of the repairs, and that the lease term needed to be cut from 12 months to three, because he was thinking about selling the house. The owner concluded the meeting by suggesting that it may be best if the tenant found another place to live.

The tenant filed a housing discrimination complaint alleging that the owner changed the terms of her lease when he found out that her husband and children were African American. The owner was charged with violations of the Act and ultimately agreed to a $10,000 fine, agreed to attend fair housing training, and agreed to pay for an advertisement in a local newspaper.

§ 25.2.4 Discriminatory Advertising

The Act prohibits a housing provider to make, print, or publish any notice, statement or advertisement with respect to the sale or rental of housing that indicates any preference, limitation, or discrimination because of race, color, religion, sex, handicap, familial status, or national origin.[2942] The prohibition covers written and oral statements or notices by any person engaged in the sale or rental of a dwelling, including, flyers, poster, brochures, deed, billboards, signs, and documents.[2943]

Specific prohibitions include, but are not limited to: (1) using words, phrases, photographs, illustrations, symbols, or forms that convey the impression that housing is available or not available to particular groups; (2) expressing to brokers, agents, employees, prospective sellers, renters or other persons a preference for or against any purchaser or renter; (3) selecting advertising media or location that deny information to certain segments of the market; and (4) refusing to publish advertising or publishing on different terms. Claims can be brought against persons engaged in the sale or rental of housing who, themselves, make, print or publish or who cause others to make, print or publish their discriminatory printings and newspapers and other advertising media that make, print or publish the offending materials of others.

2941   *Virginia Fair Housing Board v. Lineberry*, FHB File Number 2007-02592, HUD File Number 03-07-0210-8.

2942   42 U.S.C.A. § 3604(c).

2943   24 C.F.R. § 100.75(a) through 24 C.F.R. § 100.75(b).

n one case, the Court held that a newspaper violated § 3604(c) of the Act when it published a landlords classified
d for an apartment in a "white home."[2944] This is the seminal case in deciding that § 3604(c) of the Act applies
o newspaper and other media that carry discriminatory advertising, that the application of the Act to newspaper
dvertising does not violate the Freedom of Press, and whether a particular ad violates the Act is determined by how
n ordinary reader would normally interpret the ad. HUD published updated advertising guidelines that include
examples of discriminatory advertisement.[2945]

§ 25.2.4.1   Banned Terms

The Act prohibits use of terms designating national origin or other catchwords. Based on that, an ad for a "home in
nice Italian neighborhood" or "home for Asian war veterans" are prohibited. Phrases which discriminate on the basis of
religion include such statements as "Christian home" and "Jewish home."[2946]

HUD has prepared the following list of words and phrases which it believes convey either overt or tacit discriminatory
preferences or limitations. HUD will consider the use of those words to indicate a possible violation of the Act.

(a) Words descriptive of dwelling, landlord and tenants. White private home, Colored home, Jewish Home, Hispanic
     residence, adult building.

(b) Words indicative of race, color, religion, sex, handicap, familial status, or national origin

(c) Race – Negro, Black, Caucasian, Oriental, American Indian

(d) Color – White, Black, Colored

(e) Religion – Protestant, Christian, Catholic, Jew

(f) National origin – Mexican, American, Puerto Rican, Philippine, Polish, Hungarian, Irish, Italian, Chicano, African,
     Hispanic, Chinese, Indian, Latino

(g) Sex – the exclusive use of words in advertisements, including those involving the rental of separate units in a single
     or multi-family dwelling, stating or tending to imply that the housing being advertised is available to persons of
     only one sex and not the other, except where the sharing of living areas is involved. This does not apply, however, for
     advertisements of dwellings used exclusively for dormitory facilities by educational institutions.

(h) Handicap – crippled, blind, deaf, mentally ill, retarded, impaired, handicapped, physically fit

(i) Familial status – adults, children, singles, mature persons

(j) Catch words – Words and phrases used in a discriminatory context should be avoided, *e.g.*, "restricted" "exclusive,"
     "private," "integrated," "traditional," "board approval" or "membership approval"

Also advertisements which say "no wheelchairs" discriminate on the basis of handicap, advertisements that limit the
number or ages of children or state a preference for adults, couples, or single discriminate on the basis of familial
status.[2947] Even directions to a home or subdivision can be found to be in violation of the Act. Directional references
which include racially or religiously identifiable landmarks can be viewed as an unlawful signal of preference in the sale
of property.

Additionally, the Georgia Commission on Equal Opportunity has published a more comprehensive list of words
which probably violate the Act, words which may violate the Act depending upon context, and words that likely do
not violate the Act.

2944   *United States v. Hunter*, 459 F.2d 205 (4th Cir.), *cert. denied*, 409 U.S. 934 (1972).

2945   24 C.F.R. § 100.75.

2946   24 C.F.R. § 109.20(b) (1995).

2947   24 C.F.R. § 109.20(b)(6) (1995).

Words that the GCEO believes likely violate the Act include: able-bodied; adult building; adult community; adult living; adult-only swimming pool; adults; adult-only; African; agile; American Indian(s); Anglo Saxon; Asian; bachelor; bachelor pad; black(s); Caucasian; Chicano; number of children; Chinese; Christian; colored; couple; couples only; not for disabled; must be employed; empty nesters; exclusive; Filipino; foreigner(s); healthy only; Hispanic; Hungarian; no immigrants; Indian; Irish; Italian; Jewish; Korean; Latino; mature couple; mature individual; no mentally disabled; no mentally ill; mentally impaired; Mexican-American; must be employed; nationality; Negro; no alcoholics; no blind; no children; no crippled; no deaf; no disabled; no impaired; no Jews; no lesbians; no play area; no retarded; no seasonal worker; no Social Security Insurance (SSI); no unemployed; no wheelchairs; not for disabled; older person(s); one child; one person; Oriental; physically fit only; Polish; Protestant; Puerto Rican; single person; single sex club; singles; singles only, Vietnamese; white; white only; white private home.

Terms and words the GCEO may violate the act, depending upon the context in which they are used, include: active; close to; congregation; Catholic; executive; female(s) only; fisherman's retreat; gender; gentleman's farm; grandma's house; golden-agers only; handyman's dream; integrated; male(s) only; male roommate; man only; mature; membership approval required; men only; Mormon Temple; no Section 8; parish; private; restricted; retired; retiree(s); senior(s); senior citizen(s); senior housing; shrine; single man; single woman; synagogue; temple; traditional; walking distance to specified church or synagogue; woman only; women only; no students; no gays; number of persons; student(s); membership approval required; integrated; must comply with park rules; newly-weds; no more than two persons per bedroom; responsible; Spanish speaking; stable.

Words and phrases that the GCEO believes likely will not violate the Act: accessible; apartment complex with chapel; number of bedrooms; near bus; credit check required; den; desirable neighborhood; domestic quarters; no drinking; no drugs; no drug use; Easter Bunny; equal opportunity housing; great for family; family room; fixer-upper; near golf course; great view; handicapped access; Happy Easter; hobby farm/ jogging trails; kosher meals available; luxury apartment; luxury townhouse; master bedroom; Merry Christmas; mother-in-law apartment; mother-in-law suite; nanny's room; near; near country club; near church; near public transportation; near schools; specific neighborhood names; nice; no smoking; non-smoking; nursing home; play area; privacy; private; private driveway; private entrance; private property; private setting; professional; quality construction; quality neighborhood; quiet; quiet neighborhood; quiet streets; Santa Claus; specific school district; specific school name. secluded; secure; security provided; senior discount; St. Valentine's Day; square feet; townhouse; traditional-style; tranquil setting; two-bedroom; verifiable income; view of; walk-in-closet; walk to bus stop; wheel chair ramp; with view; prestigious; straight only;[2948] non-smokers; quiet tenants.

§ 25.2.4.2 Advertising

Advertisers of real estate who use only media geared toward selective groups, or who use racially identifiable human models in advertising, run the risk of being found to have violated the act. For example, a developer who exclusively uses a Korean language newspaper to advertise the sale of new homes in a housing market with a sizable non-Korean population is likely violating the Act.[2949] Similarly, if the advertisers selectively use human models based on race or national origin it likely violates the Act. Ads which show all white models, all black models, models of only one sex, adults only, and models of one national origin are all potential violations of the Act by showing a preference.[2950]

Whenever models are used in an advertisement it is good to include the following disclaimer in the marketing materials.

2948 The GCEO list was compiled in 1991, prior to HUS's expansion of the term "family" to account for actual or perceived sexual orientation and gender identity. Undoubtedly, the phrase "straight only" should not be considered one that violates the Act.

2949 24 C.F.R. § 109.20(b)(4) (1995); *Holmgren v. Little Village Community Rptr.*, 342 F.Supp. 512 (N.D. Ill. 1971).

2950 *Saunders v. General Services Corp.*, 659 F.Supp. 1042 (E.D. Va. 1987); *Spann v. Colonial Village, Inc.*, 662 F.2d 541 (D.D.C. 1987); *Ragin v. The New York Times Company*, 923 F.2d 995 (2nd Cir.), *cert. denied* 502 U.S. (1991).

Special Stipulation 353: Fair Housing Marketing Disclaimer

The models in this advertisement are included for illustrative purposes only and are not intended to indicate any preference for or against any class of persons protected under applicable fair housing laws. The housing being advertised herein is equally available to all persons regardless of their race, color, religion, national origin, familial status, sex, or handicap.

It is a violation of the Act if an ad for housing suggests to an ordinary reader that a particular race or national origin is preferred or not preferred. When models are used in advertising, the HUD regulations suggest that they should be clearly definable as reasonably representing majority and minority groups in the metropolitan area, both sexes, and when appropriate, families with children.[2951] In determining whether an ad would discourage an ordinary reader of a particular race from answering it, the court is authorized to instruct the jury to evaluate the ad from the standpoint of an ordinary reader of a protected class rather than from the standpoint of a generic ordinary reader.[2952]

§ 25.2.4.3   Restrictive Covenants

Although not considered "advertising" restrictive covenants, such as a Declaration of Condominium or a Declaration of Covenants, Conditions and Restrictions for homeowners association can violate the Act which prohibits "deeds" from containing discriminatory materials. Since the restrictive covenants are recorded in the land records, they are the equivalent of "deeds" and subject to the Act. Restrictive covenants banning persons of a certain ethnicity, banning children, banning children under a certain age, banning handicapped persons etc., are subject to challenge and subject boards of directors to liability.[2953] HUD recognizes the difficulty of amending declarations and has stated that if there are substantial legal impediments to remove language from deeds or restrictions that violate the Act, HUD will consider documented evidence of a good faith attempt to remove the language in determining if the community complies with the Act.[2954]

§ 25.2.5   Steering And Blockbusting

Real estate brokers in particular, but also lenders and other parties to real estate transactions, can have significant influence on the housing choices their clients make. For instance, it is difficult, if not impossible, for a real estate broker to show a prospective purchaser every house in a particular market. They have to pick and chose which ones to show. This can be a problem, depending upon which criteria are used to select which homes, or which neighborhoods, to show to any particular purchaser.

Steering in violation of the fair housing laws occurs when a person, through her actions, words or behaviors, encourages or directs clients toward particular neighborhoods and/or away from others based upon the client's race, color, ethnicity, sex, familial status, handicap, or religion. Steering can occur both in the initial process of identifying locations in which to look for homes, and during or after the actual showing by making comments about the home or neighborhood. It can occur in response to requests or questions from prospective buyers, or it can occur as a result of more subtle choices or unsolicited comments.

2951   24 C.F.R. § 109.30(b) (1995).

2952   *Tyus v. Urban Search Management*, 102 F.3d 256 (7th Cir. 1996), *cert. denied* 117 S.Ct. 2409 (1997).

2953   *HUD v. Paradise Gardens*, P-H: Fair Housing – Fair Lending Rptr. § 25037 (HUD ALJ 1992).

2954   62 Fed. Reg. 2003 (Jan. 14, 1997).

There are some practices that are specifically prohibited by the Act. Specifically prohibited practices include directing people to (or away from) a particular community or neighborhood because of their race or any of the other factors protected under the Act, failing to inform prospective buyers, based on their race or other prohibited factor, of desirable features of a dwelling or community in order to discourage them from buying in that area, and communicating in some way that prospective buyers would "not fit in" or "not be comfortable" in a particular community because of such prohibited factors, etc.

In the past decade, the issue of steering, particularly based on race, has come more and more into the spotlight. The Housing Discrimination Study of 2000 (HDS2000) found that while most indicators of discrimination in housing had decreased in the previous 10 years, one area that showed significant increase in that same period was that of geographically steering clients based on neighborhood racial composition. In response to concerns in this area, HUD now pays a variety of groups to "test" real estate brokerage firms and others to see if they are complying with the Act.

Possibly the greatest number of problems in the steering area arises in the interest of saving time and attempting to size-up a buyer's housing needs based upon inappropriate factors. Rather than taking the time to ask the client appropriate questions (relating to the client's desired price range, location and type of house, etc.), someone may improperly narrow the field for them by choosing not to show them houses that they think would not be right for them. The key to avoiding unlawful steering claims is to let the buyer narrow the field of available properties through their answers to legitimate questions about their housing needs, rather than guessing at what the client will like.

The following examples illustrate this point.

Example 1: Bob the Buyer asks to see homes in Alpharetta, Georgia, a city that demographically is composed of predominantly white residents. Are there any risks in showing Bob homes only in the City he has specified?

Answer: No. Steering occurs when the agent directs the buyer to a particular neighborhood. It does not occur when the buyer asks only to see homes in a given city or neighborhood. The problem arises when the client asks a broker to locate homes in reference to one of the prohibited factors (race, religion, national origin, sex, familial status or handicap).

Example 2: Betty the Buyer was born in Korea. She asks her broker to show her houses in areas where large numbers of Korean-Americans live. Betty's broker knows of two neighborhoods with large Korean-American populations. Can the broker direct Betty to these neighborhoods?

Answer: No. The broker is now being asked to steer the buyer to houses based upon the racial and ethnic make-up of a neighborhood. This would be in violation of the Act. So, what should the broker do in this situation? Explain to the buyer that under our fair housing laws, brokers cannot steer clients to neighborhoods based upon the national origin of the residents therein (or any other protected factor).

When being asked questions regarding the location of particular racial or ethnic groups, it doesn't matter that the person asking the question is a member of that group or that the group was intended to be protected under the federal law. For example, if an African-American couple asks to be steered toward neighborhoods where large numbers of other African-Americans live, a broker is no more permitted to oblige them than she would be to oblige a white buyer asking to be steered away from neighborhoods where a large number of African-Americans reside.

One frequently asked question is whether buyers can be referred to public sources where the buyer on her own might find out additional information to help them decide the specific neighborhoods where they want to live. The answer is "yes." For example, let's assume that broker A is asked to show Betty neighborhoods with large populations of Korean-Americans. The broker can refer Betty to the local Chamber of Commerce to learn more about the demographic make-up of the area. While this may seem contradictory, it really isn't. Buyers have a right to live wherever they please and to study whatever information they choose to help them make a decision. The broker simply has to make sure that, like a cab driver, she is "driving the cab" to the requested destination of the client rather than deciding the best destination for the client.

While steering relates to the buyer's side of the transaction, blockbusting applies to the seller's side. Blockbusting occurs when a property owner is encouraged, either directly or indirectly, to sell their property because of anyone or any group of people belonging to the Act's protected class moving into the neighborhood. It is a violation of the Act, for instance, for a broker to tell a potential seller that their neighborhood is undergoing a change in the race, color, religion, sex, handicap, familial status, or national origin or persons residing in it, in order to encourage the potential seller to sell the property. It is also a violation of the Act to encourage potential sellers to sell their homes through assertions that the entry or perspective entry of persons from the protected group can or will result in undesirable consequences for the neighborhood, such as a lowering of property values, an increase in criminal or antisocial behavior, or a decline in the quality of schools or other services or facilities.

§ 25.2.6   Real Estate Business Organization Discrimination

It is a violation of the Act to deny any person access to or membership or participation in any multiple-listing service, real estate brokers' organization or other service, organization, or facility relating to the business of selling or renting dwellings, or to discriminate against him in the terms or conditions of such access, membership, or participation, on account of race, color, religion, sex, handicap, familial status, or national origin.[2955] HUD took a number of internet-based real estate professional organizations to task for alleged violations of this prohibition.[2956] The websites of these organizations allegedly contained language that limited membership to people of the same faith, which is prohibited by the Act.

§ 25.2.7   Enforcement And Penalties

The Act is enforceable by private citizens and the Attorney General.[2957] Individuals can bring a civil action or an administrative law proceeding.[2958] In a civil action, if a court determines that an association violated the Act, damages may be awarded to the plaintiff. Additionally, the court may impose a public interest fine of $50,000.00 for the first offense and up to $100,000.00 for any subsequent violations.[2959]

An Administrative Law Judge may award damages and also may assess a civil penalty in an amount not to exceed $10,000.00 for the first offense, up to $25,000.00 for a second offense within five years or up to $50,000.00 for a third or more offense during a seven year period.[2960]

§ 25.3   THE AMERICANS WITH DISABILITIES ACT

The Americans with Disabilities Act of 1990 ("ADA") was signed into law on July 26, 1990[2961] with the effective date for the removal of barriers to handicapped access being January 26, 1992.[2962] It is a comprehensive civil rights law that prohibits discrimination against disabled individuals. The goal of the ADA is to insure disabled individuals' full and equal access to the same, or similar, benefits enjoyed by the general public, including access to benefits such as employment and goods and services provided to the public by private parties.[2963] Most, if not all, of the focus of the commentary regarding the ADA has been its applicability to employers. However, the applicability to employers is only one section of the ADA.

2955   42 U.S.C.A. § 3607.

2956   For example: Christian Real Estate Agents; Christian Real Estate Network; Christian Realty Network; Kingdom Real Estate Address; CatholicAgent,com, and JewishAgent.com.

2957   42 U.S.C.A. § 3612 and 42 U.S.C.A. § 3613.

2958   *See id.*, § 3612(a).

2959   *See id.*, § 3614(d)(1)(C).

2960   *See id.*, § 3612(g)(3).

2961   Pub. L. No. 101-336, 104 Stat. at 327 (codified at 42 U.S.C.A. § 12101 through 42 U.S.C.A. § 12213).

2962   *Id.* at § 108.

2963   *Id.* at § 2(b).

The ADA, in fact, is divided into five Titles. Title 3 prohibits discrimination against handicapped persons by public accommodations and commercial facilities on the basis of disability in the "full and equal enjoyment of the goods, services, facilities, privileges, advantages or accommodations."[2964] The ADA has applicability to those facilities which are open to the general public.

§ 25.3.1 The Act Applies To Commercial Facilities And Public Accommodations

§ 25.3.1.1 Commercial Facilities

Commercial facilities are defined as "facilities that are intended for nonresidential use and whose operations will affect commerce."[2965] The ADA further provides that the term "commercial facility" does not cover facilities that are covered or expressly exempted from coverage under the Fair Housing Act of 1968.[2966] The Fair Housing Act specifically applies to community associations.[2967]

Specifically, when it promulgated rules regarding the Fair Housing Amendment Act of 1988, HUD noted "that the exemption in this Section applies only to the owner of such a dwelling and that the cooperative or condominium or mobile home park would be prohibited from engaging in any discriminatory conduct with respect to the dwelling notwithstanding the fact that the conduct of the owner was not covered."[2968] The exemption it is referring to concerns the sale of single family residential dwellings.

Although not stated in the ADA, the Justice Department's interpretation of the ADA states that the definition of "commercial facilities" only includes such facilities as factories, warehouses, and office buildings which are not open to the public.[2969] Since virtually every business by definition "affects commerce" in one respect or another, almost every structure occupied by a business and not open to the public could be considered a "commercial facility."

Based on the definition of commercial facility, the Justice Department's interpretation of the ADA, and the provisions of the Fair Housing Act, the common areas of an association would not be considered a commercial facility and it is likewise unlikely that any property in an association that may be open to the public (such as a property or maintenance management office within the association's property) would be considered a commercial facility.

§ 25.3.2 Public Accommodations

The ADA defines a "public accommodation" as a private entity that owns, leases (leases to), or operates a place of public accommodation.[2970] Among other things, it is defined as "a facility operated by a private entity, whose operations affect commerce" and which falls into at least one of the following categories:

(a) places of lodging (e.g. inns, hotels, motels);

(b) establishments serving food or drink (e.g. restaurants, bars);

(c) places of public gathering (e.g. auditoriums, convention centers, lecture halls);

(d) sales or retail establishments (e.g. bakeries, grocery stores, clothing stores, hardware stores, shopping centers);

(e) places of recreation (e.g. parks, zoos, amusement parks);

2964   *Id.* at § 302 and 303 (codified at 42 U.S.C.A. § 12182 and 42 U.S.C.A. § 12183).

2965   42 U.S.C.A. § 12181(2).

2966   *Id.*

2967   *See* Implementation of the Fair Housing Amendments Act of 1988, 54 Fed. Reg. 3232, 3237 (1989) (stating that the Fair Housing Act applies "to all dwellings: including condominiums, cooperatives and mobile homes").

2968   *Id.*

2969   *See* Preamble to Regulation on Nondiscrimination on the Basis of Disability by Public Accommodations and in Commercial Facilities, 28 C.F.R. Pt. 36, App. B.

2970   42 U.S.C.A. § 12181(7).

(f) places of education (e.g. nursery schools, elementary, secondary, undergraduate, postgraduate, private schools);

(g) social service center establishments (e.g. day care facilities, senior citizen centers);

(h) places of exercise or recreation (e.g. health spas, bowling alleys, gymnasiums, golf courses);

(i) service establishments (e.g. banks, gas stations, hospitals, dry cleaners, lawyers offices);

(j) stations used for public transportation; and

(k) places of public display (e.g. museums, libraries).[2971]

In reviewing this list, it is apparent that any condominium unit or other homeowners' association property that is used for commercial purposes in the association may fall within the definition of the word "public accommodation." However, as will be described below, only in a small number of circumstances will the association's recreational facilities (places of exercise or recreation) be considered "public accommodations" and subject to the requirements of the ADA.

Although the legislative history of the ADA shows an intent to broadly construe and apply the application of the ADA to the examples of public accommodations, unless an association is selling memberships to the recreational property to individuals who do not own a home or unit or reside in that association, the recreational property should not be considered a public accommodation. However, if the association does sell memberships or allows non-members to use and enjoy the association's laundry facility, meeting room, clubhouse, swimming pool, or other recreational facilities, such an association would be required to comply with the ADA and remove all barriers for handicapped individuals, at the association's expense. This has become particularly relevant to associations with pools that are used for swimming meets. These pools are required to be outfitted with chair lifts and other accessories to render them handicap accessible.[2972]

Although the inclusion of association recreational facilities as a public accommodation is inconsistent with the underlying intent of the ADA, the result is supported by a literal construction of the term "public accommodation" since, unlike "commercial facilities," the definition of "public accommodation" does not specifically exclude the applicability of the ADA to facilities covered by the Fair Housing Act. This apparent oversight is receiving a lot of discussion and debate because, if the ADA applies to the recreational facilities of the association, as will be discussed, it would force the association to remove the barriers at the association's expense rather than merely permitting reasonable accommodations to be made by a handicapped person at their own expense as required by the Fair Housing Act.

§ 25.3.2.1 Removal Of Architectural And Structural Barriers

Under the ADA, the owners of public accommodations were to have removed, by January 26, 1992, architectural and structural barriers in existing public accommodations where the removal is "readily achievable."[2973] "Readily achievable" means that the barrier removal is "easily accomplishable and able to be carried out without much difficulty or expense."[2974] The ADA further provides that in determining whether an action is readily achievable, some of the factors to be considered include: the nature and cost of the action needed to comply with the ADA;[2975] the overall financial resources of the facility or facilities involved in the action, and the effect on expenses and resources or the impact of such action upon the operation of the facility;[2976] the overall financial resources of the covered entity;[2977] and the type of operation or operations of the covered entity.[2978]

2971 *See id.*

2972 Section 242 and 1009 of the 2010 Americans with Disability Act (ADA) Standards for Accessible Design.

2973 *Id.*, § 12182(b)(2)(A)(iv).

2974 *Id.*, § 12181(9).

2975 *Id.*, § 12181(9)(A).

2976 *Id.*, § 12181(9)(B).

2977 *Id.*, § 12181(9)(C).

2978 *Id.*, § 12181(9)(D).

What is readily achievable will have to be determined on a case-by-case basis. The final regulations accompanying the ADA provide examples of what may be readily achievable for removing barriers in appropriate circumstances. Those examples are:

(a) installing ramps;

(b) making curb cuts in sidewalks and entrances;

(c) repositioning shelves;

(d) rearranging tables, chairs, vending machines, display racks, and other furniture;

(e) repositioning telephones;

(f) adding raised markings on elevator control buttons;

(g) installing flashing alarm lights;

(h) widening doors;

(i) installing offset hinges to open doorways;

(j) eliminating a turnstile or providing an alternative accessible path;

(k) installing accessible door hardware;

(l) installing grab bars in toilet stalls;

(m) rearranging toilet partitions to increase maneuvering space;

(n) installing lavatory pipes under sinks to prevent burns;

(o) installing a raised toilet seat;

(p) installing a full length bathroom mirror;

(q) repositioning the paper towel dispenser in the bathroom;

(r) creating designated accessible parking spaces;

(s) installing an accessible paper cup dispenser at an existing inaccessible water fountain; or

(t) removing high pile, low density carpeting.[2979]

An association should conduct a survey of its property to determine what barriers exist to the free and full use and enjoyment of the property by a handicapped person.[2980] The list above provides a good basis for determining those barriers which may need to be addressed, if the association allows non-members to use and enjoy its facilities.

If an association's recreational facilities are considered public accommodations an issue arises regarding the level of compliance the association will need to achieve in order to comply with the ADA. Specifically, if the recreational facility is a public accommodation, is the association required to comply with the ADA only as it relates to the facility itself, or will the requirements extend to other portions of the common areas that contain impediments to the free use and enjoyment of the recreational facility?

For example, if the path to the recreational facility contains barriers that impede the free use and enjoyment of the recreational facility, will the association be responsible for removing the impediment or, will the owner be responsible for the common area changes, in accordance with the Fair Housing Act, and the association only responsible for the changes to the recreational facilities? Likewise, if common area barriers need to be removed to permit full access to a commercial

---

2979   28 C.F.R. § 3.304(b).

2980   The survey suggested here is not a "study" as described in the ADA. *See* 42 U.S.C.A. § 12185.

facility on the association's property (such as the management or maintenance office), will the association be responsible for the changes, even though that area of the building is not a public accommodation? Or will the owner or occupant of the commercial space be responsible for the change in accordance with the Fair Housing Act?

It appears that the association would only be responsible for the change to the recreational facility, and not portions of the condominium or subdivision that are not covered by the ADA. Similarly, based on the Fair Housing Act, the association would only be obligated to permit the owner or occupant of the commercial property to modify the association property to permit the full use and enjoyment of the commercial facility and the association would not be responsible for those costs. However, there are no cases or interpretations on these points at this time, and this conclusion is based on the Fair Housing Act and the Justice Department's interpretation of the ADA.

Additionally, the ADA does not allocate responsibility for compliance between a landlord and tenant. Instead, the ADA leaves that up to lease negotiations. Therefore, if an association leases a portion of its property to another entity, the lease must carefully define each party's obligations regarding modifications that must be made to the leased area and/or the association property, if any, in order to comply with both the Fair Housing Act and the ADA.

Like other civil rights laws, the ADA can be enforced by both private citizens and the Justice Department.[2981] Individuals have a right to bring an action to force a facility to comply with the Act. Individuals are not permitted to file a claim for damages but can recover attorneys fees and litigation expenses.[2982]

The Justice Department is authorized to file a claim for compliance and can seek monetary damages on behalf of damaged individuals.[2983] In addition, civil penalties of up to $50,000.00 can be awarded for a first violation and up to $100,000.00 for any subsequent violations.[2984]

2981   *See id.*, § 12188(a)-(b).

2982   *See id.*, §12205.

2983   *See id.*, § 12188(b)(2)(B).

2984   *See id.*, § 12188(b)(2)(C).

The **RED BOOK**

CHAPTER 26

REAL ESTATE SETTLEMENT PROCEDURES ACT ("RESPA")

OVERVIEW

This chapter discusses the Real Estate Settlement Procedures Act[2985] ("RESPA" or the "Act"). There is a cursory discussion of several Sections of RESPA, but the bulk of this chapter focuses upon the main regulatory portion of the Act, Section 8. Section 8 addresses kickbacks, fee sharing, and joint venture relationships. There are a number of practices that are clearly prohibited by RESPA. However, there are many other scenarios which may potentially violate the Act, but for which there is no clear guidance.

RESPA may be the least understood and the most violated real estate law in the country. The broad prohibitions of the law cover many practices, including some practices which are, unfortunately, engaged in by many in the real estate industry. While the Act is strict, ambiguities in the statute – and a general lack of meaningful guidance from the Department of Housing and Urban Development ("HUD") – lend to the law being regularly violated by covered individuals. Moreover, RESPA was not aggressively enforced for many years and covered individuals were essentially left to "self-police" their conduct and practices. For obvious reasons, this system did not work well and abuses naturally followed.

Over the past decade, however, HUD has made it clear that it takes violations of RESPA, specifically the anti-kickback and prohibition against unearned referral fees, very seriously. Since 2001, HUD has been on an aggressive campaign to crack down on RESPA violations. HUD has not been shy about listing the names of the parties it pursues and the amount of the fines it imposes on its website to discourage other violators from continuing to engage in illegal behavior. In addition to HUD enforcement, numerous class action civil lawsuits have been filed seeking literally millions in damages. Violations carry a high price because RESPA provides for both criminal and civil penalties and subjects the violator to treble damages. Recently, The Dodd-Frank Act granted rule-making authority under RESPA to the Consumer Financial Protection Bureau ("CFPB") and, with respect to entities under its jurisdiction, granted authority to the CFPB to supervise for and enforce compliance with RESPA and its implementing regulations.[2986] As of the time this book went to press, the CFPB had not issued any new rules relative to the RESPA issues discussed herein. As a result, rule-making references are limited to those from HUD.

Compliance with most of the RESPA requirements is simple, so long as the professional is alert and aware of the general rules. The best way for real estate professionals to avoid problems with RESPA is to follow one simple rule - pay your own way, expect others to do the same, and refer business based on the quality of the service provided rather than personal gain.

As stated in the beginning of this book, nothing contained herein is intended to be relied upon as legal advice for any particular situation. This admonishment is repeated here due to the uncertain and constantly evolving state of the law regarding RESPA. This chapter is a general guide only and anyone contemplating his own circumstances should consult competent legal counsel who is well-versed in RESPA.

§ 26.1 WHAT IS RESPA?

Congress enacted RESPA in 1974 to ensure that consumers receive greater and more timely information on the nature and costs of the real estate settlement process, and that the public is protected from unnecessarily high costs associated with real estate closings.[2987] RESPA attempts to protect borrowers by prohibiting individuals who provide services related to real estate closings from paying one another kickbacks or referral fees, especially hidden or "under the table" kickbacks and referral fees. The idea behind the law is that eliminating such payments will help keep closing costs down for borrowers.

2985   12 U.S.C.A. § 2601, *et seq.*

2986   Dodd-Frank Act §§ 1002(12)(M), 1024(b)-(c), and 1025(b)-(c); 12 USC §§ 5481(12)(M), 5514(b)-(c), and 5515(b)-(c) .

2987   12 U.S.C.A. § 2601(a).

A RESPA violation subjects a person to a fine of up to $10,000 for each offense, imprisonment for up to one year, or both.[2988] The violator may also be liable to the person who was charged for the settlement service (*i.e.*, the buyer or seller) for an amount equal to three times the amount paid for the settlement service plus attorneys fees.[2989]

HUD was charged with enforcing the Act. HUD was also empowered to draft regulations to clarify what is permitted under the law. The regulations issued by HUD are collectively known as Regulation X. The CFPB has now largely taken over these roles from HUD. It remains to be seen whether the CFPB will depart from HUD's prior actions.

The key language in RESPA is in Section 8,[2990] which provides two basic rules of prohibition and lists several exceptions to those rules. First, Section 8(a) prohibits the transfer of a thing of value pursuant to an understanding that business will be referred to any person. It states:

> No person shall give and no person shall accept any fee, kickback, or thing of value
> pursuant to any agreement or understanding, oral or otherwise, that business incident
> to or part of a real estate settlement service involving a federally related mortgage loan
> shall be referred to any person.[2991]

Second, Section 8(b) prohibits the splitting of any charge made or received for the performance of a settlement service except for services actually performed. It provides:

> No person shall give and no person shall accept any portion, split, or percentage of
> any charge made or received for the rendering of a real state settlement service in
> connection with a transaction involving a federally related mortgage loan other than
> for services actually performed.[2992]

Finally, Section 8 (c) provides a list of exceptions from the broad prohibitions contained in Sections 8(a) and (b) as follows:

> Nothing in this section shall be construed as prohibiting (1) the payment of a fee (a)
> to attorneys at law for services actually rendered or (b) by a title company to its duly
> appointed agent for services actually performed in the issuance of a policy of title
> insurance or (c) by a lender to its duly appointed agent for services actually performed
> in the making of a loan; (2) the payment to any person of a bona fide salary or
> compensation or other payment for goods or facilities actually furnished or for services
> actually performed; (3) payments pursuant to cooperative brokerage and referral
> arrangements or agreements between real estate agents and brokers; (4) affiliated
> business arrangements so long as (a) a disclosure is made of the existence of such an
> arrangement to the person being referred and, in connection with such referral, such
> person is provided a written estimate of the charge or range of charges generally made
> by the provider to which the person is referred... (b) such person is not required
> to use any particular provider of settlement services, and (c) the only thing of value
> that is received from the arrangement, other than the payments permitted under this
> subsection, is a return on the ownership interest or franchise relationship....[2993]

2988   12 U.S.C.A. § 2607(d)(1).

2989   12 U.S.C.A. § 2607(d)(2).

2990   12 U.S.C.A. § 2607.

2991   12 U.S.C.A. § 2607(a).

2992   12 U.S.C.A. § 2607(b).

2993   12 U.S.C.A. § 2607(c).

RESPA was written very broadly. Hence there are many "gray" areas in the law, making generalizations difficult and risky. However, a basic understanding of the law and following the letter of its exceptions can help to skirt some potential violations.

§ 26.2   FEDERALLY RELATED TRANSACTIONS

RESPA only applies to federally related transactions. This covers most loans, including the following: transactions that are assisted with money from the federal government: loans that are insured by the federal government; loans sold to Fannie Mae or Freddie Mac; construction to permanent loans; home equity lines of credit; and most modifications or assumptions of any of these transactions.

A limited number of exemptions exist, including: many seller-financing transactions so long as the amount financed does not exceed one million dollars; business-purpose loans, even if the business purpose is to purchase real estate; and cash transactions. To be safe, unless a transaction clearly falls into one of the exceptions, the assumption should be made that RESPA applies and the parties should proceed accordingly.

§ 26.3   RESPA SECTION 8 (A)

Section 8 (a) provides that no person shall give and no person shall accept any fee, kickback, or thing of value pursuant to any agreement or understanding, oral or otherwise, that business incident to or part of a real estate settlement service involving a federally related mortgage loan shall be referred to any person.[2994] This single sentence raises a host of questions that are more difficult to answer than one might think. These include: what is a "fee, kickback, or thing of value; what is an "agreement or understanding"; what is meant by "settlement service"; and what is a referral?

§ 26.3.1   What Is Meant By A Fee, Kickback, Or Thing Of Value?

Section 8(a) of RESPA prohibits the giving or accepting of a "thing of value" to another person for the referral of settlement business.[2995] But what is a "thing of value"? Fortunately, the answer is easy. It's virtually anything and everything.

RESPA uses the term a "thing of value" very broadly to include in its prohibition all imaginable forms of compensation for a referral. Section 3 of RESPA[2996] defines a "thing of value" to include: any payment, advance, funds, loan, service or other consideration.[2997] This term has been defined more broadly by various court decisions to include, without limitation: money; things; discounts; salaries; commissions; fees; gifts, prizes, duplicate payments of charges; stock; dividends; distributions of partnership profits; franchise royalties; credits; future opportunities; chances; retained or increased earnings; accounts; special contract terms; reduced rates; increased payments; leases or rental payments based to any degree upon the volume of business referred; the payment of someone else's expenses. A "thing of value" has also been found by HUD to include a waived fee, the opportunity to win a prize, a vacation trip, and a ticket to a baseball or football game. All of these "things of value" fall within section 8 of the Act.

Money need not be exchanged for something to be a "thing of value." Any type of consideration that has value to the recipient is covered.[2998] For example, a "chance" such as the entry in a lottery, has value, as does the making of a charitable contribution in someone's name. Other less obvious examples include: continuing education credit; a promise to refer business in the future; and providing something that has a dual use, such as a non-dedicated photocopier.

2994   12 U.S.C.A. § 2607(a).

2995   12 U.S.C.A. § 2607(a).

2996   12 U.S.C.A. § 2602.

2997   12 U.S.C.A. § 2602(2).

2998   12 U.S.C.A. § 2602(2).

There is no "*de minimus*" rule. Many people believe that there is a $25.00 safe harbor and that so long as gifts to any person do not exceed $25.00 in any year that this is permissible under RESPA. This is a prime example of the widespread misunderstanding of the Act. RESPA contains no such safe harbor. Gifts of even one penny in value trigger the Act.

§ 26.3.2   What Constitutes An Agreement Or Understanding?

An agreement for the referral of settlement service business can be oral or in writing. An agreement or understanding can also be established by a practice or pattern. For example, assume a lender decides to give a real estate agent tickets to a local sporting event after the agent sends a buyer to the lender. There is no written or oral agreement regarding this. The lender intends the tickets to be a surprise to the agent and the agent in fact receives them as an unexpected gift. This single, isolated incident may not constitute an agreement or understanding. However, let's further assume that the lender repeats this activity every time the real estate agent sends her a buyer. At some point, it just starts to look like there is an implied agreement between the lender and the agent. There is no litmus test to determine how many "surprise" tickets constitutes an agreement or understanding. It could be as many as 30 or as few as one or two. It all depends upon the circumstances.

There is an important exception to this rule. Since RESPA is intended to reduce the costs and fees paid by purchasers, a buyer by definition cannot be considered a party to an agreement or understanding related to his own loan. For example, it is permissible for a real estate agent to refund a portion of his commission to the buyer in a transaction, assuming appropriate disclosures are made so as to not violate licensure law or invoke mortgage fraud.[2999]

Agreements, in RESPA parlance, require there to be some direct or indirect benefit to the person making a referral from the person receiving the referral. The buyer-exception noted above can cause certain activities that would otherwise be prohibited to be permissible. For example, let's say a lender offers to pay the cost of a survey for any buyer that comes to it by way of a referral from a real estate broker. The payment by the lender for the survey is a benefit to the buyer, not the real estate broker. So long as there is no benefit flowing back to the real estate broker, the transaction would likely not be deemed a RESPA violation. However, if the real estate broker used the lender's payment to negotiate a higher commission for himself, then a benefit to the broker exists and the transaction is illegal.

Another example involves charities. A real estate broker cannot offer to give $100.00 to a charity for every referral that charity or its members make to the broker. However, the real estate broker can give $100.00 directly to the buyer who can then endorse the funds over to the charity. The borrower is never considered to be a party to a kickback so the payment to her (assuming full disclosure to his lender) is fine. The endorsement from the buyer to the lender is likewise permissible.

What about purchasing leads? For example, a real estate broker buys a membership list from a charity and solicits the people on the list. So long as the fee paid for the list is consistent with the normal fee charged by the charity, and the charity does not solicit its members or otherwise endorse the broker, there is no violation of the Act. However, if in conjunction with the purchase of the list the charity agrees to recommend the broker to its members, this is now likely a violation.

§ 26.3.3   What Are Settlement Services?

"Settlement service" has a broad meaning and includes most if not all services that are performed prior to or in connection with a residential real estate closing. More specifically, settlement services includes, but is not limited to, the following: title searches, title examinations, the provision of title certificates, title insurance, services rendered by an attorney, the preparation of documents, property surveys, the rendering of credit reports or appraisals, pests and fungus

---

2999   *See* Chapter 21 (Mortgage Fraud).

inspections, services rendered by a real estate agent or broker, the origination of a federally related mortgage loan,[3000] and the handling of the processing, and closing or settlement.[3001]

"Settlement service providers" include at least the following: attorneys; appraisers; surveyors; sellers, builders, credit reporting agencies; insurance companies; real estate brokers and salespersons; title insurance companies; mortgage bankers and brokers; home inspectors; pest and fungus inspectors; and even home warranty companies.

§ 26.3.4   Referrals, Required Use, And Bundled Services

Referrals are oral or written actions that have the effect of affirmatively influencing a person to use the services of a particular settlement services provider. This is the common sense definition of a referral. However, under RESPA jurisprudence, a referral is also deemed to have occurred if someone is required to use a particular settlement service provider.

"Required use" means that a person must use a specific settlement service provider in order to obtain some distinct service or property from another.[3002] For example, it would be considered a required use when a builder will sell a property if and only if the buyer uses the builder's preferred lender. If the buyer wishes to use a different lender, the builder will refuse to sell to that buyer.

While an attempt to force the use of a particular settlement service provider is prohibited by the Act, it is seemingly permissible to attempt to entice the use of the settlement service provider. For example, a builder could offer to pay $10,000 to the buyer if and only if the buyer uses the builder's preferred lender. This is permissible because HUD's definition of required use specifically exempts "the offering of a package (or combination of settlement services) or the offering of discounts or rebates to consumers [*i.e.* buyers] of multiple settlement services," provided that the bundled services are optional and the discount is a true discount (*i.e.*, not recouped elsewhere in the transaction).[3003] This concept is known as "bundling."

There is a caveat to the bundling carve-out that adds a good deal of confusion and complexity. HUD issued an informal opinion letter in which it opined that a builder can offer to pay closing costs if the buyer uses the builder's preferred lender, but that it would be a violation of RESPA if the builder's preferred lender was also the builders affiliated business partner or joint venture.[3004] Under this interpretation, it would be fine for a builder to offer to pay the buyer's closing costs if and only if the buyer used the builder's preferred lender. However, if the builder happened to own an interest in the lender, or was in a joint venture with the lender, then the offer to pay the closing costs would not be permitted.

At least some courts have simply ignored HUD's informal opinion. One court specifically held that a builder was free to offer to pay $10,000 in closing costs if and only if the buyer used the builders affiliated business partner lender.[3005] This was permissible because the buyer was free to chose another lender if she wished. HUD was not pleased with this and other similar rulings, and at one point, submitted proposed revisions to RESPA that would prohibit economic incentives or disincentives that are contingent upon the borrower using or failing to use any particular provider of settlement services. Ultimately, however, these revisions were not formally adopted.

So, is it safe to rely upon the bundled services carve-out? Unfortunately, the answer is a definitive "maybe."

3000   The origination of a federally related mortgage loan includes, but is not limited to, the taking of loan applications, loan processing, and the underwriting and funding of loans. 12 U.S.C.A. § 2602(3).

3001   12 U.S.C.A. § 2602(3).

3002   24 C.F.R. § 3500.2 (2007).

3003   Section 2 of HUD's Regulation X.

3004   HUD's May 20, 1988 informal opinion.

3005   *Spicer v. Ryland Group, Inc.*, 523 F.Supp. 2d 1356 (2007). The Court rejected the buyer's argument that the $10,000 incentive was tantamount to an economic requirement that she use the builder's preferred lender. One wonders if the court would have reached the same conclusion if the incentive had been $50,000 or $100,000.

§ 26.4 RESPA SECTION 8 (B)

Section 8 (b) provides that no person shall give and no person shall accept any portion, split, or percentage of any charge made or received for the rendering of a real state settlement service in connection with a transaction involving a federally related mortgage loan other than for services actually performed.[3006]

The questions here are: what is a portion, split or percentage, and what constitutes services actually performed.

§ 26.4.1 What Is Considered A Portion, Split Or Percentage: Mark-Ups And Overages

Mark-ups involve one party charging a fee on top of a fee charged by a third party. For example, a title examiner charges a closing attorney $125.00 to run a title search. The closing attorney marks-up this fee to $200.00 on the settlement statement, thereby making a profit of $75.00 for the work of the title examiner. If the closing attorney is not rendering any additional service for this fee, then it is considered by HUD to be a violation of Section (b).[3007] However, if instead of marking up the fee from the title examiner the closing attorney includes an additional line item fee of $75.00 for reviewing the title report, this would pass muster.

As a result of this seemingly safe way to bypass the prohibition on mark-ups, many settlement service providers charge so called "junk fees" in which an additional fee is broken out and charged for all imaginable services. For example, there could be a title review fee, a title analysis fee, and a title confirmation fee, all in the same transaction. As these itemized fees proliferate, there is an increased chance that HUD will go on the offensive and try to attack them as being disguised mark-ups. As a result, anyone charging a fee for any itemized service needs to be able to identify the specific service that was rendered and differentiate it from any other services for which there is a separate fee.

The recent United States Supreme Court ruling in Freeman v. Quicken Loans, Inc.[3008] has radically changed the landscape of Section 8(B). In Freeman, the Supreme Court addressed the long-standing issue of whether Section 8(B) applies to all mark-ups or just where there has been a fee split with another. The Court held that Section 8(B) does not prohibit a service provider from marking up a fee as long as it is not shared with another party. This has led to the dismissal of a number of class action lawsuits against real estate brokers who charged administrative brokerage commissions ("ABC's")". ABC's are a flat fee charge in addition to the percentage real estate commission typically charged by brokers. Plaintiffs claimed that ABC's constituted "junk fees" because they were in addition to the percentage commissions being charged. Under Freeman, however, the ABC's are permissible so long as they are not split with anyone.

In contrast to mark-ups, overages are where a party simply charges a very large fee for a service they actually provide. Arguments have been made that Section 8(b) mandates that charges for goods or services must be reasonably related to the market value of the goods or services rendered. However, this argument has so far been rejected by the courts, which have found that nothing in RESPA is intended to limit or regulate what someone can charge for their services.[3009]

§ 26.4.2 Services Actually Performed

In many contexts, the notion of services actually performed carries a common sense definition. In response to widespread abuse, however, HUD has taken additional measures in certain circumstance to prevent abuses of the system. These include mortgage brokerage services and title agency services.

3006   12 U.S.C.A. § 2607(b).

3007   Note, however, that not all Federal Circuits agree with HUD's position. Importantly, the 11th Circuit, of which Georgia is a part, does agree with HUD and prohibits mark-ups.

3008   *Freeman v. Quicken Loans, Inc.*, 132 S. Ct. 2034, 2039, 182 L. Ed. 2d 955 (2012)

3009   *Friedman v. Market Street Mortgage Corp.*, 520 F.3d 1289 (2008).

§ 26.4.2.1 Mortgage Brokerage Services

One area of heightened regulation involves the payment of fees for alleged mortgage brokerage services.[3010] This applies, for example, when a mortgage broker pays a real estate agent a fee for assisting with a loan origination.

Many lenders present real estate agents with alliance opportunities offering real estate salespeople the opportunity to earn revenue associated with the loan application process. One income opportunity is presented when online loan origination systems offer to pay brokers for services rendered, such as giving consumers information about various loan products, pre-qualifying prospective borrowers, and helping borrowers choose a loan product for a particular property by providing information on rates and terms. Brokers may also be asked to collect and transmit information about the borrower and the property, as well as other data necessary for a loan application to be evaluated by one or more lenders.

Section 8(a) of RESPA does not allow lenders to pay for mere referrals, but lenders may compensate real estate agents for services rendered related to loan processing. RESPA allows payment for services actually rendered. Determining where the line is between what is legal or illegal can be tricky and should not be done without the assistance of an expert on RESPA. To be legal, a payment must be for work actually performed and must be reasonably related to the value of the services performed. If the payment is not reasonable, the excess amount is considered payment for a referral and is therefore illegal.

HUD has made clear that the mere taking of a loan application is not sufficient work to justify a fee under RESPA. To determine whether sufficient loan origination work has been performed to justify a fee, HUD looks at whether the work was actually performed for the compensation paid, whether the services are necessary for the loan, and whether the services are duplicative of services performed by others.[3011] HUD generally would be satisfied that no RESPA violation had occurred if a real estate salesperson: (1) took information from the borrower and filled out the loan application; (2) performed five or more other loan origination services listed on HUD's list of application-taking services; and (3) received a fee reasonably related to the market value of the services performed. The more of the listed services a broker provides, the easier it will be to support the reasonableness of any payment received. HUD's list of "loan origination services" includes:

(a) Taking information from borrower and filling out application;

(b) Analyzing borrower's income and debt, and pre-qualifying her to determine maximum mortgage she can afford;

(c) Educating borrower in home buying and financing process, advising her about different types of loan products available, demonstrating how closing costs and monthly payments would vary under each product;

(d) Collecting financial information (tax returns, bank statements) and other related documents that are part of the application process;

(e) Collecting financial information (tax returns, bank statements) and other related documents that are part of the application process;

(f) Initiating/ordering verifications of employment and verifications of deposits;

(g) Initiating/ordering requests for mortgage and other loan verifications;

(h) Initiating/ordering appraisals;

(i) Initiating/ordering inspections or engineering reports;

(j) Providing disclosures (truth in lending, good faith estimate, etc.) to borrower;

3010   HUD Statement of Policy 1999-1.

3011   HUD Statement of Policy 2001-1.

(k) Assisting borrower in understanding credit-clearing problems;

(l) Maintaining regular contact with borrower, REALTORS® and lender between application and closing to apprise them of status of application and to gather additional information needed;

(m) Ordering legal documents;

(n) Determining whether property is located in flood zone (or ordering such service); and

(o) Participating in the loan closing.

§ 26.4.2.2 Title Agency

HUD has similarly established guidelines regarding minimum title agency services.[3012] In order for an attorney, acting as a title agent, to be paid her full share of the premium, she must provide her client with core title services for which she assumes liability. These must include, at a minimum, evaluation of the title search to determine insurability, issuance of the title commitment, clearance of underwriting objections, and the actual issuance of a title policy on behalf of the title insurance company.

§ 26.5 RESPA SECTION 8(C): EXCEPTIONS TO THE RULES

The prohibitions created by Sections 8(a) and (b) would effectively kill the real estate closing business as we currently know it but for the permitted exceptions contained in Section 8(c). This Section provides:

> Nothing in this section [RESPA Section 8] shall be construed as prohibiting (1) the payment of a fee (a) to attorneys at law for services actually rendered or (b) by a title company to its duly appointed agent for services actually performed in the issuance of a policy of title insurance or (c) by a lender to its duly appointed agent for services actually performed in the making of a loan, (2) the payment to any person of a bona fide salary or compensation or other payment for goods or facilities actually furnished or for services actually performed, (3) payments pursuant to cooperative brokerage and referral arrangements or agreements between real estate agents and brokers, (4) affiliated business arrangements so long as (a) a disclosure is made of the existence of such an arrangement to the person being referred and, in connection with such referral, such person is provided a written estimate of the charge or range of charges generally made by the provider to which the person is referred… (b) such person is not required to use any particular provider of settlement services, and (c) the only thing of value that is received from the arrangement, other than the payments permitted under this subsection, is a return on the ownership interest or franchise relationship….[3013]

Each of these exceptions is discussed in turn below.

§ 26.5.1 Payments To Attorneys, Title Companies, And Lenders For Services Actually Performed

Simply stated, lawyers, title companies, and lenders and their agents are all permitted to be paid, provided the payment is for services actually performed.[3014] There are several qualifiers:

(a) In order to qualify under this exemption, the goods or services must be bona fide; that is, they must actually exits. Simply stating that services have been rendered or that goods have been provided is not enough. They must, in fact, have actually been rendered or supplied.

3012   HUD Statement of Policy 1999-4.

3013   12 U.S.C.A. § 2607(c).

3014   *See* § 26.4.2 (Services Actually Performed) above for the definition of services actually performed.

(b) The goods and services must have been provided on a commercially reasonable basis. That is, they must be on the same terms as are generally available in the marketplace.

(c) The goods or services must be actually used.

(d) Payment for the goods or services must be on terms that are commercially available.

(e) Neither the provision of the goods or services nor the payment for them can be tied in any way to the referral of business.

§ 26.5.2   Payment of Salary or Compensation For Goods Or Facilities Actually Furnished Or For Services Actually Performed

§ 26.5.2.1   Who Qualifies As An Employee?

Section 14(g)(vii) of Regulation X permits an employer to pay its own employees for any referral activities back to the employer.[3015] But what does it mean to be an employee? As noted in the section on services actually performed,[3016] HUD regulates certain industries and activities more closely than others.

Generally, HUD evaluates twenty factors identified in IRS Revenue Ruling 87-41 to determine whether someone is a *bona fide* employee. What weight HUD assigns to these factors, however, is unknown. The factors are:

(a) Instructions. An employee must comply with instructions about when, where and how to work. The control factor is present if the employer has the right to require compliance with the instructions.

(b) Training. An employee receives ongoing training from, or at the direction of, the employer. Independent contractors use their own methods and receive no training from the purchasers of their services.

(c) Integration. An employee's services are integrated into the business operations because the services are important to the business. This shows that the worker is subject to direction and control of the employer.

(d) Services rendered personally. If the services must be rendered personally, presumably the employer is interested in the methods used to accomplish the work as well as the end results. An employee often does not have the ability to assign their work to other employees, while an independent contractor may assign the work to others.

(e) Hiring, supervising and paying assistants. If an employer hires, supervises and pays assistants, the worker is generally categorized as an employee. An independent contractor hires, supervises and pays assistants under a contract that requires her to provide materials and labor and to be responsible only for the result.

(f) Continuing relationship. A continuing relationship between the worker and the employer indicates that an employer-employee relationship exists. The IRS has found that a continuing relationship may exist where work is performed at frequently recurring intervals, even if the intervals are irregular.

(g) Set hours of work. A worker who has set hours of work established by an employer is generally an employee. An independent contractor sets his/her own schedule.

(h) Full time required. An employee normally works full-time for an employer. An independent contractor is free to work when and for whom she chooses.

(i) Work done on premises. Work performed on the premises of the employer for whom the services are performed suggests employer control, and therefore, the worker may be an employee. Independent contractors may perform the work wherever they desire as long as the contract requirements are performed.

3015   24 C.F.R. § 3500.14(g)(vii).

3016   *See* § 26.4.2 (Services Actually Performed).

(j)   Order or sequence set. A worker who must perform services in the order or sequence set by an employer is generally an employee. Independent contractor perform the work in whatever order or sequence they may desire.

(k)   Oral or written reports. A requirement that the worker submit regular or written reports to the employer indicates a degree of control by the employer.

(l)   Payments by hour, week or month. Payments by the hour, week or month generally point to an employer-employee relationship.

(m) Payment of expenses. If the employer ordinarily pays the worker's business and/or travel expenses, the worker is ordinarily an employee.

(n)   Furnishing of tools and materials. If the employer furnishes significant tools, materials and other equipment by an employer, the worker is generally an employee.

(o)   Significant investment. If a worker has a significant investment in the facilities where the worker performs services, the worker may be an independent contractor.

(p)   Profit or loss. If the worker can make a profit or suffer a loss, the worker may be an independent contractor. Employees are typically paid for their time and labor and have no liability for business expenses.

(q)   Working for more than one firm at a time. If a worker performs services for a multiple of unrelated firms at the same time, the worker may be an independent contractor.

(r)   Making services available to the general public. If a worker makes his services available to the general public on a regular and consistent basis, the worker may be an independent contractor.

(s)   Right to discharge. The employer's right to discharge a worker is a factor indicating that the worker is an employee.

(t)   Right to terminate. If the worker can quit work at any time without incurring liability, the worker is generally an employee.

§ 26.5.2.2   Control vs. Independence

Over the years, the Internal Revenue Service recognized changes in business practices and therefore created three categories of factors to assess the degree of control and independence. These factors are to be used in conjunction with the twenty factors listed above.

(a)   Behavioral Control – What type of instructions does the business gives to the worker (such as when and where to do the work), and what training does the business provide to the worker? The key consideration is whether the business has retained the right to control the details of the worker's performance or has relinquished that right.

(b)   Financial Control – What rights does the business have to control the business aspects of the worker's job?

(c)   Relationship Of Parties – Is the nature of the relationship evidenced by: a written contract describing the benefits the business provides to an worker, such as paid vacation and health coverage; the permanency of the position; and the extent to which the services performed? These are key aspects of the regular business of the company and may indicate an employer-employee relationship.

§ 26.5.3   Cooperative Brokerage, Referral Arrangements, Or Agreements Between Real Estate Agents And Brokers

RESPA permits the payment of referral fees between real estate brokers when such payments are made "pursuant to a cooperative brokerage arrangement or agreements between real estate agents and brokers."[3017] Referral fees between real estate brokers are common, for example, when a broker in one state refers a buyer or seller to a broker in another state.

3017   12 U.S.C.A. § 2607(c).

Referral fees are also commonly paid as a form of settlement and compromise when there is a dispute over whether the selling broker is entitled to a commission (such as when the selling broker may not be the procuring cause). While referral fees among real estate brokers are exempt under RESPA, they are limited to fees related to real estate brokerage services. A real estate broker could not, for example, accept a referral fee from another real estate broker who also happens to be a mortgage lender for the referral of mortgage business.

§ 26.5.4   Affiliated Business Arrangements A/K/A Joint Ventures

This exemption permits affiliated business arrangements and the formation of joint ventures,[3018] usually by and between real estate brokers, builders, and mortgage or title companies. The term "affiliated business arrangement" refers to an arrangement in which (i) a person who is in a position to refer business incident to or a part of a real estate settlement service involving a federally related mortgage loan or an associate of such person, has either an affiliate relationship with or a direct or beneficial ownership interest of more than one percent in a provider of settlement services; and (ii) either of such persons directly or indirectly refers such business to that provider or affirmatively influences the selection of that provider.[3019] The joint owners of the joint venture refer business to it and, as owners, reap the company's profits. In these instances, each owner of the venture is typical in a position to refer settlement business to a settlement service provider that is owned, in whole or in part, by the referring party.

Under a joint venture arrangement, the referring party receives no direct payment for the referral to the settlement service provider in which she has an ownership interest, but can receive indirect compensation based on the profits of the affiliated provider. For example, a real estate brokerage firm and a mortgage broker may set up a new company to do mortgage lending without violating RESPA. This arrangement, designed to provide "one stop shopping" to consumers, would qualify for the exemption only if the company is determined by HUD to be a *bona fide* provider of settlement services rather than a sham arrangement designed to illegally funnel compensation to persons who refer it business.

HUD determines whether the arrangement is legal under RESPA by (1) considering ten factors that point to whether the company is a *bona fide settlement service provider*; and (2) examining whether the company owners receive payments only in the form of a *return on ownership interest* that is not tied to the actual, estimated or anticipated volume of referrals the owners make to the company.[3020]

§ 26.5.4.1   Bona Fide Settlement Service Provider

The ten factors or questions that HUD asks in evaluating whether the jointly formed company is a bona fide settlement provider are:

(a) Does the new entity have sufficient initial capital and net worth typical in the industry to conduct the settlement service business for which it was created? Or is it undercapitalized to provide the work it purports to provide?

(b) Is the new entity staffed with its own employees to perform the services it provides? Or does the new entity have "loaned" employees of one of the parent providers?

(c) Does the new entity manage its own business affairs? Or is an entity that helped create the new entity running the new entity for the parent provider making the referrals?

(d) Does the new entity have an office for business which is separate from one of the parent providers? If the new entity is located at the same business address as one of the parent providers, does the new entity pay a general market value rent for the facilities actually furnished?

3018   12 U.S.C.A. § 2607(c).

3019   12 U.S.C.A. § 2602(7).

3020   HUD's Statement of Policy 1996-2.

(e) Is the new entity providing substantial services, i.e., the essential functions of the real estate settlement service, for which the entity receives a fee? Does it incur the risks and receive the rewards of any comparable enterprise operating in the marketplace?

(f) Does the new entity perform all of the substantial services itself or does it contract out part of the work? If contracted out, how much of the work is contracted out?

(g) If the new entity contracts out some of its essential functions, does it contract services from an independent third party? Or are the services contracted from a parent, affiliated provider, or an entity that helped create the controlled entity? If the new entity contracts out work to a parent, affiliated provider or an entity that helped create it, does the new entity provide any functions that are of value to the settlement process?

(h) If the new entity contracts out work to another party, is the party performing any contracted services receiving a payment for services or facilities provided that bears a reasonable relationship to the value of the services or goods received? Or is the contractor providing services or goods at a charge such that the new entity is receiving a thing of value for referring settlement service business to the party performing the service?

(i) Is the new entity actively competing in the market place for business? Does the new entity receive or attempt to obtain business from settlement service providers other than one of the settlement service providers that created the new entity?

(j) Is the new entity sending business exclusively to one of the settlement service providers that created it? Or does the new entity refer business to a number of entities, which may include one of the providers that created it?

HUD has indicated that a joint venture does not necessarily need to comply with all of these factors to be RESPA compliant. However, the chances that an affiliated business relationship will not pass muster increase with the number of these conditions that are not met. HUD balances the responses to all of the above questions, and no one response is determinative.

§ 26.5.4.2 Return On Ownership Interest

To qualify for the exemption, the members, as the referring party, may receive payments only in the form of a return on ownership interest. A return on ownership interest does not include (1) payments that vary by the amount of actual, estimated or anticipated referrals; or (2) payments based on ownership shares adjusted on the basis of previous referrals. When assessing whether a payment is a return on ownership interest or a payment for referrals of settlement business HUD will consider, among other things, whether or not:

(a) Each owner or participant in the new entity has made an investment of its own capital, as compared to a "loan" from an entity that receives the benefits of referrals;

(b) The owners or participants of the new entity received an ownership or participant's interest based on a fair value contribution; or the interest is based on the expected referrals to be provided by the referring owner or participant to a particular cell or division within the entity;

(c) The dividends, partnership distributions, or other payments are made in proportion to the ownership interest (proportional to the investment in the entity as a whole); or the payments vary to reflect the amount of business referred to the new entity or a unit of the new entity; and

(d) The ownership interests in the new entity are free from tie-ins to referrals of business; or there have been adjustments to the ownership interests in the new entity based on the amount of business referred.

HUD has expressed concern about settlement service providers who jointly establish a mortgage company, particularly when all the services the new company will provide are subcontracted to the existing parent settlement service providers. For example, a real estate broker and lender might agree to form a new company, joint venture, limited partnership, or other entity to receive the referrals. As joint owners of the new entity, the real estate broker and the lender would share the benefit of the referrals by receiving their returns on their ownership interests in the new entity. HUD will closely review the activities of the new company to ensure it has employees performing valuable or "core" services. If the new company merely subcontracts with someone else, such as the existing mortgage company, to perform most of the essential services, then HUD may view the company as a sham entity created to disguise illegal kickbacks for the referral of settlement services business.

§ 26.5.4.3 Disclosure Statement

Finally, RESPA requires that a referring company which is in some way financially tied to the company to whom business is being referred must provide an Affiliated Business Arrangement Disclosure Statement to the buyer or seller.[3021] The disclosure must show the nature of the relationship between the person making the referral and the service provider and an estimated charge or range of charges generally made by the provider. This disclosure form must be given to the consumers at the time that the referral is being made where the referral is made face-to-face, by electronic means, or in writing, and within 3 days if the referral is made by telephone.[3022]

If the referring company is a real estate brokerage firm, it may be a good practice for the firm to routinely get the disclosure signed by all customers and clients of the firm (*i.e.* at the time of a listing with a seller or at the time of contract with a buyer) regardless of whether an actual referral of these customers or clients will be made. The consumer is required to sign the disclosure in the space provided. If the person chooses not to sign the disclosure, a notation by the referring company must be made stating that the disclosure was provided and the consumer chose not to sign the disclosure at the time it was provided. The notation should be made in a written, electronic, or similar system of records maintained by the referring company in the regular course of business. It is important to tell the consumer that she will be required to sign such disclosure at or before closing or settlement, even if the person has chosen not to sign the disclosure when it was provided.

§ 26.6 EDUCATION AND MARKETING

RESPA provides an exception to Sections 8(a) and (b) related to payments for marketing or advertising. Specifically, under § 3500.14(g)(vi) of the regulations interpreting RESPA,[3023] settlement service providers are permitted to engage in:

> [N]ormal promotional and educational activities that are not conditioned on the referral of business and that do not involve the defraying of expenses that otherwise would be incurred by persons in a position to refer settlement services or business incident thereto.[3024]

While the payment of kickbacks and referral fees is illegal, HUD recognizes the right of settlement service providers to pay fair and reasonable fees for normal marketing and advertising efforts. For example, a lender providing real estate agents with note pads with the lender's name on them would be allowable as normal promotional items. However, if the lender gives the real estate agent note pads with the real estate agents' name on them for the agent to use to market clients for its real estate business, then the note pads could be a thing of value given for referral of loan business, because it defrays a marketing expense that the real estate agent would otherwise incur. Similarly, if a mortgage lender holds an educational program which is only open to real estate agents who refer the mortgage lender business, it would be a RESPA violation. However, an educational program open to all real estate agents in a particular geographical area, regardless of whether they referred business to the mortgage lender or not, would not be a violation of RESPA.

3021   12 U.S.C.A. § 2607(c).

3022   12 U.S.C.A. § 2607(c).

3023   Regulation X.

3024   24 C.F.R. § 3500.14(g)(vi).

A question that is frequently asked in this area is whether it is permissible for a mortgage lender to sponsor a real estate agent's luncheon at an open house without violating RESPA. An argument can be made that such an arrangement is lawful as a normal marketing expense of the mortgage lender since such a luncheon is a way for the mortgage lender to meet numerous other real estate agents who might be a source of business referrals. However, such arrangements are suspect and may be a violation if the criteria used by the mortgage lender in selecting which luncheon to sponsor is whether the agent requesting the sponsorship refers the lender a significant amount of business rather than whether the luncheon will expose the lender to the most agents.

The likelihood of an enforcement action being brought under RESPA as it relates to marketing arrangements between real estate agents and lenders is greater today than at any time in the past. In fact, HUD is currently investigating marketing agreements between mortgage lenders and real estate brokerage firms. Therefore, the risks involved in this area must be fully understood to avoid inadvertent violations of RESPA.

Another other type of marketing agreement is one in which, for example, the lender agrees to pay the real estate broker a monthly or an annual fee (usually a very significant amount) in exchange for the broker assisting the lender in marketing various loan products and programs to the broker's agents and customers. The key issue in this area is whether a specific payment made under a marketing agreement bears a reasonable relationship to the market value of the goods and services provided. While this may seem like a relatively straightforward issue, may real estate brokers have found the "devil to be in the details" in working through this issue.

Clearly, it is a violation of federal law for a mortgage lender to simply pay a real estate broker a fee for the referral of settlement services business. But if the payment is reasonable in light of the services and facilities being provided, the payment is considered a bona fide fee for services provided rather than an illegal payment for referral. Where the exact line is draw in this area is often a function of conflicting expert opinions which the broker must balance against the amount of the payment and the degree of risk the broker is willing to take in this area.

Although HUD has not provided significant guidance in determining how the reasonableness of a particular marketing fee is to be determined, in one interpretation, HUD indicated that it might be appropriate to look to fees generally charged in the marketplace for the same services (assuming the value of any referral is not included), or to the internal cost of providing the service. In other words, if placing brochures of the lender in the lobby of the broker's office results in 25 prospective homebuyers getting a copy of the brochure, HUD might ask what it would cost to get such a brochure into the hands of 25 prospective homebuyers using other means of marketing. The greater the number of marketing services and facilities performed and provided by the real estate broker on behalf of a mortgage lender, the easier it is to justify the fee paid under the marketing agreement. Further, HUD examines the purpose of the fee in determining whether it is legal and has concluded that the payment of marketing costs "in a manner that does not bear on the amount of loan business referred" is permissible.

The characterization of the purpose of the payments under a marketing arrangement generally depends on the formula for compensation. Basically, the payment should not be linked to the actual number of transactions that are generated by the arrangement. HUD has historically taken the position that fees that are not "transactionally-based" (payable on a per loan basis for loans that actually close) are fair and reasonable. Therefore, a proposed marketing agreement that does not provide for transactionally-based compensation and where the lender makes regular monthly or yearly payments at an amount fixed at the inception of the agreement will more likely survive HUD scrutiny.

§ 26.7 EXAMPLES OF WHAT MAY AND MAY NOT BE DONE UNDER RESPA

Example #1: Can a real estate agent lease office space to a mortgage lender?

Answer: Yes, but only if certain conditions are met. The rent charged must be the current general market rate for the space leased. Any discounted or inflated rental will be considered a disguised kickback. The rental cannot be tied in any way to the number of referrals between the parties. This includes disguised tying arrangements such as where a closing attorney "rents" an office from a real estate brokerage on an "as used" basis. Since the rental would only be paid when the office is used, and the office would only be used when the attorney conducts a closing in which the brokerage was involved, this would likely be deemed a disguised kickback. Similarly, the tenant cannot pay for space it does not actually use. Paying to rent space that the parties understand will not actually be occupied or used by the tenant is nothing more than a vehicle for the payment of a kickback.

In determining the fair market value of rental space, HUD looks at what a non-settlement service provider would pay for the same amount of space and services in the same or a comparable building as opposed to what a settlement service provider would pay for the office space. If the rental payments exceed the general market value of the space provided, HUD will consider the excess amount to be for the referral of business in violation of Section 8(a). This standard represents an attempt to remove the value of referrals from the determination of rent value.

Example #2: Can the closing attorney that a buyer used recently handle the same buyer's divorce for free?

Answer: No. This is a violation of Section 8 which prohibits a person from paying or receiving anything of value for the referral of settlement services business. Even though there was no agreement or understanding on either person's part that the buyer would send business to the closing attorney (in exchange for the closing attorney doing free legal work), HUD would be quick to find an implied referral agreement. In this case, unless the closing attorney is operating a free legal clinic where he advises that he handles divorce cases for anyone who walks through the door, this is likely a RESPA violation. This is because if the closing attorney is only doing this work for his real estate agent friends, HUD will likely see the attorney giving away free legal services as a thing of value being given in appreciation of past referrals and/or with the expectation of getting future referrals.

Example #3: Can a builder hold a raffle in which real estate agents receive a chance to win a prize for each buyer they bring to the builder's property?

Answer: No. This is a violation of Section 8. A raffle ticket represents a chance of winning, which is a thing of value even if the ticket is not the winning ticket. The condition that the ticket is given whenever a real estate agent brings a buyer to the builder's property is both an agreement or understanding and a referral. Note, however, that it is permissible for a builder to give the raffle ticket to prospective buyers who visit the property, provided the builder otherwise complies with Georgia's gaming law.[3025]

Example #4: Can a lender offer to include a real estate agent's card on their flyer for free?

Answer: No. Such an offer involves the lender giving a thing of value, the cost of printing and distributing the flyer, to a settlement service provider with the implicit understanding that this is in exchange for the real estate agent referring buyers to the lender. Note, however, that nothing in RESPA prevents joint advertising. The problem exists if one party is paying less than a pro-rata share for the brochure or advertisement. If the parties share the expenses evenly and on an objectively rational basis, there is likely no RESPA violation.

Example #5: Can a real estate closing firm provide free continuing education classes to real estate agents?

Answer: No. Continuing education credits are a thing of value. Even if the law firm represents the real estate brokerage, it must charge the market rate for the educational class. Curiously, it would not appear to be a RESPA violation for the law firm to give the exact same class for free, so long as it does not give away the education credits.

Example #6: Can a lender hold a holiday party to which only real estate agents who referred 3 or more buyers to the lender that year?

Answer: No. The holiday party is a thing of value and an invitation is tied to the number of referrals. The lender can, however, invite the real estate brokerage community at large.

Example #7: Can a real estate agent sent a gift basket to the closing attorney's spouse or family after the closing?

Answer. No. This is merely a thinly disguised attempt to circumvent Section 8(a).

3025   O.C.G.A. § 16-12-20, *et seq.*

§ 26.8   RESPA SECTION 5

Section 5 of RESPA requires lenders to provide and distribute special information booklets to borrowers addressing compliance with the Truth in Lending Act. This booklet is provided in order to help borrowers financing the purchase of residential real estate to better understand the nature and costs of real estate settlement services.[3026]

Under these regulations, lenders are required to provide borrowers with a Good Faith Estimate (GFE) of the amount or range of charges for specific settlement services a borrower is likely to incur from the transaction.[3027] The older version of this rule contained general disclosure requirements about these types of charges. In 2010, however, HUD issued the new RESPA rule which significantly changed the process of obtaining a mortgage loan. The first change was the revision of the GFE which now provides greater disclosures of estimated closing costs. The second change was the addition of the new HUD-1 Settlement Statement which now requires all settlement charges on the GFE to be reflected on the HUD-1 form. The use of both of these forms are required in an attempt to clarify and simply the mortgage loan process for borrowers.

The goal of the rule change was to make it easier for borrowers to comparison shop for mortgages and better understand the various closing costs they agree to pay. To promote transparency in the loan process, both the GFE and the HUD-1 spell out for the consumer the vital terms of the loan including the interest rate, term of the loan, and whether the loan has a prepayment penalty or whether the interest rate is adjustable. Therefore, when the consumer obtains her loan and at the very beginning of the closing, the consumer will be able to make sure that the loan terms are what she promised.

To help prevent surprises at the closing, there is a table on the third page of the HUD-1 which compares the charges shown on the GFE to the charges shown on the HUD-1. The borrower can tell easily if there are greater charges on the HUD-1 in all categories than she was quoted on the GFE.

However, not only are the charges compared for purposes of consistency, the new RESPA rule has put restrictions and limits on if and how much the charges may change at the closing table. The various charges for a loan closing are grouped into three categories: charges that cannot increase at all, charges that have a total tolerance of 10%, and charges that have no restriction on increases.

In the first category, state transfer fees and lender fees related by lender or mortgage broker (as opposed to third party fees such as appraisals) cannot increase at all.[3028] So, if the GFE reflects a total fee to the lender/broker of $2,000 for the transaction, for example, the HUD-1 should similarly not have a fee greater than $2,000 for the lender's fees. The fees that have an overall tolerance of 10% are those fees charged by third parties, where the lender has selected the provider or given the borrower a short list of providers.[3029] The third parties include the settlement service provider (closing attorney), owner's title insurance, government recording costs, the appraiser's fees and credit service fee.[3030] Finally, the last category is charges that can change. These are the amounts charged for all other settlement services included on the GFE.[3031] Such charges include the daily interest charge, homeowner's insurance, and initial deposit for the escrow account. It also includes those service providers that the borrowers select. In such manner, a borrower may choose to shop for one of the service providers. The lender is not responsible for the deal that the borrower reaches with such service provider.

The final way that this new rule promotes a better understanding of the loan process is by eliminating the itemization on the HUD-1 of multiple individual charges permitted under the old rule. In its place is a new requirement that fees be bundled on the HUD-1 by category or provider. For example, instead of separate lender underwriting charges,

---

3026   12 U.S.C.A. § 2604.

3027   12 U.S.C.A. § 2604.

3028   24 C.F.R. 3500.7(e)(1).

3029   24 C.F.R. § 3500.7(e)(2).

3030   24 C.F.R. § 3500.7(e)(2).

3031   24 C.F.R. § 3500.7(e)(3).

dministration costs, processing fees and loan origination fees being shown on the HUD-1, there will now be one encompassing origination fee for the entire gamut of lender charges. The hope is that by simplifying the itemization of charges to the borrower, consumers can better understand their costs and comparison shop.

The HUD-1 changed in one other significant manner. If the sales contract requires the seller to pay for certain charges and expenses, generally or specifically, and the GFE sets forth that such expense is a borrower expense, the second page of the HUD-1 will show the charge in the borrower column. However, on the first page of the HUD-1, the seller will provide a credit to the borrower/buyer for such charges.

If the charges on the HUD-1 do not match the charges on the GFE or are over the tolerance levels for the respective charges, the closing will still take place. However, the lender must reimburse the borrower within 30 days from the closing for amounts over the tolerance levels.[3032] Failure to comply with these requirements will be considered a violation of Section 5 of RESPA.[3033]

§ 26.9   RESPA SECTION 6

Section 6 of RESPA provides borrowers with consumer protections relating to the servicing of their loans. If a borrower sends a "qualified written request" to his loan servicer concerning the servicing of the loan, the servicer must provide a written acknowledgment within 20 business days of receipt of the request.[3034] Not later than 60 business days after receiving the request, the servicer must make any appropriate corrections to the borrower's account and must provide a written clarification regarding any dispute.[3035] During this 60-day period, the servicer may not provide information to a consumer reporting agency concerning any overdue payment related to such period or qualified written request.[3036] Section 6 of RESPA also provides for damages and costs for individuals or classes of individuals in circumstances where servicers are shown to have violated the requirement of that Section.[3037]

§ 26.10   RESPA SECTION 9

Section 9 of RESPA provides that no seller of property that will be purchased with the assistance of a federally related mortgage loan shall directly or indirectly require, as a condition to selling the property, that title insurance covering the property be purchased by the buyer from any particular title company.[3038]

This represents an additional limitation on joint ventures between title companies and new home builders. It is permissible for builders and title companies to enter into joint ventures, but the builder/seller cannot include language mandating which title company will be used.

§ 26.11   RESPA SECTION 10

Section 10 of RESPA limits the amount of money a lender may require the borrower to hold in an escrow account for payment of taxes, hazard insurance and other charges related to the property.[3039] RESPA does not require lenders to impose an escrow account on borrowers; however, certain government loan programs or lenders may require escrow accounts as a condition of the loan.[3040]

3032   24 C.F.R. § 3500.7(i).
3033   24 C.F.R. § 3500.7(i); see 12 U.S.C.A. § 2604.
3034   12 U.S.C.A. § 2605(e)(1).
3035   12 U.S.C.A. § 2605(e)(2).
3036   12 U.S.C.A. § 2605(e)(3).
3037   12 U.S.C.A. § 2605(f).
3038   12 U.S.C.A. § 2608.
3039   12 U.S.C.A. § 2609(a).
3040   12 U.S.C.A. § 2609(a).

RESPA also prohibits a lender from charging excessive amounts for the escrow account. The lender may require a borrower to pay into the escrow account no more than 1/12 of the total of all disbursements payable during the year, plus an amount necessary to pay for any shortage in the account.[3041] In addition, the lender may require a cushion not to exceed an amount equal to 1/6 of the total disbursements for the year.[3042] The lender must perform an escrow account analysis once during the year and notify borrowers of any shortage.[3043] Any excess of $50 or more must be returned to the borrower.

3041   12 U.S.C.A. § 2609(a).

3042   12 U.S.C.A. § 2609(a).

3043   12 U.S.C.A. § 2609(b).

The **RED BOOK**

CHAPTER 27

BANKRUPTCY

OVERVIEW

As with any financial transaction, the sale, purchase, and ownership of real estate can be significantly impacted by the bankruptcy of any of the parties involved in a transaction, whether it be the purchaser, seller, or lender. This chapter provides a basic overview of the bankruptcy process. In addition, some of the ways in which a bankruptcy petition can impact real estate transactions are also discussed.

§ 27.1 INTRODUCTION TO BANKRUPTCY

The basic ideas supporting bankruptcy laws seem, to many people, to contradict the standard that a person or entity should honor their promises. While it may be true that bankruptcy laws assist and protect a debtor who is seeking relief from contractual and legal obligations, the ultimate objectives of the bankruptcy system reach much further. The bankruptcy system seeks to: (a) preserve the ability of debtors to be economically productive by relieving them of debt they cannot pay; (b) provide a means to liquidate the debtor's assets that will generate as much value as possible for the debtor and the creditors; (c) preserve the ongoing nature of a business that is viable but cannot meet its current obligations; (d) provide court control over insolvent debtors who retain possession of assets in which there is no equity; and (e) coordinate the collection efforts of many creditors against the same debtor.

There are three main chapters of the Bankruptcy Code under which most cases proceed: Chapter 7 (liquidation), Chapter 11 (reorganization), or Chapter 13 (debt adjustment). Most debtors are eligible to file for bankruptcy protection under any of the three chapters.[3044] A particular debtor may be limited by circumstances that dictate under which chapter the case must be brought. In some circumstances, creditors may be able to control the chapter under which the case proceeds.

In general, the property of a bankrupt individual or business entity is known as the bankruptcy estate, or property of the estate. The trustee is the person appointed by the court to represent the bankruptcy estate in all matters, including the sale of real property.[3045]

§ 27.1.1 Types Of Bankruptcy Filings

§ 27.1.1.1 Chapter 7

This chapter is typically used by individual debtors whose primary purpose in filing is to obtain a discharge of their debts. Chapter 7 cases are often referred to as "straight bankruptcies." In this type of bankruptcy, the Bankruptcy Trustee[3046] liquidates the nonexempt property of the debtor through bankruptcy sales and, following bankruptcy priorities, distributes the proceeds to the creditors. Properly secured creditors receive first priority position against their own collateral.[3047] The next priority is afforded to certain types of claims that have statutory priority under the code.[3048] Any remaining funds are divided pro rata among the unsecured creditors.[3049] If the liens of valid secured creditors exceed the value of the collateral, such that a sale would result in a loss, the Bankruptcy Trustee can "abandon" the property and release it from the bankruptcy estate and allow the creditor to undertake steps to obtain or liquidate the collateral.[3050]

3044 *See generally* Bankruptcy Code § 109.

3045 11 U.S.C.A.323(a).

3046 The person appointed by the Court to oversee to collection and disposition of the debtor's assets.

3047 Bankruptcy Code § 725.

3048 Bankruptcy Code § 507(a).

3049 Bankruptcy Code § 726.

3050 Bankruptcy Code § 725.

Individuals who file under Chapter 7 emerge with most of their debts extinguished. Corporations, however, do not emerge from Chapter 7 filings. Once a corporate Chapter 7 bankruptcy proceeding has been completed, the corporation is functionally dissolved.

§ 27.1.1.2 Chapter 11

Chapter 11 is most commonly employed by a debtor company that plans to continue operation of its business. In this type of case, the debtor remains in possession of the business or property during the case and afterwards, if the business survives. Once the debtor files a Chapter 11 petition, the debtor typically has four months to prepare a "plan of reorganization" and a "disclosure statement" containing information allowing creditors to determine the feasibility of the plan.[3051] In its plan, the debtor will propose to reschedule payment of its debts over a longer period of time and to reduce the amounts to be paid. If the Bankruptcy Court finds the disclosure statement to be sufficient, the plan and disclosure statement are submitted to creditors. If the plan proposes to alter a creditor's legal or contractual rights, the creditors are given the opportunity to vote to determine whether the plan will be accepted or rejected.[3052] If approved, the plan will be confirmed and the plan will bind the debtor and creditors as if they had entered into a contract for modification of debts.[3053] If the debtor fails to meet the requirements of the plan or if the business otherwise fails during the term of the plan, the case may be converted to a Chapter 7 case for liquidation or will be dismissed.

§ 27.1.1.3 Chapter 13

A Chapter 13 bankruptcy is often referred to as a "debt adjustment" case. It is not available to corporations, partnerships, or individual debtors who owe large amounts of money. Upon filing a Chapter 13 petition or within 15 days, the debtor must file a debt adjustment plan. The plan can propose to extend time for payment of debts and reduce amounts payable. Importantly, Chapter 13 allows a debtor to reinstate a previously existing mortgage payment schedule by paying, over the period of the plan, the arrearage that existed at the time of the Chapter 13 filing.[3054] A confirmation hearing will be held and the plan will be approved by the Court if it meets the statutory requirements.[3055] If the debtor completes the payments specified under the plan, the debts that then remain unpaid are discharged, except those debts which are not dischargeable under the Bankruptcy Code.[3056]

§ 27.1.2 Automatic Stay

When a debtor who has an ownership interest in real property files for bankruptcy protection under any chapter of the Bankruptcy Code, the ownership interest in the real property automatically becomes part of the bankruptcy estate. Typically, any action thereafter taken to sell or foreclose upon the real property without the approval of the Bankruptcy Court is void. Upon the filing of a bankruptcy petition, the automatic stay prescribed by the Bankruptcy Code comes into effect.[3057] As its name suggests, the stay is automatic and immediate and precludes, among other things:[3058]

(a) The commencement or continuation, including the issuance or employment of process, of a judicial, administrative, or other action or proceeding against the debtor that was or could have commenced before the commencement of the bankruptcy, or to recover a claim against the debtor that arose before the commencement of the bankruptcy;[3059]

3051   Bankruptcy Code § 1125(a).

3052   Bankruptcy Code § 1124, Bankruptcy Code § 1129.

3053   Bankruptcy Code § 1141(a).

3054   Bankruptcy Code § 1326.

3055   Bankruptcy Code § 1324.

3056   Bankruptcy Code § 1328(a).

3057   Bankruptcy Code § 362.

3058   Bankruptcy Code § 362(a).

3059   Bankruptcy Code § 362(a)(1).

b) The enforcement, against the debtor or against property of the estate, of a judgment obtained before the commencement of the bankruptcy;[3060]

c) Any act to obtain possession of property of the estate or of property from the estate or to exercise control over property of the estate;[3061]

c) Any act to create, perfect, or enforce any lien against property of the estate;[3062]

d) Any act to create, perfect, or enforce against property of the debtor any lien to the extent such lien secures a claim that arose before the commencement of the bankruptcy;[3063]

e) Any act to collect, assess, or recover a claim against the debtor that arose before the bankruptcy;[3064]

f) The set off of any debt owing to the debtor that arose before the commencement of the bankruptcy against any claim against the debtor;[3065] and

g) The commencement or continuation of a proceeding before the United States Tax Court concerning a tax liability of a debtor that is a corporation for a taxable period the bankruptcy court may determine or concerning the tax liability of a debtor who is an individual for a taxable period ending before the date of the order for relief.[3066]

The automatic stay prohibits collection activity against the debtor or property of the debtor. It also prevents the voluntary transfer of any of the debtor's property, including real property. The stay remains in effect until the earlier of (a) the dismissal of the case; (b) the closing of the case; (c) the discharge of the debtor; or (d) order of the Court.[3067] In regard to collection activities such as foreclosures, there is now a possible routine exception involving debtors who filed a previous bankruptcy action within one-year of the pending case.

§ 27.1.2.1   Impact Of The Automatic Stay Following The Filing Of A Bankruptcy Petition

As provided by the Bankruptcy Code, the automatic stay is in place at the moment the debtor files the bankruptcy petition. The case law in the Federal Court of Appeals for the Eleventh Circuit (which governs Georgia) seems to set out that all acts taken in violation of the automatic stay are void without regard to direct knowledge of the filing of the bankruptcy case.[3068] Under this holding, any activity carried on in the face of the automatic stay is without force and effect.[3069]

This clearly impacts foreclosure proceedings and other conveyances by a debtor after the filing of the bankruptcy petition. Chapter 21 of the Real Property Law Section's Revised Title Standards provides guidance to closing attorneys: the attorney should routinely require proof at closing that no bankruptcies are pending which may affect title to the property conveyed.[3070] This is typically accomplished by the execution of affidavit by the owner.

While Georgia case law suggests that acts taken in violation of the stay are void, the Bankruptcy Code, however, sets out a possible protection to a bona fide purchaser without knowledge of the filing.[3071] It states in pertinent part:

3060   Bankruptcy Code § 362(a)(2).

3061   Bankruptcy Code § 362(a)(3).

3062   Bankruptcy Code § 362(a)(4).

3063   Bankruptcy Code § 362(a)(5).

3064   Bankruptcy Code § 362(a)(6).

3065   Bankruptcy Code § 362(a)(7).

3066   Bankruptcy Code § 362(a)(8).

3067   Bankruptcy Code § 362(c)(2).

3068   *U.S. v. White*, 466 F.3d 1241 (11th Cir. 2006).

3069   *See In re Ford*, 296 B.R. 537 (Bankr. N.D.Ga. 2003).

3070   *See* comment to Revised Title Standards § 21.1.

3071   Bankruptcy Code § 549(c).

[T]he Trustee may not avoid under subsection (a) of this section a transfer of real property to a good faith purchaser without knowledge of the commencement of the case and for present fair equivalent value unless a copy or notice of the petition was filed, where a transfer of such real property may be recorded to perfect such transfer, before such transfer is so perfected that a bona fide purchase of such real property, against whom applicable law permits such transfer to be perfected could not acquire an interest that is superior to the interest of such good faith purchaser. A good faith purchaser without knowledge of the commencement of the case and for less than present fair equivalent value has a lien on the property transferred to the extent of any present value given, unless a copy or notice of the petition was so filed before such transfer was so perfected.[3072]

Georgia courts have held that if real property is conveyed and the deed transferring title to a third party is recorded without actual or constructive notice of the bankruptcy filing, then the Bankruptcy Trustee may not avoid the conveyance.[3073]

§ 27.1.2.2   Violation Of The Stay With Knowledge Of The Bankruptcy Filing

If a foreclosure or other conveyance of real property takes place when the creditor or purchaser has knowledge of the bankruptcy, they may be subject to sanctions. The Bankruptcy Court may impose fines, award damages, including attorneys' fees and costs and even punitive damages, for knowing violations of the automatic stay.[3074] Formal notice of the filing from the Court is not required, but only actual knowledge, and a foreclosure or other conveyance in the face of such knowledge can expose all parties involved in the conveyance, including the lender and counsel, to sanctions.

§ 27.1.3   Foreclosing Creditor's Methods To Obtain Relief From Automatic Stay

§ 27.1.3.1   Relief From Automatic Stay

If there is no equity in the real property or if the debtor cannot fund a plan, the creditor can file a motion for relief from the stay.[3075] This motion will usually be heard within 30 days. The Court shall grant relief from the stay, such as terminating, annulling, modifying, or conditioning such stay for (i) cause, including the lack of adequate protection of an interest in property of such party in interest, or (ii) if the debtor does not have any equity in such property and such property is not necessary to the debtor's reorganization.[3076] In a Chapter 13 case, a debtor's residence will always be considered necessary to a reorganization. The Bankruptcy Code does not provide a definition of "cause" for which modification of the automatic stay is appropriate, other than lack of adequate protection.[3077] Courts must determine when discretionary relief is appropriate on a case by case basis. A third basis for relief applies in cases involving "single asset real estate" as below detailed.

3072   Bankruptcy Code § 549(c).

3073   *In re Kine*, 35 B.R. 530 (Bankr. N.D. Ga. 1983).

3074   *See In re Herbst*, 167 B.R. 983 (Bankr. N.D. Fla. 1994).

3075   Bankruptcy Code § 362(d).

3076   Bankruptcy Code § 362(d).

3077   Bankruptcy Code § 362(d).

27.1.3.2 Serial Bankruptcy Filings

The Bankruptcy Code provides for the stay to terminate on the 30th day with respect to any action taken with regard to the debtor if the debtor had a bankruptcy case pending within a previous one-year period.[3078] The debtor may file a motion to extend the stay. Upon motion, the Court considers whether:[3079]

a) the debtor has more than one previous case pending within the past year;[3080]

b) the previous case was dismissed for failure to amend the petition or other documents without substantial excuse (but mere inadvertence or neglect will not suffice), provide adequate protection as ordered by the court, or perform the terms of a plan confirmed by the court;[3081] or

c) there has been a substantial change in the financial or personal affairs of the debtor since the dismissal of the most previous case.[3082]

A case is presumed to be filed in bad faith as to a particular creditor if that creditor had an action pending to lift the stay as of the dismissal date of the previous case or there had been an order terminating, limiting or conditioning the stay as to that creditor in the previous case.

The Code provides a mechanism for a party-in-interest to obtain a "comfort" order confirming that the automatic stay has been terminated.[3083] In non-emergency situations, this is considered to be a best practice because there are certain exceptions that may apply. Many courts have now held that cases terminated under for failure to obtain the required credit counseling certification are not dismissed but are stricken and do not count against the debtor as cases pending within one-year. Cases dismissed for failure to meet the obligations of a "repayment plan" are not presumed to be filed in bad faith.[3084]

Where a debtor has had two or more single or joint cases pending within the previous year, the automatic stay does not go into effect and the Court can enter a "comfort order" confirming no stay is in effect upon the motion of a party-in-interest.[3085] The debtor, however, may file a motion to impose the stay as to any or all creditors. The debtor has the burden of proof to demonstrate that the latest case was filed in good faith. The stay will then only go into effect upon entry of an order.

§ 27.1.3.3 Single Asset Real Estate Cases

A secured lender can also seek to have the automatic stay lifted in regard to a bankruptcy petition which largely seeks to only protect a single piece of real property.

The Bankruptcy code defines a Single Asset Real Estate case as a case where the real property at issue is a single property or project other than residential real property with fewer than four residential units, which generates substantially all of the gross income of a debtor who is not a family farmer and on which no substantial business is being conducted by a debtor other than the business of operating the real property.[3086]

Upon motion of a secured lender in a Single Asset Real Estate case, the automatic stay terminates not later than 90 days after the entry of an Order for Relief or a later date as the Court determines for cause by Order entered within

---

3078 Bankruptcy Code § 362(c)(3)(A).

3079 Bankruptcy Code § 362(c)(3)(C).

3080 Bankruptcy Code § 362(c)(3)(C)(i)(I).

3081 Bankruptcy Code § 362(c)(3)(C)(i)(II).

3082 Bankruptcy Code § 362(c)(3)(C)(i)(III).

3083 Bankruptcy Code § 362(j).

3084 *Id.*

3085 Bankruptcy Code § 362(4).

3086 Bankruptcy Code § 101(51)(B).

that 90-day period after a debtor files bankruptcy (or 30 days after the Court determines that the realty is single asset real estate, whichever is later), unless:[3087]

(a) The debtor files a Plan of Reorganization that has a reasonable possibility of being confirmed with a reasonable time; or

(b) The debtor has commenced monthly payments to each creditor whose claim is secured by such real property, from rents or other income generated from the real property, on or after the date of the commencement of the bankruptcy, in an amount equal to the applicable non-default contract rate on the value of the creditor's interest in the real property.[3088]

§ 27.1.3.4 *In Rem* Relief

The Bankruptcy Code also provides for *in rem* relief upon motion of a party-in-interest after notice and hearing.[3089] An *in rem* action is a proceeding instituted directly against the real property rather than the debtor. In an *in rem* action, the debtor has a right to be heard but any ruling in an *in rem* action is binding only against the real property and not the individual. The Court may grant *in rem* relief to a creditor whose claim is secured by an interest in real property if the Court finds that the filing was part of a scheme to delay, hinder and defraud creditors that involved either:

(a) transfer of all or part ownership or an interest in the real property without the consent of the secured creditor or Court approval;[3090] or

(b) multiple bankruptcy filings affecting the real property.[3091]

Upon the award of the *in rem* relief, the creditor must have a certified copy of the order granting *in rem* relief properly recorded in the county in which the real property is located. This order is binding in subsequently filed cases affecting the real property for two years.

In order to grant *in rem* relief, the courts have held that three elements must be present for stay relief to be granted:[3092]

(a) The debtor's current bankruptcy must have been part of a scheme;

(b) The object of the scheme must be to delay, hinder, and defraud creditors; and,

(c) The scheme must involve either: (i) the transfer of some interest in the real property without the secured creditor's consent or Court approval; or (ii) multiple bankruptcy filings affecting the property. The court must find that the debtor's filing of the petition was part of a plan or program of action to postpone that was connected with the multiple filings affecting the real property at issue.

For example, in what appears to be the first published decision to grant relief under this provision, the Court found that the debtor, her relatives and a company controlled by them had filed seven bankruptcy petitions in three years.[3093] Each case was filed to prevent foreclosure of the same real property. The Bankruptcy Court examined all the required elements: a scheme to delay, to hinder, and to defraud. The Court held that under the circumstances, the case met all the technical requirements of the Bankruptcy Code and lifted the stay.[3094]

3087   Bankruptcy Code § 362(d)(3).

3088   Bankruptcy Code § 362(d)(3).

3089   Bankruptcy Code § 362(d)(4).

3090   Bankruptcy Code § 362(d)(4)(A).

3091   Bankruptcy Code § 362(d)(4)(B).

3092   *In re Gould*, 348 B.R. 78 (Bankr. Mass. 2006).

3093   *In re Young*, 2007 WL 128280 (Bankr. S.D.Tex. 2007).

3094   *In re Young*, 2007 WL 128280 (Bankr. S.D.Tex. 2007).

27.1.3.5 Debtor Ineligible To File And The Stay Does Not Apply

The Bankruptcy Code provides that the automatic stay does not apply to enforce a lien or security interest in real property if the debtor was ineligible to file under or if the debtor filed a new case in violation of a Bankruptcy Court order in a previous case prohibiting the debtor from filing another case.[3095]

The Bankruptcy Court has further authority to annul the stay retroactively to the filing of the case and to validate a sale which is otherwise void because it was conducted at a time when the automatic stay was in place.[3096] A motion to annul the automatic stay is ideally brought in two instances: (1) when a conveyance is conducted without knowledge of the bankruptcy filing and the facts are similar to those warranting an emergency motion for relief from stay; or (2) when foreclosure counsel has no notice of the bankruptcy until after the foreclosure is complete and the property is sold to a third-party bona fide purchaser.

§ 27.1.3.6 Discharges

A bankruptcy proceeding typically results in the "discharge" of debtors from certain debts. The effect of a discharge is to render the debt unenforceable against the debtor. A discharge, however, does not eliminate a lien or security interest against the real property or a co-signer's liability on the debt.[3097]

§ 27.1.3.7 Dismissal

In the event that a bankruptcy case is dismissed prior to a discharge of a debt, the property generally reverts to its pre-filing status.[3098] After dismissal of a bankruptcy case, it is best to record, along with any document of conveyance, a certified copy of the dismissal.

§ 27.2 WHEN THE SELLER FILES BANKRUPTCY

If a seller files for bankruptcy protection after signing a listing agreement but before the subject real property is sold, the listing agreement is an executory contract which can be dishonored by the bankruptcy trustee. The broker (or broker's attorney) may request an order directing the trustee to decide within a specified time whether to assume or reject the listing agreement. Otherwise, the broker will be in the position of having to wait 60 days (in a Chapter 7 case) or longer to determine if the listing agreement will be honored.

Another step the broker can take is to file a motion with the bankruptcy court for approval of the trustee's employment of the broker as a professional person.[3099] The trustee is empowered to employ professionals as needed to assist in carrying out the trustee's duties, which often include selling real estate. They are authorized to agree to pay a commission at a specified percentage rate, although what they agree to may be less than the original listing agreement provided. If the broker does not verify that the trustee has affirmed the listing agreement and if the broker does not apply to the court for appointment as a professional person, there is a risk that the broker could lose the commission altogether.

In the alternative, the broker may have to file a lawsuit after a sale has been made and make an equitable argument for a commission. In order to avoid this situation, the broker should try to get the listing agreement affirmed by the bankruptcy court as quickly as possible. The broker's motion for approval of employment of a professional person, if granted, will ensure that when a motion to sell the property is filed with the court the commission will be paid to the broker directly out of closing.

3095   Bankruptcy Code § 362(b)(21).

3096   Bankruptcy Code § 362(d).

3097   Bankruptcy Code § 524; *Tatnall Bank v. Smith*, 192 Ga. 89, 14 S.E. 2d 685 (1940).

3098   Bankruptcy Code § 349.

3099   11 U.S.C.A. § 3.27.

§ 27.2.1 Broker's Obligation Pending Affirmation Of Listing Agreement Or Employment Of Broker As A Professional Person

Pending a determination by the court on the above issues, what are the broker's responsibilities? By way of example, let's assume that a three-month listing agreement is signed on September 5th. Then on September 30th, the seller files a Chapter 7 bankruptcy petition. The broker files the suggested motions for affirmation of the contract or for employment as a professional person, but those will not be ruled on for several weeks. Is the broker obligated to actively market the property between the bankruptcy filing and the end of the listing period in December? The answer to this question is probably yes. Unless the trustee steps in and repudiates the contract it is still in effect, even though the broker cannot count on actually being paid under the agreement until it has been specifically affirmed by the trustee. The Brokerage Relationships in Real Estate Transactions Act ("BRRETA") requires a broker to "promote the interests of the seller by … seeking a sale…."[3100] The broker is in a catch-22 situation: she must continue to actively market the property and risk receiving no compensation, or violate BRRETA by refusing to do so until a listing agreement is affirmed by the trustee.

§ 27.2.2 When Listing Agreement Is Affirmed Or Broker Has Been Employed By Trustee

Once a listing agreement is affirmed (or the broker has been employed by the trustee) and a buyer is found, the closing attorney should be notified as soon as possible to give her time to verify that all necessary documentation is available to assure that marketable title can be conveyed. The conveyance will likely be subject to the approval of the bankruptcy judge, which may take time to obtain.

§ 27.2.3 When One Co-Owner Files For Bankruptcy But The Other Does Not

If one co-owner of property files a petition in bankruptcy, the property that is jointly owned will be affected, but any other property owned by the non-filing co-owner, individually or jointly with some other third party, will not be affected. If only one spouse files a bankruptcy action, property owned solely by the spouse who has not filed bankruptcy will not be affected. That is, if a wife owns property in her own name and her husband does not have any interest in the property, the wife's property will not be affected if the husband files the bankruptcy petition.

If husband and wife own the property jointly, however, either as joint tenants or as tenants in common, the bankruptcy petition of the husband will affect the property even if the wife does not file. In some instances, the property may be released from the bankruptcy estate due to an exemption which the debtor may claim.

In certain cases where the non-bankrupt owner does not agree to the sale, the bankruptcy trustee has the authority to sell the entire property anyway, including the interest of the non-bankrupt owner. This can happen when: partition of the property between the bankruptcy estate and co-owner(s) is impracticable; the sale of the estate's undivided interest in the property would realize significantly less for the estate than sale of the property fee of the interest of such co-owner(s); and the benefit to the estate of a sale of such property free and clear of the interests of co-owner(s) outweighs the detriments, if any, to the co-owner(s). In such cases, the co-owner(s) may purchase the property at the price at which the sale is to be consummated.

§ 27.3 SALE OF PROPERTY UNDER PROTECTION OF BANKRUPTCY

Any contract entered into by the debtor prior to filing for bankruptcy protection can be assumed or rejected by the trustee if the contract has not yet been carried out (*i.e.*, an executory contract).[3101] This includes listing agreements on real property, and any contract for sale entered into prior to the filing. In a Chapter 7 bankruptcy, the contract is deemed rejected if not specifically assumed by the trustee within 60 days of the filing of the

---

3100   O.C.G.A. § 10-6A-5.

3101   11 U.S.C.A. § 365.

petition.[3102] In Chapter 11 and 13 cases, the trustee may assume or reject an executory contract at any time before the confirmation of the Plan.[3103]

Under the Bankruptcy Code, there are many ways that real property of a debtor in bankruptcy can be conveyed. It is imperative, however, that additional inquires be made regarding such real property. Depending upon the chapter under which the debtor sought bankruptcy protection and the various orders entered by the Bankruptcy Court, there are many variables to consider. If the conveyance is proper, while it is not required, all relevant Bankruptcy Court orders should be recorded in the real property land records along with the vesting deed. Real estate professionals without detailed knowledge regarding the Bankruptcy Code should always consult with an attorney who remains abreast of the constant evolution of bankruptcy laws and rules.

In most instances, the trustee of the debtor conveying the property will first obtain an order that the sale is free and clear of all liens. Generally, in order to obtain an order authorizing the sale, the sales contract must provide for sales proceeds to be used to pay liens.

§ 27.3.1 Chapter 7 Cases

In a Chapter 7 case, the bankruptcy trustee is the party who would sign a deed of conveyance, unless the trustee abandons her interest in the property because it has little or no value to the estate. If the trustee sells the property, marketable title may be conveyed if there is (a) an order authorizing the sale of the property filed in the bankruptcy court showing notice given to all creditors and an opportunity for hearing, (b) documentation of the appointment of the trustee, and (c) proof that the property is property of the estate.

If the trustee abandons the property in a Chapter 7 bankruptcy, thereby releasing it from the estate, the debtor may sell it without obtaining prior court approval; however, it is still subject to all liens and encumbrances which must be satisfied or otherwise released when the real property is conveyed. The debtor may convey marketable title upon proof that the trustee has abandoned the property and upon satisfaction or release of liens which are not avoided under the Bankruptcy Code. Sellers should consult their attorney to determine if any exceptions apply to their situation, and the closing attorney should be kept apprised of all details as well.

Under Chapter 7 of the Bankruptcy Code, the Bankruptcy Trustee may liquidate assets of the debtor including any real property by conducting a Trustee's sale. Where the Bankruptcy Trustee seeks to convey real property of the bankruptcy estate, certain requirements must be met: (1) there must be an order authorizing the sale of the real property which is properly filed in the bankruptcy case which shows that notice was given to all creditors and that there was an opportunity to object to the sale; (2) there must be an order appointing the Bankruptcy Trustee; and (3) there must be proof that the real property was property of the bankruptcy estate and was not otherwise exempted from the estate.[3104]

§ 27.3.2 Chapter 11 Cases

Chapter 11 reorganization cases are generally more complex than Chapter 7 and Chapter 13 cases. In many Chapter 11 cases, a trustee is generally not appointed, but rather the debtor is allowed to continue to operate his, her or its business under the oversight of a committee of the largest creditors.[3105] In such a case, a debtor may sell estate property subject to certain notice requirements to credits and an opportunity for a hearing. If the sale is considered to be in the "ordinary business" of the Chapter 11 debtor, notice to creditors may not be necessary. However, to avoid

---

3102   11 U.S.C.A. § 365(d)(1).

3103   11 U.S.C.A. § 365(d)(2).

3104   Bankruptcy Code § 363.

3105   Bankruptcy Code § 1107.

disputes about whether a sale is part of the debtor's ordinary business, it is ideal to also obtain written consent for the conveyance from the Bankruptcy Trustee. If the sale is authorized as part of the confirmed Plan, marketability of the title to the property will not be impaired.

§ 27.3.3 Chapter 13 Cases

In a Chapter 13 case, marketability of the title to the property will not be impaired if the debtor has obtained a final order authorizing the sale after notice to creditors and the opportunity for a hearing. As in a Chapter 7 case where the debtor may sell the property, the sale of the property will be subject to outstanding liens and encumbrances unless the order form the court specifically provides that the sale is "free and clear of all liens." It is a best practice to obtain written consent from the Bankruptcy Trustee approving the conveyance.

§ 27.4 WHEN THE BUYER FILES BANKRUPTCY

Individuals who find it necessary to file for bankruptcy protection are not often in the market for real estate. But let's suppose that a buyer has put a property under contract and has been approved for the necessary loan so that there is no remaining financial contingency. She then suffers a major fire that destroys her business and files a Chapter 7 bankruptcy petition before the closing occurs. What then?

Here again we are dealing with the executory contract provisions of the Bankruptcy Code. The trustee has 60 days to decide whether to affirm or reject the contract for purchasing the property.[3106] Depending upon how distant is the closing date, the seller's broker in this example should consider the same motion mentioned in § 27.2 (When the Seller Files Bankruptcy) – to have the trustee make the decision to affirm or reject the contract within a specified time period. Otherwise the deal is "on" until the trustee rejects the contract or 60 days from the filing of the bankruptcy petition.

§ 27.5 LENDERS IN BANKRUPTCY

Lenders can be affected by turbulent financial markets as well as individuals, when they suffer a loss of liquidity where lines of credit to originate mortgage loans (and/or investors willing to buy mortgages) disappear. Buyers should regularly check in with their mortgage lenders to confirm that there are no problems with their deals.

If the buyer learns that the mortgage loan is not being funded, there may still be hope to complete the purchase. If the GAR Purchase and Sale Agreement form was used, the buyer is required to complete the purchase as an all-cash transaction or be in breach of the agreement. However, under the GAR Purchase and Sale Agreement, the buyer can extend the closing date *unilaterally* for a period of seven days if either the mortgage lender or closing attorney cannot fulfill their respective obligations.[3107] Since the buyer has demonstrated their credit-worthiness by qualifying once, the buyer may be able to find another lender in a short period of time. In that case, the survival of the deal may depend upon the buyer's willingness to accept a loan under perhaps less favorable terms than originally obtained.

If the seller is unwilling to extend the closing date and the buyer is unable to complete an all-cash transaction after unilaterally extending the closing date seven days, the buyer will be in breach of the agreement if the buyer does not close. At a minimum, this means that the buyer will lose the earnest money paid to the seller. The buyer may also have a claim against the lender in bankruptcy, but will need to file a creditor's claim with the bankruptcy court and stand in line with others similarly situated.

The best thing brokers can do to help buyer clients avoid these problems is to recommend that they choose a well-established lender to finance their purchase.

3106   Bankruptcy Code § 363(d).

3107   GAR Form F20.

§ 27.5.1 "Collected Funds" Law In Georgia

The closing process itself has been affected by the softer housing market in recent years. Closing attorneys have been permitted to close mortgage loan transactions after receiving the loan proceeds from a lender via either a wire, a check or draft issued by most lending institutions, or another attorney's escrow account.[3108] Unfortunately, at least one large mortgage lender in 2007 bounced checks to closing attorneys throughout Georgia after which it filed for bankruptcy protection. Since the closing attorneys did not learn of the situation until well after the loans had closed, the affected closing attorneys had to personally make up shortfalls in their escrow accounts in the millions of dollars. This has understandably resulted in most closing attorneys now refusing to close mortgage loans unless they have wired funds in their escrow account where the wire cannot be reversed.

Brokers can expect to see more closings postponed pending confirmation that the funds have been collected from the lender. It is likely that more back-to-back closings will need to be handled by the same closing firm to minimize the domino-effect of a lender bankruptcy.

In response to the issue discussed above, the Georgia General Assembly amended O.C.G.A. § 44-14-13, the Good Funds Statute, in 2008. Under the revised statute, a settlement agent may disburse settlement proceeds from its escrow account after receipt of the following: collected funds (*i.e.*, cash); a cashier's check from a federally insured bank, savings bank, savings and loan association, or credit union and issued by a lender for a closing or loan transaction (so long as the funds are immediately available and cannot be dishonored or refused when negotiated or presented for payment); a check drawn on the escrow account of a duly licensed Georgia attorney or real estate broker (so long as the settlement agent has "reasonable and prudent" grounds to believe that the check will be honored); a check issued by the United States of America or any agency thereof or by the State of Georgia or any agency or political subdivision thereof; and, a check or checks in the aggregate amount not exceeding $5,000.00 per loan closing.[3109] A more detailed discussion on good funds is located in Chapter 6 (Purchase Price).

§ 27.6 BUILDERS IN BANKRUPTCY OR FORECLOSURE

Another segment of the real estate industry that is affected by a slower real estate market is builders/developers. If a buyer has contracted to buy a house that is being built for them, it is not unusual for the buyer to advance large sums of money to builders prior to the builder beginning to construct a custom home. Many buyers do not fully consider whether the earnest money should be held by the builder or a broker, and (if held by the builder) whether the funds should be kept in an escrow account or in an operating account.

Builders have a legitimate interest in requesting a substantial deposit before they begin construction of a custom home. Many builders, particularly smaller builders, need to use the deposited funds to cover the costs of construction. Balanced against these interests is the fact that when the builder holds the funds in an operating account, the buyer is less protected against a builder default than if the funds had been held in a real estate broker's account. This is because if the earnest money is spent on the house and the builder either files bankruptcy or is foreclosed upon, there is a good chance that the buyer will lose her money.

One way to protect the buyer in this situation is to allow the builder to hold and use the earnest money, but have the builder give the buyer a note and deed to secure debt on the property for the sums advanced. While this would normally still place the buyer in second position behind the construction lender, it does give the buyer a security interest in the property. While most buyers insist on getting a security interest in the property only when large sums are being advanced to the builder, the practice may change if more builders lose their homes to foreclosure and/or bankruptcy.

3108   O.C.G.A. § 44-14-13.

3109   O.C.G.A. § 44-14-13(c).

The **RED BOOK**

TABLE OF SPECIAL STIPULATIONS

TABLE OF SPECIAL STIPULATIONS

[Note: There are no Special Stipulations in Chapters 21-24 and 26-27.]

Chapter 9: **Disclosures**

The **RED BOOK**
_____

INDEX
_____

INDEX

arbitration provision   485, 487-8, 601

arbitrator   183, 188, 353, 375, 483, 485-90, 559, 601, 691

arrangements, cooperative brokerage   575, 606, 758

as is   298, 318, 338, 342-5, 348, 351, 360, 363, 398, 469-70, 520, 526, 563, 626

asbestos   317, 339, 341, 346, 373, 508

ASHI-approved inspector   353

assessed value   688

assessments   60-1, 64-5, 113, 150-1, 363, 372-3, 375, 412, 419, 501, 630-2, 636, 657-8, 687, 690-2

assets   71, 93, 102, 122, 230, 517-18, 653, 771

association   60-1, 150-1, 161, 213, 295-6, 347, 418-19, 617-18, 620-3, 625-8, 631, 635-6, 638-40, 732, 741-5

Atlanta taxes   692-3

attorney   28, 40, 43, 64, 69, 89-91, 184-5, 384, 393-6, 406-7, 674-5, 682-3, 752-3, 756, 779

  buyer's   40-1, 246, 251, 466

  licensed   190, 393

  power of   89-91, 103, 384-5, 394-6

attorney's fees   190-1, 350, 407, 483, 547

attorneys fees   187, 191, 454, 703, 750

auction   103, 219, 526, 551, 563-4, 625, 699, 702

B

bankruptcy   64, 68-70, 75-6, 240, 362, 374, 481, 671, 769, 771-81

Bankruptcy Code   68-70, 75, 771-7, 779-80

bankruptcy court   69-70, 76, 165, 772-4, 776-7, 779-80

bankruptcy estate   68-9, 771-2, 778-9

bankruptcy protection   214, 236-7, 700-1, 771-2, 777-81

base loan amount   240

basement   153-4, 295, 298-9, 318, 344-5, 469-70, 476, 483, 507

binding agreement   4, 6-11, 13-14, 19, 21-3, 86, 188-9, 348, 381, 398, 400, 435, 439, 445, 556

Binding Agreement Date   5-6, 45-6, 181-3, 220-1, 226-8, 230, 254-5, 260, 299-301, 305-6, 340-2, 344-398-400, 520-1, 626-7

binding arbitration   484, 487, 490, 666, 670

binding contract   3-5, 7, 9, 11, 13-15, 17, 19, 21-3, 2 27, 29-31, 33, 35, 182, 551-2

blockbusting   739, 741

board members   622

  developer-appointed   623

  owner-elected   623

board of directors   60, 93-4, 151, 419, 621, 639, 728

boldface type   618-21, 624

bona fide sale, first   564, 618, 620, 623-5

bonds   12, 219, 221, 230, 262, 333-4, 423, 676-7, 694

borrower   100, 219-20, 222-3, 237-9, 241, 250, 407-9 430, 517-19, 645-8, 650-1, 653, 656, 755-6, 764-6

boundaries   44, 46-7, 65, 134-7, 140-1, 145, 150, 152-3, 156, 160, 292, 472, 687, 715, 720-1

boundary line agreement   54-5

boundary lines   46, 54, 131, 133-6, 142-3, 145, 152, 156-8, 506, 592, 595, 715

brochure   309, 311-12, 340, 620, 736, 762-3

broken seals   352

broker   6-7, 186-97, 203, 294-5, 298-9, 383-6, 388-9, 435-55, 469-72, 474-8, 571-612, 657-60, 740-1, 752-6, 777-8

  buyer's   31, 435, 443, 606, 609, 627

  commercial   453

  duties of   571, 589

broker commissions   179

broker procures   435, 443, 574

brokerage agreement   572-3, 578, 583, 587, 602-3, 605-10

  exclusive buyer   478, 605-7

  written   447, 574, 585-6, 598, 603-4

Brokerage Agreements   574, 586, 604

brokerage commission   444, 450, 455

brokerage engagement   323, 447, 478, 571-4, 585-7, 598, 602-5, 607, 665

brokerage engagement agreement   197, 435, 452, 576, 583, 610, 658

onstruction costs 60, 179, 781

onstruction defects 483, 487-8

onstruction delays 424-5

onstruction deposit 175, 178-80

onstruction lender 180, 625, 675, 781

onstruction loan 102, 222-3, 466

ontingencies 10-11, 192-3, 201-2, 210-11, 220, 35, 269-71, 273-9, 281-3, 285, 338, 340, 367-9, 425, 47-8

ontract 3-9, 14-19, 22-35, 39-43, 85-99, 103-13, 31-3, 145-9, 183-203, 219-36, 252-8, 269-75, 293-5, 25-34, 337-52

  back-up 280-1

  covered 564, 618-20, 624

  current GAR 45, 484, 528

  executory 69, 777-9

  new GAR 342, 414

  non-GAR 86, 175, 215, 485

  original 3, 19, 22, 192, 425, 466

  signed 6-7, 12, 22

  unenforceable 25, 210

  valid 4, 8, 18, 29, 148, 186, 201

contract claims 293, 463, 467, 612

contract period 113, 332, 396

contract price 273, 420, 426, 463-4, 652, 670, 672-3, 676

contract provision 233, 249-52, 264, 411, 418, 422, 426-7, 637

contract terms 191, 201, 394, 419, 422

contractor

  general 328, 402, 473, 665, 670, 673

  independent 144-5, 203, 452, 650, 757-8

contractual obligations 110, 231, 234, 320, 399, 459, 465, 626

conveyance 44, 61, 64, 68, 70, 73, 76-8, 80, 112-13, 135-6, 219, 393, 452-3, 773-4, 777-80

conveyance of property 76, 104-5

conveyance of real property 113, 136, 774

copy, conformed 18-19, 30-1

counteroffer 3, 5, 7-9, 13-15, 18, 20, 22, 31, 110, 149,

187, 338, 344-5, 348-9, 382-3

Counteroffer form 13-14, 24, 522

county land records 45-6, 60, 62, 141, 416, 453, 617, 622, 628, 640, 706

court, magistrate's 544

court order 100-2, 104, 192

covenants 30, 42-3, 45, 48, 61-3, 77, 161, 308, 361, 365, 402, 504, 617, 622, 628-37

  declaration of 42, 61-2, 627-8, 632, 634-5, 640

  recorded 62, 161, 296, 513, 628, 635

covenants of title 77-8

coverage 47, 66-7, 375, 423, 742

D

damages

  actual 95, 112, 178-9, 196-200, 202-3, 230, 503, 559, 566, 674

  seller's 197-8, 237, 511-12

date, effective 5, 332, 545-6, 731, 741

days, last 32-4, 417, 546, 553, 683, 694

death 72, 79-80, 85, 90, 106, 111, 234, 307, 399, 422, 479, 482

debtor 68-70, 75-6, 223, 415, 670, 771-80

declaration 45, 57, 61-2, 79, 150-3, 362, 374, 617-18, 621-2, 624, 627-38, 640, 725, 730

deed holder 699-702, 704-11

Deed to Secure Debt 79-80, 219, 234, 251-3

deeds 30, 41-2, 54, 60-1, 64, 77, 89, 122, 140-1, 251, 393, 416-17, 647, 739

Defect Resolution Period 344-5, 347-9, 353

defective product 351-2

defects 40-4, 66-8, 291-2, 294, 297-8, 301, 317-23, 341-54, 356, 358, 364-6, 425-6, 468-70, 472-3, 481-2

  hidden 323-4, 360, 459, 473, 489, 503-4

  latent 291, 298, 304, 321, 323, 325, 343, 469, 506, 584, 591

  repair of 281, 317, 344, 626

defendant 17, 59, 190, 449, 543, 697-701, 703-4, 706-10

defraud 295, 470, 646-7, 658, 776

DeKalb County 137, 146, 160, 668, 673, 689

delays 20, 232, 236, 419, 423-5, 502-3, 517, 547, 776

designated agency 383-4, 572, 575-6, 580-1, 583, 587, 602, 604

designated agency transactions 384, 580-1

designated agents 384, 576, 580-3, 587, 601, 612

developer control 621-2

development, mixed-use 296, 617, 640, 693

disabilities 74, 243, 727-8, 731, 742

Disabilities Act 546, 723, 725, 727, 729, 731, 733, 735, 737, 739, 741, 743, 745

disclaimers 108, 154, 294-5, 307, 329, 470, 476-80, 535

disclosure duties 322, 590-1, 594, 599

disclosure obligations 297, 299, 302-3, 312, 321, 571, 591, 593

disclosure package 618, 624-6, 635

disclosure requirements 336, 594, 597, 601

disclosure statement 168, 291-3, 295, 297-300, 344, 399, 526, 595-6, 761, 772

  seller's 294-5, 352, 470, 475

disclosures 289, 291, 293, 295, 297, 299, 301, 303, 305, 307, 309, 311, 313, 520

discretionary contingency 10-11, 269

discrimination 535-6, 546, 726-7, 729-31, 735-6, 740-2

divorce 70-1, 74, 86, 110, 222, 587-8

documents

  closing 393-5

  multiple 18, 23-4

down payment 185, 204, 241, 243-4, 257, 409, 420, 648, 652, 654

dual agency 572, 575-81, 587, 602, 604, 612

dual agency disclosures 577-8

dual agency transactions 573, 578-9

dual agent 576-80, 587, 602, 610, 612

due diligence 142, 152, 294, 298, 319, 322, 324-5, 329-30, 358, 360-1, 363, 367-9, 371, 468-70, 472-3

due diligence materials 322, 360-1, 363, 527

Due Diligence Period 12, 27, 180, 220, 276-7, 300, 317-18, 338, 342, 358-60, 363-8, 398-400, 425, 506-554

dues 418-19, 702

E

e-mail 3, 384, 387-9, 600

earnest money 39-41, 95, 112, 175-203, 229-31, 236-7, 242-3, 258-61, 366-7, 464-6, 511-12, 528-9, 559, 579, 780-1

  amount of 177, 195-6, 200

  disbursement of 193-4, 486, 601

  disputed 188, 190-3

  holding 175, 181, 183, 187, 193, 512

  payment of 11, 175, 177-8, 181, 183, 185, 198, 553

earnest money deposit 11, 149, 183-4, 186, 189, 198, 202

easement rights 58, 141, 618

easements 30, 39, 45-7, 54-9, 65, 67, 135, 140, 143, 145, 158-9, 161, 361-2, 497, 668

  recorded 55, 513

  unrecorded 56, 513

electronic signatures 30, 522

encroachments 45-6, 50, 54-5, 65, 67, 143, 145, 147

encumbrances 39, 41-3, 45-7, 49, 59, 61, 64-6, 68, 70, 77, 122, 415-16, 519-20, 564, 779-80

enforceable contract 3-5, 8, 20, 22-3, 30, 86, 95, 223, 495, 522

enhanced title insurance policies 66-7

entire agreement clause 293-5, 328-9, 470-2, 475-6

entitlement 69, 183, 242, 244, 439, 486, 606, 611, 703

EPA 308, 336, 340

escrow 182, 186-7, 189, 191, 194, 225, 241, 249, 354, 405, 408, 411-13, 689

escrow account 175, 177, 188, 194, 214, 261, 263, 394, 409, 440, 538, 729, 764-6, 781

  attorney's 185, 781

  broker's 176-7, 440-1

escrow agent 179, 184, 187-8, 191-3, 199, 673

escrow amounts 227, 239